British Sound Films
The Studio Years 1928-1959

British Sound Films

The Studio Years 1928-1959

David Quinlan

B.T. Batsford   London

To my mother

This was her era of cinemagoing

ISBN 0 7134 1874 5 (cased)

Typeset and printed in Great Britain by
Butler & Tanner Ltd,
Frome and London
for the publishers
B.T. Batsford Ltd
4 Fitzhardinge Street
London W1H 0AH

Contents

Acknowledgements

I would like to offer a special vote of thanks to Kenneth Thompson, without whose spadework on British films of the 1930s this book would have undoubtedly taken longer to write. I would also like to thank all the staff at the British Film Institute for their assistance, but particularly Linda Wood, for opening up the magic box; and Jacob Hurst, whose research on photography credits proved invaluable. My thanks to Timothy Auger, Rachel Wright, and others at Batsford, not only for their forbearance over deadlines, but for miracles performed in getting the book out on schedule.

Almost all of the illustrations in this book come from my own collection, but I would like to thank Gary Parfitt for the still from *The Secret Agent*, and the stills section of the British Film Institute for extra stills on *The Four Feathers*, *The Third Man* and *Richard III*, as well as the illustrations for *Number Seventeen* and *This Happy Breed*.

My gratitude and acknowledgement too to all the producing companies and distributors whose copyright stills are used in this book, among them Allied Artists, Anglo-Amalgamated, Associated British, ATP, BIP, British and Dominions, British Lion, British National, Butchers, Columbia, Ealing Studios, Gainsborough, Gaumont-British, Grand National, Group 3, Hammer, London Films, Mancunian, Merton Park, M-G-M, Monarch, Paramount, Pathé, The Rank Organization, Real Art, Renown, Republic, RKO Radio, Sound City, 20th Century-Fox, Twickenham, Two Cities, Universal, United Artists, Walt Disney Productions and Warner Brothers, but many more besides.

OVERLEAF
Pinewood in the 1950s

Foreword

The insularity of the British cinema has been its bane and its blessing, its pain and its pleasure. Its attempts through the studio years of 1928 to 1959 to break into the international (specifically Hollywood) market were mainly elaborate and costly failures that damaged the very industry they were intended to boost.

Yet many of the finest films from Britain in this period were distinguished by just that 'Britishness' that made them difficult to market abroad.

Consequently, the industry seemed to lurch from crisis to crisis in those years. Film producers too often made grandiose plans for the future without sufficient grip on the economics involved, or taking the time and trouble to achieve an objective overview. The wisdom of employing a sound financial mind as a studio boss only fully sank in to British studios in the 1950s – and then it was too late for the system as it existed to survive.

Before then, magnates had been too slow to react to what was wrong with the industry and insufficiently ruthless to weed out elements that were weakening the impact and future of British cinema. Nor was the lack of informed minds at government level anything but a hindrance.

The 'quota' legislation, enforcing a certain percentage of British-made films on British cinemagoers (an idea that would have had the interests of the industry more sensibly at heart had its figures been lower), contributed to the frequency of bad acting in minor pictures – a throwback to the 'over-theatrical' performances from many players in the early 1930s – that led to British films as a whole being regarded with much suspicion, and as an unacceptable risk further afield.

Exceptions to this were frequently followed by the major talents involved 'going to Hollywood' although, of those whom the domestic industry proved insufficiently high-powered to hold, it was actors rather than directors (Alfred Hitchcock excepted) who prospered in an international environment.

Thus, even though such film-makers as Carol Reed and David Lean made their best films while British-based, there was a mass exodus of acting talent in the years 1932–39 and 1946–51 which must have given directors itchy feet as well.

The British cinema's attempts to cling on to its family audience meant that its condescending view of the working-classes (who, it was felt, probably correctly, wanted to be taken out of themselves and not shown a mirror-image of their own lives) persisted almost through the entire period surveyed by this book. In consequence, upper-class accents led to much characterization that looks irritatingly phoney today. Only director John Baxter pioneered the kind of 'Love on the Dole' drama which sprang to prominence in such profusion after the success of Room at the Top in 1958.

Despite all of this, the studio years brought a continuity of production that engendered a brilliant series of successes. The Jessie Matthews musicals, the Jack Hulbert frolics, Korda's 'films of empire', the gritty realism of war films (apart from their failure to break down the class barrier), the Gainsborough costume romps (even if today some of them look pretty awful), the quality films (Brief Encounter, Odd Man Out, The Third Man, The Fallen Idol) from Britain's best directors in the immediate post-war years, Olivier's Shakespeare projects and the Ealing comedies.

This book is both an attempt to look at an era of film-making through its product, and a record of the product itself. Cast-lists and credits are as extensive as the author could contrive, even if there are infuriating examples of the 'ones that got away'. On the Jack Hulbert film Jack Ahoy!, for instance, despite extensive relevant material, it proved impossible to expand on a basic cast list of six players. The film itself is one of the few important pictures of the period – it was released in 1934 – not preserved in Britain's National Film Archive.

Only entertainment feature films are detailed in this book, that is to say no documentaries, newsreels or short cartoons, although short fictional features between 20 and 44 minutes in length are listed in brief at the end of each decade.

Photography credits on many films proved particularly difficult to trace, but were eventually identified for 99 per cent of 1940s' and 1950s' films, as well as the vast majority of those made in the 1930s. Although more photographs could have been supplied from the author's collection, it was felt that the prime factor was to expand these casts and credits as much as possible, making a permanent record for students and enthusiasts alike.

Abbreviations, however, have been used to preserve vital space and these run roughly as follows in credits and casts. Dir/Director. Prod/Producer. Scr/Screenplay. Ph/Photography. PC/Production company (those who made the film). Dis/Distributors. Cert/Certificate. Mins/Minutes. LP/Leading Players. RoC/Rest of Cast. You may also occasionally encounter Mus/Music, Ly/Lyrics and Sp Eff/Special Effects, where such credits are deemed essential. The dates are based on the copyright dates on the credits of the films.

Some production companies and distributors have also been abbreviated on occasion. Thus, ACT (Association of Cinema Technicians), ATP (Associated Talking Pictures), BIP (British International Pictures), M-G-M (Metro-Goldwyn-Mayer), and W and F (Wolfe and Freedman).

As to what constitutes a British film, Department of Trade (formerly Board of Trade) rules are both profuse and vague at the same time. But the majority of its makers should be British, and the studios used to shoot it should be in the United Kingdom. Several films made in various parts of Ireland have proved borderline cases in this respect, and some have been omitted.

In addition, three-quarters of the paid labour force on the film must be British subjects or citizens. If all these conditions are met, then the film qualifies for its 'GB' sticker, and counts towards the quota of British films that must be shown in British cinemas.

A note on the certificates of films in the period surveyed: the 'U' certificate meant that admission was unrestricted – children being able to go by themselves. To see an 'A' certificate, they would have to be accompanied by an adult. 'H' (for horror) films could not be seen by anyone under 16, the same applying to the 'X' certificate, the more general restriction which replaced the 'H' in 1952.

The 'rating system' used, indicated by numerals 1 to 6, is an amalgam of contemporary critical opinion at the time the film was first released. Readers will notice that some films were not so highly rated by critics in their time as later became the case – and, of course, vice versa. This system can be interpreted as follows:

1 = Poor
2 = Mediocre
3 = Average
4 = Good
5 = Very good
6 = Outstanding

If the British film industry did achieve an identity of its own during these crisis-ridden years, a proposition that has always given rise to challenge and controversy, then it will surely be found in the pages that follow.

D.Q., *Addington, 1984*

Dates to films may vary occasionally by a year between picture caption (referring to the release date) and text (referring to the copyright date). For reference and historical purposes the copyright date is the more appropriate.

THE TWENTIES

Jean Colin and Jameson Thomas in *The Hate Ship* (1929)

THE TWENTIES

The End of the Silents

In 1927, Al Jolson stepped before agog movie audiences and spoke the words they had been longing to hear: 'You ain't heard nothin' yet.' How right he was. In fact his audiences had been longing to hear *any* words, for this maudlin Hollywood weepie with music, entitled *The Jazz Singer*, was the first major film with whole talkie sequences. And how banal was much of what they *did* hear for the next five years - especially in Britain, with its dreaded 'quota', whose worst ramifications were yet to come.

The quota meant that the opportunities to create a prosperous British cinema in the formative years of sound were largely missed, trampled underfoot by hacks who failed to move with the times; by opportunists out to make a quick fortune; by journeymen who could not see beyond the end of their quota; by directors whose stately tempo and by actors whose stilted delivery were further hampered by the restrictions of a suddenly immobile camera; and by innovative film-makers (few enough) who could not or would not reconcile the demands of entertainment with intrinsically British subjects.

The production and distribution companies that were to dominate these early sound years - Gaumont-British, British Lion, British and Dominions, Gainsborough, ATP and BIP among them - had nearly all been set up by the late 1920s. Two more, Associated British and London Films, would soon follow. Vertical integration after the American system - companies releasing their own films - had already begun. But many of these companies, if for genuine reasons, made wrong decisions as to the shape the British film industry should take to ensure a healthy future.

Only Michael Balcon, first at Gaumont-British and later in the golden period at Ealing (the successor to ATP - Associated Talking Pictures), would forge a cinema that was both truly British and pleased the crowds at the box-office. And even he would complain in the late 1920s of 'operating in a vacuum ... making our contribution to what was no more than entertainment opium for the masses'.

But to return to the quota. In 1926 the British cinema was hardly out of the despondency into which it had slumped two years earlier when pioneer Cecil Hepworth (whose lyrical silents with Alma Taylor had lent British films some identity and pride) went broke and, for a brief period, no new British pictures were being made at all. Two years later, the position was hardly brighter. The American product dominated the home market to such an extent that only five films in every 100 shown in Britain were British - and those few were largely shunned by the cinema-going public who preferred the slicker, polished, more sophisticated entertainment Hollywood provided.

At the time, the dangers of a quota system - the requirement by law that a minimum percentage of the total annual number of films shown be British - seemed to be far outweighed by the necessity of taking some kind of step to secure the continuation of the native industry. And so the deed was done. It was named the Cinematograph Films Act of 1927.

It called for a quota of 5 per cent of British films in the first six months following its introduction. This figure was to rise to 20 per cent by successive stages over the next eight years.

The immediate effect on British film production was startling enough. The number of films produced rocketed from 26 in 1926 to 128 the following year. Money was suddenly no longer in short supply. A boom - of sorts - was on. And at exactly the right time.

While some agonised over the passing of the silents - an inevitability contested in dozens of anguished articles by the intelligentsia - others were falling over themselves in equip studios, and cinemas, for the coming craze. Some cinemas, indeed, could not afford the costly sound equipment and were forced to close.

Pictures filmed as silents were withdrawn from circulation and magically appeared a few months later with sound added, whether in Britain, or at the technically superior RCA studios in New York. Either way, the expense was considerable. Companies kept their fingers crossed - had they chosen the right system? Sound-on-film, though it slightly reduced the size of the screen, soon outpaced the more cumbersome sound-on-disc. But even then, there was the problem of whether to choose Western Electric or RCA, the two systems that led the field by mid-1928.

The coming of the talkie should have given British product a big boost. Many felt that the American accents would prove unpalatable to the British cinemagoer. And foreign-language films would be right out of court. With the variety made possible by the hugely increased film-production schedules, Britain had the capabilities to claim a bigger slice of box-office receipts than ever before.

But it did not happen. Insufficient British film-makers were men of vision and flair. Too many of its actors (and especially actresses) spoke in accents more acceptable in the regency dining-rooms of the West End and South Kensington than in the average front parlour. And the camera was not freed from its new shackles with the speed and imagination almost immediately apparent in Hollywood, whose life and drive were seldom evident in British films.

It was true that the public wanted escapist pictures, and rightly so. But at least this kind of entertainment had to *seem* rooted in reality while the lights were low. British film acting lacked conviction and 90 per cent of its product in this quota decade (1927-36) was poor by any standards, quickly and cheaply produced from the word 'Go' with too little thought given either to script or to technical departments.

The quota itself was not only achieved but surpassed in its first year. But the chances it produced were already being frittered away even as the silents died. Quantity soon exceeded (indeed almost obliterated) quality.

There were bright spots, of course. Alfred Hitchcock's *Blackmail*, the first British all-talkie, was much admired, although it is its scenes that are virtually without dialogue that work best today; and even its celebrated 'knife' sequence (repeated use of the word in a fairly ordinary conversation throws the heroine into bird-like panic) was a happy extension of an idea that 'Hitch' had already had for the silent version of the film.

The better qualities of E.A. Dupont's *Atlantic* and *Picca-dilly* also lay in their visuals, the dialogue scenes in the former seeming quite laughable now. But Balcon had an early sound success with *The Wrecker*, which contained exciting use of natural sound. And, although some careers (notably those of actresses, such as Mabel Poulton, Estelle Brody, Lilian Hall Davis - who committed suicide in 1933 - Alma Taylor, Chrissie White and, for a while, even Betty Balfour, most popular of 1920s stars) were virtually halted by sound, there were still popular idols: charismatic Ivor Novello, soon to return to the stage where he was worshipped; dark, brooding John Stuart who had the common touch and would work in the British cinema for nearly 60 years; and dominant, moustachioed, tragic Jameson Thomas, who went to Hollywood in 1931, where he never attained similar stardom, and died from tuberculosis in 1939.

Other idols, though, would soon take their places, with distinctive voices and personalities, almost all from working-class backgrounds. But for the moment, the British cinema continued on the path it had taken since the First World War - into the dark.

THE TWENTIES

ALF'S CARPET (1929) [2]
Dir *W. P. Kellino*. Scr *Val Valentine, Arthur Leclerq, Blanche Metcalf, from a novel by W. A. Darlington*. Ph *Theodor Sparkuhl*. PC *BIP*. Dis *Wardour. 65 mins. Cert U*
Fairish comedy vehicle for Danish comedians Pat (*Carl Schenstrom*) and Patachon (*Harold Madsen*), here billed as Long and Short. They play two hapless busmen who find a magic carpet, fly away on it to the kingdom of Amamikon, and rescue the heroine's father from hostile natives. A variation on Darlington's *Alf's Button*. Part-talkie only.
RoC *Janice Adair, Gerald Rawlinson, Gladys Hamer, Philip Howland, Frank Parfitt, Edward O'Neill*.

THE AMERICAN PRISONER (1929) [4]
Dir *Thomas Bentley*. Scr *Eliot Stannard, Garnett Weston*. Ph *René Guissart*. PC *BIP*. Dis *Wardour. 76 mins. Cert U*
1815: among the prisoners in Dartmoor jail during the Napoleonic wars is Stark (*Carl Brisson*), a Danish-American officer. He escapes and falls in love with a squire's daughter (*Madeleine Carroll*) whom he also saves from death.
RoC *Nancy Price, A. Bromley-Davenport, Cecil Barry, Reginald Fox, Charles Ashton, Carl Harbord, Harry Terry, John Valentine, Robert English, Edmond Dignon, Lucius Ashton*.

ATLANTIC (1929) [4]
Dir and Prod *E A. Dupont*. Scr *Victor Kendall, from a play by Ernest Raymond*. Ph *Charles Rosher*. PC *BIP*. Dis *Wardour. 91 mins. Cert A*
Creakily acted, but dramatic and well-staged story of the sinking of a great liner, which goes down after colliding with an iceberg in the Atlantic Ocean. Based, of course, on the 'Titanic' disaster of 1912. Exteriors were shot in the London Docks.
LP *Madeleine Carroll, John Stuart, Franklin Dyall, John Longden, Donald Calthrop, Sydney Lynn, Monty Banks, D. A. Clarke-Smith, Joan Barry, Helen Haye, Francis Lister, Ellaline Terriss, Arthur Hardy, Syd Crossley, Dino Galvani, Danny Green, René Ray*.

AULD LANG SYNE (1929) [3]
Dir and Prod *George Pearson*. Scr *Pearson, Hugh E. Wright, Patrick L. Mannock*. Ph *Bernard Knowles*. PC *Welsh-Pearson-Elder*. Dis *Famous-Lasky. 75 mins. Cert U*
Six songs, synchronized with earlier records, were hastily added to this silent vehicle for Sir Harry Lauder, the famous Scots entertainer. He's Sandy McTavish, a puritanical farmer, who comes to London thinking that his son Angus (*Pat Aherne*) is studying chemistry (he's a boxer) and that his daughter Marie (*Dodo Watts*) is a nurse (she's become a dancer). Ructions ensue. . . .
RoC *Dorothy Boyd, Hugh E. Wright*.

BALACLAVA (1928)
(USA: *Jaws of Hell*) [4]
Dir *Maurice Elvey, Milton Rosmer*. Prod *Michael Balcon*. Scr *V. Gareth Gundrey, W. P. Lipscomb, Boyd Cable, Angus Macphail, Milton Rosmer, Robert Stevenson*. Ph *Percy Strong*. PC *Gainsborough*. Dis *W & F. 94 mins. Cert U*
Spectacular historical adventure, set against the Crimean War, in which an army officer (*Cyril McLaglen*) is cashiered, re-enlists as a private and is instrumental in the capture of a notorious spy. Action ends with the Charge of the Light Brigade. Made in colour, but shown black and white. Silent, with sound sequences added (in New York).
RoC *Benita Hume, Miles Mander, Alf Goddard, J. Fisher White, Robert Holmes, Walter Patch, Clifford Mollison, Betty Bolton, Boris Ranevsky, Henry Mollison, H. StBarbe West, Wallace Bosco, Marian Drada, Eugene Leahy*.

BLACKMAIL (1929) [6]
Dir *Alfred Hitchcock*. Prod *John Maxwell*. Scr *Hitchcock, Charles Bennett, Benn W. Levy, Garnett Weston, from a play by Bennett*. Ph *Jack Cox*. PC *BIP*. Dis *Wardour. 96 mins. Cert A*

John Longden and Anny Ondra in Blackmail *(1929)*

Britain's first all-talkie feature, a brooding, exciting Hitchcock thriller about a girl (*Anny Ondra*), who stabs an artist (*Cyril Ritchard*) who attempts to rape her, then falls foul of a blackmailer (*Donald Calthrop*). He is pursued by the girl's detective fiancé (*John Longden*) and falls to his death through the domed roof of the British Museum. Future directors Ronald Neame and Michael Powell were clapper boy and stills cameraman respectively on this landmark production with innovative use of sound.
RoC *Sara Allgood, Charles Paton, Hannah Jones, Harvey Braban (in silent version: Sam Livesey), Phyllis Monkman, Johnny Butt, Percy Parsons, Alfred Hitchcock*. Anny Ondra's voice: *Joan Barry*.

CITY OF PLAY (1929) [3]
Dir *Denison Clift*. Prod *Michael Balcon*. Scr *Clift, Angus Macphail*. Ph *Claude MacDonnell*. PC *Gainsborough*. Dis *W & F. 80 mins. Cert A*
Melodramatic Trilby-and-Svengali-like story of a showman who has a pretty trapeze artist under his hypnotic power. A young officer tries to free the girl from his influence, but is shot and wounded by his adversary, who is finally killed by a snake unleashed by his discarded mistress. Part-talkie only.
LP *Chili Bouchier, W. Lawson Butt, Pat Aherne, James Carew, Leila Dresner, Olaf Hytten, Renée Clama, Harold Huth, Andrews Englemann*.

THE CLUE OF THE NEW PIN (1929) [4]
Dir *Arthur Maude*. Prod *S.W. Smith*. Scr *Kathleen Hayden, from the novel by Edgar Wallace*. Ph *Horace Wheddon*. PC *British Lion*. Dis *Producers' Distributing Corporation. 81 mins. Cert A*
Britain's first talking picture using sound-on-disc, a system soon to be outdistanced by sound-on-film. The body of a wealthy eccentric is found by his nephew in a locked vault, the key to which is on a table beside the corpse. A will is discovered leaving everything to the dead man's ward (*Benita Hume*). She heads the list of suspects – but the nephew turns out to be the killer.
RoC *Kim Peacock, Donald Calthrop, John Gielgud, H. Saxon-Snell, Johnny Butt, Colin Kenney, Fred Rains, Caleb Porter*.

COMETS (1929) [2]
Dir *Sasha Geneen*. Prod *Maurice J. Wilson*. PC *Alpha*. Dis *Jury-Metro-Goldwyn. 68 mins. Cert U*
A variety revue which contains early appearances by *Elsa Lanchester* and *Charles Laughton*,

as well as sketches from *Heather Thatcher*, *Jack Raine* and *Randle Ayrton* and comedy and musical acts.

RoC *Albert Sandler, Billy Merson, Flora le Breton, Rex Evans, Gus McNaughton, Noni & Horace, Marie Monighetti, Strelsky's Cossacks, Tiller Girls, Golden Serenaders.*

THE CO-OPTIMISTS (1929) [1]

Dir *Edwin Greenwood, Laddie Cliff*. Prod *Gordon Craig*. Scr *Laddie Cliff, Melville Gideon*. Ph *Sydney Blythe, Basil Emmott*. PC and Dis *New Era. 83 mins. Cert U*

Britain's first talkie revue, a version of the celebrated show which had just toured the country when the film appeared. It took a slating from the critics, who complained of poorly-chosen material.

LP *Laddie Cliff, Davy Burnaby, Stanley Holloway, Gilbert Childs, Elsa MacFarlane, Melville Gideon, Peggy Petronella, Betty Chester, Phyllis Monkman, Harry S. Pepper.*

Stanley Holloway and Elsa MacFarlane in The Co-Optimists (*1929*)

A COTTAGE ON DARTMOOR (1929)
(USA: *Escaped from Dartmoor*) [2]

Dir and Scr *Anthony Asquith*. Prod *H. Bruce Woolfe*. Ph *Stanley Rodwell, M. Lindblom*. PC *British Instructional/Swedish Biograph*. Dis *Pro Patria. 75 mins. Cert A*

Two men, a barber and a farmer, love the same girl. She marries the farmer, and the barber is jailed for accidentally wounding his rival, whom he had threatened. Three years later, he escapes, is sheltered by the girl and her husband, but decides life is not worth living without her and lets himself be shot by police. Condemned by contemporary critics as being excessively arty, the film has subsequently been re-evaluated. Sound synchronized in Berlin.

LP *Norah Baring, Uno Henning, Hans Schlettow, Judd Green.*

THE CRIMSON CIRCLE (1929) [3]

Dir *Friedrich Zelnik*. Scr *Edgar Wallace, from his novel*. Ph *Karl Püth*. PC *British Talking Pictures*. Dis *BIFD. 68 mins. Cert A*

Inspector Parr (*Stewart Rome*) pursues a blackmail gang whose mastermind works under the sign of a crimson circle. Assisted by a girl (*Lya Mara*) who is arrested for murder, escapes and pursues a vital clue, he finally unmasks the master crook. The second of three

versions of an Edgar Wallace crime thriller, shot in Berlin. Silent and sound versions made.

RoC *John Castle, Louis Lerch, Albert Steinruck, Hans Marlow, Otto Wallburg.*

THE CROOKED BILLET (1929) [4]

Dir *Adrian Brunel*. Prod *Michael Balcon*. Scr *Angus Macphail, from a play by Dion Titherage*. Ph *Claude MacDonnell*. PC *Gainsborough*. Dis *W & F. 80 mins. Cert A*

The efforts of an international spy (*Carlyle Blackwell*) to steal vital documents are thwarted by a British nobleman (*Frank Goldsmith*), his daughter (*Madeleine Carroll*) and the secret service agent (*Miles Mander*) in love with her. Filmed silent: sound added to second half of the film in 1929.

RoC *Gordon Harker, Kim Peacock, Raymond Massey, Helen Langton, Alexander Field, Margaret Yarde, Danny Green.*

DARK RED ROSES (1929) [3]

Dir *Sinclair Hill*. Scr *Leslie Howard Gordon, Harcourt Templeman*. Ph *A. Virago*. PC *British Sound Film Productions*. Dis *British Instructional. 67 mins. Cert A*

Shades of *The Hands of Orlac*, as a young pianist falls in love with the wife of a sculptor. The sculptor plans to reward him with the loss of his hands. ... Musical interludes punctuate the heated proceedings.

LP *Stewart Rome, Frances Doble, Hugh Eden, Kate Cutler, Una O'Connor, Anton Dolin, Lydya Lopokova, Sydney Morgan, Jill Clayton, Jack Clayton, Georges Balanchine.*

Stewart Rome and Jill Clayton in Dark Red Roses (*1929*)

THE DEVIL'S MAZE (1929) [2]

Dir and Prod *V. Gareth Gundrey*. Scr *Sewell Collins, from a play by G. R. Malloch*. Ph *Percy Strong*. PC and Dis *Gaumont-British. 82 mins. Cert A*

Glum drama of a girl who, to save her lover's wife's feelings, fastens the blame for her preg-

nancy on a disappeared explorer. When he returns, she loses the baby and tries (but fails) to commit suicide.

LP *Renée Clama, Trilby Clark, Hayford Hobbs, Ian Fleming, Gerald Rawlinson, Davy Burnaby.*

THE FEATHER (1929) [2]

Dir and Scr *Leslie Hiscott, from a novel by C. M. Matheson*. Prod *Julius Hagen*. Ph *Basil Emmott*. PC *Strand*. Dis *United Artists. 88 mins. Cert A*

An unhappily married insurance agent (*Jameson Thomas*) becomes infatuated with an attractive widow (*Vera Flory*) and embezzles from his firm to pay for her singing lessons in Rome to make her an opera singer.

RoC *Randle Ayrton, Mary Clare, James Reardon, W. Cronin Wilson, Charles Paton, Irene Tripod, Grace Lane.*

THE FLYING SCOTSMAN (1929) [4]

Dir *Castleton Knight*. Scr *Joe Grossman, Victor Kendall, Garnett Weston*. Ph *Theodor Sparkuhl*. PC *BIP*. Dis *Warner Bros. 61 mins. Cert U*

Engine driver Bob White (*Moore Marriott*) of the London-Edinburgh run reports his fireman Crow (*Alec Hurley*) for drunkenness. When the Flying Scotsman steams out of Kings Cross on the last day of Bob's railway service, Crow is on board. He means to wreck it. But he is spotted by Bob's daughter Joan (*Pauline Johnson*) who, with the help of her boyfriend Jim (*Raymond Milland*), saves the day. Made silent: sound added in 1930.

RoC *Dino Galvani, Billy Shine.*

THE HATE SHIP (1929) [2]

Dir *Norman Walker*. Scr *Monckton Hoffe, Eliot Stannard, Benn W. Levy, from a novel by Bruce Graeme*. Ph *René Guissart*. PC *BIP*. Dis *First National-Pathé. 83 mins. Cert A*

Ingenious but stodgy whodunnit in which a murder is intended on board a yacht when a certain key is depressed on the piano. But the attempt misfires and the captain (*Randle Ayrton*) uncovers a complicated web of hatred, death and revenge. Partly filmed on board a real yacht.

RoC *Jameson Thomas, Jean Colin, Jack Raine,*

Henry Victor, Carl Harbord, Edna Davies, Allan Jeayes, Maria Minetti, Charles Dormer, Ivo Dawson, Syd Crossley.

HIGH SEAS (1929)   3

Dir *Denison Clift.* Scr *Clift, Victor Kendall.* Ph *Claude MacDonnell.* PC *BIP.* Dis *First National-Pathé.* 71 mins. Cert A

Love, hatred, mutiny and shipwreck on the ocean, as a Press baron plots to wreck ships for the insurance money, and in so doing ruins the ship-master father of his son's fiancée. Filmed silent: sound added the following year.

LP *John Stuart, Lillian Rich, Randle Ayrton, Winter Hall, Janet Alexander, James Carew, Daisy Campbell.*

HIGH TREASON (1929)   4

Dir *Maurice Elvey.* Prod and Scr *L'Estrange Fawcett, from a play by Noel Pemberton-Billing.* PC and Dis *Gaumont-British.* 90 mins. Cert A

Critical opinion was mixed, but this futuristic drama was nothing if not imaginative in its story of a league of women trying successfully to stop the Second World War breaking out between super-powers in 1940. In life, alas, fiction did not parallel reality.

LP *Benita Hume, Jameson Thomas, Basil Gill, Humberston Wright, Henry Vibart, James Carew, Milton Rosmer, Alf Goddard, Walter Patch, Irene Rooke, Kiyoshi Takase, Hayford Hobbs, Judd Green, Clifford Heatherley, René Ray.*

I

THE INFORMER (1929)   3

Dir *Arthur Robison.* Scr *Benn W. Levy, Rolfe E. Vanlo, from a play by Liam O'Flaherty.* Ph *Werner Brandes, Theodor Sparkuhl, L. Rodgers.* PC *BIP.* Dis *Wardour.* 85 mins. Cert A

Ireland, 1920: IRA man Gypo (*Lars Hansen*) is badly in need of money to flee to America. He betrays a colleague who has killed a man to the authorities, believing (falsely) that the killer has stolen his girl. Not nearly so successful as John Ford's Hollywood-made version of the story in 1935. Critics grumbled, with some justification, that, with a German director and foreign principals, the film lacked Irish atmosphere.

RoC *Lya de Putti, Carl Harbord, Warwick Ward, Janice Adair, Dennis Wyndham, Mickey Brantford, Daisy Campbell, Craighall Sherry, Ellen Pollock, Johnny Butt.*

J

JUNO AND THE PAYCOCK (1929)   5
(USA: *The Shame of Mary Boyle*)

Dir *Alfred Hitchcock.* Prod *John Maxwell.* Scr *Alma Reville, Hitchcock, Sean O'Casey, from O'Casey's play.* Ph *Jack Cox.* PC *BIP.* Dis *Wardour.* 99 mins. Cert A

In the Irish 'Troubles' of the early twenties, a mother (*Sara Allgood*) is a helpless spectator as her family is ruined and broken. The dreams of her husband (*Edward Chapman*) are shattered, and her armless son (*John Laurie*) is shot as an informer.

RoC *Barry Fitzgerald, Kathleen O'Regan, John Longden, Donald Calthrop, Sydney Morgan, Maire O'Neill, Dave Morris, Fred Schwartz, Dennis Wyndham.*

K

KITTY (1928)   3

Dir and Prod *Victor Saville.* Scr *Violet E. Powell from a novel by Warwick Deeping.* Dialogue *Benn W. Levy.* Ph *Karl Püth.* PC *Burlington.* Dis *Wardour.* 90 mins. Cert U

Weepie about an RAF pilot (*John Stuart*) who marries a shopkeeper's daughter (*Estelle Brody*) to the fury of his snobbish mother (*Marie Ault*), whose lying letters to him while serving in France during the First World War cause him to crash. Paralysed in both legs, he is 'imprisoned' by his mother, but kidnapped by his young wife, who teaches him to walk again. Silent, with dialogue sequences (added in New York).

RoC *Dorothy Cumming, Moore Marriott, Winter Hall, Olaf Hytten, Gibb McLaughlin, Charles O'Shaughnessy, E.F. Bostwick, Rex*

John Stuart and Estelle Brody in Kitty *(1928)*

Maurice, Jerrold Robertshaw, Charles Ashton, Charles Levey.

A KNIGHT IN LONDON (1929)   3

Dir *Lupu Pick.* Prod *Ludwig Blattner.* Scr *Charles Lincoln.* Ph *Karl Freund.* PC *Blattner Pictures.* Dis *Warner Bros.* 75 mins (*British version: 74 mins*). Cert A

Made in Germany, this romantic trifle had sound added in 1930, with music by Edward Kunneke. The popular *Lilian Harvey* plays a girl staying at a London hotel, whose visit to the wrong room results in a series of complications that have a prince and a commoner vying for her hand. German title (rather strangely translated): *Eine Nacht in London.*

RoC *Ivy Duke, Robin Irvine, Bernard Nedell, Robert English, Zena Dare, The Hon. Angela Brett.*

L

THE LADY FROM THE SEA (1929)   4

Dir *Castleton Knight.* Scr *Garnett Weston, Victor Kendall.* Ph *James Rogers, Jack Cox, Theodor Sparkuhl.* PC *Famous-Lasky.* Dis *Paramount.* 62 mins. Cert U

Romantic drama of the Goodwin sands, centring on a lifeboatman who rescues an attractive French girl, falls in love with her and neglects his sweetheart. In the end he redeems himself. Filmed silent: sound added the following year.

LP *Moore Marriott, Mona Goya, Raymond Milland, Bruce Gordon, Eugenie Amami, Anita Graham, Wilfrid Shine.*

THE LADY OF THE LAKE (1928)   4

Dir *James A. Fitzpatrick.* Prod *Michael Balcon.* Scr *Fitzpatrick, Angus Macphail, from the poem by Sir Walter Scott.* PC *Gainsborough.* Dis *Select.* 57 mins. Cert U

Atmospheric picturization of Scott's epic poem, set in the West Highlands of Scotland in the sixteenth century, where Ellen (*Benita Hume*), daughter of an exiled lord (*Douglas Paine*), wins favour for her father by saving King James V of Scotland (*Percy Marmont*) from an outlaw band.

RoC *Haddon Mason, Lawson Butt, Hedda Bartlett, James Carew, Leo Dryden, J. Nelson Ramsay.*

THE LAST POST (1928)   2

Dir and Prod *Dinah Shurey.* Scr *Lydia Hayward.* Ph *D.P. Cooper.* PC *Britannia.* Dis *Gaumont.* 89 mins. Cert A

Sound was added to this silent movie late in 1929, but it can hardly have been worth the effort for what one contemporary critic described as 'sentimental sob-stuff', chiefly notable for having been written and directed by

women. *John Longden* plays a dual role, the wastrel of the two finally reforming to take his brother's place in front of a firing squad.
RoC *Cynthia Haynes, Frank Vosper, J. Fisher White, Alf Goddard, A.B. Imeson, John Butt, Agnes Brantford.*

NUMBER SEVENTEEN (1928)
Dir *Geza M. Bolvary.* Prod *Josef Somlo.* Scr *Bolvary,* from the play by *J. Jefferson Farjeon.* PC *Fellner & Somlo.* Dis *W & F. 72 mins. Cert A*
Remade four years later by Alfred Hitchcock to somewhat greater effect, this is the first film version of Farjeon's play about an itinerant seaman (*Guy Newall*) who with the assistance of a reformed girl crook, helps the police to bring a gang of jewel thieves to book. An Anglo-German film, made silent in Germany, with sound added in 1929.
RoC *Lien Dyers, Fritz Greiner, Hertha von Walter, Carl de Vogt, Craighall Sherry, Ernst Neicher, Frederick Solm.*

PICCADILLY (1929)
Dir and Prod *E.A. Dupont.* Scr *Arnold Bennett.* Ph *Werner Brandes.* PC *BIP.* Dis *Wardour. 105 mins. Cert A*
Stylized, stylish crime melodrama, much admired for its panache and impressive nightclub settings (Art director: Alfred Jünge). A cabaret owner creates jealousy between two of his female dancers, one of whom is found murdered. Suspicion falls on two innocent people until the real culprit is unmasked. Made as a silent; sound added the following year.
LP *Anna May Wong, Jameson Thomas, Gilda Gray, Cyril Ritchard, King Ho Chang, Hannah Jones, Charles Laughton, Ellen Pollock, Harry Terry, Gordon Begg, Charles Paton, Raymond Milland, Debroy Somers and His Band.*

THE PLAYTHING (1929)
Dir *Castleton Knight.* Scr *Violet E. Powell from a play by Arthur Black.* Ph *James Rogers.* PC *BIP.* Dis *Wardour. 78 mins. Cert U*
Staid and sober Wallace (*Nigel Barrie*) falls for flighty flapper Joyce (*Estelle Brody*), joins her smart set to win her heart, but finds only disillusionment. Weakish romantic drama lifted

a little by the smart production design of N. Arnold. Part-talkie only.
RoC *Heather Hatcher, Marguerite Allan, John St John, Raymond Milland.*

'Q' SHIPS (1928)
Dir *Geoffrey Barkas, Michael Barringer.* Prod *Gordon Craig.* Scr *Barringer.* Ph *Sydney Blythe.* PC *New Era.* Dis *National. 88 mins. Cert U*
First World War action drama in which British warships, disguised as merchant vessels, create havoc among German U-boats along the Flanders coastline. Lt Cdr Harold Auten and Earl Jellicoe acted as technical advisers on this lively film, with *Auten* also taking a small acting role. Filmed silent; sound added in 1932, when the film was reissued as *Blockade*.
RoC *Johnny Butt, J.P. Kennedy, Philip Hewland, Roy Travers, Charles Emerald, Val Gielgud, Alec Hurley, Lionel d'Aragon, Douglas Herald, George Turner, Terence O'Brien, Hugh Douglas.*

THE RETURN OF THE RAT (1929)
Dir *Graham Cutts.* Prod *Michael Balcon.* Scr *Angus Macphail.* Ph *Roy Overbaugh.* PC *Gainsborough.* Dis *W & F. 84 mins. Cert A*
The last of *Ivor Novello's* three films as the Paris Apaché gangster The Rat. In this story, he has deserted the underworld to marry Zelie (*Isabel Jeans*), a lady of fashion. It does not work out and he returns to his old haunts, falling in love with a barmaid (*Mabel Poulton*) and being challenged to a duel by his wife's lover (*Bernard Nedell*).
RoC *Marie Ault, Gordon Harker, Gladys Frazin, Harry Terry, 'Scotch' Kelly.*

A ROMANCE OF SEVILLE (1929)
Dir *Norman Walker.* Scr *Garnett Weston, Alma Reville.* Ph *Claude Friese-Greene.* PC *BIP.* Dis *First National-Pathé. Colour. 62 mins. Cert U*
This rare colour film, made on location in Andalusia, features the Egyptian-born actor *Alex D'Arcy,* who subsequently made films all over the world in a 45-year career. He plays a jewel thief whose mistress has a fatal fascination for

an artist prepared to throw up his own fiancée for her.
RoC *Marguerite Allan, Randle Ayrton, Eugenie Amami, Cecil Barry, Koblenzova, Hugh Eden.*

SPLINTERS (1929)
Dir *Jack Raymond.* Prod *Herbert Wilcox.* Scr *W.P. Lipscomb.* PC *British and Dominions.* Dis *W & F. 82 mins. Cert U*
A film version of the famous concert party which was formed by serving soldiers and entertained troops during the First World War. Comedian *Hal Jones* and female impersonator *Reg Stone* appear in their original roles.
RoC *Nelson Keys, Sydney Howard, George Baker, Lew Lake, Walter Glynne, Wilfred Temple, Sidney Grantham.*

TAXI FOR TWO (1929)
Dir *Alexander Esway, Denison Clift.* Prod *Michael Balcon.* Scr *Esway, Ian Dalrymple, Angus Macphail.* Ph *Jimmy Wilson.* PC *Gainsborough.* Dis *W & F. 74 mins. Cert U*
Romantic comedy, part-talkie, in which a titled lady's son (*John Stuart*) is attracted to the girl (*Mabel Poulton*) who gets a reward for returning his mother's missing necklace. He poses as a chauffeur and the girl hires him to drive the taxi she buys with the money. Store scenes shot in Harrods.
RoC *Gordon Harker, Anne Grey, Renée Clama, Grace Lane, Claude Maxten.*

TESHA (1928)
Dir and Prod *Victor Saville.* Scr *Saville, Walter C. Mycroft* (titles for silent version: *Arthur Wimperis*). Ph *Werner Brandes.* PC *BIP-Burlington.* Dis *Wardour. 87 mins. Cert A*
Hungarian star *Maria Corda* featured in this adaptation of Countess Barcynska's famous melodramatic novel about the life and loves of a Russian ballerina. Sound was added in 1929.
RoC *Jameson Thomas, Paul Cavanagh, Clifford Heatherley, Daisy Campbell, Mickey Brantford, Espinosa, Bunty Fosse, Boris Ranevsky.*

THOSE WHO LOVE (1929)
Dir *Manning Haynes.* Scr *Lydia Hayward, from a novel by Guy Fletcher.* PC *BIP.* Dis *First National-Pathé. 87 mins. Cert A*

Mary (*Blanche Adele*), fiancée of author David Mellor (*William Freshman*), dies, leaving him a broken man. He marries a prostitute (also *Blanche Adele*) because of the resemblance, but she has committed bigamy and tragedy looms. Dated melodrama filmed silent, then made into part-talkie; hardly worth it.
RoC *Lawson Butt, Carol Goodney, Hannah Jones, Dino Galvani.*

THE THREE PASSIONS (1928)   ☐3
Dir and Scr *Rex Ingram.* Prod *Ingram, Alastair Mackintosh.* Ph *L. H. Burel.* PC *St George's.* Dis *Allied Artists. 94 mins. Cert A*
Estranged from his father, a wealthy noble who owns a shipyard, young Philip Burlington (*Ivan Petrovitch*) devotes himself to helping the down-and-outs of a seaman's mission. But father and son are reunited in greater understanding after a strike at the shipyard. Filmed silent in France; sound added the following year.
Roc *Alice Terry, Shayle Gardner, Leslie Faber, Claire Eames, Andrews Englemann, Gerald Fielding.*

TO WHAT RED HELL (1929)   ☐3
Dir *Edwin Greenwood.* Prod *Julius Hagen.* Scr *Leslie Hiscott from a play by Percy Robinson.* Ph *Basil Emmott.* PC *Strand.* Dis *Tiffany. 100 mins. Cert A*
Sombre story of an epileptic (*John Hamilton*) shielded by his mother (*Sybil Thorndike*) after he kills a girl in a fit. Her lover is condemned for the crime, but at the eleventh hour the guilty man confesses and commits suicide. Silent footage scrapped, and film re-shot as talkie.
RoC *Bramwell Fletcher, Jillian Sande, Janice Adair, Arthur Pusey, Matthew Boulton, Athole Stewart, Drusilla Wills, Wyn Weaver, Sara Allgood.*

John Hamilton and Sybil Thorndike in To What Red Hell *(1929)*

UNDER THE GREENWOOD TREE (1929)   ☐4
Dir *Harry Lachman.* Scr *Lachman, Rex Taylor, Frank Launder, Monkton Hoffe.* Ph *Claude Friese-Greene.* PC *BIP.* Dis *Wardour. 101 mins. Cert U*
Thomas Hardy's multi-faceted rural drama which would surely have been ideal material for an Ealing comedy of 20 years later. The introduction of an organ into a Dorset church in 1870 leads to the dismissal of the local orchestra. . . .
LP *Marguerite Allan* (voice: *Peggie Robb-Smith*), *John Batten, Nigel Barrie, Wilfred Shine, Maud Gill, Robert Abel, Antonia Brough, Tom Coventry, Billy Shine, Robison Page, Tubby Phillips, Sid Ellery, Harry Stafford, Queenie Leighton.*

THE VAGABOND QUEEN (1929)   ☐3
Dir *Geza von Bolvary.* Scr *Rex Taylor, Val Valentine.* Ph *Charles Rosher.* PC *BIP.* Dis *Wardour. 62 mins. Cert U*
A comedy variation on *The Prisoner of Zenda*, with *Betty Balfour* as a London boarding-house skivvy who impersonates her double, a European princess, so that a plot to assassinate her at her coronation can be foiled. Filmed silent in Germany; some sound added in 1930, and film reissued as part-talkie in 1931.
RoC *Harry Terry, Glen Byam Shaw, Ernest Thesiger, Charles Dormer, Dino Galvani, Ralph Leslie.*

WHITE CARGO (1929)   ☐2
Dir and Prod *J. B. Williams, Arthur Barnes.* Scr *Williams, from a play by Leon Gordon and a novel by Vera Simonton.* Ph *Karl Püth.* PC *Neo-Art Productions.* Dis *Williams and Pritchard. 88 mins. Cert A*

More torpid than torrid, this version of the famous pot-boiler was made with rather more success by Hollywood in 1942 with Hedy Lamarr. Weston (*Leslie Faber*), manager of a West African rubber plantation, marries a half-caste girl (*Gypsy Rhouma*) and becomes a derelict. The girl is caught trying to poison him and forced to take the poison herself. A broken Weston is shipped home as 'white cargo'. Filmed in silent and sound versions.
RoC *Maurice Evans, John Hamilton, Henry de Vries, Humberston Wright, Tom Helmore, Sebastian Smith, George Turner.*

THE WOMAN HE SCORNED (1929)   ☐3
(USA: *The Way of Lost Souls*)
Dir *Paul Czinner.* Prod and Scr *Charles Whittaker.* PC *Charles Whittaker Productions.* Dis *Warner Bros. 94 mins. Cert U*
Pola Negri's first British film casts her as Louise, a prostitute who supports a gambler, but seeks a quieter married life with a lighthouse keeper in Cornwall. When the gambler becomes a fugitive, she shelters him, but he is killed and, rejected by her husband, Louise drowns herself.
RoC *Warwick Ward, Hans Rehmann, Cameron Carr, Margaret Rawlings.*

WOMAN TO WOMAN (1929)   ☐3
Dir and Scr *Victor Saville, from a play by Michael Morton.* Prod *Saville, Michael Balcon.* PC *Gainsborough/Burlington/Tiffany/Stahl.* Dis *W & F. 90 mins. Cert A*
Balcon, Saville and star *Betty Compson* shot this remake of their 1923 hit of the same name while the two Britons were in Hollywood. Miss Compson repeated her role of the French girl who has a love affair with an English officer in the First World War with tear-drenched consequences, but the story was not so successful second time round.
RoC *George Barraud, Juliette Compton, Winter Hall, Marguerite Chambers, George Billings.*

WOULD YOU BELIEVE IT! (1929)   ☐3
Dir *Walter Forde.* Prod *Archibald Nettlefold.* Scr *Forde, H. Fowler Mear.* Ph *Geoffrey Faithfull.* PC *Nettlefold.* Dis *Butchers. 56 mins. Cert U*
Unsubtle comedy lark, with *Walter Forde* as the inventor of a wireless tank control which goes wrong, so that the tank runs amok and demolishes everything in its path. Fortunately for him, it also helps him foil the plans of a gang of spies.
RoC *Pauline Johnson, Arthur Stratton, Albert Brouett, Anita Sharp Bolster, Anita O'Day.*

THE WRECKER (1928)   ☐5
Dir *Geza M. Bolvary.* Prod *Michael Balcon.* Scr *Angus Macphail, from a play by Arnold Ridley and Bernard Merivale.* Ph *Otto Kanturek.* PC *Gainsborough.* Dis *W & F. 74 mins. Cert U*
A series of spectacular train wrecks provides a strong start to this melodrama, in which railway employees Roger Doyle (*Joseph Striker*) and Mary Dalton (*Benita Hume*) prove sabotage by the railway's manager, who secretly

heads a motor-coach company in competition. Filmed silent; sound added in 1929 at RCA Studios in New York.
RoC *Carlyle Blackwell, Gordon Harker, Pauline Johnson, Winter Hall, Leonard Thompson.*

YELLOW STOCKINGS (1928)   1
Dir *Theodor Komisarjevsky.* Prod *George Pearson.* Scr *Fred Paul, Alicia Ramsay, from a novel* by *Wilson McArthur.* PC *Welsh-Pearson-Elder.* Dis *Famous-Lasky. 87 mins. Cert A*
The title seems to have been about the best thing in this dismal romantic drama, shot silent, but released as a part-talkie two years later. An adventurer pursues a woman who is unaware she is about to become an heiress.
LP *Percy Marmont, Marjorie Mars, Enid Stamp-Taylor, Marie Ault, Georges Galli, J. R. Tozer, Franklin Bellamy, Lydia Sherwood, May Calvin, Elizabeth Kerr.*

SHORTS

Sound films between 20 and 39 minutes' duration released in 1929

Josser KC (30)
More, Please (27)

Mr Smith Wakes Up (25)
Popular Pieces (23)

The Third Gun (36)
The Unwritten Law (30)

The Thirties

Eric Maturin and Trilby Clarke in *The Squeaker* (1930)

The Thirties

INTRODUCTION TO THE DECADE

About 100 British feature films were released in 1930. Of these, a mere dozen were silents. Despite continued campaigns in some periodicals for peaceful co-existence of silence and sound, the silent film was clearly in its death throes. Some stubborn producers, such as John Argyle, tried to keep the silent flag waving. But they were not among the film world's most powerful men and their small voices were soon drowned by the new sensation: talkies.

Massive new studio complexes blossomed forth as if in stop-motion photography, dotting the English countryside. Ealing was built in 1930 and opened the following year, with Basil Dean's Associated Talking Pictures (ATP) occupying its four stages. Gaumont-British Studios at Shepherd's Bush were built in 1931 and opened in 1932 with Michael Balcon in charge of production. Pinewood (its most famous days, under The Rank Organization, yet to come) and Denham (a permanent home for Alexander Korda's prospering London Films, founded four years before) were built in 1935 and their facilities well-used even before the official openings in 1936. Lesser studios were legion.

Stars for the sound era, however, were slower to emerge and even harder to keep.

The combined lure of much more money, better opportunities and facilities and a seemingly idyllic lifestyle drew numerous British players to Hollywood in the early 1930s. Many of these were actresses who combined glamour and personality: Elizabeth Allan, Binnie Barnes, Heather Angel, Margot Grahame, Valerie Hobson, Wendy Barrie, Anne Grey, Molly Lamont, Pat Paterson, Merle Oberon and many more were grazing in the greener grass of the Hollywood hills by the middle of the decade.

But there was one who stayed. A bug-eyed, buck-toothed, long-legged, lithe-figured, enchantingly unspoiled musical star called Jessie Matthews, whose sex appeal and bubbly personality radiated into the same camera which proved so hostile to her contemporary (and, in a notorious court case, rival in love), Evelyn Laye.

Under the firm but loving guidance of director Victor Saville and cameraman Glen MacWilliams, little Miss Matthews projected her unique blend of innocence and sexuality that shaped her into Britain's only world star of the decade, in a series of lavishly mounted, peculiarly British musicals that combined a high-key Hollywood gloss with an affectionate Englishness, chiefly in the portrayals of their star: *The Good Companions*, *Evergreen*, *First a Girl* and *It's Love Again* were the prime examples.

Although the critical reception for these vehicles was sometimes less than fervent, public reaction to them was ecstatic on both sides of the Atlantic.

When Saville left Gaumont-British in 1936, Matthews' feature films began to slide. She must have regretted not accepting lucrative Hollywood offers (chiefly after the smash success of *Evergreen*) that would undoubtedly have made her an even bigger star and prolonged a career that was rapidly being torpedoed in the later 1930s by the direction of her then-husband Sonnie Hale, whom she later divorced in 1944.

Matthews' only serious rivals in her peak years were Anna Neagle and Gracie Fields, neither of whom ever made as big an impact in the world arena, even when they finally went to America (Neagle in 1939, Fields in 1940). Both of these contrasting stars, however, enjoyed great bursts of popularity in Britain.

Regal Neagle, under the guidance of shrewd producer/director Herbert Wilcox, whom she would later marry, was at her best as historical characters - *Nell Gwyn* and *Peg of Old Drury* were two of her biggest popular successes. Her career temporarily slumped in the mid-1930s, and it needed two doses of Queen Victoria to restore it. It is interesting that her first film in Hollywood was as the First World War heroine Nurse Edith Cavell.

Gracie Fields was as at home in the backstreets of Blackpool as Anna Neagle was in the stately homes of England; her down-to-earth North Country friendliness and warmth, ego-deflating sense of humour and extraordinary singing voice (a cross between a chirp and an operatic trill) had made her Britain's highest-paid star by the end of the decade. Most of her best films were for Dean's ATP company, showing her as a working girl triumphing against the odds - and the bosses. A later alliance with 20th Century-Fox, intended to broaden her international appeal, had less happy results, until its last offering, *Shipyard Sally*, restored her to her natural habitat.

There were fewer home-grown male stars around in the decade, particularly of the dashing variety that appealed to female cinemagoers. Once again, the most charismatic of them - Ray Milland, Leslie Howard, Louis Hayward, George Sanders, Herbert Marshall, Brian Aherne, Charles Laughton, Patric Knowles and Ian Hunter - wasted little time in establishing themselves in Hollywood, although many of those whose love for the stage equalled their curiosity for the cinema (Laurence Olivier, Ralph Richardson, Robert Donat, John Clements, Rex Harrison, John Mills) were more frequently seen on British screens.

They were bolstered by lesser drawing-room types, Continental imports (and refugees from Nazi regimes), character stars and second-line Hollywood personalities seconded to the pursuit of the great god International Market.

The drawing-room, high-society tale, told in cultured accents and statically staged, was not least among the kind of presentations substantiating the bad name the great majority of British films had quickly built up among indigenous audiences following the coming of the quota.

Exhibitors and producers alike found that the public would only accept them in the guise of musicals or farces: thus the success of Jack Hulbert and Jack Buchanan, two upper-crust charmers who could sing and dance and clown in a likeable and entertaining, if by no means brilliant way; and the 'Aldwych farceurs', Tom Walls, Ralph Lynn and Robertson Hare (bluff, monocled and bald respectively), who transferred a long serious of Ben Travers farces - asinine capers that involved opening and closing doors, folding beds and falling trousers - lock, stock and barrel to the screen with amazing success. Hulbert's wife, angular Cicely Courtneidge, was popular too, with her endless energy, although her visit to Hollywood was pre-dictably an unhappy one.

Other comedians would soon, however, bring the accents and antics of working classes to British screens. The funniest and most timeless of these was bespectacled, befuddled Will Hay, usually seen as a charlatan quickly found out, and best when abetted by bewhiskered Moore Marriott and fat-boy Gra-ham Moffatt.

But the most successful in popular terms was Lancashire's ever-grinning George Formby, whose frantic slapstick and suggestive ditties, sung to the strumming of his ukulele, proved just the unsophisticated kind of tonic audiences required, and made him the number one British bet at the nation's box-office by the end of the decade.

Very few of these films, whether set in Mayfair or Man-chester, reflected any sort of real life, or dealt with social prob-lems in the way that Warner Brothers were doing on the other side of the Atlantic, although the Fields vehicles occasionally nudged the truth in the midst of their sentimental fervour. But something like a prison drama was unthinkable outside the context of Will Hay's *Convict 99*.

It was true that ordinary life was not what the average cinemagoer wanted to see; yet, towards the end of the decade, it became apparent that the strict divide between honest realism and entertainment *could* be breached, with the appearance of such films as *The Citadel*, *The Proud Valley* and *The Stars Look Down*.

That would have been unthinkable eight years earlier when inferior quota quickies had already glutted the market and it seemed that every other 55-minute screenplay was written by such speed specialists as Michael Barringer and Harry Fowler Mear, or directed by quota kings Leslie Hiscott and George King. They were to herald years of lost opportunities in which successes such as the Matthews musicals, the Aldwych farces, the Hitchcock thrillers and a few prestige hits from the Korda fold (such as *The Private Life of Henry VIII*) were merely the tip of an otherwise awful iceberg.

One Manchester cinema in 1935 flashed on a notice before a British 'B' picture, apologising for having to show it, as the quota compelled them to do so by law.

In a way, Charles Laughton's Oscar as Henry VIII - the first to be won by a British actor in a British film - was responsible for a false dawn: the entrée to the international film market which British movie-makers had been seeking. Money for the film industry, which had been in short supply, poured from the hands of rich investors convinced that the world was their oyster. In 1936 more than 200 British feature films were made and dumped on the home market, far more than it could hold, guaranteeing a further step towards financial disaster.

In the previous year, *128* new film-making companies were formed, many of them inevitably destined not to survive the imminent slump, which, ludicrous as it may now seem, was foreseen by only a few.

Even such relatively level-headed moguls as Alexander Korda, who scraped through the 1937 slump only to fall two years later, were blinded by the light of the 'new dawn'. Two years earlier in 1935, buoyed by financial backing from the giant Prudential company, Korda had allowed plans for his new studios at Denham to swell out of all proportion, including more than twice the number of sound stages he had originally envisaged, and with which his organisation could have coped. Walking through the finished complex, Korda is said to have sunk into a chair with his head in his hands and told a col-league: 'I have made a terrible mistake.' He had indeed, but it was too late to do anything but try to rent out enough of the white elephant to keep it going.

With Korda's London Films, as with other major studios, inferior bookkeeping and bad planning failed to draw the necessary-for-survival connections between popular success and financial profitability, or at least stability. The money in-volved was enormous for the time. In October 1936, 20 of the biggest production companies had a combined working capital of just under £1 million. Loans, mortgages and other invest-ments to the industry - the majority to these companies - totalled £12,500,000.

It was clearly a situation which placed the whole of the British film business at the mercy of its investors. Twickenham Studios called in a receiver early in 1937. Gaumont-British, well in the red, went out of business as a producer, having made, according to Balcon, 'mistaken decisions artistically, that proved financially unrewarding' (namely costly attempts to break into the international market). Balcon, a far-sighted prod-ucer, deservedly fell on his feet when called in to ATP to replace Basil Dean in 1938, after the latter had squandered thousands on disastrous vehicles for his young actress wife Victoria Hopper, in a British parallel to the W.R. Hearst-Marion Davies situation in Hollywood. The company was soon renamed Ealing Studios. BIP meanwhile made a fresh start under the title of its distributing company, Associated British.

The requirements of the quota were drastically re-shaped by a 1937 Act raising the British proportion of films to be shown, but adding stringent financial conditions which all but killed the quickie for an entire decade. For a while, late in 1937, there was almost nothing doing at all in any of the British studios.

Then, with the disappearance of foreign directors, cheap-skate producers and hack writers, new native talent began to make itself felt, to range alongside Alfred Hitchcock (firmly entrenched in the highly suspenseful thriller genre he had re-established in 1934 with *The Man Who Knew Too Much*), Victor Saville, Herbert Wilcox and the fading Walter Forde.

These younger directors, Carol Reed, Robert Stevenson, Michael Powell, David Macdonald, Arthur Woods and Pen Tennyson among them, were regarded as the coming cham-pions of the industry. But war would alter the pattern of things. Stevenson would go to America, taking his wife, actress Anna Lee, with him; Macdonald would never recapture the heights of pre-war years; Powell would prove a maverick in and out of critical favour; while Woods and Tennyson were destined to fall in the war. Only Reed would fulfil the potential of these 1937-9 years when the standard of the British film (admittedly in common with other prolific film-making nations) was of a more consistently high quality than ever before.

In September 1939, the blow fell. Britain was at war with Hitler's Germany. Suddenly, glamorous actresses accustomed to giving directions to wardrobe mistresses over their crinolines were saying that more than anything else they wanted to be ambulance drivers. Actors joined His Majesty's armed forces with alacrity, David Niven being the first to fly back from Hollywood to do so.

Those who left the country for America, or failed to return to England from trips overseas, in this darkest of hours, for whatever reasons, never quite regained the affection and esteem they had formerly enjoyed in the eyes of the British public. And, in Britain more than in Hollywood, the Forties set the cinema on a whole new course.

The Thirties
STAR OF THE DECADE

Jessie Matthews

A greengrocer's daughter born in the heart of London - Berwick Street, Soho, on 11 March 1907 - Jessie Matthews had already danced her way into the heart of millions by the time she was 21.

An early publicity shot at Gaumont-British studios in 1932

At an early age, it was apparent that she had a talent for dancing, and she was an on-stage performer at 12. Her first big breakthrough came in February 1925 when Gertrude Lawrence went down with double pneumonia and Miss Matthews, as her understudy, took over in the André Charlot Revue, then on tour in Canada. By this time, she had become an accomplished singer as well, her high, throbby tones giving emotional resonances to a song, hushing the theatre and holding audiences spellbound, especially with such a number as *My Heart Stood Still*.

By 1926 she was a West End Star, soon nicknamed 'The Dancing Divinity'. One of her great rivals was blonde Evelyn Laye whose husband, Sonnie Hale, Jessie would whisk from under her nose in a love affair that became a sensational court case in 1930. Evelyn Laye cited Miss Matthews in her divorce suit, and the judge referred to her as 'the woman Matthews' and thought her love letters revealed her as 'a person of odious mind'.

With her favourite (and best) director. Jessie Matthews and Victor Saville in 1933

The case hurt Jessie (who had already divorced her own first husband, revue star Henry Lytton Jr) in more ways than one. Her film career was at first a fairly low-key affair, musical numbers being incidental to such comedies as *There Goes the Bride* and *The Midshipmaid*. And even when her earliest film hit, *The Good Companions*, became the first talkie to be given a royal premiere, she was not presented to King George V and his wife Queen Mary.

These social barriers were not really swept aside until after the enormous success of *Evergreen*, a 1934 adaptation of her stage hit of 1930–31 (when the title was two words). The American show business magazine *Variety* called her 'Princess Personality ... the most sensational discovery in years' when the film opened to outstanding notices (and receipts) at the Radio City Music Hall in New York, making it the biggest British box-office success in America since *The Private Life of Henry VIII* a year earlier.

The score includes many of Jessie's best-remembered songs, including *Dancing on the Ceiling*, *Over My Shoulder*, *Tinkle, Tinkle, Tinkle* and *When You've Got a Little Springtime in Your Heart*.

Offers from Hollywood poured in. But Jessie, concerned for the stability of her marriage to Hale, whom she had married in 1931, decided to remain in Britain.

At first, the decision seemed justified when she followed *The Good Companions* and *Evergreen* with two more delightful musicals with the same director, Victor Saville - *First a Girl* and *It's Love Again*. Although her co-stars were negligible (perhaps deliberately so), Jessie had no difficulty in carrying the whole show with her extraordinarily charismatic vivacity, allied to the relaxed grace of her dancing and a collection of dazzlingly eye-catching costumes which showed off her exquisite figure and made even studio boss Michael Balcon nervous of public reaction.

'Hell, Mick,' Saville is said to have reassured him, 'we've got to sell that body.'

By this time, her screen image was in the loving care of American-born cinematographer Glen MacWilliams, who would photograph all of her remaining 1930s films except the last.

In 1936, a deal with M-G-M in Hollywood fell through, supposedly because Jessie was only to be one of several equally billed stars in a *Broadway Melody*-style musical. It would be her last chance to become a true world superstar. On her return to Gaumont-British, where her best musicals had been made, she found that Victor Saville had left over a pay dispute (he would direct her once more, in Hollywood in 1943, in the portmanteau movie *Forever and a Day*).

The new director of the Matthews musicals was her husband, Sonnie Hale, who had increasingly chafed at having to play second-fiddle to his wife's stardom. Under his efficient, hard-working, but uninspired guidance, the magic gradually faded. Her final film of the 1930s, *Climbing High*, was without song or dance, and was directed by Carol Reed, with whom

Jessie enjoyed a brief affair as her marriage to Hale foundered. With its release in March 1939, her British star career in films came to a close. Britain's top box-office star in 1934, 1935 and 1936, she slipped behind Gracie Fields and George Formby in 1937, the first year of her decline, but stayed in the top five for the remainder of the decade.

Her later career was a story of many ups and downs, breakdowns and comebacks, triumphs and tragedies. Her marriage to Hale finally ended in 1944, although the couple had parted for good in 1942. A later marriage also ended in divorce.

Talking to her a few months before her death in 1981 one had the impression that although her warm-hearted and extrovert personality remained bubbling on the surface, inside she still harboured considerable bitterness for the injustices with which she felt life had buffeted her. But, like all star performers, applause was life and breath to her, and most would like to remember her at her peak in the mid 1930s, as a kind of gossamer elf who wove her own fragile but enchanted web.

FILMOGRAPHY.

1923: The Beloved Vagabond. This England. 1924: Straws in the Wind. 1931: Out of the Blue. 1932: There Goes the Bride. The Midshipmaid. 1933: The Good Companions. Friday the Thirteenth. 1934: Waltzes from Vienna (USA: Strauss's Great Waltz). Evergreen. 1935: First a Girl. 1936: It's Love Again. 1937: Secrets of the Stars (short). Head Over Heels (USA: Head Over Heels in Love). Gangway. 1938: Sailing Along. Climbing High. 1943: Forever and a Day. 1944: Candles at Nine. 1947: Life is Nothing without Music. Making the Grade. 1958: Tom Thumb. 1977: The Hound of the Baskervilles. 1980: Second to the Right and On Till Morning (unreleased).

Jessie Matthews also directed a featurette, *Victory Wedding*, in 1944.

As Susie Dean, with John Gielgud as Inigo, in *The Good Companions* (1932)

As Harriet Green in *Evergreen* (1934)

Profile of Jessie in *Evergreen* (1934)

Domestication and glamour; off-set at Gaumont-British in 1938

With Robert Flemyng in *Head over Heels* (1937)

With Nat Pendleton in *Gangway* (1937)

Elegance personified in *Sailing Along* (1938)

As Susie Dean in *The Good Companions* (1932)

The Thirties
FILM OF THE DECADE

The Four Feathers

In spite of Charles Laughton's acting Oscar for *The Private Life of Henry VIII*, the finest achievement of Alexander Korda's London Films came at the end of the decade, with the release of *The Four Feathers* in April 1939.

Death in the desert

Korda himself, although a Hungarian, had fallen in love with Britain, its way of life and its traditions. He once refused to film *The Bridge on the River Kwai* because it showed British officers collaborating with the enemy, for whatever patriotic reason. He was thrilled by the concept of the British Empire and delighted in extolling its virtues and its battles against the 'ignorance' of the foreigner.

From this desire to portray a country at its best sprang some of the most notable Korda achievements of the 1930s: *Sanders of the River*, *The Scarlet Pimpernel*, *Fire Over England*, *Elephant Boy* and *The Drum*.

In his directing brother Zoltán, Korda had the ideal ally. Zoltán was a man who thrived on the spirit of adventure displayed in far-flung places; he was also a superb organizer of big action scenes.

Even, so none of this previous work quite prepares one for the magnificence of *The Four Feathers*. Britain had tried before to match Hollywood in its speciality fields, such as musicals and action films. British critics were very kind when the efforts came close, but in truth the flow, the rhythm and the spark of inspiration were never quite there, however careful the copy.

The Four Feathers nails all this to the wall. Its action scenes, pulsatingly thrilling, totally real, match anything from a like Hollywood epic, while its colour photography, by the unbeatable team of Georges Périnal, Osmond Borradaile, Jack Cardiff and Robert Krasker, three of whom were to win Academy Awards, was the best the world had seen, bringing brilliantly to life the parched landscapes or northern Africa, as well as the ancestral halls and traditional uniforms of England. Well, perhaps not quite traditional, as Korda himself insisted on one set of blue (the proper colour for a private home) uniforms being changed to red because they would look better on the screen.

A.E.W. Mason's famous novel of redemption from cowardice in the heat of action had already been filmed several times (and two more versions would follow, at very respectful intervals, in 1955 and 1978). Korda, who had acquired the rights to *Lawrence of Arabia* as early as 1934, but never filmed it because 'we are friendly with the Turks', decided that the time was right for the most patriotic version yet of Mason's seemingly failproof yarn.

The result was a triumph, although it came too late to save Korda's Denham Studios from passing, late in 1938, into other hands. Had *The Four Feathers* been made six months earlier, and its worldwide receipts settled in the London Films coffers, Korda might have been able to stave off his creditors for another year and, with war around the corner, the whole course of his career might have been altered.

Although the hero is played (and well, in the best performance of a disappointing film career) by John Clements, acting honours in the film were wholly stolen by Ralph Richardson as Durrance, one of the officers who gives our hero the white feathers of cowardice when he refuses to go to the Sudan.

Richardson is awesomely good, especially when blinded and lost in the heat of the desert – and pathetically touching in his final scenes. C. Aubrey Smith also makes an indelible impression as the old general who relieves his greatest battles on the dinner table. But the abiding memory of the film remains in its panoramas: dozens of Arabs heaving small sailing vessels along the Nile, thousands of natives charging at their enemy (nothing so blood-stirring would be achieved until *Zulu* 25 years later), the tense prison rescue, and the battle scenes themselves, full of the sweat, dust, heat, guts and desperation of desert combat. The emotive tug of such scenes is irresistible.

Said the then-film-critic Graham Greene: 'This cannot fail to be one of the best films of the year.' Even against such competition from Hollywood as *Gone With the Wind*, he was right.

Credits and cast

Dir *Zoltán Korda*. Prod *Alexander Korda*. Scr *R.C. Sherriff*, with *Lajos Biro* and *Arther Wimperis*. Ph *Georges Périnal*, *Robert Krasker*. Exterior ph *Osmond Borradaile*, *Jack Cardiff*. Technicolor. Associate prod *Irving Asher*. Prod designer *Vincent*

John Clements, C. Aubrey Smith and June Duprez

Native troops charge their enemy

Korda. Mus *Miklos Rosza*. Editors *William Hornbeck* (*supervising*), *Henry Cornelius*. Costume designers *Godfrey Brennan*, *René Hubert*. Second unit dir *Geoffrey Boothby*. Sound *A.W. Watkins*. PC *London Films*. Dis *United Artists. 130 mins. Cert A*

John Clements (Harry Faversham), Ralph Richardson (Capt. John Durrance), C. Aubrey Smith (Gen. Burroughs), June Duprez (Ethne Burroughs), Allan Jeayes (Gen. Faversham), Jack Allen (Lt Willoughby), Donald Gray (Peter Burroughs), Frederick Culley (Dr Sutton), Amid Taftazani (Karaga Pasha), Henry Oscar (Dr Harraz), John Laurie (Khalifa), Robert Rendel (Colonel), Hal Walters (Joe), Derek Elphinstone (Lt Parker), Clive Baxter (Harry, as a child), Norman Pierce (Sgt Brown), Archibald Batty (Adjutant)

John Clements as Harry . . .

. . . and in native disguise

Advertisement for the film. Note the 'C' missing from C. Aubrey Smith

Ralph Richardson and June Duprez

The *coup de grace* from a native warrior

Jack Allen as Lt Willoughby

The Thirties

ABDUL THE DAMNED (1935) [5]

Dir *Karl Grüne*, Prod *Max Schach*. Scr *Ashley Dukes, Warren Chetham Strode, Roger Burford, from the novel by Robert Neumann*. Ph *Otto Kanturek*. PC *BIP/Capitol*. Dis *Wardour. 111 mins. Cert A*

Vivid account of the last years of the rule of Abdul-Hamid II, Sultan of Turkey (*Fritz Kortner*) in the early 1900s. Abdul recalls the leaders of the Young Turk party from exile to form a democratic government, but engineers the assassination of the leader of the rival Old Turk party, so that the new government is overthrown and its leaders executed. The assassin, Kadar (*Nils Asther*) chief of police, has also wounded Talak, a Turkish officer (*John Stuart*) – a grave mistake, for Talak is eventually responsible for Abdul's downfall.

RoC *Adrienne Ames, Esme Percy, Walter Rilla, Patric Knowles, Eric Portman, Charles Carson, Clifford Heatherley, Annie Esmond, Arthur Hardy, Robert Naylor, Warren Jenkins, Alfred Woods, Henry Longhurst, George Zucco, H. Saxon-Snell, Henry Paterson, Charlotte Francis.*

ABOVE RUBIES (1931) [1]

Dir *Frank A. Richardson*. Prod *Ralph J. Pugh*. Scr *Eliot Stannard*. Ph *Geoffrey Faithfull*. PC *Ralph Pugh Films*. Dis *United Artists. 44 mins. Cert U*

Yet another comedy set in Monte Carlo, this time a pocket-sized version. Lady Wellingford is unable to redeem a valuable necklace from the jeweller from whom she has received a loan. Her daughter Joan (*Zoë Palmer*) and her three suitors devise a plan to bring the mercenary jeweller to heel.

RoC *Robin Irvine, Tom Helmore, John Deverell, Madge Snell, Franklyn Bellamy, Allan Jeayes.*

THE ACADEMY DECIDES (1937) [2]

Dir *John Baxter*. Prod *John Barter*. Scr *Stuart Jackson*. Ph *Jack Parker*. PC *UK Films*. Dis *MGM. 50 mins. Cert A*

An 'Academy of Protection' run by a group of buskers provides an 'early warning' system against the police for the more deserving criminal classes. An orphan girl 'adopted' by the Academy is seduced by their enemy, and dies in the attempt to kill him. Using its un-derground grapevine, the Academy tracks down the villain and brings him to a well-deserved death. Occasionally striking, but un-even thriller.

LP *Henry Oscar, April Vivian, John Oxford, Wensley Russell, Boris Ranevsky, Frank Birch, Walter Tobias.*

ACCUSED (1936) [2]

Dir *Thornton Freeland*. Prod *Marcel Hellman, Douglas Fairbanks Jr*. Scr *Zoë Atkins, George Barraud, Harold French*. Ph *Victor Armenise*. PC *Criterion*. Dis *United Artists. 85 mins. Cert U*

Good cast in sketchy thriller about married dancers Tony and Gaby (*Douglas Fairbanks Jr, Dolores Del Rio*) whose relations are strained when leading lady Yvette (*Florence Desmond*) is encouraged to run after him by the show's producer. When Yvette is found knifed to death, Gaby is charged, but the resulting trial clears Gaby and reveals the real murderer.

RoC *Basil Sydney, Athole Stewart, J.H. Roberts, Cecil Humphreys, Esmé Percy, Moore Marriott, Edward Rigby, Googie Withers, Roland Culver, Cyril Raymond.*

THE ACE OF SPADES (1935) [3]

Dir *George Pearson*. Prod *Julius Hagen*. Scr *Gerard Fairlie, from the novel by John Crawford Fraser*. Ph *Ernest Palmer*. PC *Real Art*. Dis *Radio. 66 mins. Cert U*

A political candidate (*Michael Hogan*) is suspected of murder on the evidence of a message written on a playing card, after a car actually driven by his brother (*Sebastian Shaw*) has knocked down and killed the peer (*Felix Aylmer*) through whose land the candidate had been advocating a railway. The brother's fiancée's sister proves to have been behind it all.

RoC *Dorothy Boyd, Jane Carr, Geraldine Fitzgerald, Michael Shepley, Richard Cooper, Bobbie Comber.*

ACTION FOR SLANDER (1937) [3]

Dir *Tim Whelan*. Prod *Victor Saville*. Scr *Miles Malleson, Ian Dalrymple, from the novel by Mary Borden*. Ph *Harry Stradling*. PC *Victor Saville Productions/London Films*. Dis *United Artists. 83 mins. Cert A*

Daviot (*Clive Brook*), whose wife has just left him, is accused of cheating at cards by Grant

Margaretta Scott and Clive Brook in Action for Slander *(1937)*

(*Antony Holles*), whom he floors. Captain Bradford (*Arthur Margetson*), husband of the woman with whom Daviot is infatuated, backs Grant's story. After being shunned by his friends, Daviot is eventually persuaded by his wife (*Ann Todd*) to take action for slander. He wins the case, and they are reunited. Stiff upper-lip drama lacks driving force.

RoC *Margaretta Scott, Ronald Squire, Athole Stewart, Percy Marmont, Frank Cellier, Morton Selten, Gus McNaughton, Francis L. Sullivan, Enid Stamp-Taylor, Kate Cutler, Felix Aylmer, Lawrence Hanray, Albert Whelan, Allan Jeayes, Googie Withers, Edgar Miles.*

ADMIRALS ALL (1935) [3]

Dir *Victor Hanbury*. Prod *John Stafford*. Scr *Stephen King-Hall, Ian Hay, from their play*. PC *Stafford*. Dis *Radio. 75 mins. Cert U*

Straight transfer to screen of the hit stage farce in which Gloria Gunn (*Wynne Gibson*), a temperamental film star, takes a trip to Chinese waters, where she meets her rejected leading man posing as the leader of Chinese bandits to prove his worth as an actor – and then some real Chinese bandits. Everyone is rescued by the timely arrival of the British fleet.

RoC *Gordon Harker, George Curzon, Anthony Bushell, Joan White, Henry Hewitt, Ben Welden, Percy Walsh, Gwynneth Lloyd, (Wilfrid) Hyde White.*

THE ADMIRAL'S SECRET (1934) [3]

Dir *Guy Newall*. Prod *Julius Hagen*. Scr *H. Fowler Mear, from a play by Cyril Campion, Edward Dignon*. PC *Real Art*. Dis *Radio. 63 mins. Cert U*

A spirited performance from *Edmund Gwenn* in this comedy-adventure as a retired admiral whose valuable diamond is pursued by crooks who try to outwit each other, but are finally outwitted by the admiral himself. He pretends to throw the gem in the sea, but actually has it attached to the end of his fishing rod.

RoC *Hope Davy, James Raglan, Aubrey Mather, Edgar Driver, Abraham Sofaer, Dorothy Black, Andrea Malandrinos, D.J. Williams, Agnes Imlay.*

ADVENTURE LIMITED (1934) [1]

Dir and Prod *George King*. Scr *George Dewhurst, from a play by Cyril Campion*. PC Dis/*British and Dominions/Paramount British. 70 mins. Cert A*

Pretty ropey comedy-thriller about three friends from 'Adventure Limited' who expose a plot against the ex-president of a South American country, after Kim (*Harry Milton*), one of the adventurers, has fallen in love with the statesman's daughter (*Pearl Argyle*). An unequal struggle for the cast.

RoC *Hugh E. Wright, Sebastian Shaw, Sam Wilkinson, Clifford Heatherley, Lawrence Hanray, Cecil Humphreys, Dorothy Buller.*

AFTER DARK (1932) [4]

Dir *Albert Parker*. Prod *Hugh Perceval*. Scr *John Barrow, from the play by J. Jefferson Farjeon*. PC *Fox British*. Dis *Fox. 45 mins. Cert U*

Mini-comedy in which stolen emeralds are

hidden in an old clock, subsequently bought by peppery old Thaddeus (*Horace Hodges*) who finds his house promptly invaded by a number of interested people searching for the hidden gems. It turns out that Thaddeus had found the emeralds himself and consigned them to the safety of a bank vault!
RoC *Grethe Hansen, Hugh Williams, George Barraud, Ian Fleming, Henry Oscar, Pollie Emery, Lucille Lisle, George Padbury, Barbara Barlow, Henry Longhurst, Reggie de Beer.*

AFTER OFFICE HOURS (1932) [5]
Dir *Thomas Bentley.* Prod *Walter C. Mycroft.* Scr *Bentley, Frank Launder, from a play by John Van Druten.* Ph *H.E. Palmer, Arthur Crabtree.* PC *BIP.* Dis *Wardour.* 78 mins. Cert U
Well-scripted story of ordinary office workers that was compared, not unfavourably, with the earlier American film *The Crowd.* Working for a firm of solicitors, Blanche (*Viola Lyel*) helps a junior (*Heather Angel*) from making the same mistakes in life as her.
RoC *Frank Lawton, Garry Marsh, Eileen Peel, Frank Royde, Katie Johnson, Nadine March, Billy Speechley.*

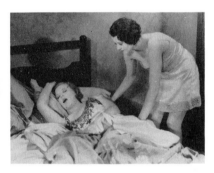

Eileen Peel and Heather Angel in After Office Hours *(1932)*

AFTER THE BALL (1932) [4]
Dir *Milton Rosmer.* Prod *Michael Balcon.* Scr *H.M. Harwood, J.O.C. Orton.* PC and Dis *Gaumont.* 70 mins. Cert A
Familiar early 1930s' comedy stuff, but done with sparkle and poking some pertinent fun at the League of Nations. American star *Esther Ralston* plays a diplomat's wife, at large in Geneva, who poses as her own maid in order to carry on a flirtation with a courier (*Basil Rathbone*).
RoC *Marie Burke, Jean Adrienne, George Curzon, Clifford Heatherley.*

AGAINST THE TIDE (1937) [2]
Dir *Alex Bryce.* Prod and Scr *Victor M Greene.* Ph *Ronald Neame.* PC and Dis *Fox British.* 67 mins. Cert U
Cornwall: Margaret (*Cathleen Nesbitt*) gives her son Jim (*Robert Cochran*) a college education, hoping to prevent him from taking to the sea that killed his father and grandfather. Returning, Jim falls in love with Mary (*Linden Travers*) and marries her. They live with Jim's mother and the two women quarrel bitterly.

One night, Mary's father's boat founders in a storm. Jim goes to the rescue and is drowned. The two women seek mutual consolation in Mary's baby son, but with the knowledge that he, too, might be a seaman.
RoC *Jimmy Mageean, Herbert Cameron, Neil Carlton, Dorothy Vernon.*

ALF'S BUTTON (1930) [3]
Dir *W.P. Kellino.* Prod and Scr *L'Estrange Fawcett, from the play by W. A. Darlington.* Ph *Percy Strong.* PC and Dis *Gaumont.* 96 mins. Some scenes in colour. Cert U
Private Alf Higgins (*Tubby Edlin*), serving in France in the First World War, is cleaning a button on his uniform when a genie appears, propelling Higgins and his friend Bill (*Alf Goddard*) into a series of fantastic adventures.
RoC *Polly Ward, Cyril McLaglen, Gypsy Rhouma, Nora Swinburne, Humberston Wright, Peter Haddon, Annie Esmond, Jimmy Nervo, Teddy Knox, Anton Dolin, Anna Ludmilla, Bruce Winston, Spencer Trevor, Stanley Cooke, Merle Oberon.*

ALF'S BUTTON AFLOAT (1938) [4]
Dir *Marcel Varnel.* Prod *Edward Black.* Scr *Marriott Edgar, Val Guest, Ralph Smart, from a play by W.A. Darlington.* Ph *Arthur Crabtree.* PC *Gainsborough.* Dis *General Film Distributors.* 89 mins. Cert U
Six busking brothers (*The Crazy Gang*), enlisted by mistake in the Marines, find a brass button that was once part of Aladdin's Lamp. A genie (*Alastair Sim*) appears, develops a taste for Hollywood gangster films and tends to misunderstand commands: people are *striped* pink; the Bank of England is robbed; the ship is turned into a harem; the brothers go fox-hunting on circus horses. Finally he returns whence he came. Quite a lot of laughs in this one.
LP *Bud Flanagan, Chesney Allen, Jimmy Nervo, Teddy Knox, Charlie Naughton, Jimmy Gold, Glennis Lorimer, Wally Patch, Peter Gawthorne, James Carney, Agnes Laughlin, Bruce Winston, Wilson Coleman, J.H. Roberts, B. John Slater.*

ALIBI (1931) [3]
Dir *Leslie Hiscott.* Prod *Julius Hagen.* Scr *H. Fowler Mear, from a play by Michael Morton and Agatha Christie.* PC *Twickenham.* Dis *W & F.* 75 mins. Cert A
Having already played A.E.W. Mason's French detective Inspector Hanaud in *At the Villa Rose* (qv), *Austin Trevor* took on Agatha Christie's Belgian sleuth Hercule Poirot in this thriller, based on the stage version of Miss Christie's novel *The Murder of Roger Ackroyd,* in which Poirot discovers the truth behind a mysterious suicide at a country house.
RoC *Elizabeth Allan, Franklin Dyall, J.H. Roberts, John Deverell, Mary Jerrold, Ronald Ward, Mercia Swinburne, Harvey Braban, Clare Greet, Diana Beaumont, Earle Grey.*

ALIBI BREAKER (1937)
See **Double Exposures.**

ALIBI INN (1935) [3]
Dir and Prod *Walter Tennyson.* Scr *Sydney Box, Muriel Box.* PC *Central Films.* Dis *MGM.* 53 mins. Cert A
A gang of jewel thieves led by Saunders (*Ben Welden*) frames Jack Lawton, an inventor (*Frederick Bradshaw*) for a murder committed while they were carrying out a robbery. Lawton breaks jail while awaiting trial and proves that the crooks are guilty and he is innocent. Fair thriller, the first film written by the husband-and-wife Box team.
RoC *Molly Lamont, Brian Buchel, Olive Sloane, Gladys Jennings, (Wilfrid) Hyde White.*

ALL AT SEA (1935) [1]
Dir *Anthony Kimmins.* Prod *John Findlay.* Scr *Kimmins, from a play by Ian Hay.* Ph *Roy Kellino.* PC and Dis *Fix British.* 60 mins. Cert U
A diffident clerk (*Tyrell Davis*), inheriting a small legacy, takes a cruise and, opposed by an aristocrat (*Rex Harrison*), poses as a well-known author to win the girl (*Googie Withers*) he has fallen for heavily. The clerk wins his 'glamour girl' – who turns out to be a humble typist. Limp.
RoC *James Carew, Cecily Byrne, Dorothy Vernon, James Harcourt, Colin Lesslie, Dorothy Hammond, Charles Delph, Georgina Esmond.*

ALL AT SEA (1939) [4]
Dir and Prod *Herbert Smith.* Scr *Gerald Elliott, Reginald Long.* Ph *Hone Glendinning.* PC and Dis *British Lion.* 76 mins. Cert U
Rambunctious *Sandy Powell* comedy, casting him as a messenger at a chemical factory who joins the navy by accident while carrying a dangerous new explosive in his pocket. Consequently, foreign spies pursue his ship to Marseilles. After various misadventures on board, Sandy encounters the spies, but gets the better of them.
RoC *Kay Walsh, John Warwick, Gus McNaughton, George Merritt, Leslie Perrins, Franklin Dyall, Robert Rendel, Aubrey Mallalieu.*

ALL IN (1936) [4]
Dir *Marcel Varnel.* Prod *Michael Balcon.* Scr *Leslie Arliss, Val Guest, from a play by Bernard Merivale and Brandon Fleming.* Ph *Jack Cox.* PC *Gainsborough.* Dis *Gaumont-British.* 71 mins. Cert A
Rollicking *Ralph Lynn* comedy in which, as sheltered Archie Slott, he inherits a racing stable which his aunt decides should be converted into a holiday home for working girls. But the hereditary Slott passion for gambling has been aroused and, in no time, thanks to two con-men, Archie finds himself with a bankrupt wrestling stadium as well. He loses the Derby and his shirt, but finds romance.
RoC *Gina Malo, Jack Barty, Claude Dampier, Sydney Fairbrother, Garry Marsh, O.B. Clarence, Gibb McLaughlin, Glennis Lorimer, Robert Nainby, Fewlass Llewellyn, W. Graham Brown, Joan Kemp-Welsh, Bryan Powley, Edwin Durer.*

ALL THAT GLITTERS (1936)   ☐3
Dir *Maclean Rogers*. Prod *A. George Smith*. Scr *Denison Clift*. Ph *Geoffrey Faithfull*. PC *GS Enterprises*. Dis *Radio. 72 mins. Cert U*
An offshoot of the Scrooge story, featuring a stingy, stuffy bank manager who accidentally takes a euphoric for his dyspepsia. Next day, he starts dispensing loans and overdrafts to all his customers, and backs a gold mine, which turns out to be as good as its name, enabling its young owner (*Jack Hobbs*) to get married and look forward to prosperity. Unpretentious but brightly done: *Aubrey Mallalieu* scores as the converted skinflint.
RoC *Moira Lynd, Kay Walsh, Annie Esmond, Fred Duprez, John Robinson, Dick Francis, Eliot Makeham*.

ALMOST A DIVORCE (1931)   ☐4
Dir *Arthur Varney Serrao*. Prod *Herbert Wilcox*. Scr *Brock Williams, Arthur Varney Serrao*. Ph *Henry Harris*. PC *British and Dominions*. Dis *W & F. 58 mins. Cert A*
This pocket-sized comedy was highly regarded in some quarters (although not all). Richard and Angela (*Nelson Keys, Marjorie Binner*) are a happy couple until Richard falls in with the habitually tipsy Mackintosh (*Sydney Howard*) at their club. Angela threatens divorce and a reconciliation attempt almost ends in disaster after Mackintosh's gold-digger friend (*Kay Hammond*) is found in Richard's hotel room!
RoC *Eva Moore, Kenneth Kove*.

ALMOST A GENTLEMAN (1938)   ☐3
Dir *Oswald Mitchell*. Prod *Sidney Morgan*. Scr *Morgan, Mitchell, Billy Bennett*. Ph *Geoffrey Faithfull*. PC and Dis *Butchers. 78 mins.*
Nightwatchman Bill Barker (*Billy Bennett*) is mistaken for a rich gum manufacturer and persuaded by two con-men to buy shares in a dud gold-mine. Large sums are subsequently invested by society shareholders, who follow the 'glue mogul's' lead. Bill is distraught when he discovers the truth, but then gold is found in the mine, making him almost a millionaire if not quite a gentleman. Robust comedy.
RoC *Kathleen Harrison, Gibb McLaughlin, Marcelle Rogez, Mervyn Johns, Basil Langton, Harry Terry, Dorothy Vernon*.

ALMOST A HONEYMOON (1930)   ☐5
Dir *Monty Banks*. Prod *John Maxwell*. Scr *Val*

Dodo Watts and Clifford Mollison in Almost a Honeymoon (*1930*)

Valentine, Banks, Walter C. Mycroft, from the play by Walter Ellis. Ph *Jack Cox*. PC *BIP*. Dis *Wardour. 100 mins. Cert U*
Funny farce about a penniless young man-about-town (*Clifford Mollison* at his 'silly ass' best) who lets his flat to an engaged couple. The girl decides to spend her wedding eve there, and the owner, returning rather more drunk than usual from a party, forgets he has let the flat and also decides to sleep there. About the best thing *Dodo Watts* did in a short-lived star career.
RoC *Donald Calthrop, Lamont Dickson, Pamela Carme, C.M. Hallard, Winifred Hall, Edward Thane*.

ALMOST A HONEYMOON (1938)   ☐3
Dir *Norman Lee*. Prod *Warwick Ward*. Scr *Kenneth Horne, Ralph Neale, from the play by Walter Ellis*. Ph *Bryan Langley*. PC *Welwyn*. Dis *Pathé. 80 mins. Cert A*
Peter (*Tommy Trinder*) is offered a colonial appointment for a married man and has 24 hours to find a bride. His old flame has taken up all-in wrestling and, drowning his sorrows in wine, he staggers home, forgetting he has let his flat to an engaged couple. In the morning, he finds the girl sleeping in the twin bed next to him. In the end, she turns out to be the bride he needs. Some fun, but treatment lacks the freshness of the original 1930 version.
RoC *Linden Travers, Edmond Breon, Frederick Burtwell, Vivienne Bennett, Arthur Hambling, Aubrey Mallalieu, Betty Jardine, Ian Fleming, Wally Patch, Julie Suedo, Beryl Meason*.

THE AMATEUR GENTLEMAN (1935)   ☐4
Dir *Thornton Freeland*. Prod *Marcel Hellman, Douglas Fairbanks Jr*. Scr *Clemence Dane, Edward Knoblock, Sergei Nolbandov, from the novel by Jeffrey Farnol*. Ph *Günther Krampf*. PC *Criterion*. Dis *United Artists. 102 mins. Cert A*
Nicely photographed historical adventure, with co-producer *Fairbanks* as Barnabas who, trained in etiquette though the poor-born son of an ex-boxer, creates a stir in fashionable London circles, falls for a high-born lady, gains a reputation as a wrestler and boxer, pleases the Prince Regent and dramatically rescues his father from hanging on a false charge, unmasking the real culprit.
RoC *Elissa Landi, Gordon Harker, Basil Sydney, Hugh Williams, Irene Browne, Coral Brown(e), Athole Stewart, Margaret Lockwood, Frank Pettingell, Esme Percy, Gilbert Davis, June Duprez, Marius Goring, Frank Bertram*.

THE AMAZING QUEST OF ERNEST BLISS (1936)   ☐4
(USA: *Romance and Riches*)
Dir *Alfred Zeisler*. Prod *Robert Garrett, Otto Klement*. Scr *John C. Balderston, from the novel by E. Phillips Oppenheim*. Ph *Otto Heller*. PC *Garrett-Klement Pictures*. Dis *United Artists. 80 mins. Cert U*
Deftly directed, if episodic, story of a bored millionaire (*Cary Grant*) who makes a bet that he can earn his own living for a year. He enjoys jobs as greengrocer, chauffeur and salesman, but loses the bet when he feels he must give

a lot of money to his girlfriend (*Mary Brian*) for an operation on her invalid sister.
RoC *Henry Kendall, Leon M. Lion, Garry Marsh, Ralph Richardson, John Turnbull, Iris Ashley, Moore Marriott, Alf Goddard, Peter Gawthorne, Charles Farrell, Arthur Hardy, Frank Stanmore, Beuna Bent, Marie Wright, Hal Gordon, Andreas Malandrinos, Alfred Wellesley, Quinton McPherson*.

THE ANGELUS (1937)
See Who Killed Fen Markham?

ANNE ONE HUNDRED (1933)   ☐2
Dir *Henry Edwards*. Prod *Herbert Wilcox*. Scr *Sewell Collins, from his play, and a novel by Edgar Franklin*. PC *British and Dominions*. Dis *Paramount. 66 mins. Cert U*
Anne Briston (*Betty Stockfeld*) returns from America to find the 'thriving' factory left to her by her father is just about on its last legs. She borrows money from a suitor, laying a wager that she will marry him if she cannot pay back in six months. Anne and her foreman (*Gyles Isham*) put the firm back on its feet, and she marries the foreman. Obvious romantic drama.
RoC *Evelyn Roberts, Allan Jeayes, Dennis Wyndham, Eric Hales, Quinton McPherson, Billy Speechley*.

ANNIE LAURIE (1936)   ☐3
Dir *Walter Tennyson*. Prod *Tennyson, Wilfrid Noy*. Scr *Frank Miller*. Ph *Jack Parker*. PC *Mondover*. Dis *Butchers. 82 mins. Cert U*
When horse-drawn barges are succeeded by motorized boats, bargee Will Laurie (*Will Fyffe*) finds himself out of work. He teams up with his friend, a travelling showman and, with the help of the singing voice of his adopted daughter Annie (*Polly Ward*), found on his barge as an abandoned baby, they become rich. Annie turns out to be the granddaughter of Will's former employer. Fyffe dominates a fair slab of music and sentiment.
RoC *Bruce Seton, Vivienne Chatterton, Romilly Lunge, Percy Walsh, Frederick Culley, Evelyn Barnard, Quinton McPherson, Horace Sheldon and His Orchestra, Rodney Hudson Girls, Doris and her Zebra*.

ANNIE, LEAVE THE ROOM! (1935)   ☐3
Dir *Leslie Hiscott*. Prod *Julius Hagen*. Scr *Michael Barringer, from a play by Norman Cannon*. Ph *William Luff*. PC *Twickenham*. Dis *Universal. 76 mins. Cert A*
Some amusing moments in this comedy about broke Lord Spendlove (*Morton Selten*) who suffers from a mother-in-law (*Eva Moore*) who holds the purse-strings. Then a film company offers him £1,000 for the loan of his baronial home. After flirting with the star (*Jane Carr*), he gets a screen test of himself taken with his dumb maid Annie (*Davina Craig*). It's Annie who gets a contract ... and the lord's discomfiture is complete when his mother-in-law proves to be a director of the film company.
RoC *Richard Cooper, Jane Welsh, Ben Welden, Arthur Finn, Edward Underdown, Alfred Wellesley*.

ANYTHING MIGHT HAPPEN (1934)   `1`
Dir *George A. Cooper*. Prod *Julius Hagen*. Scr *H. Fowler Mear, from the novel by Lady Evelyn Balfour*. Ph *Ernest Palmer*. PC *Real Art*. Dis *Radio*. 66 mins. Cert A
Reformed thief Nicholson (*John Garrick*) has turned coppers' nark, but is framed for murder. He suspects his double, a crook named Raybourn (also *Garrick*), but the killer proves to be the dead man's lawyer.
RoC *Judy Kelly, Martin Walker, Aubrey Mather, D.J. Williams, Albert Whelan.*

ANYTHING TO DECLARE? (1938)   `3`
Dir *Redd Davis*. Prod *Ralph C. Wells, Neville Carter*. Scr *Hayter Preston*. Ph *Geoffrey Faithfull*. PC *Rembrandt*. Dis *Butchers*. 76 mins. Cert U
Professor Grayson (*Eliot Makeham*) is working on an 'anti-gas' formula, and Dr Klee (*Noel Madison*), whose 'peace' propaganda masks other interests, is after it. Grayson's daughter Nora (*Belle Chrystall*) invites Klee home, to the dismay of intelligence officer Rufus Grant (*John Loder*), who is shadowing him. The professor is kidnapped, but thanks to Rufus the formula is saved. Punchy thick-ear thriller.
RoC *Leonora Corbett, Jerry Verno, Davina Craig, Alexander Sarner, Nigel Barrie, Carl Melene, Gordon Hall, Reginald Fox, Melville Crawfurd.*

AREN'T MEN BEASTS! (1936)   `5`
Dir *Graham Cutts*. Prod *Walter C. Mycroft*. Scr *Marjorie Deans, William Freshman, from the play by Vernon Sylvaine*. Ph *Roy Kellino*. PC *BIP*. Dis *Associated British*. 67 mins. Cert A
Stagebound but still funny farce about Holly (*Robertson Hare*), a querulous dentist, who is visited by a mystery woman (*Ellen Pollock*) on the morning of his son Roger's marriage. She rips her dress and screams for the police. Holly is arrested but escapes. While Roger hunts for the woman, Holly hides in a grandfather clock, then disguises himself as a woman. The woman is at last found - one of Roger's old flames out to stop the wedding.
RoC *Billy Milton, June Clyde, Alfred Drayton, Judy Kelly, Amy Veness, Ruth Maitland, Frank Royde, Kathleen Harrison, S. Victor Stanley, Charles Mortimer, Frederick Morant, Anne Boyd.*

Billy Milton, Alfred Drayton, Robertson Hare in Aren't Men Beasts! *(1937)*

AREN'T WE ALL? (1932)   `4`
Dir *Harry Lachman*. Prod *Walter Morosco*. Scr *Basil Mason, Gilbert Wakefield, from a play by Frederick Lonsdale*. PC *Paramount British*. Dis *Paramount*. 79 mins. Cert A
Two sophisticates (*Gertrude Lawrence, Owen Nares*), parted on their honeymoon, are soon flirting with others and quarrel. His father brings his own wife's lover to the scene and the honeymooners are soon reconciled. Polished comedy.
RoC *Hugh Wakefield, Harold Huth, Marie Lohr, Renée Gadd, Emily Fitzroy, Aubrey Mather, Rita Page.*

ARE YOU A MASON? (1934)   `4`
Dir *Henry Edwards*. Prod *Julius Hagen*. Scr *H. Fowler Mear, from a play by Leo Dietrichstein, Emmanuel Lederer*. Ph *Sydney Blythe*. PC *Real Art*. Dis *Universal*. 85 mins. Cert U
Frank (*Sonnie Hale*) needs a loan from his mother-in-law to clear gambling debts. He tells her he is a freemason, having followed in her husband's footsteps. But his father-in-law (*Robertson Hare*) is also a 'pretend' mason, in order to escape once a week from his wife. Frantic complications involve Frank having Lulu (*Joyce Kirby*) pose as his father-in-law's illegitimate daughter. Fast, funny comedy.
RoC *Davy Burnaby, Gwynneth Lloyd, Bertha Belmore, Lewis Shaw, Michael Shepley, Davina Craig, May Agate.*

ARMS AND THE MAN (1932)   `3`
Dir *Cecil Lewis*. Prod *Walter C. Mycroft*. Scr *Lewis, Frank Launder (uncredited) from the play by G.B. Shaw*. Ph *J.J. Cox, James Wilson*. PC *BIP*. Dis *Wardour*. 85 mins. Cert U
Disappointing screen version of Shaw's comedy play, rather restricted by the author's insistence on the retention of the original text in its entirety. *Barry Jones* plays the Swiss officer serving in the defeated Serbian army of 1885 who takes refuge in the bedroom of a lady whose father and fiancé are both officers in the victorious Bulgarian army.
RoC *Anne Grey, Maurice Colbourne, Angela Baddeley, Frederick Lloyd, Wallace Evenett, Margaret Scudamore, Charles Morgan.*

Barry Jones and Anne Grey in Arms and the Man *(1932)*

AROUND THE TOWN (1938)   `2`
Dir and Prod *Herbert Smith*. Scr *Fenn Sherie, Ingram d'Abbes*. Ph *George Stretton*. PC and Dis *British Lion*. 68 mins. Cert U
Ollie Rose (*Vic Oliver*), a theatrical agent with no work and less money, overhears a rich

American, Wyngold (*Finlay Currie*) say that he wants to find British songwriters for a show he's producing. Ollie escorts Wyngold on a tour of Britain's music publishing business. Wyngold is so delighted that he appoints Ollie his personal representative - and his daughter (*Irene Ware*) decides to marry him. Fair revue-style film.
RoC *Elisabeth Welch, Jimmy Kennedy, Michael Carr, Leslie Carew, Pat McCormack, Tin Pan Alley Trio, The Rhythm Sisters, The Three Hillbillies, Terry's Juveniles, The Two Charladies, Al & Bob Harvey, Maurice Winnick and His Band.*

THE ARSENAL STADIUM MYSTERY (1939)   `4`
Dir *Thorold Dickinson*. Prod *Josef Somlo, Richard Norton*. Scr *Dickinson, Donald Bull, from a novel by Leonard Gribble*. Ph *Desmond Dickinson*. PC *G & S Films*. Dis *General Film Distributors*. 84 mins. Cert A
In a soccer match between Arsenal and The Trojans, the visitors' brilliant but conceited striker Doyce (*Anthony Bushell*) collapses and is found to have been murdered. Chief suspects are Gwen (*Greta Gynt*), Doyce's discarded mistress, and her fiancé Morring (*Brian Worth*), and trainer Kindilett (*Wyndham Goldie*) whose daughter committed suicide on Doyce's account. During a replay of the match (The Trojans win), Inspector Slade (*Leslie Banks*) solves the mystery. Above-average of its kind, with an entertaining role for Banks.
RoC *Ian Maclean, Esmond Knight, Liane Linden, Richard Norris, Dennis Wyndham, Maire O'Neill, Frank Atkinson, Alastair McIntyre, David Keir, Johnnie Schofield, Bruce Winston, George Allison, Tom Whittaker, E.V.H. Emmett, Ted Drake, Bryn Jones, Cliff Bastin, George Swindin, other members of Arsenal Football Club.*

AS GOOD AS NEW (1933)   `2`
Dir *Graham Cutts*. Prod *Irving Asher*. Scr *Randall Faye, from the play by Thompson Buchanan*. PC and Dis *Warner Bros*. 48 mins. Cert A
'Quota' weepie about a girl who thinks her fiancé has jilted her, unaware that he has been blinded in an accident. She becomes a gold-digger but, through the good offices of the nurse who has been treating him, the couple are ultimately reunited.
LP *Winna Winifried, John Batten, Sunday Wilshin, Tonie Edgar Bruce.*

ASK A POLICEMAN (1939)   `4`
Dir *Marcel Varnell*. Prod *Edward Black*. Scr *Sidney Gilliat, Marriott Edgar, Val Guest, J.O.C. Orton*. Ph *Derek Williams*. PC *Gainsborough*. Dis *MGM*. 82 mins. Cert U
Told by their chief constable that the absence of arrests in the village of Turnbotham Round suggests no police are necessary there, the force of three (*Will Hay, Moore Marriott, Graham Moffatt*) try to manufacture a crime wave. By luck, they uncover a smuggling ring being operated by the local squire (*Charles Oliver*) under their very noses. Marriott plays his own

Herbert Lomas, Moore Marriott and Will Hay in Ask a Policeman (*1939*)

ancient father in this goodish Hay comedy. RoC *Glennis Lorimer, Peter Gawthorne, Herbert Lomas, Pat Aherne, Richard Cooper.*

ASK BECCLES (1933) [3]
Dir *Redd Davis.* Prod *Herbert Wilcox.* Scr *Cyril Campion, from a play by Campion, Edward Dignon.* PC *British and Dominions/Paramount British.* Dis *Paramount. 68 mins. Cert A*
Comedy-thriller about Beccles (*Garry Marsh*) who has various misadventures after opening an advice bureau, steals a valuable diamond to help a friend out of debt, thinks about keeping it, but then returns it when the friend himself comes under suspicion. Quite entertaining, with a rare leading role for Marsh.
RoC *Mary Newland, Allan Jeayes, Abraham Sofaer, John Turnbull, Evan Thomas, Eileen Munro, Fewlass Llewellyn, Ronald Simpson, Gordon Begg.*

AS YOU LIKE IT (1936) [4]
Dir *Paul Czinner.* Prod *Joseph M. Schenk, Czinner.* Scr *J.M. Barrie, Robert Cullen, from the play by William Shakespeare.* Ph *Hal Rosson.* PC *Inter-Allied.* Dis *20th Century-Fox. 96 mins. Cert U*
Much-chopped-about version of Shakespeare's play, greatly admired by some and reviled by others. *Elisabeth Bergner* looks well in man's clothes as Rosalind, daughter of the banished duke, and in love with Orlando, played in frenzied fashion by *Laurence Olivier.* Best things: Hal Rosson's photography, William Walton's music and Lazare Meerson's unique production design.
RoC *Sophie Stewart, Leon Quatermaine, Henry Ainley, Mackenzie Ward, Felix Aylmer, Richard Ainley, Austin Trevor, Aubrey Mather, J. Fisher White, John Laurie, Dorice Fordred, Stuart Robertson, Peter Bull, Joan White, Lional Braham.*

AT THE VILLA ROSE (1930) [5]
(USA: *Mystery at the Villa Rose*)
Dir *Leslie Hiscott.* Prod *Julius Hagen, Henry Edwards.* Scr *Cyril Twyford from a novel by A.E.W. Mason.* Ph *Sydney Blythe.* PC *Twickenham.* Dis *Warner Bros. 99 mins. Cert A*
French version: Dir *Louis Mercanton, René Herville.* Ph *Basil Emmott.*
Well-liked thriller set in France. Rich widow (*Barbara Gott*) is murdered by jewel thieves

who frame her companion (*Norah Baring*), a fake medium, for the killing. But Inspector Hanaud (*Austin Trevor*) brings them to book. RoC *Violet Farebrother, Francis Lister, Amy Brandon Thomas, Richard Cooper.*

AT THE VILLA ROSE (1939) [4]
(USA: *House of Mystery*)
Dir *Walter Summers.* Prod *Walter C. Mycroft.* Scr *Doreen Montgomery, from the novel by A.E.W. Mason.* Ph *Claude Friese-Greene.* PC and Dis *Associated British. 74 mins. Cert A*
A rich widow is murdered and suspicion falls on her young companion Celia (*Judy Kelly*), a fake medium who has vanished along with the victim's jewels. But Celia has been kidnapped as the murderer thinks she has the gems. Inspector Hanaud (*Keneth Kent*), rescuing Celia, reconstructs the seance at which the widow died, and tricks the killer into betraying himself. Well-directed third film version of reliable mystery story.
RoC *Walter Rilla, Peter Murray Hill, Antoinette Cellier, Clifford Evans, Martita Hunt, Ruth Maitland, Ronald Adam, Arthur Hambling.*

AULD LANG SYNE (1937) [2]
Dir, Prod and PC *James A. Fitzpatrick.* Scr *W.K. Williamson.* Ph *Hone Glendinning.* Dis *MGM. 72 mins. Cert A*
Sincere but ingenuous patchwork portrait of the life of Scottish poet Robert Burns. We see: his life as a farm labourer 'wasting time' writing poetry, and angering his community; his relationship with 'Highland Mary'; his love for Jean Armour; his unsuccessful attempts at farming; his experiences as an excise officer; his death to the strains of *Auld Lang Syne.*
LP *Andrew Cruickshank, Christine Adrian, Richard Ross, Doris Palette, Malcolm Graham, Marian Spencer, Ernest Templeton, Jenny Laird, Charles Howard, Anne Wilson, Lina Nasby, Winifred Willard, Frank Strickland, Kate Agnew, John Rae, Vi Kaley, Frank Webster, Anita Graham.*

AUNT SALLY (1933) [4]
(USA: *Along Came Sally*)
Dir *Tim Whelan.* Prod *Michael Balcon.* Scr *Austin Melford, Guy Bolton, A.R. Rawlinson.* Ph *Charles Van Enger.* PC *Gainsborough.* Dis *Gaumont-British. 84 mins. Cert U*
Boisterous musical comedy with *Cicely Courtneidge* well to the fore as Sally, an aspiring cabaret artist who, by posing as a French 'star', Zaza, wangles her way into a job at Mike Kelly's nightclub. On the opening night, Sally is kidnapped by gangsters, American ex-associates of Kelly (*Sam Hardy*) and out to blackmail him. But Sally escapes and comes to Mike's rescue.
RoC *Hartley Power, Ben Welden, Leslie Holmes, Phyllis Clare, Billy Milton, Enrico Naldi, Ann Hope, Ivor McLaren, Rex Evans, The Carlyle Cousins, The Three Admirals, Val Rosing, The Naldi Trio, Reilly and Comfort, Debroy Somers and His Band, Tubby Cipen.*

AUTUMN CROCUS (1934) [4]
Dir and Prod and Scr *Basil Dean, from a play by C.L. Anthony.* Ph *Robert Martin.* PC *Associated Talking Pictures.* Dis *Associated British. 85 mins. Cert A*
Sensitively handled bitter-sweet romance about Jenny Gray (*Fay Compton*) a schoolteacher pushing 40 who spends a holiday in the Tyrol with her friend Edith (*Esme Church*). She falls in love with a young innkeeper (*Ivor Novello*); he confesses he loves her too, but she learns he has a wife and daughter. On Edith's advice, Jenny declines to have an affair but returns home with her memories.
RoC *Jack Hawkins, Diana Beaumont, Muriel Aked, Mignon O'Doherty, George Zucco, Frederick Ranalow, Gertrude Gould, Alice Sandor, Pamela Blake.*

THE AVENGING HAND (1936) [2]
Dir *W. Victor Hanbury.* Prod and PC *John Stafford.* Scr *Akos Tolnay, Reginald Long.* Dis *Radio. 64 mins. Cert A*
When an old match-seller is killed by swindlers, the jury returns a verdict of suicide. But Lee (*Noah Beery*), a Chicago gangster illegally in London, takes a hand and, with the help of his hotel clerk Pierre (*Louis Borrell*) exposes the murderer and disappears in time to avoid arrest and extradition, leaving Pierre to collect a reward. Confusing thriller.
RoC *Kathleen Kelly, James Harcourt, Ben Welden, Charles Oliver, Tarver Penna, Reginald Long, Penelope Parkes, Bela Mila, Henry Longhurst, Joan Kemp Welch, Bruno Barnabe, Billie de la Volta, Frederick Bush, Peter King, Alan Keith, Ben Wright, Sidney Benson, Basil Humphries, Colin Wade, E. Stuart.*

THE AWAKENING (1938) [1]
Dir and Prod *Toni Frenguelli.* Scr *Nigel Byass.* PC *Victory.* Dis *Columbia. 64 mins. Cert A*
Two doctors (*Eric Elliott, Rex Walker*) love the same woman (*Eve Gray*). She is about to choose one, when the other changes her mind by performing a brilliant operation on his ex-fiancée. Badly acted (with the exception of *Eve Gray*) and very primitive by 1938 standards. *No supporting cast issued.*

BACHELOR'S BABY (1932) [3]
Dir and Scr *Harry Hughes, from a novel by Rolph Bennett.* PC *BIP.* Dis *Pathé. 57 mins. Cert U*
Agreeable minor comedy about a young man, Jimmy (*William Freshman*) who finds an abandoned baby while motorcycling in the country. The question of the baby's adoption subsequently unites shy wooer Capt. Rogers (*Henry Wenman*) with the love of his life Aunt

Ann Casson and William Freshman in Bachelor's Baby *(1932)*

Mary (a welcome return by silent star *Alma Taylor*) as well as furthering Jimmy's own romance.
RoC *Ann Casson, Ethel Warwick, Charles Paton, Connie Emerald, Patrick Ludlow, Helen Goss.*

BAD BLOOD (1936)
See First Offence.

BAD BOY (1938)   [3]
Dir and Scr *Lawrence Huntington*. Prod *Vaughan N. Dean*. Ph *Stanley Grant*. PC *Radius Films*. Dis *RKO Radio*. 69 mins. Cert A
Jailed as a teenager for a crime he didn't commit, Nick (*John Warwick*) has since pursued a criminal life but now, on his release after his latest sentence, plans to go to Canada. When his old gang will not part with his share of the loot from his last 'job', Nick goes on the rampage. But a detective (*John Longden*) whose life he saves gets him off with a light sentence. This time he *will* go to Canada. Capably made thick-ear drama.
RoC *Kathleen Kelly, Gabrielle Brune, Brian Buchel, Richard Norris, Edie Martin, Ernest Sefton, Gordon Edwards, Ian Fleming, Victor Hagan, Harry Lane.*

BADGER'S GREEN (1934)   [4]
Dir *Adrian Brunel*. Prod *Uncredited*. Scr *R.J. Davis, Violet Powell, from the play by R.C. Sherriff*. PC and Dis *British and Dominions/Paramount British*. 68 mins. Cert U
Refreshing and capably directed rural comedy in which the cricket-loving villagers of Badger's Green unite to fight a modern development scheme which would destroy their village green. Complications arise when the developer's daughter (*Valerie Hobson*) falls for the protesters' leader's son (*Bruce Lister*). Everything is settled in the villagers' favour when they win a crucial cricket match against powerful opponents.
RoC *Frank Moore, David Horne, Sebastian Smith, John Turnbull, Wally Patch, Elsie Irving.*

BALL AT SAVOY (1935)   [2]
Dir *W. Victor Hanbury*. Prod *John Stafford*. Scr *Akos Tolnay, Reginald Long, from a play*

by *Alfred Grunwald, Fritz Lohner-Beda*. PC *Stafford Films*. Dis *Radio*. 74 mins. Cert U
Airy musical trifle about a diplomat who pretends to be a baron posing as a waiter in order to woo an opera star (no, don't ask). In the course of the action, everybody dresses up and pretends to be someone else, a necklace is stolen or lost half-a-dozen times and the diplomat is accused of being the thief, before winning his opera star.
LP *Conrad Nagel, Marta Labarr, Fred Conyngham, Lu-Anne Meredith, Aubrey Mather, Fred Duprez, Bela Mila, Dino Galvani, Monti de Lisle, Tony de Lungo, Esther Kiss, Bruno Barnabe.*

BAND WAGGON (1939)   [4]
Dir *Marcel Varnel*. Prod *Edward Black*. Scr *Marriott Edgar, Val Guest, from the radio series by Harry S. Pepper, Gordon Crier, Vernon Harris*. Ph *Henry Harris*. PC *Gainsborough*. Dis *General Film Distributors*. 85 mins. Cert U
Ejected from their flat at the top of Broadcasting House, Arthur and his pal Stinker (*Arthur Askey* and *Richard Murdoch*) rent a castle in Sussex, complete with a ghost (*Moore Marriott*) who is really the caretaker, paid by a gang of spies to keep callers away. The spies have installed TV apparatus in the cellars for spying on Allied planes. The boys put on a show at the castle which accidentally gets broadcast, and leads to a contract for them, and jail for the spies. Good fun, just the thing for wartime audiences.
RoC *Patricia Kirkwood, Jack Hylton (and His Band), Peter Gawthorne, Wally Patch, Donald Calthorp, Freddy Schweitzer, Bruce Trent, Michael Standing, C.H. Middleton, Jasmine Bligh, Jonah Barrington, James Hayter, Michael Hordern, Bernard Miles, Forsythe, Seamon and Farrell, The Sherman Fisher Girls.*

BANK HOLIDAY (1937)   [5]
(USA: *Three on a Weekend*)
Dir *Carol Reed*. Prod *Edward Black*. Scr *Rodney Ackland, Roger Burford*. Ph *Arthur Crabtree*. PC *Gainsborough*. Dis *General Film Distributors*. 86 mins. Cert A
A nurse (*Margaret Lockwood*) tries to snatch an illicit seaside weekend with her boyfriend, but is haunted by the memory of a young husband whose wife has just died in childbirth. She cuts short her holiday just in time to save him from suicide. This main theme is interwoven with other characters, including the mishaps of a Balham beauty queen (*René Ray*) and her confidante (*Merle Tottenham*) and a harassed cockney couple (*Wally Patch, Kathleen Harrison*) whose children create havoc at every turn. Skilfully drawn, solidly acted slice of life.
RoC *John Lodge, Hugh Williams, Garry Marsh, Linden Travers, Jeanne Stuart, Wilfrid Lawson, Felix Aylmer, Alf Goddard, Michael Rennie, Arthur West Payne, David Anthony, Angela Glynne.*

THE BANK MESSENGER MYSTERY (1936)   [2]
Dir and Scr *Lawrence Huntington*. Prod *Will*

Hammer. PC *Hammer*. Dis *Renown*. 57 mins. Cert A
Embittered by what he considers his wrongful dismissal from the bank where he has worked for years, George Brown (*George Mozart*) is easy prey for a gang planning to rob the bank and becomes their pawn. Inevitably, he comes to grief.
RoC *Francesca Bahrle, Paul Neville, Marilyn Love, Kenneth Kove, Frank Tickle.*

BARNACLE BILL (1934)   [3]
Dir *Harry Hughes*. Prod *Basil Humphries*. Scr *Aveling Ginever*. PC *City*. Dis *Butchers*. 90 mins. Cert U
Sailor Bill (*Archie Pitt*) leaves the sea and makes many other sacrifices for his daughter after his wife's death. When the girl (*Joan Gardner*) reaches adulthood, she has a stormy courtship with a wealthy youth. But social barriers are eventually broken down, and Bill feels able to return to the sea.
RoC *Gus McNaughton, Jean Adrienne, Sybil Jason, Denis O'Neil, O. B. Clarence, Henrietta Watson, Minnie Rayner, Iris Darbyshire, Tully Comber, Frank Atkinson, Helen Breen, Frank Titterton, Cynthia Stock, Donna le Bourdais.*

BAROUD (1932)   [2]
(USA: *Love in Morocco*)
Dir and PC *Rex Ingram*. Prod *Ingram, Mansfield Markham*. Scr *Ingram, Benno Vigny*. Ph *L.H. Burel, Marcel Lucien*. Dis *Ideal*. 80 mins. Cert A. Bilingual versions
Slight, slow romantic adventure made on location in Morocco, with *Rex Ingram*, who also directed, co-produced and co-wrote the film, as a sergeant in the Foreign Legion, falling in love with Zinah (*Rosita Garcia*), the exotic daughter of a Berber chief.
RoC *Dennis Hoey, Arabella Fields, Pierre Batchef, Andrews Engelmann, Felipe Montes, Laura Salerni.*

THE BARTON MYSTERY (1932)   [2]
Dir *Henry Edwards*. Prod *Herbert Wilcox*. Scr *Uncredited, from a play by Walter Hackett*. PC *British and Dominions*. Dis *Paramount*. 76 mins. Cert A
Second film version of Walter Hackett's play about a man wrongly charged with murder, committed by a girl who finally admits the truth. But a fake medium helps her prove that the victim was a blackmailer and she killed him in self-defence.
LP *Ion Swinley, Ursula Jeans, Lyn Harding, Ellis Jeffreys, Wendy Barrie, Tom Helmore, O.B. Clarence, Joyce Bland, Franklyn Bellamy, Wilfred Noy.*

THE BATTLE (1934)   [4]
Dir *Nicolas Farkas*. Prod *Leon Garganoff*. Scr *Farkas, Bernard Zimmer, from a novel by Claude Farrere*. PC *Lionofilm*. Dis *Gaumont-British*. 85 mins. Cert A
Dramatic war film with some vivid battle scenes, set in Japan in the early 1900s, where the Marquis Yorisaka (*Charles Boyer*) forces his wife (*Merle Oberon*) to seduce Fergan (*John Loder*) to obtain strategic secrets. But the Mar-

quise and Fergan fall in love and the British triumph.
RoC *Betty Stockfeld, Valerie Inkijoff, Miles Mander, Henri Fabert.*

BEAUTY AND THE BARGE (1937) [2]
Dir *Henry Edwards.* Prod *Julius Hagen.* Scr *H. Fowler Mear, from the play by W.W. Jacobs.* Ph *Sydney Blythe, William Luff.* PC *Twickenham.* Dis *Wardour.* 71 mins. Cert U
Running away from an unwanted marriage, Ethel (*Judy Gunn*) is taken in by barge skipper Barley (*Gordon Harker*), to the fury of the widow he is courting. A young naval officer (*Jack Hawkins*) falls for Ethel and signs on incognito as mate on the barge. When her family catch up with her, his charm soon wins them over. Laboured comedy remake of 1914 silent.
RoC *George Carney, Margaret Rutherford, Ronald Shiner, Michael Shepley, Margaret Yarde, Sebastian Smith, Margaret Scudamore, Anne Wemyss, Frank Bertram, Hal Walters, Harry Terry.*

BE CAREFUL, MR SMITH (1935) [2]
Dir and Prod *Max Mack.* Scr *Frank Atkinson, Ernest Longstaffe.* PC *Union.* Dis *Apex.* 72 mins. Cert U
Ragged comedy about elderly Mr Smith (*Frank Atkinson*) who retires from his clerical job but, dreading full-time life with his nagging wife, buys a bookmaking business, becomes involved with a share-selling swindle and is responsible for bringing the sharpsters involved to justice, winning a new respect from Mrs Smith.
RoC *Bobbie Comber, Cecil Ramage, Bertha Belmore, (C.) Denier Warren, Bertha Ricardo, Warren C. Jenkins.*

BED AND BREAKFAST (1930) [3]
Dir *Walter Forde.* Prod *L'Estrange Fawcett.* Scr *H. Fowler Mear, from the play by Frederick Witney.* Ph *William Shenton.* PC and Dis *Gaumont.* 68 mins. Cert U
A mixed critical reception greeted this popular comedy about two honeymooners who, parted after a tiff, become involved with neighbours, burglars, a pontifical clergyman and his meek little wife, a posse of policemen and a genial Cockney bookmaker, before finally becoming reconciled.

Jane Baxter and David Hawthorne in Bed and Breakfast *(1930)*

LP *Jane Baxter, Richard Cooper, Sari Maritza, David Hawthorne, Alf Goddard, Cyril McLaglen, Muriel Aked, Frederick Volpe, Ruth Maitland, Mike Johnson, Ian Wilson, Matthew Boulton, Alexander Gilletto.*

BED AND BREAKFAST (1936) [1]
Dir and Prod and PC *Walter West.* Scr *Frank Miller.* Dis *Coronel.* 59 mins. Cert A
Bert Fink (*Barry Lupino*), an ageing actor 'resting' between assignments, helps the other people at his boarding house – a struggling composer, a writer and his wife with a baby on the way, a typist, a maid. The composer finds success and marries the typist. Bert becomes his manager. The baby arrives safely. The boarding house is left empty – possibly like cinemas playing this stodgily acted film.
RoC *Mabel Poulton, Frank Miller, Daphne Courtney, Florence leRoy.*

BEDTIME STORY (1938) [1]
Dir and Scr *Donovan Pedelty, from the play by Walter Ellis.* Prod *Victor M. Greene.* Ph *Ernest Palmer.* PC *Admiral.* Dis *Grand National.* 71 mins. Cert U
Lady Blundell's unhappy orphan niece Judy (*Lesley Wareing*) runs away from her, and impersonates a millionairess to try to get a ticket to America. The arrival of the millionairess' husband foils her plan, and she eventually goes to live on a farm with her uncle (*Eliot Makeham*), where she falls for the ex-fiancé of her selfish cousin. Poor 'story' lacks simplicity.
RoC *Jack Livesey, Dorothy Dewhurst, Margery Morris, Michael Bazalgette, Jonathan Field.*

THE BEGGAR STUDENT (1931) [3]
Dir *John Harvel, Victor Hanbury.* Prod *Harvel.* Scr *John Stafford, Hans Zerlett, from the operetta by Millöcker and Gene.* PC *Amalgamated Films Associated.* Dis *British Lion.* 64 mins. Cert U. Bilingual versions
Typical Heidelberg-type musical (music by Carl Millöcker) about an impecunious countess (*Margaret Halstan*) who is relying on her daughter (*Shirley Dale*) to make a wealthy marriage to a colonel (*Frederick Lloyd*). Following events at a masked ball, the daughter becomes free to marry her lover (*Lance Fairfax*) while mother gets the colonel.
RoC *Jerry Verno, Jill Hands, Ashley Cooper, Millicent Wolf, Mark Daly, Alfred Wellesley.*

BEHIND YOUR BACK (1937)
Dir and Scr *Donovan Pedelty, from the play by Charles Landstone.* Prod *Victor M. Greene.* Ph *Stanley Grant.* PC *Crusade.* Dis *Paramount.* 70 mins. Cert A
As opening night of a new play approaches, most of the company have problems. Archie (*Jack Livesey*) splits with stage manager Gwen (*Elizabeth Astell*) when he discovers her scarlet past. Mary (*Rani Waller*), the doorman's wife, just about rescues her husband from the clutches of predatory cashier Kitty (*Dinah Sheridan*). Then there's the playwright and the cast.... All pretty dull though, with not much real action.

RoC *Stella Bonheur, Desmond Marshall, Kenneth Buckley, Tonie Edgar Bruce, Raymond Lovell, Jimmy Mageean, Molly Hamley-Clifford, Jonathan Field, Dorothy Dewhurst.*

BELLA DONNA (1934) [3]
Dir *Robert Milton.* Prod *Julius Hagen.* Scr *H. Fowler Mear, from a play by James B. Fagan and a novel by Robert Hichens.* Ph *Sydney Blythe, William Luff.* PC *Twickenham.* Dis *Gaumont-British.* 91 mins. Cert A
Critics disagreed over the merits of this romantic drama in which a widow (*Mary Ellis*) marries an engineer (*John Stuart*) and goes with him to Egypt, where she has an affair with the fascinating Baroudi (*Conrad Veidt*). At her lover's instigation, she tries to poison her husband, but he is saved by his doctor friend (*Cedric Hardwicke*) and the price of her failure is rejection by Baroudi.
RoC *Michael Shepley, Jeanne Stuart, Rodney Millington, Eve*

THE BELLES OF ST CLEMENT'S (1935) [1]
Dir *Ivar Campbell.* Prod *Anthony Havelock-Allan.* Scr *Terence Rattigan.* PC and Dis *British and Dominions/Paramount British.* 69 mins. Cert A
Highly coloured melodrama at a girls' high school. Eileen (*Eileen Munro*) who thinks more of men than lessons, is shattered when she learns her parents are going to marry her off to an American cousin she has never seen. She runs away and is involved in a (stolen) car smash. Her friend Eve (*Evelyn Foster*) whose beret is found in the wreck, is faced with expulsion. It's the American cousin who sets things to rights.
RoC *Meriel Forbes, Isobel Scaife, Heather White, Basil Langton, Enid Lindsay, Sonia Somers, Tosca von Bissing, Don Tidbury, Arthur Metcalfe, Frederick Bradshaw.*

THE BELLS (1931) [2]
Dir *Oscar M. Werndorff, Harcourt Templeman.* Prod *Isidore Schlesinger, Sergei Nolbandov.* Scr *C.H. Dand, from a play by Erckmann and Chatrian.* Ph *Günther Krampf.* PC *British Sound Films.* Dis *Producers' Distributing Corporation.* 75 mins. Cert A. Trilingual versions
Modernized version of the play made famous on stage by Sir Henry Irving, but not up to the 1926 Hollywood version with Lionel Barrymore and Boris Karloff. Conscience gnaws at a burgomaster until, driven mad by the sound of the bells on his daughter's wedding day, he confesses before the guests to a long-forgotten murder. He goes out and drowns himself.
LP *Donald Calthrop, Jane Welsh, Edward Sinclair, O.B. Clarence, Wilfred Shine, Ralph Truman.*

BELOVED IMPOSTER (1936) [2]
Dir *W. Victor Hanbury.* Prod *John Stafford.* Scr *Connery Chappell, from a novel by Ethel Mannin.* PC *Stafford.* Dis *Radio.* 86 mins. Cert A
Wearisome musical drama somewhat enlivened

by *René Ray's* performance. George (*Fred Conyngham*) a boastful waiter, fancies himself as a cabaret star and goes to London, where he is given rooms by Mary (*Miss Ray*) but falls for the more sophisticated charms of La Chinoise (*Germaine Aussey*), a singer. When she rejects him after leading him on, he attacks her and thinks he has killed her. Mary shelters him, but the vamp proves to have survived and George is offered a cabaret contract.

RoC *Lawrence Hanray, Leslie 'Hutch' Hutchinson, Penelope Parkes, Edwin Ellis, Charles Oliver, Fred Groves, Bela Mila, Tony de Lungo, Gwen Farrar, Sydney Culver, Phil Thomas, Quinton McPherson, Reginald Long, Dino Galvani, W. Scott Harold, Bombardier Billy Wells, Bruno Barnabe, Jack Beaumont, Frederick Bush, The Caligary Brothers.*

THE BELOVED VAGABOND (1936) [3]
Dir *Kurt (Curtis) Bernhardt*. Prod *Ludovico Toeplitz*. Scr *Wells Root, Arthur Wimperis, Hugh Mills, Walter Creighton, from a novel by W.J. Locke*. Ph *Franz Planer*. PC *Toeplitz Productions*. Dis *Associated British*. 78 mins. Cert A. Bilingual versions

The critics had divided opinions on this; one of them thought it 'the best work of Maurice Chevalier's career', another found the film 'trite and tedious'. *Chevalier* plays a man who gives up his sweetheart (*Betty Stockfeld*) to enable her to marry a count and save her father from ruin. He hits the road, teaming up with Blanquette (*Margaret Lockwood*), an orphan whose grandfather founded an orchestra that he takes over. His old sweetheart, now a widow, re-emerges, but he realizes that he is in love with Blanquette.

RoC *Desmond Tester, Austin Trevor, Peter Haddon, Charles Carson, Cathleen Nesbitt, Barbara Gott, D.J. Williams, (C.) Denier Warren.*

THE BERMONDSEY KID (1933) [3]
Dir *Ralph Dawson*. Prod *Irving Asher*. Scr *W. Scott Darling*. PC *Warner Bros*. Dis *First National*. 76 mins. Cert A

Boxing drama about a fighting newsboy (*Esmond Knight*) who finally gets the chance to fight his friend and idol, Joe Dougherty (*Ellis Irving*). Strangely Dougherty is out of shape and Eddie, the newsboy, knocks him out – then finds that his manager, Lou (*Ernest Sefton*) has bribed Toots (*Eve Gray*) to keep Joe out of training as much as possible. Eddie knocks Lou out as well – and arranges a rematch.

RoC *Pat Paterson, Clifford McLaglen, Syd Crossley, Winifred Oughton, Len Harvey, George Cook, Anna Lee.*

BETRAYAL (1932) [3]
Dir, Prod and Scr *Reginald Fogwell, from a play by Hubert Griffith*. PC *Fogwell Films*. Dis *Universal*. 66 mins. Cert A

Wealthy John Armytage (*Stewart Rome*) whose wife Diana (*Marjorie Hume*) married him for his money, offers no defence to a charge of murder, lest he drag her name into disrepute, after shooting a man he believed to be her

lover. Diana perjures herself in court to clear her husband: only he will now know that she was *not* having an affair.

RoC *Leslie Perrins, Henry Hewitt, J. Fisher White, Frank Atherley, E.H. Williams, Charles Childerstone.*

BEYOND THE CITIES (1930) [3]
Dir and Prod *Carlyle Blackwell*. Scr *Blackwell, Noel Shannon*. PC *Piccadilly*. Dis *Paramount*. 70 mins. Cert A

American director-actor *Carlyle Blackwell* also starred in this melodrama, as sportsman Jim Campbell who, swindled out of his money by an unscrupulous lawyer, tries to make his fortune in Canada as a rancher. He helps Mary (*Edna Best*) whose plane crashes, the accident leaving her with amnesia. Jim advertises her whereabouts, and it turns out that her father is the crooked lawyer....

RoC *Alexander Field, Lawrence Hanray, Helen Haye, Eric Maturin, Percy Parsons.*

BIG BUSINESS (1930) [2]
Dir and Prod *Oscar M. Sheridan*. Scr *Sheridan, Hubert W. David*. PC *Sheridan Films*. Dis *Fox*. 76 mins. Cert U

Lacklustre musical, spun out to reach its 76 minutes. The story, concerning business partners who rejuvenate a night-club by staging cabarets with top-line talent, is merely a peg on which to hang a series of music-hall acts.

LP *Frances Day, Barrie Oliver, Anthony Ireland, Virginia Vaughan, Ben Welden, Jimmy Godden, Billy Fry, Elsie Percival, Leslie 'Hutch' Hutchinson, Leon Cortez with Giggie, The Sherman Fisher Girls, Arthur Roseberry and His Symphonic Syncopated Orchestra.*

BIG BUSINESS (1934) [2]
Dir *Cyril Gardner*. Prod *Irving Asher*. Scr *Gardner, Claude Hulbert*. PC and Dis *Warner Bros*. 54 mins. Cert U

Unambitious starring vehicle for *Claude Hulbert*, featuring him as Reggie Pullett, who throws in his lot with two burglars, and agrees to pose as a financier whom he resembles. He finds that the financier has swindled Sylvia (*Eve Gray*), but that his firm is on the verge of bankruptcy. By sheer luck, Reggie corrects the situation, saves the firm and wins Sylvia.

RoC *Ernest Sefton, James Finlayson, Hal Walters, Maude Zimbla.*

BIG FELLA (1937) [2]
Dir and Prod *James Elder Wills*. Scr *Fenn Sherie, Ingram d'Abbes, from a novel by Claude McKay*. Ph *Cyril Bristow*. PC *Fortune Films*. Dis *British Lion*. 73 mins. Cert U

Joe, a lazy vagabond (*Paul Robeson*), is known to all on the Marseilles waterfront through his superb singing voice. He is hired to search for a kidnapped boy and finds him, but the boy, having actually run away, threatens to name Joe as the kidnapper if he takes him back. Later, the boy really is kidnapped, but the resourceful Joe turns the situation to his advantage, and manages to retain his life of indolence. Below-par vehicle for *Robeson* with a couple of songs.

RoC *Eldon Grant, Elisabeth Welch, Marcelle Rogez, Roy Emerton, Joyce Kennedy, Eric Cowley, James Hayter, Lawrence Brown.*

THE BIG NOISE (1936) [2]
Dir *Alex Bryce*. Prod *John Findlay*. Scr *Gerard Fairlie*. Ph *Stanley Grant*. PC and Dis *Fox British*. 65 mins. Cert U

Laughs are few in this comedy about two crooked company directors who try to make a lowly employee (*Alastair Sim*) the scapegoat for their dishonesty. He's well on his way to obliging them when the company secretary (*Norah Howard*) comes to his rescue by exposing the conspirators.

RoC *Fred Duprez, (C.) Denier Warren, Grizelda Hervey, Viola Compton, Peter Popp, Howard Douglas, Edie Martin, Desmond Roberts, Reginald Forsyth and His Band, Cap the Goat.*

Alastair Sim in The Big Noise (*1936*)

THE BIG SPLASH (1935) [2]
Dir *Leslie Hiscott*. Prod *Herbert Smith*. Scr *Michael Barringer*. PC *British Lion*. Dis *MGM*. 66 mins. Cert U

Comedy about a millionaire (*Finlay Currie*) reluctantly engaged to a gold-digger (*Marguerite Allan*). He hires a married man to pose as him, but becomes involved with crooks and ends up marrying the gold-digger after all.

RoC *Frank Pettingell, Drusilla Wills, Ben Welden, Percy Parsons, Roy Royston.*

BILL AND COO (1931) [3]
Dir and Prod *John Orton*. Scr *Orton, Billy Merson*. Ph *Walter Harvey, Horace Wheddon*. PC *BIP*. Dis *Wardour*. 42 mins. Cert U

Short, revue-style entertainment as Bendo the Strong Man dreams of romance and a honeymoon with Nita, a gorgeous entertainer.

LP *Billy Merson, Nita Underwood, Hal Gordon, Leslie Hamilton, Nan Kennedy, Herman Darewski, O.K. Wise, Eddie Earle.*

BILL'S LEGACY (1931) [2]
Dir *Harry J. Revier*. Prod *Julius Hagen*. Scr *Leslie Fuller, Syd Courtenay*. PC *Twickenham*. Dis *Ideal*. 57 mins. Cert A

After paperhanger Bill Smithers (*Leslie Fuller*) has inherited a legacy, he and his wife (*Mary Clare*) move into smart society. He buys a racehorse from a countess (*Angela Joyce*), but the horse is a turkey, his bank fails and

Bill is left with nothing, except his wife who, having got fed up with his antics, is now reconciled to him. Unsubtle comedy, not one of Fuller's best.

RoC *Syd Courtenay, Ethel Leslie, Ivan Crowe, Lola Harvey.*

BIRDS OF A FEATHER (1931)   2

Dir *Ben R. Hart.* Prod and PC *P.W. Macnamara.* Dis *G & L. 52 mins. Cert A*
Romantic story of a loose-living adventurer (*Haddon Mason*) reformed by his love for the daughter (*Dorothy Bartlam*) of a widowed artist.

RoC *Edith Saville, Robert Horton, Gladys Dunham.*

BIRDS OF A FEATHER (1935)   4

Dir *John Baxter.* Prod *John Barter.* Scr *Con West, Gerald Elliott, from a play by George Foster.* Ph *Ronald Neame.* PC *Baxter and Barter.* Dis *Universal. 69 mins. Cert U*
Several noteworthy comedy performances lift this farce about a 'sausage king' (*George Robey*) with social ambitions, and the poverty-stricken earl (*Horace Hodges*) whose castle he rents. Hidden treasure is discovered, the earl poses as a servant in his own castle and a gang of burglars is rounded up before the sausage king returns to the peace of suburbia, though his son marries the earl's daughter.

RoC *Eve Lister, Jack Melford, Diana Beaumont, Sebastian Shaw, Veronica Brady, Julian Royce, (C.) Denier Warren, Ian Wilson, Fred Hearne, Billy Percy, Charles Mortimer, Eve Chapman, Maud Locker.*

BIRDS OF PREY (1930)   1
(USA: *The Perfect Alibi*)

Dir and Prod *Basil Dean.* Scr *Dean, A.A. Milne, from a play by Milne.* PC *ATP.* Dis *Radio. 98 mins. Cert A*
Another early ATP disaster, a slow-moving thriller set in a country mansion where Arthur Hilton (*C. Aubrey Smith*) is murdered by two of his guests at a house-party. The crime appears to be suicide, but Hilton's ward (*Dorothy Boyd*) and her fiancé (*Frank Lawton*) prove otherwise, after working out a vital clue involving a sheet of blotting paper.

RoC *Robert Loraine, Warwick Ward, David Hawthorne, Ellis Jeffreys, Nigel Bruce, Jack Hawkins, Tom Reynolds.*

THE BITER BIT (1937)   2

Dir *Redd Davis.* Prod *Ivor McLaren.* Scr *Al Booth.* Ph *Roy Kellino.* PC and Dis *Fox British. 49 mins. Cert A*
Fragile and far-fetched comic anecdote about a mild-mannered clerk, henpecked by his domineering wife, who seeks solitude on a South Sea island.

Briefly first released as **Calling All Ma's.**

LP *Billy Caryll, Hilda Munday, Margaret Yarde, Anthony Shaw, Julien Vedey, Charles Castella, Phillip Holles.*

BITTER SWEET (1933)   4

Dir and Prod *Herbert Wilcox.* Scr *Lydia Hayward, Wilcox, Monckton Hoffe, from the oper-*etta *by Noël Coward.* Ph *F.A. Young.* PC *British and Dominions.* Dis *United Artists. 93 mins. Cert A*
Persuasive musical weepie with *Anna Neagle* as Sarah, who marries her music teacher Carl (*Fernand Graavey*) in Vienna. To make ends meet, Carl gets a job in a café orchestra and Sarah becomes a professional dancing partner. Carl is killed in a duel, defending Sarah's honour against an amorous count (*Miles Mander*), but years later her story of happiness despite hardship enables another young girl to make a similar decision.

RoC *Ivy St Helier, Esmé Percy, Hugh Williams, Pat Paterson, Gibb McLaughlin, Stuart Robertson, Clifford Heatherley, Kay Hammond, Patrick Ludlow, Norma Whalley, Alan Napier.*

THE BLACK ABBOT (1933)   2

Dir *George A. Cooper.* Prod *Julius Hagen.* Scr *H. Fowler Mear, from a novel by Philip Godfrey.* PC *Real Art.* Dis *Radio. 56 mins. Cert U*
Weakish thriller in which wealthy Lord Jerry (*Richard Cooper*) is held to ransom in his own stately home by a gang of crooks led by Charlie (*Ben Welden*), but is rescued, initially through the efforts of his friend Frank (*John Stuart*) and finally by the police.

RoC *Drusilla Wills, Edgar Norfolk, Farren Soutar, Cyril Smith, John Turnbull.*

BLACK COFFEE (1931)   3

Dir *Leslie Hiscott.* Prod *Julius Hagen.* Scr *Brock Williams, H. Fowler Mear, from the play by Agatha Christie.* PC *Twickenham.* Dis *W and F. 78 mins. Cert U*
Austin Trevor's second screen outing as Agatha Christie's detective Hercule Poirot has him investigating the double mystery of the theft of the formula for a new explosive and the subsequent murder-by-poisoning of its inventor (*C.V. France*). As usual, Poirot triumphs; but critical reaction was mixed.

RoC *Adrianne Allen, Richard Cooper, Elizabeth Allan, Philip Strange, Dino Galvani, Michael Shepley, Melville Cooper, Marie Wright, Leila Page, Harold Meade, S.A. Cookson.*

Adrianne Allen and Elizabeth Allan in Black Coffee *(1931)*

BLACK EYES (1939)   3

Dir *Herbert Brenon.* Prod *Walter C. Mycroft.* Scr *Dudley Leslie, from a play by V. Tourjan-*sky. Ph *Günther Krampf.* PC and Dis *Associated British. 70 mins. Cert A*
Petrov (*Otto Kruger*), head waiter at a fashionable Moscow restaurant, has an unreasoned fear of his daughter (*Mary Maguire*) finding out his occupation. To provide her with luxuries, he arranges 'affairs' for clients, and makes use of their knowledge on the Stock Exchange. But she falls in love, not, as he had hoped, with her music teacher (*John Wood*), but with one of his philandering patrons (*Walter Rilla*) - and he is forced to reveal everything. Slow drama has a certain strange charm.

RoC *Marie Wright, Cecil Ramage, Kenneth Kove, Jenny Laird, O.B. Clarence, Walford Hayden and His Orchestra, Derek Farr.*

THE BLACK HAND GANG (1930)   2

Dir *Monty Banks.* Scr *Victor Kendall, from a playlet by R.P. Weston and Bert Lee.* Ph *Walter Blakeley, Ernest Palmer.* PC *BIP.* Dis *Wardour. 63 mins. Cert U*
Popular variety star *Wee Georgie Wood* in an extended film version of one of his popular music-hall sketches. He plays a rich kid who's the leader of a gang of boys who inadvertently catch a real notorious criminal, and hand him over to the police.

RoC *Violet Young, Dolly Harmer, Lionel Hoare, Junior Banks, Viola Compton, Alfred Woods.*

BLACK LIMELIGHT (1938)   4

Dir *Paul L. Stein.* Prod *Walter C. Mycroft.* Scr *Dudley Leslie, Walter Summers, from a play by Gordon Sherry.* Ph *Claude Friese-Greene.* PC and Dis *Associated British. 70 mins. Cert A*
Peter (*Raymond Massey*), wanted for the murder of his mistress, evades a police cordon and returns to his wife Mary (*Joan Marion*). His solicitor, Crawford (*Walter Hudd*) advises Peter to surrender, plead guilty and ask for mercy. Meanwhile a handkerchief gives Mary a clue to the real killer. Peter gives himself up while Mary tricks the murderer, Crawford, into revealing himself. Police re-enter the house with Peter before Crawford can add Mary to his victims. Strong melodrama, solidly made.

RoC *Henry Oscar, Coral Browne, Diana Beaumont, Elliot Mason, Dan Tobin, Leslie Bradley, Robert Beatty.*

BLACK MASK (1935)   2

Dir *Ralph Ince.* Prod *Irving Asher.* Scr *Paul Gengelin, Frank Launder, Michael Barringer, from a novel by Bruce Graeme.* Ph *Basil Emmott.* PC and Dis *Warner Bros. 67 mins. Cert A*
Poorly treated 'Raffles'-type frolic in which a gentleman crook (*Ellis Irving*) forces mean society folk to cough up for charity by stealing their valuables. When his next prospective 'victim' is found murdered, suspicion points to him. But, with the help of an old lag and his partner-in-crime, he clears himself and marries the victim's daughter.

RoC *Aileen Marson, Wylie Watson, Wyndham Goldie, Joyce Kennedy, Herbert Lomas, John Turnbull, Kate Cutler, Marjorie Rodgers.*

THE BLACK TULIP (1937) [1]

Dir *Alex Bryce.* Prod *John Findlay.* Scr *Uncredited, from the novel by Alexandre Dumas.* PC and Dis *Fox British.* 57 mins. Cert A

Bearing only the faintest of resemblances to the Dumas original, this is an unexciting period adventure in which an envious tulip merchant attempts, without success, to steal from a young cultivator three black tulip bulbs certain to bring great financial reward to the owner.

LP *Patrick Waddington, Anne Soreen, Campbell Gullan, Jay Laurier, Wilson Coleman, Bernard Lee, Florence Hunt, Ronald Shiner, Aubrey Mallalieu, W.S. Percy.*

BLARNEY (1938) [2]
(USA: *Ireland's Border Line*)

Dir *Harry O'Donovan.* Prod and Scr *O'Donovan, Jimmy O'Dea.* PC *OD Productions.* Dis *Associated British.* 68 mins. Cert U

An Irish hobo-salesman (*Jimmy O'Dea*) inadvertently takes a case of jewels in mistake for his own case filled with bottles of cough medicine. He accepts a job at the local inn, where the barmaid throws the case into the dairy. The two crooks who stole the jewels try to get their loot back but fail. Local colour swamps both the comedy and the story.

RoC *Myrette Morven, Ronald Malcolmson, Hazel Hughes, Julie Suedo, Kenneth Warrington, Noel Purcell.*

THE BLARNEY STONE (1933) [4]
(USA: *The Blarney Kiss*)

Dir *Tom Walls.* Prod *Herbert Wilcox.* Scr *A.R. Rawlinson, Lennox Robinson.* PC *British and Dominions.* Dis *W and F.* 81 mins. Cert U

A change of pace for Tom Walls as a genial Irishman in a story which, although it has a vein of comedy, is basically solid drama. Tim, the Irishman, has given shelter to Lord Breethorpe (*Robert Douglas*) and his sister Lady Anne (*Anne Grey*), who are able to repay the debt by getting him a job in the City. Tim soon makes good, but Breethorpe has been using the firm's money to pay debts and the firm crashes. Tim is briefly imprisoned, but Breethorpe clears him before ending his own life.

RoC *Haidee Wright, Zoë Palmer, Louis Bradfield, W.G. Fay, Dorothy Tetley, J.A. O'Rourke, Charles Carson, George Barrett, Robert Horton, Peter Gawthorne.*

BLIND FOLLY (1939) [2]

Dir *Reginald Denham.* Prod and PC *George Smith.* Scr *H.F. Maltby.* Ph *Geoffrey Faithfull.* Dis *RKO Radio.* 78 mins. Cert U

Oddly titled comedy about a country man, George (*Clifford Mollison*) who inherits a night club in town from his brother Fred who had been mixed up in stolen diamonds which are now hidden at the club. Crooks are after the gems but, with the aid of a pretty secretary (*Lilli Palmer*), George outwits them. Rather too long.

RoC *Leslie Perrins, William Kendall, Gus McNaughton, Elliot Mason, David Horne, Gertrude Musgrove, Roland Culver, Antony Holles, Jack Vyvyan.*

BLIND JUSTICE (1934) [2]

Dir *Bernard Vorhaus.* Prod *Julius Hagen.* Scr *Vera Allinson, from a play by Arnold Ridley.* Ph *Sydney Blythe.* PC *Real Art.* Dis *Universal.* 73 mins. Cert A

Peggy (*Geraldine Fitzgerald*) is engaged to Dick (*Frank Vosper*), a blackmailer who, when Peggy wants to break it off and marry Gilbert (*Roger Livesey*), threatens to reveal that Peggy's brother Ralph (*John Mills*) did not die a hero's death in the war but was shot for cowardice. Her older brother (*John Stuart*) plans to murder Dick, but fate takes a hand, and the housekeeper (*Eva Moore*) accidentally sends the blackmailer to eternity. Punchless drama.

RoC *Lucy Beaumont, Hay Petrie, Charles Carson.*

BLIND MAN'S BLUFF (1936) [2]

Dir and Prod *Albert Parker.* Scr *Cecil Maiden, from a play by William Foster and B. Scott-Elder.* Ph *Stanley Grant.* PC and Dis *Fox British.* 72 mins. Cert A

Dr Fairfax (*Basil Sydney*), blinded in an accident, goes on with his efforts to perfect an invention to make the human body invisible. His faithless wife (*Enid Stamp-Taylor*) steals the invention for her lover's financial gain but, unbeknown to her, Fairfax has got back his sight and, with the help of his two assistants (*James Mason, Barbara Greene*), regains the formula and kisses his wife goodbye.

RoC *Ian Colin, Iris Ashley, Wilson Coleman, E. Warburton Gamble, Betty Summers, C. Howard, Tuff de Lyle (dog).*

THE BLIND SPOT (1932) [2]

Dir *John Daumery.* Prod *Irving Asher.* Scr *Roland Pertwee, John Hastings Turner.* PC and Dis *Warner Bros.* 75 mins. Cert A

Knocked down by a car, Marilyn (*Muriel Angelus*), daughter of a gentleman crook (*Percy Marmont*), loses her memory. She marries Hugh (*Warwick Ward*), a barrister, who turns out to be prosecuting counsel when her father is arrested for theft. Hugh refuses the brief, and Marilyn's father commits suicide in his prison cell. Grim in every respect.

RoC *Laura Cowie, Ivor Barnard, George Merritt, Mary Jerrold, Eric Stanley.*

BLOCKADE
See **'Q' Ships** (1928).

BLONDES FOR DANGER (1938) [5]

Dir *Jack Raymond.* Prod and PC *Herbert Wilcox.* Scr *Gerald Elliott, from a novel by Evadne Price.* Ph *Frederick A. Young.* Dis *British Lion.* 69 mins. Cert A

A taxi-driver Alf (*Gordon Harker*), threatened by a blonde with a breach of promise suit, encounters another, Valerie (*Enid Stamp-Taylor*) who persuades him to drive a prince into the country. The prince is shot and wounded by a man determined to prevent him signing a treaty and it is only thanks to Alf's resourcefulness that he is got out of the country. Alf, richly rewarded, views blondes in a different light. Lively dialogue, seamless alter-

Enid Stamp-Taylor and Gordon Harker in Blondes for Danger (*1938*)

nation of comedy and thrills and Harker at the top of his fruitiest form.

RoC *Ivan Brandt, Janet Johnson, Percy Parsons, Everley Gregg, Charles Eaton, Henry Wolston.*

BLOSSOM TIME (1934) [4]
(USA: *April Romance*)

Dir *Paul L. Stein.* Prod *Walter C. Mycroft.* Scr *John Drinkwater, Roger Burford, Paul Perez, G.H. Clutsam.* Ph *Otto Kanturek.* PC *BIP.* Dis *Wardour.* 91 mins. Cert A

Viennese romance of great charm, with *Richard Tauber* as the composer Franz Schubert, falling in love with Vicki (*Jane Baxter*), losing her to Count Von Hohenberg (*Carl Esmond*) and helping the lovers gain the consent of the formidable archduchess (*Athene Seyler*) who is the patroness of Von Hohenberg's regiment.

RoC *Paul Graetz, Charles Carson, Marguerite Allan, Edward Chapman, Lester Matthews, Gibb McLaughlin, Frederick Lloyd, Hugh Dempster, Bertha Belmore, Ivan Samson, Cecil Ramage.*

Carl Esmond and Jane Baxter in Blossom Time (*1934*)

THE BLUE DANUBE (1931) [2]

Dir and Prod *Herbert Wilcox.* Scr *Miles Malleson.* Ph *F.A. Young.* PC *British and Dominions.* Dis *W and F.* 71 mins. Cert A. Bilingual versions

A musical romance set among Hungarian gipsies, one of whom deserts his lover for the more sophisticated attentions of a come-hither countess, but eventually returns.

LP *Brigitte Helm, Joseph Schildkraut, Dorothy Bouchier, Desmond Jeans, Patrick Ludlow, Alfred Rode (and his Tzigane Band), Massine and Nikitina.*

BLUE SMOKE (1935)   [2]

Dir *Ralph Ince.* Prod *John Barrow.* Scr *Fenn Sherie, Ingram d'Abbes.* Ph *Alex Bryce.* PC and Dis *Fox British. 74 mins. Cert U*
Romantic drama of gipsy life in which a young Romany (*Bruce Seton*) fails to win a major boxing championship thanks to the scheming of a rival, who loves the same girl (*Tamara Desni*). Ragged story with *Ralph Ince* as a tough boxing promoter, a performance far superior to his direction.
RoC *Ian Colin, Eric Hales, Hal Walters, Beryl de Querton, Wilson Coleman, Jock McKay, Billy Shine, Phil Ray, Ben Williams, Scruffy the Dog.*

THE BLUE SQUADRON (1934)   [3]

Dir *George King.* Prod *Irving Asher.* Scr *Brock Williams.* PC *Warner Bros/Steffano Pittaluga.* Dis *First National. 96 mins. Cert A*
Spectacular flying scenes compensate for a weak story. Two childhood friends become pilots in the Italian Air Force's famous Blue Squadron, then fall out over a girl. When Carlo (*Esmond Knight*) crashes in the Alps, Mario (*John Stuart*), learning that his suspicions about his girl (*Greta Hansen*) and Carlo are unfounded, flies to the rescue in the teeth of a storm. Made with the co-operation of the Italian Air Force.
RoC *Cecil Parker, Barrie Livesey, Ralph Reader, Hay Plumb, Hamilton Keene.*

THE BODY VANISHES (1939)   [2]

Dir *Walter Tennyson.* Prod *Alfred D'Eyncourt.* Scr *Ian Walker.* Ph *Desmond Dickinson.* PC *Venture.* Dis *New Realm. 45 mins. Cert U*
Rodney Paine (*Anthony Hulme*) steals a valuable painting from his partner Piper (*C. Denier Warren*), then elaborately stages his own 'death'. But his scheme backfires. Not on general release.
RoC *Ernest Sefton, Eve Foster, Wilfred Noy, Frank Atkinson.*

BOOMERANG (1934)   [2]

Dir and Prod and PC *Arthur Maude.* Scr *John Paddy Carstairs, from a play by David Evans.* Dis *Columbia. 82 mins. Cert A*
Stagebound drama about a blind man (*Lester Matthews*) and his disfigured wife (*Nora Swinburne*). When he finds out that she is being blackmailed, the husband sets out to make amends for wrongs he has committed against her in the past.
RoC *Millicent Wolf, Harvey Braban, Wallace Geoffrey, Charles Mortimer.*

BOOTS! BOOTS! (1934)   [3]

Dir *Bert Tracy.* Prod *John E. Blakeley.* Scr *George Formby, Arthur Mertz.* PC *Blakeley's Productions.* Dis *Butchers. 80 mins. Cert U*
Unsubtle but effective vehicle for *George Formby's* talkie debut. He plays John Willie, the boot-boy at a big hotel. He falls for a scul-

lery maid, Snooky, who turns out to be the long-lost niece of some wealthy residents at the hotel. 'Boots' and the maid end up as the stars of the hotel cabaret.
RoC *Beryl (Formby), Arthur Kingsley, Tonie Forde, Lilian Keyes, Donald Reid, Betty Driver, Constance Fletcher, Myfanwy Southern, Harry Hudson and His Band.*

BORN LUCKY (1932)   [3]

Dir *Michael Powell.* Prod *Jerome Jackson.* Scr *Ralph Smart, from a novel by Oliver Sandys.* Ph *Geoffrey Faithfull.* PC *Westminster.* Dis *MGM. 77 mins. Cert U*
Romantic story with music, in which a Cockney serving-girl, Mops (*René Ray*) rises to fame as a singer, and marries a successful writer (*John Longden*).
RoC *Talbot O'Farrell, Ben Welden, Helen Ferrers, Barbara Gott, Paddy Browne, Roland Gillett, Glen Pointing.*

BORN THAT WAY (1936)   [3]

Dir and Prod and PC *Randall Faye.* Scr *V.C. Clinton-Baddeley, Diana Bourbon.* Ph *Geoffrey Faithfull.* Dis *Radio. 64 mins. Cert U*
A no-nonsense but warm-hearted Scotswoman takes over the supervision of a wayward niece and nephew from her absent-minded brother-in-law. Having straightened them out, she goes back to running her business. Comedy has some funny moments, and a good performance by *Elliot Mason* as the surrogate parent.
RoC *Kathleen Gibson, Terence de Marney, Eliot Makeham, Ian Colin, Conway Palmer, John Laurie, Raymond Ellis, Robert MacLachlan.*

BORROW A MILLION (1934)   [2]

Dir and Prod *Reginald Denham.* Scr *Margaret McDonnell.* PC and Dis *Fox British. 50 mins. Cert U*
Simple, very unpretentious comedy about a teashop proprietor (*Charles Cullum*), who starts a restaurant chain as a result of backing from a millionaire (*Roland Culver*). Friends of the millionaire, seeking support for themselves, try to blacken the teashop man's name, but his secretary (*Meriel Forbes*) foils their plot.
RoC *Reginald Gardiner, Vera Bogetti, Wally Patch, Robert Rendel, Wilson Coleman, Gordon McLeod, Dania Barrigo.*

BORROWED CLOTHES (1934)   [2]

Dir and Prod *Arthur Maude.* Scr *Uncredited, from a play by Aimée and Philip Stuart.* PC *Maude Productions.* Dis *Columbia. 70 mins. Cert A*
Dull, mishandled comedy about an extravagant wife (*Anne Grey*) who learns her lesson after accidentally acquiring a dress shop that is not doing at all well, and struggling to keep it going. She is saved from bankruptcy when the original owners, impressed by the hard work and money she has poured in, in a vain effort to improve things, buy the business back.
RoC *Lester Matthews, Sunday Wilshin, Joe Hayman, Renée Macready, P.G. Clark, Philip Strange, Antony Holles, Elizabeth Inglis, Constance Shotter, Christine Adrian, Joan Ormond, Sybil Grove, H. Ardale, Ethel Ramsay, Merle Tottenham, H. O'Malley.*

BOYS WILL BE BOYS (1935)   [4]

Dir *William Beaudine.* Prod *Michael Balcon.* Scr *Will Hay, Robert Edmunds, from characters created by 'Beachcomber' (J.B. Morton).* Ph *Charles Van Enger.* PC *Gainsborough.* Dis *Gaumont-British. 75 mins. Cert A*
Will Hay hits his film stride in this hilarious piece of nonsense as 'Dr' Alec Smart, who assumes the headship of Narkover College with a forged testimonial. An ex-convict (*Gordon Harker*), father of Narkover's head boy, forces Smart to take him on as butler and plans to steal a necklace from one of the governors. The necklace ends up in the football at the annual founders' day match.
RoC *Claude Dampier, Jimmy Hanley, Davy Burnaby, Norma Varden, Charles Farrell, Percy Walsh, Peter Gawthorne.*

BOYS WILL BE GIRLS (1937)   [3]

Dir *Gilbert Pratt.* Prod *Joe Rock.* Scr *Clifford Grey, H.F. Maltby.* Ph *Cyril Bristow.* PC *Leslie Fuller.* Dis *British Independent. 66 mins. Cert U*
Leslie Fuller as boisterous as ever as Bill Jenkins, who'll inherit a legacy if he leads a strictly moral and sober life – something utterly foreign to our hero. Cigarettes and whisky and wild, wild women prove grievous temptations to Bill, but he wins through in the end – to find that the 'legacy' is a chimpanzee!
RoC *Nellie Wallace, Greta Woxholt (Greta Gynt), Judy Kelly, Tonie Edgar Bruce, Georgie Harris, D.J. Williams, Constance Godridge, Syd Crossley, Syd Courtenay, Olivette, Sybil Allen.*

BRACELETS (1931)   [3]

Dir and Scr *Sewell Collins.* Prod *L'Estrange Fawcett.* PC and Dis *Gaumont. 50 mins. Cert U*
Comedy-thriller about an old jeweller (*Bert Coote*) duped by confidence tricksters posing as a Russian countess and her secretary. For once, his lifelong absent-mindedness proves useful, leading to him foiling the crooks and receiving a reward. He is able to buy his wife a pair of bracelets to celebrate their silver wedding.
RoC *Stella Arbenina, Joyce Kennedy, Harold Huth, Margaret Emden, D.A. Clarke-Smith, Frederick Leister, George Merritt.*

THE BRAT (formerly **The Nipper**) (1930)   [1]

Dir *Louis Mercanton.* Prod *Betty Balfour.* Scr *Reginald Berkeley, Donovan Parsons, from a play by Michel Carré and A. Acremont.* PC *Betty Balfour Pictures.* Dis *United Artists. 84 mins. Cert U*
Another step on the downward path for fading superstar *Betty Balfour* – a tired musical-tragicomedy which she herself produced. She plays a Cockney waif whose songs entertain the customers at a London pub while her father is in prison. She becomes involved in a burglary, but is romanced by the owner (*John Stuart*) of the burgled house, and seems set for a stage career. But in the end she returns to the pub. Made in several language versions.

RoC *Anne Grey, Alf Goddard, Gibb McLaughlin, Helen Haye, Percy Parsons, Winifred Hall, Louis Goodrich.*

Betty Balfour and John Stuart in The Brat *(1930)*

BREAKERS AHEAD (1935) [2]

Dir and Scr *Anthony Gilkison.* Prod *Fraser Foulsham.* PC *Anglo-Cosmopolitan.* Dis *Reunion.* 58 mins. Cert U

Drama set among Cornish fishermen. Two men love the same girl, and one of them tries to drown the other – then dies to save him in a raging storm. One reviewer thought that 'The leading characters are not likely to be mistaken for Cornishmen by anyone with any experience.'

LP *Barrie Livesey, April Vivian, Billy Holland, Roddy Hughes, Cicely Oates, Richard Worth, Francis Gregory, Norman Tonkin.*

BREAK THE NEWS (1938) [3]

Dir *René Clair.* Prod and PC *Jack Buchanan.* Scr *Geoffrey Kerr, from a novel by Loic de Gouriadec.* Ph *Philip Tannura.* Dis *General Film Distributors.* 78 mins. Cert U

Small fry in Grace Gatwick's show, Teddy and François (*Jack Buchanan, Maurice Chevalier*) plan to hit the headlines by having Teddy 'murdered' and François arrested. They reckon without the redoubtable Grace (*June Knight*), who bags the lion's share of publicity at the trial. On his way to rescue François from the hangman, Teddy gets mixed up in a revolution ... but arrives in the nick of time. Comedy-musical is low-grade considering the talent involved.

RoC *Marta Labarr, Gertrude Musgrove, Garry Marsh, Felix Aylmer, C. Denier Warren, Robb Wilton, Gibb McLaughlin, Athole Stewart, Guy Middleton, George Hayes, Charles Lefeaux, Wally Patch, Wallace Douglas, D.J. Williams, Elliot Mason, J. Abercrombie, William Fazan, Mark Daly, George Benson, Joss Ambler, Hal Gordon, H.R. Hignett.*

BREWSTER'S MILLIONS (1934) [4]

Dir *Thornton Freeland.* Prod *Herbert Wilcox.* Scr *Arthur Wimperis, Douglas Furber, Clifford Grey, Paul Gangelin, Donovan Pedelty, Wolfgang Wilhelm, from the play by George Barr McCutcheon, Winchell Smith.* Ph *Henry Harris.* PC *British and Dominions.* Dis *United Artists.* 84 mins. Cert U

Vigorous musical version of the much-filmed

Jack Buchanan and Ian MacLean in Brewster's Millions *(1934)*

stage comedy about impoverished Michael Brewster (*Jack Buchanan*) who inherits two fortunes – one of half a million pounds, the other six million. But he must get rid of the former in six months to get the latter. Easier said than done ... dud investments turn out to be gold mines ... outsiders win at the races ... but he triumphs in the end.

RoC *Lili Damita, Nancy O'Neil, Amy Veness, Sydney Fairbrother, Ian MacLean, Fred Emney, Sebastian Shaw, Allan Aynesworth, Antony Holles, Henry Wenman, Dennis Hoey, Lawrence Hanray.*

BRIDES TO BE (1934) [1]

Dir and Prod *Reginald Denham.* Scr *Basil Mason, from his story 'Sign, Please'.* PC and Dis *British and Dominions/Paramount British.* 68 mins. Cert A

Shopgirl Audrey (*Betty Stockfeld*) meets rich George (*Ronald Ward*), but he falls into the clutches of a young adventuress (*Constance Shotter*) and her accomplice (*Henry Oscar*) who frame Audrey for theft. But Audrey's resourceful friend Phyllis (*Olive Sloane*) turns the tables on the crooks. Slow romantic drama. Said one critic: 'The less said about the dialogue the better.'

RoC *Ivor Barnard, Gordon McLeod, Geoffrey Goodheart, Oliver Gordon.*

BRIEF ECSTASY (1937) [2]

Dir *Edmond T. Gréville.* Prod *Hugh Perceval.* Scr *Basil Mason.* Ph *Henry Harris, Ronald Neame.* PC *Independent Films/Phoenix.* Dis *Associated British.* 71 mins. Cert A

The young wife (*Linden Travers*) of a middle-aged professor (*Paul Lukas*) had previously had a brief but passionate affair with a young aviator (*Hugh Williams*), who now comes back into her life as the professor's ward, and nearly ruins her new happiness. The professor's sex-starved housekeeper (*Marie Ney*) only narrowly fails to break up his marriage. Novelettish.

RoC *Renée Gadd, Fred Withers, Howard Douglas, Fewlass Llewellyn, Peter Gawthorne, Norman Pierce.*

BRITANNIA OF BILLINGSGATE (1932) [4]

Dir *Sinclair Hill.* Prod *Michael Balcon.* Scr *Ralph Stock, from a play by Christine Jope-*

Slade, Sewell Stokes. Ph *Mutz Greenbaum.* PC *Gaumont-British.* Dis *Ideal.* 99 mins (later 80). Cert U

A musical extravaganza spun around the talents of popular Cockney stars *Violet Loraine* and *Gordon Harker.* Miss Loraine plays the owner of a fish-and-chip shop in London's Billingsgate; her fine singing voice comes to the attention of a film company, and the family's lifestyle is soon transformed, mother having to teach her son and daughter a few hard facts of life, but retaining her new-found stardom.

RoC *Kay Hammond, John Mills, Drusilla Wills, Gibb McLaughlin, Antony Holles, Walter Sondes, Glennis Lorrimer, Joyce Kirby, Grethe Hanson, Jane Cornell, George Turner, Ernest Sefton, Jack Spree, Wally Patch, Cecil Ramage, Eliot Makeham, Ron Johnson, Gus Kuhn, Colin Watson, Tom Farndon, Roy Fox and His Band, Arthur Warwick.*

BROKEN BLOSSOMS (1936) [4]

Dir *Hans Brahm (John Brahm).* Prod *Julius Hagen.* Scr *Emlyn Williams, from a story by Thomas Burke and a screenplay by D.W. Griffith.* Ph *Curt Courant.* PC and Dis *Twickenham.* 78 mins. Cert A

Chen (*Emlyn Williams*) opens a small curiosity shop in London's Limehouse. He is fond of Lucy (*Dolly Haas*), delicate daughter of boxer Burrows (*Arthur Margetson*) who lives nearby. Finding Lucy collapsed in the snow one day, Chen takes her back to his home and nurses her. When her father hears where she is, he drags her back and thrashes her to death. Chen takes a savage revenge – but his neighbours burn down his beloved shop. Not bad, if hardly a patch on the 1919 Hollywood original.

RoC *Gibb McLaughlin, Donald Calthrop, Ernest Sefton, Jerry Verno, Bertha Belmore, Ernest Jay, C.V. France, Kathleen Harrison, Basil Radford, Edith Sharpe, Kenneth Villiers, Dorothy Minto, Sam Wilkinson.*

Dolly Haas and Emlyn Williams in Broken Blossoms *(1936)*

THE BROKEN MELODY (1934) [2]

Dir *Bernard Vorhaus.* Prod *Julius Hagen.* Scr *Vera Allinson, Michael Hankinson, H. Fowler Mear.* Ph *Sydney Blythe.* PC *Twickenham.* Dis *Associated Producers and Distributors.* 84 mins. Cert A

Somewhat unbelievable dramatic musical about a composer (*John Garrick*) who marries an opera star (*Margot Grahame*), then, after the failure of his opera, kills his wife's lover (*Austin Trevor*) in a jealous rage. Condemned to Devil's Island, he escapes some years later and goes to Germaine (*Merle Oberon*) who always loved him, and with whom he has left his child. He writes a successful opera based on his experiences and, although the governor of Devil's Island recognises him on opening night, he elects to remain silent.

RoC *Charles Carson, Harry Terry, Andrea Malandrinos, Tonie Edgar Bruce, Stella Rho, P. Kynaston Reeves.*

THE BROKEN ROSARY (1934)   4

Dir and Scr *Harry Hughes, from a poem by Adelaide Proctor.* Prod *Wilfred Noy.* PC and Dis *Butchers. 86 mins. Cert U*

Good, though very contemporary musical in which Maria (*Jean Adrienne*), betrothed to Giovanni (*Derek Oldham*) from an early age by their respective families, falls instead for his friend Jack (*Ronald Ward*). Jack becomes engaged to another girl rather than hurt his friend, but Giovanni sees that the right couple come together in the end.

RoC *Vesta Victoria, Marjorie Corbett, Dino Galvani, Margaret Yarde, Evelyn Roberts, Fred Rains, Ian Wilson, Dorothy Buller.*

BROTHER ALFRED (1932)   4

Dir *Henry Edwards.* Prod *John Maxwell.* Scr *Edwards, Claude Guerney, from a play by P.G. Wodehouse, Herbert Westbrook.* Ph *Walter Harvey, Horace Wheddon.* PC *BIP.* Dis *Wardour. 77 mins. Cert U*

Bright *Gene Gerrard* comedy casting him as a young man whose engagement is broken when his fiancée catches him kissing the maid. Subsequent complications involve him posing as his own (non-existent) twin brother and saving the life of a foreign prince, before his fiancée forgives him.

RoC *Molly Lamont, Clifford Heatherley, Elsie Randolph, Bobbie Comber, Blanche Adele, Hal Gordon, Hugh E. Wright, Henry Wenman, James Carew, Harvey Braban, Tonie Edgar Bruce, Maurice Colbourne, Jane Seymour, Marie Burke.*

BROWN ON RESOLUTION (1935)
See **For Ever England**.

BROWN SUGAR (1931)   1

Dir *Leslie Hiscott.* Prod *Julius Hagen.* Scr *Cyril Twyford, from the play by Lady Arthur Lever.* Ph *Ernest Palmer.* PC *Twickenham.* Dis *Warner Bros. 70 mins. Cert A*

Stale drawing-room drama about aristocratic parents who disapprove of their son's marriage to a showgirl. When she takes the blame for her husband's gambling debts, her stern mother-in-law realizes she was wrong, and begs the girl's forgiveness.

LP *Constance Carpenter, Francis Lister, Helen Haye, Alfred Drayton, Chili Bouchier, Allan Aynesworth, Cecily Byrne, Gerald Rawlinson, Eva Moore, Wallace Geoffrey.*

THE BROWN WALLET (1936)   2

Dir *Michael Powell.* Prod *Irving Asher.* Scr *Ian Dalrymple, from the story by Stacy Aumonier.* Ph *Basil Emmott.* PC *Warner Bros.* Dis *First National. 68 mins. Cert A*

Ruined by his profligate partner, publisher John Gillespie (*Patric Knowles*) finds a wallet full of money in a taxi. Refused help to start up in business again by his wealthy aunt, John keeps the cash. That night, his aunt is found poisoned and her safe rifled. John is accused and arrested, but goes free at the trial after the murderer confesses. Not very credible.

RoC *Nancy O'Neil, Henry Caine, Henrietta Watson, Charlotte Leigh, Shayle Gardner, Eliot Markham, Edward Dalby, Bruce Winston, Jane Millican, Louis Goodrich, Dick Francis, George Mills.*

BULLDOG DRUMMOND AT BAY (1937)   3

Dir *Norman Lee.* Prod *Walter C. Mycroft.* Scr *Patrick Kirwan, James Parrish, from the novel by Sapper (H.C. McNeile).* Ph *J. Harvey.* PC *Associated British.* Dis *Wardour. 78 mins. Cert U*

Competent, serial-like thriller, with such familiar Drummond elements as a distressed heroine, a bewildered inventor, a determined villain, a poison gas chamber and a fire at the end. Drummond (*John Lodge*) defeats a gang of foreign spies who are using a 'peace club' to cloak their nefarious activities, while they plan to steal the inventor's new radio-controlled plane.

RoC *Dorothy Mackaill, Victor Jory, Claud Allister, Richard Bird, Leslie Perrins, Hugh Miller, Brian Buchel, Jim Gerald, Maire O'Neill, Wilfrid Hyde White, Annie Esmond, Frank Cochrane, William Dewhurst.*

BULLDOG JACK (1935)   4
(USA: *Alias Bulldog Drummond*)

Dir *Walter Forde.* Prod *Michael Balcon.* Scr *J.O.C. Orton, Gerard Fairlie, Sidney Gilliat.* Ph *Mutz Greenbaum.* PC and Dis *Gaumont-British. 72 mins. Cert U*

Bulldog Drummond is injured in a car crash, and asks the passing Jack Pennington (*Jack Hulbert*) to take over the case. Ann Manders (*Fay Wray*) and her grandfather (*Paul Graetz*), both expert jewellers, are in the clutches of master criminal Morelle (*Ralph Richardson*), who is forcing them to help him replace the

jewels in a statue in the British Museum with paste stones. Crooks and heroes meet in an exciting climax in the Bloomsbury Underground.

RoC *Claude Hulbert, Gibb McLaughlin, Atholl Fleming, Cyril Smith, Harvey Braban, Ronald Curtis, Chum the Dog.*

BUSMAN'S HOLIDAY (1936)   3

Dir *Maclean Rogers.* Prod *A. George Smith.* Scr *Kathleen Butler, H.F. Maltby, from a story by Wally Patch.* Ph *Geoffrey Faithfull.* PC *GS Enterprises/Bow Bell.* Dis *Radio. 64 mins. Cert U*

Bright, entertaining Cockney comedy about Pinky and Alf (*Wally Patch, Gus McNaughton*), two suspended busmen who take up decorating. They not only practically demolish the (wrong) house, but also get involved with two crooks posing as decorators. Back on duty, they have to take a busload of old people to Scotland, end up in Sussex, get accused of being the crooks, meet the real criminals again and ensure they end up in the arms of the law.

RoC *Muriel George, H.F. Maltby, Norman Pierce, Michael Ripper, Isobel Scaife, Robert Hobbs.*

BY-PASS TO HAPPINESS (1934)   2

Dir and Scr *Anthony Kimmins.* Prod *Ivar Campbell.* Ph *Hone Glendinning.* PC *Sound City.* Dis *Fox. 74 mins. Cert A*

An ex-pilot (*Maurice Evans*) opens a garage that he expects to be a goldmine when a new by-pass is opened. When the by-pass doesn't come on time, he faces ruin, as well as the loss of his girl (*Tamari Desni*) whose guardian is opposed to the marriage. But then an old friend of the pilot's dies, leaving him a valuable work of art. The money it brings sees him through.

RoC *Kay Hammond, Mark Daly, Eliot Makeham, Nellie Bowman, John Teed, Billy Holland, Dorin Mountford, James Prior.*

CAFÉ COLETTE (1936)   2
(USA: *Danger in Paris*)

Dir *Paul L. Stein.* Prod *W. Devonport Hackney.* Scr *Eric Maschwitz, Val Gielgud, Val Valentine, Katherine Strueby, from the radio series by Maschwitz and Walford Hyden.* PC *Garrick.* Dis *Associated British. 71 mins. Cert A*

A gang of foreign spies is trying to steal formula for a new lightweight explosive from Manning (*Bruce Seton*), an intelligence officer. But they are rounded up by Ryan (*Paul Cavanagh*), a secret service man disguised as an artist. Not too successful blend of variety turns and spy melodrama.

RoC *Sally Gray, Donald Calthrop, Greta Nis-*

Jack Hulbert in Bulldog Jack *(1935)*

sen, Walford Hyden, Dino Galvani, Paul Blake, Fred Duprez, Cecil Ramage, (C.) Denier Warren, D.A. Clarke-Smith, Charles Carson, Oliver Sloane, Ronie Boyer, Cleo Nordi, Frank Atkinson, Douglas Howard, Leo von Pokorny, Tzigansky Choir, Café Colette Orchestra.

CAFÉ MASCOT (1936) [2]
Dir *Lawrence Huntington.* Prod and PC *Gabriel Pascal.* Scr *Gerald Elliott.* Ph *Stanley Grant.* Dis *Paramount. 77 mins. Cert U*

A young man comes across £1,000 in the back of a taxi. He uses the money to inspire confidence in business deals without spending a penny, and to help an Irish girl, with whom he falls in love, out of a financial mess. Romantic comedy, light but not very funny.
LP *Geraldine Fitzgerald, Derrick de Marney, George Mozart, Clifford Heatherley, Richard Norris, Paul Neville, Julien Vedey, George Turner, Geoffrey Clark, Walter Tobias, Frank Forsyth, Victor Hagen.*

THE CALENDAR (1931) [5]
(USA: *Bachelor's Folly*)
Dir *T. Hayes Hunter.* Prod *Michael Balcon.* Scr *Angus Macphail, Robert Stevenson, from the play by Edgar Wallace.* Ph *Bernard J. Knowles, Alex Bryce.* PC *Gainsborough/British Lion.* Dis *W and F. 79 mins. Cert A*

Highly regarded first version of Edgar Wallace's racetrack thriller. Double-crossed by the woman (*Anne Grey*) whom he loved, racehorse owner Garry Anson (*Herbert Marshall*) is banned from racing. With the help of his ex-burglar butler (*Gordon Harker*), Garry succeeds in regaining a £100 note that will clear him – and he falls for the bad girl's sister (*Edna Best*).
RoC *Nigel Bruce, Alfred Drayton, Allan Aynesworth, Melville Cooper, Leslie Perrins.*

Herbert Marshall and Edna Best in The Calendar *(1931)*

THE CALL BOX MYSTERY (1932) [2]
Dir *G.B. Samuelson.* Prod *Gordon Craig.* Scr *Joan Wentworth Wood.* Ph *Desmond Dickinson.* PC *Samuelson.* Dis *United Artists. 72 mins. Cert A*

Inspector Layton (*Harold French*) of Scotland Yard looks into a series of deaths believed to have been suicides. He connects the deaths with wealthy impresario Leo Mount (*Warwick Ward*). Iris (*Wendy Barrie*), sister of one of

the dead men, helps him get the evidence against Mount that he needs.
RoC *Gerald Rawlinson, Harvey Braban, Daphne Mowbray, Tom Shenton, Myno Burnet.*

CALLED BACK (1933) [2]
Dir *Reginald Denham, Jack Harris.* Prod *Julius Hagen.* Scr *Denham, from a novel by Hugh Conway.* PC *Real Art.* Dis *Radio. 50 mins. Cert A.*
Modernized adaptation of a once-famous book. A rich young Englishman, Geoffrey (*Lester Matthews*), recuperating in Spain after being temporarily blinded, falls in love with a girl (*Dorothy Boyd*) whose evil uncle (*Anthony Ireland*) has spent money left in trust and murdered his nephew. The Englishman seems in danger, but ultimately the uncle is executed in Russia. Rather far-fetched, in this version at least.
RoC *Franklin Dyall, Alexander Sarner, Francis L. Sullivan, Ian Fleming, Margaret Emden, Geoffrey Goodheart, Ralph Truman.*

CALLING ALL CROOKS (1938) [3]
Dir *George Black.* Prod *John E. Blakely.* Scr *Arthur Mertz.* Ph *Desmond Dickinson* PC and Dis *Mancunian. 85 mins. Cert A*

There's a lot going on in this occasionally funny comedy about a crooked company promoter (*Leslie Perrins*) who gets his just deserts thanks to the efforts of two disguise-mad detectives (*Duggie Wakefield, Billy Nelson*). Another north-country comedy barely seen south of the Mersey.
RoC *Helen Barnes, Dan Young, Howard Rogers, Raymond Smith, Chuck O'Neil, Jack Butler, Hal Wright and His Circus, The Seven Royal Hindustanis, The 10 Master Singers, 30 Gypsy Revellers, The Sherman Fisher Girls.*

CALLING ALL MA'S (1937)
See **The Biter Bit** (1937).

CALLING ALL STARS (1937) [3]
Dir *Redd Davis.* Prod *Herbert Smith.* Ph *George Stretton.* PC *British Lion/JH Productions.* Dis *British Lion. 75 mins. Cert U*
Spasmodically entertaining revue. Record company chief Katz (*Max Bacon*) invites some visitors to hear the master discs of the new season's releases. The messenger unfortunately drops the lot, and entertainers *Flotsam and Jetsam*, who happen to be on hand, are despatched to collect all the stars to re-record their discs.
RoC *Evelyn Dall, Ethel Revnell and Gracie West, Sam Browne, Larry Adler, Turner Layton, Elisabeth Welch, Billy Bennett, Davy Burnaby, Billy 'Popeye' Costello, The Nicholas Brothers, Buck and Bubbles, Arren and Broderick, Ambrose and His Orchestra, Carroll Gibbons and the Savoy Orpheans, The 12 Aristocrats, Whirlwind Skaters, The Bega Four, Three Canadian Bachelors.*

CALLING THE TUNE (1936) [2]
Dir *Reginald Denham.* Prod *Hugh Perceval.* Scr *Basil Mason.* Ph *Franz Weihmayer.* PC *Phoenix.* Dis *Associated British. 71 mins. Cert U*
An infusion of guest stars fails to give much

of a lift to this melodramatic musical about the development of the gramophone industry and, in particular, how one man's revolutionary idea for the making of records was stolen by another, who grew rich on it. Years later, the cheated man's son (*Clifford Evans*) proves the guilt of the record magnate, with whose daughter (*Adele Dixon*) he has fallen in love.
RoC *Sam Livesey, Sally Gray, Donald Wolfit, Eliot Makeham, Lewis Casson, Cedric Hardwicke, George Robey, Charles Penrose, Reginald Forsyth, Robert Wilton Jr, Sir Henry Wood and the Queen's Hall Light Orchestra, the English Singers Quartette, the Philharmonic String Orchestra, H.F. Maltby, Ronald Simpson.*

CALL ME MAME (1933) [1]
Dir *John Daumery.* Prod *Irving Asher.* Scr *Randall Faye.* PC and Dis *Warner Bros. 59 mins. Cert A*
Much to his embarrassment, the long-lost mother (*Edith Levey*) of Gordon (*John Batten*), heir to an earldom, turns out to be a coarse café singer from Mexico. His mother's drinking and vulgarity prove a considerable hindrance to Gordon's diplomatic career until she decides to bow out of his life again, under the pretence that she is a phoney. Crude comedy.
RoC *Dorothy Bartlam, Winifred Oughton, Julian Royce, Arthur Maude, Alice O'Day, Pat Fitzpatrick.*

THE CALL OF THE SEA (1930) [3]
Dir *Leslie Hiscott.* Prod *Julius Hagen, Henry Edwards.* Scr *H. Fowler Mear.* Ph *Sydney Blythe.* PC *Twickenham.* Dis *Warner Bros. 65 mins. Cert U*
A sentimental return to the screen for *Chrissie White*, top star of early silents. She hadn't filmed for six years when she co-starred with her husband, *Henry Edwards*, in this story of a naval officer who puts paid to the dastardly deputy governor of Pablo Island who has been kidnapping fellow officers and putting them to work in a platinum mine. Described by one reviewer as 'Stout stuff'!
RoC *Bernard Nedell, Chili Bouchier, Clifford McLagen, Alexander Field, Lewis Goodrich.*

Chili Bouchier and Henry Edwards in The Call of the Sea *(1930)*

THE CAMELS ARE COMING (1934) [2]
Dir *Tim Whelan.* Prod *Michael Balcon.* Scr *Guy Bolton, Jack Hulbert, W.P. Lipscomb.* Ph

Glen MacWilliams, Phil Tannura. PC Gainsborough. Dis Gaumont-British. 80 mins. Cert U
Jack Hulbert's first critical flop, a disappointing and rather tiresome romp, with locations in Egypt, that casts him as a blundering squadron-leader investigating drug smugglers. He disguises himself as a sheik and, with the help of Anita a girl aviator (Anna Lee), whom he at first suspects, he rounds up the gang and is saved from hostile Arabs by the timely arrival of the Flying Corps.
RoC Hartley Power, Harold Huth, Allan Jeayes, Peter Gawthorne, Norma Whalley, Peggy Simpson, Percy Parsons, Tony de Lungo.

CANARIES SOMETIMES SING (1930) [5]
Dir Tom Walls. Prod Herbert Wilcox. Scr W.P. Lipscomb, from the play by Frederick Lonsdale. Ph F.A. Young. PC British and Dominions. Dis W and F. 80 mins. Cert A
From the successful play by Frederick Lonsdale, whose brilliantly farcical conversation piece for four players is brought almost intact to the screen. Director Tom Walls also stars as the playwright who falls in love with the wife of his best friend.
RoC Yvonne Arnaud, Cathleen Nesbitt, Athole Stewart.

CAN YOU HEAR ME MOTHER? (1935) [4]
Dir Leslie Pearce. Prod Simon Rowson, Geoffrey Rowson. Scr Sandy Powell, Paul Thomson. Ph Leslie Rowson. PC New Ideal. Dis Producers' Distributing Corporation. 77 mins. Cert U
Successful comedy vehicle for comic Sandy Powell, being both human and homely. Sandy is a stagestruck Yorkshire millworker who comes to London for a trial as a comedian. In the train, he wins £50 from cardsharps, and finds a baby girl whom he 'adopts'. At first he fails as a comic, but, with the help of a girl dancer (Mary Lawson), who coaches him and minds the baby, he succeeds.
RoC Muriel Aked, Elsie Irving, Raymond Huntley, Paul Thomson, Katie Kay, Norman Pierce, Hal Walters, Henry Victors, Cingalee, Millicent Wolf, George Smith, Baby Ann Ibbitson, Bombardier Billy Wells, Denis Cowles, Roy Jeffries, Johnny Singer.

CAPE FORLORN (1930) [2]
(USA: The Love Storm)
Dir and Prod E.A. Dupont. Scr Dupont, Victor Kendall, from a play by Frank Harvey. Ph John J. Cox, Claude Friese-Greene. PC BIP. Dis Wardour. 86 mins. Cert A
Stern stuff, this, evocatively photographed and directed, but heavy going for all that. Fay Compton plays the dance-hall girl who marries a lighthouse keeper (Frank Harvey), and proceeds to have affairs with his co-keeper (Edmund Willard) and a shipwreck survivor (Ian Hunter), before shooting one when they fight over her, then finding the other is wanted by the police.
RoC Donald Calthrop.

CAPTAIN BILL (1935) [2]
Dir Ralph Ceder. Prod Joe Rock. Scr Val Valentine, Syd Courtenay, George Harris. Ph Charles Van Enger. PC Leslie Fuller. Dis Associated British. 81 mins. Cert U
A bargee becomes involved in a big race in which his barge sinks beneath him. He is involved in a brawl in a public house, but then is instrumental in the capture of a sea-going gun-running gang. Clumsy, over-long comedy.
LP Leslie Fuller, Judy Kelly, Hal Gordon, Georgie Harris, O.B. Clarence, D.J. Williams, Tonie Edgar Bruce, Ralph Truman, David Lyttle.

CAPTAIN'S ORDERS (1937) [3]
Dir and Prod Ivar Campbell. Scr Frank Shaw. PC and Dis Liberty. 75 mins. Cert U
Finding his ship, the Welcome, is to be laid up because of the Depression, Captain Trent (Henry Edwards) asks to take her out on a couple of cargo runs to give the crew some pay-off money. He organizes a concert to pay expenses, but snooty star Belle Mandeville (Jane Carr) won't come when he cannot pick her up. Ex-actress Violet Potts (Marie Levarre) fills the breach. Welcome, at sea, receives an SOS from an iceberg-stricken yacht with Belle and Violet on board. It rescues them, and still just makes it to New York. Breezy drama.
RoC Franklyn Dyall, Wally Patch, (C.) Denier Warren, Mark Daly, Roddy Hughes, Basil Radford, Kim Peacock, Joss Ambler, H.F. Maltby, Rae Collet, Jo Monkhouse, Fred Culley, Quenton McPherson, Julian Joyce, Leo von Pokorny, Frank Petley, Roy Russell, Arthur Rees, Ann Kennington, Arthur Chesney, Jack Hart and His Band, The Sherman Fisher Girls.

THE CAPTAIN'S TABLE (1936) [4]
Dir Percy Marmont. Prod James A. Fitzpatrick. Scr John Paddy Carstairs. PC Fitzpatrick Pictures. Dis MGM. 55 mins. Cert A
On a translantic cruise ship, a musician's wife is found strangled. Suspects are plentiful, but, with the help of one of them, a detective who poses as a steward, the ship's captain (Percy Marmont) finally discovers the killer. Lively pocket crime drama moves swiftly, makes one wonder why Marmont directed so little.
RoC Marian Spencer, Louis Goodrich, Mark Daly, Philip Brandon, Daphne Courtenay, Pat Fitzpatrick, Gerald Fielding.

CAPTIVATION (1931) [3]
Dir, Prod and Scr John Harvel, from the play by Edgar C. Middleton. PC John Harvel Productions. Dis W and F. 76 mins. Cert A
Romantic comedy in which a girl called Ann (Betty Stockfeld) is having the holiday of a lifetime in Monte Carlo until she loses all her money at the hotel casino and is unable to pay her bill. Ann pretends she is married to famous author Hugh Somerton (Conway Tearle), who finally ensures that the phoney marriage becomes a real one. Includes scenes shot at Monte Carlo and Cap d'Antibes.
RoC Robert Farquharson, Violet Vanbrugh, Frederick Volpe, A. Bromley Davenport, Mar-

ilyn Mawm, Louie Tinsley, Dorothy Black, George de Warfaz.

Frederick Volpe and Betty Stockfeld in Captivation *(1931)*

THE CARDINAL (1936) [3]
Dir Sinclair Hill. Prod Harcourt Templeman. Scr D.B. Wyndham-Lewis, from the play by Louis N. Parker. PC Grosvenor. Dis Pathé. 75 mins. Cert A
Rome, 1570. General Belmont (Robert Atkins), bitter enemy of Cardinal de Medici (Matheson Lang), commits a brutal killing, ties the cardinal's hands by telling him in the Confessional, then pins the murder on the cardinal's headstrong younger brother Eric (Eric Portman). But by feigning madness, and playing on the general's superstitious fears, the cardinal forces him to confess in front of witnesses. Matheson Lang's last film: he is better than his material.
RoC June Duprez, Henrietta Watson, O.B. Clarence, Douglas Jeffries, F.B.J. Sharp, Wilfred Fletcher, A. Bromley Davenport, David Horne, Rayner Barton, K. Edgar Bruce, Dora Barton.

CARNIVAL (1931) [3]
(USA: Venetian Nights)
Dir and Prod Herbert Wilcox. Scr Donald Macardle, from the play by Matheson Lang and C.M. Hardinge. Ph F.A. Young, Jack Parker. PC British and Dominions. Dis W and F. 88 mins. Cert A
Matheson Lang repeated his leading role from his silent screen (1921) success of the same name, as one half of a husband-and-wife acting team about to present Othello at carnival time

Dorothy (Chili) Bouchier in Carnival *(1931)*

in Venice. Thinking his wife is having an affair, the actor tries to strangle her (*Dorothy Bouchier*) during the performance, but collapses before he can do so. The couple are reconciled.
RoC *Joseph Schildkraut, Lilian Braithwaite, Kay Hammond, Dickie Edwards, Brian Buchel, Brember Wills, Alfred Rode and His Tzigane Band.*

CAR OF DREAMS (1935)   4
Dir *Graham Cutts, Austin Melford.* Prod *Michael Balcon.* Scr *Melford.* Ph *Mutz Greenbaum.* PC and Dis *Gaumont-British.* 72 mins. Cert U
Robert (*John Mills*), the son of the owner of a musical-instrument factory, is in love with Vera (*Grete Mosheim*) who works at the factory: neither knows about this side of the other's life. When Vera jokingly says that she would love a Rolls-Royce, Robert sees that she gets one. Then he raises her salary out of all proportion so that she will find out who he is. Bright little musical comedy has one hilarious scene with *Robertson Hare* testing trombones.
RoC *Norah Howard, Paul Graetz, Jack Hobbs, Glennis Lorimer, Mark Lester, Margaret Withers, Hay Plumb.*

CARRY ON LONDON (1937)   1
Dir *D.R. Fraser.* Prod *Frank Green.* PC and Dis *Ace Films.* 46 mins. Cert A
Another series of weak turns from the stage of the Windmill Theatre. They would have done better to have stayed there.
LP *Meggie Eaton, Gus Chevalier, Warden and West, Paddy Browne, Leslie Spurling, Ken(neth) More, Eric Barker, Lucy Loupe, Eddie Kelland, Eric Woodburn, Silvestri, Mollie Hallewell, John Stevens, Eileen, Marie and Elsie, The Windmill Girls, Alan d'Albert and the Windmill Band.*

THE CASE FOR THE CROWN (1934)   2
Dir and Prod *George A. Cooper.* Scr *Sherard Powell,* from a story by *Anthony Gittins.* PC and Dis *British and Dominions/Paramount British.* 71 mins. Cert U
Confusing crime drama about Matherson (*Whitemore Humphries*), who makes the apparent suicide of his ailing firm's boss look like murder, in order to save the boss's daughter from the stigma of suicide. Matherson is charged, and it turns out in court that it really was murder – by the firm's accountant (*Miles Mander*) who had been fiddling the books. He commits suicide in the witness box.
RoC *Meriel Forbes, Lawrence Anderson, David Horne, Gordon McLeod, John Turnbull, Sydney Monckton.*

THE CASE OF GABRIEL PERRY (1935)   3
Dir *Albert de Courville.* Prod *Herbert Smith.* Scr *L. DuGarde Peach,* from a play by *James Dale.* PC and Dis *British Lion.* 78 mins. Cert A
Meaty drama set in 1885, with *Henry Oscar* strong as hypocritical Gabriel Perry, a local JP and outwardly a benign, respected member of society – but actually vicious and grasping.

Mentally unstable, Perry is driven by greed and fear to the brutal murder of a local woman. He is brought to trial and convicted.
RoC *Olga Lindo, Margaret Lockwood, Franklin Dyall, Raymond Lovell, John Wood, Martita Hunt, Rodney Ackland, Percy Walsh, Ralph Truman, Lawrence Anderson, Mark Lester, Alastair Sim.*

CASH (1933)   4
(USA: *For Love or Money*)
Dir *Zoltan Korda.* Prod *Alexander Korda.* Scr *Arthur Wimperis.* Ph *Robert Martin.* PC *London Films.* Dis *Paramount.* 73 mins. Cert U
Applauded as 'clever and amusing', this comedy has *Edmund Gwenn* as a businessman entertaining financiers whom he hopes will lend him the money (for a 'scheme') that will help him keep up his luxury home and lifestyle. Young Paul Martin (*Robert Donat*) arrives to cut off the electricity, falls for the debtor's daughter (*Wendy Barrie*) and uses some cash they find dumped by crooks to help her father. The deal goes through, even though the 'loot' proves to be counterfeit!
RoC *Morris Harvey, Lawrence Grossmith, Clifford Heatherley, Hugh E. Wright, Antony Holles.*

Wendy Barrie and Robert Donat in Cash *(1933)*

CASTE (1930)   2
Dir *Campbell Gullan.* Prod *Jerome Jackson.* Scr *Michael Powell,* from the play by *T.W. Robertson.* PC *Harry Rowson.* Dis *United Artists.* 70 mins. Cert U
Modernized (here set in 1914) version of an old comedy play about an aristocratic Guards officer who marries a ballet dancer, daughter of an old reprobate whose passions are beer and horses. The officer goes to war and is presumed killed....
LP *Sebastian Shaw, Nora Swinburne, Hermione Baddeley, Ben Field, Alan Napier, Edward Chapman, Mabel Terry-Lewis.*

CASTLE SINISTER (1932)   3
Dir, Prod and Scr *Widgey R. Newman.* PC *Delta.* Dis *Filmophone.* 50 mins. Cert A
Early British attempt at a horror thriller: Ronald (*Haddon Mason*) and Jean (*Ilsa Kilpatrick*) find themselves in the clutches of Professor Bandov (*Eric Adney*) at his moorland castle. Pursuing a theory of longevity, Bandov is trying to cross a human with a baboon and

intends putting Jean's brain into the head of an 'ape-man'. Jean and Ronald escape and Bandov is killed by his creature.
RoC *Wally Patch, Edmund Kennedy.*

CATCH AS CATCH CAN (1937)   2
Dir *Roy Kellino.* Prod *John Findlay.* Scr *Richard Llewellyn.* Ph *Stanley Grant.* PC and Dis *Fox British.* 71 mins. Cert A
Barbara Standish (*Viki Dobson*) tries to smuggle some diamonds from France to America, but soon finds several crooks on her trail, as well as Robert Leyland (*James Mason*), a customs agent. In a madcap shootout, one of the criminals, Tony Canzari (*Eddie Pola*), a Chicago gangster, is killed by Robert, who escorts a chastened Barbara back to England and justice. Sluggish thriller.
RoC *Finlay Currie, John Warwick, Margaret Rutherford, Paul Blake, James Mageean, Paul Sheridan, Zoë Wynn, Eva Hudson, Peter Popp, Bernard Merefield, Charles Sewell, Jack Lester.*

CATHERINE THE GREAT (1934)   5
Dir *Paul Czinner, Alexander Korda* (uncredited). Prod *Korda, Ludovico Toeplitz.* Scr *Lajos Biro, Arthur Wimperis, Marjorie Deans,* from a play by *Biro* and *Melchior Lengyel.* Ph *Georges Périnal.* PC *London Films.* Dis *United Artists.* 95 mins. Cert A
Worthy, although commercially less successful follow-up to the same company's *The Private Life of Henry VIII*, with fine production values. Elizabeth of Russia orders, in 1745, a marriage between her heir, Archduke Peter (*Douglas Fairbanks Jr*) and Catherine (*Elisabeth Bergner*), an unsophisticated German girl. Although Catherine loves him, the marriage is not successful and, when Elizabeth dies and Peter ascends the throne, power goes to his head. Catherine is forced to bring about his abdication (and death) for the sake of her country.
RoC *Flora Robson, Gerald du Maurier, Irene Vanbrugh, Griffith Jones, Joan Gardner, Dorothy Hale, Diana Napier, Gibb McLaughlin, Clifford Heatherley, Lawrence Hanray, Allan Jeayes.*

THE CAVALIER OF THE STREETS (1937)   4
Dir *Harold French.* Prod *Anthony Havelock-Allan.* Scr *Ralph Neale, George Barraud,* from the story by *Michael Arlen.* Ph *Francis Carver.* PC *British and Dominions/Paramount British.* 70 mins. Cert A
Lady Avalon (*Margaret Vyner*) is seduced by Karanov (*Carl Harbord*), a blackmailer posing as a prince. His confederate, the Cavalier (*Patrick Barr*), not liking the situation, exposes Karanov's intentions to Lady A, although she does not repent until after Karanov is found dead. At the inquest, the Cavalier proves that Karanov died by accident, and, to her relief, keeps Lady Avalon out of the case before disappearing on his adventures. Wittily-scripted drama.
RoC *James Craven, Laura Smithson, Renée de Vaux, Peggy Chester, Leo Genn, Noreen Hamilton, Jack Allen.*

THE CHALLENGE (1938) [4]

Dir *Milton Rosmer, Luis Trenker*. Prod *Gunther Stapenhorst*. Scr *Emeric Pressburger, Patrick Kirwan, Rosmer*. Ph *Georges Périnal, Albert Benitz*. PC *Denham Productions/London Films*. Dis *United Artists*. 75 mins. Cert U

Carrel (*Luis Trenker*), an Italian guide, saves Whymper (*Robert Douglas*) a British mountaineer, on the Matterhorn, bringing him to an inn, where he falls in love with the innkeeper's daughter (*Joan Gardner*). Whymper joins an English party who just beat the Italian Alpine Club, guided by Carrel, to the top. On the way down, Whymper is the only survivor when a rope breaks and it takes a dangerous climb by Carrel to prove he didn't cut it to save his own life. Drama is commonplace, but mountaineering scenes are vivid and gripping.
RoC *Mary Clare, Fred Groves, Lawrence Baskcomb, Ralph Truman, Tony Simpson, Geoffrey Wardwell, Lyonel Watts, Moran Caplat, Cyril Smith, Frank Birch, Reginald Jarman, D.J. Williams, Bernard Miles, Tarva Penna, Hugo Leyner, Lloyd Pearson, Violet Hayward, Babita Soren, Max Holzber, Howard Douglas, (C.) Denier Warren, Emeric Albert*.

THE CHANCE OF A NIGHT TIME (1931) [4]

Dir *Herbert Wilcox, Ralph Lynn*. Prod *Wilcox*. Scr *W.P. Lipscomb, from a play by Ben Travers*. Ph *F.A. Young*. PC *British and Dominions*. Dis *W and F*. 74 mins. Cert U

An adaptation of Ben Travers' hit farce *The Dippers*, with *Ralph Lynn* in good form as a mild-mannered clerk who misses a train and arrives by mistake at a country house where a party is in progress. He meets a dancer (*Winifred Shotter*) there to do an act, but whose partner has not turned up. The clerk fills in – until his fiancée arrives. He decides he loves the dancer and they escape together.
RoC *Sunday Wilshin, Kenneth Kove, Robert English, Dino Galvani*.

CHANGE FOR A SOVEREIGN (1937) [2]

Dir *Maurice Elvey*. Prod *Irving Asher*. Scr *Seymour Hicks*. Ph *Basil Emmott*. PC *Warner Bros*. Dis *First National*. 72 mins. Cert A

The title is the subtlest thing about this Ruritanian-style farce about a king who likes to take an anonymous holiday while his double, a flirtatious alcoholic, occupies the throne. The double's behaviour on this occasion brings about a constitutional crisis, and the king (*Seymour Hicks*) returns just in time to thwart the wicked archduke's plans to seize the throne.
RoC *Chili Bouchier, Ralph Truman, Bruce Lister, Violet Farebrother, Aubrey Mallalieu, (Wilfrid) Hyde White, (C.) Denier Warren, Florence Vie, Daphne Raglan, George Lane, Percy Le Fré, Billy Watts*.

CHANNEL CROSSING (1933) [4]

Dir *Milton Rosmer*. Prod *Angus Macphail, Ian Dalrymple*. Scr *W. P. Lipscomb, Cyril Campion*. Ph *Phil Tannura*. PC *Gaumont*. Dis *W and F*. 70 mins. Cert A

Matheson Lang's acting, *Phil Tannura*'s photo-

Anthony Bushell and Matheson Lang in Channel Crossing (*1933*)

graphy and *Dan Birt*'s editing were among the items praised in this drama set aboard a Channel steamer bound for Calais (partly shot aboard the SS *Canterbury*). *Lang* plays a Dutch financier who has forged stock and is on the brink of exposure. After he nearly drowns his secretary's lover who has discovered his guilty secret, the voyage ends with the financier's suicide.
RoC *Constance Cummings, Anthony Bushell, Edmund Gwenn, Dorothy Dickson, Nigel Bruce, Max Miller, Douglas Jeffries, H.G. Stoker, Viola Lyel, Ellen Pollock, Cyril Smith, D. Hay Plumb, Wally Patch, (C.) Denier Warren, Gerald Barry*.

CHARING CROSS ROAD (1935) [3]

Dir *Albert de Courville*. Prod *Herbert Smith*. Scr *Con West, Clifford Grey, from a radio play by Gladys and Clay Keyes*. Ph *Philip Tannura*. PC and Dis *British Lion*. 72 mins. Cert U

Creditable musical morality tale about two entertainers, Pam and Tony (*June Clyde, John Mills*) who resolve not to marry until success comes along. Tony hits the big time first and has decided to move to grander lodgings when his landlord (*Arthur Sinclair*) tells him a cautionary tale of a singer (*Derek Oldham*) who ruined his career through conceit. Tony promises to stay with Pam.
RoC *Jean Colin, Garry Marsh, Belle Baker, Judy Kelly, Charles Heslop, Coral Browne, (C.) Denier Warren, Alfred Wellesley*.

CHECKMATE (1935) [2]

Dir *George Pearson*. Prod *Anthony Havelock-Allan*. Scr *Basil Mason, from a novel by Amy Kennedy Gould*. PC and Dis *British and Dominions/Paramount British*. 68 mins. Cert A

Philip Allen (*Maurice Evans*), a Scotland Yard detective on the trail of a gang of London jewel thieves, gets more than he bargained for when he catches up with them – the ringleader is his fiancée's father (*Felix Aylmer*). Unimaginative thriller, sometimes unintentionally funny.
RoC *Evelyn Foster, Donald Wolfit, Sally Gray, Wilfrid Caithness, Percy Walsh, Ernest Jay, John Buckmaster*.

CHEER BOYS CHEER (1939) [3]

Dir *Walter Forde*. (Associate) Prod *S.C. Balcon*. Scr *Roger Macdougall, Allan Mackinnon*.

Ph *Ronald Neame*. PC *ATP/Ealing Studios*. Dis *Associated British*. 85 mins. Cert U

Ironside (*Edmund Gwenn*), a brewing-mogul, aims to gain control of Greenleaf's (*C.V. France*) old-fashioned brewery and its chain of pubs. His son (*Peter Coke*) falls for Greenleaf's daughter (*Nova Pilbeam*), abandoning plans to ruin her father's firm. Matt (*Jimmy O'Dea*), who is always 'temperance' when drunk, provokes a crisis by selling his Greenleaf shares to Ironside; but an amalgamation is sealed under the influence of Greenleaf's best bitter. Comedy is pleasing slice of life, if not especially funny.
RoC *Moore Marriott, Graham Moffatt, Alexander Knox, Ivor Barnard, Jean Webster Brough, Sidney Monckton, Walter Forde*.

CHEER UP! (1936) [4]

Dir *Leo Mittler*. Prod and PC *Stanley Lupino*. Scr *Michael Barringer*. Dis *Associated British*. 72 mins. Cert U

Trifling but boisterous musical-comedy about an author and composer (*Stanley Lupino, Roddy Hughes*) trying to get their own show put on. Hearing that a millionaire backer of plays is staying at the Hotel Splendide, Tom (*Lupino*) tries to gatecrash his suite, is mistaken by a reporter for the millionaire's son, rescues a young actress (*Sally Gray*) from an unwanted admirer – she also thinks he's a millionaire – and finds himself backing his own production.
RoC *Gerald Barry, Kenneth Kove, Wyn Weaver, Majorie Chard, Ernest Sefton, Syd Crossley, Arthur Rigby Jr*.

CHELSEA LIFE (1933) [2]

Dir and Prod *Sidney Morgan*. Scr *Joan Wentworth Wood*. Ph *Henry Harris*. PC *British and Dominions*. Dis *Paramount*. 69 mins. Cert A

In the artists' quarter of London's Chelsea, an ambitious young English painter (*Louis Hayward*) passes off the work of an absent Italian artist as his own, and gains a certain success, deserting his girlfriend (*Molly Johnson*) for a society beauty (*Anna Lee*) – until he is found out.
RoC *Kathleen Saxon, Stanley Vilven, Gordon McLeod, Eric Hales, Patrick Ludlow, Arthur Chesney, Winifred Davies, Quinton MacPherson, Lola Duncan*.

CHICK (1936) [2]

Dir *Michael Hankinson*. Prod *Jack Raymond*. Scr *Irving Leroy, Daniel Wheddon, Gerrard Fairlie, Cyril Gardner, D. B. Wyndham-Lewis, from the novel by Edgar Wallace*. Ph *Francis Carver*. PC *British and Dominions*. Dis *United Artists*. 72 mins. Cert U

Very disappointing *Sydney Howard* vehicle casting him as Chick Beane, a college hall porter who comes into a peerage and is exploited by a gang of financial sharks. They pretend to discover oil on his newly inherited estate, but Chick's common sense comes to his rescue before he parts with his cash, and he turns the tables on the villains. Previously made as a silent in 1928 (not with Howard).
RoC *Betty Ann Davies, Fred Conyngham, Cecil*

Humphreys, Mai Bacon, Wallace Geoffrey, Aubrey Mather, Arthur Chesney, Edmund Dalby, Robert Nainby, Merle Tottenham, Aubrey Fitzgerald, Fred Rains, Jo Monkhouse, Aubrey Pollock.

CHILDREN OF CHANCE (1930) [2]
Dir *Alexander Esway*. Scr *Miles Malleson, Frank Launder*. Ph *H.E. Palmer, L. Rogers*. PC *BIP*. Dis *First National-Pathé*. 80 mins. *Cert A*
Despite a cast of popular players, this melodrama about a chorus girl (*Elissa Landi*) and her criminal double remains obstinately unconvincing. Blinnie, the dancer, is accused of the theft of some pearls but establishes not only her innocence eventually, but the fact that the pearls were fakes in any case.
RoC *John Stuart, John Longden, Mabel Poulton, Gus McNaughton, Wallace Lupino, Kay Hammond, Dorothy Minto, Gus Sharland, John Deverell, Charles Dormer, Eric Donaldson, Aileen Despard, Jack Farquhar, Anne Grey*.

CHILDREN OF THE FOG (1935) [2]
Dir *Leopold Jessner, John Quin*. Prod *Jessner*. Scr *John Cousins, Stephen Clarkson*. Ph *Eugene Schufftan*. PC *Jesba Films*. Dis *National Provincial*. 59 mins. *Cert A*
Two young people fight to escape the environment of London's dockland slums, he escaping from his drunken docker father, and taking his sweetheart and his sickly brother to live in Australia. Pretty gloomy drama.
LP *Ben Soutten, Kenneth Guthrie, Marjorie Corbett, Barbara Gott, Eric Pavitt, Linden Travers, Rani Waller, Laurence Hepworth, Vi Kaley*.

CHINATOWN NIGHTS (1938) [2]
Dir *Toni Frenguelli*. Prod *Nell Emerald*. Scr *Nigel Byass*. PC *Victory*. Dis *Columbia*. 70 mins. *Cert U*
H. Agar Lyons returns to the role of Dr Sin Fang, a low-budget rival to Fu Manchu. In this adventure, the evil Oriental mastermind again clashes with Sonia Graham (*Anne Grey*), whose brother has invented a powerful 'silver-ray' machine with which Sin Fang hopes to conquer the world. He kidnaps Sonia to force her brother's hand, but she turns the tables. Runs like an old-time serial.
RoC *Robert Hobbs, Nell Emerald, Eric Elliott, Rex Walker, Louis Darnley*.

CHIN CHIN CHINAMAN (1931) [3]
(USA: *Boat from Shanghai*)
Dir *Guy Newall*. Prod *Julius Hagen*. Scr *Brock Williams, Newall, from a play by Percy Walsh*. Ph *Basil Emmott*. PC *Real Art*. Dis *MGM*. 52 mins. *Cert U*
Stage character supremo *Leon M. Lion* gets another chance to adopt extravagant disguise as a Chinese mandarin who has jewels stolen on board a ship. On arrival in London, a countess (*Elizabeth Allan*) is accused of taking them, but it all proves to be a complicated ruse to unmask the real jewel thief - both mandarin and countess being detectives in disguise.
RoC *George Curzon, Dino Galvani, Picot Schooling, Douglas Blandford*.

THE CHINESE BUNGALOW (1930) [2]
Dir, Prod and Scr *J.B. Williams, Arthur W. Barnes, from the play by Marion Osmond, James Corbet*. PC *Neo-Art*. Dis *Williams and Pritchard*. 74 mins. *Cert A*
Stage superstar *Matheson Lang* repeated his role from the 1926 silent version of this hoary old play, as a Chinese mandarin whose English wife falls in love with another man. He tries to poison her lover, but the scheme backfires, and it is the mandarin who dies.
RoC *Jill Esmond Moore, Ballard Berkeley, Anna Neagle, Derek Williams*.

Anna Neagle and Ballard Berkeley in The Chinese Bungalow (*1930*)

THE CHINESE BUNGALOW (1939) [3]
Dir and Prod *George King*. Scr *A.R. Rawlinson, George Wellesley, from the play by Matheson Lang, Marion Osmond, James Corbet*. Ph *Hone Glendinning*. PC *Pennant*. Dis *British Lion*. 72 mins. *Cert A*
Third screen version of originally silent drama which here, though well acted, is beginning to look something of a museum piece. Yuan Sing (*Paul Lukas*), a Chinese millionaire, marries Sadie (*Kay Walsh*) and takes her to live at his luxury bungalow. Her sister Charlotte (*Jane Baxter*) comes to stay, and discovers Sadie is having an affair with a neighbouring planter, who is poisoned by Yuan Sing, by now in love with Charlotte. The planter's brother (*Robert Douglas*) also loves Charlotte and when he and Sing drink to her from goblets, one of which they know contains poison, it is the Chinese who dies.
RoC *Jerry Verno, Wallace Douglas, Mayura, James Woodburn*.

THE CHINESE PUZZLE (1932) [4]
Dir *Guy Newall*. Prod *Julius Hagen*. Scr *H. Fowler Mear, from a play by Leon M. Lion and Frances Barclay*. PC *Twickenham*. Dis *W and F*. 81 mins. *Cert A*
Chi Lung, a Chinese mandarin (*Leon M. Lion*, repeating his role from the 1919 version), has secret dealings with the British foreign office, but finds that information about a treaty is being leaked to the Press. He traces the leak to the son of an old friend and, in return for past favours, takes the blame himself and severs his links with Britain.
RoC *Lilian Braithwaite* (also repeating her 1919 role), *Elizabeth Allan, Austin Trevor,*

James Raglan, Jane Welsh, C.M. Hallard, Mabel Sealby, Francis L. Sullivan, Charles Carson, George Carr, Philip Hunt, Townsend Whitley.

CHIPS (1938) [2]
Dir and Prod *Edward Godal*. Scr *Vivian Tidmarsh*. Ph *Desmond Dickinson*. PC and Dis *British Fine Arts*. 83 mins (later 75; reissued 1939 at 66 mins). *Cert U*
Chips (*Tony Wyckham*), a boy on probation, longs to be a Sea Scout. By a lucky accident, he 'captures' a pickpocket and finds himself a local hero and welcome in the Scouts' troop. He lets them down by failing to show at a concert, and rows angrily out to sea, where he is run down and captured by smugglers. The Sea Scouts rescue him and capture the crooks. Improbable adventure for impressionable juveniles.
RoC *Robb Wilton, Davy Burnaby, Billy Merson, Peter Dawson, Joyce Bland, Bertram Wallis, Terry's Juveniles, 20 Tiny Tappers*.

CHU CHIN CHOW (1934). [3]
Dir *Walter Forde*. Prod *Michael Balcon*. Scr *Edward Knoblock, L. DuGarde Peach, Sidney Gilliat*. Ph *Mutz Greenbaum*. PC *Gainsborough*. Dis *Gaumont-British*. 103 mins. *Cert U*
Rather unimaginative version of the long-running stage musical success, with its story of Ali Baba and his 40 thieves and a slave girl (*Anna May Wong*) who foils one of the thieves (*Fritz Kortner*), posing as the mandarin he has killed. Music and lyrics by Frederic Norton.
RoC *George Robey, John Garrick, Pearl Argyle, Jetsam (Malcolm McEachern), Dennis Hoey, Francis L. Sullivan, Sydney Fairbrother, Lawrence Hanray, Frank Cochrane, Thelma Tuson, Kyoshi Takase, Constance Godridge*.

Pearl Argyle and John Garrick in Chu Chin Chow (*1934*)

THE CHURCH MOUSE (1934) [4]
Dir *Monty Banks*. Prod *Irving Asher*. Scr *W. Scott Darling, Tom Geraghty, from a play by Ladislas Fodor, Paul Frank*. PC *Warner Bros*. Dis *First National*. 77 mins. *Cert A*
Amusing romantic comedy that proves a personal triumph for American star *Laura la Plante* as a hard-up, mousy typist who gets a job with a banker (*Ian Hunter*) and goes with him to Paris. Sylvia (*Jane Carr*), his former

secretary, now his mistress, follows and unwittingly gives the 'mouse' tips on the art of fascinating men. As a result, the banker and the 'mouse' are soon married.

RoC *Edward Chapman, Clifford Heatherley, John Batten, Gibb McLaughlin, Monty Banks, Florence Wood.*

THE CITADEL (1938)   [6]

Dir *King Vidor.* Prod *Victor Saville.* Scr *Ian Dalrymple, Frank Weed, Elizabeth Hill, Emlyn Williams, John Van Druten, from the novel by A. J. Cronin.* Ph *Harry Stradling.* PC and Dis *MGM British.* 110 mins. Cert A

An idealistic young doctor (*Robert Donat*) fights slum conditions in a Welsh mining village and marries the schoolteacher (*Rosalind Russell*) there. He moves on to London where, after months of struggle, he gains an entry to society clients who rot his ideals. Only the death of a friend (*Ralph Richardson*) at the hands of a high-priced but incompetent surgeon (*Cecil Parker*) brings him to his senses. He risks being struck off by his association with a non-qualified practitioner to help save a child's life, but his own impassioned plea to the General Medical Council saves his career. Inspiring, impressively constructed, emotive drama, voted best film of 1938 by the New York Film Critics.

RoC *Rex Harrison, Emlyn Williams, Mary Clare, Nora Swinburne, Athene Seyler, Francis L. Sullivan, Edward Chapman, Felix Aylmer, Penelope Dudley-Ward, Joyce Bland, Percy Parsons, Dilys Davies, Basil Gill, Joss Ambler, Josephine Wilson, Haidee Wright, Isobel Scaife, Charles Quartermaine, Angela Baddeley, Eliot Makeham, D. J. Williams, Edgar K. Bruce, Joan Kemp-Welch, Brian Herbert, Bombardier Billy Wells, Jack James, Ben Williams, Edward Dignon, Richard Littledale, Leslie Phillips.*

THE CITY OF BEAUTIFUL NONSENSE (1935)   [3]

Dir *Adrian Brunel.* Prod *Wilfred Noy.* Scr *Donovan Pedelty, from the novel by E. Temple Thurston.* Ph *Desmond Dickinson.* PC and Dis *Butchers.* 88 mins. Cert U

Jill (*Sophie Stewart*), who is pledged to a rich man in order to save her father from ruin, is courted by Jack Grey (*Emlyn Williams*), a poverty stricken composer, who pursues her from London to Venice and eventually wins her love. Remake of a 1919 silent with Chrissie White and Henry Edwards, and quite well-developed.

RoC *George Carney, Eve Lister, Marie Wright, Eric Maturin, Derek Oldham, J. Fisher White, Daisy Dormer, Hubert Harben, Margaret Damer, Dorothy Vernon, Henry Hepworth, Francisca Moreno, Cynthia Stock, A. E. Timmis, Stanley Radcliffe, Billie Bray, Eric Marshall, Sidney Monckton, Ian Wilson, J. P. Morgan.*

CITY OF SONG (1930)   [5]
(USA: *Farewell to Love*)

Dir *Carmine Gallone.* Prod *Isidore Schlesinger.* Scr *Miles Malleson, Hans Szekely, C. H. Dand.*

PC *Associated Sound Film Industries.* Dis *Sterling.* Trilingual versions. 101 mins. Cert U

Popular musical about a young English socialite Claire (*Betty Stockfeld*) who holidays in Naples and falls in love with her guide Giovanni (*Jan Kiepura*). She brings him to London to have his fine singing voice trained, but he cannot come to grips with London society, and eventually returns to Naples and his sweetheart Carmela (*Heather Angel*).

RoC *Hugh Wakefield, Francesco Maldacea, Philip Easton, Miles Malleson.*

THE CLAIRVOYANT (1935)   [4]

Dir *Maurice Elvey.* Prod *Michael Balcon.* Scr *Charles Bennett, Bryan Edgar Wallace, Robert Edmunds, from a novel by Ernest Lothar.* Ph *Glen MacWilliams.* PC *Gainsborough.* Dis *Gaumont-British.* 80 mins. Cert A

Skilful performance by *Claude Rains* carries through this drama about a fake clairvoyant, touring music-halls, who suddenly discovers he has a real gift for it. At first he has considerable fun, but then his clairvoyancy takes a more serious turn, ending with his fight to convince authorities of an imminent mining disaster before tragedy strikes.

RoC *Fay Wray, Jane Baxter, Ben Field, Athole Stewart, Mary Clare, Felix Aylmer, Donald Calthrop, Jack Raine, Margaret Davidge, (C.) Denier Warren.*

THE CLAYDON TREASURE MYSTERY (1938)   [3]

Dir *Manning Haynes.* Prod *John Findlay.* Scr *Edward Dryhurst, from a novel by Neil Gordon.* Ph *Stanley Grant.* PC and Dis *Fox British.* 63 mins. Cert A

Three murders are committed at Claydon Manor, and Kerrigan (*John Stuart*), a novelist, is convinced the supposedly mythical Claydon treasure is behind the crimes. He and Lady Clayton (*Annie Esmond*) find its secret hiding-place, but it has already been removed by Tollemache, an art dealer (*Campbell Gullan*). He proves to be an imposter – and the killer. Neat little thriller.

RoC *Evelyn Ankers, Aubrey Mallalieu, Finlay Currie, Joss Ambler, Vernon Harris, Richard Perry, Roy Russell, Ian Fleming, Valentine Dunn, John Laurie, Ernest Borrow, Aubrey Pollock.*

CLEANING UP (1933)   [3]

Dir *Leslie Hiscott.* Prod *Herbert Smith.* Scr *Michael Barringer.* Ph *Alex Bryce.* PC and Dis *British Lion.* 70 mins. Cert U

Tony (*George Gee*), the son of a lord, becomes a vacuum-cleaner salesman to spite his father. On his rounds he meets actress Marian Brent (*Betty Astell*) and falls in love. Quite by accident and thanks to his vacuum cleaners, Tony becomes a star in variety and accepts a large order for vacuums in lieu of salary. Thus the vacuum company backs Tony and Marian's successful show.

RoC *Davy Burnaby, Barbara Gott, Alfred Wellesley, Muriel George, Joan Matheson, Dorothy Vernon, Rona Ricardo, Gilbert Davies, The Max Rivers Girls.*

Muriel George, Davy Burnaby, Joan Matheson and George Gee in Cleaning Up *(1933)*

CLIMBING HIGH (1938)   [3]

Dir *Carol Reed.* Prod *Michael Balcon.* Scr *Stephen Clarkson.* Ph *Mutz Greenbaum.* PC *Gaumont-British.* Dis *MGM.* 78 mins. Cert U

Situation comedy about Diana (a songless *Jessie Matthews*), who gets a job in a modelling agency where she meets Nicky (*Michael Redgrave*), a wealthy young man, who as 'John Smith' also gets modelling work to be near her. Lady Constance (*Margaret Vyner*) wants to marry Nicky for his money. Diana's tough Canadian brother Jim (*Torin Thatcher*) is determined Nicky shall marry his sister, but on a climbing trip the trio undertakes, finds Nicky needs no persuading.

RoC *Noel Madison, Alastair Sim, Mary Clare, Francis L. Sullivan, Enid Stamp-Taylor, Tucker McGuire, Basil Radford, Athole Stewart.*

CLOTHES AND THE WOMAN (1937)   [2]

Dir *Albert de Courville.* Prod *Julius Hagen.* Scr *F. McGrew Willis.* PC *JH Productions.* Dis *Associated British.* 70 mins. Cert A

A runaway schoolgirl (*Anne Tucker McGuire*) is taken in by a wealthy middle-aged woman (*Constance Collier*) who sets out to teach the girl how to be sophisticated and attract men, with the reluctant help of her manservant (*Alastair Sim*). The plan is so successful that the girl marries a famous airman. Good cast tries hard with low-grade material.

RoC *Rod la Rocque, George E. Stone, Dorothy Dare, Mona Goya, Renée Gadd, Mary Cole, Jim Gerald.*

COCK O' THE NORTH (1935)   [2]

Dir *Oswald Mitchell, Challis Sanderson.* Prod and Scr *Mitchell.* Ph *William Luff.* PC *Panther/Mitchell Films.* Dis *Butchers.* 84 mins. Cert U

George Barton (*George Carney*), an engine driver, is selected to drive the new locomotive *Cock o' the North*. But he is injured in a car crash and forced to take early retirement. His fellow-railwaymen stage a charity concert for him, and he gains consolation in watching the achievements of his son as a pilot. Poor film partly redeemed by very good performance by Carney. Musical guest stars.

RoC *Marie Lohr, Ronnie Hepworth, Horace*

Kenney, Eve Lister, Frederick Peisley, Peggy Novak, Johnnie Schofield, Roddy Hughes, Leslie 'Hutch' Hutchinson, Naughton and Gold, Robert Chisholm, Simone Rogers, Pearl Hay, Herbert Cameron, Stanley Kirkby, Terry Conlin, Omar.

C.O.D. (1932) [3]

Dir *Michael Powell.* Prod *Jerome Jackson.* Scr *Ralph Smart.* Ph *Geoffrey Faithfull.* PC *Westminster.* Dis *United Artists. 64 mins. Cert A*

While thinking the material ordinary, critics praised the 'brilliant direction' of Michael Powell in this crime thriller about a girl (*Hope Davy*) who discovers her stepfather's body in the library and, thinking he will be accused, hires a down-and-out thief (*Garry Marsh*) to dispose of it. Although the body 'returns', the thief exposes the girl's cousin (*Roland Culver*) as the real murderer.

RoC *Cecil Ramage, Peter Gawthorne, Bruce Belfrage, Arthur Stratton, Sybil Grove.*

COLLISON (1931) [1]

Dir and Scr *G.B. Samuelson, from a play by E.C. Pollard.* Prod *E. Gordon Craig.* PC *Samuelson.* Dis *United Artists. 88 mins. Cert A*

Unconvincing society-crime drama set on the Riviera. Young Jack Carruthers (*Gerald Rawlinson*) is in debt and suspected of the theft of a pearl necklace. His mother (*Henrietta Watson*) guesses the identity of the real thief and, by a ruse, makes an adventuress, Mrs Oliver (*Sunday Wilshin*), admit her guilt.

RoC *Wendy Barrie, Irene Rooke, A.G. Poulton, Peter Coleman, L. Tippett.*

COLONEL BLOOD (1933) [2]

Dir and Scr *W.P. Lipscomb.* Prod *Norman Loudon.* Ph *George Stretton.* PC *Sound City.* Dis *MGM. 98 mins. Cert A*

Too-long historical adventure, set in 1650. Blood (*Frank Cellier*), an Irish adventurer determined to end unjust executions of his countrymen, gains the friendship of English King Charles II (*Allan Jeayes*) through helping him perfect an invention. Trying to steal the Crown Jewels, Blood is caught and sentenced to death, but his silver tongue results in the king giving him not only a pardon, but an office of high rank.

RoC *Anne Grey, Hay Petrie, Mary Lawson, Hilda Trevelyan, Arthur Chesney, Stella Arbenina, Desmond Jeans, Robert Nainsby, Arthur Goullet, Percy Standing, Ena Grossmith, Gabriel Toyne, Peggy Evans, Vivien Reynolds, Tarver Penna.*

COME INTO MY PARLOUR (1932) [3]

Dir *John Longden.* Prod *Kenneth McLaglen, A.J. Marks.* Scr *Jean Jay, Longden.* PC *GEM Productions.* Dis *MGM. 47 mins. Cert U*

Gerry (*Pat Aherne*), a barber, jealously in love with a manicurist (*Renée Houston*), believes he has killed a man in a fight and runs away, living under an assumed name and working as a coal haulier. The manicurist eventually finds him and tells him that the man he thought he killed was a burglar at her home – and didn't die anyway.

RoC *Robert Holmes, Hal Walters, Fanny Wright, Anne Shirley.*

COME ON GEORGE (1939) [5]

Dir *Anthony Kimmins.* Prod *Jack Kitchin.* Scr *Kimmins, Leslie Arliss, Val Valentine.* Ph *Ronald Neame.* PC *ATP/Ealing Studios.* Dis *Associated British. 88 mins. Cert U*

George (*George Formby*), an ice-cream seller, makes a hurried getaway after being (falsely) accused of stealing a wallet planted in his ice-cream cart. He ends up sharing a horse-box with Maneater, an 'unmanageable' racehorse who seems to like George. George is engaged to look after Maneater and ride him in a big race. He loses his nerve (and is almost eaten by 2,000 performing fleas), but is given renewed confidence by a psychoanalyst and rides Maneater to victory after outwitting a gang of crooks. Gorgeous nonsense with slightly smutty songs thrown in: the Formby brand of fun at its best.

RoC *Pat Kirkwood, Joss Ambler, Meriel Forbes, Cyril Raymond, George Hayes, George Carney, Ronald Shiner, Gibb McLaughlin, Hal Gordon, Davy Burnaby, (C.) Denier Warren, James Hayter, Syd Crossley, Ronald Stagges, Dirk Bogarde (extra).*

George Formby and George Carney in Come On George (*1939*)

COME OUT OF THE PANTRY (1935) [2]

Dir *Jack Raymond.* Prod *Herbert Wilcox.* Scr *Austin Parker, Douglas Furber, from a play by Alice Duer Miller.* Ph *F.A. Young.* PC *British and Dominions.* Dis *United Artists. 71 mins. Cert U*

Lord Robert Brent (*Jack Buchanan*) finds himself alone and broke in New York after the bank in which he had placed family money promptly fails. He meets Eccles (*Ronald Squire*) who obtains him a position with the Beach-Howard family as footman. During a dinner at which his stodgy brother is a guest, Lord Robert proposes to Hilda (*Fay Wray*), the Beach-Howards' niece, during the soup and, much to his brother's chagrin, is accepted during the sweet course. Comedy-musical begins brightly but soon palls.

RoC *Fred Emney, James Carew, Olive Blakeney, Kate Cutler, Ethel Stewart, Ben Welden, Maire O'Neill, William T. Ellwanger.*

COMING OF AGE (1938) [2]

Dir *Manning Haynes.* Prod *A. George Smith.* Scr *Paul White, Rowan Kennedy.* Ph *Sydney*

Blythe. PC *GS Enterprises.* Dis *Columbia. 68 mins. Cert U*

Music-loving Henry (*Eliot Makeham*) timidly rebels against his bored, domineering wife (*Joyce Bland*). His chance acquaintance with a singer (*Ruby Miller*) brings about a meeting between her daughter (*Evelyn Ankers*) and his son (*Jimmy Hanley*), who fall in love. Henry's wife defiantly flirts with the singer's husband, but all complications are ironed out at their son's 21st birthday party. Comedy is well-acted but rather annoying.

RoC *Jack Melford, Annie Esmond, Aubrey Mallalieu, Michael Ripper, Isobel Scaife, Valentine Dunn.*

COMMAND PERFORMANCE (1937) [2]

Dir *Sinclair Hill.* Prod *Harcourt Templeman.* Scr *George Pearson, Michael Hankinson, Hill, from the play by Stafford Dickens.* Ph *Cyril Bristow.* PC *Grosvenor.* Dis *General Film Distributors. 84 mins. Cert U*

A star known as The Street Singer (*Arthur Tracy*), overworked to the point of exhaustion, flees the city and takes up with gipsies and hoboes, meeting gipsy Tom's daughters Susan (*Lilli Palmer*) with whom he falls in love, and little Betty (*Rae Collett*). When Susan's jealous suitor betrays him to those seeking him, Betty tries to follow him to London, but is knocked down by a car. He sings to the child on the radio, then rushes to her bedside, and is reunited with Susan. Absurdly sentimental musical.

RoC *Mark Daly, Finlay Currie, Julien Vedey, Jack Melford, Phyllis Stanley, Stafford Hilliard.*

COMMISSIONAIRE (1933) [3]

Dir *Edward Dryhurst.* Prod *Edward G. Whiting.* Scr *Herbert Ayres.* Ph *Desmond Dickinson.* PC *Granville.* Dis *MGM. 72 mins. Cert U*

George Brown (*Sam Livesey*) retires from the army and takes a commissionaire's job at the firm where his son Tom (*Barrie Livesey*) works. When Tom becomes involved with an adventuress (*Julie Suedo*), he steals money from the firm to pay her debts – and is shielded by his father who takes the blame. Ultimately, Tom comes clean, and the company agrees not to prosecute – if he joins the army.

RoC *George Carney, Betty Huntley-Wright, Robert English, Hannah Jones, Granville Ferrier, Georgie Harris, Humberston Wright.*

COMPROMISING DAPHNE (1930) [4]
(USA: *Compromised!*)

Dir *Thomas Bentley.* Prod *John Maxwell.* Scr *Val Valentine, from a play by Edith Fitzgerald.* Ph *John J. Cox.* PC *BIP.* Dis *Wardour. 86 mins. Cert A*

Saucy comedy about an engaged couple, forbidden by the girl's father to marry for a year, who hatch a plot to speed things up by having the man caught in the girl's bedroom and instructed by her stern father to 'marry her at once'. Alas, things start to go wrong in the best farcical traditions when a slinky girlfriend turns up and is given the heroine's room. ...

LP *Jean Colin, Charles Hickman, Phyllis Konstam, C.M. Hallard, Leo Sheffield, Viola Compton, Frank Perfitt, Barbara Gott, Margot Grahame.*

THE COMPULSORY HUSBAND (1930) [3]

Dir *Monty Banks.* Prod *John Maxwell.* Scr *Val Valentine, Rex Taylor, from a novel by John Glyder.* Ph *René Guissart, James E. Rogers.* PC *BIP.* Dis *Wardour.* 84 mins. Cert A

Frantically complicated *Monty Banks* comedy about a man who nearly loses his fiancée through his (innocent) involvement with two other women. The second half of the film is set at an Alpine resort: exteriors were shot at Chamonix in the South of France.

RoC *Lillian Manton, Trilby Clark, Gladys Frazin, Clifford Heatherley, Janet Alexander, Reginald Fox, Michael Powell.*

Monty Banks in The Compulsory Husband *(1930)*

THE COMPULSORY WIFE (1937) [1]

Dir *Arthur Woods.* Prod *Irving Asher.* Scr *Reginald Purdell, John Dighton, from the play by John Glyder.* Ph *Basil Emmott.* PC and Dis *Warner Bros.* 57 mins. Cert A

Rupert (*Henry Kendall*) and his girl Bobby (*Joyce Kirby*) are invited to the country for a weekend. Storms delay their friends, and Rupert and Bobby find themselves alone in the friends' cottage. A burglar breaks in and steals their clothes. Thirty years later, the ideal situation for a sex romp; here, complications are strictly within the bounds of decorum – and tedium.

RoC *Margaret Yarde, Robert Hale, Agnes Laughlan, George Merritt, Anthony Shaw, Mercia Swinburne.*

CONCERNING MR MARTIN (1937) [3]

Dir *Roy Kellino.* Prod *John Findley.* Scr *Ernest Dudley.* Ph *Stanley Grant.* PC and Dis *Fox British.* 59 mins. Cert A

Photographer *Roy Kellino* made his directorial bow with this ingenious quota thriller about crook versus crook. A gentleman thief, Leo, (*William Barrett*) pits his wits against a crooked nightclub owner (*William Devlin*) who has cheated a young man out of a large sum of money. By framing the criminal for theft, Leo achieves his objective.

RoC *Marjorie Peacock, Derek Williams, Lionel*

Montgomery, Herbert Cameron, Madge Somers, Bombardier Billy Wells, Dominick Sterlini.

CONDEMNED TO DEATH (1931) [4]

Dir *Walter Forde.* Prod *Julius Hagen.* Scr *Bernard Merivale, H. Fowler Mear, Brock Williams, from a play by George Goodchild.* Ph *Sydney Blythe, William Luff.* PC *Twickenham.* Dis *W and F.* 76 mins. Cert A

Grim crime drama about a sinister killer, Lantern (*Bernard Brunel*), sentenced to death by Sir Charles (*Arthur Wontner*), a judge. Three years after Lantern hangs, similar killings take place. Young detective Jim Wrench (*Cyril Raymond*), who loves the judge's niece (*Jane Welsh*) traces the deaths to the judge himself, who has been hypnotized by Lantern's spirit from beyond the grave.

RoC *Edmund Gwenn, Gordon Harker, Norah Howard, Griffith Humphreys, H. St Barbe West, Gordon Blythe, Gillian Lind, James Cunningham, Gilbert Davies.*

CONFIDENTIAL LADY (1939) [3]

Dir *Arthur B. Woods.* Prod *Sam Sax.* Scr *Brock Williams, Derek Twist.* Ph *Basil Emmott.* PC *Warner Bros.* Dis *First National.* 75 mins. Cert U

Jilted on her wedding day after her father (*Stewart Rome*) has been ruined, Jill (*Jane Baxter*) determines to get her own back on men. She takes an expensive flat and is soon getting presents from a publisher whose reporter, Jim (*Ben Lyon*) has been sent to see her. She discovers that the publisher and her ex-fiancé were partners in the firm that broke her father; she and Jim expose their crimes. Apart from a surplus of chat, film has nice blend of romance, comedy and drama.

RoC *Athole Stewart, Ronald Ward, Jean Cadell, Frederick Burtwell, Gibb McLaughlin, Vera Bogetti, Gordon McLeod, Leo Franklyn, Edward Orchard, Frank Tickle, Henry Hallett.*

CONGRESS DANCES (1931) [6]

Dir *Erik Charell.* Prod *Erich Pommer.* Scr *Rowland V. Lee, from an original screenplay by Norbert Falk, Robert Liebmann.* Ph *Carl Hoffman.* PC *UFA.* Dis *UFA-GB.* 92 mins. Cert A

An outstanding musical, one of the few to challenge the Hollywood supremacy in the field in the early sound years. The original was German; a French version was also made, plus this English version with some cast alterations. Full of gaiety and spectacle, the story is set in Vienna, 1814, where waltzes and women edge war into the background, and a Czar of Russia enjoys a romance with a charming girl while a double takes his place at the Kongress. (Music by Werner Richard Heymann.)

LP *Lilian Harvey, Conrad Veidt, Henri Garat, Lil Dagover, Gibb McLaughlin, Reginald Purdell, Philip Manning, Humberston Wright, Helen Haye, Spencer Trevor, Tarquini d'Or.*

CONQUEST OF THE AIR (1936) [2]

Dir *Zoltan Korda, Alexander Esway, Donald Taylor, Alexander Shaw, John Monk Saunders, William Cameron Menzies.* Prod *Alexander*

Korda. Scr *Hugh Gray, Peter Bezencenet, from stories by Saunders and Antoine de St Exupéry.* Ph *Lee Garmes, Wilkie Cooper, Hans Schneeberger, George Noble.* PC *London Films.* Dis *United Artists.* 71 mins. Cert U

Dramatized history of man's attempts to fly and aviation, from 57 AD to the present time, a mixture of newsreel footage and reconstructed dramatic scenes. Not a success in any of its several forms, the film's major plus factor is the splendid music score, written by Arthur Bliss.

LP *Laurence Olivier, Franklin Dyall, Henry Victor, Hay Petrie, John Turnbull, Charles Lefaux, Bryan Powley, Frederick Culley, Alan Wheatley, John Abbott, Ben Webster, Percy Marmont, Dick Vernon, Denville Bond, Charles Hickman, Margaretta Scott, David Horne, Michael Rennie, Charles Frend (narrator).*

THE CONSTANT NYMPH (1933) [4]

Dir *Basil Dean.* Prod *Michael Balcon.* Scr *Margaret Kennedy, Basil Dean, Dorothy Farnum, from the play by Kennedy and Dean.* Ph *Mutz Greenbaum.* PC and Dis *Gaumont-British.* 97 mins. Cert A

Poignant version – second of three – of Margaret Kennedy's story about a sickly, sensitive schoolgirl, Tessa (*Victoria Hopper*) in love with a composer (*Brian Aherne*) who marries her wealthy cousin (*Leonora Corbett*), undermining further the unhappy Tessa's already delicate health. When the composer realizes that life without Tessa is unbearable and leaves his unloving wife, it is too late: Tessa has died from a heart condition.

RoC *Lyn Harding, Mary Clare, Jane Baxter, Fritz Schultz, Tony de Lungo, Jean Cornell, Peggy Blythe, Athole Stewart, Beryl Laverick, Jim Gerald.*

CONTRABAND LOVE (1931) [3]

Dir and Prod *Sidney Morgan.* Scr *Joan Wentworth Wood.* PC *British Screenplays.* Dis *Paramount.* 67 mins. Cert U

Natural Cornish exteriors were a bonus to this adventure story about a convict on the run who turns out to be a Scotland Yard man working undercover to catch a smuggling boat-owner and his gang.

LP *C. Aubrey Smith, Haddon Mason, Janice Adair, Rosalinde Fuller, Sydney Leaward, Charles Paton, Marie Ault.*

CONVICT 99 (1938) [4]

Dir *Marcel Varnel.* Prod *Edward Black.* Scr *Marriott Edgar, Val Guest, Jack Davies Jr, Ralph Smart.* Ph *Arthur Crabtree.* PC *Gainsborough.* Dis *General Film Distributors.* 91 mins. Cert A

Appointed prison governor by an error, 'Dr' Twist (*Will Hay*) arrives in the middle of a convicts' mutiny and gets thrown into a cell. In an effort to improve conditions he goes somewhat over the top, with electric fires, armchairs, rugs, curtains and radios for the prisoners' cells. With the help of an inmate, he successfully plays the market, but has to make a perilous venture into Limehouse when his 'funds' are stolen. Usual good Hay comedy.

RoC *Moore Marriott, Graham Moffatt, Googie Withers, Garry Marsh, Peter Gawthorne, Basil Radford, Dennis Wyndham, Wilfrid Walter, Alf Goddard, Teddy Brown, Kathleen Harrison, Roy Emerton, Basil McGrail, Ben Soutten, Wilson Coleman, Charles Paton, Dick Francis, Roddy McDowall.*

COTTON QUEEN (1937) [4]

Dir *Bernard Vorhaus.* Prod *Joe Rock.* Scr *Louis Golding, Scott Pembroke.* Ph *Horace Wheddon, Cyril Bristow.* PC *Rock Studios.* Dis *British Independent.* 80 mins. Cert U

Feuding Lancashire business rivals Sam and Bill (*Stanley Holloway, Will Fyffe*) find they could secure a massive American contract if they merged their mills. Further complications come up through the romance of Bill's niece (*Mary Lawson*) with Sam's son (*Jimmy Hanley*), but everything is sorted out at the annual festival, when the Cotton Queen is chosen. Lively comedy with hearty performances.

RoC *Marcelle Rogez, Helen Haye, (C.) Denier Warren, Syd Courtenay, Gibson Gowland, Donald Calthrop.*

COUNSEL'S OPINION (1933) [4]

Dir *Allan Dwan.* Prod *Alexander Korda.* Scr *Dorothy Greenhill, Arthur Wimperis, from the play by Gilbert Wakefield.* Ph *Phil Tannura.* PC *London Films.* Dis *Paramount.* 76 mins. Cert A

Korda's burgeoning company put some sparkle into this comedy about a young barrister (*Henry Kendall*) who lets a lady-in-distress (*Binnie Barnes*) use his hotel room, only to find himself mixed up in a divorce case. Ultimately the lady proves to be a widow who was posing as a lord's adulterous wife for her own ends – and the barrister finds himself free to marry her.

RoC *Cyril Maude, Harry Tate, Lawrence Grossmith, Francis Lister, Mary Charles, Margaret Baird, J. Fisher White, (C.) Denier Warren, Stanley Lathbury.*

Henry Kendall and Binnie Barnes in Counsel's Opinion *(1933)*

CRACKERJACK (1938) [3]
(USA: *The Man With a Hundred Faces*)

Dir *Albert de Courville.* Prod *Edward Black.* Scr *A.R. Rawlinson, Michael Pertwee, Basil Mason, from the novel by W.R. Ferguson.* Ph *Jack Cox.* PC *Gainsborough.* Dis *General Film Distributors.* 79 mins. Cert A

Jack Drake (*Tom Walls*), as the burglar Crackerjack, has captured the nation's imagination by robbing the rich to help the poor (including himself). 'An old friend, the Baroness von Haltze (*Lille Palmer*) helps set a trap for him laid by other (jealous) crooks, but Crackerjack's mastery of disguise outmanœuvres the gang, and he flies off on honeymoon - with the baroness. Action comedy is okay once it gets going.

RoC *Noel Madison, Leon M. Lion, Edmund Breon, Charles Heslop, Ethel Griffies, H.G. Stoker, Michael Shepley, Henry Longhurst, Muriel George, Edmund Dalby, Tarver Penna, Fewlass Llewellyn, Tony de Lungo, Robert Nainby, Jack Lester, Andrea Malandrinos, Jack Vyvyan, Victor Fairley, Margaret Davidge, Hal Walters, Bobby Gall, Charles Hiller.*

CRAZY PEOPLE (1934) [2]

Dir *Leslie Hiscott.* Prod *Herbert Smith.* Scr *Michael Barringer, from a novel by Margot Neville.* PC *British Lion.* Dis *MGM.* 67 mins. Cert U

Comedy about idle, penniless Hippocrates Rayne (*Henry Kendall*), who loses a valuable ring entrusted to him by his aunt (*Helen Haye*). He suspects gold-digger Angela (*Vera Bogetti*) until the ring is found by his aunt's secretary (*Nancy O'Neil*) who is in love with him. The title refers to an episode in which a group of Hippo's friends pose as lunatics to gain him time with his aunt.

RoC *Kenneth Kove, Wally Patch, Hal Walters, Hugh E. Wright, Herschel Henlere, Alexander Field, Dorothy Vernon, Al Okese and The Three Stooges.*

CREEPING SHADOWS (1931) [2]
(USA: *The Limping Man*)

Dir, Prod and Scr *John Orton, from a play by Will Scott.* PC *BIP.* Dis *Wardour.* 79 mins. Cert A

Brian Nash (*Lester Matthews*) inherits a country estate where he finds strange things afoot. A limping man hangs around the place, there's a murder in the woods, a bell tolls with no-one there, mysterious footsteps are heard, telephone wires are cut and his petrol supply disappears. A detective, Disher (*Franklin Dyall*) investigates, and uncovers a plot by three people to kill the man who informed on them and sent them to prison.

RoC *Margot Grahame, Arthur Hardy, Jeanne Stuart, Gerald Rawlinson, David Hawthorne, Charles Farrell, Henrietta Watson, Matthew Boulton, Percy Parsons, Hal Gordon, Ernest Stilwell, Samuel Pringle.*

THE CRIME AT BLOSSOMS (1933) [3]

Dir and Prod *Maclean Rogers.* Scr *Mordaunt Shairp, from his play.* PC *British and Dominions.* Dis *Paramount.* 77 mins. Cert A

Chris and Valerie (*Hugh Wakefield, Joyce Bland*) let their country cottage, which is subsequently the scene of a murder. On their return, they are besieged by sightseers. The opportunist Valerie turns the situation to their 'advantage', charging admission, selling souvenirs and re-enacting the murder - the real circumstances of which, when disclosed, bring her to her senses.

RoC *Eileen Munro, Ivor Barnard, Frederick Lloyd, Iris Baker, Arthur Stratton, Maud Gill, Wally Patch, Barbara Gott, Moore Marriott, George Ridgwell.*

CRIME ON THE HILL (1933) [3]

Dir *Bernard Vorhaus.* Prod *Walter C. Mycroft.* Scr *Michael Hankinson, Vera Allinson, E. M. Delafield, Vorhaus, from the play by Jack de Leon, Jack Celestin.* PC *BIP.* Dis *Wardour.* 69 mins. Cert A

Country-house murder mystery lifted by pleasant scenes of rural England. A doctor and vicar investigate the murder of a country squire whose estate is set to go to his niece Sylvia (*Sally Blane*) until Claire (*Phyllis Dare*) reveals she has married the squire secretly. Suspicion falls on Sylvia's fiancé (*Anthony Bushell*) until the clergyman (*Lewis Casson*) reveals that his old friend the doctor (*Nigel Playfair*), in love with Claire, is the killer.

RoC *Judy Kelly, George Merritt, Gus McNaughton, Reginald Purdell, Hal Gordon, Jimmy Godden, Hay Petrie, Kenneth Kove.*

CRIME OVER LONDON (1936) [2]

Dir *Alfred Zeisler.* Prod *Marcel Hellman, Douglas Fairbanks Jr.* Scr *Norman Alexander, Harold French, from a novel by Louis de Wohl.* Ph *Victor Armenise.* PC *Criterion.* Dis *United Artists.* 80 mins. Cert A. Bilingual versions

A gang hatches an elaborate scheme to rob a store of the money it intends to distribute to its employees to celebrate its jubilee. But the store manager's double (a member of the gang) opts out of the plot and warns the store. When the crooks enter the store posing as auditors, they soon find themselves on the losing end of a pitched battle with the law. Tall story, not too happily cast.

LP *Margot Grahame, Paul Cavanagh, Joseph Cawthorn, Basil Sydney, René Ray, Bruce Lister, David Burns, Edmon Ryan, Googie Withers, Danny Green, John Darrow.*

Margot Grahame and Basil Sydney in Crime Over London *(1936)*

THE CRIMES OF STEPHEN HAWKE (1936) [3]

Dir, Prod and PC *George King.* Scr *H.F. Maltby, from the story by Jack Celestin.* Ph *Ronald Neame.* Dis *MGM.* 69 mins. Cert A

Lively entry from *Tod Slaughter*, with the old barnstormer as Hawke, apparently a kindly moneylender, but in reality a horrendous mass-murderer who enjoys breaking his victims' spines. When he is forced to kill a friend, the friend's son (*Eric Portman*) who is engaged to Hawke's adopted daughter, Julia (*Margorie Taylor*), allows Hawke to escape. Then another villain, Archer (*Gerald Barry*), blackmails Julia into agreeing to marry him. Hawke reappears, kills Archer, and crashes from a roof to his own death.
RoC *Ben Soutten, D. J. Williams, Charles Penrose, Flotsam and Jetsam, Norman Pierce, George Slater.*

CRIME UNLIMITED (1935) 3

Dir *Ralph Ince.* Prod *Irving Asher.* Scr *Brock Williams, Ralph Smart, from the novel by David Hume.* Ph *Basil Emmott.* PC *Warner Bros.* Dis *First National. 72 mins. Cert A*
Another adaptation from one of David Hume's 'Cardby' thrillers, with *Esmond Knight* as a young police college recruit who, as a face unfamiliar to the underworld, joins a gang of jewel thieves to unmask the mastermind behind their activities. He finds romance with a Russian girl (*Lilli Palmer* in a much-praised debut) who helps him in his task. Vigorous crime drama.
RoC *Cecil Parker, George Merritt, Raymond Lovell, Wyndham Goldie, Peter Gawthorne, Jane Millican, Stella Arbenina, Richard Grey, Bellenden Clarke.*

THE CRIMSON CANDLE (1934) 2

Dir, Prod, Scr and PC *Bernard Mainwaring.* Dis *MGM. 67 mins. Cert A*
Leonard Duberley (*Derek Williams*) is convinced that tonight is his last – in accordance with the family curse. Inspector Blunt (*Kynaston Reeves*) concludes that Leonard's stepmother (*Eve Gray*), her son (*Arthur Goullet*) and family doctor Gaunt (*Eliot Makeham*) are plotting to scare him to death. Leonard dies – but Gaunt proves he was killed by his ex-mistress, the maid (*Audrey Cameron*).
RoC *Kenneth Kove, Eugene Leahy.*

THE CRIMSON CIRCLE (1936) 3

Dir *Reginald Denham.* Prod *Richard Wainwright.* Scr *Howard Irving Young, from the novel by Edgar Wallace.* PC *Wainwright.* Dis *Universal. 76 mins. Cert A*
Workmanlike whodunnit in which Inspector Parr (*Alfred Drayton*), with the help of Yale (*Hugh Wakefield*), a detective who's smarter than he seems, investigates the murders of three prominent businessmen, all killed after being threatened by 'The Crimson Circle'. He arrests Sylvia (*June Duprez*), an associate of criminal Felix Marl (*Noah Beery*). When Marl is found dead, Parr releases Sylvia, and trails her to a secret meeting place on board a ship in dock, where the identity of the murderer is revealed.
RoC *Renée Gadd, Basil Gill, Niall MacGinnis, Gordon McLeod, Ralph Truman, Paul Blake, Robert Rendell.*

THE CROOKED LADY (1932) 3

Dir *Leslie Hiscott.* Prod *Julius Hagen.* Scr *H. Fowler Mear, from a novel by William C. Stone.* PC *Real Art.* Dis *MGM. 76 mins. Cert U*
A down-and-out ex-army officer (*Austin Trevor*) joins a gang of thieves, steals some pearls from under the nose of a lady detective (*Ursula Jeans*) but returns them when he finds they belong to the widow (*Isobel Elsom*) of a man who had saved his life. The lady detective is on the track of the gang chief, now wanted for murder, and the ex-officer, who has turned to writing crime stories, helps her get her man – and marries her.
RoC *George Graves, Edmund Willard, Alexander Field, Moore Marriott, Frank Pettingell, S. J. Warmington, H. B. Longhurst, Paddy Browne.*

CROSS CURRENTS (1935) 2

Dir *Adrian Brunel.* Prod *Anthony Havelock-Allan.* Scr *Brunel, Pelham Leigh Amann, from a novel by Gerald Elliott.* Ph *Francis Carver.* PC and Dis *British and Dominions/Paramount British. 66 mins. Cert U*
Indifferent comedy in which the mysterious disappearance of a man from a small English village gets all sorts of people into trouble, including the Vicar, who is suspected of having killed him over an attractive widow. The mystery is cleared up by the reappearance of the man and the arrest of a swindler who has been trying to buy his copper-mine for half its value.
LP *Frank Birch, Evelyn Foster, Ian Colin, Marjorie Hume, Aubrey Mallalieu, Kate Saxon, Aubrey Dexter, Bryan Powley, Sally Gray, Aubrey Pollock.*

CROSS MY HEART (1936) 1

Dir *Bernard Mainwaring.* Prod *Anthony Havelock-Allan.* Scr *Basil N. Keyes.* Ph *Francis Carver.* PC and Dis *British and Dominions/Paramount British. 65 mins. Cert A*
Sally (*Kathleen Gibson*) turns her boarding-house into a nightclub, but things go badly until her friends Steve (*Kenneth Duncan*) and Chesty (*Tully Comber*) add a jazz band, and – unknown to Sally – Steve also sets up a gambling room. The place is raided, and Sally ends up in court. Steve pays her fines, and Sally marries Chesty. Very thin.
RoC *Aubrey Fitzgerald, Robert Field, Muriel Johnston, Eric Hales, Sylvia Coleridge, Sam Blake, Frank Tickle.*

CROSS ROADS (1930) 2

Dir and Prod *Reginald Fogwell.* Scr *Fogwell, A. E. Bundy.* PC *British Projects.* Dis *Paramount. 58 mins. Cert A*
Wearily familiar domestic drama about a wife discovering her husband's infidelity, and shooting him, told as a cautionary tale by a woman to stop her daughter's elopement.
LP *Anne Grey, Percy Marmont, Betty Faire, Langhorne Burton, Wilfred Shine.*

THE CROUCHING BEAST (1935) 2

Dir *W. Victor Hanbury.* Prod *John Stafford.* Scr *Valentine Williams, from his novel Club-*

foot. PC *Stafford.* Dis *Radio. 80 mins. Cert A*
First World War drama, dealing with the theft of the plans of the Dardanelles' fortifications, and the attempts of Ahmed Bey (*Fritz Kortner*), head of the Turkish secret service, to get them back. When he fails, and the British fleet bombards his city, he kills himself.
RoC *Wynne Gibson, Richard Bird, Andrews Englemann, Isabel Jeans, Frederick Conyngham, Peter Gawthorne, Ian Fleming, Marjorie Mars, Gus McNaughton, A. Bromley Davenport, Margaret Yarde, Betty Shale, Bela Mira, Pegeen Mair, Pollie Emery.*

CROWN v STEVENS (1936) 2

Dir *Michael Powell.* Prod *Irving Asher.* Scr *Brock Williams, from a novel by Laurence Maynell.* Ph *Basil Emmott.* PC and Dis *Warner Bros. 66 mins. Cert A*
Desultory crime drama on the theme of the bad woman. Doris Stevens (*Beatrix Thomson*) murders a moneylender, and later tries to dispose of her husband (*Frederick Piper*) in a locked garage. She is thwarted by her husband's employee (*Patric Knowles*), who forces her to confess to the police.
RoC *Reginald Purdell, Allan Jeayes, Glennis Lorimer, Googie Withers, Mabel Poulton, Billy Watts, Morris Harvey, Davina Craig.*

THE CRUCIFIX (1934) 4

Dir *G. B. Samuelson.* Prod *Gordon Craig.* Scr *Samuelson, Roland Pertwee.* PC *New Era.* Dis *Universal. 70 mins. Cert A*
Vivid performances lift this drama about a tyrannical old woman (*Nancy Price*) whose companion (*Sydney Fairbrother*) breaks a valuable vase and has her wages stopped until the loss is made good. Ultimately, the companion steals a crucifix when her employer dies, and is caught by the police, who reveal that the old tyrant repented at the last and left her companion everything.
RoC *Farren Soutar, Brenda Harvey, Audrey Cameron, Pollie Emery, Minnie Taylor.*

A CUCKOO IN THE NEST (1933) 4

Dir *Tom Walls.* Prod *Angus Macphail, Ian Dalrymple.* Scr *Ben Travers, A. R. Rawlinson, from the play by Travers.* Ph *Glen MacWilliams.* PC *Gaumont-British.* Dis *W and F. 85 mins. Cert A*

Tom Walls and Ralph Lynn in A Cuckoo in the Nest *(1933)*

Leaving to join his wife at a party in the country, Peter (*Ralph Lynn*) misses his train through chatting to an old friend, Marguerite (*Yvonne Arnaud*), who is bound for the same party. The two go on by car, but are forced to put up at an inn which inevitably only has one room left. Pursued by his wife's parents, and caught in a series of compromising situations, Peter clears the situation up with difficulty. Slick Aldwych farce, slightly slower than usual in places.

RoC *Tom Walls, Robertson Hare, Mary Brough, Veronica Rose, Gordon James, Grace Edwin, Mark Daly, Cecil Parker, Roger Livesey, Frank Pettingell, Joan Brierley, Norah Howard.*

A CUP OF KINDNESS (1934) [4]

Dir *Tom Walls.* Prod *Michael Balcon.* Scr *Ben Travers, from his play.* PC and Dis *Gaumont-British. 81 mins. Cert A*

Despite some amusing situations, there were slight signs of staleness in this offering from the Aldwych gang, concerning a feud between two families, the Tutts and the Ramsbottoms. The feud seems to be at an end when Charlie Tutt (*Ralph Lynn*) marries Betty Ramsbottom (*Dorothy Hyson*), but when the couple come under suspicion of fraud, chaos ensues.

RoC *Tom Walls, Robertson Hare, Claude Hulbert, Marie Wright, Eva Moore, Veronica Rose, Gordon James, D. A. Clarke-Smith, J. Fisher White, Philip Carlton, Daphne Scorer.*

DANCE BAND (1935) [3]

Dir *Marcel Varnel.* Prod *Walter C. Mycroft.* Scr *Roger Burford, Jack Davies, Denis Waldock.* Ph *Bryan Langley.* PC *BIP.* Dis *Wardour. 74 mins. Cert U*

Untidily unfolded musical, but with tuneful music – by a woman, Mabel Wayne. Buddy (*Charles 'Buddy' Rogers*), a dance-band leader, falls for Pat (*June Clyde*) leader of an all-girl band. As they have both entered for a competition, Pat misunderstands his intentions, and her manager resorts to dirty work. But Buddy and his boys put things right after fighting a gang of toughs, and eventually the two bands share first prize.

RoC *Steven Geray, Magda Kun, Fred Duprez, Leon Sherkot, Richard Hearne, Jack Holland and June Hart, Albert Whelan, Hal Gordon, Fred Groves.*

THE DANCE OF DEATH (1938) [1]

Dir and Prod *Gerald Blake.* Scr *Ralph Dawson.* PC *Glenrose.* Dis *Fidelity. 68 mins. Cert A*

Ex-thief Mara (*Julie Suedo*), now a dancer, is 'called back' to crime by 'The Master' (*Stewart Rome*) who is reassembling his old gang for an assault on the legendary Lander jewels.

Mara steals the gems herself at a Lander dance after being 'shot' with blanks by accomplices, but The Master stabs her as she lies prone and makes his getaway. His car crashes over a cliff and he is burned to death. Hilariously bad thriller.

RoC *Vesta Victoria, Elizabeth Kent, Jimmy Godden, Betty Norton, Dino Galvani, Basil Broadbent, Iris Terry, Ralph Dawson, John Rowal.*

DANCE PRETTY LADY (1932) [2]

Dir and Scr *Anthony Asquith, from a novel by Compton Mackenzie.* Prod *H. Bruce Woolfe.* Ph *Jack Parker.* PC *British Instructional.* Dis *Wardour. 63 mins. Cert A*

An early version of Compton Mackenzie's tear-jerking saga (*Carnival*) of the ballet dancer (*Ann Casson*), who hits the downward path in the early 1900s after she refuses to become the mistress of the artist she loves and impulsively marries a farmer instead.

RoC *Carl Harbord, Michael Hogan, Moore Marriott, Flora Robson, Sunday Wilshin, René Ray, Leonard Brett, Norman Claridge, Eva Llewellyn, Ballet Rambert Dancers.*

DANDY DICK (1935) [3]

Dir *William Beaudine.* Prod *Walter C. Mycroft.* Scr *Frank Miller, Beaudine, Clifford Grey, Will Hay.* Ph *Jack Parker.* PC *BIP.* Dis *Wardour. 72 mins. Cert U*

Rambunctious comedy about the efforts of a country vicar (*Will Hay*) to raise money for a new church spire. He plunges all he's got on a racehorse called Dandy Dick in a (very successful) bid to increase the funds in hand – but has to clear himself of a charge of doping before he's allowed to claim his winnings.

RoC *Nancy Burne, Esmond Knight, Davy Burnaby, Mignon O'Doherty, Wally Patch, Moore Marriott, Syd Crossley, Robert Nainby, Hala Gordon, Jimmy Godden, John Singer.*

DANGEROUS FINGERS (1937) [3]
(USA: *Wanted by Scotland Yard*)

Dir *Norman Lee.* Prod *John Argyle.* Scr *Vernon Clancey, from his novel* Man Hunt. *Ph *Bryan Langley.* PC *Rialto.* Dis *Pathé. 79 mins. Cert A*

Fingers (*James Stephenson*) is a gentleman crook, equally dextrous on a piano or a safe. When he goes for a collection of rubies, he realizes that their owner, Standish (*Leslie Perrins*) was responsible for the suicide of a former flame. Letting his emotions get the better of him, Fingers is cornered by Standish, but saved by another crook, Ben (*Phil Ray*), who kills Standish before being killed by police. Fingers escapes. Leading man is good, film not so hot.

RoC *Betty Lynne, D. A. Clarke-Smith, Nadine March, Sally Stewart, George Merritt, Bryan Herbert, Florence Groves.*

DANGEROUS GROUND (1934) [3]

Dir *Norman Walker.* Prod *Uncredited.* Scr *Dion Titheradge, Dorothy Rowan.* Ph *Cyril Bristow.* PC and Dis *British and Dominions/Paramount British. 68 mins. Cert A*

Some witty dialogue gives a slight lift to this

crime story in which Claire (*Joyce Kennedy*) turns detective to unmask the killer of her fiancé (a genuine detective). The murderer turns out to be a distinguished socialite who had killed the dead man because he had found out about his 'underworld' activities as a receiver of stolen jewels.

RoC *Jack Raine, Martin Lewis, Kathleen Kelly, Henry Longhurst, Gordon Begg.*

DANGEROUS MEDICINE (1938) [3]

Dir *Arthur Woods.* Prod *Jerome Jackson.* Scr *Paul Gangelin, Connery Chappell, from the novel by Edmond Deland.* Ph *Basil Emmott.* PC *Warner Bros.* Dis *First National. 72 mins. Cert A*

Sentenced to death for a murder she did not commit, Vicky (*Elizabeth Allan*) is badly injured in a car smash returning from court. She is saved by a delicate heart operation; the surgeon, Noel Penwood (*Cyril Ritchard*) becomes convinced of her innocence and later helps her to escape. They return to the scene of the crime, a reconstruction of which reveals the killer. Grim thriller has some welcome light touches.

RoC *Edmond Breon, Antony Holles, Basil Gill, Leo Genn, Gordon McLeod, Allan Jeayes, Quinton McPherson, Frederick Burtwell, Dick Francis, Henry Caine, Aubrey Mallalieu, Patch (boy).*

DANGEROUS SEAS (1931) [2]

Dir and Scr *Edward Dryhurst.* Prod and PC *Edward G. Whiting.* Dis *Filmophone. 53 mins. Cert U*

A Cornish customs investigator (*Sandy Irving*) is torn between love and duty when he finds out that the smuggler he is after is the father of the girl he loves. Stilted melodrama.

RoC *Julie Suedo, Charles Garrey, Gerald Rawlinson, Wallace Bosco, Gladys Dunham.*

DANNY BOY (1934) [3]

Dir and Prod *Oswald Mitchell, Challis Sanderson.* Scr *Mitchell, H. Barr-Carson, Archie Pitt.* Ph *Desmond Dickinson.* PC *Panther.* Dis *Butchers. 84 mins. Cert U*

Sentimental musical, with a simple emotional story but likeable characters: Jane Kaye (*Dorothy Dickson*) searches for her estranged husband (*Frank Forbes-Robertson*), a once-successful musician, and their small son Danny (*Ronnie Hepworth*) who have become travelling buskers. Remade in 1941.

RoC *Archie Pitt, Denis O'Neil, Cyril Ritchard, Fred Duprez, Paul Neville, Herbert Cameron, Sydney Thornton, Bobbie Slater, Henry de Bray, Marcel de Haes and His Band.*

DARBY AND JOAN (1937) [1]

Dir and Scr *Syd Courtenay, from the novel by 'Rita'.* Prod *Nat Ross.* Ph *John Silver.* PC *Rock Studios.* Dis *MGM. 75 mins. Cert A*

Joan (*Peggy Simpson*), guardian of her blind young sister Darby (*Pamela Bevan*), loves rakish Yorke (*Mickey Brantford*), but marries his father, Sir Ralph (*Ian Fleming*), out of gratitude for what he has done for her and Darby. Following a bitter quarrel between Sir Ralph and his son, Yorke is found dead. But Darby's acute hearing proves that Sir Ralph is not the murderer. Dated weepie.

RoC *Tod Slaughter, Audrene Brier, Ella Retford, Harvey Braban, Charles Sewell.*

DARK EYES OF LONDON (1939)   3
(USA: *The Human Monster*)

Dir *Walter Summers.* Prod *John Argyle.* Scr *Summers, Argyle, Patrick Kirwan.* Ph *Bryan Langley.* PC *Argyle Productions.* Dis *Pathé.* 76 mins. Cert H

Britain's first 'H' certificate film is a real blood-chiller in which mysterious deaths are linked with Dr Orloff (*Bela Lugosi* in good form), head of Greenwich Insurance, and a home for the blind, run by Mrs Reaborn (*May Hallatt*). Diana Stuart (*Greta Gynt*) is convinced that her father has been murdered: Orloff offers her a job at the home. Terrorized by the blind monster Jake (*Wilfrid Walter*), Diana succeeds in revealing Orloff as a madman with a lust for killing. Jake had drowned the victims.

RoC *Hugh Williams, Julie Suedo, Edmon Ryan, Alexander Field, Arthur E. Owen, Gerald Pring, Charles Penrose, Bryan Herbert.*

Hugh Williams and Bela Lugosi in Dark Eyes of London *(1939)*

DARK JOURNEY (1937)   5

Dir *Victor Saville.* Prod *Alexander Korda.* Scr *Arthur Wimperis.* Ph *Georges Périnal, Harry Stradling.* PC *Victor Saville Productions/London Films.* Dis *United Artists.* 77 mins. Cert U

Vivid, sharply directed First World War thriller. Madeleine (*Vivien Leigh*), who runs a

Vivien Leigh and Conrad Veidt in Dark Journey *(1937)*

Stockholm dress shop, is a double agent working for the Allies. She and Baron Karl (*Conrad Veidt*) who is on the other side, form an affection for each other, leading to a love-and-duty clash. The British arrange to have Madeleine deported, but the Baron intends to have her arrested as soon as her ship leaves neutral Swedish waters. He takes her prisoner, but the tables are turned when his submarine is sunk by a Q-ship, leaving them both stranded.

RoC *Joan Gardner, Anthony Bushell, Ursula Jeans, Margery Pickard, Eliot Makeham, Austin Trevor, Sam Livesey, Cecil Parker, Edmund Willard, Charles Carson, Henry Oscar, Reginald Tate, Robert Newton, William Dewhurst, Michael Martin Harvey, Phil Ray, Percy Walsh, Laidman Browne, Antony Holles, John Justin.*

THE DARK STAIRWAY (1937)   3

Dir *Arthur Woods.* Prod *Irving Asher.* Scr *Brock Williams, Basil Dillon, from a novel by Mignon G. Eberhart.* Ph *Basil Emmott.* PC and Dis *Warner Bros.* 72 mins. Cert A.

Dr Cresswell (*Aubrey Pollock*) considers a new anaesthetic formula discovered at the Cresswell Institute to be his - but so do others. When Mortimer (*Garry Marsh*), a brilliant but unscrupulous surgeon, is murdered, Scotland Yard's Inspector Clarke (*James Stephenson*) is called in - and sorts out the killer from a tangle of suspects. Quite gripping - when one can follow the plot.

RoC *Lesley Brook, Chili Bouchier, Hugh Williams, Reginald Purdell, John Carol, Glen Alyn, Robert Rendel, Ross Landon, Elsa Buchanan, Ivy Tresmand, Muriel Pope, Katie Johnson.*

DARK WORLD (1935)   4

Dir *Bernard Vorhaus.* Prod *Leslie Laundau.* Scr *Hugh Brooke.* PC and Dis *Fox British.* 73 mins. Cert A

Philip's charm and musical talent open all doors to him, to the jealousy of his older (adopted) brother Stephen. When Stephen (*Leon Quartermaine*) and Philip (*Hugh Brooke*) both fall for the same girl, Brigitta (*Tamara Desni*), a dancer, Stephen is rejected and plots to kill his brother. But he electrocutes the wrong man, whose father finds out the truth. Gripping psychological drama.

RoC *Olga Lindo, Morton Selten, Fred Duprez, Googie Withers, Kynaston Reeves, Viola Compton, Betty Shale.*

DARTS ARE TRUMPS (1938)   4

Dir *Maclean Rogers.* Prod and PC *George Smith.* Scr *Kathleen Butler, H. F. Maltby.* Ph *Geoffrey Faithfull.* Dis *RKO Radio.* 72 mins. Cert U

Joe Stone's landlady believes him to be a bigwig at his diamond merchant's. But Joe is only a clerk there, although he still has ambitions of a partnership. His boss takes on an aristocratic ne'er-do-well as partner, and it's Joe's skill at darts that saves the day after the boss has been knocked out by his new partner's criminal associate. The clerk gets his partnership. Very nice portrayal by *Eliot Makeham* as

Joe in vivid picture of suburban life - with a touch of excitement.

RoC *Nancy O'Neil, H.F. Maltby, Paul Blake, Muriel George, Ian Colin, Johnny Singer, George Pembroke, Bryan Powley, Michael Ripper.*

DAUGHTERS OF TODAY (1933)   1

Dir and Prod *F.W. Kraemer.* Scr *Michael Barringer.* Ph *Desmond Dickinson.* PC *FWK.* Dis *United Artists.* 74 mins. Cert U

Unconvincing drama of two daughters of a puritanical farmer who revolt against his narrow-mindedness and come to London, where they work for a financier, one as a secretary, the other as a telephone girl. A shifty publisher tries to get the girls' father to invest in a mine, but he is bluffed by the financier who saves the old man's money and marries one of the girls.

LP *Betty Amann, Marguerite Allan, George Barraud, Gerald Rawlinson, Hay Petrie, Herbert Lomas, Marie Ault.*

DAVID LIVINGSTONE (1936)   1

Dir, Prod and PC *James A. Fitzpatrick.* Scr *W.K. Williamson.* Dis *MGM.* 71 mins. Cert U

Episodes in the life of Livingstone (*Percy Marmont*): his decision, from an English village, to become a missionary; his arrival in Africa, where he is mauled by a lion; his nursing by and marriage to, a girl from England; his escape from slave-dealers who burn down his mission; the death of his wife; his discovery of the Victoria Falls; his disappearance in the interior, meeting with Stanley and ultimate death. Poorly made.

RoC *Marian Spencer, James Carew, Pamela Stanley, Hugh McDermott.*

THE DAWN (1936)   2
(USA: *Dawn Over Ireland*)

Dir and Prod *Thomas G. Cooper.* Scr *Cooper, Donal O'Cahill, D.A. Moriarty.* PC *Hibernia.* Dis *Independent Producers.* 89 mins. Cert A

Drama covering three generations of those involved in the Irish Troubles, culminating in 1919 when a man expelled from the IRA joins the Royal Ulster Constabulary, and finds himself hunting his old comrades. But when he hears of a 'black and tan' raid, he hastens back to his gallant comrades and proves his worth. Gloomy.

LP *Tom Cooper, Eileen Davis, Brian O'Sullivan, Donal O'Cahill, Jerry O'Maloney, Bill Murphy, James Gleeson, Marion O'Connell.*

DEADLOCK (1931)   4

Dir and Prod *George King.* Scr *H. Fowler Mear.* PC *George King.* Dis *Butchers.* 85 mins. Cert A

One of George King's more prestigious (and better) efforts of the early 1930s: a murder is committed in a film studio, the leading man being shot dead while a scene is being played. In the end, the camera that was shooting the scene reveals the key to the mystery and the identity of the killer.

LP *Stewart Rome, Marjorie Hume, Warwick Ward, Esmond Knight, Annette Benson, Janice*

Adair, Alma Taylor, Cameron Carr, D. Hay Plumb, Pauline Peters, Kyoshi Takase, Philip Godfrey, H. Saxon-Snell

DEAD MAN'S SHOES (1939) [3]

Dir *Thomas Bentley*. Prod *Walter C. Mycroft*. Scr *Nina Jarvis, from a story by Hans Kafka*. Ph *Günther Krampf*. PC and Dis *Associated British. 70 mins. Cert A*

Roger (*Leslie Banks*), an industrialist, has no memory of his life before the First World War, when he was severely wounded. Two people blackmail him over his criminal past, but a twist of fate reveals their threats to be an elaborate hoax and Roger is able to turn the tables. Quite well done, but nowhere near as good as the French original, *Carrefour*.

RoC *Joan Marion, Wilfrid Lawson, Judy Kelly, Walter Hudd, Nancy Price, Peter Bull, Henry Oscar, Ludwig Stossel, Geoffrey Atkins, Roddy McDowall*.

DEAD MEN ARE DANGEROUS (1939) [3]

Dir *Harold French*. Prod *Warwick Ward*. Scr *Victor Kendall, Harry Hughes, Vernon Clancey, from a novel by H.C. Armstrong*. PC *Welwyn*. Dis *Pathé. 69 mins. Cert A*

Aylmer (*Robert Newton*), an unsuccessful writer, changes clothes with a corpse in the woods and starts a new life in a boarding house as Mr Jones. Then Gladys the maid is found dead in his room. Both murders were committed by Goddard (*John Warwick*), employed by Conroy (*Peter Gawthorne*), a wealthy man with a shady past. They trap Aylmer, but he has called the police. Fearing Conroy will denounce him and not Aylmer, Goddard shoots his boss, then himself dies in a hail of police gunfire. Macabre thriller sinks in quicksands of incredibility.

RoC *Betty Lynne, Merle Tottenham, John Turnbull, Aubrey Mallalieu, P. Kynaston Reeves, Googie Withers, Ian Fleming, Charles Mortimer, Winifred Oughton*.

DEAD MEN TELL NO TALES (1938) [5]

Dir *David Macdonald*. Prod *John Corfield*. Scr *Walter Summers, Stafford Dickens, Emlyn Williams, Doreen Montgomery, from a novel by Francis Beeding*. Ph *Bryan Langley*. PC *British National*. Dis *Associated British. 80 mins. Cert A*

One of Britain's grimmest and most exciting thrillers of the Thirties. Miss Haslett, matron at Dr Headlam's preparatory school, wins a French lottery prize. When she returns with the money, she is murdered by Friedberg, a hunchback moneylender. Inspector Martin (*Hugh Williams*), engaged to Elizabeth (*Lesley Brook*), cousin of Dr Headlam (*Emlyn Williams*), is given the case. A young master at the school stumbles on a vital clue – and is found hanged. A burnt-out car with a charred body in it gives Elizabeth a hint of the truth, but she is seized by Headlam (who was also Friedberg) and dragged off in his car, chased by Martin. In the school garage, before Elizabeth's horrified eyes, Headlam cuts his own throat with a piece of glass. Vividly directed.

RoC *Marius Goring, Sara Seeger, Christine Silver, Clive Morton, Anne Wilton, Hal Gordon*.

DEATH AT BROADCASTING HOUSE (1934) [4]

Dir *Reginald Denham*. Prod *Hugh Perceval*. Scr *Basil Mason, from a novel by Val Gielgud, Holt Marvel*. Ph *Günther Krampf*. PC *Phoenix Films*. Dis *Associated British. 74 mins. Cert A*

There's a fistful of suspects when ham actor Sydney Parsons (*Donald Wolfit*) is actually strangled during a murder scene in a radio play. Inspector Gregory (*Ian Hunter*) eventually unmasks the killer as mild Rodney Fleming (*Henry Kendall*), author of the play – who was being blackmailed by Parsons. Serviceable thriller with good photography and radio guest stars galore.

RoC *Austin Trevor, Mary Newland, Jack Hawkins, Val Gielgud, Peter Haddon, Betty Davies (Betty Ann Davies), Robert Rendel, Bruce Lister, Hannen Swaffer, Vernon Bartlett, Eric Dunstan, Eve Becke, Gillie Potter, Elisabeth Welch, Gordon McLeod, Ivor Barnard, Howard Douglas, Vincent Holman, George de Warfaz, Percy Rhodes, Gershom Parkington Quintet, Percival Mackey and His Band, Ord Hamilton and His Band*.

DEATH CROONS THE BLUES (1937) [2]

Dir *David Macdonald*. Prod *Julius Hagen*. Scr *H. Fowler Mear, from the novel by James Ronald*. PC *St Margarets*. Dis *MGM. 74 mins. Cert A*

A 'crooner' is found murdered, and young Viscount Brent (*Hugh Burden*) is arrested for the crime. His cousin, Lady Constance Gaye (*Antoinette Cellier*) combines with the reporter on the case, Jim Martin (*Hugh Wakefield*), to prove the nobleman's innocence and trap the real killer. Promising director was to do better than this.

RoC *George Hayes, Gillian Lind, John Turnbull, Barbara Everest*.

DEATH DRIVES THROUGH (1935) [2]

Dir *Edward L. Cahn*. Prod and PC *Clifford Taylor*. Scr *Gordon Wellesley*. Dis *Associated British. 63 mins. Cert U*

American *Edward L. Cahn*, later to make many second-features in his own country, directed this unlikely motor-racing yarn about the inventor of a new form of transmission, Kit (*Robert Douglas*), who becomes a driver to prove his invention, is involved by an unscrupulous rival in a fatal accident on the track, but recovers his nerve and wins back his reputation and a motor magnate's daughter (*Dorothy Bouchier*).

RoC *Miles Mander, Percy Walsh, Frank Atkinson, Lillian Gunns*.

DEATH ON THE SET (1935) [2]
(USA: *Murder on the Set*)

Dir *Leslie Hiscott*. Prod *Julius Hagen*. Scr *Michael Barringer, from the novel by Victor MacClure*. Ph *William Luff, Ernest Palmer*. PC *Twickenham*. Dis *Universal. 73 mins. Cert A*

Contrived, complicated thriller. Film director Caley Morden (*Henry Kendall*) murders his double, gangster Marsh (also *Kendall*), after persuading one of Marsh's molls to say he spent the night with her. Morden arranges it so that suspicion falls on his principal actress (*Jeanne Stuart*), whom he is trying to blackmail. But the moll has been strangled by Marsh before the shooting. Morden, who is now Marsh, is faced with conviction under either identity.

RoC *Eve Gray, Garry Marsh, Wally Patch, Ben Walden, Rita Helsham, Lewis Shaw, Robert Nainby, Hal Walters, Elizabeth Arkell, Arthur Wellesley*.

DEBT OF HONOUR (1936) [3]

Dir *Norman Walker*. Prod *John Corfield*. Scr *Tom Geraghty, Cyril Campion, from a story by 'Sapper'*. PC *British National*. Dis *General Film Distributors. 83 mins. Cert A*

Foolish but rousing romantic adventure about a gallant major (*Leslie Banks*) who sacrifices his army career to save the girl he loves (*Geraldine Fitzgerald*) from disgrace, after her fiancé has misappropriated mess funds to pay her gambling debts. When she discovers the truth, she follows the major to Africa, where he has gone to drown his memories in drink. She is captured by white slavers, and the major gives his life to rescue her.

RoC *Will Fyffe, Niall MacGinnis, Garry Marsh, Stewart Rome, Reginald Purdell, Phyllis Dare, Joyce Kennedy, William Kendall, Randle Ayrton, Eric Cowley, David Horne, Kathleen Davis*.

DEPARTMENT STORE (1935) [3]

Dir *Leslie Hiscott*. Prod *Julius Hagen*. Scr *H. Fowler Mear*. Ph *William Luff*. PC *Real Art*. Dis *Radio. 65 mins. Cert A*

Two young men with the same name start work in a department store. One is the nephew of the owner, and rich, the other the nephew of a friend of the manager, and an ex-convict with a penchant for safecracking. Both turn up trumps in their own ways, combining to expose the manager (*Garry Marsh*), and his hard-boiled secretary (*Eve Gray*), who have been cooking the books for years.

RoC *Sebastian Shaw, Jack Melford, Geraldine Fitzgerald, Patric Curwen, Henry Hallett, Hal Walters*.

THE DEPUTY DRUMMER (1935) [2]

Dir *Henry W. George*. Prod *Ian Sutherland*. Scr *Reginald Long, Arthur Rigby*. PC *St George's Pictures*. Dis *Columbia. 71 mins. Cert U*

Clodhopping comedy-musical in which Adolphus (*Lupino Lane*), a struggling composer (greatest hit: *Rhapsody in Pink*), gets a job as a drummer through his girlfriend (*Jean Denis*) only to lose it after a quarrel over her with the conductor. Re-engaged with the band as a rush substitute for a social function, Adolphus rounds up a gang of jewel thieves there and marries his girl.

RoC *Kathleen Kelly, Wallace Lupino, Margaret Yarde, Arthur Rigby, Syd Crossley, Reginald Long, Fred Leslie, Hal Gordon, Harold Brewer, Arthur Clayton, Brutus the Dog*.

THE DERELICT (1937) [1]

Dir and Scr *Harold Simpson*. Prod *Victor Gover, Joe Rosenthal*. PC *M.V. Gover*. Dis *In-*

dependent Film Distributors. *57 mins. Cert U*
Toby (*Malcolm Morley*), an educated but alcoholic tramp, encounters Mary (*Jane Griffiths*) and her crippled son on the road. He
offers to sell some of his drawings to rich Sir
Ben (*Frank Strickland*) to help pay for the
boy's operation. Sir Ben keeps asking Toby to
come back each day with another drawing.
Toby is furious when he finds he has been
used in an unpleasant way, but then Mary tells
him her son will walk again after the operation
which the money has bought. Amateurish sentimental drama.
RoC *Charles Penrose, Peter Kernohan.*

DEVIL'S ROCK (1938) [1]
Dir, Prod, PC and Ph *Germain Gerard Burger.*
Scr *Richard Hayward.* Dis *Columbia. 54 mins.
Cert U*
Ireland: Sam (*Richard Hayward*), a sheep-
driver, arranges a concert as part of his plans
to establish a seaside restaurant, but the tak-
ings are stolen. When a 10-year-old holiday-
maker is swept out to sea, Sam dives in and
rescues her. The thieves are caught, but Sam
decides to return to sheep-droving. Tech-
nically poor, really a non-starter.
RoC *Geraldine Mitchell, Gloria Grainger,
Nancy Cullen, Charles Fagan, Tom Casement,
Stendhal Todd, Terence Grainger, Michael
Gleason, R.L. O'Mealy, James Close, Lambeg
Folk Dance Society, St Gall's School Choir.*

DIAL 999 (1937) [2]
(USA: *Revenge of Scotland Yard*)
Dir *Lawrence Huntington.* Prod *Edward Dryhurst.* Scr *Ernest Dudley.* Ph *Stanley Grant.* PC
and Dis *Fox British. 46 mins. Cert A*
A Scotland Yard agent comes to London with
information about a gang of forgers led by a
man known as The Badger - but is killed before he can tell his colleagues a thing. A
message he has hidden in his flat leads Inspectors Waring and Morris (*John Longden, Paul
Neville*) to a wharf where The Badger, masked,
escapes by killing Morris. But The Badger's
falling out with his gang leads to his downfall.
Nicely photographed, but very mild drama.
RoC *Elizabeth Kent, Neville Brook, Ian Fleming, Ivan Wilmot, Victor Hagen, Howard Douglas, Jan Godfrey, Cecil Bishop, Jo Mott, Paul
Sheridan.*

DIAMOND CUT DIAMOND (1932) [3]
(USA: *Blame the Woman*)
Dir *Fred Niblo, Maurice Elvey.* Prod *Eric
Hakim.* Scr *Viscount Castlerosse.* PC *Cinema
House.* Dis *MGM. 70 mins. Cert U*
Adolphe Menjou's British films did not by and
large sparkle. In this comedy, he and *Claud
Allister* play international jewel thieves setting
up operation in England, the one posing as a
French count, the other as an English gentle-
man. They become involved with Marda (*Ben-
ita Hume*), a lady crook, and she completely
outwits them.
RoC *Kenneth Kove, Desmond Jeans, Tonie
Edgar Bruce, Shayle Gardner, Philip Strange,
G.B. Manetta, Roland Gillett, Stanley Vilven.*

DICK TURPIN (1933) [4]
Dir *John Stafford, Victor Hanbury.* Prod *Clyde
Cook.* Scr *Victor Kendall, from a novel by W.
Harrison Ainsworth.* Ph *Desmond Dickinson.* PC
Stoll-Stafford. Dis *Gaumont-British. 79 mins.
Cert U*
Although hardly the conventional handsome
hero, *Victor McLaglen*'s hearty interpretation
of the famous highwayman was probably closer
to historical fact than most in this refreshingly
ingenuous adventure (based on Ainsworth's
Rookwood), in which Turpin makes his famous
ride to York (which proves the death of his
beloved mare Black Bess) and rescues the
heroine (*Jane Carr*) from the villain's clutches.
RoC *Cecil Humphreys, Frank Vosper, Gillian
Lind, James Finlayson, Gibb McLaughlin,
Alexander Field, Helen Ferrers, Lewis Gilbert,
Roy Findlay.*

DID I BETRAY? (1935) [2]
Dir and Prod *Paul Martin.* Scr *John Heygate,
Peter MacFarlane.* PC *UFA.* Dis *Reunion. 93
mins. Cert A. Bilingual versions*
One of the last British films made at the UFA
studios in Berlin, and *Lilian Harvey*'s last international venture - a non-musical which
casts her as a Russian ballerina who becomes
the mistress of the Tsarist governor of Finland
in 1900 in order to save the life of the sculptor/
rebel leader (*Esmond Knight*) with whom she
has fallen in love.
RoC *Robert Rendel, Dennis Hoey, Amy Veness,
Henry Wolston, Beatrice Munro.*

DINNER AT THE RITZ (1937) [4]
Dir *Harold Schuster.* Prod *Robert T. Kane.* Scr
Roland Pertwee, Romney Brent. Ph *Philip Tannura.* PC *New World.* Dis *20th Century-Fox.
77 mins. Cert U*
Strong cast in agreeable, if hard-to-follow
caper about a French girl (*Annabella*) who refuses to believe her father committed suicide
and determines to find those responsible. Her
consequent adventures, aided by an American
detective (*Romney Brent*) and a debonair
government investigator (*David Niven*) lead to
a boat on London's Thames and finally to the
Ritz hotel, where the villain-in-chief is blackmailed into returning the money he had swindled from her father's bank.
RoC *Francis L. Sullivan, Paul Lukas, Stewart
Rome, Nora Swinburne, Tyrell Davis, Frederick*

Romney Brent and Patricia Medina in Dinner
at the Ritz (*1937*)

*Leister, William Dewhurst, Vivienne Chatterton,
Ronald Shiner, Raymond Huntley, Ralph Truman, Patricia Medina.*

DIRTY WORK (1934) [4]
Dir *Tom Walls.* Prod *Michael Balcon.* Scr *Ben
Travers, from his play.* Ph *Philip Tannura.* PC
and Dis *Gaumont-British. 78 mins. Cert A*
Tom Walls concentrated on direction in this
thin but boisterous Aldwych farce, while *Gordon Harker* proved a satisfactory replacement
in the acting trio completed by *Ralph Lynn* and
Robertson Hare. The story concerns two
assistants in a jeweller's shop who pose as
criminals to catch - more by luck than judgment - a gang of jewel thieves.
RoC *Lillian Bond, Basil Sydney, Cecil Parker,
Margaretta Scott, Gordon James, Peter Gawthorne, Louis Bradfield, Leslie Laurier.*

DISCORD (1932) [3]
Dir *Henry Edwards.* Prod *Herbert Wilcox.* Scr
Uncredited, from a play by E. Temple Thurston.
PC *British and Dominions/Paramount British.*
Dis *Paramount. 80 mins. Cert A*
Phil (*Benita Hume*), a singer married to Peter
(*Owen Nares*) a songwriter, rises to fame. Phi-
landering Lord Quilhampton (*Harold Huth*)
offers her the lead in a big new stage musical
- at a price. Phil indignantly refuses: but it
turns out that Peter is the (pseudonymous)
author of the show - and *he* has the last word
on casting! Their previous tiffs are soon for-
gotten.
RoC *Clifford Heatherley, Aubrey Fitzgerald,
O.B. Clarence, Archibald Batty, Harold Scott,
Esmé Hubbard.*

DISCOVERIES (1939) [3]
Dir and Prod *Redd Davis.* Scr *Davis, Cyril
Campion, Anatole de Grunwald.* Ph *Bryan Lan-
gley.* PC *Vogue.* Dis *Grand National. 68 mins.
Cert U*
Talent-seeker and compère *Carroll Levis,* look-
ing for radio 'discoveries', is wooed for spon-
sorship by a cheese tycoon and a spaghetti
king. They all join forces for an hour-long
radio show. Enthusiasm is main asset of revue
film based on famous radio series.
RoC *Issy Bonn, Julien Vedey, Bertha Belmore,
Ronald Shiner, Kathleen Harrison, Zoë Wynn,
Barbara Everest, Afrique, Doris Hare, Shayle
Gardner, Cyril Levis, Frank Atkinson, The
Three Ginx, Dump & Tony, George Meaton,
Pearl Venters, The Radio Rascals, Glyn Davies,
Archie Galbraith, David Delmonte, Tony
Vaughan, Ken Bonner, May Patterson, The
Scottish Sextet.*

DISHONOUR BRIGHT (1936) [4]
Dir *Tom Walls.* Prod *Herman Fellner, Max
Schach.* Scr *Ben Travers.* Ph *Phil Tannura.* PC
Cecil Films. Dis *General Film Distributors. 82
mins. Cert A*
Stephen Champion (*Tom Walls*), a 'Don Juan
and a barnacle on society' finds himself co-
respondent in the divorce case of a woman
with whom he has actually fallen in love. They
marry and go on honeymoon, where misunderstandings occur over the prosecuting coun-

Tom Walls and Betty Stockfeld in Dishonour Bright *(1937)*

sel's wife. Both the counsel and the bride assume the worst, but Stephen's practised charm saves the day. Farce has some well-written comic scenes.
RoC *Betty Stockfeld, Eugene Pallette, Diana Churchill, Arthur Wontner, Cecil Parker, George Sanders, Hubert Harben, Henry Oscar, Mabel Terry-Lewis, Basil Radford, Jeni le Gon, Bernardi, Charlotte Leigh, Michael Morel, Denis Val Norton, Mervyn Johns.*

THE DIVINE SPARK/CASTA DIVA (1935)   <u>2</u>
Dir *Carmine Gallone.* Prod *Arnold Pressburger.* Scr *Emlyn Williams, Richard Benson, from a scenario by Walter Reisch.* Ph *Franz Planer.* PC *Alleanza Cinematografica Italiana.* Dis *Gaumont-British. 81 mins. Cert U. Bilingual versions*
Ponderous Anglo-Italian biopic of the composer Bellini (*Phillips Holmes*). Studying music in Naples, he falls in love with Maddalena (*Marta Eggerth*). She is engaged to another, and refuses to run off with Bellini, fearing it will ruin his career. He misinterprets her actions, not discovering her true feelings until after her subsequent death. He resolves she will live on in his music.
RoC *Benita Hume, Donald Calthrop, Arthur Margetson, Edmund Breon, Basil Gill, Hugh Miller, Edward Chapman, John Clements, Felix Aylmer, John Deverell.*

THE DIVORCE OF LADY X (1937)   <u>3</u>
Dir *Tim Whelan.* Prod *Alexander Korda.* Scr *Ian Dalrymple, Arthur Wimperis, Lajos Biro,*

Merle Oberon in The Divorce of Lady X *(1937)*

from a play by Gilbert Wakefield. Ph *Harry Stradling.* PC *London Films/Denham Films.* Dis *United Artists. Technicolor. 92 mins. Cert A*
Remake of the 1933 film *Counsel's Opinion*, and not quite as good, despite a coat of colour and a classy cast. A young divorce lawyer gives up his hotel bed to a mystery girl in fancy dress, subsequently assuming (wrongly) that he is co-respondent in a high-powered divorce case, when a peer sues his wife for divorce on the grounds that she was in a man's bedroom at that hotel that night. The mystery girl proves to be a widow, and they are free to marry.
LP *Merle Oberon, Laurence Olivier, Binnie Barnes, Ralph Richardson, Morton Selten, J.H. Roberts, Gertrude Musgrove, Gus McNaughton, Hugh McDermott, H.B. Hallam, Eileen Peel.*

DOCTOR'S ORDERS (1934)   <u>3</u>
Dir *Norman Lee.* Prod *Walter C. Mycroft.* Scr *Clifford Grey, R.P. Weston, Bert Lee, Syd Courtenay, Lola Harvey.* Ph *Bryan Langley.* PC *BIP.* Dis *Wardour. 68 mins. Cert U*
Professor Pippin (*Leslie Fuller*) is a carnival quack who runs a fairground booth and has a son (*John Mills*) at medical school. The son's romantic rival plans to expose the 'professor' in front of the girl the two young men fancy, but his plan misfires when it turns out that Pippin has given his entire savings to aid the local hospital. Amusing comedy: *Fuller* in good form.
RoC *Mary Jerrold, Marguerite Allan, William Kendall, Ronald Shiner, Felix Aylmer, Georgie Harris, D.J. Williams.*

DODGING THE DOLE (1936)   <u>2</u>
Dir and Prod *John E. Blakeley.* Scr *Arthur Mertz.* PC and Dis *Mancunian. 95 mins. Cert U*
A north-country comedy-musical, not released in the south of England, in which 'dole-dodgers' (those who draw dole money and avoid work) ruin every attempt by the local Labour Exchange to find them jobs.
LP *Roy Barbour, Jenny Howard, Barry K. Barnes, Dan Young, Fred Walmsley, Tot Sloan, Bertha Ricardo, Hatton & Manners, The Barry Twins, The Two Jays, Steffani's Silver Songsters, Archie's Juvenile Band, Bertini and the Blackpool Tower Band.*

THE DOMINANT SEX (1936)   <u>4</u>
Dir *Herbert Brenon.* Prod *Walter C. Mycroft.* Scr *Vina de Vesci, John Fernald, from the play by Michael Egan.* Ph *Walter Harvey.* PC *BIP.* Dis *Associated British. 74 mins. Cert A*
Young marrieds Dick and Angela (*Phillips Holmes, Diana Churchill*) argue constantly: Dick wants to buy a farm and raise a family, while Angela wants to keep her smart job and work for a big city firm. Their friend Gwen, having an affair, encourages her husband to turn his attentions elsewhere. He falls for a girl in a flower shop and divorces Gwen, whose lover is already tiring of her. Their story makes Angela opt for life on the farm. Stagey but well-drawn romantic comedy.
RoC *Carol Goodner, Romney Brent, Kathleen*

Kelly, Billy Milton, Hugh Miller, Olga Edwardes, Charles Paton, Dora Gregory.*

DON'T BE A DUMMY (1932)   <u>2</u>
Dir *Frank Richardson.* Prod *Irving Asher.* Scr *Brock Williams.* PC *Warner Bros.* Dis *First National. 54 mins. Cert U*
Good idea, clumsily executed, about a racehorse owner and his jockey. Both ruined after being 'warned off' when one of their horses seems to lose a big race on purpose, they evolve a show-business act as a ventriloquist and his dummy, and get bookings in music-halls. Through overhearing a conversation by people who think he's a dummy, the jockey (*Georgie Harris*) is able to bring the crooks who framed them to book, and he and the owner are reinstated.
RoC *William Austin, Garry Marsh, Muriel Angelus, Mike Johnson, Sally Stewart, Katherine Watts, Charles Castella.*

DON'T GET ME WRONG (1937)   <u>3</u>
Dir *Arthur Woods, Reginald Purdell.* Prod *Irving Asher.* Scr *Purdell, Brock Williams, Frank Launder.* Ph *Basil Emmott.* PC *Warner Bros.* Dis *First National. 80 mins. Cert U*
Wellington (*Max Miller*), a fairground entertainer, joins up with a strange inventor and badgers a millionaire into financing his invention, a tabloid petrol substitute made of water and an unknown ingredient (which turns out to be coconut oil). The crackpot proves to be an escaped lunatic, but the millionaire, who planned a financial killing, gets all the blame. So-so comedy.
RoC *George E. Stone, Clifford Heatherley, Glen Alyn, Olive Blakeney, Wallace Evenett, Alexander Field.*

DON'T RUSH ME! (1935)   <u>3</u>
Dir *Norman Lee.* Prod and PC *Fred Karno.* Scr *Con West, Michael Barringer, from a sketch by Fred Karno.* Dis *Producers' Distributing Corporation. 72 mins. Cert U*
Cheerful, if antiquated comedy about two anti-gambling zealots (*Robb Wilton, Peter Haddon*), already secretly into greyhound racing, who come to London and get themselves deeply involved in the gambling business, one of them ending up as a dogtrack bookmaker.
RoC *Muriel Aked, Bobbie Comber, Haver & Lee, Kathleen Kelly, Kenneth Kove, Wallace Douglas, Dino Galvani, Hal Walters, Nor Kiddie, Wilson Coleman, May Beamish, Elizabeth Kent.*

DOSS HOUSE (1933)   <u>4</u>
Dir *John Baxter.* Prod *Ivar Campbell.* Scr *Herbert Ayres.* PC *Sound City.* Dis *MGM. 53 mins. Cert A*
Baxter's first film and the first of many he would make with working-class backgrounds. A reporter and a police detective (*Arnold Bell, Herbert Franklyn*) join forces to seek a wanted criminal who is believed to have taken refuge in a doss house. They pose as tramps and find their man. Atmosphere is appropriately seedy and downbeat.
RoC *Frank Cellier, Mark Daly, Edgar Driver,*

J. Hubert Leslie, Wilson Coleman, Robert Mac-Lachlan, Alec Harford, Ray Raymond, James Stadden, Cecil Clayton, Ernest Croxford.

DOUBLE DEALING (1932)   ③

Dir *Leslie Hiscott.* Prod *Julius Hagen.* Scr *Michael Barringer, H. Fowler Mear.* PC *Real Art.* Dis *Fox. 48 mins. Cert A*

Broad Yorkshire comedy featuring character star *Frank Pettingell* as a straitlaced politician who disapproves of his nephew marrying an actress, until the nephew, a reporter, uncovers his uncle's private life – including an association with the same actress.

RoC *Richard Cooper, Zoë Palmer, Sydney Fairbrother, Betty Astell, Jill Hands, Charles Groves, Eileen Despard, Gladys Hamer.*

THE DOUBLE EVENT (1934)   ④

Dir, Prod and Scr *Leslie Howard Gordon, from the play by Sidney Blow, Douglas Hoare.* PC *Triumph.* Dis *Producers' Distributing Corporation. 68 mins. Cert A*

Martingale (*O.B. Clarence*), a country vicar, secretly backs horses. His daughter Evelyn (*Jane Baxter*), supposedly an art student in London, runs a bookmaker's business. Her fiancé Dennison (*Bernard Lee*) finds a way to cure her – he makes the bookie bankrupt. Refreshing comedy.

RoC *Ruth Taylor, Alexander Field, Sebastian Smith.*

DOUBLE EXPOSURES (1937)   ①

Dir *John Paddy Carstairs.* Prod *George King.* Scr *Gerald Elliott.* PC *Triangle.* Dis *Paramount. 67 mins. Cert U*

Unintentionally funny thriller about a gambler framed for theft by his father's lawyer and secretary. When the crooks fall out, the secretary kills the lawyer, leaving clues which point to the gambler's father as murderer. A photograph taken by the gambler's inept newspaperman friend accidentally reveals the true killer. Later reissued as *Alibi Breaker.*

LP *Julien Mitchell, Ruby Miller, George Astley, Basil Langton, Mavis Clare, Brian Buchel, Frank Birch, Ivor Barnard, Fred Withers, Dennis Cowles.*

DOUBLE OR QUITS (1938)   ②

Dir *Roy William Neill.* Prod *Irving Asher.* Scr *Michael Barringer.* Ph *Basil Emmott.* PC and Dis *Warner Bros. 72 mins. Cert A*

Newspaperman Bill Brooks (*Frank Fox*), the double of master thief Scotty Tucker, is on board a transatlantic liner when he stumbles across a plot to steal some rare stamps. Sir Frederick Beal (*Ian Fleming*), the stamps' owner, is murdered. Hampered by his resemblance to Tucker, Bill finally cracks the case and gets his story. Hard to be bothered with an involved plot.

RoC *Patricia Medina, Hal Walters, Gordon McLeod, Jack Raine, Philip Ray, Charles Paton, Mai Bacon, Michael Hogarth, Scott Harold, Sam Blake, W. Edward Hodge.*

DOUBLE WEDDING (1933)   ②

Dir and Scr *Frank Richardson.* Prod *Irving Asher.* PC and Dis *Warner Bros. 50 mins. Cert U*

Two courting couples get married to silence gossip about their goings-on. But their combined honeymoon is fraught with misadventures and disasters because of the flirtatious nature of all four. Tiresome mix-up comedy.

LP *Joan Marion, Jack Hobbs, Viola Keats, Anthony Hankey, Mike Johnson, Ernest Sefton.*

DOWN OUR ALLEY (1939)   ②

Dir *George A. Cooper.* Prod and Ph *Germain Burger.* Scr *Uncredited.* PC and Dis *British Screen Services. 56 mins. Cert U*

Hughie (*Hughie Green*), who runs a music shop, falls for a girl (*Sylvia Saetre*) engaged to a singer who owns the club where her father works as commissionaire. Forced to take a job as a waiter at the club, Hughie, with the commissionaire's connivance, substitutes himself and his friends for the stage show, makes a hit and wins the girl. Strenuous musical farce.

RoC *Wally Patch, Vivienne Chatterton, Antony Holles, Daphne Raglan, Philip Morant, Johnnie Schofield, Joe Cunningham, Arnold Sellars, Sadie Corrie, Jean Ray, Danny Norton, Joey Hopkinson, Michael Appleby, Joyce Cannon, Tommy Trainer, Ron Ashen, Lily Summers, Bobby Price, Charlie Wragg, Barry Manning, Queenie Ransley, Anna Smirrell, Ray Pennington.*

DOWN OUR STREET (1932)   ④

Dir and Scr *Harry Lachman, from a play by Ernest George.* Prod *S.E. Fitzgibbon.* PC *Paramount British.* Dis *Paramount. 86 mins. Cert A*

Dramatically effective slice of life in London's East End, replete with humour, tragedy and pathos. Mrs Collins (*Nancy Pride*) opposes the romance of her daughter (*Elizabeth Allan*) to a tearaway backstreets lad, Charlie (*Hugh Williams*). Charlie reforms and buys a taxi and, although he is framed for a smash-and-grab raid by Maisie's uncle, Mrs Collins sees his worth and sorts things out.

RoC *Morris Harvey, Alexander Field, Binnie Barnes, Sydney Fairbrother, Frederick Burtwell, Merle Tottenham.*

Hugh Williams and Elizabeth Allan in Down Our Street *(1932)*

DOWN RIVER (1931)   ④

Dir *Peter Godfrey.* Prod *L'Estrange Fawcett.* Scr *Ralph Gilbert Bettinson, from a novel by*

'*Seamark*'. PC and Dis *Gaumont. 73 mins. Cert A*

Moody thick-ear thriller in which a customs investigator (*Harold Huth*) and his fiancée (*Jane Baxter*) become involved in the hunt for a gang of smugglers, whose chief (*Charles Laughton*) may also be a killer. Visiting a nightclub, the girl stumbles on a clue which she follows up, only to be kidnapped by the gang. The investigator rescues her and traps the murderer and his men.

RoC *Kenneth Kove, Arthur Goullet, Hartley Power, Norman Shelley, Cyril McLagen, Frederick Leister, Humberston Wright, Hugh E. Wright, Helen Howell.*

DRAKE OF ENGLAND (1935)   ②
(USA: *Drake the Pirate*)

Dir *Arthur Woods.* Prod *Walter C. Mycroft.* Scr *Clifford Grey, Marjorie Deans, Akos Tolnay, Norman Watson, from the play by Louis N. Parker.* Ph *Claude Friese-Greene, Ronald Neame.* PC *BIP.* Dis *Wardour. 111 mins (later 104). Cert U*

Disappointing survey of the highlights of Sir Francis Drake's adventurous career, from 1567 to 1588, including his voyages round the world, the affair of Nombre de Dios, the romance between Sir Francis (*Matheson Lang*) and Elizabeth Sydenham (*Jane Baxter*), his duel of wits with Lord Burghley (*Ben Webster*) and the defeat of the Spanish Armada. Poor dialogue, sketchy treatment.

RoC *Athene Seyler, Donald Wolfit, Henry Mollison, George Merritt, Moore Marriott, Amy Veness, Sam Livesey, Margaret Halstan, Charles Quartermaine, Allan Jeayes, Gibb McLaughlin, Helen Haye.*

DREAMING LIPS (1937)   ③

Dir *Paul Czinner, Lee Garmes.* Prod *Max Schach, Czinner.* Scr *Margaret Kennedy, Carl Meyer, Lady Cynthia Asquith, from a play by Henry Bernstein.* Ph *Roy Clark.* PC *Trafalgar.* Dis *United Artists. 94 mins. Cert A*

Selfish, neurotic Gaby (*Elisabeth Bergner*), a mixture of childlike and passionate natures, is married to a violinist (*Romney Brent*) but falls heavily for his distinguished colleague (*Raymond Massey*). Her plans to leave her husband are thwarted by his serious illness. Finally, worn out with nursing him, and by the emotional conflict in her life, she writes a despair-

Raymond Massey and Elisabeth Bergner in Dreaming Lips *(1937)*

ing note, and throws herself in the Thames. Well done in most departments (music is by William Walton) but rather laborious for all that.

RoC *Joyce Bland, Felix Aylmer, Donald Calthrop, Sydney Fairbrother, (J.) Fisher White, Charles Carson, Ronald Shiner, Cyril Raymond, George Carney, Bruno Barnabe.*

DREAMS COME TRUE (1936)   [3]
Dir *Reginald Denham.* Prod *Ilya Salkind, John Gossage.* Scr *Bruce Sevier, Donald Bull, from an opera by Franz Lehar.* PC *London and Continental.* Dis *Reunion. 78 mins. Cert A*
Musical about a father and son who go to Vienna on business and both fall heavily for the charms of Ilona (*Frances Day*), a lovely actress and singer. She elopes with the son (*Frederick Bradshaw*), but then her press agent puts out a story that makes the father believe she is his daughter from one of his youthful escapades. Serviceable film of Lehar opera *Clo-Clo.*

RoC *Nelson Keys, Hugh Wakefield, Marie Lohr, Morris Harvey, Arthur Finn, Minnie Rayner, Ivor Barnard, Molly Hamley Clifford, Charles Penrose, Roxy Russell, Arthur Brander, Leo von Pokorny, Netta Lewis, Patrick Susands, David Hawthorne.*

DREYFUS (1931)   [4]
(USA: *The Dreyfus Case*)
Dir *F.W. Kraemer, Milton Rosmer.* Prod *F.W. Kraemer.* Scr *Reginald Berkeley, Walter C. Mycroft.* Ph *W. Winterstein, Walter Harvey, Horace Wheddon.* PC *BIP.* Dis *Wardour. 90 mins. Cert U*
Early version of the much-filmed story of Captain Alfred Dreyfus, a Franco-Jewish officer who, in 1894, was charged, on the flimsiest of evidence, with high treason, convicted on false testimony, and sentenced to life imprisonment on Devil's Island. Only years later, through the efforts of Emile Zola and Georges Clemenceau, does he receive a pardon. Sterling portrayal by *Cedric Hardwicke* in the title role.

RoC *George Merritt, Garry Marsh, Charles Carson, Sam Livesey, Beatrix Thomson, Randle Ayrton, George Zucco, Abraham Sofaer, Leonard Shepherd, Henry Caine, George Skillan, Nigel Barrie, Arthur Hardy, Frederick Leister, J. Fisher White, Leslie Frith, Alexander Sarner.*

DR JOSSER KC (1931)   [3]
Dir, Prod and Scr *Norman Lee, from a revue sketch by Ernest Lotinga.* PC *BIP.* Dis *Pathé. 71 mins. Cert U*
Helter-skelter farce about a thief (*Ernie Lotinga*) who steals a handbag from Betty (*Molly Lamont*), then catches her husband in a compromising situation and blackmails him. A second thief complicates matters by stealing other things from the same people, but matters end with all parties satisfied.

RoC *Jack Hobbs, Binnie Barnes, Joan Wyndham, Harold Wilkinson, Arnold Bell.*

DR O'DOWD (1939)   [4]
Dir *Herbert Mason.* Prod *Sam Sax.* Scr *Austin Melford, Derek Twist, from the novel by L.A.G.*

Strong. Ph *Basil Emmott.* PC and Dis *Warner Bros. 76 mins. Cert A*
When the wife of Stephen O'Dowd (*Liam Gaffney*) dies after an operation by his father (*Shaun Glenville*), he accuses the older man of drunkenness and he is struck off. Years later, as an engineer in Ireland, Stephen becomes involved in a diphtheria epidemic. It is controlled through the efforts of his father, who has to perform a (successful) operation on Stephen. Stephen helps his father re-establish himself as a doctor. Moving, convincing, shrewdly made.

RoC *Peggy Cummins, Patricia Roc, Mary Merrall, James Carney, Walter Hudd, Charles Victor, Pat Noonan, Maire O'Neill, Irene Handl, Pamela Wood, Felix Aylmer, Nell Emerald.*

DR SIN FANG (1937)   [1]
Dir *Tony Frenguelli.* Prod *Nell Emerald.* Scr *Nigel Byass, Frederick Reynolds.* PC *Victory.* Dis *MGM. 60 mins. Cert A*
A sinister Oriental mastermind, Dr Sin Fang (*H. Agar Lyons*), escapes from jail, murders the judge who convicted him and, from his secret hideout, plans to gain control of a new formula for curing cancer. His efforts are foiled by the fearless work of Sonia (*Anne Grey*), whose brother had become one of Sin Fang's victims. Indescribably bad.

RoC *Robert Hobbs, George Mozart, Ernest Sefton, Nell Emerald, Arty Ash, Louis Darnley.*

DR SYN (1937)   [5]
Dir *Roy William Neill.* Prod *Michael Balcon.* Scr *Michael Hogan, Roger Burford, from the novel by Russell Thorndike.* Ph *Jack Cox, Jack Perry.* PC *Gaumont-British.* Dis *General Film Distributors. 81 mins. Cert U*
Exciting, well-handled adventure yarn. In the nineteenth century, Dymchurch parish church is invaded by revenue men hunting smugglers. The Vicar, Dr Syn (*George Arliss*) is the smugglers' leader and the parishioners his followers. After a series of clashes with the revenue officers, Syn, really Pirate Clegg, believed hanged 20 years before, destroys all evidence against him, marries his daughter to the squire's son, and escapes to continue his life of derring-do.

RoC *Margaret Lockwood, John Loder, Roy Emerton, Graham Moffatt, Frederick Burtwell, George Merritt, Athole Stewart, Wally Patch, Meinhart Maur, Muriel George, Wilson Coleman.*

THE DRUM (1938)   [4]
(USA: *Drums*)
Dir *Zoltan Korda.* Prod *Alexander Korda.* Scr *Arthur Wimperis, Patrick Kirwan, Hugh Grey, Lajos Biro, from the novel by A.E.W. Mason.* Ph *Georges Périnal, Osmond Borrodaile, Robert Krasker, Christopher Challis, Geoffrey Unsworth.* PC *London Films.* Dis *United Artists.* Technicolor. *104 mins. Cert U*
On India's turbulent north-west frontier, a young prince (*Sabu*) is forced into hiding after his wicked uncle Ghul (*Raymond Massey*) has killed his father. The prince is treated with kindness by the British garrison there, and re-

Sabu in The Drum (*1938*)

wards them by giving the alarm just before Ghul's planned massacre of them, which is foiled after a pitched battle. Standard adventure yarn, but beautifully photographed with outstanding spectacle and crowd scenes.

RoC *Valerie Hobson, Roger Livesey, Desmond Tester, Francis L. Sullivan, David Tree, Martin Walker, Roy Emerton, Edward Lexy, Julien Mitchell, Amid Taftazani, Archibald Batty, Frederick Culley, Charles Oliver, Alf Goddard, Ronald Adam, Lawrence Baskcomb, Michael Martin Harvey, Leo Genn, Guy Rolfe.*

DUSTY ERMINE (1936)   [4]
(USA: *Hideout in the Alps*)
Dir *Bernard Vorhaus.* Prod *Julius Hagen.* Scr *L. duGarde Peach, Michael Hankinson, Arthur Macrae, Paul Harvey Fox, H. Fowler Mear, from the play by Neil Grant.* Ph *Curt Courant, O. Martini.* PC *Twickenham.* Dis *Wardour. 84 mins. Cert A*
Going straight after a spell in jail for forgery, Jim Kent (*Ronald Squire*) is suspected when fake banknotes begin to circulate in his area and only his niece Linda (*Jane Baxter*) stands by him. When he finds his nephew Gilbert (*Arthur Macrae*) is part of the counterfeit gang, Jim, with Linda, follows him to Austria, hotly pursued by the police. Gilbert dies rescuing his uncle from the forgers, who are rounded up by the law. Oddly titled location-shot melodrama has no lack of thrills.

RoC *Anthony Bushell, Athole Stewart, Austin Trevor, Margaret Rutherford, Katie Johnson, Felix Aylmer, Hal Gordon, Davina Craig.*

D'YE KEN JOHN PEEL? (1934)   [3]
(USA: *Captain Moonlight*)
Dir *Henry Edwards.* Prod *Julius Hagen.* Scr *H. Fowler Mear.* Ph *Sydney Blythe.* PC *Twickenham.* Dis *Associated Producers and Distributors. 81 mins. Cert A*
Musical costume drama, set in 1815, with *John Garrick* as Major John Peel, who forces a villain to marry a girl he has betrayed, then steps in to denounce him as a bigamist when he marries another girl with whom Peel is in love. Highlight: *Stanley Holloway* delivering his famous monologue/song *Sam, Pick Up Thy Musket.*

RoC *Winifred Shotter, John Stuart, Leslie Perrins, Mary Lawson, Morris Harvey, Charles Carson, Wilfred Caithness.*

THE EARLY BIRD (1936) [2]

Dir and Scr *Donovan Pedelty, from the play by J. McGregor Douglas.* Prod *Victor M. Greene.* PC *Crusade.* Dis *Paramount. 69 mins. Cert U*
Rather boring comedy about a little Irish village which is dominated by one woman – Mrs Gordon (*Charlotte Tedlie*). She is a lady of puritanical views, which she likes to impress on everyone. Eventually, however, they land her in court on the wrong end of a libel action – and Mrs Gordon is hoist by her own petard.
RoC *Richard Hayward, Jimmy Mageean, Myrtle Adams, Nan Cullen, Elma Hayward, Terence Grainger, Charles Fagan, Pat Noonan.*

EARLY TO BED (1933) [4]

Dir *Ludwig Berger.* Prod *Erich Pommer.* Scr *Robert Stevenson.* PC *UFA/Gaumont-British.* Dis *W & F. 83 mins. Cert U*
Slight but quite charming comedy, made in Germany, about two young people sharing the same room, he (*Fernand Graavey*) sleeping by night and she (*Heather Angel*) by day – each resentful of the other. Quite unaware of their identities, they meet and fall in love.
RoC *Sonnie Hale, Edmund Gwenn, Donald Calthrop, Lady Tree, Jillian Sande, Athene Seyler, Leslie Perrins, Lewis Shaw.*

EAST LYNNE ON THE WESTERN FRONT (1931) [2]

Dir *George Pearson.* Prod *T. A. Welsh.* Scr *Donovan Parsons, Mary Parsons.* PC *Welsh-Pearson.* Dis *Gaumont. 82 mins. Cert U*
Nice idea, not too successfully executed: a group of First World War soldiers, billeted in an empty theatre, put on a performance of the famous old melodrama *East Lynne* to relieve the monotony. It gradually develops into a burlesque of the original.
LP *Herbert Mundin, Alf Goddard, Mark Daly, Harold French, Blanche Adele, Hugh E. Wright,*

Herbert Mundin and Escott Davies in East Lynne on the Western Front *(1931)*

Edwin Ellis, Wilfrid Lawson, Escott Davies, Roger Livesey, Philip Godfrey, Norman Shelley, M. Borelli.

EAST MEETS WEST (1936) [4]

Dir *Herbert Mason.* (Associate) Producer *Haworth Bromley.* Scr *Maude Howell, from a play by Edwin Greenwood.* Ph *Bernard Knowles.* PC and Dis *Gaumont-British. 74 mins. Cert A*
A small autonomous power has a harbour of strategic importance to both the British and Oriental powers. Its wily sultan (*George Arliss*) negotiates with both sides – while trying to decide whether to hang the English rum-runner with whose wife his Europeanized son has fallen in love. Arliss in decline, but story quite intriguing.
RoC *Lucie Mannheim, Godfrey Tearle, Romney Brent, Ballard Berkeley, Ronald Ward, Norma Varden, John Laurie, O.B. Clarence, Campbell Gullan, Eliot Makeham, Ralph Truman, Patrick Barr, Stella Moya, Derek Elphinstone, Peter Croft.*

EAST OF LUDGATE HILL (1937) [4]

Dir *Manning Haynes.* Prod *John Findlay.* Scr *Edward Dryhurst, Stanley Jackson.* Ph *Stanley Grant.* PC and Dis *Fox British. 47 mins. Cert U*
Nice little drama, all the better for its brevity. When bonds worth £50,000 disappear from the office safe, the staff of the firm of stockbrokers concerned see their promised £50 bonus going with them. The boss suspects his son, who had been talking of abandoning wife and firm and going abroad; it turns out the son had taken the bonds – but only to the bank for safer keeping.
LP *Robert Cochran, Nancy O'Neil, Eliot Makeham, Hal Gordon, Aubrey Mallalieu, Pamela Wood, Vernon Harris, Paul Blake, Charles Hawtrey, Annie Esmond.*

EASY MONEY (1934) [1]

Dir and Prod *Redd Davis.* Scr *Basil Mason, from his play* The Ghosts of Mr Pim. Ph *Geoffrey Faithfull.* PC *British and Dominions/Paramount British.* Dis *Paramount. 73 mins (later 69). Cert U*
Rambling comedy about Jack (*Gerald Rawlinson*), clerk to two shady bookmakers, who foils their plan to blackmail a rich colonel and falls for the latter's ward Joan (*Mary Newland*). He invites the bookies down for a weekend and scares them off for good by staging an appearance of the 'family ghost'.
RoC *Hubert Leslie, George Carney, Lawrence Hanray, Harvey Braban, Gladys Hamer, René Ray.*

EASY RICHES (1937) [1]

Dir *Maclean Rogers.* Prod *A. George Smith.* Scr *John Hunter.* Ph *Geoffrey Faithfull.* PC *GS Enterprises.* Dis *RKO Radio. 67 mins. Cert U*
Dull, phoney comedy about the rivalry between the owner of a cement works and the proprietor of a brick factory. A con-man with a bogus scheme for land developments only succeeds in uniting the lifelong feuders against

him, foiling his plans and paving the way for the son of one to marry the daughter of the other.
LP *George Carney, Gus McNaughton, Marjorie Taylor, Tom Helmore, Peter Gawthorne, Aubrey Mallalieu, Molly Hamley-Clifford, Michael Ripper.*

EBB TIDE (1932) [2]

Dir *Arthur Rosson.* Prod *Walter Morosco.* Scr *Basil Mason, Reginald Denham, from a novel by Dixie Wilson.* PC *Paramount British.* Dis *Paramount. 73 mins. Cert A*
Version of an American weepie novel, *God Gave Me 20 Cents,* already filmed by Hollywood under that title in 1926. While his mistress is in prison, a sailor falls for a shop-girl and marries her. Released, the mistress tricks him into taking her on his next voyage, but later comes good and saves his wife, whom he really loves, from suicide.
LP *Dorothy Bouchier, George Barraud, Joan Barry, Vanda Greville, Alexander Field, Annie Esmond, Merle Oberon, Anna Lee.*

THE EDGE OF THE WORLD (1937) [4]

Dir and Scr *Michael Powell.* Prod *Joe Rock.* Ph *Monty Berman.* PC *Rock Studios.* Dis *British Independent. 80 mins. Cert A*
On Hirta, a desolate Shetland island, peat supplies are giving out, and evacuation is urged by Robby (*Eric Berry*), but opposed by his father Peter (*John Laurie*) and Andrew (*Niall MacGinnis*), fiancé of Robby's sister Ruth (*Belle Chrystall*). Robby dies in a 'chicken' climb against Andrew, who leaves. Ruth has his baby. Months later, Andrew returns and saves the baby's life; by now, evacuation has been accepted as inevitable. As they are leaving, old Peter spots a rare bird's egg, climbs to get it, and falls to his death. Rugged location scenery and solid acting overcome melodramatic plot in first big success for the director.
RoC *Finlay Currie, Kitty Kirwan, Grant Sutherland, Hamish Sutherland, Campbell Robson, Francesca Reidy, George Summers, Michael Powell.*

EDUCATED EVANS (1936) [5]

Dir *William Beaudine.* Prod *Irving Asher.* Scr *Frank Launder, Robert Edmunds, from the book by Edgar Wallace.* Ph *Basil Emmott.* PC *Warner Bros.* Dis *First National. 86 mins. Cert U*
Comedian *Max Miller* never had a more successful film character than Educated Evans, a horse-racing tipster who moves into society through his friendship with some nouveau-riche people, and becomes a trainer as well. He comes into money of his own at the end when he wins a fortune by backing the wrong horse. Riotously funny and fast-moving despite its length, the film grossed four times its cost.
RoC *Nancy O'Neil, Albert Whelan, Clarice Mayne, Hal Walters, Arthur Westpayne, George Merritt, Julien Mitchell, Frederick Burtwell, Anthony Shaw, Percy Walsh, Robert English.*

18 MINUTES (1935) [4]

Dir *Monty Banks.* Prod *Gregory Ratoff.* Scr *Fred Thompson.* Ph *Geoffrey Faithfull. John J. Cox,* PC *Allied.* Dis *Pathe. 84 mins. Cert A*

Predictable but still gripping drama about a lion-tamer (*Gregory Ratoff*) who adopts an orphan girl and 'protects' her against admirers when she grows up. But he tends to treat her as he treats his lions, and marries her against her will. When he realizes that she really loves a magician, the tamer allows a lion over which he had complete domination to kill him.

RoC *Katherine Sergava, John Loder, Benita Hume, Hugh Wakefield, Paul Graetz, Carl Harbord, Richard Bennett, Rosamund Barnes, Hal Gordon, Margarde Yarde.*

THE ELDER BROTHER (1937) [1]

Dir *Frederick Hayward.* Prod *George King.* Scr *Dorothy Greenhill, from the novel by Anthony Gibbs.* PC *Triangle.* Dis *Paramount. 67 mins. Cert A*

Contemporary reviewers spoke of 'ludicrous scenes' in this negligible drama of one brother (*John Stuart*) who struggles to put the other (*Basil Langton*) through Oxford, then, although he is himself engaged, takes the blame for the death of a woman with whom his younger brother was having an affair. The younger brother eventually comes good and saves the other's life.

RoC *Marjorie Taylor, Stella Bonheur, Hilary Pritchard, Claude Horton, Fred Withers, Cecil Bevan.*

ELEPHANT BOY (1937) [4]

Dir *Robert Flaherty, Zoltan Korda.* Prod *Alexander Korda.* Scr *John Collier, Akos Tolnay, Marcia de Silva, from a novel by Rudyard Kipling.* Ph *Osmond Borradaile.* PC *London Films.* Dis *United Artists. 80 mins. Cert U*

Toomai (*Sabu*), a young stable boy in India, wins the admiration of a British government expedition by leading them to a herd of elephants. Kala-Nag, the elephant that Toomai looks after, runs away after being ill-treated; Toomai not only finds him and achieves his ambition to become a hunter, but is the first person ever to witness the fabled 'dance of the elephants'. Lovingly shot jungle goodie.

RoC *Walter Hudd, Allan Jeayes, W.E. Holloway, Bruce Gordon, D.J. Williams, (Wilfrid) Hyde White.*

Sabu and Walter Hudd in Elephant Boy *(1937)*

ELIZA COMES TO STAY (1936) [2]

Dir *Henry Edwards.* Prod *Julius Hagen.* Scr *H. Fowler Mear, from the play by H.V. Esmond.* Ph *Sydney Blythe, William Luff.* PC and Dis *Twickenham. 70 mins. Cert A*

Betty Balfour's comeback hopes received a blow from critical reaction to her performance in this comedy. The Hon. Sandy (*Seymour Hicks*), a confirmed middle-aged bachelor, accepts the guardianship of the daughter of a man who has saved his life in a car crash. She turns out to be not a little girl, but a rather unprepossessing young woman (*Miss Balfour*) who first blossoms, then marries Sandy on the rebound, when his actress girlfriend jilts him for his (richer) uncle.

RoC *Oscar Asche, Nelson Keys, Ellis Jeffreys, Vera Bogetti, A.R. Whatmore, Ben Webster, Diana Ward, Agnes Imlay, Billy Worth, Donald Burr.*

ELSTREE CALLING (1930) [3]

Dir *Adrian Brunel (supervising), Alfred Hitchcock, André Charlot, Paul Murray, Jack Hulbert.* Prod *Walter C. Mycroft.* Scr *Brunel, Mycroft, Val Valentine.* Ph *Claude Friese-Greene.* PC *BIP.* Dis *Wardour. 86 mins. Some scenes in colour. Cert U*

A patchy revue film, much after the style of Hollywood 'studio musicals' of the time (e.g. *Paramount on Parade*), with popular film personalities coming on to do their party pieces, spliced together with re-creations of music-hall acts, sketches and dancing girls. Hitchcock's section consisted of a couple of sketches with *Gordon Harker.*

RoC *Tommy Handley (compère), Anna May Wong, Donald Calthrop, Helen Burnell, Jack Hulbert, Will Fyffe, John Longden, Jameson Thomas, Lily Morris, Cicely Courtneidge, Bobbie Comber, Ivor McLaren, Hannah Jones, The Three Eddies, Teddy Brown and His Band.*

EMIL AND THE DETECTIVES (1935) [3]
(USA: *Emil*)

Dir *Milton Rosmer.* Prod *Richard Wainwright.* Scr *Cyrus Brooks, Margaret Carter, Frank Launder, from the novel by Erich Kästner and a screenplay by Billy Wilder.* Ph *Mutz Greenbaum.* PC *J.G. & R.B. Wainwright.* Dis *Gaumont-British. 70 mins. Cert U*

Sticky English version of the 1931 German film, with unconvincing child performances. Emil (*John Williams*) is the leader of a gang of children whose amateur detective work is instrumental in bringing about the capture of a bank robber.

RoC *George Hayes, Mary Glynne, Clare Greet, George Merritt, Marion Forster, Donald Pittman, Bobby Rietti, Johnny Singer, Derek Blomfield, Ricky Hyland, Roy McBane.*

THE END OF THE ROAD (1936) [3]

Dir *Alex Bryce.* Prod *John Findlay.* Scr *Edward Dryhurst.* Ph *Jack Parker.* PC and Dis *Fox British. 71 mins. Cert U*

The enthusiasm of *Harry Lauder* just about carries this weepy musical about the leader of a Scottish travelling concert party. His older daughter marries a drunken wastrel and dies

in childbirth. The old man brings the girl up and despite the return of her father, who burns the old man's marquee and caravan to the ground in a drunken fury, the granddaughter becomes a radio star and helps her grandfather start again.

RoC *Ruth Haven, Bruce Seton, Ethel Glendinning, Margaret Moffatt, Campbell Gullan, Vera Lennox, Tully Comber, Johnnie Schofield.*

ENEMY OF THE POLICE (1933) [1]

Dir *George King.* Prod *Irving Asher.* Scr *Uncredited.* PC and Dis *Warner Bros. 51 mins. Cert A*

Very poor comedy about the head of a moral reform society who is mistaken for a criminal, and given psychological treatment to make him see the error of his ways.

LP *John Stuart, Viola Keats, A. Bromley Davenport, Margaret Yarde, Violet Farebrother, Ernest Sefton, Winifred Oughton, Alf Goddard, Molly Fisher, Hal Walters, Nora Brenon.*

AN ENGLISHMAN'S HOME (1939) [2]
(USA: *Madmen of Europe*)

Dir *Albert de Courville.* Prod *Neville E. Neville.* Scr *Edward Knoblock, Ian Hay, Dennis Wheatley, Dora Nirva, Robert Edmunds, Clifford Grey, Richard Llewellyn, Rodney Ackland.* Ph *Mutz Greenbaum.* PC *Aldwych.* Dis *United Artists. 79 mins. Cert A*

Captain Brandt (*Paul von Hernried [Paul Henreid]*) is sent to England to pave the way for an air attack in time of war. He ingratiates himself with an English family, the Browns, whose daughter Betty (*Mary Maguire*) falls in love with him. When the attack comes, Father Brown (*Edmund Gwenn*), protecting his young son, kills a German officer and is taken out and shot. But a British bomber destroys the house with Brandt and dozens of enemy paratroops inside it. Shown at the beginning of the Second World War, this was not exactly a popular film.

RoC *Geoffrey Toone, Richard Ainley, Desmond Tester, John Wood, Carl Jaffe, Meinhart Maur, Mavis Villiers, Mark Lester, Kathleen Harrison, Norah Howard.*

ENTER THE QUEEN (1930) [4]

Dir *Arthur Varney-Serrao.* Prod *Harry Cohen.* Scr *Brock Williams.* PC *Starcraft.* Dis *Fox. 42 mins. Cert U*

Sprightly little comedy about a rich young man (*Richard Cooper*) told by his parents to stop his philandering ways and marry the girl of their choice. After being forced to masquerade as the fiancé of the Queen of Moravia (*Doria March*) to get his father out of his wife's bad books, Bertie finds that the girl he wants to marry is also the one his mother likes.

RoC *Chili Bouchier, Herbert Mundin, Frederick Culley, Margaret Damer, Lena Halliday, Percy Walsh.*

ESCAPE (1930) [3]

Dir, Prod and Scr *Basil Dean, from the play by John Galsworthy.* Ph *Jack Mackenzie, Robert G. Martin.* PC *ATP.* Dis *Radio. 70 mins. Cert A*

Certainly the most distinguished cast in a British talkie to this date (released April 1931) in a faithful but less than happy filming of Galsworthy's play that failed even to recover its £42,000 costs. *Sir Gerald du Maurier* stars as the man who escapes from Dartmoor, is helped by various people along the foggy way, but finally meets his nemesis in a priest (*Austin Trevor*).

RoC *Edna Best, Gordon Harker, Madeleine Carroll, Lewis Casson, Mabel Poulton, Ian Hunter, Marie Ney, Felix Aylmer, Jean Cadell, Nigel Bruce, Horace Hodges, Ben Field, Fred Groves, S.J. Warmington, Phyllis Konstam, Ann Casson, George Curzon, David Hawthorne, H. St Barbe West, Eric Cowley.*

ESCAPE ME NEVER (1935)   5

Dir *Paul Czinner.* Prod *Herbert Wilcox.* Scr *Carl Zuckerman, Robert Cullen, from the play by Margaret Kennedy.* Ph *F.A. Young.* PC *British and Dominions.* Dis *United Artists. 95 mins. Cert A*

Elisabeth Bergner was acclaimed for the 'rare perfection' of her acting in this superbly staged weepie about a waif, Gemma (*Bergner*) with a fatherless baby. She at first looks after, then is looked after by Sebastian (*Hugh Sinclair*), a struggling musician, becoming his mistress then his wife. The baby dies, but all Sebastian can think of is his new ballet, which is a success. They quarrel, but subsequently reconcile, neither prepared to escape their fate with the other, for all their weaknesses.

RoC *Griffith Jones, Penelope Dudley Ward, Irene Vanbrugh, Leon Quartermaine, Lyn Harding, Rosalinde Fuller.*

THE ETERNAL FEMININE (1931)   2

Dir and Prod *Arthur Varney.* Scr *Varney, Hugh Broadbridge, Brock Williams.* PC *Starcraft.* Dis *Paramount. 82 mins. Cert U*

Backstage romantic comedy. Michael (*Terence de Marney*), half-brother of wealthy showbiz backer Sir Charles (*Guy Newall*), marries a showgirl (*Jill Esmond Moore*). When Michael is injured in a road accident, his wife goes to work in a show which Sir Charles is backing....

RoC *Doria March, Garry Marsh, Madge Snell, Arthur Varney.*

EVENSONG (1934)   4

Dir *Victor Saville.* Prod *Michael Balcon.* Scr *Edward Knoblock, Dorothy Farnum, from a play by Knoblock and a novel by Beverley Nicholls.* Ph *Mutz Greenbaum.* PC and Dis *Gaumont-British. 83 mins. Cert U*

Slow but poignant musical with *Evelyn Laye* as Maggie, an Irish girl who elopes with a young musician (*Emlyn Williams*), is moulded into a top opera star by impresario Kober (*Fritz Kortner*), has a tempestuous affair with an archduke (*Carl Esmond*), refuses to acknowledge she is ageing and finally collapses and dies as the young star who has supplanted her is singing on stage.

RoC *Conchita Supervia, Alice Delysia, Muriel Aked, Denys Val Norton, Arthur Sinclair, Patrick O'Moore, Browning Mummery, Alec Guinness.*

Evelyn Laye in Evensong *(1934)*

EVERGREEN (1934)   4

Dir *Victor Saville.* Prod *Michael Balcon.* Scr *Emlyn Williams, Marjorie Gaffney.* Ph *Glen MacWilliams.* PC and Dis *Gaumont-British. 91 mins. Cert A*

Received cautiously by the critics, but ecstatically by the public, this became Britain's most famous musical of the 1930s, with *Jessie Matthews* ascending to world stardom as a girl posing as her own mother, a legendary music-hall star, and falling for a publicity man (*Barry Mackay*), who is understandably reluctant to declare his affection to a woman he believes to be over 50. Songs include *Dancing on the Ceiling, Over My Shoulder* and *When You've Got a Little Springtime in Your Heart.*

RoC *Sonnie Hale, Betty Balfour, Ivor McLaren, Hartley Power, Patrick Ludlow, Betty Shale, Marjorie Brooks, Richard Murdoch, Buddy Bradley Dancers.*

Jessie Matthews in Evergreen *(1934)*

EVERYBODY DANCE (1936)   3

Dir *Charles Reisner.* Prod *Michael Balcon.* Scr *Stafford Dickens, Ralph Spence, Leslie Arliss.* Ph *Arthur Crabtree.* PC *Gainsborough.* Dis *Gaumont-British. 74 mins. Cert A*

Rather incoherent comedy-musical with second-rate cabaret scenes, but a typically enthusiastic performance by *Cicely Courtneidge* as a nightclub singer who 'inherits' an orphaned niece and nephew. They believe her to be a farmer. She buys a farm, but the strain of two lives causes her to quit her club, whose manager tries to get her declared an unfit guardian. A change of heart by a local magistrate makes everyone happy.

RoC *Ernest Truex, Percy Parsons, Alma Tay-*

lor, *Charles Reisner Jr, Billie de la Volta, Peter Gawthorne, Helen Haye, Kathleen Harrison, Bruce Winston, (C.) Denier Warren, Janet Johnson, Joan Ponsford.*

EVERYTHING HAPPENS TO ME (1938)   3

Dir *Roy William Neill.* Prod *Jerome Jackson.* Scr *Austin Melford, John Dighton.* Ph *Basil Emmott.* PC and Dis *Warner Bros. 82 mins. Cert A*

Max Miller has to work hard in this comedy as a self-appointed election agent, Cromwell, who switches his loyalties half-way through the campaign, from Gusty (*H.F. Maltby*), a pompous hypocrite who runs the local orphanage, to Prodder (*Frederick Burtwell*), a mild local man whose wife has forced him to stand. In an uproarious meeting in the market-place, Cromwell and the orphanage kids show Gusty up as the double-dealer he is, and Prodder wins the election.

RoC *Chili Bouchier, Norma Varden, Winifred Izard, Adin Weeks, Ivor Barnard, Martita Hunt, Eliot Makeham, Hal Walters, Nell Emerald, Allan Jeayes, Roy Emerton, Sam Wilkinson, Phyllis Monkman.*

EVERYTHING IN LIFE (1936)   2

Dir *J. Elder Wills.* Prod *Marquis of Ely.* Scr *James E. Lewis.* PC *Tudor Films.* Dis *Columbia. 70 mins. Cert U*

A temperamental opera singer (*Gitta Alpar*) flees from her over-demanding manager and press agent, and discovers a penniless young composer-pianist (*Neil Hamilton*). She falls in love with him, helps to set up a show for his music, and keeping her identity a secret, stars in the show. Musical (*music: Hans May*) is entertaining, a bit incoherent.

RoC *Lawrence Grossmith, H.F. Maltby, Gerald Barry, Dorothy Boyd, Wyn Weaver, Clarissa Selwynne, Bruce Winston, Vera Bogetti, John Deverell, Oliver Gordon, Rosalind Rose, Judy Hallatt, Henry Ford.*

EVERYTHING IS RHYTHM (1936)   2

Dir *Alfred Goulding.* Prod and PC *Joe Rock.* Scr *Syd Courtenay, Jack Byrd, Stanley Haynes.* Dis *Associated British. 73 mins. Cert U*

Rather aimless musical entertainment said to be based on bandleader *Harry Roy*'s own life and romance. Roy keeps the film alive as the musician who falls in love with a princess and marries her in spite of the attempts of her Ruritanian-style court officials to thwart the match.

RoC *Princess Pearl (Pearl Vyner Brooke), Ivor Moreton, Davy Kaye, Dorothy Boyd, Clarissa Selwynne, Robert English, Gerald Barry, Johnnie Nit, Bill Currie, Phyllis Thackery, Mabel Mercer, Harry Roy's Band, Agnes Brantford, Syd Crossley.*

EVERYTHING IS THUNDER (1936)   3

Dir *Milton Rosmer.* (Associate) Prod *S.C. Balcon.* Scr *Marian Dix, J.O.C. Orton, from the novel by Jocelyn Hardy.* Ph *Günther Krampf.* PC and Dis *Gaumont-British. 77 mins. Cert A*

Douglass Montgomery and Constance Bennett in
Everything is Thunder *(1936)*

Canadian officer McGrath (*Douglass Montgomery*) escapes from a First World War prison camp by stabbing a sentry with wire-cutters. After several hairsbreadth escapes, he reaches Berlin and is befriended by Anna (*Constance Cummings*), an attractive streetwalker. Their plans to escape to Holland are discovered by Götz (*Oscar Homolka*) a detective in love with Anna, but he allows them to cross the Dutch border – himself being shot by a smuggler. Naïve stuff.
RoC *Roy Emerton, Frederick Lloyd, George Merritt, Peggy Simpson, H.F. Maltby, Robert Atkins, Mervyn Johns.*

EXCESS BAGGAGE (1933) [3]
Dir *Redd Davis.* Prod *Julius Hagen.* Scr *H. Fowler Mear, from the novel by H.M. Raleigh.* Ph *Sydney Blythe.* PC *Real Art.* Dis *Radio.* 59 mins. Cert U
Colonel Murgatroyd (*Claud Allister*), thinking he has shot General Brewster (*Frank Pettingell*) dead, while hunting a ghost, bundles the 'body' into a trunk he intends to heave into the river. But two trunks get mixed up, and a duchess (*Maud Gill*) unknowingly takes the general with her to a country house with a haunted bedroom. Acceptable 'spook' comedy.
RoC *René Ray, Sydney Fairbrother, Gerald Rawlinson, O.B. Clarence, Viola Compton, Finlay Currie, Minnie Rayner, Ruth Taylor, Charles Groves.*

EXCUSE MY GLOVE (1936) [3]
Dir *Redd Davis.* Prod *R. Howard Alexander, Joe Rock.* Scr *Val Valentine, Katherine Strueby.* Ph *Jack Willson.* PC *Alexander.* Dis *Associated British.* 75 mins. Cert A
Presentable vehicle for boxer *Len Harvey*, casting him as Don Carter, a meek, bespectacled collector of stained glass. When Don accidentally accepts a challenge to fight in a fairground booth, the proprietor recognizes the makings of a good boxer and becomes his manager, backed by a wealthy enthusiast. Despite crooked efforts by a rival backer, Don becomes a champion.
RoC *Betty Ann Davies, Archie Pitt, Olive Blakeney, Wally Patch, Ronald Shiner, Vera Bogetti, Arthur Finn, Bobbie Comber, Tommy Farr, Bombardier Billy Wells, Don McCorkindale, Jimmy Wilde, Gunner Moir, Benny Caplan, Dave McCleave, Frank Hough, George*

Daly, Harry Mizler, Ted Broadribb, Matt Wells, Johnny Rice, Jimmy Butler, Maurice Strickland, Syd Hull, John McAdam, Pancho Villar, André Lenglet, Moss De Young.

EXPERT'S OPINION (1935) [2]
Dir *Ivar Campbell.* Prod *Anthony Havelock-Allan.* Scr *Ivar and Sheila Campbell.* PC and Dis *British and Dominions/Paramount British.* 71 mins. Cert A
Two murders are committed and in each case the accused is freed on the evidence of a ballistics expert (*Leslie Perrins*). A ring of deadly spies is at work and their target is the expert, whose formula for a new aircraft gun is sought by foreign powers. The secret is preserved in the end by the courage of the inventor's wife (*Lucille Lisle*). Haphazard thriller.
RoC *Kim Peacock, Molly Fisher, Franklyn Bellamy, John Kevan, Lawrence Hanray, Lawrence Anderson.*

EYES OF FATE (1933) [2]
Dir *Ivar Campbell.* Prod *Norman Loudon.* Scr *Holloway Horn.* PC *Sound City.* Dis *Universal.* 59 mins. Cert A
Ingenious if incredible story – the forerunner of several other (better) films – about a shifty bookmaker (*Allan Jeayes*) forever bullying his hapless wife. A new, mysterious guest at their boarding house, Mr Oliver (*O.B. Clarence*) gives the bookie the following day's evening paper. The bookie wins a fortune on the racetrack, then checks the results in the paper – and reads of his own death.
RoC *Valerie Hobson, Terence de Marney, Faith Bennett, Nellie Bowman, Tony Halfpenny, Edwin Ellis, Edmund Cozens, May Hallatt, John Herring, Hugh René.*

THE FACE AT THE WINDOW (1932) [1]
Dir *Leslie Hiscott.* Prod *Julius Hagen.* Scr *H. Fowler Mear, from a play by F. Brooke Warren.* PC *Real Art.* Dis *Radio.* 53 mins. Cert A
A series of bank robberies in which, in each case, the night watchman or security man has been murdered by poison, stuns Paris. Famous French detective Paul le Gros (*Raymond Massey*) is called in and, by pretending that one of the victims is not dead, exposes the maniacal Count Fournal (*Eric Maturin*) as the thief and killer. Dated, theatrical stuff.
RoC *Isla Bevan, Claude Hulbert, Henry Mollison, A. Bromley Davenport, Harold Meade, Dennis Wyndham, Berenoff and Charlot, Charles Groves, David Miller.*

THE FACE AT THE WINDOW (1939) [3]
Dir *George King.* Prod *King, Randall Faye.* Scr *A.R. Rawlinson, Faye, from the play by F.*

Brooke Warren. Ph *Hone Glendinning.* PC *Pennant.* Dis *British Lion.* 65 mins. Cert A
Paris, 1880: The Wolf, a killer, stabs his victims in the back while their eyes are on a hideous face at the window. Suspicion falls on a bank clerk, Cortier (*John Warwick*) – and his rival for the bank manager's daughter, Chevalier del Gardo (*Tod Slaughter*), does his best to heighten it. It turns out that the killer is del Gardo himself, his 'monster' half-brother being the 'face'. He escapes a police trap, but is drowned in the Seine. Lurid melodrama is given full value.
RoC *Marjorie Taylor, Leonard Henry, Aubrey Mallalieu, Robert Adair, Wallace Evennett, Kay Lewis, Margaret Yarde, Harry Terry, Billy Shine.*

FACES (1933) [2]
Dir *Sidney Morgan.* Prod *Herbert Wilcox.* Scr *Joan Wentworth Wood, from a play by Patrick Ludlow, Walter Sondes.* PC *British and Dominions/Paramount British.* Dis *Paramount.* 68 mins. Cert A
Madeleine (*Anna Lee*), an assistant in a fashionable beauty shop, longs for a classier life, and neglects her boyfriend Ted (*Harold French*) when the chance comes along of an affair with a wealthy married man. She is about to agree to live with him when she learns that his wife is one of her most sympathetic clients. She decides there is more peace of mind in suburbia with Ted. Hmm.
RoC *Walter Sondes, Dorothy Tetley, Moore Marriott, Kate Saxon, Beryl de Querton, Noel Shannon, Olive Sloane, Madeleine Seymour, Peter Northcote, Mary Gaskell.*

FACING THE MUSIC (1933) [4]
Dir *Harry Hughes.* Prod *John Maxwell.* Scr *Clifford Grey, Frank Launder, Stanley Lupino.* Ph *Walter Harvey, Bryan Langley.* PC *BIP.* Dis *Wardour.* 69 mins. Cert U
To ingratiate himself with opera star Madame Calvini (*José Collins*), with whose singer niece (*Nancy Burne*) he is in love, publicist Jack Foley (*Stanley Lupino*) suggests a stunt by which Madame should wear her famous priceless jewels on stage and have them deliberately stolen. On the night, the jewels are really stolen, and the thieves only caught after a frantic chase around the theatre. Successful comedy with a couple of songs thrown in.
RoC *Doria Woodall, Lester Matthews, Morris Harvey, Dennis Hoey, Hal Gordon, Charles Gerrard, Nancy Brown, Ian Wilson, Darroll Richards, Nancy Neale.*

FAIR EXCHANGE (1936) [3]
Dir *Ralph Ince.* Prod *Irving Asher.* Scr *Brock Williams, Russell Redcraft.* Ph *Basil Emmott.* PC and Dis *Warner Bros.* 63 mins. Cert U
Unusual comedy about a criminologist who stages a fake burglary as part of his plan to discourage his son, sent down from university, from following in his footsteps. But there really has been a burglary and the son solves it, as well as falling for the niece of the criminologist's 'partner-in-crime'.

LP *Patric Knowles, Roscoe Ates, Isla Bevan, Louis Goodrich, Raymond Lovell, Cecil Humphreys, Morland Graham.*

FAITHFUL (1936)   3
Dir *Paul L. Stein.* Prod *Irving Asher.* Scr *Brock Williams.* Ph *Basil Emmott.* PC and Dis *Warner Bros. 78 mins. Cert U*
Ordinary musical romance about an American girl (*Jean Muir*) and an Austrian (*Hans Sonker*), Continental music academy students, who come to London and marry. Through her great faith in his singing voice, he becomes the rage of the nightclubs – and neglects his wife for a dazzling socialite (*Chili Bouchier*). His wife decides to leave him – but they are brought together again by the impresario (*Gene Gerrard*) who also loves her.
RoC *Margaret Yarde.*

THE FAITHFUL HEART (1932)   4
(USA: *Faithful Hearts*)
Dir *Victor Saville.* Prod *Michael Balcon.* Scr *Angus Macphail, Robert Stevenson, Lajos Biro, Saville, from a play by Monckton Hoffe.* Ph *Mutz Greenbaum.* PC *Gainsborough.* Dis *Ideal. 82 mins. Cert A*
A naval officer (*Herbert Marshall*) loves a girl (*Edna Best*) whom he is forced to leave when suddenly recalled to his ship. They lose touch. Years later, about to marry a society girl (*Anne Grey*), he is visited by his daughter, from his first love, now dead. When his fiancée refuses to accept the reality of the girl (also *Edna Best*), father and daughter go away to sea together.
RoC *Athole Stewart, Lawrence Hanray, Mignon O'Dogherty, Griffith Jones.*

Edna Best in The Faithful Heart *(1932)*

FALLING FOR YOU (1933)   4
Dir *Jack Hulbert, Robert Stevenson.* Prod *Michael Balcon.* Scr *Hulbert, Stevenson, Douglas Furber, Claude Hulbert.* Ph *Bernard Knowles.* PC *Gainsborough.* Dis *W & F. 88 mins. Cert U*
Jack and Minnie, two reporters (*Jack Hulbert* and *Cicely Courtneidge*) are in Switzerland trying to out-scoop each other on the story of a missing heiress. Jack falls in love with the heiress, saves her from the nobleman she didn't want to marry and leaves Minnie with what remains of the story. Lyrics: Furber. Music: Vivian Ellis. During the plot, Hulbert

Jack Hulbert and Tamara Desni in Falling for You *(1932)*

manages to dance on skis and on ice and get through three of the four songs.
RoC *Tamara Desni, Garry Marsh, Alfred Drayton, Ivor McLaren, Tonie Edgar Bruce, O.B. Clarence, Morton Selten, Leo Sheffield, Lillimor Schmidt, Gwenyth Lloyd.*

FALLING IN LOVE (1934)   3
(USA: *Trouble Ahead*)
Dir *Monty Banks.* Prod *Howard Welsch.* Scr *Fred Thompson, Miles Malleson, John Paddy Carstairs.* PC *Vogue.* Dis *Pathé. 81 mins. Cert U*
Hollywood film star Howard Elliott (*Charles Farrell*) arrives in London with his press agent Oscar (*Gregory Ratoff*) to make a film. He objects to his leading lady (*Margot Grahame*) who cannot act, but finds unexpected romance with an orphan girl (*Mary Lawson*) he meets on a bus. Oscar is horrified – but Howard marries his orphan.
RoC *H.F. Maltby, Diana Napier, Cathleen Nesbitt, Pat Aherne, Sally Stewart.*

FALSE EVIDENCE (1937)   2
Dir and Scr *Donovan Pedelty, from a novel by Roy Vickers.* Prod *Victor M. Greene.* PC *Crusade.* Dis *Paramount. 71 mins. Cert A*
Judy (*Gwenllian Gill*) gets a good job for her favourite cousin Gerald (*Michael Hogarth*), only to find he is marrying Annabelle (*Daphne Raglan*). Next day, his uncle is found throttled at his home and his friend, who had left him a fortune, is strangled in Paris. Judy's boss (*George Pembroke*) helps her discover Annabelle is in league with a criminal ring. Gerald is killed by a bullet meant for Judy, Annabelle is strangled, and the gang leader falls to his death from a window. Robust plot, indifferently acted.
RoC *George Pughe, Francis Roberts, Langley Howard, Ralph Michael, Dempsey Stuart, Ben Williams, Terry Conlin.*

FAME (1936)   3
Dir *Leslie Hiscott.* Prod *Herbert Wilcox.* Scr *Michael Barringer, R.P. Weston, Bert Lee, Jack Marks.* Ph *F.A. Young.* PC *Wilcox/British & Dominions.* Dis *General Film Distributors. 68 mins. Cert U*
A blundering shopwalker with eternal longings to be a Shakespearian actor wins a 'film face'

competition which entitles him to play the minor role of Oliver Cromwell in a film. On the train up to London, he has a brush with an escaped convict and further misadventures follow in the big city. As an actor, he's a disaster – but a civic reception awaits him on his return – even after the Mayor has seen his performance. *Sydney Howard* proves to be the whole show.
RoC *Muriel Aked, Guy Middleton, Miki Hood H.F. Maltby, Brian Lawrence, Geraldine Hislop, Arthur Finn, Herbert Lomas, Russel Thorndike, Frank Pettingell, Sydney Fairbrother, Maire O'Neill, Henry Victor, Frederick Piper, Geraldo and His Orchestra.*

FAREWELL AGAIN (1937)   5
(USA: *Troopship*)
Dir *Tim Whelan.* Prod *Erich Pommer.* Scr *Clemence Dane, Patrick Kirwan.* Ph *James Wong Howe, Hans Schneeberger.* PC *Pendennis/London Films.* Dis *United Artists. 85 mins. Cert U*
An old theme gets a new coat of paint in this very good study of life aboard a troopship, and the reactions and misadventures of people there after getting the news that all leave is cancelled and they have just six hours ashore before returning to active service in the Far East. Disparate elements are pulled together with remarkable skill to make a richly human film.
LP *Flora Robson, Leslie Banks, Patricia Hilliard, Sebastian Shaw, René Ray, Anthony Bushell, Robert Newton, Edward Lexy, Leonora Corbett, Wally Patch, Eliot Makeham, Robert Cochrane, Edmund Willard, Alf Goddard, Jerry Verno, Martita Hunt, Maire O'Neill, John Laurie, David Horne, J.H. Roberts, Margaret Moffatt, Gertrude Musgrove, Billy Shine, Edie Martin, Phil Ray, Janet Burnell.*

Robert Newton and René Ray in Farewell Again *(1937)*

FAREWELL TO CINDERELLA (1937)   1
Dir *Maclean Rogers.* Prod *A. George Smith.* Scr *Rogers, Kathleen Butler, H.F. Maltby.* Ph *Geoffrey Faithfull.* PC *GS Enterprises.* Dis *Radio. 64 mins. Cert U*
Margaret (*Anne Pichon*) is the drudge of a family suddenly visited by an uncle from Australia, whom mother and Margaret's sisters mistakenly imagine to be rich. Stephen (*John Robinson*), the lodger, an impoverished artist,

is fond of Margaret and, with the help of the Australian uncle and an old antique dealer, the two are brought together and the family confounded. Treacly romance.

RoC *Arthur Rees, Glennis Lorimer, Ivor Barnard, Sebastian Smith, Margaret Damer, Ena Grossmith, Robert Hobbs, Michael Ripper.*

FASCINATION (1931) [2]

Dir *Miles Mander.* Prod *Clayton Hutton.* Scr *Victor Kendall, from a play by Eliot Crawshay Williams.* Ph *Horace Wheddon, W. Winterstein.* PC *Regina.* Dis *Wardour. 70 mins. Cert A*

Stilted romantic drama about a married couple (*Dorothy Bartlam, Carl Harbord*) who have been happy for three years: then he becomes infatuated with a glamorous actress (*Madeleine Carroll*). When the wife confronts her and offers to share her husband, the actress relents and tells the man their affair is over.

RoC *Kay Hammond, Kenneth Kove, Louis Goodrich, Roland Culver, Merle Oberon, Freddie Bartholomew, Allison Van Dyke, John Kove.*

Allison Van Dyke, Freddie Bartholomew and John Kove in Fascination *(1930)*

THE FATAL HOUR (1937) [3]

Dir *George Pearson.* Prod *Anthony Havelock-Allan.* Scr *Ralph Neale, Gerald Elliott, from a novel by Cicely Frazer-Simpson.* PC and Dis *British and Dominions/Paramount British. 66 mins. Cert A*

A kindly old antique dealer, Cready (*Edward Rigby*) becomes the seemingly unsuspecting pawn of a spy ring who put a time-bomb in a clock that he is selling to a scientist whom the spies want out of the way. The villains are rounded up in a climax which reveals their leader and mastermind to be – Cready himself. Thriller is a shade threadbare: Rigby takes the acting honours.

RoC *Moira Reed, Moore Marriott, Dick Hunter, Derek Gorst, D.J. Williams, J.H. Lockwood, Ernest Sefton, Douglas Vine, Cyril Hillier.*

FATHER AND SON (1934) [1]

Dir *Monty Banks.* Prod *Irving Asher.* Scr *Randall Faye, from a novel by Ben Ames Williams.* PC and Dis *Warner Bros. 48 mins. Cert A*

Not even *Edmund Gwenn* can redeem this weak drama about a bank clerk (*Esmond Knight*) who becomes reconciled with his ex-convict father (*Gwenn*) to such an extent that he confesses to a theft he thinks the old man has committed. In the end, the real culprit comes to light.

RoC *James Finlayson, Charles Carson, Daphne Courtney, O.B. Clarence, Margaret Yarde, Roland Culver.*

FATHER O'FLYNN (1935) [3]

Dir *Wilfred Noy, Walter Tennyson.* Prod *Noy.* Scr *Tennyson.* PC and Dis *Butchers. 82 mins. Cert U*

Simple, uncomplicated melodrama with music, about an Irish priest (*Tom Burke*) who has brought up a girl, Macushla (*Jean Adrienne*) from babyhood. When she comes into some money, her crooked father turns up and takes her to London. The priest and her sweetheart (*Robert Chisholm*) follow, saving her from her father and his evil partner, who have opened a gambling den with her money.

RoC *Henry Oscar, Denis O'Neil, Ralph Truman, Johnnie Schofield, Dorothy Vernon, Ethel Revell & Gracie West, The Sherman Fisher Girls, Billy Holland, Stanley Kirkby, Louis Goodrich, Esme Lewis, Robert Hobbs, Clifford Buckton, Ian Wilson.*

FATHER O' NINE (1938) [2]

Dir *Roy Kellino.* Prod *Ivor McLaren.* Scr *Harold G. Brown.* Ph *Robert Lapresle.* PC and Dis *Fox British. 48 mins. Cert U*

Eddie Mills (*Hal Gordon*) is employed as a store's 'complaints recipient': thus he is constantly being fired (and later re-hired) to placate irate customers. Seeing Eddie 'dismissed' (for the umpteenth time), Colonel Briggs (*Jimmy Godden*) tells him he will come and see the nine children the store says he has. After getting nine kids of various races and colours together, Eddie really gets the sack – but wins the pools. Comedy is ingenious, but has few laughs.

RoC *Dorothy Dewhurst, Claire Arnold, Denis Cowles, Jo Monkhouse, William Byron, Peter Popp, Vi Kaley, Robert Field, Charles Castella, May Hallatt.*

FATHER STEPS OUT (1937) [3]

Dir *Maclean Rogers.* Prod and PC *George Smith.* Scr *Kathleen Butler.* Ph *Geoffrey Faithfull.* Dis *Radio. 64 mins. Cert U*

A self-made cheese tycoon (*George Carney*) is cheated out of his fortune by a couple of swindlers posing as society swells. But he makes himself another nest-egg with his last few pounds, with the help of his quick-witted chauffeur (*Bruce Seton*), who bests the swindlers and marries the tycoon's daughter (*Dinah Sheridan*). Nippy comedy has its moments.

RoC *Vivienne Chatterton, Basil Langton, Peter Gawthorne, Zillah Bateman, Elizabeth Kent, Isobel Scaife, Michael Ripper, Ann Wilton.*

THE FEAR SHIP (1933) [2]

Dir *James Edwards.* Prod and Scr *J. Steven Edwards (James Edwards), from a novel by R.F.W. Rees.* PC *Associated Sound.* Dis *Paramount. 66 mins. Cert A*

Some good photography distinguishes an otherwise unremarkable adventure yarn about Petrie (*Cyril McLaglen*), a seaman who has lost his ticket but who breaks the 'hoodoo' on a schooner owned by a man whose daughter he hopes to marry.

RoC *Dorothy Bartlam, Edmund Willard, William Holmes, John Blake, Hal Booth.*

THE FEATHERED SERPENT (1934) [1]

Dir *P. Maclean Rogers.* Prod *A. George Smith.* Scr *Rogers, Kathleen Butler, from the novel by Edgar Wallace.* Ph *Geoffrey Faithfull.* PC *GS Enterprises.* Dis *Columbia. 72 mins. Cert A*

Confused thriller in which an actress (*Enid Stamp-Taylor*) is accused of murdering a receiver of stolen property. But a reporter (*Tom Helmore*) sniffs out the truth, and proves she didn't do it.

RoC *D.A. Clarke-Smith, Moore Marriott, Molly Fisher, Vincent Holman, Evelyn Roberts, Iris Baker, O.B. Clarence.*

FEATHER YOUR NEST (1937) [3]

Dir *William Beaudine.* Prod *Basil Dean.* Scr *Austin Melford, Robert Edmunds, Anthony Kimmins.* Ph *Ronald Neame.* PC *ATP.* Dis *Associated British. 86 mins. Cert U*

Rather sluggish and overlong (and seldom-revived) *George Formby* comedy, although there are some laughs and he does sing the famous *Leaning on a Lamppost.* He plays Willie, a brainless bungler at a record factory, whose propensity for dropping things makes it unlikely he will achieve the rise he needs to marry his girl Mary (*Polly Ward*). Trying to replace a valuable disc he has broken, he substitutes a recording of his own voice, which becomes the hit of the year.

RoC *Enid Stamp-Taylor, Davy Burnaby, Moore Marriott, Val Rosing, Jack Barty, Clifford Heatherley, Frederick Burtwell, Ethel Coleridge, Jimmy Godden, Syd Crossley, Frank Perfitt, Frederick Piper, Mike Johnson, The Three Rhythm Sisters*

George Formby and Polly Ward in Feather Your Nest *(1937)*

FIFTY SHILLING BOXER (1937) [1]

Dir *Maclean Rogers.* Prod and PC *George Smith.* Scr *Guy Fletcher.* Ph *Geoffrey Faithfull.* Dis *Radio. 74 mins. Cert U*

Jack Foster (*Bruce Seton*), a circus clown, dreams of becoming a boxer. In London, he is spotted at a third-rate boxing club by an impresario, who offers him the part of a boxer in a play. Jack becomes entangled with the

romantic intrigues of the leading lady, Miriam (*Eve Gray*) and there is a real fist-fight on stage when Miriam's lover insults Jack's girl (*Nancy O'Neil*). Jack is fired as an actor, but hired for a big fight by a promoter in the stalls. Artless.
RoC *Moore Marriott, Aubrey Mallalieu, Charles Oliver, Michael Ripper.*

FIGHTING STOCK (1935)   4
Dir *Tom Walls.* Prod *Michael Balcon.* Scr *Ben Travers.* Ph *Philip Tannura.* PC *Gainsborough.* Dis *Gaumont-British.* 68 *mins. Cert A*
Sir Donald Rowley (*Tom Walls*) rents a country cottage, and soon finds himself squabbling over fishing rights with a neighbour, the choleric Rivers (*Hubert Harben*). Sir Donald's tactless nephew Sidney (*Ralph Lynn*) falls for Rivers' stepdaughter (*Lesley Wareing*) which makes Rivers more choleric than ever. But all ends well after the Rowleys come to the rescue of Rivers' niece (*Veronica Rose*), who is being blackmailed by a scoundrel (*Herbert Lomas*). Amusing imbroglio from the Aldwych gang.
RoC *J. Robertson Hare, Marie Lohr, Sybil Grove, Norah Howard, Margaret Davidge, Peggy Simpson.*

THE FINAL RECKONING (1931)   1
Dir, Prod and Scr *John F. Argyle.* PC and Dis *Equity British.* 65 *mins. Cert A*
Independent *John Argyle* was one of the last hold-outs in Britain against the coming of sound, and this dour crime film and *Thoroughbred* (qv) were both originally made as silents. They were released in the spring of 1932 with sound added. *The Final Reckoning* proves to be a flimsy and old-fashioned yarn about a mine-owner's son who tries to kill a miner whom he imagines is a rival for his wife's affections.
LP *James Benton, Margaret Delane, Will Marriott, Bessie Richards, Thomas Moss.*

FIND THE LADY (1936)   2
Dir *Roland Gillett.* Prod *John Findlay.* Scr *Gillett, Edward Dryhurst,* from a play by *Tod Waller.* Ph *Stanley Grant.* PC and Dis *Fox British.* 70 *mins. Cert A*
Two American crooks come to Britain and launch a faith-healing racket. One of them falls for an impecunious young man and helps him win the titled lady's daughter he loves.
LP *Jack Melford, Althea Henley, George Sanders, Viola Compton, Violet Loxley, Dorothy*

Vernon, Eric Pavitt, Nancy Pawley, Jack (*John*) Warwick, Vera Martyn, Angela Litolff, Bombardier Billy Wells, Cecil Bishop, David Keir, George Lane, Philip Ray, Billy Shine, Ben Williams, Paul Neville.

FINE FEATHERS (1937)   2
Dir *Leslie Hiscott.* Prod *Herbert Smith.* Scr *Michael Barringer.* PC and Dis *British Lion.* 68 *mins. Cert U*
Damp musical comedy about a young Scottish shopgirl (*Renée Houston*) who gets mixed up with international business adventurers. She finds herself posing as the mistress of the Crown Prince of Boravia to further the ends of an American whose oil concessions are situated in the prince's country.
RoC *Donald Stewart, Francis L. Sullivan, Robb Wilton, Jack Hobbs, Marcelle Rogez, Henry Victor, Stella Arbenina*

A FIRE HAS BEEN ARRANGED (1935)   3
Dir *Leslie Hiscott.* Prod *Julius Hagen.* Scr *H. Fowler Mear, Michael Barringer.* Ph *Sydney Blythe.* PC and Dis *Twickenham.* 70 *mins. Cert A*
Patchy vehicle for *Bud Flanagan* and *Chesney Allen* as a couple of crooks who hide some loot in a field only to find 10 years later, on their release from prison, that it has been engulfed by suburbia. The directors of the store on the spot are in dire straits and only too pleased to listen to the crooks' plans to burn it down. But the daughter of the man they had robbed gets to the booty first.
RoC *Mary Lawson, Robb Wilton, Harold French,* (C.) *Denier Warren, Alastair Sim, Hal Walters, The Buddy Bradley Girls.*

FIRE OVER ENGLAND (1936)   4
Dir *William K. Howard.* Prod *Erich Pommer.* Scr *Clemence Dane, Sergei Nolbandov,* from the novel by *A.E.W. Mason.* Ph *James Wong Howe.* PC *Pendennis/Mayflower.* Dis *United Artists.* 92 *mins. Cert U*
The late sixteenth century: Michael Ingolby (*Laurence Olivier*) escapes the sea battle in which his father is captured by the victorious Spaniards – and is later burnt to death by the Inquisition. Knowing Michael is thirsting for revenge, England's Queen Elizabeth (*Flora Robson*) assigns him to penetrate the Spanish court of King Philip (*Raymond Massey*). Dis-

covered, Michael escapes with details of the invasion by the Spanish Armada – which is defeated by the British fleet. Vigorous, quite charismatic adventure.
RoC *Leslie Banks, Vivien Leigh, Tamara Desni, Morton Selten, Lyn Harding, James Mason, Herbert Lomas, George Thirlwell, Henry Oscar, Robert Newton, Donald Calthrop, Robert Rendel, Charles Carson, Lawrence Hanray, Roy Russell, Howard Douglas, Cecil Mainwaring, Francis de Wolff, Graham Chesewright, A. Corney Grain, Evelyn Ankers.*

THE FIRE RAISERS (1933)   2
Dir *Michael Powell.* Prod *Jerome Jackson.* Scr *Jackson, Powell.* PC *Gaumont-British.* Dis *W & F.* 77 *mins. Cert A*
Not one of the best of Michael Powell's early films, even though the idea is nice. *Leslie Banks* plays Jim Bronson, an insurance assessor who is tempted to join a gang who set fire to ailing firms to help their owners collect the insurance. But Jim's conscience finally proves too much, and he helps the police bring the 'fire-raisers' to book.
RoC *Anne Grey, Carol Goodner, Frank Cellier, Francis L. Sullivan, Joyce Kirby, Laurence Anderson, Henry Caine, George Merritt.*

FIRES OF FATE (1932)   2
Dir and Prod *Norman Walker.* Scr *Dion Titheradge,* from a novel and play by *Sir Arthur Conan Doyle.* PC *BIP.* Dis *Wardour.* 74 *mins. Cert A*
A colonel (*Lester Matthews*) with only a year to live goes on a trip to Egypt and falls in love, but, knowing he's a doomed man, remains silent. When the party take a trip into the desert, they are attacked by bandits and the colonel receives a crushing blow which knocks him out. After the tourists have been rescued by the Camel Corps, he discovers he is cured(!).
RoC *Dorothy Bartlam, Donald Calthrop, Kathleen O'Regan, Garry Marsh, Jack Raine, Clifford Heatherley, Jean Cadell, Hubert Harben, Arthur Chesney.*

FIRST A GIRL (1935)   4
Dir *Victor Saville.* Prod *Michael Balcon.* Scr *Marjorie Gaffney,* from a play by *Rheinhold Schunzel.* Ph *Glen MacWilliams.* PC and Dis *Gaumont-British.* 94 *mins. Cert A*
The original version of *Victor Victoria,* a musical frowned on by some critics, but rapturously received by the public. Elizabeth (*Jessie Matthews*), a messenger girl and embryo entertainer, meets Victor (*Sonnie Hale*), a female impersonator, in a downpour. When he catches cold, she goes on in his place, as a boy impersonating a girl impersonating a boy, and becomes the rage of Europe. Songs include *Everything's in Rhythm with My Heart.*
RoC *Griffith Jones, Anna Lee, Alfred Drayton, Constance Goodridge, Martita Hunt, Eddie Gray, Donald Stewart.*

THE FIRST MRS FRASER (1932)   3
Dir *Sinclair Hill.* Prod *Louis Zimmerman.* Scr *Leslie Howard Gordon,* from the play by *St John Irvine.* PC and Dis *Sterling.* 84 *mins. Cert A*

George Sanders in Find the Lady (*1936*)

Vivien Leigh and Laurence Olivier in Fire Over England (*1936*)

Romantic drama with music: Elsie (*Joan Barry*), spoilt second wife of wealthy James Fraser (*Henry Ainley*) wants to divorce him to marry a peer. James' first wife Janet (*Dorothy Dix*), who still loves him, discovers evidence of Elsie's infidelity and forces her, much to her chagrin, to become the guilty party in the divorce. James and Janet are reunited.
RoC *Harold Huth, Richard Cooper, Gibb McLaughlin, Hargrave Pawson, Henry Hewitt, Arnold Riches, Ivan Brandt, Millicent Wolff, Oriel Ross, Eileen Peel, Naunton Wayne, Frances Day, Noel Leyland, Yvette, Edgar K. Bruce, Ellen Pollock, Billy Cotton and His Band, The Gaucho Tango Orchestra.*

FIRST NIGHT (1937)   [2]
Dir and Scr *Donovan Pedelty, from the play by Sheila Donisthorpe.* Prod *Victor M. Greene.* PC *Crusade.* Dis *Paramount.* 69 mins. Cert U
Plain-Jane Judith's (*Rani Waller*) big moment in life comes when one of her plays is accepted for production at a try-out theatre. From being the family drudge, she is suddenly an author. Her inferiority complex makes rehearsals a nightmare, but the young producer (*Jack Livesey*) helps her to see her first night through to success and, perhaps, a new life. Dullish.
RoC *Sunday Wilshin, Ernest Mainwaring, Margaret Damer, Ann Wilton, Felix Irwin.*

FIRST OFFENCE/BAD BLOOD (1936) [3]
Dir *Herbert Mason.* Prod *Michael Balcon.* Scr *Austin Melford, Stafford Dickens.* Ph *Arthur Crabtree.* PC *Gainsborough.* Dis *Gaumont-British.* 66 mins. Cert A
Fast-moving crime thriller with some good chase scenes. Johnnie (*John Mills*), rich and spoiled, joins a gang of car thieves in France after being denied a car of his own by his father (*H.G. Stoker*). Barely escaping one police pursuit, Johnnie and Jeanette (*Lilli Palmer*) resolve to quit, but he is cornered (and her brother killed) in a police attack on the gang's hideout. Johnnie's father helps him escape, and the two men come to a kind of understanding. Partly made in France.
RoC *Bernard Nedell, Michael André, Jean Wall, Paul Velsa, Judy Kelly, Maupi, George Malkine.*

THE £5 MAN (1937)   [2]
Dir and Prod *Albert Parker.* Scr *David Evans.* Ph *Stanley Grant.* PC and Dis *Fox British.* 76 mins. Cert A
Heavy comedy-drama about a man determined to find those who sent him to jail on a trumped-up counterfeiting charge. Tramping penniless through the country, the man, Fordyce (*Edwin Styles*) puts himself up for sale at a charity auction, and is bought for £5 - it's a forgery - by Margaret (*Judy Gunn*). Her father turns out to be the chief counterfeiter. Cornered, he kills himself.
RoC *Frank Allenby, Charles Bannister, Esma Cannon, G.H. Mulcaster, Paul Blake, Norman Wooland, David Arnold.*

THE FLAG LIEUTENANT (1932)   [5]
Dir *Henry Edwards.* Prod *Herbert Wilcox.* Scr *Joan Wentworth Wood, from the play by W.P.*

Drury and Leo Tover. Ph *Stanley Rodwell.* PC *British and Dominions.* Dis *W & F.* 85 mins. Cert U
Henry Edwards' reprise of perhaps his most famous role - the extrovert flag lieutenant who saves a beleaguered fort from the Bashi Bazouks, and lets his friend Major Thesiger (*Peter Gawthorne*), who has lost his memory, take the credit. The lieutenant finds himself branded a coward, but all is ultimately resolved and both officers are honoured.
RoC *Anna Neagle, Louis Goodrich, Sam Livesey, Michael Hogan, O.B. Clarence, Abraham Sofaer, Joyce Bland, Peter Northcote, Tully Comber, Sybil Grove, Annie Esmond.*

FLAME IN THE HEATHER (1935)   [1]
Dir and Scr *Donovan Pedelty, from a novel by Esson Maule.* Prod *Victor M. Greene.* PC *Crusade.* Dis *Paramount.* 66 mins. Cert A
Hilariously inept adventure set in 1745 when an English spy goes to Scotland during the Jacobite rebellion. He is entertained by the Camerons, with whose daughter he has fallen in love, rescues the girl from death and they ride off together. One writer thought that 'the scenery round the castle ... is strangely reminiscent of one of the larger London parks'.
LP *Gwen (Gwenllian) Gill, Barry Clifton, Richard Hayward, Bruce Seton, Ben Williams, Kenneth McLaglen, Rani Waller, Francis de Wolff, Donald Robertson, Margaret Duncan, Honor Magee, Jock Rae.*

THE FLAME OF LOVE (1930)   [2]
Dir *Richard Eichberg, Walter Summers.* Prod *Eichberg.* Scr *Monckton Hoffe, Ludwig Wolfe.* Ph *Jack Cox.* PC *BIP.* Dis *Wardour.* 82 mins. Cert A. Bilingual versions
Romantic drama with music, set in pre-Revolution Russia, where Lt Borisoff (*John Longden*), adjutant to the grand-duke (*George Schnell*) falls in love with an Oriental dancer (*Anna May Wong*). Later, the dancer gives herself to the duke to save her brother (*J. Ley-On*) from death, poisons herself, and dies in Borisoff's arms.
RoC *Mona Goya, Percy Standing, Fred Schwartz.*

FLAT NO. 9 (1932)   [3]
Dir *Frank Richardson.* Prod and PC *V.E. Deuchar.* Scr *Brock Williams, John Barrow.* Ph *Basil Emmott.* PC *Fox.* 49 mins. Cert A
Comedy of marital misunderstandings, concerning two couples - newlyweds having to live with her mother, and an older pair on the verge of separation. The young husband and the older wife meet many times flat-hunting and complications ensue when both unknowingly take the same apartment.
LP *Jane Baxter, Reginald Gardiner, Marjorie Brooks, Arthur Margetson, A. Bromley Davenport, Amy Vevess, Margaret Damer, W.P. Holland, Roland Culver, Joan MacLaren.*

FLAT NO. 3 (1933)   [2]
Dir *Leslie Hiscott.* Prod *Herbert Smith.* Scr *Michael Barringer.* PC *British Lion.* Dis *M-G-M.* 47 mins. Cert A

Routine thriller in which a widow (*Mary Glynne*), believing she has killed a blackmailer (*D.A. Clarke-Smith*), goes to a lawyer friend (*Cecil Parker*) for help. The lawyer helps to cover up the supposed crime, but it eventually - and unsurprisingly - transpires that the criminal is not dead.
RoC *Betty Astell, Lewis Shaw, Elizabeth English, Dorothy Vernon.*

THE FLAW (1933)   [3]
Dir *Norman Walker.* Prod and PC *Patrick K. Heale.* Scr *Brandon Fleming.* Dis *Paramount.* 67 mins. Cert A
A man devises what he imagines is the perfect crime. His intended victim, however, to whom the killer explains the whole thing after he has administered poison, shows him the flaw of his plan, and uses the rest of the murderer's scheme to turn the tables, remove the villain and save his own life. Original idea, much copied in later films.
LP *Henry Kendall, Eve Gray, Eric Maturin, Phyllis Clare, Douglas Payne, Sydney Seaward, Vera Gerald, Elsie Irving, E.A. Williams.*

FLOOD TIDE (1934)   [2]
Dir *John Baxter.* Prod *Julius Hagen.* Scr *Ernest Anson.* PC *Real Art.* Dis *Radio.* 64 mins. Cert U
Low-key, shot-on-location story of life on the Thames Estuary. After doubts all round, Ted (*Leslie Hatton*), son of a lock-keeper, decides he does want to marry Betty (*Janice Adair*), daughter of a bargee, while the bargee, Bill (*George Carney*), wins the cup at the Bargees' Regatta.
RoC *Peggy Novak, Wilson Coleman, Minnie Rayner, Mark Daly, Edgar Driver, Wilfred Benson, William Fazan, Bertram Dench.*

THE FLYING DOCTOR (1936)   [2]
Dir and Prod *Miles Mander.* Scr *J.O.C. Orton.* PC *Gaumont-British/National.* Dis *General Film Distributors.* 92 mins. Cert U
This story of the adventures of a doctor (*Charles Farrell*) who uses a helicopter to get around, and his life in the Australian bush, was greeted with more enthusiasm in Australia, where it was made, than in England, where its release was delayed for over a year. But Gaumont's Michael Balcon would try Australian film-making again, with more success, a decade on, when he headed Ealing Studios.
RoC *Mary Maguire, James Raglan, Margaret Vyner, Joe Valli, Eric Colman, Maudie Edwards, Tom Lurich, Phyllip Lytton, Andrew Beresford, Katie Towers, Phil Smith, Jack Clarke, Don Bradman.*

FLYING FIFTY-FIVE (1939)   [2]
Dir *Reginald Denham.* Prod *Victor M. Greene.* Sct *Vernon Clancy, Greene, Kenneth Horne.* Ph *Ernest Palmer.* PC *Admiral.* Dis *RKO Radio.* 72 mins. Cert U
Bill (*Derrick de Marney*), an amateur jockey, walks out on his father after a row, and takes a job with Stella (*Nancy Burne*), a rival owner. There's an attempt to blackmail him into losing a big race on a horse that only he can

manage. He loses (not on purpose), but an objection gives him the race – and Stella as a bride. Hackneyed racetrack yarn.

RoC *Marius Goring, John Warwick, Peter Gawthorne, D.A. Clarke-Smith, Amy Veness, Ronald Shiner, Billy Bray, Francesca Bahrle, Hay Plumb, John Bryning, Basil McGrail, Victor Wark, Terence Conlin, John Miller, Norman Pierce.*

THE FLYING FOOL (1931)   4

Dir, Prod and Scr *Walter Summers, from a play by Arnold Ridley and Bernard Merivale.* Ph *Claude Friese-Greene, Stanley Rodwell, J. Rosenthal, James Wilson, A.L. Fisher.* PC *BIP.* Scr *Wardour.* 76 mins. Cert U

Dashing suspense thriller about a pilot in the Secret Service (*Henry Kendall*) who is assigned to prove that the owner of a fashionable London nightclub is a murderer. The club owner's mistress (*Benita Hume*) helps the hero prove his case.

RoC *Wallace Geoffrey, Ursula Jeans, Martin Walker, Barbara Gott, Charles Farrell, Syd Crossley.*

THE FLYING SQUAD (1932)   3

Dir *F.W. Kraemer.* Prod *S.W. Smith.* Scr *Bryan Edgar Wallace, from the novel by Edgar Wallace.* PC and Dis *British Lion.* 80 mins. Cert A

Thick-ear thriller in which Ann Perryman (*Carol Goodner*) arrives from Paris to look into the murder of her brother. The killer, McGill (*Harold Huth*), leads her to believe that Bradley of the Flying Squad (*Harry Wilcoxon*) was responsible, and murders a witness who might have proved otherwise. But in the end, Bradley tricks McGill into a confession, arresting him and his drug-smuggling ring.

RoC *Edward Chapman, Abraham Sofaer, Campbell Gullan, Joseph Cunningham.*

FOLLOW THE LADY (1933)   2

Dir and Scr *Adrian Brunel.* Prod and PC *George Smith.* Dis *Fox.* 49 mins. Cert A

Low-level comedy mix-up involving two bibulous bachelors who find themselves involved with a girl and a baby – and subsequently a little blackmail – in their flat.

LP *Billy (William) Hartnell, Basil Moss, Marguerite Allen, D.A. Clarke-Smith, Marie Hemingway, Vincent Holman.*

FOLLOW YOUR STAR (1938)   3

Dir *Sinclair Hill.* Prod *Harcourt Templeman.* Scr *George Pearson, Stafford Dickens.* Ph *Cyril Bristow.* PC *Belgrave.* Dis *General Film Distributors.* 80 mins. Cert U

Arthur (*Arthur Tracy*) throws up his factory job to become a singer, to the dismay of his girlfriend Mary (*Belle Chrystall*). He is taken on in the chorus of a travelling show that folds, then stars in a revue only to see the theatre sold after a good first night. He becomes a street singer and a recording made by a BBC mobile unit makes him a star. He is reconciled with his girl and his family. Homespun,

ultra-sentimental musical is still one of Tracy's better films.

RoC *Mark Daly, Horace Hodges, Nina Boucicault, James Harcourt, Dick Tubb, Finlay Currie.*

THE FORBIDDEN TERRITORY (1934)   4

Dir *Phil Rosen.* Prod *Richard Wainwright.* Scr *Dorothy Farnum, Alma Reville, from the novel by Dennis Wheatley.* Ph *R. Goldenberg.* PC *Progress Pictures.* Dis *Gaumont-British.* 81 minutes. Cert U

Hollywood director Phil Rosen gives a professional sheen to this adventure story about an English nobleman (*Ronald Squire*) and his son Michael (*Barry Mackay*) who travel to Russia and, with the help of two Russian girls (*Binnie Barnes, Tamara Desni*), rescue Michael's elder brother (*Anthony Bushell*) from the clutches of the secret police, headed by the wily Leshkin (*Gregory Ratoff*).

RoC *Anton Dolin, Marguerite Allan, Boris Ranevsky.*

FOREIGN AFFAIRES (1935)   4

Dir *Tom Walls.* Prod *Michael Balcon.* Scr *Ben Travers.* Ph *Roy Kellino.* PC *Gainsborough.* Dis *Gaumont-British.* 71 mins. Cert U

A middle-aged gambler (*Tom Walls*) and a young car salesman (*Ralph Lynn*) nursing a sick aunt's fortune meet in Nice. The salesman becomes first a dupe, then an ally when they are both employed as touts in a bogus count's casino. They discover there's more than gambling afoot, but their belated attempts at honesty nearly land them in jail before the count is counted out. Lively farce.

RoC *J. Robertson Hare, Ivor Barnard, Norma Varden, Marie Lohr, Diana Churchill, Cecil Parker, Kathleen Kelly, Gordon James, Mervyn Johns.*

FOR EVER ENGLAND/BROWN ON RESOLUTION (1935)   5
(USA: *Born for Glory*)

Dir *Walter Forde.* Prod *Michael Balcon.* Scr *J.O.C. Orton, Gerard Fairlie, Michael Hogan, from the novel by C.S. Forester.* Ph *Bernard Knowles.* PC and Dis *Gaumont-British.* 80 mins. Cert A

Convincing naval adventure, giving *John Mills* his first major leading role as Brown, born of

John Mills in For Ever England (Brown on Resolution; *1935*)

a brief affair between his mother (*Betty Balfour*) and a naval officer (*Barry Mackay*). Serving with the Royal Navy in the First World War, Brown becomes a hero when, single-handed, he keeps a German ship in port with expert marksmanship. Thanks to his delaying action a British ship is able to sink the Germans. Brown is killed, but the commander of the British ship realizes that the dead boy was his own son. Second unit director: Anthony Asquith.

RoC *Jimmy Hanley, Howard Marion-Crawford, H.G. Stoker, Percy Walsh, George Merritt, Cyril Smith.*

FORGET-ME-NOT (1936)   3
(USA: *Forever Yours*)

Dir *Zoltan Korda.* Prod *Alexander Korda, Alberto Giacalone.* Scr *Hugh Gray, Arthur Wimperis.* Ph *Hans Schneeberger.* PC *London Films.* Dis *United Artists.* 72 mins. Cert U

Helen, a typist, falls deeply in love with a ship's officer on an Atlantic voyage, but his mistress breaks up the affair. In America, world-famous tenor Enzo Curti (*Beniamino Gigli*) proposes to her, and she accepts, hoping to forget her broken heart. When the officer reappears begging her to take him back, she finds the strength to send him away. Highlights: Gigli's singing (naturally) and his proposal with the help of a large dictionary.

RoC *Joan Gardner, Ivan Brandt, Jeanne Stuart, Hugh Wakefield, Allan Jeayes, Hay Petrie, Charles Carson, Richard Gofe.*

FORGING AHEAD (1933)   2

Dir *Norman Walker.* Prod and PC *Harry Cohen.* Scr *Brandon Fleming, from a novel by K.R.G. Browne.* Dis *Fox.* 49 mins. Cert A

Comedy about a 'haunted' house which is really the headquarters of a crime school run by Crystal Grey (*Margot Grahame*) whose main business is counterfeiting. A meek young man (*Antony Holles*) occupies the house in spite of everyone's attempts to frighten him away and unknowingly breaks up the 'school' by distributing its counterfeit money.

RoC *Garry Marsh, Clifford Heatherley, Eliot Makeham, Melville Cooper, Edgar Norfolk, Edith Saville, Arthur Chesney, George Turner, Wallace Lupino, Gus Sharland, Myles Clifton, Hamilton Keene, William Holles.*

FOR LOVE OF YOU (1933)   2

Dir *Carmine Gallone.* Prod *Frank A. Richardson.* Scr *Selwyn Jepson.* Ph *W. Goldberger.* PC *Windsor.* Dis *Sterling.* 77 mins. Cert U

Another Jack-and-Jim musical comedy (see also *Going Gay*), with *Arthur Riscoe* and *Naunton Wayne* as the two Englishmen abroad, this time in Venice, where they share an apartment adjoining that of a temperamental tenor and his discontented wife. She flirts with Jack and insists on his taking her to an impending carnival. All ends well with reconciliation between husband and wife.

RoC *Franco Foresta, Diana Napier, Pearl Osgood.*

FOR THE LOVE OF MIKE (1932)   3

Dir *Monty Banks.* Prod *Walter C. Mycroft.* Scr *Clifford Grey, Frank Launder, from a play*

Bobby Howes and Constance Shotter in For the Love of Mike *(1932)*

by *H.F. Maltby.* Ph *Claude Friese-Greene.* PC *BIP.* Dis *Wardour.* 86 mins. Cert U

Musical farce in which bungling Bobby Seymour (*Bobby Howes*) tries his hand at burglary to retrieve a power of attorney which heiress Mike (*Constance Shotter*) has signed over to her guardian, whom she no longer trusts. Seymour is caught red-handed by a detective (*Arthur Riscoe*); he turns out to be an old school chum who helps Bobby steal the document after all.

RoC *Renée Macready, Jimmy Godden, Viola Tree, Wylie Watson, Hal Gordon, Syd Crossley, Harcourt Brooke, Monty Banks, The Carlyle Cousins.*

THE FORTUNATE FOOL (1933)   [3]

Dir *Norman Walker.* Prod *Jack Eppel.* Scr *Dion Titheradge,* from his play. Ph *Alan Lawson.* PC and Dis *Associated British.* 74 mins. Cert A

Jim (*Hugh Wakefield*) falls in love with penniless Helen (*Joan Wyndham*). His haughty fiancée Mildred (*Elizabeth Jenns*) seeks to have Helen arrested on suspicion of having stolen a valuable miniature, but a rich author (*Jack Raine*) comes to the rescue of the beleaguered pair and sees that Mildred gets her just deserts. Fair romantic comedy.

RoC *Arthur Chesney, Sara Allgood, Bobbie Comber, Mary Mayfren, Griffith Humphreys.*

FOR VALOUR (1937)   [4]

Dir *Tom Walls.* Prod *Max Schach.* Scr *Ben Travers.* Ph *Phil Tannura.* PC *Capitol.* Dis *General Film Distributors.* 95 mins. Cert A

The Boer War: Private Doubleday (*Tom Walls*) saves Major Pyke (*Ralph Lynn*) who recommends him for the VC. But Doubleday is an escaped convict, and the incident only leads to his return to jail. Years later, Pyke sees Doubleday in prison and offers to bring up his son Charlie with his own grandson Willie. Charlie becomes a successful but crooked financier, Willie an unsuccessful pickpocket. After cross and double-cross, Charlie is saved from arrest only by the intervention of his wife, Willie becomes a scoutmaster, and Old Doubleday ends up wheeling Old Pyke around in a bathchair. Something a little different from the Aldwych farceurs, with Walls and Lynn playing all the Doubledays and Pykes.

RoC *Veronica Rose, Joan Marion, Hubert Har-*

ben, *Henry Longhurst, Gordon James, Reginald Tate, Alan Napier, Joyce Barbour, Romilly Lunge, Evan Thomas, Basil Lynn, Walter Lindsay.*

THE FOUR FEATHERS (1939)   [5]

Dir *Zoltán Korda.* Prod *Alexander Korda.* Scr *R.C. Sherriff, Arthur Wimperis, Lajos Biro,* from the novel by *A.E.W. Mason.* Ph *Georges Périnal, Osmonde Borrodaile, Jack Cardiff.* PC *London Films.* Dis *United Artists.* Technicolor. 130 mins (later 115). Cert A

Harry Faversham (*John Clements*) resigns his commission on the eve of being ordered abroad to fight Arabs in Sudan. He receives four white feathers (symbols of cowardice) from three fellow officers and his fiancée (*June Duprez*). Determined to redeem himself, he goes to Egypt disguised as a native and saves the lives of all three officers. Back in England, he is reinstated and his fiancée takes back the last white feather. Pulsating adventure story with magnificent Technicolor photography and a brilliant performance by *Ralph Richardson* as Durrance.

RoC *C. Aubrey Smith, Allan Jeayes, Jack Allen, Donald Gray, Frederick Culley, Henry Oscar, John Laurie, Robert Rendel, Hal Walters, Amid Taftazani, Clive Baxter, Archibald Batty, Derek Elphinstone, Norman Pierce.*

THE FOUR JUST MEN (1939)   [3]
(USA: *The Secret Four*)

Dir *Walter Forde.* (Associate) Prod *S.C. Balcon.* Scr *Roland Pertwee, Angus Macphail, Sergei Nolbandov,* from the novel by *Edgar Wallace.* Ph *Ronald Neame.* PC *Ealing Studios/CAPAD.* Dis *Associated British.* 85 mins. Cert A

The Four Just Men are opposed to all foreign plotters against Britain and her empire. One, Terry (*Frank Lawton*) goes east in search of information while the other three pose as London dress designers. They suspect Sir Hamar Ryman (*Alan Napier*) of being a traitor. Terry returns, but is poisoned at Victoria, then shot. Before he dies, he reveals his discovery of a plot to block the Suez Canal, stopping all movements of ships and troops eastwards. The other Just Men (*Hugh Sinclair, Griffith Jones, Francis L. Sullivan*) avenge him by exterminating Ryman and foiling the plot. Timely yarn has some thrills and suspense, is padded to feature length with patriotic sentiment.

RoC *Basil Sydney, Anna Lee, Edward Chapman, Athole Stewart, Lydia Sherwood, George Merritt, Garry Marsh, Ellaline Terriss, Roland Pertwee, Arthur Hambling, Eliot Makeham, Henrietta Watson, Percy Walsh, Jon Pertwee, Frederick Piper, Liam Gaffney, Manning Whiley, Neal Arden, Basil Radford, Edward Rigby, Paul Sheridan.*

THE FOUR MASKED MEN (1934)   [3]

Dir *George Pearson.* Prod *Julius Hagen.* Scr *H. Fowler Mear, Cyril Campion,* from a play by *Campion.* PC *Real Art.* Dis *Universal.* 80 mins. Cert A

Brisk, if unlikely thriller about a barrister (*John Stuart*), who swears to avenge the death of his brother, shot in a hold-up by masked bandits. The barrister poses as a thief and,

with the help of a friend (*Richard Cooper*), brings his plan to fruition.

RoC *Judy Kelly, Miles Mander, Athole Stewart, Sebastian Shaw, S. Victor Stanley.*

FP 1 (1933)   [2]

Dir *Karl Hartl.* Prod *Erich Pommer.* Scr *Kurt Siodmak, Walter Reisch, Robert Stevenson, Peter Macfarlane,* from a novel by *Siodmak.* PC *UFA.* Dis *Gaumont.* 93 mins. Cert U. Bilingual versions

Futuristic drama about a giant floating aircraft-carrier, the FP 1, which a group of financiers conspire to destroy. Not much liked even in its time and pretty creaky now. Filmed in Germany with an all-British cast.

LP *Conrad Veidt, Jill Esmond, Leslie Fenton, George Merritt, Donald Calthrop, Nicholas Hannen, Francis L. Sullivan, William Freshman, Warwick Ward, Alexander Field, Phillip Manning, Will Van Allen.*

FRAIL WOMEN (1931)   [4]

Dir *Maurice Elvey.* Prod *Julius Hagen.* Scr *Michael Barringer.* Ph *Basil Emmott.* PC *Twickenham.* Dis *Radio.* 72 mins. Cert A

Gloomy, but well-acted story of Lillian (*Mary Newcomb*) who has her illegitimate war baby adopted by a wealthy spinster. Nineteen years later, the spinster dies and the girl is forbidden to marry her sweetheart because of her illegitimacy. The girl's real father, Harvey (*Owen Nares*), now a colonel, marries Lillian to give their daughter a name. Believing she has no place in either of their lives, Lillian commits suicide.

RoC *Edmund Gwenn, Margaret Vines, Frederick Peisley, Jane Welsh, Athole Stewart, Frank Pettingell, Herbert Lomas, Miles Malleson.*

Margaret Vines and Edmund Gwenn in Frail Women *(1931)*

FREEDOM OF THE SEAS (1934)   [4]

Dir *Marcel Varnel.* Prod *Walter C. Mycroft.* Scr *Roger Burford,* from a play by *Walter Hackett.* Ph *Otto Kanturek.* PC *BIP.* Dis *Wardour.* 74 mins. Cert U

Varnel made his British directing debut with this breezy adventure comedy, set in the First World War. *Clifford Mollison* stars as Smith, a shy clerk, treated as a nonentity by his employer Harcourt (*H.F. Maltby*) and his daughter Phyllis (*Wendy Barrie*) until a friend of his late father helps him get a commission in the

Navy. In charge of a tramp steamer on which Harcourt and Phyllis are passengers, Smith outwits a group of spies and finally saves everyone by ramming and sinking a German U-boat.
RoC *Zelma O'Neal, James Carew, Frank Atkinson, Henry Wenman, Tyrell Davis, Cecil Ramage, Charles Paton, Frederick Peisley.*

FRENCH LEAVE (1930)   [2]
Dir *Jack Raymond.* Prod *Henry Defries, Sam Harrison.* Scr *Reginald Berkeley, W.P. Lipscomb, from the play by Berkeley.* PC *D & H Productions.* Dis *Sterling.* 92 mins. Cert U
Madeleine Carroll is the brightest thing in this comedy about the wife of an Army captain serving in France during the First World War, who bribes a French farmwoman to allow her to pose as her daughter. Her husband has to keep her identity secret, another officer and a general fall for her and she comes under suspicion of being a German spy! Remade in 1937.
RoC *Sydney Howard, Arthur Chesney, Henry Kendall, Haddon Mason, George de Warfaz, May Agate, George Owen.*

FRENCH LEAVE (1937)   [4]
Dir *Norman Lee.* Prod *Warwick Ward.* Scr *Vernon Clancey, from the play by Reginald Berkeley.* Ph *Bryan Langley.* PC *Welwyn.* Dis *Pathé.* 86 mins. Cert A
Amusing situation farce set in First-World-War France. Dorothy Glenister (*Betty Lynne*) goes to France to be near her husband (*John Longden*). They both pretend she is just a friend. General Root (*Edmond Breon*) and several junior officers proceed to fall in love with her, and she is also suspected of being a spy. The real spy is captured and, the truth known, the general sportingly sends Dorothy off to Paris with her husband as escort.
RoC *John Wickham, Arthur Hambling, Frederick Burtwell, Michael Morel, Margaret Yarde, Oliver Wakefield, The Roosters.*

FRENCH WITHOUT TEARS (1939)   [5]
Dir *Anthony Asquith.* Prod *David E. Rose.* Scr *Terence Rattigan, Ian Dalrymple, Anatole de Grunwald.* Ph *Bernard Knowles.* PC *Two Cities.* Dis *Paramount.* 85 mins. Cert A
At a young men's French 'cramming college', sensitive Chris (*David Tree*), hearty Brian (*Guy Middleton*) and sturdy Roger (*Roland Culver*) all fall for the wiles of Diana (*Ellen Drew*), visiting her brother. The cynical Alan (*Ray Milland*) sees through her – but ultimately becomes her fourth and final victim. Sparkling battle-of-the-sexes comedy.
RoC *Janine Darcy, Jim Gerald, Kenneth Morgan, Margaret Yarde, Toni Gable.*

FRIDAY THE THIRTEENTH (1933)   [4]
Dir *Victor Saville.* Prod *Michael Balcon.* Scr *G.H. Moresby-White, Emlyn Williams.* Ph *Charles Van Enger.* PC *Gainsborough.* Dis *Gaumont-British.* 85 mins. Cert A
Successful omnibus film about – an omnibus. At one minute to midnight on Friday the 13th, lightning strikes a crane in London and, swerving to avoid it, a bus crashes into a shop,

Ralph Richardson and Jessie Matthews in Friday the Thirteenth (*1933*)

killing two passengers. The story flashes back 24 hours and tells stories, variously dramatic and humorous, about six people – all passengers on the bus. Ultimately, we discover which two were killed.
LP (*in order of episodes*) *Sonnie Hale, Cyril Smith, Muriel Aked, Richard Hulton, Harold Warrender, John Clifford; Max Miller, Alfred Drayton, Hartley Power, Percy Parsons; Eliot Makeham, Ursula Jeans, D.A. Clarke-Smith, Gibb McLaughlin; Edmund Gwenn, Mary Jerrold, Gordon Harker; Emlyn Williams, Frank Lawton, Belle Chrystall, O.B. Clarence, Wally Patch; Robertson Hare, Martita Hunt, Leonora Corbett, Clive Morton; Jessie Matthews, Ralph Richardson, Donald Calthrop, Ivor McLaren.*

THE FRIGHTENED LADY (1932)   [4]
(USA: Criminal at Large)
Dir *T. Hayes Hunter.* Prod *Michael Balcon.* Scr *Angus Macphail, Bryan Edgar Wallace, from a play by Edgar Wallace.* PC *Gainsborough/British Lion.* Dis *Ideal.* 87 mins. Cert A
First of two decent versions (the second came in 1940) of Wallace's play *The Case of the Frightened Lady.* The lady in question is Aisla (*Belle Chrystall*), unwilling guest at the home of Lord Lebanon (*Emlyn Williams*), whose domineering mother (*Cathleen Nesbitt*) wants them to marry. Two murders by strangulation bring Scotland Yard to the scene; an attempt to strangle Aisla fails; the killer is revealed as Lord Lebanon, his unsoundness of mind the family secret concealed by his mother.
RoC *Norman McKinnel, Gordon Harker, Cyril Raymond, D.A. Clarke-Smith, Percy Parsons, Finlay Currie, Julian Royce, Eric Roland.*

THE FROG (1937)   [3]
Dir *Jack Raymond.* Prod and PC *Herbert Wilcox.* Scr *Ian Hay, Gerald Elliott, from a novel by Edgar Wallace and play by Ian Hay.* Ph *Frederick A. Young.* Dis *General Film Distributors.* 75 mins. Cert A
A powerful criminal band called The Fellowship of the Frog terrorizes the country with some new robbery, fire or murder almost every week. Richard Gordon (*Jack Hawkins*) of the CID takes over the case, assisted by the cagey, watchful Sergeant Elk (*Gordon Harker*). Gordon falls for Stella (*Vivian Gaye*) whose father and brother are involved with the Fellowship, while Elk is finally responsible for unmasking

the Frog himself. Thriller lacks the spark of urgency.
RoC *Carol Goodner, Noah Beery, Richard Ainley, Felix Aylmer, Esmé Percy, Cyril Smith, Gordon McLeod, Julien Mitchell, Harold Franklyn.*

THE FROZEN LIMITS (1939)   [5]
Dir *Marcel Varnel.* Prod *Edward Black.* Scr *Marriott Edgar, Val Guest, J.O.C. Orton.* Ph *Arthur Crabtree.* PC *Gainsborough.* Dis *General Film Distributors.* 84 mins. Cert U
Carnival group The Six Wonder Boys (*The Crazy Gang*) read about a gold rush in the (40-year-old) paper their fish and chips are in, and end up in Alaska. They try to help an aged miner (*Moore Marriott*) addicted to sleepwalking, who knows he has a goldmine if only he can remember where it is. After starting a fake gold rush, they are threatened with lynching, only to be saved at the last moment by the re-discovery of the long-lost mine. Jokes fly in all directions as the Gang are given their heads in what is probably their most successful comedy.
Gang: *Bud Flanagan, Chesney Allen, Jimmy Nervo, Teddy Knox, Charlie Naughton, Jimmy Gold.*
RoC *Eileen Bell, Anthony Hulme, Bernard Lee, Eric Clavering.*

FULL CIRCLE (1935)   [1]
Dir *George King.* Prod *Irving Asher.* Scr *Michael Barringer.* PC and Dis *Warner Bros.* 55 mins. Cert A
Confusing crime drama about an ex-Covent Garden salesman who is blackmailed into stealing a will ... but then steals it back again to return it to the girl who is the chief beneficiary. Commented one reviewer: 'None of it is very clear.'
LP *René Ray, Garry Marsh, Graham Pocket, Betty Shale, Margaret Yarde, Patricia Hilliard, Bruce Belfrage, John Wood, Elizabeth Jenns.*

FULL SPEED AHEAD (1936)   [2]
Dir, Prod and PC *Lawrence Huntington.* Scr *Gerald Elliott.* Ph *Stanley Grant.* Dis *Paramount.* 71 mins. Cert U
Jean (*Moira Lynd*), daughter of a shipowner, elopes with her father's chauffeur Tim (*Richard Norris*) and stows away on one of his ships, which turns out to have been sold to a South American politician for some shady venture. The captain and the mate plan to scuttle the ship for insurance money, but Jean and Tim foil everyone's plans. Basic thriller.
RoC *Paul Neville, George Mozart, Geoffrey Clark, Victor Hagen, George Turner, Arthur Seaton, Julien Vedey, Syd Crossley, Arthur Brander, Dorothy Dewhurst.*

FULL SPEED AHEAD (1939)   [3]
Dir and Prod *John Hunt.* Scr *'Bartimeus'.* Ph *W. Winterton.* PC *Education & General Services.* Dis *General Film Distributors.* 60 mins. Cert U
John Elwood (*Michael Osler*) joins the navy and rises to command, while his brother Michael (*Frederick Peisley*) designs a new high-

speed destroyer, which is instrumental in rescuing John's fiancée Joan (*Dinah Sheridan*) from a blazing cargo vessel far out at sea. Naval drama has first-class camerawork, but not a lot more.

RoC *Morland Graham, H.G. Stoker, Betty Shale.*

THE GABLES MYSTERY (1938) [1]

Dir *Harry Hughes.* Prod *Warwick Ward.* Scr *Victor Kendall, Hughes, from a play by Jack Celestin, Jack de Leon.* PC *Welwyn.* Dis *M-G-M. 66 mins. Cert A*

Remake of a 1931 film (*The Man at Six*), with exactly the same credits. It wasn't much good then, and this version is even worse. The plot deals with a battle of wits between an elusive international crook and a lady insurance investigator (*Antoinette Cellier*), who is aided by a plump detective (*Francis L. Sullivan*). Badly acted into the bargain.

RoC *Leslie Perrins, Derek Gorst, Jerry Verno, Aubrey Mallalieu, Sidney King, Laura Wright, Ben Williams, Charles Howard, J. Neil More, Vernon Harris, Richard Littledale.*

THE GANG'S ALL HERE (1939) [3]
(USA: *The Amazing Mr Forrest*)

Dir *Thornton Freeland.* Prod *Walter C. Mycroft, Jack Buchanan.* Scr *Ralph Spence.* Ph *Claude Friese-Greene.* PC and Dis *Associated British. 77 mins. Cert A*

Insurance investigator John Forrest (*Jack Buchanan*) is brought out of retirement to solve the theft of crown jewels from a foreign prince. He suspects Harper (*Leslie Perrins*) of the insurance company, but he is bumped off and the trail leads to a nightclub run by Chadwick (*Otto Kruger*), where John becomes a waiter. Convincing Chadwick's gang that he is an American crook, John soon brings them to book. Farce-thriller marks Buchanan's second fling as Forrest.

Googie Withers, Edward Everett Horton and Jack Buchanan in The Gang's All Here (*1939*)

RoC *Edward Everett Horton, Googie Withers, Jack La Rue, Syd Walker, Walter Rilla, David Burns, Charles Carson, Ronald Shiner, Robb Wilton, Edward Lexy, Geoffrey Atkins.*

THE GANG SHOW (1937) [3]

Dir *Alfred Goulding.* Prod and PC *Herbert Wilcox.* Scr *Marjorie Gaffney.* Ph *Ernest Palmer.* Dis *General Film Distributors. 69 mins. Cert U*

Skipper (*Ralph Reader*), a young clerk and Rover Scout, believes himself to be a second Ziegfeld when it comes to the staging of shows. He resolves to put on a huge revue with a cast entirely of Boy Scouts and, after troubles through lack of finance, and with the help of Marie (*Gina Malo*), a secretary, the show goes on – to fame. Film version of famous theatre success.

RoC *Stuart Robertson, Richard Ainley, Leonard Snelling, Syd Palmer, Roy Emerton, Percy Walsh, Sandy Williamson, Don Dalvin.*

GANGWAY (1937) [4]

Dir *Sonnie Hale.* Prod *Michael Balcon.* Scr *Lesser Samuels, Sonnie Hale.* Ph *Glen MacWilliams.* PC *Gaumont-British.* Dis *General Film Distributors. 89 mins. Cert U*

Jessie Matthews vehicle with rather less singing and dancing than heretofore. She plays Pat Wayne, a reporter who finds herself suspected of being an international jewel thief, Sparkle. To avoid arrest, she hides in a trunk, which is sent on board a ship to America. New York mobsters also think that she's Sparkle, and force her to dance at a club while they rob a wealthy guest. In a pitched battle, the crooks are rounded up and the real Sparkle unmasked. Slightly disappointing, but a good comedy performance from the star. Songs unmemorable.

RoC *Barry Mackay, Nat Pendleton, Noel Madison, Alastair Sim, Olive Blakeney, Graham Moffatt, Edmon Ryan, Danny Green, Liane Ordeyne, Patrick Ludlow, Blake Dorn.*

GAOLBREAK (1936) [4]

Dir *Ralph Ince.* Prod *Irving Asher.* Scr *Michael Barringer.* Ph *Basil Emmott.* PC and Dis *Warner Bros. 64 mins. Cert A*

Different, above-average second-feature about a convict (*Ralph Ince*) who escapes after learning that his young second wife is going with a bad crowd. He is most concerned for his young son, whom a crook is planning to take to the wealthy Kendalls, whose own child was kidnapped years before as a baby. He pursues the rich man's yacht but, when he overhears Kendall's plans for the boy, he leaves him to his new future and gives himself up.

RoC *Basil Gill, Pat Fitzpatrick, Raymond Lovell, Lorna Hubbard, Roy Findlay, Elliot Mason, Desmond Roberts, Vincent Holman, Beryl Mills, Billy Shine, Jim Regan.*

THE GAUNT STRANGER (1938) [3]
(USA: *The Phantom Strikes*)

Dir *Walter Forde.* Prod *Michael Balcon.* Scr *Sidney Gilliat, from a play and novel by Edgar Wallace.* Ph *Ronald Neame.* PC *Northwood En-*terprises/Capad/ATP/Ealing Studios. Dis *Associated British. 73 mins. Cert A*

Third of four screen versions of Edgar Wallace's *The Ringer*, with *John Longden* repeating his role of the police inspector from the 1931 film. Secret passages and suspects abound when lawyer and fence Maurice Meister's (*Wilfrid Lawson*) life is threatened by his ex-partner, a master of disguise. In spite of all police efforts, Meister is killed with a sword-stick while the lights are out. The killer (*Alexander Knox*), disguised as a doctor, escapes.

RoC *Sonnie Hale, Louise Henry, Patrick Barr, Patricia Roc, Peter Croft, George Merritt, Charles Eaton, Arthur Hambling.*

THE GAY ADVENTURE (1936) [3]

Dir *Sinclair Hill.* Prod *Harcourt Templeman.* Scr *D.B. Wyndham-Lewis, from the play by Walter Hackett.* Ph *Cyril Bristow.* PC *Grosvenor.* Dis *Pathé. 74 mins. Cert A*

A pampered young man (*Barry Jones*) gets himself involved with a couple of con artists (*Finlay Currie, Guy Middleton*), after learning from them that he is a descendant of d'Artagnan. Ultimately, he solves a murder and, using his umbrella as a sword, bests the tricksters as well. Comedy hasn't quite the vital spark.

RoC *Yvonne Arnaud, Nora Swinburne, Robert Holmes, Percy Parsons, Keith Warrington, Antony Holles, Ralph Truman, Sybil Grove, Betty Worth.*

GAY LOVE (1934) [4]

Dir *Leslie Hiscott.* Prod *Herbert Smith.* Scr *Charles Bennett, Billie Bristow, John Paddy Carstairs, from the play by Audrey and Waveney Carton.* Ph *Alex Bryce.* PC and Dis *British Lion. 77 mins. Cert A*

Tuneful and, for this producer and director, quite lavish musical which allows *Florence Desmond* scope for impersonations of Mae West, Greta Garbo and several others, as a vaudeville actress who falls in love with her sister's aristocratic fiancé. The situation is happily resolved when the sister elopes with an old suitor.

RoC *Enid Stamp-Taylor, Ivor McLaren, Sophie Tucker, Garry Marsh, Sydney Fairbrother, Ben Welden, Leslie Perrins, Finlay Currie.*

Ivor McLaren and Florence Desmond in Gay Love (*1934*)

GAY OLD DOG (1935)   2

Dir *George King*. Prod *King, Randall Faye*. Scr *Faye*. PC *Embassy*. Dis *Radio. 62 mins. Cert A*

Brothers Tom (*Edward Rigby*), a vet, and George (*Moore Marriott*), a doctor, are in partnership in a small village. When a young woman has a baby on their doorstep, they look after mother and son. Tom is ensnared by a greyhound-loving gold-digger who takes all his money. But George stays in the village, his medical student nephew saving the life of the baby after a fall. Slow.

RoC *Ruby Miller, Marguerite Allan, Annie Esmond, Patrick Barr, Joan Wyndham, Johnny Singer, Billy Holland, Vi Kaley, Norman Pierce, Ben Williams.*

GENERAL JOHN REGAN (1933)   4

Dir *Henry Edwards*. Prod *Herbert Wilcox*. Scr *Lenox Robinson, from the play by George A. Birmingham*. Ph *Cyril Bristow, G.F. Stegmann*. PC *British and Dominions*. Dis *United Artists. 74 mins. Cert U*

Genial Irish comedy, partly shot on location, that marked the last screen appearance of the great silent star *Chrissie White*, wife of star/director *Henry Edwards*. The plot has Dr O'Grady (*Edwards*) inventing an imaginary celebrity for the benefit of an American newspaper magnate (*Ben Welden*) in order to put the tiny village of Ballymoy on the map.

RoC *Pegeen Mair, W.G. Fay, Fred O'Donovan, David Horne, Denis O'Neil, Eugene Leahy, George Callaghan, Mary O'Farrell.*

A GENTLEMAN OF PARIS (1931)   4

Dir *Sinclair Hill*. Prod *Michael Balcon*. Scr *Sewell Collins, Sidney Gilliat, from a novel by Niranjan Pal*. Ph *Mutz Greenbaum*. PC and Dis *Gaumont. 76 mins. Cert A*

Old-fashioned drama but still powerful. A respected Paris judge (*Arthur Wontner*), in private life a philanderer, witnesses a murder under circumstances he would rather conceal. In time, he has to try the case. The accused is his former mistress (*Phyllis Konstam*) and the jury finds her guilty. Instead of sentencing her, the judge at last reveals the truth, at the expense of his career.

RoC *Hugh Williams, Vanda Greville, Sybil Thorndike, George Merritt, Arthur Goullet, Frederick Lloyd, George de Warfaz, Florence Wood, Millicent Wolff, Ellen Pollock, Flora Robson, Peter Lawford, Frederick Burtwell, Joan Pereira, Hector Abbas.*

GENTLEMAN'S AGREEMENT (1935)   1

Dir *George Pearson*. Prod *Anthony Havelock-Allan*. Scr *Basil Mason, from a story by Jennifer Howard*. PC and Dis *British and Dominions/Paramount British. 71 mins. Cert A*

Aimless romantic comedy about two young men, one a wealthy waster, the other a down-and-out, who exchange social positions. The latter is suspected of having business acumen, and makes good, while the former falls in love with an out-of-work typist (*Vivien Leigh*'s first leading role). Reminiscent of Hollywood's 1983 film *Trading Places*.

RoC *Frederick Peisley, Antony Holles, David Horne, Vera Bogetti, S. Victor Stanley, Ronald Shiner, Kate Saxon.*

A GENTLEMAN'S GENTLEMAN (1939)   2

Dir *Roy William Neill*. Prod *Jerome Jackson*. Scr *Austin Melford, Elizabeth Meehan*. Ph *Basil Emmott*. PC and Dis *Warner Bros. 70 mins. Cert U*

Judy (*Patricia Hilliard*) accompanies an elderly man to a dance and, when he passes out, thinks he's dead. Her friends Tony and Bassy (*Peter Coke, David Hutcheson*) hope that Heppelwhite (*Eric Blore*), Tony's resourceful butler, can help – but, after bringing the old man to, Heppelwhite tells them he's been poisoned, planning a little blackmail. However, the butler meets a wealthy widow and not only saves his skin but marries into money. Unsuccessful star vehicle for popular character-man Blore.

RoC *Marie Lohr, David Burns, Ian MacLean, Wallace Evennett, (C.) Denier Warren.*

GET OFF MY FOOT (1935)   2

Dir *William Beaudine*. Prod *Irving Asher*. Scr *Frank Launder, Robert Edmunds*. Ph *Basil Emmott*. PC *Warner Bros*. Dis *First National. 82 mins. Cert A*

First solo starring vehicle for 'cheeky chappie' *Max Miller* has the benefit only of fast-paced direction. He plays a Smithfield meat porter who thinks he has drowned a man and flees London, eventually becoming a butler. When he inherits a fortune, his 'family' plan to marry him off to their daughter. But he prefers the maid.

RoC *Chili Bouchier, Jane Carr, Norma Varden, Morland Graham, Anthony Hankey, Vera Bogetti, Reginald Purdell, Wally Patch, John Devereaux.*

GET YOUR MAN (1934)   2

Dir and Prod *George King*. Scr *George Dewhurst, from a play by Louis Verneuil*. PC and Dis *British and Dominions/Paramount British. 67 mins. Cert A*

Two business rivals plan a merger and, to cement it, marriage between their respective son (*Sebastian Shaw*) and niece (*Kay Walsh*). But the youngsters ruin their plans by running off with other partners. Good cast can't give much boost to this artificial comedy.

RoC *Dorothy Boyd, Clifford Heatherley, Hugh E. Wright, Helen Ferrers, Rex Harrison, Charles Barrett.*

THE GHOST GOES WEST (1935)   5

Dir *René Clair*. Prod *Alexander Korda*. Scr *Robert E. Sherwood, Clair, Geoffrey Kerr, from a story by Eric Keown*. Ph *Harold Rosson*. PC *London Films*. Dis *United Artists. 90 mins (USA: 85 mins). Cert A*

Delightfully whimsical comedy about a seventeenth-century Scottish ghost (*Robert Donat*) who cannot rest in peace until a member of a rival clan has conceded the ghost's clan's supremacy. An impoverished twentieth-century descendant (also Donat) sells the ghost's castle to a rich American (*Eugene Pallette*) and in America, the ghost finally finds the man he needs, while the descendant marries the new owner's daughter (*Jean Parker*).

RoC *Elsa Lanchester, Ralph Bunker, Everley Gregg, Patricia Hilliard, Morton Selten, Chili Bouchier, Mark Daly, Herbert Lomas, Elliot Mason, Jack Lambert, Hay Petrie, Colin Lesslie, Richard Mackie, J. Neil More, Neil Lester, Quinton McPherson, Arthur Seaton, David Keir.*

THE GHOST TRAIN (1931)   4

Dir *Walter Forde*. Prod *Michael Balcon*. Scr *Angus Macphail, Lajos Biro, Sidney Gilliat (uncredited), from the play by Arnold Ridley*. Ph *Leslie Rowson*. PC *Gainsborough*. Dis *W and F. 72 mins. Cert U*

Second of three film versions of Arnold Ridley's famous comedy-thriller about a ghost train that rattles through the isolated Fal Vale station at night. The 'silly ass' (*Jack Hulbert*) of the passengers stranded at Fal Vale for the night turns out to be a detective who unmasks the stationmaster (*Donald Calthrop*) as a fire-arms smuggler.

RoC *Cicely Courtneidge, Ann Todd, Cyril Raymond, Angela Baddeley, Allan Jeayes, Henry Caine, Tracy Holmes, Carol Coombe, Walter Forde.*

THE GHOUL (1933)   2

Dir *T. Hayes Hunter*. Prod *Michael Balcon*. Scr *Frank King, Leonard Hines, L. DuGarde Peach, Roland Pertwee, John Hastings Turner, Rupert Downing, from a novel by King*. Ph *Günther Krampf*. PC *Gaumont-British*. Dis *W and F. 79 mins. (USA: 73 mins). Cert A*

What should have been a triumphant return for *Boris Karloff* to his native Britain proved a major disappointment. It's a slow chiller about a professor (*Karloff*) who believes that a jewel that was once stolen from an Egyptian tomb will give him immortality. As he dies, his servant steals the gem, but the professor rises from the tomb and exacts his revenge.

RoC *Ernest Thesiger, Dorothy Hyson, Cedric Hardwicke, Anthony Bushell, Ralph Richardson, Harold Huth, D. A. Clarke-Smith, Kathleen Harrison, Jack Raine.*

Boris Karloff and Kathleen Harrison in The Ghoul *(1933)*

GIPSY BLOOD (1931)   2

(USA: *Carmen*)

Dir *G. B. Samuelson*. Prod *Cecil Lewis*. Scr *Lewis, Walter C. Mycroft, from a novel by Pros-*

per Mérimée and an opera by Georges Bizet. Ph James Wilson, Philip Grindrod. PC BIP. Dis Wardour. 79 mins. Cert U
Ineffective version of Bizet's *Carmen*, with *Thomas Burke* as the Spanish soldier who deserts both his sweetheart and the army for love of a gipsy-girl (*Marguerite Namara*). He kills for her, and dies for her.
RoC *Lester Matthews, Lance Fairfax, Mary Clare, D. Hay Petrie, Dennis Wyndham, Lewin Mannering, Winifred Dalle, Victor Fairlie, Esmé Beringer, Virginia Perry, Madam Else, Brunelleschi, Charles Morton.*

THE GIRL FROM MAXIM'S (1933)   [3]
Dir *Alexander Korda.* Prod *Korda, Ludovico Toeplitz.* Scr *Harry Graham, Arthur Wimperis, from the play by Georges Feydeau.* Ph *Georges Périnal.* PC *London Films.* Dis *United Artists.* 82 mins (later 79). Cert A. Bilingual versions
French farce with music, set at the turn of the century in Paris, where a middle-aged surgeon, Petypon (*Leslie Henson*) is unwittingly drawn into an intrigue with the notorious La Môme (*Frances Day*), singer at Maxim's nightclub. The singer is mistaken for the surgeon's wife, and they are invited to an elegant party together – at which Petypon's real wife (*Lady Tree*) turns up.
RoC *George Grossmith, Stanley Holloway, Evan Thomas, Gertrude Musgrove, Desmond Jeans, Eric Portman.*

Frances Day and Leslie Henson in The Girl from Maxim's *(1933)*

THE GIRL IN POSSESSION (1934)   [4]
Dir and Scr *Monty Banks.* Prod *Irving Asher.* PC and Dis *Warner Bros.* 72 mins. Cert U
Sprightly comedy in which Eve, an American (*Laura la Plante*) is duped by confidence tricksters into believing she has inherited an English stately home. Finding that the real owner, Sir Mortimer (*Henry Kendall*) is nearly penniless, she uses her charm to help him sell it to some Americans – then finds that some bonds she owns, thought to be of little value, are worth a fortune.
RoC *Claude Hulbert, Bernard Nedell, Monty Banks, Millicent Wolf (f), Ernest Sefton, Charles Paton, Charlotte Parry.*

THE GIRL IN THE CROWD (1934)   [4]
Dir and Scr *Michael Powell.* Prod *Irving Asher.* PC *Warner Bros.* Dis *First National.* 52 mins. Cert U

Pretty silly comedy about bachelor Bob (*Harold French*), who takes a married friend's advice: choose 'a girl from the crowd'. The girl he chooses happens to be his friend's wife, whom he has never seen. Trouble with the police follows and in the end the friend is forced to bail Bob out of jail. . . .
RoC *Patricia Hilliard, Barry Clifton, Googie Withers, Clarence Blakiston, Margaret Gunn, Richard Littledale, Phyllis Morris, Patric Knowles, Eve Lister, Betty Lynne, John Wood, Elizabeth Vaughan, Marjorie Corbett, Brenda Lawless, Barbara Waring, Melita Bell.*

THE GIRL IN THE FLAT (1934)   [2]
Dir and Prod *Redd Davis.* Scr *Violet Powell, from a story by Evelyn Winch.* Ph *Percy Strong.* PC and Dis *British and Dominions/Paramount British.* 66 mins. Cert A
Mavis (*Belle Chrystall*), a Devon girl engaged to a middle-aged barrister (*Stewart Rome*), spends a day in London and is persuaded by a friend, Girda (*Vera Bogetti*) to go to a party in Chelsea. The host is shot dead while alone with Mavis, who panics and flees. She is blackmailed by Girda, who is the real killer, but rescued by her fiancé whose experience ensures justice is done.
RoC *Jane Millican, John Turnbull, Noel Shannon.*

THE GIRL IN THE NIGHT (1931)   [3]
Dir and Prod *Henry Edwards.* Scr *Edwin Greenwood.* PC *Henry Edwards.* Dis *Wardour.* 65 mins. Cert U
A wild and rainy night: Billy (*Henry Edwards*) almost runs down, then gives a lift to Cecilie (*Dorothy Boyd*), a girl on the run from a false theft charge. The two take refuge in an apparently unoccupied house and find themselves in the middle of an extraordinary adventure which involves diamond smugglers, a gang of crooks and a scientist experimenting with dynamite.
RoC *Sam Livesey, Reginald Bach, Charles Paton, Diana Wilson, Eric Maturin, Harvey Braban.*

THE GIRL IN THE TAXI (1937)   [2]
Dir *André Berthomieu.* Prod *Kurt Bernhardt, Eugene Tuscherer.* Scr *Austin Melford, Val Valentine, Fritz Gottfurcht.* Ph *Roy Clark.* PC *British Unity.* Dis *Associated British.* 72 mins. Cert A. Bilingual versions
Over-familiar musical farce about a sugar daddy (*Lawrence Grossmith*) and his son (*Mackenzie Ward*) who both fall for the same (married) cabaret star (*Frances Day*). Both end up by spending the night in jail, where the 'daddy' finds his wife (*Helen Haye*) has known about his nocturnal activities for ages.
RoC *Henri Garat, Jean Gillie, Ben Field, Albert Whelan, Lawrence Hanray, Joan Kemp-Welch, John Deverell.*

A GIRL MUST LIVE (1939)   [4]
Dir *Carol Reed.* Prod *Edward Black.* Scr *Frank Launder, Austin Melford, Michael Pertwee (uncredited), from the novel by Emery Bonet.* Ph *Jack Cox.* PC *Gainsborough.* Dis *20th Century-Fox.* 92 mins. Cert A

Or: *Gold Diggers of Bloomsbury.* Leslie (*Margaret Lockwood*), fleeing from the Swiss finishing school for which her parents can no longer pay, poses as an actress's daughter and lands up at a theatrical boarding house where she meets Gloria and Clytie (*Renée Houston, Lilli Palmer*). She snaffles the young Earl of Pangborough (*Hugh Sinclair*) from under their noses and, by exposing Clytie's blackmail scheme, is accepted by his family.
RoC *George Robey, Naunton Wayne, Moore Marriott, Mary Clare, David Burns, Kathleen Harrison, Drusilla Wills, Wilson Coleman, Helen Haye, Frederick Burtwell, Martita Hunt, Muriel Aked, Joan White, Merle Tottenham, Kathleen Boutall, Michael Hordern.*

GIRLS PLEASE! (1934)   [3]
Dir *Jack Raymond.* Prod *Herbert Wilcox.* Scr *R. P. Weston, Bert Lee, Jack Marks.* PC *British and Dominions.* Dis *United Artists.* 73 mins. Cert A
Average *Sydney Howard* comedy (with music). Charged with keeping college girl Renée (*Jane Baxter*) and her boyfriend (*Edward Underdown*) apart, gym instructor Trampleasure (*Howard*) has a hectic time frustrating the ruses of the couple to meet. Circumstances ultimately conspire to make him masquerade as the college's headmistress!
RoC *Meriel Forbes, Peter Gawthorne, Lena Halliday, Cecily Oates, Sybil Arundale, Moore Marriott, Neva Carr-Glyn, Edna Earle.*

GIRLS WILL BE BOYS (1934)   [4]
Dir *Marcel Varnel.* Prod *Walter C. Mycroft.* Scr *Kurt Siodmak, Clifford Grey, Roger Burford, from a play by Siodmak.* Ph *Claude Friese-Greene, Ronald Neame,* PC *BIP.* Dis *Wardour.* 70 mins. Cert U
Unpretentious, amusing comedy, with an attractive performance from *Dolly Haas* as the girl-boy. The woman-hating Duke of Bridgewater sends for Pat, the heir he's never seen. But Pat is a girl, Patricia, who disguises herself as a boy and successfully carries on the deception before finally becoming engaged to the Duke's estate manager.
RoC *Cyril Maude, Esmond Knight, Irene Vanbrugh, Edward Chapman, Ronald Ward, Charles Paton, H. F. Maltby, Alfred Wellesley.*

THE GIRL WHO FORGOT (1939)   [2]
Dir *Adrian Brunel.* Prod *Daniel Birt, Louise Birt.* Scr *Louise Birt.* PC *Daniel Birt.* Dis *Butchers.* 79 mins. Cert U
On the verge of a nervous breakdown, Leonora (*Elizabeth Allan*) loses her memory while on her way to see her parents off to Iraq. She goes to a hotel and meets Tony (*Ralph Michael*). His wealthy fiancée (*Enid Stamp-Taylor*) sees her as a threat and shunts her on to Mrs Badger (*Muriel Aked*), who runs a bogus charity racket. Thanks to Mrs Badger, Leonora gets arrested. She is rescued by her parents, whose plane crash-landed, and marries Tony. Uneven yarn.
RoC *Basil Radford, Jeanne de Casalis, David Keir.*

GIVE HER A RING (1934)   4

Dir *Arthur B. Woods.* Prod *Walter C. Mycroft.* Scr *Clifford Grey, Ernst Wolff, Marjorie Deans, Wolfgang Wilhelm, from a play by H. Rosenfeld.* Ph *Claude Friese-Greene, Ronald Neame.* PC *BIP.* Dis *Pathé.* 80 mins. Cert U

A bright frolic with some tuneful music. Two girls get their dates mixed up, so that Trude (*Zelma O'Neal*) gets singer Otto (*Erik Rhodes*), while Karen (*Wendy Barrie*) finds herself paired up with own boss (*Clifford Mollison*). Romances follow after sundry complications. Set in Denmark.

RoC *Bertha Belmore, Olive Blakeney, Nadine March, Jimmy Godden, Syd Crossley, Richard Hearne, Stewart Granger, The Diamond Brothers, Maurice Winnick and His Ciro's Club Band.*

Stewart Granger in Give Her a Ring *(1934)*

GLAMOROUS NIGHT (1937)   2

Dir *Brian Desmond Hurst.* Prod *Walter C. Mycroft.* Scr *Dudley Leslie, Hugh Brooke, William Freshman, from the musical play by Ivor Novello.* Ph *Fritz Arno Wagner.* PC and Dis *Associated British.* 81 mins. Cert U

A king loves a gipsy maiden, and is plotted against by his prime minister who is eventually overthrown and disgraced, thanks to an army of gipsies led by an opera singer who is a lifetime friend of the king. Very dated musical simply doesn't convince in dramatic terms.

LP *Mary Ellis, Otto Kruger, Victor Jory, Barry Mackay, Trefor Jones, Maire O'Neill, Antony Holles, Charles Carson, Felix Aylmer, Finlay Currie, Jeanne Carpenter.*

GLAMOUR (1931)   1

Dir *Seymour Hicks, Harry Hughes.* Prod and Scr *Hicks.* PC *BIP.* Dis *Wardour.* 71 mins. Cert A

A society lady (*Margot Grahame*) is attracted by a middle-aged actor (*Seymour Hicks*). Her father, who knows the actor well, persuades him to disillusion his daughter, whom he wishes to make a wealthy marriage. The actor does so, and by so doing returns to a woman who had always loved him. Poor stuff.

RoC *Ellaline Terriss, Basil Gill, A. Bromley Davenport, Beverley Nichols, Clifford Heatherley, Naomi Jacob, David Hawthorne, Betty Hicks, Philip Hewland, Charles Paton, Arthur Stratton, Margery Binner, Eric Marshall, Irene Potter, Molly Edmunds, David Miller.*

GLAMOUR GIRL (1938)   2

Dir *Arthur Woods.* Prod *William Collier.* Scr *John Meehan Jr, Tom Phipps.* Ph *Basil Emmott.* PC and Dis *Warner Bros.* 68 mins. Cert U

Gene Gerrard's comedy talents are submerged here in the role of a conceited, quarrelsome photographer. Leaving his partner in the lurch, he attempts to become famous as a painter, but fails. His long-suffering partner takes him back and, in the bespectacled secretary (*Lesley Brook*) who adores him, the photographer finds the perfect model – and the perfect wife.

RoC *Ross Landon, Betty Lynne, Leslie Weston, Robert Rendel, Dennis Arundell, James Carew, Jimmy Godden.*

A GLIMPSE OF PARADISE (1934)   2

Dir *Ralph Ince.* Prod *Irving Asher.* Scr *Michael Barringer.* Ph *Basil Emmott.* PC *Warner Bros.* Dis *First National.* 56 mins. Cert A

Ex-convict Jim Bigsworth (*George Carney*) seeks out his long-lost daughter (*Eve Lister*), but her foster-parents pretend she is dead to keep them from meeting. Jim not only finds the girl, but saves her from a blackmailer and ensures her future happiness, all without her realizing who he was.

RoC *Robert Cochran, Winifred Oughton, Roddy Hughes, Katie Johnson, Wally Patch, Margaret Yarde, D. J. Williams, Fred Groves, Reg Marcus, Sydney Monckton, Claude Horton, Fletcher Lightfoot, Eve Llewellyn, Phyllis Baker, Quinton McPherson.*

GOING GAY (1933)   4
(USA: *Kiss Me Goodbye*)

Dir *Carmine Gallone.* Prod *Frank A. Richardson.* Scr *Selwyn Jepson, Jack Marks, K.R.G. Browne.* Ph *W. Goldberger.* PC *Windsor.* Dis *Sterling.* 79 mins *(later 72).* Cert U

Musical comedy praised for its air of 'friendly spontaneity'. Two friends, Jack and Jim (*Arthur Riscoe, Naunton Wayne*) go to Vienna. They both fall for Grete (*Magda Schneider*) who has talent both as a dancer and opera singer, and become rivals in their efforts to make her a star and win her affection.

RoC *Grete Natzler, Joe Hayman, Wilfred Noy, Ruth Maitland, Bertha Belmore, Brenda Senton, Victor Fairley, Richard Wydler.*

GOING STRAIGHT (1933)   1

Dir *John Rawlins.* Prod *Irving Asher.* PC and Dis *Warner Bros.* 51 mins. Cert U

Desperate comedy in which Peggy Edwards (*Moira Lynd*), secretary to a wealthy woman (*Helen Ferrers*) obtains jobs for two ex-convicts as butler and chauffeur. When the house is burgled, the ex-cons are suspected, but clear themselves by exposing the real thieves.

RoC *Hal Walters, Joan Marion, Tracy Holmes, Huntley Wright, Eric Stanley, George Merritt, Gilbert Davis.*

THE GOLDEN CAGE (1933)   4

Dir *Ivar Campbell.* Prod *Norman Loudon.* Scr *D. B. Wyndham-Lewis, Pamela Frankau, from the play by Lady Trowbridge.* PC *Sound City.* Dis *M-G-M.* 62 mins. Cert A

Venetia (*Anne Grey*), although going with Paul (*Anthony Kimmins*), who loves her, marries a nobleman (*Frank Cellier*) for wealth and position. Shortly, Venetia revives her affair, to the despair of Paul's new girlfriend (*Jillian Sande*). Paul and Venetia plan to run off together, but at the last moment she finds she cannot leave her 'golden cage'. Ironically, Paul then finds he has been left a large sum of money. Affecting romantic drama.

RoC *Mackenzie Ward, Cecil Parker, Andrea Malandrinos.*

GOODBYE MR CHIPS! (1939)   6

Dir *Sam Wood.* Prod *Victor Saville.* Scr *R. C. Sherriff, Claudine West, Eric Maschwitz, Sidney Franklin, from the novel by James Hilton.* Ph *Frederick A. Young.* PC and Dis *MGM British.* 113 mins. Cert U

Brimming with humanity, this four-handkerchief look at a schoolmaster's life won an Oscar for *Robert Donat* in a fiercely competitive year. Aged Mr Chipping (*Donat*) recalls his days at Brookfield, a boys' public school, from 1870 to 1928. His early difficulties and unpopularity. His disappointments. His crucial meeting with Katherine (*Greer Garson*) whom he marries and who helps him achieve a housemastership. Her death in childbirth. The many friendships with pupils and his retirement. His temporary headship in the First World War. Dying, he remembers 'all my boys'. . . .

RoC *Terry Kilburn, John Mills, Paul von Hernried (Paul Henreid), Judith Furse, Lyn Harding, Milton Rosmer, Frederick Leister, Louise Hampton, Austin Trevor, David Tree, Edmund Breon, Jill Furse, Guy Middleton, Nigel Stock, Scott Sunderland, Peter Gawthorne, Ronald Ward, Patrick Ludlow, Simon Lack, Caven Watson.*

Peter Gawthorne and Robert Donat in Goodbye Mr Chips! *(1939)*

THE GOOD COMPANIONS (1933)   4

Dir *Victor Saville.* Prod *T. A. Welsh, George Pearson.* Scr *W. P. Lipscomb, Angus Macphail, Ian Dalrymple, from the novel and play by J. B. Priestley.* Ph *Bernard Knowles.* PC *Gaumont-Welsh-Pearson.* Dis *Ideal.* 113 mins. Cert U

Phenomenally popular musical in which three people from different walks of life – a Yorkshire joiner (*Edmund Gwenn*), a middle-aged spinster with a small legacy (*Mary Glynne*) and a disillusioned music teacher (*John Gielgud*) –

become 'angels' to a failing concert party. With much hard work, it becomes a success and its young leading lady (*Jessie Matthews*) a star.
RoC *Percy Parsons, A.W. Baskcomb, Dennis Hoey, Viola Compton, Richard Dolman, Margery Binner, D.A. Clarke-Smith, Florence Gregson, Frank Pettingell, Alex Fraser, Finlay Currie, Ivor Barnard, Olive Sloane, Muriel Aked, J. Fisher White, Jack Hawkins, Max Miller, Cyril Smith, Lawrence Hanray, Annie Esmond, Ben Field, George Zucco, Arnold Riches, Wally Patch, Barbara Gott, Margaret Yarde, Pollie Emery, Hugh E. Wright, Frederick Piper, Jane Cornell, John Burch, Harold Meade, Mignon O'Doherty, Henry Crocker, Daphne Scorer, Jimmy Bishop, Gilbert Davis, Henry Adnes, John Clifford, Violet Lane, George Manship, Robert Victor, J.B. Spendlove, Mai Bacon, Tom Shale, Mike Johnson, Henry Ainley (narrator).*

GOOD MORNING, BOYS (1937)   4
(USA: *Where There's a Will*)
Dir *Marcel Varnel*. Prod *Edward Black*. Scr *Marriott Edgar, Val Guest*. Ph *Arthur Crabtree*. PC *Gainsborough*. Dis *Gaumont-British*. 79 mins. Cert A
The boys at St Michael's spend their time gambling, smoking, drinking, betting and setting traps for their headmaster, Dr Twist (*Will Hay*). A governor calls for Twist to resign, but the accidental finding of a forthcoming French exam paper means all the boys pass their exam, and win a trip to Paris. Here, they assist in the theft of the Mona Lisa, but eventually retrieve it and clear the head. Slick comedy, remade in 1953 as *Top of the Form*.
RoC *Lilli Palmer, Graham Moffatt, Charles Hawtrey, Will Hay Jr, Martita Hunt, Mark Daly, Peter Gawthorne, Basil McGrail, Peter Godfrey, Fewlass Llewellyn, (C.) Denier Warren, Charles McBain, Terry Richardson.*

GOODNIGHT VIENNA (1932)   5
(USA: *Magic Night*)
Dir and Prod *Herbert Wilcox*. Scr *Uncredited, from a radio play by Holt Marvel and George Posford*. Ph *F.A. Young*. PC *British and Dominions*. Dis *W and F*. 75 mins. Cert U
Much-loved musical, the title song from which gave *Jack Buchanan* one of his biggest hits. He plays Max, an Austrian army captain in 1913, engaged to a countess. He falls in love with Viki (*Anna Neagle*), a flowergirl – then war breaks out. After the war, they meet again: Viki has become a famous singer, while Max is a shoe salesman. But they find their love has not changed.
RoC *Gina Malo, Clive Currie, William Kendall, Joyce Bland, Gibb McLaughlin, Herbert Carrick, Clifford Heatherley, O.B. Clarence, Peggy Cartwright, Muriel Aked, Aubrey Fitzgerald.*

THE GOOD OLD DAYS (1939)   3
Dir *Roy William Neill*. Prod *Jerome Jackson*. Scr *Austin Melford, John Dighton*. Ph *Basil Emmott*. PC *Warner Bros*. Dis *First National*. 79 mins. Cert U
1840: Alexander the Greatest (*Max Miller*) and his travelling players arrange, thanks to win-

ning a pie-eating contest, to put on (illegal) shows at the King's Head tavern. The proprietor of the rival Eagle inn informs the police. Alexander, thrown in the stocks, is faced with imprisonment but wins through by collecting, after a rooftop chase, a fat reward offered for a nobleman's son kidnapped by a mad chimney-sweep. Nice idea doesn't quite work: Miller remains obdurately modern.
RoC *Hal Walters, Kathleen Gibson, H.F. Maltby, Anthony Shaw, Martita Hunt, Allan Jeayes, Sam Wilkinson, Roy Emerton, Phyllis Monkman, Ian Fleming.*

Phyllis Monkman and Max Miller in The Good Old Days (*1939*)

GRAND FINALE (1936)   1
Dir *Ivar Campbell*. Prod *Anthony Havelock-Allan*. Scr *Vera Allison*. PC and Dis *British and Dominions/Paramount British*. 71 mins. Cert A
Dud comedy-romance about a journalist pursuing a model who is in turn engaged to a pompous newspaper proprietor. All works out to everyone's satisfaction when the newspaperman's ex-wife, an actress whose other ex-husband is chasing *her*, wins him back, leaving the mannequin free to marry the reporter. Clear?
LP *Guy Newall, Mary Glynne, Glen Alyn, Eric Cowley, Douglas Rhodes, Philip Holles, Dorothy Dewhurst, Kim Peacock, Afrique.*

GRAND PRIX (1934)   3
Dir and Scr *St John L. Clowes*. Prod *L.S. Stock*. PC *Clowes and Stock*. Dis *Columbia*. 71 mins. Cert U
Longtime partners Halford (*Milton Rosmer*) and MacIntyre (*Peter Gawthorne*) are in the motor-racing business. Halford's son Jack (*John Stuart*), who loves MacIntyre's daughter Jean (*Jillian Sande*) invents a new kind of racing-car, but MacIntyre is killed testing it. Jack has to prove both himself and the car to win Jean back, and does so by winning a big race.
RoC *Wilson Coleman, Lawrence Anderson.*

THE GREAT BARRIER (1937)   5
(USA: *Silent Barriers*)
Dir *Milton Rosmer, Geoffrey Barkas*. (Associate) Prod *Gunther Stapenhorst*. Scr *Ralph Spence, Michael Barringer, Rosmer, from a novel by Alan Sullivan*. Ph *Arthur Crabtree,*

Barry Mackay, Lilli Palmer and Richard Arlen in The Great Barrier (*1937*)

Glen MacWilliams, Robert Martin. PC and Dis *Gaumont-British*. 83 mins. Cert U
Vigorous account of the building of the Canadian Pacific Railway, shot on location in British Columbia, climaxing with the battle against the Rocky Mountains themselves. This is won by the builders, led by Hickey (*Richard Arlen*), an ex-gambler, just as the mining team, desperate with lack of food and success, prepares to revolt.
RoC *Antoinette Cellier, Barry Mackay, Lilli Palmer, Jock McKay, Ben Welden, Roy Emerton, J. Farrell MacDonald, Reginald Barlow, Arthur Loft, Henry Victor, Ernest Sefton, Frank McGlynn Sr.*

THE GREAT DEFENDER (1934)   4
Dir *Thomas Bentley*. Prod *Walter C. Mycroft*. Scr *Marjorie Deans, Paul Perez*. Ph *John J. Cox*. PC *BIP*. Dis *Wardour*. 74 mins. Cert U
A husband (*Arthur Margetson*) is arrested for the murder of his mistress (*Jeanne Stuart*) after his wife (*Margaret Bannerman*) had put a private eye on his trail. Convinced of her husband's innocence, the wife provides him with an alibi, and persuades a famous, though ailing counsel (*Matheson Lang*) to defend. His brilliance leads to the unmasking of the real killer, but the strain breaks his failing health and he dies. Solid drama with dominant performance by Lang.
RoC *Richard Bird, J. Fisher White, Sam Livesey, Lawrence Hanray, O.B. Clarence, Mary Jerrold, Frank Atkinson, Kathleen Harrison, Jimmy Godden, Hal Gordon, (C.) Denier Warren, Gladys Hamer, Robert Horton, Alec Fraser.*

THE GREAT GAME (1930)   4
Dir *Jack Raymond*. Prod *L'Estrange Fawcett*. Scr *W.P. Lipscomb, Ralph Gilbert Bettinson*. Ph *Basil Emmott*. PC and Dis *Gaumont*. 79 mins. Cert U
One of the most enjoyable of the handful of British football films, with many well-known players taking part in the usual sort of story about a small team who, despite mismanagement and problems with key players, contrive to win the FA Cup in the last reel.
LP *John Batten, Randle Ayrton, Renée Clama, Jack Cock, Kenneth Kove, Neil Kenyon, A.G. Poulton, Billy Blyth, Harry Bagge, Wally Patch, Rex Harrison, Lew Lake.*

THE GREAT GAY ROAD (1931)   4
Dir and Prod *Sinclair Hill*. Scr *Leslie Howard Gordon, from the novel by Tom Gallon*. Ph *Desmond Dickinson*. PC *Stoll*. Dis *Butchers*. 88 mins. Cert A
A remake of the 1921 film, with *Stewart Rome* in his original role as gentleman tramp Hilary Kite who returns to the home he left 20 years before and resumes his place in the family. He falls in love with his cousin Nancy (*Pat Paterson*) and his father wants them to marry. But Nancy is already engaged. Hilary returns to the road. . . .
RoC *Billy Milton, Frank Stanmore, Kate Cutler, Arthur Hardy, Hugh E. Wright, Frederick Lloyd, Ethel Warwick, The Kirkby Sisters, Wally Patch, Charles Paton, Bruce Winston, Petra Charpentier, Alf Cordery, Aubrey Fitzgerald*.

GREAT STUFF (1933)   2
Dir *Leslie Hiscott*. Prod *Herbert Smith*. Scr *Michael Barringer*. PC *British Lion*. Dis *Fox*. 50 mins. Cert U
Self-made millionaire Bert Winkle and his wife try to prevent their daughter (*Betty Astell*) from marrying Archie (*Henry Kendall*) whom they fear is after their money. To test him, they pose as crooks planning to rob their own house. To their surprise, he offers to join them. However, Archie is the means of saving their valuables from real crooks – and so wins them over.
RoC *Alfred Wellesley, Barbara Gott, Hal Walters, Ernest Sefton, Gladys Hamer, Ernest Childerstone*.

GREEK STREET (1930)   4
(USA: *Latin Love*)
Dir *Sinclair Hill*. Prod *L'Estrange Fawcett*. Scr *Ralph Gilbert Bettinson, Leslie Howard Gordon*. Ph *Percy Strong*. PC and Dis *Gaumont*. 85 mins. Cert A
Polished musical with some Soho atmosphere, about café owner Rikki (*William Freshman*) and his singer (*Sari Maritza*). She becomes a star through a nightclub owner (*Martin Lewis*) who instals her in a plush apartment and provokes some jealousy before she is reunited with Rikki in a happy final fadeout.
RoC *Renée Clama, Arthur Hambling, Bert*

Sari Maritza and William Freshman in Greek Street *(1930)*

Coote, Bruce Winston, Stanelli, Rex Maurice, Peter Haddon, Max Rivers' Trocadero Girls.

THE GREEN COCKATOO/FOUR DARK HOURS (1937)   3
Dir *William Cameron Menzies, William K. Howard* (uncredited). Prod *Howard, Robert T. Kane*. Scr *Edward O. Berkman, Arthur Wimperis, from a story and screenplay by Graham Greene*. Ph *Mutz Greenbaum*. PC *New World/Fox British*. Dis *20th Century-Fox*. 65 mins. Cert A
Completed as *Four Dark Hours* in 1937, and shown as such in America, though not released in Britain until 1939 as *The Green Cockatoo*. The delay is puzzling as it's a tough little thriller that provides its star (*John Mills*) with a James Cagney-style role. Eileen (*René Ray*), from the west of England, runs into trouble in London in the form of the dying Dave (*Robert Newton*), stabbed by the racetrack crooks he double-crossed. Dave's brother Jim (*Mills*), an entertainer, overcomes his initial suspicion of Eileen to help her bring the crooks to book.
RoC *Charles Oliver, Bruce Seton, Julien Vedey, Allan Jeayes, Frank Atkinson, David Horne, Googie Withers, Aileen Marson, Alf Goddard, Clifford Heatherly, Albert Whelan Jr, Harry Terry, Stephanie James, Billy Shine, Martin Walker, Orlando Martins*.

THE GREEN PACK (1934)   3
Dir *T. Hayes Hunter*. Prod *Herbert Smith*. Scr *John Hunter, from a play by Edgar Wallace*. Ph *Alex Bryce*. PC and Dis *British Lion*. 73 mins. Cert A
Vigorous and slightly offbeat thriller. An unscrupulous businessman (*Hugh Miller*) takes on three friends (*John Stuart, Garry Marsh, Michael Shepley*) as equal partners in a goldmining venture in Africa. Finding that he intends to swindle them, the trio draws lots to decide who shall kill him. The villain dies – but the verdict returned is suicide.
RoC *Aileen Marson, J. H. Roberts, Antony Holles, Percy Walsh*.

GUEST OF HONOUR (1934)   2
Dir *George King*. Prod *Irving Asher*. Scr *W. Scott Darling, from a play by F. Anstey*. PC and Dis *Warner Bros*. 53 mins. Cert U
Although based on the successful comedy play *The Man from Blankley's*, there's little originality in material or treatment of this story of a seemingly-foppish lord (*Henry Kendall*) who poses as a professional dinner guest in order to expose a blackmailer and his schemes.
RoC *Miki Hood, Edward Chapman, Margaret Yarde, Eve Gray, Hay Plumb, Joan Playfair, Helen Ferrers, Cecil Humphreys, Louis Goodrich, Florence Woodgate, Bruce Gordon*.

GUILT (1930)   2
Dir, Prod and Scr *Reginald Fogwell*. PC *Reginald Fogwell*. Dis *Paramount*. 66 mins. Cert A
Anne Barrett (*Anne Grey*), the actress wife of a playwright (*James Carew*), hides her affair with an actor (*Harold Huth*) under the cloak of her husband's new play. But guilt eventually

drives her to admit the truth and effect a reconciliation; pretty ordinary melodrama.
RoC *Rex Curtin, James Fenton, Anne Smiley, Ernest Lester*.

GUILTY MELODY (1936)   2
Dir *Richard Potter*. Prod *Friedrich Deutschmeister*. Scr *G. F. Salmony, from the novel by Hans Rehfisch*. Ph *Jan Stallich*. PC *Franco-London*. Dis *Associated British*. 75 mins. Cert A. Bilingual versions
Rather slow and strange mixture in which spy and musical plots get in each other's way. Carter (*John Loder*), a British intelligence officer, is attracted to singer Marguerite (*Gitta Alpar*). Her husband (*Nils Asther*), an impresario, is actually a spy who sends coded messages on her records. It's Marguerite who is eventually arrested, but Carter proves her innocence.
RoC *Don Alcaide, Coral Brown(e), Ethel Griffies, Arty Ash, Robert English, F. Rendell, Clifford Buckton*.

THE GUV'NOR (1935)   3
(USA: *Mister Hobo*)
Dir *Milton Rosmer*. Prod *Michael Balcon*. Scr *Maude Howell, Guy Bolton, from a story by Paul Lafitte*. Ph *Mutz Greenbaum*. PC and Dis *Gaumont-British*. 88 mins. Cert U
George Arliss slumming it with some difficulty as a tramp being tried for poaching when it's found that his name is that of a famous banking group. He is taken into the bank and, by a series of extraordinary chances, finds himself president. But he is being used by the retiring president in his plan to swindle a girl out of a valuable mine. 'The guv'nor' learns what's afoot and scotches the plot before returning with his friend Flit (*Gene Gerrard*) to the open road.
RoC *Viola Keats, Patric Knowles, Frank Cellier, George Hayes, Mary Clare, Henrietta Watson, (Howard) Marion Crawford, Mervyn Johns*.

GYPSY (1936)   2
Dir *Roy William Neill*. Prod *Irving Asher*. Scr *Brock Williams, Terence Rattigan, from a novel by Lady Eleanor Smith*. Ph *Basil Emmott*. PC and Dis *Warner Bros*. 78 mins. Cert A
Hassina (*Chili Bouchier*), a gipsy dancer, follows her beloved, Brazil (*Hugh Williams*), a lion tamer, to England. She cannot find him, and is taken in by middle-aged bachelor Alan (*Roland Young*), whose life she turns upside down. She leaves and gets a job in a nightclub, but Alan pursues and marries her, in spite of the fact that – known to him, but unknown to her – Brazil has been found. 'Not very interesting' remarked one contemporary reviewer.
RoC *Frederick Burtwell, Glen Alyn, Brian Buchel, Andrea Malandrinos, Victor Fairley, Emilio Colombo and his Tzigane Band*.

GYPSY MELODY (1936)   2
Dir *Edmond T. Gréville*. Prod *Leon Hepner, Emil E. Reinert*. Scr *Irving Leroy, Dan Weldon, from a screenplay by Alfred Rode*. Ph *Claude*

Friese-Greene. PC *British Artistic*. Dis *Wardour*. *77 mins. Cert A*
An uninspired British version of the 1935 French film *Juanita*. Imprisoned for wounding the referee in a fogbound duel, guards officer Danilo (*Alfred Rode*) escapes and falls for a gipsy dancer. Together they join an orchestra which travels to London and enjoys great success, but on the way back their plane crashes in Danilo's duchy and he is arrested. All ends well when he is cleared, becomes Lord Chancellor and is married to his girl by gipsy rite.
RoC *Lupe Velez, Jerry Verno, Fred Duprez, Wyn Weaver, Raymond Lovell, Margaret Yarde, Monti de Lyle, Louis Darnley, Hector Abbas, G. de Joncourt.*

HAIL AND FAREWELL (1936) 4
Dir *Ralph Ince*. Prod *Paul Merzbach*. Scr *Reginald Purdell, John Dighton, Brock Williams*. Ph *Basil Emmott*. PC *Warner Bros*. Dis *First National. 74 mins. Cert A*
A prototype of 'shore leave' films, mostly entertaining comedy but with some touching scenes. A British troopship puts in to port and its men have only six hours before re-embarkation. The hours bring: tragedy to a colonel; for a sergeant-major, a taste of home that makes him thankful to be gone; for enlisted men, various joys and misadventures.
LP *Claude Hulbert, Reginald Purdell, Nicholas Hannen, Joyce Kennedy, Moira Reed, Bruce Lister, Ivan Samson, Wally Patch, Henry Caine, Marie Wright, Joyce Kirby, Helen Goss, Eve Lyntett.*

HANDLE WITH CARE (1935) 1
Dir *Redd Davis*. Prod *George King, Randall Faye*. Scr *Faye*. Ph *Geoffrey Faithfull*. PC *Embassy/Nettlefold*. Dis *Radio. 55 mins. Cert U*
'Extremely unfunny' farce about a couple of reformed crooks, a brace of spies and a country house wrestling match which one of the ex-crooks wins by taking a 'strength pill'.
LP *Molly Lamont, Jack Hobbs, James Finlayson, Henry Victor, Vera Bogetti, Margaret Yarde, Tonie Edgar Bruce, Stafford Hilliard.*

HAPPY (1933) 3
Dir and Prod *Fred (Friedrich) Zelnik*. Scr *Austin Melford, Stanley Lupino, Frank Launder, Jacques Bachrach, Alfred Halm, Karl Noti, Arthur Woods*. Ph *Claude Friese-Greene, Ronald Neame, Bryan Langley*. PC *BIP*. Dis *Wardour. 82 mins. Cert U*
English version of the German comedy-musical *Es war einmal ein Musikus*, set in Paris. Frank Brown (*Stanley Lupino*) is a jazzband conductor and songwriter, in which occupation he has no better luck than in trying to sell an invention to protect vehicles from car thieves.

He falls for a girl whose father is head of a car insurance company, poses as a millionaire to impress her and eventually manages to sell his invention.
RoC *Will Fyffe, Laddie Cliff, Dorothy Hyson, Harry Tate, Renée Gadd, Gus McNaughton, Jimmy Godden, Bertha Belmore, Hal Gordon, Elizabeth Vaughan, Norma Varden.*

HAPPY DAYS ARE HERE AGAIN (1936) 2
Dir *Norman Lee*. Prod *John Argyle*. Scr *Dan Birt, F.H. Bickerton, Alan Rennie*. PC *Argyle Talking Pictures*. Dis *Associated Producers and Distributors. 86 mins. Cert U*
Semi-autobiographical musical comedy, with the *Houston Sisters, Renée* and *Billie*, as Kitty and Mickey Seymour, who form a double act following the retirement of their parents. But they find the going tough and are forced to close their pierrot troupe. Success comes later, but each gets swollen-headed, and they fall out, only being brought back together through the good offices of Reg (*Billy Watts*), a booking agent. About as awkward as you'd suppose.
RoC *Harry Milton, Georgie Harris, Viola Compton, Shirley Houston, Sally McBride, Mark Stone, Ida Barr, Marie Kendall, Bert and Michael Kidd, Syd Seymour and His Mad Hatters, Herbert Cameron, Billie Dix, Tony Smythe.*

THE HAPPY ENDING (1931) 2
Dir *Millard Webb*. Prod *L'Estrange Fawcett*. Scr *H. Fowler Mear, Sidney Gilliat* (*uncredited*), *from the play by Ian Hay*. Ph *Percy Strong*. PC and Dis *Gaumont. 70 mins. Cert A*
Mildred (*Anne Grey*) is separated from her husband Denis (*George Barraud*) who roams the world. She has brought up her daughter to believe he died a noble death. The daughter never learns otherwise, as George makes an unsuccessful attempt to return to his wife's life and subsequently dies in hospital.
RoC *Benita Hume, Alf Goddard, Cyril Raymond, Daphne Courtenay, Alfred Drayton, Irene Russell.*

HAPPY EVER AFTER (1932) 3
Dir *Paul Martin, Robert Stevenson*. Prod *Erich Pommer*. Scr *Jack Hulbert, Douglas Furber, from a scenario by Walter Reisch, Billy Wilder*. PC *UFA*. Dis *W and F. 86 mins. Cert U. Trilingual versions*
Slight comedy-musical, made in Germany from an original which had starred Lilian Harvey (who repeated her role) and Willy Fritsch. In this English-language version, it's *Jack Hulbert* and *Sonnie Hale* as two window cleaners, both called Willie, in love with the same girl whom they help to stardom as a singer.
RoC *Cicely Courtneidge, Edward Chapman, Percy Parsons, Clifford Heatherley, Charles Redgie.*

THE HAPPY FAMILY (1936) 2
Dir *Maclean Rogers*. Prod *Herbert Smith*. Scr *Rogers, Kathleen Butler, from a play by Max

Catto*. Ph *George Stretton*. PC and Dis *British Lion. 67 mins. Cert A*
Noisy comedy about Hutt, a businessman (*Dick Francis*) who, to shake up his idle family and with the connivance of his daughter Barbara (*Leonora Corbett*) pretends that he has lost all his money. The efforts of the family to earn and economize are a catalogue of disasters – and then Mr Hutt really does lose all his money. But Barbara, who has built up a thriving business, saves the day.
RoC *Hugh Williams, Eve Gray, Maddie Hope, Ellen Pollock, Glennis Lorimer, Max Adrian, D.A. Clarke-Smith, Muriel George.*

HARMONY HEAVEN (1930) 2
Dir *Thomas Bentley*. Scr *Arthur Wimperis, Randall Faye, Frank Launder*. Ph *Theodore Sparkuhl*. Prod *BIP*. Dis *Wardour. Colour. 61 mins. Cert U*
Early colour and a few tuneful songs (including *Raggedy Romp*) were the only consolations of this woeful back-stage story about a songwriter (*Stuart Hall*) whose head is turned by success and who neglects his girl (*Polly Ward*) for a titled lady (*Trilby Clark*).
RoC *Jack Raine, Percy Standing, Philip Hewland, Gus Sharland, Aubrey Fitzgerald, Edna Prince.*

HAWLEYS OF HIGH STREET (1933) 2
Dir *Thomas Bentley*. Prod *Walter C. Mycroft*. Scr *Charles Bennett, Syd Courtenay, Frank Launder*. Ph *John J. Cox*. PC *BIP*. Dis *Wardour. 68 mins. Cert U*
Draper Hawley (*Leslie Fuller*) and Butcher Busworth (*Moore Marriott*) are bitter rivals at the local council election. Their attempted sabotage of each other's campaign results in them both ending up in court. The election ends in a tie after several recounts, but Bill Hawley has had enough of politics and decides to retire. Apart from the battle between the rivals with joints of meat, there are rather too few laughs in this Fuller comedy.
RoC *Amy Veness, Judy Kelly, Francis Lister, Wylie Watson, Hal Gordon, Syd Courtenay, Faith Bennett, Elizabeth Vaughan, Jimmy Godden, Mabel Twemlow, John Schofield, Leo Sheffield.*

HEAD OFFICE (1936) 2
Dir *Melville Brown*. Prod *Irving Asher*. Scr *Hugh Preston, from his novel*. Ph *William Luff*. PC and Dis *Warner Bros. 90 mins. Cert A*
Crossman and Dixon (*Owen Nares, Arthur Margetson*) both owe their jobs with a trading company to their wartime friendship with the boss's son, who was killed in action. When Crossman discovers Dixon stealing the firm's money, the latter threatens to tell the boss his son died a coward's death (the truth) if Crossman doesn't keep quiet. But, by a freak chance, everything is revealed anyway and Dixon goes to jail. Drama has nice office detail, but is top-heavy with dialogue.
RoC *Nancy O'Neil, Eileen Peel, Alexis France, Philip Ray, Ronald Simpson, Charles Carson, Hilda Bayley, Bruce Lister, H.F. Maltby, Wilfred Caithness, Stan Paskin.*

HEAD OF THE FAMILY (1933)   [1]

Dir *John Daumery*. Prod *Irving Asher*. Scr *Brock Williams*. PC *Warner Bros*. Dis *First National*. 66 mins. Cert A

Sir John (*Arthur Maude*), an industrialist virtually forced out of business by a new firm, is declared bankrupt and becomes night watchman for his rival, Stanmore (*John Stuart*). In this capacity, he is instrumental in preventing a robbery and things come right for him in the end, the firms amalgamating and Stanmore marrying Sir John's daughter. Too much talk drags this drama down.

RoC *Pat Paterson, Irene Vanbrugh, D.A. Clarke-Smith, Roland Culver, Alexander Field, Glen Alyn, Annie Esmond.*

HEAD OVER HEELS (1937)   [4]
(USA: *Head Over Heels in Love*)

Dir *Sonnie Hale*. (Associate) Prod *S.C. Balcon*. Scr *Dwight Taylor, Fred Thompson, Marjorie Gaffney, from a play by François de Crosset*. Ph *Glen MacWilliams*. PC and Dis *Gaumont-British*. 81 mins. Cert U

Jeanne (*Jessie Matthews*) is loved by a radio engineer, Pierre (*Robert Flemyng*) but falls for idle charmer Marcel (*Louis Borell*). But it's Pierre who helps her become a success on radio after Marcel has ditched her for a film star. After she has become famous, Marcel reappears and persuades her to 'come away' with him to Hollywood. Pierre turns up at the station, wins a terrific fight with Marcel and sweeps Jeanne back to Paris. This Matthews musical was popular although missing the light touch of director Victor Saville. Numbers include *Head Over Heels in Love, May I Have the Next Romance With You?* and *Looking Around Corners for You.*

RoC *Romney Brent, Buddy Bradley, Eliot Makeham, Helen Whitney Bourne, Paul Leyssac, Edward Cooper, Fred Duprez, Edward Wild, Leonard Berry, Arthur Denton, Paul Sheridan, David Farrar, Peter Popp, Cot d'Ordan, Molly Weeks, John Barrie, Harold Birch, Marcel Duchamps, Clement Dutto.*

Robert Flemyng and Jessie Matthews in Head Over Heels *(1937)*

HEADS WE GO (1933)   [4]
(USA: *The Charming Deceiver*)

Dir *Monty Banks*. Prod *John Maxwell*. Scr *Victor Kendall*. PC *BIP*. Dis *Wardour*. 86 mins. Cert A

Constance Cummings brightens this romantic comedy about a model, Betty, who is attracted by Toby (*Frank Lawton*), whom she thinks is a wealthy man-about-town. She follows him to France, but on the cross-channel steamer finds him to be a steward. In France, she narrowly escapes getting into hot water for posing as a film star she resembles – and re-meets Toby, who proves to be a rich man's reporter son.

RoC *Binnie Barnes, Claude Hulbert, Gus McNaughton, Fred Duprez, Ellen Pollock, Peter Godfrey, Tonie Edgar Bruce, Michael Wilding.*

HEART'S DESIRE (1935)   [5]

Dir *Paul L. Stein*. Prod *Walter C. Mycroft*. Scr *Clifford Grey, Jack Davies, L. DuGarde Peach, Roger Burford, Bruno Frank*. Ph *Jack Cox*. PC *BIP*. Dis *Wardour*. 82 mins. Cert U

Tuneful, intelligently directed musical weepie. Joseph (*Richard Tauber*), a singer in a small Viennese beer garden, is astounded by an offer from Frances Wilson (*Leonora Corbett*) to go to London. His sweetheart Anna (*Kathleen Kelly*) fears he will never return. Frances grooms him into a star and his opera is a great success. But Frances marries the composer of the opera (*Carl Harbord*) and Joseph, disillusioned by her rejection of his love, returns to Vienna.

RoC *Diana Napier, Frank Vosper, George Graves, Paul Graetz, Viola Tree, (C.) Denier Warren.*

HEARTS OF HUMANITY (1936)   [3]

Dir *John Baxter*. Prod *John Barter*. Scr *Herbert Ayres*. PC *UK Films*. Dis *Associated Producers and Distributors*. 75 mins. Cert U

Well-characterized but rather drawn-out drama about a clergyman (*Wilfred Walter*) hounded from his parish by malicious gossip. He finds a new purpose in life in helping down-and-outs, and also excitement and satisfaction in rounding up, with the help of his new friends, a gang of shipping crooks.

RoC *Bransby Williams, Cathleen Nesbitt, Pamela Randall, Eric Portman, Hay Petrie, J. Fisher White, Fred Duprez, Stanelli, Mark Daly, Ray Raymond, Patric Curwen, Edgar Driver, Leonard Morris, David Keir, Robert English, Ian Fleming, J. Hubert Leslie, Howard Douglas, Freddy Watts, Stanley Kirby, John Turnbull, Bill Percy, Teddy Joyce and His Band, Romilly Choir, Teddy Reilly.*

HEAT WAVE (1935)   [2]

Dir *Maurice Elvey*. Prod *Jerome Jackson*. Scr *Austin Melford, Leslie Arliss, Jackson*. PC *Gainsborough*. Dis *Gaumont-British*. 75 mins. Cert U

A greengrocer (*Albert Burdon*) becomes involved with a revolution in a South American country where the army is out to depose the president. He becomes mistaken for a gunrunner and accidentally puts paid to the revolution. Musical-comedy supposed to make a star of *Les Allen*, 'Britain's Bing Crosby'. It didn't.

RoC *Cyril Maude, Anna Lee, Vera Pearce, Bernard Nedell, (C.) Denier Warren, Bruce Winston, Grace Poggi, Edmund Willard, Lecuona Cuban Boys.*

THE HEIRLOOM MYSTERY (1936)   [3]

Dir *Maclean Rogers*. Prod *A. George Smith*. Scr *Kathleen Butler*. Ph *Geoffrey Faithfull*. PC *GS Enterprises*. Dis *Radio*. 72 mins. Cert A

Unpretentious but quite pleasing drama about the head of a handmade furniture firm, Marriott (*Edward Rigby*) whose agreement to copy a valuable chest which the owner does not want his wife to know he is selling leads years later to his being accused of its theft. But Marriott's son (*John Robinson*) clears his father's name.

RoC *Mary Glynne, Gus McNaughton, Marjorie Taylor, Martin Lewis, Kathleen Gibson, Louanna Shaw, Bruce Lister, H.F. Maltby, Basil Langton, Michael Ripper.*

HELLO SWEETHEART (1935)   [3]

Dir *Monty Banks*. Prod *Irving Asher*. Scr *Brock Williams, from a play by George M. Cohan*. Ph *Basil Emmott*. PC and Dis *Warner Bros*. 70 mins. Cert U

British version of Cohan's play *The Butter and Egg Man*, with *Claude Hulbert* as the young poultry farmer inveigled into financing a film. He attempts to interfere in the direction, is swindled and left in the lurch. Ultimately he turns the tables on his former associates. Left with an unfinished film, he converts it into a burlesque and it's a great success.

RoC *Gregory Ratoff, Jane Carr, Nancy O'Neil, Olive Blakeney, Cyril Smith, Morris Harvey, Felix Aylmer, Phyllis Stanley, Johnnie Nit, The Three Ginx, Marriott Edgar, Carroll Gibbons, Ernest Sefton.*

HELL'S CARGO (1939)   [3]
(USA: *Dangerous Cargo*)

Dir *Harold Huth*. Prod *Walter C. Mycroft*. Scr *Dudley Leslie, from a screenplay by Leo Joannon*. Ph *Claude-Friese-Greene, Phil Tannura*. PC and Dis *Associated British*. 82 mins. Cert U

Three naval commanders, Tomasov, a Russian (*Robert Newton*), Lesteilleur, a Frenchman (*Walter Rilla*) and Falcon (*Kim Peacock*), an Englishman, pursue an oil tanker whose skipper has committed murder in Tangier. He jettisons his cargo, a dye which generates a deadly gas and threatens the liner carrying Lesteilleur's wife and son. Lesteilleur leads a successful rescue, but Tomasov perishes in the deadly fumes. Unevenly acted version of French film *Alerte en Méditerranée*.

RoC *Penelope Dudley Ward, Geoffrey Atkins, Ronald Adam, Martin Walker, Henry Oscar, Charles Victor, Henry Morell, Louise Hampton.*

HELP YOURSELF (1932)   [3]

Dir *John Daumery*. Prod *Irving Asher*. Scr *Roland Pertwee, John Hastings Turner, from a novel by Jerome Kingston*. PC *Warner Bros-First National*. Dis *Warner Bros*. 73 mins. Cert A. Bilingual versions.

Comedy about a man who throws a Christmas party at his ancestral home, then finds the safe, containing his aunt's valuable necklace, has been tampered with. With the help of a girl for whom he has fallen, he apprehends the thieves and retrieves the necklace, only to find out that it's a fake.

LP *Martin Walker, Benita Hume, D.A.*

Clarke-Smith, Carol Coombe, Kenneth Kove, Clifford Heatherley, D. Hay Petrie, Helen Ferrers, Marie Wright, Hal Gordon, Frederick Ross.

HERE'S GEORGE (1932) [4]

Dir *Redd Davis*. Prod and PC *Thomas Charles Arnold*. Scr *Marriott Edgar, from his play* The Service Flat. Ph *Desmond Dickinson*. Dis *Producers' Distributing Company*. 64 mins. Cert U

Music-hall comedian *George Clarke* made his film debut in this fast, furious and funny farce about a man who shows his prospective in-laws his new flat, complete with all manner of labour-saving devices. In the end, it transpires he has hired the flat to impress them. Never a dull moment.

RoC *Pat Paterson, Ruth Taylor, Marriott Edgar, Syd Crossley, René Ray, Wally Patch, Merle Tottenham, Alfred Wellesley, Victor Fairlie, Jimmie Leslie.*

George Clarke and Pat Paterson in Here's George *(1932)*

HER FIRST AFFAIRE (1932) [3]

Dir *Allan Dwan*. Prod *Frank Richardson*. Scr *Dion Titheradge, Brock Williams*. Ph *Geoffrey Faithfull*. PC *St George's Productions*. Dis *Sterling*. 72 mins. Cert A

Ida Lupino, in her first film at 18, played an impetuous teenager who, much to the consternation of her boyfriend (*Arnold Riches*), becomes infatuated with a famous novelist (*George Curzon*). The boyfriend and the writer's wife (*Diana Napier*) join forces to deter her, and he decides an early marriage is the best cure.

RoC *Harry Tate, Muriel Aked, Kenneth Kove, Helen Haye, Roland Culver, Melville Gideon.*

HER IMAGINARY LOVER (1933) [3]

Dir *George King*. Prod *Irving Asher*. Scr *Uncredited, from a novel by A.E.W. Mason*. PC *Warner Bros*. Dis *First National*. 66 mins. Cert U

New York typist Celia (*Laura la Plante*) inherits a fortune and comes to England where she soon finds herself the prey of fortune-hunting young men. She and her grandmother (*Lady Tree*) invent an imaginary fiancé called Lord Michael of Ware. Alas, there really is a Lord Michael (*Percy Marmont*) and he is soon on the warpath - before, inevitably, falling for Celia himself.

RoC *Roland Culver, Bernard Nedell, Emily Fitzroy, Olive Blakeney.*

HER LAST AFFAIRE (1935) [2]

Dir *Michael Powell*. Prod *Simon Rowson, Geoffrey Rowson*. Scr *Ian Dalrymple, from a play by Walter Ellis*. Ph *Leslie Rowson*. PC *New Ideal*. Dis *Producers' Distributing Corporation*. 78 mins. Cert A

Flashbacks only confuse this turgid drama. The indiscreet wife (*Viola Keats*) of a rising politician (*Francis L. Sullivan*) is found dead at the country inn she had visited with her husband's secretary (*Hugh Williams*). He had taken her there to get information from her which would clear his father's memory. The man's innocence proved, his son marries the dead woman's daughter (*Sophie Stewart*).

RoC *Felix Aylmer, Cecil Parker, John Laurie, Eliot Makeham, Googie Withers, Shayle Gardner, Gerrard Tyrell, Henry Caine.*

HER NIGHT OUT (1932) [2]

Dir *William McGann*. Prod *Irving Asher*. Scr *W. Scott Darling*. PC and Dis *Warner Bros*. 45 mins. Cert A

Gerald Vickery (*Lester Matthews*) and his wife Kitty (*Dorothy Bartlam*) quarrel, and she packs and leaves, clad only in pyjamas and fur coat. She jumps into a taxi occupied by a man who threatens her with a revolver. Her subsequent flirtation with the man, who turns out to be a bank robber, lands her in hot water, but Gerald comes to the rescue.

RoC *Dodo Watts, Joan Marion, Jack Raine.*

HEROES OF THE MINE (1932) [3]

Dir *Widgey R. Newman*. Prod *Geoffrey Clarke*. Scr *Clarke, Commander Barwood*. PC *Delta*. Dis *Butchers*. 48 mins. Cert U

Real-life drama with a storythread of fiction, dealing with attempts to rescue men trapped in a Welsh mine disaster. Circumstances also cause one miner to confess that he framed another for a theft of which he was guilty.

LP *Moore Marriott, Walter Patch, John Milton, Terence de Marney, Eric Adeney, Agnes Brantford, Ian Wilson, George Holland, Gordon Leftwich.*

HER REPUTATION (1931) [1]

Dir, Prod and Scr *Sidney Morgan, from a play by Jean Brandon-Thomas*. PC *London Screenplays*. Dis *Paramount*. 67 mins. Cert A

Silly comedy about middle-aged Mrs Sloane (*Iris Hoey*) who craves excitement and notoriety. She decides to divorce her husband (*Frank Cellier*) naming his friend George (*Malcolm Tearle*) as co-respondent. Lawyers consider her mad and assign to the case a young clerk (*Lillian Hall-Davis*) with whom both Mrs Sloane's husband and son fall in love. Mrs Sloane is brought to heel.

RoC *Maurice Braddell, Joan Morgan, Dorothy Black, Lawrence Hanray.*

HEY! HEY! USA (1938) [4]

Dir *Marcel Varnel*. Prod *Edward Black*. Scr *Marriott Edgar, Val Guest, J.O.C. Orton*. Ph *Arthur Crabtree*. PC *Gainsborough*. Dis *General Film Distributors*. 92 mins. Cert U

Dr Ben Twist (*Will Hay*), aboard an Atlantic liner, is forced to pose as an American gangster who has fled the ship. As the crook, 'Professor' Tavistock, he is engaged as tutor to a millionaire's precocious son whom two rival gangs are out to kidnap. The boy is snatched, but Twist, chosen to deliver the ransom money, contrives to escape with both boy and money. Boisterous, offbeat Hay comedy.

RoC *Edgar Kennedy, Tommy Bupp, David Burns, Edmon Ryan, Fred Duprez, Paddy Reynolds, Peter Gawthorne, Gibb McLaughlin, Arthur Goullet, Eddie Pola, Roddy McDowall.*

Will Hay and Edgar Kennedy in Hey! Hey! USA! *(1937)*

THE HIGH COMMAND (1937) [4]

Dir *Thorold Dickinson*. Prod *Gordon Wellesley*. Scr *Katherine Strueby, Walter Meade, Val Valentine, from a novel by Lewis Robinson*. Ph *Otto Heller*. PC *Fanfare*. Dis *Renown/Associated British*. 88 mins (Later 74 mins). Cert A

Ireland, 1921: Major Sir John Sangye (*Lionel Atwill*), a war hero, shoots - in self-defence - the man who (rightly) accuses him of fathering his wife's child. Carson (*Leslie Perrins*), the medical officer, finds out. West Africa, 1937: Heverell (*James Mason*), Carson's cousin, is having an affair with Diana (*Lucie Mannheim*), wife of Cloam, a trader (*Steven Geray*). Then Carson is killed. Heverell is accused. The court-martial shows that Carson had been blackmailing Sir John for years. But Sir John believes Cloam killed Carson believing him to be Diana's lover - and proves it, at the cost of his own life. Novelettish story, but cleverly directed.

RoC *Allan Jeayes, Michael Lambart, Kathleen Gibson, Tom Gill, Wally Patch, Archibald Batty, Drusilla Wills, Cyril Howe, Evan Thomas, Aubrey Pollock, Deering Wells, Philip Strange, Frank Atkinson, Skelton Knaggs.*

HIGH FINANCE (1933) [2]

Dir *George King*. Prod *Irving Asher*. Scr *Not credited*. PC *Warner Bros*. Dis *First National*. 67 mins. Cert A

Rayburn (*Gibb McLaughlin*), a financier, is a stubborn man who not only refuses to consent to the marriage of his teenage niece (and ward) Jill (*Ida Lupino*) and Tom (*John Batten*), but also spurns the advice of Tom's lawyer father (*John H. Roberts*) about taking on the chairmanship of an 'unsound' company. The company crashes and Rayburn serves a short prison term which changes him for the better.

RoC *D.A. Clarke-Smith, Abraham Sofaer.*

HIGHLAND FLING (1936) [2]

Dir *Manning Haynes*. Prod *John Findlay*. Scr *Alan d'Egville, Ralph Stock*. Ph *Stanley Grant*. PC and Dis *Fox British*. 68 mins. Cert U

Inauspicious entry from two of the Crazy Gang, *Naughton* and *Gold*, who play defective detectives asked to find a will mislaid in a haunted Scottish castle. One fake ghost and three genuine ones appear, and the will finds itself: among rubbish intended for burning; stuffed in a clock; hidden in a prize offered at the Highland Games. One caustic critic thought it all 'hardly riotous'.
LP *Charlie Naughton, Jimmy Gold, Eve Foster, Frederick Bradshaw, Gibson Gowland, Naomi Plaskitt, Billy Shine, Peter Popp, Winifred Willard, W. S. Percy*.

HIGH SOCIETY (1932) [2]

Dir *John Rawlins*. Prod *Irving Asher*. Scr *W. Scott Darling, Randall Faye*. PC *Warner Bros*. Dis *First National*. 53 mins. Cert U

Shoddy comedy unworthy of its star, *Florence Desmond*. Mrs Cunningham-Smythe (*Margaret Damer*) wants her daughter Betty (*Joan Wyndham*) to marry Wilberforce (*William Austen*) stepson of a wealthy woman. Betty has other ideas and sends in her maid (*Florence Desmond*), while she elopes with Tommy (*Tracy Holmes*) who proves to be heir to a baronetcy. Wilberforce marries the maid.
RoC *Syd Crossley, Leo Sheffield, Emily Fitzroy*.

HINDLE WAKES (1931) [5]

Dir *Victor Saville*. Prod *Michael Balcon*. Scr *Saville, Angus Macphail, from a play by Stanley Houghton*. Ph *Mutz Greenbaum*. PC and Dis *Gaumont*. 79 mins. Cert A

Third of four screen versions (and probably the best) of *Stanley Houghton's* tale of life in a Lancashire mill town, chiefly concerning an independently minded girl (*Belle Chrystall*) who has a brief fling with the son of her father's employer, but refuses to marry him.
RoC *John Stuart, Sybil Thorndike, Norman McKinnel, Edmund Gwenn, Mary Clare, Muriel Angelus, A. G. Poulton, Ruth Peterson, Lionel Roberts, Bob Johnston*.

HIS BROTHER'S KEEPER (1939) [3]

Dir *Roy William Neill*. Prod *Sam Sax*. Scr *Neill, Austin Melford, Brock Williams*. Ph *Basil Emmott*. PC *Warner Bros*. Dis *First National*. 70 mins. Cert A

Brothers Hicky and Jack (*Peter Glenville, Clifford Evans*) have a sharpshooting act. Olga (*Tamara Desni*), a gold-digging blues singer, comes between them. Jack discards her, but the younger Hicky is infatuated, and distraught when she throws him over for a rich admirer. He fails to move correctly in the act and is shot by Jack, who then shoots Olga and himself without realizing Hicky has survived the accident. Grim tale is well cast, does just enough to hold the interest.
RoC *Una O'Connor, Reginald Purdell, Ronald Frankau, Antoinette Lupino, Aubrey Dexter, Frederick Burtwell, Kitty de Legh*.

HIS GRACE GIVES NOTICE (1933) [2]

Dir *George A. Cooper*. Prod *Julius Hagen*. Scr *H. Fowler Mear, from the novel by Lady Trow-*

bridge. Ph *Ernest Palmer*. PC *Real Art*. Dis *Radio*. 57 mins. Cert A

Arthur Margetson's butler, falling in love with the daughter of the house, is the best thing in this little romantic comedy. The butler later proves to be the heir to his master's title, but the daughter is infatuated with a ne'er-do-well man-about-town. In the end, she sees him in his true colours, and the butler wins his lady fair.
RoC *Viola Keats, Barrie Livesey, S. Victor Stanley, Ben Welden, Edgar Norfolk, Dick Francis, Lawrence Hanray, Charles Groves, O. B. Clarence, Gertrude Sterroll*.

HIS LORDSHIP (1932) [2]

Dir *Michael Powell*. Prod *Jerome Jackson*. Scr *Ralph Smart, from a novel by Oliver Heuffer*. Ph *Geoffrey Faithfull*. PC *Westminster*. Dis *United Artists*. 78 mins. Cert U

Very broad comedy-musical about a young cockney (*Jerry Verno*) who becomes a peer and agrees, to help his widowed mother, to pose as the fiancé of a tempestuous Russian Hollywood movie star (*Janet Megrew*), much to the discomfort of his girlfriend (*Polly Ward*), who finally reclaims him. Music and lyrics by *Eric Maschwitz* and *V. C. Clinton-Baddeley*.
RoC *Ben Welden, Peter Gawthorne, Michael Hogan, Muriel George, V. C. Clinton-Baddeley, Patrick Ludlow*.

HIS LORDSHIP (1936) [4]
(USA: *Man of Affaires*)

Dir *Herbert Mason*. (Associate) Prod *S.C. Balcon*. Scr *Maude Howell, Edwin Greenwood, L. duGarde Peach, from a play by Neil Grant*. Ph *Günther Krampf*. PC and Dis *Gaumont-British*. 71 mins. Cert U

Suspected of murdering a middle eastern emir, Bill (*Romilly Lunge*), helped by his older friend Richard (*George Arliss*), escapes to England, one step ahead of the real killers, two sheiks. Richard, realizing that his twin brother, the foreign secretary, will not help, kidnaps him, impersonates him, traps the sheiks into confessing their crimes and averts the danger of war. Arliss' personality steers this one through.
RoC *René Ray, Jessie Winter, John Ford, Allan Jeayes, Lawrence Anderson, John Turnbull, Basil Gill, Bernard Merefield*.

George Arliss in His Lordship *(1937)*

HIS LORDSHIP GOES TO PRESS
(1938) [2]

Dir *Maclean Rogers*. Prod *A. George Smith*. Scr *Kathleen Butler, H. F. Maltby, from a story*

by *Margaret and Gordon McDonnell*. PC *Canterbury*. Dis *RKO Radio*. 80 mins. Cert U

Lord Bill (*Hugh Williams*) pretends to be an earthy farmer in order to teach an uppity American girl (*June Clyde*) some manners, although his caddish friend (*Leslie Perrins*) was responsible for the misunderstanding that led to her getting upset. But naturally all ends in a love match. Comedy like a mile of string: thin, long and unfunny.
RoC *Romney Brent, Louise Hampton, H. F. Maltby, Zillah Bateman, Aubrey Mallalieu, Michael Ripper, Isobel Scaife*.

HIS LORDSHIP REGRETS (1938) [2]

Dir *Maclean Rogers*. Prod *A. George Smith*. Scr *Kathleen Butler, H.F. Maltby, from Maltby's play* Bees and Honey. Ph *Geoffrey Faithfull*. PC *Canterbury*. Dis *RKO Radio*. 78 mins. Cert U

Lord Reggie (*Claude Hulbert*) hard-pressed by his creditors, pays court to an heiress (*Gina Malo*), then falls for Mary (*Winifred Shotter*) at a party. Sympathetic to Lord Reggie because her father had swindled his grandfather out of a large sum of money, Mary turns out to be the real heiress, while the other is exposed as a crook. Draggy comedy.
RoC *Eve Gray, Antony Holles, Sally Stewart, Derek Gorst, Aubrey Mallalieu, Athole Stewart, Annie Esmond, Gerald Rawlinson, Michael Ripper, Paul Sheridan, Valentine Dunn*.

HIS MAJESTY AND CO (1934) [3]

Dir *Anthony Kimmins*. Prod *Uncredited*. Scr *Sally Sutherland*. PC and Dis *Fox British*. 66 mins. Cert U

John (*John Garrick*), in Poldavia on holiday, falls for the crown princess (*Barbara Waring*). Later, they meet again in London, where John is struggling to make a living as a singer, and the royal family has been exiled. As the queen is an expert cook and the king a wine connoisseur, the four start a restaurant. The venture's a great success and John gets the girl. Musical trifle has some charm.
RoC *Morton Selten, Mary Grey, Jean Gillie, Desmond Jeans, H. Saxon-Snell, Howard Douglas, Eddie Fitzmaurice, Betty le Brocke, Campbell Russell, Alfredo Campoli and His Tzigane Orchestra*.

HIS WIFE'S MOTHER (1932) [2]

Dir and Scr *Harry Hughes, from a play by Will Scott*. Prod *Walter C. Mycroft*. PC *BIP*. Dis *Wardour*. 69 mins. Cert U

Henry (*Jerry Verno*), newly-wed to Cynthia (*Molly Lamont*), is spotted with Tony (*Renée Gadd*), a showgirl, by his suspicious mother-in-law (*Marion Dawson*). His friend Eustace (*Jack Hobbs*), as keen to have Tony (his ex-girlfriend) back, as Henry is to be rid of her, devises a plan whereby Henry poses as his own double, pulling the wool over mother-in-law's eyes. Foolish comedy.
RoC *Gus McNaughton, Jimmy Golden, Hal Gordon*.

HOBSON'S CHOICE (1931) [4]

Dir *Thomas Bentley*. Prod *John Maxwell*. Scr *Harold Brighouse (uncredited), Frank Launder,*

Frank Pettingell, Viola Lyel and Jimmy Harcourt in Hobson's Choice *(1931)*

from the play by Brighouse. Ph *Walter Harvey, Bert Ford, Horace Wheddon.* PC *BIP.* Dis *Wardour. 65 mins. Cert U*
Second of three screen versions of Brighouse's famous play about a Lancashire boot-maker (*James Harcourt*) with chauvinist habits, three daughters and definite views on parental authority. But his eldest daughter (*Viola Lyel*) has a mind of her own, and when she sets her cap at Will (*Frank Pettingell*), who works for her father, the old man meets his match.
RoC *Belle Chrystall, Joan Maude, Jay Laurier, Amy Veness, Herbert Lomas, Kathleen Harrison, Reginald Bach, Basil Moss, Marie Ault, Frank Macrae, Charles Heslop.*

HOLD MY HAND (1938)   3
Dir *Thornton Freeland.* Prod *Walter C. Mycroft.* Scr *Clifford Grey, Bert Lee, William Freshman.* Ph *Otto Kanturek.* PC and Dis *Associated British. 76 mins. Cert U*
When Eddie Marston (*Stanley Lupino*) finances his ward's newspaper from his own money, she suspects he is embezzling the paper's profits. It is sorted out in the end, along with romances between Eddie and his secretary; his ward and his friend; and his fiancée and the editor of the paper, but only after the world's most ridiculous cat burglary. Much singing and fooling in fair farce.
RoC *Polly Ward, Sally Grey, Barbara Blair, Jack Melford, John Wood, Fred Emney, Bertha Belmore, Syd Walker, Arthur Rigby, Gibb McLaughlin.*

HOLIDAY LOVERS (1932)   2
Dir *Jack Harrison.* Prod and PC *Harry I. Cohen.* Scr *Leslie Arliss.* Dis *Fox. 59 mins. Cert A*
Romantic comedy set in Brighton, with both parties (*George Vollaire, Marjorie Pickard*) posing as rich somebodies, whereas they are a poor man and a lady's maid. Exposed, the two confess their deceptions and decide to marry. Inconsequential.
RoC *Pamela Carme, Boris Ranevsky, George Benson, Wyn Weaver, Vincent Holman.*

HOLIDAY'S END (1937)   3
Dir *John Paddy Carstairs.* Prod *Anthony Havelock-Allan.* Scr *Gerald Elliott.* Ph *Desmond Dickinson.* PC and Dis *British and Dominions/Paramount British. 70 mins. Cert A*
The arrival of the boy-king of a small Euro-

pean State coincides with the murder of the science master. As the boy's housemaster would ultimately become his personal tutor, there had been great rivalry among the masters, and suspicion falls on everyone. But the killer is a revolutionary: his plan to assassinate the king is discovered and foiled. Limp plot, sharp direction.
LP *Elliott Seabrooke, Beckett Bould, Sally Stewart, Wally Patch, Rosalyn Boulter, Aubrey Mallalieu, Kenneth Buckley, Leslie Bradley, Henry Victor, Robert Field, Bruce Moir, Denis Cowles.*

HOME FROM HOME (1939)   3
Dir and Prod *Herbert Smith.* Scr *Fenn Sherie, Ingram d'Abbes.* Ph *George Stretton.* PC and Dis *British Lion. 73 mins. Cert U*
After three years in jail, Sandy (*Sandy Powell*) finds the life to his liking and he is well away from his nagging wife. Then comes news that he has been cleared of the crime for which he was convicted and, protesting, he's released. Events outside go from bad to worse: Sandy determines to get back to prison and does. But he has unknowingly brought a gang of thieves to justice in the process and receives another free pardon. Well-tailored Powell comedy.
RoC *René Ray, Roy Emerton, Kathleen Harrison, Bruce Lister, Wally Patch, Norma Varden, Peter Gawthorne, George Horold, Dennis Cowles, Jack Vyvyan, The Five Harmonica Rascals, The Gaillard Brothers.*

HOME SWEET HOME (1933)   2
Dir *George A. Cooper.* Prod *Julius Hagen.* Scr *Terence Egan, H. Fowler Mear.* PC *Real Art.* Dis *Radio. 73 mins. Cert A*
Maudlin melodrama about an engineer (*John Stuart*) who, abroad for three years, receives, on board ship, a letter from his wife (*Marie Ney*) telling her she is leaving him. On return, the engineer accidentally kills his wife's lover (*Cyril Raymond*), unaware she has changed her mind. In court, he is saved from a heavy sentence when she confesses her infidelity.
RoC *Richard Cooper, Sydney Fairbrother, Eve Becke, Eliot Makeham, Felix Aylmer, Ben Welden, Joan Carter, Barbara Everest.*

A HONEYMOON ADVENTURE (1931)   4
(USA: *Footsteps in the Night*)
Dir *Maurice Elvey.* Prod *Basil Dean.* Scr *Dean, Rupert Downing, John Paddy Carstairs, from a novel by Mrs Cecily Fraser-Smith.* PC *ATP.* Dis *Radio. 67 mins. Cert U*
Zippy comedy-thriller involving an inventor and his wife (*Peter Hannen, Benita Hume*) in Scotland for their honeymoon. Crooks kidnap the husband to get their hands on the plans for one of his inventions, but the resourceful wife picks up their trail and turns the tables on them.
RoC *Harold Huth, Walter Armitage, Margery Binner, Jack Lambert, Robert English, Frances Ross Campbell, Pollie Emery.*

HONEYMOON FOR THREE
(1935)   3
Dir *Leo Mittler.* Prod *Stanley Lupino.* Scr *Frank Miller.* Ph *George Dudgeon Stretton.* PC

Gaiety Films. Dis *Associated British. 81 mins. Cert A*
Cheerful comedy about a wild playboy, Jack (*Stanley Lupino*), who accidentally compromises a French girl, Yvonne (*Aileen Marson*), whose family force her to marry him. Anxious to do the right thing, though he quite fancies her, Jack boards ship with Yvonne and her ex-fiancé, bound for America and a quickie divorce. On board, however, it's Jack who keeps the girl.
RoC *Jack Melford, Robert English, Dennis Hoey, Arty Ash, Roddy Hughes, Syd Crossley, Doris Rogers, Barry Clifton, Percival Mackey and His Band.*

HONEYMOON MERRY-GO-ROUND
(1936)   3
Dir *Alfred Goulding.* Prod *Sidney Morgan.* Scr *Goulding, Monty Banks, Joan Morgan, Warren Chetwynd Strode.* Ph *Ernest Palmer.* PC *Fanfare/ATP/London Screenplays.* Dis *RKO. 64 mins. Cert U*
Dithering Bob Bennett (*Claude Hulbert*), having fallen out with his bride on honeymoon in Switzerland, is mistaken for an ace ice-hockey player, finds himself rushed into ice-hockey gear and, despite having trouble staying on his feet, helps the English team win a vital international match - to the admiration of his bride. Fairly amusing comedy in typical Hulbert style.
RoC *Monty Banks, Princess Pearl (Pearl Vyner-Brooke), Sally Gray, Tully Comber, Bob Bowman, Wembley Lions Ice Hockey Team.*

HONOURS EASY (1935)   2
Dir *Herbert Brenon.* Prod *Walter C. Mycroft.* Scr *Roland Pertwee, from his play.* Ph *Ronald Neame.* PC *BIP.* Dis *Wardour. 62 mins. Cert A*
Barton (*Ivan Samson*) has an old score to settle against Sir Henry (*Robert Rendel*) and frames his son (*Patric Knowles*) for theft. In refuting the charge, Sir Henry accidentally reveals an affair between his son and Barton's wife (*Greta Nissen*) who could have cleared him without knowing it. In the end the two old enemies are reconciled. Heavy-handed drama.
RoC *Margaret Lockwood, Chili Bouchier, George Graves, W. H. Berry, Wallace Douglas.*

HOOTS MON! (1939)   4
Dir *Roy William Neill.* Prod *Sam Sax.* Scr *Neill, Jack Henley, John Dighton.* Ph *Basil Emmott.* PC and Dis *Warner Bros. 77 mins. Cert A*
'England's funniest comedian' Harry Hawkins (*Max Miller*) and 'Scotland's Bluebelle' Jenny McTavish, a male impersonator (*Florence Desmond*), are deadly rivals. Harry rashly accepts her dare to take a booking in Scotland, where he is such a flop the manager sends him to the local Thistle Club. His reception there lands him in hospital, where his nurse turns out to be Jenny in disguise, Slim story, but stars in magnificent fooling form.
RoC *Hal Walters, Davina Craig, Garry Marsh, Edmund Willard, Gordon McLeod, Mark Daly, Robert Gall.*

THE HOPE OF HIS SIDE (1935)
See **Where's George?**

HOTEL SPLENDIDE (1932) [2]
Dir *Michael Powell.* Prod *Jerome Jackson.* Scr *Ralph Smart.* Ph *Geoffrey Faithfull.* PC *Film Engineering.* Dis *Ideal. 52 mins. Cert U*
A publicity manager inherits a seaside hotel built on a field where crooks buried valuable pearls, the loot from a robbery. The criminals return to hunt for the treasure, but the manager (*Jerry Verno*) accidentally stumbles across the pearls, and is able to claim the reward for their return. Lacklustre comedy.
RoC *Vera Sherbourne, Antony Holles, Edgar Norfolk, Sybil Grove, Philip Morant, Paddy Browne.*

HOT NEWS (1936) [1]
Dir *W. P. Kellino.* Prod *Ian Sutherland.* Scr *Reginald Long, Arthur Rigby.* Ph *Jack Barker.* PC *St George's Pictures.* Dis *Columbia. 77 mins. Cert U*
Funny lines are few and far between in this comedy about a hapless newspaperman (*Lupino Lane*) who is somehow chosen as a 'guest reporter' on a Chicago paper. On the boat over, he mistakes ordinary people for ruthless criminals and confuses an heiress with a cabaret singer, which causes the singer to be kidnapped by real crooks. The reporter rescues the girl, but misses the scoop.
RoC *Phyllis Clare, Wallace Lupino, Barbara Kilner, Ben Welden, Glen Raynham, Reginald Long, Fred Leslie, George Pughe, Edward Pierce, Scott Harold, Geoffrey Clarke, Henry Longhurst, The Dorchester Girls.*

THE HOUND OF THE BASKERVILLES (1931) [3]
Dir *V. Gareth Gundrey.* Prod *Michael Balcon.* Scr *Edgar Wallace, Gundrey, from the novel by Sir Arthur Conan Doyle.* Ph *Bernard Knowles.* PC *Gaumont.* Dis *Ideal. 75 mins. Cert U*
Sherlock Holmes (*Robert Rendel*) and Dr Watson (*Frederick Lloyd*) journey to Dartmoor, where Holmes foresees that an attempt will be made on the life of Sir Henry (*John Stuart*) who has just inherited the Baskerville estate. The villain turns out to be a farmer who, by use of a maddened hound, coated with phosphorescent paint, hopes to gain control of the estate. This eminently filmable story has still not produced a good film and this attempt is no better than the rest.
RoC *Heather Angel, Reginald Bach, Wilfred Shine, Frederick Lloyd, Sam Livesey, Henry Hallett, Sybil Jane, Elizabeth Vaughan, Leonard Hayes.*

HOURS OF LONELINESS (1930) [2]
Dir, Prod and Scr *G. G. Glavany.* PC *Carlton.* Dis *Warner Bros. 65 mins. Cert A*
The working title of this rather dismal number, *An Obvious Situation*, is all too fitting for a Riviera-set story about Michael (*Carl Harbord*) whose shooting of an intruder leads to him being blackmailed over his affair with a married woman (*Sunday Wilshin*).
RoC *Walter Sondes, Michael Hogan, Iris Ashley, Marjorie Jennings, Mina Burnett, Harold Huth.*

HOUSE BROKEN (1936) [3]
Dir *Michael Hankinson.* Prod *Anthony Havelock-Allan.* Scr *Vera Allinson.* Ph *Francis Carver.* PC and Dis *British and Dominions/ Paramount British. 74 mins. Cert A*
When a troublesome friend, Charles (*Louis Borell*), comes to stay and won't go, Angela (*Mary Lawson*) consults newspaper sage 'Cousin Carrie' (*Enid Stamp-Taylor*). The two women plot to get rid of Charles, their schemes becoming ever wilder. But eventually he goes - he has fallen in love with Cousin Carrie. Four-hander comedy with some crisp dialogue, rather marred in the execution.
RoC *Jack Lambert.*

HOUSEMASTER (1938) [3]
Dir *Herbert Brenon.* Prod *Walter C. Mycroft.* Scr *Dudley Leslie, Elizabeth Meehan, from a play by Ian Hay.* Ph *Otto Kanturek.* PC and Dis *Associated British. 95 mins. Cert U*
The arrival of three badly behaved girls at a co-ed public school leads to a crisis in the career of their caring housemaster, Donkin (*Otto Kruger*). The severe discipline meted out by the head brings on a pupils' rebellion and, ultimately, Donkin's resignation. But Ministry intervention leads to the head being transferred and Donkin becoming his successor. Well-drawn but odd mixture of comedy and drama.
RoC *Diana Churchill, Joyce Barbour, René Ray, Phillips Holmes, Kynaston Reeves, Cecil Parker, Walter Hudd, John Wood, Henry Hepworth, Michael Shepley, Jimmy Hanley, Rosamund Barnes, Lawrence Kitchin.*

René Ray and Diana Churchill in Housemaster *(1938)*

THE HOUSE OF SILENCE (1937) [3]
Dir *R. K. Neilson-Baxter.* Prod and PC *George King.* Scr *Paul White.* Dis *MGM. 45 mins. Cert A*
Jack, a reporter (*Tom Helmore*), investigates a 'haunted' house, at the same time as Jim Hallam (*Terence de Marney*), accused of murder but innocent, and his sister Joan (*Jenny Laird*) hide there. Also in the house: a murdered woman and a gang of smugglers who blackmail the Hallams into working for them. Jim kills himself, but Jack saves Joan and unmasks the local innkeeper as the smuggler-in-chief. Deliberately paced but quite tense.
RoC *Roddy Hughes, D. J. Williams, Isobel Scaife, Howard Douglas, Dorothy Vernon, Billy Bray.*

THE HOUSE OF THE ARROW (1930) [4]
Dir *Leslie Hiscott.* Prod *Julius Hagen, Henry Edwards.* Scr *Cyril Twyford, from the novel by A. E. W. Mason.* PC *Twickenham.* Dis *Warner Bros. 76 mins. Cert A*
A famous whodunnit, set in France. Mrs Harlow (*Barbara Gott*) is poisoned, and her niece Betty (*Benita Hume*) is one of the suspects. Inspector Hanaud (*Dennis Neilson-Terry*) is called in and cracks the case.
RoC *Stella Freeman, Richard Cooper, Wilfred Fletcher, Toni de Lungo, Betty de Malero.*

THE HOUSE OF THE SPANIARD (1936) [3]
Dir *Reginald Denham.* Prod *Hugh Perceval.* Scr *Basil Mason, from the novel by Arthur Behrend.* PC *Independent Film Producers/Phoenix.* Dis *Associated British. 70 mins. Cert U*
David Gray (*Peter Haddon*), a 'silly ass' clerk, accidentally unmasks his boss as a Spanish revolutionary at a mysterious marshland house in Lancashire, also stumbling on the latter's counterfeiting racket. David is kidnapped and taken to Spain, where he is helped to escape by the Spaniard's glamorous daughter (*Brigitte Horney*). Later, he returns to help her flee the country.
RoC *Allan Jeayes, Jean Galland, Gyles Isham, Hay Petrie, Ivor Barnard, David Horne, Minnie Rayner, Fred O'Donovan.*

THE HOUSE OF TRENT (1933) [3]
Dir *Norman Walker.* Prod *W. G. D. Hutchinson.* Scr *Charles Bennett, Billie Bristow.* Ph *Robert Martin.* PC *Ensign.* Dis *Butchers. 75 mins. Cert U*
Country doctor John Trent (*John Stuart*) saves the life of a child, Angela, the daughter of press baron Lord Fairdown (*Peter Gawthorne*). When Trent dies, his son John Jnr (also *Stuart*) not only trains to be a doctor himself but coincidentally meets Angela (*Wendy Barrie*) and falls in love. Against the relationship, Fairdown is about to publish an article that will damage John's career when he finds out that it was his father who saved Angela's life.
RoC *Anne Grey, Norah Baring, Moore Marriott, Estelle Winwood, Jack Raine, Hope Davy, S. Victor Stanley, Hubert Harben, Dora Gregory, Hay Plumb, Humberston Wright.*

THE HOUSE OF UNREST (1931) [3]
Dir *Leslie Howard Gordon* (Supervising Dir *Seymour Hill*). Prod *Hill.* Scr *Gordon.* Ph *Desmond Dickinson.* PC *Associated Picture Productions.* Dis *Producers' Distributing Corporation. 58 mins. Cert U*
Busy little pot-boiler set in a remote house on a Scottish island, where a diamond and an inheritance are among the riches that may be sought by a mysterious 'Number One' who frightens everyone with warning messages, then begins bumping off those in the house. The killer proves to be the owner of the diamond, who was after the heiress' fortune.
LP *Malcolm Keen, Dorothy Boyd, Tom Helmore, Leslie Perrins, Hubert Carter, Mary Mayfren.*

Leslie Perrins and Dorothy Boyd in The House of Unrest *(1931)*

THE HOUSE OPPOSITE (1931) [2]

Dir, Prod and Scr *Walter Summers, from a play by J. Jefferson Farjeon.* PC *BIP.* Dis *Pathé.* 67 mins. Cert U

An Egyptian scientist, Fahmy (*Abraham Sofaer*) is the man behind a blackmail racket. Two detectives Dick and Nadine (*Henry Kendall, Celia Glyn*) round up Fahmy and his men, but are only rescued in the nick of time by Ben (*Frank Stanmore*), a tramp who has been helping them, when the scientist's house goes up in flames. Release delayed for a year.
RoC *Molly Lamont, Arthur Macrae, Wallace Geoffrey, Renée Macready, Charles Farrell.*

THE HOWARD CASE (1936) [2]

Dir *Frank Richardson.* Prod *Fraser Foulsham.* Scr *H.F. Maltby, from his play* Fraud. PC *Sovereign.* Dis *Universal.* 62 mins. Cert U

Pat (*Olive Melville*), a bookkeeper in her fiancé's firm, discovers discrepancies in the books, the man responsible being his partner Howard (*Arthur Seaton*) who has gambled the firm's money on gold shares. Howard tries to escape justice by killing a man who looks like him, and taking his place in a sanatorium. But the police are not taken in. Howard commits suicide. Ironically, the gold shares prove profitable.
RoC *Jack Livesey, Olive Sloane, David Keir, Jack Vyvyan, Ernest Borrand, Vincent Sternroyd, Gladys Mason, Renaud Lockwood.*

HOW'S CHANCES? (1934) [4]

Dir *Anthony Kimmins.* Prod *Norman Loudon.* Scr *Ivar Campbell, Harry Graham, from a play by E.B. Leuthege, Kurt Braun.* PC *Sound City.* Dis *Fox.* 73 mins. Cert A

Piquantly amusing musical comedy, a personal hit for *Harold French* who plays a young British ambassador with a weakness for the ladies. He has problems fending off the attentions of the flirtatious wives of two ministers whose signatures are vital to a treaty he is negotiating. But his girlfriend Helen (*Tamara Desni*) rescues him and he is able to force the ministers to sign.
RoC *Davy Burnaby, Morton Selten, Carol Rees, Peggy Novak, Reginald Gardiner, Andrea Malandrinos, Roddy Hughes.*

HUNDRED TO ONE (1932) [2]

Dir *Walter West.* Prod *Julius Hagen, Harry*
Cohen. Scr *Basil Mason.* PC *Twickenham.* Dis *Fox.* 45 mins. Cert U

Pocket racing drama about an Irish publican (*Arthur Sinclair*) who risks all his savings to fulfil his ambition of being the owner of a horse that wins the Derby. The horse he buys proves worthless, but it has a foal that grows up to win the race its owner covets.
RoC *Dodo Watts, Derek Williams, David Nichol, Edmund Hampton.*

HYDE PARK (1934) [1]

Dir and Scr *Randall Faye.* Prod *Irving Asher.* PC and Dis *Warner Bros.* 48 mins. Cert U

Outmoded comedy about a butcher's daughter falling in love with an aristocrat. Her father opposes the marriage until his father hits upon a plan by inventing an 'inheritance' so that the butcher finds he has come into money.
LP *Eve Lister, Barry Clifton, George Carney, Wallace Lupino, Charles Carson, Phyllis Morris.*

HYDE PARK CORNER (1935) [2]

Dir *Sinclair Hill.* Prod *Harcourt Templeman.* Scr *D.B. Wyndham-Lewis, from the play by Walter Hackett.* PC *Grosvenor.* Dis *Pathé.* 85 mins. Cert A

The house of Edward Chester (*Eric Portman*) in 1780; Sir Arthur Gannet (*Gibb McLaughlin*) is found to be cheating at cards. A duel is fought and Chester is killed, cursing the house as he dies. The same house, 1935: after a gambling party, a Gannet is found shot and a Chester is charged. A vital witness for the defence is also found dead. As the only man who could clear Chester, he had been shot by the last of the Gannets – who commits suicide. Dramatic subject played for comedy in strange, muddled film.
RoC *Gordon Harker, Binnie Hale, Robert Holmes, Eileen Peel, Donald Wolfit, Harry Tate.*

∭

I ADORE YOU (1933) [3]

Dir *George King.* Prod *Irving Asher.* Scr *Paul England.* PC and Dis *Warner Bros.* 74 mins. Cert U

Slender story padded out with musical comedy acts, about a young man (*Harold French*) who falls in love with a film star (*Margot Grahame*), and eventually wins her by buying up the failing film company whose contract with her forbids her to marry.
RoC *Clifford Heatherley, O. B. Clarence, Peggy Novak, Georgie Harris, Ernest Sefton, Gavin Gordon, Carroll Gibbons and the Savoy Orpheans.*

IF I WERE BOSS (1938) [1]

Dir *Malcolm Rogers.* Prod *George Smith.* Scr
Basil Mason. Ph *Geoffrey Faithfull.* PC *GS Enterprises.* Dis *Columbia.* 72 mins. Cert A

Stuck-up clerk Steve Brook (*Bruce Seton*) comes into a legacy and takes over his firm, the Biltmore Egg Company. Offering his boss his job at a trifling salary, Brook ignores his advice, and allies himself with Reeves (*Charles Oliver*), an unscrupulous rival. Biltmore (*Ian Fleming*) almost dies before Brook sees the error of his ways and realizes Reeves' eggs are rotten. Absurd drama is dull as well.
RoC *Googie Withers, Zillah Bateman, Julie Suedo, Paul Sheridan, Michael Ripper.*

IF I WERE RICH (1936) [1]

Dir, Prod and PC *Randall Faye.* Scr *Brandon Fleming, from a play by Horace Annesley Vachell.* Ph *Geoffrey Faithfull.* Dis *Radio.* 58 mins. Cert U

None-too-funny comedy about Albert Mott (*Jack Melford*), barber and socialist, who inherits an earldom. Albert swallows his principles and accepts the inheritance but in the end is glad to return to hairdressing.
RoC *Kay Walsh, Clifford Heatherley, Minnie Rayner, Henry Carlisle, Frederick Bradshaw, Ruth Haven, Quinton McPherson, Pat Noonan.*

I GIVE MY HEART (1935) [3]

Dir *Marcel Varnel.* Prod *Walter C. Mycroft.* Scr *Frank Launder, Roger Burford, Kurt Siodmak, Paul Perez (uncredited), from an operetta by Paul Knepler, J. M. Welleminsky.* Ph *Claude Friese-Greene.* PC *BIP.* Dis *Wardour.* 91 mins. Cert A

Hand-me-down musical, set in 1769. Jeanne (Hungarian soprano *Gitta Alpar*), a milliner, is first in love with René (*Patrick Waddington*), a man of her own class, but then marries a count (*Arthur Margetson*) so that, as Madame Dubarry, she can become a candidate for the post of king's mistress left vacant by the death of Madame Pompadour. Despite the efforts of a political group, she achieves her aim.
RoC *Owen Nares, Margaret Bannerman, Hugh Miller, Gibb McLaughlin, Iris Ashley, Hay Petrie, Helen Haye, Ellen Pollock.*

I KILLED THE COUNT (1939) [5]
(USA: *Who is Guilty?*)

Dir *Fred Zelnik.* Prod *Isidore Goldschmidt.* Scr *Alec Coppel, Lawrence Huntington, from Coppel's play.* Ph *Bryan Langley.* PC *Grafton.* Dis *Grand National.* 89 mins. Cert A

Inspector Davidson (*Syd Walker*) has a problem with the murder of much-hated Count Mattoni (*Leslie Perrins*) - four different people confess. All have good motives and a detailed explanation of how they did it. Davidson and his college-trained colleague (*Terence de Marney*) solve the mystery - one of the tenants in the block of flats had accidentally killed the count. Comedy murder-mystery is great fun.
RoC *Ben Lyon, Barbara Blair, Antoinette Cellier, Athole Stewart, Ronald Shiner, David Burns, Kathleen Harrison, Gus McNaughton, Aubrey Mallalieu, Robert Adair.*

I LIVED WITH YOU (1933) [5]

Dir *Maurice Elvey.* Prod *Julius Hagen.* Scr *H. Fowler Mear, from the play by Ivor Novello.* Ph

Sydney Blythe. PC *Twickenham.* Dis *W and F.* 100 mins. Cert A

Director Maurice Elvey was praised for his lightness of touch in this adaptation of a hit play, starring *Novello* himself as the exiled Russian prince lodging with an English working-class family whose shop-assistant daughter (*Ursula Jeans*) falls in love with him and follows him back to Russia when he decides he is breaking up her family.

RoC *Ida Lupino, Minnie Rayner, Eliot Makeham, Jack Hawkins, Cicely Oates, Davina Craig, Douglas Beaumont, Molly Fisher, Beryl Harrison.*

ILLEGAL (1932)   2

Dir *William McGann.* Prod *Irving Asher.* Scr *Roland Pertwee, John Hastings Turner.* PC *Warner Bros.* Dis *First National.* 81 mins. Cert A

Aggressively glum melodrama about Evelyn (*Isobel Elsom*), who deserted by her drunkard second husband, tries to care for her daughters by running a gambling club. The place is raided and Evelyn jailed. Daughter Dorothy (*Margot Grahame*) accidentally kills her sponging stepfather and is herself killed in a car crash. Evelyn, released and alone, burns down the club.

RoC *D.A. Clarke-Smith, Moira Lynd, Edgar Norfolk, Ivor Barnard.*

I'LL STICK TO YOU (1933)   2

Dir *Leslie Hiscott.* Prod *Herbert Smith.* Scr *Michael Barringer.* PC and Dis *British Lion.* 66 mins. Cert A

Supremely idiotic comedy about a girl who will inherit a fortune only if she marries a man with just as much money. As it happens, her boyfriend has invented a new super-glue formula which has been pinched by his employer. The boy and girl set a trap for the boss, a member of the Morality League, obtain a compromising snap, and force him to hand over as much money as the girl's inheritance.

LP *Betty Astell, Louis Hayward, Jay Laurier, Ernest Sefton, Hal Walters, Annie Esmond, Mary Gaskell, Charles Childerstone.*

Betty Astell and Louis Hayward in I'll Stick to You *(1933)*

I'M AN EXPLOSIVE (1933)   3

Dir and Scr *Adrian Brunel,* from a novel by *Gordon Phillips.* Prod *Harry Cohen.* Ph *Geoffrey Faithfull.* PC *George Smith Productions.* Dis *Fox.* 50 mins. Cert U

A professor (*Eliot Makeham*) has invented a mixture which, when swallowed, renders the body liable to explosion. He believes his young brother Edward (*Billy Hartnell*) has drunk some in mistake for whisky. In fact, Edward has done no such thing, but he induces the Chemical Welfare Department to settle his claim for a large sum, with which he marries his girlfriend.

RoC *Gladys Jennings, D. A. Clarke-Smith, Sybil Grove, Harry Terry, George Dillon, Blanche Adele.*

I MET A MURDERER (1939)   4

Dir *Roy Kellino.* Prod *Kellino, Pamela Kellino, James Mason.* Scr *Mason, Pamela Kellino.* Ph *Roy Kellino, Oswald Morris.* PC *Gamma Productions.* Dis *Grand National.* 78 mins. Cert A

Intelligently made, location-shot thriller in which Mark (*James Mason*), a young farmer, is driven to desperation by his nagging wife and her drunken brother. When she deliberately kills his beloved dog, he is incensed and shoots her. On the run, he meets Jo (*Pamela Kellino*), a writer living in a caravan. They have an idyllic few days together before the police close in. From a high cliff, Jo watches Mark, wounded, wade into the sea. . . .

RoC *Sylvia Coleridge, William Devlin, Peter Coke, Esma Cannon, James Harcourt, Sheila Morgan, Sheppie (dog).*

IMMEDIATE POSSESSION (1931)   3

Dir *Arthur Varney-Serrao.* Prod *Harry Cohen.* Scr *Brock Williams.* PC *Starcraft.* Dis *Fox.* 42 mins. Cert U

Comedy vehicle for *Herbert Mundin.* He plays Bootle, an estate agent whose rich partner (*Merle Tottenham*) threatens to dissolve the partnership unless he sells a 'haunted house' within 24 hours. He has a scary time until his client's fiancée proves the 'ghost' is the caretaker.

RoC *Dorothy Bartlam, Leslie Perrins, George Bellamy.*

IMMORTAL GENTLEMAN (1935)   2

Dir *Widgey R. Newman.* Prod and PC *Bernard Smith.* Scr *John Quin.* Dis *Equity British.* 61 mins. Cert U

Peculiar film, barely shown, depicting scenes from plays by Shakespeare (*Basil Gill*), who is seen in 1606 discussing his work with his friends.

RoC *Dennis Hoey, Derrick de Marney, Terence de Marney, Rosalinde Fuller, J. Hubert Leslie, Laidman Browne, Leo Genn, Anne Bolt, Edgar Owen, Fred Rains, Dennis Wyndham, Ivan Berlyn, Roy Byford.*

THE IMPASSIVE FOOTMAN (1932)   3
(USA: *Woman in Bondage*)

Dir and Prod *Basil Dean.* Scr *John Farrow, John Paddy Carstairs, Harold Dearden,* from a play by *Sapper.* Ph *Robert Martin.* PC *Associated Talking Pictures.* Dis *Radio.* 69 mins. Cert A

Grace (*Betty Stockfeld*) falls in love with Dr Daventry (*Owen Nares*) while on a sea trip with her ailing irritable husband John (*Allan Jeayes*). John, who is to have an operation per-

formed by Daventry, learns of the liaison and leaves incriminating letters with his lawyer in the event of his death. John survives, but is killed by his footman (*George Curzon*) - for reasons of revenge. Adequate drama.

RoC *Aubrey Mather, Frances Ross-Campbell, Florence Harwood.*

IMPORTANT PEOPLE (1934)   3

Dir and Scr *Adrian Brunel,* from the play by *F. Wyndham Mallock.* Prod *A. George Smith.* Ph *Geoffrey Faithfull.* PC *GS Enterprises.* Dis *M-G-M.* 48 mins. Cert A

Potted version of a successful comedy play. Tony Westcott (*Stewart Rome*), a prominent prohibitionist, has frequent petty quarrels with his young wife Margaret (*Dorothy Boyd*). When Margaret decides to stand as a candidate in a local election, Tony stands against her - on an anti-prohibition ticket. The contest ends, after several recounts, in a draw.

RoC *Jack Raine, Helen Goss, Henry Longhurst, James Carrall, Fred Withers, May Hallatt.*

THE IMPROPER DUCHESS (1935)   3

Dir *Harry Hughes.* Prod *Maurice Browne.* Scr *Hughes, Vernon Harris.* Ph *Ronald Neame.* PC *City.* Dis *General Film Distributors.* 80 mins. Cert A

The fatuous little King of Poldavia (*Hugh Wakefield*) is in America with one of the peeresses of his realm, the Duchess of Tann (*Yvonne Arnaud*) and trying to negotiate a big loan in return for oil concessions. The talks are steered to success by the wily and unconventional duchess, despite the efforts of a senator and a clergyman to frustrate the deal. Comedy sparks on and off.

RoC *James Carew, Felix Aylmer, Finlay Currie, Arthur Finn, Gerald Barry, Ben Welden, Annie Esmond, Wilfred Caithness, Andrea Malandrinos, Cynthia Stock, Honorine Catto, David Smith-Dorrien.*

IN A LOTUS GARDEN (1931)   1

Dir *Fred Paul.* Prod and Scr *Patrick K. Heale.* PC *Patrick K. Heale.* Dis *W and F.* 47 mins. Cert U

Very minor musical fare with a slender plot about a sparky girl who saves her fiancé, a naval lieutenant on duty in China, from the vengeance of an evil mandarin.

LP *Jocelyn Yeo, Roy Galloway, Harry Agar Lyons, Rita Cave, Jack Barnes, Frank Lilliput.*

IN A MONASTERY GARDEN (1932)   3

Dir *Maurice Elvey.* Prod *Julius Hagen.* Scr *H. Fowler Mear, Michael Barringer.* PC *Twickenham.* Dis *Associated Producers and Distributors.* 80 mins. Cert A

Two brothers study music in Rome and fall for the same girl, the fiancée of a prince, who is then shot dead. One of the brothers, Michael (*John Stuart*) is accused, found guilty and sentenced to life. The other brother, Paul (*Hugh Williams*) steals Michael's manuscripts to help him make good as a composer. Michael is cleared and goes to a monastery, electing to remain there even when Paul confesses to the 'theft'.

RoC *Gina Malo, Dino Galvani, Alan Napier, Humberstone Wright, Frank Pettingell.*

INCIDENT IN SHANGHAI (1937) [2]
Dir *John Paddy Carstairs.* Prod *Anthony Havelock-Allan.* Scr *A.R. Rawlinson.* Ph *Francis Carver.* PC and Dis *British and Dominions/Paramount British. 67 mins. Cert A*
Tired story grafted on to topical setting. Madeleine (*Margaret Vyner*), unhappy wife of the head of a Red Cross unit in Shanghai, falls in love with an English pilot (*Patrick Barr*) serving with the Chinese Air Force. When he is wounded, her husband (*Derek Gorst*) has to operate. ... Far East atmosphere is best thing in obviously plotted romantic melodrama.
RoC *Ralph Roberts, John Deverell, George Courtney, Lotus Fragrance, Rita Davies, Johnnie Schofield, Lloyd Pearson, Henry Woolston, Douglas Fine.*

THE INDISCRETIONS OF EVE (1932) [4]
Dir, Prod and Scr *Cecil Lewis.* Ph *James Wilson, Philip Grindrod.* PC *BIP.* Dis *Wardour. 63 mins. Cert A*
Bright and amusing mini-musical comedy about an earl who falls in love with a girl who models in a wax factory and is engaged to its manager. Hungarian dancer *Steffi Duna* is delightful as the girl who eventually marries the persistent nobleman.
RoC *Fred Conyngham, Lester Matthews, Tony Sympson, Jessica Tandy, Clifford Heatherley, Hal Gordon, Muriel Aked, Arthur Chesney, George Mozart, Teddy Brown, Stella Nelson, Marius B. Winter and His Orchestra.*

THE INNOCENTS OF CHICAGO (1932) [2]
(USA: *Why Saps Leave Home***)**
Dir and Prod *Lupino Lane.* Scr *Lane, Leslie Arliss,* from a play by *Reginald Simpson, J.W. Drawbell.* Ph *H.E. Palmer.* PC *BIP.* Dis *Wardour. 68 mins. Cert A*
Unsuccessful burlesque of an American gangster film, set in Chicago where Percy, a bland young Englishman (*Henry Kendall*), inherits a business from his uncle, unaware that it's a bootleg liquor plant. Percy finds himself caught between two rival gangs out to eliminate him.
RoC *Betty Norton, Margot Grahame, Bernard Nedell, Ben Welden, Binnie Barnes, Charles Farrell, Wallace Lupino, Cyril Smith, Val Guest, Ernest Sefton, Peter Bernard.*

Betty Norton in The Innocents of Chicago (*1932*)

INQUEST (1931) [3]
Dir *G.B. Samuelson.* Prod *Gordon Craig.* Scr *Michael Barringer,* from his play. PC *Majestic/New Era.* Dis *First National. 95 mins. Cert A*
A year after John Hamilton has died, seemingly from a weak heart, an exhumation is ordered, and he is found to have been shot. Things look black for his widow (*Mary Glynne*), especially when the coroner (*Sydney Morgan*) seems biased against her. Then a young KC (*Campbell Gullan*) comes to her defence and establishes her innocence. Remade in 1939 (see below).
RoC *Haddon Mason, G.H. Mulcaster, Lena Halliday, Peter Coleman, Reginald Tippett, Alex Hunter, Nelson Phillips.*

INQUEST (1939) [3]
Dir *Roy Boulting.* Prod *John Boulting.* Scr *Francis Miller,* from the play by *Michael Barringer.* Ph *D.P. Cooper.* PC *Charter.* Dis *Grand National. 60 mins. Cert A*
Months after the death of her husband, Margaret (*Elizabeth Allan*) is suspected of having murdered him, because a revolver has been found in her attic and weed-killer tins in the kitchen. The local coroner (*Herbert Lomas*) is convinced she is guilty and things look bad until her case is taken by a distinguished QC (*Hay Petrie*) who, by clever deduction, arrives at the unexpected truth. Standard courtroom mystery adequately maintains its tension.
RoC *Barbara Everest, Olive Sloane, Philip Friend, Harold Anstruther, Malcolm Morley, Jean Shepherd, Charles Stephenson, Basil Cunard, Richard Coke.*

INSIDE THE ROOM (1935) [2]
Dir *Leslie Hiscott.* Prod *Julius Hagen.* Scr *H. Fowler Mear,* from the play by *Marten Cumberland.* Ph *William Luff.* PC *Twickenham.* Dis *Universal. 66 mins. Cert A*
Another Continental detective for *Austin Trevor,* following his Hercule Poirot portraits. He plays French sleuth Pierre Santos, solving a series of murders at a house party, following the death of a wealthy actress, whose offspring, a singer, proves to be the avenging killer. Conventional whodunnit.
RoC *Dorothy Boyd, Garry Marsh, George Hayes, Brian Buchel, Robert Horton, Frederick Burtwell, Marjorie Chard, Vera Bogetti, Dorothy Minto, Claude Horton, Kenji Takase.*

INSPECTOR HORNLEIGH (1939) [4]
Dir *Eugene Forde.* Prod *Robert T. Kane.* Scr *Bryan Wallace, Gerald Elliott, Richard Llewellyn,* from the radio series by *Hans Wolfgang Priwin.* Ph *Derek Williams.* PC and Dis *20th Century-Fox. 87 mins. Cert A*
Hornleigh (*Gordon Harker*) and Sergeant Bingham (*Alastair Sim*) investigate a murder involving the theft of the Chancellor of the Exchequer's budget bag. Another killing leads Hornleigh to the home of Kavanos (*Steve Geray*), a foreign millionaire, then to an inn run by Bill (*Hugh Williams*), who is involved in the theft, and Ann (*Miki Hood*). Bill becomes the third murder victim, before Horn-

leigh and Bingham crack the case. Wordy but well-told comedy-thriller.
RoC *Wally Patch, Edward Underdown, Gibb McLaughlin, Ronald Adam, Eliot Makeham.*

INSPECTOR HORNLEIGH ON HOLIDAY (1939) [4]
Dir *Walter Forde.* Prod *Edward Black.* Scr *Frank Launder, Sidney Gilliat,* from a radio series by *Hans Wolfgang Priwin* and a novel by *Leo Grex.* Ph *John J. Cox.* PC and Dis *20th Century-Fox. 87 mins. Cert A*
On holiday in Brighthaven, Hornleigh (*Gordon Harker*) and his assistant Sgt Bingham (*Alastair Sim*) stumble across a murderous plot to defraud insurance companies by faking deaths of people with weighty policies and substituting other corpses for the 'victims'. The mystery is solved after Bingham disguises himself as a corpse in a hospital, and the pair return to Brighthaven, where they have missed the last fine weather of the year. Far-fetched but well-made comedy-thriller.
RoC *Linden Travers, Wally Patch, Edward Chapman, Philip Leaver, Kynaston Reeves, John Turnbull, Wyndham Goldie, Cyril Conway, Eileen Bell.*

Gordon Harker and Alastair Sim in Inspector Hornleigh on Holiday (*1939*)

INSULT (1932) [3]
Dir *Harry Lachman.* Prod *S.E. Fitzgibbon.* Scr *Basil Mason,* from a play by *Jean Fabricus.* PC *Paramount British.* Dis *Paramount. 79 mins. Cert A*
Convoluted Foreign Legion drama about a half-Arab officer (*Hugh Williams*), distrusted by a major who once had him court-martialled for insubordination. When the half-Arab, Ramon, is arrested, the major's son Henri (*John Gielgud*) takes his place in a battle against native forces. Ramon escapes and saves Henri's life at the cost of his own.
RoC *Sam Livesey, Elizabeth Allan, Sydney Fairbrother, Abraham Sofaer, Edgar Norfolk, Hal Gordon, Dinah Gilly.*

THE INTERRUPTED HONEYMOON (1936) [4]
Dir *Leslie Hiscott.* Prod *Herbert Smith.* Scr *Michael Barringer, Wyndham Brown, Neil Tyfield,* from the play by *Ernst Bach and Franz Arnold.* PC and Dis *British Lion. 72 mins. Cert A*
A friend and his blonde mistress take posses-

sion of Victor's (*Claude Hulbert*) flat while he is honeymooning in Paris. When he inadvertently kisses the wife of a jealous hotelier, Victor finds his honeymoon cut short, and all sorts of complications arise when the bickering bride and groom return home. Lively comedy.
RoC *Jane Carr, Jack Hobbs, Glennis Lorimer, Francis L Sullivan, Hugh Wakefield, Robb Wilton, David Horne, Martita Hunt, Wally Patch, Helen Haye, Hal Walters.*

IN THE SOUP (1936)   4
Dir *Henry Edwards.* Prod *Julius Hagen.* Scr *H. Fowler Mear, from the play by Ralph Lumley.* Ph *Sydney Blythe.* PC and Dis *Twickenham. 72 mins. Cert U*
Hard-up barrister Horace (*Ralph Lynn*) makes such a hash of his first case that it seems unlikely he'll ever be called again. He and his wife Kitty (*Judy Gunn*) let their flat to different people at the same time, then have to impersonate their servants (who have left after not being paid for months) at a horrendous dinner party. Kitty pours sleeping powder in the soup, and the 'guests' are all discovered in compromising positions by wives, husbands, etc., leaving Horace and Kitty with a huge rake-off in 'hush money'. Good farce.
RoC *Morton Selten, Nelson Keys, Michael Shepley, Felix Aylmer, Bertha Belmore, Mervyn Johns, Olive Sloane, Olive Melville, Margaret Yarde, Morris Harvey.*

INTIMATE RELATIONS (1937)   2
Dir *Clayton Hutton.* Prod *Herbert Wynne.* Scr *Frank Atkinson, from the play by Stafford Dickens.* Ph *John Stumar.* PC *Tudor.* Dis *Associated British. 66 mins. Cert A*
Promiscuous husband and wife George and Jane (*Garry Marsh, Vera Bogetti*) are currently trying to persuade Molly (*June Clyde*), an actress, and Freddie (*Jack Hobbs*), an old friend, to have affairs with them. The inevitable happeddie meet and fall in love with each other. Rather prolonged farce.
RoC *Moore Marriott, Cynthia Stock, Arthur Finn, Bruce Winston, Oliver Gordon, Lew Stone and His Band.*

IN TOWN TO-NIGHT (1934)   3
Dir, Prod and Scr *Herbert Smith.* PC and Dis *British Lion. 81 mins. Cert U*
A record company producer, seeking fresh talent for a new series of discs to be called *In Town To-Night*, commissions a comedian to find it for him. Fair revue with weak dialogue, but good entertainment highlights including *Stanley Holloway* reciting *Albert and the Lion*.
RoC *Jack Barty, Three Radio Rogues, Finlay Currie, Wilson, Keppel and Betty, Arthur Prince and Jim, Olive Groves, The Carson Sisters, Val Rosing, Nora Williams, Melissa Mason, Bob Lively, Tessa Deane, Beryl Orde, Howard Jacobs, The Seven Thunderbolts, The Dynamites, Dave Apollon and His Romantic Serenaders, Billy Merrin and His Commanders, Kneller Hall Military Band, The 16 Tiller Girls.*

THE INVADER (1935)   3
(USA: *An Old Spanish Custom*)
Dir *Adrian Brunel.* Prod *Sam Spiegel, Harold Richman.* Scr *Edwin Greenwood.* PC *British and Continental.* Dis *M-G-M. 61 mins. Cert U. Bilingual versions*
Buster Keaton comedy set in Spain, with Keaton as Leander Proudfoot, a guileless American tourist who falls foul of a tempestuous senorita's plan to rid herself of an unwanted suitor.
RoC *Lupita Tovar, Esmé Percy, Lyn Harding, Webster Booth, Andrea Malandrinos, Clifford Heatherley, Hilda Moreno.*

INVITATION TO THE WALTZ (1935)   3
Dir *Paul Merzbach.* Prod *Walter C. Mycroft.* Scr *Merzbach, Clifford Grey, Roger Burford, from a radio play by Eric Maschwitz, Holt Marvel, George Posford.* Ph *Claude Friese-Greene, Ronald Neame.* PC *BIP.* Dis *Wardour. 77 mins. Cert A*
Meandering musical set in 1803, about an English ballet star (*Lilian Harvey*) who uses her friendship with the Duke of Würtemberg (*Harold Warrender*) to trick him into signing a treaty with England against Napoleon. The young officer (*Carl Esmond*) who loves her fears she is the duke's mistress, but things are straightened out in the end.
RoC *Wendy Toye, Richard Bird, Esmé Percy, Gus McNaughton, Charles Carson, Alexander Field, Hay Petrie, Eric Stanley, Hal Gordon, Anton Dolin.*

IRISH AND PROUD OF IT (1936)   3
Dir *Donovan Pedelty.* Prod *Victor M. Greene.* Scr *Pedelty, David Evans, from the story by Dorothea Donn Byrne.* Ph *Geoffrey Faithfull.* PC *Crusade.* Dis *Paramount. 72 mins. Cert U*
An unpopular food-pill manufacturer is kidnapped by inhabitants of his Irish village, taken back to his native London and left there. Here, he encounters a Chicago-based gang of whisky distillers, outwits them and rounds them up for the police before returning to Ireland. Modest comedy has some charm.
LP *Richard Hayward, Dinah Sheridan, Gwen(llian) Gill, George Pembroke, Liam Gaffney, Herbert Thorpe, Jimmy Mageean, Jack Clifford, Shaun Desmond, J. Miles Merwyn, Wolf Curran, Charles Fagan.*

IRISH FOR LUCK (1936)   4
Dir *Arthur Woods.* Prod *Irving Asher.* Scr *Woods, Brock Williams, from the novel by L. A. G. Strong.* PC *Warner Bros.* Dis *First National. 68 mins. Cert U*
The Duchess (*Athene Seyler*), an impoverished noblewoman, lives on credit in a small Irish village. Her orphan niece (*Margaret Lockwood*) is horrified at her state, and goes off to England to seek fame as a singer, where she meets a busker (*Patric Knowles*) and they audition for the BBC. Unsuccessful, they return to Ireland to find that the Duchess has come into money and paid off all her creditors. Well-acted comedy of refreshing charm.
RoC *Gibb McLaughlin, Edward Rigby, Eugene Leahy, George Dillon, Terry Conlin.*

IRISH HEARTS (1934)   2
(USA: *Norah O'Neale*)
Dir and Scr *Brian Desmond Hurst, from a novel by J. Johnson Abraham.* Prod *Harry Clifton.* PC *Clifton-Hurst.* Dis *M-G-M. 71 mins. Cert A*
Publicised as 'the first all-Irish talkie', this melodrama of a doctor torn between two nurses and then thrown into fighting an outbreak of typhus in an Irish coastal town is strong on atmosphere but light on story, a rather disappointing film from Brian Desmond Hurst after his debut with *The Tell-Tale Heart*. The doctor almost dies himself from the disease, but is saved by the nurse he will marry.
LP *Nancy Burne, Lester Matthews, Patric Knowles, Molly Lamont, Sara Allgood, Kyrle Bellew, Torren Thatcher (Torin Thatcher), Mary Warren, Patrick Barr, Arthur Sinclair, Joyce Chancellor, Cathleen Drago, Maire O'Neill, Mehan Hartley, Tom Collins, Pegeen Mair, May Warren, Teresa McCormac, Mary Riley, Georgina Leech, Iya Abdy, Leo Rownson, Sean Dempsey, The Cummerford Dancers.*

THE IRON DUKE (1934)   3
Dir *Victor Saville.* Prod *Michael Balcon.* Scr *Bess Meredyth.* Ph *Curt Courant.* PC and Dis *Gaumont-British. 88 mins. Cert U*
Incidents in the life of the Duke of Wellington (*George Arliss*) from 1815 to 1816, including the great ball on the eve of Waterloo, the battle itself and the political troubles that follow. Wellington clears himself with the House of Lords, which had reviled him for not taking territory from the defeated French and settles his score with a scheming French countess (*Gladys Cooper*). Stodgy biopic never springs to life.
RoC *Emlyn Williams, Ellaline Terriss, A. E. Matthews, Allan Aynesworth, Lesley Wareing, Franklin Dyall, Felix Aylmer, Gibb McLaughlin, Peter Gawthorne, Norma Varden, Walter Sondes, Campbell Gullan, Gyles Isham, Frederick Leister, Gerald Lawrence, Edmund Willard, Farren Souter.*

A.E. Matthews and George Arliss in The Iron Duke *(1934)*

THE IRON STAIR (1932)   3
Dir *Leslie Hiscott.* Prod *Julius Hagen.* Scr *H. Fowler Mear.* PC *Real Art.* Dis *Radio. 51 mins. Cert A*
This remake of a 1920 thriller ploughs briskly through a complicated plot. George imperson-

ates his twin brother Geoffrey and forges cheques, allowing Geoffrey to go to prison for the crime. Geoffrey escapes from prison to prove his innocence, but the same night, George is killed in a fall from a horse. Geoffrey, though, clears his name through George's mistress Elsa.

LP *Henry Kendall (dual role), Steffi Duna, Dorothy Boyd, Michael Hogan, A. Bromley Davenport, Michael Sherbrooke, S. Victor Stanley, Charles Groves, Charles Paton, John Turnbull.*

I SEE ICE (1938)　　　　　　　　　　⑤

Dir *Anthony Kimmins.* Prod *Basil Dean.* Scr *Kimmins, Austin Melford.* Ph *Ronald Neame.* PC *ATP.* Dis *Associated British.* 81 mins. Cert U

George (*George Formby*), accident-prone assistant to a provincial photographer, has invented a tiny camera. He becomes 'props man' to Judy (*Kay Walsh*), a skater whom he falls for, and her sinister partner Paul (*Cyril Ritchard*). After landing himself in prison, George acts (unknowingly) as referee in an ice hockey match from which the public has been barred. The pictures he takes with his miniature camera land him a job in Fleet Street. Uproarious comedy with the star on top form.

RoC *Garry Marsh, Betty Stockfeld, Frederick Burtwell, Gordon McLeod, Gavin Gordon, Ernest Sefton, Archibald Batty, Frank Leighton, Ernest Jay, Ernest Borrow, (Dominick) Sterlini, Laura Smithson, Andrea Malandrinos, Esma Cannon, R. Meadows White, Jack Vyvyan, Roddy McDowall.*

Cyril Ritchard, Gordon McLeod, George Formby in I See Ice *(1938)*

ISLAND MAN/WEST OF KERRY (1938)　　　　　　　　　　②

(USA: *Men of Ireland*)

Dir *Dick Bird.* Prod *Victor Taylor.* Scr *Patrick Keenan Heale.* PC *Irish National.* Dis *Butchers.* 48 mins. Cert U

Neale (*Cecil Ford*), a Dublin medical student, goes to the Blasket Islands on holiday and falls for pretty islander Eileen (*Eileen Curran*), beloved of Liam (*Brian O'Sullivan*). During a fishing trip, Liam falls overboard and is dragged out by Neale. Liam dies, but before he does, gives his blessing to his girlfriend's new romance. Some pictorial value in glum Irish drama.

RoC *Gabriel Fallon, Daisy Murphy, Gerard Duffy, Josephine Fitzgerald, Eugene Leahy, Paddy Carey.*

I SPY (1933)　　　　　　　　　　②

Dir *Allan Dwan.* Prod *Walter C. Mycroft.* Scr *Dwan, Arthur Woods.* Ph *James Wilson.* PC *BIP.* Dis *Wardour.* 69 mins. Cert U

Burlesque of spy melodramas, centring on a playboy, Wally (*Ben Lyon*) who is mistaken for a spy by the secret service of tiny European country Hetzelburg. He falls for Thelma Coldwater (*Sally Eilers*) who proves to be superspy Olga whom the Hetzelburgers are after. But Olga and Wally easily escape. Pretty awful.

RoC *Harry Tate, H. F. Maltby, Harold Warrender, Andrews Engelmann, Dennis Hoey, Henry Victor, Marcelle Rogez.*

IT HAPPENED IN PARIS (1935)　　　②

Dir *Robert Wyler, Carol Reed.* Prod *Bray Wyndham.* Scr *John Huston, H. F. Maltby, from a play by Yves Mirande.* PC *Wyndham.* Dis *Associated British.* 68 mins. Cert U. Bilingual versions

Romantic comedy, none too convincing despite its credentials. *John Loder* plays Paul, a wealthy American studying painting in Paris, who pretends he is impoverished in order to win the love of a working-class girl (*Nancy Burne*).

RoC *Esmé Percy, Edward H. Robbins, Dorothy Boyd, Lawrence Grossmith, Jean Gillie, Bernard Ansell, Paul Sheridan, Warren Jenkins, Kyrle Bellew, Margaret Yarde, Minnie Rayner, Billy Shine, Denys Val Norton, Nancy Pawley, Eve Chipman, Roy Emerton, Bela Mila.*

IT'S A BET (1935)　　　　　　　　　　③

Dir *Alexander Esway.* Prod *Walter C. Mycroft.* Scr *L. DuGarde Peach, Frank Miller, Kurt Siodmak, from the novel by Marcus McGill.* PC *BIP.* Dis *Wardour.* 69 mins. Cert U

Sub-standard *Gene Gerrard* film, casting him as Rollo, an inefficient reporter sacked for attacking the police. He has a bet with Norman (*Allen Vincent*), a wealthy newspaperman, that he can disappear for a month, Norman really only being after his girl (*Judy Kelly*). Complications arise when Rollo wins a sweep and finds himself unable to claim the huge prize.

RoC *Helen Chandler, Dudley Rolph, Nadine March, Polly Ward, Alf Goddard, Jimmy Godden, Frank Stanmore, Ronald Shiner, Ellen Pollock, George Zucco, Violet Farebrother, Raymond Raikes, Charlotte Parry.*

IT'S A BOY! (1933)　　　　　　　　　　④

Dir *Tim Whelan.* Prod *Michael Balcon.* Scr *Austin Melford, Leslie Howard Gordon, John Paddy Carstairs, from a play by Melford, Franz Arnold and Ernest Bach.* Ph *Mutz Greenbaum.* PC *Gainsborough.* Dis *W and F.* 80 mins. Cert A

On his wedding day, Dudley (*Edward Everett Horton*) is confronted by a young man claiming to be his son. His best man Skippy (*Leslie Henson*) gets him through the wedding by passing the 'son' off as an author and it's later proved that the young man is nothing but a would-be blackmailer. Amusing comedy.

RoC *Albert Burdon, Heather Thatcher, Alfred Drayton, Robertson Hare, Wendy Barrie, Helen Haye, Joyce Kirby, J. H. Roberts*

Albert Burdon, Edward Everett Horton and Leslie Henson in It's a Boy! *(1933)*

IT'S A COP (1934)　　　　　　　　　　②

Dir *Maclean Rogers.* Prod *Herbert Wilcox.* Scr *R. P. Weston, Bert Lee, Jack Marks, John Paddy Carstairs, Robert Cullen.* PC *British and Dominions.* Dis *United Artists.* 85 mins. Cert A

Slackly paced comedy with *Sydney Howard* as Spry, a slow-witted constable. He is instructed to watch a house for attempted burglary, but is inveigled from his duty by the seductive Babette (*Dorothy Bouchier*), one of the gang. Sacked, he sets about earning reinstatement and succeeds, more by accident than design, in apprehending the thieves.

RoC *Donald Calthrop, Garry Marsh, Annie Esmond, Cyril Smith, John Turnbull, Ronald Simpson.*

Sydney Howard and Dorothy (Chili) Bouchier in It's a Cop *(1934)*

IT'S A GRAND OLD WORLD (1937)　②

Dir *Herbert Smith.* Prod and PC *Tom Arnold.* Scr *Arnold, Sandy Powell.* Dis *British Lion.* 71 mins. Cert U

Episodic comedy involving *Sandy Powell* as a man who, on the dole, wins £16,000 on the pools and, struck on an actress, Joan (*Gina Malo*) uses the money to help her save her ancestral home.

RoC *Cyril Ritchard, Frank Pettingell, Garry Marsh, Ralph Truman, Fewlass Llewellyn, John Turnbull, Iris Charles.*

IT'S A KING! (1932)　　　　　　　　　　④

Dir *Jack Raymond.* Prod *Herbert Wilcox.* Scr *R. P. Weston, Bert Lee, Jack Marks.* Ph *F. A. Young.* PC *British and Dominions.* Dis *W and F.* 68 mins. Cert U

Funny spoof of *The Prisoner of Zenda*, with

Sydney Howard as an insurance agent mistaken for the King of Helgia, who has taken off for a few weeks' secret holiday. Albert enjoys a romantic interlude with a princess (*Joan Maude*), becomes involved with revolutionaries intent on abducting the king and foils their plot, before the real king returns.

RoC *Cecil Humphreys, George de Warfaz, Arthur Goullet, Franklyn Bellamy, Lew Stone, Monseigneur Orchestra, Bela Berkes and His Gipsy Players.*

IT'S IN THE AIR (1938) [4]
(USA: *George Takes the Air*)
Dir and Scr *Anthony Kimmins*. Prod *Basil Dean*. Ph *Ronald Neame, Gordon Dines*. PC *ATP/Eltham Films*. Dis *Associated British*. 87 mins. Cert U

Failing to get a job as an ARP warden, George (*George Formby*) dons his despatch rider friend's RAF uniform and inevitably gets taken for an airman. Before achieving his ambition of joining the RAF, George woos the flight-sergeant's daughter (*Polly Ward*), has a disastrous encounter with her father and ends up at the controls of a new aircraft on its trial flight. Bright Formby comedy, full of good slapstick.

RoC *Garry Marsh, Julien Mitchell, Jack Hobbs, (C.) Denier Warren, Jack Melford, Hal Gordon, Michael Shepley, Frank Leighton, Ilena Sylvia, O. B. Clarence, Esma Cannon, Joe Cunningham, Scruffy (dog).*

IT'S IN THE BAG (1936) [1]
Dir *William Beaudine*. Prod *Irving Asher*. Scr *Brock Williams*. Ph *Basil Emmott*. PC and Dis *Warner Bros*. 80 mins. Cert U

Indifferent material is the downfall of this broad *Nervo and Knox* comedy, in which Jimmy and Teddy are Covent Garden porters who lose their jobs, become furniture removers, discover a bag full of £5 notes, finance a nightclub, find that the money is counterfeit and flee from the forgers, who end up in the arms of the police.

RoC *Jack Barty, George Carney, René Hunter, Ursula Hirst, Aubrey Dexter, Hal Gordon, Ernest Sefton, (C.) Denier Warren, Glen Alyn, Gaston and Andrée, Cora Beaucaire, Frederick Burtwell, The Cochran Young Ladies.*

IT'S IN THE BLOOD (1938) [2]
Dir *Gene Gerrard*. Prod *Irving Asher*. Scr *Reginald Purdell, John Dighton, J. O. C. Orton, Brock Williams, Basil Dillon, from a novel by David Whitelaw*. Ph *Basil Emmott*. PC *Warner Bros*. Dis *First National*. 56 mins. Cert U

Mild Edwin Povey (*Claude Hulbert*) is plunged into adventures galore on a day trip to Boulogne. Robbed by English thieves, Edwin gets back home on an onion boat and tries to find the gang. He and his girl (*Lesley Brook*) are trapped in a house where the crooks keep stolen valuables. But the police arrive, round up the criminals and rescue Edwin. Unpretentious romp.

RoC *James Stephenson, Max Leeds, Glen Alyn, Clem Lawrance, Percy Walsh, Reginald Purdell, George Galleon.*

IT'S LOVE AGAIN (1936) [5]
Dir *Victor Saville*. Prod *Michael Balcon*. Scr *Lesser Samuels, Marian Dix, Austin Melford*. Ph *Glen MacWilliams*. PC and Dis *Gaumont-British*. 83 mins. Cert U

Critically the most successful of *Jessie Matthews'* musicals, a vivacious show which casts her as a chorus girl who, to achieve her singing and dancing ambitions, impersonates 'Mrs Smythe-Smythe', an imaginary society woman, lately returned from the East, invented by her gossip-writer boyfriend. Eventually, she becomes a star on her own merits. The Sam Coslow-Harry Woods songs include *It's Love Again* and *Gotta Dance My Way to Heaven*.

RoC *Robert Young, Sonnie Hale, Ernest Milton, Sara Allgood, Robb Wilton, Warren Jenkins, Athene Seyler, Glennis Lorimer, Cyril Raymond, David Horne, Robert Hale, Cyril Wells.*

Athene Seyler, Robert Young and Jessie Matthews in It's Love Again *(1936)*

IT'S NEVER TOO LATE TO MEND (1937) [3]
Dir *David Macdonald*. Prod and PC *George King*. Scr *H. F. Maltby, from the play by Charles Reade, Arthur Shirley*. Dis *M-G-M*. 67 mins. Cert A

Larger-than-life old time melodrama which attempts to indict the inhuman prison system of the nineteenth century, through the story of unscrupulous Squire Meadows (*Tod Slaughter*) who plots to marry Susan (*Marjorie Taylor*) by having her betrothed (*Jack Livesey*) sent to jail. Eventually, however, the Squire gets his come-uppance and Susan gets her beloved back.

RoC *Ian Colin, Lawrence Hanray, D. J. Williams, Roy Russell, Johnny Singer.*

IT'S NOT CRICKET (1937) [3]
Dir *Ralph Ince*. Prod *Irving Asher*. Scr *Henry Kendall*. Ph *Basil Emmott*. PC *Warner Bros*. Dis *First National*. 63 mins. Cert A

Amusing trifle about a French girl (*Betty Lynne*) who determines to teach her cricket-mad husband a lesson by appearing to elope to Paris with her timid friend Willie (*Claude Hulbert*). Not only does the ruse work, but Willie, after sundry Parisian misadventures, gets engaged to his own girl (*Sylvia Marriott*) during a local cricket match that's wrecked by rain.

RoC *Henry Kendall, Clifford Heatherley, Violet Farebrother, Frederick Burtwell.*

IT'S YOU I WANT (1936) [4]
Dir *Ralph Ince*. Prod *Herbert Smith*. Scr *Cyril Campion, from the play by Maurice Braddell*. Ph *George Stretton*. PC and Dis *British Lion*. 73 mins. Cert A

Stagey but funny comedy about a middle-aged philanderer, Victor (*Seymour Hicks*) who falls in love with a young girl (*Lesley Wareing*), but is hard put to escape the attentions of an old(er) flame (*Jane Carr*), especially when he finds them both occupying his flat. Well-handled belly-laugh situations result.

RoC *Marie Lohr, Hugh Wakefield, H. G. Stoker, Gerald Barry, Ronald Waters, Dorothy Hammond.*

I'VE GOT A HORSE (1938) [4]
Dir and Prod *Herbert Smith*. Scr *Fenn Sherie, Ingram d'Abbes, Sandy Powell*. Ph *George Stretton*. PC and Dis *British Lion*. 77 mins. Cert U

Newly-wed Sandy (*Sandy Powell*) accepts a horse called Lightning in settlement of a bad debt. He hires a man from a circus to train the horse, but has to fight in court to keep it when the former owner steals the transfer deed. Comes the big race, and the horse is winning when it passes a fairground and starts to do circus tricks instead. Sandy and Lightning join the circus. Comedy provides good measure for Powell fans.

RoC *Norah Howard, Felix Aylmer, Evelyn Roberts, Leo Franklyn, D. A. Clarke-Smith, Kathleen Harrison, Edward Chapman, (Wilfrid) Hyde White, Frank Atkinson.*

I WAS A SPY (1933) [5]
Dir *Victor Saville*. Prod *Michael Balcon*. Scr *W. P. Lipscomb, Ian Hay, from a book by Marthe Cnockhaert McKenna*. Ph *William Van Engen*. PC *Gaumont-British*. Dis *W and F*. 90 mins. Cert A

Victor Saville's adroit handling of crowd scenes was praised in this widely admired true-life story of a Belgian nurse, Marthe Cnockhaert (*Madeleine Carroll*) who spied for the Allies in the First World War and, with a secret service agent (*Herbert Marshall*) who was ultimately shot (she survived), tried to blow up a big arms dump to prevent a German gas attack.

RoC *Conrad Veidt, Edmund Gwenn, Donald Calthrop, Anthony Bushell, Gerald du Maurier, Eva Moore, Nigel Bruce, May Agate, George Merritt, Martita Hunt, Gavin Gordon.*

Madeleine Carroll in I Was a Spy *(1933)*

JACK AHOY! (1934) [4]

Dir *Walter Forde*. Prod *Michael Balcon*. Scr *Sidney Gilliat, J. O. C. Orton, Jack Hulbert, Leslie Arliss, Gerard Fairlie, Austin Melford*. Ph *Bernard Knowles*. PC and Dis *Gaumont-British. 82 mins. Cert U*

Robust musical romp that gave *Jack Hulbert* another hit. He plays Able Seaman Jack Ponsonby, serving on a battleship bound for Chinese waters. He falls for Patricia (*Nancy O'Neil*), daughter of an admiral. Jack rises to the occasion after he, Patricia and her father have been kidnapped and held by revolutionaries. Hulbert's songs include *The Hat's on the Side of My Head*. Although the film has a large cast, no more than six players' names appear ever to have been issued. Remade in 1954 as *Up to His Neck.*

RoC *Alfred Drayton, Tamara Desni, Henry Peterson, Sam Wilkinson.*

Jack Hulbert in Jack Ahoy! *(1934)*

JACK OF ALL TRADES (1936) [3]
(USA: *The Two of Us*)

Dir *Jack Hulbert, Robert Stevenson*. Prod *Michael Balcon*. Scr *Hulbert, Austin Melford, J. O. C. Orton, from a play by Paul Vulpius*. Ph *Charles Van Enger*. PC *Gaumont-British*. Dis *Gaumont-British. 76 mins. Cert U*

Out-of-work Jack Warrender (*Jack Hulbert*) bluffs his way into the world of big business and, before being rumbled, sees the setting up of a company to promote his hare-brained invention. At the new shoe factory that results, Jack is employed as night watchman and helps catch a gang of arsonists. Patchy satirical comedy-musical lacks the courage of its convictions.

RoC *Gina Malo, J. Robertson Hare, Athole Stewart, Felix Aylmer, H. F. Maltby, Cecil Parker, Betty Astell, Bruce Seton, Fewlass Llewellyn, Mary Jerrold, C. M. Hallard, Ian MacLean, Peggy Simpson, Marcus Barron, Frederick Piper, Cyril Smith, Netta Westcott, Henry Crocker, Arnold Bell.*

JACK'S THE BOY (1932) [5]
(USA: *Night and Day*)

Dir *Walter Forde*. Prod *Michael Balcon*. Scr *W. P. Lipscomb*. Ph *Leslie Rowson*. PC *Gainsborough*. Dis *W and F. 89 mins. Cert U*

Comedy-musical with *Jack Hulbert* at the top of his form as the hapless son of a police commissioner. Determined to make good, he joins the police, falls for a girl called Ivy (*Winifred Shotter*) and is helped in his pursuit of jewel thieves by Ivy's old nurse (*Cicely Courtneidge*) now running the Loch Lomond Hotel. Music: Vivian Ellis. Lyrics: Douglas Furber. Choreography: Hulbert.

RoC *Francis Lister, Peter Gawthorne, Ben Field, Charles Ferrell, Ronald Curtis.*

JAIL BIRDS (1939) [3]

Dir *Oswald Mitchell*. Prod *F. W. Baker*. Scr *Con West, from the sketch by Fred Karno*. Ph *Geoffrey Faithfull*. PC and Dis *Butchers. 74 mins. Cert U*

Bill and Nick (*Albert Burdon, Charles Hawtrey*) escape from prison in drag and get a job in a bakery. A third escapee, Spike (*Charles Farrell*) joins them and gives them some stolen jewellery to hide. It ends up in a loaf of bread, which is eventually cut by the detective fiancé of Bill's daughter. Bill and Nick flee back to jail and pretend they've never left. Crazy farce, pretty riotous at times.

RoC *Shaun Glenville, Lorraine Clewes, Cyril Chamberlain, Nat Mills and Bobbie, Sylvia Coleridge, Harry Terry.*

JAMAICA INN (1939) [4]

Dir *Alfred Hitchcock*. Prod *Erich Pommer*. Scr *Sidney Gilliat, Joan Harrison, J. B. Priestley, from the novel by Daphne du Maurier*. Ph *Harry Stradling, Bernard Knowles*. PC *Mayflower*. Dis *Associated British. 108 mins. Cert A*

Sir Humphrey (*Charles Laughton*) heads a band of wreckers based at Jamaica Inn, whose landlord (*Leslie Banks*) is one of them. His niece Mary (*Maureen O'Hara*) rescues Jem (*Robert Newton*) from the gang when they accuse him of treachery. Jem, a government agent, misguidedly goes to Sir Humphrey for aid. Eventually revealed in his true colours, Sir Humphrey flees for France, taking Mary. But his boat is boarded by the military, headed by Jem. Sir Humphrey flings himself from the rigging. Lesser, rather lurid Hitchcock still has thrills a-plenty.

Charles Laughton, Maureen O'Hara and Robert Newton in Jamaica Inn *(1939)*

RoC *Emlyn Williams, Wylie Watson, Marie Ney, Morland Graham, Stephen Haggard, Mervyn Johns, Edwin Greenwood, Horace Hodges, Jeanne de Casalis, Basil Radford, John Longden, George Curzon, Hay Petrie, Frederick Piper, Herbert Lomas, Clare Greet, William Devlin, A. Bromley Davenport, Mabel Terry Lewis, Aubrey Mather, Marie Ault, O.B. Clarence, Mary Jerrold, Archibald Harradine, Harry Lane, William Fazan, Alan Lewis, Peter Scott, Philip Ray, George Smith, Robert Adair, Sam Lee.*

JANE STEPS OUT (1938) [3]

Dir *Paul L. Stein*. Prod *Walter C. Mycroft*. Scr *Dudley Leslie, William Freshman, from the play by Kenneth Horne*. Ph *Claude Friese-Greene*. PC and Dis *Associated British. 71 mins. Cert A*

Plain Jane Wilton (*Diana Churchill*), the Cinderella of her family, rebels against their treatment of her and, with the help of newly arrived Granny (*Athene Seyler*), snaffles the young man the family has earmarked for her unpleasant and spoiled sister (*Jean Muir*). Amusing anecdote with well-drawn characters.

RoC *Peter Murray-Hill, Fred Emney, Judy Kelly, Iris Hoey.*

JAVA HEAD (1934) [5]

Dir *J. Walter Ruben*. Prod *Basil Dean*. Scr *Martin Brown, Gordon Wellesley, from the novel by Joseph Hergesheimer*. Ph *Robert Martin*. PC *ATP*. Dis *Associated British. 85 mins. Cert A*

Colourful adventure-romance set in Bristol and on the high seas. Shipowner Jeremy Ammidon (*Edmund Gwenn*) has two sons: William (*Ralph Richardson*) who marries and carries on the business, and Gerrit (*John Loder*) who leads an adventurous life in far-off places, returning with a Chinese bride (*Anna May Wong*) who later commits suicide when she realizes he still loves his childhood sweetheart (*Elizabeth Allan*).

RoC *Herbert Lomas, George Curzon, Roy Emerton, John Marriner, Grey Blake, Amy Brandon Thomas, Frances Carson.*

JEALOUSY (1931) [2]

Dir and Scr *G.B. Samuelson, from a play by John McNally*. Prod *Gordon Craig*. PC *Majestic*. Dis *New Era. 56 mins. Cert A*

Small-scale drama in which tragedy results when a pretty orphan (*Mary Newland*) falls in love and her jealous guardian (*Malcolm Keen*) tries to wreck her love affair.

RoC *Harold French, Gibb McLaughlin, Sam Livesey, Henrietta Watson, Henry Carlisle, Frank Pettingell, Dino Galvani, Frederick Atwell.*

JENIFER HALE (1937) [3]

Dir *Bernard Mainwaring*. Prod *John Findlay*. Scr *Ralph Stock, Mainwaring, Edward Dryhurst, from the novel by Rob Eden*. Ph *Stanley Grant*. PC and Dis *Fox British. 66 mins. Cert A*

With stronger treatment, this drama might have made *René Ray* into the major star of the British cinema she sometimes threatened to become. She plays Jenifer, a chorus girl who is suspected of the murder of a producer whose advances she had rejected. She flees to Birmingham, where she falls for a young architect. The producer's partner tracks her down and threatens her with the police; but Jenifer has evidence of her own which eventually exposes the real killer.

RoC *Ballard Berkeley, John Longden, Paul Blake, Frank Birch, Richard Parry, Ernest Sefton, Kaye Seely, Philip Thomas, Jo Monkhouse, Raymond Ellis, (Dominick) Sterlini*

JERICHO (1937)   ▢3
(USA: *Dark Sands*)
Dir *Thornton Freeland*. Prod *Walter Futter, Max Schach*. Scr *Frances Marion, George Barraud, Robert N. Lee, Peter Ruric*. Ph *Cyril Bristow*. PC *Buckingham*. Dis *General Film Distributors*. 77 mins. Cert U

Interesting, if rather meandering adventure story which begins in the First World War, when Black US soldier Jericho Jackson (*Paul Robeson*) deserts after being court-martialled, joins forces with another deserter (*Wallace Ford*) and penetrates deep into the African jungle, where he becomes leader of a tribe and marries a native princess. The officer from whom he escaped (*Henry Wilcoxon*) tracks him down. The princess plots to kill him. Realizing Jericho is a good influence for the tribe, the officer leaves, but a bullet fired by the princess's brother tragically brings his plane down in flames.

RoC *Princess Kouka, John Laurie, James Carew, Laurence Brown, Rufus Rennell, Ike Hatch, Frank Cochrane, Frederick Cooper, George Barraud, Frank Crain, Henry Aubin*

THE JEWEL (1933)   ▢2
Dir *Reginald Denham*. Prod *Hugh Percival*. Scr *Basil Mason*, from a novel by *Edgar Wallace*. PC *Venture Films*. Dis *Paramount*. 67 mins. Cert U

Wealthy Frank Hallam (*Hugh Williams*) suspects that his cousin Maude (*Mary Newland*) and her friend Joan (*Frances Dean*) are planning to steal a valuable jewel from his aunt at a fancy dress ball. He persuades shop assistant Jenny Day to impersonate Joan, to foil the plot, but in the end it turns out that the jewel on show is a fake – Frank's aunt having wisely substituted it for the real thing.

RoC *Jack Hawkins, Eric Cowley, Annie Esmond, Geoffrey Goodheart, Clare Harris, Vincent Holman*

JEW SÜSS (1934)   ▢4
(USA: *Power*)
Dir *Lothar Mendes*. Prod *Michael Balcon*. Scr *Dorothy Farnum, A. R. Rawlinson*, from the novel by *Leon Feuchtwanger*. Ph *Bernard Knowles, Günther Krampf*. PC and Dis *Gaumont-British*. 108 mins. Cert A

Finely balanced, if rather impassionate account of the rise to power of 'Jew Süss' Oppenheimer (*Conrad Veidt*) in eighteenth-century Würtemberg in the service of a duke, so that he can further the cause of the Jewish race. Oppenheimer finds that he is, after all, a Gentile; when the duke wrongs him, he schemes his downfall, the shock of betrayal bringing on a

Conrad Veidt and Benita Hume in Jew Süss (*1934*)

seizure that kills the duke. Süss is condemned to death and hanged.

RoC *Benita Hume, Cedric Hardwicke, Frank Vosper, Gerald du Maurier, Pamela Ostrer, Joan Maude, Paul Graetz, Mary Clare, Haidee Wright, Percy Parsons, Eva Moore, James Raglan, Sam Livesey, Dennis Hoey, Campbell Gullan, Gibb McLaughlin, D. Hay Plumb, Percy Walsh, George Merritt, Frank Cellier, Francis L Sullivan, Glennis Lorimer, Diana Cotton, Jane Cornell, Robert Nainby, Helen Ferrers, Randle Ayrton, Henry Hallatt, Marcelle Rogez, P. Kynaston Reeves, Grete Hansen, Joseph Markovitch, Lucius Blake, Mickey Brantford, Selma Vaz Dias, Victor Fairley, Vittorio (Robert) Rietti, Henry Hewitt.*

JIMMY BOY (1935)   ▢2
Dir *John Baxter*. Prod *John Barter*. Scr *Con West, Harry O'Donovan*. Ph *George Dudgeon Stretton*. PC *Baxter and Barter*. Dis *Universal*. 71 mins. Cert U

Not one of the happier Baxter and Barter films, casting pint-sized Irish comedian *Jimmy O'Dea* as a lift-boy in a London hotel, where he thwarts the plans of a ring of spies plotting to blow up England's capital. Very disjointed jinks.

RoC *Enid Stamp-Taylor, Guy Middleton, Vera Sherburne, Elizabeth Jenns, Harold Williams, Edgar Driver, Harry O'Donovan, Peggy Novak, Kathleen Drago, Johnnie Schofield, Elizabeth Vaughan, J. H. Edwin, Stanley Kirby, Syd Crossley, Noel Purcell, Sherman Fisher Girls, The Mackay Twins, Reginald Forsyth and His Band.*

JOHN HALIFAX – GENTLEMAN (1938)   ▢2
Dir, Prod and PC *George King*. Scr *A. R. Rawlinson*, from the novel by *Mrs Craik*. Ph *Hone Glendinning*. Dis *M-G-M*. 69 mins. Cert U

1790: wanderer John Halifax (*John Warwick*) saves a cripple boy's life, and is taken on at the boy's father's mill where, inside a few years, he rises to become junior partner. Against a background of industrial dispute, Halifax marries the disowned ward (*Nancy Burne*) of a nobleman whose hatred he incurs, and proves a good employer who dies a respected member of the community. Lifeless period drama is a catalogue of missed chances.

RoC *Ralph Michael, D. J. Williams, Brian*

Buchel, Billy Bray, Elsie Wagstaffe, W. E. Holloway, Hugh Bickett, Roddy McDowall.

JOSSER IN THE ARMY (1932)   ▢3
Dir *Norman Lee*. Prod *John Maxwell*. Scr *Frank Launder*. PC *BIP*. Dis *Wardour*. 77 mins. Cert U

Ernie Lotinga comedy with more plot than usual, in which his character Jimmy Josser joins the Army during the First World War, becomes involved in an escape adventure, poses as a German general and unmasks an enemy agent.

RoC *Betty Norton, Jack Hobbs, Hal Gordon, Jack Frost, Arnold Bell, Harold Wilkinson.*

JOSSER JOINS THE NAVY (1932)   ▢3
Dir and Prod *Norman Lee*. Scr *Con West, Herbert Sargent*. PC *BIP*. Dis *Wardour*. 69 mins. Cert U

Fair comedy for *Ernie Lotinga* fans. Once again he is Jimmy Josser, this time a hall porter who, with his assistant Spud (*Jack Frost*) joins the Navy in order to track down a mysterious Chinaman (*H. Saxon-Snell*) and his confederate (*Cyril McLaglen*), a treacherous officer who has stolen a secret formula.

RoC *Jack Hobbs, Lesley Wareing, Renée Gadd, Charles Paton, Florence Vie, Leslie Stiles.*

JOSSER ON THE FARM (1934)   ▢2
Dir and Prod *T. Hayes Hunter*. Scr *Con West, Herbert Sargent, Ernest Lotinga*. PC and Dis *Fox British*. 63 mins. Cert U

Farmhand Jimmy Josser (*Ernie Lotinga*) outwits speculator Granby (*Garry Marsh*) who was planning to buy the farm and sell at a huge profit to the railways. Josser beats Granby in the local election, becomes a magistrate, sentences Granby and marries his sweetheart (*Betty Astell*). Comedy is practically all Lotinga, who gets in plenty of broad fooling.

RoC *Muriel Aked, John Gattrell, Hope Davy, (Wilfrid) Hyde White, Edwin Ellis, H. F. Maltby, James Craig, Franklyn Kelsey, Johnnie Schofield.*

JOSSER ON THE RIVER (1932)   ▢1
Dir and Prod *Norman Lee*. Scr *Lee, Leslie Arliss*. PC *BIP/British Instructional*. Dis *Wardour*. 75 mins. Cert A

Below-par *Ernie Lotinga* comedy in which he and *Arty Ash* are photographers who try to blackmail both a man whom they 'snap' taking a holiday away from his wife, and the couple's puritanical uncle, also caught in a compromising picture. Their attempts, however, are a dismal failure, and they end up as servants on the couple's houseboat.

RoC *Molly Lamont, Charles Hickman, Reginald Gardiner, Wallace Lupino, Joan Wyndham.*

JOURNEY'S END (1930)   ▢5
Dir *James Whale*. Prod *George Pearson*. Scr *Joseph Moncure March, V. Gareth Gundrey*, from the play by *R. C. Sheriff*. Ph *Benjamin Kline*. PC *Gainsborough-Welsh-Pearson-Tiffany*. Dis *W and F*. 120 mins. Cert A

The superior technical facilities of Hollywood tempted the producer to film this classic stage

success over there: tension mounts in the First World War trenches as, one by one, the characters go 'over the top' and die, while the captain who has become an alcoholic awaits his replacement (his girlfriend's brother) with dread. Highly praised in its time, although the acting now looks a little overwrought.
LP *Colin Clive, David Manners, Ian Maclaren, Billy Bevan, Anthony Bushell, Charles Gerrard, Werner Klinger, Tom Whiteley, Robert Adair, Jack Pitcairn.*

JOY RIDE (1935)   [3]
Dir *Harry Hughes.* Prod *Basil Humphreys.* Scr *Vernon Harris.* Ph *Ronald Neame.* PC *City Films.* Dis *Associated British.* 78 mins. Cert A
Two philanderers (*Gene Gerrard, Paul Blake*), with chorus-girl sisters (*Zelma O'Neal, Betty [Ann] Davies*) in tow, descend upon the home of an uncle of one, an admiral, using their knowledge of an indiscretion in his past to silence his protests. Auntie proves a tougher proposition, but she is won over at a garden fête after an eccentric duchess claims the girls as her godchildren. Patchy comedy.
RoC *Gus McNaughton, Charles Sewell, Amy Veness, Violet Vanbrugh, Cynthia Stock, W. G. Saunders, Vernon Harris, Bryan Farley, Molly Hamley Clifford, Robert Maclachlan, Ian Wilson, Jeanne d'Arcy.*

JUBILEE WINDOW (1935)   [1]
Dir *George Pearson.* Prod *Anthony Havelock-Allan.* Scr *Gerald Elliott, Pearson.* PC and Dis *British and Dominions/Paramount British.* 61 mins. Cert A
Poor comedy dealing with attempts to steal a valuable necklace during celebrations for King George V's Silver Jubilee in a house where several people gather to watch the procession.
LP *Frank Birch, Margaret Yarde, Sebastian Shaw, Ralph Truman, Olive Melville, Michael Shepley, Winifred Oughton, Robert Horton, Dorothy Hammond, Mark Daly, Walter Amner, Frank Bertram, Doris Hare.*

JUGGERNAUT (1936)   [2]
Dir *Henry Edwards.* Prod *Julius Hagen.* Scr *Heinrich Fraenkel, Cyril Campion, H. Fowler Mear, from the novel by Alice Campbell.* Ph *Sydney Blythe, William Luff.* PC *JH Productions/Grand National.* Dis *Wardour.* 74 mins. Cert A
Determined to pursue his experiments for a paralysis cure, Dr Sartorius (*Boris Karloff*) accedes to wealthy Lady Clifford's (*Mona Goya*) request to slowly poison her elderly husband. The old man dies, but, suspecting foul play, has transferred control of his wealth elsewhere. Sartorius kills himself, and Lady Clifford is arrested for murder. Lurid thriller, feeble by Karloff standards.
RoC *Arthur Margetson, Joan Wyndham, Morton Selten, Gibb McLaughlin, Anthony Ireland, Nina Boucicault, J. H. Roberts, Victor Rietti.*

JUMP FOR GLORY (1937)   [3]
(USA: *When Thief Meets Thief*)
Dir *Raoul Walsh.* Prod *Marcel Hellman, Douglas Fairbanks Jr.* Scr *John Meehan Jr. Harold French, from the novel by Gordon MacDonnell.*

Ph *Victor Armenise.* PC *Criterion.* Dis *United Artists.* 89 mins. Cert A
Ricky (*Douglas Fairbanks Jr*), an athletic gentleman thief, becomes enamoured of one of his 'victims', Glory (*Valerie Hobson*). Unfortunately, she is engaged to Ricky's ex-partner-in-crime Dial (*Alan Hale*), who has a hold over him. Ricky and Dial fight, Dial is killed, and Glory is accused. By convincing the court that he could have made an enormous jump into Dial's house, Ricky takes Glory's place as the accused, but both are freed when a giant crash in City shares makes Dial's death appear suicide. Okay romantic drama.
RoC *Edward Rigby, Barbara Everest, Jack Melford, Esmé Percy, Basil Radford, Leo Genn, Anthony Ireland, Ian Fleming, Frank Birch.*

JURY'S EVIDENCE (1935)   [3]
Dir *Ralph Ince.* Prod *Herbert Smith.* Scr *Ian Dalrymple, from the play by Jack de Leon, Jack Celestin.* PC and Dis *British Lion.* 74 mins. Cert A
At a murder trial, the foreman of the jury (*Hartley Power*) argues that the circumstantial evidence is too slim to convict the accused, as a vital piece of evidence is missing altogether. He reconstructs how *he* feels the crime was committed. The jury turns his theory down – but a final twist in the tale reveals the real murderer. Well-performed thriller.
RoC *Margaret Lockwood, Eve Gray, Nora Swinburne, Sebastian Shaw, Tracy Holmes, Jane Millican, Patrick Ludlow, Charles Paton, W. E. Holloway, Dick Francis, Philip Strange, Aubrey Fitzgerald.*

JUST FOR A SONG (1930)   [3]
Dir and Scr *V. Gareth Gundrey.* Prod *Michael Balcon.* PC *Gainsborough/Ideal.* Dis *W and F.* 94 mins. Black and white with colour sequence. Cert A
Fair musical about a boy and girl who seek their fortune in the music-hall, but are almost broken up by the booking manager who fancies the girl.
LP *Lillian Davis, Roy Royston, Constance Carpenter, Cyril Ritchard, Syd Crossley, Dick Henderson, Nick Adams, (Albert) Rebla, Mangan Tillerettes, Mad Hatters.*

JUST LIKE A WOMAN (1938)   [4]
Dir *Paul L. Stein.* Prod *Walter C. Mycroft.* Scr *Alec Coppel.* Ph *Claude Friese-Greene.* PC and Dis *Associated British.* 79 mins. Cert A
Tony (*John Lodge*), a jeweller's agent commissioned by his firm to find a string of black pearls, is outwitted twice by Ann (*Gertrude Michael*), acting for a smaller firm. She follows him to Argentina, on the trail of a third string, but is captured by a gang of crooks. After Tony rescues her, he finds she is his boss's daughter, out to teach her father not to undervalue a girl. Brisk comedy-thriller with some bright dialogue.
RoC *Jeanne de Casalis, Fred Emney, Arthur Wontner, Hartley Power, Anthony Ireland, David Burns, Felix Aylmer, Henry Hewitt, Ralph Truman.*

JUST MY LUCK (1932)   [3]
Dir *Jack Raymond.* Prod *Herbert Wilcox.* Scr *Ben Travers, from a play by H. F. Maltby.* Ph *F. A. Young.* PC *British and Dominions.* Dis *W & F.* 77 mins. Cert U
An Aldwych farce with *Davy Burnaby* filling in for an absent Tom Walls. *Ralph Lynn* plays a shy music teacher, pushing 40 and still unmarried, who takes a course in superiority and success. Put in charge of a new hotel by the father (*Burnaby*) of his girlfriend (*Winifred Shotter*), he accidentally catches an embezzling accountant, clearing his own name.
RoC *Robertson Hare, Vera Pearce, Frederick Burtwell, Phyllis Clare.*

JUST SMITH (1933)   [4]
(USA: *Leave It to Smith*)
Dir *Tom Walls.* Prod *Michael Balcon.* Scr *J. O. C. Orton, from a play by Frederick Lonsdale.* PC *Gaumont-British.* Dis *W and F.* 76 mins. Cert A
Gentlemen thieves Smith and Mortimer (*Tom Walls, Hartley Power*) worm their way into the confidence of a wealthy American widow (*Margaret Moffat*) with the idea of relieving her of a few of her valuables. When the widow's diamond necklace disappears at a party, Smith and Mortimer come under suspicion, until Smith proves that her daughter (*Carol Goodner*) has taken it. Smart Walls-inspired comedy of manners.
RoC *Anne Grey, Allan Aynesworth, Eva Moore, Leslie Perrins, Reginald Gardiner, Veronica Rose, Basil Radford, Peter Gawthorne.*

JUST WILLIAM (1939)   [3]
Dir *Graham Cutts.* Prod *Walter C. Mycroft.* Scr *Doreen Montgomery, Ireland Wood, Cutts, from stories by Richmal Crompton.* Ph *Walter Harvey.* PC and Dis *Associated British.* 72 mins. Cert U
Young William Brown (*Dicky Lupino*) and his gang of 'Outlaws' become involved with his father's efforts to get elected to the local council. William accidentally helps crooks get away with stolen jewels, but exposes another criminal by grabbing a bag he thinks contains a bomb. William finally achieves his personal ambition of owning an air-gun. Likeable adaptation of famous children's stories.
RoC *Fred Emney, Basil Radford, Amy Veness, Iris Hoey, Roddy McDowall, Norman Robinson, Peter Miles, David Tree, Jenny Laird, Simon Lack, Aubrey Mather, Eric Searle.*

KATE PLUS TEN (1938)   [3]
Dir *Reginald Denham.* Prod and PC *Richard Wainwright.* Scr *Jack Hulbert, Jeffrey Dell, from the novel by Edgar Wallace.* Ph *Roy Kellino.* Dis *General Film Distributors.* 81 mins. Cert U
Kate (*Genevieve Tobin*), secretary to Lord Flam-

borough, is recognized by Inspector Pemberton (*Jack Hulbert*) as the leader of a gang of crooks. When the lord's bank is robbed and details of a bullion consignment stolen, Pemberton tracks the train with the gold. Kate's 10 confederates rebel against her and take the bullion. But Pemberton, with Kate on board, chases them in the engine and blocks the getaway cars at a level crossing. Light-hearted thriller.

RoC *Noel Madison, Francis L. Sullivan, Arthur Wontner, Frank Cellier, Googie Withers, Edward Lexy, Peter Haddon, Felix Aylmer, Leo Genn, Queenie Leonard, Walter Sondes, James Harcourt, Albert Whelan, Arthur Brander, Geoffrey Clark, Vincent Holman, Paul Sheridan, Oliver Johnston, Ronald Adam, Philip Leaver.*

KATHLEEN MAVOURNEEN (1937)   [3]
(USA: *Kathleen*)
Dir *Norman Lee*. Prod *John Argyle*. Scr *Marjorie Deans, John Glen, from the novel by Clara Mulholland*. Ph *Bryan Langley*. PC *Welwyn/ Argyle-British*. Dis *Wardour*. 77 mins. Cert U
Kathleen (*Sally O'Neil*) has to earn enough in dockside Liverpool to keep her little brother and sister as well. Mike Rooney (*Tom Burke*), a singing stevedore who loves her, pays for them to go to their aunt's farm in Ireland. Their Aunt Hannah tries unsuccessfully to get the children put in an orphanage, then Kathleen falls in love with a wealthy landowner. Mike leaves for England and a singing career. 'Artless' or 'delightful' according to which critic you read.

RoC *Sara Allgood, Jack Daly, Talbot O'Farrell, Denis O'Neill, Fred Duprez, Pat Noonan, Jeanne Stuart, Ethel Griffies, John Forbes-Robertson, Arthur Lucan and Kitty McShane, Patrick O'Moore, Rory O'Connor, Sean Dempsey, Baby Brenda, J. A. O'Rourke, Mark Stone, Terry Conlin, Fred Withers, Frank Crawshaw, Guy Jones, Tara Irish Dancers, Frank Lee's Tara Ceilidh Band, Classic Symphony Orchestra.*

KEEPERS OF YOUTH (1931)   [4]
Dir *Thomas Bentley*. Prod *John Maxwell*. Scr *Bentley, Frank Launder, Walter C. Mycroft, from the play by Arnold Ridley*. Ph *James Wilson, Bert Ford*. PC *BIP*. Dis *Wardour*. 70 mins Cert A
Public-school drama about a new games master (*Garry Marsh*) who rides roughshod over his colleagues, has a mysterious hold over the headmaster and plans the seduction of the assistant matron (*Ann Todd*). Another new teacher (*Robin Irvine*) saves her from his atten-

Garry Marsh and *Ann Todd* in Keepers of Youth (*1931*)

tions, and they emigrate together to Canada. Good study of man you love to hate.

RoC *John Turnbull, O. B. Clarence, Herbert Ross, Mary Clare, John Hunt, René Ray, Ethel Warwick, Vaughn Powell, Matthew Boulton.*

KEEP FIT (1937)   [4]
Dir and Scr *Anthony Kimmins, Austin Melford*. Prod *Basil Dean*. Ph *John W. Boyle*. PC *ATP*. Dis *Associated British*. 82 mins. Cert U
George (*George Formby*), a butter-fingered barber in a department store, and Hector (*Guy Middleton*), athletic Lothario salesman, are rivals for manicurist Joyce (*Kay Walsh*). Both enter a big keep-fit competition, although the only muscles George has developed are those required for playing the ukulele. Hector wipes the floor with him in the gym trials, but George triumphs in the final event – a boxing match. Bouncy, confidently made comedy.

RoC *Gus McNaughton, Edmund Breon, George Benson, Evelyn Roberts, (C.) Denier Warren, Hal Walters, Leo Franklyn, Hal Gordon, Aubrey Mallalieu, D. J. Williams, Bob Gregory.*

KEEP IT QUIET (1934)   [2]
Dir *Leslie Hiscott*. Prod *Herbert Smith*. Scr *Michael Barringer*. PC *British Lion*. Dis *M-G-M*. 64 mins. Cert U
Joe (*Frank Pettingell*) is blackmailed by a gang of crooks into acting as their 'link man' in his nephew's house, where they plan to make a big jewel haul. But Joe, posing as the butler, manages to turn the tables. Well-played, indifferently scripted comedy.

RoC *Jane Carr, Davy Burnaby, Cyril Raymond, D. A. Clarke-Smith, Bertha Belmore.*

KEEP SMILING (1938)   [3]
(USA: *Smiling Along*)
Dir *Monty Banks*. Prod *Robert T. Kane*. Scr *Val Valentine, Rodney Ackland*. Ph *Mutz Greenbaum*. PC and Dis *20th Century-Fox*. 91 mins. Cert U
René Sidani (*Peter Coke*), a famous pianist, saves the concert party run by Gracie Gray (*Gracie Fields*) and Bert Wattle (*Roger Livesey*) from disaster by playing in their summer show, despite dirty work from competition led by Sneed (*Joe Mott*). He kidnaps the pianist, but he and his men are routed in a pitched battle with Bert. Songs include *The Holy City, Sing Your Way to Happiness, Giddy Up* and *Mrs Binns' Twins*, but proceedings have a forced air.

RoC *Jack Donohue, Mary Maguire, Eddie Gray, Edward Rigby, Tommy Fields, Hay Petrie, Gus McNaughton, Mike Johnson, Gladys Dehl, Nino Rossini, Philip Leaver, Skippy (dog).*

KEEP YOUR SEATS, PLEASE (1936)   [4]
Dir *Monty Banks*. Prod *Basil Dean*. Scr *Tom Geraghty, Ian Hay, Anthony Kimmins, from a play by Elie Ilf, Eugene Petrov*. Ph *John W. Boyle*. PC *ATP*. Dis *Associated British*. 82 mins. Cert U
One of the earliest versions of the Russian farce that has provided standard material for comics down the decades. An eccentric old lady has hidden a fortune in jewels in one of a set of antique chairs and her nephew (*George Formby*) has to track the right one down to

find the gems, aided by his girl (*Florence Desmond*) and hampered by an unscrupulous lawyer (*Alastair Sim*). Formby's songs include the title number, plus *When I'm Cleaning Windows*.

RoC *Gus McNaughton, Harry Tate, Fiona Stuart, Hal Gordon, Fred Culpitt, Margaret Moffatt, Maud Gill, Mike Johnson, Ethel Coleridge, Tom Payne, Beatrice Fielden-Kaye.*

KENTUCKY MINSTRELS (1934)   [2]
Dir *John Baxter*. Prod *Julius Hagen*. Scr *Harry S. Pepper, (C.) Denier Warren*. PC *Real Art*. Dis *Universal*. 85 mins. Cert U
Ingenuous musical entertainment in which Mott and Bayley (*Scott and Whaley*), former mainstays of a minstrel show, struggle to make a living when that kind of entertainment goes out of fashion. They sink to busking and casual labour, but finally make a successful comeback in a modern revue.

RoC *(C.) Denier Warren, April Vivian, Wilson Coleman, Madge Brindley, Roddy Hughes, Nina Mae McKinney, Terence Casey, Polly Ward, Leslie Hatton, The Eight Black Streaks, Harry S. Pepper and His White Coons, Debroy Somers and His Band, Norman Green, Edgar Driver, Jack Gerrard, Leo Sheffield.*

KEY TO HARMONY (1935)   [1]
Dir *Norman Walker*. Prod *Anthony Havelock-Allan*. Scr *Basil Mason from a book by John B. Wilson*. PC and Dis *British and Dominions/ Paramount British*. 68 mins. Cert A
Inane romantic drama that did little to boost *Belle Chrystall*'s drifting film career. She plays Mary, an actress, who marries a struggling young composer (*Fred Conyngham*) and almost loses him when success goes to his head.

RoC *Reginald Purdell, Olive Sloane, Ernest Butcher, Muriel George, D. A. Clarke-Smith, Cyril Smith, Joan Harben, Jack Knight.*

KICKING THE MOON AROUND (1938)   [4]
(USA: *The Playboy*)
Dir *Walter Forde*. Prod *Herbert Wynne*. Scr *Angus Macphail, Roland Pertwee, Michael Hogan, H. Fowler Mear*. Ph *Francis Carver*. PC *Vogue*. Dis *General Film Distributors*. 78 mins. Cert U
Finding that his fiancée Flo (*Florence Desmond*) is only after his money, young millionaire Bobbie (*Hal Thompson*) turns his attentions to record-counter assistant Pepper (*Evelyn Dall*). But Flo is out for revenge. She gets Pepper drunk just before her nightclub debut as a singer, and a wild riot ensues. Everything is sorted out in court and Pepper keeps her millionaire. Bright musical is above-average all round.

RoC *Harry Richman, Ambrose and His Orchestra, (C.) Denier Warren, Julien Vedey, Max Bacon, Leslie Carew, Davy Burnaby, George Carney, Frances Day, Edward Rigby, Maureen Fitzsimmons (Maureen O'Hara), Edgar Driver, Mike Johnson, Bill Black, Dino Galvani, Frank Atkinson.*

KING OF HEARTS (1936)   [3]
Dir, Prod and Scr *Oswald Mitchell, Walter Tennyson, from a play by Matthew Boulton*. Ph

Desmond Dickinson. PC and Dis *Butchers*. 82 mins. *Cert U*

Will Fyffe appears to advantage in this musical/weepie in which he plays a docker whose waitress daughter loves a rich boy. The boy's mother causes the girl to lose her job and tries to bribe her father to help her break up the romance. But the old man is too wily for her, and the wedding comes to pass.

RoC *Gwen (Gwenllian) Gill, Richard Dolman, Amy Veness, O.B. Clarence, Jock McKay, Googie Withers, Ronald Shiner, Margaret Davidge, Patrick Ludlow, Paul Neville, Sybil Grove, Trevor Watkins, Frakson, Java's Tzigane Band, Constance, Lilyan and Malo, Horace Sheldon's Orchestra.*

THE KING OF PARIS (1934)   3

Dir *Jack Raymond*. Prod *Herbert Wilcox*. Scr *John Drinkwater, W.P. Lipscomb, Paul Gangelin, from a play by Alfred Savoir, John Van Druten*. PC *British and Dominions*. Dis *United Artists. 75 mins. Cert A*

After his wife leaves him, egotistical actor-manager Max Till (*Cedric Hardwicke*) finds a friendless Russian girl (*Marie Glory*), makes her his new leading lady and moulds her into a star. He tricks her into marriage, but she eventually leaves him for his friend Paul (*Ralph Richardson*). Rather flat romance.

RoC *Phyllis Monkman, John Deverell, Lydia Sherwood, Jeanne Stuart, Joan Maude, O.B. Clarence.*

KING OF THE CASTLE (1936)   3

Dir *Redd Davis*. Prod *Basil Humphrys*. Scr *George Dewhurst*. PC *City*. Dis *General Film Distributors. 69 mins. Cert U*

Carefree lower-bracket comedy about a family butler (*Claude Dampier*) and his adventures in producing the missing heir to a title, and then helping the heir (*Billy Milton*) to prove his claim and win the girl (*June Clyde*) of his choice.

RoC *Cynthia Stock, Wally Patch, Arthur Finn, Paul Blake, H.F. Maltby, Mavis Villiers, Jimmy Godden, Hiram Martin, Quinton McPherson, Cecil Bevan, Johnny Singer.*

KING OF THE DAMNED (1935)   3

Dir *Walter Forde*. Prod *Michael Balcon*. Scr *Charles Bennett, A.R. Rawlinson, Sidney Gilliat, from the play by John Chancellor*. Ph *Bernard Knowles*. PC and Dis *Gaumont-British. 76 mins. Cert A*

In a Caribbean convict settlement, the brutal deputy commandant exploits the prisoners for his own ends, sending them in hordes to work on the dreaded 'Road' being constructed through malaria-infested swamp and jungle. A mutiny is eventually quelled, but the cultured Convict 83 (*Conrad Veidt*) obtains permission for a public inquiry. Vigorous stock melodrama with simplified moral issues.

RoC *Helen Vinson, Cecil Ramage, Noah Beery, Edmund Willard, Percy Parsons, Raymond Lovell, C.M. Hallard, Allan Jeayes, Percy Walsh, Peter Croft.*

KING OF THE RITZ (1933)   2

Dir and Prod *Carmine Gallone*. Scr *Clifford Grey, Ivor Montagu, from a play by Henri*

Hugh Wakefield, Gina Malo and Stanley Lupino in King of the Ritz (*1933*)

Kistemaekers. PC *Gainsborough/British Lion*. Dis *Gaumont. 81 mins. Cert U*

Rough-and-ready comedy musical: Claude King (*Stanley Lupino*), head porter at the Ritz Hotel, woos and wins a rich widow (*Betty Stockfeld*) to the discomfort of the maid (*Gina Malo*) who loves him. Claude has a title bestowed on him by an impoverished king, but when he and the widow go to inspect their ancestral home, it falls to pieces. Claude goes back to the maid – and the Ritz.

RoC *Henry Kendall, Hugh Wakefield, Gibb McLaughlin, Harry Milton, Johnny Singer.*

THE KING'S CUP (1932)   3

Dir *Herbert Wilcox, Robert J. Cullen, Sir Alan Cobham, Donald Macardle*. Prod *Wilcox*. Scr *Cobham*. Ph *F.A. Young*. PC *British and Dominions*. Dis *W and F. 75 mins. Cert U*

Dick Carter (*Harry Milton*) and his sweetheart Betty (*Dorothy Bouchier*) are both fliers. When Dick loses his nerve after a crash, Betty enters the King's Cup air race with Dick as mechanic. Taking part after being involved in a car smash on the way to the race, Betty passes out in the plane, but Dick takes over and wins the race. The only single-story film in motion picture history with four credited directors.

RoC *William Kendall, René Ray, Tom Helmore, Lewis Shaw, Sydney King, Syd Crossley, Leila Page, Anna Lee, Lew Stone and His Band.*

KING SOLOMON'S MINES (1937)   4

Dir *Robert Stevenson*. (*Associate*) Prod *Geoffrey Barkas*. Scr *Michael Hogan, Roland Pertwee, A.R. Rawlinson, Charles Bennett, Ralph Spence, from the novel by H. Rider Haggard*. Ph *Glen MacWilliams*. PC *Gaumont-British*. Dis *General Film Distributors. 80 mins. Cert U*

Brilliantly staged, but rather spottily acted (*Paul Robeson* excepted) account of the famous adventure of an African quest for a fabulously wealthy diamond mine in the heart of the jungle. The questers fall into the hands of hostile natives, but their guide Umbopa (*Robeson*) convinces the warriors he is their rightful chief, and the adventurers escape, with the help of a handy eclipse of the sun. An erupting volcano buries King Solomon's Mines for ever.

RoC *Cedric Hardwicke, Roland Young, Anna Lee, John Loder, Sydney Fairbrother, Makubalo Hlubi, Homo Toto, Robert Adams, Frederick*

Leister, Alf Goddard, Arthur Sinclair, Arthur Goullet.

KISSING CUP'S RACE (1930)   3

Dir and Prod *Castleton Knight*. Scr *Knight, Blanche Metcalfe, from a poem by Campbell Rae Brown, and a scenario by J. Bertram Brown, Benedict James*. PC and Dis *Butcher's. 75 mins. Cert A*

Uninspired remake of the 1920 film in which an impoverished lord (*John Stuart*) is forced to sell his horses to clear his debts, but keeps one promising young colt, Kissing Cup, which he hopes will win a big race, despite the machinations of a crooked rival, and restore his fortune. It does.

RoC *Stewart Rome, Madeleine Carroll, Chili Bouchier, Moore Marriott, Richard Cooper, J. Fisher White, James Knight, Gladys Hamer, Wally Patch, Charles Wade.*

KISS ME, SERGEANT (1930)   2

Dir *Monty Banks*. Prod *John Maxwell*. Scr *Val Valentine, from a play by Syd Courtenay and Lola Harvey*. PC *BIP*. Dis *Wardour, 56 mins. Cert U*

Pasted-together farce with Leslie Fuller in his customary character of soldier Bill Biggles, this time in India, where he accidentally knocks over and smashes a much-revered temple idol – and subsequently impersonates it, as well as saving its priceless jewelled eye from the villains, and helping a young lieutenant to win the colonel's daughter. The authors of the stage farce on which it was based both play roles in the film version.

RoC *Gladys Cruickshank, Syd Courtenay, Frank Melroyd, Gladys Frazin, Mamie Holland, Lola Harvey, Roy Travers, Olivette, Marika Rokk, Gotham Quartette.*

KNIGHTS FOR A DAY (1937)   2

Dir *Norman Lee, Aveling Ginever*. Prod *Ginever*. Scr *Ginever, Frank Atkinson, Charles Bray*. PC *Pearl Productions*. Dis *Pathé. 69 mins. Cert U*

An English barber (*Nelson Keys*) wins a motor-caravan in a competition and, on tour, finds himself involved with Prince Nicholas of Datria (*John Garrick*) in that country's internal disturbances. At a village pageant, rival politicians meet and decide to become co-presidents, clearing the way for the prince to wed the barber's niece (*Nancy Burne*). Fair Ruritanian comedy.

RoC *Frank Atkinson, Cathleen Nesbitt, Billy Bray, Fred Duprez, Gerald Barry, Wyn Weaver, Percy Walsh, Charles Bray, Raymond Ellis, Harry Clifford, D.J. Williams, Lawrence Hanray, Miriam Leighton, The Three Diamond Brothers.*

KNIGHT WITHOUT ARMOUR (1937)   4

Dir *Jacques Feyder*. Prod *Alexander Korda*. Scr *Frances Marion, Lajos Biro, Arthur Wimperis, from a novel by James Hilton*. Ph *Harry Stradling*. PC *London Films*. Dis *United Artists. 108 mins. Cert A*

Expensive and a little shapeless, but quite successful and well-directed romantic adventure, beginning in pre-First World War Russia, where A. J. Fotheringill (*Robert Donat*), a British secret agent posing as a Russian revolutionary, is captured by Czarist authorities and sent to Siberia. With the 1917 revolution, he is released and made commissar of a small town – then entrusted with taking the lovely Countess Alexandra (*Marlene Dietrich*) to Petrograd for trial. Instead, they flee through Russia, on foot, by train and on the River Volga, eventually escaping on an American Red Cross train.

RoC *Irene Vanburgh, Herbert Lomas, Austin Trevor, Basil Gill, John Clements, Hay Petrie, Miles Malleson, David Tree, Lyn Harding, Frederick Culley, Lawrence Hanray, Lisa d'Esterre, Dorice Fordred, Franklin Kelsey, Lawrence Kingston, Raymond Huntley, Lawrence Baskcomb, Allan Jeayes, Paul O'Brien, Edward Lexy, Evelyn Ankers.*

KNOWING MEN (1930) [2]
Dir and Prod *Eleanor Glyn.* Scr *Glyn, Edward Knoblock, from the novel by Glyn.* Ph *Charles Rosher.* PC *Talkicolor.* Dis *United Artists. Talkicolor (but shown B and W). 88 mins. Cert A. Bilingual versions*
Romantic drama set in Normandy, where an heiress (*Elissa Landi*) tries to foil those who would marry her for her money by posing as her aunt's companion.
RoC *Carl Brisson, Jeanne de Casalis, Helen Haye, C. M. Hallard, E. Vosper, Henry Mollison, Thomas Weguelin, Marjorie Loring.*

KOENIGSMARK (1935) [2]
Dir *Maurice Tourneur.* Prod *Roger Richebe, Max Schach.* Scr *Uncredited, from the novel by Pierre Benoît.* PC *Capitol.* Dis *General Film Distributors. 96 mins. Cert A*
Colourless historical epic, the release of which was delayed for several months. The marriage of convenience between Princess Aurore (*Elissa Landi*) and the Grand Duke of Lantenbourg ends when the duke is assassinated by his brother, who takes the throne. He engages a young tutor (*Pierre Fresnay*) for his son, but the tutor and the princess bring the crime to light, and the villain's reign to an end.
RoC *John Lodge, Allan Jeayes, Marcelle Rogez, Frank Vosper, Romilly Lunge, Cecil Humphreys.*

LABURNUM GROVE (1936) [4]
Dir *Carold Reed.* Prod *Basil Dean.* Scr *Gordon Wellesley, Anthony Kimmins, from the play by J. B. Priestley.* Ph *John W. Boyle.* PC *ATP.* Dis *Associated British. 73 mins. Cert A*
Amusing diversion which gave its young director another leg up the ladder. *Edmund Gwenn* plays Redfern, a pillar of local society – and a clever forger. A couple of sponging in-laws living with the Redferns go off to spend the day with money given to them by Redfern – and are terrified when they learn the cash is almost certainly counterfeit. We last see Redfern hurriedly packing for a 'holiday' on the Continent.
RoC *Cedric Hardwicke, Victoria Hopper, Ethel Coleridge, Katie Johnson, Francis James, James Harcourt, David Hawthorne, Frederick Burtwell, Terence Conlin.*

THE LAD (1935) [2]
Dir *Henry Edwards.* Prod *Julius Hagen.* Scr *Gerard Fairlie, from the novel by Edgar Wallace.* Ph *Sydney Blythe.* PC *Twickenham.* Dis *Universal. 74 mins. Cert A*
Stagy drama about a convict (*Gordon Harker*) who goes to a stately home intending to steal a necklace, is mistaken for a detective and ends up sorting out a domestic tangle, returning the necklace, and bringing happiness to the daughter of the house, in love with a man of whom her father disapproves.
RoC *Geraldine Fitzgerald, Sebastian Shaw, Betty Stockfeld, Jane Carr, Michael Shepley, Gerald Barry, John Turnbull, Ralph Truman, David Hawthorne, Barbara Everest, Wilfred Caithness.*

LADY IN DANGER (1934) [4]
Dir *Tom Walls.* Prod *Michael Balcon.* Scr *Ben Travers, from his play O Mistress Mine.* Ph *Phil Tannura.* PC and Dis *Gaumont-British. 68 mins. Cert A*
Smartly developed situation comedy-thriller, with director *Tom Walls* doubling as star. He plays a businessman dragooned into getting the exiled queen of a European country away to safety in England. Once there, his relations with the Queen (*Yvonne Arnaud*) are misconstrued by his financée (*Anne Grey*) but ultimately the King (*Hugh Wakefield*), who had fled to Paris, is reunited with his wife.
RoC *Leon M. Lion, Marie Lohr, Alfred Drayton, Leonora Corbett, Cecil Parker, O. B. Clarence, Harold Warrender, Charles Lefeaux, Hubert Harben, Dorothy Galbraith, Jane Cornell, Mervyn Johns.*

THE LADY IS WILLING (1933) [2]
Dir *Gilbert Miller.* Prod *Joseph Friedman.* Scr *Guy Bolton, from a play by Louis Verneuil.* Ph *Joseph Walker.* PC and Dis *Columbia. 74 mins. Cert A*
Disappointing first major production of Columbia British, drawn out and unworthy of its strong cast. A detective (*Leslie Howard*) is asked by friends to look into the affair of the unscrupulous financier (*Cedric Hardwicke*) who once ruined him. He falls for the villain's wife (*Binnie Barnes*) and prevents the financier from making her sign her considerable fortune over to him.
RoC *Nigel Playfair, Nigel Bruce, Claud Allister, W. Graham Browne, Kendall Lee, Arthur Howard, Virginia Field, John Turnbull.*

THE LADY VANISHES (1938) [5]
Dir *Alfred Hitchcock.* Prod *Edward Black.* Scr *Sidney Gilliat, Frank Launder, from a novel by Ethel Lina White.* Ph *Jack Cox.* PC *Gainsborough.* Dis *M-G-M. 98 mins. Cert A*
Miss Froy (*Dame May Whitty*), an elderly lady travelling on a trans-continental train, suddenly disappears. An acquaintance, Iris (*Margaret Lockwood*) tries to investigate, but nobody seems aware Miss Froy was ever on board. Helped by Gilbert (*Michael Redgrave*), she uncovers a nest of foreign spies who finally lay siege to the coach containing Iris and other Britons after it has been detached from the train. Classic Hitchcock suspense thriller.
RoC *Paul Lukas, Cecil Parker, Linden Travers, Mary Clare, Naunton Wayne, Basil Radford, Emil Boreo, Googie Withers, Philip Leaver, Catherine Lacey, Charles Oliver, Sally Stewart, Cathleen Tremayne, Zelma Vas Dias, Emile Gamba, Josephine Wilson.*

THE LAMBETH WALK (1939) [4]
Dir *Albert de Courville.* Prod *Anthony Havelock-Allan.* Scr *Clifford Grey, Robert Edmunds, John Paddy Carstairs, from a musical play by Louis Rose, Douglas Furber, Noel Gay.* Ph *Francis Carver.* PC *CAPAD/Pinebrook.* Dis *M-G-M. 84 mins. Cert U*
The original show was called *Me and My Girl*, but the popularity of its song *The Lambeth Walk* ensured the title of the film, a musical farce in which a spry little Cockney (*Lupino Lane*) inherits a title, an ancestral castle and a blue-blooded county family. He still marries his home-town sweetheart (*Sally Gray*) in spite of the efforts of a vampish distant cousin (*Enid Stamp-Taylor*).
RoC *Seymour Hicks, Norah Howard, Wallace Lupino, Wilfrid Hyde White, May Hallatt, Mark Lester, Charles Heslop.*

Lupino Lane and Sally Gray in The Lambeth Walk

LANCASHIRE LUCK (1937) [2]
Dir *Henry Cass.* Prod *Anthony Havelock-Allan.* Scr *A. R. Rawlinson.* Ph *Francis Carver.* PC and Dis *British and Dominions/Paramount British. 74 mins. Cert U*
Lancashire carpenter George Lovejoy (*George Carney*) wins a small fortune on the football pools and opens a tea-shop in a 'posh' district of the county. His daughter Betty (*Wendy Hiller*) falls in love with the son of a titled lady, who thoroughly disapproves. But George sees to it that love wins through. Predictable class-distinction comedy.
RoC *Muriel George, Nigel Stock, George Galleon, Margaret Damer, Bett Huth, Peter Popp.*

LANDSLIDE (1936)   2
Dir and Scr *Donovan Pedelty*. Prod *Victor M. Greene*. PC *Crusade*. Dis *Paramount*. *67 mins. Cert A*
Promising but muffed thriller in which a landslip entombs a company of actors in a small theatre in Wales. The cashier is murdered and the takings stolen. After a night of terror in which two further killings are attempted, the guilty party, a stage hand, is discovered. In helping the others to escape, the killer supports a beam which crashes on him and kills him.
LP *Jimmy Hanley, Dinah Sheridan, Jimmy Mageean, Ann Cavanagh, Elizabeth Inglis, Bruno Barnabe, David Arnold, Dora Mayfield, Ernie Tate, Robert Moore, Ben Williams, Edward Kennedy, Jean Scott.*

LAND WITHOUT MUSIC (1936)   4
(USA: *Forbidden Music*)
Dir *Walter Forde*. Prod *Max Schach*. Scr *Rudolph Bernauer, Marian Dix, L. duGarde Peach*. Ph *John W. Boyle*. PC *Capitol*. Dis *General Film Distributors. 80 mins. Cert U*
The best performance of *Richard Tauber*'s film career lifts this otherwise unenterprising musical about a princess (*Diana Napier*) who bans music from her country, so that her citizens will concentrate on improving the economy. A singer (*Tauber*) and an American reporter (*Jimmy Durante*) lead a revolution: the singer wins the princess, and the people win back their music.
RoC *June Clyde, Derrick de Marney, Esmé Percy, George Hayes, John Hepworth, Edward Rigby, George Carney, Ivan Wilmot, Robert Nainby, Jo Monkhouse, Quinton McPherson, Evelyn Ankers.*

Richard Tauber, June Clyde and Jimmy Durante in Land Without Music (*1937*)

THE LASH (1934)   2
Dir *Henry Edwards*. Prod *Julius Hagen*. Scr *Brock Williams, from a play by Owen Davis, Sewell Collins*. Ph *Ernest Palmer*. PC *Real Art*. Dis *Radio. 63 mins. Cert A*
Hearty morality tale about a self-made millionaire (*Lyn Harding*) and the weakling son (*John Mills*) who lets him down at every turn, even jumping a ship bound for Australia to return to England and continue an affair with a married woman (*Joan Maude*). Finally the millionaire gives his son a savage beating with a stockman's whip. Has either man learned anything? Only time will tell.
RoC *Leslie Perrins, Peggy Blythe, Aubrey*

Mather, D. J. Williams, Roy Emerton, S. Victor Stanley, Mary Jerrold.

LASSIE FROM LANCASHIRE (1938)   3
Dir *John Paddy Carstairs*. Prod *John Corfield*. Scr *Doreen Montgomery, Ernest Dudley*. Ph *Bryan Langley*. PC *British National*. Dis *Associated British. 82 mins. Cert U*
Would-be actress Jenny (*Marjorie Browne*) and her father (*Mark Daly*) are worked like slaves at his sister's boarding-house on the Isle of Man. Jenny falls for a struggling songwriter Tom (*Hal Thompson*) but nearly loses him to the jealous schemings of the star of the local pierrot troupe they both join. Then Tom and Jenny are offered a West End contract and look set for stardom.
RoC *Marjorie Sandford, Vera Lennox, Elsie Wagstaffe, Johnnie Schofield, Billy Caryll, Hilda Mundy, Joe Mott, Leslie Phillips.*

THE LAST ADVENTURERS (1937)   4
Dir *Roy Kellino*. Prod *H. Fraser Passmore*. Scr *Denison Clift*. Ph *Kellino*. PC *Conway*. Dis *Sound City. 77 mins. Cert U*
Jeremy Bowker (*Niall MacGinnis*) is rescued from a trawler wreck by skipper John Arkell (*Roy Emerton*), with whose daughter Ann (*Linden Travers*) he falls in love. But her cousin Margaret (*Kay Walsh*) also wants Jeremy and he signs on her father's new steam trawler. This, too, is wrecked; as well as rescuing Jeremy for the second time, John also rescues his own brother, ending a long-standing feud between them. Rugged romantic adventure with fine photography of storms at sea.
RoC *Peter Gawthorne, Katie Johnson, Johnnie Schofield, Norah Howard, Ballard Berkeley, Esma Cannon, Tony Wylde, Billy Shine, Howard Douglas, Bernard Ansell.*

THE LAST BARRICADE (1938)   2
Dir and Scr *Alex Bryce*. Prod *John Findlay*. Ph *Stanley Grant*. PC and Dis *Fox British. 58 mins. Cert U*
The Spanish Civil War: Michael (*Frank Fox*), a newspaperman, loves Maria (*Greta Gynt*) and wants her to leave with him, but she discovers her father is an enemy spy and plans to blow up a garrison before its soldiers have left. She rushes to warn Michael who is at the factory where the garrison is located, and they escape before it blows up. Later Michael frees her from prison and they flee to England. Wildly unlikely romantic adventure.
RoC *Meinhart Maur, Paul Sheridan, Dino Galvani, Vernon Harris, Hay Petrie, Andrea Malandrinos, Alfred Atkins, Rosarito, Dominick Sterlini.*

THE LAST CHANCE (1937)   2
Dir *Thomas Bentley*. Prod *Warwick Ward*. Scr *Harry Hughes, from the play by Frank Stayton*. Ph *Ernest Palmer*. PC *Welwyn*. Dis *Pathé. 74 mins. Cert A*
Alan Burminster (*Frank Leighton*), a Devon gunrunner, is accused of the murder of a moneylender. He goes to jail and his fiancée Mary (*Judy Kelly*) eventually marries John (*Wyndham Goldie*), the barrister who unsuccessfully defended him. Years later, Alan escapes.

He finds his case's original judge, and pieces together evidence which proves John is the killer. John commits suicide, but the judge makes sure that Alan is cleared. Static treatment of interesting plot.
RoC *Billy Milton, Aubrey Mallalieu, Jenny Laird, Franklyn Bellamy, Lawrence Hanray, Alfred Wellesley, Charles Sewell, Charles Paton, Harry Hutchinson, Arthur Hambling, Edgar Driver.*

THE LAST COUPON (1932)   4
Dir *Thomas Bentley*. Prod *John Maxwell*. Scr *Syd Courtenay, Frank Launder*. Ph *Jack Cox, Bryan Langley*. PC *BIP*. Dis *Wardour. 84 mins. Cert U*
One of Leslie Fuller's best comedies, with an amusing script from a stronger-than-usual source (a play by Ernest E. Bryan). Fuller plays a miner who thinks he has won a fortune on the football pools. Despite the efforts of his long-suffering wife (*Mary Jerrold*), he's ready to blow the lot in a week - only to discover he didn't post his coupon.
RoC *Molly Lamont, Jack Hobbs, Jimmy Golden, Marion Dawson, Harry Carr, Binnie Barnes, Hal Gordon, Gus McNaughton, Ellen Pollock, Clive Morton, Syd Crossley.*

THE LAST CURTAIN (1937)   2
Dir *David Macdonald*. Prod *Anthony Havelock-Allan*. Scr *A. R. Rawlinson*. Ph *Francis Carver*. PC and Dis *British and Dominions/Paramount British. 67 mins. Cert U*
Insurance investigator Bob Fenton (*John Wickham*), looking into a series of robberies, tracks the thieves down to a bakery, where jewels are put in doughnuts. He joins the gang, and is hired by their boss, Garsatti (*Kenneth Duncan*), to watch Sir Alan (*Campbell Gullan*), an actor who disposes of the jewels. Wearing Bob's clothes, Garsatti shoots Sir Alan, but the actor names his killer before he dies and the crooks are caught. Uneasy mixture of crime and satire.
RoC *Greta Gynt, Sara Seagar, Joss Ambler, W. G. Fay, Eric Hales, Evan John, Arthur Sinclair.*

THE LAST HOUR (1930)   3
Dir *Walter Forde*. Prod *Archibald Nettlefold*. Scr *H. Fowler Mear, from a play by Charles Bennett*. Ph *Geoffrey Faithfull*. PC *Nettlefold*. Dis *Butchers. 77 mins. Cert U*
Top silent comedian *Walter Forde* was rapidly going over to direction when he made this scrappily written thriller that makes the most of its running time in a story of an organization of foreign spies, headed by an unscrupulous prince (*Stewart Rome*), who steal the plans of a death ray and menace British shipping and airlines.
RoC *Kathleen Vaughan, Richard Cooper, Alexander Field, Wilfred Shine, James Raglan, George Bealby, Frank Arlton, Billy Shine.*

THE LAST JOURNEY (1935)   4
Dir *Bernard Vorhaus*. Prod *Julius Hagen*. Scr *John Soutar, H. Fowler Mear*. Ph *William Luff, Percy Strong*. PC and Dis *Twickenham. 66 mins. Cert A*

Exciting *Train of Events*-type story. As a result of brooding over his oncoming retirement and thinking his wife is having an affair with his fireman, an engine-driver goes mad, and drives the train at terrific speed, ignoring all signals. The story is about various people on board: an adventurer who has (bigamously) married a rich girl, a scientist, a crank, two crooks making a getaway, a brain specialist, a disguised detective and others. Disaster, incidentally, is avoided at the last moment.
LP *Hugh Williams, Godfrey Tearle, Judy Gunn, Eve Gray, Nelson Keys, Frank Pettingell, Julien Mitchell, Olga Lindo, Michael Hogan, Eliot Makeham, Sydney Fairbrother, Mickey Brantford.*

THE LAST ROSE OF SUMMER (1937) [2]
Dir, Prod and PC *James Fitzpatrick*. Scr *W. K. Williamson*. Dis *M-G-M*. 60 mins. *Cert U*
Very fragmented musical pageant based on the life and loves of the poet Lord Byron.
LP *John Garrick, Kathleen Gibson, Malcolm Graham, Marian Spencer, Cecil Ramage, R. Meadows White.*

THE LAST WALTZ (1936) [2]
Dir *Leo Mittler, Gerald Barry*. Prod *Gina Carlton*. Scr *Reginald Arkell, from an opera by Oscar Straus, Mal Wallner and Georg Weber*. PC *Warwick*. Dis *Associated Producers and Distributors*. 74 mins. *Cert U*. Bilingual versions
Tired of their prince's philandering bachelor life, the ministers of a small European country demand that he get married, and bring a countess and three of her four daughters to court. The prince (*Gerald Barry*) is attracted to Vera (*Jarmilla Novotna*), but she falls for Count Dmitri (*Harry Welchman*) their escort. The arrival of the fourth daughter resolves all problems: she marries the prince. Rather tired Viennese-style operetta.
Roc *Josephine Huntley-Wright, Tonie Edgar Bruce, Bruce Winston, Jack Hellier, Paul Sheridan, Pamela Randall, Elizabeth Arkell, MacArthur Gordon, E. Fitzclarence, Madge Snell, Bella Milo.*

LATE EXTRA (1935) [3]
Dir *Albert Parker*. Prod *Ernest Garside*. Scr *Fenn Sherie, Ingram d'Abbes*. Ph *Alex Bryce*. PC and Dis *Fox British*. 69 mins. *Cert A*
Bank robber Weinhardt (*Clifford McLaglen*) shoots a police officer in his flight. *The Daily Gazette* offers a reward for his capture. A woman informer is found, but shot down before reporter Jim Martin (*James Mason*) can reach her. Jim finally tracks down and captures Weinhardt, however, in the cellars of a Soho restaurant. Improbable thriller has some excitement.
RoC *Virginia Cherrill, Alastair Sim, Cyril Chosack, Ian Colin, Donald Wolfit, David Horne, Antoinette Cellier, Hannen Swaffer, Ralph Truman, Andrea Malandrinos, Billy Shine, Desmond Tester, Michael Wilding.*

LAUGH IT OFF (1939) [3]
Dir *John Baxter*. Prod *John Corfield*. Scr *Bridget Boland, Austin Melford*. Ph *James Wil-*

son. PC *British National*. Dis *Anglo*. 78 mins. *Cert U*
Tommy Towers (*Tommy Trinder*), an entertainer, is called up when the Second World War breaks out. He soon falls foul of Sgt-Major Slaughter (*Edward Lexy*), whose attempts to organize a camp concert, however, are a woeful mess. Tommy is called in, and the concert is such a success that he is promised a commission. Breezy comedy, ironically funniest when its star is off screen.
RoC *Jean Colin, Anthony Hulme, Marjorie Browne, Ida Barr, Charles Victor, Peter Gawthorne, Wally Patch, Warren Jenkins, John Laurie, Leonard Morris, Henry Lytton, Billy Percy, Geraldo and His Orchestra, Darville and Shires, The Three Maxwells, The Joan Davis Dancers, Sydney Burchell, The Julias Ladies' Choir, The Georgian Singers, The Scottish Sextette.*

THE LAUGHTER OF FOOLS (1933) [1]
Dir and Scr *Adrian Brunel, from a play by H. F. Maltby*. Prod and PC *George Smith*. Dis *Fox*. 47 mins. *Cert U*
Below-average comedy (but with a charming performance by *Pat Paterson*) about a harridan with an idle son, shallow daughter and henpecked husband. She tries to marry the daughter off to a rich sea captain (*Derrick de Marney*) but he prefers her niece (*Paterson*) and, encouraged by the henpecked husband (*Eliot Makeham*), runs away with her.
RoC *Helen Ferrers, D. A. Clarke-Smith, Joan Melville, George Thirlwell, Minnie Taylor.*

LAZYBONES (1934) [3]
Dir *Michael Powell*. Prod *Julius Hagen*. Scr *Gerard Fairlie, from his play*. Ph *Ernest Palmer*. PC *Real Art*. Dis *Radio*. 65 mins. *Cert U*
Reginald (*Ian Hunter*), known as Lazybones, is expected to retrieve his family's fortunes by marrying wealthy American Kitty (*Claire Luce*). But her executors have swindled her and she is penniless. Another American, Mike (*Bernard Nedell*) wants Kitty to leave Reginald, and steals some documents to raise money. Kitty refuses to help him and 'Lazybones' gets them back to their owner – on condition Mike leaves Britain. Pleasant romantic comedy.
RoC *Sara Allgood, Michael Shepley, Bobbie Comber, Denys Blakelock, Marjorie Gaskell, Pamela Carme, Harold Warrender, Miles Malleson, Fred Withers, Frank Morgan, Fewlass Llewellyn, Paul Blake.*

LEAP YEAR (1932) [3]
Dir *Tom Walls*. Prod *Herbert Wilcox*. Scr *A. R. Rawlinson*. Ph *F. A. Young*. PC *British and Dominions*. Dis *W and F*. 89 mins. *Cert A*
Sir Peter Traillon of the Foreign Office spends a weekend with a mysterious lady who refuses to tell him her name, then spends four years trying to trace her. After he has become engaged to his chief's daughter, he runs into the mystery woman again in Cannes on New Year's Day of Leap Year. He breaks his engagement and marries her. Popular Tom Walls comedy.
LP *Tom Walls, Anne Grey, Edmond Breon,*

Ellis Jeffreys, Jeanne Stuart, Charles Carson, Lawrence Hanray, Joan Brierly, Franklyn Bellamy.

LEAVE IT TO BLANCHE (1934) [2]
Dir *Harold Young*. Prod *Irving Asher*. Scr *Brock Williams*. PC *Warner Bros*. Dis *First National*. 51 mins. *Cert U*
Pedestrian comedy about the interfering friend (*Olive Blakeney*) of a young married couple (*Henry Kendall, Miki Hood*). When the husband forgets their anniversary, she persuades his wife to invent a secret lover to punish him. The husband 'kills' the lover (but thinks he really has), presents his wife with a new car and tells her to get rid of her meddling friend.
RoC *Griffith Jones, Hamilton Keene, Rex Harrison, Julian Royce, Elizabeth Jenns, Harold Warrender, Phyllis Stanley, Molly Clifford, Denise Sylvester, Margaret Gunn, Kenneth Kove, Hermione Hannen.*

LEAVE IT TO ME (1933) [3]
Dir *Monty Banks*. Prod *John Maxwell*. Scr *Gene Gerrard, Frank Miller, Cecil Lewis, from a play by P. G. Wodehouse, Ian Hay*. PC *BIP*. Dis *Wardour*. 76 mins. *Cert U*
Spirited but somewhat disappointing adaptation of an enormous stage success about a professional 'helper', Sebastian (*Gene Gerrard*) who poses as a poet while trying to safeguard his aunt's jewels, but is almost defeated by a lady crook (*Olive Borden*) posing as a poetess.
RoC *Molly Lamont, George Gee, Gus MacNaughton, Clive Currie, Tonie Edgar Bruce, Peter Godfrey, Syd Crossley, Melville Cooper, Wylie Watson.*

LEAVE IT TO ME (1937) [2]
Dir *Herbert Smith*. Prod and PC *Tom Arnold*. Scr *Fenn Sherie, Ingram d'Abbes*. Ph *George Stretton*. Dis *British Lion*. 71 mins. *Cert A*
Sent to Limehouse, special constable Sandy (*Sandy Powell*) rescues a girl (*Iris March*) from her bullying stepfather, but is drugged by Chinese crooks. Dismissed from the Constabulary, he recovers a famous stolen jewel and wins back his uniform. Powell as policeman, harem queen, all-in-wrestler, ballroom dancer, Chinese mandarin and private eye in draggy comedy.
RoC *Franklin Dyall, Garry Marsh, Davy Burnaby, Jack Hobbs, Claude Horton, Dora Hibbert, Nicholas Bird, George Pencheff, Jack Pye.*

LEND ME YOUR HUSBAND (1935) [2]
Dir *Frederick Hayward*. Prod *George King, Randall Faye*. Scr *Faye*. PC *Embassy*. Dis *Radio*. 61 mins. *Cert U*
Wearisome comedy in which Jeff (*John Stuart*) imagines himself in love with his wife's best friend Ba-Ba (*Nancy Burne*) and runs off with her. Ba-Ba's 'amusing little ways', which include smashing his car, soon change Jeff's mind, and both are glad to get back to their legal partners.
RoC *Nora Swinburne, Evan Thomas, Annie Esmond.*

LEND ME YOUR WIFE (1935) [2]
Dir *W. P. Kellino*. Prod *Fred Browett*. Scr *Kellino, Fred Duprez, Edmund Dalby, from the play*

by Duprez and Dalby. PC *Grafton*. Dis *M-G-M*. *61 mins*. *Cert A*

Typical quota quickie comedy about Tony Radford (*Henry Kendall*), anxious to claim the money promised by a rich uncle if he marries before 40, who (still a bachelor) persuades his best friend's wife to pose as Mrs Radford to fool uncle. Naturally, there are (not very hilarious) complications.

RoC *Kathleen Kelly, Cyril Smith, Jimmy Godden, Marie Ault, Hal Gordon, Gillian Maude.*

LEST WE FORGET (1934)   [3]

Dir *John Baxter*. Prod *Norman Loudon*. Scr *Herbert Ayres*. PC *Sound City*. Dis *M-G-M*. *61 mins*. *Cert U*

A reworking of the 1932 film *Reunion* (qv), by the same writer and producer - and star, *Stewart Rome*. During the First World War, four soldiers - English, Scots, Welsh and Irish - trapped in a shellhole plan a reunion if they survive the war. The Englishman (Rome) falls on hard times in peacetime, but feigns wealth when the quartet's reunion gathering takes place.

RoC *George Carney, Esmond Knight, Roddy Hughes, Ann Yates, Tony Quinn, Wilson Coleman.*

LET ME EXPLAIN, DEAR (1932)   [4]

Dir and Scr *Gene Gerrard, Frank Miller, from a play by Walter Ellis*. Prod *John Maxwell*. PC *BIP*. Dis *Wardour*. *82 mins* (later 77). *Cert A*

Typically boisterous *Gene Gerrard* vehicle, third of three screen versions of Walter Ellis' play *A Little Bit of Fluff*. The second (1928) was called *Skirts* in America. Gerrard plays a flirtatious husband who has an innocent fling with Mamie (*Jane Carr*) and subsequently not only has to feign injury to get insurance money to pay for Mamie's necklace, but has a tough time convincing wifey (*Viola Lyel*) that he's really a faithful husband.

RoC *Claude Hulbert, Amy Veness, Henry Longhurst, Hal Gordon, Reginald Bach, (C.) Denier Warren.*

LET'S BE FAMOUS (1939)   [3]

Dir *Walter Forde*. Prod *Michael Balcon*. Scr *Roger Macdougall, Allan Mackinnon*. Ph *Ronald Neame, Gordon Dines*. PC *Ealing Studios*. Dis *Associated British*. *83 mins*. *Cert U*

Jimmy (*Jimmy O'Dea*) is an Irish villager who brags about his voice, and mistakes an invitation to a spelling bee for one to sing at a concert for the BBC. After his disillusionment, he is befriended by Finch (*Sonnie Hale*), an agent. They pull various publicity stunts, and finally win a BBC contract as a double act after a 'pirate' broadcast from a French radio station. Quite lively.

RoC *Betty Driver, Patrick Barr, Basil Radford, Milton Rosmer, Lena Brown, Garry Marsh, Alf Goddard, Hay Plumb, Henry Hallett, Franklin Bellamy.*

LET'S LOVE AND LAUGH (1931)   [4]
(USA: *Bridegroom for Two*)

Dir and Prod *Richard Eichberg*. Scr *Frederick Jackson, Walter C. Mycroft, from a play by Fred Thompson and Ernest Poulton*. Ph *H.*

Gartner, B. Mondi. PC *BIP*. Dis *Wardour*. *85 mins*. *Cert A*

Musical comedy, shot in bilingual versions, with unnamed characters in the story of a wealthy young idler (*Gene Gerrard*) who wakes up after a drunken revel to find that he is married to a chorus girl. The girl he was to have married the following day is understandably miffed and complications run riot.

RoC *Muriel Angelus, George Gee, Ronald Frankau, Frank Stanmore, Denis Wyndham, Rita Page, Margaret Yarde, Henry Wenman.*

LET'S MAKE A NIGHT OF IT (1937)   [4]

Dir *Graham Cutts*. Prod *Walter C. Mycroft*. Scr *F. McGrew Willis, Hugh Brooke, from a radio play by Henrik N. Ege*. Ph *Otto Kanturek, Claude Friese-Greene*. PC and Dis *Associated British*. *94 mins*. *Cert U*

Enjoyable musical concerning Henry (*Fred Emney*), who is left a nightclub, the Silver Slipper, to cover a bad debt. He dares not tell his wife (*Iris Hoey*), but she is inveigled into buying a rival club, the Coconut Beach. Jack (*Charles 'Buddy' Rogers*), a waiter with show-biz ambitions, learns of Boydell's secret and blackmails a job out of him to be near his daughter (*June Clyde*). Both clubs are raided and all concerned end up in the cells.

RoC *Steve Geray, Zelma O'Neal, Irene Prador, Molly Picon, Jack Melford, Claud Allister, Brian Michie, Dan Donovan, Afrique, The Four Franks, Josephine Bradley, The Four Aces, Peggy and Ready, Jack Jackson and His Band, Joe Loss and His Band, Sydney Lipton and His Band, Eddie Carroll and His Band, Harry Acres and His Band, Rudy Starita's Marimba Band, The Percy Athos Follies, Bertha Belmore, Syd Walker, Oliver Wakefield, Antony Holles, Lawrence Anderson.*

LETTING IN THE SUNSHINE (1933)   [2]

Dir *Lupino Lane*. Prod *John Maxwell*. Scr *Con West, Herbert Sargent*. Ph *J.J. Cox, Bryan Langley*. PC *BIP*. Dis *Wardour*. *73 mins*. *Cert U*

A window cleaner (*Albert Burdon*) and a maid (*Renée Gadd*) get on to the track of a gang of thieves planning to steal a famous necklace, in this misfaced comedy. Tied up by the gang, our heroes escape, join a party given for Lady Anne (*Molly Lamont*) whose mother owns the necklace and expose the crooks.

RoC *Henry Mollison, Tonie Edgar Bruce, Her-*

Albert Burdon and Renee Gadd in Letting in the Sunshine (*1933*)

bert Langley, Syd Crossley, Eric Le Fré, Ethel Warwick, Henry Longhurst.

LIEUTENANT DARING RN (1935)   [3]

Dir *Reginald Denham*. Prod *Lawrence Huntington*. Scr *Gerald Elliott*. Ph *George Dudgeon Stretton*. PC and Dis *Butchers*. *85 mins*. *Cert U*

Hearty juvenile adventure which briskly disregards improbabilities. Sealed orders are stolen in Chinese waters, and Lt Daring (*Hugh Williams*) takes the blame after being framed by the captain's treacherous son (*Martin Walker*). The heroine (*Geraldine Fitzgerald*) is kidnapped by pirates, and the hero rescues her and proves his innocence at the same time. Revival of a silent film character.

RoC *Frederick Lloyd, Jerry Verno, John Rorke, Ernest Butcher, Ralph Truman, Richard Norris, Edwin Ellis, Neil McKay, George Carr, Robb Wilton, Geoffrey Clark, Eileen Tai, Grace Tai, Arthur Brander, Charles Cantley, Douglas Bell, A.E.J. Walker, Douglas Phillips, Pat Hagan, Victor Hagan, Hugh Selwyn, K. Wing, Chee Foo, Su Yee Troupe, Horace Sheldon and His Orchestra.*

LIFE GOES ON (1932)   [3]

Dir *Jack Raymond*. Prod *Herbert Wilcox*. Scr *Uncredited, from a play by Walter Hackett*. PC *British and Dominions*. Dis *Paramount*. *78 mins*. *Cert U*

Romantically attracted to a guest at her hotel, Phoebe (*Elsie Randolph*), the switchboard operator, tells him about strange happenings in the room next to his. The guest (*Hugh Wakefield*) discovers that a stockbroker has died in the room; the hotel manager and another man are keeping it quiet to manipulate the money market and plan to frame a girl for murder.

RoC *Betty Stockfeld, Warwick Ward, Wallace Geoffreys, Jeanne Stuart, Dennis Hoey, Antony Holles, Robert Horton.*

THE LIFE OF THE PARTY (1934)   [1]

Dir *Ralph Dawson*. Prod *Irving Asher*. Scr *Brock Williams, from a play by Margaret Mayo, Salisbury Field*. PC and Dis *Warner Bros*. *53 mins*. *Cert A*

Weak story about a man who is keen to move away from people for whom his wife is constantly throwing parties. But two of the wives also move to get their husbands away from *her*. Said one critic: 'There is very little life in this party.'

LP *Jerry Verno, Betty Astell, Eric Fawcett, Vera Bogetti, Kenneth Kove, Hermione Hannen, Phyllis Morris.*

LIGHTNING CONDUCTOR (1938)   [4]

Dir *Maurice Elvey*. Prod *Anthony Havelock-Allan*. Scr *J. Jefferson Farjeon, Ivor McLaren, Laurence Green*. Ph *Francis Carver*. PC *Pinebrook*. Dis *General Film Distributors*. *79 mins*. *Cert A*

Bus conductor Albert (*Gordon Harker*) goes to the Air Defence Office with his new gas-mask invention, a visit that coincides with the theft of vital plans by Anderson (*John Lodge*), who puts them in Albert's pocket. The spies almost get the plans back (a) at a busmen's concert,

(b) on Albert's bus and (c) in Epping Forest, but a swarm of bees comes to Albert's rescue in the forest and the enemy agents are routed. Comedy spy story provides suspense and rollicking excitement too.

RoC *Sally Gray, Ernest Thesiger, Steven Geray, George Moon, Charles Eaton, Arthur Hambling, Roy Findlay.*

THE LILAC DOMINO (1937)   [2]

Dir *Fred (Friedrich) Zelnick.* Prod *Max Schach, Isadore Goldschmidt, Lee Garmes.* Scr *Basil Mason, Neil Gow, R. Hutter, Derek Neame, from the play by Rudolf Bernauer, E. Gatti, B. Jenbach.* Ph *Roy Clark, Bryan Langley, (uncredited) Garmes.* PC *Grafton/Capitol/Cecil.* Dis *United Artists. 79 mins. Cert U*

Musical caper whose time had long passed. The schoolgirl daughter (*June Knight*) of a Hungarian baron is fascinated by a Hussar who gambles away a fortune. She invades his box at a masked ball, and ensnares him in her girlish web. She, known to him only as the Lilac Domino, tells him she can only be his if he changes his ways.

RoC *Michael Bartlett, Athene Seyler, Richard Dolman, Szocke Sakall, Fred Emney, Jane Carr, Morris Harvey, Paul Blake, Joan Hickson, Julie Suedo, Cameron Hall, Joan Newall, Isobel Scaife.*

LILIES OF THE FIELD (1934)   [4]

Dir *Norman Walker.* Prod *Herbert Wilcox.* Scr *Dion Titheradge, from a play by John Hastings Turner.* Ph *Cyril Bristow.* PC *British and Dominions.* Dis *United Artists. 82 mins. Cert U*

Entertaining romantic comedy about two sisters (*Winifred Shotter, Judy Gunn*) who have to compete for a man's attentions in order to win a month in London offered by their eccentric grandmother. Betty (*Miss Shotter*) wins by posing as a simple girl in crinoline, a pose she is forced to continue in London, where she sparks off a new fashion.

RoC *Ellis Jeffreys, Claude Hulbert, Anthony Bushell, Jack Raine, Bobbie Comber, Hubert Harben, Maud Gill, Tonie Edgar Bruce, Gladys Jennings, The Aspidistras (Elsie French, John Mott).*

LILY CHRISTINE (1932)   [1]

Dir *Paul Stein.* Prod *Walter Morosco.* Scr *Robert Gore-Brown, from a novel by Michael Arlen.* PC *Paramount British.* Dis *Paramount. 82 mins. Cert A*

Miserable screen farewell for *Corinne Griffith,* once Hollywood's 'most beautiful woman' of the silent screen and soon to marry the producer of this film (divorced 1934). She plays a woman threatened with divorce by her husband, who wants to marry an actress, and cites her for spending an (innocent) night with an author friend (*Colin Clive*). Despairing, she throws herself under a lorry. Maudlin, dated fare.

RoC *Jack Trevor, Miles Mander, Anne Grey, Margaret Bannerman, Barbara Everest, Peter Graves.*

LILY OF KILLARNEY (1933)   [3]
(USA: *Bride of the Lake*)

Dir *Maurice Elvey.* Prod *Julius Hagen.* Scr *H. Fowler Mear, from a play by Dion Boucicault and an operetta by Charles Benedict.* Ph *Sydney Blythe.* PC *Twickenham.* Dis *Associated Producers and Distributors. 86 mins. Cert U*

Musical, set in Ireland (actually shot in Killarney). A poor landowner (*John Garrick*), in love with a peasant girl (*Gina Malo*) who is kidnapped by a notorious smuggler (*Dennis Hoey*), mortgages his estate to Sir James (*Leslie Perrins*), who soon threatens to foreclose. But the landowner rescues the girl and keeps his land when his horse beats that of Sir James in a big race.

RoC *Stanley Holloway, Sara Allgood, Dorothy Boyd, D.J. Williams, Hughes Macklin, Pamela May, A. Bromley Davenport, John Mortimer, Pat Noonan.*

LILY OF LAGUNA (1937)   [2]

Dir *Oswald Mitchell.* Prod *Sidney Morgan.* Scr *Oswald Mitchell, Ian Walker, Joan Wentworth Wood.* Ph *Geoffrey Faithfull.* PC and Dis *Butchers. 84 mins. Cert A*

Stage star Gloria Grey (*Nora Swinburne*) gives up her career to marry a scientist. After the birth of her daughter, however, she returns to the stage and her husband divorces her. Twenty years on, mother and daughter fall for the same man, a radio producer. When Gloria realizes this, she gives him up, but is shot and wounded by a suitor she has 'used' in her schemes, an incident which causes her to be reunited with her ex-husband. Tedious.

RoC *Richard Ainley, G.H. Mulcaster, Jenny Laird, Talbot O'Farrell, Edgar Driver, Desmond Roberts, Violet Graham, Dudley Rolph, Richard Newton, Claire Arnold, Scott Harold, John Payne's Negro Choir.*

LIMELIGHT (1935)   [2]
(USA: *Backstage*)

Dir, Prod and PC *Herbert Wilcox.* Scr *Laura Whetter.* Ph *Henry Harris.* Dis *General Film Distributors. 80 mins. Cert U*

Lavish musical designed as a vehicle for *Arthur Tracy,* the popular 'Street Singer'. But the material proved poor, and Tracy no actor. He's a busker who makes the big time thanks to the efforts of the chorus girl, Marjorie (*Anna Neagle*), who loves him. But he becomes infatuated with a socialite. Marjorie also gets her big chance, but her nerve fails, and it is the Street Singer, returning from self-imposed exile, who saves her career and the show.

RoC *Tilly Losch, Jack Buchanan, Jane Winton, Ellis Jeffreys, Muriel George, Antony Holles, Ralph Reader, Alexander Field, William Freshman, Helena Pickard, Queenie Leonard, W. MacQueen Pope, Frank Boor, Ronald Shiner, Andrea Malandrinos, Geraldo and His Sweet Music, The Hippodrome Girls.*

THE LIMPING MAN (1936)   [3]

Dir, Prod and Scr *Walter Summers, from the play by Will.Scott.* Ph *Cyril Bristow.* PC *Welwyn.* Dis *Pathé. 72 mins. Cert A*

Philip Nash (*Robert Cochran*) goes to Monk's Revel, which he has inherited, dogged by a limping man (*Harry Hutchinson*) who has mistaken him for his evil twin brother. Thieves are in the house after a valuable painting, and the evil twin is out to kill Philip. Doors creak, panels slide, women scream and the twin brother is bumped off. Disher (*Francis L. Sullivan*), a criminologist staying at Monk's Revel, finally solves the mystery.

RoC *Hugh Wakefield, Patricia Hilliard, Leslie Perrins, Judy Kelly, Iris Hoey, Frank Atkinson, George Pughe, John Turnbull, Arthur Brander, Syd Crossley.*

LINE ENGAGED (1935)   [3]

Dir *Bernard Mainwaring.* Prod *Herbert Smith.* Scr *Jack de Leon, Jack Celestin, from their play.* Ph *George Dudgeon Stretton.* PC and Dis *British Lion. 68 mins. Cert A*

Quite neatly made thriller about a young author (*Bramwell Fletcher*) who finds himself in love with a married woman (*Jane Baxter*) whose unpleasant husband (*Leslie Perrins*) seems to have a hold on her. When his father (*Arthur Wontner*), an inspector, outlines a 'perfect murder' for a new novel, the author decides to use it – but his intended victim is dead when he arrives. Thinking his son guilty, the inspector only delays the capture of the real killer – the wife's mother.

RoC *Mary Clare, George Merritt, Kathleen Harrison, John Turnbull, Coral Browne, Ronald Shiner, Francis James.*

THE LION HAS WINGS (1939)   [4]

Dir *Michael Powell, Brian Desmond Hurst, Adrian Brunel.* Prod *Alexander Korda.* Scr *Adrian Brunel, E.V.H. Emmett.* Ph *Harry Stradling, Osmond Borrodaile.* PC *London Films.* Dis *United Artists. 76 mins. Cert U*

Some skilled cutting and direction helps this

Corinne Griffith in Lily Christine *(1932)*

Ralph Richardson and Merle Oberon in The Lion Has Wings *(1939)*

hectically-produced propaganda piece, showing the outbreak of the Second World War, the strength of the RAF and their Kiel Canal raid and warding off of Luftwaffe attacks. Public reception was fairly lukewarm but it is, under such exceptional circumstances, pretty well done.

LP *Ralph Richardson, Merle Oberon, June Duprez, Robert Douglas, Anthony Bushell, Derrick de Marney, Brian Worth, Austin Trevor, Ivan Brandt, G. H. Mulcaster, Herbert Lomas, Milton Rosmer, Robert Rendel, John Longden, Archibald Batty, Ronald Adam, Ian Fleming, Miles Malleson, Charles Carson, John Penrose, Frank Tickle, John Robinson, Carl Jaffe, Gerald Case, Torin Thatcher, Ronald Shiner, Bernard Miles.*

A LITTLE BIT OF BLUFF (1935) [2]

Dir *P. Maclean Rogers.* Prod *A. George Smith.* Scr *H. F. Maltby, Kathleen Butler.* PC *GS Enterprises.* Dis *M-G-M. 61 mins. Cert U*

When thieves rob old Admiral Simcox (*H. F. Maltby*) of his family heirlooms, his daughter's gadabout fiancé (*Reginald Gardiner*) seizes his chance to go up in the old man's estimation. By posing as a detective, he bluffs the thieves into panicking, and regains the admiral's valuables. Strong cast just about keeps leaky comedy afloat.

RoC *Marjorie Shotter, Clifford Heatherley, Clifford McLaglen, Margaret Watson, Molly Fisher, Peggy Novak.*

THE LITTLE DAMOZEL (1933) [3]

Dir and Prod *Herbert Wilcox.* Scr *Donovan Pedelty, from the play by Monckton Hoffe.* Ph *F. A. Young.* PC *British and Dominions.* Dis *W and F. 73 mins. Cert A*

Musical in which a gambler is bribed to marry a cabaret artist, but later falls in love with her and, although she leaves him to return to show business, feels he has wrecked her life. The gambler, Recky (*James Rennie*) makes plans to commit suicide in such a way that his estranged wife (*Anna Neagle*) will get insurance money - but the couple are reconciled by the manager of the club at which she is entertaining.

RoC *Benita Hume, Athole Stewart, Alfred Drayton, Clifford Heatherley, Peter Northcote, Franklyn Bellamy, Aubrey Fitzgerald.*

LITTLE DOLLY DAYDREAM (1938) [2]

Dir and Scr *Oswald Mitchell.* Prod *John Argyle.* Ph *Geoffrey Faithfull.* PC *Argyle British.* Dis *Butchers. 82 mins. Cert U*

Four-year-old Dolly (*Binkie Stuart*) is taken away from her unemployed actress mother and given into the care of a stern aunt. She runs away and helps Old Moe (*Talbot O'Farrell*), an organ-grinder, catch a gang of thieves. Dolly's mother gets a job at a nightclub, Dolly and Old Moe are taken on there as duettists, and the family is reunited. Simple, homely musical for the easily moved.

RoC *Jane Welsh, Warren Jenkins, Cathleen Nesbitt, Sydney Fairbrother, G. H. Mulcaster, Eric Fawcett, Arthur E. Owen, Billy Watts, Gerald Vane, Henry Adnes, Syd Crossley, Douglas Stewart, Guy Jones and His Band.*

LITTLE FELLA (1932) [3]

Dir *William McGann.* Prod *Irving Asher.* Scr *W. Scott Darling.* PC *Warner Bros.* Dis *First National. 45 mins. Cert U*

Tony (*John Stuart*), an army officer, is about to be married to a girl who is only really interested in his money, when he meets an orphan girl who has stolen a foundling baby. Their qualities make him see his fiancée in her true light: he decides to marry the orphan girl and adopt the baby.

RoC *Dodo Watts, Joan Marion, Hal Walters, Marie Ault, George Merritt, Glyn James.*

LITTLE FRIEND (1934) [5]

Dir *Berthold Viertel.* (Associate) Prod *Robert Stevenson.* Scr *Margaret Kennedy, Christopher Isherwood, Viertel, from the novel by Ernst Lothar.* Ph *Günther Krampf.* PC and Dis *Gaumont-British. 85 mins. Cert A*

This well-treated weepie about the effects of a marriage break-up on the young daughter gave Britain its first child star in some years in *Nova Pilbeam.* She plays Felicity, who tries to shield her beloved mother (*Lydia Sherwood*) in court when her father (*Matheson Lang*) sues for divorce on the grounds of adultery, and whose subsequent attempt at suicide brings her parents together again.

RoC *Arthur Margetson, Jimmy Hanley, Allan Aynesworth, Jean Cadell, Lewis Casson, Clare Greet, Cecil Parker, Finlay Currie, Gibb McLaughlin, Jack Raine, Diana Cotton.*

LITTLE MISS NOBODY (1933) [2]

Dir *John Daumery.* Prod *Irving Asher.* PC and Dis *Warner Bros. 52 mins. Cert U*

Joining the motley inhabitants of a theatrical boarding house is Norwegian Karen Bergen (*Winna Winifried*), hoping for a London stage career. Aided by her fellow boarders, she is launched as a famous Scandinavian film star and bluffs a film producer into giving her a contract. The producer discovers the deception, but is so taken with Karen, he lets matters stand.

RoC *Sebastian Shaw, Betty Huntley Wright, Alice O'Day, A. Bromley Davenport, Drusilla Wills, Ben Field, Ernest Sefton, Abraham Sofaer.*

LITTLE MISS SOMEBODY (1937) [2]

Dir *Walter Tennyson.* Prod *Tennyson, Alfred D'Eyncourt.* Scr *H. Fowler Mear, Mary Dunn.* Ph *Geoffrey Faithfull.* PC *Mondover.* Dis *Butchers. 78 mins. Cert U*

When rascally Angus Duncan (*George Carney*) learns that Binkie (*Binkie Stuart*) an orphan cared for by an engaged couple, is coming into a fortune, he contrives to adopt her and take possession of her rich relative's will. Binkie is so unhappy in the care of Duncan's nurse that the police are eventually called in, and she is restored to her original foster parents. Unabashed sentiment.

RoC *John Longden, Kathleen Kelly, Jane Carr, D. A. Clarke-Smith, Margaret Emden, Vivienne Chatterton, (C.) Denier Warren, Hal Walters, J. Fisher White, Ernest Sefton, Cynthia Stock, Roddy Hughes, Oliver Gordon.*

LITTLE STRANGER (1934) [2]

Dir, Prod, Scr and PC *George King.* Ph *Günther Krampf.* Dis *M-G-M. 51 mins. Cert A*

Maudlin weepie about middle-aged Sam (*Nigel Playfair*) who befriends his wife Jessie's boarder Millie (*Norah Baring*) after she had been seduced and is pregnant. Millie dies in childbirth, and Jessie (*Eva Moore*) accepts Sam's story that he found the baby; they adopt it as their own.

RoC *Hamilton Keene.*

LITTLE WAITRESS (1932) [3]

Dir and Scr *Widgey R. Newman.* Prod *Geoffrey Clarke.* PC *Delta.* Dis *Ace. 49 mins. Cert U*

Mini-musical, with *Claude Bailey* as John, an English tourist in Austria, who poses as a rich man to woo Trudi (*Elvi Keene*), a waitress who is really the daughter of an (impoverished) Austrian baron (*Moore Marriott*). John lands in trouble until the baron recognizes him as the son of an old English friend and gives the lovers his blessing.

RoC *Walter Patch, Noel Birkin.*

LIVE AGAIN (1936) [2]

Dir *Arthur Maude.* Prod *G. B. Morgan.* Scr *John Quin.* Ph *Horace Wheddon.* PC *Morgan Films.* Dis *National Provincial. 74 mins. Cert A*

Slow, old-fashioned musical about a once-famous opera star, Meredith (*Noah Beery*), who hopes to 'live again' through the career of his young protégé John (*John Garrick*). John falls in love and decides to switch to musical comedy to be with his girl. Meredith erupts in fury and is sent to prison for a violent attack on John. But he lives to see his dreams come true.

RoC *Bessie Love, Stan Paskin, Vi Kaley, Cecil Gray, Pamela Randall, Lynwood Roberts, Frank Stanmore, Gertrude Bibby.*

THE LIVE WIRE (1937) [3]

Dir *Herbert Brenon.* Prod *Herbert Wynne.* Scr *Stafford Dickens, from his play* Plunder in the Air. PC *Tudor/Olympic.* Dis *British Lion. 69 mins. Cert U*

In love with the manager's secretary at a near-bankrupt company, an American with a shady past (*Bernard Nedell*) saves the firm by posing as an efficiency expert. Turning the firm's one remaining asset, a seemingly worthless area of marshland, into a palatial health spa, he also exposes the manager as an embezzler. Some dull patches in generally lively comedy.

RoC *Jean Gillie, Hugh Wakefield, Arthur Wontner, Kathleen Kelly, David Burns, Felix Aylmer, Irene Ware, H. F. Maltby, C. M. Hallard.*

LIVING DANGEROUSLY (1936) [4]

Dir *Herbert Brenon.* Prod *Walter C. Mycroft.* Scr *Marjorie Deans, Geoffrey Kerr, Dudley Leslie.* PC *BIP.* Dis *Wardour. 72 mins. Cert A*

Neatly directed crime drama about a doctor (*Otto Kruger*), falsely accused of his partner's drug-dealing, who is struck off, and tries to start afresh in America. His ex-partner (*Francis Lister*), with whose ex-wife the doctor

is now involved, reappears, intent on blackmail. The doctor shoots him, and his friend the DA calls it 'justifiable homicide'. But there's a twist. . . .
RoC *Leonora Corbett, Aileen Marson, Hartley Power, Lawrence Anderson, James Carew, Iris Hoey, Jimmy Godden, Charles Mortimer, Eric Stanley, Hubert Harben.*

THE LODGER (1932) [4]
(USA: *The Phantom Fiend*)
Dir *Maurice Elvey.* Prod *Julius Hagen.* Scr *Ivor Novello, Miles Mander, Paul Rotha, H. Fowler Mear, from the novel by Mrs Belloc Lowndes.* Ph *Basil Emmott, Sydney Blythe.* PC *Twickenham.* Dis *W and F.* 84 mins. Cert A
Very serviceable modernized version of the classic Hitchcock silent of 1926, with *Ivor Novello* repeating his role of the upstairs lodger suspected of being a Jack the Ripper-style killer. An attack on the daughter of the house (*Elizabeth Allan*) ultimately reveals the homicidal maniac to be the lodger's twin brother.
RoC *Jack Hawkins, A. W. Baskcomb, Barbara Everest, Peter Gawthorne, P. Kynaston Reeves, Shayle Gardner, Drusilla Wills, Antony Holles, George Merritt, Mollie Fisher, Andrea Malandrinos, Iris Ashley.*

THE LONDONDERRY AIR (1937) [3]
Dir *Alex Bryce.* Prod *Victor M. Greene.* Scr *David Evans, Bryce, from the play by Rachel Field.* Ph *Ronald Neame.* PC and Dis *Fox British.* 47 mins. Cert U
Patrick (*Liam Gaffney*), a wandering Irish pedlar, is chased off by Widow Rafferty (*Sara Allgood*), who had engaged him to play fiddle at a party, when she sees her ward Rose Martha (*Phyllis Ryan*), engaged to her son Sheamus, is taken with his charm. Months later, Patrick returns and asks the girl to come away with him. Seeing Sheamus will never escape his mother's dominance, she goes. Pleasant Irish trifle.
RoC *Jimmy Mageean, Maurice Moore, Granville Darling, Kitty Kirwan, George Dillon, Sidney Young.*

LONDON MELODY (1930) [2]
Dir, Prod and Scr *Geoffrey Malins, Donald Stuart.* PC *British Screen Productions.* Dis *Audible Filmcraft.* 59 mins. Cert U
Very minor musical about a show business agent (*Ballard Berkeley*) who falls in love with a French music-hall star, only to find out in the end that she is as English as him.
RoC *Lorraine La Fosse, Haddon Mason, Betty Naismith, Helen Debroy Summers, Bobby Kerrigan, David Openshaw.*

LONDON MELODY (1937) [2]
(USA: *Girls in the Street*)
Dir, Prod and PC *Herbert Wilcox.* Scr *Florence Tranter, Monckton Hoffe.* Ph *F. A. Young.* Dis *General Film Distributors.* 75 mins. Cert A
Marius (*Tullio Carminati*), a diplomat, falls for Jacqueline (*Anna Neagle*), a 'street Arab', pays for her training as a dancer, and even takes the blame for the failure of a worthless colleague (*Robert Douglas*), whom he thinks she loves.

Resigning his post, Marius leaves the country, but Jacqueline, who realizes she loves him, follows. Slender musical vehicle for Miss Neagle.
RoC *Horace Hodges, Grizelda Hervey, Miki Hood, Davina Craig, Joan Kemp-Welch, Arthur Chesney, Leonard Snelling, Henry Wolston.*

THE LONELY ROAD (1936) [3]
(USA: *Scotland Yard Commands*)
Dir *James Flood.* Prod *Basil Dean.* Scr *Flood, Gerard Fairlie, Anthony Kimmins, from the novel by Nevil Shute.* Ph *Jan Stallich.* PC *ATP.* Dis *Associated British.* 80 mins. Cert A
Kicked out of the navy for drunkenness and spurned by his long-standing lady friend, Stevenson (*Clive Brook*) drives down to the coast and drunkenly interrupts a gang of gunrunners who knock him out and flee. He helps Scotland Yard track the smugglers and, with the help of Molly (*Victoria Hopper*) whose brother is a reluctant member of the gang, Stevenson rounds up the gun-runners and regains his self-respect. Thriller is quick-moving but otherwise routine.
RoC *Malcolm Keen, Nora Swinburne, Charles Farrell, Cecil Ramage, Lawrence Hanray, Frederick Peisley, Ethel Coleridge, Warburton Gamble, Dennis Wyndham.*

LONG LIVE THE KING (1933) [2]
Dir *William McGann.* Prod *Irving Asher.* Scr *W. Scott Darling.* PC *Warner Bros.* Dis *First National.* 45 mins. Cert U
Unsophisticated comedy romp, a vehicle for *Florence Desmond*, as a Cockney charwoman who wins a trip to a small European country and while there is instrumental in saving the land's baby prince from a gang of revolutionaries.
RoC *'Skipper' Glyn James, Hal Walters, Abraham Sofaer, Betty Bolton, Mike Johnson, Charles Castella.*

Gracie Fields in Looking on the Bright Side *(1932)*

LOOKING ON THE BRIGHT SIDE (1932) [4]
Dir *Basil Dean, Graham Cutts.* Prod *Dean.* Scr *Dean, Archie Pitt, Brock Williams.* Ph *Robert Martin.* PC *Associated Talking Pictures.* Dis *Radio.* 80 mins. Cert U
Familiar storyline about stage partners, in this case a singer and a songwriter (*Gracie Fields, Richard Dolman*) who split up (when he becomes infatuated with an actress). Without the

girl to sing his songs, the songwriter starts to slide, but unexpectedly she appears in his new show and they are a great success together again. *Gracie Fields'* first big film hit.
RoC *Wyn Richmond, Julian Rose, Tony de Lungo, Betty Shale, Viola Compton, Bettina Montahners.*

LOOK UP AND LAUGH (1935) [3]
Dir and Prod *Basil Dean.* Scr *Gordon Wellesley, from a story by J. B. Priestley.* Ph *Bob Martin.* PC *ATP.* Dis *Associated British.* 80 mins. Cert U
Gracie Fields just about overcomes a feeble plot about market-stallholders warding off the efforts of a chainstore to close them down by finding a Royal Charter, and beating off a siege at the Town Hall. Spirited enough, but the sort of tune played with more conviction by Michael Balcon at Ealing in the 1940s.
RoC *Douglas Wakefield, Harry Tate, Alfred Drayton, Morris Harvey, Vivien Leigh, Robb Wilton, Huntley Wright, Tommy Fields, D. J. Williams, Kenneth Kove, Billy Nelson, Jack Melford, Maud Gill, Helen Ferrers, Norman Walker, Arthur Hambling, Kenneth More.*

LOOSE ENDS (1930) [3]
Dir *Norman Walker.* Scr *Dion Titheradge, Norman Walker.* Ph *Claude Friese-Greene.* PC *BIP.* Dis *Wardour.* 95 mins. Cert A
This rather theatrical but well-acted romantic drama drew very mixed notices from the critics. *Edna Best* plays an actress who marries a man she knows nothing about and who disapproves of her 'smart' friends. Discovering he has served 15 years for murder, she leaves him, but, on learning the circumstances of his 'crime', returns.
RoC *Owen Nares, Miles Mander, Adrianne Allen, Donald Calthrop, J. Fisher White, Sybil Arundale, Edna Davies, Gerard Lyley.*

LORD BABS (1932) [3]
Dir *Walter Forde.* Prod *Michael Balcon.* Scr *Clifford Grey, Angus Macphail, Sidney Gilliat, from the play by Keble Howard.* Ph *Leslie Rowson.* PC *Gainsborough.* Dis *Ideal.* 65 mins. Cert U
Musical-comedy vehicle for stage star *Bobby Howes.* He plays ship's steward Basil 'Babs' Drayford, who learns he has inherited a peerage and a fortune, but becomes entangled with Helen (*Pat Paterson*), the daughter of a pork-

Jean Colin and Bobby Howes in Lord Babs *(1932)*

pie king. Babs' friend Dr Neville (*Hugh Dempster*), who loves Helen, persuades Babs to feign regression to babyhood in order to evade marriage.
RoC *Jean Colin, Alfred Drayton, Arthur Chesney, Clare Greet, Joseph Cunningham, Walter Forde.*

LORD CAMBER'S LADIES (1932) ③
Dir *Benn W. Levy*. Prod *Alfred Hitchcock*. Scr *Levy, Edwin Greenwood, Gilbert Wakefield, from a play by Horace Annesley Vachell*. Ph *James Wilson*. PC *BIP*. Dis *Wardour*. 66 mins. Cert *A*
Hitchcock's last chore at BIP was the production of this lurid quota drama redeemed in part by the quality of its acting. Lord Camber (*Nigel Bruce*) loves Janet (*Benita Hume*), but allows himself to be drawn into marriage with Shirley (*Gertrude Lawrence*) a vaudeville star who loves him. When Shirley dies, Janet, now working for a doctor, is briefly suspected of poisoning her, but soon cleared. Lord Camber is left alone.
RoC *Gerald du Maurier, A. Bromley Davenport, Molly Lamont, Clare Greet, Betty Norton, Harold Meade, Hugh E. Wright, Hal Gordon.*

LORD EDGWARE DIES (1934) ③
Dir *Henry Edwards*. Prod *Julius Hagen*. Scr *H. Fowler Mear, from the novel by Agatha Christie*. Ph *Sydney Blythe*. PC *Real Art*. Dis *Radio*. 82 mins. Cert *A*
Another outing for *Austin Trevor* as Agatha Christie's detective Hercule Poirot, in this workmanlike if wordy whodunnit in which Poirot proves the innocence of young Lady Edgware (*Jane Carr*) of the murders of her husband and a mystery girl, by, as usual, unmasking the real guilty party.
RoC *Richard Cooper, John Turnbull, Michael Shepley, Leslie Perrins, C.V. France, Esmé Percy.*

LORD OF THE MANOR (1933) ④
Dir *Henry Edwards*. Prod *Herbert Wilcox*. Scr *Dorothy Rowan, from the play by John Hastings Turner*. Ph *Henry Harris*. PC *British and Dominions*. Dis *Paramount*. 71 mins. Cert *U*
Well-played comedy in which a lord and a general hope that their respective offspring will marry each other. But somehow, in one week at the lord's manor, it all goes wrong. The lord's son arrives with another fiancée, but falls for a poor-born Canadian girl; while the general's daughter (*Betty Stockfeld*) falls suddenly for a complete stranger.
RoC *Fred Kerr, David Horne, Harry Wilcoxon, Kate Cutler, Frank Bertram, Joan Marion, April Dawn, Deering Wells, Frederick Ross.*

LORD RICHARD IN THE PANTRY (1930) ④
Dir *Walter Forde*. Prod *Julius Hagen, Henry Edwards*. Scr *H. Fowler Mear, from a play by Sidney Blow and Douglas Hoare*. Ph *Sydney Blythe*. PC *Twickenham*. Dis *Warner Bros*. 95 mins. Cert *U*
Presentable version of a stage success in which a lord (*Richard Cooper*), innocently involved by his partners in a swindle, becomes the but-

ler in his own stately home in order to evade arrest. When the swindlers are brought to book, he reveals his real identity to the woman (*Dorothy Seacombe*) to whom he let his home – but she has known all along.
RoC *Leo Sheffield, Frederick Volpe, Helena Pickard, Marjorie Hume, Alexander Field, Barbara Gott, Viola Lyel, Gladys Hamer, Charles Stone, Harry Terry.*

LORNA DOONE (1934) ③
Dir and Prod *Basil Dean*. Scr *Dorothy Farnum, Miles Malleson, Gordon Wellesley, from the novel by R. D. Blackmore*. Ph *Bob Martin*. PC *ATP*. Dis *Associated British*. 90 mins. Cert *A*
Lovely photography and natural settings, but weak acting in this, perhaps the best-known version of *R. D. Blackmore*'s tale of adventure and romance in early seventeenth-century Devon, where a farmer (*John Loder*) loves the daughter (*Victoria Hopper*) of a family of outlaws. After her villainous 'brother' (*Roy Emerton*) is killed, it transpires that the girl is in reality a kidnapped heiress.
RoC *Margaret Lockwood, Mary Clare, Edward Rigby, Roger Livesey, D.A. Clarke-Smith, George Curzon, Lawrence Hanray, Amy Veness, Eliot Makeham, Wyndham Goldie, Frank Cellier, Herbert Lomas, Peggy Blythe, Peter Penrose, Thea Holme, Toska von Bissing, Arthur Hambling, Alexis France, June Holden.*

THE LOST CHORD (1933) ③
Dir *Maurice Elvey*. Prod *Julius Hagen*. Scr *H. Fowler Mear*. Ph *Sydney Blythe*. PC *Twickenham*. Dis *Associated Producers and Distributors*. 91 mins. Cert *A*
David, a musician (*John Stuart*), kills a count (*Leslie Perrins*) over the countess (*Mary Glynne*), who some time later dies in his arms. Twenty years after, David falls in love with the countess' daughter (*Elizabeth Allan*) and helps her achieve her ambition to become a musical-comedy star. So-so through-the-years romance with music.
RoC *Anne Grey, Jack Hawkins, Betty Astell, Garry Marsh, Barbara Everest, Tudor Davis, Frederick Ranalow, Billy Mayerl, Eliot Makeham, Bernard Ansell.*

LOST IN THE LEGION (1934) ③
Dir *Fred Newmeyer*. Prod *Walter C. Mycroft*. Scr *Syd Courtenay, John Paddy Carstairs*. Ph *Jack Parker*. PC *BIP*. Dis *Wardour*. 70 mins. Cert *U*
Usual artless *Leslie Fuller* comedy, featuring him and *Hal Gordon* as two sea-cooks who unwittingly join the Foreign Legion, but rescue two girls from the clutches of a sheik.
RoC *Renée Houston, Betty Fields, H. F. Maltby, Alf Goddard, James Knight, Mike Johnson, A. Bromley Davenport, Syd Courtenay, Ernest Fuller, Santos Casani, Lola Harvey.*

THE LOVE AFFAIR OF THE DICTATOR (1935) ④
(USA: *The Loves of a Dictator*)
Dir *Victor Saville, Alfred Santell*. Prod *Ludovico Toeplitz*. Scr *Benn W. Levy*. Ph *Franz Planer*. PC *Toeplitz Films*. Dis *Gaumont-British*. 86 mins. Cert *A*

Clive Brook and Emlyn Williams in The Love Affair of the Dictator *(1936)*

Quite a good historical romance, though somewhat lacking in dramatic force, set in Denmark in 1776. Struensee (*Clive Brook*), a German doctor, becomes virtual dictator of the country because of his influence over the feeble King Christian VII (*Emlyn Williams*). He falls in love with the Queen (*Madeleine Carroll*) but is betrayed by their mutual enemies. Struensee is executed and the Queen banished.
RoC *Helen Haye, Isabel Jeans, Alfred Drayton, Heather Thatcher, Gibb McLaughlin, Frank Cellier, Nicholas Hannen, Ruby Miller.*

LOVE AT SEA (1936) ②
Dir *Adrian Brunel*. Prod *Anthony Havelock-Allan*. Scr *Beaufoy Milton*. Ph *Francis Carver*. PC and Dis *British and Dominion/Paramount British*. 70 mins. Cert *A*
Two middle-aged people advertise in a matrimonial paper, and arrange to go on a cruise. Neither makes it. She is forbidden by her domineering sister, and sends her niece instead. He is knocked down on the dockside, has his wallet taken by a thief, and his ticket falls into the hands of a reporter. The reporter falls for the niece, but later there's a happy ending for the older couple too. Complicated romantic comedy.
LP *Rosalyn Boulter, Carl Harbord, Aubrey Mallalieu, Maud Gill, Frank Birch, Dorothy Dewhurst, Beatrix Fielden-Kaye, Billy Bray, George Merritt, Raymond Ellis, Eve Riley, George Dewhurst, Vi Kaley, Hector McGregor.*

LOVE AT SECOND SIGHT (1934) ②
(USA: *The Girl Thief*)
Dir *Paul Merzbach*. Prod *Julius Haimann*. Scr *Frank Miller, Jack Davies*. PC *Radius/BIP*. Dis *Wardour*. 71 mins. Cert *U*
Fragile comedy with music (by Mischa Spoliansky). Allan (*Claude Hulbert*), the inventor of an inexhaustible match, falls for Juliet (*Marian Marsh*), the daughter of a 'match king' (*Ralph Ince*). Juliet falls for Allan's friend Bill (*Anthony Bushell*) and Allan, who gains due recognition for his invention, realizes he was in love with his secretary (*Joan Gardner*) all the time.
RoC *Stanley Holloway, Neil Kenyon, Vivien Reynolds.*

THE LOVE CONTRACT (1932) ④
Dir and Scr *Herbert Selpin, from a play by Letraz, Desty and Blum*. Prod *Herbert Wilcox*.

Ph *F. A. Young*. PC *British and Dominions*. Dis *W and F*. *80 mins. Cert A*

Winifred Shotter, petite feminine foil for the Aldwych farceurs, struck out on her own as the star of this bright comedy-musical about a girl who loses everything on the Stock Exchange and takes a job as chauffeur to the broker (*Owen Nares*) who bought her house. In love with her, he offers to give her back the house if she sticks the job for three months – and does his best to make her resign.

RoC *Sunday Wilshin, Miles Malleson, Gibb McLaughlin, Spencer Trevor, Frank Harvey, Cosmo Kyrle Bellew, Mangan Tillerettes*.

LOVE FROM A STRANGER (1936) 3

Dir *Rowland V. Lee*. Prod *Max Schach*. Scr *Frances Marion*, from the novel by *Agatha Christie* and the play adaptation by *Frank Vosper*. Ph *Phil Tannura*. PC *Trafalgar*. Dis *United Artists*. *90 mins. Cert A*

Slow but smoothly acted suspense drama about a woman, Carol (*Ann Harding*) who comes into a fortune, quarrels with her fiancé (*Bruce Seton*) and marries a man (*Basil Rathbone*) she hardly knows. He takes her to Europe and buys a luxury country home with her money, but a mysterious caller reveals him as a murderer of wealthy women. He prepares to kill Carol, but she tells him she has poisoned his coffee. His weak heart gives way and he dies.

RoC *Binnie Hale, Jean Cadell, Bryan Powley, Joan Hickson, Donald Calthrop, Eugene Leahy*.

Ann Harding and Basil Rathbone in Love from a Stranger *(1937)*

THE LOVE HABIT (1930) 4

Dir *Harry Lachman*. Prod *John Maxwell*. Scr *Seymour Hicks, Val Valentine*, from a play by *Louis Verneuil*. Ph *Jack Cox*. PC *BIP*. Dis *Wardour*. *90 mins. Cert A*

Director Harry Lachman, who got his early training in France, was obviously at home with this Gallic farce involving *Seymour Hicks* as an incorrigible 50-year-old roué who sets his cap at Julie (*Margot Grahame*), a young married woman. Finding that her husband, Alphonse (*Edmund Breon*) has a mistress (*Ursula Jeans*), he blackmails him into taking him on as his secretary. In the end, the roué is thwarted – for the time being. . . .

RoC *Elsa Lanchester, Clifford Heatherley, Walter Armitage*.

Walter Armitage, Seymour Hicks and Elsa Lanchester in The Love Habit *(1930)*

LOVE IN EXILE (1936) 2

Dir *Alfred L. Werker*. Prod *Max Schach*. Scr *Herman Mankiewicz, Roger Burford, Ernest Betts*, from a novel by *Gene Markey*. Ph *Otto Kanturek*. PC *Capitol*. Dis *General Film Distributors*. *78 mins. Cert A*

Creaky Ruritanian comedy, lacking in flesh and blood values, about King Regis VI (*Clive Brook*) who, having abdicated to make way for a dictator, outwits two revolutionary oil magnates and stages a surprise return to the throne of his country.

RoC *Helen Vinson, Will Fyffe, Mary Carlisle, Ronald Squire, Tamara Desni, Henry Oscar, Edmond Breon, Cecil Ramage, Barbara Everest*.

LOVE LIES (1931) 4

Dir *Lupino Lane*. Prod *Stanley Lupino*. Scr *Stanley Lupino, Arthur Rigby, Frank Miller*, from a play by *Lupino*. Ph *Walter Harvey, Horace Wheddon*. PC *BIP*. Dis *Wardour*. *70 mins. Cert U*

Brisk farce with *Stanley Lupino* re-creating the role of Jerry Walker from his own stage success. Jerry has two uncles, one of whom wants him to marry and have children, the other advising him to remain a bachelor gay. After a series of misadventures, Jerry decides to settle down with Joyce (*Dorothy Boyd*).

RoC *Jack Hobbs, Binnie Barnes, Dennis Hoey, Sebastian Smith, Wallace Lupino, Arty Ash, Charles Courtneidge*.

LOVE, LIFE AND LAUGHTER (1934) 3

Dir *Maurice Elvey*. Prod *Basil Dean*. Scr *Robert Edmunds*. PC *ATP*. Dis *Associated British*. *83 mins. Cert U*

Unlikely but quite pleasant romantic comedy about a prince (*John Loder*) who falls in love with a showgirl (*Gracie Fields*) and breaks his engagement to a princess (*Norah Howard*) to follow her, finding work in a film studio. On the death of his father, the prince is forced to return home, and the showgirl gives him up when she finds his marriage to the princess is essential for his country's well-being.

RoC *Allan Aynesworth, Esmé Percy, Veronica Brady, Horace Kenney, Robb Wilton, Fred Duprez, A. Bromley Davenport, Ivor Barnard, Eric Maturin, Elizabeth Jenns, Esmé Church*.

THE LOVE NEST (1933) 3

Dir *Thomas Bentley*. Prod *Walter C. Mycroft*. Scr *H. F. Maltby, Frank Miller, Gene Gerrard*. PC *BIP*. Dis *Wardour*. *69 mins. Cert A*

A young married woman (*Camilla Horn*) accidentally locks herself out one night in the rain and seeks help from the man (*Gene Gerrard*) opposite, who offers her shelter, although he is getting married the next day. The inevitable misunderstandings arise in this standard farce somewhat enlivened by Gerrard's energetic fooling.

RoC *Nancy Burne, Gus McNaughton, Garry Marsh, Amy Veness, Charles Paton, Judy Kelly, Marion Dawson*.

LOVE ON THE SPOT (1932) 4

Dir *Graham Cutts*. Prod *Basil Dean*. Scr *John Paddy Carstairs, Reginald Purdell*, from a novel by *Sapper*. PC *ATP*. Dis *Radio*. *64 mins. Cert A*

Musical comedy about two confidence tricksters, father and daughter (*Aubrey Mather, Rosemary Ames*). She rebels when she learns that Dad has been trying to sell crooked shares to Bill (*Richard Dolman*), a young man with whom she has fallen in love. But Bill proves to be a thief who has come to their hotel to steal the guests' jewels. All three finally reform.

RoC *Helen Ferrers, W. Cronin Wilson, Patrick Ludlow, J. Hubert Leslie, Margery Binner, Johnny Singer, Patrick Susands, Elizabeth Arkell*.

LOVE ON WHEELS (1932) 4

Dir *Victor Saville*. Prod *Michael Balcon*. Scr *Saville, Angus Macphail, Robert Stevenson, Douglas Furber*. Ph *Mutz Greenbaum*. PC *Gainsborough*. Dis *W and F*. *86 mins. Cert A*

Bright comedy-musical. To impress Jane (*Leonora Corbett*), store assistant Fred (*Jack Hulbert*) poses as the store's advertising manager. Sacked, he thwarts store thieves, gets himself re-engaged and actually becomes advertising manager for the store. He finds Jane, who had left him, earning a living as a pianist and puts her in charge of the store's music shop. Store scenes shot in London's Selfridges.

RoC *Edmund Gwenn, Gordon Harker, Tony de Lungo, Percy Parsons, Roland Culver, Miles Malleson, Martita Hunt, Lawrence Hanray*.

THE LOVE RACE (1931) 2

Dir *Lupino Lane, Pat Morton*. Prod *Stanley Lupino*. Scr *Edwin Greenwood*, from a play by *Stanley Lupino*. PC *BIP*. Dis *Pathé*. *81 mins. Cert U*

Stanley Lupino comedy in which he plays a car magnate's son, also a crack motor-racing driver. When he arrives at a party with a 'wrong' suitcase, containing lingerie, his fiancée jumps to all the wrong conclusions and only after he has defeated his great rival in the Schroeder Cup race is everything resolved.

RoC *Dorothy Boyd, Jack Hobbs, Dorothy Bartlam, Frank Perfitt, Wallace Arthur (Lupino), Artie Ash, Florence Vie, Doris Rogers*.

THE LOVES OF ARIANE (1930)   3
Dir and Prod *Paul Czinner*. Scr *Czinner, Carl Mayer*, from a novel by *Claude Anet*. PC and Dis *Nerofilm-Pathé Natan*. *70 mins. Cert A*
Somewhat fey romantic comedy, filmed in Paris (in three language versions) casting *Elisabeth Bergner* as a precocious Parisienne who invents a string of make-believe lovers to convince an older man with whom she is infatuated (*Percy Marmot*) of her worldly-wisdom. In reality, of course, she is quite inexperienced, but still contrives herself a happy ending.
RoC *Warwick Ward, Joan Matheson, Elisabeth Vaughan, Charles Carson, Oriel Ross.*

THE LOVES OF ROBERT BURNS
(1930)   3
Dir and Prod *Herbert Wilcox*. Scr *Wilcox, P. Maclean Rogers*. PC *British and Dominions*. Dis *W and F. 96 mins. Cert A*
Musical biography of Scotland's national poet, Robert Burns (*Joseph Hislop*), incorporating such songs as *Annie Laurie, Comin' thro' the Rye* and *Auld Lang Syne*. Encountered a certain amount of antagonism in Scotland through its depiction of Burns not so much as a great man, but rather as a pot-house singer and libertine.
RoC *Dorothy Seacombe, Eve Gray, Jean Cadell, Nancy Price, Neil Kenyon, C.V. France, George Baker, Wilfred Shine, Craighall Sherry, H. Saxon-Snell.*

LOVE'S OLD SWEET SONG
(1933)   3
Dir *Manning Haynes*. Prod *John Argyle*. Scr *Lydia Hayward*. Ph *Desmond Dickinson*. PC *Argyle Talking Pictures*. Dis *Butchers. 79 mins. Cert A*
Sombre romantic melodrama about a singer, Mary (*Joan Wyndham*), whose manager Paul (*John Stuart*) loves her; but she marries his worthless half-brother Eric (*Ronald Ward*), whose mistress is found dead. To shield a pregnant Mary, Paul confesses to the crime and serves a long prison term. In later developments, both Eric and Mary's old friend Jimmy (*William Freshman*) are killed in a gun battle. Mary learns the truth and promises to wait for Paul.
RoC *Julie Suedo, Moore Marriott, Marie Wright, Ivor Maxwell, Barbara Everest, Malcolm Tod, Charles Courtney, Picot Schooling, Dora Levis, Sidney Arnold.*

THE LOVE TEST (1934)   3
Dir *Michael Powell*. Prod *John Findlay*. Scr *Selwyn Jepson*. PC and Dis *Fox British. 63 mins. Cert U*
Chemists at a research laboratory, angry that a young woman, Mary (*Judy Gunn*), may be put in charge, get one of their number, John (*Louis Hayward*) to seduce her, so that she will pay more attention to emotions than chemicals. But the two fall in love. Thompson (*David Hutcheson*) steals a valuable formula and tries to blame Mary, but is found out and fired.
RoC *Morris Harvey, Aubrey Dexter, Bernard Miles, Jack Knight, Googie Withers, Eve Turner, Gilbert Davis, Shayle Gardner, James Craig.*

LOVE UP THE POLE (1936)   2
Dir *Clifford Gulliver*. Prod *Norman Hope-Bell*. Scr *Con West, Herbert Sargent, Ernest Lotinga*, from the play by *West and Sargent*. Ph *Jack Parker*. PC *British Comedies*. Dis *Butchers. 82 mins. Cert A*
Farce about two waiters, Josser (*Ernie Lotinga*) and Spud (*Jack Frost*), on the run from the police. They get on the track of some jewel thieves and, after pursuit on land, sea and even into prison, they get their men and clear their own names. Too long and sloppy even for devoted Lotinga fans.
RoC *Wallace Lupino, Vivienne Chatterton, Phyllis Dixey, Davina Craig, Lorna Hubbard, John Kevan, Harold Wilkinson, Fred Schwartz, Max Avieson, Teddy Brogden, Bobbie Slater, Clarence Blakiston, Fred Gretton, Henry Wolston, Langley Howard, Frank Tilton, Doyle Crossley, John Dudley.*

THE LOVE WAGER (1933)   2
Dir *A. Cyran*. Prod *E. A. Fell*. Scr *Moira Dale*. PC *Anglo-European*. Dis *Paramount. 64 mins. Cert U*
A general (*Morton Selten*) has wagered his son Peter (*Wallace Douglas*) that he can't make £1,500 in a year. Peter, who needs the money to marry Peggy (*Pat Paterson*) gets his chance when some of the general's jewels are stolen. Agony columnist 'Aunt Prudence' (*Moira Dale*), a friend of Peter's, advises the general to offer £1,500 reward, whereupon she, Peter and Peggy round up the thieves. Silly comedy.
RoC *Frank Stanmore, H. Saxon-Snell, Hugh E. Wright, Philip Godfrey, Harry Terry.*

LOYALTIES (1933)   3
Dir and Prod *Basil Dean*. Scr *W. P. Lipscomb*, from the play by *John Galsworthy*. Ph *Robert Martin*. PC *ATP*. Dis *ABFD. 73 mins. Cert A*
De Levis (*Basil Rathbone*), a wealthy young Jew, is trying to get ahead in society. Captain Dancy (*Miles Mander*) takes a violent dislike to him, and sees to it that he is rejected by a society club. At a house-party, De Levis is robbed of £1,000 and accuses Dancy. In a subsequent court action, it comes out that Dancy used the money to pay blackmail to a former mistress. Dancy commits suicide. Efficient but unpleasant drama.
RoC *Heather Thatcher, Joan Wyndham, Philip Strange, Alan Napier, Athole Stewart, Algernon West, Cecily Byrne, Patric Curwen, Ben Field, Marcus Barron, Griffith Humphreys, Patrick Waddington, Lawrence Hanray, Arnold Lucy, Robert Mawdesley, Mike Johnson, Stafford Hilliard, Maxine Sandra.*

THE LUCK OF A SAILOR (1934)   2
Dir *Robert Milton*. Prod *Walter C. Mycroft*. Scr *Clifford Grey, Wolfgang Wilhelm*. PC *BIP*. Dis *Wardour. 66 mins. Cert U*
Rather far-fetched Ruritanian romance in which an exiled king (*Hugh Wakefield*) marries penniless Helen (*Greta Nissen*), then is recalled to the throne. Journeying back to Europe on a British battleship, Helen and the commander (*David Manners*) fall in love. To her joy, the people of her husband's country request her to abdicate so that he can marry an heiress of their choice.
RoC *Clifford Mollison, Camilla Horn, Lawrence Grossmith, Reginald Purdell, H. F. Maltby, Jimmy Godden, Jean Cadell, Cecil Ramage, Gus McNaughton, Arnold Lucy, J. H. Roberts.*

THE LUCK OF THE IRISH (1935)   2
Dir and Scr *Donovan Pedelty*, from a novel by *Victor Haddick*. Prod *Pedelty, Richard Hayward*. Ph *Jack Willson*. PC *RH Films*. Dis *Paramount. 81 mins. Cert U*
Rather long and rambling Irish comedy about an impoverished squire who puts his hopes of financial recovery on his racehorse, putting his castle up as security to make a large wager on the animal in the English Grand National. The horse wins but is disqualified. But a wealthy American comes to the squire's rescue by buying the horse.
LP *Richard Hayward, Kay Walsh, Niall MacGinnis, J. R. Mageean (Jimmy Mageean), R. H. MacCanless, Charles Fagan, Harold Griffen, Charlotte Tedlie, Nan Cullen, John M. Henderson, Meta Grainger.*

LUCK OF THE NAVY (1938)   3
(USA: *North Sea Patrol*)
Dir *Norman Lee*. Prod *Walter C. Mycroft*. Scr *Clifford Grey*, from the play by *Clifford Mills*. PC *Associated British*. Dis *Pathé. 73 mins. Cert U*
A naval commander (*Geoffrey Toone*) has his secret orders stolen by a gang of spies led by a 'crippled' professor (*Keneth Kent*). The papers are smuggled on board an enemy Q-ship, but the commander pursues it in his destroyer and blows it out of the water. Hearty adventure for boys of all ages.
RoC *Judy Kelly, Albert Burdon, Clifford Evans, John Wood, Olga Lindo, Edmund Breon, Marguerite Allan, Leslie Perrins, Henry Oscar, Carla Lehmann, Alf Goddard, Diana Beaumont, Frank Fox, Doris Hare, Nigel Stock, Lawrence Kitchin, Daphne Raglan, Michael Ripper, Joan Fred Emney.*

LUCK OF THE TURF (1936)   3
Dir, Prod and PC *Randall Faye*. Scr *John Hunter*. Ph *Geoffrey Faithfull*. Dis *Radio. 64 mins. Cert A*
Humour with a homely touch carries this comedy about Sid Smith (*Jack Melford*) who picks winners for his friends - but never lays a bet himself. When Sid does enter the racing arena in a bid to buy a bigger shop and marry his girlfriend Letty (*Moira Lynd*), he loses. But then he finds £10, puts it on a 50-1 shot - and wins.
RoC *Wally Patch, Moore Marriott, Sybil Grove, Tom Helmore, Peggy Novak.*

LUCKY BLAZE (1933)   3
Dir, Prod and Scr *Widgey R. Newman*. PC and Dis *Ace Films. 48 mins. Cert U*
Okay racing drama, with several real-life jockeys in the cast, about a squire's daughter (*Vera Sherbourne*) who helps her gentleman rider boyfriend (*William Freshman*) outwit racecourse crooks and win the big race.
RoC *Moore Marriott, Freddie Fox, Harry Rod-*

bourne, *J. Collins, Jack Walsh, Sammy Wragg, Micky Beary, Ken Robertson, Buster Rickaby.*

LUCKY DAYS (1935) [2]

Dir *Reginald Denham.* Prod *Anthony Havelock-Allan.* Scr *Margaret MacDonnell.* Ph *Francis Carver.* PC and Dis *British and Dominions/Paramount British.* 67 mins. Cert U
Patsy (*Chili Bouchier*), as gullible as she is superstitious, tries to help her husband get ahead in big business by getting tips from an eastern astrologer (*Deering Wells*). The tips are startlingly successful - but nearly land her in the divorce court. Comedy hardly makes the most of its bright idea.
RoC *Whitmore Humphries, Leslie Perrins, Ann Codrington, Derek Gorst, Ronald Simpson, Eric Cowley, Alexander Archdale, Sally Gray, Eric Hales, Elsie Irving.*

LUCKY GIRL (1932) [4]

Dir and Scr *Gene Gerrard, Frank Miller, from a play by Reginald Berkeley, Douglas Furber, R. P. Weston and Bert Lee.* Prod *John Maxwell.* Ph *John J. Cox, Bryan Langley.* PC *BIP.* Dis *Wardour.* 75 mins. Cert U
Inconsequential musical comedy about a king and his chancellor (*Gene Gerrard, Gus McNaughton*) travelling incognito in England, who are mistaken for jewel thieves during a party at a duke's home. The king, who has fallen for the duke's daughter (*Molly Lamont*), soon clears things up.
RoC *Spencer Trevor, Tonie Edgar Bruce, Ian Fleming, Frank Stanmore, Hal Gordon.*

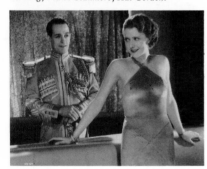

Gene Gerrard and Molly Lamont in Lucky Girl *(1932)*

LUCKY JADE (1937) [2]

Dir and Scr *Walter Summers.* Prod *Fred Browett.* Ph *Horace Wheddon.* PC *Welwyn.* Dis *Paramount.* 69 mins. Cert A
Parlourmaid Betsy Bunn (*Betty Ann Davies*) takes advantage of her employers' absence by 'borrowing' their flat for a wild party which she hopes will help her theatrical ambitions. But two crooks gatecrash and steal the owner's valuable jade. With the help of two of 'her' guests, Betsy gets the jade back. Fast but frenetic comedy-thriller.
RoC *John Warwick, Claire Arnold, Syd Crossley, Derek Gorst, Gordon Court, Richard Littledale, Tony Wylde, Leonard Shepherd, Boyer and Ravel.*

LUCKY LADIES (1932) [2]

Dir *John Rawlings.* Prod *Irving Asher.* Scr *W.*

Scott Darling, Randall Faye. PC *Warner Bros.* Dis *First National.* 74 mins. Cert U
Two squabbling middle-aged sisters run an oyster bar in this promising but disappointing comedy. One of them wins a fortune on the Irish Sweep and is swindled out of it by a bogus count who leaves her some valueless shares. Everything lost, the sisters return to the oyster bar, but subsequently find out that the shares are after all worth a fortune.
LP *Sydney Fairbrother, Emily Fitzroy, Tracy Holmes, Janice Adair, Syd Crossley, Charles Farrell.*

LUCKY LOSER (1934) [2]

Dir *Reginald Denham.* Prod *Herbert Wilcox.* Scr *Anne Smith, Basil Mason, from a play by Matthew Brennan.* PC *British and Dominions.* Dis *Paramount.* 68 mins. Cert A
A surfeit of dialogue slows this rather desperate comedy about a man (*Richard Dolman*) who sells an antique desk and then finds his winning sweepstake ticket is still inside it. The body of the film is taken up with his frenzied attempts to recover the desk.
RoC *Aileen Marson, Anna Lee, Annie Esmond, Roland Culver, Noel Shannon, Joan White, Gordon McLeod, Alice Lane, Mary Gaskell.*

THE LUCKY NUMBER (1933) [4]

Dir *Anthony Asquith.* Prod *Michael Balcon.* Scr *Franz Schultz.* Ph *Günther Krampf.* PC *Gainsborough.* Dis *Ideal.* 72 mins. Cert U
Members of the Arsenal Football Club of the time can be seen in this amusingly contrived story of a footballer (*Clifford Mollison*) who, coming back from a match in Paris, has his money stolen and is forced to pay for drinks with a lottery ticket - which of course proves to be a winner. He manages to get it back and dashes off to France, only to find that the organizers of the lottery have decamped with the prize money!
RoC *Gordon Harker, Joan Wyndham, Joe Hayman, Frank Pettingell, Esmé Percy, Alfred Wellesley, D. Hay Petrie, Betty Hartley.*

A LUCKY SWEEP (1932) [3]

Dir *A.V. Bramble.* Prod *Harry Rowson.* Scr *Uncredited.* PC *National Talkies.* Dis *Producers' Distributing Corporation.* 56 mins. Cert U
Small-scale comedy which failed to boost the faltering career of *A.V. Bramble,* a prominent actor-director in silent days, despite the presence of popular star *John Longden* as an anti-gambling fanatic who is sent an Irish Sweepstake ticket as a joke, then accused of having stolen it.
RoC *Diana Beaumont, A.G. Poulton, Marie Wright, Sybil Jane, Elsie Prince, Elsie Moore.*

LUCKY TO ME (1939) [2]

Dir *Thomas Bentley.* Prod *Walter C. Mycroft.* Scr *Clifford Grey.* Ph *Derek Williams.* PC and Dis *Associated British.* 69 mins. Cert A
Potty (*Stanley Lupino*), a solicitor's clerk, secretly marries Minnie (*Barbara Blair*), the secretary at his office. Before they can honeymoon, Potty is sent off to the country to advise Madden, a rich client, on stocks and shares. He clears up Madden's romantic problems as

---

well as his financial ones. Very elementary farce, an ignominious end to Lupino's film career.
RoC *Phyllis Brooks, Gene Sheldon, Antoinette Cellier, David Hutcheson, Bruce Seton.*

THE LURE (1933) [1]

Dir and Prod *Arthur Maude.* Scr *Uncredited, from the play by J. Sabben-Clare.* Ph *Eric Cross.* PC *Maude Productions.* Dis *Paramount.* 65 mins. Cert A
Dane (*Cyril Raymond*) and Baxter (*Alec Fraser*), guests at a houseparty, are both in love with Julia (*Anne Grey*), a widow, who is also there. Baxter stole a valuable gem from Dane's brother, so the atmosphere is tense. That night, Baxter is murdered, but Dane's ingenious scheme, involving a fake suicide, unmasks the killer. Very static thriller.
RoC *Billy (William) Hartnell, Philip Clarke, Doris Long, P.G. Clark, Jean Ormond.*

THE LYONS MAIL (1931) [3]

Dir *Arthur Maude.* Prod *Julius Hagen.* Scr *H. Fowler Mear, from a play by Charles Reade.* PC *Twickenham.* Dis *W and F.* 76 mins. Cert A
Second screen version of an adventure story set in France, where a silversmith is mistaken for his double, a notorious highwayman. He is arrested and convicted for holding up the Lyons Mail and murdering its passengers, but the truth comes out just in time to save his life.
LP *Sir John Martin Harvey, Norah Baring, Ben Webster, Moore Marriott, Michael Hogan, Sheila Wray, George Thirwell, Eric Howard, Charles Paton, Earle Grey, John Garside, Gabrielle Casartelli.*

MACUSHLA (1937) [2]

Dir *Alex Bryce.* Prod *Victor M. Greene.* Scr *David Evans.* Ph *Stanley Grant.* PC and Dis *Fox British.* 59 mins. Cert U
Ireland: Jim (*Liam Gaffney*), a young police

Pamela Wood and Liam Gaffney in Macushla *(1937)*

officer, is in love with Kathleen (*Pamela Wood*) whose brother Kerry (*Max Adrian*) and father Pat (*Jimmy Mageean*) are involved in cattle-smuggling and gun-running across the Eire-Ulster border. Kerry almost kills a policeman, then, after a fierce fight between police and rebels, a cabin hideout catches fire and Jim is trapped by a blazing beam. Kerry drags him clear, then escapes and leaves Jim with Kathleen. Gritty dialogue, but hackneyed plot.
RoC *E.J. Kennedy, Kitty Kirwan, Brian Herbert, Edgar K. Bruce*

MAD ABOUT MONEY (1937) [2]
(USA: *He Loved an Actress*)
Dir *Melville Brown*. Prod *William Rowland*. Scr *John Meehan Jr*. Ph *Jan Stumar*. PC *Morgan Films*. Dis *British Lion*. 78 mins. (USA: *75*). Cert A
Harum-scarum comedy musical (songs: Jimmy Dyrenforth, Kenneth Leslie-Smith), about Carla (*Lupe Velez*), an unemployed actress in search of work in England, who is mistaken by equally unemployed film producers for a fabulous Hollywood film star. They try to get her to finance and star in their new film, which she eventually does – thanks to an American playboy (*Ben Lyon*).
RoC *Wallace Ford, Jean Colin, Harry Langdon, Mary Cole, Cyril Raymond, Ronald Ward, Olive Sloane, Arthur Finn, Peggy Novak, Philip Pearman, Andrea Malandrinos, John Stobart, Ronald Hill, Albert Whelan, Alan Shires.*

MADAME GUILLOTINE (1931) [2]
Dir *Reginald Fogwell*. Prod *Fogwell, Mansfield Markham*. Scr *Fogwell, Harold Huth*. Ph *Roy Overbaugh*. PC *Reginald Fogwell*. Dis *W and F*. 75 mins. Cert A
Reginald Fogwell's most ambitious film to date boasted two top British stars, but failed to please the critics, who complained of 'artificial characters'. A young lawyer (*Brian Aherne*) loves the aristocratic Lucille (*Madeleine Carroll*) who rejects him. Comes the French Revolution, and Louis marries Lucille to protect her. When she learns he is willing to go to the guillotine to save her, Lucille decides to give herself up – but ultimately both are saved by a forged pardon.
RoC *Henry Hewitt, Frederick Culley, J. Fisher White, Hector Abbas, Ian MacDonald.*

MADEMOISELLE DOCTEUR (1937) [2]
Dir *Edmond T. Gréville*. Prod *Max Schach*. Scr *Jacques Natanson, Marcel Archard, Ernest Betts, from a screenplay by Georges Héreaux, Irma Von Cube*. Ph *Otto Heller*. PC *Grafton/Trafalgar*. Dis *United Artists*. 84 mins. Cert A
English-language version of a French film (and remade over 30 years later as *Fraulein Doktor*). *Dita Parlo* plays a young German doctor serving her country in the First World War, whose secret service exploits become legend. She falls in love with a British officer, Peter (*John Loder*), but it turns out he was the man she has been searching for, to avenge her lover's death. She steals plans for an Allied air attack, in which Peter is killed. Treatment is rather heavy-handed.
RoC *Erich von Stroheim, Claire Luce, Gyles*

Isham, Clifford Evans, John Abbott, Antony Holles, Edward Lexy, Raymond Lovell, Frederick Lloyd, Robert Nainby, Stewart Granger, Molly Hamley Clifford, Claud Horton.*

THE MAD HATTERS (1935) [2]
Dir *Ivar Campbell*. Prod. *Anthony Havelock-Allan*. Scr *Christine Jope-Slate, from a story by James Stewart*. Ph *Francis Carver*. PC and Dis *British and Dominions/Paramount British*. 68 mins. Cert U
Tim (*Sidney King*) throws up his military career to the fury of his mother, who has blown most of the money from a legacy intended for her daughter Ruth's medical training (on his fees). With the remainder, Ruth (*Evelyn Foster*) and some friends open a hat shop. She nearly loses her fiancé to the exotic Vicki (*Chili Bouchier*), but Tim takes the temptress off her hands. Slight comedy.
RoC *Grace James, Kim Peacock, Vera Bogetti, Toska von Bissing, H. Saxon-Snell, Bellenden Clarke, Roddy Hughes, Edgar Driver, Ralph Roberts.*

MAID HAPPY (1933) [2]
Dir and Prod *Mansfield Markham*. Scr Jack King. PC *Bendar*. Dis *Williams & Pritchard*. 75 mins. Cert U
Musical frivolity, shot in Switzerland and much along the usual 'Heidelberg' lines, as a schoolgirl, Lena (*Charlotte Ander*) poses as a high society girl in order to ensnare the diplomat (*Johannes Riemann*) for whom she has fallen.
RoC *Dennis Hoey, Marjory Mars, Sybil Grove, Gerhard Damann, Polly Luce, H. Saxon-Snell, Marie Ault.*

THE MAID OF THE MOUNTAINS
(1932) [3]
Dir *Lupino Lane*. Prod *John Maxwell*. Scr Lane, Douglas Furber, Frank Miller, Victor Kendall, Edwin Greenwood, from the play by Frederick Lonsdale*. Ph *Claude Friese-Greene, Arthur Crabtree*. PC *BIP*. Dis *Wardour*. 80 mins. Cert U
Rather creaky adaptation of the stage musical, with *Harry Welchman* (a kind of British version of America's Lawrence Tibbett) as the bandit who robs the rich to help the poor, falls in love with the Governor's daughter (*Betty Stockfeld*) and is betrayed by his jealous sweetheart (*Nancy Brown*).

Harry Welchman and Nancy Brown in The Maid of the Mountains (*1932*)

RoC *Albert Burdon, Gus McNaughton, Garry Marsh, Renée Gadd, Wallace Lupino, Dennis Hoey, Alfredo and His Gypsy Orchestra.*

MAKE IT THREE (1938) [1]
Dir *David Macdonald*. Prod *Julius Hagen*. Scr *Vernon Sylvaine*. PC *St Margarets*. Dis *M-G-M*. 78 mins. Cert U
Bank clerk Percy (*Hugh Wakefield*) is left a fortune as long as he serves three months in jail. But his imperious fiancée (*Diana Beaumont*) has told him it's off if he doesn't marry her in three months. Choosing the money, Percy commits a bungled burglary. When his cellmate, Big Ed (*Edmund Willard*) forces him to break jail, he marries the girl before going back, losing his month off for good behaviour. Terrible comedy proves director's talents lay in other directions.
RoC *Sydney Fairbrother, Jack Hobbs, Olive Sloane, Alexander Field, (C.) Denier Warren.*

MAKE UP (1937) [3]
Dir *Alfred Zeisler*. Prod *K.C. Alexander, C.M. Origo*. Scr *Reginald Long, Jeffrey Dell, from a novel by Hans Passendorf*. Ph *Phil Tannura*. PC *Standard International*. Dis *Associated British*. 70 mins. Cert U. Bilingual versions
Bux (*Nils Asther*), a former surgeon who has become a very successful clown, lives with his foster-daughter Joy (*June Clyde*), who loves him and is jealous when, on a tour of England, he is seen everywhere with a glamorous model. Joy is pestered by lion-tamer Lorenzo (*Kenneth Duncan*) and suspected of his murder when he is found dead. Bux returns to prove her innocence – and realizes he loves her.
RoC *Judy Kelly, Lawrence Grosssmith, John Turnbull, Lawrence Anderson, Norma Varden, Jill Craigie, Reginald Long, Chapman's Circus.*

THE MAN AT SIX (1931) [2]
(USA: *The Gables Mystery*)
Dir *Harry Hughes*. Scr Hughes, *Victor Kendall, from the play by Jack De Leon, Jack Celestin*. Ph *H.E. Palmer*. PC *BIP*. Dis *Wardour*. 70 mins. Cert U
Moderate thriller with the novel attraction of a lady detective (*Anne Grey*) who poses as a secretary in order to unravel a mystery at a country house, where the owner has disappeared. She suspects, correctly, that the place is being used as the headquarters of a gang of crooks, whose leader subsequently attempts to impersonate the missing owner.
RoC *Lester Matthews, Gerald Rawlinson, John Turnbull, Kenneth Kove, Charles Farrell, Arthur Stratton, Herbert Ross, Minnie Rayner.*

THE MAN BEHIND THE MASK
(1936) [3]
Dir *Michael Powell*. Prod and PC *Joe Rock*. Scr *Ian Hay, Syd Courtenay, Jack Byrd, Stanley Haynes*. Ph *Francis Carver*. Dis *M-G-M*. 79 mins. Cert A
Acting and treatment to some extent offset a dippy story in this melodrama. On the night he plans to elope from a masked ball with June (*Jane Baxter*), Nick (*Hugh Williams*) is attacked by a man who assumes his identity, steals the golden Shield of Kahm from June's

father and takes June hostage. Father and Nick find June and the Shield, but get into more hot water before the police rescue them and capture the criminal – a mad astronomer.

RoC *Maurice Schwartz, Donald Calthrop, Henry Oscar, Peter Gawthorne, Kitty Kelly, Ronald Ward, George Merritt, Reginald Tate, Ivor Barnard, Hal Gordon, Barbara Everest, Wilfred Caithness, Moyna Fagan, Henry Caine, Syd Crossley, Gerald Fielding.*

THE MAN FROM CHICAGO (1930)   4

Dir *Walter Summers.* Prod *John Maxwell.* Scr *Summers, Walter C. Mycroft, from a play by Reginald Berkeley.* PC *BIP.* Dis *Wardour. 88 mins. Cert A*

Ex-Chicago racketeer Nick Dugan (*Bernard Nedell*) comes to London, where he buys a nightclub and a garage. Organizing a gang which successfully pulls off a big bank robbery, he hides the loot in the garage. But the Flying Squad are soon on his tail. More polished and hard-hitting than the usual British crime thriller of its day.

RoC *Dodo Watts, Joyce Kennedy, Albert Whelan, Austin Trevor, Billy Milton, O.B. Clarence, Morris Harvey, Dennis Hoey, Ben Welden, Leonard Dainton, Matthew Boulton, Syd Crossley, Fred Lloyd.*

THE MAN FROM TORONTO (1932)   4

Dir *Sinclair Hill.* Prod *Michael Balcon.* Scr *W.P. Lipscomb, from the play by Douglas Murray.* Ph *Leslie Rowson.* PC *Gainsborough.* Dis *Ideal. 77 mins. Cert U*

Flimsy comedy, but charmingly played by its stars, in which Leila, a widow (*Jessie Matthews*) and Fergus, a Canadian bachelor (*Ian Hunter*) are bequeathed a fortune – if they marry within a year. Leila masquerades as Fergus' maid and they fall in love, but when he learns of her deception, Fergus angrily returns to Canada. Leila follows him....

RoC *Fred Kerr, Ben Field, Margaret Yarde, Kathleen Harrison, George Turner, Herbert Lomas, Lawrence Hanray, Kenneth Kove, Sybil Grove, Percy Parsons, George Zucco, Diana Cotton, Bob Abel, Billy Shine, Sam Wilkinson.*

THE MAN IN THE MIRROR (1936)   4

Dir *Maurice Elvey.* Prod *Julius Hagen.* Scr *F. McGrew Willis, Hugh Mills, from the novel by William Garrett.* Ph *Curt Courant.* PC *JH Productions.* Dis *Wardour. 82 mins. Cert A*

Ingenious fantasy about Jeremy (*Edward Everett Horton*), a dithering businessman whose reflection one day steps out of the mirror and does all the things Jeremy always wanted to do, but never had the courage for. The reflection ends by carrying out negotiations with a fake eastern potentate, the Bogus of Bokhara (*Aubrey Mather*) that end in triumph for the 'mirror man'.

RoC *Genevieve Tobin, Garry Marsh, Ursula Jeans, Alastair Sim, Renée Gadd, Viola Compton, Felix Aylmer, Stafford Hilliard.*

THE MAN I WANT (1934)   2

Dir *Leslie Hiscott.* Prod *Herbert Smith.* Scr *Michael Barringer.* PC *British Lion.* Dis *M-G-M. 68 mins. Cert A*

Sir George (*Davy Burnaby*) forbids his daughter Marion (*Wendy Barrie*) to marry stuffy Peter Mason (*Henry Kendall*). Sir George's family jewels are stolen by associates of gold-digger Prue Darrell (*Betty Astell*) who had also been trying to blackmail Peter. Peter unwittingly recovers the gems, and so gains Sir George's approval for the engagement. Draggy comedy.

RoC *Wally Patch, Hal Walters.*

MANNEQUIN (1933)   1

Dir *George A. Cooper.* Prod *Julius Hagen.* Scr *Charles Bennett.* PC *Real Art.* Dis *Radio. 54 mins. Cert U*

Laughable melodrama with unconvincing boxing scenes. A boxer (*Whitmore Humphries*) becomes swollen-headed and ditches his girlfriend, a model (*Judy Kelly*), for a society lady (*Diana Beaumont*), until he finds she has only been toying with him and has bet on his opponent in his next fight, which he proceeds to win, also getting back his girl.

RoC *Harold French, Richard Cooper, Ben Welden, Anna Lee, Faith Bennett, Vera Bogetti, William Pardue, Carol Lees, Tonie Edgar Bruce.*

MAN OF ARAN (1934)   5

Dir *Robert J. Flaherty.* Prod *Michael Balcon.* Scr *Robert J. Flaherty, Frances Flaherty.* Ph *Robert J. Flaherty.* PC *Gainsborough.* Dis *Gaumont-British. 75 mins. Cert U*

Brilliant dramatized documentary – although not recognized as such by all contemporary writers – about the Herculean struggles of the Aran islanders for existence on an island so barren that the soil has to be collected from rock crevices and mixed with seaweed before crops can be grown. A thrilling battle between island fishermen and a huge basking shark – essential for the supply of oil in winter – is the centrepoint of a superbly photographed film.

LP *Colman 'Tiger' King, Maggie Dirrane, Pat Mullen, Michael Dillane, Patch Ruadh, Patcheen Faherty, Tommy O'Rourke, Stephen Dirrane, Pat McDonough, 'Big Patcheen' Conneely.*

Patch Ruadh in Man of Aran *(1934)*

MAN OF MAYFAIR (1931)   3

Dir *Louis Mercanton.* Prod *Walter Morosco.* Scr *Eliot Crawshay Williams, Hugh Perceval, from a novel by May Edginton.* PC *Paramount British.* Dis *Paramount. 83 mins. Cert U*

Not one of *Jack Buchanan*'s best comedies: he plays a nobleman who falls for revue star Grace (*Joan Barry*) whose mother runs a country tea-room and believes her daughter is a dresser in the theatre. The nobleman poses as a backstage foreman and wins mother over.

RoC *Warwick Ward, Nora Swinburne, Ellaline Terriss, Lilian Braithwaite, Cyril Raymond, Charles Quartermaine, Sebastian Smith, J. Fisher White, Francis Mangan Girls.*

MAN OF THE MOMENT (1935)   4

Dir *Monty Banks.* Prod *Irving Asher.* Scr *Roland Pertwee, Guy Bolton, A.R. Rawlinson, from a play by Yves Mirande.* Ph *Basil Emmott, Leslie Rowson.* PC *Warner Bros.* Dis *First National. 82 mins. Cert A*

Engaging romantic comedy with some clever twists, well played by the stars. Tony (*Douglas Fairbanks Jr*), a hard-up man-about-town rescues Mary (*Laura la Plante*) a disillusioned working girl intent on drowning herself. In offering her a bed for the night, he torpedoes his marriage to an heiress. But he and Mary go to Monte Carlo with their remaining money and clean up at the tables.

RoC *Margaret Lockwood, Claude Hulbert, Donald Calthrop, Monty Banks, Peter Gawthorne.*

THE MAN OUTSIDE (1933)   2

Dir *George A. Cooper.* Prod *Julius Hagen.* Scr *H. Fowler Mear.* PC *Real Art.* Dis *Radio. 52 mins. Cert A*

A private detective (*Henry Kendall*) investigates a country house murder – and finds that the killer is really the police inspector (*John Turnbull*) arrived to look into the affair, who isn't a policeman at all. Standard 'quickie' thriller.

RoC *Gillian Lind, Joan Gardner, Louis Hayward, Michael Hogan, Cyril Raymond, Ethel Warwick.*

THE MAN THEY COULDN'T ARREST (1931)   3

Dir *T. Hayes Hunter.* Prod *Michael Balcon.* Scr *Arthur Wimperis, Angus Macphail, Hunter from a novel by Edgar Wallace.* Ph *Leslie Rowson.* PC *Ideal/Gainsborough.* Dis *W and F. 74 mins. Cert U*

John Dain (*Hugh Wakefield*) has developed an apparatus which enables him to listen in to conversations anywhere. He overhears a gang of thieves planning a series of robberies and determines to bring them to justice – even though his fiancée (*Renée Clama*) proves to be the daughter of a member of the gang.

RoC *Gordon Harker, Garry Marsh, Nicholas Hannen, Robert Farquharson, Dennis Wyndham.*

THE MAN WHO CHANGED HIS MIND (1936)   4
(USA: *The Man Who Lived Again*)

Dir *Robert Stevenson.* Prod *Michael Balcon.* Scr *John L. Balderston, L. duGarde Peach, Sidney Gilliat.* Ph *Jack Cox.* PC *Gainsborough.* Dis *Gaumont-British. 66 mins. Cert A*

About the best-received of *Boris Karloff*'s British ventures in the 1930s; he plays Dr Laurience, who can transpose the mind of one per-

son to the body of another. When his patron withdraws his financial support, believing the scientist to be a charlatan, Laurience exchanges the patron's brain with that of his crippled assistant and both die. After committing a murder Laurience plans to exchange his mind with that of the fiancé (*John Loder*) of the girl (*Anna Lee*) he loves, but she foils his plan and Laurience is shot down by the police. Plenty of chills.
RoC *Frank Cellier, Donald Calthrop, Cecil Parker, Lyn Harding, Clive Morton, D.J. Williams, Brian Pawley.*

THE MAN WHO CHANGED HIS NAME (1934) [3]

Dir *Henry Edwards*. Prod *Julius Hagen*. Scr *H. Fowler Mear, from the play by Edgar Wallace*. Ph *Sydney Blythe*. PC *Real Art*. Dis *Universal*. 80 mins. Cert A
A new version of the 1928 silent film thriller, in which an adulterous wife (*Betty Stockfeld*) mistakenly believes her husband (*Lyn Harding*) to be a murderer. He continues the deception in order to prevent her from running off with another man. Strong performance by *Harding* in role previously played by Stewart Rome; otherwise unexceptional.
RoC *Leslie Perrins, Ben Welden, Aubrey Mather, Richard Dolman, Stanley Vine.*

THE MAN WHO COULD WORK MIRACLES (1936) [3]

Dir *Lothar Mendes*. Prod *Alexander Korda*. Scr *Lajos Biro* (uncredited), *H.G. Wells, from the story by Wells*. Ph *Harold Rosson*. PC *London Films*. Dis *United Artists*. 82 mins. Cert U
Fotheringay, a draper's assistant in a country town, is endowed by the 'giver of Power' with the ability to work miracles, including making inanimate objects move, so that observers in Heaven can find out 'what's in the human heart'. He determines to reshape the world, but ends by commanding it to stand still, which provides such chaos, he has to make everything as it was before - including the loss of his powers. Heavier than it should have been.
LP *Roland Young, Ralph Richardson, Edward Chapman, Ernest Thesiger, Joan Gardner, Sophie Stewart, Robert Cochran, Lawrence Hanray, George Zucco, Wallace Lupino, Lady Tree, Joan Hickson, Wally Patch, Bernard Nedell, Bruce Winston, Torin Thatcher, George Sanders, Ivan Brandt, Mark Daly.*

THE MAN WHO KNEW TOO MUCH (1934) [5]

Dir *Alfred Hitchcock*. Michael Balcon Production. (Associate) Prod *Ivor Montagu*. Scr *A.R. Rawlinson, Edwin Greenwood, Emlyn Williams, from a story by Charles Bennett, D.B. Wyndham-Lewis*. Ph *Curt Courant*. PC and Dis *Gaumont-British*. 75 mins. Cert A
The thriller that re-established Hitchcock's reputation after a period of uncertainty. A secret agent is murdered in St Moritz, but before he dies passes on vital information to an English couple, Bob and Jill Lawrence (*Leslie Banks, Edna Best*) on holiday, about an assassination attempt to be made on the life of a

Frank Vosper, Leslie Banks, Nova Pilbeam and Peter Lorre in The Man Who Knew Too Much *(1934)*

foreign diplomat in London. The plotters, led by Abbott (*Peter Lorre*), kidnap the Lawrences' daughter (*Nova Pilbeam*) to ensure their silence, but the assassination is foiled and the conspirators captured after a gun battle. Ingeniously made suspenser, full of telling detail.
RoC *Frank Vosper, Hugh Wakefield, Pierre Fresnay, Cicely Oates, D.A. Clarke-Smith, George Curzon, Henry Oscar.*

THE MAN WHO MADE DIAMONDS (1937) [3]

Dir *Ralph Ince*. Prod *Irving Asher*. Scr *Michael Barringer, Anthony Hankey*. Ph *Basil Emmott*. PC *Warner Bros*. Dis *First National*. 73 mins. Cert A
Good leading performances boost this rambling chiller about a professor who invents a system for making diamonds and is killed for it by his assistant, Joseph (*Noel Madison*). His daughter (*Lesley Brook*) investigates, but is about to become Joseph's next victim when rescued by a young detective (*George Galleon*). Joseph attempts to escape by climbing a pylon but is electrocuted.
RoC *James Stephenson, Renée Gadd, Wilfrid Lawson, Philip Ray, J. Fisher White, Hector Abbas, Jim Regan, Dino Galvani.*

THE MAN WITHOUT A FACE (1935) [2]

Dir *George King*. Prod *King, Randall Faye*. Scr *Faye*. PC *Embassy*. Dis *Radio*. 62 mins. Cert A
Convicted of murder after finding £20 belonging to the victim, Bill (*Cyril Chosack*) escapes when the train taking him to prison crashes. He places a battered body in his place, runs away to the countryside and marries his girl. Hearing that the 'faceless man' is to hang in his place, Bill resolves to give himself up. By a twist of fate, the 'faceless man' proves to be the real killer. Good plot, poor treatment, bad acting.
RoC *Carol Coombe, Ronald Ritchie, Moore Marriott, Billy Howard, Ben Williams, Vi Kaley, Fred Withers.*

MANY TANKS MR ATKINS (1938) [3]

Dir *Roy William Neill*. Prod *Jerome Jackson*. Scr *Austin Melford, Reginald Purdell, John Dighton, J.O.C. Orton*. Ph *Basil Emmott*.

PC *Warner Bros*. Dis *First National*. 68 mins. Cert U
Private Nutter (*Reginald Purdell*) is transferred from one regiment to another because he will keep trying out his patent supercharger on everything - frequently damaging army property. His plans for a supercharged tank attract some German spies. Thanks to the misdirected energies of another hapless soldier, Fishlock (*Claude Hulbert*), the plans almost fall into their hands. Brisk, vigorous, topical farce.
RoC *Barbara Greene, Davy Burnaby, Jack Melford, Edward Lexy, Edmund Breon, Frederick Burtwell, Arthur Hambling, Ralph Truman, Dorothy Seacombe, Robb Wilton, André Morell.*

MANY WATERS (1931) [3]

Dir *Milton Rosmer*. Prod *J.A. Thorpe*. Scr *Monckton Hoffe, from the play by Leon M. Lion*. Ph *Henry Gerrard, Hal Young*. PC *Associated Metropolitan*. Dis *Pathé*. 76 mins. Cert A
A through-the-years story of the married life and tragedy of a couple whose daughter is seduced at an early age by a married neighbour, and who dies in childbirth. They also recall many lesser incidents that brought them joy or sadness.
LP *Lilian Hall-Davis, Arthur Margetson, Elizabeth Allan, Donald Calthrop, Sam Livesey, Robert Douglas, Mary Clare, Charles Carson, Ivan Samson, Renée Macready, Herbert Lomas, D. Hay Petrie, J. Fisher White, Monckton Hoffe, Clare Greet, S.A. Cookson, Paul Gill, E.R. Reeves, David Miller, Philip Hewland, Cecily Oates, Billy Shine.*

MARIA MARTEN: OR, THE MURDER IN THE RED BARN (1935) [2]

Dir *Milton Rosmer*. Prod and PC *George King*. Scr *Randall Faye*. Dis *M-G-M*. 67 mins. Cert A
Barnstorming version of the hoary old melodrama, telling of the seduction of a young village maiden in 1820 by the rascally squire (*Tod Slaughter*), her murder when she gets in the way of his marriage to an heiress, and the revenge taken by her gipsy lover.
RoC *Sophie Stewart, Eric Portman, Ann Trevor, D.J. Williams, Clare Greet, Quinton McPherson, Antonia Brough, Dennis Hoey, Gerrard Tyrrell.*

Eric Portman and Tod Slaughter in Maria Marten, or: The Murder in the Red Barn *(1935)*

MARIGOLD (1938) [3]

Dir *Thomas Bentley*. Prod *Walter C. Mycroft*. Scr *Dudley Leslie, from the play by Charles Garvice, Allen Harker and F. Prior*. Ph *Günther Krampf*. PC and Dis *Associated British*. 74 mins. Cert U

Sophie Stewart gave her most charming film performance in this feminist film set in 1842. She plays Marigold, who lives with a minister and his wife, believing her own mother to be dead. An officer invites her to Edinburgh to see Queen Victoria's visit, but her stern guardian says no. Rebellious Marigold packs her case and catches the coach to Edinburgh. She meets a lieutenant with whom she falls in love and an actress who proves to be her mother. RoC *Patrick Barr, Phyllis Dare, Edward Chapman, Nicholas Hannen, Hugh Dempster, Pamela Stanley, Ian MacLean, Elliot Mason, Katie Johnson, James Hayter, Jean Clyde, Mary Barton, Jack Lambert.*

MAROONED (1933) [3]

Dir *Leslie Hiscott*. Prod *Herbert Smith*. Scr *Michael Barringer*. PC *British Lion*. Dis *Fox*. 67 mins. Cert U

On a lonely lighthouse live Tom and Sarah Roberts (*Edmund Gwenn, Viola Lyel*) and their foster-daughter Mary (*Iris March*) whose father, unbeknown to her, is serving a life sentence. Then he arrives at the lighthouse – a convict on the run. For Mary's sake, Tom hides him. Ultimately it transpires that the convict was impersonating Mary's father who died in prison a year before. He falls to his death from the lighthouse.

RoC *Griffith Humphreys, Victor Garland, Wally Patch, Hal Walters, Philip Hewland, Wilfred Shine, Frances Davey, George Manship, Frederick Ross.*

THE MARRIAGE BOND (1932) [3]

Dir *Maurice Elvey*. Prod *Julius Hagen*. Scr *H. Fowler Mear*. Ph *Basil Emmott*. PC *Twickenham*. Dis *Radio*. 82 mins. Cert A

Pressured by her children, Jacqueline (*Mary Newcomb*) parts from her alcoholic husband Toby (*Guy Newall*). The children grow up hard and unfeeling and Jacqueline, although wooed by wealthy Sir Paul (*Stewart Rome*) is eventually reconciled with a reformed Toby. Good cast, ordinary film.

RoC *Ann Casson, Lewis Shaw, Florence Desmond, Denys Blakelock, Humberston Wright, Amy Veness, A. Bromley Davenport.*

THE MARRIAGE OF CORBAL (1936) [2]

(USA: *Prisoner of Corbal*)

Dir *Karl Grune*. Prod *Max Schach*. Scr *S. Fullman, from a novel by Rafael Sabatini*. Ph *Otto Kanturek*. PC *Capitol*. Dis *General Film Distributors*. 93 mins. Cert U

Archly melodramatic period piece about a young French aristocrat, Cleonie (*Hazel Terry*) rescued from the guillotine in 1790 by the Revolutionary officer Varennes (*Nils Asther*), who adores her. He disguises her as a drummer boy, and they reach the sanctuary of the Marquis of Corbal (*Hugh Sinclair*) with whom she falls in love. Varennes commits suicide,

Hugh Sinclair, Hazel Terry and Walter Sondes in The Marriage of Corbal (*1936*)

and Cleonie and Corbal escape to freedom across the border.

RoC *Noah Beery, Ernest Deutsch, Davy Burnaby, Clifford McLaglen, Ralph Truman, Brian Buchel, Walter Sondes, Arthur Rigby Jr, Moira Lynd, Gordon Begg, Vincent Sternroyd, Charles Paton, Percy Walsh, J. Hubert Leslie.*

MARRY ME (1932) [3]

Dir *William Thiele*. Prod *Michael Balcon*. Scr *Anthony Asquith, Angus Macphail (uncredited)*. PC *Gainsborough*. Dis *Ideal*. 85 mins. Cert U. *Bilingual versions*

Musical, set in Berlin, where Ann (*Renate Muller*), an employee in a gramophone factory, loves the publicity manager (*Ian Hunter*), who drops her. But she becomes his housekeeper and wins him back.

RoC *George Robey, Maurice Evans, Harry Green, Charles Hawtrey Jr, Sunday Wilshin, Billy Caryll, Viola Lyel, Charles Carson.*

Ian Hunter, Harry Green and Renate Muller in Marry Me (*1932*)

MARRY THE GIRL (1935) [3]

Dir *P. Maclean Rogers*. Prod *Herbert Smith*. Scr *Rogers, Kathleen Butler, from a play by Arthur Miller, George Arthurs*. PC and Dis *British Lion*. 69 mins. Cert A

Wealthy Wally Gibbs (*Sonnie Hale*) newly engaged to Jane (*Judy Kelly*) is sued for breach of promise by Doris (*Winifred Shotter*) who is browbeaten by her mother. Wally's barrister friend Hugh (*Hugh Wakefield*) compromises Doris, but Wally gets the blame and Jane breaks the engagement. In the end, Hugh marries Jane, and Wally decides he can't do with-

out Doris – even with her mother. Spritely performances, poor material.

RoC *Kenneth Kove, (C.) Denier Warren, Maidie Hope, Wally Patch, John Deverell, Lawrence Anderson.*

MASTER AND MAN (1934) [2]

Dir *John Harlow*. Prod *Walter C. Mycroft*. Scr *Wallace Lupino*. PC *BIP*. Dis *Pathé*. 54 mins. Cert U

Somewhat strained comedy written by *Wallace Lupino* for himself and his brother *Barry*. They play two down-and-outs who, sleeping rough on the Thames Embankment, find themselves mistaken for guests at a fancy-dress party. As the unexpected guests of Lady Sinden (*Faith Bennett*), Wally and Barry are instrumental in saving her house from arsonists. RoC *Gun McNaughton, Syd Crossley, Hal Gordon, Harry Terry, George Humphries.*

MATINEE IDOL (1933) [3]

Dir *George King*. Prod *Bray Wyndham*. Scr *Charles Bennett*. PC *Wyndham*. Dis *United Artists*. 75 mins. Cert A

A murder-mystery with a theatrical setting, as a determined young actress (German star *Camilla Horn*) proves that her sister (*Marguerite Allan*) did not murder the actor with whom she was romantically involved.

RoC *Miles Mander, Viola Keats, D. Hay Petrie, Margaret Yarde, Albert Whelan, Anthony Hankey.*

MAYFAIR GIRL (1933) [1]

Dir *George King*. Prod *Irving Asher*. Scr *Brandon Fleming*. PC and Dis *Warner Bros*. 67 mins. Cert A

Even Hollywood star *Sally Blane* could do little to improve this unconvincing crime yarn. She plays an American girl in London, who gets involved with the wrong crowd, much to the disgust of her lawyer (*John Stuart*) who loves her. But he comes to her rescue when she is framed on a murder charge while visiting a crooked gambling club.

RoC *D.A. Clarke-Smith, Roland Culver, Glen Alyn, James Carew, Charles Hickman, Winifred Oughton, Philip Strange, Anna Lee, Lawrence Anderson.*

MAYFAIR MELODY (1937) [3]

Dir *Arthur Woods*. Prod *Irving Asher*. Scr *James Dyrenforth*. Ph *Basil Emmott*. PC and Dis *Warner Bros*. 83 mins. Cert U

Brenda (*Joyce Kirby*) spoiled daughter of a car mogul, hears Mark (*Keith Falkner*), a mechanic at her father's factory, singing, and takes him to an Italian music teacher to have his voice trained. Eventually, Mark lands the lead in a new stage musical comedy in London, brings Brenda down a peg or two, and wins her love. Light musical has some amusing moments.

RoC *Chili Bouchier, Bruce Lister, Glen Alyn, Vivienne Chatterton, George Galleon, Louis Goodrich, Ian McLean, Aubrey Mallalieu.*

THE MAYOR'S NEST (1932) [2]

Dir and Scr *Maclean Rogers*. Prod *Herbert Wilcox*. Ph *F.A. Young*. PC *British and Dominions*. Dis *W and F*. 74 mins. Cert U

Comedy with music: social worker Mrs Ashcroft (*Muriel Aked*) sees possibilities in out-of-work trombonist Joe Pilgrim (*Sydney Howard*) whom she persuades to become a candidate in the local council election. Joe is eventually elected Mayor, and helps Mrs A in her campaign to clear slum houses owned by a rival candidate.
RoC *Claude Hulbert, Al Bowlly, Miles Malleson, Syd Crossley, Frank Harvey, Michael Hogan, Cyril Smith.*

McGLUSKY THE SEA ROVER (1935) [3]
(USA: *Hell's Cargo*)
Dir and Scr *Walter Summers, from the novel by A.G. Hales.* Prod *Walter C. Mycroft.* PC *BIP.* Dis *Wardour.* 58 mins. Cert U
Rough and ready sea-going adventure to exploit the personality and physical prowess of boxer *Jack Doyle.* He plays a stowaway who makes friends with the skipper and shares adventures running guns to Arabs. They fall out over an Arab girl who boards their ship, but eventually she decides to reject both of them, and their partnership is renewed.
RoC *Tamara Desni, Henry Mollison, Cecil Ramage, Frank Cochrane, Hugh Miller, Jackie Short.*

ME AND MARLBOROUGH (1935) [3]
Dir *Victor Saville.* Prod *Michael Balcon.* Scr *Ian Hay, Marjorie Gaffney, W.P. Lipscomb, Reginald Pound.* Ph *Charles Van Enger.* PC and Dis *Gaumont-British.* 84 mins. Cert U
Rather heavy masquerade, but with a typically enthusiastic performance by *Cicely Courtneidge,* singing *All for a Shilling a Day* (by Noel Gay) and playing Kit Ross who, in 1709, goes in search of her press-ganged husband, joins the ranks of Marlborough's army as a man, and proves her husband's innocence on spying charges.
RoC *Tom Walls, Barry Mackay, Alfred Drayton, Iris Ashley, Ivor McLaren, Gibb McLaughlin, Cecil Parker, Peter Gawthorne, George Merritt, Mickey Brantford, Randle Ayrton, Henry Oscar, Percy Walsh.*

ME AND MY PAL (1939) [2]
Dir *Thomas Bentley.* Prod *Warwick Ward.* Scr *Uncredited.* Ph *Ernest Palmer.* PC *Welwyn.* Dis *Pathé.* 74 mins. Cert U
Two van drivers (*Dave Willis, George Moon*) have a series of farcical adventures when a smooth crook dupes them into believing they are working for the police, when in fact he is using them in his scheme to defraud an insurance company. The action moves from a fun fair to a prison and finally to a chase climax in a theatre. Comedy doesn't hang together as a story.
RoC *Pat Kirkwood, John Warwick, Arthur Margetson, Aubrey Mallalieu, Eliot Makeham, A. Giovanni, O.B. Clarence, Ernest Butcher, Hugh Dempster, Gerry Fitzgerald, Ian Fleming, Robert Adair, Joe Mott, Agnes Laughlan,* (C.) *Denier Warren.*

THE MEDICINE MAN (1933) [3]
Dir *Redd Davis.* Prod *Julius Hagen.* Scr *Michael Barringer, Robert Edmunds.* PC *Real Art.* Dis *Radio.* 52 mins. Cert A
'Silly ass' Freddie (*Claud Allister*), inveigled into swapping identities with a doctor friend, finds himself in demand by a criminal gang: they want him to perform a leg amputation on one of their members wounded in a 'job'. Just when it looks as though Freddie's goose is cooked, a broken chloroform bottle puts all the crooks out, and the police capture the lot.
RoC *Pat Paterson, Ben Welden, Frank Pettingell, Jeanne Stuart, Viola Compton, Ronald Simpson, Betty Astell, Drusilla Wills, S. Victor Stanley, John Turnbull, Andrea Malandrinos, William Home, Syd Crossley.*

MEET MAXWELL ARCHER (1939) [3]
(USA: *Maxwell Archer Detective*)
Dir *John Paddy Carstairs.* Prod *William Sistrom.* Scr *Hugh Clevely, Katherine Strueby, from a novel by Clevely.* PC and Dis *RKO Radio.* 74 mins. Cert A
A young pilot accused of murder appeals to amateur sleuth Maxwell Archer (*John Loder*), who is on the trail of a gang of international spies. Archer is regarded with suspicion by the pilot's girlfriend (*Leueen McGrath*) and by Inspector Cornell (*George Merritt*), who believes the accused is guilty. Archer finds the real murderer and solves his own problems at the same time. Unsubtle but swift paced thriller.
RoC *Marta Labarr, Athole Stewart, Ronald Adam, Peter Halliwell Hobbes, Syd Crossley, Barbara Everest, Ralph Roberts, John Lothar.*

MEET MR PENNY (1938) [2]
Dir *David Macdonald.* Prod *John Corfield.* Scr *Victor Kendall, Doreen Montgomery, from a radio series by Maurice Moisiewitsch.* Ph *Bryan Langley.* PC *British National.* Dis *Associated British.* 70 mins. Cert U
Acacia Villas is up in arms when its residents discover that their allotment has been bought by Allgood's Kolossal Stores as a warehouse. The women arrange a produce show, and invite Mr Allgood to present the prizes. But the men, led by a the-worse-for-drink Mr Penny (*Richard Goolden*) ruin everything. Luckily, Penny is able to do Allgood a good turn and the allotment is saved. Shaky transition to film of popular radio series.
RoC *Fabia Drake, Kay Walsh, Vic Oliver, Patrick Barr, Hermione Gingold,* (*Wilfrid*) *Hyde White, Charles Farrell, Hal Walters, Joss Ambler, Jack Raine, Renée Gadd, Tom Gill, Daphne Raglan, Gilbert Davis.*

MEET MY SISTER (1933) [3]
Dir *John Daumery.* Prod *Fred Watts.* Scr *Uncredited.* Ph *Jack Parker, Gerald Gibbs.* PC *BIP.* Dis *Pathé.* 70 mins. Cert A
Unpretentious situation comedy in which a lord becomes entangled with three women – the daughter (*Frances Dean*) of a millionaire, whom he hopes to marry; his jilted girlfriend (*Enid Stamp-Taylor*); and the daughter (*Constance Shotter*) of his butler's former employer who, after occupying the lord's bedroom in his absence, is later forced to pose as his sister.

Clifford Mollison plays the harassed Lord Victor.
RoC *Fred Duprez, Jimmy Godden, Helen Ferrers, Patrick Barr, Syd Crossley, Frou-Frou.*

MELODY AND ROMANCE (1937) [3]
Dir *Maurice Elvey.* Prod *Herbert Smith.* Scr *L. duGarde Peach.* Ph *George Stretton.* PC and Dis *British Lion.* 71 mins. Cert U
Hugh (*Hughie Green*), a young Wapping bargee, at the BBC for a successful audition, strikes up a friendship with Margaret (*Margaret Lockwood*), a scientist's daughter. Finding it hard going as a single act, he enlists the help of his 'gang' and becomes a great success. On the day of rehearsals for their first radio show, the building catches fire and Hugh rescues Margaret from the flames. Fragmented musical.
RoC *Jane Carr, Alastair Sim, Garry Marsh,* (C.) *Denier Warren, Julien Vedey, Margaret Scudamore, Hughie's Gang, Joyce Cannon and Geraldine, Rex Roper and Maisie, Bobby Price, Audrey Foster, Joey Hopkinson, Mary Kelly, Connie Russell.*

THE MELODY MAKER (1933) [2]
Dir *Leslie Hiscott.* Prod *Irving Asher.* PC *Warner Bros.* Dis *First National.* 56 mins. Cert U
Slight story about a successful popular composer (*Lester Matthews*) who falls in love with a girl (*Joan Marion*) on holiday and 'modernises' her competition sonata which is rejected for failing to comply with sonata form. Later her work is bought by a theatrical producer, she learns the composer's real identity and forgives him.
RoC *Evelyn Roberts, Wallace Lupino, A. Bromley Davenport, Vera Gerald, Joan White, Charles Hawtrey, Tonie Edgar Bruce.*

MELODY OF MY HEART (1936) [2]
Dir *Wilfred Noy.* Prod *Brandon Fleming, George Barclay.* Scr *Fleming.* PC *Incorporated Talking Films.* Dis *Butchers.* 82 mins. Cert A
Undistinguished musical variation on *Carmen.* Carmel (*Lorraine la Fosse*), who works in a cigarette factory, throws over her lover for a prizefighter. A performance of *Carmen* by factory employees gives the rejected suitor an opportunity for deadly revenge. But Carmel's life is saved by her new lover.
RoC *Derek Oldham, Bruce Seton, Hughes Macklin, Dorothy Vernon, MacArthur Gordon, Colin Cunningham, Joe Veilitch, Joyce St Clair, Clelia Matania, Adriana Otero, Robert Gilbert, Wensley Russell, Mabel Twemlow, Bobbie Slater, Clarissa Selwynne, Pearl Beresford, Doris Mortlock, Mignon Marchland, Ian Wilson, Stanley Radcliffe, James Carroll, Phil Sturgess, Jack Morris, Johnnie Schofield, Jack Jarman, Bombardier Billy Wells, Eleanor Hallam, Covent Garden Chorus, Horace Sheldon's Orchestra.*

MEMBER OF THE JURY (1937) [1]
Dir *Bernard Mainwaring.* Prod *John Findlay.* Scr *David Evans, from the novel by John Millard.* Ph *Stanley Grant.* PC and Dis *Fox British.* 61 mins. Cert A
Feeble execution of promising story about

Walter (*Ellis Irving*) who finds himself on the jury hearing the trial, for murder, of his own employer, Sir John Sloane (*Franklyn Bellamy*) who had rescued Walter from months on the dole queue. Partly thinking of his own future, Walter refuses to convict Sir John on the evidence and, painstakingly reconstructing the case finds that the man really is innocent.
RoC *Marjorie Hume, Arnold Lucy, Roy Russell, Aubrey Pollock, W.E. Holloway.*

MEN ARE NOT GODS (1936)   2

Dir *Walter Reisch.* Prod *Alexander Korda.* Scr *G.B. Stern, Iris Wright.* Ph *Charles Rosher.* PC *London Films.* Dis *United Artists.* 90 mins. Cert A
Following a plea from Barbara (*Gertrude Lawrence*), wife of actor Edmond Davey (*Sebastian Shaw*), Ann (*Miriam Hopkins*) changes the review written by her boss (*A.E. Matthews*) of Edmond's play. Ann is sacked, naturally, but gets to meet Edmond, with whom she falls in love. Edmond determines to murder his wife on stage during *Othello* to clear the way for Ann and him to marry - but Ann's scream from the audience stops him. The Daveys are reunited. Ridiculous emotional drama.
RoC *Rex Harrison, Val Gielgud, Laura Smithson, Lawrence Grossmith, Sybil Grove, Wally Patch, Winifred Willard, James Harcourt, Noel Howlett, Rosamund Greenwood, Paddy Morgan, Nicholas Nadejin, Michael Hogarth.*

MEN LIKE THESE (1931)   5
(USA: *Trapped in a Submarine*)

Dir *Walter Summers.* Prod *Walter C. Mycroft.* Scr *Summers, Mycroft.* Ph *Jack Parker, Horace Wheddon.* PC *BIP.* Dis *Wardour.* 46 mins. Cert A
A little picture with a big punch. It's based on the true story of the *Poseidon,* a submarine which sank after being in collision with a battleship. The Chief Petty Officer leads the crew's agonising efforts to escape. One critic said: 'Thrilling. A masterpiece of pictorial realism.'
LP *Sydney Seaward, John Batten, James Enstone, Edward Gee, Syd Crossley, John Hunt, Charles Peachey, Athol Fleming, Lesley Wareing, Valentine White, James Watts, Chang Fat, Wang Wong*

MEN OF STEEL (1932)   3

Dir *George King.* Prod *Bray Wyndham.* Scr *Edward Knoblock, Billie Bristow, from the novel by Douglas Newton.* PC *Langham.* Dis *United Artists.* 71 mins. Cert A
Workmanlike drama about a steelworks operating with equipment known to be unsafe. Foreman James 'Iron' Harg (*John Stuart*) eventually gains sole control of the works, and employs the ruthless tactics of his predecessors until an accident to his sweetheart, a secretary, brings him to his senses - and safety to the plant.
RoC *Benita Hume, Heather Angel, Franklin Dyall, Alexander Field, Mary Merrall, Edward Ashley Cooper, Sydney Benson, Gerard Clifton, Ian Braested.*

John Stuart, Franklin Dyall and Benita Hume in Men of Steel (*1932*)

MEN OF TOMORROW (1932)   4

Dir *Leontine Sagan, Zoltan Korda.* Prod *Alexander Korda.* Scr *Arthur Wimperis, Anthony Gibbs, from a novel by Gibbs.* Ph *Bernard Browne.* PC *London Films.* Dis *Paramount.* 88 mins. Cert U
Convincing study of university life, co-directed by the German woman director, Leontine Sagan, who had made *Mädchen in Uniform* the previous year. *Maurice Braddell* plays a student who is 'sent down' after writing a scathing indictment of his university. He marries his sweetheart (*Joan Gardner*), but they separate when she becomes the breadwinner, eventually reuniting after he has written a successful book.
RoC *Emlyn Williams, Robert Donat, Merle Oberon, John Traynor, Esther Kiss, Annie Esmond, Charles Carson, Patric Knowles, Gerald Cooper.*

MEN OF YESTERDAY (1936)   4

Dir *John Baxter,* Prod *John Barter.* Scr *Gerald Elliott, Jack Francis.* PC *UK Films.* Dis *Associated Producers and Distributors.* 82 mins. Cert U
Ex-Major Radford devotes his spare time to the welfare of ex-servicemen. Currently, he is working hard on a 'reunion' that will bring English, French and German veterans of the First World War together. When he loses his job, Radford (*Stewart Rome*) loses his enthusiasm and even contemplates suicide, but his ex-batman (*Sam Livesey*) pulls him round, and his 'reunion' dream comes true. Intelligently written, poignant plea for peace.
RoC *D. Hay Petrie, Eve Lister, Cecil Parker, Roddy Hughes, Ian Colin, George Robey, Will Fyffe, Ella Shields, Dick Henderson, Edgar Norfolk, Dick Francis, Edgar Driver, Frederick Culley, Freddie Watts, Patric Curwen, Stanley Kirby, Vi Kaley, Ernest Jay, John Hepworth, Henry Hepworth, J. Neil More, Gustave Ferrari, Denis Hayden, Terry Doyle, Barbara Everest.*

MEN WITHOUT HONOUR (1939)   1

Dir *Widgey R. Newman.* Prod *Bernard Smith.* Scr *George A. Cooper.* PC *Smith and Newman.* Dis *Equity British.* 59 mins. Cert A
Crime yarn about Frank Hardy (*Ian Fleming*), a disqualified lawyer who gets involved with Fayne and Vigor (*Howard Douglas, W.T. Hodge*) and their worthless share racket. His wife and son desert him. But Frank is working with the police and Fayne and Vigor are eventually arrested, and many investors saved from ruin. Unconvincingly acted; runs like a pastiche of the real thing.
RoC *Grace Arnold, Charles Paton*

MERELY MR HAWKINS (1938)   2

Dir *Maclean Rogers.* Prod and PC *George Smith.* Scr *John Hunter.* Ph *Geoffrey Faithfull.* Dis *RKO Radio.* 71 mins. Cert U
Browbeaten by his wife, Hawkins (*Eliot Makeham*) is made President of the Henpecked Husbands' League. His daughter Betty is left money and Mrs Hawkins tries to marry her off to a rich Canadian, who involves them in a fraudulent bond scheme. But Hawkins proves the bonds are bogus, Betty becomes engaged to her bank clerk boyfriend, and Hawkins acquires a new standing in his home. Cast work hard with poor script.
RoC *Sybil Grove, Dinah Sheridan, George Pembroke, Jonathan Field, Jack Vyvyan, Max Adrian, Michael Ripper, Ann Wilton.*

MERRY COMES TO TOWN (1937)   3
(USA: *Merry Comes to Stay*)

Dir and Prod *George King.* Scr *Brock Williams.* Ph *Hone Glendinning.* PC *Embassy.* Dis *Sound City.* 79 mins. Cert U
Winnie Oatfield (*Zasu Pitts*), an American spinster, comes into enough money to enable her to visit her relations in England. They all assume she is practically a millionairess, but stingy with it. Winnie teaches them a good many home truths before returning sadder and wiser to the States. Quite pleasant light comedy, sparked by Pitts' performance.
RoC *Guy Newall, Betty Ann Davies, Stella Arbenina, Bernard Clifton, Margaret Watson, Basil Langton, Muriel George, Tom Helmore, Cecil Mannering, W.T. Ellwanger, Arthur Finn, Margaret Yarde, Hermione Gingold, George Sims, Sybil Grove, Dorothy Bush, Jack Hellier, Mabel Twemlow, Janet Fitzpatrick.*

MICHAEL AND MARY (1931)   4

Dir *Victor Saville.* Prod *Michael Balcon.* Scr *Angus Macphail, Robert Stevenson, Lajos Biro, from the play by A.A. Milne.* Ph *Leslie Rowson.* PC *Gaumont.* Dis *Ideal/Gainsborough.* 85 mins. Cert A
Deserted by her husband during the Boer War, Mary (*Edna Best*) marries aspiring author Michael (*Herbert Marshall*). Years later, the husband returns, threatens blackmail and is

Elizabeth Allan and Frank Lawton in Michael and Mary (*1932*)

accidentally killed in a fall. Michael and Mary confess everything to their son and his fiancée and find the tragedy only strengthens the bonds between them. An old theme, but sensitively handled.

RoC *Elizabeth Allan, Frank Lawton, D.A. Clarke-Smith, Sunday Wilshin, Ben Field, Margaret Yarde.*

THE MIDAS TOUCH (1939) [2]
Dir *David Macdonald.* Prod *Sam Sax.* Scr *Brock Williams, Margaret Kennedy, from the novel by Kennedy.* Ph *Basil Emmott.* PC and Dis *Warner Bros.* 68 mins. Cert A

Through Lydia (*Judy Kelly*), Evan (*Barry K. Barnes*) becomes assistant to Morgan (*Frank Cellier*) whose son David (*Philip Friend*) loves the daughter of a man money-mad Morgan has ruined. Morgan's wife's fortune-telling friend tells him he will die in a car crash involving his son. He is shot by Harkness, his chauffeur, in revenge for a beating, and his car goes over a cliff, with Evan – the long-unseen son of his first marriage – throwing himself clear. Thriller starts well but fades.

RoC *Bertha Belmore, Iris Hoey, Anna Konstam, Evelyn Roberts, Eileen Erskine, Mervyn Johns, Scott Harrold, Clayton Greene.*

THE MIDDLE WATCH (1930) [5]
Dir *Norman Walker.* Prod *John Maxwell.* Scr *Walker, Frank Launder, from the play by Ian Hay, Stephen King-Hall.* Ph *Jack Cox, Claude Friese-Greene.* PC *BIP.* Dis *Wardour.* 112 mins. Cert A

A non-stop session of inventive fun in this first screen version of the stage success, remade in 1939 under the same title and in 1958 as *Girls at Sea.* Two young ladies come aboard a ship as officers' guests and are forced to stay the night when the picket-boat breaks down. The arrival of an admiral leaves everyone, literally, at sea, in this 'cabin-room farce'.

LP *Owen Nares, Jacqueline Logan, Jack Raine, Dodo Watts, Frederick Volpe, Muriel Aked, Phyllis Loring, Syd Crossley, Henry Wenman, Margaret Halstan, Reginald Purdell, Hamilton Keene, George Carr.*

THE MIDDLE WATCH (1939) [3]
Dir *Thomas Bentley.* Prod *Walter C. Mycroft.* Scr *Clifford Grey, J. Lee Thompson, from the play by Ian Hay, Stephen King-Hall.* Ph

Fred Emney and Jack Buchanan in The Middle Watch *(1939)*

Claude Friese-Greene. PC and Dis *Associated British.* 87 mins. Cert U

Two young ladies are accidentally taken out to sea after a party aboard a battleship, and their presence must be hidden from the admiral and the woman-hating captain (*Jack Buchanan*). A hectic mix-up over cabins ensues and all the main characters find themselves compromised! Smash-hit stage farce transfers rather lamely to screen this time: not too many laughs.

RoC *Greta Gynt, Kay Walsh, Fred Emney, Leslie Fuller, Jean Gillie, David Hutcheson, Reginald Purdell, Bruce Seton, Martita Hunt, Romney Brent, Louise Hampton, Ronald Shiner.*

MIDNIGHT (1930) [4]
Dir *George King.* Prod *Harry Cohen.* Scr *Charles Bennett, Billie Bristow, from the play by Bennett.* PC *George King.* Dis *Fox.* 45 mins. Cert U

Crime comedy-drama featuring a secret service agent (*John Stuart*) disguised as a burglar, and the girl (*Eve Gray*) who helps him to save secret plans from falling into the hands of a ring of spies. One of the first (and best) of George King's long series of 'quota quickies' made to comply with Board of Trade regulations about a quota of British films in British cinemas.

RoC *George Bellamy, Ellen Pollock, Kyoshi Takase.*

John Stuart and Eve Gray in Midnight *(1931)*

MIDNIGHT AT MADAME TUSSAUD'S (1936) [1]
(USA: *Midnight at the Wax Museum*)
Dir *George Pearson.* Prod *J. Steven Edwards.* Scr *Roger Macdougall, Kim Peacock.* Ph *Jan Stallich.* PC *Premier Sound Films.* Dis *Paramount.* 66 mins. Cert A

Lacklustre chiller about a financier who accepts a bet that he can spend a night in the Chamber of Horrors at Madame Tussaud's, the famous London wax museum (where parts of the film were actually shot). An adventurer who has become engaged to the financier's ward plans to murder him that night: he wounds him but is himself killed when he falls into the torture pit.

LP *James Carew, Lucille Lisle, Charles Oliver, Kim Peacock, Patrick Barr, Billy (William) Hartnell, Bernard Miles, Lydia Sherwood.*

MIDNIGHT MENACE (1937) [3]
(USA: *Bombs Over London*)
Dir *Sinclair Hill.* Prod *Harcourt Templeman.*

Scr *G.H. Moresby-White, D.B. Wyndham-Lewis, from a story by Roger Macdougall and Alexander Mackendrick.* Ph *Cyril Bristow.* PC *Grosvenor.* Dis *Associated British.* 79 mins. Cert U

An international armaments ring plans to bomb London. A suspicious reporter is killed before he can discover the truth, but his friends, a cartoonist and an agony columnist, discover the plotters' underground laboratory and, although some bombs are dropped, smash the controls and end the raids. Hardly convincing, but packed with action and incident.

LP *Charles Farrell, Fritz Kortner, Margaret Vyner, Danny Green, Wallace Evennett, Monte de Lyle, Dino Galvani, Denys Val Norton, Arthur Finn, Lawrence Hanray, Raymond Lovell, Terence O'Brien, Andrea Malandrinos, Reyner Barton, Arthur Gomez, Billy Bray, Evan John, Victor Tandy, Sydney King.*

THE MIDSHIPMAID (1932) [4]
(USA: *Midshipmaid Gob*)
Dir *Albert de Courville.* Prod *Michael Balcon.* Scr *Stafford Dickens, from the play by Ian Hay and Stephen King-Hall* Ph *Mutz Greenbaum.* PC *Gaumont.* Dis *W & F.* 84 mins. Cert U

Comedy with musical interludes in which a pompous economy expert (*Fred Kerr*) visits the Fleet in Malta to see what cuts can be made in their expenditure. The officers all fall over themselves to woo his pretty daughter (*Jessie Matthews*): she becomes engaged to the son of the First Sea Lord and her father decides to leave economies to the Navy.

RoC *Basil Sydney, A.W. Baskcomb, Edwin Lawrence, Nigel Bruce, Anthony Bushell, Claud Allister, Jack Clewes, George Zucco, Antony Holles, John Mills, Albert Rebla, Archie Glen, Joyce Kirby, Wilma Vanne, Condos Bros, John Turnbull.*

MIDSHIPMAN EASY (1935) [4]
(USA: *Men of the Sea*)
Dir *Carol Reed.* Prod *Basil Dean, Thorold Dickinson.* Scr *Anthony Kimmins, from a novel by Captain Marryat.* Ph *Johnny Boyle.* PC *ATP.* Dis *Associated British.* 77 mins. Cert U

Robust juvenile adventure with plenty of action, based on a well-loved novel. Jack Easy (*Hughie Green*), an argumentative boy, is all for a life at sea. Captain Wilson (*Roger Livesey*), a family friend, gets him into the navy as a midshipman. His independent spirit leads him into many adventures. He is responsible for: capturing a frigate, rescuing a lady from pirates, finding treasure, fighting a duel, and discomforting a notorious buccaneer.

RoC *Margaret Lockwood, Harry Tate, (W.) Robert Adams, Lewis Casson, Dennis Wyndham, Tom Gill, Frederick Burtwell, Desmond Tester, Dorothy Holmes-Gore, Norman Walker, Arthur Hambling, Arnold Lucy, Esmé Church, Anthony Rogers, Jacky Green, Roy Sharpe, Arthur Gomez, Andrea Malandrinos, Gladys Gordon, Christine Keir.*

THE MIKADO (1938) [4]
Dir *Victor Schertzinger.* Prod *Geoffrey Toye, Josef Somlo.* Scr *Toye, from the comic opera by W.S. Gilbert and Arthur Sullivan.* Ph *Bernard*

Knowles. PC *G and S Films*. Dis *General Film Distributors*. Technicolor. 92 mins. Cert U

Nanki-Poo (*Kenny Baker*), son of the emperor of Japan in bygone days, dons the guise of a wandering minstrel to escape the rapacious attentions of a lady of court, Katisha (*Constance Willis*) and seek out the girl he loves, Yum Yum (*Jean Colin*). She is betrothed to her guardian Ko-Ko (*Martyn Green*) but Nanki-Poo arranges matters so that Katisha is married off to Ko-Ko. Technically and vocally of a high standard; Bernard Knowles' camerawork won an Academy Award.
RoC *Sydney Granville, John Barclay, Gregory Stroud, Elizabeth Paynter, Kathleen Naylor*.

MILLIONS (1936)   [3]
Dir *Leslie Hiscott*. Prod *Herbert Wilcox*. Scr *Michael Barringer*. Ph *Frederick A. Young*. PC *Wilcox*. Dis *General Film Distributors*. 70 mins. Cert U

Millionaire financier Otto Forbes (*Gordon Harker* in another of his studies of refined vulgarity), trying for a 'corner in cloves', has problems with his ne'er-do-well son Jimmy (*Richard Hearne*) who, threatened with disinheritance, passes off as his own the manuscript of an aspiring composer. Otto's rival Sir Charles (*Frank Pettingell*) tries to expose the fraud, but Otto thwarts him, and brings Jimmy to hand in his own way.
RoC *Jane Carr, Stuart Robertson, Antony Holles, Ellen Pollock, Jack Hobbs, Ernest Sefton, Queenie Leonard*.

THE MILL ON THE FLOSS (1936)   [4]
Dir *Tim Whelan*. Prod *John Clein*. Scr *John Drinkwater, Garnett Weston, Austin Melford, Whelan, from the novel by George Eliot*. Ph *John Stumar*. PC *Morgan*. Dis *National Provincial*. 94 mins. Cert A

There is a feud between the Tullivers, who own a mill on the River Floss in Lincolnshire, and the Wakems, the lawyer head of whom wins a lawsuit over the river, ruining the Tullivers. Wakem's crippled son Philip (*Frank Lawton*) falls in love with Maggie (*Geraldine Fitzgerald*), daughter of Tulliver. Through private speculation, Tom Tulliver (*James Mason*) pays all his father's debts. Old Tulliver gives Old Wakem a horse-whipping, but dies of a stroke. Maggie is manoeuvred into an affair with Stephen (*Griffith Jones*), fiancé of Tom's cousin Lucy (*Victoria Hopper*), but Philip still loves her and when he and Maggie are swept to their deaths in a flood, the feud is over. Good climax to solid, if unrelaxed filming of Eliot's epic novel.
RoC *Fay Compton, Mary Clare, Sam Livesey, Felix Aylmer, Athene Seyler. Eliot Makeham, Amy Veness, William Devlin, Ivor Barnard, David Horne, O.B. Clarence, Cecil Ramage, Pauline de Chalus, Martita Hunt, James Roberts, Philip Frost, Anna Murrell, A.W. Payne, William Holloway, Eldon Gorst, Hilary Pritchard, Beatrice Marsden, Fred Withers, A.E. Johnson, Sidney Monckton, Cynthia Stock, Geraldine Wilton, Edmund Willard*.

MIMI (1935)   [2]
Dir *Paul L. Stein*. Prod *Walter C. Mycroft*. Scr *Clifford Grey, Paul Merzbach, Jack Davies,*

Denis Waldock, from a novel by Henri Murger. PC *BIP*. Dis *Wardour*. 94 mins. Cert A

The Latin Quarter of Paris, 1850. Mimi (*Gertrude Lawrence*), mistress of a successful actor, leaves him to share a Bohemian life with struggling playwright Rodolphe (*Douglas Fairbanks Jr*) and his friends. She proves an inspiration to them all. Rodolphe has a play accepted, but the production depends on the leading lady, who finds him attractive. Mimi bows out, but her health is failing and, at the moment of Rodolphe's triumph, she dies. Lacklustre weepie.
RoC *Diana Napier, Carol Goodner, Richard Bird, Harold Warrender, Martin Walker, Austin Trevor, Lawrence Hanray, Paul Graetz, Jack Raine*.

THE MIND OF MR REEDER (1939)   [3]
(USA: *The Mysterious Mr Reeder*)
Dir and PC *Jack Raymond*. Prod *Charles Q. Steele*. Scr *Bryan Wallace, Marjorie Gaffney, Michael Hogan, from the novel by Edgar Wallace*. Ph *George Stretton*. Dis *Grand National*. 75 mins. Cert U

Mr Reeder (*Will Fyffe*), detective to the Bank of England, trails a gang of forgers to a nightclub run by Bracher (*John Warwick*) who prints the notes. Reeder meets Mr and Mrs Welford there, and discovers a printing press in the cellar. Inspector Gaylor (*Romilly Lunge*) tries to arrest Bracher, who shoots him. Some fragments of glass lead Reeder to suspect Welford (*George Curzon*) and his wife (*Chili Bouchier*), Bracher's mistress, and he tricks Welford into a confession. Bracher is killed after a battle with police. Somewhat poorly connected thriller with exciting scenes.
RoC *Kay Walsh, Lesley Wareing, Derek Gorst, Ronald Shiner, Wally Patch, Betty Astell, George Hayes, Dorothy Dewhurst, Patricia Roc*.

THE MINSTREL BOY (1937)   [2]
Dir and Prod *Sydney Morgan*. Scr *Joan Wentworth Wood*. PC *Dreadnought*. Dis *Butchers*. 79 mins. Cert A

Glum musical about a society girl, Angela (*Lucille Lisle*), who deserts her stuffy fiancé to marry an Irish bandleader, Mike (*Fred Conyngham*). Mike is still fancied by his singer Dee Dawn (*Chili Bouchier*) and, when Angela thinks they have spent the night together, she walks out. Returning to collect her things, she finds Mike unconscious in a gas-filled room. She rescues him and they are reconciled.
RoC *Kenneth Buckley, Basil Langton, Marjorie Chard, Mabel Twemlow, Granville Darling, Ronald Walters, Pat Kavanagh, Dorothy Vernon, Xenia and Boyer*.

MIRACLES DO HAPPEN (1938)   [2]
Dir *Maclean Rogers*. Prod *George Smith*. Scr *Kathleen Butler, Con West, Jack Marks*. Ph *Geoffrey Faithfull*. PC *GS Enterprises*. Dis *New Realm*. 59 mins. Cert U

Professor Gilmore (*Aubrey Mallalieu*) invents a formula for making artificial milk, and his nephew Barry (*Jack Hobbs*) assumes the guise of a financier to obtain the backing to market it, which, after a series of misadventures, he does. Watery comedy.

RoC *Bruce Seton, Marjorie Taylor, George Carney, Molly Hamley-Clifford, Antony Holles, Michael Ripper*.

MISCHIEF (1931)   [5]
Dir *Jack Raymond*. Prod *Herbert Wilcox*. Scr *W.P. Lipscomb, Maclean Rogers, from the play by Ben Travers*. PC *British and Dominions*. Dis *W and F*. 70 mins. Cert A

Rollicking adaptation of a Ben Travers farce in which Arthur Gordon (*Ralph Lynn*) comes to the aid of a friend who is having matrimonial complications with his wife – but lands in romantic trouble of his own.
RoC *Winifred Shotter, James Carew, Jeanne Stuart, Jack Hobbs, Maud Gill, A. Bromley Davenport, Kenneth Kove, Louie Emery*.

MISSING – BELIEVED MARRIED (1937)   [1]
Dir *John Paddy Carstairs*. Prod *Anthony Havelock-Allan*. Scr *A.R. Rawlinson*. Ph *Francis Carver*. PC and Dis *British and Dominions/Paramount British*. 66 mins. Cert A

Heiress Hermione (*Hazel Terry*) runs off in hysterics when she learns the count she was to marry is bogus and an adventurer. Knocked out in a market-street scuffle, she is looked after by two traders (*Wally Patch, Julien Vedey*). She loses her memory and settles with them – then the count returns and cajoles her into going to Paris. The traders follow and rescue her from his clutches. Very thin comedy whose disparate elements don't mix.
RoC *Emilio Cargher, Peter Coke, Margaret Rutherford, Charles Paton, Irene Handl, George Turner, Sheila Young*.

THE MISSING PEOPLE (1939)   [4]
Dir and PC *Jack Raymond*. Prod *Charles Q. Steele*. Scr *Lydia Hayward, from characters created by Edgar Wallace*. Ph *George Stretton*. Dis *Grand National*. 71 mins. Cert A

Bank of England investigator Mr J.G. Reeder (*Will Fyffe*) sniffs out a connection between old ladies who have recently disappeared. He traces them to an investment corporation, but walks into a trap and is imprisoned in a basement which the villains flood. Luckily Reeder is released by a burglar on business of his own, just before the Flying Squad arrives to round up the 'corporation' and the crooked solicitors running it. Discursive but still gripping thriller.
RoC *Lyn Harding, Kay Walsh, Ronald Adam, Patricia Roc, Ronald Shiner, Antony Holles, Reginald Purdell, Maire O'Neill, Lawrence Hanray, O.B. Clarence*.

THE MISSING REMBRANDT (1932)   [4]
Dir *Leslie Hiscott*. Prod *Julius Hagen*. Scr *Cyril Twyford, H. Fowler Mear, from a story by Sir Arthur Conan Doyle*. Ph *Sydney Blythe, Basil Emmott*. PC *Twickenham*. Dis *Producers' Distributing Corporation*. 83 mins. Cert A

Sherlock Holmes (*Arthur Wontner*) investigates the theft of a Rembrandt painting and suspects Baron von Guntermann (*Francis L. Sullivan*), ostensibly an art collector but in reality a crook. His suspicions are confirmed through a case of blackmail in which von Guntermann is also concerned. Solid entry in Holmes' casebook.

RoC *Ian Fleming, Miles Mander, Jane Welsh, Dino Galvani, Ben Welden, Philip Hewland, Minnie Rayner, Antony Holles, Herbert Lomas, Kenji Takase.*

MISTAKEN IDENTITY (1939) [1]

Dir *Walter Tennyson.* Prod *Alfred D'Eyncourt.* Scr *Ian Walker.* Ph *Desmond Dickinson.* PC *Venture.* Dis *New Realm. 48 mins.* Cert U

Edward Benson (*Richard Goolden*) would like to see his conjuring talent recognised – but he is too shy. He travels to London where he is mistaken for a millionaire and beset by people after his money. A producer gives him a chance on stage, the real millionaire turns up, and everything ends happily. Tame, unsophisticated comedy, not released until 1942.

RoC *Gillian Maude, Julien Vedey.*

MISTER CINDERS (1934) [4]

Dir *Fred (Friedrich) Zelnick.* Prod *Walter C. Mycroft.* Scr *Clifford Grey, Frank Miller, Jack Davies, Kenneth Western, George Western, from a play by Grey, Miller and Greatrex Newman.* Ph *Otto Kanturek.* PC *BIP.* Dis *Wardour. 72 mins.* Cert U

Musical-comedy variation on *Cinderella*, with *Clifford Mollison* as Jim, a poor relation of Sir George and Lady Lancaster, and the drudge of their household. Lady L plans to marry one of her two idle sons to Jill Kemp (*Zelma O'Neil*), daughter of an American oil baron. But Jill foils her plans by posing as a servant and marrying Jim instead. Music: *Vivian Ellis.*

RoC *Renée Houston, The Western Brothers, Edmond Breon. Esmé Church, Edward Chapman, W.H. Berry, Lorna Storm, Finlay Currie, Henry Mollison, Ellen Pollock, Sybil Grove, Julian Royce, Mabelle George.*

MIXED DOUBLES (1933) [2]

Dir *Sidney Morgan.* Prod *Herbert Wilcox.* Scr *Joan Wentworth Wood, from a play by Frank Stayton.* PC *British and Dominions/Paramount British.* Dis *Paramount. 69 mins.* Cert A

Comedy about a divorced couple who meet up again and remarry, only to discover that their divorce was never absolute.

LP *Jeanne de Casalis, Frederick Lloyd, Molly Johnson, Cyril Raymond, Athol Fleming, Rani Waller, Quinton McPherson, Gordon McLeod, George Bellamy.*

MONEY FOR NOTHING (1931) [4]

Dir *Monty Banks.* Prod *Seymour Hicks.* Scr *Victor Kendall, Walter C. Mycroft.* PC *BIP.* Dis *Pathé. 73 mins.* Cert A

Comedy of mistaken identity, attractively set in Monte Carlo and London. A financier's daughter (*Betty Stockfeld*) is asked to invite one of her father's rivals, a 'J. Cheddar', who holds the majority stock in a company the financier is after, to London. However, the Jeff Cheddar (*Seymour Hicks*) she meets is not the Jay Cheddar her father wants: she and Jeff fall in love and eventually sort out the confusion.

RoC *Edmund Gwenn, Donald Calthrop, Henry Wenman, Philip Strange, Amy Veness, Charles Farrell, Mike Johnson, Hal Gordon, Renée Gadd, Billy Shine.*

MONEY FOR SPEED (1933) [3]

Dir and Prod *Bernard Vorhaus.* Scr *Vera Allinson, Lionel Hale, Monica Ewer.* Ph *Eric Cross.* PC *Hall Mark.* Dis *United Artists. 73 mins.* Cert A

Some good thrills in this story of two motorcycle riders, Big Bill (*Cyril McLaglen*) and Mitch (*John Loder*) in love with the same girl (*Ida Lupino*). After a ferocious dirt-track contest in which Mitch is injured, Bill is warned off the track. In trying to make a comeback as a wall-of-death stunt rider he is badly hurt, but the girl helps him back to a new start.

RoC *Moore Marriott, Marie Ault, Lionel Van Praag, John Hoskins, Ginger Lees, 'Cyclone' Davis.*

MONEY MAD (1934) [1]

Dir *Frank Richardson.* Prod *Basil Humphrys.* Scr *Selwyn Jepson.* PC *Champion.* Dis *M-G-M. 68 mins.* Cert A

Bad melodrama, described by one critic as a 'monotonous melee', about a businessman (*Peter Gawthorne*) who sees a threat in the activities of a financier (*Garry Marsh*). But Linda (*Virginia Cherrill*), the businessman's niece and the financier's fiancée, prevents what could have been a disastrous inflation of the pound.

RoC *D.A. Clarke-Smith, Helen Haye, Lawrence Anderson, Dennis Wyndham.*

MONEY MEANS NOTHING (1932) [2]

Dir *Harcourt Templeman, Herbert Wilcox.* Prod *Wilcox.* Scr *Miles Malleson, Templeman, Douglas Furber.* PC *British and Dominions.* Dis *Paramount. 70 mins.* Cert U

Comedy about Bethersyde (*Gibb McLaughlin*), butler to the young Earl of Massingham (*John Loder*), who inherits a fortune, but continues his duties, steering the Earl out of the clutches of a scheming chorus girl and into the arms of his own daughter.

RoC *Irene Richards, Dorothy Robinson, Kay Hammond, Clive Currie, A. Bromley Davenport, Miles Malleson.*

MONEY TALKS (1932) [3]

Dir and Prod *Norman Lee.* Scr *Lee, Frank Miller, Edwin Greenwood.* PC *BIP* Dis *Wardour. 73 mins.* Cert U

Jewish variation on *Brewster's Millions*, with *Julian Rose* as Abe Pillstein, a hard trader but a good friend, who finds he is to inherit a fortune – provided he is a poor man by the time the legacy arrives. Losing money proves to be harder than Abe expects . . . .

RoC *Kid Berg, Gladdy Sewell, Judy Kelly, Gus McNaughton, Griffith Jones, Bernard Ansell, Lena Maitland, Hal Gordon, Mary Charles, Jimmy Godden, Rich and Galvin.*

MONTE CARLO MADNESS (1932) [2]

Dir *Hanns Schwartz.* Prod *Erich Pommer.* Scr *Franz Schulz, Hans Müller, Rowland V. Lee.* PC *UFA.* Dis *Pathé. 83 mins.* Cert U. *Bilingual versions*

Docking at Monte Carlo with insufficient funds to pay his crew, Captain Erickson (*Hans Albers*) tries his luck at the casinos, where he not only wins the money but falls in love with Yola (*Sari Maritza*), the incognito queen of a small European country. Musical of somewhat forced gaiety.

RoC *Helen Haye, John Deverall, Charles Redgie, C. Hooper Trask, Carlo Minari and His Orchestra, Comedian Harmonists.*

MOONLIGHT SONATA (1937) [2]

Dir and Prod *Lothar Mendes.* Scr *Edward Knoblock, E.M. Delafield.* Ph *Jan Stallich.* PC *Pall Mall.* Dis *United Artists. 90 mins.* Cert U

After a forced landing in Sweden, the pianist *Ignace Jan Paderewski*, with his manager and a shady Chilean, has taken refuge at the home of a baroness and her daughter. The girl is infatuated by the Chilean's charm but, with the help of Paderewski, he is revealed in his true colours before the enforced visit is over. Paderewski's piano-playing and unselfconscious performance are the only bonus factors to a stilted drama.

RoC *Charles Farrell, Marie Tempest, Barbara Greene, Eric Portman, Binkie Stuart, Graham Browne, Queenie Leonard, Lawrence Hanray, Bryan Powley.*

THE MORALS OF MARCUS (1935) [2]

Dir *Miles Mander.* Prod *Julius Hagen.* Scr *Mander, Guy Bolton, H. Fowler Mear, from a novel by W.J. Locke.* PC *Real Art.* Dis *Gaumont-British. 76 mins.* Cert A

Slowly paced comedy about Marcus (*Ian Hunter*), archaeologist and confirmed bachelor, who takes pity on stowaway half-caste Carlotta (*Lupe Velez*) fleeing from an odious marriage in Syria. He brings her to London, where her unsophisticated charms are a great success. A snooty divorcee in love with Marcus hires a playboy to entice Carlotta to Paris. But Marcus follows and rescues her.

RoC *Adrianne Allen, Noel Madison, J.H. Roberts, H.F. Maltby, D.J. Williams, Arnold Lucy, Frank Atkinson, Johnny Nit, James Raglan, Agnes Imlay.*

MOSCOW NIGHTS (1935) [3]
(USA: *I Stand Condemned*)

Dir *Anthony Asquith.* Prod *Alexis Granowski, Max Schach.* Scr *Eric Seipmann, Asquith, from the novel by Pierre Benoit.* Ph *Philip Tannura.* PC *Denham Productions/London Films/Capitol.* Dis *General Film Distributors. 75 mins.* Cert A

A young Russian officer (*Laurence Olivier*), in love with a girl engaged to a rich peasant (*Harry Baur*), loses all his money to his rival at cards. He foolishly becomes involved in spy intrigues. When the girl (*Penelope Dudley Ward*) offers to marry the peasant in return for his saving the man she now loves from being shot as a spy, the peasant gives her up to a repentant officer. Well acted by the male leads, but a little laboured in execution.

RoC *Robert Cochran, Morton Selten, Athene Seyler, Walter Hudd, Kate Cutler, C.M. Hallard, Edmund Willard, Charles Carson, Morland Graham, Hay Petrie, Richard Webster, Anthony Quayle.*

THE MOUNTAIN (1935) [2]

Dir, Prod and Scr *Travis Jackson.* PC *Jackatoon.* Dis *Equity British. 82 mins.* Cert A

Heady melodrama, made almost single-handed

by Travis Jackson on location in the Lake District. The story is about a cleric (*Alan Elliott*), who loses his young wife (*Hope Sharpe*) to a mountaineer, Rodgers (*Maurice Jones*). On a lakeland climb, the cleric goes berserk, and sends the lover hurtling to his death.
RoC *J. Vyne Clarke, Rosemary Lee Booker, Sydney Dench.*

MOUNTAINS O' MOURNE (1938) [3]
Dir and Prod *Harry Hughes.* Scr *Gerald Brosnan.* PC *Rembrandt.* Dis *Butchers.* 85 mins. *Cert U*
Lovers Paddy (*Niall MacGinnis*) and Mary (*René Ray*) are evicted from their respective farms in Ireland by landowner Finnegan. Paddy goes to London and makes a career as a singer, meeting society belle Violet Mayfair (*Betty Ann Davies*). When he goes to Dublin to give a concert, he meets Mary again. She's a café hostess being pestered by Finnegan's son, who lets slip about a secret will making her an heiress. Paddy's valet Dip (*Jerry Verno*), an ex-pickpocket, steals the will from Finnegan and the two families get their farms back. Musical has some fresh and amusing touches to enliven its well-worn theme.
RoC *Charles Oliver, Kaye Seeley, Maire O'Neill, Eve Lynd, Pat Noonan, Freda Jackson, Alexander Butler, Leonard Henry, Stanley Vilven, Johnnie Schofield, Wilfred Caithness, Vivienne Chatterton, Robert Irwin, Hamilton Keene, Langley Howard, Walter Tobias, André and Curtis, Cornelia and Eddie, Percival Mackey and His Band.*

MR BILL THE CONQUEROR (1932) [3]
(USA: *The Man Who Won*)
Dir and Prod *Norman Walker.* Scr *Dion Titheradge.* Ph *Claude Friese-Greene.* PC *BIP.* Dis *Pathé.* 86 mins. *Cert U*
Rural drama, praised for its natural Sussex backgrounds, about a society man (*Henry Kendall*) who is bequeathed a derelict farm which is coveted by a prosperous but puritanical neighbouring farmer (*Sam Livesey*). Matters are solved through a romance between the newcomer and the old farmer's daughter (*Heather Angel*).
RoC *Nora Swinburne, Moore Marriott, A. Bromley Davenport, Tonie Edgar Bruce, David Hawthorne, Louie Tinsley, Helen Ferrers, Sam Wilkinson.*

Moore Marriott and Henry Kendall in Mr Bill the Conqueror (*1932*)

MR COHEN TAKES A WALK (1935) [3]
Dir *William Beaudine.* Prod *Irving Asher.* Scr *Brock Williams, from the novel by Mary Rinehart.* Ph *Basil Emmott.* PC and Dis *Warner Bros.* 82 mins. *Cert U*
Sentimental story of Jacob Cohen (*Paul Graetz*) who starts as a pedlar, but prospers to found a large department store. His sons join the business and, when his wife dies, are virtually running it. He no longer feels useful and tramps the countryside, living rough. But there is trouble at the store and Jacob returns just in time to prevent a catastrophe.
RoC *Violet Farebrother, Chili Bouchier, Barry Livesey, Ralph Truman, Mickey Brantford, Meriel Forbes, George Merritt, Kenneth Villiers, Sam Springson.*

MR QUINCY OF MONTE CARLO (1933) [3]
Dir *John Daumery.* Prod *Irving Asher.* Scr *Brock Williams.* PC *Warner Bros.* Dis *First National.* 53 mins. *Cert U*
Quite amusing and well-observed comedy piece about a sober bank clerk, Mr Quincy (*John Stuart*) who has a windfall, goes to Monte Carlo for a holiday, and, after a few misadventures, uses the rest of his money to finance a film company.
RoC *Rosemary Ames, Ben Welden, George Merritt, Victor Fairley.*

MR REEDER IN ROOM 13 (1938) [2]
(USA: *Mystery of Room 13*)
Dir *Norman Lee.* Prod *John Corfield.* Scr *Doreen Montgomery, Victor Kendall, Elizabeth Meehan, from a novel by Edgar Wallace.* PC *British National.* Dis *Associated British.* 78 mins. *Cert A*
Ridiculously plotted crime story with Mr Reeder (*Gibb McLaughlin*), detective to the Bank of England, on the trail of a counterfeit gang. He enlists Foreign Office man Johnny Gray (*Peter Murray Hill*), who serves three years in prison in the hope of getting on to the forgery ring(!) On his release, he finds his girl (*Sally Gray*) has married the gang leader (*Leslie Perrins*). But her father, whose ex-partner was the crime chief's equally crooked father, takes a macabre revenge, while Reeder narrowly saves Gray from being hanged by the rest of the gang.
RoC *Sara Seegar, Malcolm Keen, D. J. Williams, Robert Cochran, George Merritt, Philip Ray, Rex Carvel, Florence Groves.*

MR SATAN (1938) [3]
Dir *Arthur Woods.* Prod *William Collier.* Scr *John Meehan Jr, J. O. C. Orton.* Ph *Robert La Presle.* PC *Warner Bros.* Dis *First National.* 79 mins. *Cert A*
Tim (*James Stephenson*), a war correspondent, tracks down but falls in love with Jacqueline (*Chili Bouchier*), accomplice of armaments monger Zubova (*Franklin Dyall*), who had supposedly committed suicide. Tim is captured and forced to watch Zubova sinking a ship which he hopes will start a war. Jacqueline shoots Zubova but is herself fatally wounded and dies in Tim's arms. Fast-moving melodrama on stereotyped lines.

RoC *Skeets Gallagher, Betty Lynne, Robert Rendel, Mary Cole, Eric Clavering, Dino Galvani, Cot d'Ordan, Bryan Powley, Victor Fairley.*

MRS DANE'S DEFENCE (1933) [1]
Dir *A. V. Bramble.* Prod *Harry Rowson.* Scr *Lydia Hayward, Kenelm Foss, from the play by Henry Arthur Jones.* PC *National Talkies.* Dis *Paramount.* 67 mins. *Cert A*
This very tedious drama saw the end of *Joan Barry*'s once-promising film career. She plays Felicia who, running from a scandal in Monte Carlo, comes to England and assumes the name of a dead cousin, Mrs Dane. She falls for the wealthy adopted son of a judge, who at first refuses his consent but later, after rumours about her spread, takes pity on her and gives the wedding his blessing.
RoC *Basil Gill, Francis James, Ben Field, Clare Greet, Evan Thomas. Evelyn Walsh-Hall, Tony Paynter, John H. Vyvyan.*

MR SMITH CARRIES ON (1937) [3]
Dir *Lister Laurance.* Prod *Anthony Havelock-Allan.* Scr *Ronald Gow.* Ph *Francis Carver.* PC and Dis *British and Dominions/Paramount.* 68 mins. *Cert U*
Financier Minos (*Julien Mitchell*) threatens suicide when his head clerk Smith (*Edward Rigby*) refuses to help him in a fraud. They struggle for a gun and it goes off, killing Minos. Smith hides the body and, by means of a crafty deal, saves the money of thousands of small investors. He is accused of the murder, but charges are dropped when the whole truth comes out. Drama is somewhat talky, but carries some suspense.
RoC *H. F. Maltby, Dorothy Oldfield, Basil Langton, Franklyn Bellamy, Margaret Emden, Frederick Cully, Dorothy Dewhurst, Jo Monkhouse.*

MRS PYM OF SCOTLAND YARD (1939) [4]
Dir *Fred Elles.* Prod *Victor Katona.* Scr *Elles, Nigel Morland, Peggy Barwell, from a novel by Morland.* Ph *Bryan Langley.* PC *Hurley Productions.* Dis *Grand National.* 65 mins. *Cert A*
Two women members of a psychic club are found murdered. Mrs Pym (*Mary Clare*), a detective, joins the club and, with the help of limp-witted Inspector Shott (*Edward Lexy*), reveals the medium as the killer just in time to prevent another death. Ingenious, creepy thriller with first-class role for Mary Clare.
RoC *Nigel Patrick, Janet Johnson, Anthony Ireland, Irene Handl, Vernon Kelso, Rupert English, Lionel Dymoke, Arthur Ridley, Ben Williams, Arthur Owen, Jack Jameson, Joan Halliday.*

MR STRINGFELLOW SAYS 'NO' (1937) [3]
Dir *Randall Faye.* Prod *Brandon Fleming, Reginald Gottwaltz.* Scr *Faye, Fleming.* PC *Incorporated Talking Films.* Dis *National Provincial.* 76 mins. *Cert U*
Jeremy Stringfellow (*Neil Hamilton*), a quiet Church Lads' Brigade leader, is minding his own business when a spy (in a car) crashes

through the wall of his home, insists on telling him a deadly secret, but expires before he can do so. Agents and spies are soon on Jeremy's trail. He is kidnapped, whisked off in a plane, escapes by parachute, is captured and imprisoned in the Tower of London, given a knighthood and elected to Parliament. Original satirical material not made the most of.
RoC *Marcelle Rogez, Claude Dampier, Franklin Dyall, Muriel Aked, Kathleen Gibson, Peter Gawthorne.*

MR WHAT'S-HIS-NAME (1935) [4]
Dir *Ralph Ince.* Prod *Irving Asher.* Scr *Tom Geraghty, Frank Launder, from a play by Yves Mirande, Seymour Hicks.* Ph *Basil Emmott.* PC *Warner Bros.* Dis *First National. 67 mins. Cert A*
A pickle millionaire (*Seymour Hicks*) loses his memory in a train crash. Later, he launches another (beauty) business as Monsieur Herbert Herbert, acquires another wife and eventually, by accident, find himself in the home of his original wife who, thinking him dead, has married again. His memory of his true identity comes back, and he is left with no memory of the years between. Well-written, occasionally uproarious farce.
RoC *Olive Blakeney, Tonie Edgar Bruce, Garry Marsh, Enid Stamp-Taylor, Martita Hunt, Henry Longhurst, Louis Broughton, Margaret Damer, Arthur Metcalfe, Dorothy Hammond, Eric Hales, Reg Marcus, Bombardier Billy Wells, Gunner Moir.*

MURDER (1930) [6]
Dir *Alfred Hitchcock.* Prod *John Maxwell.* Scr *Alma Reville, Walter C. Mycroft, Hitchcock, from a play by Clemence Dane and Helen Simpson.* Ph *Jack Cox.* PC *BIP.* Dis *Wardour. 108 mins. Cert A*
Hitchcock thriller in which a young actress (*Norah Baring*) in a repertory company is sentenced to death for murder. A juror (*Herbert Marshall*) who happens to be an actor-manager, is convinced of her innocence and, going to the repertory company, gradually assembles evidence which proves the girl's fiancé to be the murderer. Shot simultaneously in German, and noted for its use of impressionistic sound, especially in jury room scenes.
RoC *Phyllis Konstam, Edward Chapman, Miles Mander, Esmé Percy, Donald Calthrop, Amy Brandon Thomas, Joynson Powell, Marie*

Norah Baring and Herbert Marshall in Murder *(1930)*

Wright, Hannah Jones, Una O'Connor, Violet Farebrother, Kenneth Kove, Clare Greet, Gus McNaughton, R. E. Jeffrey.*

MURDER AT COVENT GARDEN (1932) [2]
Dir *Michael Barringer, Leslie Hiscott.* Prod *Julius Hagen.* Scr *Barringer, H. Fowler Mear, from a novel by W. J. Makin.* PC *Twickenham.* Dis *W and F. 66 mins. Cert A*
After a prominent nightclub owner is killed, a detective (*Walter Fitzgerald*) is engaged by a syndicate to track down a gang believed to be smuggling diamonds into London. He proves the gang killed the nightclub man in a fight over the gems, and unmasks its leader, in this routine crime melodrama.
RoC *Dennis Neilson-Terry, Anne Grey, George Curzon, Henri de Vries, Binnie Barnes, Fred Pease.*

MURDER AT MONTE CARLO (1934) [3]
Dir *Ralph Ince.* Prod *Irving Asher.* Scr *John Hastings Turner, Michael Barringer, from the novel by Tom Van Dyke.* PC *Warner Bros.* Dis *First National. 70 mins. Cert A*
Errol Flynn (second-billed to *Eve Gray*) made this 'quickie' thriller on his way from Tasmania to Hollywood. A professor (*Paul Graetz*) is killed after working out a system that is likely to break the banks at Monte Carlo's gambling casinos. Flynn is the star reporter who solves the case.
RoC *Molly Lamont, Lawrence Hanray, Ellis Irving, Henry Victor, Brian Buchel, Peter Gawthorne, Gabriel Toyne, James Dale, Henry Longhurst, Ernest Sefton.*

MURDER AT THE CABARET (1936) [1]
Dir *Reginald Fogwell.* Prod *Fogwell, Nell Emerald.* Scr *Fogwell, Percy Robinson.* Ph *Roy Fogwell.* PC *MB Productions.* Dis *Paramount. 67 mins. Cert A*
Disastrous combination of musical and whodunnit, in which a philandering crooner is murdered on stage by a gun which should have been loaded with blanks. The guilty party – his girlfriend – is eventually sorted out from a trio of likely suspects.
LP *Phyllis Robins, Freddie Forbes, James Carew, Frederick Peisley, Kenneth Warrington, Peggy Crawford, Miska, Douglas Phillips, Mark Daly, Chick Farr and Farland, Bernardi, Michael Ronni, Clifford Seagrave, Rosarita, Nina, Alvis and Capla, Holland's Magyar Band.*

MURDER AT THE INN (1934) [2]
Dir *George King.* Prod *Irving Asher.* Scr *Randall Faye.* PC and Dis *Warner Bros. 56 mins. Cert A*
Artificial thriller about an eloping couple (*Wendy Barrie, Harold French*) who become involved in the murder of a blackmailing publican at a country inn after their car breaks down. An additional complication is the presence of Tony's gold-digging ex-flame (*Jane Carr*) who is there to retrieve letters written to her by Angela's father.
RoC *Davy Burnaby, Nicholas Hannen, Minnie Rayner, H. Saxon-Snell.*

MURDER BY ROPE (1936) [1]
Dir *George Pearson.* Prod *Anthony Havelock-Allan.* Scr *Ralph Neale.* Ph *Ernest Palmer.* PC and Dis *British and Dominions/Paramount British. 64 mins. Cert A*
Undistinguished crime thriller about a man, supposed to have been hanged for murder, who appears to return to wreak vengeance on those responsible for his capture and punishment.
LP *D. A. Clarke-Smith, Sunday Wilshin, Constance Godridge, (Wilfrid) Hyde White, Donald Read, Daphne Courtney, Dorothy Hamilton, Guy Belmore, Philip Hewland, Alban Conway, William Collins, Charles Borrett.*

MURDER IN SOHO (1938) [2]
(USA: *Murder in the Night*)
Dir *Norman Lee.* Prod *Walter C. Mycroft.* Scr *F. McGrew Willis.* Ph *Claude Friese-Greene.* PC and Dis *Associated British. 70 mins. Cert A*
Ambitious American club owner in London, Steve Marco (*Jack La Rue*) shoots a confederate, Lane (*Francis Lister*), who tries to double-cross him. He dumps the body elsewhere but, with the help of Lane's widow Ruby (*Sandra Storme*), a hostess at the club, Inspector Hammond (*Martin Walker*) is able to prove Marco the murderer. Familiar 'quickie' nightclub thriller.
RoC *Bernard Lee, Arthur O'Connell, Edmon Ryan, Googie Withers, James Hayter, Alf Goddard, Diana Beaumont, Zillah Bateman, Renée Gadd, Diana Ward, Geoffrey Sumner, Drue Leyton, Robert Beatty, Joss Ambler.*

MURDER IN THE FAMILY (1938) [2]
Dir and Prod *Albert Parker.* Scr *David Evans, from a novel by James Ronald.* PC and Dis *Fox British. 76 mins. Cert A*
Unpleasant Aunt Octavia, finding her half-brother Stephen (*Barry Jones*) out of a job and his family in despair, not only rejects his pleas for help, but cuts him out of her Will. She leaves the £1,000 instead to her maid (*Rani Waller*) who promptly stabs her to death. Suspicion falls on Stephen who tries to commit suicide before the truth finally comes out. Ponderous thriller is well-acted but short on thrills.
RoC *Jessica Tandy, Donald Gray, Evelyn Ankers, David Markham, Glynis Johns, Roddy McDowall, Jessie Winter, Annie Esmond, Claire Arnold, A. Bromley Davenport, Stella Arbenina, W. Simpson Fraser, David Arnold, Edgar K. Bruce, Charles Childerstone.*

MURDER ON THE SECOND FLOOR (1931) [2]
Dir *William McGann.* Prod *Irving Asher.* Scr *Roland Pertwee, Challis Sanderson.* PC *Warner Bros.* Dis *First National. 70 mins. Cert A*
Never really a starter, this idea of a young playwright (*John Longden*) who imagines a murder mystery whose characters are the inhabitants of the London boarding house where he is staying. Naturally the police can't find the killer but an amateur detective (the playwright) does.
RoC *Pat Paterson, Ben Field, Sydney Fairbrother, Florence Desmond, Franklyn Bellamy, John Turnbull, Amy Veness, Oswald Skilbeck.*

MURDER TOMORROW (1938) [3]

Dir and Scr *Donovan Pedelty, from the play by Frank Harvey.* Prod *Victor M. Greene.* Ph *Ernest Palmer.* PC *Crusade.* Dis *Paramount.* 69 mins. Cert A

Jean Andrews (*Gwenllian Gill*) has a fight with her ex-husband and he is killed. She hides the body in a ditch, but has to confess to her boyfriend (*Jack Livesey*). They make it look as if the man had died the following day. Almost found out, they are saved by a helpful solicitor, and a fortunate coincidence. Dialogue not quite up to acting and plot.

RoC *Molly Hamley-Clifford, Raymond Lovell, Rani Waller, Francis Roberts, Jonathan Field, Charles Lincoln, Dempsey Stuart, Billy Bray.*

MURDER WILL OUT (1939) [2]

Dir *Roy William Neill.* Prod *Sam Sax.* Scr *Neill, Austin Melford, Brock Williams, Derek Twist.* Ph *Basil Emmott.* PC and Dis *Warner Bros.* 66 mins. Cert A

Threats are made to Paul (*John Loder*) and his wife Pam (*Jane Baxter*) after Stamp (*Jack Hawkins*) has obtained them some very valuable jade. They find Stamp's body but it disappears. A friend, Morgan (*Frederick Burtwell*), and a criminal expert, Campbell (*Hartley Power*), also vanish. Pam finally delivers a huge sum of money to prevent Paul's death, the criminals proving to be Stamp, Morgan and Campbell, who are all killed when their getaway plane crashes. Intriguing but untidily constructed thriller.

RoC *Peter Croft, Billy (William) Hartnell, Ian Maclean, Richard George, Aubrey Mallalieu, Peter Miles, Roddy McDowall.*

Frederick Burtwell, Hartley Power and Jack Hawkins in Murder Will Out (*1939*)

MUSEUM MYSTERY (1937) [1]

Dir *Clifford Gulliver.* Prod *Anthony Havelock-Allan.* Scr *Gerald Elliott.* Ph *Francis Carver.* PC and Dis *British and Dominions/Paramount British.* 69 mins. Cert U

The owner of a curio museum attempts to steal one of his own artefacts – a priceless Burmese idol – and collect the insurance money. His plans are foiled by the diligence of his own daughter and her student boyfriend. Plot is not well-written, sometimes confusing.

LP *Jock McKay, Elizabeth Inglis, Gerald Case, Tony Wylde, Charles Paton, Alfred Wellesley, Sebastian Smith, Roy Byford, J. Abercrombie, Geoffrey Clark.*

MUSIC HALL (1934) [4]

Dir and Scr *John Baxter.* Prod *Julius Hagen.* PC *Real Art.* Dis *Radio.* 73 mins. Cert U

Bright variety show encased in a flimsy story about a music-hall that fails while being run under old-fashioned ideas, but takes on a new lease of life when run by modern methods of showmanship – ironically employed by a retired old showman who renovates the hall, reopens it with a mammoth programme and puts it on its feet again.

LP *George Carney, Ben Field, Mark Daly, Helena Pickard, Olive Sloane, Derrick de Marney, Wally Patch, Peggy Novak, Edgar Driver,* (C.) *Denier Warren, Walter Amner, Wilson Coleman, Freddie Watts, Roddy Hughes, Bertram Dench, Raymond Newell, G. H. Elliott, Eve Chapman, Macari's Dutch Serenaders, Gershom Parkington Quintet, Chester's Performing Dogs, Debroy Somers and His Band, The Sherman Fisher Girls.*

MUSIC HALL PARADE (1939) [3]

Dir and Prod *Oswald Mitchell.* Scr *Con West, Mitchell.* Ph *Geoffrey Faithfull.* PC and Dis *Butchers.* 80 mins. Cert U

Smoothly made revue film in which Jean (*Glen Raynham*) tries to keep her small-time music-hall going after her father has died. A young publicity man comes to her rescue and, after a country-wide hunt for new talent, they stage a sensational show which ensures the continuation of the theatre.

RoC *Richard Norris, Charles Sewell, Rita Grant, Frank E. Franks, Hughie Green, Eve Becke, Tom Gamble, Jack Stanford, Freddie Forbes, Sid Palmer, Bill Burley, Angela Barrie, Patricia Faye. The Australian Motor Air Aces, Macari and His Dutch Accordion Serenaders, The Arnaut Brothers, The Three Jokers, Billy Cotton and His Band.*

MUSIC HATH CHARMS (1935) [4]

Dir *Thomas Bentley* (supervising), *Alexander Esway, Walter Summers, Arthur Woods.* Prod *Walter C. Mycroft.* Scr *Jack Davies, Courtney Terrett, L. DuGarde Peach.* Ph *Jack Cox, Claude Friese-Greene, Ronald Neame.* PC *BIP.* Dis *Wardour.* 71 mins. Cert U

This quirkily humorous exploitation of a popular music figure, in this case bandleader *Henry Hall,* has something in common with the Beatles' films 30 years later. Beside Hall's misadventures with his 'boys' in the studio, his music has the most startling effects – on a party of children, in saving white explorers from headhunters, in steering lost mountaineers through the fog, causing a policeman to dance on duty, saving – and breaking – marriages.

RoC *Carol Goodner, Arthur Margetson, W. H. Berry, Lorna Hubbard, Antoinette Cellier, Billy Milton, Aubrey Mallalieu, Wallace Douglas, Edith Sharpe, Gus McNaughton, Hugh Dempster, Maidie Hope, Richard Grey,* (Howard) *Marion Crawford, Norma Varden, John Turnbull, Ivan Samson, Quinton McPherson, Charles Paton.*

THE MUSIC MAKER (1936) [2]

Dir *Hugh Kairs* (*Horace Shepherd*). Prod *Shep-*

---

herd, Holt Turner. Scr *Shepherd.* PC *Inspiration.* Dis *M-G-M.* 52 mins. Cert U

Sentimental two-hander about an ageing violinist who just manages to finish his first and last symphony before he dies.

LP *Arthur Young, Violet Loxley.*

THE MUTINY OF THE *ELSINORE* (1937) [3]

Dir *Roy Lockwood.* Prod *John Argyle.* Scr *Walter Summers, Beaufoy Milton, from the novel by Jack London.* Ph *Bryan Langley.* PC *Argyle British.* Dis *Associated British.* 79 mins. Cert A

On a windjammer bound for San Francisco, a writer, Pathurst (*Paul Lukas*), finds himself siding with the first officer (*Lyn Harding*) whose harsh methods he despises when the crew, under the second officer (*Ben Soutten*), mutiny. Despite sporadic fighting, the mutineers are gradually brought to heel, and their leader is killed. Inconsistent characterization mars hearty seagoing saga.

RoC *Clifford Evans, Kathleen Kelly, Michael Martin-Harvey, Pat Noonan, Hamilton Keene, William Devlin, Conway Dixon, Tony Sympson, Alec Fraser, Jiro Soneya.*

MY FRIEND THE KING (1931) [3]

Dir *Michael Powell.* Prod *Jerome Jackson.* Scr *J. Jefferson Farjeon.* PC *Film Engineering.* Dis *Fox.* 52 mins. Cert U

Lively little trifle with *Jerry Verno* as a taxi-driver who has to masquerade as a demure countess in order to rescue a young Ruritanian prince from the hands of revolutionaries.

RoC *Robert Holmes, Phyllis Loring, Tracy Holmes, Eric Pavitt, Luli Hohenberg, H. Saxon-Snell, Victor Fairley.*

MY HEART IS CALLING (1934) [3]

Dir *Carmine Gallone.* Prod *Arnold Pressburger.* Scr *Richard Benson, Sidney Gilliat, Robert Edmunds.* Ph *Glen MacWilliams.* PC *Cine-Allianz.* Dis *Gaumont-British.* 91 mins. Cert U. Trilingual versions

Despite an entertaining performance by *Jan Kiepura,* this is an artificial and rather protracted musical about the trials and tribulations of an itinerant Italian opera company, saved by its tenor and a girl 'stowaway' with whom he falls in love.

RoC *Martha Eggerth, Sonnie Hale, Hugh Wakefield, Ernest Thesiger, Marie Lohr, Jeanne Stuart, Johnny Singer, Anthony Hankey, Parry Jones, Mickey Brantford, Hilde von Stolz, Frederick Peisley, Anton Imkamp.*

MY IRISH MOLLY (1938) [2]
(USA: *Little Miss Molly*)

Dir *Alex Bryce.* Prod *John Argyle.* Scr *Bryce, Ian Walker, W. G. Fay.* Ph *Ernest Palmer.* PC *Argyle British.* Dis *Associated British.* 69 mins (USA: 66). Cert U

Little orphan Molly (*Binkie Stuart*) comes to Ireland to live with her stern Aunt Hannah (*Maureen Moore*). Unhappy, she flees to another aunt, Mary (*Maureen O'Hara*) whose American friends Bob and Chuck (*Philip Reed,* (C.) *Denier Warren*) take the child and her singing talent to the States. Although they come back when Hannah threatens to charge Mary with abduction, everything ends happily. Pretty ingenuous musical.

RoC *Tom Burke, Maire O'Neill, Franklyn Kelsey, Leo McCabe, Paddy (dog)*.

MY LUCKY STAR (1933)   2

Dir *Louis Blattner, John Harlow*. Prod *Blattner*. Scr *Harlow*. PC *Masquerader*. Dis *W and F. 63 mins. Cert U*

Millie (*Florence Desmond*), a shop assistant, poses as a film star in order to gain the acquaintance of an artist, Dudley Collins (*Henry Longhurst*). It turns out that he too is a 'poser' – he's really a porter at a railway station. Another mediocre vehicle for the comedy talents of *Florence Desmond*.

RoC *Harry Tate, Carol Coombe, Harold Huth, Charlie Naughton and Jimmy Gold, Oscar Asche, Reginald Purdell, Herman Darewski, George Baker, Ernest Jay, Alfred Arthur, Della Rega*.

MY OLD DUTCH (1934)   4

Dir *Sinclair Hill*. (Associate) Prod *Ivor Montagu*. Scr *Marjorie Gaffney, Bryan Wallace, Mary Murillo, Michael Hogan, from the song by Albert Chevalier, and an original scenario by Chevalier, Arthur Shirley*. Ph *Leslie Rowson*. PC *Gainsborough*. Dis *Gaumont-British. 82 mins. Cert U.*

A remake of the 1915 silent (from which this includes extracts), covering 40 years in the lives of a cockney couple (*Betty Balfour, Gordon Harker*), whose happily married life is marred only when their son falls in love with a rich girl whose father disowns her, and then is killed in the First World War serving with the Royal Flying Corps. The stars breathe life into familiar characters.

RoC *Florrie Forde, Michael Hogan, Glennis Lorimer, Mickey Brantford, Frank Pettingell, Peter Gawthorne, Billy Shine, Finlay Currie, Felix Aylmer, Johnny Singer, Peggy Simpson, Ronald Shiner*.

Michael Hogan and Betty Balfour in My Old Dutch *(1934)*

MY SONG FOR YOU (1934)   4

Dir *Maurice Elvey*. Prod *Jerome Jackson*. Scr *Austin Melford, Robert Edmunds, Richard Benson, from a scenario by Ernst Marischka, Irma Von Cube*. Ph *C. Van Enger*. PC and Dis *Gaumont-British. 86 mins. Cert U*

Viennese musical of some charm, with *Aileen Marson* as a singer in the opera chorus who

Sonnie Hale and Jan Kiepura in My Song for You *(1934)*

uses the lead tenor, Gatti's (*Jan Kiepura*) infatuation for her to get a job for her fiancé, Theodore (*Emlyn Williams*). After Theodore lets her down, she agrees to marry her parents' choice, a wealthy man. But during the wedding ceremony, she changes her mind and decides to marry Gatti instead.

RoC *Sonnie Hale, Gina Malo, Muriel George, George Merritt, Reginald Smith*.

MY SONG GOES ROUND THE WORLD (1934)   2

Dir and Prod *Richard Oswald*. Scr *Clifford Grey, Frank Miller, from a scenario by Ernest Neubach*. Ph *Reinhardt Kuntze*. PC *BIP*. Dis *Wardour. 68 mins. Cert U.*

An inadequate vehicle for the tiny German tenor *Joseph Schmidt* as one of a trio of variety artists. He becomes a great stage and recording star, but loses Nina (*Charlotte Ander*) to the other member of the trio (*John Loder*).

RoC *Jack Barty, Jimmy Godden, Hal Gordon*.

THE MYSTERIOUS MR DAVIS (1936)   1

(USA: *My Partner, Mr Davis*)

Dir, Prod and Scr *Claude Autant-Lara, from a novel by Jenaro Prieto*. PC *Oxford Films*. Dis *RKO. 60 mins. Cert U*

In tight financial straits, Julian (*Henry Kendall*) invents an important but imaginary partner, Mr Davis. Crooked financiers want to meet Davis (who proves to be their undoing) and a 'vamp' tries to wheedle his whereabouts from Julian. In the end, he is glad to put Mr Davis into cold storage. Ludicrously plotted, dully photographed, weakly directed and poorly acted. Apart from that. . . . Only British film of its later-famous French director.

RoC *Kathleen Kelly, Alastair Sim, A. Bromley Davenport, Guy Middleton, Morris Harvey*.

THE MYSTERY OF THE MARIE CELESTE/THE MYSTERY OF THE MARY CELESTE (1935)   3

(USA: *Phantom Ship*)

Dir and Scr *Denison Clift*. Prod *H. Fraser Passmore*. PC *Hammer*. Dis *General Film Distributors. 80 mins. Cert A*

1872: a ship is sighted in the Atlantic with sails set, a prepared and untouched meal in the cabin and no sign of the crew. It turns out to be the revenge of Anton Lorenzon (*Bela Lu-*

gosi), a bosun shanghaied six years before and ill-treated by the brutal first mate (*Edmund Willard*) and crew. Now he dispatches everyone one by one before drowning himself. Ingenious if scarcely credible solution to a famous true-life mystery of the sea.

RoC *Arthur Margetson, Shirley Grey, Ben Welden, Dennis Hoey, Clifford McLaglen, Gibson Gowland, George Mozart, James Carew, Terence de Marney, Ben Soutten, Gunner Moir, Johnnie Schofield, D.J. Williams, Herbert Cameron, Bruve Gordon, Edgar Pierce, J.B. Williams, Charles Mortimer, Wilfred Essex, Alec Fraser, Monti de Lyle*.

MY WIFE'S FAMILY (1931)   2

Dir *Monty Banks*. Prod *John Maxwell*. Scr *Fred Duprez, Val Valentine, from a play by Duprez, Hal Stephens and Harry B. Linton*. Ph *Claude Friese-Greene*. PC *BIP*. Dis *Wardour. 80 mins. Cert A*

Debonair *Gene Gerrard* hadn't really got into his stride as a film star when he made this supremely daft comedy about confusions between a piano and a baby (both are hidden in a summerhouse).

RoC *Muriel Angelus, Jimmy Godden, Dodo Watts, Tom Helmore, Molly Lamont, Amy Veness, Charles Paton, Ellen Pollock*.

N

NAUGHTY CINDERELLA (1933)   2

Dir *John Daumery*. Prod *Irving Asher*. Scr *Randall Faye*. PC and Dis *Warner Bros. 56 mins. Cert U*

Another film in the short-lived British career of impish Danish star *Winna Winifried* who never got the material she deserved. Here she plays a schoolgirl in love with her guardian and, when they meet after some years apart, fools him by posing both as an awkward schoolgirl and a sophisticated young lady. He falls for her attractive self and they marry.

RoC *John Stuart, Betty Huntley Wright, Marion Gerth, Marie Wright, Victor Fairley, Catherine Watts*.

NELL GWYN (1934)   5

Dir and Prod *Herbert Wilcox*. Scr *Miles Malleson*. Ph *Frederick A. Young*. PC *British and Dominions*. Dis *United Artists. 85 mins. Cert A*

Well-produced slice of history, a popular vehicle for *Anna Neagle* as the actress whose wiles ensnare the reigning monarch of England, King Charles II (*Cedric Hardwicke*). Not even the schemes of the jealous Duchess of Portsmouth (*Jeanne de Casalis*) can remove Nell from the 'position' of unofficial queen, which she holds until the king dies.

RoC *Muriel George, Esmé Percy, Moore Marriott, Miles Malleson, Lawrence Anderson, Craighall Sherry, Helena Pickard, Dorothy Robinson, Julie Suedo*.

Cedric Hardwicke and Anna Neagle in Nell Gwyn (*1934*)

NEVER TROUBLE TROUBLE (1931) [2]

Dir, Prod and PC *Lupino Lane.* Scr *George Dewhurst.* Dis *Producers' Distributing Corporation.* 75 mins. Cert U

Lupino Lane comedy with a theme that would be re-worked many times by other comedians: a man arranges for his own assassination, only to find that he has inherited a fortune. Now he must find the assassin and stop him carrying out his mission.

RoC *Renee Clama, Jack Hobbs, Wallace Lupino, Iris Ashley, Dennis Hoey, Wally Patch, Lola Hunt, Barry Lupino, George Dewhurst, Tom Shale, Merle Oberon.*

THE NEW HOTEL (1932) [3]

Dir and Prod *Bernard Mainwaring.* Scr *Uncredited.* PC and Dis *Producers' Distributing Corporation.* 50 mins. Cert U

Pocket-sized musical revue against the background of the opening of a sumptuous new hotel. On the night it opens a man is 'vamped' out of his money, and a drunken resident of the hotel becomes the victim of blackmail.

LP *Norman Long, Dan Young, Hal Gordon, Mickey Brantford, Blanche Adele, Alfred Wellesley, Basil Howes, Betty Norton, Hamilton Keene, Kinsley Lark, Ruth Taylor, Bert Weston, Gilly Flower, Lindy Jeune, Frank Adey, Noel Dainton, James Croome, Myno Burnet, Percy Val, Al Davison and His Band, Barbara Dean's Girls.*

NIGHT ALONE (1938) [3]

Dir *Thomas Bentley.* Prod *Warwick Ward.* Scr *Victor Kendall, Vernon Clancy, from the play by Jeffrey Dell.* Ph *Bryan Langley.* PC *Welwyn.* Dis *Pathé.* 76 mins. Cert A

Charles (*Emlyn Williams*), a provincial solicitor, gets drunk on a night out in London, and is carried back to a girl's flat. She (*Julie Suedo*) turns out to be the accomplice of a notorious crook, and Charles is arrested. After a night in the cells, he just makes it back to his hotel before his wife (*Lesley Brook*), but then the police take him away again and he has to clear the whole mess up. Comedy is sometimes amusing but never escapes its stage origins.

RoC *Cyril Raymond, Leonora Corbett, Margot Landa, John Turnbull, Wally Patch, Basil Cunard, Joseph Cunningham, James Pirrie.*

NIGHT BIRDS (1930) [3]

Dir and Prod *Richard Eichberg.* Scr *Miles Malleson.* PC *BIP.* Dis *Wardour.* 97 mins. Cert A

Rough-and-ready but fast-moving murder story set in a nighclub where one of the customers is found poisoned. The detective in charge (*Jack Raine*) has to avoid the attentions of a mysterious knife-throwing killer before trapping the murderer – the owner of the club. RoC *Muriel Angelus, Jameson Thomas, Eve Gray, Franklyn Bellamy, Garry Marsh, D. Hay Petrie, Frank Perfitt, Harry Terry, Ellen Pollock, Margaret Yarde, Cyril Butcher, Barbara Kilner.*

Muriel Angelus and Garry Marsh in Night Birds (*1930*)

NIGHT CLUB QUEEN (1934) [4]

Dir *Bernard Vorhaus.* Prod *Julius Hagen.* Scr *H. Fowler Mear, from a play by Anthony Kimmins.* PC *Real Art.* Dis *Universal.* 88 mins. Cert A

Strong stuff about Mary Brown (*Mary Clare*) who, to keep her son at university, establishes a tea-shop without the knowledge of her crippled solicitor husband (*Lewis Casson*). The business fails, and her new partner Hale (*George Carney*) persuades her to turn it into an illicit nightclub. A police raid looms, the partners quarrel, Hale is killed, and Mary ends up being defended by her husband on a murder charge.

RoC *Jane Carr, Lewis Shaw, Marle Tottenham, Drusilla Wills, Syd Crossley, Felix Aylmer, The Eight Black Streaks, The Sherman Fisher Girls.*

A NIGHT IN MONTMARTRE (1931) [1]

Dir *Leslie Hiscott.* Prod *Michael Balcon.* Scr *Angus Macphail, from a play by Miles Malleson and Walter Peacock.* PC and Dis *Gaumont.* 70 mins. Cert A

Feeble romantic thriller which kills off its villain half-way through. A young couple who live over a Paris café owned by a notorious blackmailer come under suspicion when he is murdered, but the boy's father (*Horace Hodges*), an amateur detective, proves that the crime was committed by two waiters who worked for the dead man.

RoC *Hugh Williams, Heather Angel, Franklin Dyall, Austin Trevor, Kay Hammond, Edmund Willard, Arthur Hambling, Binnie Barnes, Reginald Purdell, John Deverell, Charles Costello.*

NIGHT JOURNEY (1938) [2]

Dir *Oswald Mitchell.* Prod *John Corfield.* Scr *Jim Phelan, Maisie Sherman, from Phelan's novel* Ten-a-Penny People. Ph *Geoffrey Faithfull.* PC *British National.* Dis *Butchers.* 76 mins. Cert A

Lorry-driver Johnny (*Geoffrey Toone*) gets a job transporting high explosives, while his girlfriend Mary (*Patricia Hilliard*) becomes involved with a gang dealing in stolen furs. It ends with the hero rescuing the girl, while the crooks and furs are blown to kingdom come. Climax is too late to relieve long, slow journey. RoC *Edward Lexy, Alf Goddard, Ronald Ritchie, Zillah Bateman, Charles Farrell, Richard Norris, Phyllis Morris, Johnnie Schofield, Charles Groves, Yolande Terrell, Douglas Stewart, George Street.*

A NIGHT LIKE THIS (1932) [5]

Dir *Tom Walls.* Prod *Herbert Wilcox.* Scr *W.P. Lipscomb, Walls, Ben Travers, from the play by Travers.* Ph *F. A. Young.* PC *British and Dominions.* Dis *W and F.* 72 mins. Cert U

Clifford Tope (*Ralph Lynn*), a man-about-town, is enamoured of a nightclub dancer (*Winifred Shotter*) who is being blackmailed by the club owner over a borrowed necklace. Irish policeman Michael Mahoney (*Tom Walls*) joins forces with Tope, retrieving the necklace and seeing the villain gets his deserts. Uproarious comedy with the Aldwych gang in full cry.

RoC *Robertson Hare, Mary Brough, Claude Hulbert, Boris Ranevsky, C.V. France, Norma Varden, Joan Brierley, Kay Hammond.*

Mary Brough and Winifred Shotter in A Night Like This (*1932*)

NIGHT MAIL (1935) [3]

Dir and Prod *Herbert Smith.* Scr *Charles Bennett, Billie Bristow.* PC *British Lion.* Dis *M-G-M.* 53 mins. Cert A

Fevered, not to say unlikely thriller set aboard the night mail train from London to Aberdeen. A mad violinist (*Henry Oscar*) tries to murder the judge (*C. M. Hallard*) who denied him divorce, but is thwarted by his own wife's lover. Assortment of interesting characters just about keeps this night train going.

RoC *Hope Davy, Garry Marsh, Jane Carr, Frank Atkinson, Doris Hare, (Wilfrid) Hyde White, Edmond Breon, Tonie Edgar Bruce, Viola Lyel, Richard Bird.*

NIGHT OF THE GARTER (1933) [4]

Dir *Jack Raymond*. Prod *Herbert Wilcox*. Scr *Austin Melford, Marjorie Gaffney* (uncredited), *from a play by Avery Hopwood, Wilson Collison*. Ph *F. A. Young*. PC *British and Dominions*. Dis *United Artists*. 86 mins. Cert U

Fast-moving, pretty funny version of the stage farce *Getting Gertie's Garter*, with *Winifred Shotter* as the bride-to-be who finds returning a jewelled garter to the former admirer whose picture is in it, to be far from easy.

RoC *Sydney Howard, Harold French, Jack Melford, Elsie Randolph, Austin Melford, Connie Ediss, Marjorie Brooks, Arthur Chesney*.

THE NIGHT OF THE PARTY (1934) [3]

Dir *Michael Powell*. Prod *Jerome Jackson*. Scr *Ralph Smart, from the play by Roland Pertwee and John Hastings Turner*. Ph *Geoffrey Faithfull*. PC and Dis *Gaumont-British*. 62 mins. Cert A

A ruthless, callous newspaper proprietor (*Malcolm Keen*) is killed at one of his own parties, where virtually every guest had good reason to want him dead. Skilled direction fights a gallant battle against poor material.

RoC *Leslie Banks, Ian Hunter, Jane Baxter, Ernest Thesiger, Viola Keats, Jane Millican, Muriel Aked, John Turnbull, Laurence Anderson, W. Graham Browne*.

THE NIGHT PORTER (1930) [3]

Dir *Sewell Collins*. Prod *L'Estrange Fawcett*. Scr *Collins, Fawcett, from a play by Harry Wall*. PC *Gaumont*. Dis *Ideal*. 45 mins. Cert U

Short-length comedy about a dim-witted hotel porter (*Donald Calthrop*) who becomes suspicious of a couple who arrive late at night, his suspicions being prompted – and stimulated – by the prospect of a reward, being offered for the arrest of a much-wanted thief. He's proved to be wrong, of course ... but not before confusion has reigned.

RoC *Trilby Clark, Gerald Rawlinson, Barbara Gott, Tom Shale*.

NIGHT RIDE (1937) [2]

Dir *John Paddy Carstairs*. Prod *Anthony Havelock-Allan*. Scr *Ralph Gilbert Bettinson*. Ph *Francis Carver*. PC and Dis *British and Dominions/Paramount British*. 70 mins. Cert U

Sacked by their shady employer, two lorry drivers find financial backing to form a trucking company of their own. But their former boss gets his daughter (*Elizabeth Kent*) to seduce the younger driver (*Jimmy Hanley*) into neglecting his work. This, together with some foul play by hired thugs, almost ruins the newly independents. But they seize their opportunity to make good when they answer an urgent call to a flooded mine. Saggy drama.

RoC *Julien Vedey, Wally Patch, Joan Ponsford, Frank Petley, Clelia Matania, Moore Marriott, Kenneth Buckley, Blake Dorn*.

NIGHT SHADOWS/A NIGHT IN MARSEILLES (1931)

Dir *Albert de Courville*. Prod *Archibald Nettlefold*. Scr *Frank Launder, from the French Grand Guignol play* The Last Tango. PC and Dis *Fox-British*. 45 mins. No certificate issued

The censor's refusal to pass this squalid crime yarn recounted by a Marseilles sailor and set in a waterfront café-cum-brothel was the death knell to the star career in films of silent leading lady *Estelle Brody*, who made no further films for two decades. The screenplay was credited to H. Fowler Mear, but in fact 'ghosted' for him by Frank Launder. (No rating.)

RoC *William Freshman, Ethel Warwick, Pat Paterson*.

NINE FORTY-FIVE (1934) [2]

Dir *George King*. Prod *Irving Asher*. Scr *Brock Williams, from a play by Owen Davis, Sewell Collins*. PC and Dis *Warner Bros*. 59 mins. Cert A

Familiar sort of murder mystery in which an inspector (*George Merritt*) and the local doctor (*Donald Calthrop*) investigate the death of a much-hated man. Three of the suspects actually confess to the 'crime' – all, as it turns out, to protect others – before the investigators eventually prove it to have been suicide.

RoC *Binnie Barnes, Violet Farebrother, Malcolm Tod, Cecil Parker, James Finlayson, Ellis Irving, Janice Adair, Margaret Yarde, René Ray*.

NINE TILL SIX (1932) [4]

Dir and Prod *Basil Dean*. Scr *Beverley Nicholls, Alma Reville, John Paddy Carstairs*. Ph *Bob Martin, Robert de Grasse*. PC *Associated Talking Pictures*. Dis *Radio*. 75 mins. Cert A

Episodic romantic drama about the lives of those who work in a fashionable dressmaker's shop. The main storyline concerns the dressmaker (*Louise Hampton*) herself, when she borrows one of her dresses to go to a swish dance with a nobleman, then finds herself accused of having stolen it.

RoC *Elizabeth Allan, Florence Desmond, Isla Bevan, Richard Bird, Kay Hammond, Sunday Wilshin, Moore Marriott, Jeanne de Casalis, Frances Doble, Alison Leggatt, George de Warfaz, Hilda Simms*.

NO ESCAPE (1934) [4]

Dir *Ralph Ince*. Prod *Irving Asher*. Scr *W. Scott Darling*. PC and Dis *Warner Bros*. 71 mins. Cert A

Unusual thriller about a rubber planter in Malaya, Jim (*Ian Hunter*), who spurns the advances of his partner's wife (*Binnie Barnes*). She tries to poison him, but kills her husband instead, ensuring, however, that Jim is arrested for murder. He escapes and flees to England where he is found to be a carrier of bubonic plague, of which the woman dies, confessing her crimes.

RoC *Molly Lamont, Ralph Ince, Charles Carson, Philip Strange, Madeleine Seymour, George Merritt*.

NO ESCAPE/NO EXIT (1936) [3]

Dir *Norman Lee*. Scr *George Goodchild, Frank Witty, from their play* No Exit. PC *Welwyn*. Dis *Pathé*. 80 mins. Cert A

A detective story writer, Wild (*Leslie Perrins*), makes a wager that he can hide a man from the police for a month without him being dis-

covered. Then the man, West (*Billy Milton*) is shot near Wild's country cottage, and the writer is suspected. The killer is Anstey (*Henry Oscar*), husband of Wild's mistress, Laura (*Valerie Hobson*). He had shot West thinking he was Laura's lover – and is now himself shot by the police. Wild emerges a sadder and wiser man. Thriller is slow to start, becomes engrossing later.

RoC *Robert Cochran, Ronald Simpson, Margaret Yarde, Hal Gordon*.

NO EXIT (1930) [3]

Dir, Prod and Scr *Charles Saunders*. Ph *Bryan Langley*. PC and Dis *Warner Bros*. 69 mins. Cert U

Lightweight romantic comedy about a penniless writer (*John Stuart*), mistaken by a publisher's daughter (*Muriel Angelus*) for a famous novelist. Romance and complications blossom, but with no problems for the publisher, who has realized all along that the famous, pseudonymous novelist was his wife.

RoC *James Fenton, Janet Alexander, John Rowal*.

NO FUNNY BUSINESS (1933) [3]

Dir *John Stafford, Victor Hanbury*. Prod *Stafford*. Scr *Hanbury, Frank Vosper*. Ph *Walter Blakeley*. PC *Stafford*. Dis *United Artists*. 76 mins. Cert A

Through a misunderstanding, professional co-respondents Anne and Clive (*Jill Esmond, Laurence Olivier* – then married in real life) think each other are clients seeking a divorce. They are mutually attracted and, after complications, the real husband and wife (*Edmond Breon, Gertrude Lawrence*) are reconciled, while the 'co-respondents' become engaged. Music: *Noel Gay*.

RoC *Gibb McLaughlin, Muriel Aked*.

NO LADY (1931) [4]

Dir *Lupino Lane*. Prod *L'Estrange Fawcett*. Scr *George Dewhurst*. Ph *Percy Strong*. PC and Dis *Gaumont*. 72 mins. Cert U

Lupino Lane comedy vehicle which made up in pace and get-up-and-go what it lacked in subtlety. He plays henpecked Mr Pog, who takes his wife and stepchildren to Blackpool on holiday. He is mistaken for an international criminal mastermind and drawn into a series of adventures that climaxes in a glider race which a foreign power aims to win by fair means or foul.

RoC *Renée Clama, Sari Maritza, Lola Hunt, Cyril McLaglen, Wallace Lupino, Charles Stone, Roy Carey, Eddie Jay, Sam Lee, Denis O'Neil, Herman Darewski and the Blackpool Tower Band*.

NO LIMIT (1935) [4]

Dir *Monty Banks*. Prod *Basil Dean*. Scr *Tom Geraghty, Fred Thompson*. Ph *Bob Martin*. PC *ATP*. Dis *Associated British*. 80 mins. Cert U

George Formby's first big studio comedy casts him as a chimney sweep's help who borrows the money to go to the Isle of Man and enter his home-made motorcycle in the famous TT races. Through a brake failure, he cracks the lap record and becomes favourite. Bribed not

George Formby in No Limit (*1935*)

to ride by rivals, he is 're-bribed' by his girl-friend's firm to ride in their colours. He wins. Songs include *Riding at the TT Races*. Breezy comedy, a big popular hit.

RoC *Florence Desmond, Edward Rigby, Jack Hobbs, Peter Gawthorne, Alf Goddard, Beatrix Fielden-Kaye, Howard Douglas, Eve Lister, Florence Gregson, Evelyn Roberts, Ernest Sefton, Arthur Young.*

NO MONKEY BUSINESS (1935)   3

Dir *Marcel Varnel.* Prod *Julius Haemann.* Scr *Roger Burford, Val Guest.* Ph *Claude Friese-Greene.* PC *Radius.* Dis *General Film Distributors.* 78 mins. Cert U

Some achingly funny moments almost over-come the basic absurdity of a man posing as an ape in this *Gene Gerrard* comedy about an anthropologist who is supposedly fooled by the masquerade.

RoC *June Clyde, Renée Houston, Richard Hearne, Claude Dampier, Hugh Wakefield, Peter Haddon, Fred Duprez, Clifford Heatherley, O.B. Clarence, Alexander Field, Robert Nainby, Charles Paton, Hal Gordon.*

NON-STOP NEW YORK (1937)   5

Dir *Robert Stevenson.* Prod *Michael Balcon.* Scr *Kurt Siodmak, Roland Pertwee, J.O.C. Orton, Derek Twist, from a novel by Ken Atti-will.* Ph *Glen MacWilliams.* PC *Gaumont-British.* Dis *General Film Distributors.* 72 mins. Cert A

English dancer Jennie Carr (*Anna Lee*) wit-nesses a gangland murder in New York and is framed for theft by the killer so that she will be sent to prison in England. Released, she learns her evidence could save an innocent man. When police refuse to believe her, she stows away on a transatlantic airliner. Inspec-tor Grant (*John Loder*) and the killer, Brandt (*Francis L. Sullivan*) are both on board. Brandt kills a man who is trying to blackmail him, nearly wrecks the plane and is himself killed. Ingenious thriller moves at a tremendous pace, is full of sharp character roles.

RoC *Frank Cellier, Desmond Tester, William Dewhurst, James Pirrie, Drusilla Wills, Jerry Verno, Athene Seyler, Ellen Pollock, Arthur Goullet, Peter Bull, Tony Quinn, Danny Green, Bryan Herbert, Tom Scott, Aubrey Pollock, Sam Wilkinson, Atholl Fleming, Alf Goddard, H.G. Stoker, Jack Lester, Hal Walters, Albert Chevalier, Phyllis Morris, Andrea Malandrinos,* *Roy Smith, Billy Watts, Frederick Piper, Edward Ryan, Percy Parsons, Alexander Sarner.*

NO PARKING (1938)   4

Dir *Jack Raymond.* Prod and PC *Herbert Wilcox.* Scr *Gerald Elliott, from a story by Carol Reed.* Ph *Francis Carver.* Dis *British Lion.* 73 mins. Cert A

Albert (*Gordon Harker*), a down-and-out with ambitions to be a car park attendant, finds a letter of introduction to Captain Sneyd (*Leslie Perrins*) who proves to be a jewel thief and believes Albert to be an American gunman. Albert survives a 'trial run' to the big job Sneyd requires of him (the theft of a new in-vention) when the real gunman turns up. Al-bert looks to be in trouble, but the lights go out, police are everywhere and Albert turns out to be an ace CID undercover man. Extra-ordinary denouement to cheerful comedy.

RoC *Irene Ware, Cyril Smith, Charles Carson, Fred Groves, George Hayes, Frank Stanmore, Blake Dorn, Alfred Atkins, George Merritt, Geraldo and His Orchestra.*

NOTHING LIKE PUBLICITY (1936)   2

Dir *Maclean Rogers.* Prod *A. George Smith.* Scr *Kathleen Butler, H.F. Maltby.* Ph *Geoffrey Faithfull.* PC *GS Enterprises.* Dis *Radio.* 64 mins. Cert U

Pedestrian comedy about a go-getting press agent (*Billy Hartnell*) who tries to build a struggling music-hall actress up into a star by first of all pretending she's an American heir-ess. Unfortunately, a lady crook is around also posing as the same heiress and, to make mat-ters worse for him, the real heiress turns up.

RoC *Marjorie Taylor, Moira Lynd, Ruby Miller, Max Adrian, Isobel Scaife, Gordon McLeod, Dorothy Hammond, Aubrey Mallalieu, Michael Ripper.*

NOT SO DUSTY (1936)   4

Dir *P. Maclean Rogers.* Prod *A. George Smith.* Scr *Kathleen Butler, H.F. Maltby, Wally Patch, Frank Atkinson.* Ph *Geoffrey Faithfull.* PC *GS Enterprises/Bow Bells Films.* Dis *Radio.* 69 mins. Cert U

Cheerful Cockney comedy about two dustmen (*Wally Patch, Gus McNaughton*) who find a valuable first edition among books thrown out as rubbish. When news gets around, several people are eager to get their hands on the book. A fake copy of the book provides for some complicated misadventures before the two 'dusties' get their rightful reward.

RoC *Muriel George, Philip Ray, Johnny Singer, Isobel Scaife, Ethel Griffies, H.F. Maltby, Raymond Lovell, Nancy Pawley, Heather White, Leonard Bullen, Aubrey Mallalieu.*

NOT SO QUIET ON THE WESTERN FRONT (1930)   3

Dir *Monty Banks.* Scr *Victor Kendall.* Ph *James Rogers.* PC *BIP.* Dis *Wardour.* 50 mins. Cert U

More frantic antics with *Leslie Fuller*, this time with music and songs thrown in, in the story of a riotous night at a French café during the First World War, with a framing story show-ing the principal characters as they are in civvy street some time after the war. Not for sophis-ticates.

RoC *Mona Goya, Wilfred Temple, Stella Browne, Gladys Cruickshank, Gerard Lyley, Dmitri Vetter, Syd Courtenay, Frank Melroyd, Marjorie Loring, Olivette.*

NOT WANTED ON VOYAGE (1936)   3
(USA: *Treachery on the High Seas*)

Dir *Emil E. Reinert.* Prod *Alexandre de Lasta.* Scr *Harold Simpson, Charles Lincoln, from a play by Maurice Messenger.* PC *Dela Films.* Dis *British Lion.* 72 mins. Cert A

Singer May Hunter (*Bebe Daniels*) and rack-eteer Johnny Hammond (*Ben Lyon*) are both after a ruby necklace on board a transatlantic liner. May attracts the collector bringing the gems to England and steals them. Her mur-derous partner Logan (*Charles Farrell*) steals fake rubies from the collector's cabin. May and Johnny abscond with each other while Logan goes to jail. Stars work hard with familiar material.

RoC *Tom Helmore, Hay Petrie, Gordon McLeod, James Carew.*

NUMBER PLEASE! (1931)   2

Dir *George King.* Prod *Harry Cohen.* Scr *H. Fowler Mear.* PC *George King.* Dis *Fox.* 4. mins. Cert A

Quota quickie with fading star *Mabel Poulton* as a hotel telephonist who quarrels with her boyfriend (*Richard Bird*) and accepts a dinner invitation from a suave hotel guest (*Warwick Ward*) who turns out to be a criminal wanted for forgery and attempted murder. Eventually her boyfriend rescues her from her foolish es-capade.

RoC *Frank Perfitt, Iris Darbyshire, Gladys Hamer, Norman Pierce.*

NUMBER SEVENTEEN (1932)   4

Dir *Alfred Hitchcock.* Prod *John Maxwell.* Scr *Hitchcock, Alma Reville, Rodney Ackland, from a play by J. Jefferson Farjeon.* Ph *Jack Cox, Bryan Langley.* PC *Wardour.* 64 mins. Cert U

Lightweight Hitchcock thriller with a brilliant chase sequence. A detective (*John Stuart*) be-lieves an empty house near a railway depot is the hideout of jewel thieves. There he finds a tramp named Ben (*Leon M. Lion*) who, with a girl gang member who falls for the detective,

John Stuart and Anne Grey in Number Sev-enteen (*1932*)

brings the crooks to justice after a sustained race between a bus and a train.
RoC *Anne Grey, Garry Marsh, Donald Calthrop, Ann Casson, Barry Jones, Henry Caine, Herbert Langley.*

THE NURSEMAID WHO DISAPPEARED (1939) [4]
Dir *Arthur B. Woods.* Prod *Jerome Jackson.* Scr *Paul Gangelin, Connery Chappell, from the novel by Philip Macdonald.* Ph *Basil Emmott.* PC and Dis *Warner Bros. 86 mins. Cert A*
After overhearing a sinister conversation, a playwright (*Peter Coke*), with the aid of a detective (*Arthur Margetson*), discovers a kidnap ring. Its headquarters is a bogus employment agency which runs a sideline in blackmail by placing its members in service to spy on their employers. Two attempts on the playwright's life, the suicide of a victim and the murder of another occur before the gang can be rounded up. Talky but still suspenseful thriller.
RoC *Lesley Brook, Edward Chapman, Coral Browne, Joyce Kennedy, Dorice Fordred, Martita Hunt, Marion Gerth, Ian Maclean, Ian Fleming, Eliot Makeham, Scott Harold, Phil Ray, Mavis Villiers.*

THE OFFICERS' MESS (1931) [2]
Dir *Manning Haynes.* Prod and PC *Harry Rowson.* Scr *Douglas Hoare, Eliot Stannard, from a play by Hoare and Sidney Blow.* Dis *Paramount. 98 mins. Cert U*
Comedy about an actress (*Elsa Lanchester*) who masquerades as a naval officer's wife in order to arouse the jealousy of his friend, with whom she is in love. Further complications arise when the actress' jewels disappear. . . .
RoC *Richard Cooper, Harold French, Mary Newland, Max Avieson, Helen Haye, George Bellamy, Margery Binner, Annie Esmond, Fewlass Llewellyn, Faith Bennett, Gordon Begg.*

Mary Newland and Richard Cooper in The Officers' Mess *(1931)*

OFF THE DOLE (1935) [3]
Dir *Arthur Mertz.* Prod *John E. Blakely.* Scr *Mertz, George Formby.* PC and Dis *Mancunian. 89 mins. Cert A*
George Formby's second and last Manchester-based comedy before he moved down south to bigger things. He plays John Willie, who makes a living queueing for his dole money, until he inherits his late uncle's investigative agency. As a detective, John Willie's a disaster, but after several misadventures, he manages to net a big local crook (*Clifford McLaglen*) the police have been after for years.
RoC *Beryl (Formby), Constance Shotter, Tully Comber, Dan Young, Wally Patch, James Plant, Stan Pell, Stan Little, The Twilight Blondes, Arthur L. Ward and His Band, The Boy Choristers, The London Babes.*

OH BOY! (1938) [1]
Dir *Albert de Courville.* Prod *Walter C. Mycroft.* Scr *Dudley Leslie.* PC and Dis *Associated British. 73 mins. Cert U*
Percy Flower (*Albert Burdon*), a chemist, takes a potion which he expects to turn him into a caveman lover. Instead, it takes him back to babyhood. While apparently a harmless tot, he overhears three American crooks planning to steal the Crown Jewels. Consequently, on regaining his adult form, he is able to foil their plans. Laughless comedy.
RoC *Mary Lawson, Bernard Nedell, Robert Cochran, Edmon Ryan, Maire O'Neill, Syd Walker, Charles Carson, Jerry Verno, John Wood, Billy Milton, Boris Ranevsky, Edmund Dalby.*

OH DADDY! (1935) [3]
Dir *Graham Cutts, Austin Melford.* Prod *Michael Balcon.* Scr *Melford, from his play.* PC *Gainsborough.* Dis *Gaumont-British. 77 mins. Cert A*
Theatrical but fast-moving comedy in which members of a Purity League miss their connection and put up at a London hotel. Their chairman, Lord Pye (*Leslie Henson*), is attracted to showgirl Benita (*Frances Day*), who proves to be the stepdaughter he had never seen and leads the League members on a wild night on the town which changes Lord Pye's views on life.
RoC *Robertson Hare, Barry Mackay, Marie Lohr, Alfred Drayton, Tony de Lungo, Daphne Courtney.*

OH, MR PORTER! (1937) [5]
Dir *Marcel Varnel.* Prod *Edward Black.* Scr *Marriot Edgar, Val Guest, J.O.C. Orton.* Ph *Arthur Crabtree.* PC *Gainsborough.* Dis *General Film Distributors. 84 mins. Cert U*
Through the offices of his influential brother-in-law, incompetent railway worker William Porter (*Will Hay*) is appointed as stationmaster to the rundown halt of Buggleskelly on the Northern Ireland-Irish Free State borders. He is driven to distraction by his two co-'workers' (*Moore Marriott* and *Graham Moffatt*) and eventually becomes involved with a gang of gun-runners. Classic comedy, full of funny things and sustained through to the end.

RoC *Sebastian Smith, Agnes Laughlan, Dennis Wyndham, Percy Walsh, Dave O'Toole, Frederick Piper.*

Will Hay (holding piglet) in Oh, Mr Porter! *(1937)*

O.H.M.S. (1936) [4]
(USA: *You're in the Army Now*)
Dir and Prod *Raoul Walsh.* Scr *Bryan Edgar Wallace, Austin Melford, A.R. Rawlinson.* Ph *Roy Kellino.* PC and Dis *Gaumont-British. 86 mins. Cert U*
Hunted for a murder he didn't commit, small-time New York racketeer Jimmy (*Wallace Ford*) flees to England where he ends up in the army. He and Bert (*John Mills*) become rivals for sergeant's daughter Sally (*Anna Lee*) – then the regiment is posted to China to fight marauding bandits. The American proves himself a hero in action – but dies saving others, including Sally. Flag-waving action adventure well up to Hollywood standards.
RoC *Frank Cellier, Grace Bradley, Frederick Leister, Lawrence Anderson, Athol Fleming, Cyril Smith, Peter Evan Thomas, Arnold Bell, William Dewhurst, Peter Croft, Arthur Chesney, Leslie Roberts, Vi Wallace, Eileen Cochrane.*

OH, NO, DOCTOR! (1934) [2]
Dir, Prod, Scr and PC *George King.* Dis *M-G-M. 62 mins. Cert A*
Haunted-house comedy: in order to carry on working on his invention, mad Dr Morrow (*Cecil Humphreys*) has been dipping into the wealth of his ward Josephine (*Dorothy Boyd*). He has to try and prevent her from marrying playwright Montague (*Jack Hobbs*) and one night tries unsuccessfully to scare him to death.
RoC *James Finlayson, Peggy Novak, Jane Carr, Abraham Sofaer, David Wilton.*

OH! WHAT A DUCHESS (1933) [1]
Dir *Lupino Lane.* Prod *Walter C. Mycroft.* Scr *Con West, Herbert Sargent.* PC *BIP.* Dis *Pathé. 66 mins. Cert U*
Rather outmoded farcical comedy, actually an extension of *Fred Karno*'s old music-hall sketch *Mumming Birds*, designed to show off *George Lacy*'s talent for female impersonation, here as a stage manager, Irving, who is forced to pose as a dowager duchess to impress a film producer.
RoC *Betty (Ann) Davies, Dennis Hoey, Fred Duprez, Renee Macready, Florence Vie, Hugh E. Wright, Pat Aherne.*

OH, WHAT A NIGHT! (1935) [1]

Dir *Frank Richardson*. Prod *Edward G. Whiting*. Scr *Ernest Denny, from his play* The Irresistible Marmaduke. PC *British Sound*. Dis *Universal. 58 mins. Cert A*

Clumsy comedy about an amnesiac persuaded that he is a missing man by the latter's relatives to ensure the vanished one (who was off getting married) being set up in business.
LP *Molly Lamont, James Carew, Valerie Hobson, Martin Walker, Nina Boucicault, Roland Culver, Kathleen Kelly, Ernest Stidwell, Stanella Perry.*

O KAY FOR SOUND (1937) [4]

Dir *Marcel Varnel*. Prod *Edward Black*. Scr *Marriott Edgar, Val Guest*. Ph *Jack Cox*. PC *Gainsborough*. Dis *General Film Distributors. 85 mins. Cert A*

Six street musicians (The Crazy Gang: *Bud Flanagan and Chesney Allen, Jimmy Nervo and Teddy Knox, Charlie Naughton and Jimmy Gold*) are spotted by a film producer and given jobs as extras in a film. Arriving in costume - bowler hats and pinstripes - they are mistaken for financiers expected at the same time, and given complete control of the studio. Utter chaos ensues. The film contains most of the Gang's best routines from the original stage show, and is pretty funny in parts. Said one reviewer: 'If you miss this, you'll be the one who's crazy.'
RoC *Enid Stamp-Taylor, Fred Duprez, Graham Moffatt, Meinhart Maur, H.F. Maltby, Patricia Bowman, Peter Dawson, Jan Gotch and Louis Pergantes, Lucienne and Ashour, The Radio Three, The Robenis, The Sherman Fisher Girls.*

Jimmy Nervo and Charlie Naughton in O Kay for Sound *(1937)*

OLD BONES OF THE RIVER (1938) [4]

Dir *Marcel Varnel*. Prod *Edward Black*. Scr *Marriott Edgar, Val Guest, J.O.C. Orton, from books by Edgar Wallace*. Ph *Arthur Crabtree*. PC *Gainsborough*. Dis *General Film Distributors. 90 mins. Cert U*

Professor Benjamin Tibbetts (*Will Hay*) comes up the river in Africa to open schools for the natives. Commissioner Sanders is just leaving and when his deputy goes down with malaria, Tibbetts is left to collect the local taxes. Abetted by the crew (*Graham Moffatt, Moore Marriott*), he manages to stir the situation up to a full-scale native revolt and barely escapes with his life. Scandalous sideshoot from *Sanders of the River* gets funnier all the time.
RoC *Robert Adams, Jack Livesey, Jack London, Wyndham Goldie, The Western Brothers* (narrators).

THE OLD CURIOSITY SHOP (1934) [3]

Dir *Thomas Bentley*. Prod *Walter C. Mycroft*. Scr *Margaret Kennedy, Ralph Neale, from the novel by Charles Dickens*. Ph *Claude Friese-Greene*. PC *BIP*. Dis *Wardour. 95 mins. Cert U*

This, always one of the Dickens novels most resistant to screen treatment, is the last of Bentley's many interpretations of the writer's books. The story, of a miserly dwarf money-lender (*Hay Petrie*) whose ruthlessness causes the deaths of Old Trent (*Ben Webster*) and Little Nell (*Elaine Benson*) who run a curiosity shop, seems slow and sentimental.
RoC *Beatrix Thompson, Gibb McLaughlin, Reginald Purdell, Polly Ward, James Harcourt, J. Fisher White, Lily Long, Roddy Hughes, Amy Veness, Peter Penrose, Dick Tubb, Wally Patch, Fred Groves, Vic Filmer.*

OLD FAITHFUL (1935) [2]

Dir *P. Maclean Rogers*. Prod *A. George Smith*. Scr *Kathleen Butler, H.F. Maltby*. PC *GS Enterprises*. Dis *Radio. 67 mins. Cert A*
Horace Hodges gives another of his likeable character studies as an old hansom cab driver who refuses to swap his horse for a new-fangled taxi. Complications arise when his daughter (*Glennis Lorimer*) falls in love with one of the hated taxi-drivers, who has to pretend to be a plumber to carry on a courtship.
RoC *Bruce Lister, Wally Patch, Isobel Scaife, Muriel George, Edward Ashley Cooper.*

OLD IRON (1938) [3]

Dir and Prod *Tom Walls*. Scr *Ben Travers*. Ph *Mutz Greenbaum*. PC *TW Productions*. Dis *British Lion. 80 mins. Cert U*
Sir Henry (*Tom Walls*), who rules his family with a rod of iron, hates the waster his daughter has married and stops her allowance. He is furious when his son Harry (*Richard Ainley*) marries Lorna (*Veronica Rose*) and kicks her father off his board of directors. Harry storms off in a rage, knocks a man down and is charged with manslaughter. The resultant trial teaches all the family a few home truths. Character drama is a change of pace for Walls and Travers, not wholly successful.
RoC *Eva Moore, Cecil Parker, Enid Stamp-Taylor, Leslie Perrins, David Tree, Arthur Wontner, Henry Hewitt, O.B. Clarence, Hubert Harben, Nancy Pawley, Frank Daly.*

THE OLD MAN (1931) [3]

Dir *Manning Haynes*. Prod *S.W. Smith*. Scr *Edgar Wallace, from his play*. PC and Dis *British Lion. 75 mins. Cert A*
Mystery about an aristocrat (*Anne Grey*) blackmailed by her house guest (*Lester Matthews*) who is stabbed to death for his pains. The charlady (*Maisie Gay*) helps reveal that the killer is the blackmailer's former associate (*D.A. Clarke-Smith*), a reformed character who returns stolen property to its owners.

RoC *Cecil Humphreys, Diana Beaumont, Gerald Rawlinson, Finlay Currie, Frank Stanmore.*

OLD MOTHER RILEY (1937) [2]

Dir *Oswald Mitchell*. Prod *Norman Hope-Bell*. Scr *Con West, John Argyle*. Ph *Jack Parker*. PC *Butchers/Hope-Bell*. Dis *Butchers. 75 mins. Cert U*
Exaggerated, stagebound farce which nonetheless set a long series of Old Mother Riley romps in motion. A 'match king' leaves his money to his family on condition they take in the first person they see selling his matches. This, of course, proves to be Mother Riley (*Arthur Lucan*), who insists on bringing her daughter (*Kitty McShane*) with her. The rich family tries everything to get rid of the unwelcome guest, but all the plans crash in ruins: Mother Riley is there to stay.
RoC *Barbara Everest, Patrick Ludlow, J. Hubert Leslie, Edith Sharpe, Syd Crossley, Edgar Driver, Dorothy Vernon, Zoë Wynn, G.H. Mulcaster, Charles Carson, Charles Paton, Charles Sewell, F.B.J. Sharp, Elma Slee, Balliol and Tiller.*

OLD MOTHER RILEY IN PARIS (1938) [4]

Dir and Prod *Oswald Mitchell*. Scr *Con West*. PC and Dis *Butchers. 76 mins. Cert U*
Kitty (*Kitty McShane*) daughter of Irish washerwoman Old Mother Riley (*Arthur Lucan*) has become engaged to Joe (*Jerry Verno*), a travel agent who is posted to Paris. With the £250 compensation she has received for breaking her leg, Mother Riley goes to Paris to keep an eye on Joe, is mistaken for a spy, ends up parachuting from a plane and is awarded a medal for counter-espionage. Hearty fun in one of the most successful Lucan and McShane comedies.
RoC *Magda Kun, (C.) Denier Warren, Stanley Vilven, George Wolkowsky, Douglas Stewart, Rex Alderman, Frank Terry, Richard Riviere, Edward Wild, Charles Castella, Harold B. Hallam.*

Arthur Lucan and George Wolkowsky in Old Mother Riley in Paris *(1938)*

OLD MOTHER RILEY JOINS UP (1939) [2]

Dir *Maclean Rogers*. Prod *John Corfield*. Scr *Jack Marks, Con West*. Ph *James Wilson*. PC *British National*. Dis *Anglo. 75 mins. Cert U*
Mother Riley (*Arthur Lucan*), a district nurse, gets mixed up in a national service demonstra-

on, finds herself in the ATS (Auxiliary Tertorial Service) and saves valuable papers from ...lling into the hands of a German spy. Rough ...nd ready farce.

...oC *Kitty McShane, Bruce Seton, Martita ...unt, H.F. Maltby, Garry Marsh, Jeanne ...tuart, Bryan Powley, Dorothy Dewhurst, Glen ...lyn.*

...LD MOTHER RILEY MP (1939) 3
...ir *Oswald Mitchell, Con West.* Ph *James Wil...n.* PC and Dis *Butchers. 77 mins. Cert U*
...other Riley (*Arthur Lucan*), a washerwoman ...cked from her laundry after a quarrel with ...e owner, a powerful landlord, is persuaded ...y some of his oppressed tenants to put up for ...arliament against him. She wins the election, ... appointed Minister for Strange Affairs and ...rces the Emperor of Rocavia to pay up a ...50,000,000 debt to Britain. Raucous farce ...ith lunatic plot.
...oC *Kitty McShane, Torin Thatcher, Henry ...onghurst, Patrick Ludlow, Dennis Wyndham, ...ynthia Stock, Rex Alderman, Kenneth Henry.*

...LD ROSES (1935) 2
...ir and Prod *Bernard Mainwaring.* Scr *An...ony Richardson.* Ph *Alex Bryce.* PC and Dis ...ox *British. 60 mins. Cert A*
...he title is the nicest thing about this not...o-convincing drama about Old Roses (*Hor...ce Hodges*) a rose-loving villager who proves ... staunch friend to two young lovers, even ...onfessing to a murder of which the young ...an is accused. Things are cleared up and the ...ld codger is able to go back to his roses.
...oC *Nancy Burne, Bruce Lister, Charles Mor...mer, Felix Aylmer, Esmé Church, Wilfrid Wal...r, Eric Portman, George Hayes, Trefor Jones, ...hilip Ray, Con Brierley, Eileen Senton.*

...LD SOLDIERS NEVER DIE (1931) 3
...ir and Prod *Monty Banks.* Scr *Val Valentine, ...yd Courtenay, Lola Harvey.* PC *BIP.* Dis ...Vardour. 58 mins. Cert U*
...ill (*Leslie Fuller*) and his pal Sam (*Max Nes...itt*) accidentally enlist in the army in 1914 and ...oon fall foul of their sergeant-major. They ...ave a tough time until they use an unexpected ...pportunity to get their enemy into hot water. ...e's reduced to the ranks while Bill is prom...ted and begins to get a bit of his own back. ...nockabout farce.
...oC *Alf Goddard, Molly Lamont, Mamie Hol...and, Wellington Briggs, Wilfred Shine, Nigel ...arrie, Harry Nesbitt, Hal Gordon.*

...LD SPANISH CUSTOMERS (1932) 3
...ir *Lupino Lane.* Prod *John Maxwell.* Scr *Syd ...ourtenay, Lola Harvey.* PC *BIP.* Dis *M-G-...M. 69 mins. Cert U*
...eslie Fuller comedy in which, in his familiar ...haracter of Bill, he wins a holiday in Spain to ...vhich he goes with his henpeck wife (*Drusilla ...Vills*). A disastrous time climaxes when Bill is ...nistaken for a famous Spanish bullfighter and ...orced to go into the arena.
...oC *Binnie Barnes, Wallace Lupino, Ernest ...efton, Hal Gordon, Syd Courtenay, Betty ...ields, Hal Walters, Lola Harvey, Allan Wood...urn.*

ON APPROVAL (1930) 5
Dir *Tom Walls.* Prod *Herbert Wilcox.* Scr *W.P. Lipscomb, from the play by Frederick Lonsdale.* Ph *F.A. Young.* PC *British and Dominions.* Dis *W and F. 98 mins. Cert A*
The 'Aldwych' farceurs in a crisp version of the smash-hit stage comedy about the stormy romance and trial marriage of an impecunious duke (*Tom Walls*, who also directed) and an eccentric millionairess (*Yvonne Arnaud*).
RoC *Robertson Hare, Mary Brough, Winifred Shotter, Edmond Breon.*

ONCE A THIEF (1935) 3
Dir *George Pearson.* Prod *Anthony Havelock-Allan.* Scr *Basil Mason.* PC and Dis *British and Dominions/Paramount British. 67 mins. Cert A*
After borrowing money from a handbag that comes into his possession, only to have a valuable necklace stolen from it by a real thief, chemist Roger Drummond (*John Stuart*) is sent to prison. While he is inside, an unscrupulous member of his firm steals his new formula for making paint. Released, Roger unmasks the culprit, and marries Marion (*Nancy Burne*), his employer's niece.
RoC *Derek Gorst, Lewis Shaw, Frederick Culley, Lola Duncan, Joan Kemp-Welch, Ronald Shiner.*

ONCE BITTEN (1932) 3
Dir *Leslie Hiscott.* Prod *Julius Hagen.* Scr *Michael Barringer, H. Fowler Mear.* PC *Real Art.* Dis *Fox. 47 mins. Cert U*
Toby (*Richard Cooper*) loses his memory after a night in which his rich father-in-law (*Frank Pettingell*) disappears after thinking he has killed the man who was blackmailing Toby. When Toby gets his memory back he is able to clear the old man, who is found working as a waiter. Doesn't sound like a comedy, but it was supposed to be.
RoC *Ursula Jeans, Dino Galvani, Jeanne Stuart, Sidney King, Antony Holles, Kathleen Kelly.*

ONCE IN A MILLION (1936) 4
(USA: *Weekend Millionaire*)
Dir *Arthur Woods.* Prod *Walter C. Mycroft.* Scr *Jack Davies, Geoffrey Kerr, Max Kester.* Ph *Ronald Neame, Ernest Steward.* PC *BIP.* Dis *Wardour. 77 mins. Cert U*
A Parisian bank clerk (*Charles 'Buddy' Rogers*) is given a vast sum of money to deposit at his bank on Saturday, but he arrives too late and has to keep the cash over the weekend. A rowdy party at his own hotel makes the money unsafe, and he hunts for a hotel with a safe deposit. He eventually finds one, but is mistaken for a millionaire. On Monday, he finds his bank has been robbed, and he earns a big reward for safeguarding the money. Bright comedy-romance owes something to René Clair's *Le million.*
RoC *Mary Brian, W.H. Berry, Billy Milton, Haver and Lee, Charles Carson, Norah Gale, Nadine March, Iris Hoey, Veronica Rose, Jimmy Godden, John Harwood, Aubrey Mallalieu, Reginald Smith.*

ONCE IN A NEW MOON (1934) 3
Dir and Scr *Anthony Kimmins, from a novel by Owen Rutter.* Prod *Uncredited.* PC and Dis *Fox British. 63 mins. Cert U*
Way-out fantasy, unusual for its time, in which an English village is hurled into space through the collision of a dead star with the Moon. The science-minded postmaster (*Eliot Makeham*) is unwillingly elected as President of the new 'country', but a government of Conservatives is set up by the nobs of the village and civil war threatens until the slice of land is returned to Earth.
RoC *René Ray, Morton Selten, Wally Patch, John Clements, Derrick de Marney, Mary Hinton, Gerald Barry, Richard Goolden, H. Saxon-Snell, John Turnbull, Cecil Landau, Ralph Howard, Vernon Kelso, Thorley Walters, Walter Roy, Charles Paton, Franklyn Kelsey, William Fazan.*

ONE GOOD TURN (1936) 2
Dir *Alfred Goulding.* Prod *Joe Rock.* Scr *Syd Courtenay, Georgie Harris, Jack Byrd.* Ph *Cyril Bristow.* PC *Leslie Fuller.* Dis *Associated British. 72 mins. Cert U*
Bill and George (*Leslie Fuller, Georgie Harris*), coffee-stall owners, have ambitions to do a comedy double-act on the halls. Their landlady's daughter (*Molly Fisher*) also has stage aspirations, and a bogus film producer persuades her mother to back a show in which she'll appear. In investigating, Bill and George become embroiled with Chinese gangsters, and are pursued round the stage by them on opening night, making the show a rip-roaring success. Unsubtle comedy.
RoC *Hal Gordon, Basil Langton, Clarissa Selwynne, Arthur Finn, Faith Bennett, Arthur Clayton, Arnold the horse.*

ONE PRECIOUS YEAR (1933) 2
Dir and Scr *Henry Edwards, from a play by E. Temple Thurston.* Prod *Herbert Wilcox.* PC *British and Dominions.* Dis *Paramount. 76 mins. Cert A*
Rather morose drama about a wife (*Anne Grey*) who, thinking she has only a year to live, and neglected by her husband, drifts into an affair with a smooth charmer (*Basil Rathbone*). The husband (*Owen Nares*) forgives her and determines to devote more time to her – then finds out that her disease is not, after all, incurable.
RoC *Flora Robson, Ben Webster, Evelyn Roberts, H.G. Stoker, Robert Horton, Olga Slade, Ronald Simpson, Jennie Robins, Violet Hopson, Western Brothers, Casa Nuova Girls.*

THE ONLY GIRL (1933) 2
(USA: *Heart Song*)
Dir *Friedrich Holländer.* Prod *Erich Pommer.* Scr *Robert Stevenson, John Heygate.* PC and Dis *UFA. 84 mins. Cert U.* Bilingual versions
Very moderate musical, actually filmed in Germany with a largely British cast. It represented another unsuccessful attempt to establish English-born *Lilian Harvey* outside the German cinema where she had made her name. She plays a hairdresser in the late nineteenth century, with whose singing voice a duke (*Charles Boyer*) falls in love.

RoC *Mady Christians, Ernest Thesiger, Maurice Evans, Friedel Schuster, Julius Falkenstein, Huntley Wright, Ruth Maitland, O. B. Clarence, Reginald Smith.*

ON SECRET SERVICE (1933)   [4]
(USA: *Secret Agent*)

Dir *Arthur Woods.* Prod *John Maxwell.* Scr *Frank Vosper, Max Kimmich, Herbert Juttke, Woods.* PC *BIP.* Dis *Wardour.* 90 *mins. Cert U*

In the First World War, an Austrian staff officer falls in love with an Italian spy. Later, when he is a counter-espionage officer, she repeatedly keeps him from arrest, before giving her life to save him; he succeeds in his mission.
LP *Greta Nissen, Carl Ludwig Diehl, Don Alvarado, Lester Matthews, Esmé Percy, C. M. Hallard, Austin Trevor, Cecil Ramage, Wallace Geoffrey.*

ON THE AIR (1933)   [3]

Dir and Prod *Herbert Smith.* Scr *Michael Barringer.* Ph *Alex Bryce.* PC and Dis *British Lion.* 79 *mins. Cert U*
Revue-style entertainment about a group of radio artists contracted to appear at a charity concert in a small village.
LP *Davy Burnaby, Reginald Purdell, Betty Astell, Anona Winn, Max Wall, Hugh E. Wright, Clapham and Dwyer, Scott and Whaley, Derek Oldham, Jane Carr, Mario de Pietro, Teddy Brown, Eve Becke, Harry Champion, Edwin Styles, Wilson, Keppel and Betty, Jimmy Jade, Roy Fox and His Band, Buddy Bradley's Rhythm Girls.*

ON THE NIGHT OF THE FIRE (1939)   [4]
(USA: *The Fugitive*)

Dir *Brian Desmond Hurst.* Prod *Josef Somlo.* Scr *Hurst, Terence Young, Patrick Kirwan, from the novel by F. L. Green.* PC *G and S Films.* Dis *General Film Distributors.* 94 *mins. Cert A*
Kobling (*Rakoh Richardson*), a barber, married to extravagant Kit (*Diana Wynyard*), steals £100. Discovering this, Kit admits she owes £75 to Pilleger (*Henry Oscar*), a draper. After the police trace the notes to Pilleger's shop, he blackmails the Koblings. On the night of a big fire nearby, Kobling kills Pilleger. He sends Kit and their baby away and goes into hiding. Police trace and surround him. Hearing Kit has been killed in a car crash, Kobling stumbles out, firing into the air, and is riddled with bullets. Grim but gripping.
RoC *Romney Brent, Mary Clare, Dave Crowley, Gertrude Musgrove, Frederick Leister, Ivan Brandt, Glynis Johns, Sara Allgood, Maire O'Neill, Mai Bacon, Phyllis Morris, Teddy Smith, Joe Mott, Joe Cunningham, Harry Terry, Irene Handl.*

ON THIN ICE (1933)   [2]

Dir and Scr *Bernard Vorhaus.* Prod *Uncredited.* Ph *Eric Cross.* PC *Hall Mark.* Dis *Equity British.* 62 *mins. Cert A*
Harry (*Kenneth Law*) is happily engaged to Lady Violet (*Ursula Jeans*), but becomes entangled with actress Mabel (*Viola Gault*) and another girl (*Dorothy Bartlam*) who claims the

first Mabel was an imposter. At length Harry realizes he is being made the dupe of crooks aiming to blackmail his rich father, and turns the tables on them. Silly thriller.
RoC *Stewart Thompson, Cameron Carr.*

ON TOP OF THE WORLD (1935)   [2]

Dir *Redd Davis.* Prod *Basil Humphrys.* Scr *Evelyn Barrie.* PC *City.* Dis *Associated Producers and Distributors.* 79 *mins. Cert U*
Doomed attempt to make a star out of Gracie Fields' younger sister *Betty.* She plays a millgirl who sells the greyhounds she has inherited from her father to make ends meet, but keeps the best, Our Betty. When the millworkers strike, she starts a food kitchen for their wives and children, into which she pours the money from Our Betty's subsequent triumph in the Greyhound Derby. Finally, she makes both sides see reason.
RoC *Frank Pettingell, Leslie Bradley, Ben Field, Charles Sewell, Wally Patch, Eileen Latham, Fewlass Llewellyn.*

ON VELVET (1938)   [1]

Dir and Prod *Widgey R. Newman.* Scr *John Quin.* PC *Associated Industries.* Dis *Columbia.* 70 *mins. Cert A*
Tedious comedy-musical about a Cockney bookmaker and a Jewish punter who sustain enormous losses at the races and, after violent quarrels with their wives, pool their remaining assets and found a TV advertising company. After a few disasters at rehearsals, their first show is brought home in triumph.
LP *Wally Patch, Joe Hayman, Vi Kaley, Mildred Franklin, Jennifer Skinner, Leslie Bradley, Nina Mae McKinney, Julie Suedo, Ambrose Day, Garland Wilson, Sidney Monckton, Olive Delmer, Bob Field, George Sims, Cleo Fauvel, Andrée Sacré, Queenie Lucy, Eric Barker, Gordon Little, Mark Stone, Collinson and Dean, Helga and Jo, Bellings' Dogs, Rex Burrows and His Orchestra, The Columbia Choir.*

OPEN ALL NIGHT (1934)   [4]

Dir *George Pearson.* Prod *Julius Hagen.* Scr *Gerrard Fairlie, from the play by John Chanellor.* PC *Real Art.* Dis *Radio.* 63 *mins. Cert A*
Anton (*Frank Vosper*), an exiled Russian grand duke, is night manager at a hotel. He becomes involved with a young couple who have quarrelled, and then with an 'accidental' murder. To save the girl from a murder charge, he kills himself. Out-of-the-rut low-budgeter with fine performance by Vosper.
RoC *Margaret Vines, Lewis Shaw, Leslie Perrins, Gillian Lind, Colin Keith-Johnston, Geraldine Fitzgerald, Michael Shepley.*

OPENING NIGHT (1935)   [2]

Dir *Alex Brown.* Prod *Charles Alexander.* PC *Olympic.* Dis *Columbia.* 68 *mins. Cert A*
Straightforward revue with no story – a succession of variety turns purporting to be the first-night cabaret at a new night spot.
LP *Douglas Byng, Reginald Gardiner, Doris Hare, Dolores Dalgarno, Walter Crisham, Edward Cooper.*

ORDERS IS ORDERS (1933)   [4]

Dir *Walter Forde.* Prod *Michael Balcon.* Sc[r] *Leslie Arliss, Sidney Gilliat, James Gleason, Ia[n] Hay, from a play by Hay, Anthony Armstrong.* Ph *Glen MacWilliams.* PC *Gaumont-British.* Dis *Ideal.* 88 *mins. Cert U*
Comedy burlesque of American film production and British Army red tape, involving [a] Hollywood director (*James Gleason*, contribut[ing] his own dialogue) taking over an arm[y] camp for what eventually turns out to be a[n] Arab epic with the colonel (*Cyril Maude*) per[s]uaded to play the lead. A court-martial loom[s] for the colonel but his bacon is saved with th[e] accidental destruction of the film.
RoC *Charlotte Greenwood, Cedric Hardwick[e,] Ian Hunter, Ray Milland, Donald Calthro[p,] Jane Carr, Eliot Makeham, Hay Plumb, Wall[y] Patch, Finlay Currie, Percy Parsons, Edwi[n] Laurence, Glennis Lorimer, Sydney Keith, Ja[n] Cornell.*

Donald Calthrop, Charlotte Greenwood, Jame[s] Gleason, Cyril Maude and Cedric Hardwicke [in] Orders Is Orders *(1933)*

OTHER PEOPLE'S SINS (1931)   [4]

Dir and Prod *Sinclair Hill.* Scr *Leslie Howar[d] Gordon.* Ph *Desmond Dickinson.* PC *Associate[d] Picture Productions.* Dis *Producers' Distributin[g] Corporation.* 63 *mins. Cert A*
Solid courtroom melodrama: barrister An[thony] Vernon (*Stewart Rome*) finds his flirta[tious] wife Ann (*Anne Grey*) with an impres[sario] (*Arthur Margetson*) after a party, an[d] storms off. Ann decides not to become the im[presario's] mistress, there is a struggle, and sh[e] kills him with a stone ash-tray. Her fathe[r] (*Horace Hodges*) insists on taking the blame and is brought to trial, defended by Vernon[.] Later, though, Ann confesses. . . .
RoC *Adeline Hayden Coffin, Arthur Hardy, A[?] Harding Steerman, Sam Wilkinson, Clifto[n] Boyne, Arthur Hambling, Arthur Bawtree, Rus[sell] Car, Laura Smithson, J. Hubert Leslie, [?] Disney Roebuck, Claude Maxted, John Hop[e.]*

THE OTHER WOMAN (1931)   [1]

Dir and Scr *G. B. Samuelson, from a story b[y] Olga Hall Brown.* Prod *Gordon Craig.* P[C] Majestic.* Dis *United Artists.* 64 *mins. Cert A*
Tired tale of a selfish and pleasure seekin[g] woman (*Isobel Elsom*) who is brought to he[r] senses when she thinks her husband (*Dav[id] Hawthorne*) guilty of a secret love affair. Sai[d]

ne contemporary reviewer: 'The players deserve sympathy.'
RoC *Eva Moore, Pat Paterson, Gladys Frazin, Jane Vaughan, Mervin Pearce, Sam Wilkinson.*

OUANGA (1934) [1]

Dir and Prod *George Terwilliger.* Scr *Uncredited.* Ph *Uncredited.* PC *GT Films.* Dis *Paramount. 68 mins. Cert A*

Set in the West Indies, this is perhaps the worst British film of its kind ever made, according to contemporary reviews. Its unintentionally hilarious story tells of the jealousy of a native woman (*Fredi Washington*) when her European lover (*Philip Brandon*) becomes engaged to a white girl (*Marie Paxton*). She calls upon her Voodoo friends to cause the girl's death, but fails.
RoC *Sheldon Leonard, Winifred Harris, Sid Easton, Babe Joyce, George Spink.*

OUR FIGHTING NAVY (1937) [2]
(USA: *Torpedoed!*)

Dir *Norman Walker.* Prod and PC *Herbert Wilcox.* Scr *Gerald Elliott, Harrison Owens.* Ph *Claude Friese-Greene.* Dis *General Film Distributors. 75 mins. Cert U*

Not exactly convincing maritime saga about a British ship sent to a powder-keg South American country to protect the British consulate. The consul's daughter is kidnapped by revolutionaries and forced aboard one of their ships. The captain of the British ship (*Robert Douglas*) helps her to escape and they jump overboard before the Britons torpedo the enemy vessel.
RoC *Hazel Terry, H.B. Warner, Richard Cromwell, Noah Beery, Esmé Percy, Richard Ainley, Binkie Stuart, Julie Suedo, Henry Victor, Frederick Culley.*

OURSELVES ALONE (1936) [4]
(USA: *River of Unrest*)

Dir *Walter Summers, Brian Desmond Hurst.* Prod *Walter C. Mycroft.* Scr *Dudley Leslie, Marjorie Deans, Dennis Johnstone, Philip Macdonald, from a play by Dudley Sturrock and Noel Scott.* Ph *Jimmy Harvey.* Dis *Wardour. 68 mins. Cert A*

Ireland, 1921: Maureen (*Antoinette Cellier*), sister of an IRA leader (*Niall MacGinnis*), is loved by both Hannay (*John Lodge*) of the Royal Irish Constabulary and his English intelligence officer Wiltshire (*John Loder*). When her brother is shot by Wiltshire, the IRA force her to help them. Hannay frustrates their plans, then tells her it was he who shot her brother, leaving her free to marry the man of her choice – Wiltshire. Strong acting from good cast.
RoC *Clifford Evans, Bruce Lister, Maire O'Neill, Jerry Verno, Pat Noonan, Fred O'Donovan, Bill Watts, Tony Quinn, Paul Farrell, Harry Hutchinson, E.J. Kennedy, Cavan O'Connor.*

THE OUTCAST (1934) [3]

Dir *Norman Lee.* Prod *Walter C. Mycroft.* Scr *Syd Courtenay, Lola Harvey.* PC *BIP.* Dis *Wardour. 74 mins. Cert U*

Two comedians, Bill and Jim (*Leslie Fuller,*

Leslie Fuller and Hal Gordon in The Outcast *(1934)*

Hal Gordon) find themselves out of work when Morton (*Wallace Geoffrey*) manager of their show, absconds with the funds. They become bookmakers at the greyhound track, but are again fleeced by Morton, and bankrupted. Things come right when Bill's pet dog The Outcast wins a big race. Amiable comedy with locations at Wembley Dog Track.
RoC *Mary Glynne, Jane Carr, Gladdy Sewell, Jimmy Godden, Pat Aherne, John Schofield.*

OUT OF THE BLUE (1931) [3]

Dir *Gene Gerrard, John Orton.* Prod *John Maxwell.* Scr *Frank Miller, R.P. Weston, Bert Lee, from a play by Caswell Garth and Desmond Carter.* Ph *Ernest Palmer, Arthur Crabtree.* PC *BIP.* Dis *Pathé. 88 mins. Cert U*

Adequate musical-comedy vehicle for *Gene Gerrard,* featuring a *Jessie Matthews* who had yet to get into her stride as a movie star. She plays a singer in love with a radio announcer (*Gerrard*) who has somehow contrived to get engaged to her sister (*Kay Hammond*) whom he doesn't love. It's sorted out when all the characters converge on a cabaret in Biarritz.
RoC *Kenneth Kove, Binnie Barnes, David Millar, Fred Groves, Averil Haley, Hal Gordon, Gordon Begg, John Reynders and His Band.*

OUT OF THE PAST (1933) [3]

Dir *Leslie Hiscott.* Prod *Irving Asher.* Scr *Uncredited.* Ph *Basil Emmott.* PC and Dis *Warner Bros. 51 mins. Cert A*

Saved from suicide, Frances (*Joan Marion*) begins a new life and within a few years has become managing director of a department store, engaged to the owner's son. At this point, the man (*Lester Matthews*) in whose divorce she had been innocently involved years before comes back into her life; eventually she decides to break her engagement and marry him.
RoC *Jack Raine, Henry Mollinson, Eric Stanley, Margaret Damer, Aubrey Dexter, Wilfred Shine.*

THE OUTSIDER (1931) [4]

Dir *Harry Lachman.* Prod *Eric Hakim.* Scr *Lachman, Alma Reville, from the play by Dorothy Brandon.* Ph *Günther Krampf.* PC *Cinema House.* Dis *MGM. 93 mins. Cert U*

Moving story of an unqualified surgeon (*Harold Huth*) who cures cripples by means of elec-

tricity, but remains an 'outsider' to the medical profession – until he takes on the case of a distinguished doctor's daughter (*Joan Barry*) who is paralysed from the waist down.
RoC *Frank Lawton, Mary Clare, Norman McKinnel, Annie Esmond, Glenore Pointin, Fewlass Llewellyn, S.J. Gillett, Randolph McLeod.*

THE OUTSIDER (1939) [3]

Dir *Paul L. Stein.* Prod *Walter C. Mycroft.* Scr *Dudley Lewis, from the play by Dorothy Brandon.* Ph *Günther Krampf.* PC and Dis *Associated British. 90 mins. Cert A*

Ragatzy (*George Sanders*), an osteopath, is sure he can cure Lalage (*Mary Maguire*), crippled daughter of a Harley Street specialist. Deserted by her boyfriend Basil (*Peter Murray Hill*), she undergoes a year of treatment; Ragatzy falls in love with her. She fails to walk but when her father denounces Ragatzy, she gets up, staggers a few paces and throws herself between them. Barely successful remake of 1931 film.
RoC *Barbara Blair, Frederick Leister, Walter Hudd, Kathleen Harrison, P. Kynaston Reeves, Edmund Breon, Ralph Truman, Martin Walker, Ian Colin, Lesley Wareing, Edward Lexy, Eddie Pola, Elaine Hamill, Zillah Bateman, Fewlass Llewellyn, Picot Schooling, Jack Lambert, Stella Arbenina, Roddy McDowall, Derek Farr.*

Joan Barry and Harold Huth in The Outsider *(1931)*

OVER SHE GOES (1937) [3]

Dir *Graham Cutts.* Prod *Walter C. Mycroft.* Scr *Elizabeth Meehan, Hugh Brooke, from the play by Stanley Lupino.* Ph *Otto Kanturek.* PC and Dis *Associated British. 74 mins. Cert A*

Pamela (*Claire Luce*) deliberately falls while out hunting, to bring Lord Harry (*John Wood*) to proposal point. This is followed by identical tumbles from her friends Kitty (*Sally Gray*) and Dolly (*Gina Malo*) to bag their men. The triple wedding comes off thanks to Harry's friends Tommy and Billy (*Stanley Lupino, Laddie Cliff*) who rout the intervention of Harry's 'ex' Alice (*Judy Kelly*). Stage show transferred to film with little subtlety.
RoC *Max Baer, Syd Walker, Bertha Belmore, Richard Murdoch, Archibald Batty.*

OVER THE GARDEN WALL (1934) [3]

Dir *John Daumery.* Prod *Walter C. Mycroft.* Scr *H.F. Maltby, Gordon Wellesley, from a play by Maltby.* Ph *Jack Cox.* PC *BIP.* Dis *Wardour.* 68 mins. Cert U

Comedy with music, in which the nephew (*Bobby Howes*) of a lady with a modern house in the country falls for the niece (*Marian Marsh*) of the sour-faced brother and sister who owns a neighbouring 'olde-worlde' cottage.

RoC *Margaret Bannerman, Viola Lyel, Bertha Belmore, Syd Crossley, Mary Sheridan, Fred Watts, Stewart Granger.*

OVER THE MOON (1937)   2

Dir *Thorton Freeland, William K. Howard.* Prod *Alexander Korda.* Scr *Anthony Pelissier, Alec Coppel, Arthur Wimperis.* Ph *Harry Stradling.* PC *London Films/Denham Films.* Dis *United Artists.* Technicolor. 78 mins. Cert A

Flimsy romantic fol-de-rol in which Jane (*Merle Oberon*) inherits £18,000,000, and, to the concern of her country doctor fiancé, Freddie (*Rex Harrison*), goes on a madcap spree on the Continent where, shunted along by dowagers and society adventuresses, she is pursued by philanderers after her money. She returns to Freddie, and they honeymoon in Italy – on a third-class rail ticket. Not released until 1940.

RoC *Ursula Jeans, Robert Douglas, Louis Borell, Zena Dare, Peter Haddon, David Tree, Mackenzie Ward, Carl Jaffe, Elisabeth Welch, Herbert Lomas, Wilfred Shine, Gerald Nodin, Bruce Winston, Lewis Gilbert, Meriel Forbes, Billy Shine, Evelyn Ankers.*

OWD BOB (1937)   5
(USA: *To The Victor*)

Dir *Robert Stevenson.* Prod *Edward Black.* Scr *Michael Hogan, J. B. Williams,* from the novel by *Alfred Olivant.* Ph *Jack Cox.* PC *Gainsborough.* Dis *General Film Distributors.* 78 mins. Cert U

Remade 10 years later by Hollywood as *Thunder in the Valley* (in Britain, *Bob, Son of Battle*), Olivant's famous animal story deals with Adam McAdam (*Will Fyffe*), a drunken, quarrelsome old Scots shepherd settled in Cumberland, and the rivalry of his dog, Black Wull, with Owd Bob, a dog owned by newly arrived David Moore (*John Loder*) who also falls for Adam's daughter Jennie (*Margaret Lockwood*). In the end, Wull not only loses the sheepdog trials to Bob, but is found to be a sheepkiller and shot. Adam gains consolation

Margaret Lockwood, John Loder and Will Fyffe in Owd Bob *(1938)*

from a litter of pups which David believes to be Bob's but which Adam knows are Wull's. Skilfully directed, moving at times, excellent sheepdog sequences.

RoC *Moore Marriott, Graham Moffatt, Wilfrid Walter, Elliot Mason, A. Bromley Davenport, H. F. Maltby, Edmund Breon, Alf Goddard, Wally Patch*

PAGLIACCI (1936)   3
(USA: *A Clown Must Laugh*)

Dir *Karl Grune.* Prod *Max Schach.* Scr *Monckton Hoffe, John Drinkwater, Roger Burford, Ernest Betts,* from the opera by *Ruggiero Leoncavallo.* Ph *Otto Kanturek.* PC *Trafalgar.* Dis *United Artists.* Two sequences in Chemicolour. 92 mins. Cert A

Despite superb singing, the cinema tends to show up the threadbare plot in Leoncavallo's famous story of a tragic clown (*Richard Tauber*) who takes his revenge on his faithless wife and her soldier lover by murdering them both on stage during a performance.

RoC *Steffi Duna, Diana Napier, Arthur Margetson, Esmond Knight, Jerry Verno, Gordon James, Harry Milton, Ivan Wilmot, John Traynor, Roy Finlay, Joe Roncoroni, Ambrose Day, Daley Cooper Jr.*

Richard Tauber, Steffi Duna in Pagliacci *(1936)*

PAID IN ERROR (1938)   3

Dir *Maclean Rogers,* Prod and PC *George Smith.* Scr *Basil Mason, H.F. Maltby.* Ph *Geoffrey Faithfull.* Dis *Columbia.* 68 mins. Cert U

Hard-up but hopeful Will (*George Carney*), who lives on the charity of his landlady, suddenly finds himself credited with a bank balance of £600 he hasn't got. Later he and the chief cashier (*Tom Helmore*) who loves the clerk (*Marjorie Taylor*) who made the error, try to recoup the cash (most of which Will has spent) to save her from the sack. A lucky bet helps them do it. Comedy has patches of amusing dialogue.

RoC *Lillian Christine, Googie Withers, Molly Hamley-Clifford, Jonathan Field, Aubrey Mallalieu, Michael Ripper.*

PARADISE FOR TWO (1937)   5
(USA: *The Gaiety Girls*)

Dir *Thornton Freeland.* Prod *Günther Stapenhorst.* Scr *Robert Stevenson, Arthur Macrae.* Ph *Günther Krampf.* PC *Denham.* Dis *United Artists.* 77 mins. Cert U

Paris: chorus girl Jeannette (*Patricia Ellis*) splashed by a millionaire's car, is given a lift home by the chauffeur. On the strength of her 'friendship' with the millionaire, Martin (*Jack Hulbert*), she is offered a star role. When Martin pays a visit to the theatre, she thinks him a reporter, and asks him to play 'her' millionaire. He plays along until the show opens – then joins her for a dance in her final triumphant number. Refreshing, capably directed musical, nicely done in all departments.

RoC *Arthur Riscoe, Googie Withers, Sydney Fairbrother, Wylie Watson, David Tree, Cecil Bevan, Antony Holles, Roland Culver, H. F. Maltby, Finlay Currie.*

PARIS PLANE (1933)   3

Dir *John Paddy Carstairs.* Prod *Ivar Campbell.* Scr *Charles Bennett.* PC *Sound City.* Dis *M G-M.* 52 mins. Cert U

A detective (*John Loder*) pursues an escaped murderer (*Allan Jeayes*) on to a plane bound from London to Le Bourget. But the killer has disguised himself and taken a false name. Just before landing, he makes a slip which enables the 'tec to unmask him and take him into custody.

RoC *Molly Lamont, Barry Livesey, Julie Suedo, Edwin Ellis, James Harcourt, Eileen Munro.*

PASSENGER TO LONDON (1937)   1

Dir and Prod *Lawrence Huntington.* Scr *David Evans.* Ph *Stanley Grant.* PC and Dis *Fox British.* 57 mins. Cert A

On a train bound from the east of Europe to London, Secret Service spies and foreign agents battle for possession of valuable documents. British agent Frank Drayton (*John Warwick*) comes out on top. Good settings but otherwise feeble thriller.

RoC *Jenny Laird, Paul Neville, Ivan Wilmot, Aubrey Pollock, Victor Hagen, Nigel Barrie, Sybil Brooke, Dorothy Dewhurst.*

THE PASSING OF THE THIRD FLOOR BACK (1935)   3

Dir *Berthold Viertel.* (Associate) Prod *Ivor Montagu.* Scr *Michael Hogan, Alma Reville,* from the play by *Jerome K. Jerome.* Ph *Curt Courant.* PC and Dis *Gaumont-British.* 90 mins. Cert A

Not-quite-successful adaptation of a famous morality play about a Bloomsbury boarding house whose tenants are a conspicuously unhappy and bickering lot. A stranger (*Conrad Veidt*) takes the back room on the third floor and changes the courses of their lives, staying only a short while, but showing them the better sides of themselves and helping them make the best of their stay on earth.

RoC *René Ray, Anna Lee, Frank Cellier, Mary Clare, Beatrix Lehmann, John Turnbull, Cathleen Nesbitt, Ronald Ward, Sara Allgood, Barbara Everest, Jack Livesey, Alexander Sarner.*

PASSING SHADOWS (1934) [2]

Dir *Leslie Hiscott.* Prod *Herbert Smith.* Scr *Michael Barringer.* Ph *Alex Bryce.* PC *British Lion.* Dis *Fox. 67 mins. Cert A*
Attacked by a thief, Jim (*Barry Mackay*), the son of a country chemist (*Edmund Gwenn*), accidentally shoots the man. It preys on his mind and affects his whole life. But his parents urge him not to give himself up, and it transpires that the man Jim shot did not die, and is himself a killer. Slowly developed drama.
RoC *Viola Lyel, Aileen Marson, D. A. Clarke-Smith, Wally Patch, John Turnbull, Barbara Everest, Barry O'Neill, Philip Hewland.*

THE PATH OF GLORY (1934) [3]

Dir and Prod *Dallas Bower.* Scr *L. DuGarde Peach, from his radio play.* PC *Triumph.* Dis *Producers' Distributing Corporation. 68 mins. Cert U*
Satirical comedy about two mythical European countries, Sardonia and Thalia, who declare war on each other – a war that each, for economic reasons, is determined to lose.
LP *Maurice Evans, Felix Aylmer, Valerie Hobson, Henry Daniell, Athole Stewart, Stafford Hilliard, John Deverell, David Burns, Frederick Burtwell, Harvey Braban, Frank Atkinson, Frank Lacey.*

PATRICIA GETS HER MAN (1937) [2]

Dir *Reginald Purdell.* Prod *Irving Asher.* Scr *Max Merritt, Maurice Kusell.* Ph *Basil Emmott.* PC *Warner Bros.* Dis *First National. 68 mins. Cert A*
Pat (*Lesley Brook*) and her father are staying at a Riviera hotel. Desperate to attract film star Brian Maxwell (*Edwin Styles*), Pat persuades local playboy Count Stephan (*Hans Sonker*) to escort her. Stephan falls for Pat, and he and Brian join forces to abduct her. Brian makes unpleasant advances to her, as they have planned, and Pat duly runs off with Stephan. Uninspired comedy.
RoC *Aubrey Mallalieu, Cissy Fitzgerald, Betty Lynne, Yoshihide Yanai, Leonard Barry, Scott Harold, Cecil Calvert, H. B. Passat.*

PAY BOX ADVENTURE (1936) [1]

Dir *W. P. Kellino.* Prod *Anthony Havelock-Allan.* Scr *Gerald Elliott.* PC and Dis *British and Dominions/Paramount British. 68 mins. Cert U*
Poor end to the directing career of W. P. Kellino, one of Britain's most prominent filmmakers of the silent era. It's a failed crime drama about the staff of a small cinema resorting to desperate measures to cut their losses by selling out to a big circuit, and the schemes of a crooked lawyer who knows that the cinema's cashier stands to inherit a fortune.
LP *Syd Crossley, Marjorie Corbett, Roxie Russell, Billy Watts, Eric Fawcett, Molly Hamley Clifford, George Turner, Billy Saunders, Harold Thorne.*

P.C. JOSSER (1930) [4]

Dir *Milton Rosmer.* Prod *Michael Balcon.* Scr *Con West, Herbert Sargent, from a play by Ernest Lotinga.* PC *Gainsborough.* Dis *W and F. 90 mins. Cert U*
Ernie Lotinga's famous comic creation Jimmy Josser, seen before in shorter-length films, made his feature-length debut in this firecracker farce about a policeman, kicked out of the force, who redeems his reputation by cracking a racehorse-doping ring with the help of the trainer who had been jailed for the offences.
RoC *Jack Frost, Maisie Darrell, Robert Douglas, Garry Marsh, Max Avieson, Elsie Percival.*

Ernie Lotinga, unknown, Jack Frost, Garry Marsh in PC Josser *(1930)*

PEACE AND QUIET (1931) [3]

Dir *Frank Richardson.* Prod *George Smith, Harry Cohen.* Scr *Brock Williams.* Ph *Basil Emmott.* PC *GS Enterprises.* Dis *Fox. 42 mins. Cert U*
Comedy for the talents of ex-music hall comic *Herbert Mundin*, soon to go to Hollywood as a character player. Discovering he is the missing heir to the Marsham peerage, Percy (*Mundin*) goes to Marsham Castle, to find it in the hands of a gang of thieves, headed by a bogus captain, who try to bump him off. But Percy is equal to them, and ends by rounding up the entire gang.
RoC *Iris Darbyshire, D. A. Clarke-Smith, Marie Ault, René Ray, George Bellamy.*

PEARLS BRING TEARS (1937) [4]

Dir *Manning Haynes.* Prod *A. George Smith.* Scr *Roy Lockwood,* Ph *Geoffrey Faithfull.* PC *GS Enterprises.* Dis *Columbia. 63 mins. Cert U*
Not knowing they have been loaned to her husband as security for a business deal, Madge (*Dorothy Boyd*) wears a string of pearls to a dance, but breaks the clasp. The pearls temporarily disappear after being taken to a friend for repair, and disaster looms when the husband (*Mark Stone*) returns. After a run of farcical incidents, the pearls go back to their owner. Ingenious comedy, neatly done.
RoC *John Stuart, Eve Gray, Googie Withers, Aubrey Mallalieu, Annie Esmond, H. F. Maltby, Hal Walters, Syd Crossley, Isobel Scaife, Michael Ripper, Elizabeth James.*

PEG OF OLD DRURY (1935) [4]

Dir and Prod *Herbert Wilcox.* Scr *Miles Malleson, from a play by Charles Reade, Tom Taylor.* Ph *F. A. Young, L. P. Williams.* PC *British and Dominions.* Dis *United Artists. 76 mins. Cert U*
Popular, lively portrait of eighteenth-century actress Peg Woffington (*Anna Neagle*). Dublin-born and jilted by Michael (*Jack Hawkins*) whom she follows to London, Peg makes a visit to Drury Lane theatre and resolves to take up acting. Under the wing of David Garrick (*Cedric Hardwicke*), she becomes the foremost theatre star of the day. Disguised as a man, she even gets her own back on Michael by tackling him in a duel. Garrick is in love with her, but does not know she has a weak heart. After a performance of *As You Like It*, she dies in his arms.
RoC *Margaretta Scott, Hay Petrie, Maire O'Neill, Arthur Sinclair, Robert Atkins, Dorothy Robinson, Aubrey Fitzgerald, Eliot Makeham, Leslie French, Tom Heslewood, Christopher Steele, Sara Allgood, Pollie Emery, Stuart Robertson, George Barratt.*

Cedric Hardwicke, Anna Neagle and Jack Hawkins in Peg of Old Drury *(1935)*

PENNY PARADISE (1938) [4]

Dir *Carol Reed.* Prod *Basil Dean, Jack Kitchin.* Scr *Thomas Thompson, W. L. Meade, Thomas Browne.* Ph *Ronald Neame, Gordon Dines.* PC *ATP.* Dis *Associated British. 72 mins. Cert U*
Merseyside tugboat skipper Joe (*Edmund Gwenn*) has won the pools. He quarrels with Widow Clegg (*Maire O'Neill*) whom he is courting, throws a hilarious party at the local pub, sees his daughter chased by a smoothie after her money and fends off a conniving aunt claiming part of the winnings. His friend Pat (*Jimmy O'Dea*) then confesses he forgot to post the coupon. But Joe gets a consolation prize: he is appointed skipper of the newest tug on the river. Hackneyed story gets new lease of life from character acting, convincing settings.
RoC *Betty Driver, Jack Livesey, Ethel Coleridge, Syd Crossley, James Harcourt.*

THE PENNY POOL (1937) [4]

Dir *George Black.* Prod *John E. Blakeley.* Scr *Arthur Mertz.* Ph *Germain Burger.* PC and Dis *Mancunian. 85 mins. Cert U*
Factory hand Renée (*Luanne Shaw*) is sacked for filling in her office coupon in working time. Her boyfriend (*Tommy Fields*) sets her up as manageress of a café, while her coupon is found by a workman who puts his name on it and posts it. It wins – but again thanks to her

boyfriend (her ex-employer's son), Renée doesn't go empty-handed. Slapstick is crude but script very funny in enthusiastic north country comedy.

RoC *Billy Nelson, Duggie Wakefield, Charles Sewell, Harry Terry, Chuck O'Neil, Jack Butler, Mascotte, The Marie Louise Sisters, Macari and His Dutch Serenaders.*

THE PERFECT CRIME (1937)   3

Dir *Ralph Ince.* Prod *Irving Asher.* Scr *Basil Woon.* Ph *Basil Emmott.* PC and Dis *Warner Bros. 69 mins. Cert A*

Tired of life as a bank clerk, Charles (*Hugh Williams*) robs the bank and flees by ship, planning to leave behind a suicide note and some money and change his identity. A steward destroys the note, steals the money and is murdered for it. Charles confesses all to a girl (*Glen Alyn*) he has met and helps a detective (*Ralph Ince*) corner the killer. Charles returns to face the music but with the hope of a light sentence. Tidily constructed little thriller.

RoC *James Stephenson, Iris Hoey, Philip Ray, Wilfrid Caithness, John Carol, Kate Cutler, Sam Springson, George Hughes, Ralph Roberts, Madge White.*

THE PERFECT FLAW (1934)   2

Dir and Prod *Manning Haynes.* Scr *Michael Barringer.* PC and Dis *Fox British. 50 mins. Cert A*

Drexel (*Ralph Truman*), junior partner in a business firm, becomes involved with ambitious clerk Maddox (*D. A. Clarke-Smith*), whose get-rich-scheme goes awry and leads to a plot to kill a wealthy stockbroker. Drexel emerges from the affair a sadder and wiser man. Standard 'quickie' drama.

RoC *Charles Carson, Hal Walters, Naomi Waters, Wally Patch, Billy (William) Hartnell, Romilly Lunge, Eric Hales.*

THE PERFECT LADY (1931)   3

Dir and Prod *Milton Rosmer, Frederick Jackson.* Scr *Jackson.* PC *BIP.* Dis *Wardour. 77 mins. Cert A*

Furious that her fiancé, Lord Tony (*Reginald Gardiner*), has become infatuated with a gold-digging French actress, Anne (*Moira Lynd*) poses as a lady's maid, gets employment with the actress, and breaks up the affair. In so doing, she falls in love with a young Canadian (*Harry Wilcoxon*): foolish Lord Tony ends with nothing. Acceptable comedy.

RoC *Betty Amann, Athene Seyler, Frederick Lloyd.*

PERFECT UNDERSTANDING (1932)   2

Dir *Cyril Gardner.* Prod *Gloria Swanson.* Scr *Miles Malleson, Michael Powell.* Ph *Curt Courant.* PC *Gloria Swanson British.* Dis *United Artists. 80 mins. Cert A*

Despite its distinguished cast, critics found this drama unpalatable and long-winded. An American (*Gloria Swanson*) marries an English aristocrat (*Laurence Olivier*). He has an affair for which she forgives him, but is less understanding himself when he thinks her guilty (she isn't) of the same sin. He sees the error of his attitude and they settle down together.

RoC *John Halliday, Genevieve Tobin, Nigel Playfair, Michael Farmer, Nora Swinburne, O. B. Clarence, Mary Jerrold, Charles Cullum.*

THE PHANTOM LIGHT (1934)   4

Dir *Michael Powell.* Prod *Jerome Jackson.* Scr *Austin Melford, Ralph Smart, from a play by Evadne Price, Joan Roy Byford.* Ph *Geoffrey Faithfull.* PC *Gainsborough.* Dis *Gaumont-British. 75 mins. Cert U*

A lighthouse off the coast of Wales is the scene of disappearances, shipwrecks and a 'phantom' light on the rocks nearby. A gang of wreckers is at work, but the lighthouse keeper, helped by a naval officer and a lady detective, rounds them up after a struggle. Above-average programme-filler with good atmosphere, tension and comic relief.

LP *Gordon Harker, Ian Hunter, Binnie Hale, Milton Rosmer, Donald Calthrop, Reginald Tate, Mickey Brantford, Herbert Lomas, Fewlass Llewellyn, Alice O'Day, Barry O'Neill, Edgar K. Bruce, Louie Emery.*

Gordon Harker and Herbert Lomas in The Phantom Light (*1934*)

PICCADILLY NIGHTS (1930)   3

Dir and Prod *Albert H. Arch.* Scr *Arch, Roger Burford.* PC *Kingsway General.* Dis *Film Booking Offices. 86 mins. Cert U*

Ramshackle musical, mostly a succession of quite presentable vaudeville turns with a threadbare storyline – the usual stand-by about the girl singer (*Billie Rutherford*) who goes out there and becomes a star when the leading lady is too drunk to appear.

RoC *Elsie Bower, Julian Hamilton, June Grey, Pat Courtney, Maurice Winnick and His Band, Ralph Goldsmith and His Band.*

PICCADILLY PLAYTIME (1936)   1

Dir and Prod *Frank Green.* PC and Dis *Ace. 50 mins. Cert U*

Dreary series of turns from the Windmill Theatre, the kind of entertainment that made the audience groan as the credits went up at the beginning.

LP *Meggie Eaton, Walden and West, Paddy Brown, Eric Woodburn, Olive Del Mar, Leslie Spurling.*

PLAY UP THE BAND (1935)   3

Dir *Harry Hughes.* Prod *Basil Humphrys.* Scr *Frank Atkinson.* PC *City.* Dis *Associated British. 71 mins. Cert U*

A Yorkshire brass band comes to London to play in a competition. The wife of the band's proprietor has her necklace stolen by a bogus count and suspicion falls on two of the bandsmen (*Stanley Holloway, Frank Atkinson*). They are cleared just in time to play. Comedy enlivened by Holloway monologues, including *Sweeney Todd.*

RoC *Betty (Ann) Davies, Leslie Bradley, Amy Veness, Charles Sewell, Julie Suedo, Cynthia Stock, Hal Gordon, Arthur Gomez, Andrea Malandrinos, Billy Bray, Ian Wilson, The London Brass Band, Louise Selkirk's Ladies' Orchestra.*

PLEASE TEACHER (1937)   3

Dir and Scr *Stafford Dickens, from the play by K. R. G. Browne, R. P. Weston, Bert Lee.* Prod *Walter C. Mycroft.* Ph *Otto Kanturek.* PC *Associated British.* Dis *Wardour. 76 mins. Cert U*

Tommy Deacon (*Bobby Howes*) has to infiltrate a girls' school to find a bust of Napoleon which he thinks contains a will that leaves him a legacy, so he poses as a pupil's explorer brother. The pupil's real brother has given her a jewelled fish stolen from a Chinese temple, and some sinister Orientals are prepared to stop at nothing to get it back. Farce with music is quite fun.

RoC *René Ray, Wylie Watson, Bertha Belmore, Vera Pearce, Lyn Harding, Aubrey Dexter, Arthur Chesney.*

PLUNDER (1930)   4

Dir *Tom Walls.* Prod *Herbert Wilcox.* Scr *W. P. Lipscomb, from the play by Ben Travers.* Ph *F. A. Young.* PC *British and Dominions.* Dis *W and F. 98 mins. Cert U*

Roisterous farce about the attempts of Freddie (*Tom Walls*) and Darcy (*Ralph Lynn*) to steal an inheritance of jewellery. Not the funniest of the Aldwych farces, although full of typical Ben Travers situations.

RoC *J. Robertson Hare, Winifred Shotter, Mary Brough, Doreen Bendix, Sydney Lynn, Ethel Coleridge, Hubert Waring.*

THE POINTING FINGER (1933)   2

Dir *George Pearson.* Prod *Julius Hagen.* Scr *H. Fowler Mear, from a novel by 'Rita'.* PC *Real Art.* Dis *Radio. 68 mins. Cert U*

Melodrama about an aristocrat (*Leslie Perrins*) who plans to have his cousin (*John Stuart*) disposed of, so that he himself will become the heir to an earldom. Complications ensue when his plans go wrong, and eventually founder.

RoC *Viola Keats, Michael Hogan, A. Bromley Davenport, Henrietta Watson, D. J. Williams, Clare Greet.*

THE POISONED DIAMOND (1934)   3

Dir and Scr *W. P. Kellino.* Prod *Fred Browett.* PC *Grafton.* Dis *Columbia. 73 mins. Cert A*

Revenge drama, in which John Reader (*Lester Matthews*) goes bankrupt and blames four people for his plight. When he discovers a diamond mine, he uses his new-found wealth to destroy the four people he hates – but has mercy on one of them.

RoC *Anne Grey, Patric Knowles, D. J. Williams, Raymond Raikes, Bryan Powley, Lucius Blake.*

POISON PEN (1939) [4]

Dir *Paul L. Stein*. Prod *Walter C. Mycroft*. Scr *Doreen Montgomery, William Freshman, N. C. Hunter, Esther McCracken, from the play by Richard Llewellyn*. Ph *Phil Tannura*. PC and Dis *Associated British*. 79 mins. Cert A

Rural Hilldale is torn apart by poison pen letters. The villagers suspect Connie (*Catherine Lacey*), a dressmaker, who is driven to suicide. But the letters go on. Sam (*Robert Newton*), a labourer, believing his young wife (*Belle Chrystall*) is having an affair, kills the 'lover'. Using forensic methods, police discover the writer to be Mary Rider (*Flora Robson*), the vicar's repressed spinster sister. She throws herself from a cliff. Slow, sordid, but striking dark drama. RoC *Ann Todd, Edward Chapman, Geoffrey Toone, Reginald Tate, Edward Rigby, Athole Stewart, Mary Hinton, Cyril Chamberlain, Wally Patch, Ella Retford, Jean Clyde, (Wilfrid) Hyde White, Marjorie Rhodes, Beatrice Varley, Peter Murray Hill, Empsie Bowman, Lawrence Kitchin, Kenneth Connor, Megs Jenkins, Esma Cannon, Eileen Beldon, Merle Tottenham, Charles Mortimer, Roddy Hughes, Roddy McDowall*.

A POLITICAL PARTY (1933) [4]

Dir *Norman Lee*. Prod *Walter C. Mycroft*. Scr *Syd Courtenay, Lola Harvey*. Ph *Claude Friese-Greene*. PC *BIP*. Dis *Pathé*. 73 mins. Cert U

Goodish *Leslie Fuller* comedy casting him as a chimney sweep standing as local Labour candidate against the Tory, a pompous local bigwig (*H. F. Maltby*). The sweep's chances are almost ruined when his son (*John Mills*) falls for Elvira (*Enid Stamp-Taylor*), who has every reason for wanting to see the Tory elected. But Bill wins in the end – only to decide not to take the seat.

RoC *Viola Lyel, Moore Marriott, Charles Gerrard, Daphne Courtenay, Hal Gordon, Marion Dawson, Rosie Howard, Dorothy Vernon, Fred Watts*.

POOR OLD BILL (1931) [2]

Dir *Monty Banks*. Prod *Walter C. Mycroft*. Scr *Val Valentine*. Ph *Claude Friese-Greene*. PC *BIP*. Dis *Wardour*. 52 mins. Cert U

An extended comedy sketch tailored to *Leslie Fuller's* own broad style. He plays a war veteran whose wife has allowed the man who saved his life in battle to stay at their home rent-free for three years. All hubby's efforts to get rid of his ex-comrade fail until it is revealed that another man really saved his life. Unfortunately, the wife insists on taking in the newcomer as a permanent guest...

RoC *Iris Ashley, Syd Courtenay, Dick Francis, Peter Lawford, Hal Gordon, Lola Harvey, Robert Brooks-Turner*.

POTIPHAR'S WIFE (1931) [3]
(USA: *Her Strange Desire*)

Dir *Maurice Elvey*. Prod *John Maxwell*. Scr *Edgar C. Middleton, from his play*. Ph *James Wilson*. PC *BIP*. Dis *First National-Pathé*. 78 mins. Cert A

Lady Diana (*Nora Swinburne*) tries to seduce her chauffeur (*Laurence Olivier*). When he re-

jects her, she brings him to court on an assault charge. The chauffeur is acquitted and receives compensation from his employer (*Norman McKinnel*), whom he suggests in future should devote a little more time to his wife.

RoC *Guy Newall, Ronald Frankau, Betty Schuster, Elsa Lanchester, Marjorie Brooks, Walter Armitage, Henry Wenman, Matthew Boulton*.

POT LUCK (1936) [4]

Dir *Tom Walls*. Prod *Michael Balcon*. Scr *Ben Travers*. Ph *Roy Kellino*. PC *Gainsborough*. Dis *Gaumont-British*. 71 mins. Cert A

Snappy Aldwych farce in which ex-inspector *Tom Walls* aids a foolish colleague (*Ralph Lynn*) and his sister (*Diana Churchill*) who have let a priceless vase be stolen. The trail leads to Wrotton Manor which the thieves use as a storehouse, unbeknown to Pye (*J. Robertson Hare*), the mild owner. Secret entrances and exits, trap doors and well shafts all play a part in the ensuing antics.

RoC *Gordon James, Martita Hunt, J. A. O'Rorke, Sara Allgood, J. H. Roberts, Peter Gawthorne, H. G. Stoker, Sam Wilkinson, T. Kirby, Charles Barrett, Cyril Smith, Louis Bradfield, James Grey, Mervyn Johns*.

PREMIERE (1938) [4]
(USA: *One Night in Paris*)

Dir *Walter Summers*. Prod *Walter C. Mycroft*. Scr *F. McGrew Willis, from an original screenplay by Max Wallner, F.D. Andam*. PC and Dis *Associated British*. 71 mins. Cert A

An impresario is murdered in his box on the first night of his new revue. A detective in the audience (*John Lodge*) tries to solve the crime without having to stop the show. There is no lack of suspects, as the leading lady had been displaced by the impresario just before the première. But when the curtain falls, the detective is ready to arrest the (left-handed) killer. Exciting thriller is well done by co-feature standards.

RoC *Judy Kelly, Hugh Williams, Joan Marion, Edward Chapman, Steven Geray, Edmund Breon, Wallace Geoffrey, Geoffrey Sumner, Joss Ambler*.

PRICE OF A SONG (1935) [3]

Dir and Prod *Michael Powell*. Scr *Anthony Gittins*. Ph *Jimmy Wilson*. PC and Dis *Fox British*. 67 mins. Cert A

Arnold Grierson (*Campbell Gullan*) is in financial difficulties and forces his daughter (*Marjorie Corbett*) to marry Nevern (*Eric Maturin*), a shallow songwriter, for money. When she decides to divorce Nevern, Grierson schemes to murder him in the hope that she will inherit his money. He does the deed but is brought to justice by his knowledge of an unpublished tune.

RoC *Gerald Fielding, Dora Barton, Charles Mortimer, Oriel Ross, Henry Caine, Sybil Grove, Felix Aylmer, Cynthia Stock, Mavis Clair*.

THE PRICE OF FOLLY (1937) [1]

Dir and Prod *Walter Summers*. Scr *J. Lee Thompson, Summers, Ruth Landon, from a play*

by *Lee Thompson*. PC *Welwyn*. Dis *Pathé*. 52 mins. Cert A

An inauspicious start to J. Lee Thompson's long association with the cinema. A crudely realized crime story about a man who is being blackmailed over the murder of a girl with whom he was having an affair. Out of money, the 'victim' stakes everything on a horse, but it loses. On the blackmailer's next visit, he shoots him dead – only to find that the girl is still alive...

LP *Leonora Corbett, Colin Keith-Johnston, Leslie Perrins, Judy Kelly, Andrea Malandrinos, Wally Patch, The Trocadero Girls*.

THE PRICE OF THINGS (1930) [2]

Dir, Prod and PC *Elinor Glyn*. Scr *Lady Rhys Williams, from the novel by Glyn*. Dis *United Artists*. 84 mins. Cert A

Real-life twins played screen twins in this otherwise undistinguished crime melodrama involving the efforts of a spy ring to gain possession of a secret document from one of the twins, a duke, with the help of a *femme fatale*. LP *Elissa Landi, Stewart Rome, Walter Tennyson, Alfred Tennyson, Mona Goya, Dino Galvani, Marjorie Loring, Muriel Minty, David Parr, Vincent Sternroyd*.

THE PRICE OF WISDOM (1935) [1]

Dir *Reginald Denham*. Prod *Anthony Havelock-Allan*. Scr *Basil Mason, George Dewhurst, from the play by Lionel Brown*. PC and Dis *British and Dominions/Paramount British*. 64 mins. Cert U

Talky drama about a country girl (*Mary Newland*) who goes to London, has adventures with a business magnate and his inventor son, designs a best-selling handbag, is loved by both men, becomes involved in a business dispute and settles it.

RoC *Roger Livesey, Robert Rendel, Mary Jerrold, Eric Cowley, Ann Codrington, Ivor Barnard, Cicely Oates*.

THE PRIDE OF THE FORCE (1933) [3]

Dir and Prod *Norman Lee*. Scr *Lee, Syd Courtenay, Arthur Woods*. Ph *Claude Friese-Greene*. PC *BIP*. Dis *Wardour*. 74 mins. Cert U

Lively *Leslie Fuller* comedy with the star as well-contrasted twins: one a policeman who joins a circus and becomes a strongman and wrestling star, the other a slow-witted farmhand who takes his brother's place in the police and, more by luck than judgment, becomes 'the pride of the force'. *Nan Bates*, who plays a supporting role, was Mrs Fuller in real life. RoC *Faith Bennett, Alf Goddard, Hal Gordon, Ben Welden, Frank Perfitt, Pat Aherne, King Curtis, Syd Courtenay, Lola Harvey, Rosie Howard, John Schofield*.

THE PRIMROSE PATH (1934) [1]

Dir and Prod *Reginald Denham*. Scr *Basil Mason, from a story by Joan Temple*. PC and Dis *British and Dominions/Paramount British*. 71 mins. Cert A

Slow-moving melodrama about a doctor's wife (*Isobel Elsom*) who falls in love with an author (*Whitmore Humphries*) on a cruise. His business partner (*Max Adrian*) falls for her daughter (*Virginia Field*). It is the author who reconciles husband and wife, and paves the way for his partner's happiness.

RoC *Gordon McLeod, Helen Ferrers, Ethel Stuart, Molly Connolly.*

PRINCE OF ARCADIA (1933) [3]

Dir *Hans Schwartz.* Prod *Archibald Nettlefold, Reginald Fogwell.* Scr *Fogwell, from the play by Walter Reisch.* Ph *Geoffrey Faithfull.* PC *Nettlefold-Fogwell.* Dis *W and F.* 80 mins. Cert A

A more-ambitious-than-usual Fogwell production, this musical deals with a ruler (*Carl Brisson*), forced to abdicate from his throne, who spends the first few weeks of his exile in pleasant Riviera surroundings. He is attracted to an actress (*Margot Grahame*) and decides to marry her, to the chagrin of his aunt, the Queen, but the delight of the princess who was his bride-to-be but didn't love him. Music: Robert Stolz.

RoC *Ida Lupino, Annie Esmond, Peter Gawthorne, (C.) Denier Warren.*

PRINCESS CHARMING (1934) [2]

Dir *Maurice Elvey.* Prod *Michael Balcon.* Scr *L. DuGarde Peach, Arthur Wimperis, Laurie Wylie.* Ph *Mutz Greenbaum.* PC *Gainsborough.* Dis *Gaumont-British.* 78 mins. Cert A

Weakly written musical with *Evelyn Laye* as a princess who, to escape revolutionaries in her small European country, marries a captain of the guard (*Harry Wilcoxon*), although she is engaged to the ruler of an adjoining state. When he refuses to annul the marriage, the captain is arrested, but the princess conceives a plan which ensures their future happiness.

RoC *Yvonne Arnaud, George Grossmith, Max Miller, Finlay Currie, Ivor McLaren, Ivor Barnard, Francis L. Sullivan, Dino Galvani.*

PRISON BREAKER (1936) [2]

Dir *Adrian Brunel.* Prod *A. George Smith.* Scr *Frank Witty, from the novel by Edgar Wallace.* Ph *George Dudgeon Stretton.* PC *GS Enterprises.* Dis *Columbia/Grand.* 69 mins. Cert A

Complicated crook drama in which a secret service agent (*James Mason*) has to bring an international crook (*Andrews Engelmann*) to book, in spite of being in love with his daughter (*Marguerite Allan*). Accidentally killing the criminal's lieutenant (*Andrea Malandrinos*), the agent is sent to prison, but effects a daring escape and brings the villains to justice.

RoC *Ian Fleming, George Merritt, Wally Patch, Vincent Holman, Tarva Penna, Neville Brook, Aubrey Mallalieu, Michael Ripper, John Counsell, Clifford Buckton.*

PRISON WITHOUT BARS (1938) [4]

Dir *Brian Desmond Hurst.* Prod *Arnold Pressburger.* Scr *Arthur Wimperis, Margaret Kennedy, from the play by Gina Kaus, E. and O. Eis, Hilde Koveloff.* Ph *Georges Périnal.* PC *London Films.* Dis *United Artists.* 80 mins. Cert A

Yvonne (*Edna Best*), new superintendent at a French reformatory, is in love with its doctor, George (*Barry K. Barnes*), but has frequent clashes with Mme Appel (*Martita Hunt*), who

believes brutality the only effective discipline. Yvonne takes an interest in hoyden inmate Suzanne (*Corinne Luchaire*) and puts her to work at the hospital, where she falls in love with George. After being cleared of causing a drunken riot, Suzanne leaves with George, leaving Yvonne to continue the battle for better conditions. Grim drama with sharply defined characters.

RoC *Mary Morris, Lorraine Clewes, Sally Wisher, Glynis Johns, Margaret Yarde, Elsie Shelton, Phyllis Morris, Nancy Roberts, Joan Ellum, Anne Crawford, Enid Lindsey, Ronald Shiner.*

THE PRIVATE LIFE OF DON JUAN (1934) [3]

Dir and Prod *Alexander Korda.* Scr *Frederick Lonsdale, Lajos Biro, from a play by Henri Bataille.* Ph *Georges Périnal, Robert Krasker.* PC *London Films.* Dis *United Artists.* 89 mins (80 in USA). Cert A

Disappointing Korda vehicle for an ageing *Douglas Fairbanks* as Don Juan, who escapes from mistresses and creditors alike by allowing himself to be thought dead, and retiring to a small village. He finds life boring, and returns to Seville. But no-one except his wife will believe he is the real Don Juan, and he has to go back to her to save himself from ridicule.

RoC *Benita Hume, Merle Oberon, Binnie Barnes, Melville Cooper, Joan Gardner, Athene Seyler, Owen Nares, Patricia Hilliard, Clifford Heatherley, Heather Thatcher, Gina Malo, Barry Mackay, Claud Allister, Diana Napier, Lawrence Grossmith, Bruce Winston, Edmund Willard, Gibson Gowland, Edmund Breon, Hindle Edgar, Florence Wood, Annie Esmond, Morland Graham, Hay Petrie, William Heughan, Natalie Lelong, Veronica Brady, Betty Hamilton, Toto Koopman, Virginia Bradford.*

Joan Gardner, Douglas Fairbanks Sr. Benita Hume, Merle Oberon and Elsa Lanchester in The Private Life of Don Juan *(1934)*

THE PRIVATE LIFE OF HENRY VIII (1933) [6]

Dir and Prod *Alexander Korda.* Scr *Arthur Wimperis, Lajos Biro.* Ph *Georges Périnal.* PC *London Films.* Dis *United Artists.* 96 mins. Cert A

The film that provided Britain with its first big breakthrough into the American market, and won an Academy Award for *Charles Laughton*, dealing with the roistering monarch and his

relationships with five of his six wives, Anne Boleyn (*Merle Oberon*), Jane Seymour (*Wendy Barrie*), Anne of Cleves (*Elsa Lanchester*), Katherine Howard (*Binnie Barnes*) and Catherine Parr (*Everley Gregg*).

RoC *Robert Donat, Lady Tree, Franklin Dyall, Miles Mander, John Loder, Claud Allister, William Austin, Gibb McLaughlin, Sam Livesey, Lawrence Hanray, Judy Kelly, John Turnbull, Frederick Culley.*

Charles Laughton and Binnie Barnes in The Private Life of Henry VIII *(1933)*

THE PRIVATE SECRETARY (1935) [3]

Dir *Henry Edwards.* Prod *Julius Hagen.* Scr *George Broadhurst, Arthur Macrae, H. Fowler Mear, from a play by Van Moser.* Ph *Sydney Blythe, William Luff.* PC and Dis *Twickenham.* 70 mins. Cert U

Famous old Victorian farce transfers shakily to 1935, despite good turns by *Edward Everett Horton* and *Alastair Sim.* Rich, philandering Cattermole (*Oscar Asche*) returns from India hoping to find his nephew a chip off the old block. The nephew, however, is fleeing his many creditors by impersonating a meek clergyman (*Horton*), who is left to bear the brunt of Cattermole's wrath.

RoC *Judy Gunn, Barry Mackay, Sydney Fairbrother, Michael Shepley, Aubrey Dexter, O. B. Clarence, Davina Craig.*

THE PROUD VALLEY (1939) [6]

Dir *Penrose Tennyson.* (Associate) Prod *Sergei Nolbandov.* Scr *Tennyson, Jack Jones, Louis Goulding, Roland Pertwee.* Ph *Glen MacWilliams, Roy Kellino.* PC *Ealing Studios/*

Edward Chapman, Rachel Thomas and Paul Robeson in The Proud Valley *(1939)*

CAPAD. Dis *Associated British*. 76 mins. Cert A

Wales. Dick (*Edward Chapman*), miner and choirmaster, hears unemployed Black stoker David Goliath (*Paul Robeson*) sing, and finds him a job down the pit. There is an explosion, Dick is killed and the mine closed. After a deputation to London led by David and Dick's son Emlyn (*Simon Lack*), the men reopen the mine themselves. A runaway truck leads to a cave-in, and David sacrifices his life to save his new friends. Considered an outstanding achievement in its time, this looks a little naïve today.

RoC *Edward Rigby, Rachel Thomas, Janet Johnson, Clifford Evans, Allan Jeayes, Jack Jones, George Merritt, Edward Lexy, Dilys Thomas, Babette Walsingham, Dilys Davies, Grant Sutherland, Charles Williams.*

THE PUBLIC LIFE OF HENRY THE NINTH (1934) [3]

Dir and Scr *Bernard Mainwaring*. Prod *Will Hammer*. PC *Hammer*. Dis *M-G-M*. 60 mins. Cert U

Henry (*Leonard Henry*), an unemployed street entertainer, becomes potman at the Henry VIII pub, where Maggie (*Betty Frankiss*) is the drudge. Henry becomes a star singer at the pub – fans call him Henry the Ninth – and Maggie the singing barmaid. The pub prospers, but when the landlord fails to show due appreciation to Henry and his friends, they accept a big stage contract and leave.

RoC *Wally Patch, George Mozart, Aileen Latham, Mai Bacon, Herbert Langley, Dorothy Vernon, Jean Lester.*

PUBLIC NUISANCE No. 1 (1936) [2]

Dir *Marcel Varnel*. Prod *Herman Fellner, Max Schach*. Scr *Roger Burford, Val Guest, Robert Edmunds*. Ph *Claude Friese-Greene*. PC *Cecil Films*. Dis *General Film Distributors*. 78 mins. Cert A

Virtually plotless farce (with music by Vivian Ellis) about an irresponsible man-about-town (*Arthur Riscoe*) set to work as a waiter at a rich uncle's hotel in the south of France. He arranges for the shopgirl (*Frances Day*) he loves to win first prize in a lottery so that she can stay at his hotel, and they become involved in various scrapes there.

RoC *Claude Dampier, Muriel Aked, Peter Haddon, Sebastian Smith, Robert Nainby, Antony Holles.*

PUPPETS OF FATE (1932) [4]
(USA: *Wolves of the Underworld*)

Dir *George A. Cooper*. Prod *Julius Hagen*. Scr *H. Fowler Mear*. PC *Real Art*. Dis *United Artists*. 72 mins. Cert A

No lack of action in this presentably acted crime thriller about a notorious forger (*Ben Welden*) who escapes from Dartmoor, sets up a gang in London's Whitechapel and blackmails a sinister doctor (*Russell Thorndike*) into helping him. It takes a determined detective (*Godfrey Tearle*) and a train smash in Devon to finally crack the gang.

RoC *Isla Bevan, Fred Groves, Michael Hogan,*

Kynaston Reeves, Roland Culver, John Turnbull, S. Victor Stanley.

PURSE STRINGS (1933) [2]

Dir *Henry Edwards*. Prod *Herbert Wilcox*. Scr *Bernard Parry, from his play*. Ph *Henry Harris*. PC *British and Dominions*. Dis *Paramount*. 69 mins. Cert A

Wealthy young Jim Willmore (*Gyles Isham*) keeps his wife Mary (*Dorothy Bouchier*) short of money, and she turns to shoplifting. When a store manager (*Allan Jeayes*) offers to drop charges against Mary in return for her 'favours', Jim takes him to court – but the case bankrupts him, and Mary makes him pay dearly for his past meanness.

RoC *G.H. Mulcaster, Joan Henley, Evelyn Roberts.*

PYGMALION (1938) [6]

Dir *Anthony Asquith, Leslie Howard*. Prod and PC *Gabriel Pascal*. Scr *Anatole de Grunwald, W.P. Lipscomb, Cecil Lewis, Ian Dalrymple, from the play by George Bernard Shaw*. Ph *Harry Stradling*. Dis *General Film Distributors*. 96 mins. Cert A

Henry Higgins (*Leslie Howard*), a professor of phonetics, turns Cockney flower girl Eliza Doolittle (*Wendy Hiller*) into a society lady thanks to an intensive course in speech, etiquette and deportment. Eliza cannot go back to her old life, and after lengthy discussions, and manœuvres on her part, Higgins duly realizes that he cannot live without her. Flawless transition of brilliant play to screen.

RoC *Wilfrid Lawson, Marie Lohr, Scott Sunderland, Jean Cadell, David Tree, Everley Gregg, Leueen MacGrath, Esmé Percy, Violet Vanbrugh, Iris Hoey, Viola Tree, O.B. Clarence, Irene Browne, Kate Cutler, Wally Patch, Ivor Barnard, H.F. Maltby, George Mozart, Stephen Murray, Anthony Quayle, Cathleen Nesbitt, Leo Genn, Cecil Trouncer, Eileen Beldon, Frank Atkinson.*

Leslie Howard and Wendy Hiller in Pygmalion *(1938)*

PYJAMAS PREFERRED (1932) [2]

Dir and Scr *Val Valentine, from a play by J.O. Twiss*. Prod *Walter C. Mycroft*. PC *BIP/ British Instructional*. Dis *Pathé*. 46 mins. Cert A

Comedy crammed with incident if not finesse in its short running time, involving various people at 'Pyjama Night' in an infamous night-club. The president of the Purity League is

there, with a cheque for £1,000 for his work in his pocket, given to him by the woman who, unbeknown to him, runs the club. The woman's philandering husband is also after the money – and he gets it.

LP *Jay Laurier, Betty Amann, Amy Veness, Kenneth Kove, Jack Morrison, Fred Schwartz, Hugh E. Wright.*

Q PLANES (1939) [5]
(USA: *Clouds Over Europe*)

Dir *Tim Whelan*. Prod *Irving Asher*. Scr *Ian Dalrymple, Brock Williams, Arthur Wimperis, Jack Whittingham*. Ph *Harry Stradling*. PC *Harefield*. Dis *Columbia*. 82 mins (USA: 79). Cert U

Major Hammond of the Yard (*Ralph Richardson*) is called in when bombers disappear on test flights. He discovers the owner's secretary Jenkins (*George Curzon*) is the 'inside man' but Jenkins is shot before he can talk. Hammond's sister Kay (*Valerie Hobson*) enlists the help of Tony McVane (*Laurence Olivier*), a test pilot whose plane is brought down by men in a salvage ship with a radio beam. After a shipboard fight, the gang is captured. Spy thriller with much good humour.

RoC *George Merritt, Gus McNaughton, David Tree, Sandra Storme, Hay Petrie, John Longden, Frank Fox, Gordon McLeod, Reginald Purdell, John Laurie, Pat Aherne, Gertrude Musgrove, Ronald Adam, Ian Fleming, Lewis Stringer, Morland Graham, Eileen Bennett, Derek Farr.*

Laurence Olivier and Valerie Hobson in Q Planes *(1939)*

QUEEN OF HEARTS (1936) [4]

Dir *Monty Banks*. Prod *Basil Dean*. Scr *Clifford Grey, H.F. Maltby, Anthony Kimmins, Douglas Furber, Gordon Wellesley*. Ph *John W. Boyle*. PC *ATP*. Dis *Associated British*. 80 mins. Cert U

Delightful comedy-musical, with *Gracie Fields* as a seamstress who works opposite a theatre

John Loder and Gracie Fields in Queen of Hearts *(1936)*

where her idol, Derek Cooper (*John Loder*) is appearing. After she saves him from the consequences of a possible drunk driving charge, she is mistaken for a wealthy woman backing the show – as long as she gets the leading part. She takes it on and, after a few setbacks, wins fame – and Derek.

RoC *Enid Stamp-Taylor, Fred Duprez, Edward Rigby, Julie Suedo, Hal Gordon, Syd Crossley, Madeleine Seymour, H.F. Maltby, Margaret Yarde, Tom Gill, Edith Fields, Vera Hilliard, Tom Payne, Vera Lennox, Mike Johnson, Pat Williams, Balliol and Merton, Jean Lister, Monty Banks.*

THE QUEEN'S AFFAIR (1934)   [3]
(USA: *Runaway Queen*)
Dir and Prod *Herbert Wilcox*. Scr *Samson Raphaelson, Monckton Hoffe, Miles Malleson, from a play by Ernst Marischa, Bruno Granichstaedten.* Ph *F.A. Young.* PC *British and Dominions.* Dis *United Artists.* 77 *mins. Cert U*
Musical romance (music by Oscar Strauss) about a shopgirl (*Anna Neagle*) who becomes heiress to a European throne, but is driven away by revolutionaries led by Carl (*Fernand Graavey*), who becomes President. When the revolution collapses, the heiress becomes Queen and falls in love with Carl, the pair arriving at a governmental compromise acceptable to all the people.
RoC *Muriel Aked, Michael Hogan, Gibb McLaughlin, Miles Malleson, Stuart Robertson, Hay Petrie, Edward Chapman, Reginald Purdell, Clifford Heatherley, David Burns, Trefor Jones, Tarva Penna, Herbert Langley, Helen Mar, Dino Galvani, Arthur Chesney.*

QUEER CARGO (1938)   [1]
(USA: *Pirates of the Seven Seas*)
Dir *Harold Schuster.* Prod *Walter C. Mycroft.* Scr *Patrick Kirwan, Walter Summers, from the play by Noel Langley.* Ph *Otto Kanturek.* PC and Dis *Associated British.* 62 *mins. Cert U*
The China Seas: tramp steamer skipper Harley (*John Lodge*) is smuggling pearls to Singapore. The crew mutinies and demands the pearls. At this moment, the ship is taken by pirates led by Cabini (*Keneth Kent*), whose life Harley had saved years before when Benson (*Louis Borell*), coincidentally also on board, had stolen his lifejacket. After the intervention of a British destroyer, Harley seemingly gives

Cabini the pearls... Too-brief, underdeveloped yarn.
RoC *Judy Kelly, Wylie Watson, Geoffrey Toone, Jerry Verno, Frank Pettingell, Bertha Belmore, Frank Cochrane.*

QUIET PLEASE! (1938)   [2]
Dir *Roy William Neill.* Prod *Irving Asher.* Scr *Reginald Purdell, Anthony Hankey.* Ph *Basil Emmott.* PC *Warner Bros.* Dis *First National.* 69 *mins. Cert A*
Two buskers (*Reginald Purdell, Wally Patch*) cross the path of some jewel thieves. One of them falls for the girl who has been arrested for the gang's latest 'job'. After adopting various disguises, the buskers free her from prison and unmask Holloway (*Julien Mitchell*), the head of the gang. Comedy is too long, even at 69 minutes.
RoC *Lesley Brook, Ian MacLean, Bruce Lister, Winifred Izard, Clem Lawrance, Ian Fleming, Brenda Harvey, Bobby Lawrence.*

RACING ROMANCE (1937)   [3]
Dir *Maclean Rogers.* Prod *A. George Smith.* Scr *John Hunter.* Ph *Geoffrey Faithfull.* PC *GS Enterprises.* Dis *Radio.* 63 *mins. Cert U*
Garage owner Harry (*Bruce Seton*), engaged to ambitious Muriel (*Elizabeth Kent*), buys a racehorse, Brownie, from Peggy (*Marjorie Taylor*) and gets her to train it. He enters it for the Oaks, and when it only finishes second, Muriel, who always hated the horse and Peggy, breaks their engagement. There is an objection and Brownie is the winner: so is Harry – he is free to marry Peggy. Good acting performances give modest sporting film a boost.
RoC *Eliot Makeham, Ian Fleming, Sybil Grove, Robert Hobbs, Charles Sewell, Michael Ripper, Jonathan Field.*

RADIO LOVER (1936)   [3]
Dir *Austin Melford, Paul Capon.* Prod *Ernest King.* Scr *Ian Dalrymple.* PC *City.* Dis *Associated British.* 64 *mins. Cert U*
Agreeable little comedy with some amusing digs at the BBC, as a plain little man with a fine singing voice (*Wylie Watson*) and his handsome but penniless friend (*Jack Melford*) invent a jointly run radio personality, the 'Radio Lover' and pull the wool over the Corporation's eyes. Even after they are exposed by snoopy Miss Oliphant (*Ann Penn*) whose previous attempts had failed, an enterprising manager is waiting with a contract for them.
RoC *Betty Ann Davies, Cynthia Stock, Gerald Barry, Max Faber.*

RADIO PARADE (1933)   [4]
Dir *Archie de Bear, Richard Beville.* Prod *John Maxwell.* Scr *Claude Hulbert, Paul England.* PC *BIP.* Dis *Wardour.* 70 *mins. Cert U*

Star-studded revue spun round a thin thread of story about a troupe of amateur actors spying on their professional counterparts, and subsequently performing with success on American radio.
LP *Christopher Stone (compère), Roy Fox and His Band, Florence Desmond, Claude Hulbert, Clapham and Dwyer, Flotsam and Jetsam, The Houston Sisters, Elsie and Doris Waters, Mabel Constanduros, Jeanne de Casalis, Elsie Carlisle, Leonard Henry, Stainless Stephen, Mario 'Harp' Lorenzi, Stanelli (with Edgar), Doris Arnold, Keith Wilbur, Harry Pepper, Reginald Gardiner, Tex McLeod, Gus McNaughton, The Carlyle Cousins, Michael Hogan.*

RADIO PARADE OF 1935 (1934)   [4]
(USA: *Radio Follies*)
Dir *Arthur Woods.* Prod *Walter C. Mycroft.* Scr *Jack Davies, Paul Perez, James Bunting, Woods.* Ph *Cyril Bristow, Philip Grindrod.* PC *BIP.* Dis *Wardour. Dufaycolour sequence.* 96 *mins. Cert A*
Occasionally funny and generally entertaining comedy-musical with guest appearances from many radio stars. Times are hard for the NBG radio station and its boss (*Will Hay*). Then its complaints manager (*Clifford Mollison*) who's in love with the boss's daughter (*Helen Chandler*) saves the day by finding new talent among the station's employees, and beaming a gala concert by television to crowds in streets and squares.
RoC *Davy Burnaby, Alfred Drayton, Billy Bennett, Lily Morris, Nellie Wallace, The Western Brothers, Clapham and Dwyer, The Three Sailors, Haver and Lee, The Carlyle Cousins, Gerry Fitzgerald, Claude Dampier, Ted Ray, Eve Becke, Georgie Harris, Arthur Young, Hugh E. Wright, Robert Nainby, Jimmy Godden, Basil Foster, Ivor McLaren, Fay Carroll, Peggy Cochrane, Yvette Darnac, Teddy Joyce and His Band, Ronald Frankau, Alberta Hunter, Joyce Richardson, Beryl Orde, Fred Conyngham, Gillie Potter, Sybil Grove, The Buddy Bradley Girls, Stanelli and His Hornchestra.*

RADIO PIRATES (1935)   [3]
Dir *Ivar Campbell.* Prod *Norman Loudon.* Scr *Donovan Pedelty.* PC *Sound City.* Dis *Associated Producers and Distributors.* 89 *mins. Cert U*
Comedy-musical in which a radio shop proprietor, a songwriter and a café proprietress start a pirate radio station to help save themselves from financial disaster. They lead the police a merry dance until they are finally cornered in the Big Ben tower.
LP *Leslie French, Mary Lawson, Warren Jenkins, Enid Stamp-Taylor, Kenneth Kove, Edgar Driver, Frederick Lloyd, John Turnbull, Fanny Wright, Hughie Green, Teddy Brown, H. Saxon-Snell, Hal Booth, Iva Gay, Arthur Mayne, Roy Fox and His Band.*

RAISE THE ROOF (1930)   [3]
Dir, Prod and Scr *Walter Summers.* PC *BIP.* Dis *First National-Pathé.* 77 *mins. Cert U*
A musical (music: *Tom Helmore*) in which Rodney, a rich man's son (*Maurice Evans*) becomes the owner of an unsuccessful touring

company, and falls for Maisie (*Betty Balfour*), one of its players. Rodney's father (*Sam Livesey*) hires a star (*Jack Raine*) to make sure the company remains a flop, but Maisie saves the day and wins the old man over.

RoC *Ellis Jeffreys, Arthur Hardy, Louie Emery, Dorothy Minto, Josephine Earle, Andrea Malandrinos, Charles Garry, Mike Johnson, Plaza Tiller Girls.*

THE RASP (1931)   [3]

Dir *Michael Powell.* Prod *Jerome Jackson.* Scr *Philip Macdonald, from his own novel.* Ph *Geoffrey Faithfull.* PC *Film Engineering.* Dis *Fox. 44 mins. Cert A*

Tidy murder mystery featuring *Claude Horton* as a reporter who becomes fascinated by the murder of a cabinet minister, for which the dead man's secretary is under suspicion. The reporter builds up evidence which suggests another man, the minister's friend and house guest, murdered him; he resorts to a bluff and tricks the killer into confessing.

RoC *Phyllis Loring, C.M. Hallard, James Raglan, Thomas Weguelin, Carol Coombe, Leonard Brett.*

THE RAT (1937)   [2]

Dir *Jack Raymond.* Prod *Herbert Wilcox.* Scr *Hans Rameau, Marjorie Gaffney, Miles Malleson, Romney Brent, from the play by Ivor Novello, Constance Collier.* Ph *Frederick A. Young.* PC *Imperator.* Dis *Radio. 72 mins. Cert A*

Doomed attempt to resuscitate the Novello-Collier play about the Paris jewel thief (*Anton Walbrook*) who milks rich ladies but is reformed by the love of the orphan daughter (*René Ray*) of another criminal. He even confesses to the killing she did in self-defence, but an old love (*Ruth Chatterton*) perjures herself to save him.

RoC *Beatrix Lehmann, Mary Clare, Felix Aylmer, Hugh Miller, Gordon McLeod, Frederick Culley, Nadine March, George Merritt, Leo Genn, Fanny Wright, Bob Gregory, Ivan Wilmot, J.H. Roberts, Aubrey Mallalieu, Paul Sheridan, Walter Schofield, Stanley Lathbury, Beatrice (Betty) Marsden.*

A REAL BLOKE (1935)   [3]

Dir *John Baxter.* Prod *John Barter.* Scr *Herbert Ayres.* Ph *Desmond Dickinson.* PC *Baxter and Barter.* Dis *Universal. 70 mins. Cert U*

Another of John Baxter's sincere slices of working-class life. Bill (*George Carney*), a navvy, is sacked for voicing his opinion on unemployment that might be created by labour-saving devices. He keeps the news from his wife until after their daughter's wedding; then his son-in-law is seriously injured in an accident. The birth of a grandson renews Bill's interest in life.

RoC *Mary Clare, Diana Beaumont, Mark Daly, Peggy Novak, Billy Holland, Wilson Coleman, Roddy Hughes, Edgar Driver, (C.) Denier Warren, Dick Francis, Johnnie Schofield, John Turnbull, Freddie Watts, Fred Wynne.*

THE REBEL SON (1939)   [2]

Dir *Adrian Brunel, Alex Granowsky.* Prod *E.C. Molinier, Charles David.* Scr *Brunel, from a story by Nicolai Gogol.* Ph *Franz Planer, Bernard Browne.* PC *Omnia Films/London Films.* Dis *United Artists. 80 mins. Cert A*

The sixteenth century: a Cossack chieftain, Tarass Boulba (*Harry Baur*) has two sons. Both of them are given a good education and one, Andrew (*Anthony Bushell*) finds himself shocked by his father's aggressive ideals. He joins sides with the Poles when Tarass makes unjustified war on them, and both Andrew and his father are killed. English-language version of 1936 French film leans heavily on spectacle for its appeal.

RoC *Roger Livesey, Patricia Roc, Joan Gardner, Frederick Culley, Joseph Cunningham, Bernard Miles, Stafford Hilliard, Charles Farrell, Amy Wemyss.*

RED ENSIGN (1934)   [3]
(USA: *Strike!*)

Dir *Michael Powell.* Prod *Jerome Jackson.* Scr *L. duGarde Peach.* Ph *Leslie Rowson.* PC and Dis *Gaumont-British. 69 mins (later 66). Cert U*

Slow but quite strong shipbuilding drama. Barr (*Leslie Banks*) plans to launch a new cargo vessel; when his board refuses to finance it, he decides to use his own money, but has also to deal with a crooked business rival (*Alfred Drayton*) who is trying to wreck the project. After forging the board chairman's signature for more money, Barr goes to prison – but the ship is eventually launched, and the woman he loves (*Carol Goodner*) stands by him.

RoC *Vosper, Donald Calthrop, Allan Jeayes, Campbell Gullan, Percy Parsons, Fewlass Llewellyn, Henry Oscar.*

RED WAGON (1933)   [5]

Dir *Paul Stein.* Prod *Walter C. Mycroft.* Scr *Roger Burford, Edward Knoblock, Arthur Woods.* Ph *Jack Cox.* PC *BIP.* Dis *Wardour. 106 mins. Cert A*

Strong emotional drama of circus life, adapted from a novel by Lady Eleanor Smith. *Charles Bickford* plays Joe Prince, orphaned son of trapeze artists, who joins a circus which he eventually inherits. Loved by Zara (*Greta Nissen*) the tiger tamer, he marries voluptuous gipsy Sheba (*Raquel Torres*), but sees her in her true colours when she absconds with her ex-lover and circus funds. Joe and Zara vow to build up the circus again – and their own relationship.

RoC *Don Alvarado, Anthony Bushell, Paul Graetz, Amy Veness, Jimmy Hanley, Frank Pettingell, Francis L. Sullivan, Alexander Field, Percy Parsons, Nancy Brown, Aubrey Mather, Stella Bonheur, Sybil Grove, Arthur Goullet, Helen Ferrers, Hay Petrie, Charles Farrell, Torin Thatcher.*

REMBRANDT (1936)   [4]

Dir and Prod *Alexander Korda.* Scr *Carl Zuckmayer, Lajos Biro, June Head, Arthur Wimperis.* Ph *Georges Périnal, Richard Angst.* PC *London Films.* Dis *United Artists. 85 mins. Cert A*

An account of the last 25 years in the life of the painter Rembrandt (*Charles Laughton*), told with dignity, subtlety and restraint. After

Charles Laughton in Rembrandt *(1936)*

the death of his wife, Rembrandt sinks towards poverty, his art no longer appreciated. He becomes entangled with his housekeeper (*Gertrude Lawrence*), then is uplifted by the love of a serving-maid (*Elsa Lanchester*). But she, too, dies, leaving him alone again.

RoC *Edward Chapman, Walter Hudd, Roger Livesey, John Bryning, Sam Livesey, Herbert Lomas, Allan Jeayes, John Clements, Raymond Huntley, Abraham Sofaer, Lawrence Hanray, Austin Trevor, Henry Hewitt, Gertrude Musgrove, Basil Gill, Edmund Willard, Marius Goring, Richard Gofe, Meinhart Maur, George Merritt, John Turnbull, William Ragan, Lewis Broughton, Frederick Burtwell, Barry Livesey, Baroness Narany, Quinton McPherson, Jack Livesey, Roger Wellesley, Byron Webber, Bellendon Powell, Charles Paton, Hector Abbas, Leonard Sharpe, Jerrold Robertshaw, Evelyn Ankers, George Pughe, James Carney.*

RETURN OF A STRANGER (1937)   [2]
(USA: *The Face Behind the Scar*)

Dir *Victor Hanbury.* Prod *John Stafford.* Scr *Akos Tolnay, Reginald Long, from the play by Rudolph Lothar.* Ph *James Wilson.* PC *Premier/Stafford.* Dis *Radio. 70 mins. Cert A*

James Martin (*Griffith Jones*), a young chemist, elopes with the boss's daughter Carol (*Rosalyn Boulter*), but a murder is committed at their hotel and Jim, under suspicion, flees. Years later he returns, a famous scientist, though disfigured in an explosion, to hunt down the killer and reclaim Carol, even though she's married. So guess who the killer is? Unlikely? Take my word for it.

RoC *Ellis Jeffreys, Athole Stewart, Constance Godridge, Cecil Ramage, Sylvia Marriott, James Harcourt, Harold Scott, Tarva Penna.*

THE RETURN OF BULLDOG DRUMMOND (1934)   [2]

Dir and Scr *Walter Summers, from a novel by 'Sapper'.* Prod *Walter C. Mycroft.* Ph *Jack Parker.* PC *BIP.* Dis *Wardour. 71 mins. Cert U*

Possibly the least successful film incarnation of Sapper's famous sleuth. Drummond's much-put-upon wife Phyllis (*Ann Todd*) is kidnapped by a gang of political crooks led by Drummond's old enemy Carl Peterson (*Francis L. Sullivan*), but Drummond (*Ralph Richardson*) rescues her and rids England of the gang.

RoC *Claud Allister, Joyce Kennedy, H. Saxon-Snell, Spencer Trevor, Charles Mortimer, Wallace Geoffrey, Pat Aherne.*

THE RETURN OF CAROL DEANE
(1938)   [1]

Dir *Arthur Woods.* Prod *Jerome Jackson.* Scr *John Meehan Jr, Paul Gangelin, Tom Phipps, from a story by Joseph Santley.* Ph *Basil Emmott.* PC and Dis *Warner Bros.* 77 mins. Cert A

Edwardian London: Carol Deane (*Bebe Daniels*) marries into the aristocracy, but is later jailed for manslaughter. On her release, she joins forces with a crooked gambler. In his casino, she encounters her son, who does not know her. She decides to keep her identity a secret from him, and to marry the gambler who loves her. Totally unbelievable weepie.

RoC *Arthur Margetson, Zena Dare, Chili Bouchier, Michael Drake, Wyndham Goldie, Peter Coke, Lesley Brook, David Burns, Ian Maclean, Aubrey Mallalieu, Ian Fleming.*

THE RETURN OF RAFFLES (1932)   [3]

Dir and Prod *Mansfield Markham.* Scr *W.J. Balef, from stories by E.W. Hornung.* Ph *Emil Schunemann, Geoffrey Faithfull.* PC *Markham.* Dis *Williams and Pritchard.* 70 mins. Cert A

Gentleman crook A.J. Raffles (*George Barraud*) visits a country house with the intention of stealing some famous emeralds there. But someone beats him to it. As he finds the lady of the house is a German girl (*Camilla Horn*) with whom he was once in love, Raffles sets out to find the real thief and get her back her gems.

RoC *Claud Allister, A. Bromley Davenport, Sydney Fairbrother, H. Saxon-Snell, Philip Strange.*

THE RETURN OF THE FROG (1938)   [4]

Dir *Maurice Elvey.* Prod *Herbert Wilcox.* Scr *Ian Hay, Gerald Elliott, from a novel by Edgar Wallace.* Ph *George Stretton.* PC *Imperator.* Dis *British Lion.* 76 mins. Cert A

A number of murders in London's dockland makes Elk of the Yard (*Gordon Harker*) suspect that the criminal gang known as The Frogs has found a new leader. Elk barely escapes death in a cellar filled with poison gas and from a bomb attached to a police launch before he locates the headquarters of the gang and unmasks the new Frog himself. Adventure is improbable but likeable and exciting.

RoC *René Ray, Hartley Power, Una O'Connor, Cyril Smith, Aubrey Mallalieu, Meinhart Maur, Charles Lefeaux, Charles Carson, George Hayes, Dennis Cowles, Patrick Parsons (Holt).*

THE RETURN OF THE SCARLET PIMPERNEL (1937)   [3]

Dir *Hans Schwartz.* Prod *Alexander Korda, Arnold Pressburger.* Scr *Lajos Biro, Arthur Wimperis, Adrian Brunel, from a novel by Baroness Orczy.* Ph *Mutz Greenbaum,* PC *London Films.* Dis *United Artists.* 94 mins. Cert A

Further (and lesser) adventures of the Pimpernel (here *Barry K. Barnes*). In Revolutionary France, the Reign of Terror is in full swing, and the infamous Citizen Chauvelin (*Francis Lister*) attempts to trap Sir Percy Blakeney, alias the Pimpernel, by kidnapping his wife Marguerite (*Sophie Stewart*), transporting her to Paris and having her condemned to death. He does not succeed.

RoC *Margaretta Scott, James Mason, Anthony Bushell, Patrick Barr, David Tree, Henry Oscar, Hugh Miller, Allan Jeayes, O.B. Clarence, George Merritt, Evelyn Roberts, Esmé Percy, Edmund Breon, John Counsell, Frank Allenby, Torin Thatcher.*

RETURN TO YESTERDAY (1939)   [3]

Dir *Robert Stevenson.* (Associate) Prod *S.C. Balcon.* Scr *Robert Stevenson, Roland Pertwee, Angus Macphail, Margaret Kennedy (uncredited), from a play by Robert Morley.* Ph *Ronald Neame.* PC *Ealing Studios/CAPAD.* Dis *Associated British.* 69 mins. Cert U

Maine (*Clive Brook*), a fading matinée idol, returns to his old seaside haunts and, unrecognized at first, is taken on at the local pier-end play when the leading man walks out. He falls in love with actress Carol (*Anna Lee*), fiancée of the playwright (*David Tree*). Maine's old landlady (*Elliot Mason*), knowing him to be married, persuades him to give Carol up and go back to reality. Sentimental story lacks length and strength.

RoC *O.B. Clarence, Dame May Whitty, Hartley Power, Milton Rosmer, Garry Marsh, Olga Lindo, Frank Pettingell, Arthur Margetson, Wally Patch, H.F. Maltby, David Horne, Alf Goddard, John Turnbull, Eliot Makeham, Mary Jerrold, Ludwig Stossel, Molly Rankin, Patric Curwen.*

REUNION (1932)   [4]

Dir *Ivan Campbell.* Prod *Norman Loudon.* Scr *Herbert Ayres, from an article by Reginald Hargreaves.* PC *Sound City.* Dis *M-G-M.* 60 mins. Cert U

Silent screen idol *Stewart Rome* had one of the best of his many roles in sound films in this quiet, restrained and moving drama. He plays a major, financially on the rocks, invited to speak at a regimental dinner. He goes to London, gives his last £1 to a collection at the dinner and walks home remembering the final words of his own speech: 'A man is never deserted until he deserts himself.'

RoC *Antony Holles, Roddy Hughes, Robert Dudley, Eric Pavitt, Fred Schwartz, George Bishop, Kit Keen, Philip Ritti, Bob Wilkins, Harry Terry, James Prior, Leonard Morris, Randolph McLeod, Bernard Dudley, Gerald Steyn, Colin Wark, Lohn Lalette, Terry Irvine, Harry Blue, Fred Watts, James Stadden, Noel Dainton, Robert Newton, Japp the dog.*

THE REVERSE BE MY LOT (1937)   [2]

Dir *Raymond Stross.* Prod *Nat Ross.* Scr *Syd Courtenay, from the novel by Margaret Morrison.* Ph *John Silver.* PC *Rock Productions.* Dis *Columbia.* 68 mins. Cert A

A down-and-out actress (*Marjorie Corbett*) volunteers as a guinea-pig for a new 'flu serum. The physician's son's fiancée dies from especially virulent flu, and the son falls for the actress. The physician also falls for the actress and is reluctant to inject her, but she does it herself, forcing him to use his antidote and prove it works. She realizes she loves the younger man, and the physician is reconciled with his wife. Dreadful title, film not much better.

RoC *Ian Fleming, Mickey Brantford, Georgie Harris, Jackie Heller, Helen Goss, Audrene Brier, Aubrey Mallalieu, Joan Ponsford.*

RHODES OF AFRICA (1936)   [5]
(USA: *Rhodes*)

Dir *Berthold Viertel.* (Associate) Prod *Geoffrey Barkas.* Scr *Michael Barringer, Miles Malleson, Leslie Arliss, from the book by Sarah Millin.* Ph *Bernard Knowles.* PC and Dis *Gaumont-British.* 92 mins. Cert U

Impressive historical epic. Diamonds are found at Kimberley in Southern Africa in 1880, where Cecil Rhodes, a man with a vision of a united southern African nation, is mining. Rhodes (*Walter Huston*) enters politics the following year, and is prime minister of the Cape Colony by 1890. He institutes far-reaching reforms, but his complicity in the infamous Jameson Raid forces him to resign in 1896. He dies at 49, with so much yet to be done.

RoC *Oscar Homolka, Basil Sydney, Peggy Ashcroft, Frank Cellier, Renee de Vaux, Bernard Lee, Lewis Casson, Glennis Lorimer, Ndaniso Kumala.*

RHYTHM IN THE AIR (1936)   [3]

Dir *Arthur Woods.* Prod *John Findlay.* Scr *Jack Donohue, Vina de Vesci.* Ph *Roy Kellino.* PC and Dis *Fox British.* 72 mins. Cert U

Unusual light musical, thin but pleasant, featuring American dancer *Jack Donohue* (who later turned director) as a riveter working on high girders who, while watching a girl practising tap dancing, falls and breaks both ankles. Visiting him in hospital, she encourages him to take up dancing to strengthen his ankles. Finding he has lost his nerve for heights, he takes her up on it, and they become partners on stage and in life.

RoC *Tutta Rolf, Vic Oliver, Leslie Perrins, Kitty Kelly, Tony Sympson.*

RHYTHM RACKETEER (1937)   [1]

Dir *James Seymour.* Prod *Joe Rock.* Scr *John Byrd.* Ph *Ernest Palmer.* PC *Rock Productions.* Dis *British Independent.* 84 mins. Cert A

Nap Connors (*Harry Roy*), a Chicago gangster on a trip to London, realizes he has a double in bandleader Harry Grand (also Roy). On board a transatlantic liner, Connors steals some jewels and frames Grand for the crime. Grand has a hard time evading the police and protecting his girlfriend from gangsters, but eventually wins through. Ineffectual crime musical.

RoC *Princess Pearl (Pearl Vyner Brooke), James Carew, Norma Varden, Johnny Hines, Johnny Schofield, Judith Wood, Georgie Harris, Pamela Randall, James Pirrie, Harry Roy's Band.*

RICH AND STRANGE (1931)   [2]
(USA: *East of Shanghai*)

Dir *Alfred Hitchcock.* Prod *John Maxwell.* Scr *Val Valentine, Alma Reville, Hitchcock, from* the novel by *Dale Collins*. Ph *Jack Cox, Charles Martin*. PC *BIP*. Dis *Wardour*. 92 mins. Cert A

Rather odd Hitchcock picture, about a young couple (*Henry Kendall, Joan Barry*) who come into some money and decide to relieve their humdrum lives by going on a cruise. While he is in his cabin, permanently sick, she is courted by a smooth Commander. Once the husband is well, he becomes infatuated by a 'princess' who proves to be an adventuress who rooks him of his money. The wife nearly leaves him for her Commander, but ultimately they survive a shipwreck and return home, sadder, wiser and still together.

RoC *Percy Marmont, Betty Amann, Elsie Randolph, Hannah Jones, Aubrey Dexter.*

Joan Barry and Henry Kendall in Rich and Strange *(1932)*

RIDING HIGH (1937)   ③

Dir *David Macdonald*. Prod *George King*. Scr *H. Fowler Mear*. Ph *Hone Glendinning*. PC *Embassy*. Dis *British Lion*. 68 mins. Cert U

Quite pleasing and inventive little comedy in period (1879) setting. Tom Blake (*John Garrick*), the husky village blacksmith, also has talents as an inventor. When he constructs a new kind of bicycle, his addle-brained solicitor friend Septimus Earwicker (*Claude Dampier*) helps him win a vital race that proves the cycle's worth.

RoC *Kathleen Gibson, Helen Haye, John Warwick, Billy Merson, Mai Bacon, Peter Gawthorne, Billy Holland, Billy Bray, Mansell and Ling, Bertie Kendrick, The Georgian Singers.*

THE RIGHT AGE TO MARRY (1935)   ③

Dir *P. Maclean Rogers*. Prod *A. George Smith*. Scr *H.F. Maltby, Kathleen Butler, from the play by Maltby*. Ph *Geoffrey Faithfull*. PC *GS Enterprises*. Dis *Radio*. 69 mins. Cert U

Good work by *Frank Pettingell* lifts this comedy-drama about Ramsden, a Yorkshire mill-owner who retires at 50, leaving his nephew Stephen (*Tom Helmore*) in control. Ramsden enters into society, but his new 'friends' make a complete ass of him, and rapidly disappear when news comes that the mill, uninsured, has burnt down. Ramsden marries his housekeeper and rebuilds the business.

RoC *Joyce Bland, Ruby Miller, Moira Lynd, Hal Walters, H.F. Maltby, Gerald Barry, Isobel Scaife, Vincent Holman, Reginald Bates.*

THE RIGHT TO LIVE (1933)   ②

Dir *Albert Parker*. Prod *Ernest Garside*. Scr *Gordon Wong Wellesley, Frank Atkinson, R.J. Davis*. PC *Fox British*. Dis *Fox*. 72 mins. Cert A

A straight role for comedian *Davy Burnaby* as a scientist who invents a formula to neutralize the effects of poison gas. Bad guys steal the formula, incriminating Fulton (*Richard Bird*) who loves the scientist's daughter (*Pat Paterson*). But Fulton clears his name and thwarts the crooks' plans to kill the scientist.

RoC *Francis L. Sullivan, Lawrence Anderson, Frank Atkinson.*

THE RINGER (1931)   ⑤

Dir *Walter Forde*. Prod *Michael Balcon*. Scr *Robert Stevenson, Angus Macphail, Edgar Wallace (uncredited), Sidney Gilliat (uncredited), from the play by Wallace*. Ph *Leslie Rowson, Alec Bryce*. PC *Gainsborough-British Lion*. Dis *Ideal*. 75 mins. Cert A

Former comedian Walter Forde gathered his best reviews so far for this second film version of Edgar Wallace's famous story (originally a novel called *The Gaunt Stranger*) about a criminal master of disguise who returns to England to carry out his revenge on the solicitor responsible for the death of his sister. Contains the classic line 'The Ringer has been seen in Deptford!' (no-one, of course, knows what The Ringer looks like without one of his disguises).

LP *Gordon Harker, Franklin Dyall, John Longden, Carol Goodner, Patrick Curwen, Dorothy Bartlam, Esmond Knight, Henry Hallett, Arthur Stratton, Kathleen Joyce, Eric Stanley.*

THE RIVER HOUSE GHOST (1932)   ②

Dir *Frank Richardson*. Prod *Irving Asher*. Scr *W. Scott Darling*. PC *Warner Bros*. Dis *First National*. 52 mins. Cert A

The personality of *Florence Desmond* gives a slight boost to a conventional haunted house thriller, in which the skeletons and apparitions prove to be the work of a syndicate anxious to get hold of River House at a low price. A young Cockney girl and two tramps expose their scheme.

RoC *Hal Walters, Joan Marion, Mike Johnson, Helen Ferrers, Erle Stanley, Shayle Gardner.*

THE RIVER HOUSE MYSTERY (1935)   ①

Dir *Fraser Foulsham*. Prod *A.B. Imeson*. Scr *F.G. Robertson*. Ph *Alex Bryce*. PC *Imeson-Foulsham*. Dis *Universal*. 56 mins. Cert U

Financier Sir John (*George (G.H.) Mulcaster*), an avid crime novel reader, becomes involved in a mystery revolving round a group of Russian refugees and a gang of crooks after emeralds possessed by a girl refugee. In protecting the girl, Sir John believes he has killed a man – but finds the whole thing was a hoax perpetrated by some of his 'friends'. Drama begins well but disintegrates.

RoC *Ena Moon, Bernard Lee, Boris Ranevsky, Roddy Hughes, Clifford Evans, A.B. Imeson, W.E. Holloway, Davy Hayward, Percy Walsh, Frank Snell.*

THE RIVER WOLVES (1933)   ②

Dir *George Pearson*. Prod *Julius Hagen*. Scr *Terence Egan, from a play by Edward Dignon, Geoffrey Swaffer*. Ph *Ernest Palmer*. PC *Real Art*. Dis *Radio*. 56 mins. Cert A

The waterfront setting is the best feature of this thick-ear melodrama about a sea captain (*Michael Hogan*) visiting dockside Tilbury for material for a novel. He meets another aspiring writer, Peter (*John Mills*) and both fall for the same girl (*Hope Davy*). A gang of crooks have a hold on Peter, but the captain deals with them, before leaving when he realizes the girl loves Peter.

RoC *Ben Welden, Helga Moray, Norman Shelley, Martin Walker, D.J. Williams, Mark Daly, Edgar Driver, Barbara Everest.*

ROAD HOUSE (1934)   ②

Dir *Maurice Elvey*. Prod *Michael Balcon*. Scr *Austin Melford, Leslie Arliss, from a play by Walter Hackett*. PC and Dis *Gaumont-British*. 76 mins. Cert A

Less successful re-teaming of *Britannia of Billingsgate* co-stars *Violet Loraine* and *Gordon Harker* in a rather disjointed low-life semi-musical about a singer at a 'road-house' who becomes a stage star, to the discomfort of her down-to-earth husband. She also clears her daughter, who had been falsely accused of killing a ne'er-do-well.

RoC *Aileen Marson, Emlyn Williams, Hartley Power, Anne Grey, Stanley Holloway, Marie Lohr, Edwin Styles, Romilly Lunge, Horace Kenney, Wylie Watson, Frank Atkinson, Geraldo and His Band.*

THE ROAD TO FORTUNE (1930)   ①

Dir and Prod *Arthur Varney-Serrao*. Scr *Hugh Broadbridge from his novel* Moorland Terror. PC *Starcraft*. Dis *Paramount*. 60 mins. Cert U

A harbinger of quota quickies to come, this was a tedious thriller about a headstrong girl (*Doria March*) whose ex-lover (*Guy Newall*) saves her from the life of crime to which her wilfulness seems to have destined her. Redeemed only by the natural beauty of its Cornish exteriors.

RoC *Florence Desmond, Stanley Cooke, J.H. Wakefield, Jean Lester, George Vollaire, Anne Kelagh.*

THE ROBBER SYMPHONY (1936)   ③

Dir *Friedrich Feher*. Prod *Robert Wiene*. Scr *Feher, Anton Kun, Jack Trendall*. Ph *Eugene Schufftan*. PC and Dis *Concordia*. 136 mins. Cert U

Long musical fairy-tale (the film is almost all music) about a band of robbers in the Tyrol who steal a fortune in gold coins and hide them in a little donkey boy's piano-organ. Evading the authorities, they pursue the boy, his dog and donkey through the countryside, but fail to get their ill-gotten gains back and are finally captured and brought to book. Made in bilingual versions.

LP *Hans Feher, Magda Sonja, Michael Martin-Harvey, Webster Booth, George Graves, Oscar Asche, Alexandre Rignault, Vinette, Ivor Wilmot.*

THE ROCKS OF VALPRÉ (1934) [2]
(USA: *High Treason*)
Dir *Henry Edwards*. Prod *Julius Hagen*. Scr *H. Fowler Mear*, from the novel by *Ethel M. Dell*. PC *Real Art*. Dis *Radio*. 73 mins. Cert A
Melodramatic adventure about a Belgian officer in 1860, Capt. Louis de Monteville (*John Garrick*) who, on the evidence of fellow-officer Capt. Rodolphe (*Leslie Perrins*), is unjustly court martialled and sent to Devil's Island. He is freed in time to save his beloved Christine (*Winifred Shotter*) from the attentions of Rodolphe, who turns out to be a spy. RoC *Michel Shepley, Lewis Shaw, Athene Seyler, Agnes Imlay, Joan Summerfield (Jean Kent)*.

RODNEY STEPS IN (1931) [3]
Dir *Guy Newall*. Prod *Julius Hagen, Harry Cohen*. Scr *Brock Williams*. Ph *Basil Emmott*. PC *Real Art*. Dis *Fox*. 42 mins. Cert U
Young Rodney Perch becomes involved with a mysterious masked lady jewel thief whose crooked activities are more apparent than real. She finds herself with her greatest prize – a rich husband. Unlikely quota quickie. LP *Richard Cooper, Elizabeth Allan, Walter Piers, Leo Sheffield, Alexander Field, John Turnbull*.

ROLLING HOME (1935) [2]
Dir *Ralph Ince*. Prod *Norman Loudon*. Scr *Frank Launder*. Ph *George Dudgeon Stretton, Hone Glendinning*. PC *Sound City*. Dis *Associated Producers and Distributors*. 69 mins. Cert U
Silly, though quite successful vehicle for *Will Fyffe*, who plays Mac, a Scottish engineer with his country's traditional passion for whisky. Mac is sacked from his ship after taking the blame for a collision (actually the captain's fault). He stows away on another ship with his pal Wally (*Ralph Ince*). There is a mutiny, foiled by Mac and Wally. He returns in triumph to the village he left in disgrace. RoC *Molly Lamont, James Raglan, Ruth Maitland, Mrs Graham Moffatt, H. Saxon-Snell, Jock McKay, Charles Castella, Douglas Stewart, Herbert Cameron*.

ROLLING IN MONEY (1934) [2]
Dir *Al Parker*. Prod *John Barrow*. Scr *R.J. Davis, Sewell Stokes, Frank Atkinson*, from a play by *R.C. Carton*. PC and Dis *Fox British*. 85 mins. Cert A
Rather wordy comedy, based on the farce *Mr Hopkinson*, and providing a showcase role for *Leslie Sarony* as the Cockney hairdresser who suddenly comes into a large amount of money and finds himself the target of Lady Eggleby (*Anna Lee*), daughter of an aristocrat (*Isabel Jeans*) whose stately home cloaks empty coffers at the bank. RoC *Horace Hodges, John Loder, Garry Marsh, René Ray, Lawrence Grossmith, C.M. Hallard, Frank Atkinson, Arnold Lucy, Elaine Inescort*.

ROMANCE À LA CARTE (1938) [2]
Dir *Maclean Rogers*. Prod *A. George Smith*. Scr *Vera Allinson*. Ph *Geoffrey Faithfull*. PC *GS Enterprises*. Dis *RKO Radio*. 72 mins. Cert U
Head chef Louis (*Leslie Perrins*) and maître d'hôtel Rudolph (*Antony Holles*) are always quarrelling. When Anne (*Dorothy Boyd*) cannot pay her bill, Rudolph threatens to call the police, but Louis gives her a job. Rudolph sacks them both, but eventually all three end up running a restaurant together. Fairly thin comedy shows up with a few laughs. RoC *Charles Sewell, Michael Bazalgette, Paul Sheridan, Betty Shale, Michael Ripper*.

A ROMANCE IN FLANDERS (1937) [3]
(USA: *Lost on the Western Front*)
Dir *Maurice Elvey*. Prod *F. Deutschmeister*. Scr *Harold Simpson*, from a novel by *Mario Fort, Ralph Vanio*. PC *Franco-London*. Dis *British Lion*. 73 mins. Cert A
A woman who believes her husband died in the first World War remarries. Twenty years later, he comes back into her life and she learns that the man she married had ordered her first husband to his death. Tragedy nearly follows when, at a reunion, the fateful events of 1917 are reconstructed. LP *Paul Cavanagh, Marcelle Chantal, Garry Marsh, Olga Lindo, Alastair Sim, Evelyn Roberts, Kynaston Reeves, (C.) Denier Warren, Frank Atkinson, Muriel Pavlow, Bobbie Comber, Andrea Malandrinos, Denise Sydney*.

ROMANCE IN RHYTHM (1934) [1]
Dir, Prod and Scr *Lawrence Huntingdon*. PC *Allied Film Productions*. Dis *M-G-M*. 73 mins. Cert A
Rough-edged look at life behind the scenes at London's cabarets, where a romance between chorus-girl Ruth (*Phyllis Clare*) and musician Bob (*David Hutcheson*) breaks up, and Bob is suspected when Ruth's new fiancé is found murdered. A nightclub manager (*David Burns*) who wanted Ruth for himself is eventually proved to be the killer. RoC *Queenie Leonard, Paul Tillett, Geoffrey Goodheart, Philip Strange, Julian Vedey, Carroll Gibbons and His Savoy Orpheans*.

ROMANY LOVE (1931) [2]
Dir *Fred Paul*. Prod, Scr and PC *Patrick K. Heale*. Dis *M-G-M*. 58 mins. Cert U
Dated attempt at a musical extravaganza against a background of gipsy life. *Esmond Knight* plays the romantic gipsy who wins the girl despite the treacherous efforts of a rival. RoC *Florence McHugh, Roy Travers, Jack Barnes, Rita Cave*.

ROME EXPRESS (1932) [6]
Dir *Walter Forde*. Prod *Michael Balcon*. Scr *Sidney Gilliat, Clifford Grey, Frank Vosper, Ralph Stock*. Ph *Günther Krampf*. PC and Dis *Gaumont*. 94 mins. Cert A
Murder and the theft of a valuable painting aboard the Paris-Rome Express are investigated by French detective Jolif (*Frank Vosper*) – and it seems that almost everyone has something to hide. This prototype train thriller attracted rave reviews. One critic even went so far as to say it was 'the best British picture

Joan Barry in Rome Express *(1933)*

ever' and Walter Forde's direction was dubbed 'outstanding'. RoC *Conrad Veidt, Esther Ralston, Gordon Harker, Joan Barry, Harold Huth, Donald Calthrop, Cedric Hardwicke, Hugh Williams, Muriel Aked, Finlay Currie, Eliot Makeham*.

THE ROOF (1933) [3]
Dir *George A. Cooper*. Prod *Julius Hagen*. Scr *H. Fowler Mear*, from a novel by *David Whitelaw*. PC *Real Art*. Dis *Radio*. 58 mins. Cert A
Rough-and-ready crime drama, but packed with incident, in which Inspector Darrow (*Leslie Perrins*) investigates the death of wealthy James Renton (*George Zucco*) and eventually proves the killer to have been lawyer John Rutherford (*Eliot Makeham*), to whom Renton had entrusted some valuable jewels. RoC *Judy Gunn, Russell Thorndike, Michael Hogan, Ivor Barnard, Barbara Everest, Leo Britt, D.J. Williams, Hector Abbas, Cyril Smith*.

ROOKERY NOOK (1930) [5]
(USA: *One Embarrassing Night*)
Dir *Tom Walls, Byron Haskin*. Prod *Herbert Wilcox*. Scr *W.P. Lipscomb, Ben Travers*, from the play by *Travers*. Ph *Dave Kessan*. PC *British and Dominions/The Gramophone Co*. Dis *W and F*. 76 mins. Cert U
The first and most famous of the 'Aldwych farces' was also the first to be made as a sound film. A girl on the run from her stepfather befriends a married man on holiday, who has to try and hide her not only from her pursuers but his own suspicious wife and mother-in-law. Complications flow fast and furious. LP *Ralph Lynn, Tom Walls, Winifred Shotter, Mary Brough, J. Robertson Hare, Ethel Coleridge, Griffith Humphreys, Margot Grahame, Doreen Bendix*.

THE ROSARY (1931) [2]
Dir *Guy Newall*. Prod *Julius Hagen*. Scr *John McNally*. PC *Twickenham*. Dis *Williams and Pritchard*. 70 mins. Cert A
Over-emotional melodrama about a girl (*Elizabeth Allan*), who sacrifices everything for her unworthy half-sister (*Margot Grahame*) after the latter has gunned down a forger. RoC *Walter Piers, Robert Holmes, Leslie Perrins, Charles Groves, Irene Rooke, Les Allen*.

ROSE OF TRALEE (1937) [2]

Dir and Scr *Oswald Mitchell*. Prod *Norman Hope-Bell*. Ph *Jack Parker*. PC and Dis *Butchers*. 80 mins. Cert U

Rather naïve musical parable, a vehicle for the child star *Binkie Stuart*. Paddy (*Fred Conyngham*), an Irish singer, goes to America in search of fame. After three years, he is successful enough to return for his wife and child, but finds he has lost touch with them. The final reunion comes in a recording studio, as the child (*Miss Stuart*) has also become a successful vocalist. Music by Debroy Somers.

RoC *Kathleen O'Regan, Talbot O'Farrell, Sydney Fairbrother, Dorothy Dare, Patrick Ludlow, Danny Malone, (C.) Denier Warren, Scott Harold, Dorothy Vernon, Paul Hanson, Jack Lester, Hamilton Keene, Henry Adnes, Harvey Brinton.*

ROYAL CAVALCADE (1935) [4]
(USA: *Regal Cavalcade*)

Dir *Thomas Bentley* (supervising), *Herbert Brenon, Norman Lee, Walter Summers, Will Kellino, Marcel Varnel*. Prod *Walter C. Mycroft* (director of productions), *Frank Mills, Roy Goddard, Jack Martin, David Horne, John Sloan*. Scr *Val Gielgud, Holt Marvell, Marjorie Deans*. Ph *Jack Cox, H. Wheddon, Bryan Langley, Leslie Rowson, Philip Grindrod*. PC *BIP*. Dis *Wardour*. 104 mins. Cert U

A survey of events in the reign of George V, seen through the fortunes of a penny – for example, it buys a programme for the Coronation, is held by a soldier who dies in the First World War and purchases a ticket from an amateur bus conductor in the 1926 general strike. Well-made historical pageant.

LP *Hermione Baddeley, Jane Baxter, Chili Bouchier, Florrie Forde, C.V. France, Reginald Gardiner, George Graves, Gene Gerrard, Jimmy Hanley, Seymour Hicks, Judy Kelly, Patric Knowles, Matheson Lang, Olga Lindo, Marie Lohr, Gus McNaughton, Arthur Margetson, John Mills, Clifford Mollison, Owen Nares, Esmé Percy, Ellen Pollock, Reginald Purdell, René Ray, George Robey, Athene Seyler, Ronald Shiner, John Stuart, Austin Trevor, Frank Vosper, (C.) Denier Warren, Marie Lohr, Robert Hale, J.H. Roberts, Charles Paton, Johnny Singer, Frederick Lloyd, Pearl Argyle, Wallace Bosco, Alice Lloyd, Amy Veness, Antoinette Cellier, Jimmy Godden, Renee Macready, Annie Esmond, Bertha Belmore, C.M. Hallard, H. Saxon-Snell, Fred Groves, Iris Ashley, Constance Shotter, Billy Caryll and Hilda Mundy, W.H. Berry, Vera Pearce, Diana Napier, Syd Walker, Elaine Benson, Leonora Corbett, Mary Glynne, Sam Livesey, Robert Nainby, Ellaline Terriss, Aileen Marson, Gyles Isham, Basil Gill, Jerry Verno, Craighall Sherry, Ivan Samson, Carol Goodner, James Carew, Ben Welden, Arthur Prince, Harry Tate, Bert Feldman, Norman Long, Stanton Jefferies, Stuart Hibberd, Leonard Henry, Debroy Somers and His Band, Sydney Baines and His Band, Band of Scots Guards; Roy Russell, Edward Chapman, D.A. Clarke-Smith (narrators).*

A ROYAL DEMAND (1933) [1]

Dir *Gustave Minzenty*. Prod *Mrs C.P. Williams*. Scr *Joan Moorland (Mrs Williams)*. PC *Moorland Productions*. Dis *Paramount*. 62 mins. Cert U

Amateurish historical drama, telling of Lord Forrest (*Cyril McLaglen*), an ardent Royalist in 1645 who outwits a Cromwellian general (*Powell Edwards*) by posing as a Roundhead, thus evading capture and securing the safety of his wife (*Marjorie Hume*) and family.

RoC *Fred Rains, Vi Kaley, Howard Fry, Tich Hunter, Gisela Leif Robinson, Cynthia Clifford.*

A ROYAL DIVORCE (1938) [3]

Dir *Jack Raymond*. Prod *Herbert Wilcox*. Scr *Miles Malleson*, from a novel by *Jacques Thery*. Ph *Frederick A. Young*. PC *Imperator*. Dis *Paramount*. 85 mins. Cert A

Josephine (*Ruth Chatterton*), an attractive widow, captivates the young Napoleon (*Pierre Blanchar*), a Corsican general, and they marry. While Napoleon is in Italy, Josephine dallies with Captain Charles (*Jack Hawkins*) and Napoleon determines to divorce her – but she wins him over with her charm. But when she cannot give him a son, they do part, only to meet once more when Napoleon brings his son for her blessing. Sympathetically directed but lacks vitality.

RoC *Frank Cellier, Carol Goodner, Auriol Lee, George Curzon, Lawrence Hanray, John Laurie, Rosalyn Boulter, Allan Jeayes, Romilly Lunge, David Farrar, Moran Caplat, Hubert Harben, Sonia Carol, Maureen Glynne, Ivy Shannon, Julien Somers, Stephen Jack, Tamara d'Etter, Daisy Thomas.*

ROYAL EAGLE (1936) [3]

Dir *George A. Cooper, Arnold Ridley*. Prod *Clive Loehnis*. Scr *Ridley*. Ph *Bryan Langley*. PC *Quality Films*. Dis *Columbia*. 69 mins. Cert A

Possibly actor-singer *John Garrick*'s best film performance, as a warehouseman who becomes suspected of a robbery and the murder of a policeman. On board a pleasure steamer, *Royal Eagle*, travelling between London and Margate, he brings one of the real crooks to book, and proves his innocence.

RoC *Nancy Burne, Edmund Willard, Lawrence Anderson, Hugh E. Wright, Muriel Aked, Fred Groves, Felix Aylmer, Betty Shale, Ian Fleming, Clare Greet.*

RUNAWAY LADIES (1935) [2]

Dir *Jean de Limur*. Prod *M. Haworth Booth*. Scr *Tristram Bernard*. PC *International Players*. Dis *Exclusive*. 56 mins. Cert A

Sticky comedy about a flighty girl (*Betty Stockfeld*) whose efforts to help the equally flighty Lady Ramsden (*Edna Searle*) to retrieve a compromising dancing shoe only result in Lady Ramsden being hauled before magistrates after she has been mistaken for an international jewel thief. Set in France, and largely shot there.

RoC *Hugh Wakefield, Roger Tréville, Raymond Cordy.*

RYNOX (1931) [4]

Dir *Michael Powell*. Prod *Jerome Jackson*. Scr *J. Jefferson Farjeon*, from a novel by *Philip Macdonald*. Ph *Geoffrey Faithfull*. PC *Film Engineering*. Dis *Ideal*. 47 mins. Cert A

One of the films that were helping to make Michael Powell's reputation as a director of quality quickies. A businessman (*Stewart Rome*) in financial difficulties is found shot dead by a bullet belonging to his enemy Boswell Marsh, who disappears. The business is carried on by the dead man's son (*John Longden*) thanks to the insurance money. In time the son learns that there was no such person as Marsh – the character was a clever invention over a period of months by his father who, learning he had only a year to live, had committed suicide.

RoC *Dorothy Boyd, Edmund Willard, Charles Paton, Fletcher Lightfoot, Sybil Grove, Leslie Mitchell, Cecil Clayton.*

SABOTAGE (1934) [2]
(USA: *When London Sleeps*)

Dir *Adrian Brunel*. Prod *Norman Loudon*. Scr *Heinrich Fraenkel, A.R. Rawlinson*. Ph *Claude Friese-Greene*. PC *Sound City*. Dis *Reunion*. 70 mins. Cert A

Originally titled *Menace*, but changed at the last moment to avoid clashing with a Hollywood film of the same name, this is a lurid melodrama about a series of train crashes which are found to have been caused by the railway chief (*D.A. Clarke-Smith*) during bouts of schizophrenia.

RoC *Joan Maude, Victor Varconi, J. Hubert Leslie, Joan Matheson, J.A. O'Rorke, Shayle Gardner, Wilfred Noy, Henry Longhurst, Cecil Bishop, George D'Arcy, Frank Barclay, Neil Boyd.*

SABOTAGE (1936) [5]
(USA: *The Woman Alone*)

Dir *Alfred Hitchcock*. (Associate) Prod *Ivor Montagu*. Scr *Charles Bennett, Alma Reville, Ian Hay, Helen Simpson, E.V.H. Emmett*, from a novel by *Joseph Conrad*. Ph *Bernard*

John Loder and Sylvia Sidney in Sabotage *(1936)*

Knowles. PC and Dis *Gaumont-British. 76 mins. Cert A*

This Hitchcock suspenser was dubbed as outstanding by most reviewers, although *Picturegoer*'s Lionel Collier described it as 'ponderous'. Verloc (*Oscar Homolka*) runs a small cinema which is a cover for his ring of dangerous anarchists. After he has been indirectly responsible for the death of his wife's young brother when the bomb the youth is carrying explodes, Verloc's wife (*Sylvia Sidney*) stabs him to death, the evidence of her crime being fortuitously destroyed in an explosion.

RoC *John Loder, Desmond Tester, Joyce Barbour, Matthew Boulton, S.J. Warmington, William Dewhurst, Austin Trevor, Torin Thatcher, Aubrey Mather, Peter Bull, Charles Hawtrey, Clare Greet, Sam Wilkinson, Sara Allgood, Martita Hunt, Arnold Bell, Albert Chevalier, Frederick Piper, Pamela Bevan, Hal Gordon.*

A SAFE AFFAIR (1931)   2

Dir *Herbert Wynne.* Prod *Franklin Dyall, J. H. Roberts.* Scr *Eliot Stannard.* PC *Langham.* Dis *M-G-M. 52 mins. Cert A*

Stars *Dyall* and *Roberts* produced this quota film themselves, but the results were disappointing. Dyall plays a millionaire who survives attempts on his life and property by a villainous financier; the latter is outwitted by the millionaire's valet and girl secretary who prove to be a resourceful pair.

LP *Franklin Dyall, John H. Roberts, Jeanne Stuart, Nancy Welford, J. Neil More, Connie Emerald, George Turner, James Knight, Douglas Jeffries.*

- SAID O'REILLY TO McNAB (1937)   4
(USA: *Sez O'Reilly to McNab*)

Dir *William Beaudine.* Prod *Edward Black.* Scr *Leslie Arliss, Marriott Edgar.* Ph *Arthur Crabtree.* PC *Gainsborough.* Dis *General Film Distributors. 85 mins. Cert U*

Malcolm McNab (*Will Fyffe*), an ultracautious Scots investor, is outwitted at every turn by Timothy O'Reilly (*Will Mahoney*), a roguish Irish 'share-pusher' who at one stage even has McNab helping to sell surefire slimming pills. But when treasury agents from America eventually catch up with O'Reilly, McNab buys up all the shares in his swindling concerns. Brightly written comedy.

RoC *Ellis Drake, Jock McKay, Jean Winstanley, James Carney, Marianne Davis, Robert Gall.*

SAILING ALONG (1938)   5

Dir *Sonnie Hale.* Prod *Michael Balcon.* Scr *Lesser Samuels, Hale.* Ph *Glen MacWilliams.* PC *Gaumont-British.* Dis *General Film Distributors. 90 mins. Cert U*

The last of the *Jessie Matthews* musicals, and probably the best directed by Sonnie Hale. Bargees Kay (*Matthews*) and Steve (*Barry MacKay*) are in love but hide it by always fighting. She dreams of becoming a stage star, he of being a financial wheeler-dealer. An eccentric millionaire (*Roland Young*) helps them both: Kay dances to stardom, while Steve makes a fortune. But they give it all up and

sail off in Steve's new boat. Songs include *My River, Your Heart Skips a Beat* and *Trusting My Luck.*

RoC *Jack Whiting, Alastair Sim, Noel Madison, Athene Seyler, Frank Pettingell, Margaret Vyner, Peggy Novak, William Dewhurst, Patrick Barr, Bruce Winston, Edward Cooper, Leslie Laurier, Charles Paton, D. Hay Plumb, Arthur Denton, Cot d'Ordan, Yvonne Dulac, Frank Fox, Bombardier Billy Wells, Clement Dutto, Eve Chipman, Alexander Ramsay, Edna Searle, Simeta Marsden, Mabel Silvester.*

THE SAINT IN LONDON (1939)   4

Dir *John Paddy Carstairs.* Prod *William Sistrom.* Scr *Lynn Root, Frank Fenton, from a novel by Leslie Charteris.* Ph *Claude Friese-Greene.* PC and Dis *RKO Radio. 77 mins. Cert A*

A ruthless gang plans a currency swindle. Called in, Simon Templar, alias The Saint (*George Sanders*), steals a document from the safe of Bruno Lang (*Henry Oscar*), whom he suspects, and rescues Count Duni (*John Abbott*), a captive at the Lang home. The gang kidnaps Penny (*Sally Gray*) and offers her in exchange for the count, who is subsequently killed. But Simon finally outwits Lang and his associates and hands them over to the harassed Inspector Teal (*Gordon McLeod*) who is relieved to close the case. Crisp, humorous thriller.

RoC *Ballard Berkeley, David Burns, Ralph Truman, Carl Jaffe, Norah Howard, Charles Carson, Athene Seyler, Ben Williams, Hugh McDermott.*

SALLY BISHOP (1932)   3

Dir *T. Hayes Hunter.* Prod *S. W. Smith.* Scr *John Drinkwater, G.E. Wakefield, from the novel by E. Temple Thurston.* Ph *Alex Bryce.* PC and Dis *British Lion. 82 mins. Cert A*

Another sad slip in the declining career of lovely *Joan Barry*, who takes the title role in this third screen version of Temple Thurston's hoary old soap opera along *Back Street* lines. Sally is the mistress of a wealthy man for three years before his sister interferes in their relationship, and manœuvres his engagement to a society girl. Sally, too, finds new romance, but in the end, her rich lover begs for forgiveness and she accepts him back.

RoC *Harold Huth, Isabel Jeans, Benita Hume, Emlyn Williams, Kay Hammond, Anthony Bushell, Diana Churchill, Annie Esmond.*

SALLY IN OUR ALLEY (1931)   2

Dir *Maurice Elvey.* Prod *Basil Dean.* Scr *Miles Malleson, Alma Reville, Archie Pitt, from a play by Charles McEvoy.* Ph *Robert G. Martin, Alex Bryce.* PC *Associated Talking Pictures.* Dis *Radio. 77 mins. Cert A*

A shaky start which *Gracie Fields'* screen career did well to survive. She plays a London coffee-shop singer who believes her sweetheart (*Ian Hunter*) dead in the First World War. But he eventually returns and all ends well, despite the vampish attentions of a rival (*Florence Desmond*) for his affections. Gracie's songs include *Sally* and *Fall in and Follow the Band.*

RoC *Ivor Barnard, Fred Groves, Gibb*

McLaughlin, Ben Field, Barbara Gott, Renee Macready, Helen Ferrers, Florence Harwood.

SAM SMALL LEAVES TOWN (1937)   3

Dir *Alfred Goulding.* Prod *Maurice J. Wilson.* Scr *Uncredited.* PC and Dis *British Screen Service. 79 mins. Cert U*

Manning (*Stanley Holloway*), a famous actor, bets a publisher that he can disappear for a week and not be found. He swaps identities with Sam Small, a jack-of-all-trades at a holiday camp. Manning has a great time but eventually allows himself to be discovered by a young reporter so that he can win the reward and marry his girlfriend. Jolly comedy, a bit long.

RoC *June Clyde, Fred Conyngham, Harry Tate, Johnnie Schofield, Robert English, James Craven, Aubrey Pollock, Molly Fisher, Brookins and Van.*

SANDERS OF THE RIVER (1935)   4
(USA: *Bosambo*)

Dir *Zoltan Korda.* Prod *Alexander Korda.* Scr *Lajos Biro, Jeffrey Dell, Arthur Wimperis, from the novel by Edgar Wallace.* Ph *Georges Perinal, Osmond Borrodaile, Louis Page, Ernst Udet.* PC *London Films.* Dis *United Artists. 98 mins (USA: 95 mins). Cert U*

Nigeria. Bosambo (*Paul Robeson*), an escaped convict, is given a probationary office as a local chief by Sanders (*Leslie Banks*), the British commissioner. Bosambo incurs the hatred of the Old King (*Tony Wane*) by stamping out slave traffic. With Sanders away, his deputy Ferguson (*Martin Walker*) sells gin and guns to the natives. The Old King sends warriors to attack Bosambo. Ferguson is killed, Bosambo captured. Sanders returns and releases Bosambo, who kills the Old King as he is about to spear Sanders. Bosambo is made king. Plot is confusing, but the film's stirring 'native' music made it a hit.

RoC *Nina Mae McKinney, Robert Cochran, Joan Gardner, Richard Grey, Marquis de Portago, Eric Maturin, Allan Jeayes, Charles Carson, Bertrand Fraser, Anthony Popafio, Orlando Martins, Beresford Gale, Lumo, Kilongalonga, Oboja, James Solomons, John Thomas.*

Paul Robeson in Sanders of the River *(1935)*

SATURDAY NIGHT REVUE (1937)   3

Dir *Norman Lee.* Prod *Warwick Ward.* Scr *Vernon Clancey.* PC *Welwyn.* Dis *Pathé. 77 mins. Cert A*

Jimmy (*Billy Milton*), singing partner of Mary (*Sally Gray*), saves a gangster, Duke (*Edward Ashley*), from being shot by his girlfriend. When Jimmy's eyes are injured in a car crash, Duke hires a top doctor who gradually restores Jimmy's sight while he hides from Mary. Wearing a mask, he partners Mary in a broadcast. She recognizes his voice, tears the mask from his face and they are reunited – for good. Many variety acts mix with slender story.

RoC *John Watt, Betty Lynne, Georgie Harris, Julien Vedey, Charles Carson, Mary Jerrold, Douglas Stuart, Gerry Fitzgerald, John Turnbull, Alvin Conway, Reg Bolton, Webster Booth, The Hillbillies, Bennett and Williams, Stanford and McNaughton, Sydney Kyte and his Band, Scots Kilties Band, John Reynders and the BBC Orchestra, Billy Reid and His Band, Strad and His Newsboys.*

SAVE A LITTLE SUNSHINE (1938)   [2]
Dir *Norman Lee.* Prod *Warwick Ward.* Scr *Victor Kendall, Vernon J. Clancey, Gilbert Gunn, from a play by W. Armitage Owen.* Ph *Ernest Palmer.* PC *Welwyn.* Dis *Pathé. 75 mins. Cert A*

Grocer's assistant Dave Smalley picks up £100 as a 'lost' reward. He is conned into becoming a partner in a run-down boarding house, where he finds himself the drudge until a girl (*Pat Kirkwood*) helps him pull himself together and turn the premises into a smart restaurant, complete with cabaret. Not an auspicious film debut for Scots comedian *Dave Willis* as Smalley.

RoC *Max Wall, Tommy Trinder, Ruth Dunning, Peggy Novak, Roger Maxwell, Annie Esmond, Marian Dawson, Aubrey Mallalieu, Annabel Maule, Rosemary Scott, Charles Lefeaux.*

SAY IT WITH DIAMONDS (1935)   [2]
Dir, Prod and PC *Redd Davis.* Scr *Jack Marks.* Dis *M-G-M. 64 mins. Cert A*

Mediocre comedy, but with a nice performance by *Frank Pettingell* as Ezra Hopkins, a brass craftsman from Manchester who is instrumental in bringing down a gang of crooks posing as policemen whose latest aim is the theft of a valuable diamond necklace.

RoC *Eve Becke, Vera Bogetti, Gerald Rawlinson, Eileen Munro, Ernest Sefton, Arthur Finn.*

SAY IT WITH FLOWERS (1933)   [3]
Dir *John Baxter.* Prod *Julius Hagen.* Scr *Wal-*

Mary Clare and Ben Field in Say It With Flowers *(1934)*

lace Orton, H. Fowler Mear. Ph *Sydney Blythe.* PC *Real Art. Radio. 71 mins. Cert U*

Two well-loved London market people, a flower-seller and her husband (*Mary Clare, Ben Field*) fall on hard times and, so that they may have a long rest at the seaside, are given a 'benefit' performance in which many old-time variety artists appear. More or less a celebration of Cockney music-hall.

RoC *George Carney, Mark Daly, Edgar Driver, Freddie Watts, Edwin Ellis, Florrie Forde, Charles Coburn, Marie Kendall, Tom Costello, Percy Honri, Kearney and Browning, Wilson Coleman.*

SAY IT WITH MUSIC (1932)   [4]
Dir *Jack Raymond.* Prod *Herbert Wilcox.* Scr *William Pollock.* PC *British and Dominions.* Dis *W and F. 69 mins. Cert U*

Tuneful musical designed to exploit the popularity of *Jack Payne* and the BBC Dance Band. Payne plays himself, helping the composer who had written his theme tune, *Say It with Music*, but is now not only down and out, but has lost his memory after a plane crash.

RoC *Percy Marmont, Joyce Kennedy, Evelyn Roberts, Sybil Summerfield, Freddy Schweitzer, Anna Lee, Billy (William) Hartnell.*

THE SCARAB MURDER CASE (1936)   [2]
Dir *Michael Hankinson.* Prod *Anthony Havelock-Allan.* Scr *Selwyn Jepson, from the novel by S.S. Van Dine.* Ph *Claude Friese-Greene.* PC and Dis *British and Dominions/Paramount British. 68 mins. Cert A*

Slightly dull mystery story in which American detective Philo Vance (*Wilfrid Hyde White*) comes to England to investigate the murder of a millionaire who was backing the archaeologist (*John Robinson*) under suspicion of killing him. The archaeologist seems to be the victim of circumstance – but Vance astutely proves him an ingenious killer.

RoC *Kathleen Kelly, Wally Patch, Henri de Vries, Wallace Geoffrey, Stella Moya, Grahame Cheesewright, Rustum Medora, Shaun Desmond.*

THE SCARLET PIMPERNEL (1934)   [5]
Dir *Harold Young (and, uncredited, Alexander Korda, Rowland V. Brown).* Prod *Korda.* Scr *S. N. Behrman, Robert E. Sherwood, Arthur Wimperis, Lajos Biro, from the novel by Baroness Orczy.* Ph *Harold Rosson.* PC *London Films.* Dis *United Artists. 98 mins (USA: 95 mins). Cert A*

Cunningly crafted adventure yarn, set in 1793. A band of English gentlemen, led by the outwardly foppish aristocrat Sir Percy Blakeney (*Leslie Howard*, ideally cast) set out to liberate as many French noblemen as possible during the purges that follow the French Revolution. Delightful dialogue exchanges between Blakeney and his chief adversary, Chauvelin (*Raymond Massey*). A great success.

RoC *Merle Oberon, Nigel Bruce, Bramwell Fletcher, Joan Gardner, Anthony Bushell, Walter Rilla, Mabel Terry-Lewis, O. B. Clarence, Ernest Milton, Edmund Breon, Melville Cooper, Gibb McLaughlin, Morland Graham, John Turnbull, Allan Jeayes, William Freshman,*

Leslie Howard in The Scarlet Pimpernel *(1934)*

Gertrude Musgrove, A. Bromley Davenport, Hindle Edgar, Derrick de Marney, Lawrence Hanray, Bruce Belfrage, Edmund Willard, Roy Meredith, Billy Shine, Brember Wills, Kenneth Kove, Renee Macready, Carl Harbord, Harry Terry, Philip Strange, Hugh Dempster, Philip Desborough, Peter Evan Thomas, Douglas Stewart, Arthur Hambling.

THE SCAT BURGLARS (1937)   [1]
Dir *Leslie Rowson.* Prod *Simon Rowson, Geoffrey Rowson.* Scr *Fenn Sherie, Ingram d'Abbes.* Ph *Leslie Rowson, H. Gillam.* PC *New Ideal.* Dis *M-G-M. 45 mins. Cert A*

Two men (*Harry Haver, Frank Lee*) set themselves up as Brains Limited, willing to tackle anything. They are commissioned by a glamorous film star (*Constance Godridge*) to steal her jewels as a publicity stunt. They carry out the burglary at the star's home, then find that the girl who hired them was an imposter. Dreadful 'comedy'.

RoC *Shayle Gardner, Baby Ann Ibbitson, Craigie Doon.*

SCHOOL FOR HUSBANDS (1937)   [4]
Dir *Andrew Marton.* Prod *Richard Wainwright.* Scr *Frederick Jackson, Austin Melford, Gordon Sherry, from the play by Jackson.* Ph *Phil Tannura.* PC *Wainwright.* Dis *General Film Distributors. 71 mins. Cert A*

Suspecting both their wives of having affairs with lothario Leonard Drummond (*Rex Harrison*), two business partners (*Henry Kendall, Romney Brent*) pretend to go to Paris, then return unexpectedly and catch their wives in seemingly compromising situations, though

June Clyde, Diana Churchill and Henry Kendall in School for Husbands *(1938)*

each is guilty merely of flirtation. Leonard concocts a flattering fiction that satisfies the men and swaggers off to yet another conquest. Nicely handled adaptation of stage farce.

RoC *Diana Churchill, June Clyde, Roxie Russell, Richard Goolden, Judith Gick, Joan Kemp-Welsh.*

THE SCHOOL FOR SCANDAL (1930) [3]

Dir and Prod *Maurice Elvey*. Scr *Jean Jay, from the play by R. B. Sheridan*. PC *Albion*. Dis *Paramount. Raycol Colour*. 76 mins. Cert U

The early use of colour was the most interesting ingredient of this relatively free, if cinematically stiff adaptation of Sheridan's famous eighteenth-century play about a wealthy man who poses as a moneylender to see which of his relations he wishes to inherit his millions. LP *Basil Gill, Madeleine Carroll, Ian Fleming, Henry Hewitt, Edgar K. Bruce, Dodo Watts, Anne Grey, Henry Vibart, Gibb McLaughlin, Hayden Coffin, Hector Abbas, John Charlton, Stanley Lathbury, May Agate, Maurice Braddell, Wallace Bosco, Rex Harrison, Constance Stevens (Sally Gray), Anna Neagle.*

SCHOOL FOR STARS (1935) [2]

Dir and Scr *Donovan Pedelty*. Prod *Anthony Havelock-Allan*. PC and Dis *British and Dominions/Paramount British*. 70 mins. Cert A

Fragile romantic comedy with charming newcomer *Jean Gillie* as a waitress who joins an academy of dramatic art, survives the jibes of some of her fellows, becomes a dancer and falls in love with another student (*Frederick Conyngham*).

RoC *Torin Thatcher, Peggy Novak, Ian Fleming, Frank Birch, Winifred Oughton, S. Victor Stanley, Rosamund Greenwood, Effie Atherton, Phyllis Calvert, Geraldo and His Music.*

THE SCHOONER GANG (1937) [1]

Dir and Prod *W. Devenport Hackney*. Scr *Frank Atkinson, Ralph Dawson, Iris Terry*. Ph *Jack Parker, Gerald Gibbs*. PC *New Garrick*. Dis *Butchers*. 72 mins. Cert U

Creaky crime story with music: former music-hall star Mrs Truman (*Vesta Victoria*) keeps a pub – and her brother Ben (*Frank Atkinson*), a reformed crook. Ben becomes involved with his old gang, who force him to crack a safe. He makes a run with the proceeds, leaving a valuable necklace in an aspidistra pot at the pub. He is killed by the gang, but Mrs T. collects the reward for finding the necklace.

RoC *Gerald Barry, Mary Honri, Billy Percy, Betty Norton, Basil Broadbent, Percy Honri, Iris Terry, Ralph Dawson, John Rowal, Tubby Hayes.*

THE SCOOP (1934) [1]

Dir and Prod *Maclean Rogers*. Scr *Gerald Geraghty, Basil Mason, from the play by Jack Heming*. PC and Dis *British and Dominions/Paramount British*. 68 mins. Cert A

On the night Mrs Banyon (*Anne Grey*) plans to elope with her lover, her husband is found dead. A reporter known as Scoop (*Tom Helmore*) is sent to cover the story. Just as the police are about to arrest Mrs Banyon's lover, Scoop makes a surprising revelation: he had killed the man himself, in self-defence. Wooden thriller.

RoC *Peggy Blythe, Roland Culver, Wally Patch, Arthur Hambling, Reginald Bach, Moore Marriott, Cameron Carr, Marjorie Shotter, Gordon Bailey.*

THE SCOTLAND YARD MYSTERY (1933) [3]
(USA: *The Living Dead*)

Dir *Thomas Bentley*. Prod *Walter C. Mycroft*. Scr *Frank Miller, from the play by Wallace Geoffrey*. PC *BIP*. Dis *Wardour*. 76 mins. Cert A

Macabre mystery; an insurance firm is worried at having to pay out large sums on the unexpected deaths of policy holders certified fit by its medical adviser, Dr Freeman (*Leslie Perrins*). Freeman's concerned fiancée (*Belle Chrystall*) asks her father, a police inspector (*Gerald du Maurier*) to investigate, and he finds a Home Office pathologist (*George Curzon*) involved in a scheme to defraud the firm by injecting policy holders with life-suspending serum.

RoC *Grete Natzler, Paul Graetz, Wally Patch, Henry Victor, Herbert Cameron, Frederick Peisley.*

SCROOGE (1935) [4]

Dir *Henry Edwards*. Prod *Julius Hagen, Hans (John) Brahm*. Scr *Seymour Hicks, H. Fowler Mear, from Charles Dickens'* A Christmas Carol. Ph *Sydney Blythe*. PC and Dis *Twickenham*. 79 mins. Cert U

Miserly Victorian businessman Ebenezer Scrooge (*Seymour Hicks*) is persuaded to change his ways one Christmas by visitations from the ghost of his former partner, and the spirits of Christmas Past, Christmas Present and Christmas Yet-to-Come. Good version of cast-iron Dickensian classic, with convincing Victorian atmosphere and settings.

RoC *Donald Calthrop, Robert Cochran, Eve Gray, Oscar Asche, C. V. France, Marie Ney, Athene Seyler, Barbara Everest, Mary Glynne, Garry Marsh, Maurice Evans, Mary Lawson, Morris Harvey, Philip Frost, D. J. Williams, Margaret Yarde, Hugh E. Wright, Charles Carson, Peggy Church, Hubert Harben.*

SCRUFFY (1938) [2]

Dir and Prod *Randall Faye*. Scr *Margaret Houghton*. Ph *Desmond Dickinson*. PC *Vulcan*. Dis *British Independent*. 61 mins. Cert U

Michael (*Michael Gainsborough*), an orphan, is parted from his dog Scruffy when he is adopted by a rich woman as companion for her spoiled son. Unhappy, he runs away – into a burglar, Jim (*Jack Melford*), who is robbing the house. He goes to live with Jim and his partner Golly (*Billy Merson*) on their barge, but the police arrest them. In court, they get off, thanks to Scruffy, who has stolen the evidence. Michael is given back to them, and they promise they will go straight. Minor weepie deserves 'bigger' treatment.

RoC *Tonie Edgar Bruce, Chris McMaster, MacArthur Gordon, Peter Gawthorne, Joan Ponsford, Roddy McDowall, Winifred Willard, Valentine Rooke, Michael Rae, E. J. Kennedy, Jenny Barclay and Scruffy.*

SECOND BEST BED (1937) [4]

Dir *Tom Walls*. Prod *Max Schach*. Scr *Ben Travers*. Ph *Jack Cox*. PC *Capitol*. Dis *General Film Distributors*. 74 mins. Cert A

Rich, middle-aged Victor (*Tom Walls*) marries fiery, spoiled Patricia (*Jane Baxter*), who is in her late twenties and immediately rebels against Victor's ideas of a dutiful wife, including taking the second-best bed. She also becomes suspicious of his aid to a girl in their village, and storms off to Monte Carlo with her 'fast' friends whom Victor hates. Eventually, this modern Kate and Petruchio settle down to (noisy) married bliss. Good fun.

RoC *Carl Jaffe, Veronica Rose, Great Gynt, Edward Lexy, Tyrell Davis, Mai Bacon, Ethel Coleridge, Davy Burnaby, Martita Hunt, Gordon James, Charlotte Leigh, (C.) Denier Warren.*

SECOND BUREAU (1936) [3]

Dir *Victor Hanbury*. Prod *John Stafford*. Scr *Akos Tolnay, from a novel by Charles Robert Dumas*. Ph *James Wilson*. PC *Premier/Stafford*. Dis *Radio*.

The First World War: a German agent (*Marta Labarr*) and a French spy (*Charles Oliver*) try to trap one another, but fall in love. They determine to escape together to a neutral country, but the woman is fatally shot and dies in her lover's arms.

RoC *Arthur Wontner, Meinhart Maur, Fred Groves, Joan White, Anthony Eustrel, G. H. Mulcaster, Leo von Pokorny, Bruno Barnabe, Fewlass Llewellyn.*

SECOND THOUGHTS (1938) [2]

Dir and Prod *Albert Parker*. Scr *David Evans*. Ph *Ronald Neame*. PC and Dis *Fox British*. 61 mins. Cert A

Research chemist Peter Frame (*Frank Allenby*) buries himself in his research at his country home, while his wife Molly (*Evelyn Ankers*) helps their writer friend Tony (*Frank Fox*) with a typescript. Peter's sister poisons his mind about Molly and Tony's relationship and, after being disfigured in a laboratory explosion, he plans to do the same to them – but comes to his senses. Dull drama.

RoC *Joan Hickson, A. Bromley Davenport, Marjorie Fielding, Alan Edmiston, Billy Shine.*

SECRET AGENT (1936) [4]

Dir *Alfred Hitchcock*. Prod *Ivor Montagu*. Scr *Charles Bennett, Ian Hay, Jesse Lasky Jr, Alma Reville, from a play by Campbell Dixon and stories by Somerset Maugham*. Ph *Bernard Knowles*. PC and Dis *Gaumont-British*. 85 mins. Cert A

Rather slow but atmospheric Hitchcock thriller. Ashenden (*John Gielgud*), a writer turned reluctant secret serviceman for the British, is sent to Switzerland in 1916 to kill an unknown German spy. He is given two assistants, one (*Madeleine Carroll*) posing as his wife, the other (*Peter Lorre*) an unscrupulous Mexican assassin. After a horrendous blunder when they kill the wrong man, the real spy is tracked down and dies (with the Mexican) in a massive train crash.

Madeleine Carroll, John Gielgud, Robert Young (face-down) and Peter Lorre in Secret Agent *(1936)*

RoC *Robert Young, Percy Marmont, Lilli Palmer, Florence Kahn, Charles Carson, Tom Helmore, Andrea Malandrinos, Michael Redgrave, Michel Saint-Denis.*

SECRET JOURNEY (1939) [2]
(USA: *Among Human Wolves*)
Dir *John Baxter.* Prod *John Corfield.* Scr *Michael Hogan, from a novel by Charles Dumas.* Ph *James Wilson.* PC *British National.* Dis *Anglo.* 72 mins. Cert U
Rival spies are after the formula for a new cartridge which is in the hands of a German chemist. A British agent and his sister arrive in Berlin and, by playing up to the chemist's son Max, she gets the formula, although she and Max have fallen in love. He pursues her and stops her train, but finds at the last moment he is unable to hand her over to the authorities. Risible spy thriller.
LP *Basil Radford, Sylvie StClaire, Thorley Walters, Peter Gawthorne, Joss Ambler, Patricia Medina, Tom Helmore, George Hayes, (C.) Denier Warren, Wilson Coleman.*

SECRET LIVES (1937) [2]
(USA: *I Married a Spy*)
Dir *Edmond T. Gréville.* Prod *Hugh Perceval.* Scr *Basil Mason, from the novel by Paul de Saint-Colombe.* Ph *Otto Heller.* PC *Independent Films/ Phoenix.* Dis *Associated British.* 80 mins. Cert A
1915: Lena, a German girl (*Brigitte Horney*) is forced to spy for the French during the First World War. Four years later she is convicted as a traitor to France by documents that derive from a German source. A French officer (*Neil Hamilton*) who makes a marriage of convenience with her, falls in love with her, and proves her innocence. Drama hasn't much excitement.
RoC *Gyles Isham, Ivor Barnard, Charles Carson, Raymond Lovell, Frederick Lloyd, Ben Field, Hay Petrie, Leslie Perrins.*

THE SECRET OF STAMBOUL (1936) [3]
Dir *Andrew Marton.* Prod *Richard Wainwright.* Scr *Wainwright, Howard Irving Young, Noel Langley, from a novel by Dennis Wheatley.* Ph *Henry Harris.* PC *Wainwright.* Dis *General Film Distributors.* 93 mins. Cert A
Thrown out of their regiment, Larry (*James Mason*) and Peter (*Peter Haddon*) find themselves, through Larry's involvement with Tania

(*Valerie Hobson*), unwilling accomplices of treacherous Kazdim (*Frank Vosper*), fighting a plot to overthrow the government of Turkey. Thanks to Tania, they succeed. Clearly developed derring-do, but none too convincing.
RoC *Kay Walsh, Cecil Ramage, Laura Cowie, Robert English, Emilio Cargher, Leonard Sachs, Andrea Malandrinos.*

THE SECRET OF THE LOCH (1934) [2]
Dir *Milton Rosmer.* Prod *Bray Wyndham.* Scr *Charles Bennett, Billie Bristow.* PC *Wyndham.* Dis *Associated British.* 80 mins. Cert U
Professor Heggie (*Seymour Hicks*) is ridiculed by fellow-scientists because of his belief in the Loch Ness monster. He is helped by a London reporter (*Frederick Peisley*) in love with his granddaughter (*Nancy O'Neill*). When a diver is killed, the reporter goes down himself and actually sees the monster. Critics complained it took a very long time to get round to this juncture.
RoC *Gibson Gowland, Eric Hales, Ben Field, Hubert Harben, Stafford Hilliard, Rosamund Jones (Rosamund John), Robb Wilton, John Jamieson, Elma Reid.*

THE SECRET VOICE (1936) [2]
Dir *George Pearson.* Prod *Anthony Havelock-Allan.* Scr *Margaret McDonell.* PC and Dis *British and Dominions/Paramount British.* 68 mins. Cert A
Conventional thriller, apart from being set two years into the future. The inventor of a non-flammable petrol (*John Kevan*) records his formula on film to send to the League of Nations. Foreign powers try to force him to reveal its content by kidnapping his pretty sister, but are thwarted by a British agent.
RoC *John Stuart, Diana Beaumont, Henry Victor, Ruth Gower, Monte de Lyle, Charles Carew, Susan Bligh.*

SEEING IS BELIEVING (1934) [1]
Dir *Redd Davis.* Prod *Uncredited.* Scr *Donovan Pedelty.* PC *British and Dominions/Paramount British.* Dis *Paramount.* 71 mins. Cert U
Tedious comedy about a would-be detective (*Billy Hartnell*) who takes the two detectives his father has hired to look after him to be jewel thieves. He is about to have them arrested when his father clears things up. At least the embryo sleuth finds romance with a girl (*Faith Bennett*) whom he - wrongly - suspected of having stolen a bracelet.
RoC *Gus McNaughton, Vera Bogetti, Fewlass Llewellyn, Joan Pereira, Elsie Irving, Pat Baring.*

SELF-MADE LADY (1932) [2]
Dir *George Brown.* Prod *George King.* Scr *Billie Bristow, from a novel by Douglas Newton.* Ph *Geoffrey Faithfull.* PC *George King Films.* Dis *United Artists.* 76 mins. Cert A
Soapy romantic drama about a poor girl (*Heather Angel*) who longs to escape her slum environment, and eventually makes a living as a fashion artist. An old enemy threatens to expose her lowly past to her high-born suitors, but the situation is rescued by a boxer (*Harry Wilcoxon*) who has long admired her and she eventually marries a doctor's son (*Louis Hay-*

ward). Although panning the film, critics were unanimous in praise of Miss Angel's performance.
RoC *Amy Veness, A. Bromley Davenport, Charles Cullum, Ronald Ritchie, Doris Gilmour, Oriel Ross, Lola Duncan, Violet Hopson.*

SENSATION (1936) [3]
Dir *Brian Desmond .Hurst.* Prod *Walter C. Mycroft.* Scr *Dudley Leslie, Marjorie Deans, William Freshman, from a play by Basil Dean, George Munro.* Ph *Walter Harvey.* PC *BIP.* Dis *Associated British.* 67 mins. Cert A
Well-handled if under-characterized crime thriller about a reporter, Pat (*John Lodge*), who discovers a vital clue to a murder in the dead girl's belongings. Working out who the killer is, he induces the wife to part with letters and family photographs on the ground that they will help her husband. Having ensured his 'scoop', Pat then hands over all evidence to the police.
RoC *Joan Marion, Diana Churchill, Francis Lister, Margaret Vyner, Athene Seyler, Richard Bird, Jerry Verno, Martin Walker, Leslie Perrins, Henry Oscar, Felix Aylmer, James Hayter, Dennis Wyndham, Antony Holles, Sybil Grove, Arthur Chesney, Billy Shine, Brian Herbert, Joe Cunningham, Michael Gainsborough.*

John Lodge and Margaret Vyner in Sensation! *(1936)*

SERVICE FOR LADIES (1931) [5]
(USA: *Reserved for Ladies*)
Dir and Prod *Alexander Korda.* Scr *Eliot Crawshay-Williams, Lajos Biro, from a novel by Ernest Vajda.* PC *Paramount British.* Dis *Paramount.* 93 mins. Cert A
Alexander Korda's first British film and the one which saw the beginning of his rise to power. It's the rags-to-riches story of Max (*Leslie Howard*), head waiter at a London hotel, whose courtship of a wealthy woman (*Elizabeth Allan*) is rather complicated by the fact that she thinks he is a prince. Although she discovers the truth and spurns Max, tips from her father enable him to win her back.
RoC *George Grossmith, Benita Hume, Morton Selten, Cyril Ritchard, Ben Field, Annie Esmond, Martita Hunt, Gilbert Davis, Merle Oberon.*

SEVEN SINNERS (1936) [4]
(USA: *Doomed Cargo*)
Dir *Albert de Courville.* Prod *Michael Balcon.*

Edmund Lowe and Constance Cummings in
Seven Sinners (*1936*)

Scr *Sidney Gilliat, Frank Launder, L. duGarde Peach, Austin Melford, from a play by Arnold Ridley and Bernard Merivale.* Ph *Mutz Greenbaum.* PC and Dis *Gaumont-British.* 70 mins. Cert A
There's plenty of snap and crackle in this train thriller about an American detective (*Edmund Lowe*) hunting the gang responsible for several rail crashes. The London insurance agent assigned to help him proves to be an attractive woman (*Constance Cummings*) and together they trap the gang through the discovery that a train wreck in which the detectives were involved was designed to cover up a murder.
RoC *Thomy Bourdelle, Henry Oscar, Felix Aylmer, Joyce Kennedy, Allan Jeayes, O. B. Clarence, Mark Lester, Antony Holles, David Home, Edwin Laurence, James Harcourt, Patrick Ludlow, Henry Hallatt, Margaret Davidge.*

77 PARK LANE (1931)

Dir *Albert de Courville.* Prod *John Harding.* Scr *Michael Powell, Reginald Berkeley, from the play by Walter Hackett.* PC *Famous Players' Guild,* Dis *United Artists.* 82 mins. Cert A. Trilingual versions
Poorly executed thriller about a lord (*Dennis Neilson-Terry*) who, celebrating Boat Race night, buys a taxi and picks up a girl (*Betty Stockfeld*) who tells him to go to 77 Park Lane - his London home. When they arrive, the lord is amazed to find the house transformed into a gambling-den. He sets the gang responsible to flight, as well as clearing the girl's brother (*Esmond Knight*) who had been gambling heavily and believed (incorrectly) he had killed a man.
RoC *Malcolm Keen, Ben Welden, Cecil Humphreys, Molly Johnson, Roland Culver, W. Molesworth Blow, John Turnbull, Percival Coyte.*

SEXTON BLAKE AND THE BEARDED DOCTOR (1935) [1]

Dir and Prod *George A. Cooper.* Scr *Rex Hardinge, from his novel* The Blazing Launch Murder. PC *Fox British.* Dis *M-G-M.* 64 mins. Cert U
Improbable crime thriller, reminiscent of a silent serial. A famous violinist is found dead, and ace detective Sexton Blake (*George Curzon*) suspects foul play. A sinister bearded doctor (*Henry Oscar*) threatens a girl and a

young insurance man with a similar fate if they refuse to sign away the dead man's effects. Blake uncovers a plot to defraud an insurance company.
RoC *Tony Sympson, Gillian Maude, Phil Ray, John Turnbull, Edward Dignon, James Knight, Donald Wolfit, Johnnie Schofield, Ben Williams.*

SEXTON BLAKE AND THE HOODED TERROR (1938) [4]

Dir Prod and PC *George King.* Scr *A. R. Rawlinson, from a novel by Pierre Quiroule.* Ph *Hone Glendinning.* Dis *M-G-M.* 70 mins. Cert A
Detective Sexton Blake (*George Curzon*) tackles The Hooded Terror, a worldwide crime organization, and its mastermind, known only as The Snake. After several brushes with death, Blake unmasks philatelist Michael Larron (*Tod Slaughter*) as The Snake. But, concentrating on rescuing the beautiful Julie (*Greta Gynt*) from a hideous fate, Blake allows The Snake to wriggle away to scheme another day. Thriller is foolish but fast and fun.
RoC *Charles Oliver, Tony Sympson, Marie Wright, Norman Pierce, David Farrar, Max Faber, Carl Melene, Alex Huber, Philip Holles, Len Sharpe, H. B. Hallam.*

SEXTON BLAKE AND THE MADEMOISELLE (1935) [3]

Dir and Ph *Alex Bryce.* Prod and Scr *Michael Barringer, from a novel by G. H. Teed.* PC *Fox British.* Dis *M-G-M.* 63 mins. Cert U
Better Sexton Blake adventure in which the lean sleuth (*George Curzon* again) is asked by a financier to recover a parcel of stolen bonds. He finds that his employer is a crook, and that the bonds were stolen by a young girl, posing as 'Mademoiselle' (*Lorraine Grey*) to avenge the ruin of her father by the financier.
RoC *Tony Sympson, Edgar Norfolk, Raymond Lovell, Ian Fleming, Vincent Holman, Wilson Coleman, Ben Williams, Henry Peterson, William Collins.*

THE SHADOW (1933) [4]

Dir *George A. Cooper.* Prod *Julius Hagen.* Scr *H. Fowler Mear, Terence Egan.* PC *Real Art.* Dis *United Artists.* 74 mins. Cert A
Suspenseful, amusing comedy-thriller in which Scotland Yard is baffled by the misdeeds of a murderous blackmailer - until the culprit is unmasked at the home of the Chief Commissioner himself, with the help of a novelist (*Henry Kendall*) and the Chief Commissioner's daughter (*Elizabeth Allan*).
RoC *Sam Livesey, Jeanne Stuart, Cyril Raymond, Viola Compton, John Turnbull.*

THE SHADOW BETWEEN (1931) [3]

Dir *Norman Walker.* Prod *John Maxwell.* Scr *Walker, Dion Titheradge, from a play by Titheradge.* Ph *Claude Friese-Greene.* PC *BIP.* Dis *Wardour.* 87 mins. Cert A
Glum drama about a wife - previously married to a suicide - and husband who both serve sentences for theft and fraud before the real culprit confesses.
LP *Godfrey Tearle, Kathleen O'Regan, Olga Lindo, Ann Casson, Haddon Mason, Mary Jerrold, Hubert Harben, Henry Wenman, Henry*

Caine, Morton Selten, Arthur Chesney, Jerrold Robertshaw, Stanley Vilven, Irene Rooke.

SHADOWED EYES (1939) [2]

Dir *Maclean Rogers.* Prod *Kurt Sternberg, A. George Smith.* Scr *Roy Carter, Herbert Hill, from a story by Arnold Ridley.* Ph *Gerald Gibbs.* PC *Savoy/GS Enterprises.* Dis *RKO Radio.* 68 mins. Cert A
After murdering his wife's lover in a mental blackout, Zander (*Basil Sydney*), a famous eye surgeon, is pronounced a criminal lunatic. When his assistant Diana's father needs a delicate eye operation, she and a colleague smuggle Zander from his asylum. He has another blackout and attacks a secretary. But the operation is a success and Diana says she will fight for his reinstatement. Absurd.
RoC *Patricia Hilliard, Stewart Rome, Dorothy Boyd, Ian Fleming, Tom Helmore, Dorothy Calve, Ruby Miller, Brian Buchel, Sidney Monckton.*

THE SHADOW OF MIKE EMERALD (1935) [2]

Dir *P. Maclean Rogers.* Prod *A. George Smith.* Scr *Kathleen Butler, Anthony Richardson.* Ph *Geoffrey Faithfull.* PC *GS Enterprises.* Dis *Radio.* 61 mins. Cert A
When crooked financier Mike Emerald (*Leslie Perrins*) tries to abscond with £20,000 in bonds, one of his associates commits suicide and the other three vow vengeance when their prison terms are up, having been unjustly accused of involvement in his crime. Emerald escapes from jail, but is traced through his wife (*Marjorie Mars*). She, however, has fallen for a wealthy bachelor (*Atholl Fleming*) who eliminates Emerald and his associates.
RoC *Martin Lewis, Vincent Holman, Neville Brook, Basil Langton, Iris Parnell, Miss Messina, Bruce Seton.*

SHADOWS (1931) [2]

Dir and Prod *Alexander Esway.* Scr *Frank Miller.* PC *BIP.* Dis *First National-Pathé.* 57 mins. Cert A
Laboured thriller about a newspaper reporter (*Derrick de Marney*) on the trail of a gangster (*Bernard Nedell*) who has murdered his mistress and is holding an heiress for ransom aboard his boat. The reporter rescues the girl and the criminal commits suicide to avoid arrest. Even at 57 minutes, it seemed to drag.
RoC *Jacqueline Logan, Gordon Harker, D. A. Clarke-Smith, Molly Lamont, Mary Clare, Wally Patch, Mark Lester, Roy Emerton.*

SHE COULDN'T SAY NO (1939) [3]

Dir *Graham Cutts.* Prod *Walter C. Mycroft.* Scr *Clifford Grey, Elizabeth Meehan, Bert Lee, from a play by Paul Smith and Fred Thompson.* Ph *Claude Friese-Greene.* PC and Dis *Associated British.* 72 mins. Cert U
Flirtatious Frankie (*Greta Gynt*) has her compromising diary locked away by her guardian (*Cecil Parker*). She asks Peter (*Tommy Trinder*), an entertainer in the RAF, and his agent (*Fred Emney*) to get it back. They attempt to burgle the safe the same night as professional burglars and flee to a sanatorium. Frankie

turns up disguised as a nurse; so do the burglars, who are after some jewels. Confusion reigns. Slim farce with lively performances.
RoC *David Hutcheson, Googie Withers, Bertha Belmore, Basil Radford, David Burns, Wylie Watson, Doris Hare, Geoffrey Sumner.*

SHE KNEW WHAT SHE WANTED
(1936)   [2]
Dir and Prod *Thomas Bentley.* Scr *Tom Gerachty, Frank Miller.* Ph *Curt Courant.* PC *Rialto.* Dis *Wardour.* 74 mins. Cert U
Frankie (*Betty Ann Davies*), a self-willed girl, expelled from her finishing college, determinedly embarks on a life of lying, cheating, publicity-seeking and libel-spreading. She gets away with it all, and even lands the dance-band leader she fancies after she helps him round up a gang of jewel thieves. Comedy with musical interludes.
RoC *Albert Burdon, Claude Dampier, W. H. Berry, Fred Conyngham, Ben Welden, Googie Withers, Hope Davy, Sybil Grove, Albert le Fré, Murray Ashford, Edgar Sawyer, Judy Shirley, Sam Costa.*

SHE SHALL HAVE MUSIC (1935)   [3]
Dir *Leslie Hiscott.* Prod *Julius Hagen.* Scr *Arthur Macrae, H. Fowler Mear.* Ph *Sydney Blythe, William Luff.* PC and Dis *Twickenham.* 91 mins. Cert U
A shipping magnate plans to present the famous *Jack Hylton* band in a cruise broadcast from out at sea, but his scheme is wrecked by a business rival. Quite a presentable showcase for the popular musician and his 'boys'.
RoC *June Clyde, Claude Dampier, Bryan Lawrence, Gwen Farrar, Marjorie Brooks, Edmond Breon, Felix Aylmer, Mathea Merryfield, Magda Neeld, Diana Ward, Two Mackeys, Carmona, Baby Terry, Freddie Schweitzer, Terry's Juveniles, Sonny Farrar, Billie Carlisle, Ernest Sefton, Leslie Carew, Langley Howard, Eddie Hooper, Billy Mann, Ken Smoothy, Leon Woizikowski Ballet, The Dalmora Can-Can Dancers.*

SHE WAS ONLY A VILLAGE MAIDEN
(1933)   [3]
Dir *Arthur Maude.* Prod *Ivar Campbell.* Scr *John Cousins, N. W. Baring-Pemberton, from a play by Fanny Bowker.* PC *Sound City.* Dis *M-G-M.* 61 mins. Cert A
Priscilla (*Anne Grey*), a romantic lady of 30 brought up by two elderly sisters, is left a fortune by one of them on condition that she leave the other sister for six months. Not surprisingly, she has no lack of suitors in the village. To stave them off, she declares she is engaged to the local lawyer (*Lester Matthews*) who, coincidentally, she eventually marries.
RoC *Carl Harbord, Barbara Everest, Julian Royce, Antony Holles, Gertrude Sterroll, Daphne Scorer, Ella Daincourt.*

SHIPMATES O' MINE (1936)   [2]
Dir *Oswald Mitchell.* Prod and PC *T. A. Welsh.* Scr *Mitchell, George Pearson.* Ph *Robert Martin.* Dis *Butchers.* 87 mins. Cert U
Through-the-years story with songs and sentiments for the unsophisticated. A sailor rises

from first officer to captain, gets married and has a son, but loses his command when his ship is rammed and he abandons ship to save passengers. For years, he lives in the country. Then his son, now grown, contacts his father's old shipmates and eventually their ship is put back into commission with its old skipper in command.
LP *John Garrick, Jean Adrienne, Wallace Lupino, Derek Blomfield, Mark Daly, John Turnbull, Frank Atkinson, Cynthia Stock, Richard Hayward, Polly Ward, Jack Hodges, Guy Dixon, Patrick Colbert, Gordon Little, Radio Male Voice Choir, Sherman Fisher Girls, Horace Sheldon and His Orchestra.*

SHIPYARD SALLY (1939)   [4]
Dir *Monty Banks.* Prod *Robert T. Kane.* Scr *Karl Tunberg, Don Ettlinger.* Ph *Otto Kanturek.* PC and Dis *20th Century-Fox.* 80 mins. Cert U
Rousing musical melodrama which restores *Gracie Fields* happily to working-class surroundings. Unemployment has hit Scotland. Shipyards lie idle, and so does the pub run by Sally (*Gracie Fields*), but she gives the men beer and food 'on tick' until her own tick runs out. Then, hindered by her cardsharp father (*Sydney Howard*), she storms up to London where, after a few disasters, she gets the investigating committee on the yards to review its findings. One of the film's songs, 'Wish Me Luck As You Wave Me Goodbye', was later adopted by the Second World War troops as a marching tune.
RoC *Morton Selten, Norma Varden, Tucker McGuire, Oliver Wakefield, MacDonald Parke, Richard Cooper, Joan Cowick, Monty Banks.*

Gracie Fields and Sydney Howard in Shipyard Sally *(1939)*

SHOOTING STARS (1937)   [2]
Dir and Prod *Eric Humphris.* Scr *Fred Duprez.* Ph *Desmond Dickinson.* PC and Dis *Viking Films.* 69 mins. Cert U
Straightforward revue entertainment, introduced by comedian/character actor *Fred Duprez,* some of his last work before his death a few months later.
RoC *Scott and Whaley, Phyllis Robins, Karina, Harry Robin, The Sherman Fisher Girls.*

A SHOT IN THE DARK (1933)   [2]
Dir *George Pearson.* Prod *Julius Hagen.* Scr *H. Fowler Mear, from the novel by Gerard Fairlie.* PC *Real Art.* Dis *Radio.* 53 mins. Cert A

A wealthy miser is found dead, having apparently committed suicide. The Rev. John Malcolm (*O. B. Clarence*), present at the reading of the will, is dissatisfied with the suicide verdict and investigates the case, finding that the old man was murdered by his worthless nephew. Typical multi-suspect whodunnit.
RoC *Dorothy Boyd, Jack Hawkins, Russell Thorndike, Michael Shepley, Davy Burnaby, A. Bromley Davenport, Hugh E. Wright, Henrietta Watson, Margaret Yarde.*

SHOULD A DOCTOR TELL? (1930)   [3]
Dir *Manning Haynes.* Prod *S. W. Smith.* Scr *Edgar Wallace.* PC and Dis *British Lion.* 59 mins. Cert A
Tangled drama about a doctor (*Basil Gill*) whose son (*Maurice Evans*) and niece (*Anna Neagle*) become involved, respectively, with an unmarried mother and her seducer.
RoC *Norah Baring, Gladys Jennings, A. G. Poulton, Harvey Braban.*

SHOW FLAT (1936)   [1]
Dir *Bernard Mainwaring.* Prod *Anthony Havelock-Allan.* Scr *Sherard Powell, George Barraud, from the play by Cecil Maiden, Martha Robinson.* PC and Dis *British and Dominions/Paramount British.* 70 mins. Cert U
Struggling playwright Paul (*Anthony Hankey*), to impress a rich aunt whom he wants to finance a play, gives his address as that of a show flat decorated by his friend. But his aunt has been financially ruined. His friend's fiancée (*Polly Ward*) persuades an impresario whom she knows to back Paul's play instead – so only the audience loses out in this hackneyed comedy.
RoC *Clifford Heatherley, Eileen Munro, Max Faber, Vernon Harris, Miki Decima, Billy Bray.*

THE SHOW GOES ON (1937)   [3]
Dir and Prod *Basil Dean.* Scr *Austin Melford, Anthony Kimmins, E. G. Valentine.* Ph *Jan Stallich.* PC *ATP.* Dis *Associated British.* 93 mins. Cert U
Composer Martin Fraser (*Owen Nares*), impressed by millgirl Sally Scowcroft's (*Gracie Fields*) singing voice, whisks her from a pierrot show to singing his own sentimental songs in the music-hall. By singing more popular songs, Sally becomes a big star. Martin dies of tuberculosis and Sally marries her childhood sweetheart. Partly based on Gracie Fields' own life story, but not one of her best films.
RoC *John Stuart, Horace Hodges, Edward Rigby, Amy Veness, Arthur Sinclair, Cyril Ritchard, Jack Hobbs, Dennis Arundell, Billy Merson, Frederick Leister, Patrick Barr, Nina Vanna, Tom Payne, Lawrence Hanray, Aubrey Dexter, Carl Randall, Andrea Malandrinos, Fred Hutchings, Queenie Leonard, Isobel Scaife, Elsie Wagstaffe, Sybil Grove, Florence Harwood, Olsen's Sea Lions.*

SIDE STREET ANGEL (1937)   [3]
Dir *Ralph Ince.* Prod *Irving Asher.* Scr *Uncredited.* Ph *Basil Emmott.* PC and Dis *Warner Bros.* 63 mins. Cert A

Silly but well-acted romantic comedy about Peter (*Hugh Williams*), a wealthy young man who, double-crossed by his society fiancée at a party, storms off into the night and runs into an ex-convict who takes him to a hostel for 'reformed' crooks. Here he meets Anne (*Lesley Brook*) who helps run the place, but is also grabbed by a gang who take him at his word that he's a gentleman thief. He is eventually rescued by Anne, who finds that Peter has bought the hostel so that its work can continue.
RoC *Henry Kendall, Reginald Purdell, Phyllis Stanley, Madeleine Seymour, Edna Davies.*

SIDE STREETS (1933)   3
Dir *Ivar Campbell*. Prod *Norman Loudon*. Scr *Philip Godfrey*. PC *Sound City*. Dis *M-G-M*. 47 mins. Cert A
Out of work, Ted (*Arnold Riches*) becomes a boxer. He is instrumental in helping his prospective mother-in-law (*Jane Wood*) cope with her ex-convict husband, who tries to blackmail her, and who is then killed while burgling her home. Ted enters a big boxing contest and wins.
RoC *Diana Beaumont, Paul Neville, Harry Terry, Dora Levis, Gunner Moir.*

THE SIGN OF FOUR (1932)   3
Dir *Rowland V. Lee, Graham Cutts*. Prod *Basil Dean*. Scr *W. P. Lipscomb, from the novel by Sir Arthur Conan Doyle*. Ph *Robert G. Martin, Robert DeGrasse*. PC *Associated Talking Pictures*. Dis *Radio*. 75 mins. Cert U
Sherlock Holmes (*Arthur Wontner*) finds himself immersed in a ruthless quest for some valuable pearls when Mary (*Isla Bevan*) daughter of a murdered man, finds her life threatened in a mysterious note which bears the Sign of Four. He discovers the protagonist is an ex-convict seeking revenge on the partners who cheated him out of his share of a robbery.
RoC *Ian Hunter, Ben Soutten, Miles Malleson, Herbert Lomas, Gilbert Davis, Kynaston Reeves, Edgar Norfolk, Roy Emerton, Clare Greet, Togo.*

THE SILENT BATTLE (1939)   4
(USA: *Continental Express*)
Dir *Herbert Mason*. Prod *Anthony Havelock-Allan*. Scr *Wolfgang Wilhelm, Rodney Ackland,*

Valerie Hobson and John Loder in The Silent Battle *(1939)*

from a novel by *Jean Bommart*. Ph *Francis Carver*. PC *Pinebrook*. Dis *Paramount*. 84 mins. Cert U
Bosnian girl Draguisha (*Valerie Hobson*) is persuaded by an armaments manufacturer that to save her imprisoned father she must assassinate the president of her country. On the Orient Express, her fiancé René (*John Loder*) and a stranger, Sauvin (*Rex Harrison*) convince her of the folly of her action, which rebels hope will start a war. Draguisha is kidnapped by the armaments king, but Sauvin, a secret service agent, and René go after them, rescue Draguisha and blow up the rebels' ammunition store. Slow to start, gets exciting at the end.
RoC *Muriel Aked, George Devine, John Salew, Kaye Seeley, Carl Jaffe, Megs Jenkins, Arthur Maude, David Keir, Joan Gibson.*

THE SILENT PASSENGER (1935)   4
Dir *Reginald Denham*. Prod *Hugh Perceval*. Scr *Basil Mason, from the novel by Dorothy L. Sayers*. Ph *Jan Stallich*. PC *Phoenix*. Dis *Associated British*. 75 mins. Cert A
Novel and ingenious thriller. Camberley (*Donald Wolfit*), a railway detective, plans the 'perfect' murder to be rid of blackmailer Windermere (*Leslie Perrins*). He kills him at his hotel, and puts the body in a trunk, unwittingly incriminating John Ryder (*John Loder*) whose wife Mollie (*Mary Newland*), another of Windermere's victims, had been travelling with him to try to retrieve some incriminating letters. Detective Lord Peter Wimsey (*Peter Haddon*) steps in and brings Camberley to justice.
RoC *Austin Trevor, Aubrey Mather, Robb Wilton, Ralph Truman, Percy Rhodes, Frederick Burtwell, Gordon McLeod, George de Warfaz, Vincent Holman, Ann Codrington, Dorice Fordred, Annie Esmond.*

SILVER BLAZE (1937)   2
(USA: *Murder at the Baskervilles*)
Dir *Thomas Bentley*. Prod *Julius Hagen*. Scr *Arthur Macrae, H. Fowler Mear, from the novel by Sir Arthur Conan Doyle*. Ph *Sydney Blythe, William Luff*. PC *Twickenham*. Dis *Associated British*. 71 mins. Cert U
Arthur Wontner returns to the role of Sherlock Holmes for the last time to solve the disappearance of a racehorse, and the murder of its groom and trainer, whom the horse is believed to have kicked to death. A low note on which to end *Wontner*'s tenure, but Basil Rathbone was soon to take up the pipe and deerstalker in the famous Hollywood series.
RoC *Ian Fleming, Lyn Harding, Judy Gunn, Lawrence Grossmith, Eve Gray, John Turnbull, Arthur Macrae, Martin Walker, Robert Horton, Arthur Goullet, Minnie Rayner.*

THE SILVER GREYHOUND (1932)   1
Dir *William McGann*. Prod *Irving Asher*. Scr *Roland Pertwee, John Hastings Turner*. PC and Dis *Warner Bros*. 47 mins. Cert U
Unconvincing comedy-thriller about a young Secret Service agent (*Anthony Bushell*) who falls in love with a girl (*Janice Adair*) in Paris. She proves to be a spy who drugs him and steals a secret document. But his chief (*Percy*

Marmont) regains the document, and the agent regains the girl.
RoC *Harry Hutchinson, J. A. O'Rourke, Dino Galvani, Eric Stanley.*

THE SILVER SPOON (1933)   1
Dir *George King*. Prod *Irving Asher*. Scr *Brock Williams*. Ph *Basil Emmott*. PC and Dis *Warner Bros*. 65 mins. Cert A
Improbable yarn about two aristocratic down-and-outs (*Ian Hunter, Garry Marsh*) who confess to the murder of Lord Perivale (*Cecil Humphreys*) to protect Lady Perivale (*Binnie Barnes*), whom they both adore. The real killer is brought to book in time to prevent them going to the gallows.
RoC *Cecil Parker, O. B. Clarence, Joan Playfair, George Merritt.*

SILVER TOP (1937)   1
Dir and Prod *George King*. Scr *Gerald Elliott, Dorothy Greenhill*. Ph *Hone Glendinning*. PC *Triangle*. Dis *Paramount*. 66 mins. Cert U
Mrs Deeping (*Marie Wright*), who runs a village sweet shop, comes into money, and a couple of crooks foist an imposter (*David Farrar*) on her as long-lost son. But the imposter falls in love with the vicar's daughter and reforms. Mrs Deeping tells the con-men at the end that she has known all along he was not her son. Over-sentimental, unconvincing.
RoC *Betty Ann Davies, Marjorie Taylor, Brian Buchel, Brian Herbert, Pollie Emery, Isobel Scaife, Alice Bolster, Fred Sinclair.*

SIMPLY TERRIFIC (1938)   2
Dir *Roy William Neill*. Prod *Irving Asher*. Scr *Anthony Hankey, Basil Dillon*. Ph *Robert Lapresle*. PC and Dis *Warner Bros*. 73 mins. Cert A
Wealthy Rodney (*Claude Hulbert*), out to impress his girlfriend's rich father, is talked by a failed businessman and his girl (*Reginald Purdell, Zoë Wynn*) into persuading the old man to back a new product, Socko, which doesn't exist. But they find a flowerseller (*Laura Wright*) who makes a home cure for that 'morning after' feeling, and market that under the new name. The flowerseller's vampish daughter (*Glen Alyn*) tries to get her hooks into Rodney but he escapes and gets the girl he wants. Comedy fails to live up to its title.
RoC *Patricia Medina, Aubrey Mallalieu, Hugh French, Ian MacLean, Frederick Burtwell.*

SING AS WE GO (1934)   4
Dir and Prod *Basil Dean*. Scr *Gordon Wellesley, from a story by J. B. Priestley*. Ph *Bob Martin*. PC *ATP*. Dis *Associated British*. 80 mins. Cert U
A millgirl (*Gracie Fields*) tries various jobs at Blackpool in the summer after her mill closes down, getting into some hair-raising scrapes. Through an accidental meeting with magnate Sir William Upton (*Lawrence Grossmith*), she is able to start negotiations to restore prosperity to the mill. Popular vehicle for its star.
RoC *John Loder, Dorothy Hyson, Stanley Holloway, Frank Pettingell, Morris Harvey, Arthur Sinclair, Maire O'Neill, Ben Field, Olive Sloane, Margaret Yarde, Evelyn Roberts, Nor-*

Gracie Fields in Sing As We Go *(1934)*

man *Walker, James R. Gregson, Richard Gray, Margery Pickard, Florence Gregson, Muriel Pavlow.*

SING AS YOU SWING (1937)   [3]

Dir *Redd Davis.* Prod *Joe Rock.* Scr *Syd Courtenay.* Ph *Jack Parker.* PC *Rock Studios.* Dis *British Independent. 82 mins. Cert U*
Slightly better than usual revue-style film which swings along quite well. A national radio station, in competing with a commercial station broadcasting from Europe, puts on an all-star variety show hosted by *Clapham and Dwyer. Claude Dampier* wanders amusingly in and out of the 'plot' as a salesman for rat poison.
RoC *Evelyn Dall, Lu-Anne Meredith, Brian Lawrence, Beryl Orde, Billie Carlisle, Edward Ashley, H.F. Maltby, Jimmy Godden, The Mills Brothers, Mantovani and His Tipicas, Nat Gonella and His Georgians, The Sherman Fisher Girls, Chilton and Thomas.*

THE SINGING COP (1937)   [2]

Dir *Arthur Woods.* Prod *Irving Asher.* Scr *Brock Williams, Tom Phipps.* Ph *Basil Emmott.* PC and Dis *Warner Bros. 78 mins. Cert U*
Scotland Yard discovers an official secrets leak. Suspicion falls on Maria (*Marta Labarr*), a prima donna, and singing policeman Jack Richards (*Keith Falkner*) is assigned to join her company. Maria and Kit (*Chili Bouchier*) both fall for Jack and, spurred on by jealousy, Kit proves Maria *is* the spy. Weak script leaves good opera sequences as film's main attraction.
RoC *Ivy StHelier, Glen Alyn, Athole Stewart, George Galleon, Ian Maclean, Bobbie Comber, Robert Rendel, Vera Bogetti, Brian Buchel, Derek Gorst, Frederick Burtwell, Covent Garden Chorus.*

A SISTER TO ASSIST 'ER (1930)   [2]

Dir *George Dewhurst.* Prod *H.B. Parkinson.* Scr *Dewhurst, from the play by John le Breton.* PC *E.A. Thompson.* Dis *Gaumont. 64 mins. Cert U*
Mrs May (*Barbara Gott*), an impoverished lodger, employs various tricks and stratagems on her landlady, Mrs McNash (*Pollie Emery*) to avoid paying her rent. The latest involves the invention of Mrs May's rich twin sister. Mrs May triumphs.
RoC *Donald Stuart, Charles Paton, Maude Gill, Alec Hunter, Johnny Butt.*

A SISTER TO ASSIST 'ER (1938)   [2]

Dir *Widgey R. Newman, George Dewhurst.* Prod *Newman.* Scr *Dewhurst, from the play by John le Breton.* PC *Associated Industries.* Dis *Columbia. 72 mins. Cert U*
Fourth of five film versions of the old comedy play, all directed or co-directed by Dewhurst. Each time landlady Mrs Getch (*Pollie Emery*) asks tenant Mrs May (*Muriel George*) for rent, she fails to get it. When Mrs Getch confiscates her trunk, over weeks of unpaid rent, Mrs May invents a rich sister, whom she impersonates, ending up not only with her trunk returned, but a handsome present for her wedding to the local fishmonger. Creaky.
RoC *Charles Paton, Billy Percy, Harry Herbert, Dorothy Vernon, Dora Levis.*

SIXTY GLORIOUS YEARS (1938)   [6]
(USA: *Queen of Destiny*)

Dir and Prod *Herbert Wilcox.* Scr *Charles de Grandcourt, Robert Vansittart, Miles Malleson.* Ph *Frederick A. Young.* PC *Imperator.* Dis *RKO Radio. Technicolor. 95 mins. Cert U*
A sequel to *Victoria the Great* (qv), depicting further events in the long reign of Queen Victoria: her wedding; the repeal of the Corn Laws; her review of the troops on horseback, despite opposition; the Great Exhibition at Crystal Palace; the Highland Games; the Crimean War; Victoria's meeting with Florence Nightingale; the death of the Prince Consort (*Anton Walbrook*); the aversion of war with America; the fall of Gordon at Khartoum; the death of the Queen (*Anna Neagle*). A stirring film, full of real humour and genuine pathos.
RoC *C. Aubrey Smith, Walter Rilla, Charles Carson, Grete Wegener, Felix Aylmer, Lewis Casson, Pamela Standish, Gordon McLeod, Stuart Robertson, Olaf Olsen, Henry Hallett, Wyndham Goldie, Malcolm Keen, Frederick Leister, Derrick de Marney, Marie Wright, Joyce Bland, Frank Cellier, Laidman Browne, Harvey Braban, Aubrey Dexter, Jack Watling.*

Anna Neagle in Sixty Glorious Years *(1938)*

THE SKIN GAME (1931)   [4]

Dir *Alfred Hitchcock.* Prod *John Maxwell.* Scr *Hitchcock, Alma Reville, from the play by John Galsworthy.* Ph *John J. Cox, Charles Martin.* PC *BIP.* Dis *Wardour. 88 mins. Cert A*
This remake of a 1921 film, with *Edmund Gwenn* and *Helen Haye* repeating their roles, seemed an odd choice for Alfred Hitchcock,

newly acclaimed as Britain's master of the thriller genre. It's a study of class confrontation, involving the battle for some valuable land, and whether it should be kept unspoiled, or used for building houses.
RoC *John Longden, Frank Lawton, C.V. France, Phyllis Konstam, Jill Esmond, Edward Chapman, Ronald Frankau, Herbert Ross, Dora Gregory, R.E. Jeffrey, George Blanchof.*

SKYLARKS (1936)   [2]

Dir *Thornton Freeland.* Prod *John Gossage.* Scr *Russell Medcraft.* PC and Dis *Reunion. 73 mins. Cert U*
Jimmy Nervo and *Teddy Knox* were only really successful in films as part of the Crazy Gang, and here's another of their threadbare solo comedies, this time casting them as Cook and Doakes, misfits in the RAF. Having become drunk one night, they steal an aeroplane and accidentally break an air endurance record. Not successful, despite a professional touch about the direction.
RoC *Nancy Burne, Eddie Gray, Queenie Leonard, Amy Veness.*

THE SKY RAIDERS (1938)   [1]

Dir, Prod and Scr *Fraser Foulsham.* PC *Sovereign.* Dis *First National. 57 mins. Cert A*
June (*Nita Harvey*) is snatched by a gang who then force her pilot brother David (*Ronald Braden*) to help hijack a bullion plane. He and June and another young pilot are held by the robbers on a remote island. Seeing the gang will kill them, the trio make a break for freedom and succeed. Thriller is terribly unconvincing, lacking in tension.
RoC *Ambrose Day, Michael Hogarth, Beatrice (Betty) Marsden, Harry Newman, David Keir, Stuart Christie, George de Brook, Rupert Mitford, Pat Keogh, Guy Waring.*

THE SKY'S THE LIMIT (1937)   [3]

Dir *Lee Garmes, Jack Buchanan.* Prod and PC *Buchanan.* Scr *Buchanan, Douglas Furber.* Ph *Garmes, Roy Clark.* Dis *General Film Distributors. 79 mins. Cert U*
Thin *Jack Buchanan* musical with the star as an aircraft designer whose best ideas are in danger of being stolen by his company, which fires him, after a riotous night with singer Isobella (*Mara Loseff*) has landed them in the headlines. But the singer proves a resourceful girl, and the designer ends up virtual head of his old company.
RoC *William Kendall, David Hutcheson, H.F. Maltby, Athene Seyler, Sara Allgood, Antony Holles, David Burns, Wally Patch, Barry Lupino, Morris Harvey, C.M. Hallard, Leslie Mitchell, Charles Stone, Andrea Malandrinos, Sam Wilkinson, Rawicz and Landauer, The Four New Yorkers.*

SLEEPING CAR (1933)   [3]

Dir *Anatole Litvak.* Prod *Michael Balcon.* Scr *Franz Schulz.* PC *Gaumont-British.* Dis *Ideal. 82 mins. Cert A*
Good cast adrift in a pretty silly comedy about an amorous sleeping car attendant (*Ivor Novello*), inveigled into marriage by a wealthy widow (*Madeleine Carroll*), who uses him as a

means to stay in France, before the couple genuinely fall in love.

RoC *Kay Hammond, Claud Allister, Stanley Holloway, Laddie Cliff, Ivor Barnard, Vera Bryer, Pat Fitzpatrick, Sam Keen, Richard Littledale, Peggy Simpson.*

THE SLEEPING CARDINAL (1931) 4
(USA: *Sherlock Holmes' Fatal Hour*)

Dir *Leslie Hiscott.* Prod *Julius Hagen.* Scr *Cyril Twyford, H. Fowler Mear, from stories by Sir Arthur Conan Doyle.* PC *Twickenham.* Dis *Warner Bros.* 84 mins. Cert U
Sherlock Holmes battles his old enemy Moriarty in an adaptation of two Conan Doyle stories, *The Empty House* and *The Final Problem.* A card cheat is pressed by the Moriarty gang to take forged notes to the Continent, but refuses and is murdered. Holmes (*Arthur Wontner*) is called in: it is almost his last case.
RoC *Norman McKinnel, Jane Welsh, Ian Fleming, Leslie Perrins, Philip Hewland, Louis Goodrich, Charles Paton, William Fazan, Sidney King, Gordon Begg, Minnie Rayner.*

Arthur Wontner and Minnie Rayner in The Sleeping Cardinal (*1931*)

SLEEPING PARTNERS (1930) 4

Dir and Scr *Seymour Hicks, from a play by Sacha Guitry.* Prod *Maurice J. Wilson, Sascha Geneen.* Ph *Claude MacDonnell.* PC *Geneen.* Dis *Paramount/Famous-Lasky.* 87 mins. Cert A
Adaptation of a famous stage farce, ingeniously spun out despite its slim premise, and with plenty of laughs. A lothario entertains a lonely wife while her husband is away, ostensibly on business, but actually on the town. They both end up asleep, the husband is out all night, and everything sorts itself out in the morning.

Edna Best and Seymour Hicks in Sleeping Partners (*1930*)

LP *Seymour Hicks, Edna Best, Lyn Harding, Herbert Waring, Marguerite Allan, David Paget.*

SLEEPLESS NIGHTS (1932) 4

Dir *Thomas Bentley.* Prod *Walter C. Mycroft.* Scr *Victor Kendall.* Ph *Jack Cox.* PC *BIP.* Dis *Wardour.* 73 mins. Cert A
Brightish *Stanley Lupino* comedy with musical interludes, casting him as a reporter in Nice to do a story about a valuable statuette. He becomes involved with a girl (*Polly Walker*) whom he saves from eloping with the thief (*Gerald Rawlinson*) who is out to lift the statuette.
RoC *Frederick Lloyd, Percy Parsons, Charlotte Parry, David Miller, Hal Gordon.*

THE SMALL MAN (1935) 4

Dir *John Baxter.* Prod *John Barter.* Scr *Con West.* Ph *Desmond Dickinson.* PC *Baxter and Barter.* Dis *Universal.* 71 mins. Cert U
Well-characterized drama of small shopkeepers whose livings are threatened by a big store. They try an intensive shopping week without success. But when Mrs Roberts (*Minnie Rayner*), the draper, finally capitulates, her obstinacy results in those shopkeepers who have to sell getting a much better price than they expected.
RoC *George Carney, Mary Newland, Ernest Butcher, Mark Daly, Edgar Driver, Charles Mortimer, Ian Colin, Roddy Hughes, (C.) Denier Warren, Haydn Wood, Thorpe Bates, Walter Amner, Stanley Kirkby, Albert Sandler and His Orchestra, The Gresham Singers, Foden's Brass Band.*

SMASH AND GRAB (1937) 4

Dir *Tim Whelan.* Prod and PC *Jack Buchanan.* Scr *Ralph Spence.* Ph *Henry Harris, Roy Clark.* Dis *General Film Distributors.* 76 mins. Cert A
John Forrest (*Jack Buchanan*), a light-at-heart private detective with a weakness for playing with model railways with his valet, is hired by an insurance firm to find a gang of smash-and-grab jewel thieves. The chase takes him to Ireland where he is helped by his wife, Alice (*Elsie Randolph*). After several murders and some excitement, the crooks are caught. Non-musical Buchanan film in *Thin Man* style.
RoC *Arthur Margetson, Antony Holles, Zoë Wynn, Edmund Willard, David Burns, Lawrence Grossmith, Edward Lexy, Lawrence Hanray, Sera Seegar, Nigel Fitzgerald.*

SMITH'S WIVES (1935) 2

Dir *Manning Haynes.* Prod *Ernest Garside.* Scr *Con West, Herbert Sargent, from a play by James Darnley.* PC and Dis *Fox British.* 60 mins. Cert A
Lesser *Ernie Lotinga* comedy in which a marital mix-up occurs through two Smiths and their respective wives living in opposite flats, one being a bookie (that's Lotinga), the other a parson.
RoC *Beryl de Querton, Tyrell Davis, Richard Ritchie, Kay Walsh, Jean Gillie, Vashti Taylor, Gilbert Davis, (Wilfrid) Hyde White, Harold Wilkinson, Daisy Brindley, Fred Gretton.*

SMITHY (1933) 3

Dir *George King.* Prod *Irving Asher.* Scr *Uncredited.* PC and Dis *Warner Bros.* 53 mins. Cert A
Smithy (*Edmund Gwenn*), a clerk in his fifties, is always dreaming of wealth and adventure. When he goes in for a mind-training course, all his fellow-clerks believe he has come into a fortune. When the truth comes out, everyone turns against him – except a cabaret singer he has befriended. Then he finds he has won £2,000 in a competition – and goes off with the singer to spend it.
RoC *Peggy Novak, Eve Gray, D. A. Clarke-Smith, Clifford Heatherley, Viola Compton, Charles Hickman.*

SOFT LIGHTS AND SWEET MUSIC (1936) 3

Dir and Prod *Herbert Smith.* Scr *Various artists.* Ph *Charles Van Enger, Harry Rose.* PC and Dis *British Lion.* 86 mins. Cert U
Straightforward musical-comedy revue, presented and compered by *The Western Brothers.* Rather on the long side and not done with much originality, but with some excellent individual turns.
RoC *Evelyn Dall, Sandy Powell, Harry Tate, Turner Layton, Billy Bennett, Elisabeth Welch, Max Bacon, Wilson, Keppel and Betty, Donald Stewart, Karina, Ambrose and His Orchestra, Three Rhythm Brothers, Four Flash Devils, Four Robinas, Five Charladies, Jimmy Fletcher, The Hollywood Beauties.*

SOLDIERS OF THE KING (1933) 4
(USA: *The Woman in Command*)

Dir *Maurice Elvey.* Prod *Michael Balcon.* Scr *Douglas Furber (also lyrics), W.P. Lipscomb, Jack Hulbert, J.O.C. Orton.* Ph *Bernard Knowles.* PC *Gainsborough.* Dis *W and F.* 80 mins. Cert U
Despite a strong cast, and a story about a family of music-hall artistes, this is virtually a one-woman show by *Cicely Courtneidge,* whose songs include 'There's Something About a Soldier' (music: Noel Gay). She plays the 'mother' of the troupe, whose own romance is doomed, and also a younger member, whose love affair she (as the 'mother') helps bring to fruition.
RoC *Edward Everett Horton, Anthony Bushell, Dorothy Hyson, Frank Cellier, Leslie Sarony, Bransby Williams, (Albert) Rebla, Herschel*

Anthony Bushell, Cicely Courtneidge and Frank Cellier in Soldiers of the King (*1933*)

Henlere, Ivor McLaren, Olive Sloane, O. B. Clarence, Arty Ash, David Deveen, André Rolet, Betty Sempsey, William Pardue.

SOMEDAY (1935) [3]

Dir *Michael Powell.* Prod *Irving Asher.* Scr *Brock Williams, from a novel by I. A. R. Wylie.* Ph *Basil Emmott.* PC and Dis *Warner Bros.* 69 mins. Cert A

Appealing, if insufficiently realized romantic drama concerning a lift-boy (*Esmond Knight*) and a cleaner (*Margaret Lockwood*) and the hot water they get into when they 'borrow' the flat of a man who is supposed to be abroad. The girl becomes ill and the boy is faced with court action, but their lives are repaired by her employer, a playboy (*Henry Mollison*), who comes to their rescue.

RoC *Sunday Wilshin, Raymond Lovell, Ivor Barnard, George Pughe, Jane Cornell.*

SOMEONE AT THE DOOR (1936) [2]

Dir *Herbert Brenon.* Prod *Walter C. Mycroft.* Scr *Jack Davies, Marjorie Deans, from the play by Dorothy and Campbell Christie.* Ph *Brian Langley.* PC BIP. Dis *Wardour.* 74 mins. Cert A

Stagebound, 'impossible' comedy-thriller about a young reporter (*Billy Milton*) who pretends to have murdered his sister (*Aileen Marson*) in order to get himself arrested and achieve a sensational scoop when she reappears. Her 'secret room' is also the hiding place of jewels various crooks are after and two real murders are committed before the case is closed and the reporter gets a genuine scoop.

RoC *Noah Beery, Edward Chapman, Hermione Gingold, John Irwin, Charles Mortimer, Edward Dignon, Lawrence Hanray, Jimmy Godden, Eliot Makeham.*

SOMETHING ALWAYS HAPPENS (1934) [4]

Dir *Michael Powell.* Prod *Irving Asher.* Scr *Brock Williams.* Ph *Percy Strong.* PC and Dis *Warner Bros.* 70 mins. Cert U

Nicely made and written comedy about Peter (*Ian Hunter*), an unemployed car salesman whose girl (*Nancy O'Neil*) suggests he approach the wealthy head of a car company – unknown to Peter also her father – with his idea for popularizing petrol stations. Father (*Peter Gawthorne*) rejects the plan, but a rival company makes it pay, and Peter gets the girl – and the forgiveness of his future father-in-law.

RoC *Johnny Singer, Muriel George, Barry Livesey, Millicent Wolf, Louie Emery, Reg Marcus.*

SOMETIMES GOOD (1934) [1]

Dir *W. P. Kellino.* Prod *Fred Browett.* Scr *Michael Barringer.* Ph *James Wilson.* PC BIP. Dis *Paramount.* 68 mins. Cert A

Novelettish comedy with *Nancy O'Neil* as shopgirl Millie, who resigns her job and goes to stay with her aunt, housekeeper to an absent explorer. Posing as the explorer's niece, Millie meets Paul (*Henry Kendall*) son of her exemployer. Her masquerade is discovered when the explorer returns unexpectedly, but her aunt, who had once known Paul's father, secures consent for their marriage.

RoC *Minnie Rayner, Hal Gordon, Charles Mortimer, Madeleine Seymour, Jimmy Godden, Edna Davies, Gladys Jennings, Millicent Wolf.*

SONG AT EVENTIDE (1934) [3]

Dir *Harry Hughes.* Prod *John Argyle.* Scr *John Hastings Turner.* Ph *Desmond Dickinson.* PC Argyle Talking Films. Dis *Butchers.* 84 mins. Cert A

Sentimental, conventional crime story with music, in which a cabaret singer (*Fay Compton*), blackmailed, acts to save her daughter (*Nancy Burne*) from scandal by first making her believe that she has died, and then entering a convent as a nun.

RoC *Lester Matthews, Leslie Perrins, Tom Helmore, Minnie Rayner, O. B. Clarence, Alfred Wellesley, Tully Comber, Barbara Gott, Charles Paton, Frank Titterton, Marie Daine, Eve Chipman, Barbara Everest, Ian Wilson, Marie Ault, Basil Atherton.*

SONG IN SOHO (1936) [2]

Dir *R. A. Hopwood.* Prod *Frank Green.* PC and Dis *Ace Films.* 49 mins. Cert A

Straightforward Windmill Theatre revue, climaxed by a take-off of a star-studded Hollywood premiere.

LP *Meggie Eaton, Edna Wood, Paddy Browne, Gus Chevalier, Olive del Mar, Warden and West, Eddie Kelland, Eddie Cooper, Gill Togo, Windmill Girls, Alan d'Albert and the Windmill Band.*

SONG OF FREEDOM (1936) [4]

Dir *J. Elder Wills.* Prod *H. Fraser Passmore.* Scr *Fenn Sherie, Ingram d'Abbes, Michael Barringer, Philip Lindsay.* Ph *Eric Cross.* PC Hammer. Dis *British Lion.* 81 mins. Cert U

John Zinga (*Paul Robeson*), a black docker taken by slave traders from a West African island years before, rises to fame through his superb singing voice. By chance, he discovers he is king of the far away island, and throws up everything to help his poor people with his wealth. He has a run-in with the witch doctor, but when he remembers the 'king's song' which has always been in his brain, everyone accepts him. Artificial but well-handled musical drama. Robeson's songs include 'Lonely Road', 'Song of Freedom', 'Sleepy River' and 'Stepping Stones'.

RoC *Elisabeth Welch, George Mozart, Esmé Percy, Joan and Fred Emney, Arthur Williams, Ronald Simpson, Robert Adams, Cornelia Smith, Alf Goddard, Will Hammer, Jenny Dean, Bernard Ansell, Sydney Benson, Ambrose Manning, Ronald Adam.*

SONG OF SOHO (1930) [3]

Dir *Harry Lachman.* Prod *John Maxwell.* Scr *Arthur Wimperis, Randall Faye, Frank Launder.* Ph *Claude Friese-Greene.* PC BIP. Dis *First National-Pathé.* 96 mins. Cert A

Carl Brisson's songs were the brightest things in this musical drama, which has him as a Legionnaire in London who helps a friend to make her Soho restaurant a success, then finds himself accused of the murder of a prostitute. His innocence is eventually proved in court by a blind beggar who, by recognizing the Legionnaire's song, establishes his alibi.

RoC *Edna Davies, Donald Calthrop, Henry Victor, Lucienne Herval, Antonia Brough, Charles Farrell, Andrea Nijinski.*

SONG OF THE FORGE (1937) [3]

Dir *Henry Edwards.* Prod *Wilfred Noy, Norman Hope-Bell.* Scr *H. Fowler Mear.* Ph *Desmond Dickinson.* PC and Dis *Butchers.* 82 mins. Cert U

Village blacksmith Joe Barrett (*Stanley Holloway*) parts company with his son William (also *Holloway*) when the latter decides to become an engineer. The two men never speak, even when the son returns 20 years later as Sir William, car magnate. Joe goes out of business. Learning that his father is about to go into the workhouse, William buys the village a fine new almshouse, and a father-son reconciliation occurs at the village Christmas fête. Holloway good in sentimental through-the-years piece.

RoC *Lawrence Grossmith, Eleanor Fayre, Davy Burnaby, (C.) Denier Warren, Arthur Chesney, Aubrey Fitzgerald, Hal Walters, Charles Hayes, Ian Wilson, Hay Plumb, Bruce Gordon, Edward Hodge, Mervyn Johns, Bert Weston, Frank Tilton, L. MacArthur Gordon, Stanley Radcliffe, Colin Kent, Wensley Russell, Shaun Desmond, Jack Morris, Ailsa Buchanan, Ambrose Day, Stanley Vine, Patrick Barry, The Rodney Hudson Dancing Girls.*

THE SONG OF THE PLOUGH (1933) [2]

Dir *John Baxter.* Prod *Ivar Campbell.* Scr *Reginald Pound.* PC *Sound City.* Dis *M-G-M.* 69 mins. Cert U

Moderate drama with music, enhanced by its photography of the English countryside. Farmer Freeland (*Stewart Rome*), having problems making ends meet, enters his dog Glen in the sheepdog trials. The animal saves Freeland from ruin when it wins the final, beating a champion dog especially imported by land-hungry Saxby (*Allan Jeayes*).

RoC *Rosalinde Fuller, Hay Petrie, Kenneth Kove, Jack Livesey, Edgar Driver, James Harcourt, Freddie Watts, Albert Richardson, Moore Marriott, Deirdre Gale.*

SONG OF THE ROAD (1937) [3]

Dir and Scr *John Baxter.* Prod *John Barter.* Ph *John Stumar.* PC *UK Films.* Dis *Sound City.* 71 mins. Cert U

Thrown out of work by the mechanical age, Old Bill (*Bransby Williams*) and his horse Polly take to the open road. After various ups and downs during their stays at a carnival and a farm, Bill and Polly finally settle down to country life. Leisurely drama has some quiet charm.

RoC *Ernest Butcher, Muriel George, Davy Burnaby, Tod Slaughter, John Turnbull, Edgar Driver, Fred Schwartz, Percy Parsons, Peggy Novak, H. F. Maltby, Johnnie Schofield, Ernest Jay, Robert English, F.B.J. Sharp, Phil Thomas.*

THE SONG YOU GAVE ME (1933) [2]

Dir *Paul Stein*. Prod *John Maxwell*. Scr *Clifford Grey, from a play by Walter Reisch*. PC *BIP*. Dis *Wardour*. 86 mins (later 83). Cert U

Rather forced romantic musical comedy about a singer (*Bebe Daniels*) who has three devoted suitors, but prefers to try to get her seemingly cold and aloof secretary (*Victor Varconi*) to propose to her. As he really loves her, but has been held back by the difference in their financial positions, this is achieved without difficulty before the end credits.

RoC *Claude Hulbert, Lester Matthews, Frederick Lloyd, Eva Moore, Iris Ashley, Walter Widdop*.

SONS OF THE SEA (1939) [3]

Dir *Maurice Elvey*. Prod *K. C. Alexander*. Scr *Elvey, Gerald Elliott, William Woolf*. Ph *Eric Cross*. PC *British Consolidated*. Dis *Grand National*. Dufaycolour. 82 mins. Cert U

Captain Hyde (*Leslie Banks*) is appointed commander of the Royal Naval College, where his son (*Simon Lack*) is a cadet. In defeating the plans of the enemy, who have laid a secret minefield, Hyde is bombed at sea and loses his memory. His son comes under suspicion of treason because of his promise to his father not to divulge his activities, but the enemy master spy is caught and all ends well. Unpretentious plug for naval life is one of more pleasant examples of a Dufaycolour film.

RoC *Kay Walsh, Mackenzie Ward, Cecil Parker, Ellen Pollock, Peter Shaw, Nigel Stock, P. Kynaston Reeves, Charles Eaton, Gordon Begg, Robert Field*.

SORRELL AND SON (1933) [5]

Dir *Jack Raymond*. Prod *Herbert Wilcox*. Scr *Lydia Hayward, from the novel by Warwick Deeping*. PC *British and Dominions*. Dis *United Artists*. 98 mins. Cert A

Sincere and tenderly observed story of an ex-captain, Sorrell (*H. B. Warner*) who devotes his whole life to his son after his wife leaves them. After many sacrifices, Sorrell sees his son grow up to be a successful surgeon. Although suffering from an incurable disease, Sorrell lives long enough to see his son marry the girl he knows will make him happy.

RoC *Hugh Williams, Winifred Shotter, Donald Calthrop, Margot Grahame, Louis Hayward, Ruby Miller, Evelyn Roberts, Arthur Chesney, Wally Patch, Hope Davy, Peter Penrose*.

Louis Hayward and H.B. Warner in Sorrell and Son *(1934)*

SO THIS IS LONDON (1939) [4]

Dir *Thornton Freeland*. Prod *Robert T. Kane*. Scr *William Conselman, Ben Travers, Tom Phipps, Douglas Furber*. Ph *Otto Kanturek*. PC and Dis *20th Century-Fox*. 89 mins. Cert A

Lord Worthing (*Alfred Drayton*), head of British Bakeries, and Hiram Draper (*Berton Churchill*), president of American Bread Inc, want to become joint owners of new Vitamin B4 flour. A solicitor, Honeycutt (*Robertson Hare*) has to get everyone together, including de Reszke, inventor of the formula. But de Reszke (*George Sanders*) falls for Honeycutt's wife, and later proves an imposter. The alliance is still consolidated – when Worthing's son marries Draper's daughter.

RoC *Fay Compton, Carla Lehmann, Stewart Granger, Ethel Revnell, Gracie West, Mavis Clair, Lily Cahill, Aubrey Mallalieu*.

Carla Lehmann and Stewart Granger in So This is London *(1938)*

A SOUTHERN MAID (1933) [3]

Dir *Harry Hughes*. Prod *Walter C. Mycroft*. Scr *Austin Melford, Arthur Woods, Frank Miller, Frank Launder, from the musical play by Dion Clayton Calthrop, Harry Graham*. Ph *Claude Friese-Greene, Philip Grindrod*. PC *BIP*. Dis *Wardour*. 85 mins. Cert U

Rather artificial musical, much troubled in the making. *Bebe Daniels* and *Clifford Mollison* play dual roles, two sets of lovers 20 years apart in Spain, the girl in each case rejecting the same man, the unfortunate Francesco (*Harry Welchman*).

RoC *Lupino Lane, Hal Gordon, Morris Harvey, Amy Veness, Nancy Brown, Basil Radford, John Beresford Cordwell, Sydney Monckton, Stewart Granger*.

SOUTHERN ROSES (1936) [3]

Dir *Fred Zelnik*. Prod *Isidore Goldschmidt, Max Schach*. Scr *Ronald Gow, from the play by Rudolph Bernauer*. Ph *Phil Tannura*. PC *Grafton*. Dis *General Film Distributors*. 78 mins. Cert U

Routine comedy-musical (music: *Hans May*), but smoothly directed. *Neil Hamilton* plays the naval officer who falls in love with a stage star, and *George Robey* carries the brunt of the comedy as his friend whom circumstances compel to pose as the star's husband.

RoC *Gino Malo, Chili Bouchier, Vera Pearce, Richard Dolman, Leslie Perrins, Sera Allgood, Athene Seyler. D. A. Clarke-Smith*.

SOUTH RIDING (1937) [4]

Dir and Prod *Victor Saville*. Scr *Ian Dalrymple, Donald Bull, from the novel by Winifred Holtby*. Ph *Harry Stradling*. PC *London Films*. Dis *United Artists*. 91 mins. Cert A

Country squire Robert Carne's (*Ralph Richardson*) rapidly diminishing fortune is largely spent keeping his wife (*Ann Todd*) in an expensive nursing home. He opposes a housing scheme fathered by socialist Astell (*John Clements*) and backed by two other council members for less honest reasons. When their duplicity is revealed, Astell feels bound to withdraw the scheme, but now Carne supports it, offering his own estate for the purpose at a knock-down price, provided the mansion itself is turned into new premises for the local school, with whose headmistress (*Edna Best*) he has fallen in love. Absorbing entertainment well made.

RoC *Edmund Gwenn, Marie Lohr, Milton Rosmer, Edward Lexy, Glynis Johns, Joan Ellum, Gus McNaughton, Josephine Wilson, Lewis Casson, Herbert Lomas, Jean Cadell, Felix Aylmer, Peggy Novak, Davina Craig, Laura Smithson, Skelton Knaggs, Florence Grosson, Arthur Hambling*.

SO YOU WON'T TALK! (1935) [4]

Dir *Monty Banks*. Prod *Irving Asher*. Scr *Russell Medcraft, Frank Launder*. Ph *Basil Emmott*. PC *Warner Bros*. Dis *First National*. 84 mins. Cert U

Snappily paced comedy about a man (*Monty Banks*) who will inherit a large fortune if he can refrain from talking – or writing – for 30 days. But three grasping female relatives, who will benefit if he breaks the conditions of the will, are determined to make him speak. They are assisted by an American gangster; but the heir wins through.

RoC *Vera Pearce, Bertha Belmore, Enid Stamp-Taylor, Muriel Angelus, Ralph Ince, Claude Dampier, A. Bromley Davenport, Julian Royce, Peter Bernard, Jack Harley*.

SPECIAL EDITION (1938) [3]

Dir, Prod and PC *Redd Davis*. Scr *Katharine Strueby*. Ph *Roy Fogwell*. Dis *Paramount*. 68 mins. Cert A

Reporter Warde (*John Garrick*) and photographer Aiken (*Norman Pierce*) are in the foyer of a theatre when a man is stabbed with a surgical knife. Police suspect Dr Pearson (*Frederick Culley*), whose daughter Sheila (*Lucille Lisle*) tells Warde he is dead, to throw him off the scent. The doctor eventually is murdered, and the killer proves to be Aiken, whose wife has died in a faulty operation for which Pearson had taken the blame. Thriller is slow but interesting, has a good roof-top climax.

RoC *Johnnie Schofield, Vera Bogetti, Mabel Twemlow, Vincent Holman, Dino Galvani, Fewlass Llewellyn*.

THE SPECKLED BAND (1931) [3]

Dir *Jack Raymond*. Prod *Herbert Wilcox*. Scr *W. P. Lipscomb, from the story by Sir Arthur Conan Doyle*. Ph *F. A. Young*. PC *British and Dominions*. Dis *W and F*. 90 mins. Cert A

Contemporary critics complained vociferously

about the modernization of Sherlock Holmes - as played by *Raymond Massey* he had an office fitted with dictaphones and a small army of typists - in a free adaptation of Conan Doyle's famous story of a mysterious death by snakebite. Once again it proves to be the work of criminal mastermind Moriarty, dominantly played by *Lyn Harding*.

RoC *Athole Stewart, Angela Baddeley, Nancy Price, Marie Ault, Stanley Lathbury, Charles Paton, Joyce Moore.*

THE SPIDER (1939) [3]

Dir *Maurice Elvey.* Prod *Victor M. Greene,* Scr *Kenneth Horne, Reginald Long, from a novel by Henry Holt.* Ph *Ernest Palmer.* PC *Admiral Wembley.* Dis *General Film Distributors.* 81 mins. Cert A

On the trail of jewel thieves headed by The Spider, Scotland Yard detective Gilbert Silver (*Derrick de Marney*) plants his wife Sally (*Diana Churchill*) with theatrical agents Bruce and Ismay, whom he suspects. Ismay (*Frank Cellier*) is killed and his body thrown from a train. His companion, Clare (*Jean Gillie*), an actress, is knocked out. When she starts to regain her memory, Bruce (*Cecil Parker*), The Spider, tries to push her off the train, but Gilbert, in the next compartment, saves her. Another sleuthing story along familiar *Thin Man* lines.

RoC *Edward Lexy, Allan Jeayes, Jack Melford, Jack Lambert, Antony Holles, Moira Lynd, Ronald Shiner, William Byron.*

SPIES OF THE AIR (1939) [3]

Dir *David Macdonald.* Prod *John Corfield.* Scr *A. R. Rawlinson, Bridget Boland, from a play by Jeffrey Dell.* Ph *Bryan Langley.* PC British National. Dis *Associated British.* 77 mins. Cert A

A well-laid scheme is afoot to pass the plans of a new plane to a foreign power. The designer (*Roger Livesey*), intent on completing and protecting the plans, neglects his wife (*Joan Marion*) who is the target of test pilot Thurloe (*Barry K. Barnes*). On the final test flight, Thurloe takes the plans aloft and photographs them. But the jig is up. He flees in the experimental plane, which runs out of fuel and crashes. Vigorous direction gives drama some punch.

RoC *Basil Radford, Felix Aylmer, John Turnbull, Henry Oscar, Edward Ashley, Wallace Douglas, Everley Gregg, Hal Walters, Santos Casani.*

SPLINTERS IN THE AIR (1937) [2]

Dir *Alfred Goulding.* Prod and PC *Herbert Wilcox.* Scr *R. P. Weston, Bert Lee, Jack Marks, K. R. G. Browne, Ralph Reader.* Ph *Eric Cross.* Dis *General Film Distributors.* 71 mins. Cert U

The 'Splinters' comedy series ground to an ignominious halt with this story of the inventor (*Sydney Howard*) of a bicycle-like helicopter who finds himself in the RAF when mistaken for his twin brother. He gets into all sorts of hot water, but covers himself with glory when he uses his helicopter to rescue the CO's wife (*Ellen Pollock*) from danger.

RoC *Richard Hearne, Stuart Robertson, Ralph*

Reader, D. A. Clarke-Smith, Franklyn Bellamy, Binkie Stuart, Ronald Ward, Lew Lake, Geraldine Hislop, George Ellisha.*

SPLINTERS IN THE NAVY (1931) [3]

Dir *Walter Forde.* Prod *Julius Hagen.* Scr *H. Fowler Mear, R. P. Weston, Bert Lee, Jack Marks.* PC *Twickenham.* Dis *W and F.* 76 mins. Cert U

The famous 'Splinters' company of ex-servicemen in drag provide the background for this farce about an able seaman (*Sydney Howard*) with a disinclination for work and exercise who amazes his mates by taking up boxing to get even with a Navy boxing champion, who has stolen his girl. The action ends in a riotous boxing match which the seaman wins.

RoC *Frederick Bentley, Helena Pickard, Paddy Browne, Alf Goddard, Rupert Lister, Harold Heath, Ian Wilson, Lew Lake, Hal Jones, Reg Stone, Wilfred Temple, Laurie Lawrence, Thomas Thurban.*

SPORTING LOVE (1936) [3]

Dir *J. Elder Wills.* Prod *H. Fraser Passmore.* Scr *Fenn Sherie, Ingram d'Abbes, from a play by Stanley Lupino.* Ph *Eric Cross.* PC *Hammer.* Dis *British Lion.* 70 mins. Cert U

Percy and Peter Brace (*Stanley Lupino, Laddie Cliff*) attempt to cure their financial blues by running a horse in the Derby. Like all their schemes it ends in disaster. They meet two girls, but the father of one proves to be one of their sternest creditors. A rich aunt comes to their rescue when they produce their 'wives' for her inspection. Rough and ready farce.

RoC *Eda Peel, Lu-Anne Meredith, Bobbie Comber, Henry Carlisle, Clarissa Selwynne, Wyn Weaver.*

THE SPORT OF KINGS (1931) [3]

Dir *Victor Saville.* Prod *Michael Balcon.* Scr *Angus Macphail, from the play by Ian Hay.* Ph *Alex Bryce.* PC *Gainsborough.* Dis *Ideal.* 98 mins. Cert U

Comedy about two racing toffs who wager that they can get puritanical anti-betting crank Amos Purdie to make a bet within a week. They manœuvre this so successfully that Purdie not only starts betting on a grand scale, but turns bookmaker to recoup his losses and welshes when the ruse fails.

LP *Leslie Henson, Hugh Wakefield, Gordon Harker, Dorothy Boyd, Renee Clama, Jack Melford,*

Gordon Harker and Leslie Henson in The Sport of Kings *(1931)*

Mary Jerrold, Barbara Gott, Wally Patch, Daphne Scorer, Willie Graham.

A SPOT OF BOTHER (1938) [3]

Dir *David Macdonald.* Prod *Anthony Havelock-Allan.* Scr *John Cousins, Stephen Clarkson, A. R. Rawlinson.* Ph *Francis Carver.* PC *Pinebrook.* Dis *General Film Distributors.* 70 mins. Cert U

The Bishop of Barchester hands over £2,000 from the Cathedral Restoration Fund to Mr Watney (*Alfred Drayton*), a 'businessman' who promises to turn it into the £3,000 the fund requires within 24 hours. The bishop's secretary, Rudd (*Robertson Hare*) is assigned to assist Watney and soon finds himself a party to smuggling silk underwear and brandy. It's the spirit that raises the money - at the bishop's jumble sale. Some laughs also raised.

RoC *Sandra Storme, Kathleen Joyce, Ruth Maitland, Gordon James, Robert Hale, Fewlass Llewellyn, Drusilla Wills, Julien Vedey, Edie Martin.*

SPRING HANDICAP (1937) [2]

Dir *Herbert Brenon.* Prod *Walter C. Mycroft.* Scr *Elizabeth Meehan, William Freshman, from a play by Ernest E. Bryan.* PC and Dis *Associated British.* 68 mins. Cert U

Vaguely based on the 1932 film *The Last Coupon*, this *Will Fyffe* vehicle has him as a miner who, inheriting a legacy, enters the horse-racing world, trying his hand with equal lack of success at betting, bookmaking, tipping and owning. His wife (*Maire O'Neill*) finally brings him to his senses. Broad comedy not really suited to Fyffe's more intimate style.

RoC *Billy Milton, Aileen Marson, Frank Pettingell, David Burns, Hugh Miller, Beatrice Varley.*

SPRING IN THE AIR (1934) [2]

Dir and Scr *S. Victor Hanbury, Norman Lee.* Prod and PC *John Stafford.* Dis *Pathé.* 74 mins. Cert A

Ilona (*Zelma O'Neal*) poses as housemaid to her friends Vilma and Max, to be near Paul (*Theo Shall*), a shy naturalist who lives at the top of their Budapest home with his frogs. Max (*Gus McNaughton*) makes advances to her, and the concierge (*Edmund Gwenn*) believes her to be his daughter - but in the end she gets Paul. Below-average comedy with music.

RoC *Lydia Sherwood, Mary Jerrold, Winifred Oughton, Jane Welsh.*

SPY FOR A DAY (1939) [4]

Dir and Prod *Mario Zampi.* Scr *Anatole de Grunwald, Hans Wilhelm, Emeric Pressburger, Ralph Block, Tommy Thompson, from a story by Stacy Aumonier.* PC *Two Cities.* Dis *Paramount.* 71 mins. Cert U

A north country farmhand, Sam (*Duggie Wakefield*) resembles a famous German spy. After nearly being shot by both the Germans and British, he is able to give the Allies the location of the real spy, who is captured. Arriving back at his village in triumph, Sam is sufficiently emboldened to propose to the local postmistress. Character comedy is agreeable surprise, with good individual scenes.

RoC *Paddy Browne, Jack Allen, Albert Lieven, Nicholas Hannen, Gibb McLaughlin, Allan Jeayes, Alf Goddard, George Hayes, Eliot Makeham, Hay Petrie, O. B. Clarence.*

THE SPY IN BLACK (1939)   [5]
(USA: *U-Boat 29*)

Dir *Michael Powell*. Prod *Irving Asher*. Scr *Emeric Pressburger, Roland Pertwee, from a novel by J. Storer Clouston*. Ph *Bernard Browne*. PC *Harefield*. Dis *Columbia*. 82 mins. Cert U

First World War: Captain Hardt (*Conrad Veidt*) is ordered to make contact in the Orkneys with a German agent posing as a schoolmistress. The British Secret Service is wise to things, and the wife (*Valerie Hobson*) of a naval officer takes the place of the German agent. Realizing the truth, Hardt escapes in disguise to a ferry-boat, frees the German prisoners there and tries to reach his fleet. He is blown out of the water by one of his own U-boats which is in turn sunk by a British submarine. Absorbing, atmospheric thriller.

RoC *Sebastian Shaw, Marius Goring, June Duprez, Athole Stewart, Agnes Lauchlan, Helen Haye, Cyril Raymond, Hay Petrie, Grant Sutherland, Robert Rendel, Mary Morris, George Summers, Margaret Moffatt, Kenneth Warrington, Torin Thatcher, Bernard Miles, Esma Cannon, Skelton Knaggs.*

Valerie Hobson and Conrad Veidt in The Spy in Black (*1939*)

SPY OF NAPOLEON (1936)   [4]

Dir *Maurice Elvey*. Prod *Julius Hagen*. Scr *L. duGarde Peach, Frederick Merrick, Harold Simpson, from the novel by Baroness Orczy*. Ph *Curt Courant*. PC *JH Productions*. Dis *Wardour*. 101 mins. Cert U

Slow but rather unusual historical adventure set in France in 1870. A dancer (*Dolly Haas*) who believes she is Louis Napoleon's illegitimate daughter and an officer (*Richard Barthelmess*) sentenced to death for plotting against him are forced to marry, so that he can give her an aristocratic name and she can spy against the aristocracy. Later they part, but years afterwards meet again while she is on a spy mission, and work together for France, living in peace after Napoleon's surrender to Bismarck.

RoC *Frank Vosper, Francis L. Sullivan, Joyce Bland, Lyn Harding, Henry Oscar, Marjorie Mars, Brian Buchel, (C.) Denier Warren,*

Wilfred Caithness, George Merritt, Stafford Hilliard.

THE SQUEAKER (1930)   [3]

Dir and Scr *Edgar Wallace, from his play*. Prod *S. W. Smith*. Ph *Horace Wheddon*. PC and Dis *British Lion*. 88 mins. Cert A

Edgar Wallace, who was chairman of British Lion Film Corporation at the time, himself directed this version of one of his most famous stories, in which Captain Leslie (*Percy Marmont*), ostensibly an ex-convict, is in reality a Scotland Yard detective on the trail of a clever fence called The Squeaker, who turns out to be the head of a philanthropic society.

RoC *Anne Grey, Gordon Harker, Trilby Clark, Alfred Drayton, Nigel Bruce, Eric Maturin, Cronin Wilson.*

Robert Newton and Edmund Lowe in The Squeaker (*1937*)

THE SQUEAKER (1937)   [4]
(USA: *Murder on Diamond Row*)

Dir *William K. Howard*. Prod *Alexander Korda*. Scr *Edward O. Berkman, Bryan Wallace, from the novel by Edgar Wallace*. Ph *Georges Périnal*. PC *Denham Productions*. Dis *United Artists*. 77 mins. Cert A

Larry Graeme (*Robert Newton*) is the latest victim of The Squeaker, a notorious jewel fence who hands over to the police, or otherwise disposes of any crooks who refuse to do business at his (cut) prices. Inspector Barrabal (*Edmund Lowe*) works undercover to reveal The Squeaker as Sutton (*Sebastion Shaw*), who uses his respectable business firm as a cover for his crooked activities. Sutton is trapped and arrested for Graeme's murder. Slick thriller.

RoC *Ann Todd, Tamara Desni, Alastair Sim, Stewart Rome, Allan Jeayes, Mabel Terry-Lewis, Gordon McLeod, Syd Crossley.*

SQUIBS (1935)   [3]

Dir *Henry Edwards*. Prod *Julius Hagen*. Scr *Michael Hogan, H. Fowler Mear*. Ph *Sydney Blythe*. PC *Twickenham*. Dis *Gaumont-British*. 77 mins. Cert U

Betty Balfour returns to the role that made her famous in silent days, but the old magic is missing. In this comedy-musical, she's again the spitfire Cockney flower-girl Squibs, whose romance with a Yorkshire policeman (*Stanley Holloway*) is threatened when her ne'er-do-well father (*Gordon Harker*) speculates with someone

else's money. A winning sweepstake ticket in Squibs' possession solves all their problems.

RoC *Margaret Yarde, Morris Harvey, Michael Shepley, Drusilla Wills, O. B. Clarence, Ronald Shiner, Thomas Weguelin.*

STAMBOUL (1931)   [1]

Dir *Dmitri Buchowetzki*. Prod *Walter Morosco*. Scr *Reginald Denham, from a play by Pierre Frondaie*. PC *Paramount British*. Dis *Paramount*. 75 mins. Cert A. Bilingual versions

Romantic intrigue runs riot in the Middle East: a German baroness falls in love with a French officer. Her husband, who is in love with a countess, plans to compromise her so that he can obtain his son in a divorce, but the French officer kills him and steals incriminating evidence against the Baroness. Ultimately, the remaining three are left empty-handed; so is the audience.

LP *Warwick Ward, Rosita Moreno, Margot Grahame, Henry Hewitt, Garry Marsh, Alan Napier, Abraham Sofaer, Stella Arbenina, Annie Esmond, Eric Pavitt.*

A STAR FELL FROM HEAVEN (1936)   [4]

Dir *Paul Merzbach*. Prod *Walter C. Mycroft*. Scr *Marjorie Deans, Dudley Leslie, Jack Davies, Gerald Elliott, Val Guest, Geoffrey Kerr*. Ph *Ronald Neame*. PC *BIP*. Dis *Wardour*. 70 mins. Cert U

Probably pocket tenor *Joseph Schmidt*'s best film vehicle. There's panic at Miracle Studios ('If it's a good film it's a Miracle') when the temperamental singer starring in their current opus loses his voice. Another voice is substituted on the soundtrack, but, in true *Singin' in the Rain* style, the hoax is exposed at the premiere. The real singer proves to be tiny Josef (*Schmidt*) whose stature makes him a star – although he loses his girl to another man.

RoC *Florine McKinney, Billy Milton, W. H. Berry, Steven Geray, Judy Kelly, George Graves, (C.) Denier Warren, Iris Hoey, Bruce Lister, Eliot Makeham, Hindle Edgar, Aubrey Mallalieu.*

STAR OF THE CIRCUS (1938)   [3]
(USA: *Hidden Menace*)

Dir *Albert de Courville*. Prod *Walter C. Mycroft*. Scr *John Monk Saunders, Hans Zerlett, Elizabeth Meehan, Dudley Leslie, from a novel by Heinrich Zeiler*. Ph *Claude Friese-Greene*. PC and Dis *Associated British*. 68 mins. Cert U

Truxa (*Patrick Barr*), a tightrope walker, loses his nerve, and offers his name and contracts to Paul (*John Clements*), a brilliant young aerialist. Paul finds himself in the same circus as Yesta (*Gertrude Michael*), a bareback dancer who would have married Truxa but for the threats of magician Garvin (*Otto Kruger*). Garvin tries to kill Paul on the high wire, but the real Truxa comes to the rescue. Far-fetched romantic drama has suspenseful tightrope scenes.

RoC *Gene Sheldon, Barbara Blair, Norah Howard, John Turnbull, Alfred Wellesley, Dora Gregory.*

THE STAR REPORTER (1931)   [2]

Dir *Michael Powell*. Prod *Jerome Jackson*. Scr *Philip Macdonald, Ralph Smart*. Ph *Geoffry*

Faithfull. PC *Film Engineering.* Dis *Fox. 44 mins.* Cert A

Reporter Michael Starr (*Harold French*) becomes chauffeur to Lady Susan (*Isla Bevan*) with the object of making his experiences the basis of an article. Instead, he gets on the trail of a thief, Mandel (*Garry Marsh*), who is out to steal the Langbourne diamond from Lady Susan's father. Starr traps the thief and marries Lady Susan.

RoC *Spencer Trevor, Antony Holles, Noel Dainton, Elsa Graves, Philip Morant.*

THE STARS LOOK DOWN (1939)   [5]

Dir *Carol Reed.* Prod *Isadore Goldschmidt.* Scr *J. B. Williams, A. J. Cronin,* Ph *Mutz Greenbaum, Ernest Palmer, Henry Harris, from the novel by Cronin.* PC *Grafton.* Dis *Grand National. 104 mins.* Cert A

Grimly realistic story set in a coal mining community in the north of England. David (*Michael Redgrave*), whose father (*Edward Rigby*) led a strike against unsafe conditions in Scupper Flats, goes to university but marries pretty, shallow Jenny (*Margaret Lockwood*), ex-girlfriend of Joe (*Emlyn Williams*), likely lad turned bookie, and bitter enemy of David, who takes a teaching job to support Jenny. She renews her affair with Joe, and David leaves her. When Joe's new coke contract entails reopening Scupper Flats, David puts the miners' protests to the union, but is overruled. The mine is flooded as soon as work begins. David's father and brother are among the dead. He dedicates his life to improving the miners' lot. This film placed Carol Reed in the forefront of young British directors.

RoC *Nancy Price, Allan Jeayes, Cecil Parker, Linden Travers, Milton Rosmer, George Carney, Ivor Barnard, Olga Lindo, Desmond Tester, David Markham, Aubrey Mallalieu, Kynaston Reeves, Clive Baxter, James Harcourt, Frederick Burtwell, Dorothy Hamilton, David Horne, Edmund Willard, Bernard Miles, Ben Williams, Frank Atkinson, Scott Harrold.*

STARS ON PARADE (1935)   [2]

Dir and Prod *Oswald Mitchell, Challis Sanderson.* PC and Dis *Butchers. 82 mins.* Cert U

Star Parade is a street where the famous and the would-be famous live, and where there's always someone 'on' at Alf's coffee stall. The acts in this revue-style entertainment are linked by episodes involving a policeman (*Robb Wilton*) and a drunk (*Jimmy James*). Moderate homespun stuff.

RoC *Edwin Lawrence, Horace Goldin, Pat O'Brien, Albert Whelan, Syd and Max Harrison, Mabel Constanduros, Arthur Lucan and Kitty McShane, John Rorke, Sam Barton, Navarre, The Act Superb, Pat Hyde, The Four Crochets, 'Dr Watson', Raymond Baird, Sherman Fisher Girls.*

STEPPING TOES (1938)   [3]

Dir *John Baxter.* Prod *John Barter, Jack Barty.* Scr *H. Fowler Mear.* PC *UK Films/Two Cities.* Dis *British Independent. 85 mins.* Cert U

Hazel Warrington (*Hazel Ascot*), a dazzling child dancer, is the granddaughter of an elderly showman who tours seaside towns in the sum-

mer season. At a child talent contest which he organizes, she not only wins the big prize, but also reconciles her father and mother, and goes on to tour in the West End of London. Teenymusical has some fresh charm.

RoC *Jack Barty, Enid Stamp-Taylor, Edgar Driver, Richard Cooper, Ernest Butcher, Ivan Samson, Wilson Coleman, John Turnbull, Gerry Fitzgerald, Billy Thorburn, Alfredo Campoli, Duggie Ascot, Freddie Watts, Wee Georgie, Marjorie Battis, Henry Latimer, Charles Sewell, Rita Linden, The Sanders Twins, The Three Dots, Cone School Girls, Duke of York's School Boys.*

THE STICKPIN (1933)   [3]

Dir *Leslie Hiscott.* Prod *Herbert Smith.* Scr *Michael Barringer.* Ph *Alex Bryce.* PC *British Lion.* Dis *Fox. 45 mins.* Cert A

Slightly above average quota quickie in which the girl victim of a blackmailer appeals to a friend (*Henry Kendall*) for help. The friend gets incriminating letters back by a spot of burglary, but then the blackmailer is found dead. A stickpin looks as though it will convict our hero, but the girl's husband revealed he was also in the blackmailer's flat that night and witnessed his (accidental) death.

RoC *Betty Astell, Francis L. Sullivan, Lawrence Anderson, Henry Caine, Pope Stamper.*

ST MARTIN'S LANE (1938)   [4]
(USA: *Sidewalks of London*)

Dir *Tim Whelan.* Prod *Erich Pommer.* Scr *Clemence Dane.* Ph *Jules Kruger.* PC *Mayflower.* Dis *Associated British. 85 mins.* Cert U

Charles (*Charles Laughton*), a London busker, is robbed by Libby (*Vivien Leigh*), out-of-work dancer turned pickpocket, and catches her when she steals a cigarette case from Harley (*Rex Harrison*). Enchanted by her, he puts her into his act with his two friends (*Tyrone Guthrie, Gus McNaughton*). Later, she meets Harley again and through his influence becomes a star. Charles, angry and hurt, is thrown in jail after a brawl, but Libby gets him an audition at her theatre. It proves to him that he was never the great performer he thought, and he returns to the streets. Flavoursome drama with good characters.

RoC *Larry Adler, Basil Gill, David Burns, Edward Lexy, Alf Goddard, Romilly Lunge, Maire O'Neill, Polly Ward, Helen Haye, Phyllis Stanley, Hal Gordon, Ronald Shiner, Cyril Smith, Clare Greet, Ronald Ward, Carroll Gibbons and His Orchestra, The Luna Boys.*

THE STOKER (1935)   [2]

Dir *Leslie Pearce.* Prod *Joe Rock.* Scr *Syd Courteney, George Harris.* Ph *Charles Van Enger.* PC *Leslie Fuller.* Dis *Gaumont-British. 70 mins.* Cert A

Ridiculous, but fast-moving *Leslie Fuller* comedy, with himself and *Georgie Harris* as stoker and steward on a P & O liner, at war with Steve (*Gibson Gowland*), the foreman stoker. Frank (*Leslie Bradley*), son of the chairman of the line, is serving an apprenticeship in the stokehole. He falls in love with an adventuress, but is saved from her clutches by his pals.

RoC *Phyllis Clare, Olive Melville, Pat Aherne, Robert English, Syd Courtenay, W. G. O'Neill.*

STOLEN LIFE (1938)   [4]

Dir *Paul Czinner.* Prod *Anthony Havelock-Allan.* Scr *Margaret Kennedy, George Barraud, from the novel by Karel J. Beneš.* Ph *Phil Tannura.* PC *Orion.* Dis *Paramount. 91 mins.* Cert A

The Alps: explorer Alan McKenzie (*Michael Redgrave*) meets Martina (*Elisabeth Bergner*) who falls in love with him. But her flighty, magnetic sister Sylvina (also *Bergner*) takes him from her and marries him. When Sylvina is drowned on holiday, Martina takes her place without Alan knowing … but finds she has to take on her sister's sins, and is threatened with divorce before her full confession throws them together. Original of weepie remade eight years later in Hollywood with Bette Davis. Good acting sees it through.

RoC *Wilfrid Lawson, Richard Ainley, Mabel Terry-Lewis, Clement McCallin, Kenneth Buckley, Dorice Fordred, Annie Esmond, Oliver Johnston, Stella Arbenina, Danielle Mendaille, Pierre Jouvenet, Kaye Seeley, Ernest Ferney, Cot d'Ordan, Roy Russell, Homer Regus, Boomsie (dog).*

THE STOLEN NECKLACE (1933)   [2]

Dir *Leslie Hiscott.* Prod *Irving Asher.* Scr *W. Scott Darling.* Ph *Basil Emmott.* PC and Dis *Warner Bros. 49 mins.* Cert A

Pocket crime thriller in which two rival gangs seek jewels stolen from an idol in a Chinese temple. But the gems bring bad luck to all who possess them until they are reclaimed by the temple's high priest.

LP *Joan Marion, Lester Matthews, Mickey Brantford, Wallace Lupino, Denis Wyndham, Charles Farrell, Victor Fairley, A. Bromley Davenport.*

STORM IN A TEACUP (1937)   [5]

Dir *Victor Saville, Ian Dalrymple.* Prod *Saville.* Scr *Dalrymple, Donald Bull, from James Bridie's adaptation of a play by Bruno Frank.* Ph *Mutz Greenbaum.* PC *Victor Saville Productions/London Films.* Dis *United Artists. 87 mins.* Cert A

A small Scottish town. The Provost (*Cecil Parker*) orders Patsy, Mrs Hegarty's beloved dog, to be destroyed because she cannot pay the licence. Newly arrived reporter Frank Burdon (*Rex Harrison*) takes up the case in the local paper. It becomes a national scandal, and the Provost's chances of becoming a Parliamentary candidate are ruined. He sues Frank, but his

Vivien Leigh, Cecil Parker and Rex Harrison in Storm in a Teacup *(1937)*

daughter Victoria (*Vivien Leigh*), in love with Frank, perjures herself to save him. Amusing, very English comedy: excellent of its kind.

RoC *Sara Allgood, Ursula Jeans, Gus McNaughton, Arthur Wontner, Edgar K. Bruce, Robert Hale, Quinton McPherson, Eliot Makeham, Ivor Barnard, W.G. Fay, Arthur Seaton, Cyril Smith, George Pughe, Cecil Mannering, Scruffy the dog.*

STORMY WEATHER (1935) [5]

Dir *Tom Walls.* Prod *Michael Balcon.* Scr *Ben Travers, from his play.* Ph *Philip Tannura.* PC *Gainsborough.* Dis *Gaumont-British. 74 mins. Cert A*

Business affairs take Sir Duncan (*Tom Walls*), boss of a chain of stores, and his two managers (*Ralph Lynn, J. Robertson Hare*) to Chinatown, where a sinister Russian (*Andrews Engelmann*), who was Sir Duncan's wife's first husband, is plotting a nasty piece of blackmail. But he is foiled during a chaotic skirmish in a Chinese opium den. Furious comedy has Aldwych gang at the top of their form.

RoC *Yvonne Arnaud, Stella Moya, Gordon James, Louis Bradfield, Fewless Llewellyn, Peter Gawthorne, Graham Moffatt.*

THE STRANGE ADVENTURES OF MR SMITH (1937) [2]

Dir *Maclean Rogers.* Prod and PC *George Smith.* Scr *H.F. Maltby, Kathleen Butler.* Ph *Geoffrey Faithfull.* Dis *Radio. 71 mins. Cert U*

Will Smith (*Gus McNaughton*) pretends to his new wife Maidie (*Eve Gray*) that he's a businessman. In fact, he's a pavement artist known as Black Patch. His mother-in-law's curiosity leads to his being unmasked, but when he is left £10,000 by one of his fond 'customers', his marriage is secured. Mediocre film does have some colourful minor characters.

RoC *Norma Varden, Aubrey Mallalieu, Billy Shine, Hal Walters, Isobel Scaife, Michael Ripper.*

STRANGE BOARDERS (1938) [4]

Dir *Herbert Mason.* Prod *Edward Black.* Scr *A.R. Rawlinson, Sidney Gilliat, from a novel by E. Phillips Oppenheim.* Ph *Jack Cox.* PC *Gainsborough.* Dis *General Film Distributors. 79 mins. Cert A*

Secret Serviceman Tommy (*Tom Walls*) is called back from honeymoon to solve the mystery of an old lady killed in a street 'accident', who has secret plans on her. Unknown to him, his bride, Louise (*Renée Saint-Cyr*) trails him – to a boarding-house, where he takes a room. A missing boarder answers the description of the dead woman and the rest, a rum lot, turn out to be spies who imprison Tommy and the newly arrived bride. Tommy turns the tables by staging a fake fire. Suspense kept up in good comedy-thriller.

RoC *Googie Withers, Ronald Adam, C.V. France, Nina Boucicault, Leon M. Lion, Tyrell Davis, (C.) Denier Warren, Irene Handl, George Curzon, Martita Hunt, John Turnbull, Douglas Stewart, Hay Plumb, Bernard Meresfield, Albert Chevalier, Arthur Goullet, Bryan Powley, Robert Nainby, Leo von Pokorny, Dino Galvani, Marie Wright, George Hayes, Maida Vanne.*

STRANGE CARGO (1936) [2]

Dir, Prod and PC *Lawrence Huntingdon.* Scr *Gerald Elliott.* Dis *Paramount. 68 mins. Cert A*

Mercenaries in a South American port plan to supply the rebels in nearby Santa Lucia with arms and ammunition – which are hidden in piano cases and shipped on to an English cargo vessel. The captain's son (*George Sanders*) rescues an English girl (*Kathleen Kelly*) falsely accused of murder; together they expose the crooks on board and find that one of them is the murderer. Colourful but punchless thriller.

RoC *Moore Marriott, George Mozart, Richard Norris, Geoffrey Clarke, Kenneth Warrington, Julien Vedey, Matt Davidson and Adele, Harry Lane, Conway Palmer, Alvin Saxon's Murray Club Band.*

STRANGE EVIDENCE (1932) [1]

Dir *Robert Milton.* Prod *Alexander Korda.* Scr *Miles Malleson.* Ph *Robert Martin.* PC *London Films.* Dis *Paramount. 71 mins. Cert A*

Gloomy, meandering drama of a girl (*Carol Goodner*) who, married to a cripple (*Leslie Banks*), has an affair with her cousin (*George Curzon*), rebuffs her husband's brother's advances, and is later accused of poisoning her husband. The brother proves to be the real culprit.

RoC *Frank Vosper, Norah Baring, Diana Napier, Haidee Wright, Lyonel Watts, Lewis Shaw, Merle Oberon, Miles Malleson.*

STRANGE EXPERIMENT (1936) [2]

Dir *Albert Parker.* Prod *John Findlay.* Scr *Edward Dryhurst, from a play by Hubert Osborne and John Golden.* PC and Dis *Fox British. 74 mins. Cert A*

James (*Donald Gray*), a chemist, becomes reluctantly involved in the theft of a formula for making pearls. He is knocked out by the robbers and left for dead when they are disturbed. A brain specialist decides to carry out an experiment on James, but it fails. It does, however, give James the chance to feign amnesia as a means of bringing the gang to justice. Heavy thriller.

RoC *Amy Wemyss, Mary Newcomb, Alastair Sim, Ronald Ward, Henri de Vries, James Carew, Eric Hales, Lilian Talbot, Joan Pereira, Henry Caine, Charles Howard, Arnold Bell.*

STRANGERS ON A HONEYMOON (1936) [3]

Dir *Albert de Courville.* (Associate) Prod *Haworth Bromly.* Scr *Laird Doyle (uncredited), Ralph Spence, Bryan Edgar Wallace, Sidney Gilliat, from a novel by Edgar Wallace.* Ph *Mutz Greenbaum.* PC and Dis *Gaumont-British. 70 mins. Cert A*

Some critics thought this breezy comedy marvellous, others a dead loss. No wonder one described it as 'a curious mixture'. October Jones (*Constance Cummings*), an orphan living with awful people, tells a snobby suitor she would rather marry a tramp. She finds herself the bride of Quigley (*Hugh Sinclair*), seemingly a hobo, but in reality a peer hunting a valuable deed, which he gets – after hairsbreadth adventures and chases. Set in Canada.

Hugh Sinclair and Constance Cummings in Strangers on a Honeymoon (*1936*)

RoC *Noah Beery, Beatrix Lehmann, David Burns, Butler Hixon, James Arnold, Ann Tucker McGuire, Edmund Breon, Maurice Freeman, Percy Parsons, Edward Ryan, Skelton Knaggs, Conway Palmer.*

STRANGLEHOLD (1931) [2]

Dir and Prod *Henry Edwards.* Scr *Hugh G. Esse.* PC *Teddington.* Dis *Warner Bros. 66 mins. Cert A*

Melodrama about a Chinese half-caste doctor (*Allan Jeayes*) out to avenge himself on Bruce (*Garry Marsh*), who seduced the Chinese girl the doctor loved. His vengeance is achieved, but he leavens it with mercy by saving the life of his enemy's son.

RoC *Isobel Elsom, Dorothy Bartlam, Derrick de Marney, Kenji Takase, Hugh E. Wright, Henry Vibart, Minnie Rayner, Frank Bertram, Pat Baring.*

THE STRANGLER (1932) [3]

Dir and Scr *Norman Lee.* Prod *Walter C. Mycroft.* PC *BIP/British Instructional.* Dis *Pathé. 45 mins. Cert A*

'Quota' whodunnit in some respects anticipating *Murder at Broadcasting House* two years later. On a darkened stage, an actor is strangled during the dress rehearsal for – a murder play. The cast are all suspect.

LP *Jack Morrison, Molly Lamont, Lewis Drayton, Moira Lynd, Cecil Ramage, Hal Gordon, Carol Coombe, Patrick Susands.*

THE STREET SINGER (1937) [3]

Dir *Jean de Marguenat.* Prod *Dora Nirva.* Scr *Reginald Arkell.* Ph *Henry Harris.* PC *British National.* Dis *Associated British. 86 mins. Cert U*

A musical comedy star, Richard King (*Arthur Tracy*), throws up his existence for the life of a busker, entertaining with Jenny (*Margaret Lockwood*), with whom he falls in love, and her father (*Arthur Riscoe*). He is 'rediscovered' and offered his old role under his new identity. His former leading lady tries to make trouble, but Richard replies by having her replaced with Jenny. Unpretentious but quite entertaining musical piece.

RoC *Ellen Pollock, Hugh Wakefield, Emil Boreo, Wally Patch, Ian MacLean, John Deverell, Rawicz and Landauer, Lew Stone and His Band, The Car Hyson Dancers.*

mott. PC *Warner Bros. Dis /*
mins. Cert U
The flirtatious Lady Foxham
adopts a big, dumb boxer (*N*
'protegé' after he has knocked
favourite in a private fight. T
land; en route the boxer's
Miller) is mistaken for a milli
digger (*Betty Lynne*) who dr
covery of the truth, and whisk
under Lady F's nose. Breezy c
RoC *Clem Lawrence, James S*
lotte Parry, Joan Miller.*

TAKE MY TIP (1937)

Dir *Herbert Mason*. Prod *Mi*
Sidney Gilliat, Michael Hoga
Ph *Bernard Knowles*. PC *Gau*
General Film Distributors. 74 m
Hilarious rapid-fire musical
Hulbert and Cicely Courtneid
Lady Pilkington, swindled ou
by a trickster (*Harold Huth*)
hotel owned by their butler, v
counter the villain again. By a
identities, including a waiter
and a couple of upper-crust c
ultimately turn the tables and
back. Songs include *I Was Ai*
timental and *I'm Like a Little I*
Cage.
RoC *Frank Cellier, Frank Pett*
ton, H.F. Maltby, Eliot N
Buchel (also co-choreography n*
ney), Paul Sheridan.

TAKE OFF THAT HAT (19.

Dir and Prod *Eric Humphri*
Dalby, (C.) Denier Warren. Ph
inson. PC and Dis *Viking Film*
59). Cert U*
A kind of British *Hellzapoppin*
comics at the centre of the cha
ful at the box-office although
vidual scenes. Pussyfoot and
and Whaley) win £10,000 on
rent an ultra-luxury flat. They
buttons that work heat, cold, t
an electric shaving machine, e
is tuned by a clown (*Noni*) wi
tools. People wander in and c
auditions are being held before
things get crazy....
RoC (C.) *Denier Warren, Inga*
Duprez, Billy Russell, Gipsy N
and His Band, The Sherman Fis*

TALKING FEET (1937)

Dir *John Baxter*. Prod *John*
Fowler Mear. PC *UK Films. I*
79 mins. Cert U
Hazel (*Hazel Ascot*), talented li
an East End fishmonger, is so
Hood (*John Stuart*) for saving
after a road accident that she
to arrange a concert at the loc
to raise funds for his failing ho
money is raised that the hosp
continue. Moderate musical. W
as Joe Barker, plus the names c
director, imagine the confusion!

STREET SONG (1935)   [2]

Dir *Bernard Vorhaus*. Prod *Julius Hagen*. Scr
Vorhaus, Paul Gangelin. PC *Real Art.* Dis
Radio. 64 mins. Cert A
Lucy (*René Ray*) and her brother Billy (*Johnny
Singer*) are struggling to make a go of their
Soho pet shop. She befriends a street singer,
Tom (*John Garrick*), without knowing that he
has got himself involved in a theft. Through
an old friend Lucy gets Tom a chance to sing
on radio, but then he is held by the police.
Billy persuades the thief to give himself up
and proves Tom's innocence. He goes on to
marry Lucy and become a well-known broad-
caster. Unattractive musical.
RoC *Wally Patch, Lawrence Hanray.*

STRICTLY BUSINESS (1932)   [2]

Dir *Mary Field, Jacqueline Logan.* Scr *Logan.*
Ph *Jack Parker.* PC *British Instructional.* Dis
Wardour. 46 mins. Cert U
A man-about-town saves an heiress, whom he
believes to be an ordinary girl, from the atten-
tions of a blackmailer. Ordinary little comedy
utilizes such genuine backdrops as the Chang-
ing of the Guard, test cricket at Lords and the
Wimbledon tennis championships.
LP *Betty Amann, Carl Harbord, Molly La-
mont, Percy Parsons, Philip Strange, C. M.
Hallard, Gordon Begg.*

Carl Harbord and Molly Lamont in Strictly
Business *(1931)*

STRICTLY ILLEGAL (1934)   [3]

Dir *Ralph Cedar.* Prod *Joe Rock.* Scr *Syd
Courtenay, Georgie Harris, from a play by Con
West, Herbert Sargent.* PC *Leslie Fuller Films.*
Dis *Gaumont-British. 69 mins. Cert U*
At-times-funny *Leslie Fuller* comedy about a
street-corner bookmaker (Fuller) who imagines
that he has killed a policeman in a fight. He
runs away and 'acquires' a parson's clothes,
being mistaken for the cleric by Lady Percival,
who wants him to marry her daughter. Another bogus clergyman appears and makes off
with the Percival jewels. The real parson puts
in a belated appearance, and chaos ensues at
a clergymen's convention on a train.
RoC *Betty Astell, Georgie Harris, Cissie Fitzgerald, Glennis Lorimer, Mickey Brantford, Ernest Sefton, Alf Goddard, Humberston Wright,
Syd Courtenay, T. Arthur Ellis.*

Gina Malo and George Gee in Strike It Rich
(1933)

STRIKE IT RICH (1933)   [2]

Dir *Leslie Hiscott.* Prod *Herbert Smith.* Scr
Michael Barringer. PC and Dis *British Lion.
72 mins. Cert U*
Rather threadbare comedy (with music by
Reggie Bristow), featuring *George Gee* as a
clerk in a hair-restorer firm who is inspired by
a phrenologist to lose his inferiority complex
and gains rapid promotion. His investment in
nutmegs looks like a blunder until it is discovered that nutmeg is the one ingredient
needed to complete the company's new, infall-
ible hair-restorer.
RoC *Betty Astell, Davy Burnaby, Gina Malo,
Ernest Sefton, Cyril Raymond, Wilfrid Lawson,
Hal Walters, Ethel Warwick.*

THE STRONGER SEX (1931)

Dir *V. Gareth Gundrey.* Prod *Michael Balcon.*
Scr *Gundrey, from a play by J. Valentine.* Ph
William Shenton. PC *Gainsborough.* Dis *Ideal.
80 mins. Cert A*
Lancashire-set triangular melodrama, ending
in a coal-pit disaster in which the central
character (*Colin Clive*) rescues his wife's lover
at the expense of his own life.
RoC *Adrianne Allen, Gordon Harker, Martin
Lewis, Renée Clama, Elsa Lanchester.*

THE STUDENT'S ROMANCE (1935)   [2]

Dir *Otto Kanturek.* Prod *Walter C. Mycroft.*
Scr *Clifford Grey, Norman Watson, Richard
Hutter, from a play by Beda and Ernst Neu-
mann.* Ph *Bryan Langley.* PC *BIP.* Dis *Wardour. 78 mins. Cert U*
Thin musical romance set in early
nineteenth-century Austria. Max and Karl
(*Patric Knowles, Mackenzie Ward*) are two
Heidelberg students. When Max is threatened
with imprisonment over debts, Veronika
(*Carol Goodner*), proprietress of the inn at
which they stay, helps him out. This leads to
gossip and almost ruins Max's chances of marrying the Princess of Westphalia.
RoC *Grete Natzler, Steven Geray, W. H.
Berry, Haver and Lee, Iris Ashley, Ivan Samson, Wallace Lupino, Hugh Dempster.*

SUCH IS LIFE (1936)   [3]

Dir *Randall Faye.* Prod *Brandon Fleming, Re-
ginald Gottwaltz.* Scr *Fleming.* Ph *Geoffrey
Faithfull.* PC *Incorporated Talking Films.* Dis
National Provincial. 80 mins. Cert A
Brightish farce about a millionaire (*Gene Ger-*

rard) who returns from a holiday, and so admires the nerve of the down-and-out (*Claude
Dampier*) who has installed himself in his flat
that he makes him his secretary. He falls
in love with a typist with ambitions to be a
singer, buys a variety agency, instals his new
secretary as manager and gets the girl a spot
in a cabaret.
RoC *Jean Colin, Eve Gray, Frank Birch, Mac-
Arthur Gordon, Aubrey Mallalieu, Paul Sheridan, Billie Carlyle, Robert Ashley, William
Daunt, John Mann, Bill Holland, Chela and
Dorvay.*

SUCH IS THE LAW (1930)   [3]

Dir *Sinclair Hill.* Prod *Oswald Mitchell.* Scr
Leslie Howard Gordon, Reginald Fogwell. Ph
Desmond Dickinson. PC *Stoll.* Dis *Butchers. 88
mins. Cert A*
An ingenious ruse that didn't quite come off.
Producer Oswald Mitchell took the pith of an
unreleased 1928 silent, *The Price of Divorce*,
and added a substantial sound framing story,
so that a cautionary tale told by a mother to
prevent her daughter eloping is seen as a silent
film. The results were fair but the public did
not bite.
LP (framing story) *Janice Adair, C. Aubrey
Smith, Kate Cutler, Lady Tree, Carl Harbord,
Bert Coote, Pamela Carme, Rex Maurice,
Aileen Despard, Frank Goldsmith, Winifred
Oughton, Charles Fancourt.*
Silent film *Wyndham Standing, Frances Day,
Miriam Seegar, Rex Maurice, Nancy Price,
Gibb McLaughlin, Maud Gill, Frances Rose
Campbell, Johnny Ashby, James Fenton*

SUMMER LIGHTNING (1933)   [4]

Dir *Maclean Rogers.* Prod *Herbert Wilcox.* Scr
*Miles Malleson, from the novel by P. G. Wode-
house.* Ph *F. A. Young.* PC *British and Dominions.* Dis *United Artists. 78 mins. Cert U*
Well-executed comedy in which Hugo (*Ralph
Lynn*), in love with his employer Lord Ems-
worth's niece Millicent (*Winifred Shotter*),
steals a prize sow for the lord (*Horace Hodges*)
to enter in a show. Complications inevitably
arise, but Hugo gets away with it: the sow
wins, is returned whence it came and Hugo
wins Millicent.
RoC *Dorothy Bouchier, Esmé Percy, Helen Ferrers, Miles Malleson, Gordon James, Joe Monkhouse.*

SUNSET IN VIENNA (1937)   [3]

(USA: *Suicide Legion*)
Dir *Norman Walker.* Prod and PC *Herbert
Wilcox.* Scr *Marjorie Gaffney, Harrison Owens.*
Ph *Frederick A. Young.* Dis *General Film Dis-
tributors. 74 mins. Cert U*
Lilli Palmer shines in this strange combination
of spy story and musical. An Italian officer
(*Tullio Carminati*) marries an Austrian girl
(*Miss Palmer*), but their happiness is blighted
by the First World War which makes their
countries enemies. She leaves him when he is
forced to shoot her brother (*John Garrick*) for
spying, but they are reunited after the war is
over.
RoC *Edgar Driver, Geraldine Hislop, Alice
O'Day, Hubert Harben, Davina Craig, Eileen
Munro.*

SUNSHINE AHEAD

Dir *Wallace Orton*. Pr[...]
West, Geoffrey Orme. P[...]
ter and Barter. Dis *Un*[...]
Musical revue, in wh[...]
manager of UK Rad[...]
broadcast variety show[...]
of a jealous critic.
LP *Eddie Pola, Betty A*[...]
Lister, Leonard Henry[...]
Band, Doris Arnold, H[...]
Leslies, Harold Ramsay[...]
Booth, Ruth Naylor, Tr[...]
The Sherman Fisher C[...]
and Santos, The Harmo[...]

SUNSHINE SUSIE (1[...]
(USA: *The Office Girl*)
Dir *Victor Saville*. Pr[...]
Angus Macphail, Rob[...]
Noel Wood-Smith, from[...]
and Franz Schulz. Ph[...]
Gainsborough. Dis *Ideal*[...]
Vivacious musical, p[...]
British success of its[...]
German star, *Renate M*[...]
from the German versio[...]
as 'Sunshine' Susie Su[...]
with a Viennese bank.[...]
with Arvay (*Owen Na*[...]
is a fellow-clerk, unawa[...]
director. Arvay toys wit[...]
as a mistress, but finally[...]
RoC *Jack Hulbert,* [...]
Grove, Gladys Hamer, I[...]
Gott.

SUSPENSE (1930)
Dir, Prod and Scr *W*[...]
play by *Patrick MacGill*[...]
Hal Young. PC *BIP*. 1[...]
Cert A
This popular First Wor[...]
for its most convincing[...]
direction by Summers,[...]
soldiers hiding out in a[...]
out to be near Germa[...]
Much excitement ensues[...]
LP *Cyril McLaglen, N*[...]
Raine, Fred Groves, D. [...]
ley, Percy Parsons, Hami[...]

SWEENEY TODD TH
BARBER OF FLEET [...]
Dir, Prod and PC *Geor*[...]
Hayward, H.F. Malth[...]
George Dibdin-Pitt. Ph[...]
M-G-M. 68 mins. *Cert A*[...]
Fiendish barber Sweene[...]
in his most famous role)[...]
chants to his dockside[...]
shaves them, murders [...]
disposes of their bodies[...]
sailor (*Bruce Seton*) is r[...]
saved thanks to a quarr[...]
and his female accompli[...]
the sailor returns – and[...]
finally caught in his own[...]
RoC *Eve Lister, Ben S*[...]
Jerry Verno, John Singer.[...]

TELL ME TONIGHT (1932)   5
(USA: *Be Mine Tonight*)
Dir *Anatole Litwak* (*Litvak*). Prod *Herman Fellner, Josef Somlo*. Scr *John Orton*. PC *Cine-Allianz*. Dis *W and F*. 91 mins. Cert U. Bilingual versions
Highly acclaimed musical-comedy set in Switzerland (although shot in Germany), where an Italian opera singer switches identities with a man on the run, and woos and wins the local Mayor's daughter.
LP *Jan Kiepura, Magda Schneider, Sonnie Hale, Edmund Gwenn, Athene Seyler, Betty Chester, Aubrey Mather*.

THE TELL TALE HEART (1934)   5
(USA: *Bucket of Blood*)
Dir *Brian Desmond Hurst*. Prod *Harry Clifton*. Scr *David Plunkett Greene, from the story by Edgar Allan Poe*. PC *Clifton-Hurst*. Dis *Fox*. 53 mins. Cert A
Pictorially distinctive treatment of the Poe horror story in which a young man (*Norman Dryden*), subject to cataleptic seizures, protests that he is not insane and describes to asylum doctors how he committed the 'perfect' murder – but was driven to confession by imagining that he heard his victim's heartbeats from beneath the floorboards.
RoC *John Kelt, Yolande Terrell, Thomas Shenton, James Fleck, Colonel Cameron, H. Vasher*.

THE TEMPERANCE FETE (1931)   3
Dir *Graham Cutts*. Prod and Scr *Reginald Fogwell, from a story by Herbert Jenkins*. PC *Fogwell Films*. Dis *M-G-M*. 45 mins. Cert A
George Robey's only appearance in the role of Bindle, the lead-swinging Cockney antique dealer created by Herbert Jenkins. In this misadventure, Bindle's wife (*Sydney Fairbrother*) volunteers him for a job looking after the lemonade stall at a temperance fete. Bindle mixes alcohol with the lemonade, and soon tipsy chaos reigns.
RoC *Connie Ediss, Gibb McLaughlin, Seth Egbert, Anita Sharp-Bolster*.

THE TEMPORARY WIDOW (1930)   3
Dir *Gustav Ucicky*. Prod *Erich Pommer*. Scr *Karl Hartl, Walter Reisch, Benn W. Levy, from a play by Curt Götz*. Ph *Werner Brandes*. PC *UFA*. Dis *Wardour*. 84 mins. Cert U
An Anglo-German comedy film, made in Berlin, with *Lilian Harvey* as the girl whose husband's career as a painter is not going well until she fakes his death in a boating accident. Suddenly, he is a celebrity – and she is rich from the sales of his work. But how is he to come back to life? Based on *Hokuspokus*, a play filmed twice before. Made in English and German – *Oscar Homolka* had a role in the German-language version.
RoC (English version) *Athole Stewart, Gillian Dean, Felix Aylmer, Frank Stanmore, Frederick Lloyd, Henry Caine*.

TEMPTATION (1934)   3
Dir and Scr *Max Neufeld, from a play by Melchior Lengyel*. PC *Milofilm*. Dis *Gaumont-British*. 77 mins. Cert U. Bilingual versions
Slowish, but colourful musical, shot in France, about Antonia (*Frances Day*), the young actress wife of a straitlaced, middle-aged farmer (*Stewart Rome*). Her harmless flirtation with a young flying officer really in love with his niece nearly causes a permanent split between husband and wife.
RoC *Anthony Hankey, Peggy Simpson, Mickey Brantford, Lucy Beaumont, (C.) Denier Warren, Effie Atherton, Molly Hamley-Clifford, Alfred Rode and His Tzigane Orchestra, Billy Watts*.

TEN DAYS IN PARIS (1939)   4
(USA: *Missing Ten Days*)
Dir *Tim Whelan*. Prod and PC *Irving Asher*. Scr *John Meehan Jr, James Curtis, from a novel by Bruce Graeme*. Ph *Otto Kanturek*. Dis *Columbia*. 82 mins. Cert A
Shot and wounded in Paris, Robert (*Rex Harrison*) wakes up to be told he has been injured in a plane crash. Ten days have elapsed between the two, days in which he has not only been chauffeur to a pretty French girl, Diane (*Kaaren Verne*), but involved with spies bent on wrecking secret fortifications of which plans are held by Diane's father. Escaping them, Robert and Diane dash to defuse the time bomb the gang has placed on a munitions train bound for the fortified area. Intricate adventure has pace and wit.
RoC *C.V. France, Leo Genn, Joan Marion, Antony Holles, John Abbott, Robert Rendel, Mavis Claire, André Morell, Hay Petrie, Frank Atkinson, Mai Bacon, Donald McLeod, Percy Walsh*.

Rex Harrison and Kaaren Verne in Ten Days in Paris (*1939*)

TEN-MINUTE ALIBI (1935)   4
Dir *Bernard Vorhaus*. Prod *Paul Soskin*. Scr *Michael Hankinson, Vera Allinson, from the play by Anthony Armstrong*. PC and Dis *British Lion*. 76 mins. Cert A
Ingenious murder mystery, a rare 1930s' example of the killer getting away with it. Playboy Philip Sevilla (*Theo Shall*) fascinates Betty (*Aileen Marson*), fiancée of Colin (*Phillips Holmes*) and persuades her to elope to Paris. Colin discovers Sevilla makes a practice of taking girls abroad, then robbing and deserting them. By manipulation of a clock, Colin makes it appear he was in his flat at the time he was actually killing Sevilla.
RoC *Morton Selten, George Merritt, Charles Hickman, Philip Hatfield, Dora Gregory, Grace Poggi*.

THE TENTH MAN (1936)   3
Dir *Brian Desmond Hurst*. Prod *Walter C. Mycroft*. Scr *Geoffrey Kerr, Dudley Leslie, Marjorie Deans, Jack Davies, from the play by W. Somerset Maugham*. Ph *Ronald Neame*. PC *BIP*. Dis *Wardour*. 68 mins. Cert A
Stodgy drama about a self-made man (*John Lodge*), now an MP, who forces his estranged wife (*Antoinette Cellier*) to stay with him through an election by involving her father in a shady financial gamble. His plottings are found out by a '10th man' (the MP's motto is '9 out of 10 men are knaves or fools') and he is ruined and almost commits suicide.
RoC *Aileen Marson, Clifford Evans, George Graves, Frank Cochrane, Athole Stewart, Iris Hoey, Bruce Lister, Barry Sinclair, Antony Holles, Hindle Edgar, Edith Sharpe, John Harwood, Aubrey Mallalieu, Kathleen Harrison, Mavis Clair*.

THE TERROR (1938)   4
Dir *Richard Bird*. Prod *Walter C. Mycroft*. Scr *William Freshman, from the play by Edgar Wallace*. Ph *Walter Harvey*. PC and Dis *Associated British*. 73 mins. Cert A
Connor and Marks (*Henry Oscar, Alastair Sim*) try to double-cross their boss, The Terror, over a gold robbery, but end in jail for their pains. Ten years later, they plan revenge and trail The Terror to 'haunted' Monks Hall Priory, where an organ is heard at night, a monk walks, maniacal laughter is heard and Connor is found dead. In an underground chapel, the police finally trap The Terror – who proves to be Goodman (*Wilfred Lawson*), a guest – and with him the gold. Very little subtlety but plenty of suspense.
RoC *Linden Travers, Arthur Wontner, Bernard Lee, Iris Hoey, Lesley Wareing, Edward Lexy, Richard Murdoch, John Turnbull, John H. Vyvyan, Jack Lambert, Stanley Lathbury*.

TERROR ON TIPTOE (1936)   2
Dir *Louis Renoir*. Prod *Reginald Fogwell, Nell Emerald*. Scr *Fenn Sherie, Ingram d'Abbes, from their play* Shadow Man. Ph *Geoffrey Faithfull*. PC *MB Productions*. Dis *New Realm*. 58 mins. Cert A
Poppy (silent star *Mabel Poulton* in one of her few sound appearances), the double of a Hollywood film star, finds herself the target for an assassin's bullet. An American detective (*Bernard Nedell*) just thwarts the killer's plans in the nick of time.
RoC *Jasper Maskelyne, Stella Bonheur, Joe Hayman, Victor Fairley*.

THANK EVANS (1938)   4
Dir *Roy William Neill*. Prod *Irving Asher*. Scr *Austin Melford, John Dighton, John Meehan Jr*. Ph *Basil Emmott*. PC *Warner Bros*. Dis *First National*. 78 mins. Cert U
Max Miller returns to his most successful film comedy character – Educated Evans, a racing tipster who, in this story, is so unpopular with his punters when he hits a long losing streak that he is forced to take refuge with a friendly barmaid at a country inn. Returning the favour, he gets involved with a crooked trainer whom he finally bests by persuading the

trainer's owner to let someone else ride his horse in the big race. It wins. Cheery farce.
RoC *Polly Ward, Hal Walters, Albert Whelan, John Carol, Robert Rendel, Glen Alyn, Freddie Watts, Harvey Braban, Aubrey Mallalieu, Charlotte Leigh, Ian Maclean, George Pughe, Charles Wade.*

Hal Walters and Max Miller in Thank Evans *(1938)*

THARK (1932) [5]
Dir *Tom Walls.* Prod *Herbert Wilcox.* Scr *Ben Travers, from his play.* Ph *F.A. Young.* PC *British and Dominions.* Dis *W and F. 80 mins. Cert A*
One of the Aldwych gang's funniest farces, a ghost comedy in which Mrs Todd (*Mary Brough*), the new owner of Thark Manor, is disturbed by eerie sounds at night. The three people responsible for selling her the house (*Tom Walls, Ralph Lynn, Evelyn Bostock*) agree to spend a night in the supposedly haunted bedroom.
RoC *Robertson Hare, Claude Hulbert, Joan Brierley, Gordon James, Beryl de Querton, Marjorie Corbett.*

THAT NIGHT IN LONDON (1932) [4]
(USA: *Overnight*)
Dir *Rowland V. Lee.* Prod *Alexander Korda.* Scr *Dorothy Greenhill, Arthur Wimperis.* Ph *Robert Martin.* PC *London Films.* Dis *Paramount. 78 mins. Cert A*
A country bank clerk (*Robert Donat*), bored with his dead-end job, decides to see London life, and absconds with £500 of the bank's funds. A crook is soon after the money, and has a dancer pose as his sister to entice the clerk into his clutches. But the dancer falls for the clerk and saves not only the money but his job as well. Effective lightweight drama.
RoC *Pearl Argyle, Miles Mander, Lawrence Hanray, Roy Emerton, Graham Soutten, James Knight, Eugene Leahy, James Bucton, The Max Rivers Girls.*

THAT'S A GOOD GIRL (1933) [4]
Dir *Jack Buchanan.* Prod *Herbert Wilcox.* Scr *Douglas Furber, Buchanan, Donovan Pedelty.* Ph *F.A. Young.* PC *British and Dominions.* Dis *United Artists. 83 mins. Cert U*
Polished musical set in the south of France (locations at Antibes, Cap Ferrat and the Alpes Maritimes) with *Jack Buchanan* as an heir who must convince his aunt he can handle the legacy due to him before he can inherit. Trying to sort out the romantic complications of cousins and friends, he nearly loses everything, but ends up with the lady detective (*Elsie Randolph*) who loves him.
RoC *Garry Marsh, Dorothy Hyson, William Kendall, Vera Pearce, Kate Cutler, Frank Stanmore, Antony Holles.*

THAT'S MY UNCLE (1935) [1]
Dir *George Pearson.* Prod *Julius Hagen.* Scr *Michael Barringer, from a play by Frederick Jackson.* PC *Twickenham.* Dis *Universal. 58 mins. Cert U*
Thin comedy about a morals reformer (*Mark Daly*), much henpecked by his wife. He becomes involved with a gang of crooks who have planted a wallet on him to evade arrest and experience great difficulty getting it back, especially when his subsequent misadventures involve him posing as a butler.
RoC *Margaret Yarde, Betty Astell, Richard Cooper, Michael Shepley, Wally Patch, David Horne, Hope Davy, Ralph Truman, Colin Lesslie, Gladys Hamer.*

THAT'S MY WIFE (1933) [3]
Dir *Leslie Hiscott.* Prod *Herbert Smith.* Scr *Michael Barringer.* PC and Dis *British Lion. 67 mins. Cert A*
Wealthy Yorkshire manufacturer Josiah Crump (*Frank Pettingell*) courts scandal when he flirts with the wife of a gouty major while spending a couple of days at a health resort. Josiah's nephew Archie (*Claud Allister*), whom he believes to be a lawyer (he actually runs a beauty parlour), keeps his uncle's nose clean – and benefits from the rich man's new invention. Hectic comedy.
RoC *Betty Astell, Davy Burnaby, Helga Moray, Hal Walters, Thomas Weguelin, Jack Vyvyan, John Morley.*

THEIR NIGHT OUT (1933) [2]
Dir, Prod and Scr *Harry Hughes, from a play by George Arthurs, Arthur Miller.* Ph *Walter Harvey.* PC *BIP.* Dis *Wardour. 73 mins. Cert U*
Good comedy cast, but a rather disappointing film in which junior partner Jimmy (*Claude Hulbert*) has to act as host to Maggie (*Renée Houston*), a lady buyer from Scotland. He takes her to a nightclub, but they both get drunk, Jimmy has his wallet stolen, is mistaken for a jewel thief, and becomes involved with a gang of crooks.
RoC *Gus McNaughton, Binnie Barnes, Ben Welden, Judy Kelly, Jimmy Godden, Amy Veness, Hal Gordon, Marie Ault.*

THERE AIN'T NO JUSTICE! (1939) [4]
Dir *Penrose Tennyson.* (Associate) Prod *Sergei Nolbandov.* Scr *Tennyson, Nolbandov, James Curtis, from Curtis' novel.* Ph *Mutz Greenbaum.* PC *Ealing Studios/CAPAD.* Dis *Associated British. 83 mins. Cert A*
Anxious to make money to impress a new girl, Tommy (*Jimmy Hanley*), a mechanic, becomes a professional boxer. He signs up with a shady manager (*Edward Chapman*) who, unknown to him, fixes fights. Tommy seems cornered when his sister needs money following her boyfriend's embezzlement. But Tommy manages

Jill Furse and Jimmy Hanley in There Ain't No Justice! *(1939)*

to win the big fight he's supposed to lose, get the money and retain his integrity. A vital-seeming slice of low life.
RoC *Edward Rigby, Mary Clare, Jill Furse, Nan Hopkins, Phyllis Stanley, Michael Wilding, Richard Ainley, Gus McNaughton, Richard Norris, Mike Johnson, Michael Hogarth, Sue Gawthorne, Patsy Hagate, Alfred Millen, Bombardier Billy Wells.*

THERE GOES SUSIE (1934) [3]
(USA: *Scandals of Paris*)
Dir, Prod and Scr *John Stafford, W. Victor Hanbury, from a novel by Charlotte Roellinghoff, Hans Jacoby.* PC *Stafford/BIP.* Dis *Pathé. 79 mins. Cert A*
The story counts for little in this musical-comedy (music: *Otto Stransky, Niklos Schwalb*) about a penniless artist (*Gene Gerrard*) and a soap king's daughter (*Wendy Barrie*) who poses for him after he has mistaken her for a model. The painting is sold as an advertisement for her father's bitterest rival.
RoC *Zelma O'Neal, Gus McNaughton, Henry Wenman, Bobbie Comber, Gibb McLaughlin, Mark Daly.*

THERE GOES THE BRIDE (1932) [4]
Dir *Albert de Courville.* Prod *Michael Balcon.* Scr *W.P. Lipscomb, Fred Raymond.* Ph *Alex Bryce.* PC *Gainsborough/British Lion.* Dis *Ideal. 79 mins. Cert U*
On the morning of an unwonted marriage, reluctant bride Annette (*Jessie Matthews*) runs away to Paris. On the train she is robbed of her purse, and meets wealthy Max (*Owen Nares*) who allows her to stay with him for 24 hours. Detectives trace the runaway and take her home, but she is followed by Max, with whom she elopes after eluding her captors. Engaging comedy.
RoC *Carol Goodner, Jerry Verno, Basil Radford, Barbara Everest, Charles Carson, Winifred Oughton, Jack Morrison, Roland Culver, Max Kirby, Gordon McLeod, Lawrence Hanray, George Zucco, Mignon O'Doherty.*

THERE WAS A YOUNG MAN (1937) [1]
Dir and Prod *Albert Parker.* Scr *David Evans.* Ph *Stanley Grant.* PC and Dis *Fox British. 63 mins. Cert U*

Very basic comedy about George Peabody (*Oliver Wakefield*), a shy, stammering, small-town investor who gets involved not only with a crooked land development scheme, but also with a gang of Orientals who are out to retrieve an ancient relic they hold sacred.

RoC *Nancy O'Neil, Clifford Heatherley, Robert Nainby, Molly Hamley Clifford, Eric Hales, Brian Buchel, John Laurie, Syd Crossley, Patric Curwen, Peter Popp, Bouncer (dog).*

THESE CHARMING PEOPLE (1931)   [4]

Dir *Louis Mercanton.* Prod *Walter Morosco.* Scr *Hugh Perceval, Irving Howard, from a play by Michael Arlen.* PC and Dis *Paramount British.* 82 mins. Cert A

A rich shipbuilder neglects his wife on account of business, and she falls in love with his secretary. Her father (*Cyril Maude*), an MP who owes his position to his son-in-law's wealth, does his best to snuff out the romance, but the adulterous couple elope to Paris before the wife finally changes her mind and returns to her husband. Well-written melodrama.

RoC *Nora Swinburne, Godfrey Tearle, Anthony Ireland, Ann Todd, Cyril Raymond, C.V. France, Billy Shine, Vincent Holman, Minnie Rayner.*

THEY DIDN'T KNOW (1936)   [1]

Dir and Prod *Herbert Smith.* Scr *Brock Williams.* Ph *Geoffrey Faithfull.* PC *British Lion.* Dis *M-G-M.* 67 mins. Cert A

An engaged couple about to be married are both, unknown to each other, menaced with blackmail over a past indiscretion each has concealed from the other. The would-be blackmailers themselves turn out to be estranged husband and wife, and all ends well. Paceless comedy.

LP *Eve Gray, Leslie Perrins, Hope Davy, Kenneth Villiers, John Deverell, Diana Beaumont, (C.) Denier Warren, Patrick Ludlow, Maidie Hope, Fred Withers, A. Scott-Gaddy, Hal Walters.*

THEY DRIVE BY NIGHT (1938)   [6]

Dir *Arthur Woods.* Prod *Jerome Jackson.* Scr *Derek Twist, from the novel by James Curtis.* Ph *Basil Emmott.* PC *Warner Bros.* Dis *First National.* 84 mins. Cert A

Shorty (*Emlyn Williams*), fresh out of prison, finds an old flame, Alice - strangled. On the run, he gets a lift from Wally (*Allan Jeayes*), a lorry driver and they save Molly (*Anna Konstam*) from being raped by another driver. Together, they investigate the people who knew Alice. The trail leads to Hoover (*Ernest Thesiger*), who invites Molly and Shorty to his flat, locks Shorty up and tries to strangle Molly. Shorty breaks out just in time to capture him and clear his name. Splendid, atmospheric black thriller: the sleeper of its year.

RoC *Antony Holles, Ronald Shiner, Yolande Terrell, Julie Barrie, Kitty de Legh, George Merritt, Billy (William) Hartnell, Jennie Hartley, Joe Cunningham.*

THINGS ARE LOOKING UP (1934)   [4]

Dir *Albert de Courville.* Prod *Michael Balcon.*

Scr *Stafford Dickens, Con West.* Ph *Glen MacWilliams.* PC and Dis *Gaumont-British.* 78 mins. Cert U

Comedy totally dominated by *Cicely Courtneidge* as a circus equestrienne who, when her twin sister elopes with a wrestler, takes her place as a teacher in a girls' school. Her methods are, to say the least, unorthodox, but, aided by the music master (*William Gargan*) she is such a success that, by the time her sister returns, she has become headmistress. Courtneidge's escapades include a hilarious tennis match with sports star *Suzanne Lenglen.*

RoC *Max Miller, Mary Lawson, Judy Kelly, Dick Henderson, Dick Henderson Jr, Mark Lester, Henrietta Watson, Alma Taylor, Cicely Oates, Danny Green, Wyn Weaver, D. Hay Plumb, Charles Mortimer, Vivien Leigh.*

THINGS TO COME (1936)   [4]

Dir *William Cameron Menzies.* Prod *Alexander Korda.* Scr *H.G. Wells, from his novel.* Ph *Georges Périnal.* Special effects *Ned Mann, Lawrence Butler, Edward Cohen, Wally Veavers, Harry Zech, Ross Jacklin.* PC *London Films.* Dis *United Artists.* 100 mins. Cert U

This costly (£300,000) science-fiction epic divided both critics and public. It begins in 1940, when a 30-year-war and black plague ruins 'Everytown'. In 1970, a brotherhood of scientists gain control over tribal communities and rebuild Everytown into a scientific city of the future. In 2036, a massed revolt fails to stop the first couple being sent to the moon.

LP *Raymond Massey, Ralph Richardson, Edward Chapman, Margaretta Scott, Sir Cedric Hardwicke, Maurice Braddell, Sophie Stewart, Derrick de Marney, Ann Todd, Pearl Argyle, Kenneth Villiers, Ivan Brandt, John Clements, Abraham Sofaer, Patrick Barr, Anne McLaren, Patricia Hilliard, Charles Carson, Antony Holles, Allan Jeayes, Paul O'Brien.*

Raymond Massey in Things to Come *(1936)*

THE THIRD CLUE (1934)   [1]

Dir *Albert Parker.* Prod *Ernest Garside.* Scr *Michael Barringer, Lance Sieveking, Frank Atkinson, from a novel by Neil Gordon.* Ph *Alex Bryce.* PC and Dis *Fox British.* 73 mins. Cert A

Over-complicated thriller about rival crooks assuming other identities to hunt for stolen

jewels, which turn out to be hidden in a sinister old house.

LP *Basil Sydney, Molly Lamont, Raymond Lovell, Frank Atkinson, Robert Cochran, Alfred Sangster, C. M. Hallard, Ernest Sefton, Ian Fleming, Quinton McPherson, Eric Fawcett, Bruce Lister, Mabel Terry-Lewis, Adela Mavis, Noel Dainton, Rani Waller.*

THE THIRD STRING (1932)   [2]

Dir *George Pearson.* Prod *Pearson, T. A. Welsh.* Scr *Pearson, James Reardon, A. R. Rawlinson.* PC *Welsh-Pearson.* Dis *Gaumont.* 65 mins. Cert U

Fairly basic comedy starring *Sandy Powell*, a music-hall comic, as a sailor on leave who falls for a barmaid, Julie (*Kay Hammond*), is forced to pose as a champion Australian boxer to impress her, then finds himself fighting her ex-boxer ex-boyfriend (*Alf Goddard*). The two men fix the fight for Sandy to win, only for Julie to go off with her boss.

RoC *Mark Daly, Charles Paton, Sydney Fairbrother, Pollie Emery, James Knight.*

THIRD TIME LUCKY (1931)   [4]

Dir *Walter Forde.* Prod *Michael Balcon.* Scr *Angus Macphail, from the play by Arnold Ridley.* Ph *William Shenton.* PC *Gainsborough.* Dis *W and F.* 85 mins. Cert A

Successful film version (Sidney Gilliat wrote additional dialogue) of Arnold Ridley's comedy-thriller about a timid cleric (*Bobby Howes*) who sets out to recover some letters which his ward Jennifer (*Dorothy Boyd*), newly engaged, had written to a suave rogue (*Garry Marsh*) who is now blackmailing her. Despite misadventures, the cleric manages to steal the letters back.

RoC *Gordon Harker, Henry Mollison, Gibb McLaughlin, Clare Greet, Margaret Yarde, Viola Compton, Marie Ault, Alexander Field, Harry Terry, Peter Godfrey, Matthew Boulton, Gunner Moir, Henry Latimer, Willie Graham.*

13 MEN AND A GUN (1938)   [4]

Dir and Prod *Mario Zampi.* Scr *Basil Dillon, Kathleen Connors.* Ph *Albertelli.* PC *Two Cities/Pisorno.* Dis *British Independent.* 64 mins. Cert U

First World War: On the Russo-Austrian front, a huge hidden gun is effectively holding up the Russian advance. The secret of its location is so closely guarded that only its 13-man crew can be suspect when the secret leaks out and the gun is destroyed. An Austrian commander orders the whole battery to be shot. But before this can be done, they unmask the traitor themselves. Unsusual, gripping drama. Made in Italy in English and Italian versions.

LP *Arthur Wontner, Clifford Evans, Howard Marion-Crawford, Allan Jeayes, Gibb McLaughlin, Wally Patch, Scott Harold, Donald Gray, Bernard Miles, André Morell, John Kevan, Kenneth Warrington, Frank Henderson, Herbert Cameron, Oscar Paterson, Roy Russell, R. Van Boolen, Joe Cunningham, Noel Dainton.*

THE THIRTEENTH CANDLE
(1933)   2

Dir *John Daumery*. Prod *Irving Asher*. Scr *Brock Williams*. PC and Dis *Warner Bros*. 68 mins. Cert A

Unlikeable Sir Charles Meeton is murdered while he has several guests in the house – but the police have reason to suspect that Lady Meeton (*Isobel Elsom*) is the killer. Captain Blyth (*Gibb McLaughlin*), an old admirer of Lady Meeton, solves the case by establishing that the thirteenth candle in a chandelier is wired to an apparatus in which a dagger was fixed, and that the chauffeur is the killer.

RoC *Joyce Kirby, Louis Hayward, D. A. Clarke-Smith, Louis Goodrich, Arthur Maude, Claude Fleming, Ernest Childerstone, Eric Hales, Hilliard Vox, Winifred Oughton*.

THE 39 STEPS (1935)   6

Dir *Alfred Hitchcock*. Prod *Michael Balcon*. Scr *Charles Bennett, Alma Reville, Ian Hay, from the novel by John Buchan*. Ph *Bernard Knowles*. PC and Dis *Gaumont-British*. 86 mins. (*USA: 81 mins*). Cert A

Excitement and suspense are skilfully maintained by Hitchcock in this atmospherically shot version of Buchan's novel. Hannay (*Robert Donat*) encounters a woman who tells him about a ring of spies and is then murdered. Handcuffed to a girl (*Madeleine Carroll*) he meets while fleeing both police and spies, Hannay eventually exposes the spy ring and clears himself, in the music hall where it all began. A pattern of telling scenes makes a memorable film.

RoC *Godfrey Tearle, Lucie Mannheim, Peggy Ashcroft, John Laurie, Helen Haye, Wylie Watson, Frank Cellier, Jerry Verno, Gus McNaughton, Hilda Trevelyan, Peggy Simpson, Frederick Piper*.

Alfred Hitchcock (right) directing Madeleine Carroll and Robert Donat in The 39 Steps *(1935)*

THIS ACTING BUSINESS (1933)   2

Dir *John Daumery*. Prod *Irving Asher*. Scr *Uncredited*. PC and Dis *Warner Bros*. 54 mins. Cert U

Actors Hugh and Joyce (*Hugh Williams, Wendy Barrie*) marry despite parental opposition from both sides. Continuing interference from his mother and her father creates quarrels between the young couple, which flare up when they co-star in a play. But they reconcile when Hugh learns Joyce is pregnant. Said one critic: 'It occasionally borders on the farcical.'

RoC *Donald Calthrop, Violet Farebrother, Marie Wright, Charles Paton, Janice Adair, Henry B. Longhurst*.

THIS GREEN HELL (1936)   4

Dir, Prod, Scr and PC *Randall Faye*. Dis *Radio*. 71 mins. Cert A

Enjoyable minor comedy with *Edward Rigby* as a humble clerk who, as a result of being injured in a train crash, believes he really *is* the famous, fire-breathing explorer of the bedtime stories he tells his son. As a result he becomes a highly paid author – even after he regains his memory.

RoC *Sybil Grove, Johnny Singer, Richard Dolman, Roxie Russell, Billy Watts, Norman Pierce, Quinton McPherson*.

THIS IS THE LIFE (1933)   4

Dir *Albert de Courville*. Prod *Herbert Smith*. Scr *Clifford Grey, R. P. Weston, Bert Lee*. PC and Dis *British Lion*. 78 mins. Cert U

Albert and Sarah (*Gordon Harker, Binnie Hale*), who run a country teashop, inherit a fortune and not only crash London society but also put paid to the activities of a group of Chicago gangsters (inevitably led by *Ben Welden* as Two Gun Mullins). But they lose their money (crookedly acquired by the uncle who left it to them) and return to their teashop, only to find that their niece and her fiancé have turned it into a fashionable roadhouse. Quite a funny comedy with the stars making a likeable team.

RoC *Betty Astell, Ray Milland, Jack Barty, Charles Heslop, Percy Parsons, Norma Whalley, Julian Royce, Percival Mackey and His Band*.

THIS'LL MAKE YOU WHISTLE
(1936)   4

Dir and Prod *Herbert Wilcox*. Scr *Guy Bolton, Paul Thompson, from their play*. Ph *F. A. Young*. PC *Wilcox/BIP*. Dis *General Film Distributors*. 79 mins. Cert A

Generally sunny mixture of songs, dancing and humour, with *Jack Buchanan* as a man engaged to two girls at once. He throws a wild party to try to offend the relatives of the girl he doesn't want to marry (they enjoy it), then poses as a forger in the south of France. This finally does the trick, and the hero ends up with the girl of his choice.

RoC *Elsie Randolph, Jean Gillie, William Kendall, David Hutcheson, Antony Holles, Marjorie Brooks, Maidie Hope, Miki Hood, Bunty Pain, Scott Harold, Irene Vere*.

THIS MAN IN PARIS (1939)   5

Dir *David Macdonald*. Prod *Anthony Havelock-Allan*. Scr *Allan Mackinnon, Roger Macdougall*. Ph *Henry Harris*. PC *Pinebrook*. Dis *Paramount*. 89 mins (later 86). Cert A

Highly successful follow-up to *This Man Is News*, with the same director and principals. Reporter Drake (*Barry K. Barnes*) is sent to Paris, where an English nobleman has been arrested in possession of fake money. Drake and his wife Pat (*Valerie Hobson*) battle to crack a code that seems the key to the mystery, are arrested by the Sûreté and kidnapped by crooks, before a showdown reveals the chief crook as a general (*Anthony Shaw*) who is killed in a gun battle with police. Action and wisecracks abound.

RoC *Alastair Sim, Edward Lexy, Garry Marsh, Jacques Max Michel, Mona Goya, Cyril Chamberlain, Charles Oliver, Paul Sheridan, Billy Watts*.

THIS MAN IS NEWS (1938)   4

Dir *David Macdonald*. Prod *Anthony Havelock-Allan*. Scr *Allan Mackinnon, Roger Macdougall, Basil Dearden*. Ph *Francis Carver*. PC *Pinebrook*. Dis *Paramount*. 78 mins. Cert A

Reporter Simon Drake (*Barry K. Barnes*) plays a joke on his editor, Mac (*Alastair Sim*), by telling him he has just seen a 'grass' murdered. Mac prints the story – which comes true. Drake is arrested, released, then finds his life constantly threatened. Each time he escapes and makes front page news. Finally the crooks concerned are caught and Drake and his wife (*Valerie Hobson*) get the glory. Successful mixture of Thin Man and Paul Temple sleuthing is good fast fun.

RoC *John Warwick, Garry Marsh, Edward Lexy, Kenneth Buckley, Philip Leaver, James Pirrie, David Keir, Tom Gill, Jack Vyvyan, Billy Watts*.

Garry Marsh, Barry K. Barnes, Edward Lexy in This Man is News *(1938)*

THISTLEDOWN (1938)   2

Dir *Arthur Woods*. Prod *Irving Asher*. Scr *Brock Williams*. Ph *Basil Emmott*. PC and Dis *Warner Bros*. 79 mins. Cert U

Opera star Therese (*Aino Bergo*) marries Scottish laird Sir Ian (*Keith Falkner*) but finds it difficult to settle to her lonely life on his estate. When Sir Ian accuses her of having an affair with a neighbouring landowner (she isn't), Therese leaves him and resumes her career. Years later, she buys the estate from the now-impoverished Sir Ian, with whom she is reunited. Scottish musical is attractive or arch, according to taste.

RoC *Athole Stewart, Sharon Lynne, Bruce Lister, Ian Maclean, Amy Veness, Vera Bogetti, Gordon McLeod, Jack Lambert, Herbert Leslie, Richard Lownes*.

THIS WEEK OF GRACE (1933)   4

Dir *Maurice Elvey*. Prod *Julius Hagen*. Scr *H. Fowler Mear, Jack Marks*. Ph *Sydney Blythe*. PC *Real Art*. Dis *Radio*. 92 mins. Cert U

Easily Real Art's most ambitious production to this date, this *Gracie Fields* comedy has her as an unemployed factory girl suddenly given charge of the estates of the eccentric Duchess of Swinford (*Nina Boucicault*) who realizes they have been mismanaged. Grace and her family soon shake things up with plenty of working-class common sense, and Grace marries the Duchess' stepsister's son (*Henry Kendall*). Skilfully contrived stuff.
RoC *John Stuart, Frank Pettingell, Helen Haye, Minnie Rayner, Douglas Wakefield, Marjorie Brooks, Vivian Foster, Lawrence Hanray.*

THOROUGHBRED (1931)   [2]
Dir *Charles Barnett*. Prod and Scr *John F. Argyle*. PC and Dis *Equity British*. 64 mins. Cert U
Racehorse trainer Smithy (*James Benton*) is a man without a past: he suffers from amnesia. It looks as though the girl he loves (*Margaret Delane*) will be forced to marry her guardian's son until a racing accident restores Smithy's memory, and he is revealed to be a man of considerable means. Filmed silent: sound added.
RoC *John F. Argyle, Jack Marriott, Thomas Moss.*

THOSE WERE THE DAYS
(1934)   [5]
Dir *Thomas Bentley*. Prod *Walter C. Mycroft*. Scr *Fred Thompson, Frank Launder, Frank Miller*. PC *BIP*. Dis *Wardour*. 80 mins. Cert U
Lively adaptation of Pinero's stage farce, which provided *Will Hay* with his feature film debut. He plays a stern magistrate, whose wife (*Iris Hoey*) has lied about her age, and dresses the 20-year-old son (*John Mills*) of her first marriage to look years younger. All the parties go to a music-hall, where a riot breaks out. The magistrate and his stepson get away, but his wife and her sister are held, and the following morning he has sentenced them before realizing who they are.
RoC *Angela Baddeley, Marguerite Allan, Jane Carr, Claud Allister, H.F. Maltby, George Graves, Lawrence Hanray, Syd Crossley, Jimmy Godden, Walter (Wally) Patch, Jimmy Hanley, Ian Wilson, Charles Hayes, Lily Morris, Harry Bedford, Gaston and Andree, G.H. Elliott, Sam Curtis, Frank Boston and Betty.*

THREADS (1931)   [1]
Dir and Scr *G.B. Samuelson, from the play by Frank Stayton*. Prod *Gordon Craig*. PC *Samuelson*. Dis *United Artists*. 76 mins. Cert A
Wynn (*Lawrence Anderson*) returns after serving 17 years for a murder he didn't commit. Finding that his son is engaged to the daughter of the judge who sentenced him, Wynn forbids the marriage, but his wife helps the lovers elope. Wynn's daughter (*Wendy Barrie*) takes the situation in hand, and brings about her parents' reconciliation. Dated morality play.
RoC *Dorothy Fane, Gerald Rawlinson, Ben Webster, Irene Rooke, Walter Piers, Leslie Cole, Aileen Despard, Pat Reid, Clifford Cobb.*

THE THREE MAXIMS (1936)   [2]
(USA: *The Show Goes On*)
Dir and Prod *Herbert Wilcox*. Scr *Herman Mankiewicz*. Ph *F.A. Young, Jack Cox*. PC *Cie Pathé Consortium*. Dis *General Film Distributors*. 87 mins. Cert U
Fragile, poorly-cast forerunner of *Trapeze*. The Three Maxims are aerialists whose daring trapeze act is the outstanding attraction of a French travelling circus. Rivalry between Mac (*Leslie Banks*) and Toni (*Tullio Carminati*) for Pat (*Anna Neagle*) culminates in Mac trying to murder Toni high above the ground. Pat faints in mid-air and there is a hair-raising rescue.
RoC *Horace Hodges, Arthur Finn, Olive Blakeney, Anthony Ireland, Miki Hood, Nicolas Koline, Gaston Palmer, Leonard Snelling, Winifred Oughton, Beatrix Fielden-Kaye, Lawrence Hanray, Tarva Penna, Vincent Holman, Henry Caine, 12 Hippodrome Girls.*

THREE MEN IN A BOAT (1933)   [3]
Dir *Graham Cutts*. Prod *Basil Dean*. Scr *Reginald Purdell, D.B. Wyndham-Lewis, from the book by Jerome K. Jerome*. Ph *Robert Martin*. PC *Associated Talking Pictures*. Dis *ABFD*. 60 mins. Cert U
Second of three adaptations of *Jerome K. Jerome*'s laughter-filled story of three friends boating down the Thames, which always seemed funnier in print or on radio than it did on screen. A romantic interest (maintained in the third film) and some music were added for this version.
LP *William Austin, Edmond Breon, Billy Milton, Iris March, Davy Burnaby, Griffith Humphreys, Stephen Ewart, Victor Stanley, Frank Bertram, Sam Wilkinson, Winifred Evans.*

THREE WITNESSES (1935)   [1]
Dir *Leslie Hiscott*. Prod *Julius Hagen*. Scr *Michael Barringer, from the novel by S. Fowler Wright*. PC *Twickenham*. Dis *Universal*. 68 mins. Cert A
Pedestrian thriller about a murder solved by solicitor Leslie Trent (*Henry Kendall*) who discovers the killer of his fiancée's brother to have been his own partner (*Garry Marsh*).
RoC *Eve Gray, Sebastian Shaw, Richard Cooper, Geraldine Fitzgerald, Noel Dryden, Ralph Truman, Gladys Hamer, Gerald Hamer, Henry Woolston.*

THUNDER IN THE CITY (1936)   [3]
Dir *Marion Gering*. Prod *Alexander Esway, Akos Tolnay*. Scr *Tolnay, Aben Kandel, Walter Hackett, from a story by Robert E. Sherwood*. Ph *Arthur Gilks*. PC *Atlantic*. Dis *United Artists*. 88 mins. Cert A
Dan Armstrong (*Edward G. Robinson*), an American publicity man, comes to Britain to 'learn the importance of dignity'. But when he falls in love with the daughter (*Luli Deste*) of the nobleman who's his distant relative, Dan uses his own methods to float the 'magnelite' mines that the duke (*Nigel Bruce*) owns. Comedy is typical not-quite-good-enough British vehicle for visiting Hollywood star.
RoC *Constance Collier, Arthur Wontner, Ralph Richardson, Nancy Burne, Annie Esmond, Eli-*

zabeth Inglis, Cyril Raymond, James Carew, Everley Gregg, Billy Bray.

TICKET OF LEAVE (1935)   [2]
Dir *Michael Hankinson*. Prod *Anthony Havelock-Allan*. Scr *Margaret McDonnell*. Ph *Francis Carver*. PC and Dis *British and Dominions/Paramount British*. 69 mins. Cert A
Rather feeble light drama about two thieves, Lucky (*John Clements*) and Lillian (*Dorothy Boyd*), who reluctantly work together after the former has tried to burgle the latter's flat, and attempt to steal a valuable necklace. When they fall in love, they decide to go straight, but find it more difficult to return the necklace than it was to steal it.
RoC *George Merritt, Max Kirby, Wally Patch, Enid Lindsay, Neil More, Molly Hamley-Clifford.*

THE TICKET OF LEAVE MAN (1937)   [1]
Dir, Prod and PC *George King*. Scr *H.F. Maltby, A.R. Rawlinson, from the play by Tom Taylor*. Dis *M-G-M*. 71 mins. Cert A
Remake of a 1918 silent, which should have been left well alone. Villainous Tiger Dalton (*Tod Slaughter*) runs a benevolent society for ex-convicts with the idea of dragging them further into a life of crime. One such man, who has got a job in a bank, is blackmailed by Tiger into robbing the safes, but his girlfriend gets a message to the police. The 'squealer' is shot dead by Tiger who is chased by police into a cemetery, falls into an open grave and breaks his neck.
RoC *John Warwick, Marjorie Taylor, Robert Adair, Peter Gawthorne, Frank Cochran, Jenny Lynn, Arthur Payne, Norman Pierce.*

TIGER BAY (1933)   [2]
Dir *J. Elder Wills*. Prod *Bray Wyndham*. Scr *John Quin*. Ph *Robert Martin*. PC *Wyndham*. Dis *Associated British*. 70 mins. Cert A
A few hearty thrills in this rather strained wharfside melodrama, with *Anna May Wong* as Lui Chang, a Chinese girl who runs a restaurant in Wales' Tiger Bay and has an English ward, Letty (*René Ray*) who is kidnapped by a Swedish gang leader (*Henry Victor*). Lui Chang kills him and commits suicide.
RoC *Lawrence Grossmith, Victor Garland, Ben Soutten, Margaret Yarde, Wally Patch, Ernest Jay, Brian Buchel.*

A TIGHT CORNER (1932)   [3]
Dir *Leslie Hiscott*. Prod *Julius Hagen*. Scr *Michael Barringer*. PC *Real Art*. Dis *M-G-M*. 49 mins. Cert A
Knockabout comedy in which two hapless enquiry agents receive a commission to gain possession of some incriminating letters held by a sinister beauty specialist. The boys pose as PT instructors and, more by luck than judgment, regain the letters from the blackmailing beauty.
LP *Harold French, Frank Pettingell, Gina Malo, Betty Astell, Madeleine Gibson, Charles Farrell, Arthur Stratton.*

TILLY OF BLOOMSBURY (1931)   [4]
Dir and Prod *Jack Raymond*. Scr *W.P. Lip-*

scomb, from the play by Ian Hay. PC and Dis *Sterling*. 69 mins. Cert U

Second of three screen versions of Ian Hay's popular play about the boarding-house keeper's daughter who falls in love with an aristocrat: his mother makes things particularly unpleasant for him. The girl tries to break off the relationship, but the boy takes the matter out of his mother's hands and wins her back. Pleasant romantic character comedy.

LP *Phyllis Konstam, Sydney Howard, Richard Bird, Ellis Jeffreys, Edward Chapman, Mabel Russell, Marie Wright, H.R. Hignett, Ena Grossmith, Sebastian Smith, Olwen Roose, Leila Page.*

TIMBUCTOO (1933)   ☐3

Dir *Walter Summers, Arthur Woods*. Prod and Scr *Summers*, from the anonymous book *Africa Dances*. Ph *James Wilson*. PC *BIP*. Dis *Wardour*. 72 mins. Cert U

Actual desert backgrounds (*Summers* made a documentary, *Across the Sahara*, at the same time) offer a small boost to this rather foolish comedy about ineffectual young Benedict (*Henry Kendall*) who quarrels with fiancée Elizabeth (*Margot Grahame*) and goes on an eventful safari to Timbuctoo with his valet (*Victor Stanley*). When he arrives, Elizabeth is waiting for him.

RoC *Jean Cadell, Rama Tahe, Emily Fitzroy, Una O'Connor, Hubert Harben, Edward Ashley Cooper.*

TIN GODS (1932)   ☐3

Dir and Prod *F.W. Kraemer*. Scr *Edgar G. Middleton*, from his play. PC *BIP*. Dis *Pathé*. 53 mins. Cert A

Melodrama set in the China Seas, where a ship is seized by Oriental pirates who hold the motley assortment of passengers to ransom, and eventually demand the death of a major (*Frank Cellier*). Everyone is saved at the last minute by the arrival of the Marines.

RoC *Dorothy Bartlam, Peter Evan Thomas, Ben Welden, Frank Royde, Alexander Field, Margaret Damer, Ruth Maitland, Athol Fleming.*

TO BE A LADY (1934)   ☐2

Dir and Prod *George King*. Scr *Violet Powell*, from a story by *C.H. Nicholson*. PC *British and Dominions/Paramount British*. Dis *Paramount*. 68 mins. Cert A

Indifferent romantic drama with *Dorothy Bouchier* as Diana, a country girl who becomes a London hairdresser, and falls in love with an entertainer, Jerry (*Bruce Lister*). Jerry is injured in a car crash, while at the same time Diana is arrested for innocently being in possession of a stolen dress. A man Diana almost marries (*Charles Cullum*) brings the young lovers together again.

RoC *Vera Bogetti, Ena Moon, Florence Vie, Tony de Lungo, Pat Ronald.*

TO BRIGHTON WITH GLADYS (1933)   ☐3

Dir and PC *George King*. Prod *Harry Cohen*. Scr *Eliot Stannard*. Dis *Fox*. 45 mins. Cert U

There can't be many films with penguins as central characters - although Bob Hope had a performing one in *My Favourite Blonde* and John Hurt thousands of 'em in *Mr Forbush and the Penguins* - but this comedy is probably the earliest, in which a nobleman (*Harry Milton*) is asked to take a penguin, Gladys, from London to Brighton. Gladys escapes, gets drunk, is mistaken for a baby and 'another woman' - and eventually arrives.

RoC *Constance Shotter, Kate Cutler, Sunday Wilshin, George Melville Cooper (Melville Cooper)* and Gladys.

TO CATCH A THIEF (1936)   ☐2

Dir *Maclean Rogers*. Prod *A. George Smith*. Scr *Kathleen Butler, H.F. Maltby*, from the play by *Margaret and Gordon MacDonnell*. Ph *Geoffrey Faithfull*. PC *GS Enterprises*. Dis *Radio*. 66 mins. Cert U

Little entertainment value in this comedy about an inventor (*John Garrick*) who fits his new 'stop thief' device to a friend's car to bring the invention to the notice of a car-factory owner. Instead it involves him with a gang of car thieves who use his friend's garage as a hideout. But he uses his invention to trap the crooks, and the factory owner is impressed enough to buy it.

RoC *Mary Lawson, H.F. Maltby, John Wood, Eliot Makeham, Vincent Holman, Max Adrian, Gordon McLeod, Bryan Powley, Ralph Teasdale, Billy Shine, Michael Ripper, Brian Herbert, Norman Pierce.*

TOILERS OF THE SEA (1936)   ☐2

Dir *Selwyn Jepson, Ted Fox*. Prod and PC *L.C. Beaumont*. Scr *Jepson*, from the novel by *Victor Hugo*. Ph *D.P. Cooper*. Dis *Columbia*. 83 mins. Cert U

Turgid adventure story, partly shot on location in the Channel Islands. Set in the early nineteenth century, it tells of the first steamship, skippered by Capt. Clubin (*Andrews Engelmann*) who abandons it for personal gain. But the ship is salvaged by Gilliatt (*Cyril McLaglen*), an adventurer.

RoC *Mary Lawson, Ian Colin, Walter Sondes, Wilson Coleman, William Dewhurst.*

TOMORROW WE LIVE (1936)   ☐2

Dir and Scr *Manning Haynes*. Prod *Clayton Hutton*. PC *Conquest Films*. Dis *Associated British*. 72 mins. Cert A

An air of unreality hangs over this drama of a financier, faced with ruin, who gives down-and-outs contemplating suicide £50 each at a dinner, to see if they feel like making something of their lives. Only one retains her intention of ending her life, but the financier (*Godfrey Tearle*) talks her round, and finds that the episode has helped him through his own crisis.

RoC *Haidee Wright, Renee Gadd, Sebastian Shaw, Eliot Makeham, Thea Holme, George Carney, Rosalind Atkinson, Jessica Black, Fred Withers, Cyril Raymond, Alfred Wellesley, Hugh Ardale, Juliet Mansell, Judith Nelmes, R.W. Steele.*

TONIGHT'S THE NIGHT - PASS IT ON (1931)   ☐3

Dir and Prod *Monty Banks*. Scr *Syd Courtenay, Leslie Arliss*. PC *BIP*. Dis *Wardour*. 73 mins. Cert U

Passable *Leslie Fuller* comedy with more serious undertones than usual. *Fuller* plays the secretary of a loan club jailed for theft when the club's funds disappear. In jail, he comes into contact with the real culprit, who confesses, unaware to whom he is talking. The innocent man escapes and manages to clear his name.

RoC *Amy Veness, Charles Farrell, Frank Perfitt, Betty Fields, Syd Crossley, Hal Gordon, Hal Walters, René Ray, Lola Harvey, Monty Banks, Syd Courtenay, Mike Johnson.*

TONS OF MONEY (1930)   ☐4

Dir *Tom Walls*. Prod *Herbert Wilcox*. Scr *Wilcox, Ralph Lynn*, from a play by *Will Evans and Arthur Valentine*. Ph *F.A. Young*. PC *British and Dominions*. Dis *W and F*. 97 mins. Cert U

Complicated but energetic comedy in which an impoverished inventor (*Ralph Lynn*) stages a bogus death to evade his creditors and returns as his long-lost Cousin George from Mexico. Then 'George' himself turns up - but is proved a phoney. Then another 'George' comes on the scene. . . .

RoC *Yvonne Arnaud, Robertson Hare, Mary Brough, Gordon James, Madge Saunders, Philip Hewland, Willie Warde, John Turnbull, Peggy Douglas.*

TO OBLIGE A LADY (1931)   ☐3

Dir *Manning Haynes*. Prod *S.W. Smith*. Scr *Edgar Wallace*, from his play. PC and Dis *British Lion*. 75 mins. Cert A

A comedy vehicle for music-hall star *Maisie Gay*, who sings a Noël Coward number, 'What Love Means to Girls Like Me', and plays the temporary cook who ruins everything when a couple hold a dinner party in a rented flat to impress an influential uncle. On top of the cooking disasters, the owner of the flat arrives home, unaware that his wife has let it.

RoC *Warwick Ward, Mary Newland, Haddon Mason, Gladys Jennings, James Carew, Annie Esmond, Gladys Hamer.*

Mary Newland and Warwick Ward in To Oblige a Lady *(1931)*

TOO DANGEROUS TO LIVE (1939)   ☐3

Dir *Anthony Hankey, Leslie Norman*. Prod *Jerome Jackson*. Scr *Paul Gangelin, Connery Chappell, Leslie Arliss*, from a novel by *David Hume*. Ph *Basil Emmott*. PC *Warner Bros*. Dis *First National*. 74 mins. Cert A

Jacques (*Sebastian Shaw*), a detective, poses as a jewel thief to win the confidence of a gang whose leader he aims to unmask. He has to steal diamonds from a safe, and falls in love with the niece (*Greta Gynt*) of his victim. Thanks to the police getting in the way, Jacques and the girl find themselves trapped by the villain (*Ronald Adam*) in a blazing garage. Jacques' knowlecge of Morse code gets them out, and the gang is caught. Remake of 1935 film *Crime Unlimited*.

RoC *Anna Konstam, Reginald Tate, Edward Lexy, Ian Maclean, Henry Caine, George Relph, Tonie Edgar Bruce, Torin Thatcher.*

TOO MANY HUSBANDS (1938)   2

Dir, Prod and Scr *Ivar Campbell, from a play by Guy Pelham Bolton.* PC and Dis *Liberty Films. 60 mins. Cert A*
The plane in which swindler Brinkway (*Jack Melford*) was to make his escape crashes. He sees the chance to change his identity. Calling himself Mr Brown he plans a massive fraud in Monte Carlo. But his wife is there, posing as a countess. She exposes his disguise and makes him promise to turn over a new leaf. Muddled quickie comedy.

RoC *Iris Baker, Geoffrey Sumner, Philip Leaver, David Baxter, Brian Oulton, Suzanne Lyle, Carol Rees, Eileen Gerald, Archie Jackson, Robert Field, Monte DeLisle.*

TOO MANY MILLIONS (1934)   1

Dir *Harold Young.* Prod *Irving Asher.* Scr *Brock Williams.* PC and Dis *Warner Bros. 57 mins. Cert U*
Short, slow and silly romantic comedy about a young millionairess (*Betty Compton*) who changes places with her maid to evade the Press, and falls in love with a penniless artist (*John Garrick*), renouncing her fortune to marry him.

RoC *Viola Keats, Athole Stewart, James Carew, Martita Hunt, Phyllis Stanley, Sybil Grove, Bruce Belfrage, Eileen Culshaw, Vincent Lawson.*

TOO MANY WIVES (1933)   2

Dir *George King.* Prod *Irving Asher.* Scr *W. Scott Darling.* PC and Dis *Warner Bros. 58 mins. Cert U*
Tiresome comedy in which a businessman (*Jack Hobbs*) whose wife has just left him gets his maid (*Viola Keats*) to pose as his wife while he entertains an important client from abroad. Complications arise when he finds the client's secretary is his estranged wife!

RoC *Nora Swinburne, Claude Fleming, Alf Goddard, John Turnbull, Charles Paton.*

A TOUCH OF THE MOON (1936)   2

Dir *P. Maclean Rogers.* Prod *A. George Smith.* Scr *Kathleen Butler, H. F. Maltby, from the play by Cyril Campion.* Ph *Geoffrey Faithfull.* PC *GS Enterprises.* Dis *Radio. 67 mins. Cert U*
Artificial romantic comedy, involving *John Garrick* as alcoholic Martin Barnaby, who makes a drunken wager than he can stop the first lady driver he sees, and persuade her to dance with him in the moonlight. The girl he stops proves to be on the run from an arranged

marriage to an elderly man. Martin puts a stop to that, bags her for himself and gives up drink.

RoC *Dorothy Boyd, Joyce Bland, David Horne, Max Adrian, Aubrey Mallalieu, W. T. Elwanger, Wally Patch, Michael Ripper, Vincent Holman.*

TRAITOR SPY (1939)   3
(USA: *The Torso Murder Mystery*)

Dir *Walter Summers.* Prod *John Argyle.* Scr *Summers, Argyle, Jan Van Lusil, Ralph Gilbert Bettinson.* PC *Rialto.* Dis *Pathé. 75 mins. Cert A*
Healey (*Bruce Cabot*), a freelance spy, has photographed some secret documents and asks a high price from the Germans, whose answer is to beat him up. He escapes to his hideout, which British agents cordon off as the Germans corner Healey inside. His wife Freyda (*Marta Labarr*) arrives and says she has burnt the documents. The house is set ablaze, the British swarm in, the Germans are taken. But Healey, having shot Freyda to save her from capture, dies in the flames. Vigorous melodrama is nothing if not colourful.

RoC *Tamara Desni, Romilly Lunge, Percy Walsh, Edward Lexy, Cyril Smith, Eve Lynd, Alexander Field, Peter Gawthorne, Fritz (Frederick) Valk, Hilary Pritchard, Davina Craig, Vincent Holman, Anthony Shaw, Bernard Jukes, Nino Rossi, Rosarita, Ken Johnson's West Indian Band.*

THE TRIUMPH OF SHERLOCK HOLMES (1935)   3

Dir *Leslie Hiscott.* Prod *Julius Hagen.* Scr *H. Fowler Mear, from a novel by Sir Arthur Conan Doyle.* Ph *William Luff.* PC *Real Art.* Dis *Gaumont-British. 84 mins. Cert A*
Brisk, if not too well told Sherlock Holmes adventure (based on *The Valley of Fear*). Holmes (*Arthur Wontner*) is tempted from retirement by a threat from his old enemy, Moriarty (*Lyn Harding*), whom he believes is behind the murder of John Douglas (*Leslie Perrins*). Holmes goes to the victim's lonely country home to investigate. The story of Douglas' early life in the USA puts Holmes on the track of a deadly secret society. In the end he and Moriarty cross swords again, with Holmes triumphant.

RoC *Jane Carr, Ian Fleming, Michael Shepley, Ben Welden, Roy Emerton, Wilfred Caithness, Charles Mortimer, Minnie Rayner, Conway Dixon, Edmund D'Alby, Ernest Lynds.*

TROPICAL TROUBLE (1936)   2

Dir *Harry Hughes.* Prod *Basil Humphrys.* Scr *Vernon Harris, from a novel and play by Stephen King-Hall.* PC *City.* Dis *General Film Distributors. 70 mins. Cert A*
Sister-pecked Sir Humphrey (*Alfred Drayton*) and his aide Masterman (*Douglass Montgomery*), of whose new wife Sir H. is unaware, soon fall under the exotic spell of Bunga-Bunga, an island to which Sir H. has been appointed governor. When extraordinary stories fly back to England, sister and wife hot-foot it to the tropics, where the men have

a hard time pretending to be pillars of sobriety. Aimless adaptation of King-Hall's classic farce *Bunga-Bunga*.

RoC *Betty Ann Davies, Sybil Grove, Natalie Hall, Marie Ault, S. Victor Stanley, Morris Harvey, Gerald Barry, Vernon Harris, Mabel Mercer, Chela and Doray, Diana Hance, Andrea Malandrinos, Billy Watts.*

TROUBLE (1933)   3

Dir *Maclean Rogers.* Prod *Herbert Wilcox.* Scr *R. P. Weston, Bert Lee, Jack Marks.* Ph *F. A. Young.* PC *British and Dominions.* Dis *United Artists. 70 mins. Cert U*
Sydney Howard comedy with the star as Hollebone, a steward on a cruise ship, who is instructed to keep an eye on a famous jewel thief aboard. Nonetheless, a valuable diamond belonging to a passenger *is* stolen, and it's more by luck than judgment that Hollebone helps the authorities get it back.

RoC *George Curzon, Dorothy Robinson, George Turner, Hope Davy, Muriel Aked, Wally Patch, Betty Shale, Abraham Sofaer, Ballard Berkeley, Frank Atherley.*

Muriel Aked and Sydney Howard in Trouble *(1934)*

TROUBLE BREWING (1939)   5

Dir *Anthony Kimmins.* Prod *Jack Kitchin.* Scr *Kimmins, Angus Macphail, Michael Hogan.* Ph *Ronald Neame.* PC *Ealing Studios.* Dis *Associated British. 87 mins. Cert U*
George Gullip (*George Formby*) is a printer who longs to be a detective. When his winnings on a horse prove to be counterfeit, he resolves to track down the forgers himself. After kidnapping the chief of police by mis-

Tiger Tasker and George Formby in Trouble Brewing *(1939)*

take, fighting an all-in wrestling champ, fingerprinting a diva and being chased round a brewery, George unmasks his editor (*Garry Marsh*) as one of the forgers, and cracks the gang. Joyous Formby romp includes the songs *Fanlight Fanny* and *Hitting the Highspots Now*. RoC *Googie Withers, Gus McNaughton, Joss Ambler, Ronald Shiner, Martita Hunt, (C.) Denier Warren, Beatrix Fielden-Kaye, Basil Radford, Esma Cannon, Tiger Tasker.*

TROUBLED WATERS (1936) [2]
Dir *Albert Parker*. Prod *John Findlay*. Scr *Gerard Fairlie*. Ph *Roy Kellino*. PC and Dis *Fox British*. 70 mins. Cert A
When a man is killed in a village car crash, the villagers get together to return a verdict of murder in the hope of gaining publicity for their failing mineral water business. An agent (*James Mason*) who investigates, finds it really was murder, and is able to round up a gang of explosives smugglers, who are after the villagers' latest notion – liquid explosive. Far-fetched thriller.
RoC *Virginia Cherrill, Alastair Sim, Raymond Lovell, Bellenden Powell, Sam Wilkinson, Peter Popp, William T. Ellwanger, Sybil Brooke, Ernest Borrow.*

TROUBLE FOR TWO (1939) [2]
Dir *Walter Tennyson*. Prod *Alfred d'Eyncourt*. Scr *Ian Walker*. Ph *Desmond Dickinson*. PC *Venture*. Dis *Anglo*. 46 mins. Cert U
Jeweller's assistant Rodney (*Anthony Hulme*) tries to deliver a priceless pearl necklace – but the buyer is out, so Rodney has to safeguard the pearls over the weekend. A lovely girl, a bogus inspector, a hidden drawer and a well-meaning neighbour combine to give him a hectic weekend which ends when a gang of gem thieves is captured at a house party. Comedy-drama staggers unconvincingly along.
RoC *Mavis Claire, (C.) Denier Warren, Jack Knight, Bryan Herbert, Douglas Stewart, Arthur Seaton.*

TRUNK CRIME (1939) [3]
(USA: *Design for Murder*)
Dir *Roy Boulting*. Prod *John Boulting*. Scr *Francis Miller, from the play by Edward Percy, Reginald Denham*. Ph *D.P. Cooper*. PC *Charter*. Dis *Anglo*. 51 mins. Cert A
Critics were sharply divided as to the merits of this early Boulting Brothers effort, a macabre little thriller in which a highly strung university student (*Manning Whiley*) plans a grim revenge for a merciless ragging by drugging its ringleader and burying him alive in a trunk. Fortunately, tenants at the student's cottage discover the dazed 'victim' just in time.
RoC *Barbara Everest, Michael Drake, Hay Petrie, Thorley Walters, Eileen Bennett, Lewis Stringer, Ian Fulton, Tom Gill, Geoffrey Gabriel.*

TRUST THE NAVY (1935) [3]
Dir *Henry W. George*. Prod *Ian Sutherland*. Scr *Reginald Long, Arthur Rigby*. PC *St George's Pictures*. Dis *Columbia*. 71 mins. Cert U
A hard-working cast makes something of this comedy about two sailors, Nip (*Lupino Lane*) and Wally (*Wallace Lupino*), on board HMS *Improbable*, who get into trouble with their chief petty officer, and a gang of smugglers, in that order.
RoC *Nancy Burne, Guy Middleton, Ben Welden, Miki Hood, Fred Leslie, Doris Rogers, Reginald Long, Arthur Rigby, Arthur Stanley, Charles Sewell.*

TUDOR ROSE (1936) [5]
(USA: *Nine Days a Queen*)
Dir *Robert Stevenson*. Prod *Michael Balcon*. Scr *Miles Malleson*. Ph *Mutz Greenbaum*. PC *Gainsborough*. Dis *Gaumont-British*. 79 mins. Cert U
A forcefully impressive and affecting piece of history: the sixteenth-century power game that placed Lady Jane Grey (*Nova Pilbeam*) on the throne of England for a few days after the death of her cousin, Edward VI the boy king (*Desmond Tester*), but resulted in her execution when her protector, Warwick (*Sir Cedric Hardwicke*) was defeated in battle by Mary I.
RoC *John Mills, Felix Aylmer, Leslie Perrins, Frank Cellier, Gwen Ffrancgon-Davies, Sybil Thorndike, Martita Hunt, Miles Malleson, John Laurie, Roy Emerton, Albert Davies, Arthur Goullet, John Turnbull, Peter Croft.*

John Mills in Tudor Rose (*1936*)

THE TUNNEL (1935) [4]
(USA: *Transatlantic Tunnel*)
Dir *Maurice Elvey*. Prod *Michael Balcon*. Scr *Kurt Siodmak, L. DuGarde Peach, Clemence Dane, from the novel by Bernhard Kellerman*. Ph *Günther Krampf*. PC and Dis *Gaumont-British*. 94 mins. Cert U
Fairly good, star-studded, futuristic (1950) fantasy. McAllan (*Richard Dix*), the brains behind a transatlantic tunnel scheme, goes to America, where he's photographed everywhere with Varlia (*Helen Vinson*), daughter of one of the millionaires backing the project. His wife Ruth (*Madge Evans*), thinking she has lost him, helps at the first aid post of the tunnel and loses her sight, through working in the dark. Their son Geoff goes to work in the tunnel, but is killed in an explosion. McAllan and Ruth are reunited in grief. The tunnel goes through.
RoC *Jimmy Hanley, Leslie Banks, C. Aubrey Smith, George Arliss, Walter Huston, Basil Sydney, Henry Oscar, Cyril Raymond, Hilda Trevelyan, Allan Jeayes, Helen Haye, Mervyn Johns.*

TURKEY TIME (1933) [4]
Dir *Tom Walls*. Prod *Michael Balcon*. Scr *Ben Travers from his play*. Ph *Charles Van Enger*. PC and Dis *Gaumont-British*. 73 mins. Cert A
Max and David (*Tom Walls, Ralph Lynn*) spend Christmas at the seaside with the Stoatts. Max, who is engaged to Mrs Stoatt's younger sister, becomes involved with another girl, Rose (*Dorothy Hyson*), but fortunately David falls for Rose, and Max is able to blame his latest indiscretion on to the hapless Stoatt (*Robertson Hare*). Seasonal Aldwych farce.
RoC *Mary Brough, Veronica Rose, Norma Varden, D. A. Clarke-Smith, Marjorie Corbett.*

Ralph Lynn and Mary Brough in Turkey Time (*1933*)

TURN OF THE TIDE (1935) [4]
Dir *Norman Walker*. Prod *John Corfield*. Scr *L. DuGarde Peach, J.O.C. Orton, from a novel by Leo Walmsley*. PC *British National*. Dis *Gaumont-British*. 80 mins. Cert U
Refreshing outdoor drama, set in a Yorkshire fishing village, where the coming of the Lunns, with their modern motorboat, is deeply resented by the Fosdycks, particularly old Isaac (*J. Fisher White*). The younger Fosdycks eventually join forces with the Lunns in buying a big boat for deep-sea fishing. Isaac is made senior partner in the new firm. John Lunn (*Niall MacGinnis*) marries Ruth Fosdyck (*Geraldine Fitzgerald*).
RoC *John Garrick, Joan Maude, Sam Livesey, Wilfrid Lawson, Moore Marriott.*

TWELVE GOOD MEN (1936) [3]
Dir *Ralph Ince*. Prod *Jerome Jackson*. Scr *Frank Launder, Sidney Gilliat, from a novel by John Rhodes*. Ph *Basil Emmott*. PC and Dis *Warner Bros*. 64 mins. Cert A
Far-fetched but well-written thriller about an escaped convict who seems to be attacking the 12 jurymen who convicted him. Two are killed, then the rest are taken to the house of another, actor Charles Drew (*Henry Kendall*). More deaths follow before Drew sniffs out the killer.
RoC *Nancy O'Neil, Joyce Kennedy, Percy Parsons, Morland Graham, Gracie Lane, Ralph Roberts, Bernard Miles, Philip Ray, Frederick Burtwell, Roddy Hughes, Sam Springson, George Hughes, Madge White.*

21 DAYS (1937) [2]
(USA: *21 Days Together*)
Dir *Basil Dean, Alexander Korda (uncredited).*

Prod *Korda*. Scr *Graham Greene, Dean, from a play by John Galsworthy*. Ph *Jan Stallich*. PC *London Films/Denham Films*. Dis *Columbia. 75 mins. Cert A*

When the husband of his girlfriend, a model (*Vivien Leigh*), turns up demanding money, Larry (*Laurence Olivier*) accidentally kills him in a struggle. His barrister brother Keith (*Leslie Banks*), fearing for his own career, begs Larry not to go to the police. A mentally deranged down-and-out ex-clergyman is accused, and his death from heart failure saves Larry from confessing in court. Very slow, seems more like 42 days. Not released until 1940.

RoC *Francis L. Sullivan, Hay Petrie, Esmé Percy, Robert Newton, Victor Rietti, Morris Harvey, Meinhart Maur, David Horne, Wallace Lupino, Muriel George, John Warwick, William Dewhurst, Frederick Lloyd, Elliot Mason, Arthur Young, Fred Groves, Aubrey Mallalieu.*

TWICE BRANDED (1935)   [3]
Dir *P. Maclean Rogers*. Prod *A. George Smith*. Scr *Kathleen Butler, from a novel by Anthony Richardson*. Ph *Geoffrey Faithfull*. PC *GS Enterprises*. Dis *Radio. 72 mins. Cert A*

One critic found this crime drama 'ridiculous', another 'real and convincing'. A man is sentenced to 12 years' jail for his (unwitting) part in a massive fraud and, on his release, finds his son in the grip of the same swindler responsible for his own downfall. The father, who has had to go incognito among his ashamed family, takes the blame, and returns to prison where such snobbery cannot be found.

LP *Robert Rendel, James Mason, Eve Gray, Lucille Lisle, Mickey Brantford, Ethel Griffies, Isobel Scaife, Paul Blake, Neville Brook, Michael Ripper, Ethel Royale.*

TWIN FACES (1937)   [1]
Dir *Lawrence Huntington*. Prod *J. Steven Edwards*. Scr *Gerald Elliott*. PC *Premier Sound Films*. Dis *Paramount. 67 mins. Cert A*

Tedious crime drama about a daring burglar, Jimmy the Climber (*Anthony Ireland*) and his double, who is pursued by the police commissioner's daughter (*Francesca Bahrle*) thinking he is the crook. She becomes embroiled in the Climber's plans, but succeeds in turning the situation to her advantage by bringing the 'twin faces' face to face.

RoC *Frank Birch, Paul Neville, Victor Hagen, George Turner, Ivan Wilmot, Frank Tickle.*

TWO CROWDED HOURS (1931)   [3]
Dir *Michael Powell*. Prod *Jerome Jackson, Harry Cohen*. Scr *J. Jefferson Farjeon, Powell (uncredited)*. Ph *Geoffrey Faithfull*. PC *Film Engineering*. Dis *Fox. 42 mins. Cert A*

Sharp direction lifts this mini-thriller about a detective (*John Longden*) hunting an escaped convict who is trying to kill the witness who sent him to prison. She (*Jane Welsh*) also happens to be the 'tec's girl, but he rescues her and the convict dies in a car crash.

RoC *Michael Hogan, Jerry Verno, Edward Barber.*

TWO DAYS TO LIVE (1939)   [2]
Dir *Walter Tennyson*. Prod *Alfred d'Eyncourt*. Scr *Ian Walker*. Ph *Desmond Dickinson*. PC *Venture*. Dis *Anglo. 47 mins. Cert U*

A hypochondriac (*Richard Goolden*) misunderstands a chat on the phone and believes he is going to die in two days. He lives life to the full, making a bizarre assortment of new friends, committing a (successful) burglary and freeing himself from all his old anxieties – before discovering he is not about to die after all. Goolden's likeable central character is film's only asset.

RoC *Phyllis Calvert, Ernest Sefton, Frank Atkinson, Andrea Malandrinos, Arthur Seaton, Douglas Stewart, Hendry White, Norman Greene, Bryan Herbert.*

TWO HEARTS IN HARMONY (1935)   [3]
Dir *William Beaudine*. Prod *John Clein*. Scr *A. R. Rawlinson, Robert Edmunds*. PC *Time Pictures*. Dis *Wardour. 75 mins. Cert A*

Slight but pleasant musical with some good directorial touches, as a singer (*Bernice Clare*) tires of the attentions of the owner of her nightclub and takes a job as governess to the young son of a widowed peer (*George Curzon*). She prises the peer away from his late-night casino habits and humanizes both him and priggish son. Finally, of course, she marries him.

RoC *Enid Stamp-Taylor, Guy Middleton, Paul Hartley, Eliot Makeham, Nora Williams, Gordon Little, Julian Royce, Charles Farrell, Chick Endor, Betty Thumling, Sheila Barrett, Rex Curtis, Victor Reith, Jack Harris and His Band.*

TWO HEARTS IN WALTZTIME (1934)   [3]
Dir *Carmine Gallone, Joe May*. Prod *Reginald Fogwell*. Scr *Fogwell, John McNally, from a scenario by Walter Reisch, Franz Schulz*. PC *Nettlefold/Fogwell*. Dis *Gaumont-British. 80 mins. Cert U*

Mittel-European musical in which Viennese composer Carl Hoffman (*Carl Brisson*), engaged to write a new operetta for producer Greenbaum (*Oscar Asche*) falls for Helene Barry (*Frances Day*) who, he later finds out, is to be the star of the show.

RoC *Bert Coote, (C.) Denier Warren, Roland Culver, William Jenkins, Peter Gawthorne, Valerie Hobson.*

Carl Brisson and Frances Day in Two Hearts in Waltztime *(1933)*

TWO MEN IN A BOX (1938)   [2]
Dir and Prod *R. A. Hopwood*. PC and Dis *Ace Films. 49 mins. Cert A*

Straightforward Windmill Theatre revue, notable only for the appearance of *Tommy Handley* in pre-ITMA days. He and *Ronald Frankau* play the men in the title, guilty of disorderly conduct in a theatre box.

RoC *Warden and West, Gus Chevalier, Meggie Eaton, Paddy Browne, Eric Woodburn, Ken Douglas, Bruno Hoffman.*

TWO MINUTES' SILENCE (1934)   [1]
Dir and Prod *Paulette MacDonagh*. Scr *Uncredited*. PC *PM Films*. Dis *Universal. 74 mins. Cert A*

Stilted and amateurish pageant in which four characters recall, while observing the two minutes' silence for those killed in the First World War, their own experiences on Armistice Day, 1918.

LP *Marie Lorraine, Ethel Gabriel, Frank Leighton, Frank Bradley, Campbell Copelin, Arthur Greenway, Leo Franklyn, Leonard Stephen, Victor Gouriet.*

TWO ON A DOORSTEP (1936)   [1]
Dir *Lawrence Huntingdon*. Prod *Anthony Havelock-Allan*. Scr *Gerald Elliott, George Barraud*. PC and Dis *British and Dominions/ Paramount British. 71 mins. Cert U*

Weak comedy about a girl, Jill (*Kay Hammond*) whose number is constantly being mistaken for that of the bookmaker with the same surname. As Derby Day approaches, she and a bailiff (*Harold French*) who is in the flat until Jill's brother has paid gambling debts, set up their own betting agency. Their winnings are in danger when Jill accepts a huge bet on a hot favourite, but a visit to the local greyhound track restores their fortunes.

RoC *Anthony Hankey, George Mozart, Dorothy Dewhurst, Frank Tickle, Walter Tobias, Tea Sanders.*

TWO'S COMPANY (1936)   [4]
Dir *Tim Whelan*. Prod *Paul Soskin*. Scr *Tom Geraghty, Roland Pertwee, 'Beachcomber' (J. B. Morton)*, Whelan, *John Paddy Carstairs, from a novel by Sidney Horler*. PC *British and Dominions/Soskin Films*. Dis *United Artists. 75 mins. Cert U*

Sparklingly written treatment of a stale old romantic comedy theme, with the stuffy son of a British noble falling for the daughter of a down-to-earth American millionaire. Their two fathers (*Gordon Harker, Ned Sparks*) also learn something about life from each other.

RoC *Mary Brian, Patric Knowles, Henry Holman, Olive Blakeney, Morton Selten, Robb Wilton, Gibb McLaughlin, H.F. Maltby, Syd Crossley, Robert Nainby.*

TWO WAY STREET (1931)   [3]
Dir *George King*. Prod *Archibald Nettlefold* Scr *Sidney Gilliat*. PC *Nettlefold*. Dis *United Artists. 43 mins. Cert A*

Quickie romantic drama about the daughter of a bird fancier: she decides to ditch her Cockney fiancé, who is a petty thief, for an aristocratic new lover. Then the thief complicates

matters by stealing a necklace belonging to the titled gent. . . .
LP *Sari Maritza, Quinton McPherson, James Raglan, Henry Wilcoxon, Peter the puppy.*

TWO WHITE ARMS (1932) 2
(USA: *Wives Beware*)
Dir *Fred Niblo.* Prod *Eric Hakim.* Scr *Harold Dearden, from his play.* PC *Cinema House.* Dis *M-G-M. 79 mins. Cert A*
Despite a strong cast, this is a stiff and unattractive comedy about a philanderer (*Adolphe Menjou*) who finds married life boring, feigns amnesia and takes a job as a car salesman. He is found by his wife's friend. Long in love with him herself, she persuades him to return to his wife, who is about to become a mother.
RoC *Jane Baxter, Margaret Bannerman, Claud Allister, Kenneth Kove, René Ray, Ellis Jeffreys, Jean Cadell, Henry Wenman, Spencer Trevor, Melville Cooper, Peter English, Archibald Batty, Arthur Stratton.*

TWO WIVES FOR HENRY (1933) 3
Dir and Scr *Adrian Brunel.* Prod and PC *George Smith.* Dis *Fox. 45 mins. Cert A*
Henry (*Garry Marsh*), a boot manufacturer, is asked by an important customer to take care of his young daughter in Brighton. After Henry's wife (*Dorothy Boyd*) refuses to go with him, circumstances demand that he take a temporary 'wife' and become involved in a plot to kidnap his charge. Director's light touch keeps this pocket comedy afloat.
RoC *Jack Raine, Millicent Wolf, Paul Sheridan, Andreas Malandrinos.*

TWO WORLDS (1930) 3
Dir and Prod *E. A. Dupont.* Scr *Miles Malleson, Norbert Falk, Franz Schulz.* Ph *Werner Brandes.* PC *BIP.* Dis *Wardour. 111 mins. Cert A*
Critics praised the technical qualities of this romantic war story – Werner Brandes' photography was especially admired – but not its pacing. *John Longden* plays a lieutenant in the Austrian Army who falls in love with the Jewish sister (*Norah Baring*) of a man he has killed. He is forced eventually to give her up, to save her father (*Randle Ayrton*) from being arrested and shot. Made in three language versions.
RoC *Donald Calthrop, C.M. Hallard, Constance Carpenter, Jack Trevor, Andrews Engelmann, Boris Ranevsky, John Harlow, Georges Marakoff, Gus Sharland, Meinhardt Jünger, Teddy Hill, Mirjam Ellis, John St John, John McMahon.*

THE UMBRELLA (1933) 2
Dir *Redd Davis.* Prod *Julius Hagen.* Scr *H. Fowler Mear.* Ph *Ernest Palmer.* PC *Real Art.* Dis *Radio. 56 mins. Cert A*
Released from prison, two pickpockets are handed their possessions, one of which is an umbrella with some jewels hidden in it. The brolly falls into the possession of Freddie (*Harold French*) and then Molly (*Kay Hammond*), a crook, whose pearls the pickpockets are after. She forestalls them at a masked ball

but, thanks to Freddie, all three are caught by the police.
RoC *S. Victor Stanley, Dick Francis, Barbara Everest, Kathleen Tremaine, John Turnbull, Syd Crossley, Ernest Mainwaring.*

UNDER A CLOUD (1937) 2
Dir and Prod *George King.* Scr *M. B. Parsons.* Ph *Hone Glendinning.* PC *Triangle.* Dis *Paramount. 67 mins. Cert A*
Edward Rigby carries this indifferent crime drama as a man who returns to England after 20 years in Australia hiding from the police. He rescues his daughter from the attentions of a dancing gigolo and his son from suspicion of murdering the blackmailer into whose clutches he had fallen. He offers his wife a divorce, but she catches the boat back to Australia with him.
RoC *Betty Ann Davies, Bernard Clifton, Renée Gadd, Hilda Bayley, Moira Reed, Brian Buchel, Peter Gawthorne, Jack Vyvyan, Billy Watts.*

UNDERNEATH THE ARCHES (1937) 4
Dir *Redd Davis.* Prod *Julius Hagen.* Scr *H. Fowler Mear.* Ph *Sydney Blythe.* PC *Twickenham.* Dis *Wardour. 72 mins. Cert U*
Two down-and-outs (*Bud Flanagan, Chesney Allen*), who sleep rough under London's arches, find a new resting-place on board a ship in the docks. Unfortunately for them, it sails to South America, where they thwart revolutionaries planning to steal a 'peace' gas, turning the revolution into a kind of Morris dance. Funny comedy triggered a series of 'Crazy Gang' films.
RoC *Stella Moya, Enid Stamp-Taylor, Lyn Harding, Edmund Willard, Edward Ashley, Aubrey Mather.*

UNDER PROOF (1936) 1
Dir *Roland Gillett.* Prod *John Findlay.* Scr *Tod Waller, from his play* Dudley Does It. Ph *Stanley Grant.* PC and Dis *Fox British. 50 mins. Cert U*
Unconvincing, unfunny comedy. A party stranded in a storm takes refuge in the house of a friend away on holiday. Unknown to all, the house is used for bootlegging liquor. Dudley (*Tyrell Davis*), a devout coward, encounters the bootleggers, gives a password (accidentally) and is mistaken for their mysterious boss. After a strong swig of brandy, he carries on the charade until the police come.
RoC *Betty Stockfeld, Guy Middleton, Judy Kelly, Charles Farrell, Viola Compton, David Horne, Edward Ashley, Henry Longhurst, Harry Watson, Andrea Malandrinos, Peter Popp, Tuff de Lyle (dog).*

UNDER THE RED ROBE (1937) 3
Dir *Victor Seastrom (Sjöström).* Prod *Robert T. Kane.* Scr *Lajos Biro, Philip Lindsay, J. L. Hodgson, Arthur Wimperis, from the play by Edward Rose, after the novel by Stanley Weyman.* Ph *Georges Perinal, Ted Pahle.* PC *New World.* Dis *20th Century-Fox. 82 mins. Cert U*
Peculiarly bloodless historical adventure (a re-make of a 1915 film). In seventeenth-century France, gambler Gil de Berault (*Conrad Veidt*) is reprieved from hanging to capture a rebel leader, the Duc de Foix. He penetrates the Duc's castle, falls in love with his sister (*Annabella*), captures the Duc, but lets him go. Rather oddly, this is seen by the king as a masterpiece of cunning, and all ends happily.
RoC *Raymond Massey, Romney Brent, Sophie Stewart, F. Wyndham Goldie, Lawrence Grant, Baliol Holloway, Haddon Mason, J. Fisher White, Ben Soutten, Anthony Eustrel, Shayle Gardner, Edie Martin, Frank Damer, James Regan, Eric Hales, Ralph Truman.*

UNEASY VIRTUE (1931) 3
Dir and Scr *Norman Walker, from a play by Harrison Owens.* PC *BIP.* Dis *Wardour. 83 mins. Cert U*
Briefly released as *Flirting Wives*, then retitled, this comedy tells of a wife's pique and determination to upset her husband's take-it-for-granted attitude towards her by pretending to have affairs with other men. But one such pretence involves her in a burglary, and more.
LP *Fay Compton, Edmund Breon, Francis Lister, Margot Grahame, Garry Marsh, Adele Dixon, Hubert Harben, Dodo Watts, Donald Calthrop, Molly Lamont, Gerard Lyley, Margaret Yarde.*

THE UNFINISHED SYMPHONY (1934) 4
Dir *Willi Forst, Anthony Asquith.* Prod *Arnold Pressburger.* Scr *Forst, Benn W. Levy.* Ph *Franz Planer.* PC *Ciné-Allianz.* Dis *Gaumont-British. 90 mins. Cert U. Bilingual versions*
Sensitive and haunting biopic of the composer Franz Schubert (*Hans Yaray*), set in Vienna, 1820, when Schubert is appointed music teacher to the family of Count Esterhazy (*Ronald Squire*). He falls for the count's daughter Caroline (*Marta Eggerth*), but loses her love and leaves a famous symphony unfinished, dying in 1828.
RoC *Helen Chandler, Paul Wagner, Esmé Percy, Hermine Sperler, Eliot Makeham, Cecil Humphreys, Beryl Laverick, Brember Wills, Frieda Richard, Vienna Boys Choir.*

THE UNHOLY QUEST (1934) 2
Dir *R. W. Lotinga.* Prod and PC *Widgey R. Newman, Reginald Wyer, Bert Hopkins.* Scr *Newman.* Dis *Equity British. 57 mins. Cert A*
British entry into the horror field. Professor Sorotoff (*Claude Bailey*) is working on a project to restore life after death. His assistant (*Terence de Marney*) and ward (*Christine Adrian*) are startled by a mysterious figure that prowls the house at night. Their ex-convict butler (*John Milton*) kills a blackmailer, whose body the professor uses to try to revive a

mummified Crusader. The experiment goes wrong and the professor dies.
RoC *Harry Terry, Ian Wilson.*

UP FOR THE CUP (1931)   [4]
Dir *Jack Raymond.* Prod *Herbert Wilcox.* Scr *Con West,* R. P. *Weston,* Bert Lee. Ph *F. A. Young.* PC *British and Dominions.* Dis *W and F.* 76 mins. Cert U
Longer-length but well-paced *Sydney Howard* comedy which casts him as a loom-inventor in London for the FA Cup Final. He is robbed of his wallet containing his money and tickets, and his sweetheart Mary (*Joan Wyndham*) disappears. All ends well when he rescues her from a fate worse than death at the hands of his employer's son and learns he's to get a large sum of money for his invention.
RoC *Stanley Kirk, Sam Livesey, Moore Marriott, Hal Gordon, Marie Wright, Herbert Woodward, Jack Raymond.*

UP FOR THE DERBY (1933)   [3]
Dir *Maclean Rogers.* Prod *Herbert Wilcox.* Scr R. P. *Weston,* Bert Lee, Jack Marks. Ph *F. A. Young.* PC *British and Dominions.* Dis *W & F.* 70 mins. Cert U
Sydney Howard comedy casting him as an eccentric stable-hand whose employer is ruined after a string of poor results. The stable-hand buys one of his old boss's horses and, after sundry misadventures on and off the turf, wins the Derby with it.
RoC *Dorothy Bartlam, Mark Daly, Tom Helmore, Frederick Lloyd, Frank Harvey, Franklyn Bellamy.*

UP TO THE NECK (1933)   [4]
Dir *Jack Raymond.* Prod *Herbert Wilcox.* Scr *Ben Travers.* Ph *Cyril Bristow.* PC *British and Dominions.* Dis *United Artists.* 73 mins. Cert U
N. B. Good (*Ralph Lynn*), a bank clerk, inherits a fortune and determines to achieve his life-long ambition of working in the theatre. He falls for a chorus girl (*Winifred Shotter*) and finances a (disastrous) production to try to make her a star. When he himself takes part in the (straight) play, the results are so hilarious it becomes a rollicking success. Fast and furious farce.
RoC *Francis Lister, Reginald Purdell, Mary Brough, Marjorie Hume, Grizelda Hervey.*

THE VANDERGILT DIAMOND MYSTERY (1935)   [1]
Dir, Prod and PC *Randall Faye.* Scr *Margaret Houghton.* Dis *Radio.* 60 mins. Cert A
A valuable diamond necklace stolen on an Atlantic liner is dropped into the golf-bag of an innocent young man. A girl who feels she has a moral right to the necklace, and the gang of thieves who stole it, all try to get their hands on it back in London. But they are rounded up by the young man's mild-mannered neighbour. Embarrassing comedy.
LP *Elizabeth* (Betty) *Astell, Bruce Seton, Charles Paton, Hilary Pritchard, Ethel Royale, Ben Graham Soutten, William Holland, Henry B. Longhurst, Brian Herbert, John Miller.*

VANITY (1935)   [2]
Dir and Scr *Adrian Brunel, from the play by Ernest Denny.* Prod *A. George Smith.* Ph *Geoffrey Faithfull.* PC *GS Enterprises.* Dis *Columbia.* 76 mins. Cert U
Ernest Denny's play about a self-obsessed actress makes rather tepid entertainment with newcomer *Jane Cain* in the title role, as the star who pretends to have died in order to mingle with her fans and wallow in their reactions. Naturally, she gets her come-uppance in the end.
RoC *Percy Marmont, H. F. Maltby, Moira Lynd, John Counsell, Nita Harvey.*

VARIETY (1935)   [3]
Dir *Adrian Brunel.* Prod *John Argyle.* Scr *Brunel, Oswald Mitchell.* Ph *Desmond Dickinson.* PC *Argyle Talking Films.* Dis *Butchers.* 84 mins. Cert U
The story of the music-hall from 1890 to 1935, centred round a show business family the Boyds (played by a real-life show business family) and their triumphs and tragedies in running their own theatre, Boyd's Empire. Unoriginal treatment, but some good variety acts of their day.
LP *Sam Livesey, Cassie Livesey, Jack Livesey, Barrie Livesey, April Vivian, George Carney, W. G. Saunders, Bertha Wilmott, Tessa Deane, Nellie Wallace, The Houston Sisters, Harry Brunning, Phyllis Robins, Olsen's Sea Lions, Denis O'Neil, Sam Barton, John Rorke, Bobbie 'Uke' Henshaw, The Sherman Fisher Girls, Billy Cotton and His Band, Horace Sheldon and His Orchestra, Bobby Slater, Sybil Wise, W. Dolphin, Ted Sanders, William Daunt, Lily Morris, Van Dock, Johnnie Schofield, Rita Cave, Roy Sharpe, John Clay, The Can Can Dancers.*

VARIETY HOUR (1937)   [2]
Dir *Redd Davis.* Prod *Herbert Smith.* PC and Dis *Fox British.* 66 mins. Cert A
Revue entertainment in which *Clapham & Dwyer,* the well-known comedians, play two hopefuls trying to make a name for themselves by posing as two radio commentators from America.
RoC *The Wiere Brothers, Jack Donohue, Helen Howard, Raymond Newell, Carson Robison and His Pioneers, Brian Lawrence and His Lansdowne Band, Kay, Katya and Kay, Norwich Trio, The Music Hall Boys.*

VARIETY PARADE (1936)   [2]
Dir *Oswald Mitchell.* Prod *Ian Sutherland, Reginald Long.* Scr *Con West.* PC *Malcolm.* Dis *Butchers.* 83 mins. Cert U
This fairly uninspired revue consists of a series of variety acts put on in a hotel owned and managed by comedian *Harry Tate.*

RoC *Sam Browne, Dave and Joe O'Gorman, G. S. Melvin, Archie Glen, Nohi and Partner, The Radio Three, Ernest Shannon, Ivor Vintnor and Ann Gordon, Ronald Tate, Harry Beasley, The Corona Kids, The Sherman Fisher Girls, The Three Nagels.*

VERDICT OF THE SEA (1932)   [1]
Dir *Frank Miller, Sydney Northcote.* Prod *Clayton Hutton.* Scr *Miller.* PC *Regina.* Dis *Pathé.* 64 mins. Cert U
Feeble maritime drama about trouble aboard a tramp steamer, and the efforts of a gang of crooks to incite mutiny and gain possession of some diamonds held by the captain, who is delivering them to their owner in Singapore. An ex-doctor helps to foil the gang.
LP *John Stuart, Moira Lynd, Cyril McLaglen, David Miller, Hal Walters, H. Saxon-Snell, Billy Shine, Fred Rains.*

VESSEL OF WRATH (1938)   [5]
(USA: *The Beachcomber*)
Dir and Prod *Erich Pommer.* Scr *Bartlett Cormack, B. Van Thal, from the story by W. Somerset Maugham.* Ph *Jules Kruger.* PC *Mayflower.* Dis *Associated British.* 93 mins. Cert A
Ginger Ted (*Charles Laughton*) is beachcomber, 'remittance man' and all-round scoundrel on a small Malay island. His drinking exploits and weakness for native girls get him into hot water with the Contrôleur (*Robert Newton*) and missionary Miss Jones (*Elsa Lanchester*). When he reluctantly accompanies her to quell a jungle epidemic, they are not only nearly murdered by natives, but discover some home truths about each other. They end up married, back in England, running the Fox and Rabbit pub, with Ginger, now teetotal, rebuking his wife for wearing a low-cut dress. Extended anecdote, but witty and brilliantly acted: priceless stuff.
RoC *Tyrone Guthrie, Dolly Mollinger, Eliot Makeham, Rosita Garcia, Fred Groves, Ley On, Mah Poo, J. Solomon, D. J. Ward, S. Alley Dudley* (dog).

Dudley the dog and Charles Laughton in Vessel of Wrath (*1938*)

THE VETERAN OF WATERLOO (1933)   [1]
Dir *A. V. Bramble.* Prod *Harry Rowson.* Scr *Uncredited, from a play by Sir Arthur Conan Doyle.* PC *National Talkies.* Dis *Paramount.* 40 mins. Cert U

Virtually the end of Bramble's directing career – a dismal drama about the last days of an old soldier, who recalls his adventures when serving with the third brigade of Guards at the Battle of Waterloo.
LP *Jerrold Robertshaw, Roger Livesey, Joan Kemp-Welch, A. B. Imeson, Minnie Rayner.*

THE VICAR OF BRAY (1937) [2]

Dir *Henry Edwards.* Prod *Julius Hagen.* Scr *H. Fowler Mear.* Ph *William Luff.* PC *JH Productions.* Dis *Associated British. 68 mins. Cert U*
Beloved of his poor Irish parishioners, the Vicar of Bray (*Stanley Holloway*) is summoned to the court of England's King Charles I, as tutor for his careless son (the future Charles II). The boy is so impressed he offers to grant any request the Vicar might make once he ascends the throne. In this way, the Vicar is ultimately able to save someone unjustly imprisoned for treason. Slice of musical history has too little style.
RoC *Lawrence Grossmith, Eleanor Fayre, Davy Burnaby, (C.) Denier Warren, Arthur Chesney, Aubrey Fitzgerald, Hal Walters, Charles Hayes, Ian Wilson, Hay Plumb, Bruce Gordon, Kitty Kirwan, Rodney Hudson Dancing Girls.*

VICTORIA THE GREAT (1937) [6]

Dir and Prod *Herbert Wilcox.* Scr *Miles Malleson, Robert Vansittart, from a play by Laurence Houseman.* Ph *Frederick A. Young.* PC *Imperator.* Dis *Radio. 112 mins. One sequence in Technicolor. Cert U*
Victoria ascends to the English throne at 18 in 1837 and, despite gloomy forebodings from ministers of the crown, proves a forthright queen throughout a turbulent era, reigning 64 years. This vivid and very successful film looks at the intimate private life of Victoria (*Anna Neagle*) and her Consort, Prince Albert (*Anton Walbrook*), rather than the events of her reign in depth. *Miss Neagle*'s simple, sincere and above all human portrait of the monarch totally revived her international star career.
RoC *Walter Rilla, Mary Morris, H. B. Warner, Grete Wegener, C. V. France, Charles Carson, Hubert Harben, Felix Aylmer, Arthur Young, Derrick de Marney, Hugh Miller, Percy Parsons, Lewis Casson, Henry Hallatt, Gordon McLeod, James Dale, Wyndham Goldie, Miles Malleson, Tom Hesslewood, Moore Marriott, Paul von Hernried (Paul Henreid), Albert*

Anton Walbrook and Anna Neagle in Victoria the Great *(1937)*

Lieven, Paul Leyssac, Joan Young, Frank Birch, William Dewhurst, Ivor Barnard.

THE VILLAGE SQUIRE (1935) [2]

Dir *Reginald Denham.* Prod *Anthony Havelock-Allan.* Scr *Sherard Powell, from the play by Arthur Jarvis Black.* PC and Dis *British and Dominions/Paramount British. 66 mins. Cert U*
A pompous squire (*David Horne*) insists on his village doing a stage production of *Macbeth*. His face is saved by a visiting film star (*Leslie Perrins*) who is trying to have an anonymous holiday. The star falls in love with the squire's daughter (*Moira Lynd*).
RoC *Vivien Leigh, Ivor Barnard, Margaret Watson, Haddon Mason, David Nichol.*

THE VILLIERS DIAMOND (1938) [2]

Dir *Bernard Mainwaring.* Prod *John Findlay.* Scr *David Evans.* Ph *Stanley Grant.* PC and Dis *Fox British. 50 mins. Cert A*
Ex-jailbird Silas Wade (*Frank Birch*) having fraudulently acquired the Villiers Diamond, finds himself badgered for money both by Barker (*Leslie Harcourt*) who got him the diamond, and his niece Joan (*Evelyn Ankers*) expelled from her Swiss finishing school. He stages a fake robbery – but his plans go wrong; he and Barker go back to prison and Joan is left penniless. Slow-moving crime yarn.
RoC *Edward Ashley, Liam Gaffney, Julie Suedo, Sybil Brooke, Billy Shine, Margaret Davidge.*

VINTAGE WINE (1935) [4]

Dir *Henry Edwards.* Prod *Julius Hagen.* Scr *Seymour Hicks, Ashley Dukes, H. Fowler Mear, from a play by Alexander Engel.* Ph *Sydney Blythe.* PC *Real Art.* Dis *Gaumont-British. 80 mins. Cert A*
Almost word-for-word copy of the stage success, a farce about a vineyard owner (*Seymour Hicks*) whose claim to be 20 years younger than he is collapses about his ears, to the dismay of his young wife (*Claire Luce*), when his family descends on him. His granddaughter (*Judy Gunn*) sides with him against his terrible relatives, and sees to it that he and his wife are reconciled.
RoC *Eva Moore, Miles Malleson, P. Kynaston Reeves, Michael Shepley, A. Bromley Davenport, Amy Brandon Thomas, Meriel Forbes, Brian Buchel, Kathleen Weston, Andrea Malandrinos, (Mary) Hayley Bell, Stella Mantovani, Sonia Somers, Tony de Lungo, Enrico Muzio.*

THE VIPER (1938) [1]

Dir *Roy William Neill.* Prod *Irving Asher.* Scr *Reginald Purdell, John Dighton, J. O. C. Orton.* Ph *Basil Emmott.* PC *Warner Bros.* Dis *First National. 75 mins. Cert U*
Criminologist C. Gull (*Claude Hulbert*) and his assistant Stiffy (*Hal Walters*) wonder why Jenny (*Lesley Brook*), Stiffy's niece, has been accused of stealing, and why Gaby (*Betty Lynne*), a dancer, is being hunted by a notorious criminal, The Viper (*Dino Galvani*), who has escaped from Devil's Island. A diamond in the heel of a dancing shoe leads C. Gull to

the solution of the mystery. Juvenile comedy runs like an extended television sketch.
RoC *Fred Groves, Boris Ranevsky, Harvey Braban, Reginald Purdell, Julian Henry, John F. Traynor.*

VIRGINIA'S HUSBAND (1934) [3]

Dir *Maclean Rogers.* Prod and PC *George Smith.* Scr *H. Fowler Mear, from the play by Florence Kilpatrick.* Dis *Fox. 72 mins. Cert U*
A certain amount of amusement is extracted from this remake of a 1928 silent comedy, with *Dorothy Boyd* as the man-hater and early women's libber who finds herself forced to take a 'temporary' husband (*Reginald Gardiner*) in order to satisfy the wealthy aunt (*Annie Esmond*) who has been sending her an ample allowance from abroad, but now suddenly descends on London.
RoC *Enid Stamp-Taylor, Ena Grossmith, Sebastian Smith, Wally Patch, Tom Helmore, Hal Walters, Andrea Malandrinos, Vi Kaley, May Hallatt.*

THE VULTURE (1937) [3]

Dir *Ralph Ince.* Prod *Irving Asher.* Scr *Stafford Dickens.* Ph *Basil Emmott.* PC *Warner Bros.* Dis *First National. 67 mins. Cert A*
The first screen adventure of Cedric Gull (*Claude Hulbert*) a correspondence course detective. Cedric trails a gang of diamond thieves, led by the mysterious 'Vulture', follows them to Chinatown, disguises himself as a Chinaman and, more by luck than judgment, rounds up the entire gang. Comedy-thriller has enough laughs to get by.
RoC *Lesley Brook, Hal Walters, Frederick Burtwell, George Merritt, Arthur Hardy, Archibald Batty, George Carr.*

WAKE UP FAMOUS (1936) [2]

Dir *Gene Gerrard.* Prod *John Stafford.* Scr *Basil Mason.* Ph *James Wilson.* PC *Premier/Stafford.* Dis *Radio. 68 mins. Cert U*
Alfred (*Nelson Keys*), a hotel clerk framed by a jewel gang, takes his wife and savings and flees to France. After misadventures involving a bogus film producer, Fink (*Gene Gerrard*), who mistakes Alfred for a songwriter, he encounters the gang again, foils their plans and captures them. A song he has composed for Fink becomes a giant hit, and Alfred finds himself famous. Frenzied comedy wears thin.
RoC *Bela Mila, Josephine Huntley Wright, Fred Conyngham, H. F. Maltby, Joan White, Leo von Pokorny, Bruno Barnabe.*

WALTZES FROM VIENNA (1934) [2]
(USA: *Strauss's Great Waltz*)

Dir *Alfred Hitchcock.* Prod and PC *Tom Ar-*

nold. Scr *Alma Reville, Guy Bolton, from a play by Heinz Reichart and a book by Ernst Marischka, D. A. Wilmer.* Ph *Glen MacWilliams.* Dis *Gaumont-British.* 81 mins. Cert U

Hardly Hitchcock's most distinguished film, and one for which his talents were totally unsuited. Set in Vienna, 1845, it concerns the feud between Johann Strauss Senior and Junior, the younger man being helped to fame by a countess (*Fay Compton*) and by Resi (*Jessie Matthews*), the pastrycook's daughter who loves him.

RoC *Esmond Knight, Edmund Gwenn, Frank Vosper, Robert Hale, Charles Heslop, Sybil Grove, Betty Huntley Wright, Cyril Smith, Berinoff and Charlot, Hindle Edgar, Marcus Barron, Bertram Dench, Billy Shine, B. M. Lewin.*

WALTZ TIME (1933) [3]
Dir *William Thiele.* Prod *Herman Fellner.* Scr *A. P. Herbert, from an opera by Johann Strauss.* PC *Gaumont-British.* Dis *W and F.* 82 mins. Cert A

Free adaptation of Strauss' *Die Fledermaus*, with Eisenstein (*Fritz Schultz*) turned into an author in Vienna to seek local colour for his books, and outwitted by his wife during a masked ball. Critical reaction to this film was especially varied.

RoC *Evelyn Laye, Gina Malo, Parry Jones, George Baker, Frank Titterton, Jay Laurier, Ivor Barnard, D. A. Clarke-Smith, Edmund Breon, Kenneth Buckley, Jane Cornell, Joe Spree, Diana Cotton, Joyce Kirby.*

THE WANDERING JEW (1933) [3]
Dir *Maurice Elvey.* Prod *Julius Hagen.* Scr *H. Fowler Mear, from the play by E. Temple Thurston.* Ph *Sydney Blythe.* PC *Twickenham.* Dis *Gaumont-British.* 111 mins. Cert A

Critics were well and truly divided over the merits of this version of the play in which the Jew (*Conrad Veidt*) who demands the release of Barabbas and the Crucifixion of Christ is condemned to wander the earth through the centuries until Christ comes to him again and grants him death. Drew comments ranging from 'wonderful' to 'boring'.

RoC *Marie Ney, Cicely Oates, Basil Gill, Anne Grey, Dennis Hoey, Jack Livesey, Bertram Wallis, Joan Maude, John Stuart, Arnold Lucy, Peggy Ashcroft, Francis L. Sullivan, Felix Aylmer, Ivor Barnard, Abraham Sofaer, Kenji Takase, Hector Abbas, Stafford Hilliard, Robert Gilbert, Conway Dixon.*

WANTED! (1937) [3]
Dir and Prod *George King.* Scr *Brock Williams, from his play.* Ph *Jack Parker.* PC *Embassy.* Dis *Sound City.* 71 mins. Cert U

Slickly made comedy in which clerk Henry and his wife Winnie (*Claude Dampier, ZaSu Pitts*) are mistaken for jewel thieves Harry the Hick and Babyface. An allied gang forces them to pose as big-game hunters at a party to steal the Buckston jewels. The real Harry the Hick and Babyface are there too. Henry puts out the lights and sets off the burglar alarm and ends with a fat reward when all the crooks are rounded up.

RoC *Finlay Currie, Norma Varden, Mark Daly, Kathleen Harrison, Billy Holland, Stella Bonheur, Arthur Wellesley, Mabel Twemlow, Billy Gray, Arthur Goullet, D. J. Williams, Brian Herbert.*

THE WARE CASE (1938) [4]
Dir *Robert Stevenson.* (Associate) Prod *S.C. Balcon.* Scr *Stevenson, Roland Pertwee, E.V.H. Emmett, from the play by George Pleydell Bancroft.* Ph *Ronald Neame.* PC *Ealing Studios/ ATP/Capad/Associated Star.* Dis *Associated British.* 79 mins. Cert A

Debonair Sir Hubert Ware (*Clive Brook*), in dire financial straits, laughs when his wife Mary (*Jane Baxter*) suggests he should curb his lifestyle. But soon he is on trial for murder when her wealthy, odious brother (*Peter Bull*) is found dead in the lake of the Wares' home. His solicitor Michael (*Barry K. Barnes*) gets him off with the help of an unexpected witness. Returning home, Sir Hubert realizes Mary and Michael are in love, declares his guilt, and throws himself from a high balcony. Strongly acted drama.

RoC *C.V. France, Francis L. Sullivan, Frank Cellier, Edward Rigby, Dorothy Seacombe, Athene Seyler, Elliot Mason, John Laurie, Wally Patch, Glen Alyn, Ernest Thesiger, Harold Goodwin, Wallace Evennett, J.R. Lockwood, Peggy Novak, Alf Goddard, Charles Paton.*

Clive Brook, Barry K. Barnes and Jane Baxter in The Ware Case *(1938)*

A WARM CORNER (1930) [4]
Dir *Victor Saville.* Prod *Michael Balcon.* Scr *Angus Macphail, Saville, from a play by Franz Arnold, Ernst Bach, Arthur Wimperis and Lauri*

Heather Thatcher and Leslie Henson in A Warm Corner *(1930)*

Wylie. Ph *Alex Bryce.* PC *Gainsborough.* Dis *Ideal.* 104 mins. Cert A

Comedian *Leslie Henson's* first talkie, casting him as Charles Corner, a millionaire maker of corn plasters who takes a holiday in Monte Carlo, and egged on by his friend Turner (*Alfred Wellesley*) enjoys a flirtation with a girl called Mimi (*Heather Thatcher*). On his return, his indiscretion is almost exposed when Mimi is a house guest, but she comes to his rescue by saying Turner was her lover.

RoC *Connie Ediss, Austin Melford, Kim Peacock, Belle Chrystall, Tonie Edgar Bruce, George de Warfaz, Merle Oberon.*

WARN LONDON! (1934) [3]
Dir *T. Hayes Hunter.* Prod *Herbert Smith.* Scr *Charles Bennett, Billie Bristow, from the novel by Denison Clift.* Ph *Alex Bryce.* PC and Dis *British Lion.* 68 mins. Cert U

Criminologist Dr Krauss (*Edmund Gwenn*) is a victim of a swindle in which he loses his life's savings. Prompted by a thief named Barraclough (*John Loder*), Krauss seeks revenge by using his specialized knowledge to plan a billion pound robbery. His plans are finally thwarted by a Scotland Yard inspector (also *Loder*) who greatly resembles Barraclough. Hearty thriller.

RoC *Leonora Corbett, Garry Marsh, D. A. Clarke-Smith, John Turnbull, Raymond Lovell, Douglas Stewart.*

THE WARREN CASE (1934) [2]
Dir and Scr *Walter Summers, from a play by Arnold Ridley.* Prod *Walter C. Mycroft.* Ph *Jack Parker.* PC *BIP.* Dis *Pathé.* 75 mins. Cert A

The photography was the only item singled out for praise in this ragged potboiler. When Hugh (*Edward Underdown*) is framed for murder, his fiancée (*Nancy Burne*) proves, with eventual help from the police, that the local crime reporter (*Richard Bird*) was the killer, the dead girl having been his mistress.

RoC *Diana Napier, Iris Ashley, A. Bromley Davenport.*

WATCH BEVERLEY (1932) [2]
Dir *Arthur Maude.* Prod *Ivar Campbell.* Scr *N.W. Baring Pemberton, John Cousins, from a play by Cyril Campion.* Ph *George Dudgeon Stretton.* PC *Sound City.* Dis *Butchers.* 80 mins. Cert U

Diplomat Victor Beverley (*Henry Kendall*), discovering that a wealthy Briton is to pay a foreign president a large sum of money for an oil concession, decides to impersonate the president to get his hands on the money for his own pet charity – the Mayfield Hospital. Laboured comedy.

RoC *Dorothy Bartlam, Francis X. Bushman, Frederic de Lara, Charles Mortimer, Patrick Ludlow, Colin Pole, Antony Holles, Ernest Stipwell, Aileen Pitt Marsden, Vincent Clive, Edith Barker Bennett.*

THE WATER GIPSIES (1932) [4]
Dir *Maurice Elvey.* Prod *Basil Dean.* Scr *Dean, Miles Malleson, Alma Reville, John Paddy Carstairs, from the novel by A. P. Herbert.* Ph *Robert Martin, Robert de Grasse.* PC *Associated*

Talking Pictures. Dis *Radio. 80 mins. Cert A*
Sensitively made version of A. P. Herbert's famous novel of bargee life. *Ann Todd* had her first showcase role as the Thames-side gipsy girl whose beauty attracts a society artist who paints her portrait. The girl's gipsy lover objects to their relationship: ultimately, in a scuffle on a barge, she accidentally drowns him.
RoC *Ian Hunter, Sari Maritza, Peter Hannen, Richard Bird, Frances Doble, Anthony Ireland, Moore Marriott, Barbara Gott, Harold Scott, Charles Garry, Betty Shale, Lilli Anne, Kenneth Carlisle, Raymond Raikes.*

THE WAY OF YOUTH (1934) [1]
Dir and Prod *Norman Walker*. Scr *Sherard Powell, from a play by Amy Kennedy Gould, Ralph Neale*. PC and Dis *British and Dominions/Paramount British. 66 mins. Cert A*
Paul (*Sebastian Shaw*) takes his fiancée Carol (*Aileen Marson*) to a gambling club run by Carol's grandmother (*Irene Vanbrugh*). Paul gets into financial difficulties gambling and the club manager (*Henry Victor*) attempts blackmail until granny scotches his plot. Said one reviewer: 'Aged plot, poor direction; stay away.'
RoC *Diana Wilson, The Western Brothers, Robert Rendel, Leslie Bradley.*

WEDDING GROUP (1936) [3]
(USA: *Wrath of Jealousy*)
Dir *Alex Bryce, Campbell Gullan*. Prod *Leslie Landau*. Scr *Selwyn Jepson, Hugh Brooke, from the radio play by Philip Wade*. Ph *Roy Kellino*. PC and Dis *Fox British. 70 mins. Cert U*
Romantic drama spanning the years 1853 to 1856. Janet (*Barbara Greene*), a minister's daughter from Scotland, falls in love with Robert (*Patric Knowles*), an army officer. They split up because of the schemings of Janet's jealous sister (*Ethel Glendinning*). Janet becomes a nurse, serving with Florence Nightingale (*Fay Compton*) in the Crimea, where she saves Robert's life.
RoC *Alastair Sim, Bruce Seton, Naomi Plaskitt, Arthur Young, Derek Blomfield, Billy Dear, David Hutcheson, Michael Wilding.*

Barbara Greene (fur-trimmed coat), Fay Compton (dark gloves) and Michael Wilding (light jacket) in Wedding Group *(1936)*

WEDDING REHEARSAL (1932) [3]
Dir and Prod *Alexander Korda*. Scr *Arthur Wimperis, Helen Gardom*. Ph *Leslie Rowson*. PC *London Films*. Dis *Ideal. 84 mins. Cert U*

Polished if facile comedy about a bachelor marquis (*Roland Young*) who survives all his grandmother's wedding plans for him by marrying off her 'candidates' to his friends, only to fall in love with his mother's secretary (*Merle Oberon*), a beauty beneath her glasses.
RoC *George Grossmith, John Loder, Maurice Evans, Lady Tree, Wendy Barrie, Joan Gardner, Kate Cutler, Edmund Breon, Morton Selten, Diana Napier, Lawrence Hanray, Rodolfo Mele.*

WEDDINGS ARE WONDERFUL (1938) [3]
Dir *Maclean Rogers*. Prod *A. George Smith*. Scr *Kathleen Butler, H.F. Maltby*. Ph *Geoffrey Faithfull*. PC *Canterbury*. Dis *RKO Radio. 79 mins. Cert A*
Henry (*Frederick Lloyd*) deceives his domineering wife with Cora (*June Clyde*), a dancer, with whom Guy (*Esmond Knight*) is also involved. When Henry's daughter (*René Ray*) is caught in a gambling raid, she flees next door – to Guy's. Their subsequent engagement party is attended by Cora, who has come to give a cabaret, and who finds several people she knows. Chaos reigns. Obvious farce, but with outstanding performance from *George Carney* as Guy's father.
RoC *Bertha Belmore, Bruce Seton, Antony Holles, Charles Paton, Michael Ripper, Valentine Dunn.*

WE DINE AT SEVEN (1931) [3]
Dir *Frank Richardson*. Prod *George Smith, Harry Cohen*. Scr *Brock Williams*. PC *GS Enterprises*. Dis *Fox. 45 mins. Cert U*
Short comedy for the talents of *Herbert Mundin*. He and *Dorothy Bartlam* play the Sweets, who become involved in a wild marital mix-up with their neighbours, the Chilworths.
RoC *Leslie Perrins, Molly Johnson, Arthur Argent.*

Herbert Mundin and Dorothy Bartlam in We Dine at Seven *(1931)*

WEDNESDAY'S LUCK (1936) [1]
Dir *George Pearson*. Prod *Anthony Havelock-Allan*. Scr *Ralph Neale*. PC and Dis *British and Dominions/Paramount British. 68 mins. Cert A*
Carfax (*Patrick Barr*), a young ex-convict, persuades benevolent old Stevens (*Wilson Coleman*) to employ him as a librarian. But Stevens is also a notorious fence, unknown to his niece

(*Susan Bligh*) who falls for Carfax. Carfax is also not what he seems: he is really a detective, and soon has Stevens behind bars. Stiff crime drama.
RoC *Moore Marriott, Paul Neville, Linden Travers, George Dewhurst, Ernest Borrow, Eric Hales, George Bailey.*

WELL DONE, HENRY (1936) [2]
Dir *Wilfred Noy*. Prod and PC *Neville Clarke*. Scr *Noy, A. Barr-Smith*. Ph *Jack Parker*. Dis *Butchers. 86 mins. Cert A*
Henry MacNabb (*Will Fyffe*) is a bank clerk with a tyrannical wife, a pain-in-the-neck son and a wailing daughter. Sent to the bank chairman's flat with valuable bearer bonds, Henry goes to the wrong flat and nips a blackmailer's schemes in the bud by quick thinking. He then hands the bonds to a crook who has bound and gagged the chairman, but turns the tables to earn the gratitude of the bank and the respect of his family. Patchy comedy.
RoC *Cathleen Nesbitt, Charles Hawtrey, Iris March, Donald Gray, Marjorie Taylor, Torin Thatcher, Edward Wild, Hugh McDermott, Paul Sheridan, Gordon Bailey, Fred Schwartz, Wensley Russell, MacArthur Gordon, Ben Wright, Gerald Pring, Douglas Stewart, Ann Campbell, Rags the dog.*

WE'RE GOING TO BE RICH (1938) [3]
Dir *Monty Banks*. Prod *Robert T. Kane, Samuel G. Engel*. Scr *James Edward Grant, Sam Hellman, Rohama Siegel*. Ph *Mutz Greenbaum*. PC and Dis *20th Century-Fox. 80 mins. Cert A*
Gracie Fields' first international venture and a big disappointment: an uninspired tale set in the 1880s. Leaving Australia after a tour, singer Kit (*Miss Fields*) finds her unreliable husband Dobbie (*Victor McLaglen*) has invested their savings in a South African goldmine which proves worthless. She sings in a saloon there, whose owner, Yankee (*Brian Donlevy*), loves her. She parts from Dobbie, but rushes back when he is injured in a prize-fight. Together again, they join the rush for a new gold strike.
RoC *Coral Browne, Ted Smith, Gus McNaughton, Syd Crossley, Charles Carson, Hal Gordon, Don McCorkindale, Robert Nainby, Charles Harrison, Tom Payne, Joe Mott, Alex Davies, D. H. Williams, Victor Fairley, Charles Castella.*

Victor McLaglen and Gracie Fields in We're Going to be Rich *(1938)*

WEST END FROLICS (1937)   [2]
Dir *R. A. Hopwood*. Prod *Frank Green*. PC and Dis *Ace Films*. 46 mins. Cert U
Dispiriting Windmill revue with all the usual turns.
LP *Meggie Eaton, Warden and West, Eric Barker, Eric Woodburn, Eddie Hooper, Edna Wood*.

WEST OF KERRY (1937)
See *Island Man* (1937)

WHAT A MAN! (1937)   [3]
Dir *Edmond T. Gréville*. Prod *Hugh Perceval*. Scr *Basil Mason, Jack Marks*. Ph *Ernest Palmer*. PC *Independent Films/Phoenix Films*. Dis *British Lion*. 74 mins. Cert U
A photographer, Pennyfeather (*Sydney Howard*), is entrusted by the Mayor (*Ivor Barnard*) with the council's slate club finds, and keeps them in an old bureau, which his wife (*Vera Pearce*) subsequently sells to a second-hand dealer. In his frantic attempts to retrieve the bureau, Pennyfeather finds an ancient charter protecting the local common against building rights. A hero, he is made mayor. Some fun, thanks to Howard, but direction stodgy.
RoC *Jenny Laird, Frederick Bradshaw, H. F. Maltby, Johnny Singer, Robert Adair, Frank Cochrane, Sybil Grove, Alfred Wellesley, Francesca Bahrle*.

WHAT A NIGHT! (1931)   [2]
Dir and Prod *Monty Banks*. Scr *Syd Courtenay, Lola Harvey*. PC *BIP*. Dis *First National-Pathé*. 58 mins. Cert U
Leslie Fuller comedy with *Fuller* as yet another character called Bill, this time though a travelling salesman who puts up for the night at a 'haunted' inn, has the fright of his life and ends a hero when he catches Grindle (*Charles Paton*), a notorious burglar. The slapstick is broad and very simple.
RoC *Molly Lamont, Frank Stanmore, Syd Courtenay, Olivette, Ernest Fuller, Molly Hamley-Clifford, Lola Harvey*.

WHAT HAPPENED THEN? (1934)   [3]
Dir and Scr *Walter Summers, from a play by Lilian Trimble Bradley*. Prod *Walter C. Mycroft*. Ph *James Wilson*. PC *BIP*. Dis *Wardour*. 62 mins. Cert A
When a sculptor (*Geoffrey Wardwell*) is wrongly convicted of the murder of his guardian, his fiancée (*Lorna Storm*) appeals to his friend, the murdered man's nephew (*Richard Bird*) to seek fresh evidence, promising to marry him if he can save the sculptor. But the friend proves to be mentally deranged and the real murderer, who had planned it all to get the girl. Average murder story with a good twist.
RoC *Francis L. Sullivan, Richard Gray, George Zucco, J. Fisher White, Cecil Ramage, Stella Arbenina, Lawrence Hanray, Kathleen Harrison, Quinton McPherson, Raymond Huntley, Alec Finter*.

WHAT HAPPENED TO HARKNESS (1934)   [3]
Dir *Milton Rosmer*. Prod *Irving Asher*. Scr

Brock Williams. PC *Warner Bros*. Dis *First National*. 53 mins. Cert U
Two village policemen (*Robert Hale, James Finlayson*) try to outdo each other in solving the apparent murder of a miser who has disappeared along with his housekeeper. Arrests are made - but then the missing pair return: they had eloped to get married. Reasonable comedy with fair rural atmosphere.
RoC *Brember Wills, John Turnbull, Walter (Wally) Patch, Clare Harris, Morland Graham, Veronica Brady, Aubrey Mallalieu, Kathleen Kelly, Douglas Jeffries, Geoffrey Wardwell, S. A. Cookson, D.J. Williams*.

WHAT'S IN A NAME? (1934)   [1]
Dir *Ralph Ince*. Prod *Irving Asher*. Scr *Uncredited*. PC *Warner Bros*. Dis *First National*. 48 mins. Cert U
Under the assumed name of Otto Krauss, clerk George Andrews (*Barry Clifton*) writes an operetta, which is selected by star Marta Radovic (*Carol Goodner*) for her next production. The producers, unable to trace the composer, hire someone else to pose as Krauss, which flushes George into the open. He also marries Marta, who proves to be a girl from the provinces. Far-fetched comedy.
RoC *Gyles Isham, Eve Gray, Ernest Sefton, George Zucco, Reginald Purdell, Winifred Oughton*.

WHAT WOULD YOU DO, CHUMS? (1939)   [4]
Dir *John Baxter*. Prod *John Corfield*. Scr *David Evans, Geoffrey Orme, Con West, from a radio series by Gordon Crier*. Ph *James Wilson*. PC *British National*. Dis *Anglo*. 76 mins. Cert A
Taking its title from its star *Syd Walker*'s radio catchphrase, this is an effective weepie drama in which a young girl (*Jean Gillie*), living on her own, falls in love with a weak young crook (*Cyril Chamberlain*), and is steered through the traumatic affair - which ends when he tries to rob a bank - by a fatherly junk dealer (*Syd Walker*).
RoC *Jack Barty, Wally Patch, Gus McNaughton, Peter Gawthorne, Julien Vedey, Leonard Morris, Andrea Malandrinos, Arthur Finn, George Street*.

WHEN KNIGHTS WERE BOLD (1936)   [4]
Dir *Jack Raymond*. Prod *Max Schach*. Scr *Austin Parker, Douglas Furber, from the play by Charles Marlow*. Ph *Frederick A. Young*. PC *Capitol*. Dis *General Film Distributors*. 75 mins. Cert U
Sir Guy (*Jack Buchanan*), home from army service in India, is horrified to find his ancestral home full of stuffy relations. He brings a tramp (*Moore Marriott*) in to dinner, imagines routing them when a suit of armour falls on him and he dreams he is back in the Middle Ages, then pays paid to them in real life on his recovery. One (*Fay Wray*) is impressed enough to stay and marry him. Efficient musical-comedy, with *Buchanan* nearly the whole show.
RoC *Garry Marsh, Kate Cutler, Martita Hunt, Robert Horton, Aubrey Mather, Aubrey Fitzgerald, Robert Nainby, Charles Paton*.

WHEN LONDON SLEEPS (1932)   [3]
Dir *Leslie Hiscott*. Prod *Julius Hagen*. Scr *Bernard Merrivale, H. Fowler Mear, from the play by Charles Darrell*. PC *Twickenham*. Dis *Associated Producers and Distributors*. 78 mins. Cert A
Tommy Blythe (*Harold French*), in debt to gambler Haines (*Francis L. Sullivan*) wins enough at Haines' gaming den to pay his debt. Then Haines finds out that Tommy's girl Mary (*René Ray*) is the daughter of his recently deceased uncle and stands between him and a fortune. Haines kidnaps Mary but his place is raided by Scotland Yard, fire breaks out and Tommy rescues Mary from the roof.
RoC *A. Bromley Davenport, Alexander Field, Diana Beaumont, Ben Field, Barbara Everest, Herbert Lomas*.

WHEN THE DEVIL WAS WELL (1937)   [3]
Dir *Maclean Rogers*. Prod *A. George Smith*. Scr *W. Lane Crawford*. Ph *Geoffrey Faithfull*. PC *GS Enterprises*. Dis *Columbia*. 67 mins. Cert U
Jack (*Jack Hobbs*) is bullied into getting engaged to rich Ann (*Eve Gray*) by his social-climbing mother. But he really loves Betty (*Vera Lennox*), a girl he met when his car conked out. At a country club, Jack and Betty get together, while his mother concedes the error of her ways, and helps his friend Bob (*Jerry Rawlinson*) to get Ann, whom he loves. Plot is unbelievable, but script provides a good many laughs.
RoC *Annie Esmond, Max Adrian, Aubrey Mallalieu, Bryan Powley*.

WHERE IS THIS LADY? (1932)   [3]
Dir *Laszlo Vajda, Victor Hanbury*. Prod *John Stafford*. Scr *Stafford, Sydney Blow, from a scenario by Billy Wilder*. PC *Amalgamated Films Associated*. Dis *British Lion*. 77 mins. Cert U
Despite music by *Franz Lehar*, this is a fairly ordinary version of a German film (*Es war einmal ein Walzer*) about failing bankers who try to make a rich marriage for their bachelor chairman (*Owen Nares*) with Lucie (*Wendy Barrie*), whose parents have also lost their money, unbeknown to the bank. Both fall in love with other partners, and convert the bank into a successful nightclub.
RoC *Marta Eggerth, George K. Arthur, Ellis Jeffreys, Gibb McLaughlin, O.B. Clarence, Robert Hale*.

WHERE'S GEORGE?/THE HOPE OF HIS SIDE (1935)   [2]
Dir *Jack Raymond*. Prod *Herbert Wilcox*. Scr *R.P. Weston, Bert Lee, Jack Marks, John Paddy Carstairs*. Ph *F.A. Young*. PC *British and Dominions*. Dis *United Artists*. 69 mins. Cert U
A henpecked blacksmith (*Sydney Howard*) who is always dreaming of Walter Mitty-style exploits, rebels against domestic tyranny, 'adopts' a little foal and joins the local rugby team. Foolishly, he stakes the foal on his team winning a vital game. The foal goes missing,

but turns up in time to provide the blacksmith with the inspiration to score the vital try.
RoC *Mabel Constanduros, Leslie Sarony, Frank Pettingell, Sam Livesey, Wally Patch.*

WHERE'S SALLY? (1936) [3]

Dir *Arthur Woods.* Prod *Irving Asher.* Scr *Brock Williams, Frank Launder.* Ph *Basil Emmott.* PC and Dis *Warner Bros. 71 mins. Cert A*

Jimmy (*Gene Gerrard*) puts his considerable bag of wild oats behind him when he marries Sally (*Renee Gadd*). But his friend Tony (*Claude Hulbert*) lets slip remarks about Jimmy's scarlet past at the wedding, which causes the groom to rush off with the indignant bride. A complicated honeymoon includes a meeting with Tony's temperamental wife Sonia (*Chili Bouchier*), who has just left him, a deaf uncle and the continual appearance and disappearance of the bride. An energetic cast works hard with quick-fire if familiar farcical situations.
RoC *Reginald Purdell, Violet Farebrother, Athole Stewart, Morland Graham, Ralph Roberts.*

WHERE'S THAT FIRE? (1939) [3]

Dir *Marcel Varnel.* Prod *Edward Black.* Scr *Marriott Edgar, Val Guest, J.O.C. Orton.* Ph *Derek Williams.* PC and Dis *20th Century-Fox. 73 mins. Cert U*

After the town hall burns down, the three-man fire brigade of Bishops Wallop, with its one-horse engine, is told to buck up or be fired. Their chief, Captain Viking (*Will Hay*), discovers a chemical extinguisher. Learning of a plot to steal the Crown Jewels, the trio goes to the Tower of London. The crooks start a fire, but Viking sets the foam going, incapacitates the gang and saves the day. One or two good individual sequences shore up below-par Hay entry.
RoC *Moore Marriott, Graham Moffatt, Peter Gawthorne, Eric Clavering, Hugh McDermott, Charles Hawtrey.*

Will Hay in Where's That Fire? *(1939)*

WHERE THERE'S A WILL (1936) [5]

Dir *William Beaudine.* Prod *Michael Balcon.* Scr *Will Hay, Robert Edmunds, Beaudine, Ralph Spence.* Ph *Charles Van Enger.* PC *Gainsborough.* Dis *Gaumont-British. 80 mins. Cert A*

Unsuccessful lawyer Benjamin Stubbins (*Will Hay*), who owes money all round, is enticed

away from his office by a gang of crooks who have realized it is over a bank. They cut through the floor and rob the bank, knocking Ben out when he returns unexpectedly. At a Christmas Eve dance held by his rich relations, Ben encounters the gang again, and is eventually able to hand them over to the police, who have fortuitously arrived in the form of a carol party. Expertly directed comedy with some very funny scenes.
RoC *Gina Malo, Hartley Power, Graham Moffatt, H.F. Maltby, Norma Varden, Peggy Simpson, Gibb McLaughlin, Hal Walters, John Turnbull, Sybil Brooke, Davina Craig, Frederick Piper, Mickey Brantford, Henry Adries, Eddie Houghton.*

WHILE PARENTS SLEEP (1935) [2]

Dir *Adrian Brunel.* Prod *Paul Soskin.* Scr *Anthony Kimmins, Edwin Greenwood, John Paddy Carstairs, Jack Marks.* Ph *Ernest Palmer.* PC *Transatlantic/British and Dominions.* Dis *United Artists. 72 mins. Cert A*

A shopgirl (*Jean Gillie*) teaches two snobbish families a few manners, declining to expose an affair between her boyfriend's brother (*Romilly Lunge*) and snooty Lady Cattering (*Enid Stamp-Taylor*), even after milady has been bitchy at her expense during a dinner party. In consequence, she finds herself accepted by her newly respectful prospective parents-in-law. Frothy but episodic comedy.
RoC *Mackenzie Ward, Ellis Jeffreys, Davy Burnaby, Athole Stewart, Albert Rebla, Wally Patch, Billy (William) Hartnell.*

WHISPERING TONGUES (1934) [2]

Dir *George Pearson.* Prod *Julius Hagen.* Scr *H. Fowler Mear.* PC *Real Art.* Dis *Radio. 55 mins. Cert A*

Alan Norton (*Reginald Tate*) returns from abroad to find that his father has been driven to suicide. He determines to make those responsible pay for it, but falls in love with the daughter (*Jane Welsh*) of the chief conspirator. In the end, the theft of some jewels is enough to ensure that honour is satisfied. Stagy drama.
RoC *Russell Thorndike, Malcolm Keen, Felix Aylmer, Charles Carson, Tonie Edgar Bruce, S. Victor Stanley.*

WHITE ENSIGN (1934) [3]

Dir and Scr *John Hunt.* Prod *Ivar Campbell.* PC *Sound City.* Dis *M-G-M. 84 mins. Cert U*

Adventure yarn with location filming at several naval stations. British cruiser *Hawk* is summoned to Santa Barbara where there is oilfield trouble involving company engineer Denton (*Anthony Ireland*) and troublemaker Cortez (*Ballard Berkeley*). The *Hawk*'s commander (*Anthony Kimmins*) puts down a revolution organized by Cortez, and wins the love of the consul's daughter (*Molly Lamont*).
RoC *Kenneth Villiers, Ivan Samson, S. Victor Stanley, Ivo Dawson, Edgar Driver.*

WHITEFACE (1932) [4]

Dir *T. Hayes Hunter.* Prod *Michael Balcon.* Scr *Angus Macphail, Bryan Edgar Wallace, from a play by Edgar Wallace.* PC *Gainsbor-*

Norman McKinnel, Gibb McLaughlin and (in window) Hugh Williams in Whiteface *(1932)*

ough/British Lion. Dis *W and F. 70 mins. Cert A*

Well-worked Edgar Wallace thriller which begins when a doctor (*John H. Roberts*) finds a man murdered in an East End side-street. Inspector Mason (*Norman McKinnel*) gets the case and finds himself hunting a blackmailer called Whiteface. The doctor reveals he has a patient answering Whiteface's description and, with the help of a reporter (*Hugh Williams*), the inspector uncovers Whiteface's identity.
RoC *Gordon Harker, Renee Gadd, Nora Swinburne, Richard Bird, Leslie Perrins, D. A. Clarke-Smith, Gibb McLaughlin, Jeanne Stuart, Clare Greet, George Merritt.*

WHITE LILAC (1935) [3]

Dir *Albert Parker.* Prod *Ernest Garside.* Scr *Uncredited, from the play by Ladislas Fodor.* Ph *Alex Bryce.* PC and Dis *Fox British. 67 mins. Cert A*

Typical multi-suspect mystery, set in a small village, in which a number of people are suspected of murdering the most unpopular man around – and all seem to have both motive and alibi.
LP *Basil Sydney, Judy Gunn, Claude Dampier, Percy Marmont, Gwenllian Gill, Leslie Perrins, Constance Travers, Billy Holland, Marjorie Hume, Edward Dignon, Edward Ashley, Vashti Taylor.*

WHO GOES NEXT? (1938) [5]

Dir *Maurice Elvey.* Prod *Ivor McLaren.* Scr *David Evans, Lawrence Green, from the play by Reginald Simpson, James W. Drawbell.* Ph *Ronald Neame.* PC and Dis *Fox British. 85 mins. Cert A*

1916: British officers in a German POW camp, digging an escape tunnel, are joined by a newcomer, Captain Beck (*Jack Hawkins*), a month before the break is planned. But another, Stevens (*Andrew Osborn*) cracks and gives the game away, and they have to go early. Beck realizes that the leader, Hamilton (*Barry K. Barnes*), is the husband of the woman with whom he has been having an affair, and sacrifices himself to let Hamilton escape. Suspenseful stiff upper lip drama foreshadows British war films of the next two decades.
RoC *Sophie Stewart, Charles Eaton, Frank Birch, Roy Findlay, Alastair Macintyre, Meinhart Maur, Viola Compton, Elizabeth Nolan,*

Charles Lancing, Kitty Kirwan, Francis James, Frances R. Mann, Wyndham Hewett.

WHO KILLED FEN MARKHAM?/ THE ANGELUS (1937) [2]

Dir *Thomas Bentley.* Prod *Julius Hagen.* Scr *Michael Barringer.* Ph *William Luff.* PC *St Margarets.* Dis *Ambassador. 76 mins. Cert A*
Briefly released as *The Angelus*, then retitled, this creaky thriller features *Nancy O'Neil* as June, an actress who has to give up Brian (*Anthony Bushell*), son of a rich banker, after getting involved in a scandal. She finds work with a small show whose manager, Fen (*Garry Marsh*), fancies her. When he is murdered, June is accused. Her aunt, a nun (*Mary Glynne*), leaves her convent and not only proves June's innocence, but reunites her with Brian.
RoC *Eve Gray, Zoë Wynn, Richard Cooper, Joy(ce) Evans, Charles Carson, Amy Veness, Alice O'Day, Ernest Sefton, Jack Allen, John Turnbull.*

WHO KILLED JOHN SAVAGE? (1937) [3]

Dir *Maurice Elvey.* Prod *Irving Asher.* Scr *Basil Dillon, from a novel by Philip Macdonald.* Ph *Basil Emmott.* PC and Dis *Warner Bros. 69 mins. Cert A*
Slightly restructured remake of the 1931 film *Rynox* (qv). Several people at a synthetic rubber firm come under suspicion when senior partner John Savage (*Nicholas Hannen*) is found dead, especially Marchetti, a mystery man whom Savage had said was threatening him. But it turns out that Savage, suffering from an incurable disease, had killed himself, making Marchetti up so that his bankrupt firm would receive the insurance.
RoC *Barry Mackay, Edward Chapman, Kathleen Kelly, Henry Oscar, Ross Landon, George Kirby, (C.) Denier Warren.*

WHOM THE GODS LOVE (1936) [3]
(USA: *Mozart*)

Dir and Prod *Basil Dean.* Scr *Margaret Kennedy.* PC *ATP.* Dis *Associated British. 82 mins. Cert U*
Although tolerably well received by the critics, this vehicle by Basil Dean for his young wife *Victoria Hopper* (as Mozart's wife) was a financial disaster. The story develops as a series of sketches in the composer's life, including his wife's resisting the attentions of a prince, and the final recognition of his genius before his tragic early death at 35.
RoC *Stephen Haggard, John Loder, Liane Haid, Marie Lohr, George Curzon, Jean Cadell, Hubert Harben, Frederick Leister, Lawrence Hanray, Richard Goolden, Muriel George, Leueen McGrath, Oda Slobodskaya, Percy Hemming, Tudor Davies, Enid James, Sylvia Nells, Norman Walker, Rowena Sanders, Sir Thomas Beecham with the London Symphony Orchestra.*

WHO'S YOUR FATHER? (1935) [2]

Dir *Henry W. George.* Prod *Lupino Lane.* Scr *Lane, Arthur Rigby, Reginald Long, from a play by Mark Melford.* PC *St George's Pictures.* Dis *Columbia. 63 mins. Cert A*

One embarrassment follows another for George (*Lupino Lane*) pending the arrival of his rich prospective father-in-law. His mother has re-married, her new husband being an undertaker. Worse, his father, believed to have died at sea, turns up and announces he has bigamously married a Negress. Tiresome comedy.
RoC *Peter Haddon, Nita Harvey, James Finlayson, Joan (Jean) Kent, Margaret Yarde, James Carew, Peter Gawthorne, Eva Hudson.*

WHO'S YOUR LADY FRIEND? (1937) [4]

Dir *Carol Reed.* Prod *Martin Sabine.* Scr *Anthony Kimmins, Julius Hoest, from a play by Österreicher and Jenbach.* Ph *Ján Stallich.* PC *Dorian.* Dis *Associated British. 73 mins. Cert A*
A plastic surgeon's secretary goes to the station to pick up his new client, but comes back with a cabaret singer. Mimi (*Margaret Lockwood*), the secretary's fiancée, sees him with the singer (*Frances Day*) and thinks the worst. The surgeon's wife (*Betty Stockfeld*) thinks likewise of her spouse (*Vic Oliver*). The secretary (*Romney Brent*), drunk with it all, ends up in the surgeon's wife's bedroom, and chaos reigns. Frothy farce.
RoC *Sarah Churchill, Marcelle Rogez, Muriel George, Frederick Ranalow.*

WHY PICK ON ME? (1937) [3]

Dir *Maclean Rogers.* Prod *A. George Smith.* Scr *H.F. Maltby, Kathleen Butler.* Ph *Geoffrey Faithfull.* PC *GS Enterprises.* Dis *Radio. 64 mins. Cert A*
Going home to celebrate his wedding anniversary, henpecked bank clerk Sam Tippet (*Wylie Watson*) finds his wife gone to visit a sick aunt. He is persuaded by younger colleagues to visit a gaudy nightclub and is quite drunk when the place is raided. As well as landing in prison on several minor offences, he finds himself charged with robbing his own home, a crime committed by his double. Much to his relief, matters are finally cleared up. Improbable comedy gets by on ingenuity.
RoC *Jack Hobbs, Sybil Grove, Max Adrian, Isobel Scaife, Elizabeth Kent, Michael Ripper.*

WHY SAILORS LEAVE HOME (1930) [2]

Dir *Monty Banks.* Prod *John Maxwell.* Scr *Val Valentine.* Ph *James Rogers.* PC *BIP.* Dis *Wardour. 69 mins. Cert U*
Big, bluff *Leslie Fuller* in his familiar character of Bill Biggles in a broad comedy which casts him as a sailor abroad who becomes involved with a sheik and ends up in charge of his harem.
RoC *Peter Barnard, Eve Gray, Syd Courtenay, Dmitri Vetter, Gladys Cruickshank, Gerard Lyley, Bob Johnson, Frank Melroyd, Lola Harvey, Marika Rokk, Olivette.*

THE WICKHAM MYSTERY (1931) [2]

Dir *G. B. Samuelson.* Prod *E. Gordon Craig.* Scr *Uncredited, from a play by John McNally.* PC *Samuelson.* Dis *United Artists. 84 mins. Cert A*
A necklace and the plans for a new kind of aircraft are stolen from the house of inventor Charles Wickham (*Lester Matthews*). Suspi-

cion falls on a neighbour, but Wickham's daughter (*Eve Gray*) proves that the thefts were the work of a gang of crooks, who hoped to sell the plans to a foreign power. Creaky.
RoC *John Longden, Sam Livesey, Walter Piers, Wally Bosco, John Turnbull, Doris Clemence, Elsie Moore, Ormonde Wynne.*

WIDOWS MIGHT (1934) [2]

Dir *Cyril Gardner.* Prod *Irving Asher.* Scr *Roland Brown, Brock Williams, from a play by Frederick Jackson.* PC and Dis *Warner Bros. 77 mins. Cert U*
Somewhat artless comedy about two merry widows (*Laura la Plante, Yvonne Arnaud*) out to get themselves new husbands. One wants her former sweetheart to renew his interest in her, and is persuaded by the other to say that a burglary has been committed. Champion the butler (*George Curzon*) agrees to confess to the burglary for £500 and indemnity against prosecution. But . . .
RoC *Garry Marsh, Barry Clifton, Margaret Yarde, Davina Craig, Joan Hickson, Hugh E. Wright, Hay Plumb, Hal Walters, Walter Amner.*

WIFE OF GENERAL LING (1937) [3]

Dir *Ladislas Vajda.* Prod *John Stafford.* Scr *Akos Tolnay, Reginald Long, from the story by Peter Cheyney, Dorothy Hope.* Ph *James Wilson.* PC *Premier/Stafford.* Dis *Radio. 72 mins. Cert A*
Secret Service agent Fenton (*Griffith Jones*) investigates the smuggling of British armaments into China. He suspects leading merchant Wong (*Inkijinoff*) of being in league with mysterious bandit leader General Ling, not knowing they are one and the same. Wong's wife Tai (*Adrianne Renn*), once in love with Fenton, discovers her husband's secret and helps lay a trap in which he is killed. Efficient 'melo' with good performance by (*Valery*) *Inkijinoff.*
RoC *Lotus Fragrance, Alan Napier, Gibson Gowland, Anthony Eustrel, Jino Soneya, Hugh McDermott, Gabrielle Brune, Marion Spencer, Billy Holland, George Merritt, Kenji Takase, Howard Douglas.*

A WIFE OR TWO (1935) [2]

Dir *P. Maclean Rogers.* Prod *Herbert Smith.* Scr *Rogers, Kathleen Butler, from the play by C. B. Poultney, Roland Daniel.* PC and Dis *British Lion. 63 mins. Cert A*
Mary and Charles (*Betty Astell, Henry Kendall*), formerly married, but now divorced and re-married to George and Margaret (*Garry Marsh, Nancy Burne*) have to pretend to be married again in order to placate a rich uncle with strong views on divorce. All five converge on a country cottage, where George is later suspected of being an escaped lunatic. Familiar sort of situation comedy.
RoC *Fred Duprez, Ena Grossmith, Wally Patch, Leo Sheffield.*

WILD BOY (1934) [4]

Dir *Albert de Courville.* Prod *Michael Balcon.* Scr *Stafford Dickens.* PC *Gainsborough.* Dis *Gaumont-British. 85 mins. Cert U*
The legendary greyhound *Mick the Miller* is

Sonnie Hale in Wild Boy *(1934)*

the star of this comedy-thriller romp about Billy (*Sonnie Hale*), secretary to the crooked Redfern (*Lyn Harding*), who helps Mick (here as the Wild Boy of the title) and his lady owner (*Gwynneth Lloyd*) win the Greyhound Derby. RoC *Leonora Corbett, Ronald Squire, Bud Flanagan and Chesney Allen, Fred Kitchen, Arthur Sinclair, Cyril Smith.*

WINDBAG THE SAILOR (1936) [3]
Dir *William Beaudine.* Prod *Michael Balcon.* Scr *Leslie Arliss, Robert Edmunds, Marriott Edgar, Val Guest.* Ph *Jack Cox.* PC *Gainsborough.* Dis *Gaumont-British.* 85 mins. Cert U
Ben Cutlet (*Will Hay*), a bogus sea captain always boring everyone at the local with his tall stories, is tricked into taking command of the unseaworthy *Rob Roy* which the owners intend to scuttle. Ben and two stowaways escape to a cannibal island and later recapture the *Rob Roy* from the crew, who have failed to sink her. Ben sails home with a real story to tell. Comedy with rather leisurely development but good individual comic scenes.
RoC *Graham Moffatt, Moore Marriott, Norma Varden, Dennis Wyndham, Amy Veness, Kenneth Warrington.*

Will Hay and friend in Windbag the Sailor *(1936)*

WINDFALL (1935) [2]
Dir *George King.* Prod *King, Randall Faye.* Scr *Faye, Jack Celestin, from the play by R.C. Sheriff.* PC *Embassy.* Dis *Radio.* 65 mins. Cert U
Sam (*Edward Rigby*), an old ironmonger, inherits £50,000 and for a time is persuaded to live like a lord. His son promptly falls into bad

company, then makes a disastrous marriage, while his brother-in-law kills a man and is sent to prison for manslaughter. Sam goes back to work to teach his family a lesson, but his decision nearly results in a fatal accident. Unconvincing drama, but some nice touches.
RoC *Derrick de Marney, George Carney, Marie Ault, Marjorie Corbett, Googie Withers.*

THE WINDJAMMER (1930) [4]
Dir *John Orton.* Prod *H. Bruce Woolfe.* Scr *Orton, A.P. Herbert, from a book by A.J. Villiers.* Ph *R.J. Walker, Alan Villiers, Jack Parker.* PC and Dis *Pro Patria.* 58 mins. Cert U
A dramatized record of a five-month voyage to and from Australia, via Cape Horn, dealing with a gentleman tramp who joins the crew of the windjammer, the *Grace Harwar*, for their journey of adventure. The film was praised for its photography and thrilling storm sequences.
LP *Michael Hogan, Tony Bruce, Hal Gordon, Charles Levey, Gordon Craig, Hal Booth, Roy Travers, J. Baker, J. Cunningham, P. Russell, C. Christie, G. Thomas.*

THE WINDMILL (1937) [2]
Dir *Arthur Woods.* Prod *Irving Asher.* Scr *Woods, from the novel by John Drabble.* Ph *Robert Lapresle.* PC *Warner Bros.* Dis *First National.* 62 mins. Cert A
Smoothly directed but rather unconvincing First World War drama. Peter (*Hugh Williams*), an English soldier, falls for Clodine (*Glen Alyn*) whose German-born fiancé turns out to be an enemy agent. When he takes her to a windmill from which his secret messages are sent, she realizes what he is, and sets fire to the mill. The agent perishes, and Clodine is rescued by Peter.
RoC *Henry Mollison, Anthony Shaw, George Galleon, William Dewhurst, Winifred Oughton, John Laurie, John Carol, Bruce Lister, Agnes Laughlan, Charlotte Parry, Robert Algar.*

WINDMILL REVELS (1936) [2]
Dir *Frank Green.* Prod *R.A. Hopwood.* PC and Dis *Ace.* 47 mins. Cert A
Straightforward Windmill Theatre revue, notable only for an early appearance on screen by *Kenneth More.*
RoC *Meggie Eaton, Gus Chevalier, Edna Wood, Paddy Browne, Warden & West, Ken Douglas, Nanette, Anita Martell, Ivor Beddoes, Eddie Hooper, The Windmill Girls, Alan d'Albert and the Windmill Orchestra.*

A WINDOW IN LONDON (1939) [4]
(USA: *Lady in Distress*)
Dir *Herbert Mason.* Prod *Josef Somlo, Richard Norton.* Scr *Ian Dalrymple, Brigid Cooper, from a screenplay by Herbert and Manet.* Ph *Glen MacWilliams.* PC *G and S Films.* Dis *General Film Distributors.* 77 mins. Cert A
From a train, Peter (*Michael Redgrave*) sees a girl being strangled in a house and goes to the police. He is embarrassed when he finds it was an illusionist, Zoltini (*Paul Lukas*) and his wife Vivienne (*Sally Gray*) rehearsing, but subsequently becomes infatuated with Vivienne. Peter thinks he has drowned Zoltini in a fight

and is relieved when he reappears. Peter goes back to his wife Pat (*Patricia Roc*). Weeks later, Pat and Peter see the same strangling scene from a train, and laugh. In the room Vivienne lies dead, throttled by the vengeful Zoltini. Different drama with good plot development.
RoC *Hartley Power, Glen Alyn, Gertrude Musgrove, George Carney, Alf Goddard, Wilfrid Walter, George Merritt, Pamela Randall, Bryan Coleman, John Salew, Kimberley and Page.*

WINGS OF THE MORNING (1937) [4]
Dir *Harold Schuster.* Prod *Robert T. Kane.* Scr *Tom Geraghty, John Meehan, Brinsley Macnamara, from a story by Donn Byrne.* Ph *Ray Rennahan.* PC *New World.* Dis *20th Century-Fox.* 85 mins. Technicolor. Cert U
A curse falls on the descendants of gipsy girl Marie (*Annabella*) when her nobleman Irish husband (*Leslie Banks*) dies in a hunting tragedy. Years later, she returns to Ireland with a horse she hopes will be a Derby winner, joined by her granddaughter Maria (also *Annabella*) who has escaped from war in Spain dressed as a boy. Maria is engaged to Don Diego (*Edward Underdown*) but falls for the Canadian (*Henry Fonda*) who trains the horse. The horse wins, Diego steps aside and, with Maria marrying her Canadian, the curse is lifted. Britain's first Technicolor feature is a thing of beauty but not quite a joy in total.
RoC *Stewart Rome, Harry Tate, Irene Vanbrugh, Helen Haye, Mark Daly, Sam Livesey, John McCormack, Steve Donohue, Hermione Darnborough, E.V.H. Emmett, D.J. Williams, Pat Noonan, Philip Frost, Emmanuelo, Nicholas Nadejine, Evelyn Ankers.*

Henry Fonda, 'Wings of the Morning' and Annabella in Wings of the Morning *(1937)*

WINGS OVER AFRICA (1936) [2]
Dir *Ladislas Vajda.* Prod *John Stafford.* Scr *Akos Tolnay.* PC *Premier.* Dis *Radio.* 63 mins. Cert U
Loose-knit, location-shot adventure about a party of four questing for hidden diamonds in the African jungle. They are joined by a prospector and a guide, each prepared to make his own claim to the treasure. One of the party is knifed to death and another wounded, making everyone suspicious of his fellows, before the culprit is revealed and the diamonds found – and shared.
LP *Joan Gardner, Ian Colin, James Harcourt,*

James Carew, Alan Napier, James Craven, Charles Oliver, Phil Thomas, Ferrule.

WISE GUYS (1937)   ③

Dir *Harry Langdon*. Prod *Ivor McLaren*. Scr *David Evans*. Ph *Stanley Grant*. PC and Dis *Fox British. 67 mins. Cert A*

Hard-up Charlie and Jimmy (*Charlie Naughton, Jimmy Gold*) must raise £500 if they want to take over their uncle's business. They try to make money at the races, but run into a gold-digger, Flo (*Audrene Brier*) and her boyfriend, who also try to take over uncle's firm. Flo wins £500 and the boys find themselves going back to London – on foot. A rare film directed by American comedian *Harry Langdon* – but nothing special.

RoC *Robert Nainby, Walter Roy, Sydney Keith, David Keir, Peter Popp.*

THE WISHBONE (1933)   ②

Dir *Arthur Maude*. Prod *Ivar Campbell*. Scr *N.W. Baring Pemberton, from a short story by W. Townend*. PC *Sound City*. Dis *M-G-M. 78 mins. Cert U*

Slender vehicle for the comedy talents of music-hall star *Nellie Wallace*. She plays a charwoman who unexpectedly receives a small legacy – £50 – has a little spree and uses the rest of the money to help a busker friend make a name for himself.

RoC *Davy Burnaby, A. Bromley Davenport, Jane Wood, Renee Macready, Geoffrey King, Fred Schwartz, Hugh Lethbridge, Joselyn Sparks, Bettina Montahners, Reggie de Beer.*

WITHOUT YOU (1934)   ②

Dir *John Daumery*. Prod *Herbert Smith*. Scr *Michael Barringer*. Ph *Alex Bryce*. PC *British Lion*. Dis *Fox. 66 mins. Cert A*

Molly (*Wendy Barrie*) splits from her composer husband Tony (*Henry Kendall*) to devote herself to becoming a playwright. After six months, Molly is being wooed by a baron (*Fred Duprez*), who coincidentally hires Tony as a 'co-respondent' with a view to Molly getting a divorce. Tony deals with the baron, and Molly's first play is a success. Not so the film.

RoC *Margot Grahame, Georgie Harris, Joe Hayman, Billy Mayerl.*

WOLF'S CLOTHING (1936)   ③

Dir *Andrew Marton*. Prod and PC *Richard Wainwright*. Scr *Evadne Price, Brock Williams, from their play* The Emancipation of Ambrose. Dis *Universal. 80 mins. Cert A*

Ambrose Girling (*Claude Hulbert*), a stumbling young diplomat in the Foreign Office, is sent on a mission to Paris, where a gang of spies mistake him for a famous assassin.

RoC *Gordon Harker, Lilli Palmer, Helen Haye, George Graves, Peter Gawthorne, Shayle Gardner, George Hayes, Joan Swinsted, Frank Birch, Ernest Sefton.*

WOLVES (1930)   ③
(USA: *Wanted Men*)

Dir *Albert de Courville*. Prod *Herbert Wilcox*. Scr *Reginald Berkeley, from a play by Georges Toudouze*. Ph *Roy Overbaugh, Dave Keesan.*

PC *British and Dominions*. Dis *Wardour. 57 mins. Cert U*

Drama of the Far North, with visiting American star *Dorothy Gish* as a near-frozen girl saved from death by a gang of outlaws who draw lots for possession of her. The softhearted leader of the gang (*Charles Laughton*) fixes the draw so that he can help the girl escape.

RoC *Malcolm Keen, Jack Ostermann, Arthur Margetson, Andrews Engelmann, Franklyn Bellamy, Betty Bolton.*

A WOMAN ALONE (1936)   ③
(USA: *Two Who Dared*)

Dir *Eugene Frenke*. Prod *Robert Garrett, Otto Klement*. Scr *Leo Lania, Warren Chetham Strode, from a scenario by Fedor Ozep*. PC *Garrett-Klement Pictures*. Dis *United Artists. 78 mins. Cert A*

Russia, late nineteenth century. Nikolai (*Henry Wilcoxon*), an army officer, is attracted to lovely peasant Maria (*Anna Sten*), but ultimately marries within his own social sphere. When her fiancé gets her a position as nurse to Nikolai's first-born, he tries to rekindle their affair. Her fiancé (*John Garrick*) tries to kill him and is sent to prison. Remorseful, Nikolai reveals all the facts, and is drummed out of his regiment. Average soaper.

RoC *Viola Keats, Romilly Lunge, Esmé Percy, Francis L. Sullivan, Guy Middleton, Peter Gawthorne, Minnie Rayner, Frank Atkinson, Ballet de Leon Woizikovski.*

THE WOMAN BETWEEN (1930)   ②
(USA: *The Woman Decides*)

Dir *Miles Mander*. Prod *John Maxwell*. Scr *Mander, Frank Launder, from a play by Mander*. Ph *Henry Gardner*. PC *BIP*. Dis *Wardour. 89 mins. Cert A*

This moderate romance may have given Frank Launder the germ of the idea for his late 1950s' comedy *Left, Right and Centre*. The mistress of a Conservative candidate falls in love with his Labour rival.

LP *Owen Nares, Adrianne Allen, C.M. Hallard, David Hawthorne, Barbara Hoffe, C. Disney Roebuck, Margaret Yarde, Winifred Oughton, Netta Westcott.*

WOMANHOOD (1934)   ③

Dir *Harry Hughes*. Prod and PC *Louis London*. Scr *Brandon Fleming*. Dis *Butchers. 62 mins. Cert A*

Reporter Jack (*Esmond Knight*) brings about the arrest of Brent (*Leslie Perrins*), a jewel thief who swears to get even on his release. Three years later, Brent plans to carry out his threat, but is killed by his discarded mistress (*Eve Gray*) in circumstances which suggest suicide.

RoC *Christine Adrian, I. MacArthur Gordon, Charles Castella.*

WOMEN WHO PLAY (1932)   ④

Dir *Arthur Rosson*. Prod *Walter Morosco*. Scr *Gilbert Wakefield, Basil Mason, from a play by Frederick Lonsdale*. PC *Paramount British*. Dis *Paramount. 78 mins. Cert A*

Drawing-room comedy. Finding that his wife is falling in with a set of social parasites and

believing one of them, a philanderer, is in love with her, Richard (*George Barraud*) hires an actress (*Mary Newcomb*) to pose as a prostitute at a dinner party. From the situations that result, he gets his wife back, a sadder and wiser woman.

RoC *Benita Hume, Joan Barry, Barry Jones, Edmond Breon, Gerald Lyley, Sylvia Lesley, Peter Evan Thomas, Mary Hamilton, Frank Lacy.*

THE WONDERFUL STORY (1932)   ③

Dir, Prod, Scr and PC *Reginald Fogwell, from a novel by I. A. R. Wylie*. Dis *Sterling. 79 mins (later 70). Cert A*

Second screen version of I. A. R. Wylie's novelettish story about two brothers in love with the same girl. She marries one but he becomes a cripple, and she marries the other. Her first husband eventually accepts the situation after she has his brother's baby. Stout acting just about saves it.

LP *Wyn Clare, Eric Bransby Williams, John Batten, Sam Livesey, J. Fisher White, Ernest Lester.*

THE WORLD, THE FLESH AND THE DEVIL (1932)   ③

Dir *George A. Cooper*. Prod *Julius Hagen*. Scr *H. Fowler Mear, from the play by Lawrence Cowen*. PC *Real Art*. Dis *Radio. 53 mins. Cert A*

The imposing title to this ordinary drama is merely the name of a London dockland pub, where a shady criminal lawyer, the illegitimate son of a baronet, makes plans – but fails – to oust the lawful son and heir.

LP *Harold Huth, Isla Bevan, S. Victor Stanley, Sara Allgood, James Raglan, Fred Groves, Felix Aylmer, Frederick Leister, Barbara Everest.*

THE 'W' PLAN (1930)   ③

Dir and Prod *Victor Saville*. Scr *Saville, Miles Malleson, Frank Launder, from a novel by Graham Seton*. Ph *F. A. Young, Werner Brandes, René Guissart*. PC *BIP-Burlington*. Dis *Wardour. 104 mins. Cert U*

Entertaining, if rather incredible spy thriller in which a British agent (*Brian Aherne*) undertakes a dangerous mission behind enemy lines. His task: to find the meaning of the 'W' plan, a strange document found on a dead German officer during the First World War. In the end the agent combines with prisoners-of-war to abort the enemy plan, which involves the building of secret tunnels.

RoC *Madeleine Carroll, Mary Jerrold, Gordon Harker, Gibb McLaughlin, George Merritt, C. M. Hallard, Clifford Heatherley, Frederick Lloyd, Milton Rosmer, Alfred Drayton, Norah Howard, Robert Harris, Charles Paton, Cameron Carr, Austin Trevor, B. Gregory, Walter Koenig, Arthur Hambling.*

THE WRITTEN LAW (1931)   ②

Dir and Scr *Reginald Fogwell*. Prod *Fogwell, Mansfield Markham*. PC *Fogwell*. Dis *Ideal. 79 mins. Cert A*

Another sluggish Fogwell film, this one about a wife (*Madeleine Carroll*) about to leave her doctor husband (*Percy Marmont*) for another man when he loses his sight in a car accident. The lover soon turns up again, but the doctor regains his sight and conceals the fact from his wife, turning it to his advantage and saving the marriage.

RoC *Henry Hewitt, James Fenton, Barbara Barlow, Ernest Lester.*

A YANK AT OXFORD (1937)   [5]

Dir *Jack Conway.* Prod *Michael Balcon.* Scr *John Monk Saunders, Leon Gordon, Sidney Gilliat, Michael Hogan, Roland Pertwee, Malcolm Stuart Boylan, Walter Ferris, George Oppenheimer* and *(all uncredited) John Paddy Carstairs, F. Scott Fitzgerald, Frank Wead, Angus Macphail.* Ph *Harold Rosson, Cyril Knowles.* PC and Dis *M-G-M British.* 105 mins. Cert U

Lee Sheridan (*Robert Taylor*), arrogant son of an American small-town publisher, is sent to Oxford to complete his education. A crack sportsman, he is convinced that the university has much to learn from him. He is brought down a few pegs before falling in love with Molly (*Maureen O'Sullivan*) and stroking Oxford to victory in the Boat Race. *Boy's Own* stuff which the public eagerly lapped up. Certainly there is never a dull moment.

RoC *Lionel Barrymore, Vivien Leigh, Edmund Gwenn, Griffith Jones, C.V. France, Edward Rigby, Morton Selten, Claude Gillingwater, Tully Marshall, Walter Kingsford, Robert Coote, Peter Croft, Edmund Breon, Noel Howlett, Norah Howard, John Warwick, Ronald Shiner, Syd Saylor, Doodles Weaver, Richard Wattis, Anthony Hulme, Peter Murray-Hill, Jon Pertwee, Kenneth Villiers, Philip Ridgeway Jr, John Varley.*

Maureen O'Sullivan and Robert Taylor in A Yank at Oxford (1938)

THE YELLOW MASK (1930)   [3]

Dir *Harry Lachman.* Prod *John Maxwell.* Scr *Val Valentine, Miles Malleson, George Arthurs, Walter C. Mycroft, W. David,* from a play by

Edgar Wallace. Ph *John J. Cox.* PC *BIP.* Dis *Wardour.* 95 mins. Cert U

Edgar Wallace's play *Traitor's Gate* resisted the combined efforts of five scriptwriters, emerging as an indigestible, and according to one critic 'very silly' mixture of slapstick, melodrama, chases, music and dancing. The story concerns the efforts of a Chinese nobleman to steal the Crown Jewels from the Tower of London.

LP *Lupino Lane, Dorothy Seacombe, Warwick Ward, Haddon Mason, William Temple, William Shine, Winnie Collins, Frank Cochrane, Wallace Lupino.*

YELLOW SANDS (1938)   [5]

Dir *Herbert Brenon.* Prod *Walter C. Mycroft.* Scr *Michael Barringer, Rodney Ackland,* from a play by *Eden* and *Adelaide Philpotts.* Ph *Walter Harvey.* PC and Dis *Associated British.* 68 mins. Cert U

In a little Cornish village, an old lady (*Marie Tempest*) who knows her own mind and those of people around her, sees to it that those in whom she takes an interest and whom she feels have a future benefit by her will. She dies as she had wished, looking at the sun rising over the sea, and content that her last wishes will bring about the results she intended. Unusual little film is packed with rich humour and gentle wit.

RoC *Wilfrid Lawson, Belle Chrystall, Robert Newton, Patrick Barr, Edward Rigby, Amy Veness, Coral Browne, Drusilla Wills, Muriel Johnston, Roddy McDowall.*

YES, MADAM (1933)   [3]

Dir *Leslie Hiscott.* Prod *Herbert Smith.* Scr *Michael Barringer,* from a novel by *K.R.G. Browne.* PC *British Lion.* Dis *Fox.* 46 mins. Cert U

Quota quickie comedy in which Bill (*Harold French*), to comply with the terms of his uncle's will, becomes chauffeur-valet to nouveau-riche Mr Peabody (*Frank Pettingell*). If he gets the sack within two months, his uncle's fortune goes to his cousin Hugh (*Peter Haddon*). Hugh does his best to ensure Bill's dismissal, but Bill's girlfriend Pansy (*Kay Hammond*) sees to it that he gets the money.

RoC *Muriel Aked, Wyn Weaver, Hal Walters.*

YES, MADAM? (1938)   [3]

Dir *Norman Lee.* Prod *Walter C. Mycroft.* Scr *Clifford Grey, Bert Lee, William Freshman,* from the novel by *K.R.G. Browne.* Ph *Walter Harvey.* PC and Dis *Associated British.* 77 mins. Cert U

To inherit £80,000 apiece, cousins Bill and Sally (*Bobby Howes, Diana Churchill*) have to go into service for a month without getting sacked. A third cousin, Tony (*Billy Milton*), who's next in line for the legacy, tries to get Bill fired by telling his employer he's a burglar. But the employer asks Bill if he can get back some incriminating letters. The resultant burglary is a disaster, no-one gets the legacy, but Bill and Sally get each other. Spirited musical farce. Remake of 1933 film.

RoC *Wylie Watson, Bertha Belmore, Fred Emney, Vera Pearce, Cameron Hall.*

YES, MR BROWN (1932)   [2]

Dir *Herbert Wilcox, Jack Buchanan.* Prod *Wilcox.* Scr *Douglas Furber* (also lyrics), from a play by *Paul Frank, Ludwig Hershfield.* Ph *F.A. Young.* PC *British and Dominions.* Dis *W and F.* 94 mins (later 86). Cert A

Below-par *Jack Buchanan* musical comedy. He's Nicky, manager of a store in Vienna, awaiting the owner, Mr Brown (*Hartley Power*), whom he hopes will offer him a partnership. When Nicky's wife (*Margot Grahame*) walks out, he gets his secretary Ann (*Elsie Randolph*) to act as his wife. The deception is discovered, but Brown marries Ann – and Nicky gets the partnership, and his wife back.

RoC *Vera Pearce, Clifford Heatherley, Anna Lee.*

YOU'D BE SURPRISED! (1930)   [3]

Dir *Walter Forde.* Prod *Archibald Nettlefold.* Scr *Walter Forde, H. Fowler Mear.* Ph *Geoffrey Faithfull.* PC *Nettlefold.* Dis *Butcher's.* 64 mins. Cert U

Minor comedy, directed by its star, *Walter Forde,* who plays an aspiring songwriter and singer, whose efforts to gain recognition lead to his being mistaken, while he is in 'fancy dress', for an escaped convict.

RoC *Frank Stanmore, Joy Windsor, Frank Perfitt, Douglas Payne, Donald Russell, Sidney Gilliat.*

YOU LIVE AND LEARN (1937)   [2]

Dir *Arthur Woods.* Prod *Irving Asher.* Scr *Brock Williams, Tom Phipps,* from a novel by *Norma Patterson.* Ph *Basil Emmott.* PC and Dis *Warner Bros.* 80 mins. Cert U

Peter (*Claude Hulbert*) meets and marries Mamie (*Glenda Farrell*), an American showgirl, who thinks he is a rich landowner. At Peter's tumbledown farm, Mamie finds he is a widower with three children. The straightlaced schoolma'am, Miss Tanner, hates Mamie and tries to turn her reunion with showbiz friends into an orgy through gossip, but Peter helps put her to flight and a new life for all at the farm begins. Obvious, leisurely comedy, but with a very funny turn by *Charlotte Leigh* as Miss Tanner.

RoC *Glen Alyn, John Carol, James Stephenson, Arthur Finn, Margaret Yarde, Gibb McLaughlin, Pat Fitzpatrick, Anna Murrell, Muriel Blatcher, Wallace Evennett.*

YOU MADE ME LOVE YOU (1933)   [3]

Dir *Monty Banks.* Prod *John Maxwell.* Scr *Frank Launder.* Ph *John J. Cox.* PC *BIP.* Dis *Wardour.* 70 mins. Cert U

Musical comedy take-off of *The Taming of the Shrew.* A songwriter (*Stanley Lupino*) meets a beautiful girl (Hollywood star *Thelma Todd*) in a traffic jam and writes a song about her: it becomes a hit. Through a ruse of her father's, the couple marry, but the 'shrew' will not be tamed until her new husband decides to give her grounds for divorce.

RoC *John Loder, Gerald Rawlinson, James Carew, Charles Mortimer, Hugh E. Wright, Charlotte Parry, Arthur Rigby Jr, Syd Crossley, Monty Banks.*

YOU MUST GET MARRIED (1936)   [3]

Dir *Leslie Pearce*. Prod *Basil Humphrys*. Scr *F. McGrew Willis, Richard Willis, from a novel by David Evans*. Ph *Claude Friese-Greene*. PC *City*. Dis *General Film Distributors*. 68 mins. Cert A

Entertaining piece of frivolity in which Fenella (*Frances Day*), an American film star, marries Captain Brown (*Neil Hamilton*) to avoid extradition from England. Indignant at the idea that he should leave after the ceremony, Brown abducts her and sails off on his steamer. Some wife taming is attempted at sea, but, in port, Fenella slips away to find a big film contract awaiting her. Before she can sign, Brown arrives and sweeps her off again.

RoC *Robertson Hare, Wally Patch, Gus McNaughton, Fred Duprez, Dennis Wyndham, (C.) Denier Warren, James Carew, Bryan Powley, Hilary Pritchard*.

YOUNG AND INNOCENT (1937)   [5]
(USA: *The Girl Was Young*)

Dir *Alfred Hitchcock*. Prod *Edward Black*. Scr *Charles Bennett, Alma Reville, Antony Armstrong, Edwin Greenwood, Gerald Savory, from a novel by Josephine Tey*. Ph *Bernard Knowles*. PC *Gainsborough*. Dis *General Film Distributors*. 82 mins. Cert A

Seen running away from the body of a murdered actress on a lonely beach, Robert (*Derrick de Marney*) is hauled in for murder. Escaping from the courthouse, he enlists the initially unwilling help of Chief Constable's daughter Erica (*Nova Pilbeam*) and, after a

George Merritt, Nova Pilbeam, Derrick de Marney (being revived) and John Longden in Young and Innocent *(1937)*

hectic cross-country flight, she helps him trap the real murderer, Guy (*George Curzon*) in a crowded ballroom. Much-praised thriller now looks lesser Hitchcock, but is lean, spare, consistently holding.

RoC *Percy Marmont, Edward Rigby, Mary Clare, John Longden, Basil Radford, George Merritt, J.H. Roberts, Jerry Verno, H.F. Maltby, Pamela Carme, Torin Thatcher, Gerry Fitzgerald, Anna Konstam, Peggy Simpson, Frederick Piper, John Miller, Billy Shine, Alfred Hitchcock*.

YOUNG MAN'S FANCY (1939)   [5]

Dir *Robert Stevenson*. (Associate) Prod *S.C. Balcon*. Scr *Roland Pertwee, E.V.H. Emmett, Rodney Ackland*. Ph *Ronald Neame*. PC *Ealing Studios/CAPAD*. Dis *Associated British*. 77 mins. Cert A

A young nobleman (*Griffith Jones*) rebels against marriage with a wealthy brewery heiress and falls in love with the human cannonball (*Anna Lee*) who lands in his lap at the circus. The adventurous Miss Lee is said to have been cross at not being allowed to be fired out of the cannon herself, but must have been consoled by the best notices of her career in this

Anna Lee and Griffith Jones in Young Man's Fancy *(1939)*

refreshing, touching and funny romantic comedy.

RoC *Seymour Hicks, Billy Bennett, Edward Rigby, Francis L. Sullivan, Martita Hunt, Meriel Forbes, Felix Aylmer, Aimos, Phyllis Monkman, Morton Selten, George Carney, Violet Vanbrugh, Athene Seyler, Irene Eisinger, Allan Aynesworth, Peter Bull, Aubrey Dexter, Harry Terry*.

YOUNG WOODLEY (1930)   [5]

Dir *Thomas Bentley*. Scr *John Van Druten, Victor Kendall, from the play by Van Druten*. Ph *William Shenton*. PC *Regal Films*. Dis *Wardour*. 80 mins. Cert A

Nicely handled *Tea and Sympathy*-style story about a teenage boy (*Frank Lawton*) who falls in love with the beautiful young wife (*Madeleine Carroll*) of an elderly, pompous schoolmaster.

RoC *Sam Livesey, Billy Milton, Gerald Rawlinson, Aubrey Mather, John Teed, Tony Halfpenny, René Ray*.

YOU'RE THE DOCTOR (1938)   [3]

Dir *Roy Lockwood*. Prod *A. George Smith*. Scr *Beaufoy Milton, H.F. Maltby*. Ph *Geoffrey Faithfull*. PC *New Georgian*. Dis *British Independent*. 78 mins. Cert U

Heiress Helen (*Googie Withers*) refuses to go with her parents on a cruise with the man of their choice because she cannot stand him. She persuades a young scientist (*Barry K. Barnes*) staying at their hotel to pose as a doctor and certify her too ill to travel. She makes him drive her off into the country and eventually, though hotly pursued by her mother, marries him. Story is old hat but this treatment of it quite bright.

RoC *Norma Varden, Joan White, Gus McNaughton, Paul Blake, James Harcourt, Margaret Yarde, Aubrey Mallalieu, Bruce Seton, Eliot Makeham, Bryan Powley, Jack Vyvyan, Billy Shine, Julian Vedey, Michael Ripper*.

YOUTHFUL FOLLY (1934)   [2]

Dir *Miles Mander*. Prod *Norman Loudon*. Scr *Heinrich Frankel, from a play by Gordon Daviot*. PC *Sound City*. Dis *Columbia*. 72 mins. Cert A

An ambitious young working-class musician deserts his Balham sweetheart for a society girl. His sister persuades the girl to give him up and the London lovers are reunited. Unconvincing romantic drama.

LP *Irene Vanbrugh, Grey Blake, Jane Carr, Belle Chrystall, Mary Lawson, Arthur Chesney, Betty Ann Davies, Kenneth Kove, Eric Maturin, Merle Tottenham, Fanny Wright*.

SHORTS

Entertainment films of the 1930s between 20 and 44 minutes' duration

1930
Amateur Night in London (34)
Ashes (23)
Bedrock (39)
The Cockney Spirit in the War No. 1: All Riot on the Western Front (22)
The Cockney Spirit in the War No. 2 (30)
The Cockney Spirit in the War No. 3 (21)
Eve's Fall (34)

His First Car (35)
Infatuation (35)
The Jerry Builders (30)
Leave It to Me (39)
The Message (28)
The Musical Beauty Shop (35)
The New Waiter (35)
OK Chief (20)
Stranger Than Fiction (27)
Thread o' Scarlet (35)
Too Many Crooks (38: featuring Laurence Olivier)

1931
Aroma of the South Seas (35)
Bull Rushes (37)
Harry Lauder Songs (24)
Hot Heir (39)
How He Lied to Her Husband (33)
Lloyd of the CID (USA: Detective Lloyd. Serial in 12 episodes, each approximately 20 minutes)
M'Blimey (36: not generally released)
Morita (39)
My Old China (35)

The Other Mrs Phipps (38)
Who Killed Doc Robin? (36)
The Wrong Mr Perkins (38)

1932
Account Rendered (32)
The Bad Companions (43)
The Bailiffs (24)
The Changing Year (30)
Dual Control (20)
Flat No 9 (42)
A Letter of Warning (33)
The Merry Men of Sherwood (36)
Partners Please (34)
Postal Orders (24)
The Safe (20)
A Safe Proposition (43)
Smilin' Along (38)
The Spare Room (34)
Strip, Strip, Hooray! (36)
*A Voice Said Goodnight (35)
Women Are That Way (22)
A Yell of a Night (42)

1933
Double Bluff (35)
Hiking with Mademoiselle (40)
House of Dreams (41: not generally released)
In Our Time (23)
*Little Napoleon (44)
A Moorland Tragedy (38)
Poste Haste (20)
Screen Vaudeville No 1 (24)
Send 'Em Back Half Dead (44)
Skipper of the Osprey (29: in Raycolour: featuring Ian Hunter)
Song Birds (36)
Strictly in Confidence (42)
The Television Follies (44)
Till the Bells Ring (44)
Trouble in Store (39)

1934
Bagged (40)
The Black Skull (21)
Dangerous Companions (44)
Eight Cylinder Love (42)
Lost Over London (38)
The Man Downstairs (20)
*The Medium (38)

The Office Wife (43)
Part-Time Wife (43: not generally released)
Pathetone Parade (40)
Tell Me If It Hurts (20)
Wishes (35)
Ysani the Priestess (32)

1935
The Ghost Walks (22)
The Half-Day Excursion (30)
Kiddies on Parade (34)
*Miss Bracegirdle Does Her Duty (20: featuring Elsa Lanchester)
The Obvious Thing (20)
Old-Timers (24)
Pity the Poor Rich (22)
Polly's Two Fathers (23)
Riders to the Sea (40)
The Strange Case of Mr Todmorden (20)
Wedding Eve (39)
We've Got to Have Love (35)
*What the Parrot Saw (39)
When the Cat's Away (34)

1936
Apron Fools (34)
Bottle Party (44)
Chinese Cabaret (44)
Cocktail (27: in Spectracolour)
Digging for Gold (43)
The Dream Doctor (41)
Faust (43: in Spectracolour)
Full Steam (42)
International Revue (40)
Pal o' Mine (41)
Pathetone Parade of 1936 (36)
Pictorial Revue (40)
Railroad Rhythm (43: in Spectracolour)
Servants All (34)
Talking Hands (20: in Harmonicolour)
21 Today (34)
Unlucky Jim (44)
The Voice of Ireland (42)
What the Puppy Said (39)

1937
The Bells of St Mary's (44)
Concert Party (44)
Double Alibi (40: directed by David Macdonald)

A Dream of Love (37)
Footlights (44)
*The Gap (38)
George Bizet, Composer of Carmen (37)
Heavily Married (35)
The Inspector (34)
The Life of Chopin (36)
*Overcoat Sam (43)
*Pathétone Parade of 1938 (36)
Screen Struck (38)
Starlight Parade (38)
Uptown Revue (44)
When the Poppies Bloom Again (44)

1938
Behind the Tabs (43)
Breakers Ahead/As We Forgive (37)
*Consider Your Verdict (37: directed by Roy Boulting)
Crown Trial (20)
*Horse Sense (39)
The Interrupted Rehearsal (39)
The Landlady (35)
The Light (20)
The Mistletoe Bough (25)
Mother of Men (20: in Dufaycolour)
Revue Parade (35)
Smugglers' Harvest (43)
Spotlight (39)
Swing (37)
Take Cover (27)

1939
All Living Things (22)
Beyond Our Horizon (42)
*Happy Event (36: in Dufaycolour)
Hospital Hospitality (25)
Oh Dear Uncle! (22)
Pandamonium (27)
Pathétone Parade of 1939 (39)
*Pathétone Parade of 1940 (42)
Prince of Peace (23)
Shadow of Death (23)
Two Minutes (USA: The Silence: 42)
What Men Live By (42)

*indicates a film of above-average merit
Minutes in brackets

The Forties

Celia Johnson and Trevor Howard in *Brief Encounter* (1945)

The Forties
INTRODUCTION TO THE DECADE

The war, of course, changed everything. Matinée idols, already falling from public favour, disappeared completely from the cinema scene with the turn of the decade (the most elegant of them, Noël Coward, would next be seen begrimed and clinging to a liferaft during *In Which We Serve*), and the kind of star that appealed to the public changed completely.

Gracie Fields had fled to America with her Italian-born husband, director-comedian Monty Banks, who had been threatened with internment. Jessie Matthews, who *should* have gone there five years earlier, had her British theatrical comeback thwarted by the start of hostilities. She did go to Hollywood in 1941, but turned down the chance of starring in a musical with Fred Astaire (Rita Hayworth took over) because of a prior stage commitment, thereby finally dooming her career as an international film star.

The third of the late 1930s box-office heavyweights, George Formby, would continue in popularity until 1941, when a move from ATP/Ealing to Columbia British signalled the beginning of his decline in popularity. Formby's vehicles for his new studio lacked the technical discipline of his greatest hits, and he was out of films by 1946.

By that time an entirely new hierarchy of actors had taken over. The accent was on youth and determination, two qualities which would help to save the day in Britain's darkest wartime hours. Among those who reflected them were James Mason, who had hovered sullenly on the fringes of the film industry, but was suddenly the beast every wife wanted to be beaten by; John Mills, whose film career had wavered in the late 1930s, but who now projected sincerity that cut through social distinctions, enabling him to play upper- and working-classes with equal facility, a quality only the dangerous-looking Robert Newton could match; Stewart 'Jimmy' Granger, whose lithe good looks were undercut by a certain rakish streak that again appealed to women; and Michael Wilding, the limitations of whose upper-class image suddenly disappeared when teamed (fortuitously; a Hollywood star was unavailable) with Anna Neagle, who had resoundingly re-established her British career following a series of inconsequential musicals in Hollywood.

Despite Miss Neagle's praiseworthy resurgence, the leading female star of the decade, a flamboyant mayfly soaring from the depths of an English rose, was Margaret Lockwood.

Her role in Carol Reed's *The Stars Look Down*, released in December 1939, had given her the confidence to play bad girls, after a period of increasingly resourceful heroines. She began the decade quietly, but the heartless Hesther in *The Man in Grey* gave her the chance to project amorality with rare relish, and she continued plotting and scheming her way through the 1940s, with an occasional sidestep into a full-blooded weepie, which the public lapped up with almost equal fervour.

The Man in Grey also started the vogue, which its studio, Gainsborough, was only too happy to spearhead, for rampant period melodrama, a fashion that continued through the de-

cade, but had already reached its ultimate absurdity by 1945 in *The Wicked Lady*, with Miss Lockwood as a tempestuous, self-centred highwayman, and her *Man in Grey* co-star, James Mason, again following her path to self-destruction.

The critics were apathetic to the film and, despite its box-office takings, it was also helping to sow seeds of destruction. For too many of the heady yarns of this time were actually not very good films, their lack of scriptual intelligence being only one of the follies perpetrated in a decade which produced many excellent films, without laying the proper foundations for a flourishing industry.

Thus the British cinema never moved forward as a whole, and opportunities offered and initially built on were lost, finally swept away by yet another series of industry crises towards the end of the decade. The parable of the sower and his seed might well have been applied to the continuing state of the British film world, and never more so than in the 1940s.

Nonetheless, there were many glittering individual successes, even if the decade began with the uncertainty one would expect from a nation taking a battering from its wartime enemy. Seven of the major studios were idle at the beginning of 1940. Alexander Korda had departed for America, not to return in earnest for five years. Herbert Wilcox, too, was in Hollywood, directing Anna Neagle films. Even so, at home, loins *were* being girded. New patterns of power were being established that would govern the paths of the British cinema until well into the 1950s.

At Ealing Studios, with its family atmosphere, Michael Balcon and his team were gearing themselves up for a programme of war films, fantasies and comedies – although not yet the distinctive 'Ealing' comedies which would take shape in post-war years. And there were other producers – John Argyle (still battling on), John Corfield, Paul Soskin and Edward Black (initially with Fox British, but soon to take the reins at Gainsborough before a tragically early death at 48) willing and eager to listen to the cries of millions like the lady who wrote in to a national magazine in 1940 to say that 'I never miss a week. I find myself taken away from the war into a make-believe world, and I thank God for it.'

But the dominant figure in production was a man whose greatest asset (although one that could backfire) was, according to his associates, that he knew nothing about the making of motion pictures, thus leaving his staff and directors free from interference on the creative side. J. (for Joseph) Arthur Rank, the son of a millionaire miller, had entered the film world regrettably late in life (he was born in 1888). Initially producing religious shorts, Rank was soon seized both by evangelical enthusiasm – he was a devout Methodist – and a sense that the fate of his remaining years was to be inextricably linked with the triumphs and disasters of the British film industry.

Starting (with Lady Yule) British National films in 1934, Rank found his first major presentation, *The Turn of the Tide*, denied a booking by the major circuits. He was not a man who took such slights easily, and this was a decision he would make them regret. He gained a foothold in Gaumont-British in 1935, secured Pinewood Studios for his use in 1936 and, in 1939, combined it with Korda's Denham, which he had just taken over. He also bought Amalgamated Studios, foiling a bid by John Maxwell of Associated British, one of the men who had blocked general release of *The Turn of the Tide*, and acquired a large interest in C.M. Woolf's General Film Distributors, soon to become the largest outfit of its kind.

Illness and death were now to play roles in the final consolidation (and shaky future) of the Rank empire. John Maxwell died suddenly at the beginning of 1941, leaving Rank's business rivals in disarray. Isidore Ostrer moved to America for his wife's health, and Rank was thereby made chairman of Gaumont-British. Only weeks later, Oscar Deutsch, who had built up the Odeon circuit to over 300 cinemas (as opposed to Gaumont-British's 250 and Associated British's 350) discovered that, at 48, he had terminal cancer and only a short time to live. In a momentous decision, he asked Rank to act as chairman of the Odeon group.

It was a meteoric rise – and Rank by now had grandiose plans for British films and the final conquering of the American market.

In 1942, however, stars as well as funds were in short supply. Producers had to rely on leading actors being granted leave, or – as happened to John Mills and Stewart Granger – being invalided out early in the war, and unable to return. Thus such distinctive character actors as Wilfrid Lawson, Mervyn Johns, Edward Rigby, Alastair Sim, Basil Radford and Naunton Wayne, and, in a slightly different category, Eric Portman, Bernard Miles and William Hartnell, found themselves often elevated to a rather precarious star status.

Lawson it was, in fact, who starred in Rank's biggest film to date, *The Great Mr Handel*, a Technicolor disappointment based on the composer's life. But Rank's most successful releases for the 1940s were to come from the outposts of his now far-flung empire.

By 1944 he controlled the product of Gainsborough (with its big box-office stars), Two Cities (with directors Carol Reed and Anthony Asquith), Cineguild (including directors David Lean and Ronald Neame), Individual (the Frank Launder-Sidney Gilliat outfit), The Archers (Michael Powell and Emeric Pressburger) and Wessex, as well as British National. In the same year, he took over distribution of Balcon's Ealing Films. He now had additional studios at Shepherd's Bush and Islington, as well as the country's biggest releasing company. He controlled over 600 cinemas – although ABPC had also increased its houses to run close to the 450 mark.

Rank was different in one important aspect from almost all the Hollywood moguls, and most of the British, including Korda: he was not Jewish. Millionaire he may have been, but he lacked the innate business sense and the capacity for personal supervision of the purse strings that made so many Hollywood studios tick; all too often he locked the farmyard gate after the golden goose had flown. It was a hard lesson and Rank, who unfortunately lost the wise counsel of C.M. Woolf (who died on the last day of 1942), learned it the hard way.

At one dinner held in the early 1940s he told an audience of film-makers that he knew nothing about films, but could get the money to make them, a generalization greeted with despair in saner quarters of the industry. It was a despair well founded, as proven by the Rank extravagance that followed, bringing him to the brink of disaster before better counsels prevailed and saved the day. But, in 1942, anything looked possible. . . .

The early 1940s saw the end of the *Thin Man*-style comedy-thrillers which had featured such popular players as Barry K. Barnes, Diana Churchill, Derrick de Marney, Valerie Hobson, Margaret Vyner, Hugh Williams, Judy Kelly and Geoffrey Toone, few of whom would be the same force in post-war years. Nor would the directors of these films, most prominent among them David Macdonald, fare much better.

War films arrived, moving quickly from naivety to the grimmest of reality. *In Which We Serve* (1942, co-directed by Noël Coward and David Lean) was the first great British war film; besides being the country's top money-maker for 1943, it con-

tained in its cast many of the names coming to the forefront of British films in the 1940s: John Mills, Celia Johnson, Michael Wilding, Philip Friend, Kathleen Harrison, James Donald, Bernard Miles and Richard Attenborough among them.

Mills was also in *We Dive at Dawn*, which brought home the claustrophobic tension of war in a submarine, and in *The Way to the Stars*, a nostalgic look at the desperate wartime role played by the RAF – in both films character engrossed the audience as much as action. Mills completed a trio of huge wartime hits with his (more marginal) participation in *This Happy Breed*, directed by Lean from Coward's play, in which Ronald Neame's Technicolor photography proved the most sophisticated to date in a British film, and actually lent warmth to the subject, the life of an ordinary London family through the years.

These were all Two Cities films (sometimes in conjunction with Lean's Cineguild), a company set up by an Italian refugee, Filippo del Giudice. Rank took over control of Two Cities early in 1944, when furnishing the funds for one of their more expensive projects, *Henry V*, but del Giudice stayed on until 1947 when the two men fell out over the budgeting of another Olivier Shakespeare film, *Hamlet*.

Of these two, *Henry V*, made in Technicolor with thrilling stylized battle scenes shot in Ireland, was the most successful Shakespeare to date with the public, and Olivier won Academy Awards for both. Other Cineguild and/or Two Cities successes were *Brief Encounter* and *Blithe Spirit*, two more Lean films from Coward plays, if in very different vein not only from each other but from most wartime offerings; and Carol Reed's contribution to the war film effort, *The Way Ahead*. All of these were fine films which gave a distinctive top coating to the 15 per cent British quota now required.

Rank, however, had meanwhile caught a crab with the acquisition of Bernard Shaw nut Gabriel Pascal, and furthermore one that would not let go of his trousers pocket. Pascal's long, dreary and inordinately expensive production of *Caesar and Cleopatra*, apart from sending audiences to sleep, accounted for a large slice of Rank's dismaying loss of £1,700,000 on film production between 1945 and 1946. Worse, much worse, was to follow. And, as certain areas of the British cinema reached a peak, the fabric of the industry was collapsing behind the glittering façade.

Good, often innovative work was done by Thorold Dickinson, who made *Gaslight* and *The Queen of Spades*, the on-off Anthony Asquith, the Launder-Gilliat team (who between them contributed *Millions Like Us*, *Waterloo Road*, *Green for Danger*, *London Belongs to Me* and *The Blue Lagoon*) and the Powell-Pressburger combination, which continued to delight their devotees and infuriate their detractors. But the key names of the 1946-9 period are those of David Lean, Carol Reed and Ealing Studios.

Lean broke away from Noël Coward (although retaining John Mills, now at his peak as an actor and a box-office attraction) with *Great Expectations*, the first of two Charles Dickens adaptations which rank with *Brief Encounter* as the cream of his work. These films (*Oliver Twist* followed two years later) have almost a feel of Dickensian Gothic, as if the best of English literary tradition had been combined with the Universal horror cycle of the 1930s. The performances drip memorably with character, especially those of Finlay Currie and Martita Hunt (as Magwitch and Miss Havisham in *Expectations*) and Alec Guinness and Robert Newton (as Fagin and Bill Sikes in *Twist*), something that stems not only from fine acting and clever direction, but also from having the perfect actors available at the right time.

Lean then embarked on a series of films starring his then-wife Ann Todd, moving towards ever-more ambitious projects in which style was to outweigh effect.

Carol Reed's films are of the twentieth century, and pay careful attention to the way in which angle, shadow, editing and the pacing of dialogue scenes can add weight and effect to a narrative. They are stories of betrayal and disillusionment, yet they do not in any way have a downbeat effect on the viewer.

Reed was greatly aided by his brilliant cameramen, Robert Krasker (who had so evocatively shot the railway scenes in Lean's *Brief Encounter*) and Georges Périnal. Krasker, who also photographed *Odd Man Out*, Reed's famous story of an IRA gunman on the run through a forbidding Belfast, won an Oscar for his work on *The Third Man*, while Périnal shot *The Fallen Idol*. *The Third Man* is probably the best of this striking trio. It has the most enduring characters, some purple patches of dialogue written by Orson Welles for himself, unique theme music on zither by Anton Karas, and a director at the peak of his confidence: the whole sequence of Welles' first appearance as Lime is one of the most remarkable and dazzlingly edited in all cinema.

Meanwhile, the Ealing comedies had sparked to life almost by mistake with the taste for post-war realism. Previous Ealing comedies had been carried on from the ATP regime, with George Formby and Will Hay; Tommy Trinder had been rather uneasily converted into a character star. But suddenly, with *Hue and Cry*, there was a new whiff of laughing gas in the air, a regional flavour, if you like, as Balcon's boys moved from England to Scotland, Ireland and Wales to give their audiences a fit of the giggles. The year 1949 produced *Whisky Galore!*, *Passport to Pimlico*, *Kind Hearts and Coronets* and *A Run for Your Money*, all made by different directors, but each bearing the identifiably irreverent stamp of the same studio.

Perhaps most popular of all post-war British films, for a brief, heady time, were the high-society 'place name' affairs of Anna Neagle and Michael Wilding, directed by Herbert Wilcox. Only one of them, *Spring in Park Lane*, sparklingly scripted by Nicholas Phipps, is worthy of such adulation, but they were all hefty queue-fodder at the box-office.

Many of the profits accruing from the Ealing successes, however, were to be swallowed up at Rank by the even more costly failures. Chastened by the *London Town* affair - a spectacular comedy-musical that had cost a million pounds all barring spit and lost a sizeable portion of it after a mauling from the critics - Rank went to America to sell personally the many successful films he had been handling. It was a brave move, but it came at the wrong time. The post-war backlog of American films was flooding the country, and the dreaded Quota of British films, which had been raised from 15 to 20 per cent with the cessation of hostilities, was upped to a stunning 45 per cent in 1947, a government move which only riled the public, who had to put up with an increasingly mediocre bottom half of British production at all their major cinemas. Attendances, which had reached a peak in 1946, began gradually to fall away.

Rank, though, was near to agreements in America when, on hearing a rumour that Hollywood product was about to be subjected to tax at a fixed rate of 25 per cent, he rushed back to England, to find that, from August 1947, American films would be subject to a ridiculous 75 per cent duty - a misguided effort by the government to stem the 'dollar drain'. The result was inevitable: American stopped the export of all new films to Britain. Rank, Korda and the other moguls stepped up production, only to find themselves stepping up their losses.

The tax was repealed in May 1948 (although the Quota was not reduced until March 1949, and then only by a paltry 5 per cent), but irreparable damage had been done. Rank, never the most reliable of producers, was, without the American market deal which had been stillborn, forced to declare loans and overdrafts of more than £13,000,000, a figure which rose to more than £16,000,000 by the end of the decade, including a loss of close to £5,000,000 on actual film production.

Korda's London Films-British Lion set-up, which had also had some major disasters, including *Bonnie Prince Charlie* and *Anna Karenina* (though the latter might have benefited from the Technicolor that early publicity stills suggested) to offset its Carol Reed successes, lost over £2,000,000 in 1948 and, despite a government loan of £3,000,000, had to admit a loss of £700,000 in 1949.

By March 1949 the tremors had reached even the fan magazines. 'There is a crisis in the British film world,' *Picturegoer* told its readers. 'Studios are closing down [Highbury, Twickenham - rebuilt after destruction by a flying bomb - British National's Elstree, Shepherd's Bush and several smaller concerns had all gone under]. Reissues are being played to make up Quota. The Gainsborough and Two Cities bubbles are bursting. Technicians are out of work.'

Eight months later, things were worse. *Picturegoer* lashed out, in a *cri de coeur*. 'Some of our remaining studios [26 in 1946, nine by the end of the decade] are in an appalling mess. The film world is reeling under a series of severe blows. British film production cannot go on in the Never Never Land of the last few years. The people to blame for the economic collapse of British films are the producers.'

Well, maybe. But not without a little help from their friends. At the end of the 1940s, the government at least cut the crippling 38 per cent Entertainment Tax, and reduced British Quota to 30 per cent.

Meanwhile, British stars were taking to the lifeboats. Rex Harrison and Lilli Palmer sailed to Hollywood in November 1945. They were joined the following year by Peggy Cummins, James Mason (one of the British cinema's most outspoken critics), Philip Friend and Patricia Roc (who later returned until 1949).

Deborah Kerr went to M-G-M in 1947 and the following year saw the (temporary) departure of Phyllis Calvert. Greta Gynt and Stewart Granger left in 1949; and within another year they had been joined by Jean Simmons (following husband-to-be Granger), Michael Rennie, David Farrar and Richard Burton.

Perhaps the saddest loss, both from the British cinema's point of view and his own, was that of Michael Wilding, who probably would not have gone to Hollywood had it not been for his marriage to Elizabeth Taylor. He was totally unsuited both to the film capital and to the ridiculous roles they expected him to play, but by the time this unhappy period, and the marriage, was over, he was unable to revive his British film career.

The stars that replaced them would not go to Hollywood in such numbers; the crumbling film capital would no longer seem such an attractive proposition.

In desperation at the loss of such assets (and such cash), the beleaguered Rank turned to John Davis, an accounts wizard, to dig him out of what John Mills' Mr Polly, in one of the more successful films of 1949, would have called 'a beastly, rotten 'ole.'

Korda and others would never fully recover from the slings and arrows of the times. It would be left to the much-maligned J. Arthur Rank to carry the flag through the last of the studios years - the 1950s.

The Forties

Margaret Lockwood

As Blanquette in *The Beloved Vagabond* (1936)

A magazine, writing about three of the greatest Gainsborough ladies of the 1940s, once said that, if one wandered into Phyllis Calvert's dressing room, one might find things for the home, shopping lists and memo pads; Patricia Roc's would probably be filled with make-up and beautiful clothes. But in Margaret Lockwood's dressing room, there would be nothing but her latest script and a portrait of her daughter.

The labels of practical Phyllis, glamorous Pat and workaholic Margaret are, in each case, less than a complete portrait of the actress concerned. Even so, the remarkable Miss Lockwood, whom one still associates today with wicked ladies and beauty spots (the kind you wear), has always lived and breathed acting.

This compulsion to keep working probably led her to accept far too many inferior scripts, both in the cinema and theatre. The fact that she made only one really good film (*A Place of One's Own* in 1945) after 1943, speaks volumes for her attractive personality and the loyalty of her many thousands of fans, something emphasized by the sad truth that many of these films from the last 12 years of her major film career aren't even average, and some of them downright bad.

When doors were closed to her in films after the failure of *Cast a Dark Shadow* in 1955 (ironically, one of her better pictures), she tenaciously carved out a new career in television.

Born in Karachi, India, in 1911 or 1916, according to which biography you read, Margaret Lockwood was dead set from a

very early age on being a musical comedy star. From the age of 10 she was appearing in what she has described as 'cabarets and tea dances', making her London stage debut at 16 shortly before enrolling simultaneously at RADA and a school of dancing.

Her time at RADA encouraged her to concentrate on straight acting. Basil Dean spotted her potential when she was playing a bit part in his *Lorna Doone* (1934), and promoted her to second lead when the actress concerned, Dorothy Hyson, fell ill. Even at that early stage, Lockwood provided more than enough competition for Dean's young wife Victoria Hopper, who was playing the lead.

She was pretty and appealing as a succession of fresh, wide-eyed *ingénues* in British films of the 1930s, attracting praise both in smaller films like *Some Day* (1935) and opposite Maurice Chevalier in *The Beloved Vagabond* (1936).

Her new standing was confirmed by her touching portrayal of the nurse in Carol Reed's *Bank Holiday* and Hitchcock promptly chose her as his leading lady in *The Lady Vanishes*. She was the lynch pin in that (projecting a believable, sympathetic personality that was to stand her in good stead through her years of villainy) and was swept off to Hollywood late in 1938.

She played a couple of minor leads in Fox pictures, but could not settle in the film capital, and returned to England to play progressively more forthright roles.

She had married a businessman, Rupert Leon, in 1937, but the couple drifted apart during the war and divorced in 1949. 'He hated my films,' she said, 'and could not bear me to do love scenes.' She has not remarried, declaring that she would 'never stick my head into that noose again'.

There was a daughter, though, Margaret Julia, nicknamed Toots, who was soon appearing in her mother's films, making her debut at five in *Hungry Hill* (1946). Later, as Julia Lockwood, she played a few leads in British comedies of the 1960s.

Small wonder that the little girl was much in the limelight,

As George Arliss's daughter in *Dr Syn* (1937)

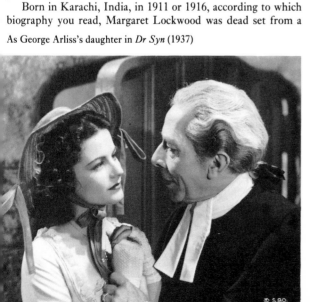

With Will Fyffe in *Owd Bob* (1937), released in 1938

As the nurse in Carol Reed's *Bank Holiday* (1937)

for her mother was Britain's top female actress for almost all of the 1940s, and actually No. 1 box-office star in 1945 and 1946, years in which national polls put her among the top five attractions in the world on British screens.

The film which started such adulation was *The Man in Grey*, in which Lockwood played her first truly unsympathetic schemer since *The Stars Look Down*, four years previously in 1939. As the actress who becomes mistress to her best friend's husband, she icily allows the friend (Phyllis Calvert) to die from pneumonia, before being whipped to death by the husband (James Mason). Audiences loved it all.

There was hardly a critic to be found willing to give *The Wicked Lady* (1945) a good review, but its production company, Gainsborough, was able to laugh all the way to the bank, as the 'risqué' theme and Lockwood's low-cut seventeenth-century dresses caused queues all round wartime cinemas.

The beauty spot on her left cheek, first seen in *A Place of One's Own*, a charmingly chilling ghost story, became a fixture from here on, as Lockwood rampaged all over the screen as the rotten apple whose marriage to her best friend's rich fiancé proves so dull that she takes to highway robbery, coming to a sticky end after shooting her lover-accomplice (Mason again).

After poisoning several husbands in *Bedelia*, and playing tempestuous girls from the wrong side of the tracks in *Hungry Hill* and *Jassy*, Lockwood handed over the role of 'bad girl of the British cinema' to Googie Withers and Jean Kent, while she resuscitated the tear-jerkers that had begun with *Love Story* in 1944. The trouble was that *Look Before You Love* and *Madness of the Heart* were simply too silly to have any chance as great cinema.

Clearly, Lockwood didn't think it mattered. 'I've never liked film critics,' she confessed. 'I don't think there was one of them that ever gave me or Phyllis or James Mason a decent notice for those Gainsborough films, even though the public adored the stuff.

'In those days, people believed anything. We never had any location shooting on *The Man in Grey* or *The Wicked Lady*. A couple of strategically placed trees and a plant or two, stuck in the studio, made a forest, and nobody asked questions.'

She was hurt, though, by critical reaction to her performance in *Cardboard Cavalier*. The film, a moderately successful vehicle for comedian Sid Field, only proved how ill-at-ease she was in farce, a genre she had never attempted before, nor since. But this time, her popularity was on the slide at last, and her film career virtually came to a standstill after a sublimely silly comedy-thriller, *Highly Dangerous*, in which a 'truth drug' torture makes her imagine she's an intrepid agent who can do anything.

Her 1950s roles were, by and large, singularly ill-advised. And so the film career of Britain's greatest woman star since Gracie Fields slipped quietly into obscurity. In retrospect, her ladies, wicked or otherwise were, by 1955, a deal too unreal for post-war audiences to take.

But, for a giddy while, those flashing, liquid eyes had a hypnotic effect on the public, proving themselves as adept at expressing love and hatred as suffering, deviousness, pity or determination. In the end she paid the penalty for the British passion for youthful stars. Hollywood, which she never liked, could well have prolonged her star career. In her peak years there was an excitement about a Lockwood film that drew the public in droves. They were sure of one thing: it wouldn't be dull.

FILMOGRAPHY.

1934: Lorna Doone. 1935: The Case of Gabriel Perry. Honours Easy. Some Day. Man of the Moment. Midshipman Easy (USA: Men of the Sea). Jury's Evidence. The Amateur Gentleman. 1936: The Beloved Vagabond. Irish for Luck. 1937: The Street Singer. Who's Your Lady Friend? Dr Syn. Melody and Romance. Owd Bob (USA: To the Victor). Bank Holiday (USA: Three on a Weekend). 1938: The Lady Vanishes. 1939: Rulers of the Sea. Susannah of the Mounties. A Girl Must Live. The Stars Look Down. 1940: Night Train to Munich (USA: Night Train). The Girl in the News. 1941: Quiet Wedding. 1942: Alibi. 1943: Dear Octopus (USA: The Randolph Family). The Man in Grey. 1944: Give Us the Moon. Love Story (USA: A Lady Surrenders). 1945: A Place of One's Own. I'll Be Your Sweetheart. The Wicked Lady. 1946: Bedelia. Hungry Hill. 1947: Jassy. The White Unicorn (USA: Bad Sister). 1948: Look Before You Love. Cardboard Cavalier. 1949: Madness of the Heart. 1950: Highly Dangerous. 1952: Trent's Last Case. 1953: Laughing Anne. 1954: Trouble in the Glen. 1955: Cast a Dark Shadow. 1976: The Slipper and the Rose.

In a few years hence to be two of the best bad girls in British films, Margaret Lockwood and Googie Withers flank director Alfred Hitchcock on the set of *The Lady Vanishes* (1938). Extreme left is Sally Stewart.

Bags and baggage: Margaret Lockwood arrives at James Mason's home in the film that established her as a bad lot – *The Man in Grey* in 1943

In the first big Gainsborough weepie, *Love Story*, with Stewart Granger in 1944

Out to poison Ian Hunter in *Bedelia* (1946)

The 1940s villainess par excellence in *The Wicked Lady* (1945)

A change to comedy was not for the better. As Nell Gwynne, she protects Sid Field's *Cardboard Cavalier* (1948)

A Rank studio portrait of 1950

The Forties

FILM OF THE DECADE

The Third Man

The British cinema has produced a select number of films that stick in the mind long after they first came out; *The Third Man* is one such, eagerly anticipated with each successive showing.

Holly (Joseph Cotten) waits for Harry at the fairground

The film's title (and its meaning), the name 'Harry Lime', the zither music of Anton Karas and the final chase through the sewers of Vienna are all fragments of movie history that have embedded themselves in our memories.

The film's genesis lies in a meeting over dinner in 1948 between author Graham Greene, film mogul Alexander Korda and director Carol Reed. Korda wanted to set a drama in war-ravaged Vienna and Reed was struck by the atmospheric possibilities. Greene contributed two sentences, which he had scribbled on the back of an envelope some time before as the thought came to him, but never followed up.

They read: 'I had paid my last farewell to Harry a week ago, when his coffin was lowered into the ground. So it was with some incredulity that I saw him pass by, without a hint of recognition, amongst the host of strangers in the Strand.'

Those sentences were enough for Korda to send Greene off to Italy, where he wrote the screenplay for *The Third Man* in eight weeks. Very little of it was in fact changed, apart from the ending. Reed's insistence that Valli walk past Joseph Cotten

instead of into his arms (after he has betrayed her lover to the police) won out over the happier ending favoured by Greene and David O. Selznick, whose business tie-up with Korda had added Cotten and Valli to the cast.

Although Noël Coward was at one time well in the running to play the engaging drug racketeer and killer Lime, Reed was lucky enough to secure the services of Orson Welles, on the run from Hollywood following *Lady from Shanghai* and *Macbeth*. Lime is still the character, above even Citizen Kane, in which moviegoers seem to remember Welles best, whether calmly crossing verbal swords with Cotten in the fairground, desperately trying to escape from the sewers, or (smiling smugly as a cat) revealing his physical presence to Cotten for the first time, his face in shadow until suddenly lit up in a doorway.

This use of light and dark, shape and shade, tilted cameras and unusual angles (cinematographer Robert Krasker deservedly won an Academy Award) helps to give the film its unique identity. Although Reed has said that his lurching cameras merely existed 'to suggest that something crooked was going on, to give the audience a feeling of unease and discomfort', the effect is more menacing than that. Krasker's use of darkness to outline the set features of a character-full group of European actors who make up the supporting cast emphasizes their hostility and the seeming hopelessness of Cotten's quest (especially as his character is not the brightest man alive) in an unfamiliar city full of hidden danger.

Valli as Anna

Joseph Cotten and Orson Welles on the big wheel

Trevor Howard, Joseph Cotten and Bernard Lee in the sewers

Orson Welles as Harry Lime

Lime (Orson Welles) trapped in the sewers

The Third Man is a film in which the behind-the-scenes factors - the style, the settings, the editing and the music, make a bigger than usual contribution. The music to form the background was something yet to be decided when Reed went to Vienna to scout locations - and discovered Anton Karas playing his zither in a small Viennese restaurant. Karas's subsequent *Harry Lime Theme* hooked itself into the minds of millions and wouldn't let go. Its enormous success as a popular record undoubtedly added to the film's potential at the box-office, the music itself reflecting the enigmatic mystery qualities of the plot.

Greene's story is a deceptively simple classic of corruption, evasion and disillusionment, the treatment placing it head and shoulders above Hollywood *noir* films of the 1940s, but bringing that particular cycle in the cinema to a shatteringly satisfactory crescendo.

Credits and Cast

Dir/Prod *Carol Reed*. Scr *Graham Greene*. Ph *Robert Krasker*. Additional ph *John Wilcox, Stan Pavey, Denys Coop, Ted Scaife*. Editor *Oswald Hafenrichter*. Mus *Anton Karas*. Design *Vincent Korda, Joseph Bato, John Hawkesworth*. Assistant dir *Guy Hamilton*. PC *London Films. Presented by Alexander Korda, David O. Selznick. 104 mins. Cert A*

Joseph Cotten (Holly Martins), Valli (Anna Schmidt), Orson Welles (Harry Lime), Trevor Howard (Major Calloway), Bernard Lee (Sergeant Paine), Ernst Deutsch (Baron Kurtz), Erich Ponto (Dr Winkel), Paul Hoerbiger (Porter), Siegfried Breuer (Popescu), Geoffrey Keen (British policeman), Wilfrid Hyde White (Crabbin), Hedwig Bleibtreu (Anna's landlady), Annie Rosar (Porter's wife), Eric Pohlmann (Proprietor), Harbut Helbek (Hansl), Alexis Chesnakov (Brodsky), Paul Hardtmuth (Porter at Sacher's), Frederick Schrecker (Hansl's father), Jenny Werner (Maid), Nelly Arno (Kurzt's mother), Leo Bieber (Barman), Martin Boddey (Man).

Valli, Joseph Cotten and Trevor Howard

Joseph Cotten relaxes off set with director Carol Reed

The Forties

A

ADAM AND EVELYNE (1949) [4]
(USA: *Adam and Evalyn*)
Dir and Prod *Harold French*. Scr *Noel Langley, Lesley Storm, George Barraud, Nicholas Phipps.* Ph *Guy Green*. PC *Two Cities*. Dis *General Film Distributors*. 92 mins. Cert A
Rich gambler Adam (*Stewart Granger*) is dismayed to find that Evelyne (*Jean Simmons*), an orphan, has been brought up with the mistaken belief that he is her father. He leaves the task of telling her the truth to his fiancée Moira (*Helen Cherry*), then sends Evelyne to a Swiss school, from which she returns a beautiful young woman with whom he falls in love, even when she calls up police to put an end to his gambling. Light romantic comedy carried well by its stars.
RoC *Joan Swinstead, Edwin Styles, Raymond Young, Beatrice Varley, Wilfrid Hyde White, Peter Reynolds, Irene Handl, Fred Johnson, Geoffrey Denton, John Forrest, Sally Newson, Jimmy Holland, Keith Falkner, Lionel Grose, Anthony Eustrel, Francis de Wolff, Brenda Hogan, Dora Bryan, Betty Blackler, Joy Harrington, Mona Washbourne, Dino Galvani, Patrick Barr, Johnnie Schofield, Edie Martin, Dennys Taylor, Max Kirby, Philip Ray, Fred Davies, Ernest Metcalfe, Patrick Baring, Elsie Wagstaffe, Bruce Waller, John Kelly.*

THE ADVENTURES OF JANE (1949) [1]
Dir *Edward G. Whiting, Alfred Goulding*. Prod *Whiting*. Scr *Whiting, Goulding, Con West*. Ph *Jack Rose*. PC *New World/Keystone*. Dis *Eros*. 55 mins. Cert A
The adventures of the famous strip-cartoon characters (created by Norman Pett) who was forever losing her clothes. In this very poor tribute to her long-running popularity, Jane (*Christabel Leighton-Porter*) is a variety artist used by a crook to smuggle diamonds into England. Jane finds out and tracks the smugglers to Brighton, where they kidnap her. Her pet dachshund carries a message under his collar which saves his mistress.
RoC *Michael Hogarth, Ian Colin, Stanelli, Wally Patch, Sebastian Cabot, Sonya O'Shea, Peter Butterworth, Sidney Benson, Charles Irwin, George Crawford, Joan Grindley.*

THE ADVENTURES OF PC 49: THE CASE OF THE GUARDIAN ANGEL (1949) [3]
Dir *Godfrey Grayson*. Prod *Anthony Hinds*. Scr *Alan Stranks, Vernon Harris, from the radio series by Alan Stranks*. Ph *Cedric Williams*. PC *Hammer*. Dis *Exclusive*. 67 mins. Cert A
A very well-bred policeman, Archibald Berkeley-Willoughby (*Hugh Latimer*), tracks down a hi-jacking gang specializing in cargoes of whisky. Trailing them to their roadside café hideout, he becomes one of the gang, and, with the help of his girlfriend Joan (*Patricia Cutts*) turns gangleader Ma Brady (*Pat Nye*) and her evil henchmen over to the arms of the law. Unconventional radio character somewhat straitjacketed in conventional plot.
RoC *John Penrose, Annette Simmonds, Arthur Brander, Eric Phillips, Martin Benson, Michael Ripper, Billy Thatcher.*

THE ADVENTURES OF TARTU (1943) [4]
(USA: *Tartu*)
Dir *Harold S. Bucquet*. Prod *Irving Asher*. Scr *Howard Emmet Rogers, John Lee Mahin, Miles Malleson*. Ph *John J. Cox*. PC and Dis *MGM British*. 103 mins. Cert A
Terence Stevenson (*Robert Donat*), a British agent, is assigned to blow up a poison gas plant in Czechoslovakia. He takes the name Tartu, and contacts the Czech underground, who prove more hindrance than help. Eventually he achieves his objective, escaping from the factory as it goes up in flames. Maruschka (*Valerie Hobson*), beautiful guerilla leader, goes with him back to England. Familiar, straightforward thriller, lifted a bit by its star performance.
RoC *Walter Rilla, Glynis Johns, Phyllis Morris, Martin Miller, Anthony Eustrel, Percy Walsh, Frederick Richter, John Penrose, Mabel Terry Lewis, David Ward, Hubert Leslie, Alexander Karden, John Boxer.*

AGAINST THE WIND (1948) [3]
Dir *Charles Crichton*. (Associate) Prod *Sidney Cole*. Scr *T. E. B. Clarke, Michael Pertwee, P. Vincent Carroll*. Ph *Lionel Banes*. PC *Ealing Studios*. Dis *General Film Distributors*. 96 mins. Cert A
Five Allied saboteurs are parachuted into Belgium to try to free a fellow saboteur in the hands of the Germans. One (*Jack Warner*)

Simone Signoret in Against the Wind (*1948*)

proves to be a traitor and has to be shot. Another (*Gordon Jackson*) loses his life through a moment's hesitation. The remaining three, after several hairsbreadth escapes, succeed in their mission. Quite exciting, but rather implausible and spottily cast.
RoC *Robert Beatty, Simone Signoret, Paul Dupuis, Gisèle Préville, John Slater, Peter Illing, James Robertson Justice, Sybilla Binder, Helen Hanson, Eugene Deckers, André Morell, Gilbert Davis, Andrew Blackett, Arthur Lawrence, Leo de Pokorny, Rory MacDermott, Olaf Olsen, Kenneth Hyde, Guy Deghy, Philo Hauser, Robert Wyndham, Kenneth Villiers, Martin Bradley, Sheila Carty, Duncan Lewis, John Boxer.*

THE AGITATOR (1945) [3]
Dir *John Harlow*. Prod *Louis H. Jackson*. Scr *Edward Dryhurst, from a novel by William Riley*. Ph *James Wilson*. PC *British National*. Dis *Anglo-American*. 104 mins. Cert U
Pettinger (*Billy Hartnell*), a young mechanic at Overend's, is angry because he feels his father was cheated out of money for an invention. Old Mr Overend (*Frederick Leister*) hears of this, and leaves the works to Pettinger who, after six turbulent months as managing director, learns to be more tolerant of his fellow man. Thought-provoking drama becomes too light in later stages.
RoC *Mary Morris, John Laurie, Moore Marriott, George Carney, Edward Rigby, Elliot Mason, J. H. Roberts, Cathleen Nesbitt, Moira Lister.*

ALIBI (1942) [4]
Dir *Brian Desmond Hurst*. Prod *Josef Somlo*. Scr *Lesley Storm, from a screenplay by Jacques Companeez, Justine and R. Carter and the novel by Marcel Archard*. Ph *Otto Heller*. PC *Corona*. Dis *British Lion*. 82 mins. Cert A
Pre-war Paris: a nightclub owner, Hélène (*Margaret Lockwood*), in need of money, accepts a huge bribe to supply an alibi to her star turn, a mind-reader (*Raymond Lovell*), after he has killed a man. Inspector Calas (*Hugh Sinclair*) has an idea she is lying and uses one of his men, Laurent (*James Mason*), to make her fall in love with him, then pretends to arrest him for the murder. Hélène is furious at first, but eventually forgives Laurent, whom she really loves. Quite creditable remake of French thriller *L'alibi*.
RoC *Enid Stamp-Taylor, Jane Carr, Hartley Power, Rodney Ackland, Edana Romney, Elisabeth Welch, Olga Lindo, Muriel George, George Merritt, Judy Grey, Philip Leaver, Derek Blomfield, Clarie Wear's Embassy Orchestra.*

ALL OVER THE TOWN (1948) [3]
Dir *Derek Twist*. Prod *Ian Dalrymple*. Scr *Twist, Michael Gordon, Inez Holden, Stafford Byrne, from a story by R. F. Delderfield*. Ph *C. M. Pennington-Richards*. PC *Wessex*. Dis *General Film Distributors*. 88 mins. Cert U
Nat (*Norman Wooland*) becomes part-owner of the paper for which he works. He investigates a proposed housing scheme, causing Councillor Baines (*James Hayter*) to push his (shady) plans through fast. He also causes most

of Nat's workforce to desert him, but the story is printed against all odds and Nat and his girlfriend Sally (*Sarah Churchill*) soon have the support of the town. Pleasant, rather rambling drama.

RoC *Cyril Cusack, Fabia Drake, Edward Rigby, Patric Doonan, Eleanor Summerfield, Bryan Forbes, John Salew, Henry Edwards, Sandra Dorne, Frederick Leister, Ronald Adam, Trefor Jones, Anthony Oliver, J. Hubert Leslie, Erik Chitty, Patrick Macnee, Walter Horsbrugh, Lydia Bilbrook, Stanley Baker.*

THE ANGEL WITH THE TRUMPET (1949) [3]

Dir *Anthony Bushell*. Prod *Karl Hartl*. Scr *Hartl, Franz Tassie, Clemence Dane, from a novel by Ernst Lothar*. Ph *Robert Krasker*. PC *London Films*. Dis *British Lion*. *98 mins*. *Cert U*

1888. The Alts are Viennese piano-makers. Francis Alt (*Basil Sydney*) announces he is to marry half-Jewish Henrietta Stein (*Eileen Herlie*), ex-mistress of Crown Prince Rudolf; the prince is found dead that night at Mayerling. Wars and tragedies intervene, but the Alts go on. Francis is paralysed in the First World War. His son becomes a Nazi. The Nazis come to Vienna, and Henrietta takes her own way out.... In 1946, the youngest Alt and his wife decide to start making pianos again, from their bomb-hit factory. Long, languorous saga, an English-language version of *Der Engel mit der Posaune* (1948).

RoC *Norman Wooland, Maria Schell, Olga Edwardes, John Justin, Oskar Werner, Andrew Cruickshank, Anthony Bushell, Wilfred Hyde White, Campbell Cotts, Dorothy Batley, John Van Eyssen, Jane Henderson, Jill Gibbs, Brian Crown, Allan Woolstan, John Corbett, Titia Brookes, Anton Edthofer, Alfred Neugebauer, Joan Schofield, R. Meadows White, Jack Faint, David Davies, Nigel Neilson, Derrick Penley, Olive Gregg, Marc Anthony.*

ANNA KARENINA (1947) [3]

Dir *Julien Duvivier*. Prod *Alexander Korda*. Scr *Duvivier, Jean Anouilh, Guy Morgan, from the novel by Leo Tolstoy*. Ph *Henri Alekan*. PC *London Films*. Dis *British Lion*. *139 mins (later 123)*. *Cert A*

Anna (*Vivien Leigh*), wife of Karenin (*Ralph Richardson*), a civil servant in 1875 Moscow, falls for Czarist officer Vronsky (*Kieron Moore*). They eventually become lovers, and Karenin resolves to divorce her, taking his son. Anna gives birth to Vronsky's stillborn son. Shunned by society, Vronsky decides to leave Moscow, alone. Convinced she has lost him, Anna boards her train. When it stops, she wanders distraught along the line and is killed by an oncoming train. Lavishly produced, but slow, dull and bloodless.

RoC *Sally Ann Howes, Niall MacGinnis, Martita Hunt, Marie Lohr, Michael Gough, Hugh Dempster, Mary Kerridge, Heather Thatcher, Helen Haye, Austin Trevor, John Longden, Leslie Bradley, Ruby Miller, Michael Medwin, Jeremy Spenser, Gino Cervi, Frank Tickle, Mary Martlew, Ann South, Guy Verney, Beckett Bould, Judith Nelmes, Valentina Murch, Ther-*

esa Giehse, John Salew, Patrick Skipwith, Michael Gough, Barbara Murray.

ANOTHER SHORE (1948) [3]

Dir *Charles Crichton*. (Associate) Prod *Ivor Montagu*. Scr *Walter Meade, from the novel by Kenneth Reddin*. Ph *Douglas Slocombe*. PC *Ealing Studios*. Dis *General Film Distributors*. *91 mins*. *Cert U*

Irishman Gulliver (*Robert Beatty*) dreams of a life on the South Sea Islands. He assists an old man in an accident, who is rich enough to help him fulfil his dream. They make plans to go to the Pacific, but the love of Jennifer (*Moira Lister*) keeps Gulliver on a more familiar shore. Nicely photographed whimsy is otherwise none too successful.

RoC *Stanley Holloway, Michael Medwin, Maureen Delany, Fred O'Donovan, Sheila Manahan, Desmond Keane, Dermot Kelly, Michael Golden, W. A. Kelley, Wilfrid Brambell, Irene Worth, Bill Shine, Edie Martin, Michael Dolan, Michael O'Mahoney, Madame Kirkwood Hackett.*

Moira Lister, Robert Beatty and Michael Medwin in Another Shore (*1948*)

APPOINTMENT WITH CRIME (1946) [4]

Dir and Scr *John Harlow*. Prod *Louis H. Jackson*. Ph *James Wilson*. PC *British National*. Dis *Anglo-American*. *97 mins*. *Cert A*

A falling shutter traps the wrists of petty criminal Leo Martin (*William Hartnell*) in a robbery, and his 'friends' leave him to his fate. On release from prison, he murders one and frames the other, Loman (*Raymond Lovell*), who turns to gang leader Lang (*Herbert Lom*) for help. Lang kills him. Martin gets in with the gang, but when he asks Lang for money to go off to a new life, Lang refuses. There is a fight and Lang is shot. Martin tries to escape, but is ironically trapped again by the wrists. Strong, credible thriller.

RoC *Joyce Howard, Robert Beatty, Alan Wheatley, Cyril Smith, Ivor Barnard, John Rorke, Ernest Butcher, Kenneth Warrington, Wilfrid Hyde White, Albert Chevalier, Elsie Wagstaffe, Ian Fleming, Ian MacLean, Harry Lane, Paul Croft, Alfred A. Harris, Howard Douglas, Frederick Morant, Joe Cunningham, Anders Timberg, Victor Weske, James Knight, Harry Terry, James Robertson (Justice), Percy Coyte, André Belhomme, Elizabeth London, John Clifford, Jimmy Rhodes, Gaston and Helen, Elizabeth Webb, Lew Stone and His Band, Buddy Featherstonehaugh and His Sextette.*

ASKING FOR TROUBLE (1942) [3]

Dir *Oswald Mitchell*. Prod *Wallace Orton*. Scr *Mitchell, Con West*. Ph *Jimmy Wilson*. PC *British National*. Dis *Anglo-American*. *81 mins*. *Cert U*

Fishmonger Dick Smith (*Max Miller*) is jailed for bookmaking, but escapes. Finding a girl locked in his flat, he agrees to help her out of a fix by posing as a white hunter. He arrives at her home with his fellow-escapee blacked up as his servant, and an elephant in tow. The real hunter turns up, but Dick talks his way out of trouble and flees, still one jump ahead of the law. Chatterbox comedy: the plot deserves a mark for cheek.

RoC *Carole Lynne, Mark Lester, Wilfrid Hyde White, Billy Percy, Aubrey Mallalieu, Kenneth Kove, Eleanor Hallam, Chick Elliott, Raymond Glendenning, Wally Patch, Esma Cannon, Lesley Osmond.*

THE ASTONISHED HEART (1949) [2]

Dir *Antony Darnborough, Terence Fisher*. Prod *Darnborough*. Scr *Noël Coward, from his play*. Ph *Jack Asher*. PC *Gainsborough*. Dis *General Film Distributors*. *89 mins*. *Cert U*

A psychiatrist (*Noël Coward*) falls for his wife's beautiful friend (*Margaret Leighton*). He loses his grip at work, develops jealous fits about his mistress. His wife (*Celia Johnson*) gives him up and sends them on a trip round Europe. After a final quarrel on their return, he throws himself from a high building. Dreary triangle drama in very dated style. Coward replaced Michael Redgrave during filming.

RoC *Joyce Carey, Graham Payn, Amy Veness, Ralph Michael, Michael Hordern, Patricia Glyn, Everley Gregg, Alan Webb, John Salew, Gerald Anderson, John Warren.*

ATLANTIC FERRY (1941) [4]
(USA: *Sons of the Sea*)

Dir *Walter Forde*. Prod *Max Milder*. Scr *Gordon Wellesley, Edward Dryhurst, Emeric Pressburger*. Ph *Basil Emmott*. PC and Dis *Warner Bros*. *108 mins*. *Cert U*

The saga of the first regular steamship service between England and America, depicting the horrendous below-decks conditions of early 'coffin ships'. Two brothers join rival firms after their first joint venture fails. In an 1840 race between a steamship and a fast sailing-vessel, one brother dies. Stirring stuff, although the model work leaves something to be desired by later standards.

LP *Michael Redgrave, Griffith Jones, Valerie Hobson, Margaretta Scott, Bessie Love, Hartley Power, Milton Rosmer, Frederick Leister, Henry Oscar, Edmund Willard, Charles Victor, Leslie Bradley, Felix Aylmer, Frank Tickle, Joss Ambler, Ian MacLean, Joe Cunningham, James Harcourt, David Keir, Jean Lester, Roddy Hughes, Aubrey Mallalieu, James Knight.*

B

BACK ROOM BOY (1942) [3]

Dir *Herbert Mason*. Prod *Edward Black*. Scr *Val Guest, Marriott Edgar*. Ph *Jack Cox*. PC *Gainsborough*. Dis *General Film Distributors*. 82 mins. *Cert U*

Bored BBC backroom boy Arthur Pilbeam (*Arthur Askey*) syncopates the news 'pips', and finds himself banished to the weather station at an isolated lighthouse. To his delight, a boatload of models is shipwrecked – then the girls start to vanish one by one. Nazi spies are behind it, but Arthur gets the better of them, also posing as a mermaid to lure an enemy battleship into a minefield. Askey comedy doesn't quite have the courage of its craziness. RoC *Moore Marriott, Graham Moffatt, Googie Withers, Vera Frances, Joyce Howard, John Salew, George Merritt.*

Arthur Askey in Back Room Boy *(1942)*

BADGER'S GREEN (1948) [3]

Dir *John Irwin*. Prod *John Croydon*. Scr *William Fairchild, from the play by R. C. Sherriff*. Ph *Walter Harvey*. PC *Production Facilities*. Dis *General Film Distributors*. 62 mins. *Cert U*

Pocket version of Sherriff's hit play about a businessman who tries to buy up the cricketing village of Badger's Green to build bungalows and an amusement park. Even long-standing feuds are forgotten as the villagers not surprisingly present a united front against him. Everything is finally settled on the result of a cricket match. Gently paced, mild little comedy-drama, filmed previously in 1934. LP *Barbara Murray, Brian Nissen, Garry Marsh, Kynaston Reeves, Laurence Naismith, Mary Merrall, Jack McNaughton, Norman Pierce, Duncan Lewis, Grace Arnold, Linda Grey, Sam Kydd, James Lomas, Patience Rentoul, Richard Gilbert.*

THE BAD LORD BYRON (1948) [1]

Dir *David Macdonald*. Prod *Aubrey Baring*. Scr *Terence Young, Anthony Thorne, Peter Quennell, Lawrence Kitchin, Paul Holt*. Ph *Stephen Dade*. PC *Triton*. Dis *General Film Distributors*. 85 mins. *Cert A*

The poet Byron (*Dennis Price*) has his life and loves reviewed by a heavenly tribunal, his vices and virtues expounded by a stream of witnesses. His sundry love affairs are recounted in detail. Ultimately, the audience is left to decide for itself whether George Gordon, Lord Byron, was hero, genius or libertine – or all three. Dull, fragmented and embarrassingly unconvincing. Bad is the word. RoC *Mai Zetterling, Joan Greenwood, Linden Travers, Sonia Holm, Raymond Lovell, Leslie Dwyer, Denis O'Dea, Nora Swinburne, Ernest Thesiger, Irene Browne, Barry Jones, Henry Oscar, Archie Duncan, John Salew, Wilfrid Hyde White, Liam Gaffney, Betty Lynne, Ronald Adam, Zena Marshall, Cyril Chamberlain, Robert Harris, Natalie Moya, John Stone, Gilbert Davis, Richard Molinas, Vincent Holman, Guy le Feuvre, Aubrey Mallalieu, Desmond Roberts, Lena Lanare, Leo (Virgilio) Texera, Gerard Heinz, Bernard Rebel.*

BAIT (1949) [1]

Dir and Prod *Frank Richardson*. Scr *Mary Bendetta, Francis Miller, from a play by Richardson*. Ph *Ernest Palmer*. PC *Advance*. Dis *Adelphi*. 73 mins. *Cert A*

The adventures of a gang of jewel thieves, led by a woman, Eleanor (*Diana Napier*, slumming it in extraordinary fashion) who frames her enemy for the murder of his half-brother. With the help of his girlfriend, he turns the tables. Dreary quota picture, badly made. RoC *John Bentley, Patricia Owens, John Oxford, Kenneth Hyde, Sheila Robins, Willoughby Goddard, Douglas Trow, Richard Gatehouse, Jack Gracey.*

THE BALLOON GOES UP (1942) [2]

Dir *Redd Davis*. Prod *E.J. Fancey*. Scr *Val Valentine*. Ph *Stephen Dade*. PC and Dis *New Realm*. 58 mins. *Cert U*

Combination of music and comedy, with *Ethel Revnell* and *Gracie West* as two entertainers who masquerade as WAAFs on a balloon site in order to help the authorities round up a group of fifth columnists. Modest in aim and execution, this balloon barely rises. RoC *Donald Peers, Ronald Shiner, Elsie Wagstaffe, Gertrude Maesmore Morris, Gordon McLeod.*

BANANA RIDGE (1941) [3]

Dir and Prod *Walter C. Mycroft*. Scr *Mycroft, Lesley Storm, Ben Travers, from the play by Travers*. Ph *Claude Friese-Greene*. PC *Associated British*. Dis *Pathé*. 87 mins. *Cert A*

Business associates Pink and Pound (*Robertson Hare, Alfred Drayton*) are horrified when adventuress Sue Long (*Isabel Jeans*) arrives and says that one of them is the father of her 23-year-old son. Pound blackmails Pink into taking the boy away to their plantation in Malaya. But Sue finds the boy's real father there, and the boy marries Pound's daughter. Spirited but unfunny farce. RoC *Patrick Kinsella, Nova Pilbeam, Adèle Dixon, Stewart Rome, John Stuart, Gordon McLeod, Mignon O'Doherty, Valentine Dunn, Basil Lynn, Wally Patch, Lloyd Pearson, Ley On, Audrey Boyes, Charles Stewart.*

BATTLE FOR MUSIC (1943) [4]

Dir and Prod *Donald Taylor*. Scr *St John L. Clowes*. PC *Strand Films*. Dis *Anglo-American*. 79 mins (later 75). *Cert U*

The story of the London Philharmonic Orchestra. Thanks to various backers, the orchestra carries on through numerous wartime crises, even surviving the loss of all its instruments in the burning of the Queen's Hall in 1941. Unusual, appealing film, a treat for music lovers. LP *Hay Petrie, Mavis Clair, Joss Ambler, Charles Carson, Dennis Wyndham, Ben Williams, Antony Holles, Clifford Buckton, Jack Hylton, David Keir, Thomas Russell, Charles Gregory; and J.B. Priestley, Bryan Michie, Eileen Joyce, Moiseiwitch, Sir Adrian Boult, Sir Malcolm Sargent, Warwick Braithwaite, Constant Lambert, London Philharmonic Orchestra.*

BEDELIA (1946) [3]

Dir *Lance Comfort*. Prod *Isadore Goldsmith*. Scr *Vera Caspary, Herbert Victor, Goldsmith, Moie Charles, Roy Ridley, from the novel by Caspary*. Ph *Frederick A. Young*. PC *John Corfield*. Dis *General Film Distributors*. 90 mins. *Cert A*

1938. Bedelia (*Margaret Lockwood*) has bumped off three husbands and, having persuaded the fourth (*Ian Hunter*) to insure himself up to the neck, prepares to poison him. When she realizes that detective Ben (*Barry K. Barnes*) is on to her, she tries to poison him instead. Her husband realizes the truth, confronts her with it, and leaves her with the poison. Hasn't much depth or conviction, but the public swallowed the potion whole. RoC *Anne Crawford, Jill Esmond, Barbara Blair, Louise Hampton, Ellen Pollock, Julien Mitchell, Kynaston Reeves, Beatrice Varley, Olga Lindo, John Salew, Claude Bailey, Paul Bonifas, Marcel Poncin, (Michael) Martin Harvey, Sonia Sergyl, Aubrey Mallalieu, Oscar Nation, David Keir, Jill Bardi, Elizabeth Maude, Madoline Thomas, Claude Frederic, Yvonne André, Alice Gachet, John Allen, Charles Paton, John Serret, Michelle de Lys, Paul Hardtmuth, George Pelling, Dermot Walsh, Al Gold and Lola Cordell.*

BEES IN PARADISE (1944) [1]

Dir *Val Guest*. Prod *Edward Black*. Scr *Guest, Marriott Edgar*. Ph *Phil Grindrod*. PC *Gainsborough*. Dis *General Film Distributors*. 75 mins. *Cert A*

A ferry-boat crew is stranded on a South Atlantic island ruled by women. Arthur (*Arthur Askey*), in love with Jani (*Jean Kent*), has to marry Rouana (*Anne Shelton*), tries to escape and is sentenced to jump from a high rock, or paddle a canoe out into the ocean. He chooses the latter, but Rouana pursues him over the horizon. After this disastrously unprofessional comedy, Askey quit films for 10 years. RoC *Peter Graves, Max Bacon, Ronald Shiner, Antoinette Cellier, Joy Shelton, Beatrice Varley, Joy Millan, Pat(ricia) Owens.*

BELL-BOTTOM GEORGE (1943) [3]

Dir *Marcel Varnel*. Prod *Ben Henry*. Scr *Peter Fraser, Edward Dryhurst, John L. Arthur*. Ph

Roy Fogwell. PC and Dis *Columbia British. 97 mins. Cert U*

When a sailor friend 'borrows' his clothes, George (*George Formby*) is forced to don the naval uniform. Picked up by the shore patrol, he has to masquerade as his friend. After many farcical misfortunes, he becomes a hero by exposing a nest of spies at the naval base. Hardly one of the star's best; tunes include the title song and *Swim Little Fish.*

RoC *Anne Firth, Reginald Purdell, Peter Murray Hill, Charles Farrell, Eliot Makeham, Manning Whiley, Hugh Dempster, Dennis Wyndham, Jane Welsh, Peter Gawthorne, Felix Aylmer, Ian Fleming.*

THE BELLS GO DOWN (1943) [4]

Dir *Basil Dearden.* (Associate) Prod *S. C. Balcon.* Scr *Roger Macdougall, from the novel by Stephen Black.* Ph *Ernest Palmer.* PC *Ealing Studios.* Dis *United Artists.* 90 mins. Cert U

Bob Matthews (*Philip Friend*) postpones his wedding to join the Auxiliary Fire Service in the war. Other 'part-timers' under Leading Fireman Robbins (*James Mason*) are Sam (*Mervyn Johns*), a petty thief, and Tommy (*Tommy Trinder*), greyhound fan and self-termed wit. Bob gets married only to watch his house burn down while he fights a warehouse blaze. Sam saves the life of the policeman who was after him. Tommy dies in a fruitless attempt to save the fire chief. Fairly authentic wartime camaraderie yarn had the misfortune to be released at the same time as the classic documentary *Fires Were Started.*

RoC *Finlay Currie, Philippa Hiatt, Billy (William) Hartnell, Meriel Forbes, Beatrice Varley, Muriel George, Norman Pierce, Lesley Brook, Julien Vedey, Richard George, Victor Weske, Leslie Harcourt, Frederick Culley, Stanley Lathbury, Johnnie Schofield, Leslie Dwyer, Alfie Bass, Sydney Tafler, Patricia Dainton.*

BEWARE OF PITY (1946) [4]

Dir *Maurice Elvey.* Prod *W. P. Lipscomb.* Scr *Lipscomb, Elizabeth Baron, Margaret Steen, from the novel by Stefan Zweig.* Ph *Derek Williams.* PC *Two Cities.* Dis *Eagle-Lion. 106 mins. Cert A*

Out of pity, a young Austrian officer (*Albert Lieven*) allows the hopelessly crippled daughter (*Lilli Palmer*) of a wealthy baron to fall in love with him. He at first tries to escape without hurting her but, seeing how the girl's doctor (*Cedric Hardwicke*) and his blind wife (*Gladys Cooper*) have faced their own problems, recognizes the depth of his involvement and returns. But the girl has committed suicide. Spun out, but makes the most of what it has.

RoC *Linden Travers, Ernest Thesiger, Emrys Jones, Gerhardt Kempinski, Ralph Truman, John Salew, Peter Cotes, Godfrey Parker, Freda Jackson, Jenny Laird, Kenneth Warrington, Miles Malleson, Frederick Wendhausen, David Ward, Tony Dawson, Cameron Hall, Hannah Norbert, Miki Iveria, Harold Norway, Gordon Phillott, Miles Silverton, Alan Jennings, Lea Court, Vida Hope, Derek Gorst, John Howard, Anders Timberg.*

THE BIG BLOCKADE (1941) [4]

Dir *Charles Frend.* (Associate) Prod *Alberto Cavalcanti.* Scr *Angus Macphail,* (uncredited) *Frend.* Ph *Wilkie Cooper, Douglas Slocombe.* PC *Ealing Studios.* Dis *United Artists.* 73 mins (later 68). Cert U

Propaganda film, effective as such, about the use of economic warfare, together with strikes by the Royal Navy and RAF. The climax is a reconstruction of a giant night-time bomber raid, following the fortunes of one plane, its pilot (*Michael Rennie*) and navigator (*John Mills*). The plane is hit by anti-aircraft fire, but its bombs reach their target.

RoC *Leslie Banks, Michael Redgrave, Will Hay, Frank Cellier, Robert Morley, Alfred Drayton, Bernard Miles, Marius Goring, Austin Trevor, Morland Graham, Albert Lieven, John Stuart, Joss Ambler, Michael Wilding, David Evans, George Woodbridge, Leif Konow, Peter de Greff, Cyril Chamberlain, Percy Walsh, George Merritt, Bernard Rebel, Charles Minor, Lawrence Kingston, Quentin Reynolds, Hon. David Bowes-Lyon, Hugh Dalton, James Knight, Griffith Jones, Stewart Rome, Elliot Mason, Frank Owen* (commentator).

Michael Rennie and John Mills in The Big Blockade *(1941)*

BLACK MEMORY (1947) [4]

Dir *Oswald Mitchell.* Prod *Gilbert Church.* Scr *John Gilling.* Ph *S. D. Onions.* PC *Bushey.* Dis *Ambassador.* 73 mins. Cert A

Danny (*Michael Atkinson*) runs away from reform school, tormented by Johnny (*Michael Medwin*), a boy who had given evidence that had sent Danny's father to the gallows. Years later, Danny returns. Johnny tries to get him involved in a warehouse robbery, but Danny gets an old friend's daughter out of trouble before extracting a confession from Johnny that clears his father's name. Gripping street-level thriller.

RoC *Myra O'Connell, Jane Arden, Frank Hawkins, Winifred Melville, Betty Miller, Sidney James, Michael Conry, Arthur Brander, Gerald Pring, Valerie Hulton, Maurice Nicholas, Malcolm Sommers.*

BLACK NARCISSUS (1947) [5]

Dir, Prod and Scr *Michael Powell, Emeric Pressburger, from the novel by Rumer Godden.* Ph *Jack Cardiff.* PC *The Archers/Independent Producers.* Dis *General Film Distributors.* Technicolor. 100 mins. Cert A

Five nuns open a school and hospital in a disused palace in the Himalayas. The young local ruler (*Sabu*) attends school, but later runs off with a beautiful native girl (*Jean Simmons*). After a nun treats a child that dies, the villagers desert the convent. Sister Ruth (*Kathleen Byron*) goes mad, throws herself unsuccessfully at the local agent (*David Farrar*), then attacks Sister Clodagh (*Deborah Kerr*) in the bell tower, falling to her death. Sister Clodagh leaves with the remaining nuns, humbled but spiritually stronger. Very stately, but striking, at times memorable film. Oscars for best colour photography, best art direction.

RoC *Flora Robson, Jenny Laird, Judith Furse, Esmond Knight, Shaun Noble, May Hallatt, Nancy Roberts, Eddie Whaley Jr, Ley On.*

THE BLACK SHEEP OF WHITEHALL (1941) [4]

Dir *Will Hay, Basil Dearden.* Prod *Michael Balcon.* Scr *Angus Macphail, John Dighton.* Ph *Gunther Krampf.* PC *Ealing Studios.* Dis *United Artists.* 80 mins (later 77). Cert U

Professor Davis (*Will Hay*), who runs an unsuccessful correspondence course, is mistaken for economics expert Professor Davys and is interviewed about his part in a trade agreement. The 'real' Davys arrives, but the Prof and his pupil Bobby (*John Mills*) discover he's a fake: the genuine Davys has been kidnapped by Nazi sympathisers. They rescue him and escape in a motor-cycle, sidecar and bathchair. The Prof gets a 'highly placed' position as a reward – on a rooftop looking out for enemy planes. More slapstick than usual in Hay comedy, but it's fast and funny.

RoC *Basil Sydney, Felix Aylmer, Henry Hewitt, Owen Reynolds, Frank Cellier, Joss Ambler, Frank Allenby, Thora Hird, Dorothy Hamilton, Margaret Halstan, Barbara Valerie, Agnes Laughlan, Leslie Mitchell, Ronald Shiner, Kenneth Griffith, Cyril Chamberlain.*

BLANCHE FURY (1948) [3]

Dir *Marc Allegret.* Prod *Anthony Havelock-Allan.* Scr *Audrey Erskine Lindop, Hugh Mills, Cecil McGivern.* Ph *Guy Green, Geoffrey Unsworth.* PC *Cineguild/Independent Producers.* Dis *General Film Distributors.* Technicolor. 95 mins. Cert A.

Blanche (*Valerie Hobson*) is asked by her rich uncle, Simon Fury (*Walter Fitzgerald*) to be governess to his widowed son Lawrence's (*Michael Gough*) daughter. Blanche agrees to marry Lawrence, although in love with Philip (*Stewart Granger*), an illegitimate Fury who believes the estate to be rightfully his. Philip shoots both Simon and Lawrence in the guise of a gipsy, but when he decides to kill the daughter too, Blanche gives him to the law. Philip is hanged and Blanche dies giving birth to his child. Another happy story, typical of its period.

RoC *Maurice Denham, Sybilla Binder, Edward Lexy, Allan Jeayes, Suzanne Gibbs, Ernest Jay, George Woodbridge, Arthur Wontner, Amy Veness, Bryan Herbert, W. E. Clifton James, Cherry London, Townsend Whitling, Lionel Grose, Margaret Withers, Norman Pierce, Wilfred Caithness, James Dale, Roddy Hughes, John Marquand, J. H. Roberts, Lance George, Roy Arthur, Hilary Pritchard, Michael Brennan, Charles Saynor, Alexander Field.*

BLESS 'EM ALL (1948) [3]

Dir and Prod *Robert Jordan Hill*. Scr *C. Boganny, Hal Monty*. Ph *S. D. Onions*. PC *Advance*. Dis *Adelphi*. 79 mins. Cert U
1939. Skimpy, Tommy and Jock (*Hal Monty, Max Bygraves, Jack Milroy*) pal up on joining the army, but soon fall foul of bellowing Sergeant Willis (*Les Ritchie*), especially when Tommy falls for Willis's friend Val (*Patricia Linova*), an ENSA entertainer. Tommy is wounded at Dunkirk and the comrades don't meet again until D-Day. Val proves to be Willis's daughter and marries Tommy. Pretty sketchy but very funny in parts.
RoC *Stanley White, Sybil Amiel, Vic Ford, Christopher Sheen.*

THE BLIND GODDESS (1948) [4]

Dir *Harold French*. Prod *Betty Box*. Scr *Muriel Box, Sydney Box, from the play by Patrick Hastings*. Ph *Ray Elton*. PC *Gainsborough*. Dis *General Film Distributors*. 87 mins. Cert A
Derek (*Michael Denison*), secretary to Lord Brasted (*Hugh Williams*) is told by a friend that Brasted has been converting funds of the International Relief Organization to his own use – but there is no proof. Derek, who was once in love with Lady Brasted (*Anne Crawford*) quizzes Lord Brasted, who offers him £10,000 and a job in West Africa. Derek has a hard time proving the case against his employer, but eventually does so in the high court, with the help of a brilliant KC (*Eric Portman*). A lot of talk, but most of it engrossing.
RoC *Nora Swinburne, Raymond Lovell, Claire Bloom, Frank Cellier, Clive Morton, Elspet Gray, Maurice Denham, Martin Benson, Carl Jaffe, Cecil Bevan, John Stone, Philip Saville, Martin Benson, Cyril Chamberlain, Thora Hird, Rosemary Treston, Marcel Poncin, Martin Miller, Geoffrey Denton, Noel Howlett.*

BLITHE SPIRIT (1945) [5]

Dir *David Lean*. Prod *Anthony Havelock-Allen*. Scr *Noël Coward, Lean, Havelock-Allen, Ronald Neame, from Coward's play*. Ph *Neame*. PC *Two Cities/Cineguild*. Dis *General Film Distributors*. Technicolor. 96 mins. Cert A
Charles Condomine's dead wife Elvira (*Kay Hammond*) materializes at a seance held at the Condomines' home by Madame Arcati (*Margaret Rutherford*). Ruth, his second wife (*Constance Cummings*) eventually gets wise to

Rex Harrison, Margaret Rutherford and Constance Cummings in Blithe Spirit *(1945)*

this, although only Charles (*Rex Harrison*) can see Elvira. Ruth tries to get Madame Arcati to send the troublesome Elvira back, while Elvira 'fixes' the car for Charles to join her; but it is Ruth who is killed. Now the wives gang up on Charles, who flees, only to crash in another 'fixed' car and join them for eternity. Beautifully produced farce won an Oscar for best special effects (photographic).
RoC *Hugh Wakefield, Joyce Carey, Jacqueline Clark.*

THE BLUE LAGOON (1948) [4]

Dir *Frank Launder*. Prod *Launder, Sidney Gilliat*. Scr *Launder, John Baines, Michael Hogan*. Ph *Geoffrey Unsworth*. PC *Individual*. Dis *General Film Distributors*. Technicolor. 103 mins. Cert A
Two children, Emmeline and Michael, are shipwrecked on a Pacific island with an old sailor (*Noel Purcell*) who soon dies on a drunken binge. They grow up (*Jean Simmons, Donald Houston*), fall in love, have a baby and try to escape in a home-made boat. They are picked up. Beautifully photographed version of the novel by H. de Vere Stacpoole, the plot beefed up by storms, a fight with a giant octopus, and two evil traders (*James Hayter, Cyril Cusack*) who force the boy to dive for pearls before killing each other off. A box-office rather than critical hit, but a masterpiece compared to the 1980 version.
RoC *Susan Stranks, Peter Jones, Maurice Denham, Patrick Barr, Russell Waters, Nora Nicholson, Philip Stainton, Lyn Evans, John Boxer, Bill Raymond, Kathleen Boutall, Gladys Boot, Edwin Styles, Peter Wood. W. A. Kelley, Anthony Verney, R. Stuart Lindsell, Frank Coburn, Captain Gray.*

Donald Houston and Jean Simmons in The Blue Lagoon *(1948)*

THE BLUE LAMP (1949) [5]

Dir *Basil Dearden*. Prod *Michael Relph*. Scr *T. E. B. Clarke, Alexander Mackendrick*. Ph *Gordon Dines, Lionel Banes*. PC *Ealing Studios*. Dis *General Film Distributors*. 84 mins. Cert A
Two young hoodlums and their moll rob a cinema and one (*Dirk Bogarde*) guns down a veteran policeman (*Jack Warner*) on the eve of his retirement. He gets rid of the gun and strangles the girl (*Peggy Evans*) to ensure her silence. But he is hunted down not only by police but also by old lags who despise the use of guns. Archetypal British police film, the be-

getter of many other films and TV series. Won British Oscar for best 1950 film. The critic who deplored its 'spurious attempt at characterization' was a voice crying in the wilderness.
RoC *Jimmy Hanley, Patric Doonan, Robert Flemyng, Bernard Lee, Gladys Henson, Bruce Seton, Meredith Edwards, Clive Morton, Frederick Piper, Dora Bryan, Norman Shelley, Campbell Singer, Tessie O'Shea, William Mervyn, Charles Saynor, Gwynne Whitby, Sidney Pointer, Michael Golden, Gene Neighbors, Betty Ann Davies, Glen Buckland, Jennifer Jayne, Doris Yorke, Renee Gadd, Muriel Aked, Cameron Hall, Glyn Houston, John Salew, Anthony Steel, Sam Kydd; Basil Radford and Glynis Johns (walk-ons).*

Jack Warner and Dirk Bogarde in The Blue Lamp *(1949)*

BLUE SCAR (1948) [3]

Dir and Scr *Jill Craigie*. Prod *William McQuitty*. Ph *Jo Jago*. PC *Outlook*. Dis *British Lion*. 90 mins. Cert U
Olwen (*Gwyneth Vaughan*), a miner's daughter, turns down Tom (*Emrys Jones*), an ambitious miner, after winning a music scholarship. She marries a white-collar worker while Tom, although injured in a pit accident, works on to become mine manager. She is almost ready to leave her husband and go back to Tom but he, hating her 'smart set' circle, marries the village girl who has always loved him. Simple story skirts any real issues involved.
RoC *Rachel Thomas, Anthony Pendrell, Prysor Williams, Madoline Thomas, Jack James, Kenneth Griffith, Francis Lunt, Dilys Jones, D. L. Davies, Phil Burton, David Keir, Winston Edwards, Dan Bevan, Pauline Bentley, Patsy Drake, Prudence Hyman, Anthony Verney, Pearl Evans, Julian Somers, Ernest Beck, Michael Stankiewicz, John Williams, Tom Thomas, Douglas Jones, Harry Waters, Isaac Parry.*

BOB'S YOUR UNCLE (1941) [3]

Dir *Oswald Mitchell*. Prod *F. W. Baker*. Scr *Mitchell, Vera Allinson*. Ph *Stephen Dade*. PC and Dis *Butchers*. 76 mins. Cert U
Porter Albert Smith (*Albert Modley*) falls for Dolly Diehard (*Jean Colin*), daughter of his local Home Guard commander. After being uprooted from his cushy HG job of tea-boy to take part (disastrously) in manœuvres, Albert proves himself worthy of Dolly by organizing a 'buy your own tank' campaign. Simple broad comedy, quite good of its kind.

RoC *Wally Patch, H. F. Maltby, George Bolton, Bert Linden, Clifford Cobbe, Johnnie Schofield.*

BOND STREET (1948)   3

Dir *Gordon Parry.* Prod *Anatole de Grunwald.* Scr *de Grunwald, Terence Rattigan, Rodney Ackland.* Ph *Otto Heller.* PC *Associated British/World Screenplays.* Dis *Pathé. 108 mins. Cert A*

Stories behind various items being prepared for a wedding, all in London's Bond Street. There's a crisis at the dressmakers, blackmail at the invisible menders and murder at the jewellers. The linking story concerns the attempts of the bride's father (*Roland Young*) to stop an old flame of the bridegroom from ruining the marriage. Some good acting, but scripting as variable as in Rattigan's later portmanteau films. Apart from the central theme, a bit dreary.

RoC *Jean Kent, Derek Farr, Paula Valeska, Kathleen Harrison, Hazel Court, Ronald Howard, Patricia Plunkett, Kenneth Griffith, Joan Dowling, Adrianne Allen, Charles Goldner, James McKechnie, Leslie Dwyer, Mary Jerrold, Robert Flemying, Marian Spencer, Ian Wilson, Ian Carmichael, Martin Miller.*

BONNIE PRINCE CHARLIE (1948)   3

Dir *Anthony Kimmins.* Prod *Edward Black.* Scr *Clemence Dane.* Ph *Robert Krasker.* PC *London Films.* Dis *British Lion. Technicolor. 136 mins. Cert A*

1745. Prince Charles Stuart (*David Niven*) lands in the Highlands after exile in Rome, intent on regaining the English throne. With an army of Highlanders he invades England, and reaches Derby before his officers make the fatal decision to turn back and fight in Scotland. Later he is routed at Culloden, but with the help of Flora MacDonald (*Margaret Leighton*) evades capture. Subject is approached with too much care and reverence; has no magnetism. A famous flop.

RoC *Jack Hawkins, Judy Campbell, Morland Graham, Finlay Currie, Elwyn Brook-Jones, John Laurie, Hector Ross, Hugh Kelly, Charles Goldner, Henry Oscar, Martin Miller, Franklin Dyall, Herbert Lomas, Ronald Adam, John Longden, James Hayter, Julien Mitchell, Guy le Feuvre, G. H. Mulcaster, Tommy Duggan, R. Stuart Lindsell, Simon Lack, Kenneth Warrington, Nell Ballantyne, Patricia Fox, Antony Holles, Lola Duncan, John Rae, Molly Rankin, John Forrest, Jane Gill-Davis, Edward Lexy, Louise Gainsborough, Bruce Seton, Mark Daly, Jean Stuart, Blanche Fothergill, Margaret Gibson, Alan Judd, Frederick Hearn, Bill Allison, Charles Cullum, Norman Maitland, Harry Schofield.*

A BOY, A GIRL AND A BIKE (1948)   3

Dir *Ralph Smart.* Prod *Ralph Keene.* Scr *Ted Willis.* Ph *Ray Elton.* PC *Gainsborough.* Dis *General Film Distributors. 92 mins. Cert U*

Sam and Susie (*Patrick Holt, Honor Blackman*) belong to a Yorkshire cycling club. David (*John McCallum*), a rich boy who, like Sam, fancies Susie, joins to be near her and stays to help the club win an important race. A bicycle

thief is chased and caught; Sam wins Susie; and veteran secretary Steve (*Leslie Dwyer*) pairs up with the lady (*Thora Hird*) who runs the 'club café'. Homespun humour and romance, with a variety of accents from the Rank Charm School.

RoC *Diana Dors, Anthony Newley, John Blythe, Margaret Avery, Barry Letts, Megs Jenkins, Maurice Denham, Alison Leggatt, Julien Mitchell, Amy Veness, Hal Osmond, Cyril Chamberlain, Vera Cook, Joan Seton, Lyn Evans, Margot Bourke, Dennis Peck, Vera Williams, Geoffrey Best, John Howlett, Jennifer Jayne, Patrick Halstead.*

Diana Dors in A Boy, a Girl and a Bike *(1948)*

BOYS IN BROWN (1949)   4

Dir and Scr *Montgomery Tully, from the play by Reginald Beckwith.* Prod *Antony Darnborough.* Ph *Gordon Lang, Cyril Bristow.* PC *Gainsborough.* Dis *General Film Distributors. 85 mins. Cert A*

After a raid on a jeweller's shop, Jackie (*Richard Attenborough*) finds himself sent to a Borstal correction centre. He encounters the stern but benign governor (*Jack Warner*), as well as unregenerate companions, including Alfie (*Dirk Bogarde*), who leads an abortive escape, in which Jackie nearly kills a man and is finally led to see the error of his ways. Quite an exciting film, even if some of the 'boys' are a trifle mature.

RoC *Jimmy Hanley, Patrick Holt, Andrew Crawford, Barbara Murray, Thora Hird, Michael Medwin, Graham Payn, John Blythe, Alfie Bass, Cyril Chamberlain, Stanley Escane, Robert Desmond, Martin Tiffen, Philip Stainton, Tony Quinn, Elspeth March, Frederick Leister, Edward Judd.*

BREACH OF PROMISE (1941)   3
(USA: *Adventure in Blackmail*)

Dir *Harold Huth, Roland Pertwee.* Prod *Richard Norton, Michael Brooke.* Scr *Pertwee, Emeric Pressburger.* Ph *John J. Cox.* PC *British Mercury.* Dis *MGM. 79 mins. Cert A*

Pamela (*Judy Campbell*) brings a fake breach of promise suit against playwright Peter (*Clive Brook*) in revenge for an alleged injustice to her brother. To teach her a lesson, Peter marries her, expecting a quick divorce. Pamela has no intention of letting him off that easily but, after numerous complications, they find they love each other in any case. Ordinary comedy, stiffly played.

RoC *C. V. France, Marguerite Allan, Percy Walsh, Dennis Arundell, George Merritt, David Horne, Charles Victor, Aubrey Mallalieu, Tony Bozell.*

BRIEF ENCOUNTER (1945)   6

Dir *David Lean.* Prod *Anthony Havelock-Allan, Ronald Neame.* Scr *Noël Coward, Lean, Neame, Havelock-Allan, from Coward's play* Still Life. Ph *Robert Krasker.* PC *Cineguild.* Dis *General Film Distributors. 86 mins. Cert A*

Laura (*Celia Johnson*), a housewife on her weekly shopping trip to town, and Alec (*Trevor Howard*), a doctor on weekly duty at the town hospital, meet at the railway station, then meet again by chance and strike up a friendship that gradually turns to love. They cannot bring themselves to consummate the affair. He realizes he must go away, and they part for ever at the station. Laura momentarily contemplates suicide, but returns to her husband. Touchingly understated, brilliantly photographed love story; the critics were bowled over, the public somewhat less enthusiastic.

RoC *Stanley Holloway, Joyce Carey, Cyril Raymond, Everley Gregg, Margaret Barton, Dennis Harkin, Valentine Dyall, Marjorie Mars, Irene Handl, Nuna Davey, Edward Hodge, Sydney Bromley, Avis Scott, Wilfred Babbage, Henrietta Vincent, Richard Thomas, George V. Sheldon, Wallace Bosco, Jack May.*

THE BRIGGS FAMILY (1940)   2

Dir *Herbert Mason.* Prod *A. M. Salomon.* Scr *John Dighton.* Ph *Basil Emmott.* PC and Dis *Warner Bros. 69 mins. Cert U*

Bob Briggs (*Peter Croft*), injured in a car accident, is embittered because he is useless for work or war, and falls in with ne'er-do-wells. Mr Briggs (*Edward Chapman*), a special constable, finds Bob trapped in a stolen car, with stolen goods in the back. As a solicitor's clerk, he undertakes Bob's defence and proves his innocence. Thoughts of a series of 'Briggs' films were dropped after criticisms that the characters were not true to life.

RoC *Jane Baxter, Oliver Wakefield, Lesley Brook, Mary Clare, Felix Aylmer, Jack Melford, Austin Trevor, George Carney, Glynis Johns, Muriel George, Aubrey Mallalieu, Joss Ambler, Kitty de Legh, Ian Fleming, Vincent Holman, Francis L. Sullivan, Esma Cannon, Johnnie Schofield, Hamilton Keene, Pat McGrath, Stan Paskin.*

BRIGHTON ROCK (1947)   4
(USA: *Young Scarface*)

Dir *John Boulting.* Prod *Roy Boulting.* Scr *Graham Greene, Terence Rattigan, from the novel by Graham Greene.* Ph *Harry Waxman.* PC *Associated British.* Dis *Pathé. 91 mins. Cert A*

A journalist dies at Brighton in a revenge killing by teenage hoodlum Pinkie (*Richard Attenborough*) and his gang. Pinkie has an alibi, but has to marry Rose (*Carol Marsh*), the young waitress who could destroy it; he intends to kill her too. Ida (*Hermione Baddeley*), a pier entertainer friend of the dead reporter, saves Rose at the point of death and Pinkie falls from the pier and drowns. Sordid, but strong, tense and realistic thriller.

RoC *William Hartnell, Nigel Stock, Wylie Watson, Harcourt Williams, Alan Wheatley, George Carney, Charles Goldner, Reginald Purdell, Virginia Winter, Basil Cunard, Hector Ross, Constance Smith, Campbell Copelin.*

BRITANNIA MEWS (1948)   [3]
(USA: *Forbidden Street*)

Dir *Jean Negulesco.* Prod *William Perlberg.* Scr *Ring Lardner Jr, from the novel by Margery Sharp.* Ph *Georges Périnal.* PC and Dis *20th Century-Fox. 91 mins. Cert A*

When her dissolute husband Lambert (*Dana Andrews*) crashes to his death down the outside stairs of their home in squalid Britannia Mews, well-bred Adelaide (*Maureen O'Hara*) is blackmailed by a witness, the raddled Mrs Mounsey (*Fay Compton*) into staying. Two years later, she takes an ex-barrister, Lauderdale (also *Andrews*) as a lodger. He deals summarily with Mrs Mounsey, finds Lambert's puppets and opens a puppet theatre. It is a great success. Adelaide marries Lauderdale, now calling himself Lambert. . . . Attractively bizarre story, spoiled by Hollywoodization and central miscasting.

RoC *Sybil Thorndike, Fay Compton, A. E. Matthews, Anne Butchart, Diane Hart, Wilfrid Hyde White, Anthony Tancred, Herbert C. Walton, Mary Martlew, Neil North, Suzanne Gibbs, Gwen Whitby, June Allen, Scott Harold, Anthony Lamb, Heather Latham, Joan Wright's Marionettes.*

BROKEN JOURNEY (1947)   [3]

Dir *Ken Annakin.* Prod *Sydney Box.* Scr *Robert Westerby.* Ph *Jack Cox.* PC *Gainsborough.* Dis *General Film Distributors. 89 mins. Cert A*

Thirteen people, including a top boxer, a star singer and an iron lung patient, are on a charter plane that crashes in the Alps. Their care makes the air hostess (*Phyllis Calvert*) forget her own tragic love affair. The iron lung man (*Grey Blake*) gives up his batteries so that distress signals might go on. The nurse (*Sonia Holm*) who loved him walks out into the snow and joins him in death. An old refugee (*Gerard Heinz*) going to Switzerland for reunion with his wife dies with rescue in sight of the rest. Prototype disaster film has its moments.

RoC *Margot Grahame, James Donald, Francis L. Sullivan, Derek Bond, Raymond Huntley, Guy Rolfe, David Tomlinson, Andrew Crawford, Charles Victor, Sybilla Binder, Amy Frank, Bonar Colleano, Michael Allan, Stuart Lindsell, Mary Hinton, Jan van Loewen, Arthur Goullet, Leo Bieber, Ferdy Mayne.*

THE BROTHERS (1947)   [4]

Dir *David Macdonald.* Prod *Sydney Box.* Scr *Macdonald, Box, Muriel Box, Paul Vincent Carroll, from the novel by L. A. G. Strong.* Ph *Stephen Dade.* PC *Triton.* Dis *General Film Distributors. 98 mins. Cert A*

Skye 1900. A tempestuous orphan girl (*Patricia Roc*) becomes servant to a crofting family and soon sets brother against brother in their passion for her. John (*Duncan Macrae*), one of the few who have no luck with her, says she

is an ill omen and orders brother Fergus (*Maxwell Reed*) to take her fishing and kill her. He does so, then kills himself. The islanders take revenge on John, tying him up and setting him adrift for wild geese to peck to death. Heady mixture of sex, superstition and murder.

RoC *Will Fyffe, Finlay Currie, Andrew Crawford, Morland Graham, Megs Jenkins, James Woodburn, Patrick Boxall, Donald McAllister, David Keir, John Laurie.*

'BULLDOG' SEES IT THROUGH (1940)   [4]

Dir *Harold Huth.* Prod *Walter C. Mycroft.* Scr *Doreen Montgomery, from a novel by Gerard Fairlie.* Ph *Claude Friese-Greene.* PC and Dis *Associated British. 77 mins. Cert A*

Test pilot 'Bulldog' Watson (*Jack Buchanan*) becomes involved in the mysterious sabotaging by enemy agents of the British armaments programme. Returning from dinner with Jane (*Greta Gynt*), an old friend, he finds a body in Jane's husband's study. Before police arrive, the body disappears. The trail leads to a plan to blow up the Houses of Parliament, a threat which is averted by 'Bulldog' after a desperate air battle over the Thames. Hectic comedy-melodrama.

RoC *Sebastian Shaw, David Hutchinson, Googie Withers, Robert Newton, Arthur Hambling, Wylie Watson, Polly Ward, Nadine March, Ronald Shiner, Aubrey Mallalieu, Danny Green, Raymond Huntley.*

BUSH CHRISTMAS (1947)   [4]

Dir, Prod, Scr and PC *Ralph Smart.* Ph *George Heath.* Dis *General Film Distributors. 77 mins. Cert U*

A family of Australian children and their English evacuee are riding home for Christmas holidays when they chat to two strangers about their mare and new foal. As a result, mare and foal are snatched and the kids, together with an Aborigine boy, set out to get them back from the thieves. They go through many scrapes before succeeding. Children's adventure has both charm and excitement.

LP *Chips Rafferty, John Fernside, Stan Tolhurst, Helen Grieve, Nicky Yardley, Michael Yardley, Morris Unicombe, Clyde Combo, Neza Saunders, Pet Penny, Thelma Grigg, John McCallum (narrator).*

BUSMAN'S HONEYMOON (1940)   [4]
(USA: *Haunted Honeymoon*)

Dir *Arthur B. Woods.* Prod *Harold Huth.* Scr *Monckton Hoffe, Angus Macphail, Harold Goldman, from the play by Dorothy L. Sayers, Muriel St Claire Byrne.* Ph *Frederick A. Young.* PC and Dis *M-G-M British. 99 mins. Cert A*

Charmingly described as 'a love story with detective interruptions'. On their marriage Lord Peter Wimsey and his bride Harriet (*Robert Montgomery, Constance Cummings*) vow not to get involved with crime again. Then murder is committed on their honeymoon in Devon. They try to keep out of it, but cannot resist sniffing out the criminal in the end. Not exactly thrilling, but good fun.

RoC *Leslie Banks, Seymour Hicks, Robert Newton, Googie Withers, Frank Pettingell, Joan Kemp-Welch, Aubrey Mallalieu, James Carney, Roy Emerton, Louise Hampton, Eliot Makeham, Reginald Purdell.*

THE BUTLER'S DILEMMA (1943)   [2]

Dir *Leslie Hiscott.* Prod *Elizabeth Hiscott.* Scr *Michael Barringer.* Ph *Erwin Hillier.* PC *British National/Shaftesbury.* Dis *Anglo-American. 83 mins. Cert U*

In debt to gamblers, Rodney (*Richard Hearne*) agrees to pose as butler at his fiancée's house, to enable his friend Carmichael (*Henry Kendall*) to use it for a gambling party. He's in trouble when his fiancée (*Judy Kelly*) rumbles the deception; then he discovers the real butler is also a jewel thief wanted by the police. Potential for hilarity is here, but only silliness results.

RoC *Francis L. Sullivan, Hermione Gingold, Wally Patch, Ronald Shiner, Ralph Truman, Marjorie Rhodes, Ian Fleming, Wilfrid Hyde White, André Randall, Frank Pettingell, Alf Goddard, Arthur Denton.*

BUT NOT IN VAIN (1948)   [2]

Dir *Edmond T. Gréville.* Prod *Guus E. Ostwalt, Geoffrey Goodheart.* Scr *Ben Van Eeslyn, from his play.* Ph *William McLeod, Hone Glendinning, Ernest Palmer.* PC *Anglo-Dutch.* Dis *Butchers. 73 mins. Cert A. Bilingual versions*

1943. Dutch underground fighters hiding out on a farm face a 'doubting Thomas' who may betray them all. The troublemaker's father makes a supreme sacrifice to ensure the work of the movement will go on. Gréville also directed the Dutch version of this rather dull and sombre, and distinctly odd, film.

LP *Raymond Lovell, Carol Van Derman, Martin Benson, Agnes Bernelle, Julian Dallas, Bruce Lister, Ben Van Esselsteyn (Eeslyn), Jordan Lawrence, Harry Croizet, Geoffrey Goodheart, Victor Colane, Henry Almar, Gerhard Alexander.*

CAESAR AND CLEOPATRA (1945)   [3]

Dir and Prod *Gabriel Pascal.* Scr *George Bernard Shaw, Marjorie Deans, W. P. Lipscomb.* Ph *Frederick A. Young, Jack Hildyard, Robert Krasker, Jack Cardiff.* PC *Independent Producers/Pascal.* Dis *Eagle-Lion.* Technicolor. *138 mins. Cert A*

45 BC: Egypt's voluptuous young queen Cleopatra (*Vivien Leigh*) entrances the Roman emperor Caesar (*Claude Rains*). Under his guidance, she escapes from the domination of her severe native servant Ftatateeta (*Flora Robson*) and becomes a ruling queen in her own right. At a million and a half pounds, Britain's most expensive film to date, this emerged over-

Vivien Leigh and Claude Rains in Caesar and Cleopatra *(1945)*

loaded with talk and hopelessly posed, but with brilliant colour photography and set design. Several embryo stars can be seen strumming lutes and carrying spears.

RoC *Stewart Granger, Francis L. Sullivan, Renee Asherson, Olga Edwardes, Basil Sydney, Cecil Parker, Ernest Thesiger, Raymond Lovell, Stanley Holloway, Anthony Eustrel, Leo Genn, Alan Wheatley, Esmé Percy, Gibb McLaughlin, James McKechnie, Anthony Harvey, Robert Adams, Harde Swanhilde, Antony Holles, Charles Victor, Ronald Shiner, John Bryning, Michael Rennie, Jean Simmons, John Laurie, Charles Rolfe, Felix Aylmer, Ivor Barnard, Vaentine Dyall, Charles Deane, Peter Lord, Hamilton Humphries, Shaun Noble, Gerald Case, Russell Thorndyke, Basil Jason, Peter Bayliss, Gerhardt Kempinski, André Belhomme, Don Stannard, Peter Lilley, Virginia Keiley, Zena Marshall, Agnes Bernelle, Toni Gable, Margaret Harvey, Kay Kendall, Renee Gilbert, Olwyn Brookes, Anne Moore, Cathleen Nesbitt, Ena Burrill, Marie Ault, Michael Martin-Harvey, Harry Lane, MacKenzie Ward, Michael Cacoyannis, Roy Russell, Wilfrid Walter, Charles Paton, Dorothy Bramhall, H.F. Maltby, George Luck, Paul Crift, Roger Moore, Bob Cameron.*

THE CALENDAR (1948)   [4]
Dir *Arthur Crabtree.* Prod *Antony Darnborough.* Scr *Geoffrey Kerr, from the play by Edgar Wallace.* Ph *Reginald Wyer.* PC *Gainsborough.* Dis *General Film Distributors. 80 mins. Cert A*
Garry Anson's (*John McCallum*) fiancée Wenda (*Greta Gynt*) leaves him when he loses all his money horse-racing. While drunk, a depressed Garry agrees to 'pull' one of his horses. He sends Wenda a telegram asking her not to back it. Sober, he changes his mind, revoking the 'gram on the back of £100 note. Wenda refuses to back him at a stewards' inquiry, but his trainer Mollie (*Sonia Holm*) burgles Wenda's safe, and tricks her into admitting the truth. Another adaptation of Wallace play; quite exciting and not too long.
RoC *Raymond Lovell, Leslie Dwyer, Charles Victor, Barry Jones, Felix Aylmer, Sydney King, Diana Dors, Fred Payne, Noel Howlett, Claude Bailey, Desmond Roberts, Cyril Chamberlain, O.B. Clarence, Constance Smith.*

CALLING PAUL TEMPLE (1948)   [4]
Dir *Maclean Rogers.* Prod *Ernest G. Roy.* Scr

Francis Durbridge, A.R. Rawlinson, Kathleen Butler, from a radio serial by Durbridge. Ph *Geoffrey Faithfull.* PC *Nettlefold.* Dis *Butchers. 92 mins. Cert A*
The mysterious Rex murders several women. Blackmail seems to be involved, and novelist Paul Temple (*John Bentley*), helping the police, discovers the victims were all patients of Dr Kohima (*Abraham Sofaer*). Paul and his wife Steve (*Dinah Sheridan*), answering an SOS from Kohima's secretary Mrs Trevelyan (*Margaretta Scott*), are nearly blown up, and narrowly escape drowning in a vault where they had hoped to trap the killer, who turns out to be Latham (*Alan Wheatley*). An improvement on the ace radio sleuth's first film adventure, *Send for Paul Temple.*
RoC *Jack Raine, Hugh Pryse, Michael Golden, Celia Lipton, Wally Patch, John McLaren, Ian MacLean, Shaym Bahadur, Merle Tottenham, Aubrey Mallalieu, Hugh Miller, George Merritt, Harry Herbert, Maureen Glynne, Gerald Rex, Paul Sheridan, Marion Taylor, David Keir, Sydney Tafler.*

CALL OF THE BLOOD (1947)   [2]
Dir *John Clements, Ladislas Vajda.* Prod *John Stafford, Steven Pallos.* Scr *Clements, Akos Tolnay, Basil Mason, from the novel by Robert Hichens.* Ph *Wilkie Cooper.* PC *Pendennis.* Dis *British Lion. 88 mins. Cert A*
Anne (*Kay Hammond*) a doctor, gives up her career to marry David (*John Justin*) and go with him to his Sicilian villa. They meet the strange Julius Ikon (*John Clements*) who seems upset that they intend to return to England. Anne goes off to help fight an epidemic; David becomes involved with a Sicilian girl. On Anne's return, the girl kills herself and David is shot by her drunken father. Heavily over-acted morality play.
RoC *Lea Padovani, Robert Rietti, Carlo Ninchi, Hilton Edwards, Eliot Makeham, Michael Medwin, H.G. Stoker, Mariesa Facincani, Valentino Bruchi, Islo Sebastini, Keith Pyott, Dora Gregory, Jelo Filippo.*

CANDLELIGHT IN ALGERIA (1943)   [4]
Dir, Prod and PC *George King.* Scr *Katherine Strueby, Brock Williams.* Ph *Otto Heller.* Dis *British Lion. 85 mins. Cert U*
Allied and German agents seek a priceless piece of film, deposited in Algeria, which reveals the exact location of a meeting of Allied leaders to determine the counter-invasion of North Africa. British agent Alan Thurston (*James Mason*) shoots his way out of the Casbah with the film; his warning to Allied officers on the coast saves the lives of patriots liaising with a British submarine in readiness for the invasion. Slick tough-hero thriller.
RoC *Carla Lehmann, Walter Rilla, Raymond Lovell, Enid Stamp-Taylor, Pamela Stirling, Leslie Bradley, Lea Seidl, Michel Morel, Meinhart Maur, Albert Whelan, Harold Berens, Hella Kurty, MacDonald Parke, Paul Bonifas, Richard George, Bart Norman, John Slater, Berkeley Schultz, Jacques Metadier, Graham Penley, Richard Molinas, Cecile Chevreau, Cot d'Ordan, Paul Sheridan, Eric L'Epine Smith.*

CANDLES AT NINE (1944)   [1]
Dir *John Harlow.* Prod *Wallace Orton.* Scr *Harlow, Basil Mason, from a novel by Anthony Gilbert.* Ph *Jimmy Wilson, Arthur Grant.* PC *British National.* Dis *Anglo-American. 86 mins (later 83). Cert A*
Miserly old Everard Hope (*Eliot Makeham*) teases his relatives about his will. That night, he is murdered. His money goes to an unknown relative, Dorothea (*Jessie Matthews*), an actress. Before she even gets to the home, she is saved from death twice by Gordon (*John Stuart*), a CID man on the case. Further attempts on her life inside the house are foiled; the killer turns out to be the housekeeper (*Beatrix Lehmann*). Suspenseless thriller with musical numbers; a disaster that finished Matthews' star career in films.
RoC *Winifred Shotter, Reginald Purdell, Hugh Dempster, Joss Ambler, Vera Bogetti, Ernest Butcher, Guy Fielding, Gerry Wilmott, John Salew, André Van Gyseghem, C. Denier Warren, Patricia Hayes, Antony Holles.*

A CANTERBURY TALE (1944)   [3]
Dir, Prod and Scr *Michael Powell, Emeric Pressburger.* Ph *Erwin Hillier.* PC *The Archers Independent Producers.* Dis *Eagle-Lion. 124 mins. Cert U*
More than one critic confessed himself baffled as to quite what was going on in this fey tale of an American army sergeant, a British soldier and a land girl (*John Sweet, Dennis Price, Sheila Sim*) who solve the mystery of a man who pours glue on village girls' hair when they go out at night. It proves to be the local JP (*Eric Portman*). Afterwards they go on a pilgrimage to Canterbury.
RoC *Esmond Knight, Charles Hawtrey, Hay Petrie, George Merritt. Edward Rigby, Freda Jackson, Betty Jardine, Eliot Makeham, Harvey Golden, Leonard Smith. James Tamsitt, David Todd, Esma Cannon.*

CAPTAIN BOYCOTT (1947)   [4]
Dir *Frank Launder.* Prod *Launder, Sidney Gilliat.* Scr *Launder, Wolfgang Wilhelm, Paul Vincent Carroll, Patrick Campbell, from the novel by Philip Rooney.* Ph *Wilkie Cooper.* PC *Individual/Independent Producers.* Dis *General Film Distributors. 93 mins. Cert A*
1800. Poor Irish tenant farmers are rebelling against harsh landlords. The Land League suggests ostracizing landlords, and those willing to take over from farmers unjustly evicted. Landlord Captain Boycott (*Cecil Parker*) and his bailiff (*Mervyn Johns*) defy the edict by installing Mark Killain (*Niall MacGinnis*) and his daughter Anne (*Kathleen Ryan*) in an 'evicted' farm. Even though villagers' leader Hugh (*Stewart Granger*) is in love with Anne, Boycott has to get military help to get his harvest in. Ruined by the expense, he admits defeat; the word 'boycott' has been added to the language. Nicely-handled historical theme, largely made on location in southern Ireland.
RoC *Alastair Sim, Noel Purcell, Robert Donat, Maureen Delaney, Eddie Byrne, Liam Redmond, Liam Gaffney, Edward Lexy, Maurice Denham, Joe Linane, Bernadette O'Farrell, Ian Fleming, Reginald Purdell, Harry Webster, Eddie Golden,*

Harry Hutchinson, Phyllis Ryan, Cavan Malone, John Kelly, Anne Clery, Shelagh Carty, Michael Ripper, Norrie Duff, Harry Bailey, Norah O'Mahoney, Bill Shine, James Hayter, Nora Finn, Michael Brennan, Anthony Verney, Brian Smith, Beth Ross, Rosheen Boland, Jim Phelan, Lyn Evans, John McDarby, Jim Winter, Norma Moore, Richard Courtney, Brian Peck, Paddy Layoe, Edward Mulhare, Kathleen Murphy, Martin Macdonald, Peter Murray.

THE CAPTIVE HEART (1946) [5]

Dir *Basil Dearden*. (Associate) Prod *Michael Relph*. Scr *Angus Macphail, Guy Morgan*. Ph *Douglas Slocombe*. PC *Ealing Studios*. Dis *General Film Distributors. 104 mins. Cert A*
In a German prisoner camp a Czech officer (*Michael Redgrave*) who has assumed the identity of a dead English officer to save himself from the Gestapo, finds himself forced to write to the dead man's wife (*Rachel Kempson*): he pretends his writing hand is injured. She is surprised by the warmth of the letters as her marriage had been unhappy but, after her initial horror when he comes to England, they face the future together. Other stories of the camp's inmates are also unfolded in this moving film.
RoC *Mervyn Johns, Basil Radford, Jack Warner, Jimmy Hanley, Gordon Jackson, Karel Stepanek, Ralph Michael, Derek Bond, Guy Middleton, Jack Lambert, Frederick Leister, Meriel Forbes, Robert Wyndham, Jane Barrett, Gladys Henson, Rachel Thomas, Margot Fitzsimmons, James Harcourt, Frederick Richter, Peter Reynolds, Elliot Mason, David Keir, Frederick Schiller, Jill Gibbs, David Wallbridge, Torin Thatcher, Sam Kydd.*

Michael Redgrave in The Captive Heart *(1946)*

CARAVAN (1946) [4]

Dir *Arthur Crabtree*. Prod *Harold Huth*. Scr *Roland Pertwee, from the novel by Lady Eleanor Smith*. Ph *Stephen Dade*. PC *Gainsborough*. Dis *General Film Distributors. 122 mins. Cert A*
When Richard (*Stewart Granger*) goes to Spain on business, his rival for Oriana (*Anne Crawford*), Sir Francis (*Dennis Price*), sends a man after him to kill him. Left for dead, Richard is nursed by Rosal (*Jean Kent*), a gypsy. Oriana marries Sir Francis; hearing of it, Richard marries Rosal. When Oriana leaves Sir Francis, he follows her to Richard and accidentally shoots Rosal, after which he sinks in quicksands. Richard marries Oriana. Florid stuff, but pretty pacy for a long film.

RoC *Robert Helpmann, Gerard Heinz, Enid Stamp-Taylor, David Horne, John Salew, Arthur Goullet, Julian Somers, Peter Murray, Sylvie StClair, Mabel Constanduros, Jusef Ramart, Gypsy Petulengro, Joseph O'Donohue, Patricia Laffan, Merle Tottenham, H. R. Hignett, Victoria Campbell, Dick Dunn, Erin De Selfa, Brookes Turner, Johnny Roman, Cecil Brock.*

CARDBOARD CAVALIER (1948) [3]

Dir and Prod *Walter Forde*. Scr *Noel Langley*. Ph *Jack Hildyard*. PC *Two Cities*. Dis *General Film Distributors. 96 mins. Cert U*
1658. Sidcup (*Sid Field*), is enrolled to take a secret letter to a Royalist leader in a plot against Oliver Cromwell. Assisted by Nell Gwynne (*Margaret Lockwood*), he encounters a castle ghost before getting to the top Royalist. Everyone escapes pursuing Roundheads in a coach – except for Sidcup, who is left behind by accident. Mainly mild period farce.
RoC *Mary Clare, Jerry Desmonde, Claude Hulbert, Brian Worth, Anthony Hulme, Edmund Willard, Irene Handl, Miles Malleson, Joan Young, Jack McNaughton, Alfie Dean, Michael Brennan, Peter Bull, Vincent Holman, John Salew, Edie Martin, Wensley Pithey, Patrick Troughton.*

CARNIVAL (1946) [2]

Dir *Stanley Haynes*. Prod *John Sutro, William Sassoon*. Scr *Haynes, Peter Ustinov, Eric Maschwitz, Guy Green*. Ph *Green*. PC *Two Cities*. Dis *General Film Distributors. 93 mins. Cert A*
1890: Ballet dancer Jenny Pearl (*Sally Grey*) falls in love with a young sculptor (*Michael Wilding*). When she refuses to live with him, he leaves. She rejects an offer of marriage from a painter for the security of marriage to a dour Cornish farmer (*Bernard Miles*), who makes her life a misery. The sculptor comes back to take her away, but the farmer blasts her with a shotgun. She dies in the sculptor's arms. Like winter weather: dull and wet.
RoC *Stanley Holloway, Jean Kent, Catherine Lacey, Nancy Price, Hazel Court, Brenda Bruce, Antony Holles, Ronald Ward, Dennis Arundell, Amy Veness, Mackenzie Ward, Phyllis Monkman, Bebe de Roland, Carpenter Corps de Ballet.*

THE CASE OF CHARLES PEACE (1948) [3]

Dir *Norman Lee*. Prod and PC *John Argyle*. Scr *Doris Davison, Lee*. Ph *Joseph Ambor*. Dis *Monarch. 88 mins. Cert A*
1879. The trial of notorious criminal Charles Peace (*Michael Martin-Harvey*) shows how he became cracksman, seducer and killer of policemen. Peace shoots and kills a neighbour, with whose wife Katherine (*Chili Bouchier*) he is in love. Fleeing, he eludes police time and again by his mastery of disguise. But he is finally arrested, brought to trial and sentenced to death. Good central performance holds the attention.
RoC *Valentine Dyall, Bruce Belfrage, Ronald Adam, Roberta Huby, Peter Forbes-Robertson, Richard Sjayne, Peter Gawthorne, Kathleen Rooney, Jean Shepheard, Robert Cameron, John*

Kelly, Hamilton Deane, Robert McLachlan, Gordon Court, Bartlett Mullins, Rose Howlett, Liam Gaffney, Howard Douglas.

THE CASE OF THE FRIGHTENED LADY (1940) [4]
(USA: *The Frightened Lady*)

Dir and Prod *George King*. Scr *Edward Dryhurst, from the novel by Edgar Wallace*. Ph *Hone Glendinning*. PC *Pennant*. Dis *British Lion. 81 mins. Cert A*
At Marks Priory, where the Dowager Lady Lebanon (*Helen Haye*) is anxious for her son Willie (*Marius Goring*) to marry his reluctant cousin Isla (*Penelope Dudley Ward*), Isla is terrified by an attempt on her life in a dark passage. Before Scotland Yard can get too far, the chauffeur and a doctor are strangled. Finally, Isla acts as a terrified trap for the killer: it proves to be the mentally unstable Willie, the house's two sinister butlers being male nurses in constant attendance. Remake of 1932 film does its job well as chilly thriller.
RoC *Patrick Barr, Felix Aylmer, John Warwick, George Merritt, Ronald Shiner, Roy Emerton, George Hayes, Elizabeth Scott, Torin Thatcher.*

CASTLE SINISTER (1947) [1]

Dir *Oscar Burn*. Prod *W. Howard Borer*. Scr *Mary Cathcart Borer*. PC *Unicorn*. Dis *Equity British. 49 mins. Cert A*
A bizarre group of people assembles at Glennye Castle, including a Nazi spy masquerading as a doctor, who aims to dispatch stolen plans to Germany. Lady Glennye threatens to expose him, although he is her son's real father. A British agent arrives. The Glennye phantom walks. Lady G. dies and the Nazi is shot. A muddled plot is only one of this film's many deficiencies.
LP *Mara Russell-Tavernan, Robert Essex, Karl Mier, Alistair Hunter, John Gauntley, James Liggatt, Maureen O'Moor.*

CELIA (1949) [3]

Dir *Francis Searle*. Prod *Anthony Hinds*. Scr *Searle, Edward J. Mason, A.R. Rawlinson, from the radio serial by Mason*. Ph *Cedric Williams*. PC and Dis *Exclusive. 67 mins. Cert A*
Celia (*Hy Hazell*), an attractive but hard-up actress, takes an assignment as a detective to earn money to buy an expensive hat. By impersonating a charwoman, she prevents the murder of a wealthy woman by her husband. Lively little thriller, quite tidily made.
RoC *Bruce Lister, John Bailey, James Raglan, Elsie Wagstaffe, Lockwood West, John Sharp, Joan Hickson, Jasmine Dee, Charles Paton, Olive Walter, Grace Denbigh-Russell, Ferdy Mayne.*

CHAMPAGNE CHARLIE (1944) [5]

Dir *Alberto Cavalcanti*. (Associate) Prod *John Croydon*. Scr *Austin Melford, Angus Macphail, John Dighton*. Ph *Wilkie Cooper*. PC and Dis *Ealing Studios. 105 mins. Cert A*
The 1860s: music-hall rivalry between belligerent George Leybourne (*Tommy Trinder*) and conceited The Great Vance (*Stanley Holloway*) to lay hands on the 'most popular

drinking song of the era', goes up the social scale from *Old Ale* to *Champagne Charlie*. When the existence of the halls is menaced by jealous theatre owners, the rivals combine forces to oppose them. Invigorating semi-musical with good period detail.

RoC *Betty Warren, Austin Trevor, Jean Kent, Guy Middleton, Frederick Piper, Harry Fowler, Robert Wyndham, Peter de Greeff, Andrea Malandrinos, Drusilla Wills, Eddie Phillips, Norman Pierce, Joe Carr, Vida Hope, Phyllis Morris, Paul Bonifas, Hazel Court, James Robertson (Justice), Eric Boon, Vernon Greeves, George Hirste, Aubrey Mallalieu, Billy Shine, Patricia Gennett, Ted Finch, Monte de Lyle, Kay Kendall, Richard Harrison.*

CHARLEY'S (BIG-HEARTED) AUNT (1940)   [4]

Dir *Walter Forde.* Prod *Edward Black.* Scr *Marriott Edgar, Val Guest, from the play by Brandon Thomas.* Ph *Arthur Crabtree.* PC *Gainsborough.* Dis *General Film Distributors. 76 mins. Cert U*

Arthur, Stinker and Albert (*Arthur Askey, Richard Murdoch, Graham Moffatt*), three undergraduates, find themselves in a serious scrape. Learning that the Dean (*J. H. Roberts*) is interested in Egyptology, Arthur invents a South American aunt with the same interest, then is forced to impersonate her, involving some hectic changes of costume and personality. In the end, all three are sent down, while the senior proctor (*Felix Aylmer*) marries Arthur's real aunt. Plot is thin, but laughs come thick and fast.

RoC *Moore Marriott, Phyllis Calvert, Jeanne de Casalis, Wally Patch, Elliot Mason, Peggy Evans.*

Arthur Askey, Richard Murdoch and Graham Moffatt in Charley's (Big-Hearted) Aunt *(1940)*

CHILDREN OF CHANCE (1949)   [2]

Dir *Luigi Zampa.* Prod *Ludovico Toeplitz, John Sutro.* Scr *Piero Tellini, Michael Medwin.* Ph *Carlo Montuori.* PC *Ortus.* Dis *British Lion. 99 mins. Cert A*

On the island of Ischia the local priest (*Manning Whiley*) founds a home for the illegitimate daughters of Allied soldiers, with funds sent to his predecessor for safe keeping, by a girl black marketeer (*Patricia Medina*). She returns to the island, with an ambitious friend (*Yvonne Mitchell*) to claim her fortune, but eventually

agrees to use it for the cause the priest intended. Unconvincing; protracted, too.

RoC *Eliot Makeham, Barbara Everest, George Woodbridge, Eric Pohlmann, Edward Lexy, Carlo Giustini (Justini), Frank Tickle, Catherine Paul, Richard Molinas, Denis Carey, Peter Illing, Peter Ducrow, Vittoria, Febe.*

THE CHILTERN HUNDREDS (1949)   [4]
(USA: *The Amazing Mr Beecham*)

Dir *John Paddy Carstairs.* Prod *George H. Brown.* Scr *William Douglas Home, Patrick Kirwan, from the play by Douglas Home.* Ph *Jack Hildyard.* PC *Two Cities.* Dis *General Film Distributors. 84 mins. Cert U*

Young Viscount Pym (*David Tomlinson*) gets army leave to stand as a Tory candidate. Engaged to an American heiress (*Helen Backlin*), he has no intention of standing but is cornered into doing it – and beaten by the Labour man. When that worthy is made a peer, Pym stands again, as a Socialist, but is beaten by Beecham, the family butler (*Cecil Parker*), for the Tories. Original, well-paced, popular comedy.

RoC *A. E. Matthews, Lena Morris, Marjorie Fielding, Tom Macaulay, Joyce Carey, Charles Cullum, Anthony Steel, Bill Shine, Gerald Andersen, Michael Brennan.*

A. E. Matthews, Marjorie Fielding, David Tomlinson, Helen Backlin and Tom Macaulay in The Chiltern Hundreds *(1949)*

CHORUS GIRL (1947)   [3]

Dir and Prod *Randolph Tomson.* Scr *Raphael Knappett.* Ph *Alan Cullimore.* PC *St James's Pictures/R. J. Thomson.* Dis *Renown. 46 mins. Cert U*

Valerie (*Jacquelyn Dunbar*) wants to be a dancer. Encouraged by her mother and grandmother, she goes through various stages of training before getting a position in the chorus at the London Palladium. Her father, who had opposed her ambition, is now proud of her. Pretty slight mini-feature does at least give a good idea of the hard work involved.

RoC *Alex Wright, Maud Long, Charmian Innes, Beth Ross, Beryl Trent.*

CHRISTOPHER COLUMBUS (1948)   [2]

Dir *David Macdonald.* Prod *A. Frank Bundy.* Scr *Cyril Roberts, Muriel and Sydney Box.* Ph *Stephen Dade.* PC *Gainsborough.* Dis *General Film Distributors. Technicolor. 104 mins. Cert U*

1492. Christopher Columbus (*Frederic March*),

delayed for years by the Spanish court, finally sails for the western hemisphere with three ships. After quelling a mutiny, he arrives in Cuba three months later and thence to America. Then, returning in triumph, he sails for new discoveries, but court intrigues have him sent back to Spain, where he dies an embittered man. A notable disaster, long and tedious. Said one critic: 'I have rarely felt so bored.'

RoC *Florence Eldridge, Francis L. Sullivan, Linden Travers, Kathleen Ryan, Derek Bond, James Robertson Justice, Felix Aylmer, Nora Swinburne, Edward Rigby, Francis Lister, Niall McGinnis, Abraham Sofaer, Dennis Vance, Ralph Truman, Sonia Holm, Arthur Hambling, Richard Ahearne, Ronald Adam, Guy le Feuvre, Lyn Evans, David Cole, Hugh Pryse, Anthony Steel, R. Stuart Lindsell, Gordon Dainton, Valentine Dyall (narrator).*

CIRCUS BOY (1947)   [3]

Dir *Cecil Musk.* Prod *Frank Hoare.* Scr *Musk, Mary Cathcart Borer.* Ph *A. T. Dinsdale, C. Marlborough.* PC *Merton Park.* Dis *General Film Distributors. 50 mins. Cert U*

Michael (*James Kenney*) is a boy swimmer overcome by nerves on big occasions. He spends a summer holiday with a circus, makes friends with two young tightrope walkers, Florence and George, and performs as a clown. George is burned rescuing an aunt from a blazing caravan, and Michael takes his place with great success. Newly confident, he wins back his place in the school swim team.

RoC *Florence Stephenson, George Stephenson, Denver Hall, Dennis Gilbert, Peter Scott, Gwen Bacon, Jock Easton, Robert Raglan, Bertram Mills' Circus.*

THE CLOUDED CRYSTAL (1948)   [1]

Dir and Scr *Alan J. Cullimore.* Prod *Ben Arbeid, A. Grossman.* Ph *Phil Grindrod.* PC *Grossman-Arbeid-Cullimore.* Dis *Butchers. 57 mins. Cert A*

When Paula (*Dorothy Bramhall*) and her husband Jack (*Patrick Waddington*) are told by two different fortune-tellers that a man in their house is to die in a month, they take steps to prevent that man being Jack. After a false alarm on the last night of the month, all ends happily. Amateur-night comedy.

RoC *Dino Galvani, Lind Joyce, Frank Muir, Ethel Coleridge.*

COLONEL BOGEY (1947)   [3]

Dir *Terence Fisher.* Prod *John Croydon.* Scr *William Fairchild, John Baines.* Ph *Gordon Lang.* PC *Production Facilities.* Dis *General Film Distributors. 51 mins. Cert U*

On a visit to Aunt Mabel and Uncle James, Wilfred (*John Stone*) and his suffragette fiancée Alice (*Jane Barrett*) are puzzled by the non-appearance of their uncle who, it transpires, has died 11 years previously. His ghost, however, is very much around (voiced by *Jack Train*) and Wilfred's efforts to drive it out only rebound on him. Then Alice tells it that its old regiment is required to fight suffragettes.

The ghost is shamed into going for good. Mild comedy.

RoC *Mary Jerrold, Ethel Coleridge, Heidi Anderson, Bertram Shuttleworth, Sam Kydd, Dennis Woodford, Charles Rolfe.*

COMIN' THRO' THE RYE (1947)   2

Dir *Walter C. Mycroft.* Prod *Arthur Dent.* Scr *Gilbert McAllister.* PC *Advance.* Dis *Adelphi.* 61 *mins. Cert U*

A musical biography of the Scottish ploughman and poet Robbie Burns (*Terence Alexander*), told almost entirely in song (19 of them). Well-known radio singers exercise their lungs, but the film has little entertainment vaue. The scenario, such as it is, was written by the then Labour MP for Rutherglen.

RoC *Trefor Jones, Sylvia Welling, Olivia Barley, Patricia Burleigh, Walter Saull's Scotia Singers.*

THE COMMON TOUCH (1941)   3

Dir and Prod *John Baxter.* Scr *Barbara K. Emary, Geoffrey Orme.* Ph *James Wilson.* PC *British National.* Dis *Anglo-Amalgamated.* 104 *mins. Cert U*

Taking over his father's firm at 18, Peter Henderson (*Geoffrey Hibbert*) disguises himself as a down-and-out to look around the buildings his managing director Cartwright (*Raymond Lovell*) wants to demolish in a poor part of London. By befriending derelicts at a hostel, Peter is able to discover Cartwright's ulterior motives and remove him from the board. Director Baxter returns to the scene of his first film (*Doss House*).

RoC *Greta Gynt, Joyce Howard, Harry Welchman, Edward Rigby, George Carney, Bransby Williams, Wally Patch, Eliot Makeham, John Longden, Percy Walsh, Bernard Miles, Charles Carson, Bill Fraser, Arthur Maude, Jerry Verno, Mark Hambourg, Carroll Gibbons, Sandy McPherson, Scott Sanders, John Slater, Hector Abbas, Edgar Driver, Arthur Hambling, Eric Lugg, Margaret Lang, Rowland Douglas, Cyril Chamberlain, Elizabeth Hunt, Iris Vandeleur, Gerald Moore, Freddie Watts, Ben Williams, Edwin Ellis, John Turnbull, Marion Spencer, Grant Tyler, Dennis Wyndham, Sydney Shaw.*

CONSPIRATOR (1949)   2

Dir *Victor Saville* Prod *Ben Goetz, Arthur Hornblow Jr.* Scr *Gerard Fairlie, Sally Benson, from the novel by Humphrey Slater.* Ph *F. A. Young.* PC and Dis *M-G-M British.* 87 *mins. Cert U*

Michael (*Robert Taylor*), a Guards officer, takes a lovely teenage bride (*Elizabeth Taylor*). Before long, she discovers he belongs to a subversive political party to whom he is giving military secrets. He is ordered to kill her. For his failure to do so, he has to kill himself – and he does. Not an auspicious return for the director; lacklustre film has neither life nor credibility.

RoC *Robert Flemyng, Harold Warrender, Honor Blackman, Marjorie Fielding, Marie Ney, Thora Hird, Jack Allen, Wilfrid Hyde White, Helen Haye, Karel Stepanek, Cyril Smith, Cicely Paget-Bowman, Nicholas Bruce, Janette Scott, Bill Travers.*

Elizabeth Taylor and Robert Taylor in Conspirator (1949)

CONTRABAND (1940)   5
(USA: *Blackout*)

Dir *Michael Powell.* Prod *John Cornfield.* Scr *Powell, Emeric Pressburger, Brock Williams.* Ph *Frederick Young.* PC *British National.* Dis *Anglo-American.* 92 *mins. Cert U*

Danish merchant skipper Andersen (*Conrad Veidt*) tries to evade Britain's wartime contraband control, but is forced to put into port, where his shore leave passes are stolen by 'Pidgeon' and 'Mrs Sorenson', two passengers. He trails Mrs Sorenson (*Valerie Hobson*), a British naval intelligence agent, and they both fall into the clutches of German spies operating from a cinema before escaping to help round them up. Thriller is hardly believable, but topical, polished and exciting.

RoC *Esmond Knight, Hay Petrie, Raymond Lovell, Harold Warrender, Charles Victor, Manning Whiley, Peter Bull, Stuart Lathom, Leo Genn, Dennis Arundell, Julien Vedey, Paddy Browne, Henry Wolsten, Sydney Monckton, Hamilton Keene, Molly Hamley Clifford, Eric Berry, Olga Edwardes, Desmond Jeans, Eric Hales, John Roberts, Eric Maturin, John Longden, *Deborah Kerr, Toni Gable, Phoebe Kershaw, Joss Ambler, Cameron Hall.*

* scenes deleted from final release print

CONVOY (1940)   6

Dir *Pen Tennyson.* (Associate) Prod *Sergei Nolbandov.* Scr *Tennyson, Patrick Kirwan.* Ph *Roy Kellino, Wilkie Cooper, Leslie Rowson, Gordon Dines.* PC *Ealing Studios.* Dis *Associated British.* 90 *mins. Cert A*

Captain Armitage (*Clive Brook*) of the cruiser *Apollo* is in charge of a convoy heading for England across the North Sea. News comes that a German pocket battleship has located the convoy. Armitage engages the enemy, but is heavily outgunned. First officer Cranford (*John Clements*), with whom Armitage's wife had been having an affair, is killed, and the *Apollo* crippled. But the convoy is saved. Epic emotion-tugger was hailed as 'the most exciting, lifelike and restrained account of the navy in war yet seen'.

RoC *Judy Campbell, Edward Chapman, Edward Rigby, Penelope Dudley Ward, Allan Jeayes, Albert Lieven, Michael Wilding, Charles Williams, Harold Warrender, David Hutcheson, George Carney, Al Millen, Charles Farrell, John*

Director Pen Tennyson (to die a year later in an air crash) with Clive Brook on 'the bridge' in Convoy (1940)

Laurie, Hay Petrie, Mervyn Johns, Edward Lexy, John Glyn Jones, Stewart Granger, George Benson, Hans (John) Wengraf, James Knight, Patrick Parsons (Holt), John Boxer.

CORRIDOR OF MIRRORS (1948)   3

Dir *Terence Young.* Prod *Rudolph Cartier.* Scr *Cartier, Edana Romney.* Ph *André Thomas.* PC *Apollo Films.* Dis *General Film Distributors.* 105 *mins. Cert A*

Paul (*Eric Portman*), an artist, is obsessed with a girl in a 400-year-old picture; he believes himself to be the reincarnation of her lover, and that Mifanwy (*Edana Romney*) is the re-embodiment of the girl. His mistress (*Joan Maude*) is later found strangled; Paul hangs for the murder. Years later his housekeeper (*Barbara Mullen*) realizes Mifanwy is the killer, and that there is something very strange about her. She runs from her, but is killed by a car. A rum do and no mistake, and very arty; the players seem unsure how to react.

RoC *Hugh Sinclair, Bruce Belfrage, Alan Wheatley, Leslie Weston, Lois Maxwell, Valentine Dyall, Christopher Lee, Mavis Villiers, Hugh Latimer, John Penrose, Gordon McLeod, Noel Howlett, Thora Hird.*

COTTAGE TO LET (1941)   4
(USA: *Bombsight Stolen*)

Dir *Anthony Asquith.* Prod *Edward Black.* Scr *Anatole de Grunwald, J. O. C. Orton, from the play by Geoffrey Kerr.* Ph *Jack Cox.* PC *Gainsborough.* Dis *General Film Distributors.* 90 *mins. Cert A*

At his Scottish country-home Barrington (*Leslie Banks*) and his assistant Trently (*Michael Wilding*) complete a new bombsight for the Air Ministry. His cook is a fifth column spy, his butler a detective, and Dimble (*Alastair Sim*), who has rented the cottage in his grounds, an MI5 agent. Barrington is kidnapped by agents acting for Perrey (*John Mills*), a German posing as an RAF pilot, but rescued by Dimble, who guns Perrey down in a hall of mirrors. Fast-paced comedy-thriller with good characters.

RoC *Carla Lehmann, Jeanne de Casalis, George Cole, Frank Cellier, Catherine Lacey, Wally Patch, Hay Petrie, Muriel Aked, Muriel George.*

COUNTERBLAST (1948)　[3]

Dir *Paul L. Stein*. Prod *Louis H. Jackson*. Scr *Jack Whittingham*. Ph *James Wilson*. PC *British National*. Dis *Pathé*. 99 mins. Cert A

Murdering a British bacteriologist, Nazi scientist Dr Bruckner (*Mervyn Johns*) takes his identity and uses his laboratory to carry on his experiments in germ warfare. Ordered by Nazi Martha (*Sybilla Binder*) to kill his English assistant Tracy (*Nova Pilbeam*), of whom he is fond, Bruckner kills Martha instead. Found out, he flees, but in the hold of a boat leaving for Holland he is killed by poisonous fumes. Holes in plot spoil nicely constructed idea.

RoC *Robert Beatty, Margaretta Scott, Marie Lohr, Karel Stepanek, Alan Wheatley, Gladys Henson, John Salew, Anthony Eustrel, Carl Jaffe, Ronald Adam, Martin Miller, Aubrey Mallalieu, Horace Kenney, Archie Duncan, Kynaston Reeves, Jack Melford, Peter Madden, Frederick Schiller, Olive Sloane, Stevins Chambers, John England, Kenneth Keeling, H.G. Guinle.*

THE COURTENEYS OF CURZON STREET (1947)　[4]
(USA: *The Courtney Affair*)

Dir and Prod *Herbert Wilcox*. Scr *Nicholas Phipps*. Ph *Max Greene (Mutz Greenbaum)*. PC *Imperadio*. Dis *British Lion*. 120 mins. Cert U

Aristocratic Sir Edward (*Michael Wilding*) marries the parlour maid (*Anna Neagle*). Ostracized by Victorian society, she leaves him, bearing him a son. Later she makes good on the stage, sends his son to his old school, and they are reunited. Their son, who marries an aristocratic miss, is killed, but their grandson marries a factory girl in 1944. Pot-boiling *Cavalcade* of incident and sentiment. Tops at the box-office in its year.

RoC *Gladys Young, Coral Browne, Michael Medwin, Daphne Slater, Jack Watling, Helen Cherry, Bernard Lee, Percy Walsh, Thora Hird, Max Kirby, Terry Randall, Kenneth Warrington, James Kavanagh, Peter Hobbes, Martin Case, Ethel O'Shea. Alice Gatchet, Madge Brindley.*

CRIMES AT THE DARK HOUSE (1940)　[4]

Dir and Prod *George King (uncredited dir: David Macdonald)*. Scr *Edward Dryhurst, Frederick Hayward, H. F. Meltby, from a novel by Wilkie Collins*. Ph *Hone Glendinning*. PC *Pennant*. Dis *British Lion*. 69 mins. Cert A

Tongue-in-cheek version of *The Woman in White* put across in high melodramatic style, and certainly more enjoyable than the later Hollywood version. *Tod Slaughter* does perhaps his best film work as Sir Percival Glyde, who marries Laura (*Sylvia Marriott*) for her money, is thwarted by her sister, but seizes the opportunity provided by 'the woman in white', vengeful but deranged and dying daughter of the real Glyde (one of 'Sir Percival's' several murder victims), to put Laura in an asylum. She is rescued by an admirer, and 'Sir Percival' perishes in a church set ablaze by himself.

RoC *Hilary Eaves, Hay Petrie, Geoffrey Wardwell, David Horne, Margaret Yarde, Rita Grant, David Keir, Elsie Wagstaff.*

CROOKS' TOUR (1940)　[3]

Dir *John Baxter*. Prod *John Corfield*. Scr *John Watt, Max Kester, from a radio serial by Frank Launder, Sidney Gilliat (uncredited)*. Ph *James Wilson*. PC *British National*. Dis *Anglo-American*. 84 mins. Cert U

Charters (*Basil Radford*) and Caldicott (*Naunton Wayne*), upper-crust Englishmen touring the Near East, visit a Baghdad café to see La Palermo (*Greta Gynt*), a dancer. Accidentally given a record which, unknown to them, has on it information vital to Britain's enemies, they are pursued by German agents to Istanbul and Budapest. The Germans are bested - but Caldicott catches La Palermo with the disc and they tussle, to the concern of his fiancée, who bursts in, and La Palermo, who is a British agent. Comedy-thriller makes no demands on credulity.

RoC *Abraham Sofaer, Charles Oliver, Gordon McLeod, Bernard Rebel, Cyril Gardner, Morris Harvey, Leo de Pokorny, Noel Hood, Billy Shine, Peter Gawthorne, Andrea Malandrinos.*

CUP-TIE HONEYMOON (1947)　[1]

Dir and Prod *John E. Blakeley*. Scr *Anthony Toner, Harry Jackson*. Ph *Geoffrey Faithfull*. PC and Dis *Mancunian*. 93 mins. Cert A

Joe (*Sandy Powell*) runs a successful football team, and his talented son Eric (*Pat McGrath*) is torn between playing for the school side and his father's. A girl settles this case of divided loyalties - and Joe's team, with Pat's help, wins the Cup Final. Painful comedy; disastrous comeback for *Powell*.

RoC *Dan Young, Betty Jumel, Violet Farebrother, Frank Groves, Joyanne Bracewell, Vic Arnley, Harold Walden.*

THE CURE FOR LOVE (1949)　[3]

Dir and Prod *Robert Donat*. Scr *Walter Greenwood, Donat, Alexander Shaw, Albert Fennell, from Greenwood's play*. Ph *Jack Cox*. PC *Island Productions/London Films*. Dis *British Lion*. 98 mins. Cert U

War hero Jack Hardacre (*Robert Donat*) returns to his native Lancashire for 21 days' leave. He falls in love with Milly (*Renee Asherson*), a refugee from London. But a local girl (*Dora Bryan*) announces that *she* is engaged to Jack and privately vows to get him by fair means or foul. Although Jack has a rival for Milly, he manages to get out of his 'engagement' and marry the girl he loves. Leisurely, sometimes amusing comedy can't shake off its stage origins.

RoC *Marjorie Rhodes, Charles Victor, Thora Hird, Gladys Henson, John Stratton, Francis Wignall, Norman Partridge, Edna Morris, Michael Dear, Tonie MacMillan, Lilian Stanley, Margot Bryant, Lucille Gray, Jack Howarth, Sam Kydd, Jack Rodney, Reginald Green, Johnnie Catcher, Jan Conrad.*

THE CURSE OF THE WRAYDONS (1946)　[1]

Dir *Victor M. Gover*. Prod *Gilbert Church*. Scr *Michael Barringer*. Ph *S. D. Onions*. PC *Bushey Films*. Dis *Ambassador*. 94 mins. Cert A

After years in France, Philip Wraydon (*Tod Slaughter*) returns to England as head of Napoleon's spy system and with an insane hatred of the English. He invents contrivances designed to crush the life out of members of his own family. He tries to put the blame for the resultant killings on 'Trueblue' Jack (*Bruce Seton*), his nephew, but meets his doom in one of his own fiendish contraptions. Lurid horror-thriller is much too long and slow.

RoC *Gabriel Toyne, Lorraine Clewes, Andrew Laurence, Pearl Cameron, Ben Williams, Barry O'Neill, Alan Lawrence.*

D

DANCING WITH CRIME (1947)　[4]

Dir *John Paddy Carstairs*. Prod *James Carter*. Scr *Brock Williams*. Ph *Reginald Wyer*. PC *Coronet/Alliance*. Dis *Paramount*. 83 mins. Cert A

Ted Peters (*Richard Attenborough*), a young taxi-driver recently demobbed, nearly gets mixed up with a gang of crooks, then one night finds the body of the ringleader (*Bill Rowbotham - Bill Owen*), an ex-army pal, in his taxi. With the help of his girlfriend Joy (*Sheila Sim*), Ted tracks down the murderer, a slimy black marketeer (*Barry K. Barnes*), even though it places his own life in danger. Not exactly convincing, but a confident piece of filmcraft.

RoC *Garry Marsh, John Warwick, Judy Kelly, Barry Jones, Cyril Chamberlain, John Salew, Hamish Menzies, Peter Croft, Norman Shelley, Dennis Wyndham, Diana Dors, Patricia Dainton, Dirk Bogarde, Johnnie Schofield.*

THE DANCING YEARS (1949)　[3]

Dir *Harold French*. Prod *Warwick Ward*. Scr *Ward, Jack Whittingham, from the musical play by Ivor Novello*. Ph *Stephen Dade*. PC *Associated British*. Dis *AB-Pathé*. Technicolor. 96 mins. Cert A

Rudi (*Dennis Price*), a young composer in 1910 Vienna, finds fame with the help of Maria (*Gisèle Préville*), a musical comedy star, and he falls in love with her. But he loses her when she overhears his mock proposal of marriage to a youthful sweetheart (*Patricia Dainton*), and marries a prince (*Anthony Nicholls*). Rudi lives contented alone, with his music and his memories. Rather treacly operetta transferred straight to film for better or worse.

RoC *Olive Gilbert, Grey Blake, Muriel George, Jeremy Spenser, Martin Ross, Moyra Fraser, Gerald Case, Carl Jaffe, Sylvia Clark, Cynthia Teale, Diana Wilding, Jean Lodge, Pat Russell, Mary Midwinter, Arthur Lawrence, Russ Allen, Stanley Beard, Martin Boddey, John Howard, Delysia Blake, Janet Aleisser, John Williams, André Cordova, James White, Pamela Foster, Igo Barcinszki, Barry Ashton.*

DANGEROUS MOONLIGHT (1941) [4]
(USA: *Suicide Squadron*)

Dir *Brian Desmond Hurst*. Prod *William Sistrom*. Scr *Shaun Terence Young, Hurst, Rodney Ackland*. Ph *Georges Périnal*. PC and Dis *RKO Radio British*. 98 mins. *Cert U*

Stefan (*Anton Walbrook*), a Polish pianist, escapes to America in 1938, meeting and marrying a journalist, Carole (*Sally Gray*). By 1940, he feels compelled to suspend his musical career and join a Polish air squadron forming in England. Carole says she will leave him if he goes. He is badly wounded in the Battle of Britain and loses his memory, but regains it when he starts playing the piano. Carole comes back to him. Rather talky story redeemed by spectacular air combat shots, and a memorable theme in Richard Addinsell's *Warsaw Concerto*.

RoC *Derrick de Marney, Cecil Parker, Percy Parsons, Keneth Kent, J. H. Roberts, Guy Middleton, John Laurie, Frederick Valk, Philip Friend, Michael Rennie, Robert Beatty*.

DANNY BOY (1941) [3]
Dir *Oswald Mitchell*. Prod *Hugh Perceval*. Scr *Mitchell, A. Barr-Carson*. Ph *Stephen Dade*. PC *Signet*. Dis *Butchers*. 80 mins. *Cert U*

Remake of the director's own 1934 film, here with *Ann Todd* as the singer who leaves America and success (a hint to some of Britain's Hollywood stars?), returning to London in the blitz to seek her former husband Nick (*John Warwick*) and their son Danny. Nick, who has been playing his violin in the streets, gets a cabaret date, and the three are reunited at the same cabaret when Nick conducts a 'street orchestra'. Sincere playing gets it by.

RoC *Wilfrid Lawson, David Farrar, Wylie Watson, Grant Tyler, Albert Whelan, Tony Quinn, Norah Gordon, Percy Manchester, Pat Lennox, Harry Herbert*.

THE DARK ROAD (1947) [1]
Dir *Alfred Goulding*. Prod *Henry Halstead*. Scr *Uncredited*. Ph *Stanley Clinton*. PC *Marylebone*. Dis *Exclusive*. 72 mins. *Cert A*

A thriller novelist is commissioned to write a tale of a petty thief: he tells of a young boy who, through lack of parental guidance, drifts into a life of crime. He rises to a position of power in the underworld, but is unexpectedly laid low by a stroke of fate. Very raggedly made morality thriller.

LP *Charles Stuart, Joyce Linden, Antony Holles, Roddy Hughes, Patricia Hicks, Mackenzie Ward, Veronica Rose, Maxine Taylor, Michael Ripper, Rory McDermott, Sefton Yates, Joanna Carter, Cyril Chamberlain, Gale Douglas, Peter Reynolds, Sydney Bromley*.

DARK SECRET (1949) [1]
Dir *Maclean Rogers*. Prod *Ernest G. Roy*. Scr *A. R. Rawlinson, Moie Charles, from a play by Mordaunt Shairp*. Ph *W. J. Harvey*. PC *Nettlefold*. Dis *Butchers*. 85 mins. *Cert A*

Chris and Valerie Merryman, a hard-up young couple, let their country cottage, and the woman tenant is murdered there. When they return, Valerie (*Dinah Sheridan*) becomes obsessed with the crime, eventually believing

herself possessed by the spirit of the dead woman. Chris (*Emrys Jones*) brings her to her senses by discovering the truth of the crime. A remake of *The Crime at Blossoms* (1933), made by the same director. Not a good idea.

RoC *Irene Handl, Hugh Pryse, Barbara Couper, Percy Marmont, Geoffrey Sumner, MacKenzie Ward, Charles Hawtrey, John Salew, George Merritt, Stanley Vilven, Grace Arnold, Edgar Driver, Laurence Naismith, Esmé Beringer, Molly Hamley-Clifford, Terry Randall, Johnnie Schofield*.

THE DARK TOWER (1943) [2]
Dir *John Harlow*. Prod *Max Milder*. Scr *Brock Williams, Reginald Purdell, from the play by Alexander Woolcott, George S. Kaufman*. Ph *Otto Heller*. PC and Dis *Warner Bros*. 93 mins. *Cert A*

The circus run by Phil Danton (*Ben Lyon*) is in a bad way until Torg (*Herbert Lom*), a mysterious stranger, saves it by hypnotizing Mary (*Anne Crawford*) into doing a sensational act. To her brother's dismay, she is soon completely in the stranger's power, but her friends kill Torg to break his evil spell. Tawdry drama with eye-catching performance by Lom.

RoC *David Farrar, Billy (William) Hartnell, Frederick Burtwell, Josephine Wilson, Elsie Wagstaffe, J. H. Roberts*.

A DATE WITH A DREAM (1948) [1]
Dir *Dicky Leeman*. Prod *Robert S. Baker, Monty Berman*. Scr *Leeman, Baker, Berman*. Ph *Berman*. PC *Tempean*. Dis *Grand National*. 55 mins. *Cert U*

The Second World War ends, and a concert party breaks up after a triumphant Middle East tour. Finding at a reunion a year later that none of them has done too well, they decide to re-form. Jean (*Jean Carson*) joins them, and Terry (*Terry-Thomas*), Len (*Len Lowe*) and Bill (*Bill Lowe*) become rivals for her. She chooses Terry. Popular cast can't save bittily constructed comedy.

RoC *Norman Wisdom, Wally Patch, Elton Hayes*.

DAUGHTER OF DARKNESS (1947) [3]
Dir *Lance Comfort*. Prod *Victor Hanbury*. Scr *Max Catto, from his play* They Walk Alone. Ph *Stan Pavey*. PC *Alliance/Kenilworth*. Dis *Paramount*. 91 mins. *Cert A*

Emmy (*Siobhan McKenna*), a brooding Irish girl, is a homicidal nymphomaniac, as her admirers find out to their cost. She murders three times before herself meeting a grisly death at the jaws of her first victim's dog. Grim, sombre melodrama, not very credible, but pretty unusual for its time.

RoC *Maxwell Reed, Anne Crawford, Barry Morse, George Thorpe, Liam Redmond, Honor Blackman, Grant Tyler, David Greene, Denis Gordon, Arthur Hambling, George Merritt, Alexis Milne, Nora O'Mahoney, Ann Clery*.

DAYBREAK (1946) [3]
Dir *Compton Bennett*. Prod *Sydney Box*. Scr *Box, Muriel Box, from the play by Monckton Hoffe*. Ph *Reginald Wyer*. PC *Triton*. Dis *General Film Distributors*. 81 mins. *Cert A*

Eddie (*Eric Portman*), barber and public hangman, inherits a barge business. He meets and marries Frankie (*Ann Todd*), a lovely waif, and they live on one of the barges. His assistant Olaf (*Maxwell Reed*) wants Frankie and sets out to seduce her. Returning unexpectedly one night, Eddie finds them together. There is a fight and Eddie goes overboard. Frankie kills herself and Olaf is charged with Eddie's death. But Eddie has survived and eventually saves Olaf from hanging by revealing his identity. Held up for two years, this emerged much cut by the censor; what is left is unrelievedly glum.

RoC *Edward Rigby, Bill Owen, John Turnbull, Eliot Makeham, Maurice Denham, Jane Hylton, Milton Rosmer, Margaret Withers, Lyn Evans*.

THE DAY WILL DAWN (1942) [5]
(USA: *The Avengers*)

Dir *Harold French*. Prod *Paul Soskin*. Scr *Terence Rattigan, Anatole de Grunwald, Patrick Kirwan*. Ph *Bernard Knowles*. PC *Niksos Films*. Dis *General Film Distributors*. 98 mins. *Cert U*

1940. Colin (*Hugh Williams*), a rakish reporter, soon changes when, thanks to his friend Lockwood (*Ralph Richardson*), he is sent to Norway. A seaman and his daughter Kari (*Deborah Kerr*) show Colin the site of a U-boat base, to which, after escaping his German captors and witnessing Lockwood's death, he is able to guide British bombers. He and Kari, about to be shot, are rescued by commandos. Fine espionage melodrama has excellent direction.

RoC *Griffith Jones, Francis L. Sullivan, Roland Culver, Niall MacGinnis, Finlay Currie, Bernard Miles, Patricia Medina, Elizabeth Mann, Henry Oscar, John Warwick, David Horne, Jack Watling, Henry Hewitt, Alan Haines, Ann Farrer, George Merritt*.

Deborah Kerr and Hugh Williams in The Day Will Dawn (*1942*)

DEADLOCK (1943) [1]
Dir and Prod *Ronald Haines*. Scr *Uncredited*. Ph *Uncredited*. PC *British Foundation*. Dis *International Film Renters*. 59 mins. *Cert A*

Allan (*John Slater*), after feigning insanity to escape hanging, is sent to jail as a criminal lunatic. He escapes with the help of his twin brother Fred, whom he then murders. He is set to resume life with his wife, Eileen (*Cecile Chevreau*), but she has become embroiled with an old flame. Allan is about to kill them both when he is shot by a vengeful friend of Fred's. Very uninspired.

RoC *Hugh Morton, Molly Hamley-Clifford*.

DEAD OF NIGHT (1945) [6]

Dir *Cavalcanti, Basil Dearden, Robert Hamer, Charles Crichton.* (Associate) Prod *Sidney Cole, John Croydon.* Scr *Angus Macphail, John V. Baines, T.E.B. Clarke from stories by E.F. Benson, Macphail, Baines, H.G. Wells.* Ph *Douglas Slocombe, Stan Pavey.* PC *Ealing Studios.* Dis *Eagle-Lion. 102 mins. Cert A*

Architect Craig (*Mervyn Johns*) is, in a nightmare, summoned to a villa whose occupants tell him bizarre tales: a teenager at a Christmas party (*Sally Ann Howes*) meets a child ghost; a haunted mirror almost compels a repeat of a murder that happened in the room it reflects; an apparition saves a man from a fatal crash; a golfer commits suicide after a bet, but returns to haunt the partner who cheated; a ventriloquist (*Michael Redgrave*) is possessed by his own dummy. Craig is driven to strangle a psychiatrist (*Frederick Valk*) at the house. He awakes, but is summoned to *the* villa: this time, there can be no escape for him. Ghost-story telling *par excellence*, flawed only by the lighter 'golfing' story.

RoC *Roland Culver, Mary Merrall, Renee Gadd, Barbara Leake; Michael Allan, Robert Wyndham; Googie Withers, Ralph Michael, Esmé Percy; Antony Baird, Judy Kelly, Miles Malleson; Basil Radford, Naunton Wayne, Peggy Bryan; Hartley Power, Elisabeth Welch, Magda Kun, Garry Marsh, Allan Jeayes, John Maguire.*

DEAR MR PROHACK (1949) [3]

Dir *Thornton Freeland.* Prod *Ian Dalrymple.* Scr *Dalrymple, Donald Bull, from the play by Edward Knoblock and a novel by Arnold Bennett.* Ph *H.E. Fowle.* PC *Wessex.* Dis *General Film Distributors. 91 mins. Cert U*

Arnold Prohack (*Cecil Parker*), a Treasury official, comes into a fortune and finds he has less success handling his own finances than those of the nation. He is persuaded to make dubious investments and gamble on the stock market. He moves into a grand new home, and his wife, son and daughter are also financially foolish. A fortuitous stroke of fate returns him to the Treasury. Amusing central situation gradually wears thin.

RoC *Hermione Baddeley, Dirk Bogarde, Sheila Sim, Glynis Johns, Heather Thatcher, Frances Waring, Charles Goldner, Denholm Elliott, Campbell Cotts, Henry Edwards, Frederick Valk, Russell Waters, James Hayter, Bryan Forbes, Jon Pertwee, Ada Reeve, Judith Furse, Lloyd Pearson, Frederick Leister, Jerry Verno, Charles Perry, Janet Burnell, Ian Carmichael.*

DEAR MURDERER (1947) [4]

Dir *Arthur Crabtree.* Prod *Betty Box.* Scr *Muriel and Sydney Box, Peter Rogers, from the play by StJohn Legh Clowes.* Ph *Stephen Dade.* PC *Gainsborough.* Dis *General Film Distributors. 94 mins. Cert A*

Lee Warren (*Eric Portman*) returns after six months on business to find that his wife has had an affair with her solicitor. He murders him, making it appear suicide – then learns his wife (*Greta Gynt*) has a new lover, Jimmy (*Maxwell Reed*). He alters the death to look like murder, with Jimmy as the killer. The

Dennis Price in Dear Murderer *(1947)*

police suspect Lee, but his wife poisons him – only to find Jimmy has returned to his former fiancée. Unpleasant characters in intelligent, suspenseful drama.

RoC *Dennis Price, Jack Warner, Hazel Court, Andrew Crawford, Jane Hylton, John Blythe, Ernest Butcher, Charles Rolfe, Helen Burke, Valerie Ward, Vic Hagan, Howard Douglas.*

DEAR OCTOPUS (1943) [4]
(USA: *The Randolph Family*)

Dir *Harold French.* Prod *Edward Black.* Scr *R.J. Minney, Patrick Kirwan, from the play by Dodie Smith.* Ph *Arthur Crabtree.* PC *Gainsborough.* Dis *General Film Distributors. 86 mins. Cert A*

The 'octopus' is the family. Dora and Charles Randolph (*Helen Haye, Frederick Leister*) are celebrating their golden wedding. Three generations meet at their country home. Many problems are sorted out, but Dora and Charles lose their companion, Cynthia (*Celia Johnson*), who is an unofficial 'secretary' to the family, to an author relative, Nicholas (*Michael Wilding*). Lots of talk but some moving moments too.

RoC *Margaret Lockwood, Roland Culver, Basil Radford, Athene Seyler, Jean Cadell, Nora Swinburne, Antoinette Cellier, Kathleen Harrison, Madge Compton, Ann Stephens, Muriel George, Graham Moffatt, Derek Lansiaux, Alastair Stewart, Evelyn Hall, Annie Esmond, Irene Handl, Arthur Denton, Pamela Western, Arty Ash, Henry Morrell, Jane Gill-Davis, Frank Foster, Thelma Rea, Helen Goss, Noel Dainton, Barbara Douglas, Bobby Bradfield, Virginia Vernon, Jack Vyvyan, Leonard Sharp, James Lomas, Sidney Young, Amy Dalby, Jack Leslie.*

DEATH IN HIGH HEELS (1947) [1]

Dir and Scr *Lionel Tomlinson, from the novel by Christianna Brand.* Prod *Henry Halstead.* Ph *Stanley Clinton.* PC *Marylebone.* Dis *Exclusive. 47 mins. Cert A*

An imperious mannequin, Magda Doon (*Patricia Laffan*), who queens it over a small Bond Street dress salon, is killed by poison intended for the even more disliked Agnes Gregory (*Veronica Rose*). Detective Inspector Charlesworth eventually unmasks the guilty party in this unconvincing thriller that hardly does justice to the author's original novel.

RoC *Bill Hodge, Denise Anthony, Elsa Tee,*

Diana Wong, Leslie Spurling, Kenneth Warrington, Norah Gordon.

THE DEMI-PARADISE (1943) [4]
(USA: *Adventure for Two*)

Dir *Anthony Asquith.* Prod and Scr *Anatole de Grunwald.* Ph *Bernard Knowles.* PC *Two Cities.* Dis *General Film Distributors. 115 mins. Cert U*

Ivan (*Laurence Olivier*), Russian inventor of an icebreaker propeller, comes to pre-war England to get it made. He finds the people hard to know and, despite an attraction for Ann (*Penelope Dudley Ward*), the shipbuilder's granddaughter, goes back home. Returning in wartime, Ivan's view of the people changes. English persistence makes his invention a success and he decides to stay and marry Ann. Pleasantly satirical view of English ways.

RoC *Leslie Henson, Marjorie Fielding, Margaret Rutherford, Felix Aylmer, George Thorpe, Guy Middleton, Michael Shepley, Edie Martin, Joyce Grenfell, Jack Watling, Muriel Aked, Everley Gregg, Aubrey Mallalieu, Johnnie Schofield, John Laurie, Brian Nissen, Hay Petrie, Miles Malleson, John Boxer, Marian Spencer, Margaret Withers, Josephine Middleton, Wilfrid Hyde White, Alexis Chesnakoff, Mavis Clair, Charles Paton, George Street, Ben Williams, Beatrice Harrison, Inga Perten, Harry Fowler, George Cole, David Keir.*

DEMOBBED (1944) [2]

Dir and Prod *John E. Blakeley.* Scr *Roney Parsons, Anthony Toner.* Ph *Stephen Dade.* PC *Mancunian.* Dis *Butchers. 96 mins. Cert U*

Demobbed from the army, four trouble-making soldiers take jobs in an instrument-making factory where the foreman proves to be their old sergeant. Instruments are being stolen, but the famous four catch the thieves. Another long Mancunian comedy, slapstick and variety its mainstay. One critic felt that the cast 'spent most of their factory time doing weak variety acts'.

LP *Nat Jackley, Norman Evans, Dan Young, Jimmy Plant, Betty Jumel, Tony Dalton, Anne Firth, Neville Mapp, George Merritt, Fred Kitchen Jr, Gus McNaughton, Arthur Hambling, Marianne Lincoln, Kay Lewis, Fred Watts, Sydney Bromley, Edgar Driver, Noel Dainton, Marjorie Gresley, Angela Glynne, Anne Ziegler and Webster Booth, Felix Mendelssohn and His Hawaiian Serenaders.*

DIAMOND CITY (1949) [3]

Dir *David Macdonald.* Prod *A. Frank Bundy.* Scr *Roger Bray, Roland Pertwee.* Ph *Reginald Wyer.* PC *Gainsborough.* Dis *General Film Distributors. 90 mins. Cert U*

The opening of the South African diamond fields in the 1870s brings a flood of illicit diamond buyers. A diggers' community is formed in Klipdrift, where Parker (*David Farrar*), a tough adventurer, gets a concession for mining ahead of Muller (*Niall MacGinnis*), an unscrupulous rum trader. The rivalry between them leads to bloodshed and a republic is proclaimed before the British government takes over. Rough-and-tumble costume adventure.

RoC *Honor Blackman, Diana Dors, Andrew*

Crawford, Mervyn Johns, Phyllis Monkman, Bill Owen, Philo Hauser, Hal Osmond, John Blythe, Reginald Tate, Ronald Adam, Dennis Vance, Norris Smith, John Salew, Tony Quinn, Slim Harris, Julian Somers, Harry Quashie, Arthur Lane, John Warren, Ernest Butcher.

DICK BARTON – SPECIAL AGENT
(1948)   2

Dir *Alfred Goulding.* Prod *Henry Halstead.* Scr *Alan Stranks, Goulding,* from a radio serial by *Edward J. Mason.* Ph *Stanley Clinton.* PC *Marylebone.* Dis *Exclusive.* 70 mins. Cert U
Detective Dick Barton (*Don Stannard*) and his aides Jock (*Jack Shaw*) and Snowy (*George Ford*) arrive at a Cornish fishing village. The locals suspect that Dick is on to their smuggling, but he is after bigger fish. Via a subterranean passage, he tracks down Dr Caspar, who plans to destroy England with germ bombs. Very disappointing effort to film phenomenally popular radio show; poor casting.
RoC *Gillian Maude, Colin Douglas, Geoffrey Wincott, Beatrice Kane, Ivor Danvers, Arthur Bush, Alec Ross, Janice Lowthian, Morris Sweden, Farnham Baxter, Ernest Borrow, Beatrice Kane.*

DICK BARTON STRIKES BACK
(1949)   3

Dir *Godfrey Grayson.* Prod *Anthony Hinds, Mae Murray.* Scr *Ambrose Grayson,* from a radio serial by *Edward J. Mason.* Ph *Cedric Williams.* PC and Dis *Exclusive.* 71 mins. Cert U
An improvement on the radio sleuth's first film adventure; here Dick (*Don Stannard*) roots out a gang of criminals in possession of an atomic apparatus which has already destroyed two villages. Escaping from a cage of poisonous snakes, he pursues the arch-criminal, Forracuda (*Sebastian Cabot*) up Blackpool Tower, from which the fiend falls to his death. Enthusiastic juvenalia.
RoC *Jean Lodge, James Raglan, Bruce Walker, Humphrey Kent, John Harvey, Morris Sweden, Sydney Vivian, Toni Morelli, George Crawford, Laurie Taylor, Flash (dog).*

DON CHICAGO (1945)   2

Dir *Maclean Rogers.* Prod *Louis H. Jackson.* Scr *Austin Melford,* from the novel by *C.E. Bechhofer-Roberts.* Ph *Gerald Gibbs.* PC *British National.* Dis *Anglo-American.* 79 mins. Cert A
Don Chicago (*Jackie Hunter*), a timid tough, is chased out of America. Introduced to English society as a big-shot gangster, he wrecks a fake seance, tries to steal the Crown Jewels (and is thwarted by a comic cop) and opens a nightclub. His mother arrives to tell him that America has made him Public Enemy No. 1001. Possibilities of comedy defeated by quality of the material.
RoC *Joyce Heron, Claud Allister, Amy Veness, Wylie Watson, Donald (Don) Stannard, Charles Farrell, Finlay Currie, Cyril Smith, Ellen Pollock, Moira Lister, Wally Patch, Henry Wolston, Inga Anderson, C. Denier Warren, George Merritt, Charles Doe, Eric Winstone and His Band, The Modernaires.*

DON'T EVER LEAVE ME (1949)   2

Dir *Arthur Crabtree.* Prod *Sydney Box.* Scr *Robert Westerby,* from a novel by *Anthony Armstrong.* Ph *Stephen Dade.* PC *Triton.* Dis *General Film Distributors.* 85 mins. Cert U
Sheila (*Petula Clark*), bored young daughter of a famous actor (*Hugh Sinclair*), is thrilled when old lag Harry Denton (*Edward Rigby*) steals not only her father's car but her as well. Her father revels in the publicity, and Sheila is reluctant to return home, especially after meeting Harry's grandson (*Jimmy Hanley*). After a few hectic days she goes, making a spectacular return in front of her father's audience. Pleasant cast tries hard, but script is largely unfunny.
RoC *Linden Travers, Anthony Newley, Barbara Murray, Brenda Bruce, Maurice Denham, Sandra Dorne, Anthony Steel, Frederick Piper, Dandy Nichols, John Salew, Cyril Chamberlain, Michael Balfour, James Hayter, Russell Waters, Philip Stainton, Barbara Leake, Arthur Hambling, Ben Williams, Patricia Dainton, Elizabeth Blake, Douglas Herald, Lyn Evans.*

DON'T TAKE IT TO HEART (1944)   4

Dir and Scr *Jeffrey Dell.* Prod *Sydney Box.* Ph *Eric Cross.* PC *Two Cities.* Dis *General Film Distributors.* 91 mins. Cert U
Sightseeing lawyer Peter (*Richard Greene*), enchanted by Lord Chanduyt's daughter Mary (*Patricia Medina*), stays in the nearby hamlet to study old manuscripts uncovered by a bomb which has also released the ghost (*Richard Bird*) of one of the wilder Chanduyt ancestors. Trying to spike the guns of Pike, a profiteer (*Alfred Drayton*), Peter, with ghostly help, proves in court that Lord Chanduyt has no claim to the title, which belongs to the village poacher. The villager moves into the manor, Peter marries Mary and Chanduyt becomes a poacher. Fun, with gentle mockery of tradition.
RoC *Edward Rigby, Wylie Watson, Moore Marriott, Brefni O'Rorke, Amy Veness, Claude Dampier, Joan Hickson, Joyce Barbour, Ronald Squire, Ernest Thesiger, David Horne, Esma Cannon, Ivor Barnard, Patric Curwen, Margaret Withers, Harry Fowler, George Merritt, George Bailey, Edie Martin, Ernest Jay, Peter Cotes, John Salew, John Turnbull.*

Brefni O'Rourke, Richard Greene and Wylie Watson in Don't Take It To Heart *(1944)*

THE DOOR WITH SEVEN LOCKS
(1940)   4
(USA: *Chamber of Horrors*)

Dir *Norman Lee.* Prod *John Argyle.* Scr *Lee, Argyle, Gilbert Gunn,* from the novel by *Edgar Wallace.* Ph *Desmond Dickinson.* PC *Rialto.* Dis *Pathé.* 89 mins. Cert A
A rich man leaves his fortune in the family vault (sealed by a door with seven locks) where his body is buried. Sinister Dr Manetta (*Leslie Banks*), a descendant of Spanish Inquisitors, has his own private torture chamber and commits three murders in his hunt for the fortune; finally he is trapped in one of his own torture devices and reveals the secret of the seven-lock door. Robust blood and thunder, eerie and well-acted.
RoC *Lilli Palmer, Romilly Lunge, Gina Malo, David Horne, Richard Bird, Cathleen Nesbitt, J.H. Roberts, Aubrey Mallalieu, Harry Hutchinson, Ross Landon.*

DOWN MELODY LANE (1943)   3

No credits issued. PC and Dis *New Realm.* 60 mins. Cert U
Sam Mitchell (*Johnnie Schofield*), stage manager at a music-hall theatre, recalls how he met his wife, Trixie (*Lesley Osmond*), a barmaid at the music-hall, and some of the stars they saw over the years. This film includes excerpts from earlier movies.
RoC *Naughton and Gold, The Houston Sisters, Phyllis Robins, Leslie 'Hutch' Hutchinson, G.S. Melvin, The Australian Air Aces, The Sherman Fisher Girls.*

DREAMING (1944)   3

Dir, Prod and PC *John Baxter.* Scr *Bud Flanagan, Reginald Purdell.* Ph *Stan Pavey.* Dis *Ealing Studios.* 78 mins. Cert U
Private *Bud Flanagan* and Captain *Chesney Allen* are giving their idea of first aid to a fainted Wren when a heavy bag falls on Flanagan's head, causing him to dream he is (a) a white hunter in Africa pursued by natives but rescued by Allen and glamorous Tondelayo; (b) taking part in a raid over Berlin; (c) a jockey winning an important race in improbable circumstances; (d) running a stage door canteen where Goebbels appears to make a speech. Cheerful fooling.
RoC *Hazel Court, Dick Francis, Philip Wade, Gerry Wilmott, Ian MacLean, Roy Russell, Robert Adams, Sam Blake, Noel Dainton, Maurice Sweden, George Street, Kay Kendall, Teddy Brown, Reginald Foort, Gordon Richards, Raymond Glendenning, Bobby Jones, Alfredo Campoli, Donald McCullough, Band of HM Coldstream Guards, Peter Bernard.*

DR MORELLE – THE CASE OF THE MISSING HEIRESS (1949)   2

Dir *Godfrey Grayson.* Prod *Anthony Hinds.* Scr *Ambrose Grayson, Roy Plomley,* from the radio series by *Ernest Dudley* and a play by *Wilfred Burr.* Ph *Cedric Williams.* PC and Dis *Exclusive.* 73 mins. Cert A
Miss Frayle (*Julia Lang*), secretary to investigator Dr Morelle (*Valentine Dyall*), goes to find an old school friend, an heiress, who has vanished. She gets a job as a maid and per-

suades the sinister butler to help her search for clues. After she discovers her friend's charred remains, she sends for Dr Morelle, who arrives in time to trap the killer and save Miss Frayle from the same fate as the heiress. Good radio characters wasted in story built on absurdities.
RoC *Philip Leaver, Jean Lodge, Peter Drury, Bruce Walker, James Raglan.*

DUAL ALIBI (1947) [3]

Dir *Alfred Travers.* Prod *Louis H. Jackson.* Scr *Travers, Stephen Clarkson, Vivienne Ades.* Ph *James Wilson.* PC *British National.* Dis *Pathé. 81 mins. Cert A*
France. Twin trapeze artists Georges and Jules (*Herbert Lom*) win a million francs in the national lottery. Bergen (*Terence de Marney*) sets his girlfriend Penny (*Phyllis Dixey*) to get the winning ticket. She fails, but Bergen later manages to switch it for a worthless one. The twins vow vengeance, trace Bergen and kill him. A witness cannot prove which one of them did it. Good performance by Lom in dual role just keeps cheapie thriller going.
RoC *Ronald Frankau, Abraham Sofaer, Eugene Deckers, Ben Williams, Clarence Wright, Beryl Measor, Harold Berens, Sebastian Cabot, Marcel Poncin, Margaret Withers, Gerald Rex, Cromwell Brothers.*

Herbert Lom in dual role in Dual Alibi *(1947)*

THE DUMMY TALKS (1943) [3]

Dir *Oswald Mitchell.* Prod *Wallace Orton.* Scr *Michael Barringer.* Ph *Jimmy Wilson.* PC *British National.* Dis *Anglo-American. 85 mins. Cert A*
CID detective Piers Harriman (*G. H. Mulcaster*) visits the Empire theatre, where he suspects one of the performers of being a forger. Just after a mindreader's act, when Piers contrives to get one of the forged banknote numbers called out, a blackmailing ventriloquist is murdered backstage. Before the curtain rises on the second act, Piers holds a seance and finds the killer by having a midget pretend to be the dummy. Thriller could do with more story, less music-hall.
RoC *Claude Hulbert, Jack Warner, Manning Whiley, Beryl Orde, Derna (Hy) Hazell, John Carol, Charles Carson, Gordon Edwards, Max Earle, Leonard Sharp, Vi Kaley, Harry Herbert, Pamela Hesbitt, Wendy Welling, Arthur Denton, Olive Sloane, Ian Wilson, Barry Morse, Leslie Bradley, Patricia Hayes, Dorothy Gordon, Ivy Benson and Her All-Ladies Orchestra,* *Manley and Austin, Sylvester and Nephew, Skating Avalons, Five Lai Founs, Evelyn Darvell.*

EAST OF PICCADILLY (1940) [3]
(USA: The Strangler)

Dir *Harold Huth.* Prod *Walter C. Mycroft.* Scr *Lesley Storm, J. Lee Thompson, from the novel by Gordon Beckles.* Ph *Claude Friese-Greene.* PC *Associated British.* Dis *Pathé. 79 mins. Cert A*
Crime reporter Penny Sutton (*Judy Campbell*) and detective writer Tamsie Green (*Sebastian Shaw*) get on the case of the nylon stocking murders, in which London prostitutes are being strangled. An American millionaire, found to have been leading a double life, is convicted on circumstantial evidence; but, on the eve of his execution, Penny and Tamsie trap the real killer. Densely atmospheric murder thriller.
RoC *Henry Edwards, Niall MacGinnis, George Pughe, Martita Hunt, George Hayes, Cameron Hall, Edana Romney, Bunty Payne, Charles Victor, Frederick Piper, June Corda.*

EASY MONEY (1947) [3]

Dir *Bernard Knowles.* Prod *A. Frank Bundy.* Scr *Muriel and Sydney Box, from the play by Arnold Ridley.* Ph *Jack Asher.* PC *Gainsborough.* Dis *General Film Distributors. 94 mins. Cert A*
There's a jackpot on the football pools. The suburban Staffords believe their daughter has forgotten to post their coupon – but it was the coupon of the week before; they have won. A henpecked clerk (*Mervyn Johns*) is also a winner – but dies from a heart attack trying to give in his notice. A singer (*Greta Gynt*) seduces a pools checker (*Dennis Price*), but her attempt to win by fraud fails. Third winner is an old double-bass player (*Edward Rigby*) who buys up his orchestra and maddens the conductor he hates by putting the double-basses in front of the violins. Predictably variable portmanteau movie.
RoC *Marjorie Fielding, Jack Warner, Petula Clark, Yvonne Owen, Jack Watling, Mabel Constanduros, Maurice Denham; Joan Young, Gordon McLeod, David Horne, Grey Blake; Bill Owen, Dennis Harkin, Frederick Piper, Jack Raine, John Blythe, Freddie Carpenter, London Casino dancers; Guy Rolfe, Raymond Lovell, Frank Cellier.*

THE ECHO MURDERS (1945) [2]

Dir and Scr *John Harlow, from characters by Harry Blyth.* Prod *Louis H. Jackson.* Ph *James Wilson.* PC *British National/Strand.* Dis *Anglo-American. 75 mins. Cert A*
Detective Sexton Blake (*David Farrar*) is called to Cornwall by James Duncan (*Julien Mitchell*) who has been killed by the time he gets there. Acting on information supplied by two petty thieves whom he blackmails, Blake not only unmasks the murderer, but links Duncan's death and another with a Nazi plot to set up a base on the English coast. Enthusiastic but juvenile thick-ear thrills.
RoC *Pamela Stirling, Dennis Price, Dennis Arundell, Ferdi Mayne, Cyril Smith, Kynaston Reeves, Patric Curwen, Johnnie Schofield, Paul Croft, Desmond Roberts, Danny Green, Tony Arpino, Vincent Holman, Howard Douglas, Billy Howard, Anders Timberg, Victor Weske, Gerald Pring, Noel Dainton, Charles Hersee, Olive Walter.*

EDWARD MY SON (1948) [4]

Dir *George Cukor.* Prod *Edwin H. Knopf.* Scr *Donald Ogden Stewart, from the play by Robert Morley, Noel Langley.* Ph *F. A. Young.* PC and Dis *M-G-M British, 112 mins. Cert A*
Obsessed with the success of his son, Edward, Arnold Boult (*Spencer Tracy*) becomes a monster. He commits fraud and arson and drives two people to suicide. His wife (*Deborah Kerr*) drinks herself to death. Boult ends up with millions and a peerage, but Edward is killed in a plane crash after abandoning the girl expecting his son. Family friends wisely prevent Boult from locating his illegitimate grandson. Poignantly acted morality play with satirical undertones. Edward is never seen.
RoC *Ian Hunter, Leueen McGrath, James Donald, Mervyn Johns, Harriette Johns, Felix Aylmer, Walter Fitzgerald, Ernest Jay, Colin Gordon, Tilsa Page, Julian d'Albie, Clement McCallin.*

ELIZABETH OF LADYMEAD (1948) [3]

Dir and Prod *Herbert Wilcox.* Scr *Frank Harvey, from his play.* Ph *Max Greene (Mutz Greenbaum).* PC *Imperadio.* Dis *British Lion. Technicolor. 97 mins. Cert A*
When John (*Hugh Williams*) comes home from the Second World War and finds mother-in-law has moved in, he has a row with his wife Liz (*Anna Neagle*). She hits her head and is knocked out, dreaming of similar situations in 1854, 1903 and 1919. The first wife has become a feminist, the second has learned to run the estate herself, the third has become a wanton who drives her husband to suicide. Liz wakes up and they make up. Tedious repetition: Michael Wilding sorely missed.
RoC *Bernard Lee, Michael Laurence, Nicholas Phipps, Isobel Jeans, Hilda Bayley, Michael Shepley, Jack Allen, Catherine Paul, Kenneth Warrington, Claude Bailey.*

THE END OF THE RIVER (1947) [2]

Dir *Derek Twist.* Prod *Michael Powell, Emeric Pressburger.* Scr *Wolfgang Wilhelm, from the novel by Desmond Holdridge.* Ph *Christopher G. Challis.* PC *The Archers/Independent Producers.* Dis *General Film Distributors. 83 mins. Cert A*
Manuel (*Sabu*), an Amazon Indian, is banished by his tribe when he fails to take revenge for the killing of his family by a chieftain. He is looked after by an English prospector, a brutal trader and a kindly ship's master. He marries

an Indian girl (*Bibi Ferreira*), joins a sort of fascist union, is nearly sent to prison, loses his job, becomes a docker and kills a man in a brawl. Thanks to a persuasive lawyer, he is sent back to his homeland to till the land. Tedious.

RoC *Esmond Knight, Robert Douglas, Antoinette Cellier, Orlando Martins, Raymond Lovell, Torin Thatcher, James Hayter, Maurice Denham, Nicolette Bernard, Alan Wheatley, Charles Hawtrey, Zena Marshall, Dennis Arundell, Milton Rosmer, Minto Cato, Eva Hudson, Peter Illing, Nino Rossini, Basil Appleby, Milo Sperber, Andrea Malandrinos, Arthur Goullet, Russell Napier.*

ENGLISH WITHOUT TEARS (1944) [4]
(USA: *Her Man Gilbey*)
Dir *Harold French.* Prod *Anatole de Grunwald, Sydney Box, William Sassoon.* Scr *Terence Rattigan, de Grunwald.* Ph *Bernard Knowles.* PC *Two Cities.* Dis *General Film Distributors. 89 mins. Cert A*

Joan (*Penelope [Dudley] Ward*) is the susceptible niece of Lady Beauclerk (*Margaret Rutherford*), a defender of migratory birds, who goes to Switzerland to plead her cause, taking with her a Foreign Office man, and her butler Gilbey (*Michael Wilding*), with whom Joan falls in love. The war seals the romance when the butler becomes an officer and a gentleman. Charming, cleverly directed comedy.

RoC *Lilli Palmer, Claude Dauphin, Roland Culver, Albert Lieven, Peggy Cummins, Felix Aylmer, Guy Middleton, Martin Miller, Beryl Measor, Judith Furse, Gerard Heinze (Heinz), André Randall, Louise Lord, Joan Misseldine, Irene Handl, Frederick Richter, Antony Holles, Esma Cannon, David Keir, Ivor Barnard, Beryl Laverick, Primula Rollo, Heather Boys, Vida Hope, Margaret McGrath, J. A. Brimstone, Andrea Malandrinos, Johnnie Schofield, Peggy Carlisle, Brian Nissen, Pat(ricia) Owens.*

ESCAPE (1948) [3]
Dir *Joseph L. Mankiewicz.* Prod *William Perlberg.* Scr *Phillip Dunne, from the play by John Galsworthy.* Ph *Frederick A. Young.* PC and Dis *20th Century-Fox. 79 mins. Cert A*

Matt Denant (*Rex Harrison*), an ex-RAF man, accidentally kills a man who was bothering a young girl, and pays with a three-year sentence. Escaping to Dartmoor, he meets Dora (*Peggy Cummins*), who gives him food and clothes. When the police surround the church

Rex Harrison in Escape (*1948*)

in which he is hiding, she persuades him to surrender. He does so knowing she will be waiting for him. Fair thriller with good performances and atmosphere.

RoC *William Hartnell, Betty Ann Davies, Norman Wooland, Jill Esmond, Frederick Piper, Cyril Cusack, Marjorie Rhodes, John Slater, Frank Pettingell, Maurice Denham, Walter Hudd, Frederick Leister, George Woodbridge, Michael Golden, Frank Tickle, Jacqueline Clarke, Peter Croft, Stuart Lindsell, Ian Russell, Patrick Troughton, Cyril Smith.*

ESCAPE DANGEROUS (1947) [2]
Dir *Digby Smith.* Prod *Smith, John Denny.* Scr *Oswell Blakeston.* PC *DS Films.* Dis *H and S. 62 mins. Cert A*

1793. Dr Belhomme (*Beresford Egan*) is making himself a rich man by aiding wanted aristocrats to escape the guillotine for a fat fee, then betraying them to the Revolution for an even fatter one. His game is, not surprisingly, soon rumbled, and he gets his just deserts. Cardboard historical drama.

RoC *Mary (Marianne) Stone, Lily Lapidus, Peter Noble, Daphne Day, Humberston Wright.*

ESCAPE TO DANGER (1943) [4]
Dir *Victor Hanbury, Lance Comfort, Mutz Greenbaum.* Prod *William Sistrom.* Scr *Wolfgang Wilhelm, Jack Whittingham.* Ph *Guy Green.* PC and Dis *RKO Radio British. 92 mins. Cert A*

Joan (*Ann Dvorak*), a schoolmistress in Denmark, gets in with the Gestapo, though really working for the Danish underground. Sailing for England on a Nazi mission, she is torpedoed. Her drunken companion, Lawrence (*Eric Portman*) is revealed as a British agent and, after being picked up by a destroyer, they devise a plan to fool the Germans into misplacing vital coastal defences. The plan works but at the last moment Joan is shot down by a German agent. Solid thriller with good characters.

RoC *Karel Stepanek, Ronald Ward, Ronald Adam, Lilly Kann, David Peel, Felix Aylmer, Brefni O'Rorke, A. E. Matthews, Charles Victor, Marjorie Rhodes, Frederick Cooper, Ivor Barnard, Hay Petrie, George Merritt, Anthony Shaw, John Ruddock, Richard George.*

ESTHER WATERS (1948) [2]
Dir *Ian Dalrymple, Peter Proud.* Prod *Dalrymple.* Scr *Michael Gordon, William Rose, Gerard Tyrrell.* Ph *C. M. Pennington-Richards, H. E. Fowle.* PC *Wessex.* Dis *General Film Distributors. 109 mins. Cert A*

1873. Esther (*Kathleen Ryan*), a servant-girl, is seduced by a young groom, William Latch (*Dirk Bogarde*), and her child is born in a workhouse. After much suffering and hard work, she again meets William, and they marry. He becomes a bookmaker and for a while they prosper. Then comes a bad season, and his health begins to fail. Grappling with his assistant when he tries to welsh after a big race, William has an attack and eventually dies. Esther finds peace at the house where she began as a servant. Dreary drama.

RoC *Cyril Cusack, Ivor Barnard, Fay Comp-*

ton, *Mary Clare, Julian d'Albie, Morland Graham, Shelagh Fraser, Margaret Withers, Lalage Lewis, George Hayes, Alex Parker, Margaret Diamond, Joseph Dillon, Philip Ashley, Harry Ross, Billy Rees, Fred Lane, Nuna Davey, Barbara Shaw.*

EUREKA STOCKADE (1948) [4]
(USA: *Massacre Hill*)
Dir *Harry Watt.* (Associate) Prod *Leslie Norman.* Scr *Watt, Walter Greenwood, Ralph Smart.* Ph *George Heath.* PC *Ealing Studios.* Dis *General Film Distributors. 103 mins. Cert U*

1835. The discovery of gold in Australia brings a series of clashes between miners, government and the law. After riots and a lynching, the authorities act, and the miners are comprehensively beaten in a pitched battle at Eureka Hill. The surviving leaders, however, are acquitted, and public pressure brings all miners improved rights. Their leader, Lalor (*Chips Rafferty*) becomes an MP. Sprawling, brawling period adventure.

RoC *Jane Barrett, Gordon Jackson, Jack Lambert, Peter Illing, Ralph Truman, Sydney Loder, John Fernside, Grant Tyler, Peter Finch, Frederick Vern, Kevin Brennan, John Fegan, Al Thomas, Perk Allison, Reg Wykeham, Betty Ross, John Wiltshire, Nigel Lovell, Charles Tasman, Mary Ward, John Cazabon, Ron Whelan.*

Chips Rafferty and Gordon Jackson in Eureka Stockade (*1948*)

EYES THAT KILL (1947) [1]
Dir and Scr *Richard M. Grey.* Prod *Harry Goodman.* Ph *Ray Densham.* PC *Condor Films.* Dis *Butchers. 55 mins. Cert A*

Nazi war criminal Martin Bormann (*Robert Berkeley*) flees to Britain, sets up a secret organization called The Eyes That Kill, kidnaps a German atomic scientist, and tortures him for his secrets. But thanks to Medway (*William Price*) and his girlfriend Joan (*Sandra Dorne*), Bormann comes to a sticky end. Breathless thriller tries to cram too much in.

No supporting cast issued.

F

FACING THE MUSIC (1941) [2]

Dir and Prod *Maclean Rogers*. Scr *Rogers, Kathleen Butler*. Ph *Stephen Dade*. PC and Dis *Butchers*. 79 mins. Cert U

Sacked from job after job, Wilfred Hollebone (*Bunny Doyle*) is the obvious candidate for the managership of a 'dummy' munitions factory set up to fool the Germans. Spies duly raid the factory and are caught and Wilf is told to his amazement that he has been a success at something at last. Stodgy comedy.

RoC *Betty Driver, H. F. Maltby, Chili Bouchier, Wally Patch, Gus McNaughton, Ruby Miller, Eliot Makeham, Gordon McLeod, Ronald Chesney, Paddy Drew, Aubrey Mallalieu, Gerald Rex, Kenneth Henry, Eric Clavering, Dorothy Dewhurst, Rita Grant, Jack Vyvyan, Bryan Herbert, Paul Martin, John Slater, Marjorie Day, Norah Gordon, Vi Kaley, Percival Mackey's Band.*

THE FALLEN IDOL (1948) [6]

Dir *Carol Reed*. Prod *David O. Selznick, Reed*. Scr *Graham Greene, Lesley Storm, William Templeton*, from a story by *Greene*. Ph *Georges Périnal*. PC *London Films*. Dis *British Lion*. 95 mins. Cert A

Felipe (*Bobby Henrey*), eight-year-old son of a London-based ambassador, is left alone for the weekend with his pet snake MacGregor and Baines the butler (*Ralph Richardson*) and his harridan wife (*Sonia Dresdel*), who kills the snake. She later tricks the boy into revealing a conversation between Baines and his mistress (*Michèle Morgan*). The Baineses quarrel and Mrs Baines accidentally falls down a stairway to her death. Felipe attempts to protect Baines when police come; the very piece of evidence he tries to withhold proves the butler's innocence. Tense, moving, brilliantly scripted and ingeniously directed film; won British best picture Oscar for 1948.

RoC *Denis O'Dea, Jack Hawkins, Dora Bryan, Walter Fitzgerald, Bernard Lee, Karel Stepanek, Joan Young, Geoffrey Keen, James Hayter,*

Bobby Henrey and Ralph Richardson in The Fallen Idol (*1948*)

Hay Petrie, John Ruddock, Torin Thatcher, George Woodbridge, Dandy Nichols, Gerard Heinz, Norah Gordon, Ethel Coleridge, Ralph Norman, James Swan.

FALL OF THE HOUSE OF USHER (1949) [2]

Dir and Prod (*George*) *Ivan Barnett*. Scr *Kenneth Thompson, Dorothy Catt*, from the story by *Edgar Allan Poe*. PC *GIB Films*. Dis *Vigilant*. 70 mins. Cert H

Early 1800s. A curse is put on Roderick Usher (*Kay Tendeter*) and his sister Madeleine (*Gwendoline Watford*) by their mother's lover, who swears before he is beheaded that they shan't live past 30. A month before her 30th birthday, Madeleine dies from an undiagnosed illness. Roderick imagines she has been put prematurely in her coffin, and that she escapes to confront him. But is it imagination? Disjointed and hard to follow, but at times it *is* frightening.

RoC *Irving Steen, Lucy Pavey, Vernon Charles, Gavin Lee, Connie Goodwin, Tony Powell-Bristow, Robert Woollard, Keith Lorraine.*

FAME IS THE SPUR (1947) [4]

Dir *Roy Boulting*. Prod *John Boulting*. Scr *Nigel Balchin*, from the novel by *Howard Spring*. Ph *Günther Krampf*. PC *Two Cities*. Dis *General Film Distributors*. 116 mins. Cert A

1870: Hamer Radshaw (*Michael Redgrave*) is determined to fight for better conditions for his north-country fellows. He becomes a Labour MP, and stirs striking miners up to fury against their employers; a miner is killed. His wife Ann (*Rosamund John*) becomes a suffragette and goes to prison: Hamer disapproves. On her release, she dies from TB. The miners' strike of 1914 shows that they have lost confidence in Hamer: he is changing. Finally, be becomes Lord Radshaw in 1935, alone and friendless, a man who has not been true to his ideals. Thoughtful, well-made; might perhaps have stirred the blood more.

RoC *Bernard Miles, Carla Lehmann, Hugh Burden, Marjorie Fielding, Seymour Hicks, Anthony Wager, Brian Weske, Gerald Fox, David Tomlinson, Milton Rosmer, Wylie Watson, Jean Shepheard, Kenneth Griffith, Guy Verney, Percy Walsh, Charles Wood, Honor Blackman.*

FANNY BY GASLIGHT (1944) [4]
(USA: *Man of Evil*)

Dir *Anthony Asquith*. Prod *Edward Black*. Scr *Doreen Montgomery, Aimée Stuart*, from the novel by *Michael Sadleir*. Ph *Arthur Crabtree*. PC *Gainsborough*. Dis *General Film Distributors*. 108 mins. Cert A

Fanny (*Phyllis Calvert*) illegitimate daughter of a cabinet minister, goes to live with him in 1870 after her foster-father is killed in a brawl by evil Lord Manderstoke (*James Mason*). Her father's wife (Manderstoke's mistress) threatens a scandal over Fanny: the minister commits suicide. His secretary (*Stewart Granger*) loves Fanny, but is challenged to a duel by Manderstoke, who is killed. Period is nicely evoked, though only Mason really brings his character to life. A big box-office success.

RoC *Wilfrid Lawson, Margaretta Scott, Jean*

Kent, John Laurie, Stuart Lindsell, Nora Swinburne, Amy Veness, Ann Wilton, Helen Haye, Cathleen Nesbitt, Ann Stephens, Gloria Sydney, John Turnbull, Guy le Feuvre, Helen Goss, Peter Jones, Maureen O'Brien, Beryl Laverick, Virginia Keiley, Guy Gy-Mas.

THE FARMER'S WIFE (1940) [3]

Dir *Norman Lee, Leslie Arliss*. Prod *Walter C. Mycroft*. Scr *Lee, Arliss, J. E. Hunter*. Ph *Claude Friese-Greene*. PC *Associated British*. Dis *Pathé*. 82 mins. Cert U

Widower farmer Sam Sweetland (*Basil Sydney*) decides to re-marry and, with his farmhand Churdles (*Wilfrid Lawson*) and his housekeeper Araminta (*Nora Swinburne*) draws up a list of three candidates: a horsey widow, a spinster and the local barmaid, none of whom works out. After he stops a runaway bull, all three renew their interest. But he has decided to marry Araminta. Stock dose of rural humour.

RoC *Patricia Roc, Bunty Payne, Enid Stamp-Taylor, Betty Warren, Michael Wilding, Viola Lyel, Edward Rigby, Kenneth Griffith, A. Bromley Davenport, Jimmy Godden, Gilbert Gunn, James Harcourt, Mark Daly, Davina Craig.*

THE FATAL NIGHT (1948) [5]

Dir and Prod *Mario Zampi*. Scr *Gerald Butler, Kathleen Connors*, from a story by *Michael Arlen*. Ph *Cedric Williams*. PC *Anglofilm*. Dis *Columbia*. 50 mins. Cert A

Cyril and Tony (*Leslie Armstrong, Patrick Macnee*) dare Puce (*Lester Ferguson*), a young American, to spend a night in a haunted house. He is given a loaded revolver, a candle and a match. They leave a horror thriller as bedside reading. It tells the story of two young girls who come to a grisly end in a house of fear. The ghost walks, Puce fires, screaming…. Months later, Cyril and Tony, who had played the ghost and loaded the gun with blanks, meet Puce, who had vanished. Two men in white coats appear to take him back to the lunatic asylum. Genuinely frightening chiller made on record low budget; the best second-feature of its year.

RoC *Jean Short, Brenda Hogan, Aubrey Mallalieu.*

FIDDLERS THREE (1944) [2]

Dir *Harry Watt*. (Associate) Prod *Robert Hamer*. Scr *Watt, Diana Morgan, Angus Macphail*. Ph *Wilkie Cooper*. PC and Dis *Ealing Studios*. 88 mins. Cert A

Cycling back from leave, Tommy (*Tommy Trinder*) and The Prof (*Sonnie Hale*) pick up a Wren (*Diana Decker*). A storm breaks out, and they take shelter under the altar stone at Stonehenge. Struck by lightning they are, as per legend, transported back to ancient Rome. At first they save their necks by making prophecies. Just as they are to be thrown to the lions, lightning strikes again, and they are transported back. Could have been more sparkling.

RoC *Frances Day, Francis L. Sullivan, Elisabeth Welch, Mary Clare, Ernest Milton, Frederick Piper, Robert Wyndham, Russell*

Thorndike, Alec Mango, Danny Green, James Robertson (Justice), Kay Kendall, Frank Tickle.

FINGERS (1940)   [2]
Dir *Herbert Mason*. Prod *A.M. Salomon*. Scr *Brock Williams*. Ph *Basil Emmott*. PC and Dis *Warner Bros*. 69 mins. Cert A
A famous jewellery fence, Fingers (*Clifford Evans*) deserts his native East End to mingle with high society – and discovers he has made a mistake. He walks out on his high-class girlfriend Bonita (*Leonora Corbett*), forgets his life of crime, and returns to Meg (*Elizabeth Scott*), the working-class girl who loves him. About as much in story as synopsis suggests.
RoC *Edward Rigby, Esmond Knight, Roland Culver, Reginald Purdell, Joss Ambler, Peter Cotes.*

THE FIRST GENTLEMAN (1947)   [4]
(USA: *Affairs of a Rogue*)
Dir *Cavalcanti*. Prod *Joseph Friedman*. Scr *Nicholas Phipps, Reginald Long, from the play by Norman Ginsbury*. Ph *Jack Hildyard*. PC and Dis *Columbia British*. 111 mins. Cert A
1814. The Prince Regent (*Cecil Parker*), envious of his daughter Charlotte's (*Joan Hopkins*) popularity, tries to marry her off to William of Orange. She refuses and, after 18 months as a virtual prisoner in Windsor Castle, she outmanoeuvres him and marries the man of her choice, Prince Leopold of Saxe-Coburg (*Jean-Pierre Aumont*). 18 months later, she dies giving birth to a stillborn son. Good performances and re-creation of past; but pretty lumbering withal.
RoC *Margaretta Scott, Ronald Squire, Athene Seyler, Jack Livesey, Hugh Griffith, Anthony Hawtrey, Gerard Heinz, George Curzon, Betty Huntley-Wright, Tom Gill, Lydia Sherwood, Frances Waring, Amy Frank, Joan Young, Richard Shayne, Judy Beaumont, Olwen Brookes, Melissa Stribling, Drusilla Wills, Judith Nelmes, Dorothy Hammond.*

Jean-Pierre Aumont, Joan Hopkins and Cecil Parker in The First Gentleman *(1948)*

THE FIRST OF THE FEW (1942)   [5]
(USA: *Spitfire*)
Dir *Leslie Howard*. Prod *Howard, George King, John Stafford, Adrian Brunel*. Scr *Anatole de Grunwald, Miles Malleson*. Ph *Georges Périnal*. PC *Misbourne/British Aviation*. Dis *General Film Distributors*. 118 mins. Cert U

The life story of aircraft designer R. J. Mitchell, starting with his failures and successes in Schneider Trophy races. A visit to Germany in the 1930s resolves Mitchell (*Leslie Howard*) to build Britain the best and fastest fighter in the world. In the face of government apathy, he nears his ambition, then is told he has a year to live unless he quits work. Sacrificing himself to the project, Mitchell dies as the first Spitfires roar overhead. Inspiring tribute, with great music from *William Walton*.
RoC *David Niven, Rosamund John, Roland Culver, Anne Firth, David Horne, J. H. Roberts, Filippo del Giudice, Derrick de Marney, Rosalyn Boulter, Tonie Edgar Bruce, Gordon McLeod, Erik Freund, Brefni O'Rorke, Bernard Miles, Miles Malleson, Gerry Wilmott, Patricia Medina, Herbert Cameron, George Skillan, F.R. Wendhausen, John Chandos, Victor Beaumont, Suzanne Clair, Robert Beatty, Jack Peach.*

THE FLAMINGO AFFAIR (1947)   [2]
Dir and Prod *Horace Shepherd*. Scr *Maurice Moisiewitch*. Ph *Freddie Ford*. PC *Inspiration*. Dis *Grand National*. 66 mins. Cert A
Demobbed from the commandos, Frank (*Dennis Webb*) gets a job in a garage. Infatuated with glamorous Paula (*Colette Melville*), he agrees to help burgle his employer's safe. But the early arrival of two thieves prompts the garage owner to entrust Frank with the money. Changing his mind, Frank knocks the crooks out and bids a determined farewell to Paula. Undistinguished.
RoC *Arthur Chesney, Eddie Matthews, Michael Anthony, Geoffrey Wilmer, Charmain Innes, Stephane Grappelly and His Quintet, Eugene Pini and His Tango Orchestra.*

THE FLEMISH FARM (1943)   [4]
Dir *Jeffrey Dell*. Prod *Sydney Box*. Scr *Dell, Jill Craigie*. Ph *Eric Cross*. PC *Two Cities*. Dis *General Film Distributors*. 82 mins. Cert U
Escaping from occupied Belgium, Matagne (*Philip Friend*) and Duclos (*Clifford Evans*), burying the flag of the Belgian Air Force on Matagne's farm, flee to England and join the RAF. Matagne is killed in the Battle of Britain and Duclos is dropped by parachute to retrieve the flag. With the help of Matagne's wife (*Jane Baxter*), he achieves his aim. Restrained heroics.
RoC *Clive Brook, Brefni O'Rorke, Wylie Watson, Ronald Squire, Mary Jerrold, Charles Compton, Richard George, Lilly Kann, Irene Handl, Martin Walter, Wendy Hall, Basil Cunard, Neville Mapp, Valerie Forrest, Peter Tennant, John Boxer.*

FLIGHT FROM FOLLY (1945)   [3]
Dir and Prod *Herbert Mason*. Scr *Basil Woon, Lesley Storm, Katherine Strueby, from a story by Edmund Goulding*. Ph *Otto Heller*. PC and Dis *Warner Bros*. 94 mins. Cert A
Out-of-work showgirl Sue Brown (*Pat Kirkwood*) poses as a nurse and lands the job of looking after Clinton Clay (*Hugh Sinclair*), a neurotic and alcoholic composer deserted by his wife. Sue puts up with his tantrums and goes with him to Majorca, where he hopes to

effect a reconciliation with his wife. Events there convince him that his true love is – Sue. Quite lively, tuneful if lower-bracket musical.
RoC *Sydney Howard, Jean Gillie, A. E. Matthews, Tamara Desni, Leslie Bradley, Marian Spencer, Charles Goldner, Mildred Shay, Halamar and Konarski, Edmundo Ros and His Rhumba Band.*

FLOODTIDE (1949)   [3]
Dir *Frederick Wilson*. Prod *Donald B. Wilson*. Scr *George Blake, the Wilsons*. Ph *George Stretton*. PC *Aquila*. Dis *General Film Distributors*. 90 mins. Cert A
Spurning family farming traditions, David Shields (*Gordon Jackson*) gets a job in the Glasgow shipyards. He achieves his ambition to design ships by hard work, falling in love with Mary (*Rona Anderson*), the boss's daughter. They quarrel, but reconcile after David has saved a new ship from damage by storm on the eve of its launching. Fair romantic drama with good settings and exciting moments.
RoC *John Laurie, Jack Lambert, Jimmy Logan, Elizabeth Sellars, Janet Brown, Gordon McLeod, Ian MacLean, Archie Duncan, Molly Weir, Ian Wallace, Kitty Kirwan, Alexander Archdale, Peter Illing, Grace Garvin, Alastair Hunter, Norah Gordon, Molly Urquhart, Sam Kydd, James Fraser, Arthur Lowe, Hugh Munro.*

FLY AWAY PETER (1948)   [3]
Dir *Charles Saunders*. Prod *Henry Passmore*. Scr *Arthur Reid, from the play by A. P. Dearsley*. Ph *Roy Fogwell*. PC *Production Facilities*. Dis *General Film Distributors*. 60 mins. Cert U
The middle-class Hapgood family is gradually splitting up, despite fresh opposition from mother (*Kathleen Boutall*) as each offspring leaves home, to get married or go abroad. But when she sees her youngest daughter is willing to stay at home, and forget her own happiness, just to please her, Mrs Hapgood is moved to accept the inevitable. Rather stagey but agreeable little picture.
RoC *Frederick Piper, Margaret Barton, Patrick Holt, Elspet Gray, Peter Hammond, Nigel Buchanan, John Singer, Sam Kydd, Josephine Stuart.*

FLYING FORTRESS (1942)   [3]
Dir *Walter Forde*. Prod *Max Milner*. Scr *Gordon Wellesley, Edward Dryhurst, Brock Williams*. Ph *Basil Emmott*. PC and Dis *Warner Bros*. 109 mins. Cert U
An irresponsible millionaire, Jim (*Richard Greene*), after causing the death of a passenger in his private plane – Jim's pilot, Kelly (*Donald Stewart*), is held to blame – reforms and joins the Air Ferry Service in Canada: his instructor proves to be Kelly. In a London air-raid, they finally bury the hatchet, and both take part in an RAF bombing raid on Berlin. Good action scenes, novelettish script.
RoC *Carla Lehmann, Betty Stockfeld, Charles Heslop, Sidney King, Basil Radford, Joss Ambler, Edward Rigby, Billy (William) Hartnell, John Boxer, Peter Croft, Tommy Duggan, Hubert Gregg, Robert Beatty, Andrea Malandrinos.*

THE FLYING SQUAD (1940)　　[2]
Dir *Herbert Brenon.* Prod *Walter C. Mycroft.* Scr *Doreen Montgomery, from the novel by Edgar Wallace.* Ph *Claude Friese-Greene, W. Harvey.* PC and Dis *Associated British.* 64 mins. Cert A
The adventures of a Scotland Yard man (*Sebastian Shaw*) on the trail of a gang of smugglers, whose leader makes no bones about disposing of those who might make life awkward for him. The sister (*Phyllis Brooks*) of one of these victims joins the gang to get inside information and, working with the detective, brings the villains to justice. Not very good.
RoC *Jack Hawkins, Basil Radford, Ludwig Stossel, Manning Whiley, Kathleen Harrison, Cyril Smith, Henry Oscar, Kynaston Reeves.*

THE FOOL AND THE PRINCESS (1948)　　[3]
Dir and Scr *William C. Hammond, from the novel by Stephen Spender.* Prod *Frank Hoare.* Ph *A. T. Dinsdale.* PC *Merton Park.* Dis *General Film Distributors.* 73 mins. Cert A
Kate's husband Harry (*Bruce Lester*) cannot settle to civilian life after the war. Telling Kate (*Lesley Brook*) that he met a princess in Germany whom he loves, he returns there on business, straightens things out with the 'princess' (who isn't) and flies back to England determined to make a fresh start – with Kate. Well-acted, intelligent comedy-romance, a shade too unambitious.
RoC *Adina Mandlova, Murray Matheson, Irene Handl, MacDonald Parke, Vi Kaley, Millicent Russell, Sylvia Harker, Gordon Phillott, Julian Henry, Paul Erikson, Richard Nelson.*

FOOLS RUSH IN (1948)　　[2]
Dir *John Paddy Carstairs.* Prod *Aubrey Baring.* Scr *Geoffrey Kerr, from the play by Kenneth Horne.* Ph *Geoffrey Unsworth.* PC *Pinewood.* Dis *General Film Distributors.* 82 mins. Cert A
Pamela (*Sally Ann Howes*) panics on the morning of her wedding, which she postpones, as much as anything else because of the arrival of her father (*Guy Rolfe*): she cannot see why her mother (*Nora Swinburne*) divorced him. Indeed, her parents decide to re-marry. Mother's fiancé flies off to Peru in a huff and Pamela is able to go through with her own ceremony at last. A few funny moments, but rather tiresome.
RoC *Nigel Buchanan, Raymond Lovell, Thora Hird, Patricia Raine, Nora Nicholson, Peter Hammond, Charles Victor, Esma Cannon, Guy Verney, Jonathan Field, David Lines, George Mansfield.*

FORBIDDEN (1948)　　[4]
Dir and Prod *George King.* Scr *Katherine Strueby.* Ph *Hone Glendinning.* PC *Pennant Pictures.* Dis *British Lion.* 87 mins. Cert A
Jim (*Douglas Montgomery*), patent medicine man at a fair, falls for Joan (*Hazel Court*), the ice-cream girl. She is upset on finding he is married. When his wife refuses to divorce him, Jim increases her pills to play on her weak heart. Remorseful, he rushes home. She is dead. He buries her – then finds the extra pills, untaken. Fleeing, he is cornered by police on

Blackpool tower, only to find that they knew all along his wife died from a heart attack. Dark little drama keeps its suspense going, creates believable characters.
RoC *Patricia Burke, Garry Marsh, Kenneth Griffith, Ronald Shiner, Eliot Makeham, Frederick Leister, Richard Bird, Michael Medwin, Andrew Cruickshank, William Douglas, Dora Stevening, Erik Chitty, Peggy Ann Clifford, Dennis Hawkins, Peter Jones.*

THE FOREMAN WENT TO FRANCE (1942)　　[5]
(USA: *Somewhere in France*)
Dir *Charles Frend.* (Associate) Prod *Alberto Cavalcanti.* Scr *John Dighton, Angus Macphail, Leslie Arliss, Roger Macdougall, Diana Morgan, from a story by J. B. Priestley.* Ph *Wilkie Cooper.* PC *Ealing Studios.* Dis *United Artists.* 87 mins. Cert A
Fred (*Clifford Evans*), a British foreman, journeys to France in 1940 to prevent vital machinery from falling into enemy hands. Befriended by two soldiers (*Tommy Trinder, Gordon Jackson*) and an American girl (*Constance Cummings*), he outwits fifth columnists and succeeds in shipping the machinery home after a hazardous lorry journey to the coast. Engaging blend of comedy and thrills, based on a real-life character, Melbourne Johns, to whom the film is dedicated.
RoC *Robert Morley, Paul Bonifas, Ernest Milton, Charles Victor, John Williams, Anita Palacine, François Sully (Francis L. Sullivan), Ronald Adam, Mervyn Johns, Bill Blewett, Mrs Blewett, John Boxer, Owen Reynolds, Eric Maturin, Tony Ainley, Michèle Forbes-Fraser, Edward Lisle, Robert Bendall, Nora Herman, Irone Kirilloff, Madeleine Rive, Thora Hird.*

Clifford Evans, Tommy Trinder, Constance Cummings and Gordon Jackson in The Foreman Went to France (*1942*)

FOR FREEDOM (1940)　　[5]
Dir *Maurice Elvey, Castleton Knight.* Prod *Edward Black, Knight.* Scr *Miles Malleson, Leslie Arliss.* Ph *Arthur Crabtree.* PC *Gainsborough.* Dis *General Film Distributors.* 87 mins. Cert U
A newsreel chief and his son, Will and Steve Ferguson (*Will Fyffe, Anthony Hulme*) agree to make a film on human achievement, but Will reverts to his original idea of *Shadow Over Europe* when Hitler invades Czechoslovakia. Steve resigns and goes to South America, where he captures the story of the

battle of the River Plate, in which the German battleship *Graf Spee* is sunk by the British ships *Exeter* and *Ajax*. Excellent semi-documentary strikes just the right note.
RoC *Guy Middleton, Albert Lieven, Hugh McDermott, E. V. H. Emmett, Billy Russell, Arthur Goullet, Millicent Wolf, Pat Williams, Jack Raine, Arthur Denton, Capt Dove, Capt Pottinger, F. O. Murphy, Engineers Walker and Angel, Vice-Admiral J. E. T. Harper (narrator).*

FOR THEM THAT TRESPASS (1949)　　[3]
Dir *Cavalcanti.* Prod *Victor Skutezky.* Scr *J. Lee Thompson, William Douglas Home, from the novel by Ernest Raymond.* Ph *Derek Williams.* PC and Dis *Associated British-Pathé.* 95 mins. Cert A
Writer Christopher Drew (*Stephen Murray*) crosses to 'the other side of the tracks' to associate with Frankie (*Rosalyn Boulter*). When she is murdered by Heal (*Michael Laurence*), Drew withholds vital information and ex-convict Herb Logan (*Richard Todd*) takes the rap. Released after ten years, Logan extracts a deathbed confession from Heal, then tricks Drew into revealing the facts that prove his innocence. Story holds its grip despite basically unconvincing characters.
RoC *Patricia Plunkett, Joan Dowling, Mary Merrall, Frederick Leister, Helen Cherry, Michael Medwin, Vida Hope, Harry Fowler, Irene Handl, James Hayter, George Curzon, Valentine Dyall, Robert Harris, Harcourt Williams, John Salew, Kynaston Reeves, George Hayes, Ian Fleming, Edward Lexy, Michael Brennan.*

Rosalyn Boulter and Richard Todd in For Them That Trespass (*1949*)

FOR THOSE IN PERIL (1944)　　[4]
Dir *Charles Crichton.* (Associate) Prod *S. C. Balcon.* Scr *Harry Watt, J. O. C. Orton, T. E. B. Clarke.* Ph *Douglas Slocombe, Ernest Palmer.* PC and Dis *Ealing Studios.* 67 mins. Cert U
Rawlings (*Ralph Michael*) joins Murray's (*David Farrar*) air-sea rescue unit in wartime, unhappy as his heart is in flying. Sent out after a dinghy near the French coast, they encounter a minefield, fog and attack by an armed trawler, after picking up the drifting aircrew. The navy rescues them but, when the trawler is sunk, German shore batteries open fire. Going back through the minefield, they are strafed by planes and Murray is killed. A changed Rawl-

ings brings the rescue craft home. Variably acted, but gripping, vivid, brilliantly photographed wartime realism.

RoC *Robert Wyndham, John Slater, John Batten, Robert Griffiths, Anthony Bushell, William Rodwell, Anthony Bazell, Leslie Clarke, James Robertson (Justice), Peter Arne.*

FORTUNE LANE (1947)   3

Dir and Prod *John Baxter.* Scr *Geoffrey Orme, Mary Cathcart Borer.* Ph *Jo Jago, Brendan Stafford.* PC *Elstree Independent.* Dis *General Film Distributors. 60 mins. Cert U*

Young Peter (*Douglas Barr*) wants to be an engineer and needs money to develop an invention. His father says he must raise it himself – or join the family market gardening business. He and an Irish friend, Tim (*Brian Weske*) become window cleaners. Tim needs money to see his sick grandfather in Ireland; Peter gives him all they have earned. But virtue has its reward ... and eventually he is hailed as a budding genius. Pleasant, simple film for children.

RoC *Billy Thatcher, Angela Glynne, George Carney, Nail Ballantyne, Antony Holles.*

49TH PARALLEL (1941)   5
(USA: The Invaders)

Dir *Michael Powell.* Prod *John Sutro, Powell.* Scr *Emeric Pressburger, Rodney Ackland.* Ph *Frederick A. Young.* PC *Ortus Films.* Dis *General Film Distributors. 123 mins. Cert U*

With their U-boat trapped and sunk in the Gulf of St Lawrence, six Germans try to escape across Canada to then-neutral America. One by one they are captured or killed, one by his own comrades when he defends a Hutterite settlement against them. The Nazi leader (*Eric Portman*, rising to stardom) is finally dispatched on board a train by a Canadian soldier (*Raymond Massey*). Out-of-the-rut propaganda thriller.

RoC *Leslie Howard, Laurence Olivier, Anton Walbrook, Glynis Johns, Niall MacGinnis, Finlay Currie, Raymond Lovell, John Chandos, Basil Appleby, Eric Clavering, Charles Victor, Ley On, Richard George, Frederick Piper, Tawera Moana, Charles Rolfe, Theodore Salt, O. W. Fonger, *Robert Beatty.*

* scene deleted from final release print

Glynis Johns in 49th Parallel (*1941*)

FOR YOU ALONE (1945)   3
Dir *Geoffrey Faithfull.* Prod *F. W. Baker.* Scr

Montgomery Tully. Ph *Ernest Palmer.* PC and Dis *Butchers. 105 mins (later 98). Cert U*

Lt John Bradshaw (*Robert Griffith*) loves vicar's daughter Katherine (*Lesley Brook*), but she feels she must look after her father, since her brother (*Jimmy Hanley*) is missing in Malaya. Her brother returns with a half-blind (from injuries) friend Max (*Manning Whiley*) who falls for the sympathetic Katherine. With his eyesight improving, he realizes she loves John, and leaves. Weepie with music: too long, but with some touching moments.

RoC *Dinah Sheridan, G. H. Mulcaster, Olive Walter, Irene Handl, George Merritt, Muriel George, Hay Petrie, Aubrey Mallalieu, Billy Shine, Helen Hill, Heddle Nash, Albert Sandler, London Symphony Orchestra.*

FREEDOM RADIO (1941)   4
(USA: A Voice in the Night)

Dir *Anthony Asquith.* Prod *Mario Zampi.* Scr *Basil Woon, Gordon Wellesley, Louis Golding, Anatole de Grunwald, Bridget Boland, Jeffrey Dell, Roland Pertwee.* Ph *Bernard Knowles.* PC *Two Cities.* Dis *Columbia. 95 mins*

Austrian throat specialist Dr Karl Roder (*Clive Brook*) opposes Nazism, while his wife Irena (*Diana Wynyard*) accepts a post in Berlin. With the help of Hans (*Derek Farr*), a young engineer, whose girlfriend Elly (*Joyce Howard*) has been raped by a stormtrooper and sent to a concentration camp, Karl founds Freedom Radio, denouncing Nazism and sabotaging Hitler speeches. He is reconciled with a disillusioned Irena, but her fanatical brother (*John Penrose*) betrays Freedom Radio. Karl and Irena are killed, but Hans and Elly, who has escaped, ensure that Freedom Radio lives on. Gripping, more subtle than most anti-Nazi melodramas.

RoC *Roland Squire, Raymond Huntley, Bernard Miles, Howard Marion Crawford, Morland Graham, Clifford Evans, Reginald Beckwith, Gibb McLaughlin, Muriel George, Martita Hunt, Hay Petrie, Manning Whiley, Abraham Sofaer, Katie Johnson, George Hayes.*

Diana Wynyard and Clive Brook in Freedom Radio (*1941*)

FRIEDA (1947)   5
Dir *Basil Dearden.* (Associate) Prod *Michael Relph.* Scr *Ronald Millar, Angus Macphail, from Miller's play.* Ph *Gordon Dines.* PC *Ealing Studios.* Dis *General Film Distributors. 98 mins. Cert A*

To save Frieda (*Mai Zetterling*), a German girl, from reprisals, after she helps him escape from a POW camp, Robert (*David Farrar*) marries her. In England, she suffers from the hostility of the local town, and his aunt (*Flora Robson*), a fanatical anti-German MP. Frieda's pro-Nazi brother (*Albert Lieven*) appears, and is given a beating by Robert when he implies Frieda is also pro-Nazi. But Robert has lost faith in her, and she attempts suicide. He prevents her, but they face an uncertain future together. Sensitive, forceful and uncompromising.

RoC *Glynis Johns, Barbara Everest, Gladys Henson, Ray Jackson, Patrick Holt, Milton Rosmer, Barry Letts, Barry Jones, Garry Marsh, Gilbert Davis, Renee Gadd, Douglas Jefferies, Eliot Makeham, Norman Pierce, John Ruddock, D. A. Clarke-Smith, Aubrey Mallalieu, John Molecey, Stanley Escane, Gerhard Hinze (Gerard Heinz), Arthur Howard.*

FRONT LINE KIDS (1942)   3
Dir *Maclean Rogers.* Prod *Hugh Perceval.* Scr *Kathleen Butler, H. F. Maltby.* Ph *Stephen Dade.* PC *Signet.* Dis *Butchers. 80 mins. Cert U*

The leaders of a gang of street urchins are found jobs as page boys by Nobby Clarkson (*Leslie Fuller*), a hotel head porter. The rest are evacuated. The hotel manager, a crook, is, with his female accomplice, hoping to double-cross jewel thieves coming to the hotel. The boys get on to both sides and, aided by the return of the evacuees, fed up with country life, put paid to them both. Smooth-running farce is fair family fun.

RoC *Marion Gerth, Antony Holles, Gerard Rex, John Singer, George Pughe, Ralph Michael, Eric Clavering, Kay Lewis, O. B. Clarence, David Keir, Norman Pierce, Vi Kaley, Douglas Stewart, Ben Williams, Vincent Holman, Norah Gordon, Gerald Moore, John Tacchi, David Anthony, Michael John, Brian Fitzpatrick, Derek Prendergast.*

G

GAIETY GEORGE (1946)   3
(USA: Showtime)

Dir and Prod *George King.* Scr *Katherine Strueby,* Ph *Otto Heller.* PC *Embassy.* Dis *Warner Bros. 98 mins. Cert U*

Irishman George Howard (*Richard Greene*) comes to London in the 1890s and buys the lease of a theatre. He puts on 'musical comedies', a new type of entertainment, and enjoys great success, marrying his original leading lady. In Austria when the First World War breaks out, he is interned for most of its duration. Broken in health, he is helped by his wife and friends to make a West End comeback before he dies. Period well caught, but characters uninteresting.

RoC *Ann Todd, Peter Graves, Hazel Court, Leni Lynn, Ursula Jeans, Morland Graham, Frank Pettingell, Charles Victor, Maire O'Neill, Jack Train, Daphne Barker, Phyllis Robins, John Laurie, Frederick Burtwell, Antony Holles, David Horne, Patrick Waddington, Claud Allister, Wally Patch, Graeme Muir, Evelyn Darvell, Paul Blake, John Miller, Richard Molinas, Gerhardt Kempinski, Carl Jaffe, Maxwell Reed, Roger Moore.*

GARRISON FOLLIES (1940)   [3]

Dir *Maclean Rogers.* Prod *Hugh Perceval, Ernest Gartside.* Scr *Rogers, Kathleen Butler, H.F. Maltby.* Ph *Geoffrey Faithfull.* PC *Signet.* Dis *Butchers. 64 mins. Cert U*

Rastminster aerodrome little knows what it has let itself in for when a retired Indian army major (*H.F. Maltby* in tremendous form) is put in charge and arranges a concert party which includes Alf (*Barry Lupino*), a cornet-playing plumber who, via the order of the wrong kind of tanks for a water carnival, becomes involved in an incredible profusion of plumbers and Mr Plummers. Music hall-style skit: good wartime blues-chaser.

RoC *Nancy O'Neil, John Kevan, Hugh Dempster, Gabrielle Brune, Neville Brook, Denys Val Norton, Harry Herbert, Jack Vyvyan, David Tomlinson, Rita Grant, Martyn Box, Sylvia Kellaway and Leslie, Ann Lenner, Joan Davis' Eight Rose Petals, Dorothy Lloyd, Percival Mackey's Band.*

GASBAGS (1940)   [4]

Dir *Marcel Varnel.* Prod *Edward Black.* Scr *Val Guest, Marriott Edgar.* Ph *Arthur Crabtree.* PC *Gainsborough.* Dis *General Film Distributors. 77 mins. Cert U*

The Crazy Gang (*Bud Flanagan, Chesney Allen, Jimmy Nervo, Teddy Knox, Charlie Naughton, Jimmy Gold*) tie a barrage balloon to their fish-and-chip stall and land on the Western Front. In a prison camp, they meet Jerry (*Moore Marriott*) a very old prisoner with plans of a secret weapon drawn on his back. They decide to find the weapon, a tank that burrows underground. Teddy impersonates Hitler, not knowing there is a plot to assassinate him. They stumble on the tank and return with it to England, where they are arrested for misappropriating a balloon. Crazy is the word.

RoC *Wally Patch, Peter Gawthorne, Frederick Valk, Eric Clavering, Anthony Eustrel, Carl Jaffe, Manning Whiley, Torin Thatcher, Irene Handl, Mavis Villiers, Gerik Schjelderup, Richard Morell, Theodore Zichy, Gerald Cooper, Frank Henderson, Felicity Andrae, Rowland Douglas, Rolf Brandt, George Merritt, John Lothar, Pat Noonan.*

GASLIGHT (1940)   [5]
(USA: *Angel Street*)

Dir *Thorold Dickinson.* Prod *John Corfield.* Scr *A.R. Rawlinson, Bridget Boland.* Ph *Bernard Knowles.* PC *British National.* Dis *Anglo-American. 88 mins. Cert A*

1880: Paul and Bella Mallen (*Anton Walbrook,*

Anton Walbrook and (blurred in foreground) Frank Pettingell in Gaslight *(1940)*

Diana Wynyard) buy an old house where a widow was murdered 15 years before. Paul soon begins a campaign to drive his wife to madness, and orders her helpful cousin Ullswater (*Robert Newton*) from the house. Bella's mind begins to crumble, but she is reached by a dogged policeman (*Frank Pettingell*), who brings evidence that Mallen not only married her bigamously, but killed his rich aunt 15 years ago, and has returned to hunt for the rubies he never found. Mallen, now completely mad himself, is taken into custody. Gripping, harrowing essay in fear.

RoC *Cathleen Cordell, Jimmy Hanley, Minnie Rayner, Marie Wright, Mary Hinton, Jack Barty, Aubrey Dexter, Angus Morrison, The Darmora Ballet.*

GENTLEMAN OF VENTURE (1940)   [3]
(USA: *It Happened to One Man*)

Dir *Paul L. Stein.* Prod *Victor Hanbury.* Scr *Paul Merzbach, Nina Jarvis, from the play by Roland Pertwee, John Hastings Turner.* Ph *Walter Harvey.* PC *British Eagle.* Dis *RKO Radio. 80 mins. Cert A*

Shady financier Felton Quair (*Wilfrid Lawson*) goes to jail, thanks to a treacherous partner, Ackroyd (*Reginald Tate*), serves his sentence and leaves for South America, where he kills Ackroyd in a fight. Returning, he finds his family living under an assumed name. Rather than ruin their new life, he abandons an (above-board) venture and leaves, promising his son he will return for him when successful.

RoC *Nora Swinburne, Marta Labarr, Ivan Brandt, Brian Worth, Edmund Breon, Patricia Roc, Athole Stewart, Thorley Walters, Ruth Maitland, Ian Fleming.*

THE GENTLE SEX (1943)   [5]

Dir *Leslie Howard, Maurice Elvey.* Prod *Howard, Derrick de Marney.* Scr *Moie Charles, Aimée Stuart, Roland Pertwee, Phyllis Rose.* Ph *Robert Krasker.* PC *Two Cities/Concanen.* Dis *General Film Distributors. 93 mins. Cert U*

Seven girls from very varied backgrounds join the ATS in the Second World War. They are trained for different jobs, part company to face separate dangers, but later come together again, helping to ward off an enemy bombing blitz at an anti-aircraft station. A well-made film: the emotional contest rings true, and the action scenes - the air-raid, an all-night lorry convoy - are vividly done.

LP *John Gates, Jean Gillie, Joan Greenwood, Joyce Howard, Rosamund John, Lilli Palmer, Barbara Waring, John Justin, Frederick Leister, Mary Jerrold, Everley Gregg, Anthony Bazell, Elliot Mason, John Laurie, Rosalyn Boulter, Meriel Forbes, Harry Welchman, Peter Cotes, Jimmy Hanley, Ronald Shiner, Miles Malleson, Noreen Craven, Roland Pertwee, Nicholas Stuart, Frank Atkinson, Maud Dunham, Amy Dalby, Grace Arnold, Claude Bailey, Richard George, Clifford Buckton, Frederick Peisley, James Sadler, Leslie Howard (and narrator).*

GEORGE AND MARGARET (1940)   [4]

Dir *George King.* Prod *A.M. Salomon.* Scr *Brock Williams, Rodney Ackland, from the play by Gerald Savory.* Ph *Basil Emmott.* PC and Dis *Warner Bros. 77 mins. Cert U*

An announcement that the dreaded George and Margaret are coming to dinner throws the Garth-Binders into a panic. All the family tries to make excuses, but Mrs G-B (*Marie Lohr*) has hysterics.... Frankie G-B (*Judy Kelly*) breaks her lunch date with Roger (*Oliver Wakefield*), who storms out. Claude G-B (*John Boxer*) declares he's marrying the maid. Mrs G-B has hysterics. ... The maid pulls everyone round. Witty comedy of chaos from successful play. (George and Margaret are never seen.)

RoC *Noel Howlett, Ann Casson, Arthur Macrae, Irene Handl, Margaret Yarde, Gus McNaughton.*

GEORGE IN CIVVY STREET (1946)   [2]

Dir *Marcel Varnel.* Prod *Varnel, Ben Henry.* Scr *Peter Fraser, Ted Kavanagh, Max Kester, Gale Pedrick.* Ph *Phil Grindrod.* PC and Dis *Columbia British. 79 mins. Cert A*

Demobbed, George (*George Formby*) and his ex-pickpocket pal Fingers (*Ronald Shiner*) go to The Unicorn, the village pub George owns. He loves Mary (*Rosalyn Boulter*), of the Lion, but finds she now has a manager, Jed (*Frank Drew*), who becomes George's rival. Jed sends a stripper along to ruin George's jazzband reopening, and lose him his licence. After a free-for-all, George wins the day. Despite a formidable array of new writers, this stale comedy ended Formby's film career.

RoC *Wally Patch, Philippa Hiatt, Ian Fleming, Enid Cruickshank, Mike Johnson, Moore Raymond, Robert Ginns, Daphne Elphinstone, Rita Varien, John Coyle, Roddy Hughes, Lyn Evans, Johnny Claes and His Claepigeons.*

GERT AND DAISY CLEAN UP (1942)   [3]

Dir *Maclean Rogers.* Prod *F.W. Baker.* Scr *Kathleen Butler, H.F. Maltby.* Ph *Stephen Dade.* PC and Dis *Butchers. 85 mins. Cert U*

Cockneys Gert and Daisy (*Elsie and Doris Waters*) are fired from their café after soap gets mixed up with cheese. Their efforts to start a salvage campaign are not much more successful, but they do manage to expose the activities of Perry (*Joss Ambler*), a leading local light whose grocery and philanthropic concerns are a cloak for black marketeering. Rumbustious farce with ebullient performances from the stars.

RoC *Iris Vandeleur, Elizabeth Hunt, Ralph*

Michael, Tonie Edgar Bruce, Douglas Stewart, Harry Herbert, Angela Glynne, Uriel Porter.

GERT AND DAISY'S WEEKEND (1941)   ③

Dir *Maclean Rogers.* Prod *F. W. Baker.* Scr *Rogers, Kathleen Butler, H. F. Maltby.* Ph *Stephen Dade.* PC and Dis *Butchers. 79 mins. Cert U*

Gert and Daisy (*Elsie and Doris Waters*) are put in charge of a party of tearaway evacuee children. The kids contrive to wreck Lady Plumtree's country seat at Little Pipham Hall, but also unmask two jewel thieves. Pretty wild comedy goes at a fair old pace; material is broad but the stars play it with gusto.

RoC *Iris Vandeleur, John Slater, Wally Patch, Elizabeth Hunt, Annie Esmond, Aubrey Mallalieu, Gerald Rex.*

GET CRACKING (1943)   ⑤

Dir *Marcel Varnel.* Prod *Ben Henry.* Scr *L. duGarde Peach.* Ph *Stephen Dade.* PC and Dis *Columbia British. 96 mins. Cert U*

Rivalry between the Major Wallop and Minor Wallop Home Guards comes to a head when the War Office sends a machine gun by rail, and both sides try to get it. Furious at losing his stripe when Major Wallop pinch the gun, garage mechanic George (*George Formby*) converts his repair lorry into a tank, leads Minor Wallop to victory in an exercise and recaptures the gun single-handed. Formby's last really good film, full of crazy almost-impossibilities.

RoC *Dinah Sheridan, Edward Rigby, Frank Pettingell, Wally Patch, Ronald Shiner, Mike Johnson, Irene Handl, Vera Frances, Desmond Jeans, Pauline Winter, Jack Vyvyan, Harry Fowler.*

THE GHOST OF ST MICHAEL'S (1941)   ④

Dir *Marcel Varnel.* (Associate) Prod *Basil Dearden.* Scr *Angus Macphail, John Dighton.* Ph *Derek Williams.* PC *Ealing Studios.* Dis *Associated British. 82 mins. Cert A*

Incompetent William Lamb (*Will Hay*), new master at St Michael's, is the butt of the boys. With war, the school is evacuated to a gloomy Scottish castle. The caretaker tells of phantom pipes when anyone is about to die. The pipes play: the head (*Felix Aylmer*) dies; so does his successor (*Raymond Huntley*), whom Lamb had suspected. Will's friend Hilary (*Claude Hulbert*) is made head, but the pipes wail again. But the real murderer, the matron (*Elliot Mason*), in the pay of the Germans and engaged in signalling to enemy submarines, is this time fortuitously trapped. Happy mixture of Hay's best character and a topical comedy-thriller.

RoC *Charles Hawtrey, John Laurie, Hay Petrie, Roddy Hughes, Manning Whiley, Derek Blomfield, Brefni O'Rorke.*

THE GHOSTS OF BERKELEY SQUARE (1947)   ③

Dir *Vernon Sewell.* Prod *Louis H. Jackson.* Scr *James Seymour, from a novel by Caryl Brahms and S. J. Simon.* Ph *Ernest Palmer.* PC *British National.* Dis *Pathé. 89 mins. Cert A*

Two ghosts of military men (*Robert Morley, Felix Aylmer*) are doomed to haunt their Mayfair mansion until it is visited by a reigning monarch. All their efforts with successive tenants come to naught. When the house is bombed in the First World War, it seems they are condemned to roam the earth for eternity. But Queen Mary visits it while inspecting war damage, and saves their spectral skins. Episodic comedy, amusingly developed, but a bit stretched to reach feature length.

RoC *Yvonne Arnaud, Claude Hulbert, Abraham Sofaer, Ernest Thesiger, Marie Lohr, Martita Hunt, John Longden, A. E. Matthews, Ronald Frankau, Wilfrid Hyde White, Martin Miller, Wally Patch, Esmé Percy, Mary Jerrold, Robert Beaumont, Madge Brindley, Strelsa Brown, Ronald Shiner, Harry Fine, James Hayter, Gerhardt Kempinski, Edward Lexy, Aubrey Mallalieu, Anthony Marlowe, Mary Martlew, J. H. Roberts, Pamela Roberts, Tom Walls Jr.*

THE GHOST TRAIN (1941)   ④

Dir *Walter Forde.* Prod *Edward Black.* Scr *Marriott Edgar, Val Guest, J. O. C. Orton, Sidney Gilliat, from the play by Arnold Ridley.* Ph *John J. Cox.* PC *Gainsborough.* Dis *General Film Distributors. 85 mins. Cert A*

Eight people find themselves stranded at Fal Vale junction in Cornwall. Forced to stay the night, they are regaled by the stationmaster's tales of The Ghost Train that hurtles through the station. The 'ghost' turns out to be a gang of fifth-columnists running arms (smugglers in earlier film versions of the story), who are routed by comedian Tommy Gander (*Arthur Askey*) and his friend Teddy (*Richard Murdoch*). Slow to start, but lots of laughs and thrills later.

RoC *Kathleen Harrison, Morland Graham, Linden Travers, Peter Murray Hill, Carole Lynne, Herbert Lomas, Raymond Huntley, Betty Jardine, Stuart Latham, D. J. Williams, Wallace Bosco, Sydney Monckton, George Merritt.*

Herbert Lomas and Arthur Askey in The Ghost Train *(1941)*

A GIRL IN A MILLION (1946)   ④

Dir *Francis Searle.* Prod *Sydney Box.* Scr *Muriel and Sydney Box.* Ph *Reginald H. Wyer.* PC *Boca Productions.* Dis *British Lion. 90 mins. Cert A*

Freed by divorce from a relentlessly nagging wife, scientist Tony (*Hugh Williams*) settles down to a bachelor existence at his laboratory in the country. He is beguiled by a dumb girl (*Joan Greenwood*) and marries her; she recovers her voice and proves just as bad a nag as his first wife. So he divorces her too. Then she loses her voice again. ... Amusing light entertainment; made Miss Greenwood a star.

RoC *Basil Radford, Naunton Wayne, Wylie Watson, Yvonne Owen, Hartley Power, Garry Marsh, Edward Lexy, Eileen Joyce, James Knight, Charles Rolfe, Gwen Clark (Jane Hylton), Millicent Wolf, Aubrey Mallalieu, Michael Hordern, Julian d'Albie, John Salew, John Olson.*

THE GIRL IN THE NEWS (1940)   ④

Dir *Carol Reed.* Prod *Edward Black.* Scr *Sidney Gilliat, from the novel by Roy Vickers.* Ph *Otto Kanturek.* PC *Twentieth Century.* Dis *M-G-M. 78 mins. Cert A*

Anne (*Margaret Lockwood*), a nurse, is charged with murder when an elderly patient who had left her money dies mysteriously. Stephen Farringdon (*Barry K. Barnes*), though thinking her guilty, successfully defends her. When she takes a new nursing post under an assumed name, circumstances repeat themselves. Stephen, seeing she has been framed, proves her innocence and unmasks the guilty party. Neat combination of romance, suspense and thrills.

RoC *Emlyn Williams, Roger Livesey, Margaretta Scott, Wyndham Goldie, Basil Radford, Irene Handl, Mervyn Johns, Betty Jardine, Kathleen Harrison, Felix Aylmer, Roland Culver, Edward Rigby, Jerry Verno, Allan Jeayes, Richard Bird, Michael Hordern, V. R. Bateson, Ben Williams, Pauline Winter, Bryan Herbert, Roddy Hughes, Aubrey Mallalieu.*

THE GIRL WHO COULDN'T QUITE (1949)   ③

Dir *Norman Lee.* Prod and PC *John Argyle.* Scr *Lee, Marjorie Deans, from the play by Leo Marks.* Ph *Geoffrey Faithfull.* Dis *Monarch. 85 mins. Cert A*

Ruth (*Elizabeth Henson*) hasn't smiled since she was a little girl. But the friendship of Tim (*Bill Owen*), a tramp, makes her laugh again. After she tells him about her unhappy childhood, she suffers an attack of amnesia. He cures that, too, but she then forgets all about him and what he has done. Tim goes unhappily out of her life. Blend of laughter and tears isn't as unbearable as it might have been.

RoC *Betty Stockfeld, Iris Hoey, Stuart Lindsell, Vernon Kelso, Rose Howlett, Fred Groves.*

GIVE ME THE STARS (1944)   ②

Dir *Maclean Rogers.* Prod *Fred Zelnik.* Scr *Rogers, Austin Melford.* Ph *James Wilson.* PC *British National.* Dis *Anglo-American. 90 mins. Cert A*

Toni Martin (*Leni Lynn*), an American orphan, comes to England in search of her uncle Hector MacTavish (*Will Fyffe*), once a famous music-hall star. She finds him drowning in whisky and tries to reform him. When he is knocked down in an accident, she takes his place entertaining a theatre queue, is engaged by a nearby nightclub and becomes a great success. MacTavish takes the pledge and gets

a chance in pantomime. Further unsuccessful attempt to launch American songbird.
RoC *Jackie Hunter, Olga Lindo, Emrys Jones, Margaret Vyner, Antony Holles, Grace Arnold, Patric Curwen, Joss Ambler, Hilda Bayley, Angela Glynne, Robert Griffith, Johnnie Schofield, Janet Morrison, Hal Gordon, David Trickett, George Merritt, David Keir, Alan Johnstone, Stanley Paskin, Harry Herbert, Sidney Arnold, George Spence, Larry Jay, Ben Williams, Vi Kaley, Desmond Roberts, Kenneth Mosely, Peter Lowry, Jack Williams, George Pughe, Jack May, Trixie Scales, Philip Hillman, Brookes Turner, Keith Shepherd.*

GIVE US THE MOON (1944)   3
Dir and Scr *Val Guest, from a novel by Caryl Brahms, S.J. Simon.* Prod *Edward Black.* Ph *Phil Grindrod.* PC *Gainsborough.* Dis *General Film Distributors. 95 mins. Cert U*
The future. Three years after the war is over, a young man (*Peter Graves*) stumbles into a Soho society, the Elephants, whose qualification for membership is a total disregard for work. Nevertheless, they decide to help him run a hotel. Chaos inevitably follows. Satirical farce of sorts with *Jean Simmons* as 'a hard-boiled child of 11'.
RoC *Margaret Lockwood, Vic Oliver, Roland Culver, Max Bacon, Frank Cellier, Eliot Makeham, Iris Lang, George Relph, Gibb McLaughlin, Irene Handl, Henry Hewitt, Jonathan Field, John Salew, Rosamund Greenwood, Arty Ash, Frank Atkinson, George Hirste, Dorothy Bramhall, Jean Capra, Monte de Lyle, Gertrude Kaye, Pat(ricia) Owens, Harry Fowler, Charles Paton, Joy Millan, Lysbeth Sydney, Owen Fellows, Arthur Denton.*

GIVE US THIS DAY (1949)   3
(USA: *Salt to the Devil*)
Dir *Edward Dmytryk.* Prod *Rod E. Geiger, Nat A. Bronsten.* PC *Ben Barzman, John Penn, from a novel by Pietro di Donato.* Ph *C. M. Pennington-Richards.* PC *Plantagenet.* Dis *General Film Distributors. 120 mins. Cert A*
Brooklyn 1921. Geremio (*Sam Wanamaker*) sends for Lucrezia (*Lea Padovani*) to come to America, saying he has a house. He has lied; they settle down to life in a slum. 1929: for the sake of their children, he takes a job on a safety-last building site. His friend is crippled in an accident and Geremio seeks solace in drink and an old flame (*Kathleen Ryan*). Finally a building collapses and he is drowned in liquid concrete. Strong dose of tragedy.
RoC *Bonar Colleano, Charles Goldner, Bill (William) Sylvester, Sidney James, Karel Stepanek, Nino Pastellides, Philo Hauser, Ina de la Haye, Rosalie Crutchley, Ronan O'Casey, Robert Rietty, Charles Moffat.*

THE GLASS MOUNTAIN (1948)   4
Dir *Henry Cass.* Prod *John Sutro, Fred Zelnik, Joseph Janni.* Scr *Janni, Cass, John Hunter, Emery Bonnet, John Cousins.* Ph *William McLeod.* PC *Victoria.* Dis *Renown. 98 mins. Cert A*
Shot down in Italy during the Second World War, Richard (*Michael Denison*), a composer, is helped by an Italian girl, Alida (*Valentina*

Cortesa). He falls in love with her. She tells him the legend of the Glass Mountain. When he returns to his wife (*Dulcie Gray*) in England, he writes an opera based on it. He goes back to Italy to see Alida, but returns to his wife for good after she has been hurt in an air crash. Rather slow love story boosted considerably by its striking direction, photography and especially music (*Nino Rota* wrote the hit theme).
RoC *Tito Gobbi, Sebastian Shaw, Antonio Centa, Sidney King, Elena Rizzieri, Arnold Marle, Ferdinand Terschack.*

GOLDEN ARROW (1949)   2
(USA: *The Gay Adventure*)
Dir *Gordon Parry.* Prod and PC *Anatole de Grunwald.* Scr *Paul Darcy, Sid Colin, de Grunwald.* Ph *Otto Heller.* Dis *Renown. 82 mins. Cert U*
Three men and a girl travel in the same section of the Golden Arrow express from Paris. Each of the men daydreams a story involving himself and the girl - the French bus-driver that she is a model on the Riviera, the American officer that she is a Berlin club singer, and the British businessman that she is a film star on the run from the Press. Hard to tell why this ordinary film was held up for nearly four years, finally getting a circuit release in 1953, by which time *Kathleen Harrison*, who only appears in one episode, had been promoted from supporting player to star. Made under title *Three Men and a Girl.*
RoC *Jean-Pierre Aumont, Burgess Meredith, Richard Murdoch, Paula Valeska, Julian d'Albie, José de Almeyda, Karel Stepanek, Edward Lexy, Hilda Bayley, Ernest Jay, Colin Gordon, Natasha Parry, Sandra Dorne, Philip Slessor.*

THE GOLDEN MADONNA (1948)   2
Dir *Ladislas Vajda.* Prod *John Stafford.* Scr *Akos Tolnay.* Ph *Anchise Brazzi, Otello Martelli.* PC *Independent Film Producers.* Dis *Warner Bros. 88 mins. Cert A*
A British girl, Patricia (*Phyllis Calvert*), who inherits property in Italy, accidentally throws away a painting which symbolizes prosperity to the local villagers. Her efforts to retrieve it are complicated by the fact that it has fallen into the hands of a black market gang. With the help of an art collector, the painting is eventually found in Capri. Romantic comedy is heavy going.
RoC *Michael Rennie, Tullio Carminati, David Greene, Aldo Silvani, Pippo Bonucci, Francesca Bondi, Franco Coop, Claudio Ermelli.*

GOLDEN SALAMANDER (1949)   3
Dir *Ronald Neame.* Prod *Alexander Galperson.* Scr *Victor Canning, Neame, Lesley Storm, from the novel by Canning.* Ph *Oswald Morris.* PC *Pinewood.* Dis *General Film Distributors. 87 mins. Cert U*
David Redfern (*Trevor Howard*), an archaeologist, is sent to North Africa to collect valuable antiques housed in the home of wealthy Serafis (*Walter Rilla*). He witnesses a gun-running incident, but keeps quiet. He falls for Anna (*Anouk*), who runs a cafe with her bro-

ther (*Jacques Sernas*) whose involvement in the guns racket leads to his death. Now David swears to crack the ring which includes many of the locals and is led by Serafis, whom David captures in a ferocious fight. Slow in getting to the nub of things, then quite exciting.
RoC *Herbert Lom, Miles Malleson, Wilfrid Hyde White, Peter Copley, Marcel Poncin, Kathleen Boutall, Eugene Deckers, Sybilla Binder, Henry Edwards, Percy Walsh, Valentine Dyall.*

GOOD TIME GIRL (1948)   4
Dir *David Macdonald.* Prod *Sydney Box, Samuel Goldwyn Jr.* Scr *Box, Muriel Box, Ted Willis, from a novel by Arthur la Bern.* Ph *Stephen Dade.* PC *Triton.* Dis *General Film Distributors. 93 mins. Cert A*
Caught stealing, Gwen (*Jean Kent*) is sacked by her boss and beaten by her father. She is found a job in a nightclub, where the owner, Max (*Herbert Lom*), gets her to pawn stolen jewellery. She is arrested in the flat of a friend, Red (*Dennis Price*). Sent to a reformatory, she escapes and gets to Brighton, becoming the mistress of Danny, a racketeer (*Griffith Jones*). After a car smash in which a policeman dies, Gwen breaks with Danny and ends up with two GI deserters. In a holdup, they shoot a man - Red. For her involvement, Gwen gets 15 years. Convincing thriller based on a true story. Held up by censor trouble until a new opening was added.
RoC *Flora Robson, Bonar Colleano, Hugh McDermott, Peter Glenville, Nora Swinburne, Elwyn Brook-Jones, Jill Balcon, Beatrice Varley, Margaret Barton, Garry Marsh, John Blythe, Diana Dors, George Carney, Amy Veness, Zena Marshall, Harry Ross, Orlando Martins, Jack Raine, Michael Hordern, George Merritt, Renee Gadd, Joan Young, Phyllis Stanley, Betty Nelson, Danny Green.*

THE GOOSE STEPS OUT (1942)   3
Dir *Will Hay, Basil Dearden.* (Associate) Prod *S. C. Balcon.* Scr *John Dighton, Angus Macphail.* Ph *Ernest Palmer.* PC *Ealing Studios.* Dis *United Artists. 79 mins. Cert U*
William Potts (*Will Hay*), double of an infamous Nazi spy, is dropped over Germany to steal a secret weapon. At Altenburg University he is put in charge of the spies' class, teaching them that a V-sign to Hitler is the finest form of salute. He steals an empty bomb instead of the real one, but pinches that from General von Goltz (*Julien Mitchell*) en route to Berlin, returns to Britain and crash-lands in Whitehall. Patchy wartime fun.
RoC *Frank Pettingell, Charles Hawtrey, Anne Firth, Raymond Lovell, Leslie Harcourt, Barry Morse, Peter Ustinov, Jeremy Hawk, Aubrey Mallalieu, Lawrence O'Madden, Peter Croft.*

THE GORBALS STORY (1949)   2
Dir and Scr *David MacKane, from a play by Robert McLeish.* Prod *Ernest Gartside.* Ph *Stanley Clinton.* PC *New World.* Dis *Eros. 74 mins. Cert A*
Life in the tenements of a Glasgow slum area, where the vicissitudes of life almost drive a sensitive young man (*Howard Connell*) to mur-

der. Eventually he escapes his environment and becomes an artist. Well-intentioned drama; execution of it is on the amateurish side.

RoC *Betty Henderson, Russell Hunter, Marjorie Thomson, Roddy McMillan, Isobel Campbell, Jack Stuart, Archie Duncan, Sybil Thomson, Eveline Garrett, Lothar Lewinsohn.*

THE GRAND ESCAPADE (1946) 3

Dir and Prod *John Baxter.* Scr *Geoffrey Orme, Barbara K. Emary.* Ph *Jo Jago.* PC *Elstree Independent.* Dis *British Lion. 70 mins. Cert U*
Three boys travel to London with an old junk dealer whose son was drowned while smuggling. As they pass through London and the south to the sea, the junkman collects evidence on the smuggling gang and finally exposes the leader. Serviceable children's film with pleasant travelogue aspects thrown in.

LP *Peter Artemus, Philip Artemus, Jackie Artemus, Patric Curwen, James Harcourt, Peter Bull, Ernest Sefton, Edgar Driver, Ben Williams, Bobbie and Nornie Dwyer.*

GREAT DAY (1945) 4

Dir *Lance Comfort.* Prod *Victor Hanbury.* Scr *Wolfgang Wilhelm, John Davenport, from the play by Lesley Storm.* Ph *Uncredited.* PC and Dis *RKO Radio British. 79 mins. Cert U*
Mrs Ellis (*Flora Robson*), chairwoman of Denley Women's Institute, heads the preparations for the visit of Mrs Roosevelt to the village. Her out-of-work husband (*Eric Portman*), acutely embarrassed by his poor health and lack of money, finds himself cadging money to buy rounds of drinks and is eventually driven to steal. Their daughter declines the chance to retrieve the family fortunes by refusing to marry a rich farmer. Story has its own charm; caring performances.

RoC *Sheila Sim, Philip Friend, Isabel Jeans, Walter Fitzgerald, Marjorie Rhodes, Margaret Withers, Maire O'Neill, Beatrice Varley, Joan Maude, Ivor Barnard, John Laurie, Patricia Hayes, Irene Handl, Kathleen Harrison, Leslie Dwyer.*

GREAT EXPECTATIONS (1946) 6

Dir *David Lean.* Prod *Anthony Havelock-Allan, Ronald Neame.* Scr *Neame, Lean, Havelock-Allan, Kay Walsh, Cecil McGivern, from the book by Charles Dickens.* Ph *Guy Green.* PC *Cineguild/Independent Producers.* Dis *General Film Distributors. 118 mins. Cert A*
Pip (*Anthony Wager*), an orphan, has a scary encounter with escaped convict Magwitch (*Finlay Currie*) on the moors. He brings him food. Scarcely less daunting is old Miss Havisham (*Martita Hunt*), whom he visits in the vast cobweb-ridden rooms of her mansion - although he worships her haughty ward Estella (*Jean Simmons*). Grown (*John Mills*), Pip becomes recipient of a mysterious legacy. Miss Havisham dies in a fire; Magwitch, Estella's real father, also dies as Pip tries to help him escape police on his return from Australia. Pip returns to the mansion to help Estella (now *Valerie Hobson*) escape Miss Havisham's spinsterly fate. Double Oscar-winner (photography;

art direction). Perfectly made encapsulation of Dickens' novel, enthralling from start to finish.
RoC *Bernard Miles, Francis L. Sullivan (repeating his role, Jaggers, from 1934 Hollywood version), Alec Guinness, Freda Jackson, Torin Thatcher, Ivor Barnard, Eileen Erskine, Hay Petrie, George Hayes, Richard George, Everley Gregg, John Burch, Grace Denbigh-Russell, O. B. Clarence, John Forrest, Michael Hordern, Anne Holland, Frank Atkinson, Gordon Begg, Edie Martin, Walford Hyden, Roy Arthur.*

THE GREAT MR HANDEL (1942) 3

Dir *Norman Walker.* Prod *James B. Sloan.* Scr *Gerald Elliott, Victor MacClure.* Ph *Claude Friese-Greene, Jack Cardiff.* PC *Independent Producers/GHW.* Dis *General Film Distributors. Technicolor. 103 mins. Cert U*
George Frederick Handel (*Wilfrid Lawson*), Britain's most successful composer at the beginning of the eighteenth century, falls out of favour with the foppish Prince of Wales, loses the royal patronage, and suffers a series of misfortunes. Although ill, he finds fresh inspiration in composing *The Messiah* which, when completed, wins him back his reputation. Standard biopic with no outstanding performances.
RoC *Elizabeth Allan (singing voice: Gladys Ripley), Malcolm Keen, Michael Shepley, Morris Harvey, Hay Petrie, Max Kirby, A. E. Matthews, Frederick Cooper, Robert Atkins, H.F. Maltby, Andrew Leigh, Michael Hunt, Alan Wren, Ivan Samson, Charles Groves, Alfred Sangster, D.J. Williams, Amy Dalby, Trefor Jones, Alfred Harris, Dorothy Vernon, Charles Doe, Frank Atkinson, Len Sharr, Judith Nelmes, Victor MacClure, Jean Stanley.*

Wilfrid Lawson in The Great Mr Handel *(1942)*

THE GREED OF WILLIAM HART (1948) 4

Dir *Oswald Mitchell.* Prod *Gilbert Church.* Scr *John Gilling.* Ph *D.P. Cooper, S.D. Onions.* PC *Bushey.* Dis *Ambassador. 78 mins. Cert A*
Graverobbers Hart and Moore (*Tod Slaughter, Henry Oscar*) move on to murder in nineteenth-century Edinburgh when they cannot supply corpses fast enough to medical students. Tramps, drunks and prostitutes are among their victims before the police get suspicious. When they kill Daft Jamie (*Aubrey Woods*), a local character, mob fury erupts. Hart tries to throw the blame on to Moore, but they cannot escape their fate. Full-

blooded, well-lit Tod Slaughter version of the Burke and Hare story.
RoC *Jenny Lynn, Arnold Bell, Mary Love, Winifred Melville, Patrick Addison, Ann Trego, Janet Brown.*

GREEN FINGERS (1947) 3

Dir *John Harlow.* Prod *Louis H. Jackson.* Scr *Jack Whittingham, from a novel by Edith Arundel.* Ph *Ernest Palmer.* PC *British National.* Dis *Anglo-American. 83 mins. Cert A*
Fisherman Tom Stone (*Robert Beatty*), who has 'the gift of healing', decides to become an osteopath. He cures his landlady's crippled daughter Jeannie (*Carol Raye*) and marries her. He has an affair with upper-crust Alexandra (*Nova Pilbeam*), who shoots herself when he tries to end it. Severely censured he returns to the sea. Jeannie is crippled again in an accident; he cures her again and returns to his practice. Women's magazine stuff; quite well acted.
RoC *Felix Aylmer, Moore Marriott, Brefni O'Rorke, Charles Victor, Harry Welchman, Edward Rigby, Ellis Irving, Olive Walters, Wally Patch, Howard Douglas, Gerald Moore, Leslie Weston, Daisy Burrell, Felicity Devereaux, Doreen Lawrence, George Pelling, Patric Curwen, Carol Lawton, Arsene Kirilloff, John England, Frederick Morant, Paul Blake, Richard Barclay, Doris Bloom, Brookes Turner, Charles Paton, Roddy Hughes, Percy Coyte, Robert Moore, Norah Gordon, Ernie Priest.*

GREEN FOR DANGER (1946) 5

Dir *Sidney Gilliat.* Prod *Gilliat, Frank Launder.* Scr *Gilliat, Claude Guerney, from the novel by Christianna Brand.* Ph *Wilkie Cooper.* PC *Individual/Independent Producers.* Dis *General Film Distributors. 91 mins. Cert A*
At a wartime emergency hospital, a mysterious killer strikes by switching cylinders during an operation. Sister Bates (*Judy Campbell*) gets on to the killer but becomes the next victim. Nurse Linley (*Sally Gray*) is almost gassed to death, but saved by Nurse Sanson (*Rosamund John*). The quirky Inspector Cockrill (*Alastair Sim*) gets on to the killer - Nurse Sanson - but bungles the denouement, allowing her to commit suicide. Delightful comedy-thriller, creepy and amusing at different times.
RoC *Trevor Howard, Leo Genn, Megs Jenkins, Moore Marriott, Henry Edwards, Ronald Adam, George Woodbridge, Wendy Thompson, Elizabeth Sydney, John Rae, Frank Ling, Hattie Jacques.*

THE GUINEA PIG (1948) 4
(USA: *The Outsider*)

Dir *Roy Boulting.* Prod *John Boulting.* Scr *Warren Chetham Strode, Bernard Miles, Roy Boulting, from the play by Chetham Strode.* Ph *Gilbert Taylor.* PC *Pilgrim.* Dis *Pathé. 97 mins. Cert U*
As an experiment, an elementary school boy (*Richard Attenborough*) is accepted at a public school, where life quickly becomes a living hell for him. The other boys mock his ways and his London accent, and his housemaster, Hartley (*Cecil Trouncer*), is no help. But, with the help of Hartley's sympathetic daughter

Richard Attenborough in The Guinea Pig
(1948)

(*Sheila Sim*), the guinea pig finds his own salvation. Skilful human dialogue made this film a big popular success.
RoC *Bernard Miles, Robert Flemyng, Edith Sharpe, Joan Hickson, Peter Reynolds, Timothy Bateson, Clive Baxter, Basil Cunard, John Forrest, Maureen Glynne, Brenda Hogan, Herbert Lomas, Anthony Newley, Anthony Nicholls, Wally Patch, Hay Petrie, Oscar Quitak, Percy Walsh, Norman Watson, Robert Desmond, Kynaston Reeves, Jack McNaughton, Judy Manning, Lionel Stevens, Ambrose Day, Digby Wolfe, James Kenney, Peter Howes, Richard Hart, Michael Braisford, Michael McKeag, Edward Judd, Colin Stroud, Desmond Newling, George Bryden, Olive Sloane.*

A GUNMAN HAS ESCAPED (1948)   3
Dir *Richard Grey*. Prod *Harry Goodman, Grey*. Scr *John Gilling*. Ph *Cedric Williams*. PC *Condor Films*. Dis *Monarch*. 58 mins. Cert A
Three armed robbers kill a Soho jeweller in a robbery. Fleeing the city, they work on a farm. When the farmer gets suspicious, they get away in his car. One kills the other two then, cornered in their original London hideout, he shoots himself. Thriller has little subtlety, but plenty of action; based on a true story.
LP *John Harvey, Robert Cartland, John Fitzgerald, Frank Hawkins, Jane Arden, Maria Charles, Hope Carr, Ernest Brightmore, Manville Tarrant, Patrick Westwood, George Self, Dennis Lehrer, Melville Crawfurd, Hatton Duprez.*

H

THE HALFWAY HOUSE (1944)   4
Dir *Basil Dearden*. (Associate) Prod *Alberto Cavalcanti*. Scr *Angus Macphail, Diana Morgan, T.E.B. Clarke, from a play by Denis Ogden*. Ph *Wilkie Cooper*. PC and Dis *Ealing Studios*. 95 mins. Cert A
To The Halfway House, a Welsh inn, come a number of people, each with personal problems. They find the atmosphere strange; news-

papers and radio broadcasts are a year old. The innkeeper's daughter (*Glynis Johns*) casts no shadow. She and her father (*Mervyn Johns*) are ghosts, killed when their home was bombed, as it is again now, when its tenants' problems are solved. Chilly fantasy, well made.
RoC *Françoise Rosay, Tom Walls, Alfred Drayton, Esmond Knight, Richard Bird, Guy Middleton, Sally Ann Howes, Valerie White, Philippa Hiatt, Pat McGrath, C.V. France, John Boxer, Joss Ambler, Eliot Makeham, Jack Jones, Rachel Thomas, Roland Pertwee, Moses Jones.*

HAMLET (1948)   6
Dir and Prod *Laurence Olivier*. Text editor *Alan Dent, from the play by William Shakespeare*. Ph *Desmond Dickinson*. PC *Two Cities*. Dis *General Film Distributors*. 155 mins. Cert U
Denmark, centuries ago. Hamlet (*Laurence Olivier*), prince of Denmark, learns from a ghost that his father was murdered, and that the queen has married the killer, his uncle (*Basil Sydney*), now king. The king sets Laertes (*Terence Morgan*) to kill Hamlet in a duel, but a poisoned sword wounds them both, and the queen (*Eileen Herlie*) drinks poison also meant for Hamlet. Before he dies, Hamlet stabs the king with the deadly sword. Decidedly shivery, atmospheric version which won Oscars for best film, best actor (*Olivier*), best black-and-white photography, best art direction, best costume design.
RoC *Jean Simmons, Norman Wooland, Felix Aylmer, Stanley Holloway, John Laurie, Esmond Knight, Anthony Quayle, Niall MacGinnis, Harcourt Williams, Peter Cushing, Russell Thorndike, Patrick Troughton, Tony Tarver, Christopher Lee, Patrick Macnee.*

Laurence Olivier in Hamlet *(1948)*

HANGMAN'S WHARF (1949)   2
Dir, Prod, Scr and Ph *Cecil H. Williamson, from the radio serial by John Beldon*. PC and Dis *DUK Films*. 73 mins. Cert U
A young doctor, Galloway (*John Witty*), urgently called to a ship lying off Hangman's Wharf, is later suspected of the murder there of a wealthy man. Aided by a woman reporter, Alison (*Genine Graham*), Galloway manages to clear himself and disclose the real murderer. Filmization of radio serial shows up all its less likely aspects.
RoC *Patience Rentoul, Gerald Nodin, Campbell Singer, Max Brimmell, Patricia Laffan, Molly*

Looe, Tom Masson, Frederick Allen, Barry Faber, John Walker, Harry Hearn, R.C. Huggins, Maureen Williamson.

THE HANGMAN WAITS (1947)   3
Dir and Scr *A. Barr-Smith*. Prod *Barr-Smith, Roger Proudlock*. Ph *Denys Coop, Fred Langdon*. PC *Five Star*. Dis *Butchers*. 64 mins. Cert A
A cinema organist murders an usherette, dismembers the body and puts the remains in a trunk at Victoria Station. Reporters and police close in on him. The chase goes on until he kills a country church organist who had reported his whereabouts to the police. Finally he is trapped in the office of the very newspaper which had led the hunt. Documentary-style study of the pursuit of a killer; burly character actor *John Turnbull*'s only leading role in the films (he's the inspector).
RoC *Anthony Baird, Kenneth Warrington, Michael Bazalgette, Edwin Ellis, Leonard Sharp, Robert Wyndham, Hylton Allen, Bessie Courtney, Vi Kaley, Arthur Mack, Stanley Jay, Beatrice Campbell, Jeanette Green.*

HAPPIDROME (1943)   2
Dir *Phil Brandon*. Prod *Harold Boxall, Jack Buchanan, Tom Arnold*. Scr *Arnold, James Seymour, from the radio series by Harry Korris*. Ph *Geoffrey Faithfull*. PC *Aldwych*. Dis *M-G-M*. 87 mins. Cert U
A group of struggling performers suddenly finds success after rich Mr Mossup (*Joss Ambler*) sponsors his daughter Bunty (*Bunty Meadows*) to star in a 'great tragedy' which her fellow-players accidentally turn into the comedy hit of the year. Enormously popular radio show looks uncomfortable on screen. Plot vaguely reminiscent of 1933s *Up to the Neck*.
RoC *Harry Korris, Robbie Vincent, Cecil Frederick, Lisa Lee, Jennie Gregson, Valentine Dunn, Muriel Zillah, Connie Creighton, Marie Lawson, Olga Stevenson, Arthur Hambling, Bombardier Billy Wells, Leslie 'Hutch' Hutchinson, The Cairoli Brothers.*

HARD STEEL (1941)   3
Dir *Norman Walker*. Prod *James B. Sloan*. Scr *Lydia Hayward, from a novel by Roger Dataller*. Ph *Claude Friese-Greene*. PC *GHW Productions*. Dis *General Film Distributors*. 86 mins. Cert A
Walter Haddon (*Wilfrid Lawson*) is a ruthless steelworks foreman. Given the overseeing of three mills, his ambitions assume dictatorial proportions. He alienates his wife (*Betty Stockfeld*), antagonizes the work force and indirectly causes the death of one of his men. He prepares to leave, but his friend Bert (*George Carney*), a lay preacher, convinces him to stay, face the men, and admit his mistakes. Direction brings a human touch to rather trite material.
RoC *John Stuart, Joan Kemp-Welch, James Harcourt, Frank Atkinson, Arthur Hambling, John Turnbull, Hay Petrie, Clifton Boyne, Angela Glynne, Mignon O'Doherty, Philip Godfrey, Cameron Hall, Charles Rolfe, Kenneth Griffith, Harry Riley, Victor Weske, Charles Groves, D.J. Williams, Len Sharp, Roberta*

Read, Roddy Hughes, Arthur Seaton, Dane Gordon, David Crickett.

THE HASTY HEART (1949) [4]

Dir and Prod *Vincent Sherman*. Scr *Ranald Macdougall, from the play by John Patrick*. Ph *Wilkie Cooper*. PC and Dis *Associated British-Pathé*. 107 mins. Cert U
1945. An embittered Scotsman (*Richard Todd*) in a Burma military hospital rejects the friendship of his fellow-patients. They know what he doesn't: that he is dying. He mistakes the pity of his nurse (*Patricia Neal*) for love, and retreats further into his shell. But eventually, the rest of the ward breaks down his reserve by their genuine kindness and generosity and his faith in human nature is restored. Weepie carries a powerful emotional charge.
RoC *Ronald Reagan, Anthony Nicholls, Howard Marion Crawford, Ralph Michael, Orlando Martins, John Sherman, Alfie Bass, Sam Kydd*.

Richard Todd, Orlando Martins, John Sherman, Anthony Nicholls, Howard Marion Crawford, Ronald Reagan in The Hasty Heart *(1949)*

HATTER'S CASTLE (1941) [5]

Dir *Lance Comfort*. Prod *Isadore Goldsmith*. Scr *Paul Merzbach, Rudolf Bernauer, Rodney Ackland, from the novel by A.J. Cronin*. Ph *Max Greene (Mutz Greenbaum)*. PC and Dis *Paramount British*. 102 mins. Cert A
1879: Tyrannical Scottish hatter Brodie (*Robert Newton*) rules his family by fear. His daughter Mary (*Deborah Kerr*), torn between Dr Renwick (*James Mason*) and Dennis (*Emlyn Williams*), ne'er-do-well ex-lover of Brodie's mistress, is driven out by Brodie and, rejected by Dennis, throws herself from a train. Brodie goes bankrupt, his wife dies from cancer and his son Angus (*Anthony Bateman*) commits suicide after being pressurized into cheating in an exam. Brodie burns down his palatial home, nicknamed Hatter's Castle, burying himself and the body of Angus with it. Mary, who has survived, attends the funeral, leaving with Dr Renwick. Newton dominates a grim story that holds the interest.
RoC *Beatrice Varley, Henry Oscar, Enid Stamp-Taylor, June Holden, Brefni O'Rorke, George Merritt, Lawrence Hanray, Roddy Hughes, Claude Bailey, Stuart Lindsell, Mary Hinton, Ian Fleming, David Keir, Aubrey Mallalieu*.

HEADLINE (1943) [3]

Dir *John Harlow*. Prod and PC *John Corfield*. Scr *Ralph Gilbert Bettinson, Maisie Sharman, from a novel by Ken Attiwill*. Ph *James Wilson*. Dis *Ealing Studios*. 76 mins. Cert A
Sent to discover the identity of a mystery woman involved in a murder, reporter Brookie (*David Farrar*) finds out it was his boss's wife – and has to catch the killer without exposing the frightened witness, or telling his chief (*John Stuart*) the truth. Pretty unlikely story.
RoC *Anne Crawford, Antoinette Cellier, Billy (William) Hartnell, Anthony Hawtrey, Nancy O'Neill, Joss Ambler, Richard Goolden, Merle Tottenham, Lorna Tarbat, Ian MacLean*.

HEAVEN IS ROUND THE CORNER (1944) [3]

Dir *Maclean Rogers*. Prod *Fred Zelnik*. Scr *Austin Melford*. Ph *James Wilson*. PC *British National*. Dis *Anglo-American*. 94 mins. Cert U
When her father remarries, Joan (*Leni Lynn*) leaves her home farm and goes to Paris, where an uncle helps to have her singing voice trained. She falls for a British Embassy man, but they are parted by the outbreak of war, and she does not realize he returns her love. She goes back to her father's farm and three years later meets her man again, thanks to the efforts of her father's bailiff. Stickily acted vehicle for new songthrush.
RoC *Will Fyffe, Austin Trevor, Magda Kun, Peter Glenville, Barbara Waring, Leslie Perrins, Barbara Couper, Tonie Edgar Bruce, Hugh Dempster, Paul Bonifas, Jan van Loewen, Rosamund Greenwood, Elsa Tee, Neville Brook, Louis Lord, Suzy Marquis, Christine Silver, Hal Gordon, Marcel de Haes*.

HE FOUND A STAR (1941) [3]

Dir *John Paddy Carstairs*. Prod and PC *John Corfield*. Scr *Austin Melford, Bridget Boland*. Ph *Ernest Palmer*. Dis *General Film Distributors*. 88 mins. Cert U
Stage manager Lucky Lyndon (*Vic Oliver*) starts a theatrical employment agency for all the 'little people' in show business in whom no-one takes much interest. His venture is a success, turning into a kind of club, but his weakness for blondes alienates his girl Friday Ruth (*Sarah Churchill*). She still saves him when the star walks out on the first night of his new show. Slight but quite pleasing musical comedy.
RoC *Evelyn Dall, Robert Sansom, Robert Atkins, George Merritt, Uriel Porter, Raymond Lovell, J.H. Roberts, Barbara Everest, Joan Greenwood, Peter Saunders, Charles Victor, David Evans, Jonathan Field, Mignon O'Doherty, Peggy Novak, The Kellaways*.

HELD IN TRUST (1948) [2]

Dir, Prod, Scr and Ph *Cecil H. Williamson*. PC *Productions Number 1*. Dis *Do-U-Know Film Productions*. 58 mins. Cert A
Captain Lovell persuades petty crook Charlie (*Ian Proctor*) to give up crime and develop his painting talents. Charlie becomes an artist of repute, but his old gang force him to help them with the theft of art treasures from a country villa. Thanks to Charlie, the robbery

is foiled. He kills the gang leader (*Guy Verney*) in self-defence. Good leading performance, not much more.
RoC *Dorothy Shaw (no further cast issued)*.

HELTER SKELTER (1949) [1]

Dir *Ralph Thomas*. Prod *Antony Darnborough*. Scr *Patrick Campbell, Jan Read, Gerard Bryant*. Ph *Jack Asher*. PC *Gainsborough*. Dis *General Film Distributors*. 84 mins. Cert A
Susan Graham (*Carol Marsh*) suffers an attack of hiccups in a quarrel. Shock treatment fails to cure her. A psychiatrist prescribes laughter and various famous people try to amuse her. A 'ghost' finally effects a cure, but the shock of a proposal of marriage brings on another attack. One of the best casts ever wasted on a terrible film; gets worse the harder it tries.
RoC *David Tomlinson, Mervyn Johns, Peter Hammond, Richard Hearne, Henry Kendall, Jon Pertwee, Terry-Thomas, Jimmy Edwards, Zena Marshall, Colin Gordon, Harry Secombe, Wilfrid Hyde White, Glynis Johns, Dennis Price, Valentine Dyall, Geoffrey Sumner, Peter Haddon, Patricia Raine, Judith Furse, Robert Lamouret, Shirl Conway, Anthony Steel, George Benson*.

HENRY STEPS OUT (1940) [2]

Dir and Prod *Widgey R. Newman*. Scr *Uncredited*. Ph *Uncredited*. PC *Clive Films*. Dis *Anglo-International*. 52 mins. Cert U
Henpecked Henry (*George Turner*) finds the loot from a bank robbery. He is about to get a reward when his wife insists on him joining the army. He fails, but somehow lands in the ATS as a bathroom orderly. Before he can have too good a time girl-watching, his wife turns up as a corporal and discovers him. He is kicked out, but collects the original reward. Runs like an extended music-hall sketch.
RoC *Margaret Yarde, Wally Patch*.

HENRY V (1944) [6]

Dir and Prod *Laurence Olivier*. Scr *Olivier, Alan Dent, from the play by William Shakespeare*. Ph *Robert Krasker, Jack Hildyard*. PC *Two Cities*. Dis *Eagle-Lion*. Technicolor. 137 mins. Cert U
Henry V (*Laurence Olivier*), King of England in 1415, invades France and enjoys successes in battle. Attempting to withdraw his outnumbered troops to Calais for an honourable return, he is blocked by the French army at Agincourt and forced to fight a battle which

Laurence Olivier in Henry V *(1944)*

e wins against all the odds. Later he woos nd wins the French princess, Katherine (*Renée Asherson*), but dies at only 35. Olivier took a special Oscar for his work on this enthralling and thrillingly successful effort to put Shakespeare on screen, which combines deliberate sets with naturalistic backgrounds and contains dazzling battles and brilliant colour. RoC *Robert Newton, Leslie Banks, Esmond Knight, Leo Genn, Ralph Truman, Jimmy Hanley, John Laurie, Niall MacGinnis, George Robey, Roy Emerton, Griffith Jones, Harcourt Williams, Ivy StHelier, Ernest Thesiger, Max Adrian, Francis Lister, Valentine Dyall, Russell Thorndike, Morland Graham, George Cole, Felix Aylmer, Nicholas Hannen, Robert Helpmann, Freda Jackson, Frederick Cooper, Michael Warre, Gerald Case, Brian Nissen, Janet Burnell, Vernon Greeves, Arthur Hambling, Frank Tickle.*

HERE COMES THE SUN (1945)   3

Dir, Prod and PC *John Baxter.* Scr *Geoffrey Orme, from a story by Bud Flanagan, Reginald Purdell.* Ph *Stan Pavey.* Dis *General Film Distributors. 91 mins. Cert U*
Two film extras (*Bud Flanagan, Chesney Allen*) decide to rewrite the script as social melodrama. When his partner dies, Bradshaw (*Joss Ambler*) forges a will which disinherits everyone except him. He frames Corona (*Flanagan*) who is sent to prison but escapes. It is not until he is re-arrested, however, that he finds the original will. Some laughs for the unsophisticated.
RoC *Elsa Tee, Dick Francis, John Dodsworth, Gus McNaughton, Roddy Hughes, Horace Kenney, Edie Martin, Peter Bernard, Harry Terry, A. A. Harris, 'Peter', Ernest Sefton, Walter Roy, Freddie Watts, Vic Hagen, Jack Buckland, Ian MacLean, Iris Kirkwhite Dancers, Dudley and His Midgets.*

HERE COME THE HUGGETTS (1948)   4

Dir *Ken Annakin.* Prod *Betty Box.* Scr *Mabel and Denis Constanduros, Muriel and Sydney Box, Peter Rogers.* Ph *Reg Wyer.* PC *Gainsborough.* Dis *General Film Distributors. 93 mins. Cert A*
Their glamorous blonde niece Diana (*Diana Dors*) upsets the Huggetts' well-ordered household and nearly loses father Joe (*Jack Warner*) his job. After spending seven days in jail following a crash in the family car, Diana leaves. Other problems, mostly romantic, are also solved. Lacks tightness of structure, but has some bright dialogue; quite good fun. Characters first introduced in *Holiday Camp*. RoC *Kathleen Harrison, Jane Hylton, Susan Shaw, Petula Clark, Jimmy Hanley, David Tomlinson, Peter Hammond, John Blythe, Amy Veness, Clive Morton, Maurice Denham, Doris Hare, Dandy Nichols, Hal Osmond, Esma Cannon.*

HE SNOOPS TO CONQUER (1944)   2

Dir *Marcel Varnel.* Prod *Ben Henry, Varnel.* Scr *Stephen Black, Norman Lee, Howard Irving Young, Michael Vaughan, Langford Reed.* Ph *Roy Fogwell.* PC and Dis *Columbia British. 103 mins. Cert U*
Reporters from London visit Tangleton and, with the unwitting help of George (*George*

Formby), the town hall oddjob man, discover the corrupt council is doing nothing about post-war planning. The council orders George to burn forms complaining about housing, but he gets them blown about the town streets instead. An eccentric inventor (*Robertson Hare*) helps George oust the dishonest councillors. Unsuccessful departure from Formby comedy format.
RoC *Elizabeth Allan, Claude Bailey, Gordon McLeod, James Harcourt, Aubrey Mallalieu, Vincent Holman, William Rodwell, James Page, Robert Clive, Frank Atkinson, Hugh Dempster, Ian Fleming, Richard Harrison, Charles Paton, John Coyle, Katie Johnson, Jack Vyvyan, John Rae, Arthur Hambling, Jack Williams, Ted Venables, Frank Raymond, Gerald Moore.*

HI, GANG! (1941)   4

Dir *Marcel Varnel.* Prod *Edward Black.* Scr *Val Guest, Marriott Edgar, J.O.C. Orton, Howard Irving Young, from the radio series originated by Bebe Daniels, Ben Lyon.* Ph *Jack Cox, Guy Green.* Dis *General Film Distributors. 100 mins. Cert U*
Husband-and-wife entertainers *Bebe Daniels* and *Ben Lyon* are great radio rivals in America. Both have British evacuee boys on their shows, but Bebe's boy (*Graham Moffatt*) is believed to be a lord's son because he lives at The Castle, Amersham (a pub). Bebe flies to England to restore the castle, pursued by Ben who has discovered the truth. Getting together to stage a British radio show, they cause a fake invasion alarm and flee back to America. Brightish lark.
RoC *Moore Marriott, Vic Oliver, Felix Aylmer, Sam Browne, Georgina Mackinnon, Maurice Rhodes, Percy Parsons, Diana Beaumont, Jacques Brown, Mavis Villiers, The Green Sisters, Jay Wilbur and His Band.*

HIGH JINKS IN SOCIETY (1949)   3

Dir and Prod *Robert Jordan Hill.* Scr *Hill, John Guillermin.* Ph *Gerald Gibbs.* PC *Advance.* Dis *Adelphi. 78 mins. Cert U*
After accidentally foiling a smash-and-grab raid, Ben (*Ben Wrigley*), a window-cleaner, is hired by Lady Barr-Nunn (*Netta Westcott*) to guard her valuables. He invents anti-burglar devices which only trap members of the family, dresses up as a duchess at a reception, exposes a fake seance and catches crooks who include Lady Barr-Nunn's original detective. Big-nosed, long-necked new comedy star provides clean, crazy, modestly inventive fun.
RoC *Barbara Shaw, Moore Marriott, Basil Appleby, Ivan Craig, Michael Ward, Peter Gawthorne, Myrette Morven, Russell Westwood, Jean Lodge, Pamela van Dale, Bill Benny, The Radio Revellers, The Squadronaires, Otto (dog).*

THE HILLS OF DONEGAL (1947)   2

Dir and Prod *John Argyle.* Scr *John Dryden.* Ph *Arthur Grant.* PC and Dis *Butchers. 85 mins. Cert A*
Eileen Hannay (*Dinah Sheridan*), an Irish girl, gives up her singing career to marry Terry (*John Bentley*), her partner Michael's cousin. They try to settle down on her family estate in Donegal, but Terry does not like Ireland.

He is blackmailed by a girl from his past, and his efforts to get rid of her only result in his own death. Eileen turns to Michael. Musical with all the predictable Irish songs (*Believe Me, If All Those Endearing Young Charms*, etc.) and an overcrowded plot.
RoC *James Etherington, Moore Marriott, Brendan Clegg, Irene Handl, Tamara Desni, Maire O'Neill, Bob (Robert) Arden.*

THE HISTORY OF MR POLLY (1948)   4

Dir and Scr *Anthony Pelissier, from the novel by H.G. Wells.* Prod *John Mills.* Ph *Desmond Dickinson.* PC *Two Cities.* Dis *General Film Distributors. 95 mins. Cert A*
1900. Tired of his miserable life and nagging wife (*Betty Ann Davies*), draper Alfred Polly (*John Mills*) sets fire to his own store, leaves his wife and takes to the high road, ending up at the Potwell Inn, where he has to battle against fearsome Uncle Jim (*Finlay Currie*) before settling down with the Plump Woman (*Megs Jenkins*) who runs the inn. Pleasant, sunny version of classic book, with nicely captured rural atmosphere.
RoC *Sally Ann Howes, Edward Chapman, Diana Churchill, Gladys Henson, Miles Malleson, Moore Marriott, Shelagh Fraser, David Horne, Ernest Jay, Edie Martin, Dandy Nichols, Wally Patch, Lawrence Baskcomb, Juliet Mills, Wylie Watson, Doris Hare, Irene Handl, Grace Arnold, Cyril Smith, Dennis Arundell, Victor Platt, Cameron Hall, Michael Ripper, Muriel Russell.*

Megs Jenkins and John Mills in The History of Mr Polly *(1949)*

HOLIDAY CAMP (1947)   4

Dir *Ken Annakin.* Prod *Sydney Box.* Scr *Box, Peter Rogers, Muriel Box, Mabel Constanduros, Denis Constanduros, Ted Willis.* Ph *Jack Cox,* PC *Gainsborough.* Dis *General Film Distributors. 97 mins. Cert A*
Stories of characters in a holiday camp: a bus driver and his wife, young son and war-widowed daughter; a sailor who has been jilted; a homicidal maniac posing as an RAF officer; a spinster taking a holiday after years of devotion to her invalid mother; a man-chasing waitress; two card-sharps; a composer and the girl he can't marry because of family opposition. Some find romance, but the spinster finds death at the hands of the 'mannequin murderer' who is caught by police. Popular picture of post-war Britain. The Huggetts

(*Jack Warner* and *Kathleen Harrison*) soon had a series of their own.

RoC *Flora Robson, Dennis Price, Hazel Court, Emrys Jones, Esma Cannon, Yvonne Owen, Esmond Knight, Jimmy Hanley, Peter Hammond, John Blythe, Dennis Harkin, Beatrice Varley, Jeannette Tregarthen, Susan Shaw, Maurice Denham, Jane Hylton, Jack Raine, Alfie Bass, Patricia Roc, Reginald Purdell, Diana Dors, Gerry Wilmott, Charlie Chester, Pamela Braman, John Stone, Phil Fowler, Jack Ellis.*

HOLIDAYS WITH PAY (1948) [2]

Dir and Prod *John E. Blakeley.* Scr *Harry Jackson, Frank Randle.* Ph *Ben Hart.* PC and Dis *Mancunian.* 115 mins. Cert A

Jack Rogers (*Frank Randle*) and his family visit Blackpool, where daughter Pam (*Sally Barnes*) makes friends with Michael (*Sonny Burke*) whose evil cousin Jasper (*Frank Groves*) is trying to kill him for the family estate. The Rogers plan a campaign against Jasper, and, after a night in a 'haunted' house, put him to flight. Phenomenally long North Country comedy with too many crosstalk routines.

RoC *Tessie O'Shea, Dan Young, Josef Locke, Joyanne Bracewell, Bert Tracy, Pat Heywood and Her Troupe.*

HOME SWEET HOME (1945) [3]

Dir and Prod *John E. Blakeley.* Scr *Roney Parsons, Anthony Toner, Frank Randle.* Ph *Geoffrey Faithfull.* PC *Mancunian.* Dis *Butchers.* 92 mins. Cert A

Orphan evacuee Jacqueline (*Nicolette Roeg*) falls for Eric (*Tony Pendrell*), the son of the colonel to whom she is chauffeuse. The colonel's wife vetoes the romance and Jacqueline leaves to be a singer in a club. In the Channel Islands, Eric discovers she is an heiress. Randle (*Frank Randle*), with whom she had been staying, brings her back, but makes sure the colonel's wife is humbled first. Unsophisticated farce-musical, sometimes quite funny.

RoC *H. F. Maltby, Hilda Bayley, Cecil Fredericks, Stan Little, Bunty Meadows, Gerhardt Kempinski, George Merritt, Howard Douglas, Iris Vandeleur, Esme Lewis, Vincent Holman, Lily Lapidus, Ben Williams, Max Melford.*

HOTEL RESERVE (1944) [2]

Dir *Victor Hanbury, Lance Comfort, Max Greene (Mutz Greenbaum).* Prod *Hanbury.* Scr *John Davenport, from a novel by Eric Ambler.* Ph *Max Greene.* PC and Dis *RKO Radio British.* 89 mins. Cert U

Ambler's *Epitaph for a Spy* adapted as a very lightweight thriller about an Austrian tourist (*James Mason*) in the south of France in 1938. His camera containing pictures of lizards is switched for a spy's camera containing pictures of shore defences. He has to hunt down the real spy himself to prove his innocence. With a lot of help from the police, he does so.

RoC *Lucie Mannheim, Raymond Lovell, Julien Mitchell, Clare Hamilton, Martin Miller, Herbert Lom, Frederick Valk, Ivor Barnard, Valentine Dyall, Patricia Medina, David Ward, Hella Kurty, Anthony Shaw, Lawrence Hanray, Patricia Hayes, Josef Ulmas, Ernest Ulman, Mike Johnson, Hugo Schuster, Henry T. Russell, John Baker.*

HOUSE OF DARKNESS (1948) [3]

Dir *Oswald Mitchell.* Prod *Harry Reynolds.* Scr *John Gilling, Robin Estridge, from a play by Betty Davies.* Ph *Cyril Bristow.* PC *International Motion Pictures.* Dis *British Lion.* 77 mins. Cert A

Francis (*Laurence Harvey*) is obsessed with possessing his stepbrother John's house in Dorset. Playing subtly on John's weak heart, he brings on a fatal attack by smashing his stepbrother's violin. He drives his own wife and John's other stepbrother from the house but, once again, starts hallucinating. He hears the violin playing and, crazed with fear, tries to drown it by playing the piano. But he crashes to the keyboard, felled by the family weak heart. Rather hackneyed in treatment, chiller nonetheless has eerie atmosphere.

RoC *Lesley Brook, Lesley Osmond, John Stuart, Alexander Archdale, Henry Oscar, George Melachrino.*

THE HOUSE OF THE ARROW (1940) [2]
(USA: *Castle of Crimes*)

Dir *Harold French.* Prod *Walter C. Mycroft.* Scr *Doreen Montgomery, from the novel by A. E. W. Mason.* Ph *Walter Harvey.* PC and Dis *Associated British.* 66 mins. Cert A

Wealthy eccentric Madame Harlowe is poisoned with South American curare. Inspector Hanaud (*Keneth Kent*) finds that several people have various reasons for wanting her dead – but picks the right one at a masked ball. Kent is not an ideal Hanaud in a film that moves in fits and starts.

RoC *Diana Churchill, Belle Chrystall, Peter Murray Hill, Clifford Evans, Catherine Lacey, James Harcourt, Louise Hampton, Aubrey Dexter, Ivor Barnard, Athene Seyler.*

HUE AND CRY (1947) [5]

Dir *Charles Crichton.* (Associate) Prod *Henry Cornelius.* Scr *T.E.B. Clarke.* Ph *Douglas Slocombe, J. Seaholme.* PC *Ealing Studios.* Dis *General Film Distributors.* 82 mins. Cert U

15-year-old Joe Kirby (*Harry Fowler*) and his East End gang suspect that their favourite weekly, *The Trump*, is being used for communication by a gang of fur thieves. They set a trap, but snare police instead, and flee through sewers. Capturing the blonde mistress (*Valerie White*) of the gang leader (*Jack Warner*), they force her to talk by using a white mouse. Joe is cornered, but summons boys of all ages to a terrific dockland free-for-all, in which all the crooks are captured. Real backgrounds help make this exhilarating stuff.

RoC *Alastair Sim, Jack Lambert, Vida Hope, Frederick Piper, Gerald Fox, Grace Arnold, Joan Dowling, Douglas Barr, Stanley Escane, Ian Dawson, Paul Demel, Bruce Belfrage, Joey Carr, Robin Hughes, Howard Douglas, Heather Delane, David Simpson, Albert Hughes, John Hudson, David Knox, Jeffrey Sirett, James Crabbe, Alec Finter, Arthur Denton.*

THE HUGGETTS ABROAD (1949) [3]

Dir *Ken Annakin.* Prod *Betty Box.* Scr *Mabel and Denis Constanduros, Ted Willis, Gerard Bryant.* Ph *Reginald Wyer.* PC *Gainsborough.* Dis *General Film Distributors.* 87 mins. Cert U

Joe Huggett (*Jack Warner*), fed up with his job, throws it up to emigrate with his family to South Africa. En route they become involved with a Canadian diamond smuggler (*Hugh McDermott*). They get stranded in the desert and French officers arrest them all, including the Canadian crook. Finally, the offer of his old job back makes Joe give up the trek. Just a few smiles in meandering Huggett film: the series went no further.

RoC *Kathleen Harrison, Susan Shaw, Petula Clark, Jimmy Hanley, Dinah Sheridan, Peter Hammond, Amy Veness, John Blythe, Esma Cannon, Everley Gregg, Brian Oulton, Olaf Pooley, Martin Miller, Meinhart Maur, Philo Hauser, Peter Illing, Frith Banbury, Marcel Poncin, Ferdy Mayne.*

THE HUNDRED POUND WINDOW (1943) [3]

Dir *Brian Desmond Hurst.* Prod *Max Milder.* Scr *Abem Finkel, Brock Williams, Rodney Ackland.* Ph *Otto Heller.* PC and Dis *Warner Bros.* 84 mins. Cert U

Losing badly at roulette, Ernest Draper (*Frederick Leister*), a clerk in charge of the Tote's £100 window at the racetrack, jeopardizes his own future plans, the buying of a wedding-gift home for his daughter (*Anne Crawford*) and the financing of his son's (*Richard Attenborough*) engineering career. A lucky long-odds win retrieves the money and he also helps to net the black marketeers hunted by his detective future son-in-law (*David Farrar*). Modest, well-acted comedy-drama.

RoC *Mary Clare, Niall MacGinnis, David Hutcheson, Francis Lister, Claud Allister, Claude Bailey, Peter Gawthorne, John Slater, David Horne, Anthony Hawtrey, Ruby Miller, C. Denier Warren, John Salew, Hazel Bray.*

HUNGRY HILL (1946) [3]

Dir *Brian Desmond Hurst.* Prod *William Sistrom.* Scr *Daphne du Maurier, Terence Young Francis Crowdy, from the novel by du Maurier* Ph *Desmond Dickinson.* PC *Two Cities.* Di *General Film Distributors.* 109 mins. Cert A

'There is trouble at the mines' seems to be th most oft-used line in this epic about two feud ing Irish families over several generations. Th Donovans are dispossessed of Hungry Hill an see the Brodricks sink a successful copper min there. 200 years on, the last Brodricks, Wil Johnnie (*Dermot Walsh*) and his mother Fann

Douglas Barr, Alastair Sim and Harry Fowler in Hue and Cry *(1947)*

Jean Simmons and Dennis Price in Hungry Hill
(1946)

Rosa (*Margaret Lockwood*), close the mine: Johnnie is killed by an angry mob, and Fanny, who had married Greyhound John (*Dennis Price*), who was sympathetic to the miners, but died from typhoid contracted from the Donovans, reopens the mine, and ends the feud.
RoC *Cecil Parker, Michael Denison, F.J. McCormick, Eileen Crowe, Peter Murray, Eileen Herlie, Jean Simmons, Siobhan McKenna, James Robertson (Justice), Guy Rolfe, Patrick Holt, Dan O'Herlihy, Barbara Waring, Arthur Sinclair, Anthony Wager, Henry Mollison, Tony Quinn, Hector MacGregor, Eddie Byrne, Julia Lockwood, Seamus Locke, Ingrid Forrest.*

I

AN IDEAL HUSBAND (1947) [4]
Dir and Prod *Alexander Korda*. Scr *Lajos Biro, from the play by Oscar Wilde*. Ph *Georges Périnal*. PC *London Films*. Dis *British Lion*. Technicolor. 96 mins. Cert A
1895. Adventuress Mrs Cheveley (*Paulette Goddard*) blackmails upright politician Sir Robert (*Hugh Williams*), whose wife (*Diana Wynyard*) believes he can do no wrong, over an early moral lapse. She wants support for an Argentine canal scheme, which he is about to attack in the Commons. Thanks to cunning play by Sir Robert's friend Lord Goring (*Michael Wilding*), the schemer is thwarted. Wildean wit is preserved but an overdose of Technicolor drowns the production.
RoC *C. Aubrey Smith, Glynis Johns, Constance Collier, Christine Norden, Harriette Johns, Michael Medwin, Michael Anthony, Fred Groves, Peter Hobbes, Johns Clifford, Michael Ward.*

I DIDN'T DO IT (1945) [4]
Dir *Marcel Varnel*. Prod *Varnel, Ben Henry*. Scr *Norman Lee, Peter Fraser, Howard Irving Young, Stephen Black, Michael Vaughan*. Ph *Roy Fogwell*. PC and Dis *Columbia British*. 97 mins. Cert A

Entertainer George Trotter (*George Formby*), seeking fame in London, books in at a theatrical boarding house, just before an Australian acrobat is murdered in the room next to his. At first the killer tries to pin it on George, then to poison him, finally to shoot him in a hall of mirrors. George escapes each time, also winning success in a cabaret. Quite amusingly dotty comedy.
RoC *Marjorie Browne, Billy Caryll, Hilda Mundy, Gaston Palmer, Jack Daly, Carl Jaffe, Wally Patch, Ian Fleming, Vincent Holman, Dennis Wyndham, Jack Raine, Gordon McLeod, Merle Tottenham, Georgina Cookson, The Boswell Twins.*

THE IDOL OF PARIS (1948) [2]
Dir *Leslie Arliss*. Prod *R.J. Minney*. Scr *Norman Lee, Stafford Dickens, Harry Ostrer*. Ph *Jack Cox*. PC *Premier*. Dis *Warner Bros*. 105 mins. Cert A
1860. Therese (*Beryl Baxter*), daughter of a rag-and-bone man, runs off to Moscow with a rich man's son. He deserts her. She marries a poor but honest tailor. When she falls in love with Hertz (*Michael Rennie*), a famous pianist, her husband leaves, writing a suicide note. Hertz meets a violent end and Therese goes back to the gutter. She marries a marquis for his name, and lures the emperor away from his mistress. Offenbach is inspired by her to compose *La Belle Hélène*. One critic summed it up as 'a complete farrago of nonsense'.
RoC *Christine Norden, Margaretta Scott, Keneth Kent, Andrew Osborn, Henry Oscar, Andrew Cruickshank, Miles Malleson, Sybilla Binder, Leslie Perrins, Patti Morgan, Donald Gray, Genine Graham, Campbell Cotts, John Penrose, Frederick Bradshaw, April Stride, June Holden.*

I KNOW WHERE I'M GOING (1945) [4]
Dir, Prod and Scr *Michael Powell, Emeric Pressburger*. Ph *Erwin Hillier*. PC *The Archers/Independent Producers*. Dis *General Film Distributors*. 92 mins. Cert U
On her way to a Hebridean island, Kiloran, to marry an elderly company director, money-minded Joan (*Wendy Hiller*) is stranded by fog on Mull, and thrown into the company of Torquil (*Roger Livesey*), laird of Kiloran. She tries to leave by bribing a young sailor to take her out in a storm, but when Torquil brings her back, she realizes she loves him. Good characters and marvellous scenery, although the plot has its oddities.
RoC *Pamela Brown, Nancy Price, Finlay Currie, John Laurie, George Carney, Walter Hudd, Murdo Morrison, Jean Cadell, Petula Clark, Margot Fitzsimmons, Norman Shelley, Valentine Dyall, Catherine Lacey, Herbert Lomas, Graham Moffatt, Duncan MacKechnie, Ian Sadler, C.W.R. Knight, John Rae, Duncan McIntyre, Ivy Milton, Anthony Eustrel, Alec Faversham, Kitty Kirwan, Boyd Stevens, Maxwell Kennedy, Jean Houston, Arthur Chesney, Donald Strachan.*

I LIVE IN GROSVENOR SQUARE (1945) [4]
(USA: *A Yank in London*)
Dir and Prod *Herbert Wilcox*. Scr *Nicholas*

Phipps, William D. Bayles. Ph *Otto Heller*. PC *Associated British*. Dis *Pathé*. 113 mins. Cert U
An American sergeant (*Dean Jagger*) and a British major (*Rex Harrison*) become rivals for Lady Patricia (*Anna Neagle*) at whose home the American is billeted during the war. The American wins her, but shortly afterwards is killed in an air crash. The major leaves for France not knowing whether he and Lady Patricia still have a future. Rather long but very successful romantic drama.
RoC *Robert Morley, Jane Darwell, Nancy Price, Irene Vanbrugh, Edward Rigby, Walter Hudd, Elliott Arluck, Francis Pierlot, Aubrey Mallalieu, Michael Shepley, Charles Victor, Irene Manning, Ronald Shiner, H.R. Hignett, Brenda Bruce, John Slater, Peter Hobbs, Frank Webster, William Murton, Cecil Ramage, Percy Walsh, Shelagh Fraser, Helen Lowry, Neville Mapp, Norman Williams, David Horne, Arvid O. Dahl, Alvar Liddell, Gerry Wilmott, Carroll Gibbons and His Orchestra.*

I'LL BE YOUR SWEETHEART (1945) [4]
Dir *Val Guest*. Prod *Louis Levy*. Scr *Val Valentine, Guest*. Ph *Phil Grindrod*. PC *Gainsborough*. Dis *General Film Distributors*. 104 mins. Cert A
1900: London songwriters Kahn (*Vic Oliver*), le Brunn (*Moore Marriott*) and Kelly (*Jonathan Field*) are hard-hit by pirates who publish their songs without paying royalties. Le Brunn later starves to death in tragic circumstances. Bob Fielding (*Michael Rennie*) and Jim Knight (*Peter Graves*), rivals in publishing and for the music-hall star Edie Story (*Margaret Lockwood*), join forces against the pirates. Eventually a copyright law is brought in. Interesting period musical: Miss Lockwood's songs include *The Honeysuckle and the Bee*, *Oh Mr Porter* and *Little Wooden Hut*.
RoC *Frederick Burtwell, Maudie Edwards, Garry Marsh, George Merritt, Muriel George, Eliot Makeham, Ella Retford, Alf Goddard, Barry Lupino, David Crowley, Joss Ambler, Wendy Toye.*

I'LL TURN TO YOU (1946) [4]
Dir *Geoffrey Faithfull*. Prod *F.W. Baker*. Scr *David Evans, Kathleen Butler*. Ph *Arthur Grant*. PC and Dis *Butchers*. 96 mins. Cert U
Roger (*Don Stannard*) finds it hard to settle down to his pre-war job after years as a sergeant-pilot. He decides to leave his wife (*Terry Randall*) so that she can marry an old admirer, rich Henry (*Ellis Irving*) who has already offered them a flat at a nominal rent. Henry finds Roger again and talks him into coming back. Good performances by young leads in topical film with music thrown in.
RoC *Harry Welchman, Ann Codrington, George Merritt, Irene Handl, Nicolette Roeg, Tony Pendrell, Leslie Perrins, John McHugh, Cameron Hall, Aubrey Mallalieu, Jonathan Field, Janet Morrison, Olive Kirby, Michael Gainsborough, Melville Crawfurd, Peter Penn, David Keir, John Allen, Hamilton Keene, Grace Arnold, Hal Gordon, Arthur Denton, Jack Vyvyan, Davina Craig, Evelyn Laye, Albert Sandler and the Palm Court Orchestra, Sylvia Welling, Sandy MacPherson, Choir of the Welsh Guards, London Symphony Orchestra.*

I'LL WALK BESIDE YOU (1943)   ③

Dir *Maclean Rogers*. Prod *F.W. Baker*. Scr *Kathleen Butler*. Ph *Geoffrey Faithfull*. PC and Dis *Butchers*. 88 mins. Cert U

John (*Richard Bird*) and Ann (*Lesley Brook*), who share a love of music, are parted by the war, and he goes missing on service with the navy. Ann becomes a nurse in a children's hospital and is engaged to a doctor when she meets John again; he has lost his memory of everything that happened before his ship was sunk. With the help of a song, Ann helps him remember it – and their love. Sincere performance by Miss Brook helps.

RoC *Percy Marmont, Leslie Bradley, Sylvia Marriott, Hugh Miller, Beatrice Varley, Irene Handl, George Merritt, Hilda Bayley, John McHugh, St David's Singers, London Symphony Orchestra.*

INSPECTOR HORNLEIGH GOES TO IT (1941)   ④
(USA: *Mail Train*)

Dir *Walter Forde*. Prod *Edward Black*. Scr *Frank Launder, Val Guest, J.O.C. Orton*. Ph *John J. Cox, Arthur Crabtree*. PC *Twentieth Century*. Dis *20th Century-Fox*. 87 mins. Cert U

Inspector Hornleigh (*Gordon Harker*), disappointed at not being entrusted with a spy case, is assigned to find out who is stealing army stores. This accidentally leads him and Sergeant Bingham (*Alastair Sim*) to a nest of fifth columnists. A dentist whom they suspect is murdered ... the trail leads to a school and finally to a mail train where Hornleigh, posing as a sorter, finds evidence that finishes the spies. Very British and good fun.

RoC *Phyllis Calvert, Edward Chapman, Raymond Huntley, Charles Oliver, Percy Walsh, David Horne, Peter Gawthorne, Wally Patch, Betty Jardine, O.B. Clarence, John Salew, Cyril Cusack, Bill Shine, Sylvia Cecil, Edward Underdown, E. Turner, Marie Makine, Richard Cooper.*

THE INTERRUPTED JOURNEY (1949)   ③

Dir *Dan Birt*. Prod *Anthony Havelock-Allan*. Scr *Michael Pertwee*. Ph *Erwin Hillier*. PC *Valiant*. Dis *British Lion*. 80 mins. Cert A

John (*Richard Todd*), a young married author, runs away with another woman, only to change his mind on the train journey. He pulls the communication cord and jumps out. As an indirect result, the train crashes. His mistress is dead, but shot – by her husband. An investigation follows, but the whole thing proves only to have been a minatory dream; no wonder the plot lacks plausibility.

RoC *Valerie Hobson, Christine Norden, Tom Walls, Ralph Truman, Vida Hope, Alexander Gauge, Dora Bryan, Arnold Ridley, Gwyneth Vaughan, Cyril Smith, Dora Sevening, Elsie Wagstaffe, Nigel Neilson, Arthur Lane, Vincent Ball, Jack Vyvyan.*

IN WHICH WE SERVE (1942)   ⑥

Dir *Noël Coward, David Lean*. Prod and Scr *Coward*. Ph *Ronald Neame*. PC *Two Cities*. Dis *British Lion*. 114 mins. Cert U

Noël Coward in In Which We Serve *(1942)*

1941. The British destroyer *Torrin*, commanded by Captain Kinross (*Noël Coward*), has already been torpedoed and towed back to port, successful in battle and involved in bringing troops back from Dunkirk. In the Battle of Crete, the *Torrin* is dive-bombed and sinks. Clinging to a raft, strafed by enemy bombers, the captain and his men remember loved ones back home. Most of them make it back. Inspiring, expertly scripted war drama.
RoC *John Mills, Bernard Miles, Celia Johnson, Joyce Carey, Kay Walsh, Michael Wilding, Robert Sansom, Philip Friend, James Donald, Derek Elphinstone, Ballard Berkeley, Chimmo Branson, Kenneth Carten, George Carney, Kathleen Harrison, Wally Patch, Richard Attenborough, Penelope Dudley Ward, Hubert Gregg, Frederick Piper, Caven Watson, Johnnie Schofield, Geoffrey Hibbert, John Boxer, Leslie Dwyer, Walter Fitzgerald, Ann Stephens, Daniel Massey, Gerald Case, Dora Gregory, Lionel Grose, Norman Pierce, Jill Stephens, Eileen Peel, Barbara Waring, Kay Young, Jeremy Hawk, Everley Gregg, Baby Juliet Mills.*

I SEE A DARK STRANGER (1946)   ④
(USA: *The Adventuress*)

Dir *Frank Launder*. Prod and Scr *Launder, Sidney Gilliat*. Ph *Wilkie Cooper*. PC *Individual*. Dis *General Film Distributors*. 111 mins. Cert A

British-hating Bridie Quilty (*Deborah Kerr*) leaves her home village hoping to join the IRA, but instead becomes the pawn of a Nazi agent (*Raymond Huntley*). Involved in the escape of a Nazi spy from an English prison, Bridie goes on to the Isle of Man, but encounters British naval officer David Baynes (*Trevor Howard*) who changes her mind about Englishmen and helps her evade arrest when hostilities cease. Delicately handled comedy-thriller with a battery of fascinating characters.
RoC *Michael Howard, Norman Shelley, Liam Redmond, Brefni O'Rorke, James Harcourt, W.G. O'Gorman, George Woodbridge, Garry Marsh, Tom Macauley, Olga Lindo, Kathleen Harrison, Harry Webster, Eddie Golden, Marie Ault, Tony Quinn, John Salew, Humphrey Heathcote, David Ward, Kenneth Buckley, David Tomlinson, Torin Thatcher, Everley Gregg, Kathleen Boutall, Katie Johnson, Pat Leonard, Gerald Case, Dorothy Bramhall, Cameron Hall, Joan Hickson, Doreen Percheron, Harry Hutchinson, Albert Sharpe, Eddie Byrne,* *Bob Elson, Brenda Bruce, Austin Meldon Kathleen Murphy, Leslie Dwyer, Sydney Tafler Josephine Fitzgerald, Ethel O'Shea, Frank Atkinson, John Vere, Patricia Laffan, Peter Jones Hugh Dempster, Jack Lester, Clifford Buckton Peter Cotes, Michael Dunne.*

IT ALWAYS RAINS ON SUNDAY (1947)   ⑤

Dir *Robert Hamer*. (Associate) Prod *Henry Cornelius*. Scr *Angus Macphail, Hamer, Cornelius*. Ph *Douglas Slocombe*. PC *Ealing Studios* Dis *General Film Distributors*. 92 mins. Cert A
Escaped convict Tommy Swann (*John McCallum*) makes for the home of Rose (*Googie Withers*), his mistress from years before, now the discontented wife of a middle-aged man (*Edward Chapman*). He begs her to hide him Eventually, Tommy's hideout is discovered Rose, fearing arrest, tries to gas herself but fails. Tommy flees from the police headed by Sergeant Fothergill (*Jack Warner*) and, after a desperate chase through railway yards, he is recaptured. Bleak view of East End life, but rich in human touches. Gripping all through
RoC *Jimmy Hanley, John Carol, John Slater Susan Shaw, Patricia Plunkett, David Lines Sydney Tafler, Alfie Bass, Betty Ann Davies. Michael Howard, Jane Hylton, Frederick Piper Hermione Baddeley, Gladys Henson, Nige. Stock, Meier Tzelniker, John Salew, Edie Martin, Betty Baskcomb, Gilbert Davis, Al Millen Vida Hope, Arthur Hambling, Grace Arnold John Vere, Patrick Jones, Joe E. Carr, Free Griffiths, Francis O'Rawe, David Knox.*

Googie Withers, Patricia Plunkett, Edwar Chapman, David Lines, Susan Shaw in It Always Rains on Sunday *(1947)*

I THANK YOU (1941)   ②

Dir *Marcel Varnel*. Prod *Edward Black*. Scr *Howard Irving Young, Val Guest, Marriott Edgar*. Ph *Jack Cox, Arthur Crabtree*. PC *Gainsborough*. Dis *General Film Distributors*. 8 mins. Cert U

Lady Randall (*Lily Morris*) refuses to go on backing a theatrical company. To explain why she should, two of them (*Arthur Askey Richard Murdoch*) take positions as cook/maid and butler in her household. Lady Randall goes away and her old father (*Moore Marriott*) takes charge, creating chaos and ending by firing at barrage balloons from the roof. Back in the air-raid shelter where the action started, Lady Randall, a former music-hall star, is persuaded to sing and finds herself as popular as ever. She finances the show with herself as star. Halting comedy.

RoC *Graham Moffatt, Kathleen Harrison, Wally Patch, Felix Aylmer, Cameron Hall, Peter Gawthorne, Roberta Huby, Issy Bonn, Phyllis Morris, Forsythe, Seamon and Farrell.*

IT HAPPENED IN LEICESTER SQUARE (1946) [2]

Dir and Scr *Geoffrey Benstead.* Prod *Norman Sharp.* Ph *Brooks-Carrington.* PC *Benstead and Sharp.* Dis *Benstead. 49 mins. Cert U*

Two working lads from Yorkshire come to London for the day, make fools of themselves seeing the sights, take in a variety show, and visit a snooker hall, where they meet world champion Joe Davis. Mercifully brief programme-filler.

LP *Harry Tate Jr, Slim Allen.*

IT HAPPENED IN SOHO (1948) [1]

Dir and Prod *Frank Chisnell.* Scr *Terry Sanford.* Ph *Ronnie Pilgrim.* PC *FC Films.* Dis *Associated British. 55 mins. Cert A*

A girl is strangled in Soho one dark night, and Bill Scott (*Richard Murdoch*), a reporter on the case, tries to beat the police to the killer. There is another killing, and the reporter's country girlfriend (*Patricia Raine*), who helps him sniff out clues, narrowly escapes a similar fate before the killer is caught. Poor dialogue, amateurish treatment; players struggle to little avail.

RoC *John Bailey, Henry Oscar.*

IT HAPPENED ONE SUNDAY (1944) [3]

Dir *Karel Lamac.* Prod *Victor Skutezky.* Scr *Skutezky, Frederick Gotfurt, Stephen Black, from a play by Skutezky.* Ph *Basil Emmott.* PC *Associated British.* Dis *Pathé. 99 mins. Cert A*

Moya (*Barbara White*), a pretty Irish girl in Liverpool, is told by the romantically minded Mrs Buckland (*Marjorie Rhodes*) that she has a secret admirer, Mr Brown. Later, Mrs B. tells Moya her imaginary suitor is in hospital. Hurrying to the hospital, Moya finds a Mr Brown (*Robert Beatty*), comforts him and, after he cuts himself free from crooked company, marries him. Pleasantly ingenuous if overlong fable.

RoC *Ernest Butcher, Judy Kelly, Irene Vanbrugh, Kathleen Harrison, C.V. France, Paul Demel, Marie Ault, Brefni O'Rorke, Charles Victor, Moore Marriott, Robert Adams, Frederick Piper, Philip Godfrey, Kathryn Beaumont, Arthur Hambling, David Keir, Vic Wise, Patric Curwen, Hal Gordon, Tonie Edgar Bruce.*

IT'S A WONDERFUL DAY (1948) [2]

Dir, Prod and Scr *Hal Wilson.* Ph *Brooks-Carrington, Stanley Clinton.* PC *Knightsbridge.* Dis *Equity British. 50 mins. Cert U*

A young band leader (*John Blythe*), in need of a rest, makes a leisurely tour of the West Country, and finally settles at a farmhouse, where he and his band encourage local talent, and he falls in love with a local girl. Minimusical has a few bright moments.

RoC *Dorothee Baroone, Eva Benyon, Jack Hodges, Lew Sherman, Yvonne Griffiths, The Seven Imeson Brothers, George Mitchell and His Swing Choir.*

IT'S HARD TO BE GOOD (1948) [1]

Dir and Scr *Jeffrey Dell.* Prod *John Gossage.* Ph *Laurie Friedman.* PC *Two Cities.* Dis *General Film Distributors. 93 mins. Cert U*

Captain Gladstone Wedge VC (*Jimmy Hanley*) leaves the army after the Second World War resolved to spread peace and goodwill among men. This leads to consecutive disasters at home, at a local paper and at a political meeting. He falls in love with Mary (*Anne Crawford*), who intends to make the Captain try less hard to be good. Promising idea; embarrassingly inept execution.

RoC *Raymond Huntley, Lana Morris, Edward Rigby, Elwyn Brook-Jones, David Horne, Joyce Carey, Muriel Aked, Geoffrey Keen, Cyril Smith, Leslie Weston.*

IT'S IN THE BAG (1943) [3]

Dir *Herbert Mason.* Prod *F. W. Baker.* Scr *Con West.* PC and Dis *Butchers. 80 mins. Cert U*

Cockney sisters Gert and Daisy (*Elsie and Doris Waters*) find that an old dress, left to them by Granny, has £20,000 sewn in the bustle. They have just sold it. Joe (*Reginald Purdell*), their landlady's son, is determined to get it first. In search of the dress, Gert and Daisy have to impersonate the leading lady and child roles in a repertory play. Only after a delayed action bomb has exploded in the theatre do they get the dress back. Slight story moved along at great speed, yet another variant on *The 12 Chairs*.

RoC *Lesley Osmond, Ernest Butcher, Gordon Edwards, Irene Handl, Antony Holles, Tony Quinn, Vera Bogetti, Megs Jenkins, Margaret Yarde, Edie Martin, Esma Cannon, Benita Lydell, Jonathan Field, Richard Molinas, Jack Vyvyan, Terry Conlin, Noel Dainton, Hugh Stewart.*

IT'S NOT CRICKET (1948) [4]

Dir *Alfred Roome, Roy Rich.* Prod *Betty Box.* Scr *Bernard McNab, Gerard Bryant, Lyn Lockwood.* Ph *Gordon Lang.* PC *Gainsborough.* Dis *General Film Distributors. 77 mins. Cert U*

For letting a dangerous Nazi (*Maurice Denham*) escape, Major Bright (*Basil Radford*) and Captain Early (*Naunton Wayne*) are 'retired' from the army. They set up as private detectives, but the Nazi still dogs their tracks, popping up in every case and finally involving them in a lunatic cricket match where the ball contains a stolen diamond. Funny second-feature with a riotous climax.

RoC *Susan Shaw, Alan Wheatley, Nigel Buchanan, Jane Carr, Leslie Dwyer, Diana Dors, Patrick Waddington, Edward Lexy, Frederick Piper, Mary Hinton, Margaret Withers, Brian Oulton, Cyril Chamberlain, Charles Cullum, John Mann, Hal Osmond, Sheila Huntington, John Warren, Viola Lyel, Arthur Hambling, Hamilton Keene, Meinhart Maur, John Boxer.*

IT'S SAM SMALL AGAIN (1942)

Reissue title of **Sam Small Leaves Town** (1937).

IT'S THAT MAN AGAIN (1943) [4]

Dir *Walter Forde.* Prod *Edward Black.* Scr *Howard Irving Young, Ted Kavanagh, from the* radio series by *Kavanagh.* PC *Gainsborough.* Dis *General Film Distributors. 84 mins. Cert U*

The Mayor (*Tommy Handley*) of Foaming-at-the-Mouth invests money from the rates in the purchase of the Olympic Theatre (virtually gutted by bombs) and a dramatic academy, all of whose pupils are owed money by the ex-principal. Fleeing from his creditors, the Mayor appropriates a play from a drunken playwright. But, on its first night, the academy performers turn up and wreck the show. A good many laughs, but radio show's unique appeal not captured.

RoC *Jack Train, Greta Gynt, Sidney Keith, Horace Percival, Dorothy Summers, Dino Galvani, Clarence Wright, Leonard Sharp, Claude Bailey, Vera Frances, Jean Kent, Richard George, Raymond Glendenning, Peter Noble, Franklin Bennett.*

I WAS A DANCER (1949) [2]

Dir, Prod, Scr and PC *Frank Richardson.* Ph *Ernest Palmer.* Dis *Adelphi. 49 mins. Cert A*

Murder mystery set in a ballet school, initially in 1920. It is nearly 30 years later before the killer is unmasked. The kind of film that guts-and-gore directors would revel in 30 years later still, here rather more decorously made. And duller.

LP *Diana Napier, Patricia Owens, Sheila Robins, Primrose Rhead.*

THE JACK OF DIAMONDS (1948) [4]

Dir *Vernon Sewell.* Prod *Walter d'Eyncourt.* Scr *Nigel Patrick, Cyril Raymond.* Ph *Moray Grant.* PC *VS Productions.* Dis *Exclusive. 73 mins. Cert U*

Hard-up Roger (*Cyril Raymond*) and his wife Joan (*Joan Carol*) charter their last major asset, a yacht, to treasure-seeker Alan Butler (*Nigel Patrick*). Sailing to the French coast, they hunt for a sunken chest full of diamonds. Meeting the rightful owner of the chest, they find that Butler is up to no good. His attempt to flee with the gems in their yacht is foiled. Minor adventure story is cleanly, plausibly made by its little team.

RoC *Darcy Conyers, Vernon Sewell.*

JASSY (1947) [2]

Dir *Bernard Knowles.* Prod *Sydney Box.* Scr *Dorothy and Campbell Christie, Geoffrey Kerr, from the novel by Norah Lofts.* Ph *Jack Asher.* PC *Gainsborough.* Dis *General Film Distributors. Technicolor. 102 mins. Cert A*

Jassy (*Margaret Lockwood*), a gipsy with second sight, is taken into the home of Nick Helmar (*Basil Sydney*) by his daughter Dilys (*Patricia Roc*). Barney (*Dermot Walsh*), who wants back the mansion his father Chris (*Dennis Price*) lost to Helmar, at cards, is attracted to Dilys. Jassy marries Helmar with the mansion as dowry, intending to give it to Barney. Dilys marries into money. Helmar is found poisoned and Jassy is suspected, but the killer turns out to be her dumb, devoted maid, whose confession clears the way for Jassy and Barney to wed. Old-time period melodrama is not very good, even of its kind.

RoC *Nora Swinburne, Linden Travers, Ernest Thesiger, Cathleen Nesbitt, Jean Cadell, John Laurie, Grey Blake, Clive Morton, Torin Thatcher, Beatrice Varley, Maurice Denham, Alan Wheatley, Esma Cannon, Grace Arnold, Bryan Coleman, Eliot Makeham, Joan Haythorne, Hugh Pryse, Stewart Rome, Susan Shaw, Dennis Harkin, Constance Smith.*

JEANNIE (1941)
(USA: *Girl in Distress*) [4]

Dir *Harold French.* Prod *Marcel Hellman.* Scr *Anatole de Grunwald, Roland Pertwee, from the play by Aimee Stuart.* Ph *Bernard Knowles.* PC *Tansa Films.* Dis *General Film Distributors.* 101 mins. Cert U

Appealing romantic comedy about a Scots lass (*Barbara Mullen*), left exactly £277 by her skinflint father. She spends it on a trip to Vienna, where she is rescued from various pitfalls by Stanley Smith (*Michael Redgrave*), there to sell his new washing machine at a trade fair. Back in England, her laundry asks her to demonstrate at Olympia, where she finds her stand next to Smith's washing machines. She flees, and takes up domestic service, but Stanley finds her and makes her agree to marry him.

RoC *Wilfrid Lawson, Kay Hammond, Albert Lieven, Edward Chapman, Googie Withers, Gus McNaughton, Phyllis Stanley, Hilda Bayley, Marjorie Fielding, Frank Cellier, Anne Shelton, Percy Walsh, Philip Godfrey, Meinhart Maur, Esmé Percy, Rachel Kempson, Joan Kemp-Welch, Joss Ambler, Katie Johnson, Lynn Evans, Ian Fleming, James Knight.*

JIM THE PENMAN (1947) [2]

Dir and Prod *Frank Chisnell.* Scr *Terry Sanford, Edward Eve.* Ph *Fred Ford.* Dis *New Realm.* 45 mins. Cert A

Documentary-style thriller about an impecunious nineteenth-century barrister, James Townsend Saward (*Mark Dignam*), who becomes the greatest forger of all time, known as Jim the Penman. He is eventually tracked down by Atwell (*Alec Ross*), a private investigator. Somewhat amateurish presentation of fascinating subject.

RoC *Beatrice Kane, Campbell Singer, George Street, Daphne Maddox, Theodore Tree, Colin Gordon.*

JOHNNY FRENCHMAN (1945) [4]

Dir *Charles Frend.* (Associate) Prod *S.C. Balcon.* Scr *T.E.B. Clarke.* Ph *Roy Kellino.* PC *Ealing Studios.* Dis *Eagle-Lion.* 105 mins. Cert U

Bretons Lanec Florrie (*Françoise Rosay*) and her son Yan (*Paul Dupuis*) launch pre-war fish-poaching expeditions into Cornish waters. The feud that results is broken when the French help the Cornishmen land a giant catch

Paul Dupuis and Ralph Michael in Johnny Frenchman (*1945*)

of mullet, is on again when Bob (*Ralph Michael*) breaks Yan's leg in a wrestling match, but is buried in war when the French become refugees. Lanec and her men net a dangerous mine and tow it to sea, setting the seal on the new friendship. Unusual, interesting film rather lacking in dramatic tension.

RoC *Tom Walls, Patricia Roc, Frederick Piper, Richard George, Bill Blewett, Arthur Hambling, James Harcourt, Grace Arnold, Beatrice Varley, Judith Furse, Stan Paskin, James Knight, George Hirste, Carroll O'Connor, Franklin Bennett, Leslie Harcourt, Bernard Fishwick, Herbert Thomas, Denver Hall, Vincent Holman, Alfie Bass, Drusilla Wills, Paul Bonifas, Marcel Poncin, Henri Bollinger, Jean-Marie Balcon, Louise Gournay, Charles Jezequel, Pierre Richard, Jean-Marie Nacry, Joseph Menou.*

JOURNEY AHEAD (1947) [3]

Dir and Prod *Peter Mills.* Scr *Warren Tute.* PC *Random.* Dis *Independent Film Renters.* 62 mins. Cert U

Ann Franklin (*Ruth Haven*), a war widow on the edge of a nervous breakdown, goes for a rest cure to a little Cornish fishing village. She meets two brothers just out of the navy and falls in love with one of them, worrying because they seem to be involved in a smuggling racket. But they are really undercover policemen aiming to bring the smugglers to book, and Ann's new romance is secure. Modest drama with refreshing settings.

RoC *John Stevens, Howard Douglas, Norah Gordon.*

JOURNEY TOGETHER (1945) [5]

Dir, Prod and Scr *John Boulting, from a story by Terence Rattigan.* Ph *Harry Waxman.* PC *RAF Film Unit.* Dis *RKO Radio.* 95 mins. Cert U

David Wilton (*Richard Attenborough*), a working-class RAF corporal, and his friend John (*Jack Watling*), a university graduate, train to be wartime pilots. Wilton fails his final test, actually crashing a plane through lack of judgment. Disillusioned, he goes to a Canadian navigation school, where his instructor impresses how important he will be to an air crew. In a raid over Berlin, Wilton's new skills are tested and not found wanting. Documentary-style war drama with a human touch.

RoC *Edward G. Robinson, Bessie Love, David Tomlinson, John Justin, George Cole, Ronald Squire, Hugh Wakefield, Stuart Lathom, Sid Rider, Bromley Challoner, Z. Persankski, Sebastian Shaw, Leslie Nixon, Norvell Crutcher, Patrick Waddington, Miles Malleson.*

JUST WILLIAM'S LUCK (1947) [3]

Dir and Scr *Val Guest, from stories by Richmal Crompton.* Prod *David Coplan, James Carter.* Ph *Bert Mason.* PC *Diadem/Alliance.* Dis *United Artists.* 92 mins. Cert U

Young tearaway William (*William Graham*) and his gang decide to become Knights of the Square Table. Through some weird process of logic, they decide that the path to the bicycles their hearts desire is by haunting an old manor house and scaring off its inhabitants. But the manor houses a gang of thieves. William and the boys put the thieves to flight and become heroes. Quite lively schoolboy romp that could have done with a scruffier William.

RoC *Brian Roper, James Crabbe, Brian Weske, Garry Marsh, Jane Welsh, Leslie Bradley, A.E. Matthews, Muriel Aked, Hugh Cross, Kathleen Stuart, Jack Raine, Hy Hazell, Audrey Manning, Ivan Hyde, Michael Balfour, Michael Medwin, Patricia Cutts, John Powe, Leslie Hazell, Peter Davis, John O'Horo, Joan Hickson, Anna Marie, John Martel, Ivan Craig, Jumble (dog).*

K

KIND HEARTS AND CORONETS (1949) [6]

Dir *Robert Hamer.* (Associate) Prod *Michael Relph.* Scr *Hamer, John Dighton, from a novel by Roy Horniman.* Ph *Douglas Slocombe.* PC *Ealing Studios.* Dis *General Film Distributors.* 106 mins. Cert A

1900. When his mother is denied interment in the family vault, Louis Mazzini (*Dennis Price*), son of a penniless Italian and a duke's daughter, vows vengeance, murdering six of those who stand between him and the dukedom. Others die fortuitously and Louis is duke. But

Dennis Price and Clive Morton in Kind Hearts and Coronets (*1949*)

he is arrested and condemned for a murder he did not commit. Reprieved and pardoned, he is about to choose between the women in his life when he realizes he has left his telltale memoirs in the condemned cell. Brilliant black comedy, with a *tour de force* by *Alec Guinness* as all eight of the crumbling aristocrats who stand in Mazzini's way.

RoC *Valerie Hobson, Joan Greenwood, Audrey Fildes, Miles Malleson, Clive Morton, Cecil Ramage, John Penrose, Hugh Griffith, John Salew, Eric Messiter, Lyn Evans, Peggyann Clifford, Barbara Leake, Arthur Lowe, Anne Valery.*

KING ARTHUR WAS A GENTLEMAN (1942) [3]

Dir *Marcel Varnel.* Prod *Edward Black.* Scr *Val Guest, Marriott Edgar.* Ph *Arthur Crabtree.* PC *Gainsborough.* Dis *General Film Distributors.* 99 mins. Cert U

Arthur King (*Arthur Askey*) gets into the army at last and is posted to 'King Arthur' country. He is obsessed with the Camelot legend, and his friends jokingly present him with a sword, which he imagines to be Excalibur. Ordered out East, Arthur gains courage from the possession of the sword and performs heroic deeds. When he is told the truth, his illusions are shattered. Some funny scenes and good songs, but overlong and missing opportunities to indulge in fantasy.

RoC *Evelyn Dall, Anne Shelton, Max Bacon, Jack Train, Peter Graves, Vera Frances, Al Burnett, Brefni O'Rorke, Ronald Shiner, Freddie Crump, Ernie Feldman, John Wynn, Veronica Turleigh, Elizabeth Flateau, Margot Hunter, Sonia Somers, Virginia Keiley, Cameron Hall, Vincent Holman, Clifford Cobbe, Clifford Buckton, Bryan Herbert.*

KIPPS (1941) [4]

Dir *Carol Reed.* Prod *Edward Black.* Scr *Sidney Gilliat, from the novel by H. G. Wells.* Ph *Arthur Crabtree.* PC *20th Century.* Dis *20th Century-Fox.* 112 mins *(later 108).* Cert U

Kipps (*Michael Redgrave*), a draper's assistant, comes into a fortune, and rejects an impoverished society girl (*Diana Wynyard*) to marry his childhood sweetheart (*Phyllis Calvert*). But their ideas clash, and each is thoroughly miserable until news comes that Kipps' friend Ronnie (*Michael Wilding*) has lost the fortune. The play that Kipps has backed is a great success, leaving the young couple enough money to buy

Michael Redgrave and Diana Wynyard in Kipps *(1941)*

a draper's store and live the kind of life they want. Although somewhat truncated and dubiously cast, this is still a well-told story. A prologue featuring *H. G. Wells* was cut before general release.

RoC *Arthur Riscoe, Max Adrian, Helen Haye, Lloyd Pearson, Edward Rigby, MacKenzie Ward, Hermione Baddeley, Betty Ann Davies, Betty Jardine, Frank Pettingell, Beatrice Varley, George Carney, Irene Browne, Peter Graves, Kathleen Harrison, Muriel Aked, Philip Frost, Viscount Castlerosse, Diana Calderwood, Arthur Denton, Robert McCarthy, Felix Aylmer, Marda Shannon, Carol Gardiner.*

KISS THE BRIDE GOODBYE (1944) [3]

Dir and Prod *Paul L. Stein.* Scr *Jack Whittingham.* Ph *Geoffrey Faithfull.* PC and Dis *Butchers.* 89 mins. Cert A

Joan's (*Patricia Medina*) mother eggs her on to get engaged to her pompous boss (*Claud Allister*), although she loves a soldier (*Jimmy Hanley*) overseas. When he turns up and finds Joan betrothed, he storms off to Scotland. Joan follows. They visit her aunt and uncle at Rugby (the first stop on the train journey) who assume they are on their honeymoon. After another quarrel, there's a happy ending. Broad romantic farce but well played.

RoC *Ellen Pollock, Frederick Leister, Marie Lohr, Wylie Watson, Jean Simmons, Muriel George, Irene Handl, Aubrey Mallalieu, Hay Petrie, C. Denier Warren, Ben Williams, Hal Gordon, Noel Dainton, Vi Kaley, Beatrice Marsden, Ann Kennington, Frank Atkinson, Ethel Beal, Julie Suedo, Eve Llewellyn.*

L

LADY FROM LISBON (1942) [4]

Dir *Leslie Hiscott.* Prod *Elizabeth Hiscott.* Scr *Michael Barringer.* Ph *Erwin Hillier.* PC *British National/Shaftesbury.* Dis *Anglo-American.* 75 mins. Cert U

Minghetti (*Francis L. Sullivan*), a South American racketeer living in Lisbon, asks for the Mona Lisa in exchange for working for the Nazis. They plan to give him a copy. The real painting has, unknown to the Germans, been stolen by another crook, Anzoni (*Antony Holles*). He plans to sell it to Minghetti, who is offered another fake by an English spinster who believes it to be the real thing. The Nazis get the Mona Lisa from Paris but this is, of course, also a fake. Minghetti gives up in despair and, when the real painting is picked out by a British agent, agrees to work for the Allies. Lively, amusing comedy-thriller.

RoC *Jane Carr, Martita Hunt, Charles Victor, George Street, Gerhardt Kempinski, Leo de Pokorny, Wilfrid Hyde White.*

THE LAMP STILL BURNS (1943) [4]

Dir *Maurice Elvey.* Prod *Leslie Howard.* Scr *Elizabeth Baron, Roland Pertwee, Major Neilson, from a novel by Monica Dickens.* Ph *Robert Krasker.* PC *Two Cities.* Dis *General Film Distributors.* 90 mins. Cert A

Architect Hilary Clarke (*Rosamund John*) decides in wartime to become a nurse. She undergoes her training and at first finds the strict discipline rather hard to take. She becomes a fighter for better hospital conditions, and falls for a wounded airman (*Stewart Granger*) whose fiancée (*Margaret Vyner*) agrees to step aside. But it's Hilary who steps aside – to devote her life to nursing. Sincere, moving tribute to overworked profession.

RoC *Godfrey Tearle, Sophie Stewart, John Laurie, Cathleen Nesbitt, Eric Micklewood, Joyce Grenfell, Joan Maude, Grace Arnold, Jenny Laird, Megs Jenkins, Wylie Watson, Ernest Thesiger, Brefni O'Rorke, John Howard, Mignon O'Doherty, Leslie Dwyer, Max Earle, Gordon Begg, Althe Parker, Paul Merton, Aubrey Mallalieu, Jane Gill-Davis, David Keir, Patrick Curwen, Janette Scott.*

LANDFALL (1949) [3]

Dir *Ken Annakin.* Prod *Victor Skutezky.* Scr *Talbot Jennings, Gilbert Gunn, Anne Burnaby, from the novel by Nevil Shute.* Ph *Wilkie Cooper.* PC and Dis *Associated British-Pathé.* 88 mins. Cert U

1940. Rick (*Michael Denison*), a young flight lieutenant attached to coastal command, sinks what he believes to be a German U-boat. Later, he is told it was a British submarine. His girlfriend (*Patricia Plunkett*), a barmaid, after listening to some careless talk in the pub, is able to prove Rick right and remove the shadow from his career. Good book reduced to average film.

RoC *Kathleen Harrison, David Tomlinson, Joan Dowling, Maurice Denham, A. E. Matthews, Denis O'Dea, Margaretta Scott, Sebastian Shaw, Nora Swinburne, Charles Victor, Laurence Harvey, Paul Carpenter, Frederick Leister, Hubert Gregg, Walter Hudd, Margaret Barton, Edith Sharpe, Stanley Rose, Ivan Samson, Gerald Case, Bryan Coleman, Norman Watson, James Carney, Moultrie Kelsall, Dennis Vance, Caven Watson, Andrew Leigh, Harry Fowler, Andrea Lea.*

THE LAST DAYS OF DOLWYN (1949) [3]
(USA: *Woman of Dolwyn*)

Dir and Scr *Emlyn Williams.* Prod *Anatole de Grunwald.* Ph *Otto Heller.* PC *London Films.* Dis *British Lion.* 95 mins. Cert U

1892. The Welsh village of Dolwyn is to be flooded to make a reservoir, thanks to Rob (*Emlyn Williams*), who was driven out of Dolwyn as a boy for thieving and now returns to destroy it. He gets villagers to sell land rights, but one old woman, Merri (*Edith Evans*) holds out, even persuading Rob's bosses that an alternative scheme is on. He determines to flood Dolwyn anyway, but is killed after a fight with Merri's stepson, Gareth (*Richard Burton*). Merri floods the valley to hide the body. Slow; good village detail though.

RoC *Anthony James, Barbara Couper, Allan*

Anthony James, Edith Evans, Richard Burton in The Last Days of Dolwyn (*1949*)

Aynesworth, Andrea Lea, Hugh Griffith, Roddy Hughes, David Davies, Tom Jones, Sam Hinton, Prysor Williams, Pat Glyn, Joan Griffiths, Betty Stanley, Dudley Jones, Aubrey Richards, Madoline Thomas, Dorothy Langley, Doreen Richards, Bryan V. Thomas, Frank Dunlop, Dafydd Havard, Eileen Dale, Betty Humphries, Rita Crailey, Emrys Leyshon, Constance Lewis, Hywel Wood, Edmund Rees, Kenneth Evans, Maurice Browning.

THE LAST LOAD (1948)   3

Dir and Prod *John Baxter*. Scr *Geoffrey Orme, Mary Cathcart Borer*. Ph *Jo Jago*. PC *Elstree Independent*. Dis *General Film Distributors*. 57 mins. Cert U
The respective fathers of David (*Douglas Barr*) and Susan (*Angela Glynne*) each own a fleet of lorries. The kids discover a plot to steal a whole convoy-load of goods on its way to the docks. David's father contacts the police and the gang is rounded up, before Susan and David sit in on an exciting race to get the cargo to the docks on time. Rousing children's film.
RoC *Ivor Bowyer, Angela Foulds, David Hannaford, Ian Colin, John Longden, Frank Atkinson.*

LATE AT NIGHT (1946)   1

Dir *Michael Chorlton*. Prod *Herbert Wynne*. Scr *Henry C. James*. Ph *Jan Sikorski*. PC *Bruton Films*. Dis *Premier*. 76 mins (later 69). Cert A
Reporter Dave Jackson (*Barry Morse*), on the trail of a wood alcohol gang, is helped by singer Jill (*Daphne Day*), who knows that her nightclub boss Tony (*Noel Dryden*) is involved. When one of the gang is murdered, Tony draws the line and, thanks to him and Dave, the leader, The Spider (*Paul Demel*), is run to earth - but not before he has killed Tony. Unintentionally funny thriller.
RoC *Don Avory, Monica Mallory, Paul Sheridan.*

LATIN QUARTER (1945)   3

Dir and Scr *Vernon Sewell, from a play by Pierre Mills, C. de Vylars*. Prod *Louis H. Jackson, Derrick de Marney*. Ph *Günther Krampf*. PC *British National*. Dis *Anglo-American*. 79 mins. Cert A
Sculptor Charles Garrie (*Derrick de Marney*)

rents, in 1893, a Paris studio previously let to sculptor Minetti, who died in a madhouse. His friend Lucille (*Joan Seton*) worried at the effect the studio has on him, calls in Dr Krasner (*Frederick Valk*) who discovers Garrie had been in love with Minetti's vanished wife (*Joan Greenwood*). A seance reveals that Minetti had killed her and hidden her body inside a clay statue. Heavy melodrama, remake of the director's first film, *The Medium*, (1934).
RoC *Beresford Egan, Lilly Kann, Martin Miller, Valentine Dyall, Anthony Hawtrey, Bruce Winston, Sybilla Binder, Gerhardt Kempinski, Espinosa, Margaret Clarke, Rachel Brodbrar, Billy Holland, Cleo Nordi.*

THE LAUGHING LADY (1946)   4

Dir *Paul L. Stein*. Prod *Louis H. Jackson*. Scr *Jack Whittingham, from the musical play by Ingram d'Abbes*. Ph *Geoffrey Unsworth*. PC *British National*. Dis *Anglo-American*. Technicolor. 93 mins. Cert A
1790: Robespierre promises to spare the Duchess of Lorraine's life if her son André (*Webster Booth*) can restore to France a valuable necklace called The Pearls of Sorrow. In England, though, he falls in love with Denise (*Anne Ziegler*), owner of the pearls. He returns to France and is condemned to death. But Denise goes to Robespierre, taking the pearls. Touched, he frees André to marry her. Opulent musical vehicle for popular radio duettists.
RoC *Peter Graves, Felix Aylmer, Francis L. Sullivan, Paul Dupuis, Chili Bouchier, Ralph Truman, Charles Goldner, John Ruddock, Jack Melford, Hay Petrie, Frederick Burtwell, Anthony Nicholls, D. Whittingham, George de Warfaz, John Serret, Clare Lindsay, Harry Fine, Griffiths Moss, Mary Martlew, Geoffrey Wilmer, Laurence Archer, James Hayter, John Clifford, André Belhomme, Hugh Owens, Harry Terry, Beatrice Campbell, Robert Conner, George Dudley, Maurice Bannister.*

LAW AND DISORDER (1940)   3

Dir *David Macdonald*. Prod *K.C. Alexander*. Scr *Roger Macdonald*. PC *British Consolidated*. Dis *RKO Radio*. 74 mins. Cert A
Young lawyer Larry Preston (*Barry K. Barnes*) successfully defends thugs accused of sabotage - to the annoyance of the police, the anger of his senior partner Samuel Blight (*Alastair Sim*) and the curiosity of both his wife (*Diana Churchill*) and the man who employs the heavies (*Austin Trevor*). Larry is called up when war starts, but just has time to foil the villains' plans to use portable radios to guide enemy bombers to important targets. Too much wisecracking in Thin Man style holds up plot.
RoC *Edward Chapman, Ruby Miller, Leo Genn, Geoffrey Sumner, Glen Alyn, Torin Thatcher, Carl Jaffe, Cyril Smith.*

LET GEORGE DO IT (1940)   5

Dir *Marcel Varnel*. (Associate) Prod *Basil Dearden*. Scr *John Dighton, Austin Melford, Angus Macphail, Dearden*. Ph *Ronald Neame*. PC *Ealing Studios/ATP*. Dis *Associated British*. 82 mins. Cert U
Dinkie Doo concert performer George (*George Formby*) goes to Bergen (Norway) instead of

Blackpool and is mistaken for a British intelligence agent. With the help of hotel receptionist Sally (*Phyllis Calvert*), a real agent, George finds the code by which bandleader Mendez (*Garry Marsh*) is sending shipping information to U-boats. Taken prisoner on board a U-boat, George gets a message out, and a destroyer depth-charges the sub. George is rescued after being blown out of a torpedo tube. Topical Formby comedy moves along nicely.
RoC *Romney Brent, Bernard Lee, Coral Browne, Diana Beaumont, Torin Thatcher, Hal Gordon, Donald Calthrop, Ronald Shiner, Albert Lieven, Helena Pickard, Percy Walsh.*

LET THE PEOPLE SING (1942)   2

Dir and Prod *John Baxter*. Scr *Baxter, Barbara K. Emary, Geoffrey Orme, from the novel by J. B. Priestley*. Ph *Jimmy Wilson*. PC *British National*. Dis *Anglo-American*. 105 mins. Cert U
A group of travelling players decides to help local people battle against the takeover of their entertainments hall by two groups, one a commercial company, the other fuddy-duddies who want to build a museum. A government arbitrator is appointed and recognized by two of the players, who get him drunk and win the day for the people of the town. Good idea, but execution lacks mobility.
LP *Alastair Sim, Fred Emney, Edward Rigby, Patricia Roc, Oliver Wakefield, Annie Esmond, Marian Spencer, Olive Sloane, Maire O'Neill, Gus McNaughton, Charles Hawtrey, Peter Gawthorne, Aubrey Mallalieu, G. H. Mulcaster, Wally Patch, Horace Kenney, Morris Harvey, Spencer Trevor, David Keir, Ida Barr, Charles Doe, Eliot Makeham, Alexander Field, Leopold Glasspoole, Ian Fleming, Robert Aitken, Mignon O'Doherty, Michael Martin-Harvey, Richard George, Diana Beaumont, Stanley Paskin, George Merritt.*

THE LIFE AND DEATH OF COLONEL BLIMP (1943)   5

(USA: *Colonel Blimp*)
Dir, Prod and Scr *Michael Powell, Emeric Pressburger*. Ph *Georges Périnal, Jack Cardiff*. PC *Independent Producers/The Archers*. Dis *General Film Distributors*. Technicolor. 163 mins. Cert U
Clive Candy (*Roger Livesey*), a young Boer War VC, goes to Berlin to counter anti-British propaganda. He becomes friends with a German officer, Theo (*Anton Walbrook*) after they fight a duel. Theo marries the girl (*Deborah Kerr*) Candy loved. In the First World War, Candy marries a girl (*Kerr* again) who resembles his lost love and helps get Theo, a POW, repatriated. He retires, comes back in the Second World War as a brigadier, is axed, meets Theo, who has fled the Nazis, and vouches for him. His wife dies. On a Home Guard exercise, Candy is captured in the Turkish bath of his club, threatens to break the officer concerned, but is dissuaded by Theo, and by his ATS driver (*Kerr's* third role), who is the image of his dead wife. Warmly human, skilfully acted, if rather shapeless epic.
RoC *Roland Culver, James McKechnie, Albert*

Lieven, Arthur Wontner, David Hutcheson, Ursula Jeans, John Laurie, Harry Welchman, Reginald Tate, A. E. Matthews, Carl Jaffe, Valentine Dyall, Muriel Aked, Felix Aylmer, Frith Banbury, Eric Maturin, David Ward, Nevill Mapp, Vincent Holman, Spencer Trevor, James Knight, Dennis Arundell, Jan van Loewen, Robert Harris, Theodore Zichy, Jane Millican, Phyllis Morris, Diana Marshall, Yvonne André, Marjorie Gresley, Helen Debroy (Summers), Norman Pierce, Edward Cooper, Joan Swinstead, Thomas Palmer, Patrick Macnee.

LISBON STORY (1946)   3

Dir *Paul L. Stein*. Prod *Louis H. Jackson*. Scr *Jack Whittingham, from the musical play by Harold Purcell, Harry Parr-Davis*. Ph *Ernest Palmer*. PC *British National*. Dis *Anglo-American. 103 mins. Cert A*

David Warren (*David Farrar*), English intelligence officer betrothed to French actress Gabrielle (*Patricia Burke*), has to track down an atom bomb scientist and save him from the attentions of the Nazis, led by von Schriner (*Walter Rilla*), whom David outwits by having Gabrielle pose as a collaborator. Script stacked with clichés; score includes *Pedro the Fisherman*.
RoC *Richard Tauber, Lawrence O'Madden, Austin Trevor, Paul Bonifas, Harry Welchman, Esmé Percy, Noele Gordon, John Ruddock, Joan Seton, Allan Jeayes, Ralph Truman, Martin Walker, Michelle de Lys, Jan van Loewen, Uriel Porter, Hannah Watt, F. Wendhausen, Morgan Davies, Leo de Pokorny, Stephane Grappelly, Lorely Dyer, Halamar and Konarski.*

THE LITTLE BALLERINA (1947)   2

Dir *Lewis Gilbert*. Prod *Geoffrey Barkas*. Scr *Gilbert, Michael Barringer, Mary Cathcart Borer*. Ph *Frank North*. PC *Gaumont-British Instructional*. Dis *General Film Distributors. 60 mins. Cert U*

Joan (*Yvonne Marsh*), a London schoolgirl, pulls through ballet school with the help of friends after their parents' income fails. She is chosen to dance before *Margot Fonteyn*, but nearly misses her chance thanks to the schemings of a jealous rival. But she goes on and triumphs. Children's film is for junior balletomanes only.
RoC *Beatrice Varley, George Carney, Martita Hunt, Eliot Makeham, Leslie Dwyer, Anthony Newley, Herbert C. Walton, Marian Chapman, Doreen Richards, Kay Henderson, Michael Somes, Sydney Tafler.*

LONDON BELONGS TO ME (1948)   5
(USA: *Dulcimer Street*)

Dir *Sidney Gilliat*. Prod *Frank Launder, Gilliat*. Scr *Gilliat, J. B. Williams, from the novel by Norman Collins*. Ph *Wilkie Cooper*. PC *Individual*. Dis *General Film Distributors. 112 mins. Cert A*

In a South London boarding house, 1939, live: Mr and Mrs Josser (*Wylie Watson, Fay Compton*); their daughter Doris (*Susan Shaw*); Connie Coke (*Ivy StHelier*), a sad cloakroom attendant; Mrs Boon and her son Percy (*Gladys Henson, Richard Attenborough*); Mr Squales (*Alastair Sim*), a fake medium; Mrs Vizzard (*Joyce Carey*), the lonely landlady. Percy gets involved in the killing of a girl. He is tried and

sentenced to hang. His boarding-house friends rally round and eventually win him a reprieve. Very human drama with fine London atmosphere.
RoC *Stephen Murray, Andrew Crawford, Eleanor Summerfield, Hugh Griffith, Maurice Denham, Jack McNaughton, Henry Edwards, Arthur Howard, Hatton Duprez, Ivor Barnard, Kenneth Downey, Cecil Trouncer, Lionel Grose, Russell Waters, John Salew, Michael Kent, Basil Cunard, Cyril Chamberlain, Edward Evans, Fabia Drake, Myrette Morven, Alexis France, Aubrey Dexter, Henry Hewitt, J. H. Roberts, Wensley Pithey, Stanley Rose, John Boxer, Manville Tarrant, George Cross, Owen Reynolds, Sydney Tafler, D.A. Mehan, Susan Buret, Frank Ling, Alan Saynes, Frederick Knight, Ewen Solon, Leonard Morris, Ivy Collins, Joe Clark, Ewan Roberts, Lala Lloyd, Nellie Sheffield, Stanley Beard, Arty Ash, Paula Young, Grace Allardyce, Alexander Field, Elsie Bernard, Arthur Lowe, John Gregson.*

LONDON TOWN (1946)   2
(USA: *My Heart Goes Crazy*)

Dir, Prod and PC *Wesley Ruggles*. Scr *Elliot Paul, Sigfried Herzig, Val Guest*. Ph *Erwin Hillier*. Dis *Eagle-Lion. Technicolor. 126 mins. Cert U*

Jerry (*Sid Field*), a provincial comic, comes to London to appear in a revue, but finds he is only to be an understudy. When his daughter (*Petula Clark*) plays a trick on the principal comedian, ensuring his non-appearance, Jerry goes on and is a great success. More than can be said for the film which, much too long and ponderous, was one of the great British postwar flops.
RoC *Greta Gynt, Tessie O'Shea, Claude Hulbert, Sonnie Hale, Mary Clare, Jerry Desmonde, Kay Kendall, Beryl Davis, Scotty McHarg, Reginald Purdell, W.G. Fay, Lucas Hovinga, Marion Saunders, Jack Parnell, Pamela Carroll, Alfie Dean, Charles Paton, James Kennedy, Susan Shaw.*

Sid Field and Petula Clark in London Town (*1946*)

THE LONE CLIMBER (1949)   4

Dir *William C. Hammond*. Prod *Mary Field*. Scr *Patricia Latham*. Ph *Walter Riml*. PC *GB Instructional*. Dis *General Film Distributors. 59 mins. Cert U*

A party of town children go on an Alpine holiday. One boy is anxious to climb a mountain

and sets off alone. The remaining children, having delayed their teacher, go to bring him back. One child falls and injures a leg, search parties are sent out and all ends happily with the children rescued. Straightforward film for youngsters with excitements efficiently arranged. German dialogue, English commentary.
LP *Fritz von Friedl, Gerty Jobstmann, Eleanore Kulicek, Herbert Nitsch, Herbert Navratil, Elfriede Kaspar, Ernestine Frauenberger.*

LOOK BEFORE YOU LOVE (1948)   2

Dir *Harold Huth*. Prod *John Corfield, Huth*. Scr *Reginald Long, from a story by Ketti Frings*. Ph *Harry Waxman*. PC *Burnham*. Dis *General Film Distributors. 96 mins. Cert A*

Ann (*Margaret Lockwood*), an embassy secretary, marries smooth Charles (*Griffith Jones*), an international con-man, blackmailer and drunkard. He sells her to a fortyish millionaire (*Norman Wooland*) for £10,000 and, knowing that the man has six months to live, tries to win her back. Ann, who is fond of her new husband, tells Charles where to go, and the millionaire's doctors decide he has a lot longer to live than they thought. Farce played as romantic drama: pretty silly.
RoC *Phyllis Stanley, Michael Medwin, Maurice Denham, Frederick Piper, Violet Farebrother, Bruce Seton, Peggy Evans, June Elvin, Joan Rees, Nigel Lawlor, Alan Adair, Giselle Morlais, Stanley Quentin, Daphne Arthur, Dorothy Bramhall, Edwin Palmer, Peter Fontaine.*

Griffith Jones, Norman Wooland and Margaret Lockwood in Look Before You Love (*1949*)

THE LOST PEOPLE (1949)   3

Dir *Bernard Knowles, Muriel Box*. Prod *Gordon Wellesley*. Scr *Bridget Boland, Box, from a play by Boland*. Ph *Jack Asher*. PC *Gainsborough*. Dis *General Film Distributors. 88 mins. Cert A*

A disused German theatre serves as a dispersal centre for displaced persons. The inexperienced British officer in charge (*Dennis Price*) battles to keep order among the various nationalities and political factions. A suspected outbreak of plague makes everyone comrades, while the murder of an innocent woman by a fanatic teaches them about tolerance. Poor transition of stage play to screen; some critics liked it, not so the public.
RoC *Mai Zetterling, Richard Attenborough, Siobhan McKenna, Maxwell Reed, William*

Hartnell, Gerard Heinz, Zena Marshall, Olaf Pooley, Harcourt Williams, Philo Houser, Jill Balcon, Grey Blake, Marcel Poncin, Tutte Lemkow, Paul Hardtmuth, Nelly Arno, Pamela Stirling, Peter Bull, George Benson.

LOVE IN WAITING (1948) [2]

Dir *Douglas Pierce*. Prod *Henry Passmore*. Scr *Arthur Reid, Martin Lane, from a story by Monica Dickens*. Ph *Roy Fogwell*. PC *Production Facilities*. Dis *General Film Distributors. 60 mins. Cert U*

Golly (*Peggy Evans*) and her friend Brenda (*Elspet Gray*) become waitresses at a restaurant. Golly's involvement with the shy manager Clitheroe (*David Tomlinson*) incurs the enmity of the manageress, who plants 'hot' money in Golly's coat. Thanks to an unexpected witness, it's the manageress who goes to jail, while the girls end up in charge. Foolishly handled comedy wastes its cast.

RoC *Andrew Crawford, John Witty, Patsy Drake, George Merritt, Johnnie Schofield, Eliot Makeham, Linda Grey, Diana Chesney, James Lomas, Duncan Lewis, Grace Arnold, Richard Gilbert, Charles Paton, Sam Kydd, Patricia Dainton, Patience Rentoul*.

LOVE ON THE DOLE (1941) [5]

Dir and Prod *John Baxter*. Scr *Walter Greenwood, Barbara K. Emary, Rollo Gamble, from the novel by Greenwood and play by Ronald Gow*. Ph *James Wilson*. PC *British National*. Dis *Anglo-American. 100 mins. Cert A*

Sally (*Deborah Kerr*), a mill girl in Lancashire during the Depression, is in love with Larry (*Clifford Evans*), a militant factory worker who loses his job and refuses to marry Sally on dole money. Leading a demonstration against pay, conditions and unemployment, Larry is wounded in a scuffle with police and later dies. Sally, crushed, gives herself to a rich old admirer to get jobs for her father and brother. Gloomy but convincing, an early forerunner of kitchen sink dramas 20 years on.

RoC *Joyce Howard, Frank Cellier, Mary Merrall, George Carney, Geoffrey Hibbert, Maire O'Neill, A. Bromley Davenport, Peter Gawthorne, Martin Walker, Iris Vandeleur, Marie Ault, Marjorie Rhodes, Kenneth Griffith, B. John Slater, Muriel George, Charles Williams, Colin Chandler, Jordan Lawrence, Dennis Wyndham, Ben Williams, James Harcourt, Terry Conlin, Charles Groves*.

Deborah Kerr and Clifford Evans in Love on the Dole *(1941)*

THE LOVES OF JOANNA GODDEN (1947) [4]

Dir *Charles Frend*. (Associate) Prod *Sidney Cole*. Scr *H. E. Bates, Angus Macphail, from a novel by Sheila Kaye-Smith*. Ph *Douglas Slocombe*. PC *Ealing Studios*. Dis *General Film Distributors. 89 mins. Cert U*

1905. Strong-willed Joanna Godden's (*Googie Withers*) father leaves her his Romney Marsh sheep farm. She refuses the aid of neighbour Arthur Alce (*John McCallum*), hiring an Australian shepherd (*Chips Rafferty*) who nearly ruins her pedigree flock by cross-breeding. Her fiancé Martin (*Derek Bond*) drowns in an accident. Her spoilt young sister (*Jean Kent*) marries Alce, but deserts him when foot-and-mouth decimates his flock. Joanna and Alce realize that, after all, their future lies together. Human, well-acted; not quite the emotiontugger it might have been.

RoC *Henry Mollison, Sonia Holm, Josephine Stuart, Edward Rigby, Frederick Piper, Alec Faversham, Fred Bateman, Douglas Jefferies, Grace Arnold, Barbara Leake, Ronald Simpson, Ethel Coleridge, William Mervyn, Betty Shale, Ernie Flisher, Charles Whiteley, David Turk, Albert Thompson*.

LOVE STORY (1944) [3]
(USA: *A Lady Surrenders*)

Dir *Leslie Arliss*. Prod *Harold Huth*. Scr *Arliss, Doreen Montgomery, Rodney Ackland, from the novel by J. W. Drawbell*. Ph *Bernard Knowles*. PC *Gainsborough*. Dis *Eagle-Lion. 108 mins. Cert U*

Lissa (*Margaret Lockwood*), a composer-pianist with a few months to live, goes to Cornwall and meets Kit (*Stewart Granger*), a mining engineer going blind. He has promised his fiancée Judy (*Patricia Roc*) not to undergo a dangerous operation with a small chance of success. He and Lissa fall in love; she tells Judy she will go away if Kit has the operation. It succeeds. Judy releases him from their engagement the night Lissa plays her *Cornish Rhapsody* at the Albert Hall. Sounds ridiculous and it was, but pure gold at the box office.

RoC *Tom Walls, Reginald Purdell, Moira Lister, Dorothy Bramhall, Vincent Holman, Joan Rees, Walter Hudd, A. E. Matthews, Beatrice Varley, Harriet Cohen, Bryan Herbert, Josephine Middleton, Lawrence Hanray, Sydney Beer*.

LOYAL HEART (1946) [3]

Dir *Oswald Mitchell*. Prod *Louis H. Jackson*. Scr *George A. Cooper, from a novel by Ernest Lewis*. Ph *Arthur Grant, Gerald Gibbs*. PC *British National/Strand*. Dis *Anglo-American. 80 mins. Cert U*

The story of a farmer and his sheepdog, which another farmer tries to buy, but is refused. The two men quarrel, and the dog's owner finds himself unjustly charged with sheep-stealing, so that the other may get his hands on the dog. But the intervention of the farmer's son and the local squire brings about an amicable end to the feud. Quite a nice little picture, in spite of the reservations of one critic who thought the dog 'far and away the best actor in the film'.

LP *Percy Marmont, Harry Welchman, Patricia Marmont, Philip Kay, Eleanor Hallam, Beckett Bould, Valentine Dunn, Cameron Hall, Alexander Field, James Knight, Sydney Bromley, Mac Harry Picton, Gerald Pring, Joseph Ralph, Harry Herbert, John England, Arthur E. Owen, Charles Doe, Carl Lacey, Dorothy Dark, Fleet (dog)*.

LUCKY MASCOT (1948) [2]

Dir *Thornton Freeland*. Prod *Nat A. Bronsten, David Coplan*. Scr *Alec Coppel, Freeland, C. Dennis Freeman*. Ph *Bert Mason*. PC *Diadem/Alliance*. Dis *United Artists. 84 mins. Cert A*

Radio personality *Carroll Levis* becomes involved with a Buddhist connoisseur who will stop at nothing to get his hands on a rare brass monkey. Levis and his 'discoveries' (new talent) put a stop to the villain's nefarious plans. Rough-and-tumble comedy-thriller, also called *Brass Monkey*.

RoC *Carole Landis, Herbert Lom, Avril Angers, Terry-Thomas, Ernest Thesiger, Henry Edwards, Edward Underdown, Carole Lester (Lesley), Albert and Les Ward, Leslie 'Hutch' Hutchinson*.

M

MADELEINE (1949) [3]

Dir *David Lean*. Prod *Stanley Haynes*, Scr *Haynes, Nicholas Phipps*. Ph *Guy Green*. PC *Cineguild*. Dis *General Film Distributors. 114 mins. Cert A*

1857. Madeleine (*Ann Todd*), daughter of a prosperous Glasgow merchant, falls for French adventurer Emile (*Ivan Desny*). Soon after Emile threatens to show her letters to her family unless she introduces him to them, he is found dead from poison. Madeleine is arrested and tried for murder, but her counsel (*André Morell*) puts up a brilliant defence and the verdict is Not Proven. As Madeleine drives away in a cab, she permits herself a small smile. Cold, clinical account of real-life case. Not too good by anyone's standards, let alone this director's.

RoC *Norman Wooland, Leslie Banks, Edward Chapman, Barbara Everest, Barry Jones, Elizabeth Sellars, Jean Cadell, Ivor Barnard, Patricia Raine, Eugene Deckers, Amy Veness, John Laurie, Irene Browne, Henry Edwards, Susan Stranks, David Horne, Kynaston Reeves, Cameron Hall, Douglas Barr, Alfred Rodriguez, Moyra Fraser, James McKechnie (narrator)*.

MADNESS OF THE HEART (1949) [3]

Dir and Scr *Charles Bennett, from a novel by Flora Sandstrom*. Prod *Richard Wainwright*. Ph *Desmond Dickinson*. PC *Two Cities*. Dis *General Film Distributors. 105 mins. Cert A*

Lydia (*Margaret Lockwood*) loves Paul (*Paul Dupuis*) but, going blind, enters a convent. It does not work out, and she leaves and marries Paul. His family do not consider her a fit wife and jealous Verité (*Kathleen Byron*) tries to kill her. Lydia goes back to England, where an operation cures her; Verité kills herself in a car smash. Unrestrained melodrama quite enjoyable.

RoC *Maxwell Reed, Thora Hird, Raymond Lovell, Maurice Denham, David Hutcheson, Cathleen Nesbitt, Peter Illing, Jack McNaughton, Pamela Stirling, Marie Ault, Marie Burke, Kynaston Reeves, Joy Harrington, Sheila Raynor, Marcel Poncin, Stafford Byrne, Pat(ricia) Cutts, Betty Blake, Cynthia Teale, Muriel Russell, Sam Lysons, Paul Anthony, George de Warfaz, Gordon Littman, Gillian Maude, Ann Heffernan, Arthur Reynolds, Fletcher Lightfoot, H.G. Stoker, Frank Ling, Peter Dunlop, Sam Kydd, Lionel Grose.*

MADONNA OF THE SEVEN MOONS (1944) [2]

Dir *Arthur Crabtree.* Prod *R.J. Minney.* Scr *Roland Pertwee, Brock Williams, from the novel by Margery Lawrence.* Ph *Jack Cox.* PC *Gainsborough.* Dis *Eagle-Lion.* 110 mins. Cert A

Maddalena (*Phyllis Calvert*), wife of an Italian wine merchant (*John Stuart*), has a split personality which causes her to periodically flee to the 'Seven Moons' in Florence as mistress of Nino (*Stewart Granger*), a notorious jewel thief. Her daughter (*Patricia Roc*), trying to find her, is trapped by Nino's brother, Sandro (*Peter Glenville*). Finding them together, Maddalena mistakes Sandro for Nino and stabs him. But he gets her, too, before he dies. Lurid melodrama unconvincingly enacted by upper-class accents.

RoC *Jean Kent, Nancy Price, Peter Murray Hill, Dulcie Gray, Reginald Tate, Amy Veness, Hilda Bayley, Alan Haines, Evelyn Darvell, Danny Green, Eliot Makeham.*

THE MAGIC BOW (1946) [2]

Dir *Bernard Knowles.* Prod *R.J. Minney.* Scr *Roland Pertwee, Norman Ginsbury, from the novel by Manuel Komroff.* Ph *Knowles.* PC *Gainsborough.* Dis *General Film Distributors.* 106 mins. Cert U

Paganini (*Stewart Granger*), a poor-born violinist, is tricked into helping the father of aristocratic Jeanne (*Phyllis Calvert*) to break jail. The money he is paid enables him to buy a Stradivarius, but a subsequent gambling spree sends it to the pawnshop. Wounded in a duel over Jeanne, Paganini loses interest in the violin she redeems - until she arranges for him to play for the Pope. Soppy biography for the very credulous. The film that drew C.A. Lejeune's famous one word review: 'Fiddlesticks'.

RoC *Dennis Price, Jean Kent, Cecil Parker, Felix Aylmer, Frank Cellier, Marie Lohr, Henry Edwards, Mary Jerrold, Betty Warren, Antony Holles, David Horne, Charles Victor, Eliot Makeham, Stewart Rome, Robert Speaight, O.B. Clarence, Yehudi Menuhin (violinist).*

MAJOR BARBARA (1941) [4]

Dir *Gabriel Pascal* and (*uncredited*) *Harold French, David Lean.* Prod *Pascal.* Scr *Anatole*

Rex Harrison and Wendy Hiller in publicity shot for Major Barbara (*1941*)

de Grunwald, George Bernard Shaw, from the play by Shaw. Ph *Ronald Neame.* PC *Pascal.* Dis *General Film Distributors.* 121 mins. Cert A

Adolphus Cusins (*Rex Harrison*), a young professor, joins the Salvation Army to be near its Major Barbara Undershaft (*Wendy Hiller*). They are soon engaged. Barbara's father (*Robert Morley*) offers to visit her SA shelter in Limehouse if she will see his armaments factory. When he comes, he gives the SA general £50,000, and Barbara resigns. Adolphus agrees to be Undershaft's successor at the factory, and Barbara, too, changes her mind, seeing it as a new opportunity, in its own way, of saving souls. Good entertainment, though nowhere near the popular and critical success of *Pygmalion. Robert Newton* shot to stardom as a slum ne'er do-well.

RoC *Emlyn Williams, Sybil Thorndike, Deborah Kerr, David Tree, Penelope Dudley-Ward, Marie Lohr, Walter Hudd, Marie Ault, Donald Calthrop, Felix Aylmer, Cathleen Cordell, Stanley Holloway, Torin Thatcher, S.I. Hsiung, Kathleen Harrison, Mary Morris, Ronald Squire, O.B. Clarence, Miles Malleson, Edward Rigby, Bombardier Billy Wells.*

A MAN ABOUT THE HOUSE (1947) [4]

Dir *Leslie Arliss.* Prod *Edward Black.* Scr *Arliss, J.B. Williams, from the novel by Francis Brett Young and the play by John Perry.* Ph *Toni Day.* PC and Dis *British Lion.* 99 mins. Cert A

1907. The Misses Isit (*Margaret Johnston, Dulcie Gray*) unexpectedly inherit a large villa in Naples. Salvatore (*Kieron Moore*), the handyman there, longs to own the villa and marries Agnes (*Johnston*) to do so, importing his family, planting vineyards and slowly poisoning his wife. Ellen's doctor friend gets on to his game; Salvatore throws himself from a cliff. Agnes, who never knew the truth, devotes herself to continuing her husband's work on the land. Unusual theme is nicely developed.

RoC *Guy Middleton, Felix Aylmer, José Salinas, Lilian Braithwaite, Maria Fimiani, Reginald Purdell, Fulvia de Priamo, Nicola Esposito, Wilfred Caithness, Victor Rietti, Andrea Malandrinos.*

THE MAN AT THE GATE (1940) [2]

Dir *Norman Walker.* Prod *James B. Sloan.* Scr

Manning Haynes, Lydia Hayward, Harold Simpson, from a poem by Louise Haskin. Ph *Eric Cross.* PC *GHW Productions.* Dis *General Film Distributors.* 48 mins. Cert U

Mrs Foley (*Mary Jerrold*) wife of a Cornish fisherman, has lost two sons to the sea. She persuades her husband to retire after his ship is wrecked and not to join the lifeboat crew. But he does join it when war comes and her last son, George, joins the navy. Embittered and alone, Mrs Foley hears that George's ship has been sunk. Later, he is reported rescued and safe. Rather theatrical sentiment.

RoC *Wilfrid Lawson, William Freshman, Kathleen O'Regan.*

THE MAN FROM MOROCCO (1945) [3]

Dir *Max Greene (Mutz Greenbaum).* Prod *Warwick Ward.* Scr *Ward, Edward Dryhurst, Margaret Steen.* Ph *Basil Emmott.* PC *Associated British.* Dis *Pathé.* 115 mins. Cert A

Karel (*Anton Walbrook*), Czech leader of the remains of the International Brigade fighting in Spain in 1939, escapes to Morocco, and is given a list of Allied sympathizers in North Africa to get to England. His Spanish sweetheart, Maria (*Margaretta Scott*), has to marry his old enemy, Ricardi (*Reginald Tate*), now in the pay of the Nazis, so that the list may reach its destination. But all comes out well in the end. Meandering adventure picks up pace in later stages.

RoC *Mary Morris, Reginald Tate, Peter Sinclair, David Horne, Hartley Power, Sybilla Binder, Charles Victor, Dennis Arundell, Orlando Martins, Josef Almas, John McLaren, Paul Demel, David Baxter, Paul Bonifas, Margaret Emden, Jan van Loewen, Paul Sheridan, Gwen Bateman, Henry Morrell, Stuart Lindsell, André Randall, Carl Jaffe, Roger Snowden, Robert Arden, Harold Berens, Glyn Rowland, Marie Ault.*

THE MAN FROM YESTERDAY (1949) [2]

Dir *Oswald Mitchell.* Prod *Harry Reynolds.* Scr *John Gilling.* Ph *Cyril Bristow.* PC *International Motion Pictures.* Dis *Renown.* 68 mins. Cert A

Mysterious Julius Rickman (*Henry Oscar*) from India descends on the Amersley home. Doris Amersley (*Marie Burke*), impressed by his 'spiritual powers', asks him to put her in touch with her dead fiancé Cedric. Later she is found dead; Rickman accuses Gerald Amersley (*John Stuart*) of killing both Cedric and Doris. Infuriated, Gerald pushes Julius out of a window. The story turns out to be a dream; but then the Amersleys hear that Rickman has died - on his way to them from India. Good idea; but development barely satisfactory.

RoC *Gwyneth Vaughan, Laurence Harvey, Grace Arnold, Cherry Davis.*

THE MAN IN BLACK (1949) [2]

Dir *Francis Searle.* Prod *Anthony Hinds.* Scr *John Gilling, Searle, from a radio series by John Dickson Carr.* Ph *Cedric Williams.* PC *Hammer.* Dis *Exclusive.* 75 mins. Cert A

By using yoga, a rich man (*Sidney James*) pretends to be dead, in order to expose the villainy of his second wife, Bertha (*Betty Ann*

Davies), who is trying to drive his heiress daughter out of her mind. Ridiculous chiller at least moves along at a fair rate.

RoC *Valentine Dyall, Anthony Forwood, Sheila Burrell, Hazel Penwarden, Courtenay Hope, Lawrence Baskcomb, Molly Palmer, Gerald Case.*

THE MAN IN GREY (1943)   4

Dir *Leslie Arliss.* Prod *Edward Black.* Scr *Margaret Kennedy, Arliss, Doreen Montgomery, from the novel by Lady Eleanor Smith.* Ph *Arthur Crabtree.* PC *Gainsborough.* Dis *General Film Distributors. 116 mins. Cert U*

Miserable in a loveless marriage to the sadistic Lord Rohan (*James Mason*), Clarissa (*Phyllis Calvert*) engages former schoolfriend Hesther (*Margaret Lockwood*) as governess to her child. Hesther becomes Rohan's mistress, and schemes to become his wife by encouraging Clarissa's friendship with Rokeby (*Stewart Granger*), an actor. The Prince Regent (*Raymond Lovell*) persuades Clarissa not to leave Rohan; Hesther, furious, allows her to die from a severe cold. Rohan thrashes her to death. Crowd-pulling Regency melodrama (in modern framework) started Gainsborough 'wicked ladies' series, made Mason and Lockwood big stars.

RoC *Nora Swinburne, Helen Haye, Martita Hunt, Amy Veness, Diana King, Beatrice Varley, Roy Emerton, A.E. Matthews, Ann Wilton, Drusilla Wills, Jane Gill-Davis, Stuart Lindsell, Celia Lamb, Lupe Maguire, Harry Scott, Gertrude Maesmore, Hargrave Pawson, James Carson, Babs Valerie, Wally Kingston, Glyn Rowland, Patric Curwen, Lola Hunt, Mary Naylor, Kathleen Boutall, Ruth Woodman.*

MAN ON THE RUN (1948)   3

Dir, Prod and Scr *Lawrence Huntington.* Ph *Wilkie Cooper.* PC and Dis *Associated British-Pathé. 82 mins. Cert A*

Peter Burdon (*Derek Farr*), an army deserter, tries to sell his revolver, becomes indirectly involved in a robbery and has to try to find the thieves while on the run from both the police and the army. Though he catches up with them, they take him prisoner. Jean (*Joan Hopkins*), a girl who had helped him before being arrested, leads police to the gang's hideout, where Peter's vital participation in rounding the crooks up clears his name. He goes back to face the army. Pacy thrills and spills if not much credibility.

RoC *Edward Chapman, Lawrence Harvey, John Stuart, Edward Underdown, Leslie Perrins, Kenneth More, John Bailey, Eleanor Summerfield, Martin Miller, Anthony Nicholls, Alfie Bass, Howard Marion Crawford, Cameron Hall, Valentine Dyall, Howard Douglas, Laurence Ray, Bruce Belfrage, Robert Adair, Charles Paton, Basil Cunard, Jack McNaughton, Margaret Goodman, Virginia Winter, Lalage Lewis, Patrick Barr, Gerald Case, John Boxer, Roy Russell, R. Stuart Lindsell.*

A MAN'S AFFAIR (1948)   1

Dir and Prod *Jay Gardner Lewis.* Scr *Lewis, Harold Stewart.* Ph *Douglas Ransome, Norman*

Johnson. PC *Concord.* Dis *Exclusive. 62 mins. Cert U*

Two miners (*Hamish Menzies, Cliff Gordon*) pick up two girls (*Diana Decker, Joan Dowling*), on holiday at the seaside. A playboy friend, however, trails dissatisfaction in his wake, and both couples quarrel and part. It takes the precocious younger sister of one of the miners to get them together again. Never-Never-Land comedy.

RoC *Wallas Eaton, Bruce Walker, Joyce Linden.*

THE MAN WITHIN (1947)   3
(USA: *The Smugglers*)

Dir *Bernard Knowles.* Prod and Scr *Muriel and Sydney Box.* Ph *Geoffrey Unsworth.* PC *Production Film Service.* Dis *General Film Distributors. Technicolor. 90 mins. Cert A*

1820. When his father dies, young Francis (*Richard Attenborough*) reluctantly embarks on a seagoing life under his smuggling guardian Carlyon (*Michael Redgrave*). Falsely accused of theft, Francis is flogged, subsequently betraying Carlyon to the authorities and running away in the ensuing fight. Later Francis redeems himself, refusing to condemn Carlyon despite torture, and his guardian gives up his own life so that he might go free. Artificial adventure almost redeemed by Attenborough's performance.

RoC *Joan Greenwood, Jean Kent, Francis L. Sullivan, Felix Aylmer, Ronald Shiner, Ernest Thesiger, Basil Sydney, David Horne, Ralph Truman, Allan Jeayes, George Merritt, Maurice Denham, Charles Rolfe, Lyn Evans, Herbert Lomas, Danny Green, Torin Thatcher, Andrew Crawford, John Olson, Allan McClelland.*

THE MAN WITH THE MAGNETIC EYES (1945)   2

Dir, Prod and Scr *Ronald Haines, from the novel by Roland Daniel.* Ph *Stanley Fletcher.* PC and Dis *British Foundation. 52 mins. Cert A*

Wilbur (*Peter Lilley*) is jailed for stealing plans of a secret weapon. Believing there is a mastermind behind him, Inspector Wade (*Robert Bradfield*), in love with Wilbur's sister (*Joan Carter*), who is kidnapped, initially suspects Van Deerman (*Henry Norman*), a mysterious foreigner, but finally shoots the villain, a bogus count (*André Belhomme*) who hypnotizes his dupes and victims. Unconvincing harbinger of post-war 'B' features to come.

RoC *Charles Penrose, Mabel Twemlow.*

THE MARK OF CAIN (1947)   2

Dir *Brian Desmond Hurst.* Prod *W.P. Lipscomb.* Scr *Lipscomb, Francis Crowdy, Christianna Brand, from a novel by Joseph Shearing.* Ph *Erwin Hillier.* PC *Two Cities.* Dis *General Film Distributors. 88 mins. Cert A*

Sarah (*Sally Gray*), raised in France, marries John (*Patrick Holt*), a Northern businessman, but is little more than his housekeeper. When his brother Richard (*Eric Portman*) tells her she should bring 'French ways' to the home, he and John have a stand-up row. John falls ill, Richard kills him with an overdose, and Sarah is accused. Richard's plan to save her

fails, and he himself is found out by another of her admirers. Fashionable gloom and doom.

RoC *Dermot Walsh, Denis O'Dea, Edward Lexy, Helen Cherry, Therese Giehse, Maureen Delany, Vida Hope, James Hayter, Andrew Cruickshank, Miles Malleson, Dora Sevening, Janet Kay, Helen Goss, Beryl Measor, Marjorie Gresley, May MacDonald, Susan English, John Warren, Noel Howlett, Arthur Howard, Hope Matthews, Olwen Brookes, Rose Howlett, Johnnie Schofield, Sydney Bromley, Fred Johnson, Albert Ferber, John Hollingsworth, Willoughby Gray, James Carson, Michael Logan, Norah Gordon, Christiana Forbes, Sheila Raynor, Wensley Pithey, Mary Daniels, Jean Bowler, Colleen Nolan, Jean Anderson.*

MARRY ME! (1949)   2

Dir *Terence Fisher.* Prod *Betty Box.* Scr *Lewis Gilbert, Denis Waldock.* Ph *Ray Elton.* PC *Gainsborough.* Dis *General Film Distributors. 97 mins. Cert A*

Couples meet through a marriage bureau. A reporter and a waitress, both romantic liars, are ideally suited. A manservant decides a teacher is not for him, but his employer falls for her. A dance hostess falls for a parson, but feels he's too good for her. A French girl seeking British nationality to escape her cruel husband is traced by him; in a struggle with her British friend, he falls to his death. Cast defeated by their material.

LP *Susan Shaw, Derek Bond, Carol Marsh, Patrick Holt, Zena Marshall, Guy Middleton, David Tomlinson, Nora Swinburne, Brenda Bruce, Jean Cadell, Denis O'Dea, Mary Jerrold, Yvonne Owen, Beatrice Varley, Anthony Steel, Alison Leggatt, Anthony Neville, George Merritt, Sandra Dorne, Judith Furse, Tamara Lees, Esma Cannon, Mary (Marianne) Stone, Everley Gregg, J.H. Roberts, Lyn Evans, Hal Osmond, Cyril Chamberlain, John Warren, Ann Valery, John Boxer, Herbert C. Walton, Dan Yarranton, Jill Allen.*

Anthony Steel and David Tomlinson in Marry Me! *(1949)*

MASTER OF BANKDAM (1947)   4

Dir *Walter Forde.* Prod *Nat Bronsten, Forde, Edward Dryhurst.* Scr *Dryhurst, Moie Charles, from a novel by Thomas Armstrong.* Ph *Basil Emmott.* PC *Holbein.* Dis *General Film Distributors. 105 mins. Cert A*

1854. Simeon Crowther (*Tom Walls*) makes his fortune with the smallest mill in Yorkshire's

Bankdam. Of his sons, Zebediah (*Stephen Murray*) weds Clara (*Linden Travers*), a schemer; Joshua (*Dennis Price*) marries Annie (*Anne Crawford*), a weaver. Zeb installs heavy looms too high in the old mill; it collapses and Josh is killed. His son Simeon (*Jimmy Hanley*) becomes master of Bankdam after Zeb's pampered son Lancelot (*David Tomlinson*) has bungled the business. Family saga is a bit ponderous at times, but grippingly effective in the end.

RoC *Nancy Price, Patrick Holt, Herbert Lomas, Frederick Piper, Beatrice Varley, Raymond Rollett, April Stride, Avis Scott, Amy Veness, Nicholas Parsons, Maria Var, Kenneth Buckley, Lyn Evans, Bertram Shuttleworth, Edgar K. Bruce, Frank Henderson, Aubrey Mallalieu, Shelagh Fraser.*

A MATTER OF LIFE AND DEATH
(1946)
(USA: *Stairway to Heaven*) [5]
Dir, Prod and Scr *Michael Powell, Emeric Pressburger*. Ph *Jack Cardiff*. PC *The Archers/ Independent Producers*. Dis *General Film Distributors*. Technicolor with black-and-white sequences. 104 mins. Cert A

Pilot Peter Carter (*David Niven*) bales out of a blazing plane and is washed ashore apparently unharmed. He falls for the American WAC (*Kim Hunter*) he was talking to before the crash, but starts having hallucinations in which he sees people from 'another world'. During a brain operation, a battle for his life goes on in his mind between 'Heaven' and earth – which his new love helps him to win just as the operation is successfully completed. Beautiful, bizarre, highly imaginative fantasy. Not surprisingly, critical reception was mixed. The first Royal Performance film.

RoC *Roger Livesey, Raymond Massey, Marius Goring, Robert Coote, Kathleen Byron, Richard Attenborough, Bonar Colleano, Joan Maude, Robert Atkins, Abraham Sofaer, Edwin Max, Betty Potter, Bob Roberts.*

Roger Livesey and David Niven in A Matter of Life and Death *(1946)*

A MATTER OF MURDER (1949) [2]
Dir and Scr *John Gilling*. Prod *Roger Proudlock, Sam Lee*. Ph *S.D. Onions*. PC *Vandyke*. Dis *Grand National*. 59 mins. Cert A

A man embezzles funds to keep his greedy girlfriend in luxuries. She is found murdered and he is the fall guy. He flees to Cheltenham, where he hides away in a boarding-house run by a detective and his daughter. The latter befriends him, but he is ultimately shot by his girlfriend's killer, who is in turn captured by the detective. Tatty programme-filler.

RoC *John Barry, Maureen Riscoe, Ivan Craig, Charles Clapham, Ian Fleming, John le Mesurier, Sonya O'Shea, Peter Madden, Blanche Fothergill.*

MAYTIME IN MAYFAIR (1949) [3]
Dir and Prod *Herbert Wilcox*. Scr *Nicholas Phipps*. Ph *Max Greene (Mutz Greenbaum)*. PC *Imperadio*. Dis *British Lion*. Technicolor. 96 mins. Cert U

Man-about-town Michael Gore-Brown (*Michael Wilding*) inherits a dress shop run by Eileen (*Anna Neagle*). A rival firm, headed by D'Arcy Davenport (*Peter Graves*) is trying to put them out of business. Michael's cousin leaks new fashion designs; this torpedoes Michael's budding romance with Eileen who, believing he did it, storms off to France. Learning the truth, she returns just in time to stop him selling the business. Inconsequential escapism.

RoC *Tom Walls, Nicholas Phipps, Thora Hird, Michael Shepley, Max Kirby, Desmond Walter-Ellis, Tom Walls Jr, Teddy Lane, David Ellis, David Gardiner, Pat Clare, Sabina Gordon, Cynthia Williams, Eugenie Sivyer, Paddy Johnston, Pam Kail, Monica Francis, Pat Dare, Josephine Ingram.*

MEDAL FOR THE GENERAL (1944) [3]
Dir *Maurice Elvey*. Prod *Louis H. Jackson*. Scr *Elizabeth Baron, from the novel by James Ronald*. Ph *James Wilson*. PC *British National*. Dis *Anglo-American*. 99 mins. Cert U

Old General Church (*Godfrey Tearle*), finding no wartime work, contemplates suicide. But he finds new interests in life when slum children are evacuated to his home. He takes special interest in a cripple boy, and helps him get cured. He wins his medal for helping to rescue the pilot of a crashed plane. Sincere and well-acted with moving moments; rather slow.

RoC *Jeanne de Casalis, Morland Graham, Mabel Constanduros, John Laurie, Maureen Glynne, Gerald Moore, Brian Weske, Petula Clark, Patric Curwen, Thorley Walters, H.F. Maltby, Alec Faversham, Michael Lambart, Janette Scott, Irene Handl, Rosalyn Boulter, Gerald Moore, David Trickett, Pat Geary.*

MEET ME AT DAWN (1946) [2]
Dir *Thornton Freeland*. Prod *Marcel Hellman*. Scr *James Seymour, Lesley Storm, Maurice Cowan*. Ph *Günther Krampf*. PC *Excelsior*. Dis *20th Century-Fox*. 99 mins. Cert A

1900: Charles, a professional duellist (*William Eythe*) is hired to insult a French senator and put him out of action. He uses an attractive girl (*Hazel Court*) as pretext for the challenge. She is given wide coverage by newspaperman Vernorel (*Basil Sydney*) who does not realize the mystery girl is his daughter. The result is another duel, but Charles allows Vernorel to slightly wound him. Poorly cast comedy.

RoC *Stanley Holloway, Margaret Rutherford, Irene Browne, George Thorpe, Ada Reeve, Graham Muir, Beatrice Campbell, John Salew, Charles Victor, Hy Hazell, Wilfrid Hyde White, James Harcourt, Diana Decker, Lind Joyce, Percy Walsh, John Ruddock, Joan Seton, Katie Johnson, O.B. Clarence, Aubrey Mallalieu, Guy Rolfe, Charles Hawtrey.*

MEET SEXTON BLAKE (1944) [2]
Dir and Scr *John Harlow, from characters by Harry Blyth*. Prod *Louis H. Jackson*. Ph *Geoffrey Faithfull*. PC *British National/Strand*. Dis *Anglo-American*. 80 mins. Cert A

Detective Sexton Blake (*David Farrar*) and his assistant Tinker (*John Varley*) are asked to recover photographs and a ring stolen from a man killed in an air-raid. They discover the pictures contain the formula for a vital metal, of which the ring is made, for aeroplane construction. They defeat the villain in the hunt: he proves to be their employer's stepbrother. Blood, thunder and unintentional laughs.

RoC *Magda Kun, Gordon McLeod, Manning Whiley, Kathleen Harrison, Dennis Arundell, Cyril Smith, Ferdi Mayne, Betty Huntley-Wright, Roddy Hughes, Charles Farrell, Jean Simmons, Tony Arpino, Charles Rolfe, Philip Godfrey, Billy Howard, John Powe, Mark Jones, Jack Vyvyan, Henry Wolston, David Keir, Elsie Wagstaffe, Brookes Turner, Alfred Harris, Margo Johns, Olive Walter.*

MEET SIMON CHERRY (1949) [3]
Dir *Godfrey Grayson*. Prod *Anthony Hinds*. Scr *Gale Pendrick, Grayson, A.R. Rawlinson, from a radio series by Pedrick*. Ph *Cedric Williams*. PC *Hammer*. Dis *Exclusive*. 67 mins. Cert A

There are strange goings-on at Harling Manor, where the invalid daughter (*Jeanette Tregarthen*) of Lady Harling (*Courtenay Hope*) is found dead, providing a case for sleuthing parson Simon Cherry (*Hugh Moxey*), who clears a young lady suspected of murder by proving the dead girl had a heart attack. Serviceable, no-frills version of popular radio serial *Meet the Rev.*

RoC *Zena Marshall, John Bailey, Anthony Forwood, Ernest Butcher, Arthur Lovegrove, Gerald Case.*

MEET THE DUKE (1948) [2]
Dir *James Corbett*. Prod *Link Neale*. Scr *Farnham Baxter, from a play by Temple Saxe*. Ph *Ernest Palmer*. PC *New Park*. Dis *Associated British*. 64 mins. Cert U

An American ex-boxer inherits an English dukedom, complete with family mansion where treasure is rumoured to be hidden. A Dutch gang is after the treasure; its members pose as servants to the new duke, but the American finds the hidden riches and donates them to houses for the aged and playing fields for children, himself returning to America. Ham-fisted comedy thriller.

LP *Farnham Baxter, Heather Chasen, Gale Douglas.*

MEET THE NAVY (1946) [3]
Dir *Alfred Travers*. Prod *Louis H. Jackson*. Scr *Lester Cooper, James Seymour*. Ph *Ernest Palmer*. PC *British National*. Dis *Anglo-American*. Technicolor sequence. 82 mins. Cert U

In a Royal Canadian Navy shore camp, a show is produced which tours Canada and then Europe. Despite personal problems for various members of the cast, the show is booked for a season in London, and plays before the Royal Family. Film version of successful forces' stage show is rather hampered by confused narrative. Some of the turns are good though.
LP *Lionel Murton, Margaret Hurst, John Pratt, Bob Goodier, Bill Oliver, Phyllis Hudson, Oscar Natzke, Percy Haynes, Jeanette de Huek, Alan Lund, Mae Richards.*

MEIN KAMPF – MY CRIMES (1940) [4]
Dir *Norman Lee.* Prod *Walter C. Mycroft.* Scr *Alec Dyer.* Ph *Walter James Harvey.* PC and Dis *Associated British.* 75 mins. Cert A
A reworking of a French film, *Après Mein Kampf – Mes Crimes*, being a semi-documentary reconstruction of Hitler's rise to power, ridiculing him as well as detailing his atrocities. A dramatized sequence shows how a son betrays his father to the Gestapo for criticizing Hitler. Not surprisingly, this was well received in Britain at the time.
LP *Herbert Lom, Robert Beatty, Peter Ustinov.*

MELODY CLUB (1949) [1]
Dir *Monty Berman.* Prod *Robert S. Baker, Berman.* Scr *Carl Nystrom.* Ph *Peter Newbrook.* PC *Tempean.* Dis *Eros.* 65 mins. Cert A
Freddy Forrester (*Terry-Thomas*), a nitwit detective, is on the trail of a gang of jewel thieves. He traces them to a nightclub and ultimately, more by luck than judgment, rounds them up. Collection of well-worn jokes stitched together to make a plot.
RoC *Gwyneth Vaughan, Len Lowe, Bill Lowe, Michael Balfour, Lilian Grey, Arthur Gomez, Anthony Shaw, Sylvia Clark, Jack Mayne, Ida Patlanski.*

MELODY IN THE DARK (1948) [2]
Dir and Prod *Robert Jordan Hill.* Scr *John Guillermin.* Ph *Jo Jago.* PC *Advent.* Dis *Adelphi.* 68 mins. Cert A
A company of entertainers, out of work, 'rest' in a mansion inherited by their leading lady. They put on a show for the locals, but are beset by 'ghosts' at the mansion. They find the heroine's 'dead' uncle locked away, by his housekeeper and her husband who thought that they would inherit his fortune. *Ben Wrigley* does raise some laughs in below-average comedy-musical.
RoC *Eunice Gayson, Richard Thorp, Dawn Lesley, Myrette Morven, Russell Westwood, Lionel Newbold, Ida Patlanski, Neville Sidney, Alan Dean, Carl Carlisle, Maisie Weldon, The Keynotes, The Stardusters, The London Lovelies.*

MEN OF TWO WORLDS (1946) [3]
(USA: *Kisenga*)
Dir *Thorold Dickinson.* Prod *John Sutro.* Scr *Dickinson, Herbert W. Victor.* Ph *Desmond Dickinson (no relation to director).* PC *Two Cities.* Dis *General Film Distributors.* Technicolor. 109 mins. Cert A
After 15 years in Europe, making his way as a composer, Kisenga (*Robert Adams*) returns to help the District Commissioner (*Eric Port-*

man) in his native Africa. He finds his tribe in the grip of the witch doctor Magole (*Orlando Martins*). Seeing the threat, Magole says Kisenga will die with the full moon. Only with the help of his friends does Kisenga break the hold heredity has on him, and with it Magole's power. Sincerely told; could do with a bit more guts.
RoC *Phyllis Calvert, Arnold Marle, Cathleen Nesbitt, David Horne, Cyril Raymond, Sam Blake, Uriel Porter, George Cooper, Cicely Dale, Brenda Davies.*

MERRY-GO-ROUND (1948) [1]
Dir *Josh Binney.* Prod *Margaret Cordin.* Scr *Uncredited.* Ph *Jo Jago.* PC and Dis *Federated.* 53 mins. Cert U
A film producer hunts for new ideas for his upcoming comedy-musical film. Melange of unfunny comedy and badly recorded music is a complete waste of time.
LP *Bonar Colleano, Beryl Davis, Leon Sherkot.*

MILLIONS LIKE US (1943) [4]
Dir and Scr *Frank Launder, Sidney Gilliat.* Prod *Edward Black.* Ph *Jack Cox, Roy Fogwell.* PC *Gainsborough.* Dis *General Film Distributors.* 103 mins. Cert U
The Crowson family is split up by the war. The married daughter gets her old job back, another joins the ATS, and Celia (*Patricia Roc*), the youngest, is drafted into a plane factory. Working with her is a socialite (*Anne Crawford*), who at first falls out with the foreman (*Eric Portman*) but later falls *for* him. Celia meets a young air gunner (*Gordon Jackson*) and marries him, but he is killed in action. Quite realistic and unsentimental war drama of emotional appeal.
RoC *Joy Shelton, Basil Radford, Naunton Wayne, Valentine Dunn, Megs Jenkins, Terry Randall, Moore Marriott, John Boxer, John Salew, Irene Handl, Amy Veness, Hilda Davies, Angela Foulds, Terence Rhodes, Paul Drake, John Wynn, Albert Chevalier, Frank Webster, Beatrice Varley, Courtney Luck, Amy Dalby, Johnnie Schofield, Jack Vyvyan, Arthur Denton, Jonathan Field, Avis Scott, Clifford Cobbe, Grace Allardyce, Barry Steele, Gordon Edwards, Brenda Bruce, Stanley Paskin, Bertha Willmott, John Slater, Hugh Cross, Alan Haines, George Hirste.*

MINE OWN EXECUTIONER (1947) [5]
Dir *Anthony Kimmins.* Prod *Kimmins.* Jack Kitchin. Scr *Nigel Balchin, from his novel.* Ph *Wilkie Cooper.* PC *London Films/Harefield.* Dis *British Lion.* 108 mins. Cert A
Lay psychiatrist Felix Milne (*Burgess Meredith*) treats Adam (*Kieron Moore*), a schizophrenic ex-RAF officer who has already tried to kill his wife. At odds with his own wife (*Dulcie Gray*), Felix has an affair with his friend (*Christine Norden*), neglecting Adam, who murders his wife, escaping to a high roof. Felix goes up on a ladder and tries to reason with him, but Adam jumps. Felix is severely censured at the inquest. Nail-biting thriller, stylishly made; tension on high virtually throughout.
RoC *Barbara White, John Laurie, Michael*

Shepley, Lawrence Hanray, Walter Fitzgerald, Martin Miller, Jack Raine, Helen Haye, John Stuart, Clive Morton, Edgar Norfolk, Joss Ambler, Ronald Simpson, Gwynne Whitby, Malcolm Tremayne, Michael Hordern.

MIRANDA (1948) [4]
Dir *Ken Annakin.* Prod *Betty Box.* Scr *Peter Blackmore, Denis Waldock, from Blackmore's play.* Ph *Ray Elton.* PC *Gainsborough.* Dis *General Film Distributors.* 80 mins. Cert A
On a Cornish holiday, Dr Paul Marten (*Griffith Jones*) is trapped by Miranda (*Glynis Johns*), a mermaid, who threatens to keep him in her cave unless he shows her the sights of London. Arriving as a wheelchaired invalid, Miranda soon has hordes of male admirers. Only her custodian, Nurse Cary (*Margaret Rutherford*) knows the truth. Miranda fulfils all her ambitions before flopping off to the sea again via the Embankment. Engaging, witty fantasy, gave Gainsborough a much-needed box office hit.
RoC *Googie Withers, John McCallum, David Tomlinson, Sonia Holm, Yvonne Owen, Brian Oulton, Maurice Denham, Zena Marshall, Charles Penrose, Lyn Evans, Anthony Drake, Stringer Davis, Hal Osmond, Charles Rolfe, Charles Paton, Frank Webster, Toni McMillan, Thelma Rea, Joan Ingram, Gerald Campion.*

THE MISSING MILLION (1942) [2]
Dir *Phil Brandon.* Prod *Hugh Perceval.* Scr *James Seymour, from the novel by Edgar Wallace.* Ph *Stephen Dade.* PC *Signet.* Dis *Associated British.* 84 mins. Cert A
A young millionaire disappears on the eve of his wedding. His sister (*Linden Travers*) enlists a Scotland Yard detective (*John Stuart*) to trace him. Murders strew their path, being members of a gang who have tried to double-cross their leader, The Panda. The millionaire's fiancée is an unwilling member of the gang and offers to turn them in. The Panda kidnaps her and hunts the million pounds the millionaire had withdrawn. The detective gets there first, and The Panda bites the dust. Thriller lacks speed and slickness.
RoC *John Warwick, Patricia Hilliard, Ivan Brandt, Brefni O'Rorke, Charles Victor, Marie Ault, Jim (James) Donald.*

MISS LONDON LTD (1943) [3]
Dir *Val Guest.* Prod *Edward Black.* Scr *Val Guest, Marriott Edgar.* Ph *Basil Emmott.* PC *Gainsborough.* Dis *General Film Distributors.* 99 mins. Cert U
Terry (*Evelyn Dall*), daughter of the American owner of an escort agency, Miss London Ltd, finds on a visit that business is bad. With the help of manager Arthur Bowman (*Arthur Askey*), she launches a number of schemes which put the business back on its shapely feet again. Good songs (lyrics by director *Val Guest*) and some amusing moments; a bit long.
RoC *Anne Shelton, Richard Hearne, Jack Train, Max Bacon, Peter Graves, Jean Kent, Virginia Keiley, Ronald Shiner, Iris Lang, Una Shepherd, Sheila Bligh, Noni Brooke, Pat(ricia) Owens.*

MISS PILGRIM'S PROGRESS (1949) [3]
Dir and Scr *Val Guest*. Prod *Daniel M. Angel, Nat Cohen*. Ph *Bert Mason*. PC *Angel Productions*. Dis *Grand National*. 82 mins. Cert U
Laramie Pilgrim (*Yolande Donlan*), a factory girl from America, comes to England on an exchange scheme. She finds herself in a picture postcard village, and, hooked on such English traditions as fish and chips, joins in a campaign to preserve the village from town and country planners who want to tear it down. Modest comedy; bright central performance.
RoC *Michael Rennie, Garry Marsh, Emrys Jones, Reginald Beckwith, Valentine Dyall, Jon Pertwee, Helena Pickard, Richard Littledale, Bruce Belfrage, Peter Butterworth, Avril Angers, Barry Faber, Arthur Hill, Ivan Craig, Trevor Hill, Marianne Stone, Mary Vallange, Terry Randall, Frances Marsden, Frederick Bradshaw, Basil Lord, Raymond Waters*.

THE MONKEY'S PAW (1948) [2]
Dir *Norman Lee*. Prod *Ernest G. Roy*. Scr *Lee, Barbara Toy, from the play by W.W. Jacobs*. Ph *Bryan Langley*. PC *Kay Films*. Dis *Butchers*. 64 mins. Cert A
A curio dealer who sells a monkey's paw warns that, although it can grant three wishes, disaster follows. The paw passes to Trelawne (*Milton Rosmer*) who wishes his gambling debts paid. His son is killed in a motorcycle race; the compensation pays the debt. Mrs Trelawne (*Megs Jenkins*) wishes her son restored to life, but Trelawne counters by asking that he rest in peace, thus using the last wish. Old chiller loses most of its sting in this version.
RoC *Joan Seton, Norman Shelley, Michael Martin-Harvey, Eric Micklewood, Brenda Hogan, MacKenzie Ward, Alfie Bass, Hay Petrie, Rose Howlett, Sydney Tafler, Patrick Ward, Vincent Lawson*.

MORNING DEPARTURE (1949) [4]
(USA: *Operation Disaster*)
Dir *Roy Baker*. Prod and PC *Jay Lewis* (administrator: *Leslie Parkyn*). Scr *W.E.C. (William) Fairchild, from the play by Kenneth Woollard*. Ph *Desmond Dickinson*. Dis *General Film Distributors*. 102 mins. Cert A
A submarine hits an electric mine, which explodes, sending the sub to the sea-bed and killing all but 12 of her crew. The captain, Armstrong (*John Mills*) gets eight out through the conning tower and gun hatch – but no more escape sets are left. Stoker Snipe (*Richard Attenborough*) becomes hysterical; Armstrong has to knock him out. After seven days, a salvage ship lifts the sub in a heavy storm. A cable snaps, plunging the sub back to the bottom. Armstrong reads the two remaining men the Naval Prayer. Poignant, sturdily acted, stiff upper-lip drama in the best tradition.
RoC *Helen Cherry, Nigel Patrick, George Cole, Bernard Lee, Lana Morris, James Hayter, Kenneth More, Andrew Crawford, Michael Brennan, Wylie Watson, Jack Stuart, Roddy McMillan, Frank Coburn, Peter Hammond, Victor Maddern, Alastair Hunter, George Thorpe, Zena Marshall, Arthur Sandifer*.

MR EMMANUEL (1944) [4]
Dir *Harold French*. Prod *William Sistrom*. Scr *Gordon Wellesley, Norman Ginsburg, from the novel by Louis Golding*. Ph *Otto Heller*. PC *Two Cities*. Dis *Eagle-Lion*. 97 mins. Cert A
1938: Mr Emmanuel (*Felix Aylmer*), an elderly Jew, goes to Germany to discover the mother of an evacuee boy housed by a friend. He falls into the clutches of the Gestapo and is tortured. Released through the intervention of an old friend, Elsie Silver (*Greta Gynt*), now the mistress of a high Nazi official, he finds the woman he seeks, but she renounces her son in favour of her new Nazi husband. Aylmer makes the most of a rare leading role.
RoC *Walter Rilla, Peter Mullins, Ursula Jeans, Elspeth March, Frederick Richter, Frederick Schiller, Maria Berger, Charles Goldner, Irene Handl, Meier Tzelniker, Arnold Marle, David Baxter, Norman Pierce, Guy Deghy, Neil Ballantyne, Oscar Ebelsbacher, Eric Freund, Milo Sperber, Lyonel Watts, Margaret Vyner, Louis de Wohl, Jean Simmons*.

MR PERRIN AND MR TRAILL (1948) [4]
Dir *Lawrence Huntington*. Prod *Alexander Galperson*. Scr *L.A.G. Strong, T.J. Morrison, from the novel by Hugh Walpole*. Ph *Erwin Hillier*. PC *Two Cities*. Dis *General Film Distributors*. 92 mins. Cert A
David Traill (*David Farrar*), a new master at a Cornish coastal school, has a progressively chilly relationship with another master, Vincent Perrin (*Marius Goring*); matters come to a head when David wins Isobel Lester (*Greta Gynt*), the school nurse, with whom Perrin was in love. Faced with oppression from the head (*Raymond Huntley*), Perrin's control gradually crumbles. Finally, he attacks Traill with a knife. David goes over a cliff and Perrin dies rescuing him. Capable, well-cast version of popular novel.
RoC *Edward Chapman, Mary Jerrold, Finlay Currie, Ralph Truman, Lloyd Pearson, Viola Lyel, Archie Harradine, Donald Barclay, David Spencer, Roddy Hughes, Maurice Jones, May McDonald, Pat Nye, Brendan Clegg, John Campbell, David Lines, Cavan Malone, Brian McDermott, Roy Sargent, Sheila Huntington, Howard Douglas, Johnnie Schofield, John Warren*.

MRS FITZHERBERT (1947) [3]
Dir *Montgomery Tully*. Prod *Louis H. Jackson*. Scr *Tully, from a novel by Winifred Carter*. Ph *James Wilson*. PC *British National*. Dis *Pathé*. 99 mins. Cert A
The 1780s. Catholic widow Maria Fitzherbert's affair with the Prince Regent has caused so much gossip that she leaves him. He attempts suicide, she returns and they marry. But the marriage is publicly denied, and the king is so pleased he pays off the prince's debts. When the prince refuses to declare the marriage, they part. When Lady Jersey (*Margaretta Scott*) convinces the prince (*Peter Graves*) that Maria (*Joyce Howard*) is having an affair, the split is complete. The marriage is declared void, and he remarries Princess Caroline of Brunswick – but many years later dies with

Peter Graves (seated) in Mrs Fitzherbert *(1947)*

Maria's name on his lips. Humdrum history with uncharismatic leads.
RoC *Leslie Banks, Wanda Rotha, Mary Clare, Frederick Valk, John Stuart, Chili Bouchier, Helen Haye, Ralph Truman, Lilly Kann, Lawrence O'Madden, Frederick Leister, Julian Dallas, Barry Morse, Ivor Barnard, Eugene Deckers, Moira Lister*.

MUCH TOO SHY (1942) [3]
Dir *Marcel Varnel*. Prod *Ben Henry*. Scr *Ronald Frankau*. Ph *Arthur Crabtree*. PC *Gainsborough*. Dis *Columbia*. 92 mins. Cert U
George (*George Formby*), a handyman with a talent for portrait painting, is too shy to draw human bodies. On a commercial art course, other students add nude bodies to three heads he's drawn, the painting is used by accident in a soap commercial, and the three village women concerned sue George for damages. He proves their reputations haven't suffered, and is fined a farthing. Bit of a yawn for a Formby farce.
RoC *Kathleen Harrison, Hilda Bayley, Eileen Bennett, Joss Ambler, Jimmy Clitheroe, Frederick Burtwell, Brefni O'Rorke, Eric Clavering, Gibb McLaughlin, Peter Gawthorne, Gus McNaughton, D.J. Williams, Valentine Dyall*.

MURDER AT THE WINDMILL (1949) [3]
(USA: *Murder at the Burlesque*)
Dir and Scr *Val Guest*. Prod, PC and Dis *Daniel Angel, Nat Cohen*. Ph *Bert Mason*, 70 mins. Cert A
At the Windmill theatre, after the curtain has fallen on the last show, a man is found shot dead in the stalls. Police establish the fatal shot was fired from the stage and suspicion falls on the leading man (*Donald Clive*) whose girlfriend (*Jill Anstey*) had been pestered by the dead man. But the culprit turns out to be the old property man (*Eliot Makeham*), who shoots himself. Bright if silly musical-comedy-mystery.
RoC *Garry Marsh, Jack Livesey, Jon Pertwee, Diana Decker, Margo Johns, Genine Graham, Peter Butterworth, Jimmy Edwards, Pamela Deeming, Ivan Craig, John Powe, Mary Valange, Constance Smith, Barry O'Neil, Robin Richmond, Christine Welsford, Johnnie Gale, Ron Perriam, Anita d'Ray, Johnnie McGregor, The Windmill Girls*.

MURDER IN REVERSE (1945) [4]
Dir and Scr *Montgomery Tully, from a novel*

by 'Seamark'. Prod *Louis H. Jackson*. Ph *Ernest Palmer*. PC *British National*. Dis *Anglo-American*. 88 mins. Cert A

Stevedore Tom Masterick (*Billy Hartnell*) chases Smith (*John Slater*), who had seduced his wife (*Chili Bouchier*), up a crane, from which Smith falls into the quay. His body is not found; Masterick is convicted of murder. On his release 15 years later, and with the help of Sullivan, a reporter (*Brefni O'Rorke*) who had helped him and fostered his daughter, Masterick finds Smith alive, and shoots him dead. Harsh, well-directed thriller.

RoC *Dinah Sheridan, Jimmy Hanley, Wylie Watson, Edward Rigby, Maire O'Neill, Ellis Irving, Petula Clark, Kynaston Reeves, John Salew, Aubrey Mallalieu, Scott Sanders, Maudie Edwards, Ben Williams, Ethel Coleridge, Cyril Smith, K. Lung, Mary Norton, Henry White, Alfred Harris, Sonny Miller, Johnny Catcher, Ivor Barnard, Dick Francis, Peter Gawthorne, Goeffrey Dennis, Cyril Luckham*.

MY AIN FOLK (1944)   [2]

Dir *Germain Burger*. Prod *F.W. Baker*. Scr *Kathleen Butler*. Ph *Ernest Palmer*. PC and Dis *Butchers*. 75 mins. Cert U

Jean (*Moira Lister*), engaged to naval officer Malcolm (*Norman Prince*), leaves her Highland home to work in a war factory. Malcolm is reported missing at sea but, convinced he is safe, Jean returns to the factory just in time to avert a strike. She is asked to organize a radio show for the factory workers and, as she is singing in this, Malcolm returns for a joyous reunion. (Over) sentimental, (over) loaded with Scottish songs.

RoC *Mabel Constanduros, Herbert Cameron, Nicolette Roeg, John Turner, Ben Williams, Charles Rolfe, Walter Midgeley, Lorna Martin, Desmond Roberts, Harry Angers, David Keir, Ben Williams, Herbert Thorpe, Gordon Begg, Lowry and Richardson*.

MY BROTHER JONATHAN (1947)   [4]

Dir *Harold French*. Prod *Warwick Ward*. Scr *Leslie Landau, Adrian Arlington, from the novel by Francis Brett Young*. Ph *Derick (Derek) Williams*. PC *Associated British*. Dis *Pathé*. 107 mins. Cert A

Jonathan Dakers (*Michael Denison*) dreams both of becoming a great surgeon and marrying Edie Martyn (*Beatrice Campbell*). But he has to work as a partner in a small industrial practice to help his brother Harold (*Ronald Howard*) through university. Harold wins Edie, but is killed in the First World War. She is pregnant and Jonathan, who is fighting to improve conditions in his town, marries her, although attracted to Rachel (*Dulcie Gray*), his partner's daughter. Edie dies in childbirth; Rachel and Jonathan marry and adopt the child. Solidly crafted version of bestseller really packs in a lot of story.

RoC *Stephen Murray, Mary Clare, Finlay Currie, Arthur Young, Beatrice Varley, James Robertson Justice, James Hayter, Jessica Spencer, John Salew, Peter Murray, Wylie Watson, Hilda Bayley, Josephine Stuart, Wilfrid Hyde White, R. Stuart Lindsell, Fred Groves, Kath-*

Michael Denison and Ronald Howard in My Brother Jonathan *(1948)*

leen Boutall, Felix Deebank, Eric Messiter, Paul Farrell, Jack Melford, David Ward, Peter Hobbes, George Woodbridge, Leslie Watson, Merle Tottenham, Grace Denbigh-Russell, Howard Douglas, Hilary Pritchard, Derek Farge, Eunice Gayson, Norah Gordon, Cameron Hall, Kathleen Heath, Paul Blake, Thora Hird, Maureen Jones, Vi Kaley, Fred Kitchen, Daniel King, Ruth Lodge, Johnnie Schofield, Elsie Wagstaffe, Hazel Adair, Grace Arnold, Ernest Borrow, Ernest Butcher, Basil Cunard, Andrea Malandrinos, Beatrice Marsden, Sydney Monckton, Paul Sheridan, Janet Morrison, Ray Cooney, Elizabeth Maude, Jane Shirley, Wendy Thompson, Desmond Newling, Alan Goodwin, Michael Caborne.

MY BROTHER'S KEEPER (1948)   [4]

Dir *Alfred Roome, Roy Rich*. Prod *Antony Darnborough*. Scr *Frank Harvey*. Ph *Gordon Lang*. PC *Gainsborough*. Dis *General Film Distributors*. 91 mins. Cert A

Handcuffed together, two convicts, George (*Jack Warner*), a hardened criminal, and Willie (*George Cole*), a simple youth, escape. An ex-girlfriend of George's gives them food and shelter, but George later kills a man who finds them sawing the 'cuffs apart. Willie gives himself up and is accused of the killing. A police cordon closes in on George, who makes a last desperate gamble on fleeing through a minefield. Almost through, he makes an error and is blown to pieces. Slow-moving thriller but with human and suspenseful moments.

RoC *Jane Hylton, David Tomlinson, Bill Owen, Yvonne Owen, Raymond Lovell, Brenda Bruce, Susan Shaw, John Boxer, Beatrice Varley, Amy Veness, Garry Marsh, Wilfrid Hyde White, Maurice Denham, Frederick Piper, Jack Raine, Fred Groves, Arthur Hambling, Valentine Dyall, George Merritt, Christopher Lee*.

MY HANDS ARE CLAY (1948)   [1]

Dir *Lionel Tomlinson*. Prod *Patrick McCrossan*. Scr *Paul Trippe*. PC *Dublin Films*. Dis *Monarch*. 60 mins. Cert U

Sculptor Michael (*Robert Dawson*) is obsessively jealous of his benefactor Peter (*Cecil Brook*), especially when he sees him dancing with their mutual friend Mary (*Bernadette Leahy*). Michael and Mary wed, but when Peter calls with a present for their first child, Michael almost destroys his finest sculpture,

being redeemed only by the power of prayer. Religion-slanted Irish feature lacks professionalism in all departments.

RoC *Richard Ahearne, Sheila Richards, Terry Wilson, Francis Riedy*.

MY LEARNED FRIEND (1943)   [4]

Dir *Will Hay, Basil Dearden*. (Associate) Prod *S.C. Balcon*. Scr *John Dighton, Angus Macphail*. Ph *Wilkie Cooper*. PC and Dis *Ealing Studios*. 76 mins. Cert U

Forger Grimshaw (*Mervyn Jones*) comes out of prison and starts killing off everyone responsible for putting him there. Last on the list, as a kind of tit-bit, is William Fitch (*Will Hay*), the incompetent barrister who defended him. One by one the others are bumped off, until Fitch and his equally incompetent barrister friend (*Claude Hulbert*) are pursued across the face of Big Ben by the vengeful Grimshaw, who dies in the attempt. Hay's last film: a crazy, fluidly made farce.

RoC *Ernest Thesiger, Charles Victor, Derna (Hy) Hazell, Lloyd Pearson, Maudie Edwards, G.H. Mulcaster, Gibb McLaughlin, Aubrey Mallalieu, Leslie Harcourt, Lawrence Hanray, Eddie Phillips, Valerie White*.

Claude Hulbert and Will Hay in My Learned Friend *(1943)*

MY SISTER AND I (1948)   [2]

Dir *Harold Huth*. Prod *Huth, John Corfield*. Scr *A.R. Rawlinson, Joan Rees, Michael Medwin, Robert Westerby, from a novel by Emery Bonnet*. Ph *Harry Waxman*. PC *Burnham*. Dis *General Film Distributors*. 97 mins. Cert A

Robina (*Sally Ann Howes*), a set designer, finds lodgings with wealthy Mrs Camelot (*Martita Hunt*), who owns the local theatre and takes a shine to Robina. When Mrs Camelot is murdered, suspicion falls on Robina, who is left all her money. But the revelation that Mrs Camelot's adored dead husband was not a paragon of virtue leads to the discovery of the real killer. Novelettish; characters have names like Hypatia Foley and Ardath Bondage.

RoC *Barbara Mullen, Dermot Walsh, Hazel Court, Patrick Holt, Jane Hylton, Michel Medwin, Diana Dors, Stewart Rome, Joan Rees, Helen Goss, Hugh Miller, James Knight, Ian Wilson, Rory McDermott, Niall Lawlor, Elizabeth Sydney, Olwen Brookes, Jack Vyvyan, Wilfred Caithness, John Miller, Amy Dalby, Barbara Leake*.

THE MYSTERIOUS MR NICHOLSON (1946) [2]

Dir *Oswald Mitchell*. Prod *Gilbert Church*. Scr *Francis Miller*, *Mitchell*. Ph *S.D. Onions*. PC *Bushey*. Dis *Ambassador*. 79 mins. Cert A

Sent by her employers to deliver the will of Sir James Carteris, Peggy (*Lesley Osmond*) finds him slain. Nicolson (*Anthony Hulme*), a gentleman thief, is suspected, but he helps her track down the real murderer: his double. Rough-and-ready thriller.

RoC *Frank Hawkins, Andrew Laurence, Douglas Stewart, George Bishop, Josie Bradley, Ivy Collins*.

THE MYSTERIOUS POACHER (1949) [4]

Dir *Don Chaffey*. Prod *Mary Field*. Scr *Patricia Latham*. Ph *Walter Riml*. PC *GB Instructional*. Dis *General Film Distributors*. 49 mins. Cert U

In a deer forest in Austria an elusive poacher is hunting and stealing deer. But a group of children run him to earth and capture him (with a little help from their adult friends). Shot in Austria, this fresh, lively little children's film has German dialogue and English commentary.

LP *Herbert Leidinger, Herbert Navratil-Edgar, Vera Kulicek, Fritz von Friedl, Karl Gallasch, Leontine (Loni) von Friedl, Toni Lamprecht-Ehret, Gertrude (Gerty) Jobstmann, Gustaf Dennert*.

MY WIFE'S FAMILY (1941) [2]

Dir and Prod *Walter C. Mycroft*. Scr *Norman Lee, Clifford Grey, from the play by Fred Duprez*. Ph *Walter Harvey*. PC *Associated British*. Dis *Pathé*. 82 mins. Cert A

Jack's (*John Warwick*) plans for a happy leave with his wife Peggy (*Patricia Roc*) are dashed by the arrival of his dominant mother-in-law (*Margaret Scudamore*) and her husband Noah (*Wylie Watson*); Doc Knott (*Charlie Clapham*), a travelling cheapjack; a glamorous actress (*Chili Bouchier*) caught in compromising circumstances with Noah; and the discovery of a baby in the summerhouse where Jack had hidden a piano as a surprise for his wife. Unimaginative presentation of a catalogue of old jokes.

RoC *Peggy Bryan, David Tomlinson, Joan Greenwood, Leslie Fuller*.

N

NEUTRAL PORT (1940) [2]

Dir *Marcel Varnel*. Prod *Edward Black*. Scr *J.B. Williams, T.J. Morrison*. Ph *Arthur Crabtree*. PC *Gainsborough*. Dis *General Film Distributors*. 92 mins. Cert U

Captain Ferguson (*Will Fyffe*) skippers a battered old cargo boat which is sunk by a German U-boat. He determines to replace it with one of the German vessels lying in a neutral port. The first ship he steals is torpedoed, the second is a submarine supply vessel which he uses to ram a U-boat, two more being sunk thanks to his radio message. Gilbert-and-Sullivan-type war story; director should have stuck to comedy.

RoC *Leslie Banks, Phyllis Calvert, Hugh McDermott, Yvonne Arnaud, John Salew, Frederick Valk, Albert Lieven, Cameron Hall, Antony Holles, Wally Patch, Dennis Wyndham, Jack Raine, Sigurd Lohde, Noel Dainton, Len Sharpe, Ernest Metcalfe, Charles Rolfe, Stuart Lathom, Keith Shepherd, John Rae, Sam Lee, Mignon O'Doherty, Eric Clavering, Yvonne André, Cot d'Ordan, Rowland Douglas, Gerik Schjelderup, Frank Henderson, Hugh Griffith*.

NEXT OF KIN (1942) [6]

Dir *Thorold Dickinson*. (Associate) Prod *S.C. Balcon*. Scr *Dickinson, John Dighton, Angus Macphail, Captain Sir Basil Bartlett*. Ph *Ernest Palmer*. PC *Ealing Studios*. Dis *United Artists*. 102 mins. Cert A

What started as a propaganda film on careless talk was expanded into an outstanding commercial film, gripping throughout. An English-born German (*Mervyn Johns*) is sent to Britain and gathers vital pieces of information from unwary servicemen, one of whom has his briefcase, with its aerial photographs, stolen. German officials piece it all together, and get wise to an impending attack by commandos which, although successful, proves costly in lives. The German agent continues his work....

RoC *Nova Pilbeam, Stephen Murray, Geoffrey Hibbert, Reginald Tate, Philip Friend, Phyllis Stanley, Mary Clare, Basil Sydney, Jack Hawkins, Brefni O'Rourke, Joss Ambler, David Hutcheson, Alexander Field, Frederick Leister, Torin Thatcher, Charles Victor, John Chandos, Thora Hird, Basil Radford, Naunton Wayne, Peter de Greff, Pat Hagan, Frank Allenby, Sandra Storme, Owen Reynolds*.

Stephen Murray in Next of Kin *(1942)*

NICHOLAS NICKLEBY (1947) [4]

Dir *Cavalcanti*. (Associate) Prod *John Croydon*. Scr *John Dighton, from the book by Charles Dickens*. Ph *Gordon Dines*. PC *Ealing Studios*. Dis *General Film Distributors*. 108 mins. Cert A

Taking the job his father Ralph (*Cedric Hardwicke*) has got him, a master at Dotheboys Hall, a monstrous institution, Nicholas (*Derek Bond*) ends up beating Wackford Squeers (*Alfred Drayton*) with his own cane. He joins some travelling players, accompanied by Smike (*Aubrey Woods*) from the Hall. Squeers kidnaps Smike, but Nicholas, assisted by his father's clerk Noggs (*Bernard Miles*), rescues him. Smike dies, after Nicholas has discovered he was Ralph's unwanted son. He saves his sister (*Sally Ann Howes*) from a loveless marriage and marries his sweetheart Madeleine (*Jill Balcon*). Not exactly attention-grabbing, but nicely adapted.

RoC *Stanley Holloway, Cyril Fletcher, Mary Merrall, Sybil Thorndike, Vera Pearce, Cathleen Nesbitt, Athene Seyler, Cecil Ramage, George Relph, Emrys Jones, Fay Compton, James Hayter, Vida Hope, Roddy Hughes, Timothy Bateson, Frederick Burtwell, Roy Hermitage, Patricia Hayes, Una Bart, June Elvin, Drusilla Wills, Michael Shepley, Lawrence Hanray, Hattie Jacques, Eliot Makeham, John Salew, Arthur Brander, Guy Rolfe, Dandy Nichols, John Chandos*.

NIGHT BEAT (1947) [2]

Dir and Prod *Harold Huth*. Scr *T.J. Morrison, Roland Pertwee*. Ph *Vaclav Vich*. PC and Dis *British Lion*. 91 mins. Cert A

Andy and Don (*Ronald Howard, Hector Ross*) leave the army and try the police; Andy later resigns. Don is engaged to Julie (*Anne Crawford*), but she marries Felix (*Maxwell Read*), a 'spiv'. Andy has a spell in jail, and is involved in the murder of Felix, but all ends well, after the suicide of Jackie, a malicious blonde whom Julie bluffs into confessing to the killing. Weakish thriller with unsympathetic characters.

RoC *Christine Norden, Fred Groves, Sidney James, Nicholas Stuart, Frederick Leister, Michael Medwin, Philip Stainton, Michael Hordern*.

NIGHT BOAT TO DUBLIN (1945) [4]

Dir *Lawrence Huntington*. Prod *Hamilton G. Inglis*. Scr *Huntington, Robert Hall*. Ph *Otto Heller*. PC *Associated British*. Dis *Pathé*. 99 mins. Cert A

A Swedish scientist working on the atom bomb is battled for by British and German agents. He thinks he is working for Britain, but information on the project is being sent to German agents in Ireland, via the night boat to Dublin. Grant (*Robert Newton*) leads a British intelligence bid to recapture him for good, which succeeds after Grant thrashes the chief Nazi, Faber (*Raymond Lovell*) at the monastery where the scientist is held. Well-developed spy thriller, a catalogue of breathless excitements.

RoC *Muriel Pavlow, Guy Middleton, Herbert Lom, Marius Goring, John Ruddock, Martin Miller, Brenda Bruce, Gerald Case, Julian Dallas, Leslie Dwyer, Olga Lindo, Joan Maude, Derek Elphinstone, Bruce Gordon, George Hirste, Hubert Leslie, Gordon McLeod, Hay Petrie, Wilfrid Hyde White, Stuart Lindsell, Lawrence O'Madden, Valentine Dyall, Carroll Gibbons, Edmundo Ros and His Rhumba Band*.

NIGHT COMES TOO SOON (1947) [2]

Dir *Denis Kavanagh.* Prod *Harold Baim.* Scr *Pat Dixon, from a play by Lord Lytton.* Ph *Ray Densham.* PC *Federated/British Animated.* Dis *Butchers.* 52 mins. Cert A

Phyllis and her husband tell friends that they have seen ghosts, spirits which their mysterious friend Dr Clinton (*Valentine Dyall*) had identified as a sailor's wife and her lover, shot by the sailor. Since Clinton, on finding an old book and crystal belonging to a 'necromancer' who also had lived there, had broken the crystal, the hauntings had stopped. There is the sound of breaking glass; Clinton and the book vanish. Dreary chiller with no scares.

RoC *Anne Howard, Alec Faversham, Beatrice Marsden, Howard Douglas, Anthony Baird, Arthur Brander, David Keir, Frank Dunlop, Monte de Lyle, Nina Erber, John Desmond.*

THE NIGHT HAS EYES (1942) [3]
(USA: *Terror House*)

Dir *Leslie Arliss.* Prod *John Argyle.* Scr *Argyle, Arliss, Alan Kennington, from a story by Kennington.* Ph *Günther Krampf.* PC *Associated British.* Dis *Pathé.* 79 mins. Cert A

Teachers Marian and Doris (*Joyce Howard, Tucker McGuire*) go to Yorkshire, where their friend Evelyn disappeared a year earlier on the moors. Caught in a storm, they are sheltered by reclusive composer Stephen (*James Mason*), who is subject to fits. Evelyn's killers turn out to be his housekeeper and her husband (*Mary Clare, Wilfrid Lawson*) who themselves die in quicksands on the moors. Hard to believe, but quite powerfully done.

RoC *John Fernald.*

THE NIGHT INVADER (1942) [3]

Dir *Herbert Mason.* Prod *Max Milder.* Scr *Brock Williams, Edward Dryhurst, Roland Pertwee, from a novel by John Bentley.* Ph *Otto Heller.* PC and Dis *Warner Bros.* 81 mins. Cert U

RAF intelligence man Dick Marlow (*David Farrar*) is ordered to get a secret document out of Holland. Parachuting in, he poses as an American reporter, stays with a pro-British baroness (*Sybilla Binder*) and falls in love with, but suspects, the sister (*Anne Crawford*) of the man with the document. Both in turn are suspected by the Nazis, but finally manage to get out with the secrets. Unconvincing but fast-moving thriller.

RoC *Carl Jaffe, Marius Goring, Jenny Lovelace, Martin Walker, John Salew, George Carney, Kynaston Reeves, Philip Godfrey, Ernest Verne, Ronald Shiner, Harry Charman, Walter Gotell.*

A NIGHT OF MAGIC (1944) [1]

Dir *Herbert Wynne.* Prod *Burt Hyams.* Scr *Eversley Bracken.* Ph *W. Richards.* PC *Berkeley.* Dis *Premier.* 56 mins. Cert U

Reggie (*Robert Griffith*) dreams that his uncle has sent him a sarcophagus containing the mummy of a 3,000-year-old Egyptian princess. He finds the princess (*Marian Olive*) alive, and they paint pre-war London red. The princess says they had an even better time in Egypt in her day, and whisks him off to prove it. Sloppy revue-style film.

RoC *Billy 'Uke' Scott, Vera Bradley, Dot Delavine, Gordon Ray, The Broadway Boys, The Gordon Ray Girls.*

NIGHT TRAIN TO MUNICH (1940) [5]
(USA: *Night Train*)

Dir *Carol Reed.* Prod *Edward Black.* Scr *Frank Launder, Sidney Gilliat, from a story by Gordon Wellesley.* Ph *Otto Kanturek.* PC *20th Century Productions.* Dis *M-G-M.* 95 mins (*US:* 90). Cert A

In a concentration camp, Anna Bomasch (*Margaret Lockwood*) meets a young German Karl (*Paul von Hernried*) and they escape together to England. It is a ruse of the Gestapo to trace Anna's father, whose invention they are determined to steal. Tricking agent Gus Bennett (*Rex Harrison*), they seize Dr Bomasch. But Anna, Gus and Dr Bomasch, aided by two English cricketing enthusiasts (*Basil Radford* and *Naunton Wayne* repeating their *Lady Vanishes* roles), escape on a night train to Munich and later flee to Switzerland on a funicular railway across a chasm. Gus kills Karl. Humorous thriller keeps suspense going to the last.

RoC *James Harcourt, Felix Aylmer, Wyndham Goldie, Roland Culver, Eliot Makeham, Raymond Huntley, Austin Trevor, Keneth Kent, C.V. France, Morland Graham, Billy Russell, Fritz (Frederick) Valk, Irene Handl, Pardoe Woodman, Albert Lieven, Edward Baxter, J.H. Roberts, David Horne, G.H. Mulcaster, Ian Fleming, Wilfrid Walter, Jane Cobb, Charles Oliver, Torin Thatcher, Pat Williams, Winifred Oughton, Hans (John) Wengraf.*

Margaret Lockwood and Albert Lieven in Night Train to Munich *(1940)*

NINE MEN (1943) [5]

Dir *Harry Watt.* (Associate) Prod *Charles Crichton.* Scr *Watt.* Ph *Roy Kellino.* PC *Ealing Studios.* Dis *United Artists.* 68 mins. Cert A

A bunch of new recruits is told the story of nine British army men stranded in the north African desert. When their officer dies, Sergeant Watson (*Jack Lambert*) takes command, and gets the survivors to a derelict tomb where they hold out for a day and a night against enemy attacks until relieved. Gripping yarn based on a Russian film, *The 13*, the same theme being used for a 1943 Hollywood film, *Sahara*.

RoC *Gordon Jackson, Frederick Piper, Grant Sutherland, Bill Blewett, Eric Micklewood, John Varley, Jack Horsman, Richard Wilkinson, Giulio Finzi, Trevor Evans.*

NO ORCHIDS FOR MISS BLANDISH (1948) [2]

Dir and Scr *StJohn L. Clowes, from the novel by James Hadley Chase.* Prod *Clowes, A.R. Shipman, Oswald Mitchell.* Ph *Gerald Gibbs.* PC *Alliance/Tudor.* Dis *Renown.* 104 mins (later 102). Cert A

Heiress Barbara Blandish (*Linden Travers*) is kidnapped by small-time crooks who beat her fiancé to death. In turn, she is 'stolen' from them by the even tougher Grisson gang. A love affair develops between Barbara and Slim Grisson (*Jack La Rue*), the mother-dominated gangleader. The police track them to Slim's log cabin hideout, and he dies in a hail of gunfire. Harsh, unpleasant, tedious crime drama, banned by several countries and watch committees.

RoC *Hugh McDermott, Walter Crisham, Leslie Bradley, Zoë Gail, Charles Goldner, MacDonald Parke, Lily Molnar, Danny Green, Percy Marmont, Michael Balfour, Frances Marsden, Irene Prador, Jack Lester, Bart Norman, Bill O'Connor, Gibb McLaughlin, John McLaren, Sidney James, Richard Nelson, Annette Simmonds, Jack Durant, Halama and Konarski, Tony and Wing.*

Jack La Rue, Linden Travers and Walter Crisham in No Orchids for Miss Blandish *(1948)*

NOOSE (1948) [3]
(USA: *The Silk Noose*)

Dir *Edmond T. Gréville.* Prod and PC *Edward Dryhurst.* Scr *Richard Llewellyn, Dryhurst, from Llewellyn's play.* Ph *Hone Glendinning.* Dis *Pathé.* 95 mins. Cert A

Captain Jumbo Hoyle (*Derek Farr*) comes to the aid of a girl reporter Linda (*Carole Landis*) in her efforts to smash the black market racket of Soho nightclub owner Sugiani (*Joseph Calleia*). With the help of a group of Hoyle's ex-commando friends, they eventually succeed. British imitation of an American gangster film. Not bad, but hardly authentic.

RoC *Stanley Holloway, Nigel Patrick, John Slater, Edward Rigby, Ruth Nixon, Leslie Bradley, Reginald Tate, Hay Petrie, John Salew, Carol Van Derman, Brenda Hogan, Robert Adair, Ella Retford, Michael Golden, Sydney Monckton, Howard Douglas, Uriel*

Porter, *John Harvey, Michael Ripper, Michael Brennan, Arthur Lovegrove, Monte de Lyle, W.E. Hodge, Dennis Harkin, Diana Hope, Arthur Gomez, Kenneth Buckley, Ben Williams, Vi Kaley, John Martell, Ernest Metcalfe, Maria Berry, Ronald Boyer and Jeanne Ravel, Olive Lucius.*

NO PLACE FOR JENNIFER (1949)   ☐3
Dir *Henry Cass.* Prod *Hamilton G. Inglis.* Scr *J. Lee Thompson, from a novel by Phyllis Hambledon.* Ph *William McLeod.* PC *Associated British.* Dis *AB-Pathé.* 90 mins. Cert A
Nine-year-old Jennifer (*Janette Scott*) is torn between divorcing parents. When her father (*Leo Gunn*) is remarried, to her schoolteacher (*Rosamund John*), Jennifer becomes unmanageable and is sent to a home for maladjusted children. More fights between her parents nearly drive the girl to suicide, but she finds happiness away from both parents with a caring family that has always loved her. Rather slow weepie that found a very big audience thanks to its young star.
RoC *Beatrice Campbell, Guy Middleton, Megs Jenkins, Philip Ray, Anthony Nicholls, Jean Cadell, Edith Sharpe, Ann Codrington, Brian Smith, André Morell, Chris Castor, Viola Lyel, William Simon, William Fox, Ruth Lodge, Jean Shepheard, Arnold Bell, Stanley Lorimer, MacDonald Hobley, Lockwood West, Billy Thatcher, Anthony Wager.*

NO ROOM AT THE INN (1948)   ☐4
Dir *Dan Birt.* Prod *Ivan Foxwell.* Scr *Foxwell, Dylan Thomas, from a play by Joan Temple.* Ph *James Wilson.* PC *British National.* Dis *Pathé.* 82 mins. Cert A
Wartime child evacuees suffer at the hands of sluttish, alcoholic Mrs Voray (*Freda Jackson*). One girl, Mary (*Ann Stephens*) appeals to the local church and council for help, but with no success. After Mrs Voray locks one child in the coalhole for some trifling offence, Mary and her friend rescue him. Mrs Voray wakes up, comes down a rickety staircase to investigate, and crashes to her death. Self-consciously sordid, but strongly put across.
RoC *Joy Shelton, Hermione Baddeley, Joan Dowling, Niall MacGinnis, Harcourt Williams, Sydney Tafler, Frank Pettingell, Robin Netscher, Betty Blackler, Jill Gibbs, Wylie Watson, Beatrice Varley, Cyril Smith, James Hayter, Eliot Makeham, Billy Howard, Jack Melford, Bartlett Mullins, Frederick Morant, Dora Bryan, Harry Locke, Bee Adams, Marie Ault, Vera Bogetti, Basil Cunard, O.B. Clarence, Eleanor Hallam, Jack May, Robert McLachlan, Ernie Priest, Vi Kaley, Stanley Escane, Joyce Martyn, Pamela Deacon, Veronica Haley.*

NOTHING VENTURE (1947)   ☐2
Dir, Prod and PC *John Baxter.* Scr *Geoffrey Orme.* Ph *Jo Jago.* Dis *British Lion.* 73 mins. Cert U
Helping a girl whose horse had been startled by a shot, three boys stumble across a criminal plot to steal the plans for a secret ray invented by the girl's father. Helped by a CID man, they bring the criminals responsible to justice, freeing the girl and her father, who have been

snatched and held captive underground. Improbable children's adventure.
LP *Peter Artemus, Philip Artemus, Jackie Artemus, Terry Randal(l), Patric Curwen, Michael Aldridge, Paul Blake, Wilfred Caithness, Howard Douglas, Ben Williams, Peter Gawthorne, Jack Simpson and His Sextet.*

NO WAY BACK (1949)   ☐3
Dir *Stefan Osiecki.* Prod *Derrick de Marney.* Scr *Osiecki, de Marney, from a story by Thomas Burke.* Ph *Robert Navarro.* PC *Concanen.* Dis *Eros.* 72 mins. Cert A
His sight damaged in a big fight, 'The Croucher' (*Terence de Marney*) is forced to give up boxing. Sliding downhill, he loses his money, then his wife, but is rescued from oblivion by his childhood friend Beryl (*Eleanor Summerfield*). They become involved with Sleet (*Jack Raine*), a racketeer, thanks to whom all three are eventually shot down by police. Competent acting in undistinguished thriller.
RoC *John Salew, Shirley Quentin, Denys Val Norton, Gerald C. Lawson, Tommy McGovern.*

NOW BARABBAS was a robber ...
(1949)   ☐5
Dir and Scr *Gordon Parry, from the play by William Douglas Home.* Prod and PC *Anatole de Grunwald.* Ph *Otto Heller.* Dis *Warner Bros.* 87 mins. Cert A
Downbeat story of various prisoners in jail: a seemingly nice young man under sentence of death; an Irish nationalist; a bigamist; a bank clerk led astray through a girl; and others. Some are released at the end of the story; but there is no reprieve for the 'pleasant killer'. ... Characters clearly drawn, emotions skilfully played upon.
LP *Richard Greene, Cedric Hardwicke, Ronald Howard, Stephen Murray, William Hartnell, Richard Burton, Kathleen Harrison, Beatrice Campbell, Betty Ann Davies, Leslie Dwyer, Alec Clunes, Kenneth More, Harry Fowler, Dora Bryan, Constance Smith, Lily Kahn (Lilly Kann), Julian d'Albie, David Hannaford, Peter Doughty, Percy Walsh, Glyn Lawson, Gerald Case, Victor Fairley, Dandy Nichols.*

O

OBSESSION (1948)   ☐4
(USA: *The Hidden Room*)
Dir *Edward Dmytryk.* Prod *Nat A. Bronsten.* Scr *Alec Coppel, from his novel* A Man About a Dog. Ph *C.M. Pennington-Richards.* PC *Independent Sovereign.* Dis *General Film Distributors.* 98 mins. Cert A
Incensed by his wife's (*Sally Gray*) continual affairs, Dr Riordan (*Robert Newton*) decides to murder her latest lover (*Phil Brown*). He kidnaps him, hides him in a cellar room, and

Robert Newton in Obsession (*1948*)

gradually prepares an acid bath. ... The plan begins to go astray when his wife's dog follows him to the hideout. Police eventually get on his trail and rescue the trapped man just in time. Solid suspense value.
RoC *Naunton Wayne, Olga Lindo, Ronald Adam, James Harcourt, Allan Jeayes, Russell Waters, Michael Balfour, Betty Cooper, Roddy Hughes, Lyonel Watts, Stanley Baker, Monty (dog).*

THE OCTOBER MAN (1947)   ☐4
Dir *Roy Baker.* Prod *Eric Ambler, Filippo del Giudice.* Scr *Ambler, from his novel.* Ph *Erwin Hillier.* Dis *Eagle Lion.* 110 mins (later 95). Cert A
After an accident in which a child was killed and he sustained brain injuries, Jim (*John Mills*) develops suicidal tendencies. Molly (*Kay Walsh*), a model at his hotel, is sympathetic, although it's Jenny (*Joan Greenwood*) he starts dating. Shortly after he lends Molly some money, she is found strangled. Jim is suspected. The real killer (*Edward Chapman*) taunts him. He begins to crack up. Then the police get on the right track just as Jenny stops Jim throwing himself under a train. Suspenseful psychological thriller with good background detail.
RoC *Joyce Carey, Felix Aylmer, Catherine Lacey, Patrick Holt, Frederick Piper, Adrianne Allen, Jack Melford, George Benson, John Salew, John Boxer, Esme Beringer, Ann Wilton, Philip Ray, George Woodbridge, John Miller, Kathleen Boutall, Edward Underdown, James Hayter, Juliet Mills.*

ODD MAN OUT (1946)   ☐5
Dir and Prod *Carol Reed.* Scr *F.L. Green, R.C. Sherriff, from Green's novel.* Ph *Robert Krasker.* PC *Two Cities.* Dis *General Film Distributors.* 116 mins. Cert A
IRA man Johnny McQueen (*James Mason*) escapes from prison, but is shot and wounded in a raid on a linen mill. Pursued through Belfast by police, he finds himself painted by a crazy artist (*Robert Newton*) and operated on by a failed medical student (*Elwyn Brook-Jones*). Trying to reach the docks, he meets his girl (*Kathleen Ryan*), but the police are closing in, and she fires so that they will both be killed together. Claustrophobic, skilfully made study of a man on the run; goes just a little astray towards the end.

James Mason in Odd Man Out *(1946)*

RoC *Robert Beatty, F.J. McCormick, William Hartnell, Fay Compton, Beryl Measor, Cyril Cusack, Dan O'Herlihy, Roy Irving, Maureen Delany, Kitty Kirwan, Min Milligan, Joseph Tomelty, W.G. Fay, Arthur Hambling, Denis O'Dea, Anne Clery, Maura Milligan, Eddie Byrne, Maureen Cusack, Dora Bryan, Guy Rolfe, Geoffrey Keen, *Beatrice Campbell.*
* scene deleted from final release print.

OLD BILL AND SON (1940)   ③

Dir *Ian Dalrymple.* Prod *Josef Somlo, Harold Boxall.* Scr *Bruce Bairnsfather, Dalrymple, Arthur Wimperis, from cartoons by Bairnsfather.* Ph *Georges Périnal.* PC *Legeran Films.* Dis *General Film Distributors. 96 mins. Cert U*
Old Bill (*Morland Graham*), after grumbling his way through the First World War, tries to get into the 1939–45 conflict jealous of his son, Young Bill (*John Mills*), who has already enlisted and is in France. He manages to get into the Pioneer Corps near Young Bill – who goes missing on a night-time raid. Old Bill goes to the rescue, only to find Young Bill – who lets him share the glory – has captured a whole platoon of enemy soldiers. Good acting, nice dialogue, but a bit slow.
RoC *Mary Clare, Renée Houston, René Ray, Janine Darcey, Roland Culver, Gus McNaughton, Ronald Shiner, Manning Whiley, Nicholas Phipps, Allan Jeayes, Donald Stewart, Percy Walsh.*

OLD MOTHER RILEY AT HOME
(1945)   ②

Dir *Oswald Mitchell.* Prod *Louis H. Jackson.* Scr *Mitchell, George A. Cooper.* Ph *James Wilson.* PC *British National.* Dis *Anglo-American. 76 mins. Cert A*
Mother Riley (*Arthur Lucan*) makes such a scene over her daughter Kitty's (*Kitty McShane*) new boyfriend Bill (*Willer Neal*) that Kitty leaves. She gets a job at a gambling den, pursued by Mother Riley and her lodger Dan (*Richard George*) who loves Kitty. Mother Riley mistakenly sets off the alarm there for a police raid; she and Dan, who KOs Bill, escape with Kitty. (Very) rough and tumble romp.
RoC *Freddie Forbes, Wally Patch, Kenneth Warrington, Angela Barrie, Janet Morrison, Elsie Wagstaffe.*

OLD MOTHER RILEY DETECTIVE
(1942)   ②

Dir *Lance Comfort.* Prod ~~*John Baxter.*~~ Scr

Austin Melford, Geoffrey Orme. Ph *James Wilson.* PC *British National.* Dis *Anglo-American. 80 mins. Cert U*
Old Mother Riley (*Arthur Lucan*), an office cleaner, is frogmarched to the police station on a trumped up charge, so that police can enlist her help in tracking down black marketeers. After many adventures, Mother Riley corners the leader of the gang in a haystack and pounds him into submission with a pitchfork. Not much story in a below-par Riley romp.
RoC *Kitty McShane, Ivan Brandt, Owen Reynolds, George Street, Johnnie Schofield, Hal Gordon, Valentine Dunn, Marjorie Rhodes, H.F. Maltby, Peggy Cummins, Edgar Driver, Michael Lynd, Nellie Bowman, Jimmy Rhodes, Eddie Stern, Pat Kavanagh, Gerry Wilson, Pat Keogh, Charles Paton, Jack Vyvyan, Eve Chipman, Frank Webster, Charles Doe, Vi Kaley, Ernest Metcalfe, Mike Johnson, Louise Nolan, Mary Norton, Hilde Palmer, Bryan Herbert, Nino Rossini, Alfredo Campoli, Noel Dainton, Ben Williams, Harry Terry, Bombardier Billy Wells, Leo de Pokorny, Arthur Dent, Stanley Paskin, Geoffrey Roberts.*

OLD MOTHER RILEY IN BUSINESS
(1940)   ③

Dir *John Baxter.* Prod *John Corfield.* Scr *Geoffrey Orme.* Ph *James Wilson.* PC *British National.* Dis *Anglo-American. 80 mins. Cert U*
Willingdon's village shopkeepers face new competition – from Golden Stores, a conglomerate. Storemistress Old Mother Riley (*Arthur Lucan*) spurs them to action, organizing a pirate radio station to advertise their wares. Accidentally pushing the Golden Stores manager in the river, Mother Riley takes refuge from the police in a hospital and escapes dressed as a nurse. At a board meeting of Golden Stores, Mother Riley finally triumphs.
RoC *Kitty McShane, Cyril Chamberlain, Charles Victor, Wally Patch, Ernest Butcher, Ernest Sefton, O.B. Clarence, Edgar Driver, Edie Martin, Roddy Hughes, Morris Harvey, Ruth Maitland.*

OLD MOTHER RILEY IN SOCIETY
(1940)   ②

Dir *John Baxter.* Prod *John Corfield.* Scr *Austin Melford, Barbara K. Emary, Mary Cathcart Borer, Kitty McShane.* Ph *James Wilson.* PC *British National.* Dis *Anglo-American. 81 mins. Cert U*
Kitty Riley (*Kitty McShane*) star of a pantomime disrupted by her harridan mother (*Arthur Lucan*) marries a society swell (*John Stuart*). Old Mother Riley introduces herself as Kitty's dresser and later becomes their maid. After various comic disasters, Kitty confesses their relationship, and Mother Riley assumes her proper place in the household. Another washerwoman's bundle of well-worn gags.
RoC *Dennis Wyndham, Minnie Rayner, Athole Stewart, Charles Victor, Ruth Maitland, Margaret Halstan, Peggy Novak, Diana Beaumont, Aubrey Dexter, Cyril Chamberlain.*

OLD MOTHER RILEY OVERSEAS
(1943)   ③

Dir and Prod *Oswald Mitchell.* Scr *H. Fowler*

Mear, Arthur Lucan. Ph *James Wilson.* PC *British National.* Dis *Anglo-American. 80 mins. Cert U*
Tricked out of the licenseeship of the Ship Inn by a rival, Old Mother Riley (*Arthur Lucan*) follows her daughter Kitty (*Kitty McShane*), who has gone to Portugal to work for a wine importer. After being mistaken for a famous pianist, Mother Riley foils a bid to steal the famous port from the Quantas warehouse, and saves Kitty from kidnappers. Simple fun but plenty of it.
RoC *Morris Harvey, Fred Kitchen Jr, Magda Kun, Antony Holles, Ferdi Mayne, Freddie William Breach, Bob Lloyd, Jack Vyvyan, Paul Erikson, Eda Bell, Ruth Meredith, Stanelli, Rosarito and Paula.*

OLD MOTHER RILEY'S CIRCUS
(1941)   ③

Dir *Thomas Bentley.* Prod *Wallace Orton.* Scr *Con West, Geoffrey Orme, Barbara K. Emary, Arthur Lucan.* Ph *James Wilson.* PC *British National.* Dis *Anglo-Amalgamated. 80 mins. Cert U*
Hearing that Santley's Circus is about to close after the disappearance of its owner, Old Mother Riley (*Arthur Lucan*), a former music-hall star, takes over as ringmaster. Putting on a good show, she clears off the circus's debts and discovers that Kitty (*Kitty McShane*), its star, is her long-lost daughter. An attempt by Santley to regain control is foiled. Good circus acts the main attraction.
RoC *John Longden, Roy Emerton, Edgar Driver, Beckett Bould, O.B. Clarence, Syd Crossley, Hector Abbas, W.T. Holland, John Turnbull, Iris Vandeleur, Norah Gordon, Jennie Gregson, Lawrence Hanray, Ernest Sefton, Ben Williams, The Hindustans, The Balstons, Harry Koady, Jean Black, The Carsons, Reading and Grant, Medlock & Marlow, Speedy, Isabel and Emma, Eve and Joan Banyard.*

OLD MOTHER RILEY'S GHOSTS
(1941)   ③

Dir, and Prod *John Baxter.* Scr *Con West, Geoffrey Orme, Arthur Lucan.* Ph *James Wilson.* PC *British National.* Dis *Anglo-American. 82 mins. Cert U*
Charwoman Old Mother Riley (*Arthur Lucan*) finds herself the owner of a 'haunted' castle plagued not only by ghosts, but also by spies seeking the plans of an inventor working there. Inventing her own ghosts, Mother Riley puts the spies to flight. Crude but quite effective comedy, with Lucan working overtime.
RoC *Kitty McShane, John Stuart, A. Bromley Davenport, Dennis Wyndham, John Laurie, Peter Gawthorne, Henry B. Longhurst, Ben Williams, Charles Paton, Henry Woolston, Eric Stuart.*

OLD MOTHER RILEY'S NEW
VENTURE (1949)   ③

Dir *John Harlow.* Prod and PC *Harry Reynolds.* Scr *Con West, Jack Marks.* Ph *James Wilson.* Dis *Renown. 79 mins. Cert U*
Mother Riley (*Arthur Lucan*), washer-up at a hotel, is left in charge by the proprietor when he goes away to rest his nerves after a series of

robberies. Further developments include the theft of a huge diamond from a foreign potentate. Mother Riley is thrown into prison, but escapes in time to witness the unmasking of the villains. Lively slapstick comedy just keeps on coming.

RoC *Kitty McShane, Chili Bouchier, Maureen Riscoe, Willer Neal, Sebastian Cabot, Wilfred Babbage, John le Mesurier, C. Denier Warren, Fred Groves, Paul Sheridan, Arthur Gomez.*

OLIVER TWIST (1948) [5]

Dir *David Lean.* Prod *Anthony Havelock-Allan.* Scr *Lean, Stanley Haynes, from the novel by Charles Dickens.* Ph *Guy Green.* PC *Cineguild.* Dis *General Film Distributors. 116 mins. Cert A*

Son of a girl who dies in childbirth, young Oliver (*John Howard Davies*) suffers the cruel discipline of a parish workhouse in the early 1800s. He runs away from his sadistic first employer, an undertaker, and falls in with a gang of pickpockets, led by Fagin (*Alec Guinness*). When he is found to be the son of a rich man, the relative he will disinherit pays Fagin to have a man kill him. It turns out to be murderous Bill Sikes (*Robert Newton*) who strangles his kind-hearted mistress Nancy (*Kay Walsh*), but fails to despatch Oliver, falling to his death in a rooftop chase with police. Fagin goes to the gallows and Oliver starts a new life. The best version of the story, teeming with detail and excitement.

RoC *Francis L. Sullivan, Henry Stephenson, Mary Clare, Anthony Newley, Ralph Truman, Josephine Stuart, Kathleen Harrison, Gibb McLaughlin, Amy Veness, Diana Dors, Frederick Lloyd, Maurice Denham, W.G. Fay, Henry Edwards, Hattie Jacques, Betty Paul, Ivor Barnard, Deidre Doyle, Edie Martin, Fay Middleton, Michael Dear, Graveley Edwards, Peter Bull, John Potter, Maurice Jones, Kenneth Downey.*

Alec Guinness, John Howard Davies and Anthony Newley in Oliver Twist (*1948*)

ON APPROVAL (1944) [5]

Dir *Clive Brook.* Prod *Sydney Box, Brook.* Scr, *Brook, Terence Young, from the play by Frederick Lonsdale.* Ph *Claude Friese-Greene,* PC *Independent Producers.* Dis *General Film Distributors. 80 mins. Cert A*

Idle, conceited George, Duke of Bristol (*Clive Brook*) and weak, good-natured Richard (*Roland Culver*) are stranded on a Scottish coastal

island with an American heiress (*Beatrice Lillie*) and a dominant English widow (*Googie Withers*). In their attempts to keep home unaided, the two fortune-hunting men have a hard time. Sparkling comedy of manners that entertains uproariously throughout.

RoC *O.B. Clarence, Lawrence Hanray, Elliot Mason, Hay Petrie, Marjorie Rhodes, Molly Munks, E.V.H. Emmett (narrator).*

ONCE A CROOK (1941) [4]

Dir *Herbert Mason.* Prod *Edward Black.* Scr *Roger Burford.* Ph *Arthur Crabtree.* PC *Twentieth Century.* Dis *20th Century-Fox. 81 mins. Cert A*

Charlie, a reformed cracksman (*Gordon Harker*), now runs an East End pub. His ex-partner, Duke (*Bernard Lee*), lures Charlie's son (*Cyril Cusack*) into burglary, then frames him and his girlfriend. Charlie allows himself to be suspected and even tried for murder to shield his son, but fresh evidence crops up and he is cleared. Crime drama with lots of character: *Sydney Howard* is very effective as a Bible-thumping pickpocket, Hallelujah Harry.

RoC *Carla Lehmann, Frank Pettingell, Kathleen Harrison, Diana King, Joss Ambler, Raymond Huntley, Felix Aylmer, Wally Patch, Charles Lamb, John Salew.*

ONCE A JOLLY SWAGMAN (1948) [4]
(USA: *Maniacs on Wheels*)

Dir *Jack Lee.* Prod *Ian Dalrymple.* Scr *Lee, William Rose, Cliff Gordon, from the novel by Montagu Slater.* Ph *H.E. Fowle.* PC *Wessex.* Dis *General Film Distributors. 100 mins. Cert A*

1935. Bill Fox (*Dirk Bogarde*) becomes a top speedway rider. His Australian friend Lag (*Bill Owen*) is badly injured and ends up in a mental home. Bill has an affair with a society lady (*Moira Lister*) but marries Lag's sister Pat (*Renee Asherson*): she leaves him when he refuses to retire. He joins up in wartime, returning to win a race against a brilliant newcomer. Now he decides to quit. Pat drops divorce proceedings. Story a bit long and routine, but still a graphic portrait of a dangerous sport.

RoC *Bonar Colleano, Thora Hird, James Hayter, Patric Doonan, Cyril Cusack, Sandra Dorne, Sidney James, Anthony Oliver, Dudley Jones, Pauline Jameson, Russell Waters, Stuart Lindsell, Frederick Knight, Michael Kent, June Bardsley, Cyril Chamberlain, Jennifer Jayne, Graham Doody, Joyce Tyler, Jill Allan, Edward Judd.*

ONCE UPON A DREAM (1948) [2]

Dir *Ralph Thomas.* Prod *Antony Darnsborough.* Scr *Patrick Kirwan, Victor Katona.* Ph *Jack Cox.* PC *Triton.* Dis *General Film Distributors. 84 mins. Cert A*

Jackson (*Griffith Jones*), Major Gilbert's (*Guy Middleton*) wartime batman, becomes his domestic servant, working with Mrs Jackson (*Googie Withers*). She takes a mild fancy to him and dreams of their having a romantic affair, waking up believing it to be true. Predictable complications arise but are sorted out. Daft comedy, a damper on the careers of those involved.

RoC *Raymond Lovell, Agnes Lauchlan, Hubert Gregg, Maurice Denham, Betty Lynne, David Horne, Gibb McLaughlin, Dora Bryan, Geoffrey Morris, Noel Howlett, Mirren Wood, Mona Washbourne, Nora Nicholson, Hal Osmond, Arthur Denton, Eric Messiter, Cecil Bevan, Wilfred Caithness, Anthony Steel.*

ONE EXCITING NIGHT (1944) [3]
(USA: *You Can't Do Without Love*)

Dir *Walter Forde.* Prod *Ben Henry, Culley Forde.* Scr *Howard Irving Young, Peter Fraser, Margaret Kennedy, Emery Bonnet.* Ph *Otto Heller.* PC and Dis *Columbia British. 89 mins. Cert A*

Vera (*Vera Lynn*) plans to get Thorne (*Donald Stewart*), impresario and temporarily government official, to give her an audition; instead she gets mixed up in a gang's plans to steal a valuable painting from him. She is invited to sing at a charity concert where he is to be kidnapped (and subsequently impersonated), but contrives to foil the gang's plans and further her own career. Not unpleasant mixture of thrills, songs and fun.

RoC *Mary Clare, Frederick Leister, Richard Murdoch, Phyllis Stanley, Cyril Smith, Mavis Villiers, Peggy Anne, Jeanette Redgrave, Pat(ricia) Owens.*

ONE NIGHT WITH YOU (1948) [3]

Dir *Terence Young.* Prod *Josef Somlo.* Scr *Caryl Brahms, S.J. Simon.* Ph *André Thomas.* PC *Two Cities.* Dis *General Film Distributors. 92 mins. Cert U*

Missing his train to Rome, singing film star Giulio (*Nino Martini*) is stranded, along with English girl Mary (*Patricia Roc*). His clothes are stolen by a tramp who goes to Rome to impersonate him. After a night of adventure, Giulio and Mary end up in prison, but he escapes, goes to Rome, and catches the tramp. Mary arrives to see him singing in a film. She runs towards the screen, he lifts her into it, and they 'fade-out' together. Critics were very divided on this slight musical with bright comic moments.

RoC *Bonar Colleano, Guy Middleton, Stanley Holloway, Hugh Wakefield, Charles Goldner, Irene Worth, Willy Feuter, Miles Malleson, Richard Hearne, Stuart Lathom, Judith Furse, Brian Worth, Christopher Lee.*

ONE OF OUR AIRCRAFT IS MISSING (1942) [4]

Dir, Prod and Scr *Michael Powell, Emeric Pressburger.* Ph *Ronald Neame.* PC *British National.* Dis *Anglo-Amalgamated. 102 mins. Cert U*

The Second World War: after raiding Stuttgart, the oddly assorted six-man crew of a British bomber has to bale out when their plane is hit over Holland. They are befriended by children, almost caught by Nazis, then passed from friend to friend across the country. After more hairsbreadth escapes, they get back to England, and return to operational duty. Well-acted realistic drama designed to show how people from all walks of life were fighting together.

LP *Godfrey Tearle, Eric Portman, Hugh*

Bernard Miles and Eric Portman in One of Our Aircraft is Missing (*1942*)

Williams, Bernard Miles, Hugh Burden, Emrys Jones, Pamela Brown, Googie Withers, Joyce Redman, Hay Petrie, Arnold Marle, Robert Helpmann, Peter Ustinov, Alec Clunes, Roland Culver, Stewart Rome, David Evans, Selma Vaz Dias, Hector Abbas, James Carson, Bill Akkerman, Joan Akkerman, Peter Schenke, Valerie Moon, John Salew, William D'Arcy, David Ward, Robert Duncan, Robert Beatty.

OPERATION DIAMOND (1948) [3]
Dir and Ph *Ronnie Pilgrim*. Prod *Patrick Matthews*. Scr *Anthony Richardson*. PC *Cine-Industrial Productions*. Dis *Renown*. *53 mins. Cert U*
After relating the details of the discovery of the world's largest diamond in 1905, the story develops into a secret mission to Holland during the Second World War, to save her stock of diamonds falling into Nazi hands. An English officer and a Dutchman between them manage to spirit the gems away from under the Germans' noses. Little film stages its events with some conviction and excitement. LP *Frank Hawkins, Michael Medwin, Beth Moss, Campbell Singer, Gerik Schjelderup, Archie Duncan, Donald Ferguson, Toni McMillan, Alastair Hunter, Martin Wyldeck, Hamish Menzies, Arthur Mullard, Fred Beck, Sydney Benson, Cyril Conway.*

OTHELLO (1946) [2]
Dir *David Mackane*. Prod and PC *Henry Halstead*. Ph *Stanley Clinton*. Dis *Exclusive*. *46 mins. Cert A*
Four players in a précis version of Shakespeare's play about the jealous Moor who strangles his wife. Not very useful to schools or general audiences, although *John Slater* gives a powerful account of the title role.
RoC *Luanne Shaw, Sebastian Cabot, Sheila Raynor.*

THE OVERLANDERS (1946) [5]
Dir and Scr *Harry Watt*. (Associate) Prod *Ralph Smart*. Ph *Osmond Borradaile*. PC *Ealing Studios*. Dis *Eagle-Lion*. *91 mins. Cert U*
1942: Japan menaces northern Australia, which decides on a scorched earth policy. But drover Dan McAlpine (*Chips Rafferty*) resolves to save 1,000 head of cattle by driving them to Queensland nearly 2,000 miles away. He takes one family and a few volunteers, sets out, and,

after a hazardous passage, achieves his aim. Flying back, he sees thousands more cattle on the overland trail he blazed. The best of Ealing's Australian films, with exciting, almost documentary like thrills and remarkable sequences of cattle on the run.
RoC *Daphne Campbell, John Nugent Hayward, Jean Blue, John Fernside, Helen Grieve, Peter Pagan, Frank Ransome, Clyde Combo, Stan Tolhurst, Marshall Crosby, John Fegan, Henry Murdoch.*

Chips Rafferty in The Overlanders (*1946*)

P

PACK UP YOUR TROUBLES (1940) [3]
Dir *Oswald Mitchell*. Prod *F.W. Baker*. Scr *Reginald Purdell, Milton Hayward*. Ph *Geoffrey Faithfull*. PC and Dis *Butchers*. *75 mins. Cert U*
Garage proprietor Tommy joins up to fight the Germans, but he and his pal Eric are captured in France. By a trick (Eric is a ventriloquist), they capture the commandant and a Gestapo officer and lock them in a safe. They are granted leave in reward for valuable information found in the officer's uniform and Tommy decides to marry Sally (*Patricia Roc*), a girl in the ATS. Story is nothing, but *Reginald Purdell* and *Wylie Watson* are quite funny together and score includes title number, plus *Roll Out the Barrel* and *Goodbye Sally*.
Roc *Wally Patch, Muriel George, Ernest Butcher, Manning Whiley, George (G.H.) Mulcaster, Meinhart Maur, Leonie Lamartine, Yvonne André.*

PAINTED BOATS (1945) [3]
(USA: *The Girl on the Canal*)
Dir *Charles Crichton*. (Associate) Prod *Henry Cornelius*. Scr *Stephen Black, Michael McCarthy, Louis MacNeice* (commentary). Ph *Douglas Slocombe*. PC and Dis *Ealing Studios*. *63 mins. Cert U*
The Smiths and the Stoners are bargee families of Britain's canals. The horse-drawn Smiths are soon forced to join the Stoners in having motor-power. Pa Smith (*Bill Blewett*)

falls ill and dies. Ted Stoner (*Robert Griffith*) is called up and has to postpone his wedding to Mary Smith (*Jenny Laird*) who, unknown to him, is pregnant. Without Ted, the Stoners give up their boat. Their youngest son joins the Smiths. Leisurely film of some charm.
RoC *Harry Fowler, May Hallatt, Madoline Thomas, Megs Jenkins, Grace Arnold, John Owers, James McKechnie* (narrator).

PANIC AT MADAME TUSSAUD'S (1948) [1]
Dir *Peter Graham Scott*. Prod *Roger Proudlock*. Scr *Proudlock, Scott, Sam Lee*. Ph *S.D. Onions*. PC *Vandyke*. Dis *Exclusive*. *49 mins. Cert A*
A thief hides the proceeds of a jewel robbery under the feet of a model at Madame Tussaud's waxworks. Various people try to get their hands on the gems, including a burglar, the jewels' owner, two crooks, a night watchman and the police. Their paths converge in a free-for-all in the Chamber of Horrors. Fourth-rate comedy.
LP *Harry Locke, Harry Fine, Patricia Owens, Ivan Craig, Frances Clare, Sam Lee.*

PAPER ORCHID (1949) [2]
Dir *Roy Baker*. Prod *William Collier, John R. Sloan*. Scr *Val Guest, from the novel by Arthur la Bern*. Ph *Basil Emmott*. PC *Ganesh*. Dis *Columbia*. *86 mins. Cert A*
When the *Daily National* changes hands, many of its staff go to the rival *World Record*. The two papers are soon in hot competition over the story of a man found murdered in the flat of gossip writer Stella Mason (*Hy Hazell*), known as The Orchid. Freddy Evans (*Sidney James*), *National* crime reporter, finally admits to having killed the man while drunk; he throws himself under a train. Thriller has good credentials, but carries little conviction.
RoC *Hugh Williams, Garry Marsh, Andrew Cruickshank, Ivor Barnard, Hughie Green, Vida Hope, Walter Hudd, Ella Retford, Frederick Leister, Kenneth Morgan, Vernon Greeves, Patricia Owens, Rolf Lefebvre, Roger Moore, The Ray Ellington Quartet.*

THE PASSIONATE FRIENDS (1948) [4]
(USA: *One Woman's Story*)
Dir *David Lean*. Prod *Eric Ambler*. Scr *Ambler, Lean, Stanley Haynes, from the novel by H.G. Wells*. Ph *Guy Green*. PC *Cineguild*. Dis *General Film Distributors*. *95 mins. Cert A*
Mary (*Ann Todd*) and Steven (*Trevor Howard*) have been lovers before her marriage to Howard (*Claude Rains*) and again five years later. Howard has forgiven her, on condition she does not see Steven again. They meet by accident nine years later, and spend an innocent day together. Howard finds out and says he will divorce her. Mary tries to throw herself under a tube train, but Howard, contrite, saves her. Sensitive, entertaining romantic drama.
RoC *Betty Ann Davies, Isabel Dean, Arthur Howard, Wilfrid Hyde White, Guido Lorraine, Marcel Poncin, Natasha Sokolova, Helen Burls, Jean Serret, Frances Waring, Wanda Rogerson, Helen Piers, Ina Pelly, John Hudson, Max Earl.*

PASSPORT TO PIMLICO (1948)   6

Dir *Henry Cornelius*. (Associate) Prod *E.H. Emmett*. Scr *T.E.B. Clarke, Cornelius*. Ph *Lionel Banes*. PC *Ealing Studios*. Dis *General Film Distributors. 85 mins. Cert U*

An unexploded bomb is detonated in Pimlico, revealing secret documents saying Pimlico belongs to Burgundy. The inhabitants declare themselves Burgundians. Pubs are open day and night. Black marketeers flourish. The Home Office can't cope: the United Nations is called in. Water, electricity and other supplies are cut but, putting up barbed wire and accepting food parcels from friends, Pimlico holds out until an honourable settlement is reached. Delightfully inventive comedy, brilliantly executed: funny too.

LP *Stanley Holloway, Barbara Murray, Margaret Rutherford, Paul Dupuis, Betty Warren, Jane Hylton, Basil Radford, Naunton Wayne, Raymond Huntley, Hermione Baddeley, John Slater, Frederick Piper, Sydney Tafler, Charles Hawtrey, James Hayter, Philip Stainton, Roy Carr, Nancy Gabrielle, Stuart Lindsell, Gilbert Davis, Michael Hordern, Arthur Howard, Bill Shine, Sam Kydd, Joey Carr, Lloyd Pearson, Arthur Denton, Tommy Godfrey, Masoni, Fred Griffiths, Grace Arnold, Paul Demel, Michael Knight, Roy Gladdish, Harry Locke, E.H. Emmett, Bernard Farrel, Michael Craig (extra).*

Barbara Murray and Stanley Holloway in Passport to Pimlico *(1949)*

PASTOR HALL (1940)   5

Dir *Roy Boulting*. Prod *John Boulting*. Scr *Leslie Arliss, Anna Reiner, Haworth Bromley, from the play by Ernst Toller*. Ph *Mutz Greenbaum*. PC *Charter*. Dis *Grand National. 97 mins. Cert A*

In the German village of Altdorf in 1934, oppression by the new Nazi regime causes Lina (*Lina Barrie*) to commit suicide. The pastor (*Wilfrid Lawson*) denounces the Nazis and urges the village to resist. He is arrested and sent to a concentration camp. A former villager (*Bernard Miles*) helps him escape, but he returns to his church to preach a last sermon. As he leaves, he is shot by stormtroopers 'while trying to escape'. Vividly tragic drama.

RoC *Nova Pilbeam, Seymour Hicks, Marius Goring, Percy Walsh, Peter Cotes, Brian Worth, Hay Petrie, Eliot Makeham, Manning Whiley, Edmund Willard, J. Fisher White, Barbara Gott, Raymond Rollett.*

THE PATIENT VANISHES (1941)

See *This Man is Dangerous* (1941).

PENN OF PENNSYLVANIA (1941)   3
(USA: *The Courageous Mr Penn*)

Dir *Lance Comfort*. Prod *Richard Vernon*. Scr *Anatole de Grunwald, from a book by C.E. Vulliamy*. Ph *Ernest Palmer*. PC *British National*. Dis *Anglo-American. 79 mins. Cert A*

The political activities of Quaker William Penn (*Clifford Evans*) get him thrown into prison. Granted land in America on his release, he and his followers cross the Atlantic, fighting a smallpox epidemic on the way. Returning to England, Penn finds his wife (*Deborah Kerr*) dying, and has to be persuaded to return to America, where he organizes law and order, makes peace with the Indians, and completes the building of the city of Philadelphia. Biopic is worthy, a bit dull.

RoC *Dennis Arundell, Aubrey Mallalieu, O.B. Clarence, James Harcourt, D.J. Williams, Charles Carson, Henry Oscar, Max Adrian, John Stuart, Maire O'Neill, Edward Rigby, Joss Ambler, J.H. Roberts, Edmund Willard, Percy Marmont, Gibb McLaughlin, Herbert Lomas, Gus McNaughton, David Farrar, Mary Hinton, Vincent Holman, G.H. Mulcaster, Lawrence Hanray, John Slater, David Keir, Frank Atkinson, Arthur Goullet, Boy Raynor, Hwfa Pryse, Andrea Troubridge, Nina Alvis, Henry Hewitt, W.E. Holloway, Manning Whiley, Drusilla Wills, Arthur Dent, Gordon Begg, Amy Dalby, Escott Davis, Arthur Hambling, Rosamund Greenwood, Ben Williams, Tom Quinn, James Knight, Sam Kydd, Henry Hallett, Angela Glynne, Pat Sawyer.*

PENNY AND THE POWNALL CASE (1947)   2

Dir *Slim Hand*. Prod *John Corfield*. Scr *William Fairchild*. Ph *Jimmy Harvey*. PC *Production Facilities*. Dis *General Film Distributors. 47 mins. Cert A*

Model Penny (*Peggy Evans*) is a keen amateur 'tec. Learning that Pownall, a secret serviceman, has been murdered, she goes to Spain, scene of the crime. She is accompanied by her boss, Blair (*Christopher Lee*), whom she discovers to be a traitor working for the escape of Nazi war criminals. Aided by Inspector Carson (*Ralph Michael*), she exposes Blair's network and unmasks Pownall's killer. First of many Rank-backed 'B' features for quota purposes.

RoC *Diana Dors, Frederick Piper, Olaf Pooley, Ethel Coleridge, Sam Costa, Dennis Vance, Duncan Carse, Shaun Noble, Philip Saville, John Lorrell, Peter Madden.*

PERFECT STRANGERS (1945)   4
(USA: *Vacation from Marriage*)

Dir and Prod *Alexander Korda*. Scr *Clemence Dane, Anthony Pelissier*. Ph *Georges Périnal*. PC *M-G-M/London Films*. Dis *M-G-M. 102 mins. Cert A*

War interrupts the staid marriage of Robert (*Robert Donat*) and Catherine (*Deborah Kerr*). He joins the navy, she the Wrens. They become different people, each having a fling with another partner. Neither looks forward to seeing the other again after three years, each

Deborah Kerr and Robert Donat in Perfect Strangers *(1945)*

thinking of divorce. But, during a long night together, they surprise each other, part and come together again. Topical theme, handled with kid gloves. Academy Award for Best Original Story.

RoC *Glynis Johns, Ann Todd, Roland Culver, Elliot Mason, Eliot Makeham, Brefni O'Rorke, Edward Rigby, Muriel George, Allan Jeayes, Henry Longhurst, Billy Shine, Billy Thatcher, Brian Weske, Rosamund Taylor, Harry Ross, Vincent Holman, Leslie Dwyer, Caven Watson, Jeanne Carre, Molly Munks, Roger Moore, Bill Rowbotham, Ivor Barnard.*

THE PERFECT WOMAN (1949)   4

Dir *Bernard Knowles*. Prod *George and Alfred Black*. Scr *Knowles, George Black, J.B. Boothroyd, from the play by Wallace Geoffrey, Basil Mitchell*. Ph *Jack Hildyard*. PC *Two Cities*. Dis *General Film Distributors. 89 mins. Cert A*

Professor's niece Penelope (*Patricia Roc*) decides to take the place of his invention, a robot woman modelled on herself. Two men (*Nigel Patrick, Stanley Holloway*) have been engaged to take 'Olga' to a hotel. The situation is soon out of hand, and Penelope phones her father's housekeeper (*Irene Handl*) for the real robot. She is found out, but falls for one of her 'escorts'. Good rollicking fun that never lets up; successfully silly.

RoC *Miles Malleson, Anita Sharp-Bolster, Fred Berger, David Hurst, Pamela Devis, Constance Smith, Patti Morgan, Noel Howlett.*

THE PETERVILLE DIAMOND (1942)   3

Dir *Walter Forde*. Prod *Max Milner*. Scr *Gordon Wellesley, Brock Williams*. Ph *Basil Emmott*. PC and Dis *Warner Bros. 85 mins. Cert U*

Teri (*Anne Crawford*) longs for romance, but, although they travel through exotic South American republics, her husband (*Donald Stewart*) is obsessed with business. He does, however, buy her the fabulous Peterville Diamond. But a charming thief (*Oliver Wakefield*) locks Teri's husband and friend in a strong room: he wants the diamond and Teri, although he ultimately emerges with neither. Some bright dialogue keeps this fragile enterprise afloat.

RoC *Renee Houston, Charles Heslop, Bill Hartnell, Felix Aylmer, Charles Victor, Joss Ambler, Paul Sheridan, Jeremy Hawk, Julian Somers, Rosamund Greenwood, Leo de Pokorny.*

THE PHANTOM SHOT (1947)   3

Dir and Prod *Mario Zampi*. Scr *Walter C. Mycroft, Norman Lee*. Ph *Bryan Langley*. PC *International Talking Pictures*. Dis *International Film Renters*. 49 mins. Cert A
Cheeky little thriller in which the audience is invited to spot the murderer of unpleasant Caleb Horder (*Ronald Adam*) before the police, led by Inspector Webb (*John Stuart*). There is no lack of suspects, all with motives. But it's Angus the poacher (*Jock McKay*) who proves to hold the key to the mystery! Not great, but confidently made and a pleasant change.
RoC *Olga Lindo, Howard Marion Crawford, Louise Lord, John Varley, Cyril Conway, Leslie Armstrong*.

PICCADILLY INCIDENT (1946)   3

Dir and Prod *Herbert Wilcox*. Scr *Nicholas Phipps*. Ph *Max Greene (Mutz Greenbaum)*. PC *Associated British*. Dis *Pathé*. 102 mins. Cert A
A Wren, Diana (*Anna Neagle*), and Royal Marine officer (*Michael Wilding*) meet during an air-raid and marry. After the fall of Singapore, she is reported missing at sea. Three years later he marries again, and has a son. Diana returns, having been marooned on an island, but soon sees her presence is a disaster and pretends she wants a divorce. She dies in another air-raid. Slow, but at times movingly done. A big box-office hit, it established the stars as one of Britain's most potent post-war teams.
RoC *Michael Laurence, Frances Mercer, Coral Browne, A.E. Matthews, Edward Rigby, Brenda Bruce, Leslie Dwyer, Maire O'Neill, Neville Mapp, Duncan McIntyre, Michael Medwin, Madge Brindley, Roger Moore, Harry Locke*.

A PIECE OF CAKE (1948)   2

Dir *John Irwin*. Prod *Adrian Worker*. Scr *Bernard McNab, Lyn Lockwood, Dick Pepper*. Ph *Walter Harvey*. PC *Production Facilities*. Dis *General Film Distributors*. 46 mins. Cert U
Cyril (*Cyril Fletcher*) dreams that a magician he created in fiction has come to life. Supplied with several forbidden post-war luxuries, Cyril finds himself in trouble with the police, food inspectors and black-marketeers alike. Getting ambitious, the sorcerer kidnaps Cyril's wife (*Betty Astell*). Cyril rescues her, then wakes up. Heavy little comedy with a few bright moments.
RoC *Laurence Naismith, Jon Pertwee, Sam Costa, Harry Fowler, Sam Kydd, Tamara Lees, Duncan Lewis, Sandra Dorne, Anthony Steel*.

PIMPERNEL SMITH (1941)   4
(USA: *Mister V*)

Dir and Prod *Leslie Howard*. Scr *Anatole de Grunwald, Roland Pertwee, Ian Dalrymple, from a novel by A.G. MacDonnell*. Ph *Mutz Greenbaum*. PC *British National*. Dis *Anglo-Amalgamated*. 121 mins. Cert U
Under a veneer of absent-mindedness, university professor Horatio Smith (*Leslie Howard*) helps refugees escape the Gestapo. After he is wounded, the undergraduates, whose Swiss archaeological 'dig' has been his cover, realize his identity and help him rescue more people. Smith later goes alone to Berlin to bring out a girl who is helping the Nazis to (she thinks) save her father, and succeeds. Excellent acting, especially from Howard, cloaks the holes in the plot.
RoC *Francis L. Sullivan, Mary Morris, Hugh McDermott, Raymond Huntley, Manning Whiley, Peter Gawthorne, Allan Jeayes, Dennis Arundell, Joan Kemp-Welch, Philip Friend, Lawrence Kitchen, David Tomlinson, Basil Appleby, Percy Walsh, Roland Pertwee, Suzanne Claire, A.E. Matthews, Charles Paton, Aubrey Mallalieu, George Street, Oriel Ross, Bryan Herbert, Arthur Hambling, Ronald Howard, Ben Williams, Roddy Hughes*.

PINK STRING AND SEALING WAX (1945)   3

Dir *Robert Hamer*. (Associate) Prod *S.C. Balcon*. Scr *Diana Morgan, Hamer, from the play by Roland Pertwee*. Ph *Richard Pavey*. PC *Ealing Studios*. Dis *Eagle-Lion*. 89 mins. Cert A
1880. Brighton chemist Edward Sutton (*Mervyn Johns*) rules his family with a rod of iron. Rebelling, David Sutton (*Gordon Jackson*) goes to the seafront pub run by Pearl (*Googie Withers*), faithless wife of the proprietor Joe (*Garry Marsh*). David is as fascinated by her as she is by the strychnine in his father's shop. Joe dies from poison. The body is exhumed and Pearl threatens to involve David if Sutton talks. He refuses and she throws herself into the sea. Slow but strong stuff.
RoC *Sally Ann Howes, Mary Merrall, John Carol, Catherine Lacey, Jean Ireland, Frederick Piper, Maudie Edwards, Pauline Letts, Margaret Ritchie, Don Stannard, Colin Simpson, David Wallbridge, John Owers, Helen Goss, John Ruddock, Ronald Adam, Charles Carson, Valentine Dyall, David Keir*.

Googie Withers and Gordon Jackson in Pink String and Sealing Wax *(1945)*

A PLACE OF ONE'S OWN (1945)   5

Dir *Bernard Knowles*. Prod *R.J. Minney*. Scr *Brock Williams, from the novel by Osbert Sitwell*. Ph *Stephen Dade*. PC *Gainsborough*. Dis *Eagle-Lion*. 92 mins. Cert A
Mr and Mrs Smedhurst (*James Mason, Barbara Mullen*) retire and buy a splendid country house which has a reputation for hauntings. Their companion/secretary Annette (*Margaret Lockwood*) is the centre of strange happenings which culminate in her being laid low by a

James Mason, Margaret Lockwood and Barbara Mullen in A Place of One's Own *(1945)*

mystery illness. Delirious, she asks for Dr Marsham (*Ernest Thesiger*) who attended the dead girl murdered there 40 years before. Dr Marsham comes and Annette is cured. Later the Smedhursts are told that Marsham was found dead several hours before he appeared at the house. Eerie spinechiller with elegant, light touch.
RoC *Dennis Price, Helen Haye, Michael Shepley, Dulcie Gray, Moore Marriott, Gus MacNaughton, O.B. Clarence, John Turnbull, Clarence Wright, Helen Goss, Edie Martin, Muriel George, Henry Longhurst, Aubrey Mallalieu*.

PLAYTIME FOR WORKERS (1943)   2

Dir and Prod *Harold Baim*. *No further credits issued*. PC and Dis *Federated*. 51 mins. Cert U
Gerry Wilmott is compère of a series of turns from regulars on the radio show *Workers' Playtime*. Most of them lack confidence in front of a camera.
RoC *Kay Cavendish, Scott Sanders, Bill Smith, Stan Shedden and His Orchestra*.

POET'S PUB (1949)   3

Dir *Frederick Wilson*. Prod *Donald B. Wilson*. Scr *Diana Morgan, from the novel by Eric Linklater*. Ph *George Stretton*. PC *Aquila*. Dis *General Film Distributors*. 79 mins. Cert U
Saturday Keith (*Derek Bond*), rowing blue and would-be poet, takes over the management of an old inn, the Downy Pelican. With the help of a friend, Quentin (*Peter Croft*), it's a great success. While Professor Benbow (*James Robertson Justice*), who condemned Saturday's first poems, and his daughter Joanna (*Rona Anderson*) are staying there, two crooks arrive in search of a jewelled gauntlet. Joanna is kidnapped, but Saturday rescues her and defeats the criminals. Mild character comedy-thriller.
RoC *Leslie Dwyer, John McLaren, Barbara Murray, Joyce Grenfell, Fabia Drake, Iris Hoey, Andrew Osborn, Kay Cavendish, Maurice Denham, Leslie Weston, Geoffrey Dunn, Roddy Hughes, Philip Stainton, Joan Sterndale-Bennett, Alexander Field, Sam Kydd, Dorothy Green, Ann Codrington, Olwen Brookes, Arthur Lowe, Mona Harris, Anthony Steel*.

PORTRAIT FROM LIFE (1948)   4
(USA: *The Girl in the Painting*)

Dir *Terence Fisher*. Prod *Antony Darnborough*. Scr *Muriel and Sydney Box, Frank Harvey*. Ph

Jack Asher, Len Harris. PC Gainsborough. Dis General Film Distributors. 90 mins. Cert A
An Austrian professor (Arnold Marle) believes a girl in a painting to be his missing daughter. A British officer (Guy Rolfe) tries to help him find her, but the artist (Robert Beatty) dies in an alcoholic fit. Searching European displaced persons' camps, the officer finds the girl (Mai Zetterling) by chance. She had been forcibly adopted by a war criminal (Herbert Lom) – but a childhood memory restores her identity. Imaginative, well-acted drama with realistic detail.
RoC Patrick Holt, Sybilla Binder, Thora Hird, Gerard Heinz, Yvonne Owen, Ernest Thesiger, John Blythe, George Thorpe, Philo Hauser, Cyril Chamberlain, Betty Lynne, Nellie Arno, Richard Molinas, Donald Sinden, Hugo Schuster, Eric Messiter, Dorothea Glade, Michael Hordern, Peter Murray, Gordon Bell, Sam Kydd, Eric Pohlmann, Anthony Steel.

THE PRIME MINISTER (1941) [3]
Dir Thorold Dickinson. Prod Max Milder. Scr Brock Williams, Michael Hogan. Ph Basil Emmott. PC and Dis Warner Bros. 109 mins. Cert U
Events in England 1837–78, centring on Benjamin Disraeli (John Gielgud). Originally a novelist, he becomes a politician and, under the loving guidance of his wife (Diana Wynyard), prime minister in 1868 and again from 1874 to 1880, his greatest triumph being to bring England back from the brink of war in 1878. Soporific history lesson lacks flesh and blood characters.
RoC Stephen Murray, Owen Nares, Fay Compton, Will Fyffe, Lyn Harding, Pamela Standish, Leslie Perrins, Vera Bogetti, Anthony Ireland, Irene Browne, Frederick Leister, Nicholas Hannen, Barbara Everest, Kynaston Reeves, Gordon McLeod, Glynis Johns, Margaret Johnston, Joss Ambler, Nadine March, Andrea Troubridge, John Patience, Hugh Beckett, J. Walters.

PRIVATE ANGELO (1949) [2]
Dir and Scr Peter Ustinov, Michael Anderson, from the novel by Eric Linklater. Prod Ustinov. Ph Erwin Hillier. PC Pilgrim. Dis Associated British-Pathé. 106 mins. Cert A
An Italian private, Angelo (Ustinov) spends the Second World War trying to escape it, and to get back to his home town and his girlfriend Lucrezia (Maria Denis). He and she are eventually married after the surrender of Italy, despite the fact that she has a son whose father, a British corporal, is best man at the wedding. Angelo has to fight again, but loses a hand and his military career is mercifully over. A few funny moments, but not enough.
RoC Godfrey Tearle, James Robertson Justice, Robin Bailey, Marjorie Rhodes, Moyna McGill, Harry Locke, Bill Shine, John Harvey, Norman Watson, Peter Humphries, Peter Jones, Rupert Davies, Diana Graves, Arthur Howard, Dervis Ward, Philo Hauser, Ernest Clark, George Bradford, Conrad Tom, John McKnight, John Garson, William C. Tubbs, Brenda Hogan.

QUARTET (1948) [4]
Dir Ralph Smart, Harold French, Arthur Crabtree, Ken Annakin. Prod Antony Darnborough. Ph Ray Elton, Reg Wyer. PC Gainsborough/Sydney Box. Dis General Film Distributors. 120 mins. Cert A
Four stories from the works of W. Somerset Maugham: in The Facts of Life, Henry (Basil Radford) allows his son Nicky (Jack Watling) to play tennis in Monte Carlo, warning him about gambling and women. But Nicky proves successful with both. In The Alien Corn, George (Dirk Bogarde) trains to be a concert pianist. Told he will never make the grade, he commits suicide. In The Kite, Herbert (George Cole) and Betty (Susan Shaw) split up because of his passion for kites, but are reunited at the end of one. In The Colonel's Lady, a colonel (Cecil Parker) who worries over love poems published by his wife (Nora Swinburne) finds that the object of her affections was his younger self. Well-made portmanteau movie.
RoC Naunton Wayne, Mai Zetterling, James Robertson Justice, Angela Baddeley, Jean Cavall, Ian Fleming, Jack Raine, Nigel Buchanan; Françoise Rosay, Raymond Lovell, Honor Blackman, Irene Browne, George Thorpe, Mary Hinton, Maurice Denham, James Hayter, Russell Barry, Henry Morrell, Ben Williams, Marcel Poncin, Molly Mainwaring, Cecil Paul, Harman Phelps; Mervyn Johns, Hermione Baddeley, Bernard Lee, Frederick Leister, George Merritt, David Cole, Cyril Chamberlain; Linden Travers, Ernest Thesiger, Felix Aylmer, Henry Edwards, Claud Allister, J.H. Roberts, Lyn Evans, Cyril Raymond, Wilfrid Hyde White, John Salew, Margaret Withers, Yvonne Owen, Margaret Thorburn, Hal Osmond, Ernest Butcher, Clive Morton, Harcourt Williams, Mary Eaton.

THE QUEEN OF SPADES (1948) [4]
Dir Thorold Dickinson. Prod Anatole de Grunwald. Scr Rodney Ackland, Arthur Boys, from the novel by Alexander Pushkin. Ph Otto Heller. PC Associated British/World Screenplays. Dis Associated British-Pathé. 95 mins. Cert A
1806. Herman (Anton Walbrook), a Russian officer, is determined to wrench from an aged countess (Edith Evans) the secret of winning at cards, for which she has sold her soul to the devil. Seducing her companion (Yvonne Mitchell), he gains admittance by a secret stairway – but frightens the countess to death without gaining the secret. Dreaming that he has it, he plays cards – and his winning ace turns into the Queen of Spades with the grinning face of the countess. Baroque chiller with richly decadent decor.
RoC Mary Jerrold, Ronald Howard, Anthony Dawson, Miles Malleson, Athene Seyler, Michael Medwin, Pauline Tennant, Ivor Barnard,

Valentine Dyall, Yusef Ramart, Gibb McLaughlin, Jacqueline Clarke, Gordon Begg, Aubrey Mallalieu, Drusilla Wills, George Woodbridge, Pauline Jameson, Hay Petrie, Brown Derby, Ian Colin, Clements McCallin, John Howard, Aubrey Woods, David Paltenghi, Violetta Elvin, Maroussia Dmitravitch.

QUIET WEDDING (1941) [5]
Dir Anthony Asquith. Prod Paul Soskin. Scr Terence Rattigan, Anatole de Grunwald, from the play by Esther McCracken. Ph Bernard Knowles. PC Conqueror. Dis Paramount. 80 mins. Cert A
Janet (Margaret Lockwood) and Dallas (Derek Farr) would like a quiet wedding. But their romance is nearly wrecked by all the preparations. Wise Aunt Mary (Athene Seyler) encourages Dallas to 'kidnap' Janet and take her to the flat where they are to live. This settles all their differences and, despite their arrest by the local policeman and appearance in court, the wedding goes through. Nice film, full of comic subtlety, kindly caricature and spiky wit.
RoC Marjorie Fielding, A.E. Matthews, Margaretta Scott, Peggy Ashcroft, Frank Cellier, Roland Culver, Jean Cadell, David Tomlinson, Sydney King, Michael Shepley, Roddy Hughes, Muriel Pavlow, O.B. Clarence, Margaret Rutherford, Wally Patch, Bernard Miles, Martita Hunt, Muriel George, Margaret Halstan, Hay Petrie, Valentine Dunn, Amy Dalby, Viola Lyel, Charles Carson, Lawrence Hanray, Mark Stone, R. Brodis-Turner, Peter Bull, Ivor Barnard, Mike Johnson, Esma Cannon.

QUIET WEEKEND (1946) [3]
Dir Harold French. Prod Warwick Ward. Scr Ward, Victor Skutezky, Stephen Black, T.J. Morrison, from the play by Esther McCracken. Ph Eric Cross. PC Associated British. Dis Pathé. 93 mins. Cert U
Sequel to Quiet Wedding. Mr and Mrs Royd (George Thorpe, Marjorie Fielding) arrive with their son Denys (Derek Farr), a married daughter, her husband and baby at their country cottage. Denys, however, has invited a frightful girlfriend (Helen Shingler) who upsets everyone before the 'quiet weekend' is over. Not bad, but pretty thin and uninspired compared to the original.
RoC Barbara White, Frank Cellier, Edward Rigby, Josephine Wilson, Gwen Whitby, Ballard Berkeley, Judith Furse, Pat Field, Helen Burls, George Merritt, Christopher Steele, Mary Matthew, Conway Palmer, Brian Weske, Richard George.

RAINBOW ROUND THE CORNER (1943) [1]
Dir Victor M. Gover. Prod Burt Hyams. Scr

Robin Richmond, Edward Eve. PC Berkeley. Dis *Premier*. 52 mins. (later 47). Cert U

Inspired by a statement from then Foreign Secretary Anthony Eden about 'a highway from Edinburgh to Chunking', this failed documentary/revue puts musical backgrounds and numbers to the countries along this route.
LP *Daphne Day, Billy 'Uke' Scott, Vera Bradley, The Boswell Twins, Chappie d'Amato, Robin Richmond, The Gordon Ray Girls.*

THE RAKE'S PROGRESS (1945)   4
(USA: *Notorious Gentleman*)
Dir *Sidney Gilliat*. Prod and Scr *Gilliat, Frank Launder*. Ph *Wilkie Cooper*. PC *Individual*. Dis *Eagle-Lion*. 124 mins. Cert A

Sent down from Oxford, Old Etonian Vivian (*Rex Harrison*) is found a job on a coffee plantation by his father, but muffs it. He seduces his best friend's (*Griffith Jones*) wife (*Jean Kent*), swindles an Austrian (*Lilli Palmer*) after marrying her for money and drives her to attempt suicide over his affair with his father's secretary (*Margaret Johnston*), whom he leaves to go to war where he is unheroically killed. Polished, sometimes touching catalogue of cadsmanship. Had troubles with the Hollywood censors.
RoC *Godfrey Tearle, Guy Middleton, Marie Lohr, Garry Marsh, David Horne, Alan Wheatley, Brefni O'Rorke, Charles Victor, Joan Maude, Patricia Laffan, Emrys Jones, Howard Marion Crawford, John Salew, Olga Lindo, David Wallbridge, John Dodsworth, Jack Vyvyan, Frederick Burtwell, George Cross, Kynaston Reeves, Jan van Loewen, Howard Douglas, Joy Frankau, Maureen McDermot, Jack Melford, David Ward, Sheila Huntington, Frank Phillips and Sidney Gilliat (voices only).*

THE RED SHOES (1948)   5
Dir and Prod *Michael Powell, Emeric Pressburger*. Scr *Pressburger, Keith Wilbur, partly from the story by Hans Christian Andersen*. Ph *Jack Cardiff*. PC *The Archers/Independent Producers*. Dis *General Film Distributors*. 134 mins. Cert A

Ballerina Vicky Page (*Moira Shearer*) and composer Julian Craster (*Marius Goring*) join the famous Lermontov (*Anton Walbrook*) ballet company. Vicky falls in love with Julian and is groomed for the lead in his ballet *The Red Shoes*, which is a great success. But Lermontov demands she choose between her career and her lover. The strain is too great. Vicky throws herself in the path of a train. Commonplace plot, but brilliant ballet scenes. The whole film is superb to look at. Oscars for best colour, art direction and best background score.
RoC *Robert Helpmann, Leonide Massine, Albert Basserman, Ludmilla Tcherina, Esmond Knight, Irene Browne, Austin Trevor, Marcel Poncin, Jerry Verno, Jean Short, Gordon Littman, Julia Lang, Bill Shine, Eric Berry, Derek Elphinstone, Madame Rambert, Joy Rawlins, Michael Bazalgette, Yvonne André, Hay Petrie.*

RHYTHM SERENADE (1943)   3
Dir *Gordon Wellesley*. Prod *Ben Henry, George Formby*. Scr *Marjorie Deans, Basil Woon, Mar-*

garet Kennedy, Edward Dryhurst. Ph *Bert Mason, Erwin Hillier, Geoffrey Faithfull*. PC and Dis *Columbia British*. 87 mins. Cert U

Teacher Ann Martin (*Vera Lynn*) is persuaded to run a nursery school for a munitions factory. She tries to rent the empty house next door to her flat for the school, but finds a man (*Peter Murray Hill*) living in a cottage in the garden. Unknown to her, he owns the house, and arranges for the nursery to be run there. After a few misunderstandings, Ann agrees to marry him. Direction holds together unstable mixture of propaganda, music, sentiment and comedy.
RoC *Julien Mitchell, Charles Victor, Jimmy Jewel, Ben Warriss, Joss Ambler, Rosalyn Boulter, Betty Jardine, Irene Handl, Lloyd Pearson, Jimmy Clitheroe, Joan Kemp-Welch, Aubrey Mallalieu, Maurice Rhodes, Peter Madden.*

RIVER PATROL (1947)   2
Dir *Ben R. Hart*. Prod *Hal Wilson*. Scr *James Corbett*. Ph *Brooks-Carrington*. PC and Dis *Knightsbridge*. 45 mins. Cert A

A young customs agent (*John Blythe*) and his girlfriend (*Lorna Dean*) get on to the scent of a gang of nylon smugglers. Thanks to a clue in the form of a gambling chip, they trace the gang's headquarters to a waterfront dive. After a fight in a burning warehouse, the gang is rounded up. Unambitious pocket thriller.
RoC *Wally Patch, Stan Paskin, Cyril Collins, Wilton West, Johnny Doherty, George Crowther, Tony Murray, Iris Keen, Andrew Sterne, George Lane, Dolly Gwynne.*

THE ROCKING HORSE WINNER (1949)   4
Dir and Scr *Anthony Pelissier, from the story by D.H. Lawrence*. Prod *John Mills*. Ph *Desmond Dickinson*. PC *Two Cities*. Dis *Rank*. 90 mins. Cert A

Hester (*Valerie Hobson*) is an ambitious woman resolved to live as extravagantly as she can. Her son Paul (*John Howard Davies*) sees that money is the thing that could restore stability to a marriage threatened by the loss of his father's job. His imagination fired by Bassett (*John Mills*), the groom, Paul rides his rocking horse, imagining himself a jockey, and naming horses which all prove winners. The money piles up, but Paul cracks, dying even as his last horse wins £80,000. An embittered Hester orders the rocking horse burnt and the money given to charity. A bit stretched from a short story, but generally absorbing, superbly photographed drama.
RoC *Ronald Squire, Hugh Sinclair, Charles Goldner, Susan Richards, Cyril Smith, Antony Holles, Melanie McKenzie, Caroline Steer, Michael Ripper.*

THE ROMANTIC AGE (1949)   2
(USA: *Naughty Arlette*)
Dir *Edmond T. Gréville*. Prod *Edward Dryhurst, Eric l'Epine Smith*. Scr *Dryhurst, Peggy Barwell, from a novel by Serge Weber*. Ph *Hone Glendinning*. PC *Pinnacle Productions*. Dis *General Film Distributors*. 86 mins. Cert A

A teacher (*Hugh Williams*) at a girls' finishing school is seduced by his daughter's classmate (*Mai Zetterling*) who feels that he has slighted

her. He eventually emerges sadder and wiser, his marriage still intact. Blundering comedy with over-age schoolgirls discomforts a lot of people, including the audience.
RoC *Margot Grahame, Petula Clark, Carol Marsh, Raymond Lovell, Paul Dupuis, Margaret Barton, Marie Ney, Mark Daly, Judith Furse, Betty Impey, Adrienne Corri, May Hallatt, Dorothy Latta, Jean Anderson, Viola Johnstone, Colette Melville, Brenda Cameron, Margaret Anderson, June Charlier, Christina Forrest, Christine Finn, Ann Smith, Mary Merritt, Betty Leslie Smith, Howard Douglas, Joan Kirkpatrick, Cecily Walper, Charlotte Mitchell, Margaret Ridgway, Walter Horsbrugh, Jacqueline Allerton, Susan Dudley.*

ROOM FOR TWO (1940)   2
Dir *Maurice Elvey*. Prod *Victor Catona*. Scr *Uncredited, from the play by Gilbert Wakefield*. Ph *Bernard Browne, Bryan Langley*. PC *Hurley*. Dis *Grand National*. 77 mins. Cert A

Michael (*Vic Oliver*) falls heavily for Clare (*Frances Day*), whose friend Hilda (*Greta Gynt*) is having an affair with Clare's husband Robert (*Basil Radford*). Michael dons drag and is engaged by Robert as Clare's new maid Sophie. Clare finds out about Hilda and decides to divorce Robert and marry Michael. Robert is upset by Hilda's dressmaker's bill and she has to start chasing him anew. Tired farce with dislikeable characters.
RoC *Hilda Bayley, Leo de (von) Pokorny, Magda Kun, Victor Rietti, Andrea Malandrinos, Rosamund Greenwood, Charles Goldner, Glenys Mortimer.*

Vic Oliver and Frances Day in Room for Two *(1940)*

ROOM TO LET (1949)   3
Dir *Godfrey Grayson*. Prod *Anthony Hinds*. Scr *John Gilling, Grayson, from a radio play by Margery Allingham*. Ph *Cedric Williams*. PC *Hammer*. Dis *Exclusive*. 68 mins. Cert A

1900. A strange doctor (*Valentine Dyall*) - at a home for mental cases - lodges with crippled Mrs Musgrave (*Christine Silver*) and her daughter Molly (*Constance Smith*). Gradually, he dominates the two women, making them virtual prisoners in their own home. They suspect he may be Jack the Ripper. A cub reporter (*Jimmy Hanley*) is finally successful in proving the man no doctor or Ripper, but an escaped lunatic. Well-acted; tedious at times
RoC *Merle Tottenham, Charles Hawtrey, J.*

Anthony la Penna, Reginald Dyson, Laurence Naismith, Aubrey Dexter, John Clifford, Stuart Sanders, Cyril Conway, Charles Houston, Harriet Petworth, Charles Mander, H. Hamilton Earle, F.A. Williams, Archie Callum.

THE ROOT OF ALL EVIL (1947) [1]

Dir and Scr *Brock Williams, from the novel by J.S. Fletcher.* Prod *Harold Huth.* Ph *Stephen Dade.* PC *Gainsborough.* Dis *General Film Distributors.* 110 mins. Cert A

By threatening a breach of promise action, Jeckie Farnish (*Phyllis Calvert*) gets enough money to start a rival business that ruins the man who refused to be her father-in-law. Next she buys land from a poor farmer, taking a partner (*Michael Rennie*) and exploiting the oil under the ground. She is attracted to her partner, but finds he is married. Then the ex-farmer sets fire to the refineries which are destroyed. Jeckie settles down with a farmhand (*John McCallum*) she has known since childhood. Dated histrionics.

RoC *Moore Marriott, Brefni O'Rorke, Hazel Court, Arthur Young, Hubert Gregg, Reginald Purdell, George Carney, George Merritt, Pat Hicks, Bryan Herbert, Rory McDermott, Diana Decker, Michael Medwin.*

ROSE OF TRALEE (1942) [2]

Dir *Germain Burger.* Prod *F.W. Baker.* Scr *Kathleen Butler, H.F. Maltby.* Ph *Jack Parker, Robert Krasker.* PC and Dis *Butchers.* 77 mins. Cert U

Remake of the 1937 musical weepie about an Irishman (*John Longden*) who, unable to support his wife and daughter, goes to America, where he succeeds as a singer. Returning to England at the outbreak of war, he finds that the wealthy uncle who was supporting the family has died, and his wife has vanished. He joins the RAF and, through a series of coincidences, the family is reunited. Hard to sit through.

RoC *Lesley Brook, Angela Glynne, Mabel Constanduros, Talbot O'Farrell, Gus McNaughton, George Carney, Virginia Keiley, Iris Vandeleur, Morris Harvey.*

ROVER AND ME (1948) [2]

Dir, Prod and Ph *Frank Chisnell.* Scr *Terry Sanford.* PC *FC Films.* Dis *Equity British.* 46 mins. Cert U

Orphan Tommy finds a thoroughbred dog. His foster-parents let him keep it - until they think it has killed one of their chickens. Tommy flees, staying with a tramp in an empty house. One night Tommy, the dog Rover and Tommy's friends Susan and Arnold get on the trail of smugglers and help the police catch them. Tommy and Rover find a new home with Susan and her father. Camera-conscious children spoil this one-man show.

LP *Keith Bartlett, Edward Rigby, Judy Edwards, Campbell Singer, Ninian Brodie, Pat Nye, Janet Borrow, Rover (the dog).*

A RUN FOR YOUR MONEY (1949) [4]

Dir *Charles Frend.* (Associate) Prod *Leslie Norman.* Scr *Frend, Norman, Richard Hughes, Diana Morgan, from a story by Clifford Evans.*

Ph *Douglas Slocombe.* PC *Ealing Studios.* Dis *General Film Distributors.* 85 mins. Cert A

Two Welsh miners (*Donald Houston, Meredith Edwards*) win a competition and come to London to collect their prize - £100 each and a visit to the England v Wales rugby match. One goes on a pub crawl, the other falls in with a con-girl (*Moira Lister*). They spend the money and don't get to see the match. Agreeable, friendly romp with the occasional very funny moment.

RoC *Alec Guinness, Hugh Griffith, Clive Morton, Leslie Perrins, Joyce Grenfell, Edward Rigby, Julie Milton, Peter Edwards, Dorothy Bramhall, Desmond Walter-Ellis, MacKenzie Ward, Patric Doonan, Andrew Leigh, R. Meadows White, Gabrielle Brune, Charles Cullum, Ronnie Haines, Diana Hope, Dudley Jones, David Davies, Tom Jones, Richard Littledale.*

S

SABOTAGE AT SEA (1942) [2]

Dir *Leslie Hiscott.* Prod *Elizabeth Hiscott.* Scr *Michael Barringer.* Ph *Günther Krampf.* PC *Shaftesbury/British National.* Dis *Anglo-American.* 74 mins. Cert U

Captain Tracey (*Dave - David - Hutcheson*) discovers his ship has been sabotaged. Suspecting several people, he puts to sea in the hope that the guilty party will confess if he thinks the ship is going down. His plan fails, but when a rigger is murdered, Tracey succeeds in connecting him with the saboteur and traps the guilty man into betraying himself. Too much not-very-good dialogue sinks thrills.

RoC *Jane Carr, Margaretta Scott, Wally Patch, Felix Aylmer, Martita Hunt, Billy (William) Hartnell, Ronald Shiner, Ralph Truman, Arthur Maude, Ian Fleming.*

SAILORS DON'T CARE (1940) [3]

Dir and Scr *Oswald Mitchell, from a story by W.W. Jacobs.* Prod *F.W. Baker.* Ph *Stephen Dade.* PC and Dis *Butchers.* 79 mins. Cert U

Boatbuilding father and son Joe and Nobby Clark (*Edward Rigby, Tom Gamble*) join the River Patrol service. They are 'vamped' by two nightclub girls mixed up, with their manager, in spy work. Manning a 'listening post' on the ship *Terrific*, Joe and Nobby see a parachutist landing in the river with a time bomb in his hands. They rescue him; Scotland Yard arrives and arrests the spy trio; the bomb blows up, drenching everyone. Simple, broad fooling.

RoC *Jean Gillie, Marion Gerth, Mavis Villiers, Michael Wilding, G.H. Mulcaster, John Salew, Henry B. Longhurst, Dennis Wyndham, Ian Maclean.*

SAILORS THREE (1940) [4]
(USA: *Three Cockeyed Sailors*)

Dir *Walter Forde.* (Associate) Prod *Culley*

Forde. Scr *Angus Macphail, John Dighton, Austin Melford.* Ph *Gunther Krampf.* PC *Ealing Studios.* Dis *Associated British.* 86 mins. Cert U

A comedy with music. Stranded in a South American port on a foggy night after a drunken spree, three British sailors (*Tommy Trinder, Michael Wilding, Claude Hulbert*) board a German pocket battleship in mistake for their own vessel. With the help of an Austrian sailor, they end up capturing the entire ship for the British fleet. Slow to get under way, but pretty funny in the end.

RoC *Carla Lehmann, Jeanne de Casalis, James Hayter, Henry Hewitt, John Laurie, Harold Warrender, John Glyn Jones, Julien Vedey, Manning Whiley, Robert Rendel, Allan Jeayes, Alec Clunes, Brian Fitzpatrick, Eric Clavering, Hans (John) Wengraf, Victor Fairley, Derek Elphinstone, Danny Green, Olaf Olsen, Jonny Bloor, E.V.H. Emmett.*

THE SAINT MEETS THE TIGER (1941) [3]

Dir *Paul L. Stein.* Prod *William Sistrom.* Scr *Leslie Arliss, Wolfgang Wilhelm, James Seymour, from a novel by Leslie Charteris.* Ph *Bernard Knowles, Robert Krasker.* PC and Dis *RKO Radio British.* 79 mins. Cert A

After a murder on his own doorstep, Simon Templar, alias The Saint (*Hugh Sinclair*), tracks down a Cornwall-based gang who steal a million in bullion and plan to smuggle it to South Africa. The Saint is trapped, but saved when crooks fall out and all shoot each other. Routine invincible-hero thriller.

RoC *Jean Gillie, Clifford Evans, Wylie Watson, Gordon McLeod, Dennis Arundell, Charles Victor, Louise Hampton, Eric Clavering, Ben Williams.*

SAINTS AND SINNERS (1949) [3]

Dir and Prod *Leslie Arliss.* Scr *Arliss, Paul Vincent Carroll.* Ph *Osmond Borradaile.* PC *London Films.* Dis *British Lion.* 85 mins. Cert A

Michael Kissane (*Kieron Moore*), having served two years for theft, returns home to clear himself and finds his fiancée Sheila (*Sheila Manahan*) now engaged to the local bank manager. Old Ma Murnahan foretells the end of the world and the villagers rush to confess their sins. Rescued by Michael from a fire, the bank manager does *his* penance by admitting the theft for which Michael went to jail. Uneven mixture of Irish whimsy and suburban drama.

RoC *Maire O'Neill, Michael Dolan, Christine Norden, Tom Dillon, Noel Purcell, Pamela Arliss, Tony Quinn, Eddie Byrne, Liam Redmond, Eric Gorman, Cecilia McKevitt, Austin Meldon, Minnie McKittrick, Godfrey Quigley, Edward Byrne, Sheila Ward, Joe Kennedy, Dave Crowley, Vincent Ellis, Gabrielle Daye, Harry Hutchinson, James Neylin, Sam Kydd, Glenville Darling, Vic Hagan, Maurice Keary, Maureen Delaney.*

THE SAINT'S VACATION (1941) [3]

Dir *Leslie Fenton.* Prod *William Sistrom.* Scr *Jeffrey Dell, from a novel by Leslie Charteris.*

Ph *Bernard Knowles*. PC and Dis *RKO Radio British*. 57 mins. Cert A

Persistent reporter Mary Langdon (*Sally Gray*) trails Simon Templar, 'The Saint', on his Swiss holiday. At an inn, he becomes embroiled in the attempts of an international gang to steal a musical box containing a vital code. The Saint (*Hugh Sinclair*) and Mary are cornered, but his friend Monty (*Arthur Macrae*) unwittingly helps turn the tables on Rudolph (*Cecil Parker*), the chief conspirator. Brisk, if very minor thriller.

RoC *Leueen McGrath, Gordon McLeod, John Warwick, Ivor Barnard, Manning Whiley, Felix Aylmer*.

SALOON BAR (1940) [4]

Dir *Walter Forde*. (Associate) Prod *Culley Forde*. Scr *Angus Macphail, John Dighton, from the play by Frank Harvey Jr*. Ph *Ronald Neame*. PC *Ealing Studios*. Dis *Associated British*. 76 mins. Cert A

When Eddie (*Alec Clunes*), boyfriend of Queenie (*Elizabeth Allan*), barmaid at the Cap and Bells, is sentenced to hang for a murder he didn't commit, the regulars, led by bookie Joe Harris (*Gordon Harker*) decide to act. A note from the murdered woman leads to the real criminal (*Cyril Raymond*) who, cornered by the Cap and Bells crowd, tries to leap from one balcony to another, but fails. Verbose but winning mixture of mystery and comedy, with nice pub atmosphere.

RoC *Mervyn Johns, Joyce Barbour, Judy Campbell, Anna Konstam, Al Millen, Norman Pierce, Mavis Villiers, Felix Aylmer, O.B. Clarence, Manning Whiley, Torin Thatcher, Aubrey Dexter, Lawrence Kitchin, Helena Pickard, Gordon James, Annie Esmond, Roddy Hughes, Judy Kelly, Eliot Makeham, Julie Suedo, Roddy McDowall, Robert Rendel*.

Alec Clunes and Elizabeth Allan in Saloon Bar *(1940)*

SALUTE JOHN CITIZEN (1942) [4]

Dir *Maurice Elvey*. Prod *Wallace Orton*. Scr *Clemence Dane, Elizabeth Baron, from novels by Robert Greenwood*. Ph *Jimmy Wilson*. PC *British National*. Dis *Anglo-American*. 98 mins. Cert A

1938: on the brink of retirement, Bunting (*Edward Rigby*), with the same firm for almost 50 years, is sacked. His sons Chris and Ernest (*Eric Micklewood, Jimmy Hanley*), who have good jobs, rally round. With war, Bunting is reinstated, and becomes an ARP warden too. Ernest marries his girl in the ruins of a bombed church. Chris joins up and is killed. Ernest hates war but, after a fierce blitz in which his wife gives birth, he too joins up. New Year's Eve finds the Buntings alone with their baby grandson. Sincere, human, nicely detailed family saga. Said one critic: 'There is no doubt at all that it is British.'

RoC *Stanley Holloway (and narrator), Mabel Constanduros, George Robey, Dinah Sheridan, Peggy Cummins, Charles Deane, Stewart Rome, June Willock, David Keir, Henry Hallett, Christine Silver, Jonathan Field, Gordon Begg, Ian Fleming, Valentine Dunn, Harry Fowler*.

SAN DEMETRIO, LONDON (1943) [6]

Dir *Charles Frend*. (Associate) Prod *Robert Hamer*. Scr *Hamer, Frend, from the factual account by F. Tennyson Jesse*. Ph *Ernest Palmer*. PC and Dis *Ealing Studios*. 105 mins. Cert U

Blasted by a German battleship, the crew of the oil tanker *San Demetrio* abandon ship. One of the boats drifts for three days. Then they sight a ship. A burning ship. The *San Demetrio*. . . . They reboard her, put the fires out. In appalling conditions and against all odds, they bring her home. Outstanding, uplifting and unforgettable epic of the sea that proves truth indeed stranger than fiction.

LP *Walter Fitzgerald, Mervyn Johns, Ralph Michael, Robert Beatty, Charles Victor, Frederick Piper, Gordon Jackson, Arthur Young, Barry Letts, James McKechnie, Nigel Clarke, Lawrence O'Madden, David Horne, James Knight, John Coyle, Neville Mapp, Michael Allen, Herbert Cameron, Duncan McIntyre, Diana Decker, Rex Holt, James Donald, James Sadler, Peter Miller Street*.

SARABAND FOR DEAD LOVERS (1948) [4]
(USA: *Saraband*)

Dir *Basil Dearden, Michael Relph*. (Associate) Prod *Relph*. Scr *John Dighton, Alexander Mackendrick, from the novel by Helen Simpson*. Ph *Douglas Slocombe*. PC *Ealing Studios*. Dis *General Film Distributors*. Technicolor. 96 mins. Cert A

Unhappy in her marriage to the dissolute George Louis of Hanover (later George I of England), Sophie Dorothea (*Joan Greenwood*) falls in love with Count Philip Konigsmark (*Stewart Granger*). But the lovers have a powerful enemy in his ex-mistress, Countess Platen (*Flora Robson*) who, hearing they plan to flee, has him attacked and killed. Sophie Dorothea is sent to an isolated castle, where she spends the rest of her wretched life. Well-mounted, rather stolid period drama, but with several striking moments.

RoC *Françoise Rosay, Frederick Valk, Peter Bull, Anthony Quayle, Megs Jenkins, Michael Gough, Jill Balcon, Cecil Trouncer, David Horne, Mercia Swinburne, Miles Malleson, Allan Jeayes, Guy Rolfe, Aubrey Mallalieu, Noel Howlett, Barbara Leake, Anthony Lang, Rosemary Lang, Edward Sinclair, Margaret Vines, Peter George, W.E. Holloway, Myles Eason, Victor Adams, Peter Albrecht, Janet Howe, Anthony Steel, Christopher Lee, John Gregson, Sandra Dorne, Barbara Murray*.

SCHOOL FOR RANDLE (1949) [3]

Dir and Prod *John E. Blakeley*. Scr *Blakeley, Anthony Toner, Frank Randle*. Ph *Ernest Palmer*. PC *Film Studios Manchester*. Dis *Mancunian*. 90 mins. Cert A

Flatfoot Mason (*Frank Randle*) and his friends Clarence (*Dan Young*) and Blackhead (*Alec Pleon*) are the bane of the staff of the school at which Flatfoot is janitor, and where one of the pupils is his long-lost daughter. Usual Randle slapstick antics; some good belly-laughs, but on the longish side.

RoC *Terry Randal(l), Maudie Edwards, John Singer, Hilda Bayley, Elsa Tee, Jimmy Clitheroe*.

SCHOOL FOR SECRETS (1946) [5]
(USA: *Secret Flight*)

Dir and Scr *Peter Ustinov*. Prod *Ustinov, George H. Brown*. Ph *Jack Hildyard*. PC *Two Cities*. Dis *General Film Distributors*. 108 mins. Cert A

A group of 'boffins' quarrel among themselves as they battle to perfect radar. One, Watlington (*David Tomlinson*) is killed in the attempt. Another, shy zoologist Professor Heatherington (*Ralph Richardson*), plays a key role in a commando attack on a German radio station. Dropped with others from a plane with only a short time to spare, he gets the job done and returns a hero. Script admirably combines humour with moving and exciting moments.

RoC *Raymond Huntley, Richard Attenborough, Marjorie Rhodes, John Laurie, Ernest Jay, David Hutcheson, Finlay Currie, Michael Hordern, Pamela Matthews (Lana Morris), Joan Young, Cyril Smith, Hugh Dempster, Peggy Evans, Edward Lexy, Bill Rowbotham (Owen), Paul Carpenter, Robin Bailey, Alvar Liddell, Norman Webb, Joan Haythorne, Ann Wilton, Patrick Waddington, Cyril Smith, James Hayter, D. Bradley Smith, Kenneth Buckley, Anthony Dawson, Robert Lang, Richard Mantell, Murray Matheson, Anthony Wyckham, Ingrid Forrest, Geraldine Keyes, Vida Hope, Sonia Elverson (Holm), Robert Wyndham, Andrew Blackett, Tony Arpino, Peter March, Robert Elson, Roger Keyes, Trevening Hill, Edward Lodge, Joseph Alman, Arthur Rieck, Ernest Urbank, Karl Morel, Hugh Pryse, Kenneth More, O.B. Clarence, Aubrey Mallalieu, Desmond Roberts, Guy Belmore*.

SCHWEIK'S NEW ADVENTURES (1943) [2]

Dir *Karel Lamac*. Prod *Walter Sors, Edward G. Whiting*. Scr *Lamac, Con West, from characters created by Jaroslav Hasek*. PC *Eden Films*. Dis *Coronel*. 84 mins. Cert U

Schweik (*Lloyd Pearson*), a Czech humourist, is sent to find a card in a pack that will give patriots the position of German ammunition dumps. He gets himself arrested, released, made butler to a drunken Gestapo chief, lays hands on secret plans, helps saboteurs, is mistaken for a Russian parachutist and arrested again, but finally achieves his goal. Laboured comedy.

RoC *Julien Mitchell, George Carney, Richard Attenborough, Margaret McGrath, Jan Masaryk*.

SCOTT OF THE ANTARCTIC (1948) [5]

Dir *Charles Frend.* (Associate) Prod *Sidney Cole.* Scr *Walter Meade, Ivor Montagu, Mary Hayley Bell.* Ph *Jack Cardiff, Osmond Borradaile, Geoffrey Unsworth.* PC *Ealing Studios.* Dis *General Film Distributors.* Technicolor. *111 mins. Cert U*

1912. English explorer Robert Falcon Scott (*John Mills*) and his team are beaten in a race to the South Pole by Norwegians. On their return, blizzards delay them and stores run low. Evans (*James Robertson Justice*), badly frostbitten, dies. Oates (*Derek Bond*) walks out into the storm to allow the others more food. But they are unable to travel through the blizzard and Scott, Wilson (*Harold Warrender*) and Bowers (*Reginald Beckwith*) die only 11 miles from base camp. Honest but still inspiring account of doomed expedition. Royal Performance film of 1948.

RoC *Kenneth More, John Gregson, James McKechnie, Norman Williams, Barry Letts, Clive Morton, Anne Firth, Diana Churchill, Dennis Vance, Bruce Seton, Christopher Lee, Larry Burns, Edward Lisak, Melville Crawfurd, Sam Kydd, John Owens, Mary Merrett, Percy Walsh, Noel Howlett, Philip Stainton, Desmond Roberts, Dandy Nichols, David Lines.*

John Mills in Scott of the Antarctic *(1948)*

THE SECOND MR BUSH (1940) [3]

Dir *John Paddy Carstairs.* Prod *John Corfield.* Scr *Doreen Montgomery, Leslie Arliss, from the play by Stafford Dickens.* Ph *Jimmy Wilson.* PC *British National.* Dis *Anglo-American. 56 mins. Cert U*

Tony (*Derrick de Marney*), a writer, offers to help timid Mr Bush, a butterfly farmer who has inherited £500,000 and is being chased by reporters, by posing as him, and pretending to give the money away. Tony gets in with a grasping family, and falls in love with their nice daughter (*Kay Walsh*), but the arrival of Mrs Bush upsets all his plans. Amusing, if somewhat truncated version of the play.

RoC *Barbara Everest, Evelyn Roberts, Wallace Evennett, Margaret Yarde, Robert Rendel, Vi Kaley.*

SECRET MISSION (1942) [3]

Dir *Harold French.* Prod *Marcel Hellman.* Scr *Anatole de Grunwald, Captain Sir Basil Bartlett.* Ph *Bernard Knowles.* PC *Independent Producers/Excelsior.* Dis *General Film Distributors. 94 mins. Cert U*

Four British intelligence men are sent to assess the strength of German defences in occupied France. With the help of forged papers, they succeed and, as the Germans hunt them, information is sent by the Resistance to British paratroops who destroy German munitions and fortifications. One of the four infiltrators, Raoul (*James Mason*) is killed on the brink of escape. Good performances in slowish melodrama.

RoC *Hugh Williams, Michael Wilding, Roland Culver, Carla Lehmann, Nancy Price, Percy Walsh, Anita Gombault, David Page, Betty Warren, Nicholas Stuart, Brefni O'Rourke, Karel Stepanek, Herbert Lom, John Salew, Beatrice Varley, F.R. Wendhausen, Yvonne André, Stewart Granger, Oscar Ebelsbacher.*

THE SECRET TUNNEL (1947) [3]

Dir and Scr *William C. Hammond, from a novel by Mary Cathcart Borer.* Prod *Frank A. Hoare.* Ph *A.T. Dinsdale.* PC *Merton Park.* Dis *General Film Distributors. 49 mins. Cert U*

Two boys discover that their father's housekeeper is in with a gang of thieves who have already stolen a Rembrandt and plan to swipe more valuables by means of a secret tunnel. One of the boys hides himself in the crooks' van and brings about their ultimate capture. Competent children's film; lots of mystery.

LP *Anthony Wager, Ivor Bowyer, Murray Matheson, Thelma Rea, Gerald Pring, Frank Henderson, John H. Sullivan, Michael Kelly.*

SEND FOR PAUL TEMPLE (1946) [2]

Dir and Prod *John Argyle.* Scr *Francis Durbridge, Argyle, from characters created by Durbridge.* Ph *Geoffrey Faithfull.* PC and Dis *Butchers. 83 mins. Cert A*

Scotland Yard calls in novelist and amateur detective Paul Temple (*Anthony Hulme*) to help track down a gang of diamond robbers. Steve (*Joy Shelton*), a girl reporter, whose detective brother has been killed by the gang, joins forces with Temple to unmask the gang leader, posing as a police-inspector. Inauspicious, penny-dreadful film start for radio's favourite sleuth of the 1940s. But better Temple films would follow.

RoC *Tamara Desni, Jack Raine, Beatrice Varley, Hylton Allen, Maire O'Neill, Phil Ray, Olive Sloane, Michael Golden, Richard Shayne, Edward V. Robson, Leslie Weston, Victor Weske, Norman Pierce, Melville Crawfurd, Charles Wade.*

THE SEVENTH SURVIVOR (1941) [4]

Dir *Leslie Hiscott.* Prod *Elizabeth Hiscott.* Scr *Michael Barringer.* Ph *Basil Emmott, Laurie Freeman.* PC *Shaftesbury/British National.* Dis *Anglo-American. 75 mins. Cert U*

A German agent with Allied secrets is one of six passengers on board a ship which is torpedoed. On a lifeboat, the six survivors are joined by Hartzmann, captain of a sunken U-boat, who proceeds to take charge when they reach a lighthouse, saying a U-boat is on its way. When the German agent begs him to take him with her, Hartzmann is revealed as a British counter-agent. Minor but fast-moving, well-cast thriller.

LP *Austin Trevor, Linden Travers, John Stuart, Martita Hunt, Frank Pettingell, Jane Carr, Wally Patch, Henry Oscar, Felix Aylmer, Ralph Truman, Ronald Shiner.*

THE SEVENTH VEIL (1945) [5]

Dir *Compton Bennett.* Prod *John Sutro, Sydney Box.* Scr *Sydney and Muriel Box.* Ph *Reginald H. Wyer.* PC *Theatrecraft/Ortus.* Dis *General Film Distributors. 94 mins. Cert A*

Under the care of a psychiatrist (*Herbert Lom*), pianist Francesca (*Ann Todd*) strips away the veils concealing a traumatic life. Caned so badly she is unable to play in her music exam, she is put in the care of Svengali-like guardian Nicholas (*James Mason*) who ruthlessly ends her affairs with a bandleader (*Hugh McDermott*) and a painter (*Albert Lieven*). The psychiatrist restores her to the man she really wants – Nicholas. Very well made melodrama contains Miss Todd's best performance and was a giant popular hit. Also took an Academy Award for Best Original Screenplay.

RoC *Yvonne Owen, David Horne, Manning Whiley, Grace Allardyce, Ernest Davies, Beatrice Varley, John Slater, Margaret Withers, Arnold Goldsborough, Muir Matheson, Eileen Joyce (piano).*

Ann Todd and James Mason in The Seventh Veil *(1945)*

SHEEPDOG OF THE HILLS (1941) [3]

Dir and Ph *Germain Burger.* Prod *F.W. Baker.* Scr *Kathleen Butler, Vera Allinson.* PC and Dis *Butchers. 77 mins. Cert U*

All Devonshire farmers around Collington are losing sheep, except Riggy (*Dennis Wyndham*) whose immunity is put down to Moss, 'the best sheepdog in the land'. In reality, Moss has been trained to steal sheep for Riggy, swelling his flock. Trying to escape, Riggy is drowned. A secondary story ends when the Vicar (*David Farrar*) marries the girl he loves (*Helen Perry*) to his best friend (*Philip Friend*). Moss makes them a present of four sheep. Sentimental drama rather over-dominated by its doggy star.

RoC *Len Sharp, Jack Vyvyan, Arthur Denton, Philip Godfrey, Johnnie Schofield, Moss (the dog).*

THE SHIPBUILDERS (1943) [4]

Dir and Prod *John Baxter.* Scr *Gordon Wellesley, Reginald Pound, Stephen Potter.* Ph *Jimmy Wilson.* PC *British National.* Dis *Anglo-American. 89 mins. Cert A*

With the launching of the *Milano* in 1932, Pagan (*Clive Brook*) closes his shipyard for lack of orders. On the dole are Pagan's wartime batman (*Morland Graham*) and his son Peter (*Geoffrey Hibbert*), arrested for murder but acquitted; Pagan steers him into the navy. About to sell up in the mid 1930s, Pagan foresees world war and reopens the yard. In 1943, working at full pressure, the shipyard hears of Peter's death in an action fought by the *Milano*. Conventional filming of a fine, well-structured idea.
RoC *Nell Ballantyne, Finlay Currie, Maudie Edwards, Allan Jeayes, Moira Lister, Frederick Leister, Gus McNaughton, John Turnbull, Ian Sadler, Bertram Wallis, Caven Watson, James Woodburn, Beckett Bould, Patric Curwen, Michael Gainsborough, Emrys Jones, David Keir, Ian MacLean, Dudley Paul, Walter Roy, David Trickett, C. Denier Warren, Alec Faversham.*

SHIPS WITH WINGS (1941)   [3]

Dir *Sergei Nolbandov.* (Associate) Prod *S.C. Balcon.* Scr *Nolbandov, Patrick Kirwan, Austin Melford, Diana Morgan.* Ph *Mutz Greenbaum, Roy Kellino, Wilkie Cooper, Eric Cross.* PC *Ealing Studios.* Dis *United Artists.* 103 mins. Cert A
Stacey (*John Clements*), one of three Fleet Air Arm pilots in love with admiral's daughter Celia (*Jane Baxter*), is responsible for her brother's death in a crash. Dismissed the service, he joins a Greek air line. When war breaks out, the Germans overrun his Greek island, killing his mistress, Kay (*Ann Todd*) and his friend (*Edward Chapman*) who ran the line. Learning that Celia has married one of his friends, he goes to his death by crashing his plane on a strategically vital dam. Melodrama moves fast, but has poor model shots.
RoC *Leslie Banks, Basil Sydney, Hugh Williams, Frank Pettingell, Michael Wilding, Michael Rennie, Hugh Burden, Cecil Parker, John Laurie, John Stuart, Frank Cellier, Morland Graham, Charles Victor, Betty Marsden, Graham Penley, Charles Russell, Elizabeth Pengally.*

THE SHOP AT SLY CORNER (1946)   [4]
(USA: *The Code of Scotland Yard*)

Dir and Prod *George King.* Scr *Katherine Strueby, from the play by Edward Percy.* Ph *Hone Glendinning.* PC *Pennant Pictures/London Films.* Dis *British Lion.* 92 mins. Cert A
Heiss (*Oscar Homolka*), a London antique dealer, is in fact a convict escaped from Devil's Island, a secret shared only by his partner Morris (*Manning Whiley*) and hidden from his violinist daughter Margaret (*Muriel Pavlow*). His assistant Archie (*Kenneth Griffith*) finds out and blackmails him. Heiss and Morris kill Archie, but Morris dies in a car crash. Cornered by police, Heiss commits suicide on the night of Margaret's concert debut. Absorbing drama with fine leading performance.
RoC *Derek Farr, Kathleen Harrison, Garry Marsh, Irene Handl, Johnnie Schofield, Diana Dors, Jan van Loewen.*

SILENT DUST (1948)   [3]

Dir *Lance Comfort.* Prod *Nat A. Bronsten.* Scr

Michael Pertwee, from the play by himself and Roland Pertwee. Ph *Wilkie Cooper.* PC *Independent Sovereign.* Dis *Associated British-Pathé.* 82 mins. Cert A
Blind Sir Robert (*Stephen Murray*) plans a memorial to his shiftless son Simon (*Nigel Patrick*), reported killed in action. But the man who breaks into his house, wanted for murder, is Simon, a deserter. The family hide Simon - but Sir Robert ultimately learns the truth. There is a bitter row followed by a struggle - and Simon falls to his death from a balcony. Pretty average.
RoC *Sally Gray, Derek Farr, Beatrice Campbell, Seymour Hicks, Marie Lohr, Yvonne Owen, James Hayter, Maria Var, Edgar Norfolk, George Woodbridge, Irene Handl.*

THE SILVER DARLINGS (1947)   [3]

Dir *Clarence Elder, Clifford Evans.* Prod *Karl Grune, William Elder.* Scr *Clarence Elder.* Ph *Francis Carver.* PC *Holyrood.* Dis *Pathé.* 84 mins. Cert U
Good photography distinguishes this slow-moving story of how the Hebridean people turned from their unfertile land and took to herring-fishing as a way of life, finally turning it into an industry. Sub-plots include a slight romantic story, a dramatic sea rescue, a hazardous cliff climb and the battle against a cholera epidemic.
LP *Clifford Evans, Helen Shingler, Carl Bernard, Norman Shelley, Simon Lack, Norman Williams, Murdo Morrison, Josephine Stuart, Hugh Griffith, Carole Lester (Lesley), Wilfred Caithness, Michael Martin-Harvey, Roddy Hughes, Iris Vandeleur, Christopher Capon, Stanley Jay, Harry Fine, Phyllis Morris, Jean Shepheard, Jack Fant, Anne Allan, Paula Clyne, Peter Illing, Hamilton Deane, Kenneth Warrington.*

THE SILVER FLEET (1943)   [5]

Dir and Scr *Vernon Sewell, Gordon Wellesley.* Prod *Michael Powell, Emeric Pressburger, Ralph Richardson.* Ph *Erwin Hillier.* PC *Independent Producers/The Archers.* Dis *General Film Distributors.* 87 mins. Cert U
Building two submarines in a Dutch shipping port now occupied, van Leyden (*Ralph Richardson*) agrees to complete them for the Nazis - a collaborationalist cloak for his guerilla activities. The townsfolk hate him and the Germans are fooled. Under his secret orders, patriots steal a submarine and get it to England. Finally, van Leyden destroys the second, taking with it himself and several high-ranking German officers. On-target acting and direction boost film's emotional appeal.
RoC *Googie Withers, Esmond Knight, Beresford Egan, Frederick Burtwell, Kathleen Byron, Willem Akkerman, Charles Victor, John Longden, Dorothy Gordon, Joss Ambler, Ivor Barnard, Margaret Emden, Valentine Dyall, Gerik Schjelderup, Neville Mapp, John Carol, John Arnold, Philip Leaver, Laurence O'Madden, Anthony Eustrel, Charles Minor.*

A SISTER TO ASSIST 'ER (1948)   [2]

Dir and Scr *George Dewhurst, from the play by John le Breton.* Prod *W. L. Trytel.* Ph *Reggie*

Pilgrim. PC *Bruton/Trytel.* Dis *Premier.* 60 mins. Cert A
Yet another Dewhurst-made version of the old stage chestnut, really no better than all the rest. Once again we meet Mrs May (*Muriel George*), a cunning old dear always trying to get out of paying the rent. When a ruse involving her nephew posing as her long-lost son fails, she invents a rich twin sister who swigs the landlady's gin, leaves her a dud cheque and flees, returning as herself in time to see her bags safely out of the house.
RoC *Muriel Aked, Michael Howard.*

SKIMPY IN THE NAVY (1949)   [1]

Dir *Stafford Dickens.* Prod *David Dent.* Scr *Aileen Burke, Leone Stuart, Hal Monty.* Ph *Gerry Moss.* PC *Advance.* Dis *Adelphi.* 84 mins. Cert A
Skimpy (*Hal Monty*) and his friends Tommy (*Max Bygraves*) and Lickett (*Les Ritchie*), demobbed from the army, join the navy to help Sheila (*Avril Angers*), a pretty girl, find buried treasure on a Mediterranean island. Series of songs and gags allied to a slapdash story. Second and last of the 'Skimpy' films.
RoC *Susan Page, Bob Trent, Vic Ford, Chris Sheen, Terence Downing, Derrick Penley, Bart Allison, Ivan Craig, Billy Rhodes, Chick Lane, Arthur Mullard, Patricia Hayes.*

SLEEPING CAR TO TRIESTE (1948)   [4]

Dir *John Paddy Carstairs.* Prod *George H. Brown.* Scr *Allan Mackinnon, William Douglas Home, from a story by Clifford Grey.* Ph *Jack Hildyard.* PC *Two Cities.* Dis *General Film Distributors.* 95 mins. Cert A
Zurta (*Albert Lieven*) and Valya (*Jean Kent*) board the Orient Express as it leaves Paris. They are after Poole (*Alan Wheatley*), who has double-crossed them over the theft of a diary containing political secrets. Others become involved, with problems of their own. Poole is killed, but M Jolif (*Paul Dupuis*) of the Paris police sees that the diary does not end in the hands of Zurta, who also dies. Serviceable remake of *Rome Express* (1932), with more comedy counter-balance to the thrills.
RoC *Derrick de Marney, David Tomlinson, Rona Anderson, Bonar Colleano, Finlay Currie, Alan Wheatley, Hugh Burden, Gregoire Aslan, Zena Marshall, David Hutcheson, Eugene Deckers, Claude Larue, Leslie Weston, Michael Ward, Dino Galvani, Jefferson Searles, George de Warfaz, Michael Balfour.*

THE SMALL BACK ROOM (1948)   [4]
(USA: *Hour of Glory*)

Dir and Prod *Michael Powell, Emeric Pressburger.* Scr *Powell, Presburger, Nigel Balchin, from Balchin's novel.* Ph *Christopher Challis.* PC *The Archers/London Films.* Dis *British Lion.* 108 mins. Cert A
Bomb disposal boffin Sammy Rice's (*David Farrar*) artificial foot gives him constant pain. Only the love of Susan (*Kathleen Byron*) keeps him from drowning his sorrows in drink more often than he does. At the end, he proves his life worthwhile when dismantling the intricate mechanism of a new and deadly kind of Ger-

Jack Hawkins, Robert Morley, Milton Rosmer and David Farrar in The Small Back Room *(1948)*

man booby bomb. Moving study of human nature, with tense climax.

RoC *Jack Hawkins, Leslie Banks, Cyril Cusack, Emrys Jones, Renee Asherson, Robert Morley, Walter Fitzgerald, Anthony Bushell, Milton Rosmer, Michael Gough, Michael Goodliffe, Henry Caine, James Dale, Sam Kydd, Elwyn Brook-Jones, June Elvin, David Hutcheson, Sidney James, Roderick Lovell, James Carney, Roddy Hughes, Geoffrey Keen, Bryan Forbes.*

THE SMALL VOICE (1948)   4
(USA: *Hideout*)
Dir *Fergus McDonnell.* Prod *Anthony Havelock-Allan.* Scr *Derek Neame, Julian Orde, George Barraud, from the novel by Robert Westerby.* Ph *Stan Pavey.* PC *Constellation.* Dis *British Lion.* 85 mins. Cert A
The victims of a car crash helped by Murray Birne (*James Donald*) and his wife (*Valerie Hobson*), prove to be two convicts who hold the Birnes captive at their house. A third convict arrives with two child hostages. Murray applies psychological pressure to Boke (*Harold Howard*) *Keel*), the convicts' leader, not only getting him to spare the life of a sick child, but ultimately allowing Murray to kill him. Tense drama with unexpected developments.
RoC *David Greene, Michael Balfour, Joan Young, Norman Claridge, Edward Evans, Bill Shine, Michael Hordern, Edward Palmer, Lyn Evans, Glyn Dearman, Angela Foulds, Alan Tilvern, Hugh Owens, Frederic Steger, Godfrey Barrie, Edward Hodge, Barry Wicks, Kathleen Michael, Sidney Benson, Edward Judd, Grace Denbigh-Russell.*

SNOWBOUND (1948)   4
Dir *David Macdonald.* Prod *Aubrey Baring.* Scr *David Evans, Keith Campbell, from a novel by Hammond Innes.* Ph *Stephen Dade.* PC *Gainsborough.* Dis *RKO Radio.* 86 mins. Cert A
Seven people converge on a lonely Alpine hut. They are all ostensibly on holiday, but in fact are there to hunt for wartime gold buried by Nazis under the hut. The 'holiday' becomes a game of deadly cat and mouse when snow traps them. Boxes are dug up, but there is no gold in them. Finally the hut collapses, and only three are left alive. Claustrophobic thriller is slow developing, gets more exciting towards the end.
LP *Robert Newton, Dennis Price, Herbert Lom, Mila Parely, Marcel Dalio, Stanley Holloway,*

Guy Middleton, Willy Feuter, Richard Molinas, Catherine Ferraz, William Price, Zena Marshall, Massimo Coen, Gilbert Davis, Lionel Grose, Rossiter Shepherd.

SO EVIL, MY LOVE (1948)   3
Dir *Lewis Allen.* Prod *Hal B. Wallis.* Scr *Leonard Spiegelglass. Ronald Millar, from the novel by Joseph Shearing.* Ph *Max Greene (Mutz Greenbaum).* PC and Dis *Paramount British.* 109 mins. Cert A
Victorian London: missionary's widow Olivia (*Ann Todd*) returns to the city only to fall into the clutches of an immoral artist (*Ray Milland*) and his companions. When she falls in love with him, he involves her in blackmail and the murder of the husband (*Raymond Huntley*) that her old school friend (*Geraldine Fitzgerald*), now an alcoholic, hates but hasn't the courage to do away with. Well-acted and -set, the picture remains at a distance.
RoC *Leo G. Carroll, Martita Hunt, Raymond Lovell, Moira Lister, Finlay Currie, Roderick Lovell, Muriel Aked, Ivor Barnard, Hugh Griffith, Guy le Feuvre, Clarence Bigge, Leonie Lamartine, Zena Marshall.*

Ray Milland in So Evil, My Love *(1948)*

SOLDIER, SAILOR (1944)   4
Dir *Alexander Shaw.* Prod *John Taylor.* Scr *Frank Launder, StJohn L. Clowes, Al Lloyd.* Ph *A. E. Jeakins, Raymond Elton.* PC *Realist.* Dis *United Artists.* 61 mins. Cert U
A merchant ship is attacked by enemy planes and motor boats but survives, blazing, to join a convoy setting out from Gibraltar. The ship is subsequently torpedoed, and several of its crew join a troopship carrying New Zealand soldiers. Subsequently they take part in a dramatic action against Nazi E-boats and Dornier fighter planes. Again, their ship is set on fire - but they survive. Documentary footage helps realistic thrills.
LP *Sgt Ted Holliday, Gun Slayer Al Beresford, Engineer David Sime, Rosamund Jarn, Jean Kent, Charles Victor, George Carney, Jean Cadell, Jimmy Knight, Bill Elliot, John Rae, Neville Mapp, Jimmy Plant, Esme Lee, men of the New Zealand Expeditionary Force.*

SOMEWHERE IN CAMP (1942)   3
Dir and Prod *John E. Blakeley.* Scr *Roney Parsons, Anthony Toner, Frank Randle.* Ph *Stephen Dade.* PC *Mancunian.* Dis *Butchers.* 88 mins. Cert U

Further escapades of Privates Randle, Enoch and Young (*Frank Randle, Robbie Vincent, Dan Young*) and their sergeant (*Harry Korris*) in helping young private Trevor (*John Singer*) to win the CO's daughter in spite of the adjutant's rivalry, involving the sergeant posing as an amorous housekeeper. In other words, the plot as before. More music-hall nonsense.
RoC *Toni Lupino, Peggy Novak, Clifford Buckton, Gus Aubrey, Betty Wheatley, Evie Carcroft.*

SOMEWHERE IN CIVVIES (1943)   1
Dir *Maclean Rogers.* Prod and PC *T. A. Welsh.* Scr *Con West.* Ph *Geoffrey Faithfull.* Dis *Butchers.* 87 mins. Cert U
Wangling his discharge from the army on medical grounds, Randle (*Frank Randle*) finds his crooked cousin trying to rob him of a legacy from a rich uncle which he will lose if proved of unsound mind. Despite some bizarre trials in a mental home, and as nightwatchman to a magician, Randle collects the money - but is glad to return to army life. Weak comedy: situations just too ridiculous.
RoC *George Doonan, Suzette Tarri, Joss Ambler, H. F. Maltby, Nancy O'Neil, Grey Blake, Gus Aubrey.*

SOMEWHERE IN ENGLAND (1940)   3
Dir and Prod *John E. Blakeley.* Scr *Arthur Mertz, Roney Parsons.* Ph *Geoffrey Faithfull.* PC *Mancunian.* Dis *Butchers.* 79 mins. Cert U
At a North of England army training camp, popular Lance-Corporal Kenyon (*Harry Kemble*) is framed by a jealous rival, found guilty and reduced to the ranks. Eventually his friends (*Harry Korris, Frank Randle, Dan Young, Robbie Vincent*) manage not only to clear his name but also to win the adjutant's daughter. First of several broad, homespun comedies with this quartet, here with music.
RoC *Winki Turner, John Singer, Sydney Monckton, Stanley King, The Eight Master Singers, Percival Mackey's Orchestra.*

Winki Turner and Harry Korris in Somewhere in England *(1940)*

SOMEWHERE IN POLITICS (1949)   3
Dir and Prod *John E. Blakeley.* Scr *Harry Jackson, Arthur Mertz, Frank Randle.* Ph *Ernest Palmer, Ben Hart.* PC and Dis *Mancunian.* 110 mins. Cert A
Joe Smart (*Frank Randle*), a wireless repair

man, decides to fight his own boss for a vacant seat on the town council. Joe wins the election, but nearly gets into very hot water by letting the same house to two different tenants at once. Better than some of its kind, speedily paced despite the inordinate length.
RoC *Tessie O'Shea, Josef Locke, Sally Barnes, Jimmy Clitheroe, Bunty Meadows, Sonny Burke, Syd and Max Harrison.*

SOMEWHERE ON LEAVE (1942)　[2]
Dir and Prod *John E. Blakeley.* Scr *Roney Parsons, Anthony Toner, Frank Randle.* Ph *Geoffrey Faithfull.* PC *Mancunian.* Dis *Butchers. 96 mins. Cert U*
Wealthy private Roy Desmond (*Pat McGrath*) takes his soldier friends (*Frank Randle, Robbie Vincent, Dan Young*) and their tough but tender-hearted sergeant (*Harry Korris*) to his palatial home for a leave. While the hapless quartet misbehave themselves with indefatigable gusto, Roy wins ATS girl Toni Beaumont (*Toni Lupino*) whose worries about being an adopted child prove groundless. Old hat high jinks.
RoC *Noel Dainton, Tonie Edgar Bruce, Percival Mackey and His Orchestra.*

A SONG FOR TOMORROW (1948)　[2]
Dir *Terence Fisher.* Prod *Ralph Nunn-May.* Scr *William Fairchild.* Ph *Walter Harvey.* PC *Production Facilities.* Dis *General Film Distributors. 62 mins. Cert A*
Wounded in the Second World War, the last voice Derek (*Shaun Noble*) hears is that of contralto Helen Maxwell (*Evelyn McCabe*), a friend of the surgeon, Roger Stanton (*Ralph Michael*). Recovering, he has amnesia, with Helen's voice the only link with his past. They fall in love, but when Derek's memory is restored, he proves to be engaged and returns to his fiancée. Stanton consoles Helen.
RoC *Valentine Dunn, James Hayter, Christopher Lee, Conrad Phillips, Sam Kydd, Yvonne Forster, Carleen Lord, Ethel Coleridge, Martin Boddey, Lockwood West.*

SOUTH AMERICAN GEORGE (1941)　[3]
Dir *Marcel Varnel.* Prod *Ben Henry.* Scr *Leslie Arliss, Norman Lee, Austin Melford.* Ph *Arthur Crabtree.* PC and Dis *Columbia British. 92 mins. Cert U*
The double of a famous South American tenor, George (*George Formby*) agrees to switch places (to prevent the singer's contract being broken) through love for the tenor's press agent (*Linden Travers*). He finds himself fleeing from gangsters employed by the singer's manager to bump him off. Then the manager recognizes George's comedy talents and offers him a contract. 'Extremely disappointing' or 'extremely funny' according to which reviewer you were reading.
RoC *Enid Stamp-Taylor, Jacques Brown, Felix Aylmer, Ronald Shiner, Alf Goddard, Gus McNaughton, Mavis Villiers, Eric Clavering, Beatrice Varley, Herbert Lomas, Muriel George, Cameron Hall, Charles Paton, Rita Grant, Norman Pierce.*

SO WELL REMEMBERED (1947)　[3]
Dir *Edward Dmytryk.* Prod *Adrian Scott.* Scr *John Paxton, from the novel by James Hilton.* Ph *Freddie A. Young.* PC *Alliance/RKO Radio British.* Dis *RKO Radio. 114 mins. Cert A*
In the mill town that sent her extortionist father to jail, ambitious Olivia (*Martha Scott*) marries editor George Boswell (*John Mills*), persuading him to run for Parliament. Dr Whiteside (*Trevor Howard*) adopts Julie, orphan of an epidemic that kills the Boswells' son. Olivia leaves George, who gives up his candidacy to fight for better local homes. Years later, as Mayor, he sees her return, politically scheme, and fight the romance of Julie (*Patricia Roc*) and Charles (*Richard Carlson*), disfigured son of her second marriage. George intervenes, Olivia leaves for good and the youngsters marry. Slow saga: Mills very good.
RoC *Beatrice Varley, Reginald Tate, Ivor Barnard, Sydney Benson, Roddy Hughes, Julian d'Albie, Frederick Leister, John Turnbull, Juliet Mills, Lyonel Watts, Kathleen Boutall, Rhona Sykes, James Hilton (narrator).*

SPARE A COPPER (1940)　[3]
Dir *John Paddy Carstairs.* (Associate) Prod *Basil Dearden.* Scr *Roger Macdougall, Dearden, Austin Melford.* Ph *Bryan Langley.* PC *Ealing Studios/ATP.* Dis *Associated British. 77 mins. Cert U*
A gang is out to sabotage the new battleship *Hercules* before its launching. George Carter (*George Formby*), a War Reserve policeman, though chased by police who think he is one of the gang, manages to bring its members to book, and help launch the *Hercules* down a slipway which is blown up seconds later. Below-par Formby comedy with weaker-than-usual material.
RoC *Dorothy Hyson, Bernard Lee, John Warwick, John Turnbull, Eliot Makeham, Warburton Gamble, Ellen Pollock, Edward Lexy, Jack Melford, Hal Gordon, Jimmy Godden.*

SPELLBOUND　[4]
(USA: *The Spell of Amy Nugent*)
Dir *John Harlow.* Prod *R. Murray Leslie.* Scr *Miles Malleson, from a novel by Robert Benson.* Ph *Walter Harvey.* PC *Pyramid Amalgamated.* Dis *United Artists. 82 mins. Cert A*
At first banned by the censors, this film was passed with the addition of a foreword from the Spiritualist church. Laurie (*Derek Farr*), brought up with Diana (*Vera Lindsay*), whom his mother hopes he will marry, falls for Amy, a grocer's daughter, who suddenly dies. Attending seances, Laurie, already distraught, goes mad when possessed by an evil spirit, and is only brought back to sanity by the prayers of Diana, who loves him. Interesting, dramatically strongly developed.
RoC *Frederick Leister, Hay Petrie, Felix Aylmer, Diana King, W. G. Fay, Gibb McLaughlin, Marian Spencer, Hannen Swaffer, Winifred Davis, Enid Hewitt, Joyce Redman, Cameron Hall, Irene Handl, Stafford Hilliard.*

THE SPIDER AND THE FLY (1949)　[4]
Dir *Robert Hamer.* Prod *Maxwell Setton, Aubrey Baring.* Scr *Robert Westerby.* Ph *Geoffrey*

Unsworth. PC *Mayflower.* Dis *General Film Distributors. 95 mins. Cert A*
1913, France. The chief of police (*Eric Portman*) knows the crimes committed by Philippe (*Guy Rolfe*), a brilliant safecracker, but cannot pin them on him: he admires their audacity. Just before the First World War, the chief leaves to do espionage work. He persuades Philippe to undertake a dangerous mission, the theft of vital papers. It is accomplished ... with cruelly ironic consequences for them both. Gripping, suspenseful, poignant drama.
RoC *Nadia Gray, Edward Chapman, Maurice Denham, George Cole, John Carol, Harold Lang, May Hallatt, James Hayter, Jeremy Spenser, Sebastian Cabot, Natasha Sokolova, John Salew, Arthur Lowe, Hal Osmond, Philip Stainton, Patrick Young, Alistair Hunter, Frederic Steger, Wallace Douglas, Madge Brindley, Keith Pyott, Ann Gunning, Andrea Malandrinos, Howard Douglas, Hattie Jacques.*

SPRING IN PARK LANE (1948)　[6]
Dir and Prod *Herbert Wilcox.* Scr *Nicholas Phipps, from a play by Alice Duer Miller.* Ph *Max Greene (Mutz Greenbaum).* PC *Imperadio.* Dis *British Lion. 92 mins. Cert U*
Judy (*Anna Neagle*) niece/secretary of wealthy art collector Joshua Howard (*Tom Walls*) has her doubts about his new footman's humble origins – and she's right. He is Richard (*Michael Wilding*), a nobleman on the run from his family after accepting a dud cheque for their art collection. He and Judy fall in love, and it later turns out that the cheque was good after all. Sparkling script and all concerned on top form; best of the Wilcox-Neagle-Wilding films.
RoC *Peter Graves, Marjorie Fielding, Nicholas Phipps, G.H. Mulcaster, Nigel Patrick, Josephine Fitzgerald, Lana Morris, H.R. Hignett, Catherine Paul, Cyril Conway, Tom Walls Jr.*

Anna Neagle, Tom Walls and Michael Wilding in Spring in Park Lane (*1948*)

SPRING MEETING (1940)　[3]
Dir and Prod *Walter C. Mycroft.* Scr *Mycroft, Norman Lee, from the play by M.J. Farrell, John Percy.* Ph *Walter Harvey.* PC *Associated British.* Dis *Pathé. 93 mins. Cert U*
An English widow, Tiny (*Enid Stamp-Taylor*), and her son Tony (*Michael Wilding*) decide to visit an old flame of hers, Sir Richard (*Henry Edwards*), in Ireland. Romantic complications run riot in his eccentric household, but Tiny

finally gets her man, Tony marries Sir Richard's daughter Baby (*Nova Pilbeam*) and Baby's sister Joan (*Sarah Churchill*) marries the stablehand. Pleasantly amusing, with *Margaret Rutherford* wonderful as decrepit Aunt Bijou who backs horses on the sly.
RoC *Basil Sydney, Hugh McDermott, W.G. Fay, Kieran Tunney*.

SPRING SONG (1946) [4]
(USA: *Springtime*)
Dir *Montgomery Tully*. Prod *Louis H. Jackson*. Scr *Tully, James Seymour*. Ph *Ernest Palmer*. PC *British National*. Dis *Anglo-American*. 86 mins. Cert *A*
Group Captain Tony Winster (*Peter Graves*) gives Janet Ware (*Carol Raye*) a brooch. Tony has a row with her comedian father (*Lawrence O'Madden*) but explains the history of the brooch: in Edwardian times it was given to an actress by an undergraduate who went to the bad and deserted her. They were her mother and his uncle. It looks as though Janet has lost Tony when he disappears - but he has gone to attempt a new speed record in a jet. Medium-budget musical with a degree of freshness; competent in all departments.
RoC *Leni Lynn, Alan Wheatley, George Carney, Finlay Currie, Jack Billings, Maire O'Neill, Netta Westcott, David Horne, Lois Maxwell, Diana Calderwood, Peter Penn, Howard Douglas, Harold Franklin, Melville Crawfurd, Kathleen Heath, Albert Chevalier, Alan Reed, Gordon Edwards, Griffiths Moss, Charles Paton, Horace Kenney, Gerhardt Kempinski, David Keir, Richard Molinas, Roy Sergeant, Charles Banks, Emanuel François, Joseph Fisher, Walter Anton, John Serret*.

SQUADRON LEADER X (1942) [5]
Dir *Lance Comfort*. Prod *Victor Hanbury*. Scr *Wolfgang Wilhelm, Miles Malleson, Emeric Pressburger*. Ph *Mutz Greenbaum*. PC and Dis *RKO Radio British*. 100 mins. Cert *A*
Ace Luftwaffe pilot Erich Kohler (*Eric Portman*) dons RAF uniform to bomb a Belgian town, bale out and spread the word that the Allies are attacking civilian targets. But he lands in the arms of the underground, and has to accept their offer of passage to England. Here, he blackmails his American ex-fiancée (*Ann Dvorak*) into helping him steal a plane, but is shot down over the Channel by German aircraft. Improbable but exciting spy melodrama.
RoC *Walter Fitzgerald, Barry Jones, Henry Oscar, Beatrice Varley, David Peel, Martin Milller, Frederick Richter, Charles Victor, Marjorie Rhodes, Mary Merrall, John Salew, Carl Jaffe, Aubrey Mallalieu*.

STOP PRESS GIRL (1949) [1]
Dir *Michael Barry*. Prod *Donald B. Wilson*. Scr *T. J. Morrison, Basil Thomas*. Ph *Cyril Bristow*. PC *Aquila*. Dis *General Film Distributors*. 78 mins. Cert *U*
Teenage Jennifer (*Sally Ann Howes*) can stop any kind of machinery after being near it for 15 minutes. Her fiancé Roy (*Nigel Buchanan*), a clock and watch maker, breaks the engagement. Reporters Angela (*Sonia Holm*) and Jock

(*Gordon Jackson*) follow her around as she creates havoc. Eventually, she falls in love with Jock and the power leaves her. Comedy almost as silly as anyone who thought it could make a film. One critic 'wished her strange power had caused the film to stop earlier than it did'.
RoC *Basil Radford and Naunton Wayne* (both in several roles), *James Robertson Justice, Joyce Barbour, Julia Lang, Kenneth More, Michael Goodliffe, Campbell Cotts, Cyril Chamberlain, Humphrey Lestocq, Betty Cooper, Fred Griffiths, Oliver Burt, Arthur Lowe, Olive Walter, Ann Valery, Vincent Ball, Alex Field, Stanley Rose, Olwen Brookes, Percy Walsh, Sam Kydd, Michael Balfour, Desmond Keith, Patti Morgan, Christine Silver, Patrick Waddington, Denys Val Norton, William Mervyn, Michael Ward, Frederick Owen, John Boxer, Jimmy Rhodes, Richard Vernon*.

THE STORY OF SHIRLEY YORKE [3]
(1948)
Dir *Maclean Rogers*. Prod *Ernest G. Roy*. Scr *A. R. Rawlinson, Kathleen Butler, Rogers*. Ph *Geoffrey Faithfull*. PC *Nettlefold*. Dis *Butchers*. 92 mins. Cert *A*
As the only person capable of effecting a new treatment perfected by her boss, Dr Napier (*John Robinson*), Nurse Shirley Yorke (*Dinah Sheridan*) has to stay with sick Alison (*Margaretta Scott*), wife of a man who once jilted her. Alison's companion Muriel (*Barbara Couper*) tells all. Alison collapses and is later found dead. Shirley is arrested and tried, but Dr Napier proves Muriel killed Alison. Hackneyed plot given good value by cast.
RoC *Derek Farr, Beatrix Thomson, Ian MacLean, Jack Raine, Lesley Osmond, Valentine Dyall, Bruce Seton, Eleanor Summerfield, Hugh Pryse, Charles Hawtrey*.

THE STRANGERS CAME (1949) [2]
(USA: *You Can't Fool an Irishman*)
Dir *Alfred Travers*. Prod *Roger Proudlock, Michael Healy*. Scr *Healy, Travers, Tommy Duggan*. Ph *Cyril Aradoff*. PC *Vandyke*. Dis *Grand National*. 71 mins. Cert *A*
A Hollywood producer (*Tommy Duggan*) comes to Ireland to film the life of St Patrick. He finds his backer is broke but a waiter, Tom O'Flaherty (*Shamus Locke*) can lay his hands on £500. He makes O'Flaherty a star, but Tom spends all the money on a celebration party. Along comes a widow (*Josephine Fitzgerald*) who is ready to back the movie as long as it is made in Scotland! Very minor relation to Ealing comedies.
RoC *Shirl Conway, Reed de Rouen, Tony Quinn, Ivan Craig, Eve Eacott, Sheila Martin, Geoffrey Goodheart, Seamus Harty, Gabriel Fallon, Robert Mooney*.

STRAWBERRY ROAN (1944) [3]
Dir *Maurice Elvey*. Prod *Louis H. Jackson*. Scr *Elizabeth Baron, from the novel by A. G. Street*. Ph *James Wilson*. PC *British National*. Dis *Anglo American*. 84 mins. Cert *U*
Farmer Chris Lowe (*William Hartnell*) marries showgirl Molly (*Carol Raye*) and brings her to his farm. Her extravagant tastes cause him to neglect his work and get into debt.

When Chris asks her to settle down a bit, she rides off in anger and is killed when thrown from her horse. Chris sells the farm and goes to work for the new owner as foreman. Well-photographed film loses some subtlety in transference from book to screen.
RoC *Walter Fitzgerald, Sophie Stewart, John Ruddock, Wylie Watson, Petula Clark, Joan Maude, Joan Young, Ellis Irving, Kynaston Reeves, Norman Shelley, Pat Geary, Charles Doe, Gordon Begg, Percy Coyte, Charles Paton, Patric Curwen, Richard Turner, Janet Morrison, Josie Huntley Wright, Patricia Stainer, Ernest Barrow, Vi Gould*.

SUSPECTED PERSON (1942) [4]
Dir and Scr *Lawrence Huntington*. Prod *Warwick Ward*. Ph *Günther Krampf*. PC *Associated British*. Dis *Pathé*. 75 mins. Cert *A*
American bank robbers Franklin (*Robert Beatty*) and Dolan (*Eric Clavering*) kill their partner, but find the loot has landed in the unwitting lap of an English reporter, Jim (*Clifford Evans*), who has gone back home. In England, they trace him through his girl Carol (*Annae Firth*), but Scotland Yard's Inspector Thompson (*David Farrar*) also moves in and, with the help of Jim's sister (*Patricia Roc*), saves him making a fool of himself, and nabs the crooks. Smartly made suspense thriller.
RoC *Leslie Perrins, Eliot Makeham, John Salew, Terry Conlin, Anthony Shaw*.

SWISS HONEYMOON (1947) [2]
Dir *Jan Sikorski, Henry C. James*. Prod and Scr *W. M. Sibley*. Ph *Sikorski*. PC *International Artists*. Dis *New Realm*. 64 mins. Cert *U*
The adventures of a couple on honeymoon in Switzerland. They visit Interlaken, Lucerne and the Wagner Museum at Triebschen. They see a storm on the Jungfrau, village life in the Rhone Valley and, of course, the Matterhorn. Makers should have stuck with the lovely scenery and photography and turned in a 30-minute documentary. Story is less than negligible, even with a mountain rescue at the end.
LP *Percy Marmont, Patricia Mainwaring*.

TAKE MY LIFE (1947) [4]
Dir *Ronald Neame*. Prod *Anthony Havelock-Allan*. Scr *Winston Graham, Valerie Taylor, Margaret Kennedy*. Ph *Guy Green*. PC *Cineguild/Independent Producers*. 79 mins. Cert *A*
Nicholas (*Hugh Williams*) and his opera star wife Philippa (*Greta Gynt*) row over his renewed friendship with Liz (*Rosalie Crutchley*), a violinist, who is later found dead. Nicholas is held as, in the row with his wife, he got a cut on his head similar to that inflicted on the killer. Philippa investigates and traces the mur-

derer by a tune written by Elizabeth. She is saved by a plainclothes man on the same track. Sound thriller, intelligently made.

RoC *Marius Goring, Ronald Adam, Francis L. Sullivan, Henry Edwards, Marjorie Mars, Maurice Denham, Leo Bieber, Herbert Walton, Leo Britt, Henry Morrell, David Wallbridge, Mavis Villiers.*

TALK ABOUT JACQUELINE (1942) [3]

Dir *Harold French.* Prod *Marcel Hellman.* Scr *Roland Pertwee, Marjorie Deans, from the novel by Katherine Holland.* Ph *Bernard Knowles.* PC *Excelsior.* Dis *M-G-M. 84 mins. Cert A*

Pre-war days. Playgirl Jacqueline (*Carla Lehmann*) marries a doctor (*Hugh Williams*) and is afraid to tell him of her scarlet past. When he begins to ask questions about the notorious 'Marlow girl', her sister June (*Joyce Howard*) insists it is her. June finds it difficult to live up to Jacqueline's reputation without ruining her own life, so Jacqueline confesses. Her husband only forgives her after she almost dies in a car crash. Light, inconsequential comedy.

RoC *Roland Culver, John Warwick, Mary Jerrold, Guy Middleton, Max Adrian, Antony Holles, Katie Johnson, Martita Hunt, Eileen Peel, Percy Walsh, Ian Fleming, Joan Kemp-Welch, Beatrice Varley, Roland Pertwee, Gerhardt Kempinski.*

TAWNY PIPIT (1944) [4]

Dir, Prod and Scr *Bernard Miles, Charles Saunders.* Ph *Ray Sturgess.* PC *Two Cities.* Dis *General Film Distributors.* Sepiatone. *85 mins. Cert U*

Rare birds nest near an English village and involve its inhabitants in a war against tanks and soldiers, farmers who want to plough the site and egg thieves. A nurse, the vicar and a convalescent pilot lead the fight, but finally the Ministry of Agriculture has to be called in to save the tawny pipits. Pleasant little comedy gently mocks idiosyncrasies of village life.

LP *Rosamund John, Niall MacGinnis, Bernard Miles, Jean Gillie, Christopher Steele, Lucie Mannheim, Brefni O'Rorke, George Carney, Wylie Watson, John Salew, Marjorie Rhodes, Ernest Butcher, Grey Blake, Joan Sterndale-Bennett, Lionel Watson, Scott Harrold, Arthur Burne, Billy Bridget, John Rae, Ann Wilton, Stuart Lathom, Johnnie Schofield, Katie Johnson, Ian Fleming, Sam Wilkinson, David Keir, Sydney Benson, Jenny Weaver.*

TEHERAN (1947) [2]
(USA: *The Plot to Kill Roosevelt*)

Dir *William Freshman.* Prod *Steven Pallos, John Stafford.* Scr *Akos Tolnay, Freshman.* Ph *U Arata.* PC *Pendennis.* Dis *General Film Distributors. 86 mins. Cert U*

Pemberton Grant (*Derek Farr*), a young British war correspondent, with the help of Natalie (*Marta Labarr*), a Russian ballet dancer who is at first forced to aid his enemies, foils a plot to assassinate US President Roosevelt in Persia 1943. Second-rate pot-boiler.

RoC *Manning Whiley, John Slater, John Warwick, Pamela Stirling, MacDonald Parke, Sebastian Cabot, Philip Ridgeway Jr, Enrico Glori, Anthony Sharpe.*

TEMPTATION HARBOUR (1947) [3]

Dir *Lance Comfort.* Prod *Victor Skutezky.* Scr *Skutezky, Frederic Gotfurt, Rodney Ackland, from a novel by Georges Simenon.* Ph *Otto Heller.* PC *Associated British.* Dis *Pathie. 104 mins. Cert A*

Signalman Bert Mallinson (*Robert Newton*) sees two men fighting over a suitcase on the quayside near the boat train. One, plus the case, falls in the water. Bert fails to save him, but rescues the case, which is full of money. He decides to keep it on account of his young daughter (*Margaret Barton*), but ends up having to fight and kill the other man (*William Hartnell*) and giving himself up for manslaughter. Leisurely but gripping drama with rather unpleasant characters.

RoC *Simone Simon, Marcel Dalio, Edward Rigby, Joan Hopkins, Charles Victor, Kathleen Harrison, Irene Handl, Wylie Watson, Leslie Dwyer, W.G. Fay, Edward Lexy, George Woodbridge, Kathleen Boutall, Dave Crowley, Gladys Henson, John Salew.*

THE TEMPTRESS (1949) [2]

Dir *Oswald Mitchell.* Prod *Gilbert Church.* Scr *Kathleen Butler, from a novel by Alice Campbell.* Ph *S.D. Onions.* PC *Bushey.* Dis *Ambassador. 85 mins.*

Dr Leroy (*Arnold Bell*) needs money to perfect his cure for infantile paralysis. Lady Clifford (*Joan Maude*), wife of one of his patients, suggests Leroy murder her husband, and split his fortune with her. When Sir Charles (*John Stuart*) dies, his son Derek (*Don Stannard*), who loves his father's nurse (*Shirley Quentin*), inherits the lot. Leroy tries to kill Derek, but is thwarted by the nurse and commits suicide. Gloomy thriller with unpleasant characters.

RoC *Ferdy Mayne, Conrad Phillips, Michael Bazalgette, Roy Russell, Richard Leech, John Serret, Rita Varian.*

THAT DANGEROUS AGE (1949) [3]
(USA: *If This Be Sin*)

Dir and Prod *Gregory Ratoff.* Scr *Gene Markey, from a play by Margaret Kennedy, Ilya Surgutchoff.* Ph *Georges Périnal.* PC *London Films.* Dis *British Lion. 98 mins. Cert A*

Sir Brian Brooke (*Roger Livesey*) suffers a breakdown and temporary blindness. His second wife Cathy (*Myrna Loy*) and daughter Monica (*Peggy Cummins*) take him to Capri, where they are later joined by Michael (*Richard Greene*), a young barrister with whom Cathy had had an affair while Sir Brian was immersed in his work. This comes to light, but Michael falls in love with Monica and Sir Brian forgives his wife for her indiscretion. Quite well made, but a bit stodgy.

RoC *Elizabeth Allan, Barry Jones, George Curzon, Gerard Heinz, Jean Cadell, Wildrid Hyde White, G.H. Mulcaster, Margaret Withers, Robert Atkins, Phyllis Stanley, Ronald Adam, Henry Caine, Patrick Waddington, Edith Sharpe, Daphne Arthur, Martin Case, Louise Lord, Nicholas Bruce, William Mervyn.*

THAT'S THE TICKET (1940) [2]

Dir *Redd Davis.* Prod *A.M. Salomon.* Scr *Jack Henley, John Dighton, Sid Field.* Ph *Basil*

Emmott. PC and Dis *Warner Bros. 63 mins. Cert A*

Sid Field's first film is an unsuccessful comedy casting him and *Hal Walters* as cloakroom attendants who trap a gang of foreign agents in Paris, after starting by mistaking three British secret service men for German spies.

RoC *Betty Lynne, Gus McNaughton, Gordon McLeod, Charles Castella, Gibb McLaughlin, Ian Maclean, Ernest Sefton.*

THEATRE ROYAL (1943) [4]

Dir and Prod *John Baxter.* Scr *Bud Flanagan, Austin Melford, Geoffrey Orme.* Ph *Jimmy Wilson.* PC *British National.* Dis *Anglo-American. 101 mins (later 92). Cert U*

Maxwell (*Chesney Allen*), owner of the Theatre Royal, is on the point of having to sell to a rival. Bob (*Bud Flanagan*), the theatre's props man, organizes a show from among the talented staff, which looks so good in rehearsal that an American backer promises his financial support. A grateful Maxwell makes Bob a partner in the theatre. Make-do plot backs some amusing comedy sketches, including an hilarious Elizabethan dream sequence.

RoC *Peggy Dexter, Lydia Sherwood, Horace Kenney, Marjorie Rhodes, Finlay Currie, Owen Reynolds, Maire O'Neill, Gwen Catley, Buddy Flanagan, Charles Mortimer, Ben Williams.*

THEY CAME BY NIGHT (1940) [3]

Dir *Harry Lachman.* Prod *Edward Black.* Scr *Frank Launder, Sidney Gilliat, Michael Hogan, Roland Pertwee, from the play by Barré Lyndon.* Ph *J.J. Cox.* PC and Dis *20th Century-Fox. 72 mins. Cert A*

A priceless ruby is stolen and a fake substituted. Jeweller Fothergill (*Will Fyffe*) finds that his brother, who has committed suicide, was the gang's fence. Forced to take his brother's place with the gang, Fothergill discovers how the burglar alarm works in the bullion store they are robbing, and the thieves are caught. Made-to-measure part for Fyffe in confusing drama.

RoC *Phyllis Calvert, Anthony Hulme, George Merritt, John Glyn Jones, Athole Stewart, Cees Laseur, Kathleen Harrison, Wally Patch, Hal Walters, Kuda Bux, Sylvia StClaire, Peter Gawthorne, Leo Britt, Sam Kydd, Pat Williams.*

THEY CAME TO A CITY (1944) [3]

Dir *Basil Dearden.* (Associate) Prod *Sidney Cole.* Scr *Dearden, Cole, from the play by J.B. Priestley.* Ph *Stan Pavey.* PC and Dis *Ealing Studios. 78 mins. Cert U*

Conversation piece. Nine people come to an 'ideal' city, where there is no poverty, overcrowding or overwork. They are: a philosophical seaman; a society widow and her repressed daughter; a waitress; a shady financier; a bank clerk and his neurotic wife; a baronet; a charwoman. Only the daughter and the char stay. Five leave in bitterness. The seaman and the waitress leave to tell the world about the city. Uncinematic conversion of play; not box-office either.

LP *John Clements, Mabel Terry-Lewis, Frances Rowe, Googie Withers, Norman Shelley, Ray-*

mond Huntley, Renee Gadd, A.E. Matthews, Ada Reeve, Ralph Michael, Brenda Bruce, J.B. Priestley.

THEY FLEW ALONE (1941) [4]
(USA: *Wings and the Woman*)
Dir and Prod *Herbert Wilcox*. Scr *Miles Malleson*. Ph *Frederick A. Young*. PC *Imperator*. Dis *RKO Radio*. 103 mins. Cert U

Amy Johnson and Jim Mollison, brilliant flyers both, break records separately, but fail when together, and finally find their marriage has drifted on to the rocks. With the Second World War, they both join the Air Transport Auxiliary, and Amy disappears on a flight over the English Channel in 1941. Quite an exciting biopic, although the miscasting of principals *Anna Neagle* and *Robert Newton* was much criticized.

RoC *Edward Chapman, Nora Swinburne, Joan Kemp-Welch, Charles Carson, Brefni O'Rorke, Muriel George, Martita Hunt, Eliot Makeham, Ronald Shiner, David Horne, Charles Victor, Miles Malleson, Anthony Shaw, Ian Fleming, George Merritt, Arthur Hambling, Aubrey Mallalieu, Hay Petrie, Charles Maxwell, Anne Crawford, Leslie Dwyer, Billy (William) Hartnell, John Slater.*

THEY KNEW MR KNIGHT (1945) [2]
Dir *Norman Walker*. Prod *James B. Sloan*. Scr *Walker, Victor MacClure, from the novel by Dorothy Whipple*. Ph *Erwin Hillier*. PC *GHW Productions*. Dis *General Film Distributors*. 93 mins. Cert A

The Midlands. Unassuming Mr Blake (*Mervyn Johns*) is rescued from a financial mess by powerful financier Mr Knight (*Alfred Drayton*). The Blakes move up in the world – but Knight has dabbled in fraudulent speculation and Blake is ruined. He forges a bank return and goes to prison. Knight commits suicide. Blake's daughter marries a rich playboy. The rest of the family await his release. All pretty depressing.

RoC *Nora Swinburne, Joyce Howard, Joan Greenwood, Olive Sloane, Joan Maude, Marie Ault, Peter Hammond, Frederick Cooper, Grace Arnold, Kenneth Kove, Frederick Burtwell, Winifred Oughton, Tarva Penna, Patric Curwen, Muriel Aked, Antony Holles, Gordon Begg, Ian Fleming, Sheila Raynor, Pat Stevens, Doyley John.*

THEY MADE ME A FUGITIVE (1947) [4]
(USA: *I Became a Criminal*)
Dir *Cavalcanti*. Prod *Nat Bronston, James Carter*. Scr *Noel Langley, from a novel by Jackson Budd*. Ph *Otto Heller*. PC *Gloria/Alliance*. Dis *Warner Bros*. 103 mins. Cert A

Clem Morgan (*Trevor Howard*), just out of the RAF, is drawn into a gang of black marketeers led by Narcy (*Griffith Jones*). When he discovers they peddle dope, Clem wants out, but they arrange for his capture on a job. Sent to prison, he escapes. Helped by Narcy's discarded mistress (*Sally Gray*), he has a terrific fight with the gangleader. Narcy is killed. Clem returns to prison but with hopes of a retrial. Good brutal thriller with occasional silly moments.

Trevor Howard in They Made Me a Fugitive *(1947)*

RoC *René Ray, Mary Merrall, Vida Hope, Ballard Berkeley, Phyllis Robins, Charles Farrell, Eve Ashley, Jack McNaughton.*

THEY MET IN THE DARK (1943) [3]
Dir *Karel Lamac*. Prod *Marcel Hellman*. Scr *Anatole de Grunwald, Miles Malleson, from a scenario by Basil Bartlett, Victor McClure and James Seymour, and a novel by Anthony Gilbert*. Ph *Otto Heller*. PC *Independent Producers/Excelsior*. Dis *General Film Distributors*. 104 mins. Cert U

Commander Heritage (*James Mason*) is dismissed from the navy – framed by Nazi agents. He goes to a cottage at night to meet a girl who was involved in the plot, but is surprised by Laura (*Joyce Howard*), a Canadian hoping to find relatives there. Heritage flees and all Laura finds is a murdered girl. Later they team up to prove that a theatrical agency run by Child (*Tom Walls*) is the cover for the spy network that disgraced Heritage and killed the girl. Old-hat plot grafted to topical subject.

RoC *Phyllis Stanley, Edward Rigby, David Farrar, Karel Stepanek, Ronald Ward, Betty Warren, Walter Crisham, George Robey, Peggy Dexter, Ronald Chesney, Finlay Currie, Brefni O'Rorke, Jeanne de Casalis, Patricia Medina, Eric Mason, Herbert Lomas, Charles Victor, Robert Sansom, Alvar Lidell, Ian Fleming.*

THEY WERE SISTERS (1945) [4]
Dir *Arthur Crabtree*. Prod *Harold Huth*. Scr *Roland Pertwee, Katherine Streuby, from the novel by Dorothy Whipple*. Ph *Jack Cox*. PC *Gainsborough*. Dis *General Film Distributors*. 115 mins. Cert A

The lives of sisters Lucy (*Phyllis Calvert*), Charlotte (*Dulcie Gray*) and Vera (*Anne Crawford*) change dramatically when they marry. Lucy has a daughter who dies, Vera embarks on a series of affairs with younger men, while Charlotte marries Geoffrey (*James Mason*) who turns out to be a sadistic beast. Lucy tries to get Charlotte help, but Vera messes things up by failing to keep a vital appointment. Geoffrey beats Charlotte unmercifully; she rushes out and throws herself under a car. Geoffrey is severely censured by the coroner, and Lucy and her husband gain custody of his two children. Emotional pot-boiler strongly acted.

RoC *Hugh Sinclair, Pater Murray Hill, Pamela*

Kellino, Barry Livesey, Ann Stephens, Helen Stephens, John Gilpin, Brian Nissen, David Horne, Brefni O'Rorke, Roland Pertwee, Amy Veness, Thorley Walters, Joss Ambler, Roy Russell, Edie Martin, Dora Sevening, Helen Goss.

THE THIEF OF BAGHDAD (1940) [4]
Dir *Michael Powell, Ludwig Berger, Tim Whelan and (uncredited) Zoltan Korda, Alexander Korda, William Cameron Menzies*, Prod *Alexander Korda*. Scr *Lajos Biro, Miles Malleson*. Ph *Georges Périnal, Osmond Borrodaile*. PC *London Films*. Dis *United Artists*. Technicolor. 106 mins. Cert U

Ahmad (*John Justin*), King of Baghdad, is thrown in prison by his wicked vizier (*Conrad Veidt*). Here he meets a little street thief Abu (*Sabu*). They escape and flee to Basra, where Ahmad falls for the daughter (*June Duprez*) of the sultan. She is sold to the vizier who blinds Ahmad and turns Abu into a dog. With the help of a genie (*Rex Ingram*), Abu steals the All-Seeing Eye and, with Ahmad, rides into Baghdad on a magic carpet, slaying the vizier before he can marry the princess. Academy Awards for colour cinematography, art direction and special effects, although not too well liked by British critics. Completed in Hollywood.

RoC *Miles Malleson, Morton Selten, Mary Morris, Bruce Winston, Hay Petrie, Roy Emerton, Allan Jeayes, Adelaide Hall, Miki Hood.*

John Justin, June Duprez and Sabu in The Thief of Bagdad *(1940)*

THINGS HAPPEN AT NIGHT (1948) [2]
Dir *Francis Searle*. Prod *A.R. Shipman, James Carter*. Scr *StJohn Legh Clowes, from a play by Frank Harvey*. Ph *Leslie Rowson*. PC *Tudor/Alliance*. Dis *Renown*. 79 mins. Cert A

Wilfred (*Alfred Drayton*) persuades Joe (*Gordon Harker*), an insurance assessor, to stay at his home and help get rid of a poltergeist. After a hectic night, Spender (*Garry Marsh*) of the Psychical Research College finds that Audrey (*Gwyneth Vaughan*), Wilfred's youngest daughter, is the carrier of the evil spirit, which transfers itself to Joe. Slow-paced throwback to Aldwych farces, with stars who have seen better (and funnier) days.

RoC *Robertson Hare, Olga Lindo, Wylie Watson, Beatrice Campbell, Joan Young, Grace Denbigh-Russell, Judith Warden, June Elvin, Eric Micklewood, Charles Doe, Michael Callin, George Bryden, L. Franks, Marilyn Williams,*

Ernest Borrow, Esmé Lewis, Lilian Stanley, Peter Reynolds, Patricia Owens.

THE THIRD MAN (1949)   6

Dir *Carol Reed.* Prod *Reed, David O. Selznick, Alexander Korda.* Scr *Graham Greene, from his novel.* Ph *Robert Krasker.* PC *London Films.* Dis *British Lion. 104 mins. Cert A*
Writer Holly Martins (*Joseph Cotten*) arrives in post-war Vienna to be told by police that his friend Harry Lime has been killed in a street accident and that he was mixed up in drug-dealing. Holly meets Anna (*Valli*), Lime's mistress, a frightened lady with forged papers, and finally Lime (*Orson Welles*) himself, who proves very much alive and indifferent to his life of crime. Reluctantly, Holly helps police trap Lime in the sewers beneath the city. Anna shuns him. Masterly thriller in which every cinematic trick works. One Oscar, for best black-and-white photography; but Anton Karas's zither theme music was a hit around the world. Also British Film Oscar for Best Film.
RoC *Trevor Howard, Bernard Lee, Paul Hoerbiger, Ernst Deutsch, Erich Pomto, Siegfried Breuer, Wilfrid Hyde White, Paul Hardtmuth, Hedwig Bleibtreu, Annie Rosar, Herbert Halbik, Alexis Chesnakov, Eric Pohlmann, Frederick Schreicher, Leo Bieber, Nelly Arno, Jenny Werner, Geoffrey Wade, Thomas Gallagher, Walter Hortner, Martin Miller, Rona Grahame, Holga Walrow, Harry Belcher, Michael Connor, Lilly Khan (Kann).*

THIRD TIME LUCKY (1948)   2

Dir *Gordon Parry.* Prod *Mario Zampi.* Scr *Gerald Butler, from his novel* They Cracked Her Glass Slipper. Ph *Cedric Williams.* PC *Alliance/Kenilworth.* Dis *General Film Distributors. 91 mins. Cert A*
Joan (*Glynis Johns*) falls for gambler Lucky (*Dermot Walsh*) who regards her as his mascot. They tour the casinos successfully; but then he begins to lose. Tangling with a dangerous crook, Flash (*Charles Goldner*), Lucky is shot in the back. After tricking Flash into parting with cash (and an IOU) to patch Lucky up, Joan accidentally kills him when he turns on her. Lucky swears off gambling. Low-grade thriller.
RoC *Harcourt Williams, Yvonne Owen, John Stuart, Helen Haye, Ballard Berkeley, Sebastian Cabot, Harold Berens, Millicent Wolf, Bruce Walker, Marianne Deeming, Jean Short, Michael Hordern, Edna Kaye, Jack Tottenham, Tom Block.*

THIS ENGLAND (1941)   2
(Scotland: *Our Heritage*)

Dir *David Macdonald.* Prod *John Corfield.* Scr *Emlyn Williams.* Ph *Mutz Greenbaum.* PC *British National.* Dis *Anglo-American. 84 mins. Cert U*
The story of threats against English freedom made through the ages. An American journalist (*Constance Cummings*) is told the history of the English village she visits by its squire (*John Clements*), through the Norman invasion, the Spanish Armada, the Napoleonic wars and the First World War. A well-meant

parade of aphorisms, model shots and prop beards. Supposedly good for morale.
RoC *Emlyn Williams, Frank Pettingell, Esmond Knight, Roland Culver, Morland Graham, Leslie French, Martin Walker, Ronald Ward, James Harcourt, Walter Fitzgerald, Charles Victor, Roddy McDowall, Norman Wooland, David Keir, Robert Warwick, A.E. Matthews, Dennis Wyndham, Kynaston Reeves, Judy Ross, Leslie French, Andrea Troubridge, William Humphries.*

THIS HAPPY BREED (1944)   5

Dir *David Lean.* Prod *Noël Coward, Anthony Havelock-Allan.* Scr *Coward, Lean, Havelock-Allan, Ronald Neame, from Coward's play.* Ph *Neame.* PC *Two Cities/Cineguild.* Dis *Eagle-Lion. Technicolor. 114 mins (later 110). Cert A*
A sentimental and nostalgic look at the lives of an average British working-class family through the years 1919 to 1939. The Gibbonses (*Robert Newton, Celia Johnson*) have a son (*John Blythe*) who is killed in an accident, and a daughter (*Kay Walsh*) who runs off with a married man, but eventually settles for the boy next door (*John Mills*) and follows his naval career to Singapore. The critics weren't bowled over, but the public went for the film in a big way.
RoC *Stanley Holloway, Amy Veness, Alison Leggatt, Eileen Erskine, Guy Verney, Merle Tottenham, Betty Fleetwood, Laurence Olivier (narrator).*

Robert Newton and Celia Johnson in This Happy Breed *(1944)*

THIS MAN IS DANGEROUS/THE PATIENT VANISHES (1941)   4

Dir *Lawrence Huntington.* Prod *John Argyle.* Scr *Argyle, Edward Dryhurst, from a novel by David Hume.* Ph *Bryan Langley.* PC *Rialto.* Dis *Pathé. 82 mins. Cert A*
The death of a policeman in Hyde Park leads Mick Cardby (*James Mason*), private eye son of a Scotland Yard man, on to the track of Lena (*Barbara James*), kidnapped daughter of a millionaire. The trail leads to a sinister nursing home and ultimately to a vast old house in Wales, where Mick's inspector father saves both him and Lena from a fate worse than death. Thick-ear thriller with lots of action.
RoC *Margaret Vyner, Gordon McLeod, Mary Clare, Frederick Valk, Barbara Everest, G.H. Mulcaster, Eric Clavering, Brefni O'Rorke, Terry Conlin, W.G. Fay, Viola Lyel, Anthony Shaw, Michael Rennie, B. John Slater.*

THIS MAN IS MINE (1946)   4

Dir and Prod *Marcel Varnel.* Scr *Doreen Montgomery, Nicholas Phipps, Reginald Beckwith, David Evans, Mabel Constanduros, Val Valentine, from a play by Beckwith.* Ph *Phil Grindrod.* PC and Dis *Columbia British. 103 mins. Cert A*
Extraordinarily dramatic title for bright comedy about a Canadian soldier (*Hugh McDermott*) billeting with a middle-class English family for Christmas, He finds he has walked into a madhouse. Mother (*Jeanne de Casalis*) is leaving Father (*Tom Walls*) for the twentieth time. Cook (*Agnes Laughlan*) has renounced food and locked herself away to write a novel. He sorts these and other members of the household out, with the unexpected help of some black marketeers. The director's last film before his early death.
RoC *Glynis Johns, Barry Morse, Nova Pilbeam, Ambrosine Philpotts, Rosalyn Boulter, Mary Merrall, Bernard Lee, Charles Victor, Peter Gawthorne, King Whyte, Bryan Herbert, Leslie Dwyer, Charles Farrell, John Coyle, Natalie Lynn, Johnnie Schofield, Mai Bacon, Paul Carpenter, Olwen Brookes, Captain Bob Farnon and the Canadian Army Orchestra.*

THIS WAS A WOMAN (1947)   4

Dir *Tim Whelan.* Prod *Marcel Hellman.* Scr *Val Valentine.* Ph *Günther Krampf.* PC *Excelsior.* Dis *20th Century-Fox. 104 mins. Cert A*
Domineering Sylvia Russell (*Sonia Dresdel*) wrecks her daughter's happy marriage, humiliates her husband whenever she can, and finally poisons him so that she can marry a wealthy man in her pursuit of power. Her son Terry (*Emrys Jones*), a brain specialist, eventually backs her into an inescapable corner, and she is forced to give herself up to the police. Strong acting and direction gloss over unlikelihood of plot.
RoC *Barbara White, Walter Fitzgerald, Cyril Raymond, Marjorie Rhodes, Celia Lipton, Lesley Osmond, Kynaston Reeves, Julian Dallas, Noel Howlett, Joan Hickson, Clive Morton, Percy Walsh.*

THIS WAS PARIS (1941)   3

Dir *John Harlow.* Prod *Max Milder.* Scr *Brock Williams, Edward Dryhurst.* Ph *Basil Emmott.* PC and Dis *Warner Bros. 88 mins. Cert U*
Paris, 1940. Bill (*Griffith Jones*), a British agent, suspects that Anne (*Ann Dvorak*), American dress designer for Florian's, is a spy. But Anne is a pawn in the hands of the real spies, unwittingly carrying messages to the enemy in the ambulance her employer has bought. Bill hides in the ambulance and knocks out the Nazi motor-cyclist come to collect a message, taking it and Anne to French headquarters with the prisoner. But it is too late: thousands are fleeing Paris as the Germans advance. Okay espionage drama with some light touches.
RoC *Ben Lyon, Robert Morley, Harold Huth, Mary Maguire, Vera Bogetti, Harry Welchman, Frederick Burtwell, Marian Spencer, Miles Malleson, Hay Petrie.*

THOSE KIDS FROM TOWN (1942) 3

Dir *Lance Comfort.* Prod *Richard Vernon.* Scr *Adrian Arlington, from his novel* These Our Strangers. Ph *Jimmy Wilson.* PC *British National.* Dis *Anglo-American. 82 mins. Cert U*

This comedy contained early roles for *George Cole* and *Harry Fowler* as Cockney evacuee boys who move from the slums of London to the country home of an earl (*Percy Marmont*). Their scrapes and exploits prove that each has something to learn from the other.

RoC *Shirley Lenner, Jeanne de Casalis, D.J. Williams, Angela Glynne, Maire O'Neill, Charles Victor, Olive Sloane, Sydney King, Bransby Williams, Ronald Shiner, Josephine Wilson, A. Bromley Davenport.*

THREE SILENT MEN (1940) 3

Dir *Daniel Birt.* Prod *F.W. Baker.* Scr *Dudley Leslie, John Byrne, from the novel by E.P. Thorne.* Ph *Geoffrey Faithfull.* PC and Dis *Butchers. 72 mins. Cert A*

Zaroff (*Meinhart Maur*), the inventor of a deadly secret weapon to be used against the Allies, is injured in a crash. He is saved by Sir James (*Sebastian Shaw*), a surgeon who then learns of Zaroff's activities. Next day Zaroff is found dead from an overdose of ether. Sir James comes under suspicion, but his daughter and her fiancé work to clear his name. Poor dialogue, but action and thrills hold the interest.

RoC *Derrick de Marney, Patricia Roc, Arthur Hambling, John Turnbull, Peter Gawthorne, André Morell, Cameron Hall, Jack Vyvyan, Scott Harrold, Cynthia Stock, Basil Cunard, F.B.J. Sharp, Charles Oliver, Hugh Dempster, Ian Fleming, Billy Watts, Kay Lewis, Marjorie Taylor, Barbara Lott.*

THE THREE WEIRD SISTERS (1947) 2

Dir *Dan Birt.* Prod *Louis H. Jackson.* Scr *Louise Birt, David Evans, Dylan Thomas, from a novel by Charlotte Armstrong.* Ph *Ernest Palmer.* PC *British National.* Dis *Pathé. 82 mins. Cert A*

Owen (*Raymond Lovell*) goes to see his three elderly half-sisters (*Nancy Price, Mary Clare, Mary Merrall*) who need money to restore some local houses. After a series of accidents, his secretary Claire (*Nova Pilbeam*) realizes the sisters are trying to kill him. Confined to bed with injuries, Owen makes a new will leaving his money to Claire. The sisters then try to kill her and are about to succeed when the collapse of an old mine brings the house crashing down. Owen and Claire escape; the sisters are killed. Heavy melodrama.

RoC *Anthony Hulme, Elwyn Brook-Jones, Edward Rigby, Hugh Griffith, Marie Ault, David Davies, Hugh Pryse, Lloyd Pearson, Doreen Richards, Bartlett Mullins, Frank Dunlop, Frank Crawshaw, Elizabeth Maude, Belinda Marshall, D.J. Tawe-Jones, Wilfred Boyle, Lionel Gadsden, John Humphreys, Ursula Granville, Ethel Beale, Dora Levis, Elizabeth Allen, Helen Lee.*

THUNDER ROCK (1942) 5

Dir *Roy Boulting.* Prod *John Boulting.* Scr *Jeffrey Dell, Bernard Miles, Wolfgang Wilhelm,* *Anna Reiner, from the play by Robert Ardrey.* Ph *Mutz Greenbaum.* PC *Charter Films.* Dis *M-G-M. 112 mins. Cert A*

To escape a world of which he has despaired, author David Charleston (*Michael Redgrave*) becomes lighthouse keeper at isolated Thunder Rock. Here, he finds himself living in a dream world, conversing with people shipwrecked nearly a century before. They bring him inspiration and strength to face the real world again, with its threat of imminent world war. Sensitive, unusual film, excellent in technical departments.

RoC *Barbara Mullen, James Mason, Lilli Palmer, Finlay Currie, Frederick Valk, Sybilla Binder, Frederick Cooper, Jean Shepeard, Barry Morse, George Carney, Miles Malleson, A.E. Matthews, Olive Sloane, Bryan Herbert, James Pirrie, Tommy Duggan, Tony Quinn, Harold Anstruther, Alfred Sangster, Gerhard Hinze (Gerard Heinz), Andrea Malandrinos.*

THURSDAY'S CHILD (1943) 3

Dir *Rodney Ackland.* Prod *John Argyle.* Scr *Donald Macardle, Ackland, from Macardle's novel.* Ph *Desmond Dickinson.* PC *Associated British.* Dis *Pathé. 81 mins. Cert U*

Fennis Wilson (*Sally Ann Howes*) by chance becomes a child film star. Her mother's reaction causes her elder sister to leave home, and her parents to fall out. Finally, having earned £500 for 10 weeks' work, Fennis throws up her new career to spend the money on the boarding school education she has always wanted. Well-plotted film somewhat spoiled in the execution.

RoC *Wilfrid Lawson, Kathleen O'Regan, Eileen Bennett, Stewart Granger, Felix Aylmer, Marianne Davis, Gerhardt Kempinski, Margaret Yarde, Vera Bogetti, Percy Walsh, Ronald Shiner, Pat Aherne, Michael Allen, Margaret Drummond, Antony Holles, Terry Randall.*

Stewart Granger, Sally Ann Howes and Eileen Bennett in Thursday's Child (*1943*)

TILLY OF BLOOMSBURY (1940) 4

Dir *Leslie Hiscott.* Prod *Kurt Sternberg, A. Barr-Smith.* Scr *Nils Holstius, Jack Marks, from the play by Ian Hay.* Ph *Bernard Browne.* PC *Hammersmith.* Dis *RKO Radio. 83 mins. Cert U*

When Tilly (*Jean Gillie*), a poor girl, falls in love with gadabout aristocrat Dick (*Michael Denison*), her parents, who run a boarding-house, are dismayed – the broker's man (*Syd-* *ney Howard*) has just arrived. He agrees to play butler when the aristocrats come to call. The results are disastrous – but Dick defies his snobbish mother to marry Tilly anyway. Leisurely, unsubtle comedy with a cameo gem from Howard.

RoC *Henry Oscar, Athene Seyler, Michael Wilding, Kathleen Harrison, Athole Stewart, Martita Hunt, Joy Frankau, Eve Shelley, Ian Fleming, Lloyd Pearson, Mavis Raeburn, Hendry White, Ben Williams, Charles Hersee, Reg Mankin.*

TIME FLIES (1943) 3

Dir *Walter Forde.* Prod *Edward Black.* Scr *Howard Irving Young, J.O.C. Orton, Ted Kavanagh.* Ph *Basil Emmott.* PC *Gainsborough.* Dis *General Film Distributors. 88 mins. Cert U*

Tommy (*Tommy Handley*), a New York valet whose boss is away, spends the days promoting an inventor's time machine, then transports himself and two friends back to Elizabethan times. They soon become court favourites, but commit heresy and are condemned to be burnt. They escape in the nick of time and land back in New York three months before they started. Not bad, but good idea should have been more brightly treated.

RoC *Evelyn Dall, George Moon, Felix Aylmer, Moore Marriott, Graham Moffatt, John Salew, Leslie Bradley, Olga Lindo, Roy Emerton, Iris Lang, Stephane Grappelly, Peter Murray, Lloyd Pearson, Vincent Holman, Paul Morton, Nicholas Stuart, Tommy Duggan, Sydney Young, Noel Dainton, Glyn Rowlands, Brooks Turner, Wallace Bosco.*

TINKER (1949) 2

Dir *Herbert Marshall.* Prod and Scr *Marshall, Fredda Brilliant.* Ph *Günther Krampf.* PC *Citizen.* Dis *Eros. 70 mins. Cert U*

Tinker (*Derek Smith*), a gipsy's son, runs away and joins a group of mining trainees, with whom he is taught to read and write. Unjust suspicion of theft causes him to move on again, before his new comrades rescue him from drowning and he is welcomed back. Well-intentioned and -photographed film hasn't much more to offer.

No supporting cast issued.

TOMORROW WE LIVE (1942) 4
(USA: At Dawn We Die)

Dir *George King.* Prod *King, John Stafford.* Scr *Anatole de Grunwald, Katherine Strueby.* Ph *Otto Heller.* PC *British Aviation.* Dis *British Lion. 85 mins. Cert U*

Bent on reaching England, Jean (*John Clements*) becomes involved with the freedom fighters of a French river town, where the Mayor and his daughter Marie (*Greta Gynt*) appear to support the Nazis. When the patriots wreck an ammunition train, killing the commandant, 50 hostages, including the Mayor, are arrested and shot. Germaine (*Judy Kelly*), a waitress working for the Nazis, betrays the patriots' leader – Marie, who escapes to England with Jean. Eventful war film.

RoC *Hugh Sinclair, Godfrey Tearle, Yvonne Arnaud, Bransby Williams, Gabrielle Brune, Karel Stepanek, F.R. Wendhausen, Allan*

Jeayes, Brefni O'Rorke, Gibb McLaughlin, Margaret Yarde, David Keir, Victor Beamont, Antony Holles, Cot d'Ordan, Olaf Olsen, D.J. Williams, Herbert Lom, John Salew, Walter Hertner, Walter Gotell, Townsend Whitling.

TORMENT (1949)   [2]
(USA: Paper Gallows)
Dir and Scr *John Guillermin*. Prod *Guillermin, Robert Jordan Hill*. Ph *Gerald Gibbs*. PC *Advance*. Dis *Adelphi*. 78 mins. Cert A
Two brothers, both authors of crime novels, live with their secretary in a big, gloomy house. Jim (*John Bentley*) is outgoing, Cliff (*Dermot Walsh*) neurotic – and homicidally jealous when Jim falls for the secretary (*Rona Anderson*). Cliff is bent on killing his brother, but he himself comes to a timely end. Hackneyed script, heavy playing: torment for the audience.
RoC *Michael Martin-Harvey, Valentine Dunn, Dilys Lay(e).*

TO THE PUBLIC DANGER (1948)   [2]
Dir *Terence Fisher*. Prod *John Croydon*. Scr *T.J. Morrison, Arthur Reid, from the play by Patrick Hamilton*. Ph *Harry Waxman, Roy Fogwell*. 45 mins. Cert A
Capt Cole (*Dermot Walsh*) and Reggie (*Roy Plomley*) call at a roadhouse where Fred (*Barry Letts*) and his girl Nan (*Susan Shaw*) are drinking. Fancying Nan, Cole orders scotches all round, and suggests a drive in his car. Nan takes the wheel. A cyclist is knocked down. Fred protests, but is subdued in a fight. The drive goes even faster. Fred escapes. A final crash kills the other three. Interesting but finally undistinguished.
RoC *Frederick Piper, Betty Ann Davies, Sydney Bromley, Cliff Weir, Sam Kydd, Barbara Murray, Patricia Hayes, John Lorrell, Patience Rentoul.*

THE TOWER OF TERROR (1941)   [2]
Dir *Lawrence Huntington*. Prod *John Argyle*. Scr *Argyle, John Reinhart*. Ph *Bryan Langley*. PC *Associated British*. Dis *Pathé*. 78 mins. Cert A
Marie (*Movita*), fugitive from a concentration camp, jumps into a dock and swims to the Westrode Island lighthouse, where she is picked up by the demented German lighthouse keeper Kristan (*Wilfrid Lawson*). Hale (*Michael Rennie*) gets to the tower by kidnapping the assistant keeper, and saves Marie, whom a now completely mad Kristan had planned to bury in his wife's grave. Overheated melodrama.
RoC *Morland Graham, George Woodbridge, Edward Sinclair, Richard George, Charles Rolfe, John Longden, Victor Weske, Olive Sloane, Davina Craig, Noel Dainton, Rita Grant, Eric Clavering, Joe Welch, Charles Minor, Kieran Tunney, Robert Cameron, Sam Lee, Daley Cooper.*

TRAIN OF EVENTS (1949)   [3]
Dir *Sidney Cole, Charles Crichton, Basil Dearden*. (Associate) Prod *Michael Relph*. Scr *Dearden, T.E.B. Clarke, Angus Macphail, Ronald Millar*. Ph *Lionel Banes, Gordon Dines*. PC

Jack Warner and Miles Malleson in Train of Events (*1949*)

Ealing Studios. Dis *General Film Distributors*. 88 mins. Cert A
A train crashes. On it are: (1) an engine driver (*Jack Warner*) thinking of his wife and their daughter's romance; (2) a composer-conductor (*John Clements*) who has amorous adventures; (3) a German (*Laurence Payne*) who doesn't want to go back, and the girl (*Joan Dowling*) who befriends him; (4) an actor (*Peter Finch*) who has murdered his wife. Some die, some survive. Not one of the better British portmanteau films.
RoC *Gladys Henson, Susan Shaw, Patric Doonan, Miles Malleson, Philip Dale, Leslie Phillips, Wylie Watson, Arthur Hambling, Percy Walsh, Will Ambro; Valerie Hobson, Irina Baronova, John Gregson, Gwen Cherrell, Jacqueline Byrne, Neal Arden, Thelma Grigg; Olga Lindo, Dennis Webb; Mary Morris, Laurence Naismith, Doris Yorke, Michael Hordern, Charles Morgan, Mark Dignam, Guy Verney, Lyndon Brook, Philip Ashley, Bryan Coleman, Henry Hewitt, Johnnie Schofield.*

TRAPPED BY THE TERROR (1948)   [1]
Dir *Cecil Musk*. Prod *Frank Hoare*. Scr *Sherard Powell, Mary Cathcart Borer*. Ph *A.T. Dinsdale*, PC *Merton Park*. Dis *General Film Distributors*. 56 mins. Cert U
1790, France. A refugee count returns from England to rescue his wife and son Philippe. That night, his chateau is stormed and his wife taken in a coach. Philippe hides in the coach's boot. In the prison yard, he escapes, but sees his father brought in. With the help of an old family servant and some bakers' children, Philippe gets into the prison and helps his family escape. Well-intentioned children's film is embarrassingly unprofessional.
LP *James Kenney, Colin Stephens, Valerie Carlton, Ian Colin, Louise Gainsborough, Alastair Bannerman, John Longden, Martin Benson.*

TRAVELLER'S JOY (1949)   [2]
Dir *Ralph Thomas*. Prod *Antony Darnborough*. Scr *Bernard Quayle, Allan Mackinnon, from the play by Arthur Macrae*. Ph *Jack Cox*. PC *Gainsborough*. Dis *General Film Distributors*. 78 mins. Cert A
Bumble Pelham (*Googie Withers*) and her ex-husband Reggie (*John McCallum*) both find themselves stranded in Sweden without any money. Their various bright ideas bring them

together again, but infuriate the Swedes and fail to raise any money, until a Swedish businessman steps in with a novel notion for an exchange.... This film was held up until 1951 when the play had finished its run, but the McCallums are not happy in comedy and the wait was hardly worth it.
RoC *Yolande Donlan, Maurice Denham, Geoffrey Sumner, Gerard Heinz, Dora Bryan, Colin Gordon, Peter Illing, Anthony Forwood, Sandra Dorne, Eric Pohlmann.*

THE TRIAL OF MADAME X (1948)   [2]
Dir and Scr *Paul England, from a play by Alexandre Bisson*. Prod *Wyndham T. Vint*. Ph *Hone Glendinning*. PC *Invicta*. Dis *Equity British*. 55 mins. Cert A
Little-known minor version of the famous weepie, filmed five times on more lavish scale by Hollywood producers. *Mara Russell-Tavernan* plays Jacqueline, who pays dearly for an indiscretion, loses her husband, goes on a long downhill slide, shoots her blackmailer and is defended in court by her son – who does not know her. She dies.
RoC *Paul England, Edward Leslie, Frank Hawkins, Hamilton Deane, Hamilton Keene, Jean le Roy.*

THE TROJAN BROTHERS (1945)   [3]
Dir *Maclean Rogers*. Prod *Louis H. Jackson*. Scr *Rogers, Irwin Reiner, from the novel by Pamela Hansford-Johnson*. Ph *Ernest Palmer*. PC *British National*. Dis *Anglo-American*. 86 mins. Cert A
Sid Nichols (*David Farrar*), front legs of a horse in a music-hall act called The Trojan Brothers and Maggie, falls for a married socialite he insults while she is sitting in the audience. His parents save him from making a fool of himself, and later celebrate the tenth anniversary of their team. Interesting theme marred by inferior dialogue.
RoC *Barbara Mullen, Bobby Howes, Patricia Burke, Lesley Brook, David Hutcheson, Finlay Currie, George Robey, Wylie Watson, Gus McNaughton, Hugh Dempster, Annette D. Simmonds, H.F. Maltby, Bransby Williams, Joyce Blair, Joan Hickson, Carol Lawton, Roma Milne, Grace Arnold, Shirley Renton, Vincent Holman, Vi Kaley, Doorn van Steyn, Joy Frankau, Patricia Fox, Olive Kirby, Anders Timberg, Dawn Bingham.*

TROTTIE TRUE (1948)   [4]
(USA: Gay Lady)
Dir *Brian Desmond Hurst*. Prod *Hugh Stewart*. Scr *C. Denis Freeman, from the novel by Caryl Brahms, S.J. Simon*. Ph *Harry Waxman*. PC *Two Cities*. Dis *General Film Distributors*. Technicolor. 96 mins. Cert A
Trottie True begins her theatrical career as the Great Little Trottie of Camden Town. Her first romance is with Sid (*Andrew Crawford*), a young balloonist who crashes in her garden. 'Discovered' by an impresario, she triumphs at London's Gaiety Theatre and becomes a star. She marries Lord Digby (*James Donald*) but, after a tiff, runs off and joins Sid in a balloon race. They crash into a stream, and Trottie decides it's safer being a duchess. Very enter-

taining romp never quite reaches the gaiety to which it aspires.

RoC *Hugh Sinclair, Lana Morris, Bill Owen, Hattie Jacques, Michael Medwin, Harcourt Williams, Joan Young, Heather Thatcher, Mary Hinton, Francis de Wolff, Harold Scott, Dilys Laye, Daphne Anderson, Carol(e) Lesley, Irene Browne, Gladys Young, Anthony Halffpenny, Patricia Deane, Shirley Mitchell, David Lines, Campbell Cotts, Elspet Gray, Mary Jones, Ian Carmichael, Christopher Lee, Roger Moore, Anthony Steel, Sam Kydd.*

TROUBLE IN THE AIR (1948) [1]

Dir *Charles Saunders.* Prod *George and Alfred Black.* Scr *Michael Pertwee, Martin Lane, Jack Davies.* PC *Production Facilities.* Dis *General Film Distributors. 55 mins. Cert A*

The bellringing team in a small English village is to broadcast on the BBC. Spivs try to cash in on the occasion, but a radio commentator (*Jimmy Edwards*) puts paid to their racket. Crude comedy proves more than popular radio comedians are needed for film success.

RoC *Freddie Frinton, Joyce Golding, Sam Costa, Bill Owen, Jon Pertwee, Dennis Vance, Laurence Naismith, Malcolm Russell, Lionel Murton, David Lines, Stella Hamilton, Lisa Lee, Gerald Kent, Patsy Drake, Sam Kydd, Harry Fowler.*

TURNED OUT NICE AGAIN (1941) [4]

Dir *Marcel Varnel.* (Associate) Prod *Basil Dearden.* Scr *Austin Melford, John Dighton, Dearden, from a play by Hugh Mills, Wells Root.* Ph *Gordon Dines.* PC *ATP/Ealing Studios.* Dis *United Artists. 81 mins. Cert U*

George (*George Formby*), foreman of Dawson's underwear factory, is tricked by a rival into buying an untried material. George is fired. His wife (*Peggy Bryan*), tired of her mother-in-law's nagging, vanishes and, at a London convention, displays lingerie made of the new yarn. Its success means hot competition between Dawson's and their rivals. George sells to Dawson's and is made their London representative. Ealing influence makes this more of a character comedy than usual for its star.

RoC *Edward Chapman, Elliot Mason, MacKenzie Ward, O.B. Clarence, Ronald Ward, John Salew, Wilfrid Hyde White, Hay Petrie, Michael Rennie, Bill Shine.*

Peggy Bryan and George Formby in Turned Out Nice Again *(1941)*

THE TURNERS OF PROSPECT ROAD (1947) [3]

Dir *Maurice J. Wilson.* Prod *Victor Katona.* Scr *Katona, Patrick Kirwan.* Ph *Freddie Ford.* PC and Dis *Grand National. 88 mins. Cert A*

A London taxi-driver Will Turner (*Wilfrid Lawson*) finds an unwanted greyhound puppy in his cab and gives it to his daughter Betty (*Maureen Glynne*), who trains it to be a racer. In spite of the efforts of rival owners and race-track crooks, the dog wins the Greyhound Derby. Faintly unbelievable story has homely, natural atmosphere.

RoC *Helena Pickard, Jeanne de Casalis, Leslie Perrins, Peter Bull, Amy Veness, Shamus Locke, Desmond Tester, Gus McNaughton, Christopher Steele, Giselle Morlaix, Joy Frankau, Andrew Blackett, Charles Farrell.*

29 ACACIA AVENUE (1945) [2]
(USA: *The Facts of Love*)

Dir *Henry Cass.* Prod *Sydney Box.* Scr *Muriel and Sydney Box, from a play by Mabel and Denis Constanduros.* Ph *Ernest Palmer, Nigel Duke.* PC *Boca.* Dis *Columbia. 83 mins. Cert A*

Family crisis occurs when Mr and Mrs Robinson (*Gordon Harker, Betty Balfour*) go off on a Mediterranean cruise but get no further than Bognor. Arriving back early, they find their daughter about to embark on a trial marriage and their son involved in a divorce suit between his girlfriend and her husband. Even the maid has problems. Embarrassingly stagy version of West End success.

RoC *Carla Lehmann, Jimmy Hanley, Dinah Sheridan, Hubert Gregg, Jill Evans, Henry Kendall, Guy Middleton, Megs Jenkins, Noele Gordon, Aubrey Mallalieu.*

THE TWENTY QUESTIONS MURDER MYSTERY (1949) [3]

Dir *Paul L. Stein.* Prod *Steven Pallos, Victor Katona.* Scr *Patrick Kirwan, Katona.* Ph *Ernest Palmer.* PC *Pax-Pendennis.* Dis *Grand National. 95 mins. Cert A*

An anonymous question and a £5 note challenging the panel (*Jack Train, Richard Dimbleby, Daphne Padel and Jeanne de Casalis*) of radio's *Twenty Questions* to find the solution lead to a series of murders in which the killer uses the programme to name his victims in advance. Two reporters spot a link between them, and enlist the aid of the panel in trapping the guilty party. Polished if easy-to-solve mystery with novel background.

RoC *Robert Beatty, Rona Anderson, Clifford Evans, Edward Lexy, Wally Patch, Frederick Leister, Olga Lindo, Harold Scott, R. Meadows White, Kynaston Reeves, Stewart MacPherson, Norman Hackforth, Gordon McLeod, Liam Redmond, John Salew, Howard Douglas, Arthur Young, Merle Tottenham, Sonya O'Shea, Homi D. Bode, Philip King.*

TWILIGHT HOUR (1944) [3]

Dir *Paul L. Stein.* Prod *Louis H. Jackson.* Scr *Jack Whittingham, from the novel by Arthur Valentine.* Ph *James Wilson. 85 mins. Cert U*

Major John Roberts (*Mervyn Johns*) had lost his memory when buried alive in the First World War. He is employed as a gardener by

kind-hearted Earl Chetwood (*Basil Radford*) whose guardsman son (*Grey Blake*) is engaged to Virginia (*Lesley Brook*), an actress. Under the strain of answering a false charge of theft, Roberts regains his memory and realizes that Virginia is his daughter. Sterling sincerity by Mervyn Johns keeps stodgy story going.

RoC *Marie Lohr, A.E. Matthews, Ian MacLean, Barbara Waring, Brefni O'Rorke, Margaret Vyner, Olive Walter, *Joyce Heron, Christopher Steele, Tonie Edgar Bruce, Roy Russell, Sybil Wise, Ethel Royale, John Howard, Marjorie Caldicott, Rita Varian, Elsa Tee, Gabrielle Day, Victor Wood, Noel Dainton, C. Denier Warren, David Ward, Ruby Miller, Richard Turner, Bertram Wallis, Margaret Emden, Edward Stirling, Violet Gould, Alfred Harris, Marie Ault, Cecil Bevan.*

* scene deleted from final release print

TWO FOR DANGER (1940) [3]

Dir *George King.* Prod *A.M. Salomon.* Scr *Brock Williams, Basil Woon, Hugh Gray.* Ph *Basil Emmott.* PC and Dis *Warner Bros. 73 mins. Cert A*

With the theft of a a priceless gem from the Frencham collection, suspicion falls on the three Frencham brothers and their curator. Police Commissioner's son Tony (*Barry K. Barnes*) becomes interested in the case – and in Diana (*Greta Gynt*), the curator's secretary. The criminal warns of further thefts, and carries them out, killing an employee in the process. Tony tracks him down and proves him to be Sir Richard Frencham (*Cecil Parker*), trying to fly to a richer life with his high-priced mistress. He fails. Good teamwork in unconvincing but action-filled comedy-thriller.

RoC *George Merritt, Henry Oscar, Vera Bogetti, Peter Gawthorn, Gus McNaughton, P. Kynaston Reeves, Ian Maclean, Leslie Weston, Gordon McLeod, Wilfred Caithness, David Keir, Peter Glenville, Jean Capra, Katie Johnson, Leon Lindos, Alec Waugh, Sam Wolsey.*

TWO SMART MEN (1940) [1]

Dir and Prod *Widgey R. Newman.* Scr *Uncredited.* Ph *Uncredited.* PC *Clive Films.* Dis *Anglo-International. 52 mins. Cert U*

Wally and Jim, partners in an unsuccessful casting bureau, act as butler and cook for a friend's social-climbing sister, who holds a party where a duchess can meet her designer friend. But the designer is only interested in meeting the duchess's jewels, and it's Wally and Jim, with the help of a bright little girl, who save the jewels and everyone's blushes. Hardly funny at all, a far cry from star *Leslie Fuller's* hearty comedies of the 1930s.

RoC *Wally Patch, Margaret Yarde, Pamela Bevan, George Turner.*

2,000 WOMEN (1944) [3]

Dir and Scr *Frank Launder.* Prod *Edward Black.* Ph *Jack Cox.* PC *Gainsborough.* Dis *General Film Distributors. 97 mins. Cert A*

The Germans set up a women's internment camp at a former French spa hotel. Two of the girls, Freda (*Phyllis Calvert*) and Rosemary (*Patricia Roc*), form a group of English prisoners against the Nazis, going into action after

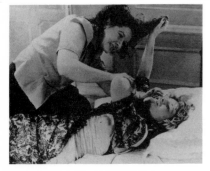

Betty Jardine and Jean Kent in 2,000 Women *(1944)*

three British airmen bale out in the camp grounds. The men are hidden in an attic, and got away during a camp concert, as Freda and Rosemary sing *There'll Always Be an England*. Light-hearted treatment of familiar theme.

RoC *Flora Robson, Renee Houston, Anne Crawford, Jean Kent, Thora Hird, Dulcie Gray, Reginald Purdell, James McKechnie, Robert Arden, Carl Jaffe, Muriel Aked, Kathleen Boutall, Hilda Campbell-Russell, Christina Forbes, Joan Ingram, Christiane de Maurin, Betty Jardine, Paul Sheridan, Dora Sevening, Walter Gotell, Wallace Bosco, William Hatton, Guy le Feuvre, Janette Scott, Anders Timberg, John England, Hazel Bray, John Snagge (voice).*

U

UNCENSORED (1942)   2

Dir *Anthony Asquith.* Prod *Edward Black.* Scr *Wolfgang Wilhelm, Terence Rattigan, Rodney Ackland, from the novel by Oscar Millard.* Ph *Arthur Crabtree.* PC *Gainsborough.* Dis *General Film Distributors. 108 mins. Cert U*
1940. The Germans overrun Belgium and print their own newspaper, edited by Lanvin (*Frederick Culley*), a former pro-Nazi who, unknown to the Germans, has switched sides and now runs an underground paper, which has all the Nazi paper's news - given a different slant. When his brother turns informer, he is almost trapped. But his narrow escape not only serves to ensure the continuation of the paper - but also the release of those who *were* caught. Muddled drama, surprisingly poorly made.
RoC *Eric Portman, Phyllis Calvert, Griffith Jones, Peter Glenville, Raymond Lovell, Carl Jaffe, Irene Handl, Eliot Makeham, J.H. Roberts, Felix Aylmer, Walter Hudd, Phyllis Monkman, Stuart Lindsell, Aubrey Mallalieu, Ben Williams, Arthur Goullet, John Slater, Philip Godfrey, Lloyd Pearson, Kathleen Boutall, Josephine Wilson, Allan Jeayes, Clifford Cobbe, Johnnie Schofield, John Snowden, Ian Kenyon, Antony Holles, Corey Ellison, Everley Gregg,* Charles Paton, Charlton Morton, Charles Doe, Norman Pierce, Lawrence O'Madden, Arthur Denton, Peter Cozens, James Carson.

UNCLE SILAS (1947)   2
(USA: *The Inheritance*)
Dir *Charles Frank.* Prod *Josef Somlo, Laurence Irving.* Scr *Ben Travers, from the novel by J. Sheridan le Fanu.* Ph *Robert Krasker.* PC *Two Cities.* Dis *General Film Distributors. 103 mins. Cert A*
1890. With the death of her father, 17-year-old Caroline Ruthyn (*Jean Simmons*) goes to live with her grasping Uncle Silas in his run-down old house. Eventually, she realizes Silas is trying to acquire her considerable inheritance by bringing about her demise. After some nightmarish experiences, Caroline is saved from Silas (*Derrick de Marney*) and his house-keeper (*Katina Paxinou*). Facing the gallows, Silas poisons himself. Creepily shot but over-ripe melodrama is laughable in parts.
RoC *Derek Bond, Esmond Knight, Sophie Stewart, Manning Whiley, Reginald Tate, Marjorie Rhodes, John Laurie, Frederick Burtwell, George Curzon, O.B. Clarence, Guy Rolfe, Frederick Ranalow, Patricia Glyn, Robin Netscher, John Salew, Patricia Dainton.*

Derrick de Marney, Jean Simmons and Katina Paxinou in Uncle Silas *(1947)*

UNDER CAPRICORN (1948)   2
Dir *Alfred Hitchcock.* Prod *Sydney M. Bernstein.* Scr *James Bridie, Hume Cronyn, from the novel by Helen Simpson, and play by John Colton, Margaret Linden.* Ph *Jack Cardiff.* PC *Transatlantic/Capricorn.* Dis *Warner Bros. Technicolor. 116 mins. Cert A*
1830s Australia. An aristocratic Irish girl (*Ingrid Bergman!*) elopes with a stable boy (*Joseph Cotten!*), killing her brother, who tries to stop them. Her new husband atones for her crime with seven years' hard labour. Years later, they are still together, he cruel and hard, she an alcoholic. A girlhood friend (*Michael Wilding*), despite his love for her and the machinations of a treacherous maid (*Margaret Leighton!*), cures her, and brings them together again. Muffled Hitchcock, with principals ludicrously miscast.
RoC *Cecil Parker, Denis O'Dea, Jack Watling, Harcourt Williams, John Ruddock, Ronald Adam, Francis de Wolff, G.H. Mulcaster, Olive Sloane, Maureen Delaney, Billy Shine, Victor Lucas, Julia Lang, Betty McDermott.*

UNDERCOVER (1943)   2
(USA: *Underground Guerillas*)
Dir *Sergei Nolbandov.* (Associate) Prod *S.C. Balcon.* Scr *John Dighton, Nolbandov, Monja Danischewsky, Milosh Sokulich.* Ph *Wilkie Cooper.* PC *Ealing Studios.* Dis *United Artists. 88 mins (later 80). Cert A*
When Belgrade is bombed, Milosh Petrovitch (*John Clements*) takes to the hills as a Yugoslav guerilla leader. His brother Stefan (*Stephen Murray*), a doctor, remains behind as an apparent Nazi sympathiser, passing information to Milosh. Despite saving a German general's life in an operation, Stefan dies after a mistake by his father (*Tom Walls*), and the Petrovitch home is besieged. Only courage survives. Probably Ealing's least convincing war film.
RoC *Godfrey Tearle, Michael Wilding, Mary Morris, Robert Harris, Rachel Thomas, Charles Victor, Niall MacGinnis, Finlay Currie, Ivor Barnard, Ben Williams, George Merritt, Stanley Baker, Eynon Evans, Norman Pierce, Eric Micklewood, John Slater, Terwyn Jones, Brynmore Thomas.*

UNDER NEW MANAGEMENT (1946)   1
Dir and Prod *John E. Blakeley.* Scr *Roney Parsons, Anthony Toner.* Ph *Geoffrey Faithfull.* PC *Mancunian.* Dis *Butchers. 90 mins. Cert A*
Joe (*Norman Evans*), a sweep, inherits a posh hotel, which he takes over with his daughter Brenda (*Nicolette Roeg*) and ex-servicemen and women. Two land speculators try to buy the hotel and estate cheaply, to make a mint when a planned airport is built nearby, but Joe and his friends foil their plans. Long, unsubtle musical farce outstays its welcome.
RoC *Nat Jackley, Dan Young, Betty Jumel, Tony Dalton, Marianne Lincoln, Bunty Meadows, Aubrey Mallalieu, G.H. Mulcaster, John Rorke, Hay Petrie, Babs Valerie, Michael Taylor, Lily Lapidus, Gordon McLeod, Joss Ambler, David Keir, Marcel Vallée, André Genin, Jacques Varennes, John Allen.*

UNDER YOUR HAT (1940)   4
Dir *Maurice Elvey.* Prod *Jack Hulbert.* Scr *Rodney Ackland, Anthony Kimmins, L. Green, from the play by Hulbert, Archie Menzies, Geoffrey Kerr, Arthur Macrae.* Ph *Mutz Greenbaum.* PC *Grand National.* Dis *British Lion. 79 mins. Cert U*
To keep an eye on her actor husband Jack (*Jack Hulbert*) when he is sent abroad on a secret mission, his actress wife Kay (*Cicely Courtneidge*) gets herself a job as maid to Carole Markoff (*Leonora Corbett*) whom she suspects Jack fancies. Jack, however, is more concerned with recovering a new airplane component stolen by enemy agents. The chief spy (*Austin Trevor*) fits the device to his plane, but Kay and Jack, posing as mechanics, force the pilot to bale out and fly back to England. Stars enjoy a number of disguises in cheerful lark.
RoC *Cecil Parker, Charles Oliver, H.F. Maltby, Glynis Johns, Myrette Morven, Tony Hayes, Mary Barton, The Rhythm Brothers.*

UNEASY TERMS (1948) [2]

Dir *Vernon Sewell*. Prod *Louis H. Jackson*. Scr *Uncredited, from the novel by Peter Cheyney*. Ph *Ernest Palmer*. PC *British National*. Dis *Pathé*. 91 mins. Cert A

Private eye Slim Callaghan (*Michael Rennie*) finds his client, Col Stenhurst, murdered. An anonymous letter seems to indicate Viola (*Faith Brook*), eldest of the colonel's three stepdaughters, may have done the deed, but Callaghan threads his way through a maze of jealousy to discover the real killer. The critic who declared 'A disgrace!' was perhaps over the top, but this is a disappointingly stiff adaptation of a best-selling pulp thriller.

RoC *Moira Lister, Joy Shelton, Patricia Goddard, Barry Jones, Marie Ney, Nigel Patrick, Paul Carpenter, Sydney Tafler, J.H. Roberts, Joan Carol, John Robinson, Tony Quinn, Mary Horn, George Street, John England, Chick Rolfe, Roy Russell, Harry Brooks, Etienne Bonichon, Mark Stone, Lionel Newbold, Gordon Plunkett, Kathleen Heath, George Rigby, Raphael Norman, William Forbes, Robert Moore, Clifford Buckton, William Bridger, Delia Digby, Margaret Allworthy, Alec Bernard, Doreen English*.

Michael Rennie and Nigel Patrick in Uneasy Terms (*1947*)

UNPUBLISHED STORY (1942) [3]

Dir *Harold French*. Prod *Anthony Havelock-Allan*. Scr *Anatole de Grunwald, Patrick Kirwan, (uncredited) Sidney Gilliat, Lesley Storm*. Ph *Bernard Knowles*. PC *Two Cities*. Dis *Columbia*. 92 mins. Cert A

War correspondent Bob Randall (*Richard Greene*) uncovers a 'peace organization' that he believes to be Nazi-backed. Before he is kidnapped, the innocent secretary of the organization gets a note to Carol (*Valerie Hobson*), Bob's reporter girlfriend. She barely escapes a Nazi trap. The organization is finally broken, but the editor decides the story cannot be published. Spirited melodrama.

RoC *Basil Radford, Roland Culver, Brefni O'Rorke, Miles Malleson, George Carney, Muriel George, André Morell, Renee Gadd, Frederick Cooper, Aubrey Mallalieu, George Thorpe, Henry Morrell, Claude Bailey, Ronald Shiner, Wally Patch, D.J. Williams, Anthony Shaw, John Longden, Peter Cozens, Townsend Whitling, Tony Quinn, Edie Martin, John Ojerholm*.

THE UPTURNED GLASS (1947) [4]

Dir *Lawrence Huntington*. Prod *Sydney Box,*

James Mason, Betty Box. Scr *Jno (John) P. Monaghan, Pamela Kellino*. Ph *Reginald Wyer*. PC *Triton*. Dis *General Film Distributors*. 86 mins. Cert A

Michael (*James Mason*), a brain specialist, strangles a woman responsible for the death of his fiancée. He plans to hide the body, but, in fogbound roads, is stopped by a doctor needing a lift to a road accident, where a child (*Ann Stephens*) lies with a fractured skull. The distraught mother (*Rosamund John*) persuades him to operate; it is a brilliant success. The doctor (*Brefni O'Rorke*) sees the body in Michael's car and says he must be mad. Michael flees and throws himself from a cliff. Psychological thriller with charismatic performance from the star. The title is meaningless.

RoC *Pamela Kellino, Henry Oscar, Morland Graham, Jane Hylton, Sheila Huntington, Jno P. Monaghan, Susan Shaw, Peter Cotes, Cyril Chamberlain, Richard Afton, Maurice Denham, Beatrice Varley, Howard Douglas, John Stone, Nuna Davey, Janet Burrell, Margaret Withers, Helen Burls, Lyn Evans, George Merritt, Glyn Rowland*.

UP WITH THE LARK (1943) [1]

Dir *Phil Brandon*. Prod *E.J. Fancey*. Scr *Val Valentine*. Ph *Stephen Dade*. PC and Dis *New Realm*. 83 mins. Cert U

In the guise of land girls, amateur sleuths Ethel and Gracie (*Ethel Revnell, Gracie West*) pursue a gang of black marketeers to their secret headquarters in the country. Despite, rather than because of, their ham-fisted efforts, the villains are eventually captured. Broad comedy with musical interludes: pretty unbearable, even in wartime.

RoC *Anthony Hulme, Lesley Osmond, Alan Kane, Antony Holles, Ian Fleming, Alma and Bobby, Van Straten's Piccadilly Dance Band*.

V

VARIETY JUBILEE (1943) [3]

Dir *Maclean Rogers*. Prod *F.W. Baker*. Scr *Kathleen Butler*. Ph *Geoffrey Faithfull*. PC and Dis *Butchers*. 92 mins. Cert U

Kit Burns (*Ellis Irving*) and Joe Swan (*Reginald Purdell*) are variety stars at the turn of the century. Kit becomes manager of a music-hall, Joe his employee and later partner. Kit's son is killed in First World War air combat, but he in turn leaves a son who carries on both family traditions by reviving the music-hall and enlisting in the RAF in wartime, watched by the elderly Swan, last survivor of a bygone age. Musical consists mainly of variety acts.

RoC *Lesley Brook, Marie Lloyd Jr, Tom E. Finglass, George Robey, Charles Coborn, John Rorke, Betty Warren, George Merritt, Arthur Hambling, Pat McGrath, Louis Bradfield, Ella Retford, Charles Shadwell, Joan Winters, Nat*

D. Ayer, Slim Rhyder, Tessa Deane, Wilson Keppel and Betty, Ganjou Bros and Juanita, Band of HM Coldstream Guards, Six Can Can Dancers, Jubilee Girls, Plantation Girls.

VENGEANCE IS MINE (1948) [1]

Dir and Scr *Alan Cullimore*. Prod *Ben Arbeid*. Ph *Bill Oxley*. PC *Cullimore-Arbeid*. Dis *Eros*. 59 mins. Cert A

Told he has six months to live, Heywood (*Valentine Dyall*) hires a man to kill him, intending to frame Kemp (*Arthur Brander*), the man responsible for his recent, unjustified prison sentence. Told the diagnosis was incorrect, Heywood searches frenziedly for the assassin, who turns out to have died. Menaced by Kemp, he shoots him in self-defence and is able to start life anew. Absurd thriller: even the cast don't seem enthusiastic.

RoC *Anne Firth, Richard Goolden, Sam Kydd, Alex Wright, Ethel Coleridge, Bob Connor, Jack Hart, Alex Graham, Michael Darbyshire, Bart Allison, Betty Taylor, Manville Tarrant, Pat Drake, Russell Westwood*.

VICE VERSA (1947) [2]

Dir and Scr *Peter Ustinov, from the novel by F. Anstey*. Prod *Ustinov, George H. Brown*. Ph *Jack Hildyard*. PC *Two Cities*. Dis *General Film Distributors*. 111 mins. Cert U

Thanks to unthinking wishes on a magic stone, pompous Edwardian Paul Bultitude (*Roger Livesey*) and his tearaway son Dickie (*Anthony Newley*) change places with each other. Dickie's friends are shocked. The headmaster (*James Robertson Justice*) is bewildered. But they are only too pleased to return to their old selves in the end. Funny idea, too long in the telling.

RoC *Kay Walsh, Petula Clark, David Hutcheson, Joan Young, Patricia Raine, Kynaston Reeves, Vida Hope, James Kenney, Harcourt Williams, Robert Eddison, James Hayter, Alfie Bass, Hugh Dempster, Peter Jones, Vi Kaley, Ernest Jay, Bill Shine, Andrew Blackett, John Willoughby, Stanley Van Beers, Michael McKeag, Timothy Bateson, Malcolm Summers, John Glyn-Jones, Frank Tickle*.

THE VOICE WITHIN (1945) [2]

Dir *Maurice J. Wilson*. Prod *Isadore Goldsmith*. Scr *Stafford Dickens, Herbert Victor, B. Charles-Deane*. Ph *R. Francke, Jan Sikorski*. PC and Dis *Grand National*. 74 mins. Cert A

Ireland, the 1920s. Denis (*Kieron O'Hanrahan*) and his IRA brother Roy (*Shaun Noble*) both love their adopted sister Kathleen (*Barbara White*). When Roy needs money to leave the country, Denis, for selfish motives, undertakes smuggling to get it. He is caught by a constable and kills him. Roy is arrested for the crime, but the constable's dog follows Denis until he feels forced to confess. Indifferent film, but O'Hanrahan continued his star career as Kieron Moore.

RoC *Violet Farebrother, Olive Sloane, Brefni O'Rorke, George Merritt, Paul Merton, Hay Petrie, Johnnie Schofield*.

THE VOLUNTEER (1943) [4]

Dir, Prod and Scr *Michael Powell, Emeric*

Pressburger. Ph *Erwin Hillier*. PC *The Archers*. Dis *Anglo-American. 46 mins. Cert U*
Fred Davy (*Pat McGrath*), dresser to a star (*Ralph Richardson*), volunteers for the Fleet Air Arm and becomes a skilled engineer. The star, who becomes a pilot in the same service, is amazed at Fred's abilities in aircraft maintenance, and proud when his courage in action wins the Distinguished Service Medal. Fascinating, human, charmingly made featurette.
No supporting cast.

VOTE FOR HUGGETT (1948)   [3]
Dir *Ken Annakin*. Prod *Betty Box*. Scr *Mabel and Denis Constanduros, Allan Mackinnon*. Ph *Reginald Wyer*. PC *Gainsborough*. Dis *General Film Distributors. 84 mins. Cert A*
Up for election as a borough councillor, Joe Huggett (*Jack Warner*) suggests a new lido as a war memorial. A suitable site is part-owned by his wife (*Kathleen Harrison*). She refuses to sell, but her niece Diana (*Diana Dors*) forges her signature, and Joe is in hot water. Luckily, his daughter Susan (*Susan Shaw*) discovers the forgery and all ends well, with Joe winning the election. Standard Huggett shenanigans, quite entertaining.
RoC *Petula Clark, David Tomlinson, Peter Hammond, Amy Veness, Hubert Gregg, John Blythe, Anthony Newley, Charles Victor, Adrianne Allen, Frederick Piper, Eliot Makeham, Clive Morton, Norman Shelley, Lyn Evans, Hal Osmond, Elizabeth Hunt, Empsie Bowman, Isa Bowman, Nellie Bowman, Ferdy Mayne*.

WALKING ON AIR (1946)   [2]
Dir *Aveling Ginever*. Prod and PC *Michael H. Goodman*. Scr *Ginever, John Worthy, Val Guest*. Ph *Stanley Clinton*. Dis *Piccadilly. 61 mins. Cert U*
A pretty skater (*Susan Shaw*) plays the part of a horse's back legs in an ice pantomime, but longs to be a ballerina. She seems set for success, but a swollen head is nearly her downfall. Rather indigestible mixture of dancing, skating, revue and a slight dramatic story.
RoC *Bertie Jarrett, Johnny Worthy, Jasmine Dee, Billy Thatcher, Maudie Edwards, Miki Hood, Gordon Edwards, Freddie Crump, Sunny Thomas, Jill Allen, Lauderic Caton, Coleridge Good, The Skating Avalons, The Ray Ellington Quartet*.

WALTZ TIME (1945)   [4]
Dir *Paul L. Stein*. Prod *Louis H. Jackson*. Scr *Montgomery Tully, Jack Whittingham*. Ph *Ernest Palmer*. PC *British National*. Dis *Anglo-American. 100 mins. Cert A*
Old Vienna. Empress Maria (*Carol Raye*) wants to marry an officer in her imperial guard, but the Council of Ministers say he's a philanderer. When he (*Peter Graves*) does indulge in a flirtation with Maria's friend Cenci (*Patricia Medina*), Maria teaches him a lesson, rids herself of the Council, and sees that the ban on dancing the waltz at court is lifted. Gay musical trifle could do with a dash of colour.
RoC *Thorley Walters, Richard Tauber, Harry Welchman, George Robey, Brefni O'Rorke, Hugh Dempster, John Ruddock, Wylie Watson, Tonie Edgar Bruce, Kay Kendall, Ferdi Mayne, Hay Petrie, Cecil Bevan, David Keir, Billy Matthews, Charles Paton, Roy Russell, Ivan Samson, Marie Ault, Dick Francis, Charles Doe, Basil Jason, Charles Peters, John Howard, Gordon Edwards, Joyce Linden, Ruthene Leclerc, Eileen Moore, Dawn Bingham, Anne Ziegler and Webster Booth, Albert Sandler, Hans May*.

WANTED FOR MURDER (1946)   [4]
Dir *Lawrence Huntington*. Prod *Marcel Hellman*. Scr *Emeric Pressburger, Rodney Ackland, Maurice Cowan, from the play by Percy Robinson, Terence de Marney*. Ph *Max Greene (Mutz Greenbaum)*. PC and Dis *Excelsior. 103 mins. Cert A*
Victor (*Eric Portman*), a descendant of a public hangman of Victorian times, lives with his mother (*Barbara Everest*), is mentally disturbed and strangles young women. He meets Anne (*Dulcie Gray*) and falls in love with her, but is driven to kill her like the rest. Before he can, the police surround him, but Victor drowns himself. Good, complex portrayal by Portman in otherwise straightforward thriller.
RoC *Derek Farr, Roland Culver, Stanley Holloway, Bonar Colleano, Jenny Laird, Kathleen Harrison, Viola Lyel, John Ruddock, Moira Lister, George Carney, Bill Shine, John Salew, Edna Wood, Wilfrid Hyde White, Gerhardt Kempinski, Mary Mackenzie, Caven Watson, Beatrice Campbell, Wally Patch*.

WARNING TO WANTONS (1948)   [4]
Dir and Prod *Donald B. Wilson*. Scr *Wilson, James Laver, from the novel by Mary Mitchell*. Ph *George Dudgeon Stretton*. PC *Aquila*. Dis *General Film Distributors. 104 mins. Cert A*
Capricious René (*Anne Vernon*) runs away from a convent to embarrass her mother who is having an affair with Count Karnak (*Harold Warrender*), a middle-aged flame. René goes off with the count to his castle, where she also captivates his son Max (*David Tomlinson*), to the discomfort of his sports-loving fiancée Maria (*Sonia Holm*) who gives René more competition than she bargained for. Fluffy sex comedy, dated but well done.
RoC *Judy Kelly, Marie Burke, Ellen Pollock, Hugh Cross, André van Gyseghem, Bruce Belfrage, Dennis Vance, Jack Melford, Brian Oulton, Stanley Ratcliffe, Aletha Orr, Ida Patlanski, Olwen Brookes, Kenneth Firth, Vincent Ball, John Warren, Mela White, Alexander Field, Betty Thomas, Frank Cochrane, Nancy Roberts, Grace Denbigh-Russell, Margaret Damer, Michael Bazalgette, Patricia Davidson, David Keir, Herbert C. Walton, Peter Faber, Pauline Loring, Mary Midwinter, Claud Frederic, Joan Denver, Caldwell Mason, Harriet Petworth*.

WARN THAT MAN (1943)   [3]
Dir *Lawrence Huntington*. Prod *Warwick Ward*. Scr *Vernon Sylvaine, Huntington, from the play by Sylvaine*. Ph *Günther Krampf*. PC *Associated British*. Dis *Pathé. 82 mins. Cert A*
German parachutists seize Buckley Hall. Lord Buckley (*Raymond Lovell*) and his staff are locked up: he is imitated by a German actor. But Buckley's niece Frances (*Jean Kent*) is hidden in an upstairs room. With help from friends who evade the Nazis, she gets a message out to stop 'that man' (presumably Churchill) from coming. The army moves in and the invaders are wiped out. Thriller thrills but can't overcome its unlikeliness.
RoC *Gordon Harker, Finlay Currie, Philip Friend, Frederick Cooper, Carl Jaffe, John Salew, Veronica Rose, Anthony Hawtrey, Antony Holles, Pat Aherne, Frederick Richter, Leonard Sharp, Frank Bagnall*.

WATERLOO ROAD (1944)   [4]
Dir and Scr *Sidney Gilliat*. Prod *Edward Black*. Ph *Arthur Crabtree, Phil Grindrod*. PC *Gainsborough*. Dis *General Film Distributors. 76 mins. Cert A*
London 1940. Tillie (*Joy Shelton*) lives with her mother-in-law and sister-in-law while her husband Jim (*John Mills*) is in the army. She falls under the influence of the local Romeo, Purvis (*Stewart Granger*), who has evaded army service through a forged medical certificate. Jim, hearing of it from his sister, breaks camp, is arrested, but escapes again. Beaten up by some of Purvis's friends, Jim still runs Purvis and Tillie to earth in the middle of an air-raid. There is a terrific fight with Jim the winner. He and Tillie sort out their problems. Slight theme, sincerely and satisfyingly played.
RoC *Alastair Sim, Beatrice Varley, Alison Leggatt, Arthur Denton, Vera Frances, Leslie Bradley, Ben Williams, George Carney, Anna Konstam, Dennis Harkin, Jean Kent, Johnnie Schofield, Frank Atkinson, Wylie Watson, Mike Johnson, Dave Crowley, John Boxer, George Merritt, Wallace Lupino, Amy Dalby, Nellie Bowman*.

Joy Shelton and Stewart Granger in Waterloo Road *(1944)*

THE WAY AHEAD (1944)   [6]
Dir *Carol Reed*. Prod *John Sutro, Norman Walker*. Scr *Eric Ambler, Peter Ustinov*. Ph *Guy Green*. PC *Two Cities*. Dis *Eagle-Lion. 115 mins. Cert U*

Seven civilians, all none too willing, are conscripted into the British army in 1940. After grumbling and sweating through long training under Lt Jim Perry (*David Niven*) and Sgt Fletcher (*Billy Hartnell:* the role made him a leading actor), they take part in the invasion of North Africa. Finally, bayonets fixed, they move forward together to face death in a German smokescreen. Lively script, good characterizations, inspiring theme.

RoC *Raymond Huntley, Stanley Holloway, James Donald, John Laurie, Leslie Dwyer, Hugh Burden, Jimmy Hanley, Renee Ascherson (Asherson), Penelope Dudley-Ward, Reginald Tate, Leo Genn, Mary Jerrold, Raymond Lovell, Alf Goddard, A.E. Matthews, Peter Ustinov, Tessie O'Shea, John Ruddock, A. Bromley Davenport, Johnnie Schofield, Jack Watling, John Salew, Lloyd Pearson, Grace Arnold, Eileen Erskine, Esma Cannon.*

THE WAY TO THE STARS (1945) [5]
(USA: *Johnny in the Clouds*)
Dir *Anthony Asquith*. Prod *Anatole de Grunwald*. Scr *Terence Rattigan, de Grunwald*. Ph *Derek Williams*. PC *Two Cities*. Dis *United Artists. 109 mins. Cert U*
1940: Peter (*John Mills*), a newly trained pilot, arrives at a bomber station for duty. He is helped by David (*Michael Redgrave*), already a veteran flier. David is in love with Toddy (*Rosamund John*), manageress of the Golden Lion. They marry and have a son. Later, David is killed, and his death makes Peter reluctant to commit himself to his own girl Iris (*Renee Asherson*). The Americans arrive: one is Johnny (*Douglass Montgomery*) who befriends Toddy. He too is killed. Toddy intervenes to bring Peter and Iris back together. The war in the skies goes on. Inspiring, understated war film; poems for it were written by *John Pudney*.
RoC *Stanley Holloway, Basil Radford, Felix Aylmer, Bonar Colleano, Trevor Howard, Joyce Carey, Tyron Nichol, Bill Rowbotham (Owen), Grant Miller, David Tomlinson, Hugh Dempster, Charles Victor, Jean Simmons, Johnnie Schofield, Hartley Power, Vida Hope, Anthony Dawson, Murray Matheson, John McLaren, Charles Farrell, Bill Logan, John Howard, Jacqueline Clarke, Alf Goddard, Caven Watson, Sydney Benson, Peter Cotes, Ian Warner McGilvray, Ann Wilton, Alan Sedgewick, O.B. Clarence.*

John Mills and Michael Redgrave in The Way to the Stars (*1945*)

THE WAY WE LIVE (1946) [4]
Dir, Prod and Scr *Jill Craigie*. Ph *Laurie Friedman*. PC *Two Cities*. Dis *General Film Distributors. 64 mins. Cert U*
Quasi-documentary about the re-creation of a blitzed city (Plymouth), seen through the adventures of a bombed-out family. We see them go through the tribulations of billeting and temporary housing. Finally, thousands go on the march demanding that the Watson-Abercrombie plan (an expenditure of £20,000,000 on land alone) be carried out. It is. Solidly crafted.
LP *Peter Willes, Francis Lunt, Verena Chaffe, Patsy Scantlebury, June Riddolls, Beryl Rose-kelly, Mrs MacMillan, Pat Lang, James Robson, Lt Hutchinson, Sir Patrick Abercrombie, James Paton-Watson.*

THE WEAKER SEX (1948) [5]
Dir *Roy Baker*. Prod *Paul Soskin*. Scr *Esther McCracken, Soskin, from a play by McCracken*. Ph *Erwin Hillier*. PC *Two Cities*. Dis *General Film Distributors. 84 mins. Cert U*
1944. Middle-class Martha (*Ursula Jeans*) is mother, housewife, firewatcher and canteen worker. Her two daughters (*Joan Hopkins, Lana Morris*), though living at home, are serving in the Wrens. Her son Ben (*Digby Wolfe*) is in the navy. Two other soldiers (*Cecil Parker, Derek Bond*) are billeted at her home. But they too leave when D-Day comes. The war ends and this family, at least, is reunited. Nicely human story, well handled: sentimental but convincingly so.
RoC *John Stone, Marian Spencer, Thora Hird, Kynaston Reeves, Eleanor Summerfield, Bill Owen, Gladys Henson, Dorothy Bramhall, Basil Appleby, Vi Kaley, Campbell Cotts, Merle Tottenham, Rosemary Lomax, Evelyn Moore, Helen Goss, Joan White, Kathleen Boutall, Josephine Ingram.*

WE DIVE AT DAWN (1943) [5]
Dir *Anthony Asquith*. Prod *Edward Black*. Scr *J.B. Williams, Val Valentine, (uncredited) Frank Launder*. Ph *Jack Cox*. PC *Gainsborough*. Dis *General Film Distributors. 98 mins. Cert U*
Clever study in mounting excitement, focusing first on the shore-leave lives of the crew of the submarine *Sea Tiger* – Hobson (*Eric Portman*) finds his wife has left him – then on their secret mission to torpedo a Nazi battleship before she can reach the Kiel canal. Skipper Taylor (*John Mills*) has to go through a minefield to the other end of the canal to get a shot in at the German ship. Pressed for oil, they spy a tanker on a Danish island and refuel while holding off occupying Germans. Making for England, they hear that they sank the enemy ship. Among relatives on the quayside is Hobson's wife who has come back.
RoC *Reginald Purdell, Niall MacGinnis, Louis Bradfield, Ronald Millar, Caven Watson, Leslie Weston, Norman Williams, Lionel Grose, David Peel, Philip Godfrey, Robert Wolton, John Slater, Joan Hopkins, Josephine Wilson, Beatrice Varley, Frederick Burtwell, Marie Ault, John Salew, Philip Friend, Kenneth Evans, Charles Russell, Gerik Schjelderup, Molly Johnson, Jack*

Watling, Franklin Bennett, Bryan Powley, Merle Tottenham, Joan Sterndale, George Cross, John Redmond, Johnnie Schofield, Victor Beaumont.

WELCOME MR WASHINGTON (1944) [4]
Dir *Leslie Hiscott*. Prod *Elizabeth Hiscott*. Scr *Jack Whittingham, from a story by Noel Streatfeild*. Ph *Erwin Hillier*. PC *British National/Shaftesbury*. Dis *Anglo-American. 90 mins. Cert U*
Pleasant drama about the impact of a US Army unit on an English village. Just outside the village, Jane and Sarah (*Barbara Mullen, Peggy Cummins*), penniless after their father's death, decide to stay on in their ancestral home and farm its land. For their airstrip, the Yanks choose land belonging to Selby (*Roy Emerton*), a nasty tenant-farmer, who believes the girls have fixed it. He tries to blacken the Americans' name, but the villagers are won over by Jane and duck Selby in the millpond.
RoC *Donald Stewart, Leslie Bradley, Martita Hunt, Graham Moffatt, Arthur Sinclair, Shelagh Frazer, Louise Lord, Paul Blake, Beatrice Varley, George Carney, Herbert Lomas, Johnnie Schofield, Drusilla Wills, Irene Handl, Julian d'Albie, Alexander Field, Victor Woods, Tony Quinn, Tommy Palmer, Hal Gordon, John MacLaren, Danny Green, Gordon Begg, Elsie Wagstaffe.*

WE'LL MEET AGAIN (1942) [3]
Dir *Phil Brandon*. Prod *Ben Henry, George Formby*. Scr *James Seymour, Howard Thomas*. Ph *Stephen Dade*. PC and Dis *Columbia British. 84 mins. Cert U*
Peggy Brown (*Vera Lynn*) gets her first big chance through singing to an audience one night in an air-raid. With help from her friend Frank (*Ronald Ward*), a composer, she is hired by the BBC and becomes a radio sensation. She falls in love with Bruce (*Donald Gray*), a Scottish soldier, but loses him to her best friend, and leaves London to entertain the forces. Conventional show business musical, loosely based on Vera Lynn's own career.
RoC *Geraldo, Patricia Roc, Frederick Leister, Betty Jardine, Brefni O'Rorke, Marian Spencer, Lesley Osmond, John Watt, John Sharman, Alvar Liddell, Molly Raynor, Aubrey Mallalieu.*

WE'LL SMILE AGAIN (1942) [4]
Dir and Prod *John Baxter*. Scr *Austin Melford, Barbara K. Emary, Bud Flanagan*. Ph *Jimmy Wilson*. PC *British National*. Dis *Anglo-American. 93 mins. Cert U*
Film star Gordon Maxwell (*Chesney Allen*) is fascinated by down-and-out Bob Parker (*Bud Flanagan*) and hires him as his dresser. Finding that German spies are using Gordon's films to send coded messages, Bob enlists a stand-in (*Phyllis Stanley*) and a make-up man (*Horace Kenney*) to ruin the Huns' schemes. He is fired, but then the spies are caught, and Gordon finds him again after a city-wide search. Full of bright gags and human touches.
RoC *Meinhart Maur, Charles Austin, Wally Patch, Peggy Dexter, C. Denier Warren, Julian Vedey, Gordon McLeod, Gwen Catley, Billy*

Mayerl, Malcolm 'Mr Jetsam' McEachern, Edgar Driver, Nuala Barrie, Trevor Denis, Charles Doe, Mary Eaton, Buddy Flanagan, Hal Gordon, Harry Herbert, Henry Hilliard, Gerhardt Kempinski, Joe E. Lee, Patrick Ludlow, Ruth Maitland, Andrea Malandrinos, Ernest Metcalfe, Peter Newman, Hilde Palmer, Stanley Paskin, Ethel Royale, Brookes Turner, Bombadier Billy Wells, Ben Williams, Horace Kenney, George Merritt.

WENT THE DAY WELL? (1942)   [3]
(USA: *48 Hours*)

Dir *Alberto Cavalcanti*. (Associate) Prod *S.C. Balcon*. Scr *John Dighton, Diana Morgan, Angus Macphail, from a story by Graham Greene*. Ph *Wilkie Coooper*. PC *Ealing Studios*. Dis *United Artists. 92 mins. Cert A*
The lorry-loads of Royal Engineers eagerly billeted by the villagers of Bramley are in fact German paratroops. They are helped by the squire, Wilsford (*Leslie Banks*), a fifth columnist, but the villagers' suspicions are aroused (the visitors cross their sevens) and they have to be rounded up. The alarm is eventually given and the Germans are wiped out in a battle with British troops. Wilsford is dispatched by the vicar's daughter. Innovative, but only barely convincing.
RoC *Elizabeth Allen, Frank Lawton, Basil Sydney, Valerie Taylor, Mervyn Johns, Edward Rigby, Marie Lohr, C.V. France, David Farrar, Muriel George, Thora Hird, Harry Fowler, John Slater, Johnnie Schofield, Patricia Hayes, Eric Micklewood, Norman Pierce, Edward Rigby, Grace Arnold, James Donald, Gerhard Hinze (Gerard Heinz), Janette Scott*.

Valerie Taylor, C.V. France, Leslie Banks and Basil Sydney in Went the Day Well?

WHAT A CARRY ON! (1949)   [1]

Dir and Prod *John E. Blakeley*. Scr *Anthony Toner*. Ph *Ernest Palmer*. PC *Film Studios Manchester*. Dis *Mancunian. 94 mins. Cert U*
Jimmy Jervis and Ben Watts (*Jimmy Jewel and Ben Warriss*) join the army, encounter a singing sergeant-major (*Josef Locke*) and a pretty lady corporal (*Terry Randall*) and generally create havoc in a series of slapstick episodes. Top radio comics prove the old *Abbott and Costello* plot no sure route to film stardom.
RoC *Anthony Pendrell, Eve Eacott, Kitty Bluett*.

WHEN THE BOUGH BREAKS (1947)   [3]

Dir *Lawrence Huntington*. Prod *Betty Box*. Scr *Muriel and Sydney Box, Peter Rogers*. Ph *Bryan Langley*. PC *Gainsborough*. Dis *General Film Distributors. 81 mins. Cert A*
Young mother Lily (*Patricia Roc*) learns her husband had married her bigamously. A wealthy worker (*Rosamund John*) at the day nursery persuades Lily to let her adopt the child, Jimmy, although Lily won't sign any papers and, when she marries a shopkeeper, takes the boy back. But he is unhappy and Lily returns him. Soon afterwards, she becomes pregnant. Uninspired weepie; disappointing performances.
RoC *Bill Owen, Patrick Holt, Brenda Bruce, Leslie Dwyer, Sonia Holm, Cavan Malone, Torin Thatcher, Catherine Lacey, Jane Hylton, Muriel George, Ada Reeve, Edith Sharpe, Joan Haythorne, Edie Martin, Mary Stone, Sheila Huntington, Gerald Case, Noel Howlett*.

WHEN WE ARE MARRIED (1943)   [4]

Dir *Lance Comfort*. Prod *John Baxter*. Scr *Austin Melford, Barbara K. Emary, from the play by J.B. Priestley*. Ph *Jimmy Wilson*. PC *British National*. Dis *Anglo-American. 98 mins. Cert U*
Three big noises in a small Yorkshire town are shaken out of their complacent shells by the news, on their respective silver wedding days, that their marriages were not legal. They plan to keep it quiet, but one of their cleaning women has heard. The mess is finally sorted out by a drunken photographer (*Sydney Howard*), but not before a few home truths have been aired. Entertaining version of Priestley play with some amusing characters.
RoC *Raymond Huntley, Olga Lindo, Marian Spencer, Ethel Coleridge, Lloyd Pearson, Ernest Butcher, Barry Morse, Lesley Brook, Marjorie Rhodes, Charles Victor, Cyril Smith, George Carney, A. Bromley Davenport, Charles Doe, Patricia Hayes, Charles Mortimer, Lydia Sherwood, Terry Randall*.

WHEN YOU COME HOME (1947)   [2]

Dir and Prod *John Baxter*. Scr *David Evans, Geoffrey Orme, Frank Randle*. Ph *Geoffrey Faithfull*. PC and Dis *Butchers. 98 mins. Cert U*
At his birthday party, Grandpa (*Frank Randle*) tells his granddaughter (*Lesley Osmond*) the story of his life, beginning in 1908 when he was handyman at the Empire theatre, and helped the owner of the music-hall there to outwit a couple of financial crooks and save her fortune. Enormously long and artless comedy with musical numbers.
Ph *Leslie Sarony, Leslie Holmes, Diana Decker, Fred Conyngham, Lynda Parker, Jack Melford, Hilda Bayley, Tony Heaton, Lily Lapidus, Gus Aubrey, Ernest Dale*.

WHILE I LIVE (1947)   [2]

Dir *John Harlow*. Prod and PC *Edward Dryhurst*. Scr *Harlow, Doreen Montgomery*. Ph *F.A. Young*. Dis *20th Century-Fox. 85 mins. Cert A*
After the fall from a cliff of her sister Olwen, a musician whom she had driven to death by overwork, Julia (*Sonia Dresdel*) refuses to believe she has been killed, a belief mistakenly encouraged by her servant Nehemiah (*Tom Walls*). Many years later, a girl pianist suffering from amnesia wanders into Julia's house and history almost tragically repeats itself. Julia, who was convinced the girl was Olwen, is eventually left alone. Not much to commend this except its popular theme, *The Dream of Olwen*.
RoC *Clifford Evans, Carol Raye, Patricia Burke, John Warwick, Edward Lexy, Audrey Fildes, Charles Victor, Ernest Butcher, Sally Rogers, Enid Hewit, Johnnie Schofield, John Martyn, Brenda Cameron, Diana Lake, Doreen Fischer*.

WHILE THE SUN SHINES (1946)   [3]

Dir *Anthony Asquith*. Prod *Anatole de Grunwald*. Scr *Terence Rattigan, de Grunwald, from Rattigan's play*. Ph *Jack Hildyard*. PC *Associate British/International Screenplays*. Dis *Pathé. 81 mins. Cert A*
Lady Elisabeth (*Barbara White*) is about to marry Ordinary Seaman Lord Harpenden (*Ronald Howard*) and end her father's money worries. But Harpenden's friends, a high-powered American (*Bonar Colleano*) and a young Frenchman (*Michael Allan*), give him hot competition, especially as Lady E has developed suspicions about some of his earlier girlfriends. However, he gets her to the altar in the end. Frothy, rather theatrical trifle.
RoC *Ronald Squire, Margaret Rutherford, Brenda Bruce, Cyril Maude, Miles Malleson, Garry Marsh, Joyce Grenfell, Charles Victor, Wilfrid Hyde White, Geoffrey Sumner, O.B. Clarence, Gordon Begg, Amy Frank, Judith Furse, Clive Morton, Cecil Trouncer, Vida Hope, Aubrey Mallalieu, Tamara Beck, Andrea Malandrinos, Beryl Measor, Eric Messiter, Pat(ricia) Owens, Brian Peck, Patrick Bloomfield, Wilfred Caithness, Hugh Dempster, Hamilton Keene, David Keir, Richard Turner, Geoffrey Dunn, Russell Barry*.

WHISKY GALORE! (1948)   [5]
(USA: *Tight Little Island*)

Dir *Alexander Mackendrick*. (Associate) Prod *Monja Danischewsky*. Scr *Compton Mackenzie, Angus Macphail, from Mackenzie's novel*. Ph *Gerald Gibbs*. PC *Ealing Studios*. Dis *General Film Distributors. 82 mins. Cert A*
Todday in the Outer Hebrides is, in 1943, an island out of its favourite tipple: whisky. Then a ship laden with export Scotch runs aground. The crew abandons her and the islanders seize their chance. The local Home Guard captain (*Basil Radford*) calls in excise men, but the islanders are too wily. While whisky takes the place of water in the taps, the captain is left to take the blame. Imaginatively directed, always amusing, sometimes side-splitting comedy.
RoC *Joan Greenwood, James Robertson Justice, Gordon Jackson, Wylie Watson, Gabrielle Blunt, Jean Cadell, Morland Graham, Catherine Lacey, Bruce Seton, Henry Mollison, John Gregson, Duncan Macrae, James Woodburn, Compton Mackenzie, A.E. Matthews, James Anderson, Jameson Clark, Mary MacNeil, Norman MacOwan, Alistair Hunter, Frank Webster, Finlay Currie (narrator)*.

WHITE CRADLE INN (1947) [4]
(USA: *High Fury*)
Dir *Harold French*. Prod *Ivor McLaren, A.E. Hardman*. Scr *French, Lesley Storm*. Ph *Derek Williams*. PC *Peak Films*. Dis *British Lion*. 83 mins. Cert *A*

In the Swiss Alps lies the White Cradle Inn, owned by Magda (*Madeleine Carroll*), who wants to adopt Roger (*Michael McKeag*), a French refugee boy. Her philandering husband Rudolph (*Michael Rennie*) is against it. But Roger jumps the train taking him back to France and returns. To gain Rudolph's permission to adopt, Magda signs over the White Cradle Inn. Man and boy go climbing, and Rudolph gives his life to save Roger. Exciting climax to box-office flop.

RoC *Ian Hunter, Anne Marie Blanc, Arnold Marle, Willy Feuter, Max Haufler, Margarete Hoff, Gerhardt Kempinski*.

THE WHITE UNICORN (1947) [3]
(USA: *Bad Sister*)
Dir *Bernard Knowles*. Prod *Harold Huth*. Scr *Robert Westerby, A.R. Rawlinson, Moie Charles*, from a novel by *Flora Sandstrom*. Ph *Reginald H. Wyer*. PC *John Corfield*. Dis *General Film Distributors*. 97 mins. Cert *A*

Lucy (*Margaret Lockwood*), first married to a cold, calculating lawyer (*Ian Hunter*), then a romantic lover (*Dennis Price*) killed in a car accident, and Lottie (*Joan Greenwood*), a slum girl who has tried to gas both herself and her illegitimate child, meet at the remand home where Lucy is superintendent. Her passionate defence of Lottie in court (the judge is her first husband) wins Lottie back her child. Rather slack drama with the accent on costume and long speeches.

RoC *Guy Middleton, Catherine Lacey, Mabel Constanduros, Paul Dupuis, Eileen Peel, Toots (Julia) Lockwood, Lilly Kann, Valentine Dyall, Stewart Rome, Bryl Wakely, Elizabeth Maude, Noel Howlett, Joan Rees, Isola Strong, Anna Marita, Jan van Loewen, John Howard, Kyra Vane, Jean Shepheard, Clifford Cobbe, John Boxer, Thelma Rea, Vernon Conway, Amy Dalby, Desmond Roberts, Cecil Bevan, Robert Moore, Dorothy Bramhall, David Evans, Paul Sheridan, Alexis Milne*.

WHO KILLED VAN LOON? (1948) [4]
Dir *Gordon Kyle, Lionel Tomlinson*. Prod *Kyle, James Carreras*. Scr *Peter Cresswell*. PC *Kyle*. Dis *Exclusive*. 52 mins. Cert *A*

Schmidt (*Raymond Lovell*) rescues a diamond cutter from a Nazi camp, locks him up and kills his ex-partner, Van Loon, stealing a priceless collection of uncut gems. To force his prisoner to cut the stones, he frames his daughter Anna (*Kay Bannerman*) for the murder. But, thanks to the efforts of a young detective (*Robert Wyndham*), he doesn't get away with it. Intelligent script; capable direction; good second-feature.

RoC *Patricia Laffan, Milton Rosmer, Paul Sheridan, John Dodsworth, Beth Ross, Graham Russell*.

THE WICKED LADY (1945) [2]
Dir *Leslie Arliss*. Prod *R.J. Minney*. Scr *Leslie*

Margaret Lockwood and James Mason in The Wicked Lady *(1945)*

Arliss, Aimee Stuart, Gordon Glennon, from a novel by Magdalen King-Hall. Ph *Jack Cox*. PC *Gainsborough*. Dis *Eagle-Lion*. 104 mins. Cert *A*

Ambitious, self-centred Barbara (*Margaret Lockwood*), a seventeenth-century adventuress, takes Sir Ralph Skelton (*Griffith Jones*) away from her friend Caroline (*Patricia Roc*), but soon becomes bored with his life and takes to highway robbery. She has a passionate affair with highwayman Jerry Jackson (*James Mason*), who is nearly hanged as a result of her treachery. He escapes, only for Barbara to shoot him. She is badly wounded in return and barely gets back to her room before dying under the eyes of Kit (*Michael Rennie*), another of Caroline's beaux, with whom she was really in love. Lurid melodrama acted with gusto. Hated by the critics, it became Britain's top moneymaking film of 1946.

RoC *Enid Stamp-Taylor, Felix Aylmer, David Horne, Martita Hunt, Emrys Jones, Jean Kent, Amy Dalby, Beatrice Varley, Helen Goss, Francis Lister, Ivor Barnard*.

WILLIAM COMES TO TOWN (1948) [3]
Dir and Scr *Val Guest*, from stories by *Richmal Crompton*. Prod *John R. Sloan, David Coplan*. Ph *Bert Mason*. Ph *Diadem/Alliance*. Dis *United Artists*. 89 mins. Cert *U*

Scruffy William's (*William Graham*) parents (*Garry Marsh, Jane Welsh*) agree to take him to the circus – but only if he's good. This is like asking for the moon, especially as William and his cronies are in the middle of a campaign for shorter school hours and more pocket money that takes him to the Prime Minister himself. Gifts from admirers include a chimpanzee that creates havoc. William does get to the circus, but not quite in the way he expected.

RoC *Hugh Cross, Kathleen Stuart, Muriel Aked, A.E. Matthews, Brian Weske, James Crabbe, Brian Roper, Michael Medwin, Jon Pertwee, David Paige, Michael Balfour, Norman Pierce, Eve Mortimer, John Powe, Mary Vallange, Peter Butterworth, Donald Clive, John Warren, Alan Goford, Basil Gordon, Claude Bonsor, Ivan Craig, John Martell, Pinkie Hannaford, Jumble (dog), Marquis (chimpanzee)*.

THE WINSLOW BOY (1948) [5]
Dir *Anthony Asquith*. Prod *Anatole de Grun-*

wald. Scr *Terence Rattigan, de Grunwald, Asquith*, from Rattigan's play. Ph *Frederick Young, Osmond Borradaile*. PC *Anatole de Grunwald Productions/London Films*. Dis *British Lion*. 117 mins. Cert *U*

Accused of stealing a postal order, Ronnie Winslow (*Neil North*) is expelled from naval college. His father (*Cedric Hardwicke*), a retired bank official, is convinced of his innocence. He takes the case to the Admiralty and the House of Commons, wrecking his health. A famous QC, Sir Robert Morton (*Robert Donat*) takes up the fight and, after a tense court hearing, Ronnie is exonerated. Sir Robert indicates to the Winslows' suffragette daughter (*Margaret Leighton*) that she has not seen the last of him. Directed with a nice insight into English character by Asquith, who keeps tension on high throughout.

RoC *Basil Radford, Kathleen Harrison, Francis L. Sullivan, Marie Lohr, Jack Watling, Frank Lawton, Walter Fitzgerald, Wilfrid Hyde White, Kynaston Reeves, Ernest Thesiger, Lewis Casson, Stanley Holloway, Cyril Ritchard, Nicholas Hannen, Evelyn Roberts, Mona Washbourne, Billy Shine, Anthony Baird, Barry Briggs, Cecil Bevan, Wilfred Caithness, Hugh Dempster, Archibald Batty, Philip Ray, Edward Lexy, Gordon McLeod, W.A. Kelley, Lambert Ensom, George Bishop, Charles Groves, Ian Colin, Ivan Samson, Dandy Nichols, Vera Cook, Jane Gill-Davis, Frank Tickle, Honor Blake, Margaret Withers, Noel Howlett, Aubrey Mallalieu, Mary Hinton, Nicholas Hawtrey, Beatrice Marsden, Hilary Pritchard*.

WOMAN HATER (1948) [3]
Dir *Terence Young*. Prod *William Sistrom*. Scr *Robert Westerby, Nicholas Phipps*, from a story by *Alec Coppel*. Ph *André Thomas*. PC *Two Cities*. Dis *General Film Distributors*. 105 mins. Cert *A*

Film star Colette Marly (*Edwige Feuillere*) declares she is off men and wants to be alone. To prove it's a publicity stunt, woman-hating Lord Datchett (*Stewart Granger*) rents her a house, poses as the estate agent, and tries to contrive romantic situations. By the time he realizes she is sincere, she has rumbled his game, turns the situation to her advantage and eventually marries him. Not exactly sparkling; seems rather long.

RoC *Ronald Squire, Jeanne de Casalis, Mary Jerrold, David Hutcheson, W.A. Kelley, Georgina Cookson, Henry Edwards, Stewart Rome, Valentine Dyall, Richard Hearne, Cyril Ritchard, Graham Moffatt, Miles Malleson, Dino Galvani, Vernon Greeves, Rosemary Treston, Diana Chandler, Margaret Thorburn, Barbara Gurnhill, Diana Hope, Doreen Lawrence, Jeremy Annett, Peter Cotten, Vida Hope, H.G. Stoker, Michael Medwin, John Stevens, Anne Holland*.

THE WOMAN IN THE HALL (1947) [4]
Dir *Jack Lee*. Prod *Ian Dalrymple*. Scr *G.B. Stern, Dalrymple, Lee*, from Stern's novel. Ph *C.M. Pennington Richards, H.E. Fowle*. PC *Wessex/Independent Producers*. Dis *General Film Distributors*. 93 mins. Cert *A*

Jay (*Jean Simmons*) is a girl whose mother,

Lorna (*Ursula Jeans*), lives on begging letters and phoney appeals to rich, charitable people. Jay's older sister Molly (*Jill Raymond*) tries to protect her from this influence, but Jay is arrested for the forgery of a cheque and Lorna, who has succeeded in hooking an elderly suitor, turns her back on her. In court, however, it is explained that Jay was trying to reverse her mother's lifestyle by giving, and Lorna is shown up for what she is. Good script helps refreshingly original story.
RoC *Edward Underdown, Cecil Parker, Joan Miller, Nigel Buchanan, Ruth Dunning, Russell Waters, Terry Randal(l), Lilly Kann, Martin Walker, Barbara Shaw, Dorothy (Totti) Truman Taylor, Hugh Pryse, Everley Gregg, Alexis France, Susan Hampshire, Tania Tipping.*

WOMAN TO WOMAN (1946) [4]
Dir *Maclean Rogers*. Prod *Louis H. Jackson*. Scr *James Seymour, Marjorie Deans, from the play by Michael Morton*. Ph *James Wilson*. PC *British National*. Dis *Anglo-American*. 99 mins. Cert A

Third film version of Michael Morton's play. About to be dropped behind enemy lines, married officer David Anson (*Douglass Montgomery*) has an affair with a dancer (*Joyce Howard*). After the liberation of Paris, he finds her again, with their son, but also with a heart condition. His wife (*Adele Dixon*) refuses a divorce. The dancer goes back to the stage, has a heart attack, and dies. A bit creaky, but still touching at the right moments.
RoC *Yvonne Arnaud, Paul Collins, John Warwick, Eugene Deckers, Lilly Kann, Martin Miller, George Carney, Carol Coombe, Ralph Truman, Charles Victor, Finlay Currie, Daisy Burrell, Agnes Bernelle, Kay Young, Gerhardt Kempinski, Marcel de Haes, Therese Carroll, Alan Sedgwick, René Poirier, Eric Lindsay, H.G. Guinle, Daphne Day, Molly Raynor, Griffiths Moss, Ballet Rambert.*

WOMEN AREN'T ANGELS (1942) [4]
Dir *Lawrence Huntington*. Prod *Warwick Ward*. Scr *Vernon Sylvaine, Bernard Mainwaring, Huntington, from the play by Sylvaine*. Ph *Günther Krampf*. PC *Associated British*. Dis *Pathé*. 85 mins. Cert A
Randle and Popday (*Alfred Drayton, Robertson Hare*) are partners in business and – while their wives are away with the ATS – pleasure. On their Home Guard duties, they lose their clothes, wear their wives' uniforms, round up some fifth columnists, and are acclaimed as heroines. When the wives return, *they* take the glory. Ridiculous but fun; direction is slick.
RoC *Polly Ward, Joyce Heron, Mary Hinton, Peggy Novak, Ethel Coleridge, John Stuart, Ralph Michael, Leslie Perrins, Charles Murray, George Merritt, Michael Shepley, Peter Gawthorne, Sydney Monckton.*

THE WORLD OWES ME A LIVING (1944) [2]
Dir *Vernon Sewell*. Prod *Louis H. Jackson*. Scr *Sewell, Erwin Reiner, from the novel by John Llewellyn-Rhys*. Ph *Gerald Gibbs, Geoffrey Faithfull*. PC *British National*. Dis *Anglo-American*. 91 mins. Cert A

Paul Collyer (*David Farrar*) crash-lands, losing his memory. Seeing Moira (*Judy Campbell*) at his bedside, he recalls meeting her when he worked in a 'flying circus', then as an amateur flier keen to make a record flight. Collyer designs and Moira finances a troop-carrying glider, but the authorities take over the project. In hospital, he begs her to marry him – but they are already married, with three children. Jerkily developed drama.
RoC *Sonia Dresdel, Jack Livesey, Jack Barker, John Laurie, Anthony Hawtrey, Wylie Watson, Roy Minear, Alan Keith, Howard Douglas, Humphrey Kent, Amy Veness, MacKenzie Ward, Stewart Rome, Ian MacLean, Max Melford, Richard Clarke, Terence O'Brien, Joss Ambler.*

WOT! NO GANGSTERS? (1946) [2]
Dir *E.W. White*. Prod and Scr *Cecil H. Williamson*. Ph *Adolphe Burger, Oscar Burns*. PC *Cinefilm*. Dis *New Realm*. 46 mins. Cert A
The inventors of a super TV set with worldwide scope give a demonstration before the president of a TV broadcasting company. At first, he can hardly be bothered to listen. But, by the end of the 'show' he has become enthusiastic enough to agree to the inventors' terms. Ragbag of items from earlier films and what look like scraps from the cutting room floor.
LP *Claude Dampier, Ronald Frankau, Mark Hambourg, Billie Carlisle, George Pughe, Miki Decima, Bettina Richman, Corona Babes, Harry Owen and His Band, The Mini-Piano Ensemble.*

THE YEARS BETWEEN (1946) [3]
Dir *Compton Bennett*. Prod and PC *Sydney Box*. Scr *Muriel and Sydney Box, from the play by Daphne du Maurier*. Ph *Reginald H. Wyer*. Dis *General Film Distributors*. 100 mins. Cert A
When her husband Michael (*Michael Redgrave*) is reported killed in action, Diana (*Valerie Hobson*) is persuaded by her friends to stand for his seat in Parliament, which she does successfully. She is about to re-marry when Michael returns from a POW camp. Instead of the wife he left, he finds a budding career woman. Diana gives up the seat, but is re-elected elsewhere. Michael learns that he must accept the changes in his wife if he is to keep her. Not too convincing portrayal of upper-class problems.
RoC *Flora Robson, Felix Aylmer, Dulcie Gray, Edward Rigby, James McKechnie, John Gilpin, Yvonne Owen, Wylie Watson, Esma Cannon, Muriel George, Ernest Butcher, Lyn Evans, Joss Ambler, Katie Johnson, Maxwell Reed, Michael Hordern, Gwen Clark (Jane Hylton).*

THE YELLOW CANARY (1943) [3]
Dir and Prod *Herbert Wilcox*. Scr *Miles Malle-*

son, DeWitt Bodeen. Ph *Mutz Greenbaum*. PC *Imperator*. Dis *RKO Radio*. 98 mins. Cert U
1940: Nazi sympathizer Sally Maitland (*Anna Neagle*) goes to Canada, shadowed by intelligence man Jim Garrick (*Richard Greene*). She liaises with Nazi agents planning to blow up the harbour in Halifax, Nova Scotia. Being in reality a British agent, she is able, with the help of Jim, really her assistant, to sabotage the German plot. Although shot and wounded, she survives. Thriller not as smart as it thinks.
RoC *Lucie Mannheim, Albert Lieven, Nova Pilbeam, Margaret Rutherford, Cyril Fletcher, Claude Bailey, Patric Curwen, Marjorie Fielding, Aubrey Mallalieu, David Horne, Franklin Dyall, George Thorpe, Gordon McLeod, John Longden, Hedley Goodall, Winifred Oughton, David Ward, Eliot Makeham, Ian Fleming, Valentine Dyall, MacDonald Parke, John Kannowin, Gerry Wilmott, Clifford Buckton, Grace Allardyce, Anthony Eustrel, Tatiana Lieven, Leslie Dwyer, Edgar Driver, Grizelda Hervey.*

THE YOUNG MR PITT (1941) [4]
Dir *Carol Reed*. Prod *Edward Black*. Scr *Frank Launder, Sidney Gilliat, Viscount Castlerosse*. Ph *Frederick A. Young*. PC *Twentieth Century*. Dis *20th Century-Fox*. 118 mins. Cert U
Prime Minister of Britain at only 24, William Pitt (*Robert Donat*) gradually overcomes the bitter opposition of C.J. Fox (*Robert Morley*), but his career is thrown into turmoil when France declares war on Britain in 1793. His health begins to fail and in 1801 he is compelled to resign, following a series of British defeats. Recalled in 1804, Pitt sees Napoleon (*Herbert Lom*) defeated at Trafalgar. His popularity regained, Pitt dies the following year at 46.
RoC *Phyllis Calvert, Raymond Lovell, John Mills, Max Adrian, Felix Aylmer, Albert Lieven, Stephen Haggard, Geoffrey Atkins, Jean Cadell, Agnes Laughlan, Ian MacLean, A. Bromley Davenport, John Salew, Stuart Lindsell, Henry Hewitt, Frederick Culley, Frank Pettingell, Leslie Bradley, Roy Emerton, Hugh McDermott, Alfred Sangster, Kathleen Byron, Jack Watling, Ronald Shiner, John Slater, Leslie Dwyer, Hugh Ardele, Frederick Leister, Esma Cannon, Merle Tottenham, Aubrey Mallalieu, Margaret Vyner, Austin Trevor, Leo Genn, James Harcourt, Muriel George, Dalla Black, Louis Diswarte, Townsend Whitling, Kynaston Reeves, Johnnie Schofield, Ann Stephens, Bruce Winston, Owen Reynolds, Billy Holland, Gerald Cooper, Ralph Roberts, Edgar Vosper, Edmund Willard, Alf Goddard, Frederick Valk, J.H. Roberts, Esmé Percy, Gibb McLaughlin, D.J. Williams, Morland Graham, Lloyd Pearson, W.E. Holloway, Charles Paton, Neal Arden, Gordon James, Stanley Escane, Leslie Harcourt, James Kenney, Sydney Tafler.*

YOU WILL REMEMBER (1940) [3]
Dir and PC *Jack Raymond*. Prod *Charles Q. Steele*. Scr *Lydia Hayward*. Ph *Henry Harris*. Dis *British Lion*. 87 mins. Cert U
Musical biography of poor-born Tom Barrett (*Robert Morley*), who becomes 1890s' composer Leslie Stuart and, with the help of his bootblack friend (*Emlyn Williams*) and others,

rises to fame with such songs as *Lily of La-guna*, *Little Dolly Daydream* and *Soldiers of the King*. Through over-confidence and over-generosity, he lands in debtors' prison when the Jazz Age sends his career into decline. But his friends come to his rescue. Well-acted but low-key biopic.

RoC *Dorothy Hyson, Tom E. Finglass, Nicholas Phipps, Allan Jeayes, Charles Victor, Maire O'Neill, Maurice Kelly, Roddy McDowall, Marie Ault, Gertrude Musgrove, Charles Lefeaux, Muriel George, Mary Merrall, Band of HM Grenadier Guards.*

Emlyn Williams and Robert Morley in You Will Remember *(1940)*

SHORTS

Entertainment films of the 1940s between 20 minutes' and 44 minutes' duration

1940
At the Havana (28)
Hullo Fame! (44) with Jean Carr (Kent), Peter Ustinov
John Smith Wakes Up (43) with Joan Greenwood

1941
Dangerous Acquaintance (27)
Pathétone Parade of 1941 (35)

1942
Escape to Justice (44)
Pathétone Parade of 1942 (41)
The Safe Blower (20)
Soldiers Without Uniform (39) with Tod Slaughter

1943
*I Want to be an Actress (36)
Pictorial Revue of 1943 (39)
Starlight Serenade (44)
Strange to Relate (33)
There's a Future In It (36)

1944
Browned Off (35)
The Man from Scotland Yard (36)
*Victory Wedding (20) with John Mills, Dulcie Gray. Director: Jessie Matthews

1945
Bad Company (44)
Bothered by a Beard (36) with Tod Slaughter

Camera Reflections (38)
Dumb Dora Discovers Tobacco (40); director: Charles Hawtrey
Echo of Applause (41)
*Hands Across the Ocean (37)
Here We Come Gathering (21) with Nanette Newman
Men of the Mines (42)
Sports Day (24) with Jean Simmons
Sweethearts for Ever (33)
The Tell Tale Taps (20)
Trouble at Townsend (23) with Petula Clark

1946
The Adventures of Parker (35)
Amateur Night (35)
The Clock Strikes Eight (27)
Dancing Thru (35)
The Gong Cried Murder (29)
*A Great Failure (40)
Happy Family (39)
The House in Rue Rapp (31)
Jean's Plan (30)
Musical Masquerade (39)
Riders of the New Forest (serial, five episodes, 15 mins each)
Those Were the Days (38)
The Voyage of Peter Joe (serial, six episodes, 20 mins each)

1947
*Bank Holiday Luck (42)
*Crime Reporter (36)
Dusty Bates (serial, five episodes, 20 mins each)
*A Journey for Jeremy (34) released 1949

Life is Nothing Without Music (34) with Jessie Matthews
Making the Grade (33)
Musical Romance (35)
*Punch and Judy (35)
Stage Frights (34)
The Way of the World (33)
We Do Believe in Ghosts (36)

1948
Born of the Sea (38)
*Death in the Hand (44)
Escape from Broadmoor (37)
For Old Times' Sake (34)
The Gentlemen Go By (39)
*The Girl from Scotland Yard (35)
The Goodwin Sands (34)
Tails You Lose (35)
*Under the Frozen Falls (44)

1949
Artful Dodgers (39)
The Greedy Boy's Dream (22)
The Haunted Palace (34)
The Last Wish (34)
Movie-Go-Round (44)
The Nitwits on Parade (42)
Slick Tartan (37)
Three Bags Full (serial, three episodes, 19 mins each)
A Touch of Shamrock (30)
Which Will You Have? (36) (USA: *Barabbas the Robber*) with Niall MacGinnis

*indicates a film of above average merit
Minutes in brackets

The Fifties

Kay Kendall and Kenneth More in *Genevieve* (1953)

The Fifties

INTRODUCTION TO THE DECADE

After the financial gloom and doom of the post-war 1940s, it was expected that most British studios thereafter would face a struggle to stay alive. In fact, the major studios were kept in a modest state of buoyancy until towards the end of the decade, thanks to a more intelligent appraisal of economics from the men in charge of their accounts.

It brought a golden era of 'pop' cinema to the Rank Organization and to Associated British, as well as to British Lion, who probably made bigger popular hits than their rivals, especially in the second half of the decade, but lacked the financial cushion control of a circuit of cinemas would have provided.

In 1951, Rank, London Films and Associated British all showed small profits (although London Films chief Alexander Korda would lose control of British Lion in 1954, when the government called in the notorious £3,000,000 loan it had perhaps unwisely allowed Lion in 1949). Blinkered to the onset of television, studios began to don an outer coat of prosperity. Players were put under contract, although many of the lesser lights would soon leave over dissatisfaction with the work they had been offered. Few of these defectors, alas, moved on to greater heights in their careers.

Many of the new stars who did come to the fore proved less durable than those who had gone to Hollywood. Conversely, some of those who had been unhappy or unsuccessful in Hollywood returned, only to find themselves unable to regain their former stature in the British industry.

As the decade began, the great female stars of the 1940s, Margaret Lockwood, Anna Neagle and Phyllis Calvert, were clearly beginning to lose their drawing-power at the box-office. Of those who had not gone to Hollywood, some, such as Patricia Roc and Jean Kent, elected to freelance in search of better roles - not always to their advantage.

It quickly became obvious that the 1950s would become the first wholly male-dominated decade of the British cinema, whether by 'pin-up' stars, high-powered character actors or popular comedians. And the vast majority of them would blossom in films from The Rank Organization.

Anna Neagle, Michael Wilding, Laurence Olivier, John Mills and Margaret Lockwood were still high in popularity polls as the decade opened. Although Mills was to soldier on (appropriately!) on the fringe of the polls for the rest of the decade, the picture had changed dramatically as early as 1953.

The unlikely trio of Alec Guinness, Alastair Sim and Ronald Shiner had come to the fore, and were joined in the 'top five' by two dominant figures of the 1950s, the contrasting Jack Hawkins and Dirk Bogarde.

The weakening of female stars as a box-office factor was given additional impetus when Britain's highest-ranked actress in films, Dinah Sheridan, who had risen to prominence after a long apprenticeship, retired at the peak of her popularity to marry John Davis, the one-time accountant whose financial wizardry had made him the power behind the Rank throne. The marriage was to end in divorce. She had, in fact, been in films almost as long as Ronald Shiner, whose unexpected popularity after years of character roles was thanks to two hugely successful versions of stage farces - *Worm's Eye View* and *Reluctant Heroes*.

Shiner then perhaps unwisely crossed from Associated British to Rank, whose publicity for him was tremendous, but who neglected to provide him the material to keep him at the top, their Shiner films being mainly uninspired reworkings of scripts that had served other comedians in the 1930s.

By 1954, Rank's golden goose of comedy came from another nest, and Shiner was dropped, perhaps unfairly, although he certainly floundered outside the aegis of a big studio, and was out of films by the end of the decade, after playing second-fiddle to the man who had been his stooge - Brian Rix.

The queues that stretched round cinemas, and out into the streets, in the winter of 1953, for an 85-minute comedy called *Trouble in Store* provided Rank with both a godsend and a warning. For the star of the film was Norman Wisdom, a diminutive comedian fond of too-tight suits, falls down stairs and paroxysms of laughter. He could sing, appear genuinely wretched in misfortune and play musical instruments.

His popularity, however, had been built up by television, the 'gains' from which, in terms of star players, would never be sufficient to offset the inroads it would make into the cinema's ever-decreasing audience.

By now, after the resounding success of *Genevieve* and *Doctor in the House*, two of Rank's biggest financial winners of the early 1950s, affable Kenneth More, who proved a versatile and likeable leading man, had joined Bogarde, Hawkins and Wisdom at the top.

These two films - Rank lost no time in reissuing them as 'the Doc and the Crock' (*Genevieve* being about the 'old crocks' rally to Brighton) in a double-bill - highlighted two other trends of the decade.

Firstly, they were both in Technicolor, and colour began to be used from 1953 with much greater frequency by the two major distributors, sometimes even for films that hardly seemed to call for it. But then colour was a thing that, for the moment, British television was unable to offer.

The other trend lay in the acceptance of comedy series as a formula for box-office success. Both the Boulting Brothers and the Launder-Gilliat team, all releasing through British Lion, were turning to comedy by the middle of the decade, the former with their series of institutional lampoons starring Ian Carmichael, another unexpected star of the 1950s, the latter with the St Trinian's films and other farces featuring the lugubrious Alastair Sim. The 'Doctor' comedies continued apace with an increasingly unhappy Bogarde (see *Star of the Decade*), while Anglo-Amalgamated got into the act in 1958 with the first of the biggest and broadest comedy series of all - the 'Carry On' films.

By then, though, many people had slipped away from the cinema compared to 1953, a year in which John Davis had cut Rank's overdraft to £6 million - £11 million less than in 1949, an additional incentive, perhaps, to splash out on colour films.

Popular throughout this period was big, burly, reliable Jack Hawkins, as rugged in character as his big box-office rival, Bogarde, was vulnerable. After an awkward apprenticeship in juvenile roles of the 1930s, Hawkins marked time in the kind of roles that, say, Bernard Lee might have been playing.

Hawkins' big breakthrough came as late as 1952, with his

roles as the teacher of deaf-and-dumb children in *Mandy*, and the ebullient group-captain in *Angels One Five*. His role as Erickson in Ealing Studios' *The Cruel Sea* the following year made Hawkins the number one British box-office star, a position that would also be enjoyed by Bogarde and More before the decade was out.

Despite a couple of costume flops (*The Seekers* and *Land of the Pharaohs* - the latter, which Hawkins termed 'perfectly ridiculous', probably put him off Hollywood for years), Hawkins held his place well at the top, through to the 1960s. His last good leading role, in *The League of Gentlemen*, was seen early in 1960, and it was practically the last time he enjoyed top billing. In any case, an operation for throat cancer in 1966 removed his vocal chords and with them the wonderful Hawkins voice that in films it seemed could rip through an inadequate subordinate at 20 yards.

The eclipse of Kenneth More, who was four years younger, was more sudden and is less easy to explain. He had begun as a stand-up comic at the Windmill Theatre, taking part in a few of their makeshift films of the mid-1930s. It was not until the late 1940s that he began to take films seriously as a character player, but it seemed that More, now in his late thirties, was destined to be no more than a pleasant part of the supporting cast.

The turning point was a little film that More made for Group 3, a vaguely Ealing-style outfit inspired by the great documentarist John Grierson. In their short lifespan (1951-5), Group 3's best films were probably dramas - *The Brave Don't Cry*, *Conflict of Wings* and *The Blue Peter* among them - but they produced a number of whimsical comedies along Ealing lines, of which *Brandy for the Parson* (1951) was one of the first.

For the first time More, second-billed as a genial brandy-smuggler, attracted personal interviews and magazine articles. Predictions of stardom became more widely heard after his quietly effective father in *The Yellow Balloon* (1952). In 1953, he completely ran away with the otherwise undistinguished desert-island farce *Our Girl Friday*, against competition from George Cole, Joan Collins and Robertson Hare; when he followed this with *Genevieve* and *Doctor in the House* (winning a British Oscar for the latter), the home cinema clearly had a major star on its hands.

Subsequently, More brought his genial personality to light up a number of minor projects, most of which he turned into solo shows. Proving himself a versatile actor in *The Deep Blue Sea* and *Reach for the Sky*, he was successfully teamed in the 1958-61 period with such disparate actresses as Jayne Mansfield, Lauren Bacall, Dana Wynter, Danielle Darrieux and Susannah York. His performances began to lose some of their joie-de-vivre after that, although the film that ended his star career, *The Comedy Man*, is ironically one his best. The subject - an ageing, womanizing actor reaching out for stardom before old age grabs him first - and the certificate (X) did not please a Rank Organization used to jolly More romps, and they offered the film only a minimal release some two years after its completion.

The X certificate had become a thorny problem for both circuits as they fought (and gradually lost) a battle to retain the family audience. The certificate, which had been introduced (to replace the old H certificate) as a cloak for genuinely adult drama, had soon become tarnished by a morass of continental sex sagas, and both Rank and Associated British for a time outlawed it from their cinemas.

As the industry fought a decline in audiences that was re-latively slight in the early 1950s, showy double-bills, often all in colour, were seen to be one answer, even quite major films often being afforded substantial support in this manner.

Rank's arrangements with Universal-International, and Associated British's with Allied Artists, Warner Brothers and, for a while, Fox's Panoramic Productions brought the undemanding mid-1950s' cinemagoer rich value on some occasions.

It meant, for example, that Rank were able to twin *Trouble in Store* with an Edward G. Robinson thriller *The Glass Web*, while Associated British could offer *For Better, For Worse* (with Dirk Bogarde, on loan from Rank) in harness with *The Raid*, a good Civil War drama with Van Heflin, Anne Bancroft and Lee Marvin. An Ealing Studios comedy could crop up in company with an Audie Murphy western, widening the range of audience to which the complete programme might appeal. In this way, British cinema was seen to be not only prosperous, but also part of the international scene.

The independent cinemas not belonging to the two major circuits were quick to jump on this band wagon. The usual ploy was to take the top feature from the local Odeon or Gaumont (whichever was farthest away) and team it with an attractive reissue. The drawback to this was that it stretched programmes to ever greater lengths, sometimes as much as four hours, which in turn restricted the number of daily programmes that could be provided for paying customers.

The independents were given a temporary boost when Rank fell out with 20th Century-Fox at the time of the introduction of CinemaScope (over the number of cinemas to be equipped with stereophonic sound), and big new Fox pictures also became available.

The Fox-Rank rift was healed, however, after a couple of years, and Rank further stifled competition in 1958 when doing away with Odeons and Gaumonts as separate circuits, replacing them with the Rank (main release) and National (secondary release) circuits. The independents were now usually able to play only the National, or inferior release, which few people wanted to see, and gradually reverted to being repertory cinemas to survive for a few more years.

Ealing Studios continued to release through Rank until 1956. Michael Balcon's 'Academy for Young Gentlemen', as it has been described by one of its producers, Monja Danischewsky, had begun the decade well with two vintage Ealing comedies, *The Lavender Hill Mob* and *The Man in the White Suit*, both starring Alec Guinness, then the nation's top box-office star.

Of the Ealing dramas, however, only *Mandy* was a big success, and comedy was perhaps unwisely left alone until the studio decided to splash out colour on *The Titfield Thunderbolt*, a pleasant comedy about rural railways. It paled by comparison with *Genevieve*, made at Rank by one-time Ealing man Henry Cornelius, who had regretfully been turned down by Balcon who had neither time nor space to fit the film in.

Although Ealing immediately had another giant hit with *The Cruel Sea*, its only remaining comedy successes were *The Maggie*, about the wily crew of an old Scottish puffer boat, and the classic black farce *The Ladykillers*.

A demand for a new broader type of comedy was prevailing, part of a general pattern. The public now preferred a less subtle approach - something that would, in the late 1950s, bring about both the revival of the horror film with Hammer Studios and the new wave of realist dramas, led by *Room at the Top*, that dug deep into the problems of the working classes.

On 13 January 1956, Ealing Studios were taken over by

BBC Television. Balcon rejected an offer from Rank by which two new sound stages would have been built at Pinewood for Ealing's (non-exclusive) use, and the Ealing distribution pact with Rank was terminated, although 'Ealing Films' continued (downward) for a few more years.

As Ealing fell, Hammer rose. The company had originally been founded in the 1930s by producer Will Hammer (appropriately, Bela Lugosi starred in one of its earlier films), but was little heard from until the beginning of the 1950s, when it began to produce a number of quite lengthy second-features, starring fading Hollywood figures, clearly aimed for double-bills on the international market.

The breakthrough to the bigtime came when Hammer acquired the rights to film the hugely successful television serial *The Quatermass Experiment*, which had glued millions to their screens for weeks. Buoyed by the resultant profits, the company decided not only to make a sequel, but to plunge into a new series of horror films on old themes – to be made, for the first time since the two-colour Technicolor chillers from Hollywood's Warner Brothers in the early 1930s, in colour.

After a hesitant start with *The Curse of Frankenstein* in 1957, Hammer hit the jackpot the following year with a stylish and scary remake of *Dracula*. The gore flowed unabated from then on, and the company sailed along quite happily on its river of blood until the mid-1970s, the locations around its small studio at Bray turning up unashamedly in one film after another.

When all other avenues were exhausted, a *Hammer House of Horror* series appeared on television in the 1980s, bringing the company full circle to the origin of its success.

The onslaught of television had, of course, proved the killer blow to an industry already weakened by decreasing audiences and rising costs. It is also true that the sheer number of really good entertainment films from Britain and Hollywood had declined from its 1938–41 peak, a gradual erosion of quality that had gone unnoticed in the entertainment-starved war years.

A slip in attendances after the 'captive audience' days of 1939–45 was to be expected, and the industry's price rises, coupled with adjustments in Entertainments Tax, for a while kept heads above water. There were 1,585 million admissions to Britain's cinemas in 1945, 1,396 million in 1950 and 1,182 million in 1955 – not too disastrous if a levelling-out could be swiftly achieved.

But quality was ignored in favour of ever-widening screens, 3-D, stereophonic sound and other gimmicks. Commercial television arrived in the London area in 1955, and in a few short years, the battle for the British film industry as it then existed was won and lost. At the beginning of the 1960s admissions had dropped to 501 million – an irreparable collapse. Cinemas, too, which had held steady from 1935 to 1955 at around 4,500, now began to close.

By 1960, their numbers were down to just over 3,000. Admission money, too, started to fall rapidly from 1957. Entertainments Tax was slashed from 1957 and abolished altogether by 1960 – but it was too late, and it is doubtful even if much earlier action on this front could have improved the ultimately black prospect.

Observers of the disaster have accurately noted that television bit deep into the working-class family audience on which the cinema had relied. But the senior members of those families, who had been film fans since at least the beginning of sound, were now nearing retirement age, and only too willing to put their feet up in front of the mint-new magic of the box,

especially in the winter months, when film programmers found it increasingly difficult to drag their once-enthusiastic patrons away from the now more attractive fireside. After all, as cinemas emptied, so they grew colder – and more expensive to heat for the faithful few who remained.

At Rank, the rot for the film side of what, thanks again to John Davis, had become a profitably diversified group of companies, had set in by the middle of 1957. Eighteen films were personally produced by Rank productions – now out in the open after masquerading as British National in the 1940s, British Film Makers in the early 1950s and then Group Film Productions in 1953–4.

Another 20 films were announced for 1958, but those schedules were reduced in December 1957, the month in which a number of major studio stars, such as John Gregson and Donald Sinden, found that their contracts were not being renewed. Most of these stars had done nothing wrong – Rank simply couldn't afford to keep them. Early in 1958, 300 workers at Pinewood were laid off after the termination of four films budgeted at around £250,000 each.

By 1959, independents using Pinewood outnumbered Rank's minimal production line-up. In June of that year, rumours were rife that the studio was going to withdraw from film-making altogether – but that was not to happen, for the time being.

The company was in fact now well into the black, announcing profits of more than £7,000,000 for 1959/60. But it was Davis' shrewd ventures into copying machines, bingo halls, bowling alleys, motorway service areas, commercial TV and electronic and computer equipment that had brought prosperity. Had it not been for this diversification and cut-backs in film-making, the Rank empire could not have survived.

Austerity days had also arrived at Associated British's Elstree Studios, where the crowded schedules of 1957 were halved in the two following years. By 1961, TV series were being made there; that was the year in which the number of British films began to drop dramatically after remaining fairly constant through the 1950s.

The ambitious Warwick film outfit, releasing through Columbia, had at last discovered that importing such major Hollywood stars as Victor Mature, Robert Mitchum, Rita Hayworth, Robert Taylor and Jack Lemmon for high-budget action epics was not enough without a decent script to go with them. Warwick films were reviled by the critics, although they did gradually make a star of Anthony Newley, and many of the men associated with the company had the last laugh when, under another banner, they began the phenomenally successful James Bond films in 1962.

The last Ealing film, *The Siege of Pinchgut*, was released in August 1959, and with it Britain's greatest independent went out of existence. Universal and Gaumont-British newsreels were closed by Rank as an economy measure and, with the replacement of AB-Pathé as a distributor by Warner-Pathé in December 1959, the days of Pathé News, too, were numbered.

Britain's two great weekly fan magazines, *Picturegoer* and *Picture Show*, had been struggling for advertising since 1958, and now looked doomed. *Picturegoer* closed in April 1960, and *Picture Show* in July 1960, taking with them the studio news columns once so eagerly turned to by thousands of readers.

The day of the big studio in Britain, financed by its proprietor's own films, was clearly over.

The Fifties
STAR OF THE DECADE

Dirk Bogarde

In the title role of *The Spanish Gardener* (1956)

Although others were more admired as actors – a situation that would change in succeeding decades – no actor's bag of fanmail was heavier in the 1950s than that of Dirk Bogarde. Whether as unreliable ne'er-do-wells, men on the run or embryo doctors, Bogarde exuded a faintly 'lost' quality which his audiences, particularly women, found attractive.

For a while, at the time of *Penny Princess* and *So Long at the Fair*, it seemed that he might get typecast as ineffectual heroes; but Bogarde was always too interesting for that; there were too many facets of his character still be explored. From 1952 to 1958, he was top dog at Britain's premier studio, the Pinewood of The Rank Organization, but, even here, in the prime pin-up days before respect made him perhaps a shade sombre, he managed to get through a surprising variety of roles.

Born Derek Van Den Bogaerde (of Dutch extraction) in London, 1921, he was never far away from the world of the arts. His godmother was actress Yvonne Arnaud, while his father was art editor of *The Times*. Bogarde made his first stage appearance in Glasgow at 13 and was with Newick Amateur Dramatic Society at 17.

The next step was repertory at Amersham, during which period he appeared as an extra in a George Formby comedy. But at that stage World War II intervened, and Bogarde became an officer in Air Photographic Intelligence, spending most of his time as a sketch artist, a reflection of his early career in commercial art after studies at Chelsea Polytechnic.

Success on the London stage in post-war years soon led to his being offered a contract by Ian Dalrymple's Wessex Films (releasing through Rank's General Film Distributors) and he played his first major role for them in *Esther Waters* (1948).

Producers seemed to see shifty qualities in Bogarde that led him to be cast as callow characters. Although he fought against such casting, later events proved that he was always at his most fascinating as men of flawed, devious or mysterious character. Thus the most memorable of his early roles came late in 1949, as the young hoodlum who shoots down Jack Warner's police constable in *The Blue Lamp*.

Rank now took him under its wing. At first his enigmatic qualities caused him to be cast as fugitives, for instance in *Hunted*, *The Gentle Gunman*, *Desperate Moment* and *The Sleeping Tiger*, but, after *Doctor in the House* was released early in 1954, he became sure-fire at the box-office for the rest of the decade, despite increasing dissatisfaction with his commitment to the 'Doctor' comedies, a commitment which actually lasted until 1963, when he made his last appearance as Simon Sparrow, in *Doctor in Distress*.

Bogarde had always resisted offers from Hollywood, and his brief flirtation there at the end of the 1950s only proved how right he had been. None of these 'international' films, *The Doctor's Dilemma*, *Libel!* and *Song Without End* (in which, as

With Betty Warren in *Esther Waters* (1948)

With Jean Simmons in *So Long at the Fair* (1950)

As the doomed pianist in *Quartet* (1948)

With Jon Whiteley in *Hunted* (1951)

Liszt, he had to master a long and complicated series of piano fingerings), did as well as the Rank offerings with the public and, indeed, they marked the end of Bogarde's days as a 'pin-up' male lead.

Now, he played three interesting 'villain' roles – as the Mexican bandit, clad in black leather, in *The Singer Not the Song*, as the sadistic lieutenant in *HMS Defiant* and, most notably, as the corrupt butler in *The Servant*, a role that set the pattern for the later stages of his career, as he became a favourite of such distinguished directors as Losey and Visconti.

These latter-day films have mainly been studies in gloom and suffering, although Bogarde has lightened the burden on his admirers by also writing three very readable volumes of autobiography and several best-selling novels, mostly written at the villa in France where he now lives.

Of those Rank days in the 1950s, Bogarde has said: 'I loved the camera, and the camera seemed to love me – well, half of

With Dinah Sheridan in *Appointment in London* (1952)

me, at any rate. Every set in my Rank films was built with a view to showing off my left profile. Nobody ever saw the other side of my face in something like 30 pictures. I was the Loretta Young of Pinewood.'

FILMOGRAPHY:

1939: Come On George (as extra). 1947: Dancing with Crime. 1948: Esther Waters. Quartet. Once a Jolly Swagman (US: Maniacs on Wheels). 1949: Dear Mr Prohack. Boys in Brown. The Blue Lamp. 1950: So Long at the Fair. Blackmailed. The Woman in Question (US: Five Angles on Murder). 1951: Hunted (US: The Stranger in Between). 1952: Penny Princess. The Gentle Gunman. Appointment in London. 1953: Desperate Moment. They Who Dare. 1954: Doctor in the House. For Better, For Worse (US: Cocktails in the Kitchen). The Sleeping Tiger. The Sea Shall Not Have Them. 1955: Simba. Doctor at Sea. Cast a Dark Shadow. 1956: The Spanish Gardener. Ill Met by Moonlight (US: Night Ambush). 1957: Doctor at Large. Campbell's Kingdom. 1958: A Tale of Two Cities. The Wind Cannot Read. 1959: Libel! The Doctor's Dilemma. 1960: Song Without End. The Singer Not the Song. The Angel Wore Red. 1961: Victim. 1962: HMS Defiant (US: Damn the Defiant!). The Password is Courage. We Joined the Navy (cameo role). The Mind Benders. 1963: I Could Go On Singing. Doctor in Distress. The Servant. Hot Enough for June (US: Agent 8¾). 1964: King and Country. The High Bright Sun (US: McGuire, Go Home!). 1965: Darling. 1966: Modesty Blaise. 1967: Accident. Our Mother's House. Sebastian. 1968: The Fixer. Return to Lochaver (short). 1969: Oh! What a Lovely War. Justine. La caduta degli dei (GB and US: The Damned). 1970: Upon This Rock (short). 1971: Death in Venice. 1973: The Serpent. 1974: The Night Porter. 1975: Permission to Kill. 1977: Providence. A Bridge Too Far. 1978: Despair. 1981: The Patricia Neal Story (TV).

With Donald Sinden and Kenneth More in *Doctor in the House* (1954)

With Barbara Murray in *Campbell's Kingdom* (1957)

As Simon Sparrow in
Doctor at Large (1957)

As Sydney Carton in
A Tale of Two Cities (1958)

With Michael Redgrave in *The Sea Shall Not Have Them* (1954)

As an undercover Intelligence officer in *Ill Met By Moonlight* (1956)

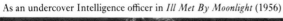

With Leslie Caron in *The Doctor's Dilemma* (1959)

Richard III

Not even in the same actor-director's *Henry V* had Shakespeare ever made such dazzling, hypnotic screen entertainment as in Laurence Olivier's *Richard III*. Affectionately

Portrait in evil. Laurence Olivier as the malignant fifteenth-century English king.

known by most of its cast as 'Dickie Three-Eyes', the historical spectacular, a super-epic by almost any standards, took just 17 weeks to shoot – inside schedule and budget – thanks to the boundless energy of Olivier himself.

Olivier's brilliant Richard Crookback, an extension of the interpretation he had first brought to a stage performance in 1944, provided material for a thousand imitators with his unique delivery of the famous 'Now is the winter of our discontent' and 'My kingdom for a horse' speeches.

His power-hungry king is a ruthless, dominant, unstoppable and unforgettable gross black spider of a figure that devours or possesses everything in its path.

No character in the film, nor actor in the cast is a match for him, despite sterling, thoughtful portrayals from John Gielgud, as the hapless Clarence drowned in a butt of malmsey, Claire Bloom as Lady Anne, seduced by Richard over her husband's coffin, and Ralph Richardson as the cunning, ever-scheming Duke of Buckingham.

During the shooting of the Battle of Bosworth Field (filmed first, in Spain, although the climax of the story), Olivier was accidentally shot in the leg by the film's master archer, with a bolt intended for the much-cushioned horse beneath him, which had been trained to roll over and 'play dead' on its impact.

Laurence Olivier and Ralph Richardson

Deeming the scene too important to stop, Olivier calmly asked co-director Anthony Bushell if it were all satisfactorily 'in the can' before calling for a doctor. The consequent delay meant that the limp which Oliver had intended to affect as Richard turned out to be very genuine.

The project to film Olivier's stage triumph in the first place had been initiated by film mogul Alexander Korda, whose death the following year (1956) rendered stillborn similar plans to film Olivier's *Macbeth* (with Vivien Leigh as Lady Macbeth).

The work then began of adapting Shakespeare's text in such a way as to make it accessible to the average cinemagoer. In fact the job done by Alan Dent, with assistance from Olivier himself, was nothing short of brilliant – a rare case of the right decisions on excisions and omissions from the original being made on every occasion.

Some characters were omitted entirely (notably the murderous Queen Margaret), as were some passages of dialogue. Very few of the lines that were left in, however, were shortened or re-phrased, while the film's 'crown' motif, which reaches its climax in the final battle, was reinforced by Olivier's 'pinching' of the coronation of Edward IV (Richard's adult predecessor) from another Shakespeare play, *Henry VI, Part III*.

This telescoping and adaptation added greatly to the power of the dialogue, particularly that spoken by the king. Olivier's awesome appearance undoubtedly helped in this respect. His make-up – not dissimilar from the stage original 11 years earlier – took three hours to apply each day. Besides the unprepossessing black 'fright wig', Olivier's Richard had long, thin rattrap lips, a deformed, two-fingered left hand, usually blackgloved and bejewelled, an elongated, icicle-like nose, plus the famous crooked back and sidling walk – making a man to be feared but never trusted, and one for all the world like a male equivalent of the wicked stepmother in *Snow White*.

The air of magnetic unreality that resulted was heightened by the bizarre Technicolor photography of Otto Heller, almost cartoon-like in its effect, like such over-bright Hollywood colour processes of the past as Supercinecolor or Trucolor.

It certainly brought the larger-than-life characters into sharp focus, and it is much to the credit of some of the supporting performances, especially those of Alec Clunes (as Hastings) and Norman Wooland (as Catesby) that they emerge from under the giant shadow of Olivier's cloak as definite characters in their own right.

Still, it was Olivier, and rightly so, who took the best actor award at the British film Oscars for 1956, which also named *Richard III* as best British film and, indeed, best film from any source.

Credits and Cast

Dir/prod *Laurence Olivier*. Co-dir *Anthony Bushell*. Scr *Alan Dent (with Olivier uncredited), from the play by William Shakespeare*. Ph *Otto Heller*. PC/dis *London Films. Technicolor. Vista Vision*. Art design *Carmen Dillon*. Prod design *Roger Furse*.

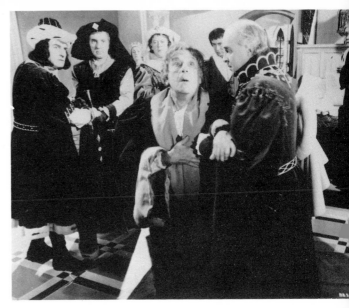

The death of Edward IV. Laurence Naismith holds Cedric Hardwicke while Olivier and Richardson look on like vultures

Director Olivier (minus wig) prepares John Gielgud for a scene

Editor *Helga Cranston*. Mus *Sir William Walton*. Mus dir *Muir Mathieson*. Assistant dir *Gerry O'Hara*. Assistant ph *Denys Coop*. *161 mins. Cert U*

Laurence Olivier (Richard III), Ralph Richardson (Buckingham), Claire Bloom (Lady Anne), John Gielgud (Clarence), Cedric Hardwicke (Edward IV), Mary Kerridge (Queen Elizabeth), Pamela Brown (Jane Shore), Alec Clunes (Hastings), Stanley Baker (Henry Tudor), Michael Gough (Dighton), Laurence Naismith (Stanley), Norman Wooland (Catesby), Helen Haye (Duchess of York), John Laurie (Lovel), Esmond Knight (Ratcliffe), Andrew Cruickshank (Brakenbury), Clive Morton (Rivers), Nicholas Hannen (Archbishop), Russell Thorndike (Priest), Paul Huson (Prince of Wales), Douglas Wilmer (Dorset), Dan Cunningham (Grey), Michael Ripper (Second murderer), Stewart Allen (Page), Wally Bascoe (Monk), Norman Fisher (Monk), Terence Greenridge (Scrivener), Andy Shine (Young Duke of York), Roy Russell (Abbot), George Woodbridge (Lord Mayor), Willoughby Gray (Second priest), Peter Williams (Messenger to Hastings), Timothy Bateson (Ostler), Anne Wilton (Scrubwoman), Bill Shine (Beadle), Derek Prentice (Clergyman), Deering Wells (Clergyman), Richard Bennett (George Stanley), Patrick Troughton (Tyrell), John Phillips (Norfolk), Bernard Hepton (Knight), John Greenwood (Knight), Brian Nissen, Alexander Davion, Lane Meddick and Robert Bishop (Messengers)

Richard III prepares to do battle with Henry Tudor's army at Bosworth Field

Olivier in his original stage performance as Richard III in 1944

On the field of battle: Olivier's Richard with Norfolk (John Phillips) and Catesby (Norman Wooland)

Olivier off set with Ralph Richardson

Hundreds of Spanish extras clash on 'Bosworth Field' – just outside Madrid

The Fifties

ABDULLA THE GREAT (1954)
(USA: *Abdulla's Harem*)

Dir/Prod *Gregory Ratoff*, Scr *George St George, Boris Ingster*, Ph *Lee Garmes*. PC *Sphinx*. Dis *Independent Film Distributors/ British Lion. Technicolor. 103 Mins. Cert A.*
King Abdulla of Banderia (*Gregory Ratoff*) desperately desires Ronnie (*Kay Kendall*), an English model. When she icily ignores him, he has her kidnapped and brought to his yacht. An officer (*Sydney Chaplin*) who also loves Ronnie tries to assassinate Abdulla, and the whole situation causes such unrest in the country that Abdulla is finally forced to abdicate, leaving Ronnie free to go with her officer. Anglo-Egyptian comedy co-production, strident in the Ratoff manner.
RoC *Marina Berti, Alex D'Arcy, Marti Stevens, Mary Costes.*

THE ABOMINABLE SNOWMAN
(1957)

Dir *Val Guest*. Prod *Aubrey Baring*. Scr *Nigel Kneale*, from his TV play *The Creature. Ph Arthur Grant. PC Hammer. Dis Warner Bros. 90 mins. Cert A*
Adventurer Tom Friend (*Forrest Tucker*) and botanist Dr Rollason (*Peter Cushing*) team up on a Himalayan expedition to find the giant creature known as the Yeti, or 'abominable snowman'. Friend shoots a Yeti, but the expedition is trapped by the creature's comrades, who reclaim the dead body and dispatch Friend in an avalanche. Rollason survives, though he cannot remember how. Decently made shocker misses out on the chills.
RoC *Maureen Commell, Richard Wattis, Robert Brown, Michael Brill, Wolfe Morris, Arnold Marle, Anthony Chinn.*

ABOVE US THE WAVES (1955)

Dir *Ralph Thomas*. Prod *Sydney Box, William MacQuitty*. Scr *Robin Estridge*, from the book by *C.E.T. Warren and John Benson*. Ph *Ernest Steward. PC London Independent. Dis General Film Distributors. 99 mins. Cert U*
In World War II, the German battleship *Tirpitz* is a constant menace to Allied shipping, always lurking in a Norwegian fjord. Commander Frazer (*John Mills*) persuades his superiors that the answer lies with midget submarines. A first attempt is foiled by a storm; a second results in the planting of bombs, but the capture of two of the subs and their crews; while the third is blown up with the *Tirpitz*. Studio-bound war, but excitingly put together.
RoC *Donald Sinden, John Gregson, James Robertson Justice, Michael Medwin, James Kenney, O.E. Hasse, Lee Patterson, Lyndon Brook, William Russell, Theodore Bikel, Thomas Heathcote, Harry Towb, Anthony Newley, Cyril Chamberlain, John Horsley, Anthony Wager, William Franklyn, Leslie Weston, Guido Lorraine, Raymond Francis, Basil Appleby.*

ACCOUNT RENDERED (1957)

Dir *Peter Graham Scott*. Prod *John Temple-Smith, Francis Edge*. Scr *Barbara S. Harper*, from the novel by *Pamela Barrington*. Ph *Walter J. Harvey. PC Major. Dis Rank. 61 mins. Cert A*
Trying to identify his wife's lover, banker Robert Ainsworth (*Griffith Jones*) is knocked out. When he recovers, he finds she has been murdered, and he is one of four suspects, the others being Clive (*John Van Eyssen*), her discarded lover, Goodman (*Vernon Smythe*), who was paying her gambling debts and Morgan, Ainsworth's partner (*Carl Bernard*), whom she was blackmailing. The murderer is Clive who crossed railway lines to establish an alibi. Efficient thriller.
RoC *Honor Blackman, Ewen Solon, Mary Tenes, Philip Gilbert, Robert Raikes, Gordon Phillott, Doris Yorke, Gerda Larson, Harry Ross, Barry Steele, Edwin Richfield.*

THE ACCUSED (1953)

Dir *Lawrence Huntington, Charles Saunders*. Prod/PC *Douglas Fairbanks Jr*. Scr *John and Gwen Bagni, Robert Westerby; Larry Marcus and Guy Murgan*. Ph *Gerry Gibbs, Brendan J. Stafford. Dis British Lion. 52 mins. Cert A*
Two stories. (1) A quiet insurance salesman (*Clifford Evans*) out for a walk finds himself accused of assault and later murder. He loses everything before hitting the road to find the only woman who can clear him. (2) 1946: a mute German girl (*Ingeborg Wells*) is married for her money by a man who tries to make her kill herself. At the last moment, she turns the tables. ... Capable twist-in-the-tail, partly-for-TV thrillers.
LP *Mary Laura Wood, Jean Lodge, Robert Adair, John Warwick, Edwin Styles, Peter Reynolds, Irene Handl, Gerard Heinz, Frederick Berger, George Ruck, Douglas Fairbanks Jr.*

ACROSS THE BRIDGE (1957)

Dir *Ken Annakin*. Prod *John Stafford*. Scr *Guy Elmes, Denis Freeman*, from the story by *Graham Greene*. Ph *Reginald Wyer*. PC/Dis *Rank. 103 mins. Cert A*
Schaffner (*Rod Steiger*), a financier on the run from a £3,000,000 embezzlement, meets a man on the train to Mexico who bears a resemblance to him; Schaffner drugs him, takes his papers and throws him from the train. Later, he finds the Mexican was wanted for murder but, once across the border, he produces his own papers, and the Mexican, who survived, is killed resisting arrest. Schaffner, lured across a frontier bridge by his love for a dog, is also killed, by a Scotland Yard inspector's car. Overlong but powerful drama; Steiger gives it all he's got.
RoC *David Knight, Marla Landi, Noel Willman, Bill Nagy, Bernard Lee, Eric Pohlmann, Alan Gifford, Ingeborg Wells, Faith Brook, Stanley Maxted, Marianne Deeming, Mark Baker, Jack Lester, Jon Farrell, Betty Cooper.*

ACTION OF THE TIGER (1957)

Dir *Terence Young*. Prod *Kenneth Harper*. Scr *Robert Carson, Peter Myers*, from the novel by *James Wellard*. Ph *Desmond Dickinson*. PC *Claridge. Dis M-G-M. Technicolor. Cinema-Scope. 93 mins. Cert U*
Carson (*Van Johnson*), an adventurer, is hired by Tracy (*Martine Carol*) in Greece, to cross into Communist Albania and rescue her brother. Once there, they are captured by militia, but released by a bandit gang led by Trifon (*Herbert Lom*) who is later killed. Now joined by refugee children and the remains of Trifon's men, the fugitives make it across the border. Clichéd adventure; the cast has a defeated look.
RoC *Gustavo Rocco, Tony (Anthony) Dawson, Anna Gerber, Yvonne Warren (Romain), Helen Haye, Sean Connery, Pepé Nieto, Helen Goss, Norman MacOwan, José Nieto.*

ACTION STATIONS (1956)

Dir/Scr/Ph *Cecil H. Williamson*. Prod *E.J. Fancey*. PC *Aqua*. Dis *New Realm. 50 mins. Cert U*
When a counterfeiting gang stoops to murder, the forger who makes their plates decides to quit the racket. He goes to Spain, but the gang kidnaps his daughter and threatens to kill her unless he co-operates. Her father's smuggling friends (*Paul Carpenter, Joe Robinson*) move into action and rescue the girl, the gang's car crashing over a cliff. Shoestring thriller, not released until 1959.
RoC *Mary Martin* (not US star), *Ronald Leigh-Hunt, Jack Taylor, Jacques Labreque.*

THE ADMIRABLE CRICHTON
(USA: *Paradise Lagoon*)

Dir *Lewis Gilbert*. Prod *Ian Dalrymple*. Scr *Vernon Harris*, from the play by *J.M. Barrie*. Ph *Wilkie Cooper. PC Modern Screenplays. Dis Columbia. Technicolor. VistaVision. 93 mins. Cert U*
1905. When a noble family is shipwrecked on a desert island, Crichton (*Kenneth More*), the butler, being the only practical member of the party, gradually assumes authority. Lord Loam (*Cecil Parker*) is happy as a kitchen hand, and Crichton is about to marry Lady Mary (*Sally Ann Howes*) when a rescue ship is sighted. Back home, Crichton spares the family embarrassment by leaving – with his new fiancée, the maid (*Diane Cilento*), and a small souvenir of the island: a bag, containing a fortune in pearls. ... Sunny, amusing version of Barrie's play, previously filmed in 1918.
RoC *Martita Hunt, Jack Watling, Peter Graves, Miles Malleson, Eddie Byrne, Gerald Harper, Mercy Haystead, Miranda Connell, Toke Townley, Joan Young, Beth Rogan, Peter Welch, Roland Curram, Brenda Hogan, John le Mesurier.*

ADVENTURE IN THE HOPFIELDS
(1954)   4

Dir *John Guillermin*. Prod *Roger Proudlock*. Scr *John Cresswell, from a novel by Nora Lavin and Molly Thorp*. Ph *Kenneth Talbot*. PC *Vandyke/ Children's Film Foundation*. Dis *Associated British*. 60 mins. Cert U

Jenny (*Mandy Miller*) panics when she breaks her mother's prize china ornament and follows families in her street to the hopfields, hoping to earn money for a replacement. She buys another ornament, but it is stolen by the ragamuffin Reillys, who tie her up when she chases them to an old mill. The mill is struck by lightning and set ablaze. The Reillys rescue Jenny and she is reunited with her parents. Good children's film with genuine characters. RoC *Melvyn Hayes, Leon Garcia, Hilda Fenemore, Harold Lang, Russell Waters, Mona Washbourne, Molly Osborne, Wallas Eaton, Jane Asher, Edward Judd*.

THE ADVENTURERS (1950)   2
(USA: *The Great Adventure*)

Dir *David Macdonald*. Prod *Maxwell Setton, Aubrey Baring*. Scr *Robert Westerby*. Ph *Oswald Morris*. PC *Mayflower*. Dis *General Film Distributors*. 86 mins. Cert A

After the South African war, four men set out to find diamonds hidden by one of them. They are Pieter (*Jack Hawkins*) and his young friend Hendrik (*Peter Hammond*), Dominic (*Gregoire Aslan*) and Hunter (*Dennis Price*), who has taken Pieter's girl as his wife and won Dominic's hotel in a card game. The diamonds are found, Hendrik is injured and Hunter killed – by Pieter, who tries to kill the others, too, before dying under a cave-in. Derivative but still interesting thriller; clumsy handling spoils it. RoC *Siobhan McKenna, Bernard Lee, Ronald Adam, Charles Paton, Martin Boddey, Philip Ray, Walter Horsbrugh, Cyril Chamberlain*.

Jack Hawkins in The Adventurers (*1950*)

THE ADVENTURES OF HAL 5 (1957)   4

Dir/Scr *Don Sharp, from a novel by Henry Donald*. Prod *Gilbert Church*. Ph *Jo Jago*. PC *Bushey/Children's Film Foundation*. Dis *British Lion*. 59 mins. Cert U

'Hal 5' is a car, always breaking down, and sold at an exorbitant price by its shady owner (*John Glyn-Jones*) to a vicar (*William Russell*). The vicar is forced to sell it at a loss, but its former owner decides to get greedy, steal Hal

5 and launch an insurance fiddle. Hal 5 won't co-operate and exposes its former owner's chicanery. British relative of *The Love Bug* is charming, full of fun. RoC *Janina Faye, Peter Godsell, John Charlesworth, Edwin Richfield, David Morrell, Kathleen Williams*.

THE ADVENTURES OF QUENTIN DURWARD (1955)   5
(USA: *Quentin Durward*)

Dir *Richard Thorpe*. Prod *Pandro S. Berman*. Scr *Robert Ardrey, George Froeschel, from the novel by Sir Walter Scott*. Ph *Christopher Challis*. PC/Dis *MGM British*. Eastman Colour. CinemaScope. 100 mins. Cert U

Isabelle (*Kay Kendall*), ward of the Duke of Burgundy (*Alec Clunes*) in 15th-century France, is betrothed to elderly Lord Crawford (*Ernest Thesiger*). Crawford sends his nephew, Quentin Durward (*Robert Taylor*) for her, but Isabelle runs away and places herself under the wing of King Louis XI (*Robert Morley*), a situation which allows Burgundy to threaten civil war. Panicking, Louis arranges for Isabelle to be kidnapped by de la Marck (*Duncan Lamont*). Quentin engages and kills de la Marck and later marries Isabelle. First-rate, fast-moving action film, with a wicked sense of humour and a splendid final duel in a belltower. RoC *George Cole, Marius Goring, Laya Raki, Wilfrid Hyde White, Eric Pohlmann, Michael Goodliffe, Harcourt Williams, Nicholas Hannen, John Carson, Moultrie Kelsall, Frank Tickle, Bill Shine, Arthur Howard*.

THE AFRICAN QUEEN (1951)   5

Dir *John Huston*. Prod *Sam Spiegel*. Scr *Huston, James Agee, from the novel by C.S. Forester*. Ph *Jack Cardiff*. PC *Romulus/Horizon*. Dis *Independent Film Distributors*. Technicolor. 105 mins. Cert U

Central Africa, 1914. German troops overrun a village; the missionary (*Robert Morley*) dies from shock; his zealous sister Rose (*Katherine Hepburn*) is left alone. Despite her dislike of him, she joins gin-swilling Charlie Allnutt (*Humphrey Bogart*) going up-river in his launch *The African Queen*. Rose has a mad scheme to destroy a German gunboat blocking the mouth of the river to British forces. The unlikely partners fall in love and survive hazards and hardships to make an attempt on the

Humphrey Bogart and director John Huston making The African Queen (*1951*)

gunboat. They are captured and the captain marries them (as they are about to be hanged) before an explosive-loaded *African Queen* rams the gunboat. Rose and Charlie survive. Unique romantic comedy-adventure; Bogart took the year's Oscar as best actor. RoC *Peter Bull, Theodore Bikel, Walter Gotell, Peter Swanwick, Richard Marner, Gerald Onn*.

AFTER THE BALL (1957)   3

Dir *Compton Bennett*. Prod *Peter Rogers*. Scr *Hubert Gregg, Peter Blackmore, from a book by Lady de Frece and the TV play by Gregg*. Ph *Jack Asher*. PC *Romulus/Beaconsfield*. Dis *Independent Film Distributors/British Lion*. Eastman Colour. 89 mins. Cert U

Matilda (*Pat Kirkwood*), daughter of an emcee at an English music-hall, develops into a singer with a striking voice and, taking the name Vesta Tilley, becomes a great star of Victorian days, touring America with equal success. Marrying Walter (*Laurence Harvey*), an architect who makes himself her manager, she becomes the best-known voice of World War I before Walter goes into politics and she retires in 1920, living to be 88. Rather dull life-story enlivened by a well-sung collection of the star's numbers.

RoC *Clive Morton, Jerry Verno, Jerry Stovin, June Clyde, Charles Victor, Marjorie Rhodes, Tom Gill, Peter Carlisle, George Margo, Leonard Sachs, Mark Baker, Terry Cooke, Ballard Berkeley, Margaret Sawyer, Franklyn Scott, Concepta Fennell, Una Venning, David Hurst, Roland Brand, Philip Ashley, John Kelly, Rita Stevens, Cyril Chamberlain, Barbara Graley, Jane Hardie, Graham Stewart, Geoffrey Tyrell, Margo Johns, Sydney Keith, Erik Chitty, Howard Greene, Marjorie Lawrence, Olwen Brookes, Stella Bonheur, John Mott, The Television Toppers*.

ALBERT, RN (1953)   5
(USA: *Break to Freedom*)

Dir *Lewis Gilbert*. Prod *Daniel M. Angel*. Scr *Guy Morgan, Vernon Harris, from the play by Morgan, Edward Sammis*. Ph *Jack Asher*. PC *Dial Films*. Dis *Eros*. 88 mins. Cert U

World War II. With the help of a lifelike dummy, Albert, Allied officers are escaping from a German P-o-W camp. The dummy's maker, Lt Ainsworth (*Anthony Steel*) lets others escape because he fears facing the girl pen-friend he has never met. But when one such hesitation leads to a colleague's death, Ainsworth makes the break, killing a treacherous German (*Anton Diffring*) on the way. Solid, emotive war film with original appeal. RoC *Jack Warner, Robert Beatty, William Sylvester, Eddie Byrne, Paul Carpenter, Guy Middleton, Michael Balfour, Moultrie Kelsall, Frederick Valk, Frederick Schiller, Peter Jones, Geoffrey Hibbert, Walter Gotell, Peter Swanwick, Arthur Howard*.

ALF'S BABY (1952)   2

Dir *Maclean Rogers*. Prod *John Harlow*. Scr *A.P. Dearsley, from his play* It Won't Be a Stylish Marriage. Ph *Ted Lloyd*. PC *ACT Films*. Dis *Adelphi*. 75 mins. Cert U

Three bachelor brothers 'inherit' a baby; she

grows up to be a beautiful young girl who falls in love with a smart-alec young garage-manager. When he is trapped by a young detective, the girl turns her attentions to the right side of the law, to the relief of the now-aged brothers. Rudimentary comedy; cast tries hard, gets a few laughs.

LP *Pauline Stroud, Jerry Desmonde, C. Denier Warren, Mark Daly, Sandra Dorne, Peter Hammond, Olive Sloane, Roy Purcell, Roddy Hughes, Sebastian Cabot, Michael Ripper.*

ALIAS JOHN PRESTON (1956) [1]

Dir *David Macdonald.* Prod *Sid Stone.* Scr *Paul Tabori.* Ph *Jack Smith.* PC *Danziger Photoplays.* Dis *British Lion.* 67 mins. Cert *A*

Suave John Preston (*Christopher Lee*) moves into town and steals Sally (*Betta St John*) from her sweetheart Bob (*Peter Grant*). However, he is soon forced to consult a psychiatrist, Walton (*Alexander Knox*), about recurring nightmares in which he kills a girl and bludgeons Walton with a poker. It transpires that Preston is a schizophrenic and the nightmares are true stories of the past. Dreary, turgid drama: seems much longer than it is.

RoC *Patrick Holt, Sandra Dorne, John Longden, John Stuart, Betty Ann Davies, Bill Fraser, Guido Lorraine, Dinah Ann Rogers, Leonard Sharp, Gabrielle Gay, Ben Williams, Mona Washbourne, Nicholas Hill.*

Estelle Winwood, Sybil Thorndike and Kathleen Harrison in Alive and Kicking *(1958)*

ALIVE AND KICKING (1958) [3]

Dir *Cyril Frankel.* Prod *Victor Skutezky.* Scr *Denis Cannan, from the play by William Dinner, William Morum.* Ph *Gilbert Taylor.* PC *Associated British.* Dis *AB-Pathé.* 95 mins. Cert *U*

Three elderly ladies (*Sybil Thorndike, Kathleen Harrison, Estelle Winwood*) flee from an old folks' home and escape (by Russian trawler) to a remote Irish island, where they take over three cottages (from a landlord who is – wrongly – presumed dead) and start up a sweater industry. The landlord (*Stanley Holloway*) returns and decides to become their partner. Fey comedy.

RoC *Liam Redmond, Marjorie Rhodes, Richard Harris, Olive McFarland, Joyce Carey, Eric Pohlmann, Colin Gordon, John Salew, Anita Sharp Bolster, Paul Farrell, Patrick McAlinney, Raymond Manthorpe, Tony Quinn, Harry Hutchinson, Brendan O'Dowda, Joseph MacNally.*

ALIVE ON SATURDAY (1954) [1]

Dir *Alfred Travers.* Prod *Geoffrey Goodhart, Brandon Fleming.* Scr *Fleming.* Ph *Hilton Craig.* PC *Pan.* Dis *AB-Pathé.* 58 mins. Cert *U*

Penniless George Pilbeam (*Guy Middleton*) is baffled when offered a large sum of money if he is still alive three days after registering at a London hotel. He soon finds why, when he becomes the target for Pagodian revolutionaries. He falls in love with the daughter (*Patricia Owens*) of the millionaire behind the rebellion in Pagoda, and all three narrowly escape being blown up before George earns his fortune. Comedy lacks the style to smooth over its foolishness. Not released until 1957.

RoC *John Witty, John Salew, Jessica Cairns, Geoffrey Goodhart, Charles Lloyd Pack, Wallas Eaton.*

ALL FOR MARY (1955) [2]

Dir *Wendy Toye.* Prod *Paul Soskin.* Scr *Soskin, Peter Blackmore, Alan Melville, from the play by Harold Brock, Kay Bannerman.* PC/Dis *Rank.* Eastman Color. 79 mins. Cert *U*

Two Britons (*Nigel Patrick, David Tomlinson*), on a skiing holiday in Switzerland, both fall for the innkeeper's daughter Mary (*Jill Day*). While Gaston (*Leo McKern*) pays court to Mary, both 'invalids' are treated by Nannie (*Kathleen Harrison*) who used to look after Humphrey (*Tomlinson*) when he was a child. She sees to it that Humphrey gets Mary in the end. Very barren comedy slopes; a song, a smile or two, no more.

RoC *Joan Young, Lionel Jeffries, David Hurst, Nicholas Phipps, Paul Hardtmuth, Fabia Drake, Tommy Farr, Shirley Ann Field.*

AN ALLIGATOR NAMED DAISY (1955) [3]

Dir *J. Lee Thompson.* Prod *Raymond Stross.* Scr *Jack Davies, from the novel by Charles Terrot.* Ph *Reginald Wyer.* PC *Group/Raymond Stross Productions.* Dis *Rank.* Technicolor. VistaVision. 88 mins. Cert *U*

Songwriter Peter (*Donald Sinden*) finds himself landed with a pet alligator and Moira, an Irish girl (*Jean Carson*) who loves all animals. Neither of them pleases his heiress fiancée Vanessa (*Diana Dors*) but, after the alligator wrecks a rally designed to popularize reptiles as pets, Vanessa settles for Moira's handsome brother (*Stephen Boyd*) and leaves Peter, Moira and Daisy the alligator together. Enjoyable frolic with song-and-dance numbers (though not up to much) thrown in.

RoC *James Robertson Justice, Margaret Rutherford, Stanley Holloway, Roland Culver, Avice Landone, Richard Wattis, Henry Kendall, Michael Shepley, Charles Victor, Ernest Thesiger, Wilfrid Lawson, George Moon, Jimmy Edwards, Gilbert Harding, Frankie Howerd, Martin Miller, Colin Freer, Bill Shine, Harry Green, Maurice Kaufmann, George Woodbridge, Patrick Cargill, Ronnie Stevens, Don Cameron, Arnold Bell, Charles Carson, Myrette Morven, Joan Young, John Vere.*

ALWAYS A BRIDE (1953) [4]

Dir *Ralph Smart.* Prod *Robert Garrett.* Scr *Smart, Peter Jones.* Ph *C. Pennington-Richards.*

PC *Clarion.* Dis *General Film Distributors.* 83 mins. Cert *A*

Father-and-daughter tricksters Victor (*Ronald Squire*) and Clare (*Peggy Cummins*), playing a roué and his bride, home in on a Monte Carlo hotel and Treasury man Terence (*Terence Morgan*). When Clare is 'deserted', the guests shower her with gifts and, though in love with Terence, she joins her father in Nice. Their next swindle misfires and, when the pursuing Terence catches up, Victor delays the law long enough for the lovebirds to marry and escape. He requests a cell with a view. Silly comedy comes off, thanks to polished production, amusing characterization, neat script.

RoC *James Hayter, Marie Lohr, Geoffrey Sumner, Charles Goldner, David Hurst, Jacques Brunius, Sebastian Cabot, Jacques Brown, Dino Galvani, Jill Day, Jacques Cey, Eliot Makeham, Mary Hinton.*

ANASTASIA (1956) [5]

Dir *Anatole Litvak.* Prod *Buddy Adler.* Scr *Arthur Laurents, from Guy Bolton's adaptation of the play by Marcelle Maurette.* Ph *Jack Hildyard.* PC and Dis *20th Century-Fox.* Eastman Colour. CinemaScope. 105 mins. Cert *U*

Eager to get their hands on £10,000,000 deposited by the late Czar of Russia in the Bank of England, a group of exiled White Russians in Paris in 1928 find a destitute girl whom they groom to be 'Anastasia' (*Ingrid Bergman*), youngest daughter of the Czar, and supposed to have escaped the massacre that ended his family's lives. She may well *be* Anastasia, and passes the acid test of acceptance by the aged Dowager Empress (*Helen Hayes*). However, she elects to disappear with the man who found her, Bounine (*Yul Brynner*). Miss Bergman won an Oscar for this polished, affecting film.

RoC *Akim Tamiroff, Martita Hunt, Felix Aylmer, Sacha Pitoeff, Ivan Desny, Natalie Schafer, Gregoire Gromoff, Karel Stepanek, Ina de la Haye, Katherine Kath, Hy Hazell, Olga Valery, Tamara Shayne, Peter Sallis, Polycarpe Pavloff.*

AND THE SAME TO YOU (1959) [3]

Dir *George Pollock.* Prod *William Gell.* Scr *John Paddy Carstairs, John Junkin, Terry Nation.* Ph *Stan Pavey.* PC *Monarch.* Dis *Eros.* 70 mins. Cert *U*

When an addled vicar (*Leo Franklyn*) takes over his new parish, he finds himself sharing the church hall with a shady boxing promoter (*Dick Bentley*). After the vicar's nephew Dickie (*Brian Rix*) knocks out the promoter's prize fighter, the vicar sees a chance of raising money for a new church-hall roof. The Archdeacon (*John Robinson*) threatens to stop the fights, but is neatly blackmailed over his wife's gambling – and the roof, after a scare or two for Dickie, is saved. Speedy farce for once doesn't run too long; expert cast works well.

RoC *Tony Wright, William Hartnell, Sidney James, Vera Day, Renee Houston, Miles Malleson, Shirley Anne Field, Tommy Cooper, Larry Taylor, Terry Scott, Arthur Mullard, Jean Clarke, Ronald Adam, Tommy Duggan, Rupert Evans, George Leech, Lindsay Hooper, Jennifer*

Phipps, Jack Taylor, Mickey Wood, Bob Simmons.

AND WOMEN SHALL WEEP (1959) [2]

Dir *John Lemont.* Prod *Norman Williams.* Scr *Lemont, Leigh Vance.* Ph *Brendan J. Stafford.* PC *Ethiro/Alliance.* Dis *Rank.* 65 mins. Cert A
Mrs Lumsden (*Ruth Dunning*), a widow, is determined to prevent her younger son Godfrey (*Richard O'Sullivan*) from following in the footsteps of his criminal older brother Terry (*Max Butterfield*). When she learns that a man has been killed during Terry's gang's latest 'job' (robbing a pawnbroker), she breaks Terry down and hands him over to the police. Overwrought domestic drama.
RoC *Gillian Vaughan, Claire Gordon, David Gregory, David Rose, Leon Garcia, Keith Smith, Julie Shearing, Prudence Bury, John Pike, Joyce Gregg, Robert Moore, Arthur Lovegrove, Gerald Case, Reginald Hearne, Mary Jones.*

ANGELS ONE FIVE (1952) [5]

Dir *George More O'Ferrall.* Prod *John W. Gossage, Derek Twist.* Scr *Twist.* Ph *Christopher Challis* (*ground*), *Stanley Grant* (air). PC *Templar.* Dis *AB-Pathé.* 98 mins. Cert U
1940, on a Kent fighter station. 'Septic' Baird (*John Gregson*), a volunteer reserve pilot, has his enthusiasm dampened by Group Captain 'Tiger' Small (*Jack Hawkins*) because he is rigidly guided by the textbook, not experience. 'Septic' becomes friendly with an ambulance driver (*Veronica Hurst*) and settles down to squadron discipline. He proves himself a brilliant fighter pilot, but in the end is shot down by a German ace. No heroics, downbeat, but exciting and very successful war film.
RoC *Michael Denison, Dulcie Gray, Cyril Raymond, Andrew Osborn, Humphrey Lestocq, Ronald Adam, Harold Goodwin, Norman Pierce, Geoffrey Keen, Harry Locke, Philip Stainton, Vida Hope, Amy Veness, Richard Dunn, Russell Hunter, Richard Levin, Donald McLisky, Harold Siddons, Anthony Moore, Gordon Bell, Thorp Devereaux, Neil Wilson, Rosemary Lomax, Colin Tapley, John Sharp, Ewan Roberts, Hugh Moxey, John Phillips, John Harvey, Sam Kydd, Peter Jones, Josephine Douglas, Freda Bamford, Karen Grayson, Joan Sterndale Bennett, Marianne Stone, Gillian Maude, Vari Falconer, Helen Stirling, Ann Lancaster, Harry Fowler, Russell Waters, Victor Maddern.*

John Gregson and Jack Hawkins in Angels One Five (*1952*)

THE ANGEL WHO PAWNED HER HARP (1954) [3]

Dir *Alan Bromly.* Prod *Sidney Cole.* Scr *Charles Terrot, Cole, from a TV play by Terrot.* Ph *Arthur Grant.* PC *Group 3.* Dis *British Lion.* 76 mins. Cert U
An angel (*Diane Cilento* in her film debut) comes to the Angel district of Islington to sort out people's lives. She has to pawn her harp before softening the heart of the pawnbroker (*Felix Aylmer*), straightening out his assistant's love-life, freeing a woman from her nagging companion, and putting paid to two crooks and a con-man. Minor whimsy, a bit plodding but quite acceptable.
RoC *Jerry Desmonde, Joe Linnane, Sheila Sweet, Philip Guard, Genitha Halsey, Edward Evans, Elaine Wodson, Alfie Bass, Thomas Gallagher, David Kossoff, Raymond Rollett, Phyllis Morris, June Ellis, Herbert C. Walton, Freddie Watts, Cyril Smith, Jean Aubrey, Maurice Kaufman(n), Thomas Moore, Robert Eddison* (voice), *Nelson's Gift* (horse).

THE ANGRY HILLS (1959) [2]

Dir *Robert Aldrich.* Prod/PC *Raymond Stross.* Scr *A.I. Bezzerides, from the novel by Leon Uris.* Ph *Stephen Dade.* Dis *M-G-M.* 105 mins. Cert A
Mike (*Robert Mitchum*), an American war correspondent in 1940 Greece, comes into possession of a list of resistance agents needed by MI5, but is wounded by Nazis. Nursed by Eleftheria (*Gia Scala*), a peasant, he is aided by Lisa (*Elisabeth Müller*), a Greek underground agent, who is tempted to betray him when her children are taken hostage by Heisler (*Stanley Baker*), her Gestapo ex-lover. She changes her mind, and Mike and the children escape. Laughable war story gets sillier by the minute.
RoC *Donald Wolfit, Kieron Moore, Theodore Bikel, Sebastian Cabot, Marius Goring, Leslie Phillips, Peter Illing, George Pastell, Jackie Lane, Patrick Jordan, Stanley Van Beers, Marita Constantiou, Tom Chatto, Alec Mango, Andrea Malandrinos.*

Elisabeth Müller and Stanley Baker in The Angry Hills (*1959*)

ANIMAL FARM (1954) [5]

Dir/Prod *John Halas, Joy Batchelor.* Scr *Halas, Batchelor, Lothar Wolff, Borden Mace, Philip Stapp, from the novel by George Orwell.* Animation dir *John Reed.* PC *Halas and Batch-*elor. Dis *AB-Pathé.* Technicolor. 72 mins. Cert U
A full-length cartoon version of Orwell's political fable, though with altered ending. The animals take over the running of Manor Farm from the cruel Farmer Jones. Led by the intelligent pigs Napoleon and Snowball, they set up their own constitution, proclaiming: 'All animals are equal.' But Napoleon eliminates Snowball and, quelling further revolt, declares: 'All animals are equal - but some are more equal than others.' Farmer Jones dynamites the mill, and deteriorating conditions, especially following the death of Boxer the horse, lead to a mass attack on Napoleon and his pig-leaders. ... Strongly dramatic animated feature, just about Britain's best in the field. All voices: *Maurice Denham.*

ANOTHER MAN'S POISON (1951) [4]

Dir *Irving Rapper.* Prod *Daniel Angel, Douglas Fairbanks Jr.* Scr *Val Guest, from a play by Leslie Sands.* Ph *Robert Krasker.* PC *Daniel Angel.* Dis *Eros.* 89 mins. Cert A
The Yorkshire moors. Janet (*Bette Davis*), having an affair with Larry (*Anthony Steel*), her secretary's fiancé, is menaced by the return of her husband, on the run from a robbery. She poisons him with a horse pill, but his partner Bates (*Gary Merrill*) turns up; after failing to kill him in a car crash, she eventually despatches him with horse serum in alcohol. When the doctor (*Emlyn Williams*) tells her he knew Bates was a threat and had informed the police, Janet faints. Unknowing, he feeds her the poisoned alcohol. Laughing hysterically, she dies. Rampaging overacting by the star saves ridiculous script.
RoC *Barbara Murray, Reginald Beckwith, Edna Morris.*

ANOTHER TIME, ANOTHER PLACE (1958) [2]

Dir *Lewis Allen.* Prod *Allen, Smedley Aston, Joseph Kaufman.* Scr *Stanley Mann, from the novel by Lenore Coffee.* Ph *Jack Hildyard.* PC *Kaydor.* Dis *Paramount. VistaVision.* 95 mins. Cert A
1944. British and American war correspondents Mark and Sara (*Sean Connery, Lana Turner*) fall deeply in love, although he is already married to Kay (*Glynis Johns*). When Mark is killed in an air crash, Sara is distraught to the brink of breakdown. She goes to see Kay, telling her that, although she loved Mark dearly, to him she was just a passing affair. Unaffecting soap opera.
RoC *Barry Sullivan, Sidney James, Terence Longdon, Doris Hare, Martin Stephens, John le Mesurier.*

APPOINTMENT IN LONDON (1952) [4]

Dir *Philip Leacock.* Prod *Maxwell Setton, Aubrey Baring.* Scr *John Wooldridge, Robert Westerby.* Ph *Stephen Dade.* PC *Mayflower.* Dis *British Lion.* 96 mins. Cert U
1943. Mason (*Dirk Bogarde*), a wing commander showing the strain of too many 'sorties', is relaxed by his friendship with Eve (*Dinah Sheridan*), a Wren officer and war widow. But Mason's squadron keeps losing men, among them Greeno (*Bryan Forbes*), whose widow is

befriended by Eve. Told he is grounded, Mason, with his friend Mac (*William Sylvester*) takes off again on a big raid when replacements are needed. He gets back, but is reprimanded and posted overseas. Familiar characters and situations still carry conviction; exciting climax. Co-writer *Wooldridge* also composed the film's music.

RoC *Ian Hunter, Bill Kerr, Anne Leon, Walter Fitzgerald, Charles Victor, Richard Wattis, Terence Longdon, Sam Kydd, Campbell Singer, Donovan Winter, Don Sharp, Anthony Shaw, Tom Walls Jr, Harold Siddons, Arnold Bell, Allan McClelland, Peter Rendall, Michael Ripper, Eric Corrie, Desmond Roberts, Gillian Maude, John Colicos, John Fabian, Edward Evans, Stephen Vercoe, John Martin, Carl Jaffe, Carl Duering, Wolf Frees, Lloyd Lamble.*

APPOINTMENT WITH VENUS (1951) [4]
(USA: *Island Rescue*)

Dir *Ralph Thomas.* Prod *Betty Box.* Scr *Nicholas Phipps, from the novel by Jerrard Tickell.* Ph *Ernest Steward.* PC *British Film Makers.* Dis *General Film Distributors. 89 mins. Cert U*
World War II. Venus, a pedigree cow, is stranded on the Channel island of Armorel – a captive of the Nazis! In view of the cow's great value, a major (*David Niven*), a sergeant (*Patric Doonan*), and an ATS girl (*Glynis Johns*) who knows the cow, are sent to the rescue in a submarine. After many adventures and the birth of a calf to Venus, they get back to England following a final battle with an E-Boat. Fast-moving, original comedy thriller; quite exciting, quite funny.

RoC *George Coulouris, Barry Jones, Noel Purcell, Kenneth More, Bernard Lee, Jeremy Spenser, Richard Wattis, David Horne, Geoffrey Sumner, Peter Butterworth, Martin Boddey, Anton Diffring, John Horsley, George Benson, Raymond Young, Richard Marner, Herbert C. Walton, Malcolm Farquhar, Charles Cullum, Stanley Rose, John Stratton, Peter Martyn, Neil Wilson, Geoffrey Denton, Michael Ward, Pat Nye, Marianne Stone, Betty Cooper, Noel Johnson, Jeanne Pali, Oscar Nation, Helen Goss, Michael Evans, Philip Stainton, Derek Blomfield, Harold Goodwin, Basil Dignam, Olwen Brookes, Charles Lamb, Michael Ritterman, Henrik Jacobsen, Fritz Krenn, Johnnie Schofield, Terence Longden.*

THE ARMCHAIR DETECTIVE (1951) [2]

Dir *Brendan J. Stafford.* Prod *Donald Ginsberg, Derek Elphinstone.* Scr *Ernest Dudley, Elphinstone, from a radio series by Dudley.* Ph *Gordon Lang.* PC *Meridian.* Dis *Apex. 60 mins. Cert A*
Radio's famous Armchair Detective (*Ernest Dudley*) tries to help a pretty girl beset by a blackmailer, but the villain is found dead and the girl confesses. Scotland Yard pronounces it suicide. Dudley visits the scene of the crime, and deduces a third explanation. His theory enables the police to set a trap by which the real murderer is caught. Harmless mystery with priggish central character.

RoC *Sally Newton, Hartley Power, Derek Elphinstone, Iris Russell, David Oxley, Lionel Grose, David Jenkins, Anna Korda, Charles Hunt, Gordon Foster, Arthur Lovegrove.*

AS LONG AS THEY'RE HAPPY (1955) [4]

Dir *J. Lee Thompson.* Prod *Raymond Stross.* Scr *Alan Melville, from the play by Vernon Sylvaine.* Ph *Gilbert Taylor.* PC *Raymond Stross/Group.* Dis *General Film Distributors. Eastman Colour. 91 mins. Cert U*
When an American crooner (*Jerry Wayne*) stays at a British home, the three daughters of the house (*Janette Scott, Jean(nie) Carson, Susan Stephen*) go wild – so does father (*Jack Buchanan*), but in a different way. In the end, though, the singer is responsible for reuniting father and mother, as well as revealing the secret of his 'crying crooner' technique – a hidden onion. Good-natured semi-musical romp in good colour, with lots of middle-sized laughs.

RoC *Brenda de Banzie, Diana Dors, Hugh McDermott, Nigel Green, Athene Seyler, David Hurst, Gilbert Harding, Joan Sims, Dora Bryan, Charles Hawtrey, Joan Hickson, Leslie Phillips, Jean Aubrey, Edie Martin, Susan Lyall-Grant, Peter Illing, Arnold Bell, Pauline Winter, Hattie Jacques, Vivienne Martin, Charles Ross, Ronnie Stevens, John Blythe, Bill Shine, Norman Wisdom.*

Jack Buchanan and Diana Dors in As Long As They're Happy (*1955*)

ASSASSIN FOR HIRE (1951) [3]

Dir *Michael McCarthy.* Prod *Julian Wintle.* Scr *Rex Rienits, from his TV play.* Ph *Robert Lapresle.* PC *Merton Park.* Dis *Anglo-Amalgamated. 67 mins. Cert A*
A Soho killer (*Sydney Tafler*) finances his brother's musical training with the money he receives as a hired assassin. The police know which underworld figures he has despatched, but cannot prove a thing. Finally a wily inspector (*Ronald Howard*) brings about the killer's downfall by making him believe he has killed his own brother. Slowish, quite well-made thriller with impressive central performance.

RoC *John Hewer, Katherine Blake, June Rodney, Gerald Case, Ian Wallace, Martin Benson, Ewen Solon, Reginald Dyson, Sam Kydd.*

ASSIGNMENT REDHEAD (1956) [2]

Dir/Scr *Maclean Rogers.* Prod *W.G. Chalmers.* Ph *Ernest Palmer.* PC/Dis *Butchers. 79 mins. Cert A*
An international crime ring is after 12 million counterfeit dollars printed by the Nazis in World War II. Keen (*Richard Denning*) is among those assigned to stop them. He falls

for Hedy (*Carole Mathews*), a member of the ring, but she switches her allegiances when her colleagues stoop to murder. Hedy is killed by the criminals' boss (*Ronald Adam*), who falls to his own death from the top of a warehouse. Bustling, highly unlikely thriller.

RoC *Danny Green, Brian Worth, Jan Holden, Hugh Moxey, Elwyn Brook-Jones, Peter Swanwick, Alex Gallier, Bill Nagy, Robert O'Neil, Robert Crewdson, Robert Bruce, Paul Hardtmuth, Ronald Leigh-Hunt, Edward Forsyth, James Cairns, Theodore Wilhelm.*

AT THE STROKE OF NINE (1957) [2]

Dir *Lance Comfort.* Prod *Harry Booth, Michael Deeley, Jon Pennington.* Scr *Booth, Pennington, Deeley, Tony O'Grady.* Ph *Gerald Gibbs.* PC *Tower.* Dis *Grand National. 72 mins. Cert A*
A maniac pianist (*Stephen Murray*) with a grudge against the press kidnaps a young reporter (*Patricia Dainton*) and forces her to send to her paper daily despatches of the ordeal she is suffering without revealing his name. At the end of five days, he intends to kill her, but a piano concerto heard in the background to a phone call sets the police on his track, and he is killed in a struggle with one of them. Pretty implausible – it took four men to write this?

RoC *Dermot Walsh, Patrick Barr, Clifford Evans, Leonard White, Reg Green, Frank Atkinson, Alexander Doré, Leonard Sharp, Robert Hartley, William Moore, George Lee, William Hepper, Donald B. Edwards.*

AUNT CLARA (1954) [4]

Dir *Anthony Kimmins.* Prod *Colin Lesslie, Anthony Kimmins.* Scr *Kenneth Horne, Roy Miller, from the novel by Noel Streatfeild.* PC *Lesslie.* Dis *British Lion. 84 mins. Cert U*
An old reprobate (*A.E. Matthews*) leaves all his money and dubious holdings – five greyhounds, a brothel, a racecourse racket and a low dive – to ultra-religious Clara (*Margaret Rutherford*). His outspoken valet (*Ronald Shiner*) stays to help Clara clean up everything, turning the racing racket into a moneymaker for her missionary charities. She endears herself to the shadiest of characters before passing gently on. Familiar-type comedy, carried by its excellent cast.

RoC *Fay Compton, Nigel Stock, Jill Bennett, Raymond Huntley, Eddie Byrne, Reginald Beckwith, Sidney James, Garry Marsh, Diana Beaumont, Gillian Lind, Ronald Ward, Jessie Evans, Eileen Way, George Benson, Stringer Davis, Jean St Clair, Vivienne Martin, Joss Ambler.*

B

THE BABY AND THE BATTLESHIP (1956) [4]

Dir/PC *Jay Lewis.* Prod *Antony Darnborough.*

Scr *Lewis, Gilbert Hackforth-Jones, Bryan Forbes, from the novel by Anthony Thorne.* Ph *Harry Waxman.* Dis *British Lion. Eastman Colour. 95 mins. Cert U*

During shore leave in Naples, Puncher (*John Mills*) and Knocker (*Richard Attenborough*) have to take along the baby brother of one of the local popsies (*Lisa Gastoni*). Puncher finds himself holding the baby, alone, and smuggles it on board ship, where it is kept out of sight by his shipmates, until it provides a convenient excuse for the captain (*Michael Hordern*) to disengage from a mock battle that he was losing. Broad farce, strenuously played for all it's worth.

RoC *Bryan Forbes, Lionel Jeffries, André Morell, Michael Howard, Ernest Clark, Harry Locke, Clifford Mollison, Thorley Walters, Duncan Lamont, Cyril Raymond, D.A. Clarke-Smith, Kenneth Griffith, John le Mesurier, Gordon Jackson, Harold Siddons, Patrick Cargill, John Forbes-Robertson, Ferdy Mayne, Martin Miller, Barry Foster, Vincent Ball, Robert Ayres, Sam Kydd, Michael Dear, Jacinta Dicks, Carlo Justini, Vince Barbi, Vittorio Vittori, Mark Sheldon, Martyn Garrett (baby), Yvonne Romain.*

BACHELOR OF HEARTS (1958) [3]

Dir *Wolf Rilla.* Prod *Vivian A. Cox.* Scr *Leslie Bricusse, Frederic Raphael.* Ph *Geoffrey Unsworth.* PC/Dis *Rank. Eastman Colour. 94 mins. Cert U*

It takes German exchange student Wolf (*Hardy Kruger*) some time to get used to the 'rags' at Cambridge University, especially when he is doused in paraffin, set alight and thrown into the river. His friendship with Ann (*Sylvia Syms*) is somewhat strained when he has to date all his friends' girls while they are studying for exams – but all ends well. Harmless, likeable romantic comedy with several star hopefuls.

RoC *Ronald Lewis, Jeremy Burnham, Peter Myers, Philip Gilbert, Charles Kay, John Richardson, Gillian Vaughan, Sandra Francis, Catherine Feller, Barbara Steele, Miles Malleson, Eric Barker, Newton Blick, Monica Stevenson, Pamela Barreaux, Beatrice Varley, Ronnie Stevens, Hugh Morton.*

Hardy Kruger and Sylvia Syms in Bachelor of Hearts (*1958*)

BACKGROUND (1953) [4]
(USA: *Edge of Divorce*)
Dir *Daniel Birt.* Prod *Herbert Mason.* Scr

Warren Chetham-Strode, Don Sharp, from the play by Chetham-Strode. Ph *Arthur Grant.* PC/*Group 3.* Dis *Associated British. 83 mins. Cert A*

John and Barbie Lomax (*Philip Friend, Valerie Hobson*) decide to divorce after 16 years of marriage. Barbie is set to marry an old friend Bill (*Norman Wooland*). Of their children, 15-year-old Jess (*Janette Scott*) is excited and nine-year-old Linda (*Mandy Miller*) miserable. Twelve-year-old Adrian (*Jeremy Spenser*) tries to kill Bill with an airgun, wounding him. John and Barbie decide to stay together. Sincere, down-to-earth drama.

RoC *Lilly Kann, Helen Shingler, Richard Wattis, Thora Hird, Jack Melford, Louise Hampton, Joss Ambler, Brian Harding, Lloyd Lamble, Barbara Hicks, Ernest Butcher, Rory.*

THE BANDIT OF ZHOBE (1959) [3]

Dir/Scr *John Gilling.* Prod *Irving Allen, Albert R. Broccoli.* Ph *Ted Moore.* PC *Warwick.* Dis *Columbia. Technicolor. CinemaScope. 81 mins. Cert U*

The 19th century. Kasim (*Victor Mature*), an Indian tribal chief, turns bandit when his wife, baby and people are massacred by an enemy chief, Azhad (*Walter Gotell*), who has dressed his men in British uniforms. Kasim raids the British garrison, where Zena (*Anne Aubrey*), the CO's daughter, having been kidnapped by Kasim, brings both parties to see the truth. Kasim kills Azhad, but is killed in turn by one of Ahzad's henchmen. Rip-roaring adventure makes no sense, but keeps coming at you.

RoC *Anthony Newley, Norman Wooland, Dermot Walsh, Sean Kelly, Paul Stassino, Laurence Taylor, Denis Shaw, Maya Koumani, Murray Kash, Maxwell Shaw, Harold Goodwin, Anthony Jacobs, Barbara Joyce, Eve Eden.*

BANG! YOU'RE DEAD (1954) [3]
(USA: *Game of Danger*)
Dir/Prod *Lance Comfort.* Scr *Guy Elmes, Ernest Borneman.* Ph *Brendan J. Stafford.* PC *Wellington.* Dis *British Lion. 88 mins. Cert A*
Tearaway bombsite kid Cliff (*Anthony Richmond*) plays 'Bang! You're Dead' with his slow-witted friend Willy (*Sean Barrett*), using toy guns. One day, he finds a loaded revolver, points it at a man and kills him. The man had just had a quarrel with Carter (*Michael Medwin*), who is suspected of murder, but the truth comes out after Willy tries to sell the dead man's watch. Unusual drama, but not too well made.

RoC *Jack Warner, Derek Farr, Gordon Harker, Veronica Hurst, Philip Saville, Beatrice Varley, John Warwick, Toke Townley, Fred Griffiths, Larry Burns, Arnold Bell, Leo Phillips.*

THE BANK RAIDERS (1958) [1]
Dir *Maxwell Munden.* Prod *Geoffrey Goodhart.* Scr *Brandon Fleming.* Ph *Henry Hall.* PC *Film Workshop.* Dis *Rank. 60 mins. Cert U*
Terry (*Peter Reynolds*), a flashy crook, gets a job as getaway driver at a bank robbery. Afterwards, he splashes about his share of the proceeds and Shelton (*Sydney Tafler*), the gang leader, is forced to kidnap a witness. Egged on by his girl (*Sandra Dorne*), Terry decides to

rob Shelton, opens his safe, but is killed by a mechanical gun there. The police catch Shelton. Rock-bottom 'B' film, very badly acted with the exception of the three stars.

RoC *Rose Hill, Lloyd Lamble, Arthur Mullard, Tim Ellison, Ann King, Dennis Taylor, Robert Bruce, Jeanne Kent, Roberta Wooley.*

BARBADOS QUEST (1955) [2]
(USA: *Murder on Approval*)
Dir *Bernard Knowles.* Prod *Robert S. Baker, Monty Berman.* Scr *Kenneth R. Hayles.* Ph *Berman.* PC *Cipa.* Dis *RKO Radio. 70 mins. Cert U*

Employed by a millionaire to investigate his purchase of a rare stamp which seems to be a forgery, private eye Duke Martin (*Tom Conway*) finds pretty well everyone he meets involved in the deception: Coburn, the dealer (*Campbell Cotts*); Gordini, an engraver (*Ronan O'Casey*); Jean (*Delphi Lawrence*), secretary to the stamp's original owner; and Blake (*Brian Worth*), the owner's nephew. Blake kills Coburn and Gordini (who made fake plates), but is shot by Jean as he tries to kill Duke. Tired thriller, not very well acted.

RoC *Michael Balfour, John Horsley, Colin Tapley, Launce Maraschal, Alan Gifford, Grace Arnold, John Colicos, Mayura, John Watson, Reg Morris, Marianne Stone, Derrick Whittingham, Frank Pemberton, Neil Wilson, Olive Kirby, Rosamund Waring, Margaret Rowe, Maureen Connell.*

BARNACLE BILL (1957) [3]
(USA: *All at Sea*)
Dir *Charles Frend.* (Associate) Prod *Dennis Van Thal.* Scr *T.E.B. Clarke.* Ph *Douglas Slocombe.* PC *Ealing Films.* Dis *M-G-M. 87 mins. Cert U*

Captain William Horatio Ambrose (*Alec Guinness*), last in a line of distinguished naval men, has a fatal flaw: he gets seasick. So he takes charge of a pier, calls it the *Arabella*, and plans to turn it into an entertainment centre. When the council opposes him, he registers the pier as a ship – a pleasure liner for the seasick. The council sends a dredger to tear down the pier, but are defeated by Ambrose leading a fleet of children's pedal-boats. He crosses the Channel on the wreck of the *Arabella*. Sounds hilarious, but isn't quite – more an echo of Ealing's golden days. Guinness also plays the hero's six ancestors.

Frank Burdett and Alec Guinness in Barnacle Bill (*1958*)

RoC *Irene Browne, Maurice Denham, Victor Maddern, Percy Herbert, George Rose, Lionel Jeffries, Harold Goodwin, Lloyd Lamble, Warren Mitchell, Jackie Collins, Richard Wattis, Frederick Piper, Eric Pohlmann, Donald Pleasence, Miles Malleson, Max Butterfield, Mike Morgan, Donald Churchill, Joan Hickson, Junia Crawford, Susan Gibson, Charles Cullum, Alexander Harris, G.H. Raines, Edith Jewell, Peggy Williamson, George McIntyre, Sam Kydd, Harry Locke, Newton Blick, George Butler, John Benn, Frank Burdett, Allan Cuthbertson.*

THE BARRETTS OF WIMPOLE STREET (1956) [2]
Dir *Sidney Franklin.* Prod *Sam Zimbalist.* Scr *John Dighton, from the play by Rudolf Besier.* Ph *F.A. Young.* PC/Dis *M-G-M British.* Metrocolor. CinemaScope. 105 mins. Cert U
1845. Banker Edward Moulton-Barrett (*John Gielgud*) rules his six sons and three daughters by fear. Elizabeth (*Jennifer Jones*), who suffers from rheumatic fever, meets and falls in love with Robert Browning (*Bill Travers*), a poet. Her health improves, but her father turns on her when he finds she has been abetting the love affair of one of her sisters. Horrified to find that her father's feelings transcend the mere parental, Elizabeth flees the house and marries Browning. Very slow and boring romantic drama, with a few laughs in the wrong places. Remake of the 1934 Hollywood film, which had the same director.
RoC *Virginia McKenna, Susan Stephen, Vernon Gray, Maxine Audley, Laurence Naismith, Leslie Phillips, Michael Brill, Moultrie Kelsall, Kenneth Fortescue, Nicholas Hawtrey, Richard Thorp, Keith Baxter, Brian Smith, Jean Anderson.*

THE BATTLE OF THE RIVER PLATE (1956) [4]
(USA: *Pursuit of the Graf Spee*)
Dir/Prod/Scr *Michael Powell, Emeric Pressburger.* Ph *Christopher Challis.* PC *Arcturus.* Dis *Rank.* Technicolor. VistaVision. 119 mins. Cert U
A menace to Allied shipping, and sinker of several British ships in the early months of World War II, the German pocket battleship *Admiral Graf Spee* is pursued by three British cruisers and badly damages one of them before holing up in the Uruguayan harbour of Montevideo. Outwitted by British intelligence, the Germans are convinced *Graf Spee* is trapped by a massive naval force. The captain (*Peter Finch*) takes his men off and the ship is scuttled. Workmanlike, poker-faced war film, the Royal Film Performance of its year.
RoC *John Gregson, Anthony Quayle, Ian Hunter, Bernard Lee, Jack Gwillim, Lionel Murton, Anthony Bushell, Peter Illing, Michael Goodliffe, William Squire, Andrew Cruickshank, Christopher Lee, Patrick Macnee, John Chandos, Douglas Wilmer, Roger Delgado, Edward Atienza, Brian Worth, April Olrich, Maria Mercedes, Barry Foster, Edward Judd.*

THE BATTLE OF THE SEXES (1959) [4]
Dir *Charles Crichton.* Prod/Scr *Monja Danischewsky, from a story by James Thurber.* Ph

Freddie Francis. PC *Prometheus.* Dis *British Lion/Bryanston.* 84 mins. Cert U
When an American efficiency expert (*Constance Cummings*) moves in on an old-fashioned Scots tweed company, its chief accountant (*Peter Sellers*) sabotages her plans at every opportunity. Desperate when she plots to turn the firm over to synthetic automation, he at first tries (unsuccessfully) to murder her, then (more successfully) to have her declared insane. Eventually, she gives up and leaves the firm in peace. Comedy of constant chuckles; not quite a joy, but certainly a pleasure.
RoC *Robert Morley, Donald Pleasence, Ernest Thesiger, Moultrie Kelsall, Jameson Clark, Alex Mackenzie, Roddy McMillan, Michael Goodliffe, Norman MacOwan, William Mervyn, James Gibson, Noel Howlett, Abe Barker, Gordon Phillott, MacDonald Parke, Patricia Hayes, Eric Woodburn, Donald Bisset, Sam Wanamaker (voice only).*

BATTLE OF THE V1 (1958) [3]
(USA: *V1/Unseen Heroes*)
Dir *Vernon Sewell.* Prod *George Maynard, Sewell, John Bask.* Scr *Jack Hanley, Eryk Wlodek, from a book by Bernard Newman.* Ph *Basil Emmott.* PC *Criterion.* Dis *Eros.* 109 mins. Cert A
Two Poles (*Michael Rennie, David Knight*) conscripted by the Germans as labourers during World War II not only give information to the British raid on Peenemunde, but discover an unexploded V1 rocket in a field and arrange to have it got back in its entirety to England, which is thus able to destroy most of the rockets when they attack. True-life war exploits trivialized into conventional action film.
RoC *Patricia Medina, Milly Vitale, Esmond Knight, Christopher Lee, Carl Jaffe, John G. Heller, Peter Madden, Gordon Sterne, George Pravda, Julian Somers, Carl Duering, Harold Siddons, George Pastell, Henry Vidon, Stanley Zevic, Gregory Dark, Jan Conrad, Tom Clegg, Robert Raikes, Valerie White, Geoffrey Chater.*

THE BEACHCOMBER (1954) [4]
Dir *Muriel Box.* Prod *William MacQuitty.* Scr *Sydney Box, from a story by W. Somerset Maugham.* Ph *Reginald Wyer.* PC *London Independent.* Dis *General Film Distributors.* Technicolor. 90 mins. Cert A
The Hon Ted (*Robert Newton*), drunken outcast of the Welcome Islands, hated by the missionary (*Paul Rogers*) and his sister Martha (*Glynis Johns*), is exiled by the Resident (*Donald Sinden*) to a nearby island. Here, Martha operates both on the Headman (*Michael Hordern*) and an elephant, and sees Ted in a different light, seeking his help when cholera breaks out. She and Ted are condemned by natives, but the elephant she saved will not trample her, and they escape and marry. Rather less tasty remake of *Vessel of Wrath* (1938); critics were split on the respective merits of the two films.
RoC *Donald Pleasence, Walter Crisham, Ronald Lewis, Auric Lorand, Tony Quinn, Ah Chong Choy, Jean Rollins, Ronald Adam, Kim Parker, Wanda Sinclair, Lysbeth Rollins.*

'BEAT' GIRL (1959) [1]
(USA: *Wild for Kicks*)
Dir *Edmond T. Gréville.* Prod *George Willoughby.* Scr *Dail Ambler.* Ph *Walter Lassally.* PC/Dis *Renown.* 85 mins. Cert X
Precocious teenager Jennifer (*Gillian Hills*), who hangs around Soho coffee bars, finds out that her father's (*David Farrar*) new French wife Nichole (*Noelle Adam*) was once a dancer. She tells club-owner Kenny (*Christopher Lee*), who uses the knowledge to block Nichole when she tries to warn him off Jennifer. A wild party at her home ends with Jennifer running away after doing a striptease. Kenny attempts to seduce her but is stabbed by a stripper. Dreary exploitation film with cast of embryo stars.
RoC *Adam Faith, Shirley Ann Field, Peter McEnery, Claire Gordon, Nigel Green, Delphi Lawrence, Oliver Reed, Carol White, Christina Curry, Pasqualine Justano.*

BEAT THE DEVIL (1953) [4]
Dir *John Huston.* Prod *Huston, Jack Clayton.* Scr *Truman Capote, Huston.* PC *Romulus/Santana.* Dis *Independent Film Distributors/British Lion.* 100 mins. Cert A
A group of people on a Mediterranean tramp steamer becomes involved in cross and double-cross over (fictitious) uranium deposits, invented by imaginative Gwendolen (*Jennifer Jones*), who is being squired, unknown to her husband Harry (*Edward Underdown*), by Dannreuther (*Humphrey Bogart*), an associate of the Peterson gang, also on board. Harry vanishes and is believed dead. After a brush with Arabs on arrival in Africa, Peterson (*Robert Morley*) and his gang are held for murder. Gwendolen receives a message from Harry saying he has swum ashore and bought up the 'uranium' land. Jokey, involved comedy. Fun and might have been more so.
RoC *Gina Lollobrigida, Peter Lorre, Ivor Barnard, Bernard Lee, Marco Tulli, Mario Perroni, Alex Pochet, Aldo Silvani, Manual Serano, Giulio Donnini, Saro Urzi, Juan de Landa, Mimo Poli.*

BEAU BRUMMELL (1954) [4]
Dir *Curtis Bernhardt.* Prod *Sam Zimbalist.* Scr *Karl Tunberg, from the play by Carl Fitch.* Ph *Oswald Morris.* PC/Dis *M-G-M British.* Technicolor. 111 mins. Cert U
The elegant Beau Brummell (*Stewart Granger*) becomes a great favourite at the Regency court of George III (*Robert Morley*) and a close friend of the Prince Regent (*Peter Ustinov*). But he loves and loses Lady Patricia (*Elizabeth Taylor*), quarrels with the prince, and is forced to flee to France one step ahead of creditors. His health collapses and he dies, reconciled on his deathbed with the Prince, now George IV. Fine performances in largely enjoyable, occasionally moving film – the Royal Film Performance of its year. Outrageously inaccurate history though.
RoC *James Donald, James Hayter, Rosemary Harris, Paul Rogers, Noel Willman, Peter Dyneley, Charles Carson, Finlay Currie, Peter Bull, Ernest Clark, Mark Dignam, Desmond Roberts, David Horne, Ralph Truman, Elwyn Brook-Jones, George de Warfaz, Henry Oscar, Harold Kasket.*

BEAUTIFUL STRANGER (1954)   3
(USA: *Twist of Fate*)

Dir *David Miller*. Prod *Maxwell Setton, John R. Sloan*. Scr *Robert Westerby, Carl Nystrom*. Ph *Ted Scaife*. PC *Marksman*. Dis *British Lion*. 89 mins. Cert A

Stunned by the realization that Galt, her wealthy Riviera lover (*Stanley Baker*), – secretly mixed up in a coining racket – does not intend to divorce his wife (*Margaret Rawlings*) and marry her, Johnny (*Ginger Rogers*) contemplates suicide until she meets Pierre (*Jacques Bergerac*). They become implicated in Galt's murder, but the real killer, Landosh (*Herbert Lom*), shot by police, unintentionally clears them. Tortuous thriller, played for rather more than its worth.

RoC *Eddie Byrne, Lilly Kann, Coral Browne, Lisa Gastoni, Ferdy Mayne, John Chandos, Keith Pyott, Rudolph Offenbach, Olive Lucius, Yves Aysage, John le Mesurier, Tony Spear, Dino Galvani, Bernard Rebel, Marcella De Cleve, Elizabeth Digby-Smith, Alexis Chesnakov, Marianne Stone, Nicholas Bruce.*

BEFORE I WAKE (1955)   3
(USA: *Shadow of Fear*)

Dir *Al Rogell*. Prod *Steven Pallos, Charles A. Leeds*. Scr/(uncredited) *Robert Westerby, from the novel by Hal Debrett*. Ph *Jack Asher*. PC *Gibraltar*. Dis *Grand National*. 78 mins. Cert A

April (*Mona Freeman*) returns from America to her native England and soon suspects that her stepmother (*Jean Kent*) did away with April's alcoholic mother, to whom she was nurse, and father, whom she subsequently married. She's dead right, and stepmother, who appears an angel of mercy to the locals, plans to kill April too when she discovers April will inherit, at 21, all that she herself plotted to gain. No-one will believe April, who has to battle grimly to escape her fate. Barnstorming melodrama, played with enthusiasm by the two protagonists.

RoC *Maxwell Reed, Frederick Leister, Hugh Miller, Gretchen Franklin, Alexander Gauge, Josephine Middleton, Frank Forsyth, Stanley Van Beers, Frank Atkinson, Philip Ray, Robert Sansom, Phyllis Cornell.*

THE BEGGAR'S OPERA (1952)   3

Dir *Peter Brook*. Prod *Laurence Olivier, Herbert Wilcox*. Scr *Dennis Cannan, Christopher Fry, from the musical play by John Gay*. Ph *Guy Green*. PC *Imperadio*. Dis *British Lion*. Technicolor. 94 mins. Cert U

1741. Awaiting execution in Newgate Jail, highwayman Macheath (*Laurence Olivier*) hears an 'opera' of his colourful life composed by a beggar, telling of his hair-raising escapes, both from the law and the numerous doxies who pursue him, one of whom is responsible for his ultimate betrayal. As the opera ends, Macheath is improbably granted a reprieve, and gallops away to freedom. Vivid and vigorous 'opera' lacks cinematic rhythm. Olivier sings quite well though.

RoC *Dorothy Tutin, Stanley Holloway, Daphne Anderson, Hugh Griffith, Sandra Dorne, Yvonne Furneaux, George Devine, Mary Clare,*

Margot Grahame, Athene Seyler, George Rose, Kenneth Williams, Denis Cannan, Edith Coates, Eric Pohlmann, Laurence Naismith, Bombardier Billy Wells. Singers: Olivier, Holloway, Coates, Adele Leigh, Joan Cross, Bruce Boyce, Jennifer Vyvyan, John Cameron.

BEHEMOTH THE SEA MONSTER (1958)   4
(USA: *The Giant Behemoth*)

Dir *Douglas Hickox, Eugene Lourié*. Prod *Ted Lloyd, David Diamond*. Scr *Lourié*. Ph *Ken Hodges*. PC *Artistes Alliance*. Dis *Eros*. 70 mins. Cert X

Marine biologist Steve Karnes (*Gene Evans*) believes that increased radioactivity from atomic tests could have created a giant sea monster which is attacking shipping and causing thousands of dead fish – and a few dead people. Identified as a palaeosaurus, the creature invades London, wrecking the Woolwich Ferry and storming up the Thames before being despatched by a radium-tipped torpedo from a midget submarine. Superior creature feature has good effects, is convincingly acted.

RoC *André Morell, Leigh Madison, Henry Vidon, John Turner, Jack MacGowran, Maurice Kaufmann, Leonard Sachs, Neal Arden.*

BEHIND THE HEADLINES (1953)   3

Dir/Scr *Maclean Rogers*. Prod/PC *E.J. Fancey*. Ph *Geoffrey Faithfull, Ian Barnes*. Dis *New Realm*. 51 mins. Cert U

A crime reporter (*Gilbert Harding*) goes into the detailed activities of Scotland Yard for a writer (*John Fitzgerald*). He lists the numerous behind-the-scenes activities that lead to the tracing and apprehension of a gang of lorry-thieves, and the trial of the ringleader for the murder of a caretaker. Fairly interesting semi-documentary drama.

RoC *Adrienne Scott, Vi Kaley, Michael McCarthy, Jack May, Howell Evans, Pat Hagan.*

BEHIND THE HEADLINES (1956)   2

Dir *Charles Saunders*. Prod *Guido Coen*. Scr *Allan Mackinnon, from a novel by Robert Chapman*. Ph *Geoffrey Faithfull*. PC *Kenilworth*. Dis *Rank*. 67 mins. Cert U

Reporter Paul Banner (*Paul Carpenter*) determines to solve the mystery surrounding a blackmailing blonde's murder. Pam (*Adrienne Corri*) beats Paul to the scoop when the killer is unmasked, but loses him to Maxine (*Hazel Court*), his ex-fiancée, with whom he is still in love. Another Banner comedy-thriller (the third); only fitfully effective.

RoC *Alfie Bass, Ewen Solon, Harry Fowler, Trevor Reid, Olive Gregg, Marianne Brauns, Gaylord Cavallaro, Marian Collins, Sandra Colville, Tom Gill, Magda Miller, Arthur Rigby, Colin Rix.*

BEHIND THE MASK (1958)   4

Dir *Brian Desmond Hurst*. Prod *Sergei Nolbandov, Josef Somlo*. Scr *John Hunter, from a novel by John Rowan Wilson*. Ph *Robert Krasker*. PC *GW Films*. Dis *British Lion*. Eastman Colour. 98 mins. Cert A

Sir Arthur (*Michael Redgrave*), a wealthy,

John Gale, Ian Bannen and Tony Britton in Behind the Mask (*1958*)

deeply-caring surgeon, is constantly at odds with his dispassionate associate (*Niall MacGinnis*). Selwood (*Tony Britton*), a brilliant new surgeon in love with Sir Arthur's daughter (*Vanessa Redgrave*) becomes involved with a drug-addicted Polish anaesthetist (*Carl Mohner*) and, trying to help, neglects a patient who dies. He tenders his resignation, but Sir Arthur, seriously ill, persuades him to stay on and continue the fight for caring treatment. Serious-minded hospital drama.

RoC *Ian Bannen, Brenda Bruce, Lionel Jeffries, Miles Malleson, John Welsh, Ann Firbank, Jack Hedley, Hugh Miller, John Gale, Jack Hedley, Mary Skinner, Margaret Tyzack.*

THE BELLES OF ST TRINIAN'S (1954)   4

Dir *Frank Launder*. Prod *Launder, Sidney Gilliat*. Scr *Launder, Gilliat, Val Valentine, from cartoons by Ronald Searle*. Ph *Stanley Pavey*. PC *London Films*. Dis *British Lion*. 91 mins. Cert U

Clarence Fritton (*Alastair Sim*), bookie brother of the headmistress (also *Sim*) of the terrifying St Trinian's School for Girls, sneaks his daughter into the sixth form to pick up racing tips from the daughter of a racehorse owner, whose horse, Arab Boy, is backed by the Fourth Form, Miss Fritton and the school funds to win a fortune. The horse is kidnapped by the Sixth, but rescued and wins. St Trinian's is saved from bankruptcy. Rollicking comedy, a big commercial hit.

RoC *Joyce Grenfell, George Cole, Hermione Baddeley, Betty Ann Davies, Beryl Reid, Mary*

Alastair Sim, Peter Jones and Sidney James in The Belles of St Trinian's (*1954*)

Merrall, Renee Houston, Irene Handl, Joan Sims, Balbina, Guy Middleton, Sidney James, Arthur Howard, Richard Wattis, Eric Pohlmann, Lloyd Lamble, Andree Melly, Belinda Lee, Jerry Verno, Jack Doyle, Jane Henderson, Diana Day, Jill Braidwood, Annabelle Covey, Pauline Drewett, Jean Langston, Michael Ripper, Martin Walker, Noel Hood, Vivienne Martin, Elizabeth Griffiths, Michael Kelly, Tommy Duggan, Paul Connell, Lorna Henderson, Cara Stevens, Vivienne Wood, Stuart Saunders, Jim Tyson, Bill O'Malley, Arthur Sandifer, Henry Longhurst, Barry Steele, Michael Balfour, Pat Hagan, Gilbert Harrison, Raymond Glendenning, Barbara Denney, Marigold Russell, Shirley Burniston, Shirley Eaton, Lillimor Knudsen, Barbara Deeks (Windsor), Gloria Turower, Dilys Lay(e), Damaris Hayman, Ann Way, Susan Kester, Doreen Dawne, Wendy Adams, Gillian Gordon-Inglis, Gillian Town, Catherine Feller, Mildred Gordon, Sandra Alfred, Cherry White, Madeleine Yates, Stella Mandler, Jennifer Beach, Sandra Scott Kerr, Dominica More O'Ferrall, Alanna Boyce, Pauline Coe, Amanda Coxill, Lynn Courtney, Marcia Manolescu, Mavis Sage, Jacqueline Wall, Pamela Ballard, Carole Boom, Heather Bradley, Valerie Winer, Eileen Dudley, Irene French, Gloria Richards, Barbara Sharman, Carole Hicks, Myrette Morven, Ronald Searle, Sally Lahee, Norman Maitland, Bob Gregory, Kaye Webb, Beryl Hyslop, Peggy O'Farrell, Rita Pettet, Carole Riches, Jill Stewart, Virginia Jameson, Patricia Jameson, Windsor Cottage (horse).

BERMUDA AFFAIR (1956) [1]

Dir *Edward Sutherland*. Prod *Coolidge Adams*. Scr *Sutherland, Robert J. Shaw*. Ph *Harry W. Smith*. PC *Bermuda*. Dis *Columbia*. 77 mins. Cert *A*

Korean War buddies Bob and Chuck (*Gary Merrill, Ron Randell*) stay together to run a Bermuda-based airline. Chuck's wife Chris (*Zena Marshall*) has an affair with Bob, who gives his life to save his friend in a mid-air crisis. Turgid, lifeless drama.
RoC *Kim Hunter, Don Gibson, Robert Arden, Elspeth Hoffman, James McLaughlin, Wilbert Smith, Alfred Wagstaff, William Rewalt.*

THE BETRAYAL (1957) [3]

Dir *Ernest Morris*. Prod *Edward J. Danziger, Harry Lee Danziger*. Scr *Brian Clemens, Eldon Howard*. Ph *Jimmy Wilson*. PC *Danzigers*. Dis *United Artists*. 82 mins. Cert *U*

Ten years after being betrayed, shot and blinded in a World War II escape bid, Michael McCall (*Philip Friend*) hears the voice of his betrayer again at a London party. A friend, Janet (*Diana Decker*) helps him draw up a list of guests, but forgets to list her boss, who held the party and is the man for whom McCall is looking. He tries to frame McCall for murder, but is on the point of being choked by the blind ex-PoW when police break in and hear his confession. Almost believable offbeat thriller doesn't quite make it.
RoC *Philip Saville, Peter Bathurst, Peter Burton, Ballard Berkeley, Harold Lang.*

BEYOND MOMBASA (1956) [3]

Dir *George Marshall*. Prod *Adrian Worker, M.J. Frankovitch*. Scr *Richard English, Gene Levitt, from a novel by James Eastwood*. Ph *Frederick A. Young*. PC *Hemisphere*. Dis *Columbia*. Technicolor. 90 mins. Cert *U*

Matt Campbell (*Cornel Wilde*) comes to East Africa to avenge his brother's death at the hands of the Leopard Men, an anti-white organization. He also sets off in search of a uranium mine discovered by his brother, accompanied by Ann (*Donna Reed*), an anthropologist; Hoyt (*Leo Genn*), her missionary uncle; Rossi (*Christopher Lee*), a hunter; and Hastings (*Ron Randell*), the dead man's partner. Several more killings occur before Hoyt is unmasked as the Leopard Men's leader, and killed. Clean, improbable fun in the jungle; no surprises.
RoC *Dan Jackson, Bartholomew Sketch, Clive Morton, Eddie Calvert, MacDonald Parke, Virginia Bedard, Ed Johnson Purcell, Julian Sherrier.*

BEYOND THIS PLACE (1959) [3]
(USA: *Web of Evidence*)

Dir *Jack Cardiff*. Prod *Maxwell Setton, John R. Sloan*. Scr *Kenneth Taylor, from the novel by A.J. Cronin*. Ph *Wilkie Cooper*. PC *Georgefield*. Dis *Renown*. 89 mins. Cert *A*

Arriving from America to enquire into the death of his father in World War II, Paul (*Van Johnson*) is stunned to find him still alive, serving a life sentence for the murder of a girl in 1940. The authorities are unsympathetic to Paul's requests to have the case reopened, but when he gets the support of a newspaper, public opinion is aroused, Paul's father is released (though shattered by imprisonment) and the real killer found. Rather lackadaisical sentimental mystery.
RoC *Vera Miles, Emlyn Williams, Bernard Lee, Jean Kent, Leo McKern, Rosalie Crutchley, Moultrie Kelsall, Vincent Winter, Ralph Truman, Geoffrey Keen, Jameson Clark, Oliver Johnston, Henry Oscar, Joyce Heron, Anthony Newlands, John Glyn-Jones, Hope Jackman, Michael Collins, Danny Green, Eira Heath, Thomas Baptiste, Lynda King, Emma Young, Frank Atkinson, John Carson.*

BHOWANI JUNCTION (1955) [3]

Dir *George Cukor*. Prod *Pandro S. Berman*. Scr *Sonya Levien, Ivan Moffat, from the novel by John Masters*. Ph *F.A. Young*. PC/Dis *MGM British*. Eastman Colour. CinemaScope. 109 mins. Cert *A*

British India, 1947. Half-caste Victoria Jones (*Ava Gardner*) is torn between a British officer (*Stewart Granger*), an Anglo-Indian railway boss (*Bill Travers*) and a Sikh (*Francis Matthews*). Killing a British lieutenant (*Lionel Jeffries*) who tries to rape her, Victoria becomes involved with terrorist Ghanshayam (*Peter Illing*) who kidnaps her, but is eventually killed by the rail chief, who is also killed. The officer Victoria loves decides to leave the service and marry her. Long, sprawling saga in muddy colour.
RoC *Abraham Sofaer, Freda Jackson, Marne Maitland, Edward Chapman, Alan Tilvern.*

THE BIG CHANCE (1957) [3]

Dir *Peter Graham Scott*. Prod *John Temple-Smith, Francis Edge*. Scr *Graham Scott, Barbara S. Harper, from a novel by Pamela Barrington*. Ph *Walter J. Harvey*. PC *Major*. Dis *Rank*. 61 mins. Cert *U*

Bill (*William Russell*), an embezzler, meets Diana (*Adrienne Corri*), as he is trying to get his stolen money through the customs. Through a chance, she rumbles his game but, in return for silence, agrees to helps him. The flight out is delayed by fog, a series of complications ensues which ends in the death of Diana's husband, and Bill is ultimately only too glad to return the money and go back to his wife. Very minor, but the playing and direction create some moments of tension.
RoC *Ian Colin, Penelope Bartley, Ferdy Mayne, John Rae, Douglas Ives, Robert Raglan, Mary Jones, Doris Yorke, John Walters.*

Adrienne Corri, John Walters and William Russell in The Big Chance (*1957*)

THE BIG MONEY (1956) [2]

Dir *John Paddy Carstairs*. Prod *Joseph Janni*. Scr *John Baines, Patrick Campbell*. Ph *Jack Cox*. PC/Dis *Rank*. Technicolor. VistaVision. 86 mins. Cert *U*

The motto of the Frith family is: we never got caught. Father (*James Hayter*) is a pickpocket, mother and daughter (*Kathleen Harrison, Jill Ireland*) run a successful shoplifting swindle. The only problem is son Willie (*Ian Carmichael*), who finally manages to swipe a suitcase full of banknotes, only to find they are as fake as the clergyman (*Robert Helpmann*) who had them. Further complications culminate in Willie's arrest and conviction – and the removal of his portrait from the Frith family album. Uneasy farce has shakily cast stars forcing for laughs. Not released until 1958.
RoC *Belinda Lee, George Coulouris, Renee Houston, Michael Brennan, Leslie Phillips, Harold Berens, Digby Wolfe, Hugh Morton, Ferdy Mayne, Digby Wolfe, Michael Balfour, Desmond Jeans.*

THE BIRTHDAY PRESENT (1957) [4]

Dir *Pat Jackson*. Prod/PC/Scr *Jack Whittingham*. Co-prod *George Pitcher*. Ph *Ted Scaife*. Dis *British Lion*. 100 mins. Cert *U*

Attempting to smuggle a watch for his wife (*Sylvia Syms*) back from a trip to Germany, Simon (*Tony Britton*) is caught and sentenced to six months' imprisonment. Faced with the fact that an appeal would be ruinously expensive, Simon serves his time, but finds it impossible to get a job on his release, until Colonel Wilson (*Geoffrey Keen*), a director of his old firm, persuades them to take Simon back. Small-scale but well-acted, effective drama.

RoC *Jack Watling, Walter Fitzgerald, Howard Marion Crawford, Lockwood West, Harry Fowler, John Welsh, Ian Bannen, Thorley Walters, Malcolm Keen, Frederick Piper, Cyril Luckham, Ernest Clark.*

BITTER SPRINGS (1950) [4]

Dir *Ralph Smart*. (Associate) Prod *Leslie Norman*. Scr *W.P. Lipscomb, Monja Danischewsky*. Ph *George Heath*. PC *Ealing Studios*. Dis *General Film Distributors*. 89 mins. Cert U
Australia, 1900. Wally King (*Chips Rafferty*) and his family buy land from the government and trek 600 miles to reach it. They fall out with Aborigines who see the land as theirs. After a native is killed, the Kings' home is destroyed and they are rescued by police from a native siege. Wally realizes that the only way to pioneer is to work peaceably hand in hand with the Aborigines. Quite liked by critics at the time, but the end of Ealing's Australian ventures for some years.

RoC *Tommy Trinder, Gordon Jackson, Jean Blue, Nonnie Piper, Charles Tingwell, Nicky Yardley, Henry Murdoch, Michael Pate.*

BLACK ICE (1957) [3]

Dir *Godfrey Grayson*. Prod *Jacques de Lane Lea*. Scr *Roger Proudlock, John Sherman*. Ph *Jimmy Harvey*. PC *Parkside*. Dis *Archway*. 51 mins. Cert U
A trawler goes to the rescue of a ship adrift in fog, but itself becomes trapped by the onset of ice. Several seamen are killed in attempts to free the vessels before the survivors are winched off by helicopter. Good team effort raises some suspense on a very low budget.

LP *Paul Carpenter, Gordon Jackson, Ewen Solon, David Oxley, Maureen Davis, Claude Kingston, Barry Keegan, Tony Doonan, Michael Peake, Arnold Bell, Hilda Fenemore, Ronald Fraser, George Tovey, Ben Williams, Edwin Richfield, Robert Robinson, Errol Mackinnon.*

THE BLACK KNIGHT (1954) [2]

Dir *Tay Garnett*. Prod *Irving Allen, Albert R. Broccoli*, (uncredited) *Phil C. Samuel*. Scr *Alec Coppel*. Ph *John Wilcox*. PC *Warwick*. Dis *Columbia*. 85 mins. Cert U
Sixth-century England. King Arthur (*Anthony Bushell*) gives armourer John (*Alan Ladd*) three months to prove that renegade Sir Palamides (*Peter Cushing*) is the leader of 'Viking' raiders sacking English castles. Disguised as 'The Black Knight', John reveals Palamides as the agent of rival King Mark of Cornwall (*Patrick Troughton*) and wins an earl's daughter (*Patricia Medina*). Frightful foray into English history, the end of Ladd's love affair with British films. Among his dialogue: 'Lemme speak, sire. You gotta lissen. England's gonna be invaded.'

RoC *André Morell, Harry Andrews, Laurence Naismith, Ronald Adam, Basil Appleby, Jean Lodge, John Laurie, Elton Hayes, David Paltenghi, Olwen Brookes, Bill Brandon, Thomas Moore, Pauline Jameson, Claudia Carr, Susan Swinford, John Kelly.*

BLACKMAILED (1950) [2]

Dir *Marc Allegret*. Prod *Harold Huth*. Scr *Hugh Mills, Roger Vadim*, from a novel by *Elizabeth Myers*. Ph *George Stretton*. PC *HH Films*. Dis *General Film Distributors*. 85 mins. Cert A
A blackmailer (*James Robertson Justice*) is shot dead in an argument at which several of his victims are present. They conspire to conceal the crime, but the decision brings nothing but tragedy for those involved. One of them, an army deserter (*Dirk Bogarde*), tries to collect the reward on the killer (*Fay Compton*), but is chased by police and falls to his death. She decides to confess. Slow-paced story's threads are not well knitted together.

RoC *Mai Zetterling, Robert Flemyng, Michael Gough, Joan Rice, Harold Huth, Bruce Seton, Wilfrid Hyde White, Norah Gordon, Cyril Chamberlain, Charles Saynor, Derrick Penley, Peter Owen, Dennis Brian, Arthur Hambling, Shirley Wright, Michael Ingham, Johnnie Schofield, Betty Cooper, Vernon Greeves, Lilian Shaw, Helen Goss, Constance Smith, Dorothy Bramhall, Joan Schofield, Edie Martin, Valentine Dunn, Marianne Stone, John Horsley, Ballard Berkeley, Patricia Glyn, Sally Lahee, Don Lidell.*

BLACK ORCHID (1952) [3]

Dir *Charles Saunders*. Prod *Robert S. Baker, Monty Berman*. Scr *Francis Edge, John Temple-Smith*. Ph *Eric Cross*. PC *Kenilworth-Mid-Century*. Dis *General Film Distributors*. 60 mins. Cert A
A doctor (*Ronald Howard*) is in love with his wife's sister (*Olga Edwardes*) but, even though his scheming wife (*Mary Laura Wood*) agrees to a divorce, the law forbids the prospective marriage. Then the wife is knocked down by a lorry and killed, but a post-mortem finds poison. The doctor is accused, but new evidence about his wife clears him. Easily guessed whodunnit, quite well made.

RoC *John Bentley, Patrick Barr, Russell Napier, Sheila Burrell, Mary Jones.*

BLACKOUT (1950) [3]

Dir *Robert S. Baker*. Prod *Baker, Monty Berman*. Scr *Baker, John Gilling*. Ph *Berman*. PC *Tempean*. Dis *Eros*. 73 mins. Cert A
Chris (*Maxwell Reed*), handsome but blind, comes to London for a party, goes to the wrong house and stumbles over a dead body. He picks up a signet ring and is bashed over the head. The resultant operation cures his blindness. Returning to the scene of the crime, he meets Patricia (*Dinah Sheridan*) and together they launch an investigation which rounds up a ruthless contraband gang led by Patricia's supposedly dead brother. Slightly different approach to an old story: acceptable thriller.

RoC *Patric Doonan, Eric Pohlmann, Annette Simmonds, P. Kynaston Reeves, Michael Brennan, Michael Evans.*

Maxwell Reed and Dinah Sheridan in Blackout *(1950)*

THE BLACK RIDER (1954) [3]

Dir *Wolf Rilla*. Prod/Scr *A.R. Rawlinson*. Ph *Geoffrey Faithfull*. PC *Balblair*. Dis *Butchers*. 66 mins. Cert U
Trying to prove that a 'ghost' rider is in fact a smuggler, local reporter Jerry (*Jimmy Hanley*) gets himself knocked out for his pains. Careering round the country in pursuit of the story, with the boss's daughter (*Rona Anderson*) on the pillion, he discovers a nest of enemy 'atomic agents', secures a scoop with its destruction and lands a job on a national paper. Very modestly done, but fast-paced crime drama.

RoC *Lionel Jeffries, Leslie Dwyer, Beatrice Varley, Michael Golden, Valerie Hanson, Vincent Ball, Edwin Richfield, Kenneth Connor, Frank Atkinson.*

THE BLACK ROSE (1950) [3]

Dir *Henry Hathaway*. Prod *Louis D. Lighton*. Scr *Talbot Jennings*, from the novel by *Thomas B. Costain*. Ph *Jack Cardiff*. PC/Dis *20th Century-Fox*. Technicolor. 121 mins. Cert U
Walter (*Tyrone Power*) a Saxon scholar in 1250, seeks adventure in the Far East, together with Tristram (*Jack Hawkins*), a famous bowman. Joining the caravan of Boyan (*Orson Welles*), a fierce Mongol, they become friendly with Maryam (*Cecile Aubry*), his charming captive, known as The Black Rose. She follows them when they go to China as Boyan's emissaries and they make a bid for freedom. Tristram is killed, but Walter makes it back to England where, thanks to the ultimately softhearted Boyan, he is joined by Maryam. Spectacular adventure, moderately scripted.

RoC *Michael Rennie, Herbert Lom, Finlay Currie, Mary Clare, James Robertson Justice, Laurence Harvey, Alfonso Bedoya, Gibb McLaughlin, Henry Oscar, Valery Inkijinoff, Bobby Blake, Alfonso Bedoya, Torin Thatcher, Hilary Pritchard, Ley On, Carl Jaffe, Madame Phang, Rufus Cruickshank, George Woodbridge, Ben Williams, Peter Drury, Alexis Chesnakov, Alan Tilvern, Thomas Gallagher, John Penrose.*

THE BLACK TENT (1956) [3]

Dir *Brian Desmond Hurst*. Prod *William MacQuitty*. Scr *Robin Maugham, Bryan Forbes*. Ph *Desmond Dickinson*. PC/Dis *Rank*. Technicolor. VistaVision. 93 mins. Cert U
1942. David (*Anthony Steel*), a wounded

British officer in North Africa, is cared for by, and falls in love with, the daughter (*Anna Maria Sandri*) of a Libyan sheik. They marry, but David rejoins his unit and is killed. Years later, his brother Charles (*Donald Sinden*) journeys to Libs to persuade David's son to come back and claim a sizeable fortune. But the boy prefers to remain with his people. Unusual story, not very well treated.

RoC *André Morell, Donald Pleasence, Ralph Truman, Anthony Bushell, Michael Craig, Anton Diffring, Frederick Jaeger, Paul Homer, Derek Sydney, Terence Sharkey.*

BLACK 13 (1953)   2

Dir/Scr *Ken Hughes* (*scr uncredited*), *from a screenplay by Pietro Germi.* Prod *Roger Proudlock.* Ph *Gerry Gibbs.* PC *Vandyke.* Dis *Archway. 77 mins. Cert A*

Following a horrendous car smash, Stephen (*Peter Reynolds*) takes to a life of crime, robbing, breaking gates and shooting a caretaker. His sister (*Rona Anderson*) falls in love with the detective (*Patrick Barr*) on this latter case. Betrayed by a nightclub singer (*Genine Graham*), Stephen ironically is killed in a car crash. Excellent performance by Reynolds totally wasted in ham-fisted situations. A remake of the 1948 Italian film *Gioventu Perduta.*

RoC *Lana Morris, Michael Balfour, John Forrest, Viola Lyel, Martin Walker, John le Mesurier, Martin Benson.*

BLACK WIDOW (1951)   1

Dir *Vernon Sewell.* Prod *Anthony Hinds.* Scr *Allan Mackinnon, from a radio serial by Lester Powell.* Ph *Walter Harvey.* PC *Hammer.* Dis *Exclusive. 62 mins. Cert A*

Hit over the head by a 'body' that turns out to be a man out to rob him (subsequently killed in a crash), Mark (*Robert Ayres*) loses his memory. Recovering some days later, he finds his wife (*Christine Norden*) happily identifying the body from the crash as his, so that she can marry her lover (*Anthony Forwood*). Horrified at Mark's emergence, she plots to murder him, but he turns the tables and she is forced to kill herself. Shabby thriller in which the cast, as one critic put it, 'act as if they wished it were over'.

RoC *John Longden, Jennifer Jayne, John Harvey, Reginald Dyson, Madoline Thomas, Joan Carol, Jill Hulbert, Jack Stewart, Bill Hodge.*

BLIND DATE (1959)   4

Dir *Joseph Losey.* Prod *David Deutsch.* Scr *Ben Barzman, Millard Lampell, from the novel by Leigh Howard.* Ph *Christopher Challis.* PC *Independent Artists.* Dis *Rank. 95 mins. Cert A*

Jan (*Hardy Kruger*), an impoverished Dutch artist in London, falls for a married woman, Jacqueline (*Micheline Presle*), who becomes his mistress. Told she has been killed, and grilled by Inspector Morgan (*Stanley Baker*), Jan learns she was the mistress of diplomat Sir Howard Fenton. But his portrait of her is at odds with that Morgan gets from other sources and it turns out that Lady Fenton was Jan's 'Jacqueline', hoping to frame him for the mur-

der of the real Jacqueline. Intelligent nightmare thriller.

RoC *Robert Flemyng, Gordon Jackson, John Van Eyssen, Jack MacGowran, George Roubicek, Redmond Phillips, David Markham, Tom Naylor, Lee Montague.*

BLIND MAN'S BLUFF (1951)   2

Dir *Charles Saunders.* Prod *Charles Reynolds.* Scr *John Gilling.* Ph *Ted Lloyd.* PC *Present Day.* Dis *Apex. 67 mins. Cert A*

Roger (*Anthony Pendrell*), thriller-writer son of a police inspector, seeking background colour for his next novel, solves a mystery that has baffled Scotland Yard – namely, who killed Hugh Penfold, leader of a gang of jewel thieves. He tracks down the gang, which was operating from a boarding house, and brings it to justice. Few thrills here.

RoC *Zena Marshall, Sydney Tafler, Russell Napier, Norman Shelley, John le Mesurier, Anthony Doonan, Barbara Shaw.*

BLIND SPOT (1958)   3

Dir *Peter Maxwell.* Prod *Robert S. Baker, Monty Berman.* Scr *Kenneth R. Hayles.* Ph *Arthur Graham.* PC/Dis *Butchers. 71 mins. Cert U*

Blind Dan Adams (*Robert Mackenzie*) goes to the wrong house to a party, and stumbles over a body before being knocked out. After an operation has restored his sight, he tracks down the killers, uncovering a diamond-smuggling racket operated by June Brent (*Anne Sharp*) and her brother Johnny (*Michael Caine*), whom the police had thought was dead. Thriller is briskly paced and intriguing, but limply written and acted. A remake of *Blackout* (1950).

RoC *Gordon Jackson, Delphi Lawrence, John le Mesurier, George Pastell, Ernest Clark, Ronan O'Casey, Andrew Faulds, Robert Gallico, John Crawford, Kerrigan Prescott, Paulle Clarke, Tom Gill, Leigh Madison, Stuart Saunders, Angela Krefeld, Dianne Potter, Jane Sothern.*

BLOOD OF THE VAMPIRE (1958)   3

Dir *Henry Cass.* Prod *Robert S. Baker, Monty Berman.* Scr *Jimmy Sangster.* Ph *Berman.* PC *Tempean.* Dis *Eros. Eastman Colour. 85 mins. Cert X*

Installed as a doctor in charge of an asylum for the criminally insane, Callistratus (*Donald Wolfit*) was previously executed as a vampire but restored to life by Carl (*Victor Maddern*), a one-eyed hunchback. He now uses his inmates as a blood supply. Dr Pierre (*Vincent Ball*), his unwilling accomplice, tries to escape with his fiancée (*Barbara Shelley*), adored by Carl. Callistratus captures them, but Carl revolts against harming the girl and the vampire is torn to pieces by his own dogs. Gory horror film, played with great enthusiasm.

RoC *William Devlin, Andrew Faulds, John le Mesurier, George Murcell, Bryan Coleman, Colin Tapley, Bernard Bresslaw, Denis Shaw, John Sullivan, Hal Osmond, Max Brimmell, Henry Vidon, John Stuart, Cameron Hall, Muriel Ali, Otto Diamant, Sylvia Casimir, Yvonne Buckingham, Julian Strange, Bruce Wightman, Richard Golding, Milton Reid, Theodore Wilhelm, Gordon Honey, Carlos Williams.*

BLOOD ORANGE (1953)   3

Dir *Terence Fisher.* Prod *Michael Carreras.* Scr *Jan Read.* Ph *Jimmy Harvey.* PC *Hammer.* Dis *Exclusive. 76 mins. Cert A*

A London fashion house. A model (*Delphi Lawrence*) and a rich client (*Margaret Halstan*), both wearing copies of the new 'blood orange' dress, are murdered. Private eye Tom Conway (*Tom Conway* - sic) suspects a connection between their deaths and jewel robberies. A shady jeweller involved is murdered with a pair of dressmaking scissors. The killer turns out to be model Gina (*Naomi Chance*), to whom Tom was attracted. Thriller is smartly styled but low-cut on excitement.

RoC *Mila Parely, Eric Pohlmann, Andrew Osborn, Richard Wattis, Eileen Way, Thomas Heathcote, Michael Ripper, Betty Cooper, Alan Rolfe, Roger Delgado, Reed de Rouen, Christina Forrest, Ann Hanslip, Leon Davey, Leo Phillips, Dorothy Robson, Robert Moore, Dennis Cowles, John Watson, Cleo Rose.*

BLOW YOUR OWN TRUMPET (1958)   4

Dir/Prod *Cecil Musk.* Scr *Mary Cathcart Borer.* Ph *Jo Jago.* PC *Film Producers' Guild/ Children's Film Foundation.* Dis *British Lion. 57 mins. Cert U*

In a northern colliery town, young Jim Fenn (*Michael Crawford*) is mustard-keen to get a place playing cornet in the local brass band. His rival hides his cornet on the day of the competition for a vacancy, but Jim's sister gets it back and rushes it to the concert hall just in time. Jim wins. Polished, refreshing children's film.

RoC *Peter Butterworth, Gillian Harrison, Martyn Shields, J.W. Brotherhood, Arley Welfare Band.*

BLUE MURDER AT ST TRINIAN'S (1957)   4

Dir *Frank Launder.* Prod *Launder, Sidney Gilliat.* Scr *Launder, Gilliat, Val Valentine.* Ph *Gerald Gibbs.* PC *John Harvel/Launder-Gilliat/ British Lion.* Dis *British Lion. 86 mins. Cert U*

With its headmistress (*Alastair Sim*) in prison, and the army unable to control its girls, a rampant St Trinian's wins a European tour by its pupils' usual method – cheating. The tour is headed by Joe Mangan (*Lionel Jeffries*), hotly pursued by a policewoman (*Joyce Grenfell*) in disguise. He attempts to get away with a fortune in gems hidden in a water-polo ball, but

Lionel Jeffries in Blue Murder at St Trinian's *(1957)*

the girls run him to earth and bring (most of) the reward money back to the jailed head. Noisy romp with some good comic performances. Plot bears a resemblance to that of *Good Morning, Boys!* (1937).

RoC *Terry-Thomas, George Cole, Eric Barker, Richard Wattis, Sabrina, Thorley Walters, Lisa Gastoni, Dilys Laye, Judith Furse, Lloyd Lamble, Kenneth Griffith, Guido Lorraine, Peter Jones, Raymond Rollett, Terry Scott, Ferdy Mayne, Cyril Chamberlain, Alma Taylor, Michael Ripper, Lisa Lee, Peter Elliott, Charles Lloyd Pack, José Read, Rosalind Knight, Patricia Lawrence, Marigold Russell, Vikki Hammond, Nicola Braithwaite, Amanda Coxell, Moya Francis, Marianne Brauns, Edwina Carroll, Janet Bradbury, Bill Shine.*

THE BLUE PARROT (1953) [3]

Dir *John Harlow.* Prod *Stanley Haynes.* Scr *Allan Mackinnon,* from a story by *Percy Haskins.* Ph *Bob Navarro.* PC *ACT Films.* Dis *Monarch.* 69 mins. Cert A

A car-hire operator is murdered after receiving a mysterious phone call in a Soho nightclub, The Blue Parrot. An American detective, Bob (*Dermot Walsh*), studying methods of crime detection in England, joins the club to help, and Maureen (*Jacqueline Hill*), a policewoman, is installed as a hostess. She nearly loses her life at the hands of the killer, Carson (*John le Mesurier*), the club owner, before the case is closed. Efficient thriller with a bit more sting in the action than usual.

RoC *Ferdy Mayne, Edwin Richfield, Valerie White, June Ashley, Derek Prentice, Richard Pearson, Arthur Rigby, Diane Watts, Cyril Conway.*

THE BLUE PETER (1954) [4]
(USA: *Navy Heroes*)

Dir *Wolf Rilla.* Prod *Herbert Mason.* Scr *Don Sharp, John Pudney.* Ph *Arthur Grant.* PC *Group 3/Beaconsfield.* Dis *British Lion.* Eastman Colour. 94 mins. Cert U

A straggler from Group 3, but a good one. Brainwashed in Korea, Mike (*Kieron Moore*), a Merchant Navy officer, is asked to become an instructor at a school for sea cadets. In dealing with the problems of the boys, Mike overcomes his own and, when the course is finished, agrees to run a similar venture in Malaya. Persuasive story has genuine warmth, grips and thrills in the right places.

RoC *Greta Gynt, Sarah Lawson, Mervyn Johns, John Charlesworth, Brian Roper, Harry Fowler, Ram Gopal, Anthony Newley, Mary Kerridge, Russell Napier, Vincent Ball, Edwin Richfield, William Ingram, Donald McCorkindale, Keith Faulkner, Michael Bennett, Harold Siddons.*

BOBBIKINS (1959) [2]

Dir *Robert Day.* Prod *Oscar Brodney, Bob McNaught.* Scr *Oscar Brodney.* Ph *Geoffrey Faithfull.* PC/Dis *20th Century-Fox.* 89 mins. Cert U

Hard-up variety artist Barnaby (*Max Bygraves*) suddenly finds his 14-month-old baby Bobbikins (*Steven Stocker*) can talk lucidly – but only to him. Bobbikins is befriended in the park by the Chancellor of the Exchequer, and the tips he picks up enables his father to make a fortune. But it corrupts him and Bobbikins, seeing this, soon restores the status quo. Preposterous and over-sentimental comedy just about gets by on the charm of the baby and stars.

RoC *Shirley Jones, Billie Whitelaw, Barbara Shelley, Colin Gordon, Charles Tingwell, Lionel Jeffries, Charles Carson, Rupert Davies, Charles Lloyd Pack, Noel Hood, David Lodge, Murray Kash, Arnold Diamond, Trevor Reid, John Welsh, Michael Ripper, Ronald Fraser, John Downing.*

THE BODY SAID NO! (1950) [3]

Dir/Scr *Val Guest.* Prod *Daniel M. Angel.* Ph *Bert Mason.* PC *New World/Angel.* Dis *Eros.* 75 mins. Cert U

Mikki (*Yolande Donlan*), a beautiful, blonde, but not-too-bright cabaret star, overhears a 'plot' to murder film star *Michael Rennie* (himself). She tries to warn the intended 'victim', but the whole thing turns out to have been an after-hours rehearsal for a radio play. Rennie lets Mikki off lightly. Trivial comedy boosted by delightful central performance.

RoC *Hy Hazell, Valentine Dyall, Arthur Hill, Jon Pertwee, Reginald Beckwith, Cyril Smith, Jack Billings, Peter Butterworth, Margaret McGrath, Joyce Heron, Eddie Vitch, Ivan Craig, Winifred Shotter, Barry O'Neil, Jack Faint.*

THE BOLSHOI BALLET (1957) [4]

Dir *Paul Czinner.* Prod *Czinner, I.R. Maxwell.* Ph *S.D. Onions.* PC *Harmony.* Dis *Rank.* Eastman Colour. 100 mins. Cert U

A film record of the Bolshoi Ballet's repertoire for their 1956 visit to England. The programme consists of Tchaikovsky's *Spanish Dance,* Rachmaninov's *Spring Water,* Glinka's *Polonaise and Cracovienne,* Gounod's *Walpurgisnacht,* Saint-Saens' *The Dying Swan* and, perhaps most notably, Adam's *Giselle.* A treat for balletomanes.

LP *Galina Ulanova, Nikolai Fadeyechev, Taisia Monakhova, Alexander Radunsky, Erik Volodin, Irina Makedonskaya, Vladimir Levashev, Rimma Karelskaya, Raissa Struchkova.*

BOND OF FEAR (1956) [2]

Dir *Henry Cass.* Prod *Robert S. Baker, Monty Berman.* Scr *John Gilling.* Ph *Berman.* PC *Mid-Century.* Dis *Eros.* 66 mins. Cert A

A man and his family on a caravan holiday in France are terrorized by an escaped convict. He thwarts their every attempt to resist until, back at Dover, the wife manages to slip a note into another car, whose driver notifies the police. The convict is recaptured. Repetitive drama just about passes the time.

LP *Dermot Walsh, Jane Barrett, John Colicos, Marilyn Baker, Anthony Pavey, Jameson Clark, John Horsley, Avril Angers, Alan MacNaughtan, Hal Osmond.*

BONJOUR TRISTESSE (1957) [3]

Dir/Prod *Otto Premiger.* Scr *Arthur Laurents,* from the novel by *Françoise Sagan.* Ph *Georges Perinal.* PC *Wheel Films.* Dis *Columbia.* Technicolor. CinemaScope. 93 mins. Cert A

Raymond, a wealthy widower (*David Niven*) and his daughter Cécile (*Jean Seberg*) live a life of spoiled luxury on the Riviera, in return for which Cécile is happy to put up with her father's sundry mistresses. When a widow, Anne (*Deborah Kerr*), comes along, and Raymond, failing to seduce her, proposes, Cécile quickly sees the threat to her lifestyle and breaks up the relationship. Distraught, Anne drives off, crashes her car and is killed. Rather tedious morality play in sumptuous settings.

RoC *Mylène Demongeot, Geoffrey Horne, Juliette Gréco, Walter Chiari, Martita Hunt, Jean Kent, David Oxley, Elga Andersen, Jeremy Burnham, Roland Culver, Evelyn Eyfel.*

BOOBY TRAP (1956) [3]

Dir *Henry Cass.* Prod *Bill Luckwell, D.E.A. Winn.* Scr *Peter Bryan, Luckwell.* Ph *James Wilson.* PC *Jaywell.* Dis *Eros.* 72 mins. Cert A

A doddery professor (*Tony Quinn*) invents a fountain pen bomb, timed to explode at a stroke of Big Ben. It is stolen by a spiv (*Harry Fowler*), who pawns it, loses it, and joins the professor in the hunt for the mini-bomb, which ends in the hands of a narcotics king (*Sydney Tafler*) whose drugs are kept in mock fountain pens. The big crook escapes with the drugs, but his car explodes as Big Ben chimes. Bright comedy thriller, fast and amusing, misses on the thrills.

RoC *Patti Morgan, Richard Shaw, Jacques Cey, John Watson, Michael Moore, Fred McNaughton.*

BORN FOR TROUBLE (1955) [1]

Dir *Desmond Davis.* Prod *Victor Hanbury.* Scr *Doreen Montgomery, Derek Frye.* Ph *Geoffrey Faithfull.* PC *Mid Ocean.* Dis *Eros.* 77 mins. Cert A

Adventures of an American fashion buyer (*Joan Shawlee*) in London. She tracks down a gang illegally copying dress designs; breaks a ring of counterfeiters; and foils a strangler by throwing itching powder over him. Very weak, made with an eye to TV.

RoC *Peter Reynolds, Greta Gynt, Elizabeth Allan, Stephen Boyd, Peter Illing, Harold Kasket, John McLaren, Bill Nagy.*

THE BOY AND THE BRIDGE (1959) [2]

Dir/Prod *Kevin McClory.* Scr *Geoffrey Orme, McClory, Desmond O'Donovan,* from the story by *Leon Ware.* Ph *Ted Scaife.* PC *Xanadu.* Dis *Columbia.* 90 mins. Cert U

Running away after his father is arrested in a pub brawl, little Tommy (*Ian MacLaine*) finds his way into a small room in one of the towers of London's bridge and, with a pet seagull, makes it his home. He saves a woman from suicide by calling to her and becomes known as the 'Phantom of the Bridge'. Eventually, father and son are reconciled. Flimsy whimsy much too long for its content.

RoC *Liam Redmond, James Hayter, Norman MacOwan, Geoffrey Keen, Jack MacGowran, Royal Dano, Rita Webb, Bill Shine, Jocelyn Britton, Andrea Malandrinos, Chili Bouchier, Arthur Lowe, Nigel Arkwright, Stuart Saun-*

ders, Brian Sunners, R. Meadows White, Paddy Kennedy, Neil Wilson, Ivor Salter, Charles Saynor, Martin Boddey, Winifrede Kingston, Jimmy Herbert, Jack Stewart.

THE BRAIN MACHINE (1954)   4

Dir/Scr *Ken Hughes*. Prod *Alec C. Snowden*. Ph *Josef Ambor*. PC *Merton Park*. Dis *Anglo-Amalgamated*. 83 mins. Cert A

Dr Roberts (*Elizabeth Allan*), a hospital psychiatrist, is alarmed to find that the brain patterns of Smith (*Maxwell Reed*) are similar to those of a psychopath she has examined before. She tells the police, but is kidnapped by Smith, who is part of a large-scale drugs ring. He falls out with his associates, however, when they kill his wife, and kills the gang leader before Dr Roberts is rescued. Pretty lively thriller; situations are familiar but directed with zest and ingenuity.

RoC *Patrick Barr, Russell Napier, Gibb McLaughlin, Edwin Richfield, Neil Hallett, Vanda Godsell, Bill Nagy, Mark Bellamy, Anthony Valentine, John Horsley, Donald Bisset, Gwen Bacon, Clifford Buckton, Cyril Smith, Thomas Gallagher, Ian Wilson, Henry Webb, Joan Tyrell.*

Maxwell Reed and Elizabeth Allan in The Brain Machine *(1954)*

BRANDY FOR THE PARSON (1951)   4

Dir *John Eldridge*. Prod *John Grierson, Alfred O'Shaughnessy*. Scr *John Dighton, Walter Meade, from the novel by Geoffrey Household*. Ph *Martin Curtis*. PC *Group 3*. Dis *Associated British*. 79 mins. Cert U

A young couple on a yachting holiday become involved with brandy smugglers operating between France and the Kent coast. Somehow, they find themselves seconded into transporting some of the liquor and, after one narrow escape, are caught by the authorities. They find that two of the justices are customers of the smugglers, so their fines are paid for them and they return to yachting. Fairly amusing comedy in Ealing style; a leg up the stardom ladder for *Kenneth More* as the smuggler-in-chief.

RoC *James Donald, Jean Lodge, Frederick Piper, Charles Hawtrey, Michael Trubshawe, Alfie Bass, Reginald Beckwith, Wilfred Caithness, Arthur Wontner, Lionel Harris, Richard Molinas, Stanley Lemin, Frank Tickle, Walter Hodges, Hamlyn Benson, W.E. Holloway, Wensley Pithey, Sam Kydd, Patience Rentoul, Grace*

Arnold, Amy Dalby, Edmund Gray, Douglas Ives, Stanley van Beers, Gaston Richer, John Powe, Fred Dornom, Robert Hay-Smith, Tony Lyons, Brian Weske, André Griveau, Denzil Highmore, E.M. Smith.

THE BRAVE DON'T CRY (1952)   5

Dir *Philip Leacock*. Prod *John Grierson, John Baxter*. Scr *Montagu Slater*. Ph *Arthur Grant, Ken Hodges*. PC *Group 3*. Dis *Associated British*. 90 mins. Cert U

A documentary-like reconstruction of the Knockshinnoch mine disaster 18 months earlier. 118 men are trapped below ground by a subsidence and subsequent flooded shaft. Everything seems hopeless; even a glimmer of hope is extinguished by a gas threat. Finally, the men are saved by pumping through oxygen which enables them to last out the necessary hours for rescue to come. Nail-biting drama.

LP *John Gregson, Meg Buchanan, John Rae, Fulton Mackay, Russell Waters, Wendy Noel, Jack Stewart, Andrew Keir, Jameson Clark, Archie Duncan, Jock McKay, Eric Woodburn, Anne Butchart, Mac Picton, Jean Anderson, John Singer, Chris Page, Kelty MacLeod, Hal Osmond, Guthrie Mason, Howard Connell, Russell Hunter, Sam Kydd.*

BREAKAWAY (1956)   2

Dir *Henry Cass*. Prod *Robert S. Baker, Monty Berman*. Scr *Norman Hudis, from a story by Manning O'Brine*. Ph *Berman*. PC *CIPA*. Dis *RKO Radio*. 72 mins. Cert U

After Johnny (*Brian Worth*) whisks a secret formula from under the noses of Berlin agents, he and his girlfriend Paula (*Honor Blackman*) are attacked in London. She is kidnapped, but her handbag – and the formula – is found by private eye Duke Martin (*Tom Conway*) who becomes involved in the case, and helps Johnny root out both spies and a criminal ring. Tedious thriller with regulation car chases.

RoC *Bruce Seton, Michael Balfour, Freddie Mills, John Horsley, Alexander Gauge, Paddy Webster, John Colicos, Larry Taylor, Arthur Lowe, Frederick Schrecker, Marianne Waller, Russell Westwood.*

BREAK IN THE CIRCLE (1955)   4

Dir *Val Guest*. Prod *Michael Carreras*. Scr *Guest, (uncredited) Robert Westerby, from the novel by Philip Lorraine*. Ph *Walter Harvey*. PC *Hammer*. Dis *Exclusive*. Eastman Colour. 92 mins. Cert U

Seaman-turned-smuggling-adventurer Morgan (*Forrest Tucker*) accepts an assignment from financier Baron Keller (*Marius Goring*) to get a Polish scientist out of East Germany. In Hamburg, Morgan falls victim to the gang holding the scientist, but is rescued by Lisa (*Eva Bartok*) and completes his mission only to learn Keller is a crook. The baron drowns after a fight with Morgan, who surrenders to the law. Robust thriller with a vein of humour.

RoC *Eric Pohlmann, Guy Middleton, Arnold Marle, Reginald Beckwith, Fred Johnson, David King-Wood, Guido Lorraine, André Mikhelson, Stanley Zevic, Marne Maitland, Arthur Lovegrove, Derek Prentice.*

BREAKOUT (1959)   4

Dir *Peter Graham Scott*. Prod *Julian Wintle, Leslie Parkyn*. Scr *Peter Barnes, from a novel by Frederick Oughton*. Ph *Eric Cross*. PC *Independent Artists*. Dis *Anglo-Amalgamated*. 62 mins. Cert U

George Munro (*Lee Patterson*), a local government employee, builds up his bank account by arranging prison breaks. His idea to 'spring' an embezzler is unique – and goes like clockwork. But a small detail puts the police on to the escaper's truck, and everyone gets caught. Quite exciting vest-pocket thriller with edgy performances.

RoC *Hazel Court, Terence Alexander, John Paul, Billie Whitelaw, William Lucas, Estelle Brody, Dermot Kelly, George Bishop, Robert Cawdron, George Woodbridge, Neil McCarthy, Alene Daniels, Rupert Davies, Robert McBain, Benny Nightingale, Tom Naylor, Lloyd Lamble.*

THE BRIDAL PATH (1959)   4

Dir *Frank Launder*. Prod *Launder, Sidney Gilliat*. Scr *Launder, Geoffrey Willans, from the novel by Nigel Tranter*. Ph *Arthur Ibbetson*. PC *Vale*. Dis *British Lion*. Technicolor. 95 mins. Cert U

Ewan McEwan (*Bill Travers*), a Hebridean farmer forbidden by the elders of his Hebridean island to marry a first cousin (almost all the island people are first cousins), goes to the mainland to find a wife. His roving eye gets him mistaken for a white slaver, accused of poaching, pursued by irate husbands and arrested. He also disrupts the local Highland Games before finding out that his island sweetheart (*Fiona Clyne*) is not his cousin after all. Pleasant enough; sex comedy with no sex but gorgeous scenery.

RoC *Bernadette O'Farrell, Patricia Bredin, George Cole, Gordon Jackson, Charlotte Mitchell, Dilys Laye, Elizabeth Campbell, Alex Mackenzie, Vincent Winter, Eddie Byrne, Duncan Macrae, Eric Woodburn, Jack Lambert, Joan Fitzpatrick, Pekoe Ainley, Joan Benham, Annette Crosbie, Nancy Mitchell, Lynda King, Robert James, Terry Scott, Jameson Clark, John Dunbar, Andrew Downie, John Rae, Roddy McMillan, Jefferson Clifford, Neil Ballantyne, Molly Weir, Myrette Morven, Abe Barker, Edward Evans, Hope Jackman, Ewan McDuff, Arthur Lawrence, Ian McNaughtan, Hamish Roughead, Bluey (dog).*

Bernadette O'Farrell and Bill Travers in The Bridal Path *(1959)*

THE BRIDGE ON THE RIVER KWAI (1957) [6]

Dir *David Lean*. Prod *Sam Spiegel*. Scr *Pierre Boulle, from his novel*. Ph *Jack Hildyard*. PC *Horizon*. Dis *Columbia*. Technicolor. Cinema-Scope. 161 mins. Cert *U*

Burma, 1943. Sticking to his guns over a matter of principle, Nicholson (*Alec Guinness*), colonel of a group of British prisoners working on a bridge over the River Kwai, is subjected to horrendous deprivation before winning his point, whereupon he determines to make the best bridge possible to show the Japanese what British soldiers can do. When a group of Allied saboteurs, led by Warden (*Jack Hawkins*) and Shears (*William Holden*), an American seaman who had escaped from the camp, launch a sabotage attack, Nicholson orders defence of the bridge. He, Shears and many others are killed before Warden blows the bridge to pieces. Big, bitter, enthralling war story. Oscars for film, director, actor (*Guinness*), screenplay, photography, editor (*Peter Taylor*) and music (*Malcolm Arnold*). British Oscars for film, screenplay and actor. Box-office champion of 1958. RoC *Sessue Hayakawa, James Donald, Geoffrey Horne, Ann Sears, André Morell, Peter Williams, John Boxer, Percy Herbert, Harold Goodwin, Henry Okawa, Tsai Chin (voice only)*.

THE BROKEN HORSESHOE (1953) [3]

Dir *Martyn C. Webster*. Prod *Ernest G. Roy*. Scr *A.R. Rawlinson, from a radio series by Francis Durbridge*. Ph *Gerald Gibbs, Noel Rowland*. PC *Nettlefold*. Dis *Butchers*. 79 mins. Cert *U*

Through operating on a Frenchman (*Ferdy Mayne*) who has been hit by a car and is later murdered, Dr Fenton (*Robert Beatty*), who has to deliver a letter for the man, finds himself involved with a dope ring and under suspicion of murder. He is saved by the girl member (*Elizabeth Sellars*) of the gang, who has fallen in love with him. Rare coincidence of director, writer (Durbridge) and star (*Peter Coke*) from radio's famous Paul Temple series. But thriller is fairly ordinary. RoC *Vida Hope, James Raglan, Hugh Pryse, Hugh Kelly, Janet Butler, George Benson, Ronald Leigh-Hunt, Roger Delgado, Toke Townley, Marc Sheldon, Marguerite Brennan, Jean Hardwicke*.

BROTHERS IN LAW (1956) [5]

Dir *Roy Boulting*. Prod *John Boulting*. Scr *Frank Harvey, Jeffrey Dell, Roy Boulting, from the novel by Henry Cecil*. Ph *Max Greene (Mutz Greenbaum)*. PC *Charter Tudor*. Dis *British Lion*. 94 mins. Cert *U*

Episodic adventures of Roger (*Ian Carmichael*), a new barrister distinctly lacking in confidence. Junior to an absent-minded QC (*Miles Malleson*) who has to be introduced to him at each meeting, Roger is flung to the lions on his first (disastrous) day, helped by a smart-alec fellow barrister (*Richard Attenborough*) who becomes his rival for the 'girl upstairs' (*Jill Adams*) and finally triumphs in a case held in his home town. Funny follow-up to *Private's Progress*, wittily written and confidently played.

Ian Carmichael and Nicholas Parsons in Brothers in Law (1956)

RoC *Terry-Thomas, Raymond Huntley, Eric Barker, Nicholas Parsons, Kynaston Reeves, John le Mesurier, Irene Handl, Olive Sloane, Edith Sharpe, Leslie Phillips, Brian Oulton, George Rose, Kenneth Griffith, Basil Dignam, Henry Longhurst, Michael Ward, Everley Gregg, Robert Griffiths, Ian Wilson, John Schlesinger, Margaret Lacey, John Boxer, John Warren, Norma Shebbear, Peggyann Clifford, Stuart Saunders, Penny Morell, Maurice Colbourne, Wyndham Goldie, Rolf Lefebvre, Ian Colin, Brian Oulton, Brian Fox, Ronald Cardew, John Van Eyssen, Bob Gregory, John Welsh, Llewellyn Rees, Bob Vosler, Jack McNaughton, Susan Marryot*.

BROTH OF A BOY (1958) [3]

Dir *George Pollock*. Prod *Alec C. Snowden*. Scr *Patrick Kirwan, Blanaid Irvine, from a play by Hugh Leonard*. Ph *Walter J. Harvey*. PC *Emmet Dalton*. Dis *British Lion/Britannia*. 77 mins. Cert *U*

Tony Randall (*Tony Wright*), a TV man touring Ireland in search of material, is anxious to televise the 110th birthday of Patrick Farrell (*Barry Fitzgerald*), believed to be Europe's oldest man. Patrick, having falsified his age years before over a pension, has no wish for publicity, but when he is caught poaching, he agrees to the show in return for being let off. Palatable dose of Irish, lent sparkle by Fitzgerald. RoC *June Thorburn, Harry Brogan, Maire Kean, Eddie Golden, Godfrey Quigley, Dermot Kelly, Josephine Fitzgerald, Bart Bastable*.

THE BROWNING VERSION (1951) [5]

Dir *Anthony Asquith*. Prod *Teddy Baird*. Scr *Terence Rattigan, from his play*. Ph *Desmond Dickinson*. PC *Javelin*. Dis *General Film Distributors*. 90 mins. Cert *A*

Crocker-Harris (*Michael Redgrave*), teacher at a public school for nearly 20 years, has to retire through ill-health, to the annoyance of his shrewish wife Millie (*Jean Kent*) who is glorying in an affair with the science master (*Nigel Patrick*). Crocker-Harris has never been able to 'get through' to his pupils, but one boy gives him a farewell present and the incident triggers him into making a passionate speech to the school (in which he lists his faults) which draws loud applause. He leaves Millie

Michael Redgrave, Jean Kent and Nigel Patrick in The Browning Version (1951)

behind for a new life. Affecting, strongly-acted drama. RoC *Ronald Howard, Wilfrid Hyde White, Brian Smith, Bill Travers, Paul Medland, Ivan Samson, Josephine Middleton, Peter Jones, Sarah Lawson, Scott Harold, Judith Furse, Vivienne Gibson, Josephine Middleton, Johnnie Schofield, Russell Waters*.

BURNT EVIDENCE (1954) [2]

Dir *Daniel Birt*. Prod *Ronald Kinnoch*. Scr *Ted Willis*. Ph *Jo Jago*. PC *ACT Films*. Dis *Monarch*. 61 mins. Cert *A*

Heavily in debt, Jack (*Duncan Lamont*) is attempting suicide when confronted by Jimmy (*Donald Gray*), whom Jack thinks is having an affair with his wife (*Jane Hylton*). They fight, Jimmy is killed and Jack's paint factory burns down. He runs away, but both himself and his wife come under suspicion of murder before they are free to start life again. Glum, plodding, low-budget thriller. RoC *Meredith Edwards, Cyril Smith, Irene Handl, Hugo Schuster, Kynaston Reeves, Hugh Moxey, Tony Hilton, Stanley Vilven, Hamilton Keane*.

C

CAGE OF GOLD (1950) [3]

Dir *Basil Dearden*. (Associate) Prod *Michael Relph*. Scr *Jack Whittingham*. Ph *Douglas Slocombe*. PC *Ealing Studios*. Dis *General Film Distributors*. 83 mins. Cert *A*

About to become engaged to Alan (*James Donald*), Judith (*Jean Simmons*) runs into her schoolgirl crush, Bill (*David Farrar*), now an ex-pilot, and is again swept off her feet. When she becomes pregnant, they marry, but Bill deserts her on finding she has no money. He is reported dead, and Judith later marries Alan. Then Bill turns up, threatening blackmail. When he is killed, Judith and Alan are both suspect, but the killer is Bill's French mistress (*Madeleine Lebeau*), whom he had also deserted. Hokum presented with some slickness and punch.

RoC *Herbert Lom, Bernard Lee, Gladys Henson, Maria Mauban, Gregoire Aslan, Hercourt Williams, Leo Ferré, George Benson, Martin Boddey, Arthur Hambling, Campbell Singer, Guy Verney, Arthur Howard, Arthur Lowe.*

CAIRO ROAD (1950) [2]

Dir *David Macdonald*. Prod *Aubrey Baring*. Scr *Robert Westerby*. Ph *Oswald Morris*. PC *Mayflower*. Dis *AB-Pathé*. 95 mins. Cert A

Cairo's police chief, Col Youssef Bey (*Eric Portman*), wages a constant war against narcotics smugglers, with the help of his keen but inexperienced aide, Lt Mourad (*Laurence Harvey*). Thanks to the colonel's astute strategies, the 'big fish' is eventually landed. Perceptive performance by Portman fails to lift the gloom of humdrum production.

RoC *Maria Mauban, Karel Stepanek, Harold Lang, Camelia, Coco (Gregoire) Aslan, John Bailey, Martin Boddey, John Gregson, Marne Maitland, Abraham Soflaer, Oscar Quitak.*

CALLING BULLDOG DRUMMOND (1951) [2]

Dir *Victor Saville*. Prod *Hayes Goetz*. Scr *Gerard Fairlie, Howard Emmett Rogers, Arthur Wimperis, from the novel by Fairlie*. Ph *Graham Kelly*. PC/Dis *MGM British*. 80 mins. Cert U

Ex-officer Bulldog Drummond (*Walter Pidgeon*) is called in by Scotland Yard to track down a gang of thieves operating with military precision. A lady police sergeant (*Margaret Leighton*) is assigned to work with him. Drummond joins the gang, but is recognized by the leader, and he and the sergeant are imprisoned; they escape and round up the crooks. Sober Bulldog in silly plot.

RoC *Robert Beatty, David Tomlinson, Peggy Evans, Charles Victor, James Hayter, Bernard Lee, Patric Doonan, Harold Lang, Michael Allan, Anthony Oliver.*

CAMPBELL'S KINGDOM (1957) [4]

Dir *Ralph Thomas*. Prod *Betty E. Box*. Scr *Robin Estridge, from the novel by Hammond Innes*. PC/Dis *Rank*. Eastman Colour. 100 mins. Cert U

Bruce Campbell (*Dirk Bogarde*), given six months to live, goes to Canada to take over land inherited from his grandfather, who believed there was oil there. Morgan (*Stanley Baker*), a crooked contractor, wants to flood the land for his hydro-electric dam – which he cannot do if oil is found there. He attempts to kill Bruce, but is himself drowned. Told by doctors that he is no longer dying, Bruce grows rich from the land, and marries a local girl. Action, acting and scenery help to atone for pretty silly script.

RoC *Barbara Murray, Michael Craig, James Robertson Justice, Athene Seyler, Robert Brown, John Laurie, Sidney James, Mary Merrall, George Murcell, Roland Brand, Finlay Currie, Peter Illing, Stanley Maxted, Gordon Tanner, Richard McNamara.*

THE CAMP ON BLOOD ISLAND (1958) [4]

Dir *Val Guest*. Prod *Anthony Hinds*. Scr *Jon Manchip White, Guest*. Ph *Jack Asher*. PC *Hammer*. Dis *Columbia*. MegaScope. 82 mins. Cert X

Subjected to daily atrocities by their Japanese commandant, who has sworn to kill them all if Japan surrenders, the Allied P-o-Ws at the camp on Blood Island try desperately to keep that news from him when it happens. Some escape and make for a nearby partisan HQ, while Col Lambert (*André Morell*) leads the prisoners, with home-made weapons, into a last frenzied battle. Allied relief planes find few survivors on either side. Sordid, savage war film stirred up controversy – and box office.

RoC *Carl Mohner, Edward Underdown, Walter Fitzgerald, Phil Brown, Barbara Shelley, Michael Goodliffe, Richard Wordsworth, Mary Merrall, Michael Gwynn, Ronald Radd, Marne Maitland, Wolfe Morris, Edwin Richfield, Lee Montague, Peter Wayn, Michael Brill, Barry Lowe, Max Butterfield, Alan McNaughtan, Michael Ripper, Howard Williams, Michael Dea, Anthony Chinn, Tagaki, S. Goh, Jimmy Raphael, David Goh, Don Lee, Liliane Sottane, Grace Denbigh-Russell, Geoffrey Bayldon, Jacqueline Curtiss, Jan Holden, Betty Cooper, Anne Ridler.*

CAPTAIN HORATIO HORNBLOWER R.N. (1951) [4]

Dir and Prod *Raoul Walsh*. Scr *Ivan Goff, Ben Roberts, Aeneas Mackenzie, from novels by C. S. Forester*. Ph *Guy Green*. PC and Dis *Warner Bros*. Technicolor. 118 mins. Cert U

The early 1800s. Setting out for the Pacific on a secret mission, Capt. Hornblower (*Gregory Peck*) captures a Spanish ship by superior cunning, gives it away to an ally, then retakes it when Spain enters the war on Britain's side. He sinks four French men o' war, is captured, escapes, steals a British ship from a French harbour and sails home with Lady Barbara (*Virginia Mayo*) and a crew of English prisoners. Expensive, enjoyable action, for those who haven't read the books. Dialogual drama remains landbound.

RoC *Robert Beatty, James Robertson Justice, Denis O'Dea, Terence Morgan, Richard Hearne, James Kenney, Stanley Baker, Christopher Lee, Michael Goodliffe, Richard Johnson, Moultrie Kelsall, Michael Dolan, John Witty, Kynaston Reeves, Ingeborg Wells, Ronald Adam, Amy*

Robert Beatty and Gregory Peck in Captain Horatio Hornblower R.N. (*1951*)

Veness, Howard Connell, Sam Kydd, Raymond Sherry, Stuart Pearless, Jack Stewart, Russell Waters, Alec Mango, Alan Tilvern, Alexander Davion, Miguel Delgado, Michael Mellinger, Julio Monterde, Derek Sydney, Basil Bartlett, Anthony Marlowe, Anthony Forwood, Eugene Deckers, Arthur Gomez, Patrick Young, Andrea Malandrinos, Gavin Dyer, André Belhomme, Robert Cawdron, Howard Lang.

THE CAPTAIN'S PARADISE (1953) [4]

Dir and Prod *Anthony Kimmins*. Scr *Alec Coppel, Nicholas Phipps*. Ph *Ted Scaife*. PC *London Films*. Dis *British Lion*. 77 mins. Cert A

Some seamen have a girl in every port. Captain Henry St James (*Alec Guinness*) has a girl in only two. But he is married both to ever-dancing Nita (*Yvonne de Carlo*) in Kalik in north Africa, and quiet, home-making Maud (*Celia Johnson*) in Gibraltar. Unfortunately, Nita longs to be conventional, while Maud has secret desires to go wild on the dance floor. Eventually, both leave him. Often witty and enjoyable comedy hasn't quite the required zip.

RoC *Charles Goldner, Miles Malleson, Bill Fraser, Walter Crisham, Ferdy Mayne, Nicholas Phipps, Sebastian Cabot, Claudia Gray, George Benson, Joss Ambler, Joyce Barbour, Peter Bull, Tutte Lemkow, Henry Longhurst, Bernard Rebel, Ambrosine Phillpotts, Ann Heffernan, Arthur Gomez, Michael Balfour, Robert Adair, Jacinta Dicks, Alejandro Martinez, Andrea Malandrinos, Amando Guinle, Paul Armstrong, Roy Purcell, Raymond Hoole, Catherina Ferraz, Roger Delgado, Bill Fraser.*

THE CAPTAIN'S TABLE (1958) [2]

Dir *Jack Lee*. Prod *Joseph Janni*. Scr *John Whiting, Bryan Forbes, Nicholas Phipps, from the novel by Richard Gordon*. Ph *Christopher Challis*. PC and Dis *Rank*. Eastman Colour. 89 mins. Cert A

To his surprise, Albert Ebbs (*John Gregson*), a cargo-boat skipper, is put in charge of a luxury liner. He finds the first officer (*Donald Sinden*) is an incompetent, girl-chasing snob and the purser a smuggler. Ebbs, in fact, upsets nearly everybody, but when an influential passenger (*Maurice Denham*) resolves to report him, an adventuress (*Nadia Gray*) who has taken a liking to Ebbs comes to his rescue. Episodic farce, some way behind *Doctor at Sea*.

RoC *Peggy Cummins, Richard Wattis, Reginald Beckwith, Bill Kerr, Nicholas Phipps, John le Mesurier, Lionel Murton, Joan Sims, Miles Malleson, James Hayter, Joseph Tomelty, June Jago, Nora Nicholson, John Warner, Harry Locke, Ed Devereaux, Rosalie Ashley, Donald Churchill, Oliver Reed, Sam Kydd.*

THE CARD (1952) [4]
(USA: *The Promoter*)

Dir *Ronald Neame*. Prod *John Bryan*. Scr *Eric Ambler, from the novel by Arnold Bennett*. Ph *Oswald Morris*. PC *British Film Makers*. Dis *General Film Distributors*. 91 mins. Cert U

The Potteries, 1890. Denry Machin (*Alec Guinness*), a washerwoman's son, progresses by his wits. They gain him a scholarship (by for-

Alec Guinness, Glynis Johns and Petula Clark in The Card *(1952)*

gery) but later lose him a job. Undaunted, he becomes rent-collector and moneylender, sets up a thrift club and becomes the toast of the Five Towns – he revives Bursley football club by bringing them a big-name player. He becomes Bursley's youngest mayor, and turns away from a countess (*Valerie Hobson*) and a golddigger (*Glynis Johns*) to marry the local girl (*Petula Clark*) of his choice. Engagingly cheeky central character carries all before him. RoC *Edward Chapman, Veronica Turleigh, Gorge Devine, Joan Hickson, Frank Pettingell, Gibb McLaughlin, Michael Hordern, Alison Leggatt, Wilfrid Hyde White, Peter Copley, Deirdre Doyle, Harold Goodwin, Lyn Evans, Michael Trubshawe, Paul Hopkins, Matthew Guinness.*

CARLTON-BROWNE OF THE F.O. (1958) [4]
(USA: *Man in a Cocked Hat*)
Dir and Scr *Roy Boulting, Jeffrey Dell.* Prod *John Boulting.* Ph *Max Greene (Mutz Greenbaum).* PC *Charter.* Dis *British Lion.* 88 mins. Cert U
Confined to the harmless corner of the Foreign Office known as 'miscellaneous territories', Cadogan deVere Carlton-Browne (*Terry-Thomas*), the world's worst diplomat, is suddenly lifted out of mothballs and flown out to a long-forgotten island ally where rich mineral deposits have been found. Continually falling foul of oily premier Amphibulous (*Peter Sellers*), C-B blunders from one disaster to another – and is finally decorated for his services to international peace! Uneasy mix of farce and satire is still very funny in places.
RoC *Luciana Paoluzzi (Paluzzi), Ian Bannen, Thorley Walters, Miles Malleson, Raymond Huntley, John le Mesurier, Kynaston Reeves, Marie Lohr, Marne Maitland, John Van Eyssen, Nicholas Parsons, Irene Handl, Kenneth Griffith, Ronald Adam, Basil Dignam, Sam Kydd, Robert Bruce, Michael Ward, Michael Partridge, Alexis Chesnakov, Billy Rayment, André Charisse, John Glyn-Jones, Julie Hopkins, Kathryne Keeton, Harry Locke, Marianne Stone, Mike Ward, John Payne, Maurice Colbourne, James Dyrenforth, Robert Young.*

CARRINGTON VC (1954) [5]
Dir *Anthony Asquith.* Prod *Teddy Baird.* Scr *John Hunter, from the play by Dorothy and*

Campbell Christie. Ph *Desmond Dickinson.* PC *Romulus/Remus.* Dis *Independent Film Distributors/British Lion.* 105 mins. Cert A
Desperate for money the Army owes him, Major Carrington (*David Niven*), warns his CO (*Allan Cuthbertson*) he'll take part of it from the battery safe. But, at his subsequent court-martial, both the CO and Carrington's shrewish wife (*Margaret Leighton*), for reasons of their own, deny prior knowledge. Carrington is dismissed the service and, crushed, refuses to appeal – until a telephonist reveals hearing a phone conversation which confirms his story. Quietly strong, touching drama with distinguished performances.
RoC *Noelle Middleton, Maurice Denham, Laurence Naismith, Geoffrey Keen, Clive Morton, Victor Maddern, Mark Dignam, John Glyn-Jones, Newton Blick, Raymond Francis, John Chandos, Michael Bates, Robert Bishop, Stuart Saunders, Johnnie Schofield, Basil Dignam, Deryck Barnes, Vivienne Martin, Ann Heffernan, Elizabeth Digby-Smith, Reginald Hearne, Timothy Bateson, Fred Griffiths, RSM Brittain.*

CARRY ON ADMIRAL (1957) [2]
(USA: *The Ship Was Loaded*)
Dir and Scr *Val Guest, from a play by Ian Hay and Stephen King-Hall.* Prod/PC *George Minter.* Ph *Arthur Grant.* Dis *Renown.* SpectaScope. 82 mins. Cert U
A naval officer (*Brian Reece*) and a parliamentary private secretary (*David Tomlinson*) get drunk together and accidentally change places. After the PPS has fired a torpedo at the First Sea Lord and the naval officer has got himself arrested, their girl-friends (*Peggy Cummins, Eunice Gayson*) manage to get them switched back again. Hoary old naval farce, played with vigour but pretty antiquated.
RoC *A. E. Matthews, Joan Sims, Lionel Murton, Reginald Beckwith, Desmond Walter-Ellis, Ronald Shiner, Peter Coke, Derek Blomfield, Ronald Adam, George Moon, Alfie Bass, Tom Gill, Howard Williams, Joan Hickson, Toke Townley, Arthur Lovegrove, Sam Kydd, Philip Ashley, Donald Pickering, Everley Gregg, David Hannaford, Jimmie Rae, Emrys Leyshon, James Sharkey, Walter Horsbrugh.*

CARRY ON NURSE (1959)
Dir *Gerald Thomas.* Prod *Peter Rogers.* Scr *Norman Hudis.* Ph *Reg Wyer.* PC *Beaconsfield.* Dis *Anglo-Amalgamated.* 86 mins. Cert U
The men's surgical ward at Haven Hospital. The escapades of the patients there provide a nightmare for the matron (*Hattie Jacques*) that culminates in an 'unofficial' operation for the removal of a bunion from a patient who wants to be away for the weekend. The operation fails after all concerned succumb to laughing gas. The British public, too, succumbed to this quickfire collection of venerable medical gags.
RoC *Shirley Eaton, Kenneth Connor, Charles Hawtrey, Kenneth Williams, Terence Longdon, Leslie Phillips, Bill Owen, Wilfrid Hyde White, Michael Medwin, Joan Sims, Susan Stephen, Susan Beaumont, Ann Firbank, Joan Hickson, Cyril Chamberlain, Harry Locke, Irene Handl, Brian Oulton, Ed Devereaux, Frank Forsyth,*

John Matthews, Graham Stewart, David Williams, Patrick Durkin, Rosalind Knight, Marita Stanton, Leigh Madison, Stephanie Schiller, Christine Ozanne, Shane Cordell, John Van Eyssen, John Horsley, Lucy Griffiths, Anthony Sagar, Fred Griffiths, Charles Stanley, Susan Shaw, Jill Ireland, Martin Boddey, June Whitfield, Marianne Stone, Hilda Fenemore, Norman Rossington.

CARRY ON SERGEANT (1958) [3]
Dir *Gerald Thomas.* Prod *Peter Rogers.* Scr *Norman Hudis, John Antrobus, from a story by R. F. Delderfield.* Ph *Peter Hennessy.* PC *Insignia.* Dis *Anglo-Amalgamated.* 83 mins. Cert U
About to retire from the army, tough Sergeant Grimshawe (*William Hartnell*) swears his last National Service platoon must win the Star Squad Award. But he is landed with a bunch of no-hopers. Shout as loud as he might, they seem to get worse than ever. On the eve of the final parade, they are surprised to find Grimshawe actually kinder than the other drill sergeants. Making a supreme effort, they win the Star Squad prize. Rough-and-ready, rat-a-tat compendium of old army jokes, with a talented cast of farceurs, started the ball rolling for the enormously successful Carry On films.
RoC *Bob Monkhouse, Shirley Eaton, Eric Barker, Dora Bryan, Bill Owen, Kenneth Connor, Charles Hawtrey, Kenneth Williams, Hattie Jacques, Terence Longdon, Norman Rossington, Gerald Campion, Cyril Chamberlain, Gordon Tanner, Frank Forsyth, Basil Dignam, John Gatrell, Arnold Diamond, Martin Boddey, Ian Whittaker, Anthony Sagar, Joanne Stewart, Edward Judd, Helen Gross.*

Gerald Campion, Bob Monkhouse and William Hartnell in Carry On Sergeant *(1958)*

CARRY ON TEACHER (1959) [3]
Dir *Gerald Thomas.* Prod *Peter Rogers.* Scr *Norman Hudis.* Ph *Reginald Wyer.* PC *Beaconsfield.* Dis *Anglo-Amalgamated.* 86 mins. Cert U
William Wakefield (*Ted Ray*), popular acting head of Maudlin Street Secondary School, plans to move schools. But his pupils don't want him to. So, when two school inspectors descend, the kids resort to every conceivable prank to show their head is unfit for promotion. His poor staff get floured, glued, electrified, blown up and infested with itching powder. Touched by the efforts to keep him,

Wakefield agrees to stay. Fair example of blossoming series; Ray nicely in the footsteps of Will Hay.

RoC *Kenneth Connor, Charles Hawtrey, Leslie Phillips, Joan Sims, Kenneth Williams, Hattie Jacques, Rosalind Knight, Cyril Chamberlain, Richard O'Sullivan, Diana Beevers, George Howell, Carol White, Jacqueline Lewis, Roy Hines, Paul Cole, June White, Larry Dann.*

CARVE HER NAME WITH PRIDE (1958) [4]

Dir *Lewis Gilbert.* Prod *Daniel M. Angel.* Scr *Gilbert, Vernon Harris, from the book by R.J. Minney.* Ph *John Wilcox.* PC *Keyboard.* Dis *Rank. 119 mins. Cert U*

After Violette Szabo's (*Virginia McKenna*) French husband is killed in World War II, she is amazed to find herself seconded to the British secret service. Subjected to rigorous training, she is parachuted into Germany and proves herself a valuable and resourceful agent. On a second mission, she is captured when her ammunition runs out. Torture fails to break her, and she is finally shot. Quite inspiring war film with moving ending and a vivid account of Violette's training.

RoC *Paul Scofield, Jack Warner, Maurice Ronet, Bill Owen, Denise Grey, Avice Landone, Nicole Stephane, Anne Leon, Billie Whitelaw, William Mervyn, Michael Goodliffe, Sydney Tafler, Noel Willman, Alain Saury, André Maranne, Harold Lang, Michael Caine.*

A CASE FOR PC 49 (1951) [3]

Dir *Francis Searle.* Prod *Anthony Hinds.* Scr *Alan Stranks, Vernon Harris, from characters created in their radio series.* Ph *Walter Harvey.* PC *Hammer.* Dis *Exclusive. 80 mins. Cert A*

To evade being suspected of the crime she plans, model Della (*Christine Norden*) asks for police protection – and gets upper-crust copper Archibald Berkeley-Willoughby (*Brian Reece*). She then bumps off a millionaire and disguises it as an accident – but Archie's fiancée Joan (*Joy Shelton*) smells a rat. She and Archie risk their lives with even more dangerous criminals before the case is closed. Hectic comedy-thriller acting better than first 'PC 49' for having radio cast aboard.

RoC *Leslie Bradley, Gordon McLeod, Campbell Singer, Jack Stewart, Michael Balfour, Michael Ripper, Joan Seton, Edna Morris, John Sharp, Frank Hawkins, John Barry, John Warren.*

CAST A DARK SHADOW (1955) [4]

Dir *Lewis Gilbert.* Prod *Herbert Mason.* Scr *John Cresswell, from a play by Janet Green.* Ph *Jack Asher.* PC *Frobisher.* Dis *Eros. 82 mins. Cert A*

Edward Bare (*Dirk Bogarde*) has no compunction in murdering his middle-aged wife (*Mona Washbourne*) when he thinks she is altering her will. But he is mistaken, and his second wife (*Margaret Lockwood*), a prosperous widow of working-class background, is more resilient. When he meets wealthy Charlotte (*Kay Walsh*), Edward plans another killing. He turns his attentions to Charlotte when he finds she is his first wife's sister, but meets his own

death in a car with which he has tampered. Stagy thriller, played with panache.

RoC *Kathleen Harrison, Robert Flemyng, Walter Hudd, Philip Stainton, Myrtle Reed, Lita Roza.*

CASTLE IN THE AIR (1952) [4]

Dir *Henry Cass.* Prod *Edward Dryhurst, Ernest Gartside.* Scr *Alan Melville, Dryhurst, from Melville's play.* Ph *Erwin Hillier.* PC *Hallmark.* Dis *AB-Pathé. 90 mins. Cert U*

The penniless Scottish Earl of Locharne, failing to make a go of turning his draughty castle into a hotel, gets involved with an American cousin who wants to buy it, a Coal Board man who wants to turn it into a miners' hostel, and a genealogist who tries to prove that the earl (*David Tomlinson*) is the rightful heir to the Scottish throne. In the end, the American gets the castle, the earl gets his secretary. A good few chuckles, mainly from *Margaret Rutherford* as the genealogist.

RoC *Helen Cherry, Barbara Kelly, A. E. Matthews, Patricia Dainton, Brian Oulton, Ewan Roberts, Clive Morton, Gordon Jackson, Russell Waters, Stringer Davis, Winifred Willard.*

CAT AND MOUSE/THE DESPERATE ONES (1958) [4]

Dir/Prod/Scr *Paul Rotha, from a novel by Michael Halliday.* Ph *Wolfgang Suschitzky.* PC *Anvil.* Dis *Eros. 79 mins. Cert A*

Knowing that a fortune in diamonds is at stake, a US Army deserter, Fenner (*Lee Patterson*), kills a man who was blackmailing him but makes Ann (*Ann Sears*), whose father stole the diamonds and was hanged for murder, believe she did it. She helps him and falls for him, but later he finds out the diamonds are at her bank and holds her hostage. He is trapped trying to get them. Offbeat thriller with good atmosphere and performances.

RoC *Victor Maddern, Hilton Edwards, George Rose, Roddy McMillan, Diana Fawcett.*

THE CAT GANG (1959) [2]

Dir *Darrel Catling.* Prod *Arthur T. Viliesid.* Scr *John Eldridge from a story by G. Ewart Evans.* Ph *Leslie Dear.* PC *Realist/Children's Foundation.* Dis *British Lion. 51 mins. Cert U*

A series of events linked by the motif of a cat leads a trio of teenagers to a smuggling racket in their coastal village. They help to lure the smugglers into the waiting arms of local customs men, and, after a hand-to-hand struggle, the crooks are captured. Poorly-scripted children's film, awkwardly acted.

LP *Francesca Annis, John Pike, Jeremy Bulloch, John Gabriel, John Stacy, Paddy Joyce.*

CAT GIRL (1957) [3]

Dir *Alfred Shaughnessy.* Prod *Herbert Smith.* Scr *Lou Rusoff.* Ph *Peter Hennessy.* PC *Insignia.* Dis *Anglo-Amalgamated. 76 mins. Cert X*

By night, the spirit of Leonora (*Barbara Shelley*) enters a leopard, which does her murderous bidding. Thus she has got rid of an unwanted husband, and now gets her claws into psychiatrist Dr Marlowe (*Robert Ayres*) who believes her affliction is just an obsession. Leonora's obsession is to get rid of Marlowe's wife

Dorothy (*Kay Callard*), but her plan misfires, and Marlowe runs over her – as the leopard – in his car. Britain's scream-queen-to-be's first taste of horror: fairly silly, it has some chills.

RoC *Paddy Webster, Ernest Milton, Lilly Kann, Jack May, Martin Boddey.*

CHAIN OF EVENTS (1958) [3]

Dir *Gerald Thomas.* Prod *Peter Rogers.* Scr *Patrick Brawn, from a radio play by Leo McKern.* Ph *Peter Hennessy.* PC *Beaconsfield.* Dis *British Lion. 62 mins. Cert A*

To avoid conviction for not paying his fare, Clarke (*Kenneth Griffith*) a bank clerk, tells a lie which starts a chain of events that leads to his own death. Killed at the same time is a blackmailer who came on to the scene with the court case that arose from the incident. Circular story is packed with improbabilities but keeps up a good pace.

RoC *Susan Shaw, Dermot Walsh, Jack Watling, Alan Gifford, Harold Lang, Lisa Gastoni, Ballard Berkeley, Frank Forsyth, Cyril Chamberlain, Freddie Mills, Anthony Sagar, John Stuart, Myrtle Reed, Martin Wyldeck, Martin Boddey, Joan Hickson, James Raglan.*

THE CHALLENGE (1959) [2]

Dir and Scr *John Gilling.* Prod *John Temple-Smith.* Ph *Gordon Dines.* PC *Alexandra/Alliance.* Dis *Rank. 89 mins. Cert A*

Glamorous gang boss Billy Lacross (*Jayne Mansfield*) decides to persuade widower Jim Maxton (*Anthony Quayle*), who is infatuated with her, to hide the loot from a bullion robbery in return for a share. But Jim is caught and goes down for five years. On his release, he is determined to claim his money to give his son an education. But he has to face the kidnap of his son by greedy gang members before, with the aid of Billy, he wins through. Lively but fairly laughable crook drama.

RoC *Carl Mohner, Peter Reynolds, Barbara Mullen, Dermot Walsh, Patrick Holt, Robert Brown, Edward Judd, John Bennett, John Stratton, Percy Herbert, Lorraine Clewes, Peter Pike, Bill McGuffie, Liane Marelli, Lloyd Lamble, John Wood, Wally Patch, Arthur Brough, Bryan Pringle, Marigold Russell, Victor Brooks, Bill Shine, Richard Shine, Richard Shaw, David Davenport.*

CHANCE OF A LIFETIME (1950) [3]

Dir *Bernard Miles, Alan Osbiston.* Prod *Miles, John Palmer.* Scr *Miles, Walter Greenwood.* Ph *Eric Cross.* PC *Pilgrim.* Dis *British Lion. 89 mins. Cert U*

When his factory hands strike, Dickinson (*Basil Radford*), an industrialist, hands over his business to employees Stevens (*Bernard Miles*) and Morris (*Julien Mitchell*). The new bosses win a big foreign order, but currency troubles cause its cancellation. Dickinson returns to bring his experience to their aid and all concerned look forward to the future with renewed confidence and trust. A bit preachy, but acting and direction are nicely relaxed. However, it was denied a circuit release.

RoC *Niall MacGinnis, Kenneth More, Geoffrey Keen, Josephine Wilson, John Harvey, Russell*

Waters, *Patrick Troughton, Hattie Jacques, Amy Veness, Compton Mackenzie, Peter Jones, Stanley van Beers, Bernard Rebel, Eric Pohlmann, Leonard Sharp, Erik Chitty, Norman Pierce, Molly Palmer, Gordon McLeod, Alistair Hunter, George Street, Stanley Rose, Charles Houston, Nigel Fitzgerald, Basil Cunard, John Boddington, Jim Watts, Tony Halfpenny, Doris Dellingpole.*

CHARLEY MOON (1956) [3]

Dir *Guy Hamilton.* Prod *Aubrey Baring.* Scr *Leslie Bricusse, John Creswell, from the novel by Reginald Arkell.* Songs *Bricusse, Robin Beaumont.* Ph *Jack Hildyard.* PC *Colin Lesslie Productions.* Dis *British Lion. Eastman Colour. 92 mins. Cert U*

Two ex-service buddies, Charley (*Max Bygraves*) and Harold (*Dennis Price*), try their hands at show business. Charley reluctantly leaves Harold behind on his successful way to the bright lights. But he is sickened by the hangers-on and fair-weather friends, joins a travelling circus and eventually returns to his countryside sweetheart (*Patricia Driscoll*). Meandering, rather tiresome musical, with one outstanding hit song – *Out of Town.*

RoC *Michael Medwin, Shirley Eaton, Florence Desmond, Charles Victor, Reginald Beckwith, Cyril Raymond, Peter Jones, Newton Blick, Vic Wise, Eric Sykes, Bill Fraser, Vida Hope, Harold Goodwin, Jane Asher, Anthony Bygraves, Lou Jacobi, Brian Oulton, Stuart Saunders, Michael Dear.*

CHASE A CROOKED SHADOW (1957) [5]

Dir *Michael Anderson Jr.* Prod *Douglas Fairbanks Jr, Thomas Clyde.* Scr *David D. Osborn, Charles Sinclair.* Ph *Erwin Hillier.* PC *Associated Dragon.* Dis *AB-Pathé. 87 mins. Cert U*

Kim (*Anne Baxter*), an heiress whose brother has been killed in a car crash and whose father committed suicide, returns to her Costa Brava villa to find a stranger (*Richard Todd*) claiming to be her brother. Her uncle and the local police chief, to her horror, back his story. Terrified by a web of intrigue from which there seems to be no escape, Kim finally reveals herself as a thief and a murderess – the whole idea of a plot wrought against her by the authorities. Suspenseful, hair-raising thriller.

RoC *Alexander Knox, Herbert Lom, Faith Brook, Alan Tilvern, Thelma D'Aguiar.*

Richard Todd, Herbert Lom and Anne Baxter in Chase a Crooked Shadow (*1957*)

CHECKPOINT (1956) [3]

Dir *Ralph Thomas.* Prod *Betty E. Box.* Scr *Robin Estridge.* Ph *Ernest Steward.* PC and Dis *Rank. Eastman Colour. 83 mins. Cert U*

Explosions shake an Italian car-designing factory, as British saboteur O'Donovan (*Stanley Baker*) acting for racing mogul Warren Ingram (*James Robertson Justice*) makes off with secret new blueprints. Ingram plans to get him out of Italy as co-driver to Bill Fraser (*Anthony Steel*) but Fraser, realising O'Donovan intends to kill him when they are across the border, flings himself clear as the car and O'Donovan go over a cliff. Phoney action film moves in fits and starts.

RoC *Odile Versois, Maurice Denham, Michael Medwin, Paul Muller, Lee Patterson, Anne Heywood, Anthony Oliver, Jill Dixon, Philip Gilbert, McDonald Hobley, Robert Rietty, Andrea Malandrinos, Dino Galvani, Harold Ayer.*

CHEER THE BRAVE (1951) [3]

Dir and Scr *Kenneth Hume.* Prod *John Sutro, David Webster.* Ph *Uncredited.* PC *Piccadilly.* Dis *Apex. 62 mins. Cert U*

Browbeaten by his domineering wife (*Elsie Randolph*), peace-loving William Potter (*Jack McNaughton*) seizes his chance to leave her when her thought-dead first husband (*Geoffrey Keen*) pops up and tries to blackmail them. William is able to flee the coop and marry someone else. Competent comedy.

RoC *Vida Hope, Marie Ault, Douglas Ives, Manville Tarrant, Mavis Villiers, Violet Gould, Eileen Way, David Dunn, Jimmy Bruce, Frank Hawkins, Gordon Mulholland, Sam Kydd, Rose Howlett, Helen Goss, Michael Ward, John Bull, Elizabeth Saunders, Jennifer Duncan, Molly Weir.*

CHELSEA STORY (1951) [2]

Dir *Charles Saunders.* Prod *Charles Reynolds.* Scr *John Gilling.* Ph *Ted Lloyd.* PC *Present Day.* Dis *Apex. 65 mins. Cert A*

Mike Harvey (*Henry Mollison*), one-time crime reporter now out of work, goes to a Chelsea party and accepts a bet of £100 from a sinister man (*Sydney Tafler*) that he won't break into a house. With another man who has taken the wager, Harvey does the break-in, but they are caught and his partner kills the owner. Escaping from the police, Harvey hopes to revenge himself on the sinister man, whom he believes has entrapped him; but the police nail him before he can do so. Dreary, unconvincing 'B'.

RoC *Ingeborg Wells, Lesley Osmond, Michael moore, Wallas Eaton, Laurence Naismith, Michael Ward, Andrea Malandrinos, Mercy Haystead, John Bell, Ian Fleming.*

THE CHILD AND THE KILLER (1959) [3]

Dir *Max Varnel.* Prod *Edward J. Danziger, Harry Lee Danziger.* Scr *Brian Clemens, Eldon Howard.* Ph *Jimmy Wilson.* PC *Danzigers.* Dis *United Artists. 65 mins. Cert A*

An American army camp in England. Captain Joe Marsh (*Robert Arden*) would like to marry Peggy (*Patricia Driscoll*), a widow, but her seven-year-old son Tommy (*Richard Williams*) dislikes him. Joe is questioning Mather (*Ryck Rydon*), a deserter, when the man grabs his

Ryck Rydon and Richard Williams in The Child and the Killer (*1959*)

gun, kills a man and escapes. He is discovered by Tommy, who at first befriends the man, but is later made a virtual hostage by him, before Joe shoots him and earns Tommy's friendship. Some tension raised in non-dialogue scenes.

RoC *John McLaren, Robert Raglan, Gary Thorne, Gordon Sterne, Frank Ellement.*

CHILD IN THE HOUSE (1956) [3]

Dir *C. Raker Endfield, Charles de la Tour.* Prod *S. Benjamin Fisz.* Scr *Endfield, from the novel by Janet McNeill.* Ph *Otto Heller.* PC *Golden Era.* Dis *Eros. 88 mins. Cert U*

Elizabeth (*Mandy Miller*), aged 12, is sent to live with her aunt (*Phyllis Calvert*) and uncle (*Eric Portman*) when her mother is taken to hospital – for her father (*Stanley Baker*) is on the run from the police. Her aunt tricks her into revealing her father's whereabouts; he decides to flee the country, but changes his mind and gives himself up. Elizabeth's influence ultimately has a softening effect on her relatives. Standard weepie with stars uneasily cast.

RoC *Dora Bryan, Joan Hickson, Victor Maddern, Percy Herbert, Joan Benham, Martin Miller, Alfie Bass, Christopher Toyne, Molly Urquhart, Bruce Beeby, Peter Burton.*

CHILDREN GALORE (1954) [2]

Dir *Terence Fisher.* Prod *Henry Passmore.* Scr *John and Emery Bonett, Peter Plaskitt.* Ph *Jonah Jones.* PC *Grendon.* Dis *General Film Distributors. 60 mins. Cert U*

A lord and lady build a cottage in their ancestral village and offer it to the couple with the most grandchildren. In the end, after fierce local rivalry that drags numerous skeletons out from cupboards, the winners are Zacky (*Eddie Byrne*) and Mrs Gedge (*Grace Arnold*) whose marriage – their former partners having died – combines two lots of grandchildren together. Group 3-style comedy has neither depth nor taste; the cast works hard.

RoC *RoC Marjorie Rhodes, June Thorburn, Peter Evan Thomas, Marjorie Hume, Lucy Griffiths, Betty Ann Davies, Jack McNaughton, Richard Leach (Leech), Violet Gould, Henry Caine, Olive Milbourne, Anna Turner, John Peters, Jack Hartman, John Lothar, Patrick Ludlow.*

CHILD'S PLAY (1954) [4]

Dir *Margaret Thomson.* Prod *Herbert Mason.*

Scr *Peter Blackmore.* Ph *Denny Densham.* PC *Group 3.* Dis *British Lion.* 68 mins. Cert U
The children of two scientists at the new atomic research station near an English village join the village kids' secret society and become Holy Terrors. Their sworn object: to blow up the local PC (*Peter Martyn*). They almost achieve this when the boffins' kids construct a mini-atom bomb, but happily turn their hands to exploding breakfast cereal instead. Fun, natural children's fantasy.
RoC *Mona Washbourne, Dorothy Alison, Carl Jaffe, Ingeborg Wells, Ballard Berkeley, Joan Young, Christopher Beeny, Patrick Wells, Wendy Westcott, Ian Smith, Anneke Willys, Ernest Scott, Elain Sykes, Robert Raglan.*

CIRCLE OF DANGER (1951) [3]
Dir *Jacques Tourneur.* Prod *David E. Rose, Joan Harrison.* Scr *Philip Macdonald, from his novel.* Ph *Oswald Morris.* PC *Coronado.* Dis *RKO Radio.* 86 mins. Cert U
American Clay Douglas (*Ray Milland*) comes to England to investigate the mysterious death of his commando brother during World War II. He eventually establishes that the shot that killed him was fired by his commanding officer, MacAllan (*Hugh Sinclair*). The latter refuses to explain, and Clay comes close to killing him before it is revealed that his brother was shot for disobeying orders. Book is quite well filmed, but plot lacks build-up in tension.
RoC *Patricia Roc, Marius Goring, Naunton Wayne, Edward Rigby, Marjorie Fielding, John Bailey, Colin Gordon, Dora Bryan, Michael Brennan, Reginald Beckwith, David Hutcheson, Philip Dale, Archie Duncan, Norah Gordon, George Margo, Ben Williams.*

Hugh Sinclair and Ray Milland in Circle of Danger *(1951)*

CIRCUMSTANTIAL EVIDENCE (1952) [2]
Dir *Dan Birt.* Prod *Phil Brandon.* Scr *Allan Mackinnon, from his story* The Judge Sees the Light. Ph *Brendan J. Stafford.* PC *ACT Films.* Dis *Monarch.* 62 mins. Cert A
On the point of divorcing her ne'er-do-well husband (*John Arnatt*) to marry Michael (*Patrick Holt*), the son of a judge, Linda Harrison (*Rona Anderson*) finds herself blackmailed by her spouse. He and Michael fight, and Harrison is found murdered. Even Michael's father (*Frederick Leister*) thinks him guilty, but

Linda's dogged investigation proves otherwise. Ordinary pocket 'meller'.
RoC *John Warwick, Ronald Adam, June Ashley, Peter Swanwick, Lisa Lee, Ballard Berkeley, Leonard White, Roy Russell, Frederick Morant, Grace Arnold, Ben Williams, Thais Jobling, Henry Longhurst, Dorothy Coleman, Ian Fleming.*

CIRCUS FRIENDS (1956) [4]
Dir *Gerald Thomas.* Prod and Scr *Peter Rogers.* Ph *Otto Heller.* PC *Femina/Children's Film Foundation.* Dis *British Lion.* 63 mins. Cert U
When two circus children (*Carol White, Alan Coleshill*) discover that their performing pony, Pinto, has been given to their landlord in lieu of rent in a poor season, they determine to get him back. But their dog Judy has beaten them to it. The landlord's every attempt to recapture the pony is thwarted until a solo performance by Pinto before a record crowd brings in enough takings to settle everything. Both animals and youngsters do well in this children's adventure.
RoC *Meredith Edwards, Sam Kydd, John Horsley, David Tilley, Pat Belcher.*

CLOAK WITHOUT DAGGER (1955) [2]
(USA: *Operation Conspiracy*)
Dir *Joseph Sterling.* Prod and Scr *A.R. Rawlinson.* Ph *Gerry Gibbs, Eric Williams.* PC *Balblair.* Dis *Rank.* 69 mins. Cert U
World War II. Kyra (*Mary Mackenzie*) unknowingly causes her lover, Major Gretton (*Philip Friend*) to miss out on the capture of a spy. Years later, they meet at a fashion show, which Kyra is reporting. Gretton, ostensibly a waiter, but really still working for intelligence, refuses to believe her story that dress designer Gilroudian (*John G. Heller*) is the wartime spy. Circumstances prove her to be right and Gilroudian, trying to escape by helicopter, is trapped. Some thrills, some unintentional laughs.
RoC *Leslie Dwyer, Allan Cuthbertson, Chin Yu, Bill Nagy, Patrick Jordan, Patricia Haines, Stuart Mitchell, Ivor Dean, Marianne Stone, Maria Mercedes, Frank Thornton, Gerry Levey, Boris Ranevsky.*

CLOUDBURST (1951) [3]
Dir *Francis Searle.* Prod *Anthony Hinds.* Scr *Searle, Leo Marks, from Marks' play.* Ph *Walter Harvey.* PC and Dis *Exclusive.* 92 mins. Cert A
When the wife of Foreign Office cipher expert Graham (*Robert Preston*) is killed by hit-and-run robbers making their escape, Graham, a wartime officer in the resistance movement, gets his ex-colleagues to trace the criminals (*Harold Lang, Sheila Burrell*) and runs them down in his own car. He attempts suicide, but is prevented by the police, and led away to stand trial. Grim, violent thriller takes some believing.
RoC *Elizabeth Sellars, Colin Tapley, Mary Germaine, Edward Lexy, Lyn Evans, Daphne Anderson, George Woodbridge, Thomas Heathcote, Edith Sharpe, Noel Howlett, James Mills, Martin Boddey, Robert Brown, Charles Saynor, Stanley Baker, Gerald Case, Frederic Steger.*

THE CLOUDED YELLOW (1950) [4]
Dir *Ralph Thomas.* Prod *Betty Box.* Scr *Eric Ambler.* Ph *Geoffrey Unsworth.* PC *Carillon.* Dis *General Film Distributors.* 96 mins. Cert A
Somers (*Trevor Howard*), a disgraced Secret Service agent, gets a job classifying butterflies for eccentric Nicholas Fenton (*Barry Jones*), whose wife (*Sonia Dresdel*) is having an affair with the shady Nick (*Maxwell Reed*), who also molests Sophie (*Jean Simmons*), their niece, a girl unbalanced by the believed suicide of her parents. Nick is murdered and Sophie suspected. With the help of Somers, she evades the police until the real killer, Fenton, is unmasked. Trying to kill her, he falls to his death from a roof. Thriller grips in later stages.
RoC *Kenneth More, André Morell, Geoffrey Keen, Michael Brennan, Gerard Heinz, Lilly Kann, Sandra Dorne, Gabrielle Blunt, Eric Pohlmann, K.C. Ooi, Marianne Stone, Anthony Oliver, Richard Wattis, Maire O'Neill, Sam Kydd, Cyril Chamberlain, Glyn Houston.*

THE CLUE OF THE MISSING APE (1953) [4]
Dir and Scr *James Hill.* Prod *Frank Wells,* Ph *James Allen.* PC *Gaumont-British/Children's Film Foundation.* Dis *Associated British.* 58 mins. Cert U
Rewarded for bravery by a trip to Gibraltar, sea cadet Jimmy (*Roy Savage*) becomes embroiled in a plot to blow up Her Majesty's fleet, which involves killing the Barbary apes of Gibraltar as well. After some hectic chases, Jimmy and his friend Pilar (*Nati Banda*) finally convince the authorities, who deactivate limpet mines and round up the saboteurs. Fast and furious children's film is good value for adults too.
RoC *George Cole, Patrick Boxill, William Patrick, Marcus Simpson, John Ocello, Peter Copley, Bill Shine, Evelyn Roberts, John Welsh, Harold Siddons, Julian Somers, Wilfrid Walter, Luis Ellul, Carla Challoner.*

COCKLESHELL HEROES (1955) [4]
Dir *José Ferrer.* Prod *Phil C. Samuel.* Scr *Bryan Forbes, Richard Maibaum, from the book by George Kent.* Ph *John Wilcox, Ted Moore.* PC *Warwick.* Dis *Columbia.* Technicolor. CinemaScope. 97 mins. Cert U
Major Stringer (*José Ferrer*) plans to train a small group to man cockleshell canoes, so that they may break the blockade of Bordeaux by limpet-mining German ships. He adjusts his unorthodox methods to compromise with those favoured by Captain Thompson (*Trevor Howard*) and 10 men are trained. The desperately hazardous raid is carried out successfully, but only two of the 10 'heroes' survive. Character is ignored in favour of action, but the 'training' section is very good.
RoC *Victor Maddern, Anthony Newley, David Lodge, Peter Arne, Percy Herbert, Dora Bryan, Graham Stewart, Walter Fitzgerald, Beatrice Campbell, Karel Stepanek, Sydney Tafler, Gladys Henson, Patric Doonan, Judith Furse, Christopher Lee, John Fabian, John Van Eyssen, Robert Desmond, Jacques Brunius, Andrea Malandrinos.*

THE COLDITZ STORY (1954) [4]

Dir *Guy Hamilton*. Prod and PC *Ivan Foxwell*. Scr *Hamilton, Foxwell, William Douglas Home, from the book by P. R. Reid*. Ph *Gordon Dines*. Dis *British Lion*. 97 mins. Cert U

World War II. Colditz Castle houses hardened Allied escapers of all nationalities. It is supposedly impregnable. At first, escape bids fail: tunnels collapse, an informer is discovered. Then British, French, Polish and Dutch get together and a mass break-out takes place beneath the stage of a camp concert. Only a few make it to freedom. More important, the escape route remains undiscovered. Quintessential 'great escape story' with the accent on humour.

LP *John Mills, Eric Portman, Christopher Rhodes, Lionel Jeffries, Bryan Forbes, Ian Carmichael, Richard Wattis, David Yates, Frederick Valk, Denis Shaw, Anton Diffring, Ludwig Lawinski, Carl Duering, Keith Pyott, Eugene Deckers, Rudolf Offenbach, Theodore Bikel, Frederick Schiller, Peter Swanwick, Guido Lorraine, Arthur Butcher, Leo Bieber, Claude Le Sache, Zygmunt Rewkowski, John Heller*.

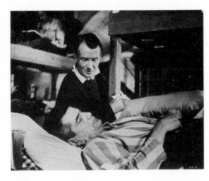

John Mills and Christopher Rhodes in The Colditz Story *(1954)*

COLONEL MARCH INVESTIGATES (1953) [3]

Dir *Cyril Endfield*. Prod *Donald Ginsberg*. Scr *Leo Davis*. Ph *Jonah Jones*. PC *Criterion*. Dis *Eros*. 70 mins. Cert A

Three cases from the Department of Queer Complaints, run by blackpatched Colonel March (*Boris Karloff*) at Scotland Yard. A robber hides his loot so successfully that a police search of his hiding-place cannot find it; a nightclub manager sets up a 'foolproof' alibi when he kills a dancer; a magician deceives people into thinking he has committed murder. Smoothly produced conundrums; solutions fairly obvious.

RoC *Ewan Roberts, Richard Wattis, Sheila Burrell, Patricia Owens, Hubert Gregg, Joan Sims, John Hewer, Anthony Forwood, Ronald Leigh Hunt, Roger Maxwell, Dagmar (Dana) Wynter, Sonya Hana, Bernard Rebel*.

COME BACK PETER (1952) [3]

Dir *Charles Saunders*. Prod *Charles Reynolds*. Scr *Saunders, from the play by A. P. Dearsley*. Ph *Ted Lloyd*. PC *Present Day*. Dis *Apex*. 80 mins. Cert U

A sequel to *Fly Away Peter* (1948), with many of the same cast. The Hapgoods (*Kathleen Boutall, Charles Lamb*) move to a small country cottage now that their offspring have flown. But they all come back, most of them with marital problems, and Mr Hapgood finds himself sleeping in the broom cupboard with the dog. The Hapgoods, who had felt sad before, heave a sigh of relief when domestic crises are settled and they can call their home their own. Light fun with lots of incident.

RoC *Patrick Holt, Peter Hammond, John Singer, Humphrey Lestocq, Pamela Bygrave, Aud Johansen, Dorothy Primrose, Doris Groves, Anthony Doonan, Howard Douglas, Joan Hickson, Avice Landone, Ian Fleming, Paul Hilliker, Lindy Jane Moore, Dandy Daniel (dog)*.

COME DANCE WITH ME (1950) [1]

Dir and Prod *Mario Zampi*. Scr *Cyril Roberts*. Ph *James Wilson*. PC *Anglofilm*. Dis *Columbia*. 58 mins. Cert U

To get into a smart night club, a valet (*Gordon Humphris*) and a maid (*Yvonne Marsh*) pose as a baronet and the 'Hon. Francesca'. They fall in love there, and are eventually asked to join the show. Not much more than a peg for variety turns. Too thin even to sustain an hour.

RoC *Max Wall, Barbara Hamilton, Vincent Ball, Anne Shelton, Derek Roy, Anton Karas, The Marquis Trio, The Aida Foster Girls*.

COMPANIONS IN CRIME (1954) [2]

Dir *John Krish*. Prod *William N. Boyle*. Scr *Kenneth Hayles, Patricia Latham, Lester Powell*. Ph *Basil Emmott*. PC and Dis *Republic*. 70 mins. Cert U

Two cases for Inspector Stryker (*Clifford Evans*) of the Yard. A man working for his crooked brother is convicted of a murder he didn't commit. But his fiancée proves his innocence. A yachtsman smuggles stolen jewels – but the councillor who puts Stryker on to him proves himself to be head of the smuggling ring. Not two of the best stories in the series; though competent, they seem too slight for a feature.

RoC *George Woodbridge; Kenneth Haigh, Maurice Kaufmann, Christine Silver, Billie Whitelaw, Gaylord Cavallaro, Ian Fleming, Cyril Chamberlain, Jack Lambert, Fred Griffiths, Russell Napier, Patrick Jordan, Gillian Lutyens; Eliot Makeham, Dorothy Alison, Tim Turner, David Perrin, Guy Deghy, Philo Hauser*.

CONFESSION (1955) [4]
(USA: *The Deadliest Sin*)

Dir and Scr *Ken Hughes*. Prod *Alec C. Snowden*. Ph *Philip Grindrod*. PC *Anglo Guild*. Dis *Anglo-Amalgamated*. 90 mins. Cert A

Robbers Nelson and Corey (*Sydney Chaplin, Patrick Allen*) flee to England, where Nelson's sister (*Audrey Dalton*) and father (*Jefferson Clifford*) live, not knowing him to be a crook. Nelson and Corey fight over the loot and the sister's boyfriend Alan (*Peter Hammond*) accidentally shoots Corey. A Catholic, he feels compelled to tell a priest. Nelson shoots him dead in the confessional booth, but Inspector Kessler (*John Bentley*) traps Nelson in a belltower, whence he falls to his death. Gripping, nicely constructed thriller; well-acted.

RoC *John Welsh, Pat McGrath, Robert Raglan, Betty Wolfe, Richard Huggett, Eddie Stafford, Alan Robinson, Edward Dane, Sheila Allen, Hugh Munro, Dorinda Stevens, Percy Herbert*.

CONFLICT OF WINGS (1954) [4]
(USA: *Fuss Over Feathers*)

Dir *John Eldridge*. Prod *Herbert Mason*. Scr *Don Sharp, John Pudney, from Sharp's novel*. Ph *Arthur Grant*, (aerial) *Martin Curtis*. PC *Group 3*. Dis *British Lion*. Eastman Colour. 84 mins. Cert U

Norfolk locals are horrified to learn that a piece of waste land known as the Island of Children, and regarded by them as a bird sanctuary, is to be used by the RAF as a rocket firing range. Protests fail, but a local historian discovers the land belongs to the church and the RAF has no right to it. Villagers crowd the site, prevent the RAF from opening the range, and set a public enquiry in motion. A sort of serious Ealing film, well thought out and argued. Credit marks in all departments.

LP *John Gregson, Muriel Pavlow, Kieron Moore, Niall MacGinnis, Guy Middleton, Harry Fowler, Sheila Sweet, Campbell Singer, Frederick Piper, George Woodbridge, Russell Napier, William Mervyn, Charles Lloyd Pack, Howard Connell, Barbara Hicks, Brian Moorehead, Bartlett Mullins, Edwin Richfield, Dorothea Rundle, Harold Siddons, David Spenser, Peter Swanwick, Gwenda Wilson, Margaret Withers, William Mervyn, Hugh Moxey, Beryl Cooke, Brian Harding, Humphrey Lestocq, Guy Verney, Tony Doonan*.

THE CONSTANT HUSBAND (1955) [4]

Dir *Sidney Gilliat*. Prod *Gilliat, Frank Launder*. Scr *Gilliat, Val Valentine*. Ph *Ted Scaife*. PC *Individual/London Films*. Dis *British Lion*. Technicolor. 88 mins. Cert U

Charles Hathaway (*Rex Harrison*) gradually recovers from amnesia to discover that he is married to seven different wives. The barrister (*Margaret Leighton*) who defends him on the charge of multiple bigamy falls for him too. He insists on pleading guilty and goes to prison. On his release, he succeeds in evading the seven waiting wives - but not his barrister. Bright (perhaps over-bright) comedy with good ration of chuckles. First British film to have its US première on TV.

RoC *Kay Kendall, Nicole Maurey, Cecil Parker, George Cole, Raymond Huntley, Michael Hordern, Robert Coote, Eric Pohlmann, Jill Adams, Valerie French, Muriel Young, Marie Burke, Ursula Howells, Roma Dumville, Arthur Howard, John Robinson, Eric Berry, Derek Sydney, Guy Deghy, Charles Lloyd Pack, Stephen Vercoe, Sally Lahee, Norah Gordon, Noel Hood, Myrette Morven, Sam Kydd, Paul Connell, Jill Melford, Michael Ripper, Alfred Burke, Stuart Saunders, George Woodbridge, Paul Whitsun-Jones, Arnold Diamond, Leslie Weston, George Thorne, Doreen Dawne, Pat Kenyon, Monica Stevenson*.

CONTRABAND SPAIN (1955) [2]

Dir and Scr *Lawrence Huntington*. Prod *Ernest Gartside*. Ph *Harry Waxman*. PC *Diadem*. Dis *AB-Pathé*. Eastman Colour. 82 mins. Cert U

Lee Scott (*Richard Greene*), an FBI agent whose brother has been murdered, and Ricky Metcalfe (*Michael Denison*), a British customs agent, track down gold-money-and-watches smugglers operating along the Franco-Spanish border. Draggy melodrama.

RoC *Anouk (Aimée), José Nieto, John Warwick, Philip Saville, Antonio Almoros, Alfonso Estella, Arnold Bell, George (G. H.) Mulcaster, Conrado San Martin, Olive Milbourne, Robert Ayres.*

CORRIDORS OF BLOOD (1958) [4]

Dir *Robert Day.* Prod *John Croydon.* Scr *Jean Scott Rogers.* Ph *Geoffrey Faithfull.* PC *Producers' Associates.* Dis *M-G-M. 86 mins. Cert X* 1840. Sickened by the anguish inflicted by operations (before the invention of anaesthetics), Dr Bolton (*Boris Karloff*), in his attempts to eliminate pain, becomes addicted to drugs and falls into the clutches of bodysnatchers Resurrection Joe (*Christopher Lee*) and Black Ben (*Francis de Wolff*). He is forced to sign bogus death certificates for drugs. After the murder of a hospital guard, Ben and Joe are chased and killed. Bolton dies too, but his son (*Francis Matthews*) continues his original work. Nicely atmospheric thriller, not released until 1961.

RoC *Betta St John, Finlay Currie, Adrienne Corri, Basil Dignam, Frank Pettingell, Carl Bernard, Marian Spencer, Nigel Green, Charles Lloyd-Pack, Robert Raglan, Yvonne Warren (Romain), John Gabriel, Howard Lang.*

COSH BOY (1952) [3]
(USA: *The Slasher*)

Dir *Lewis Gilbert.* Prod *Daniel M. Angel.* Scr *Gilbert, Vernon Harris, from a play by Bruce Walker.* Ph *Jack Asher.* PC *Romulus/Daniel M. Angel.* Dis *Independent Film Distributors. 75 mins. Cert X*

Roy Walsh (*James Kenney*) is the leader of a gang of vicious teenage hoodlums, who beat up an old woman and a prostitute. Roy fancies his friend's sister (*Joan Collins*). He seduces her one night on a bombsite while his gang beats up her boyfriend. Pregnant, she tries to do away with herself. A dance-hall raid fails after Roy attempts to shoot the doorman; he goes on the run. His stepfather finds and thrashes him; the police are not far behind. Brutal crime drama heavily criticized for its sensationalist slant.

James Kenney and Joan Collins in Cosh Boy *1952*

RoC *Betty Ann Davies, Robert Ayres, Hermione Baddeley, Hermione Gingold, Nancy Roberts, Ian Whittaker, Stanley Escane, Sean Lynch, Michael McKeag, Edward Evans, Laurence Naismith, Frederick Piper, Walter Hudd, Sidney James, John(ny) Briggs, Cameron Hall, Arthur Howard, Peter Swanwick, Toke Townley, Anthony Oliver, Sheila McCormack, Vi Kaley, Marian Chapman, Fred Powell, Roy Bentley, G. Crossman.*

THE COUNTERFEIT PLAN (1956) [2]

Dir *Montgomery Tully.* Prod *Alec C. Snowden.* Scr *James Eastwood.* Ph *Phil Grindrod.* PC and Dis *Anglo-Amalgamated. 87 mins. Cert A* Fleeing from France, counterfeiter Max (*Zachary Scott*) sets up operations in England, with the reluctant help of ex-forger Louie (*Mervyn Johns*), and makes a fortune in forged fivers until an infatuation for Louie's daughter (*Peggie Castle*) puts the skids under him. Louie goes to the police and is shot for his pains. Max and his henchman Duke (*Lee Patterson*) escape, but their jeep crashes over a cliff. Heavily Americanized thriller with repetitive plot.

RoC *Sydney Tafler, Robert Arden, Chili Bouchier, Eric Pohlmann, John Welsh, Aubrey Dexter, David Lodge, Martin Wyldeck, Mark Bellamy, Arthur Lovegrove, Charles Mortimer, Bernard Fox, Basil Dignam, Alvar Liddell.*

COUNTERSPY (1953) [3]
(USA: *Undercover Agent*)

Dir *Vernon Sewell.* Prod *W. H. Williams.* Scr *Guy Elmes, Michael Le Fevre, from a novel by Julian Symons.* Ph *A. T. Dinsdale.* PC *Merton Park.* Dis *Anglo-Amalgamated. 68 mins. Cert U*

An author (*Dermot Walsh*), asked to deliver a package, finds a man dead in a bath. He posts the packet, which contains secret jet plans, to himself, but is grabbed by crooks before he can phone the police. Escaping, he is recaptured with his wife (*Hazel Court*), and taken to a bogus nursing home. But police have been tracking her, and the gang is captured. Comedy-thriller has a bit more life than average 'B'.

RoC *James Vivian, Hermione Baddeley, Archie Duncan, Alexander Gauge, Frederick Schrecker, Bill Travers, Hugh Latimer, Beryl Baxter, John Penrose, Gwen Bacon, Maxwell Foster, Howard Lang, Monti de Lyle, Stuart Saunders, Ann Wrigg, Fred Buckland.*

COUNT FIVE AND DIE (1957) [5]

Dir *Victor Vicas.* Prod *Ernest Gartside.* Scr *Jack Seddon, David Pursall.* Ph *Arthur Grant.* PC *Zonic.* Dis *20th Century-Fox. CinemaScope. 92 mins. Cert A*

Things begin to go wrong in 1944 with an Allied plan to fool the Germans about the location of the D-Day invasion. When two of his agents are killed in Holland, Major Howard (*Nigel Patrick*) suspects a new radio operator Rolande (*Annemarie Düringer*). His second-in-command Ranson (*Jeffrey Hunter*), is in love with her. After saving a child hostage from Gestapo agents, Ranson catches her sending a

message to the Nazis, and she shoots him. But she is herself shot by a German spy who did not trust her. Stylish war film with striking climax.

RoC *David Kossoff, Larry Burns, Rolf Lefebvre, Wolf Frees, Arthur Gross, Philip Bond, Otto Diamant, Claude Kingston, Marianne Walla, Beth Rogan, Robert Raglan, Peter Prowse.*

COUNT OF TWELVE (1955) [1]

Dir *Paul Gerrard.* Prod *Edward J. Danziger, Harry Lee Danziger.* Scr *Rex Rienits; Paul Tabori.* Ph *Jimmy Wilson.* PC *Danzigers.* Dis *AB-Pathé. 51 mins. Cert A*

Two stories. (1) A ruthless financier is told he will die one night on the stroke of twelve. He does so, believing his maid has poisoned him. In fact his weak heart has given way – as the maid hoped it would. (2) A famous surgeon persuades a friend's wife to run away with him. But, as her husband pursues, they are both killed in a car crash. Stories are indifferently made, with little entertainment value.

LP *Ron Randell; John Longden, Genine Graham, Jill Adams, Garrard Green, Mona Washbourne, Enid Lorrimer; John Bentley, Eunice Gayson, Leonard Sachs, Patrick Holt.*

COVER GIRL KILLER (1959) [3]

Dir and Scr *Terry Bishop.* Prod *Jack Parsons.* Ph *Gerald Gibbs.* PC *Parroch/Butchers.* Dis *Eros. 61 mins. Cert A*

Mason (*Spencer Teakle*), publisher of a spicy magazine, finds that his cover girls are ending up dead. The killer (*Harry H. Corbett*) is a man with a lethal complex about girls who strip for pin-ups, but his murderous run is ended after attractive June (*Felicity Young*) agrees to be a cover-girl and act as bait – a risk that almost costs her her life. Plenty of suspense for a minor thriller.

RoC *Victor Brooks, Tony Doonan, Bernadette Milnes, Christina Gregg, Charles Lloyd-Pack, Denis Holmes, Dermot Kelly, Tony Thawnton, Julie Shearing, Paddy Joyce, Alan Edwards, John Barrard, Claude Jones, John Baker.*

CRASH DRIVE (1959) [2]

Dir *Max Varnel.* Prod *Edward J. Danziger, Harry Lee Danziger.* Scr *Brian Clemens, Eldon Howard.* Ph *Jimmy Wilson.* PC *Danzigers.* Dis *United Artists. 65 mins. Cert A*

Parted from his wife Ann (*Wendy Williams*), racing driver Paul Dixon (*Dermot Walsh*) crashes and finds himself condemned to a wheelchair. He is full of self-pity, but Ann comes back and he gains courage from her, and from Tomson (*Anton Rodgers*), a crippled dancer determined to recover. When Tomson kills himself, Paul's new world crumbles, but Ann takes him to the racetrack where his old firm want him as team manager. Excellent plot very indifferently treated; maudlin and disappointing.

RoC *Ian Fleming, Grace Arnold, Ann Sears, George Roderick, Rolf Harris, Geoffrey Hibbert, Garard Green, Hal Osmond, Diana Daneman, Hazel Wright, Victor Maring, Malcolm Ranson, Russell Cardon.*

THE CRIMSON PIRATE (1952)   [4]

Dir *Robert Siodmak*. Prod *Harold Hecht*. Scr *Roland Kibbee*. Ph *Otto Heller*. PC/Dis *Warner Bros*. Technicolor. *104 mins. Cert U*

The 18th century. In the Caribbean, pirates Vallo (*Burt Lancaster*) and Ojo (*Nick Cravat*) become involved in an island power struggle. Vallo, who was to sell arms to the rebel leader then betray him, falls in love with his daughter (*Eva Bartok*) and switches sides – to the fury of his crew, who desert. With the aid of a balloon, a submarine and a new explosive, Vallo helps the rebels defeat the tyrant Gruda (*Leslie Bradley*), frees his crew whom Gruda double-crossed, and sails away. Spirited pirate farce with excellent battle scenes; the humour is less effective.

RoC *Torin Thatcher, James Hayter, Margot Grahame, Noel Purcell, Eliot Makeham, Frederick Leister, Frank Pettingell, Dagmar (Dana) Wynter, Christopher Lee, George Woodbridge.*

Burt Lancaster, Nick Cravat and Eva Bartok in The Crimson Pirate *(1952)*

THE CROOKED SKY (1957)   [2]

Dir *Henry Cass*. Prod *Cass, Derek Winn, Bill Luckwell*. Scr *Norman Hudis*. Ph *Phil Grindrod*. PC *Luckwin*. Dis *Rank*. *77 mins. Cert U*

Fake pound notes are flooding Britain. A US treasury man (*Wayne Morris*) and a Scotland Yard detective (*Bruce Seton*) centre their enquiries on an airline company whose radio operators have a curious habit of getting murdered. This leads to a London gambling den whose boss, Fraser (*Anton Diffring*) is the leader of the counterfeiters. He flees the country, only to have a mid-air battle with the pilot (*Sheldon Lawrence*) and fall from the plane. Patchwork of familiar crime-plot elements.

RoC *Karin Booth, Collette Barthrop, Seymour Green, Frank Hawkins, Murray Kash, Wally Peterson, Richard Shaw, Bill Brandon, Guy Kingsley Poynter.*

CROSS CHANNEL (1955)   [1]

Dir *R. G. Springsteen*. Prod *William N. Boyle*. Scr *Rex Rienits*. Ph *Basil Emmott*. PC and Dis *Republic*. *61 mins. Cert A*

Tex (*Wayne Morris*), a charter-boat skipper, unwittingly becomes involved with diamond-smugglers, one of whom tries to murder him. Thrown overboard, he reaches the French coast and falls in love with a girl (*Yvonne Furneaux*) from a fishing village. The crooks eventually shoot it out, and Tex finds his name

cleared. Unappetizing mélange of cross and double-cross.

RoC *Patrick Allen, Carl Jaffe, Arnold Marle, Michael Golden, Charles Laurence, Peter Sinclair.*

THE CROWDED DAY (1954)   [4]

Dir *John Guillermin*. Prod *David Dent*. Scr *Talbot Rothwell*. Ph *Gordon Dines*. PC *Advance*. Dis *Adelphi*. *82 mins. Cert A*

Romantic comedy about the lives of six girls working in a large department store at Christmas time. Chief among them are Peggy (*Joan Rice*) who quarrels with her boyfriend, but eventually gets him back – with a job for him in publicity; and Yvonne (*Josephine Griffin*), pregnant mistress of an aristocrat, who almost commits suicide before her missing lover returns. Quite nicely done in its routine and episodic way.

RoC *John Gregson, Freda Jackson, Patricia Plunkett, Sonia Holm, Patricia Marmont, Vera Day, Dora Bryan, Rachel Roberts, Sydney Tafler, Richard Wattis, Cyril Raymond, Edward Chapman, Thora Hird, Sidney James, Kynaston Reeves, Brian Oulton, Arthur Hill, Joan Hickson, Mary Hinton, Prunella Scales, Nora Nicholson, Dandy Nichols, Jill Dixon, Peter Hammond.*

CROW HOLLOW (1952)   [1]

Dir *Michael McCarthy*. Prod *W. H. Williams*. Scr *Vivian Milroy*. Ph *Bob Lapresle*. PC *Bruton*. Dis *Eros*. *69 mins. Cert A*

Ann (*Natasha Parry*) goes to live with her new husband (*Donald Houston*) at his gloomy ancestral mansion, Crow Hollow, where she soon feels herself terrorized by his three eccentric aunts. He assures her that her fears are groundless; then the maid is found stabbed to death. Ann takes matters into her own hands and solves the mystery. Gloomy yarn, poorly made, performed without conviction. Best thing's the title.

RoC *Nora Nicholson, Esma Cannon, Susan Richmond, Pat(ricia) Owens, Melissa Stribling, R. Meadows White.*

THE CROWNING TOUCH (1958)   [3]

Dir *David Eady*. Prod *Jon Penington, Charles A. Leeds*. Scr *Margot Bennett*. Ph *Ernest Palmer*. PC *Crescent*. Dis *Butchers*. *75 mins. Cert U*

Four stories connected with a hat that has been sold but is uncollected, three of them accounts of what might have happened. A boy and girl quarrel when she wins the hat in a TV quiz. A rich woman intends to leave her husband for an old flame but changes her mind. A 'wide boy' hopes to use it to seduce the ex-barmaid wife of an acquaintance – but is unsuccessful. The real truth about the hat lies elsewhere. Passes the time agreeably; nothing special.

LP *Ted Ray, Greta Gynt, Sydney Tafler, Diane Hart, Maurice Kaufmann, Dermot Walsh, Griffith Jones, Maureen Connell, Allan Cuthbertson, Irene Handl, Colin Gordon, Joan Benham, Richard Pearson, Shaun O'Riordan, Damon D'Esti.*

THE CRUEL SEA (1953)   [6]

Dir *Charles Frend*. Prod *Leslie Norman*. Scr *Eric Ambler, from the novel by Nicholas Monsarrat*. Ph *Gordon Dines, Jo Jago, Paul Beeson*. PC *Ealing Studios*. Dis *General Film Distributors*. *140 mins (later 130 and 126). Cert U*

The men of the corvette *Compass Rose* are introduced head-on to the horrors of war, especially when their skipper, Ericson (*Jack Hawkins*) has to kill his own countrymen in the water in order to attack a lurking enemy sub. The *Compass Rose* herself is later torpedoed and only a few survive. Ericson and his second-in-command Lockhart (*Donald Sinden*), now both on a frigate, come to a better understanding after picking up survivors from a German U-boat. Unrelenting war film with a sense of constant danger; brilliantly made.

RoC *John Stratton, Denholm Elliott, Stanley Baker, Virginia McKenna, Moira Lister, Liam Redmond, Meredith Edwards, Bruce Seton, June Thorburn, Megs Jenkins, Glyn Houston, Alec McCowen, John Warner, Andrew Cruickshank, Walter Fitzgerald, Leo Phillips, Dafydd Havard, Fred Griffiths, Laurence Hardy, John Singer, Sam Kydd, Barry Steele, Barry Letts, Gerard Heinz, Gerik Schjelderup, Gaston Richer, Kenn Kennedy, Harold Goodwin, George Curzon, Anthony Snell, Ronald Simpson, Don Sharp, Herbert C. Walton, Jack Howard, Russell Waters, Harold Jamieson, Warwick Ashton.*

Jack Hawkins in The Cruel Sea *(1953)*

A CRY FROM THE STREETS (1958)   [5]

Dir *Lewis Gilbert*. Prod *Ian Dalrymple*. Scr *Vernon Harris, from a novel by Elizabeth Coxhead*. Ph *Harry Gillan*. PC *Film Traders*. Dis *Eros*. *100 mins. Cert U*

Ann, a welfare officer (*Barbara Murray*) enlists Bill (*Max Bygraves*), a radio mechanic, in her work with deprived children. His fears in her over-confidence are justified when the dipsomaniac mother of one of her charges commits suicide, triggering off a chain of events which results in the boy (*Colin Petersen*) and three young children of a murderer running away with a gun. Bill brings them back. More children arrive. Refreshing, captivating slice of life, outstandingly scripted.

RoC *Dana Wilson, Kathleen Harrison, Sean Barrett, Eleanor Summerfield, Mona Washbourne, Toke Townley, Gillian Vaughan, Dandy Nichols, Avice Landone, Charles McShane, David Bushell, Tony Baker, Jennifer Tafler,*

Robert Howell, Pauline Challoner, John Moulder-Brown, Glyn Houston, Paul Alsford, Mark Mileham, Alastair Hunter, John Watson, Marianne Stone, Basil Dignam, Julia Nelson, Vi Stevens, Fred Griffiths.

CRY, THE BELOVED COUNTRY
(1951)   [3]
(USA: *African Fury*)
Dir *Zoltan Korda.* Prod *Korda, Alan Paton.* Scr *Paton, from his novel.* Ph *Robert Krasker.* PC *London Films.* Dis *British Lion.* 103 mins. Cert *A*

South Africa: a poor black priest (*Canada Lee*) learns that his son (*Lionel Ngakane*) has murdered the son of his wealthy white neighbour (*Charles Carson*). The dead man had been working for racial harmony, and his father comes together in friendship with the priest, whose own son is sentenced to death. Sincerity not quite enough in the face of some indifferent performances, but film is still touching at times.

RoC *Sidney Poitier, Joyce Carey, Edric Connor, Geoffrey Keen, Vivien Clinton, Michael Goodliffe, Albertina Temba, Charles MacRae, Henry Blumenthal, Ribbon Dhlamani, Cyril Kwaza, Max Dhlamani, Shayiwa Riba, Evelyn Nayati, Jsepo Gugushe, Reginald Ngcobo, Emily Pooe, Bruce Meredith Smith, Bruce Anderson, Berdine Grunewald, Cecil Cartwright, Andrew Kay, Danie Adrewmah, Clement McCallin, Michael Golden, Stanley Van Beers, John Arnatt, Scott Harrold.*

THE CURSE OF FRANKENSTEIN
(1957)   [3]
Dir *Terence Fisher.* Prod *Anthony Hinds.* Scr *James Sangster, from the book by Mary Shelley.* Ph *Jack Asher.* PC *Hammer.* Dis *Warner Bros.* Eastman Colour. 83 mins. Cert *X*

Brilliant scientist Victor Frankenstein (*Peter Cushing*) uses sections of stolen corpses to make a creature. When Victor murders a scientist for his brain, his associate (*Robert Urquhart*) rebels and, in the ensuing struggle, the brain is damaged, leaving the finished creature with homicidal tendencies. This proves Victor's undoing, as he goes to the guillotine for crimes that the creature (*Christopher Lee*) has committed. Gory re-working of the old horror classic opened a new vein of horror for British films.

Peter Cushing in The Curse of Frankenstein *(1957)*

RoC *Hazel Court, Valerie Gaunt, Noel Hood, Melvyn Hayes, Paul Hardtmuth, Fred Johnson, Sally Walsh, Claude Kingston, Marjorie Hume, Henry Caine, Michael Mulcaster, Patrick Troughton, Joseph Behrman, Anne Blake, Raymond Rollett, Alex Gallier, Ernest Jay, J. Trevor Davis, Bartlett Mullins, Eugene Leahy.*

CURTAIN UP (1952)   [3]
Dir *Ralph Smart.* Prod *Robert Garrett.* Scr *Michael Pertwee, Jack Davies, from a play by Philip King.* Ph *Stanley Pavey, Ted Moore.* PC *Constellation.* Dis *General Film Distributors.* 82 mins. Cert *U*

The man who is financing the Drossmouth Repertory Company has an aunt (*Margaret Rutherford*). The aunt has written a play. And the company, to the fury of its producer, Harry Blacker (*Robert Morley*) *has* to put it on. Chaos reigns until Blacker falls into the orchestra pit and the aunt takes over the production. Further problems ensue, culminating in the play's unexpected success. Buoyed up by its stars, this is still less funny than the hit stage farce on which it is based.

RoC *Joan Rice, Kay Kendall, Michael Medwin, Olive Sloane, Liam Gaffney, Charlotte Mitchell, Lloyd Lamble, Constance Lorne, Margaret Avery, Charles Lamb, Diana Calderwood, Stringer Davis, Joan Hickson, John Cazabon, Ben Williams.*

D

THE DAM BUSTERS (1954)   [5]
Dir *Michael Anderson.* Prod *Robert Clark, W. A. Whittaker.* Scr *R. C. Sherriff, from books by Paul Brickhill and Guy Gibson.* Ph *Erwin Hillier, Gilbert Taylor (effects).* PC *Associated British.* Dis *AB-Pathé.* 124 mins. Cert *U*

World War II. To breach the Ruhr dams and crush Nazi industrial potential, Dr Barnes Wallis (*Michael Redgrave*) invents five-ton mines that must be bounced along the water of a lake to embed themselves in the walls of the dams, launched by planes flying suicidally low. A hand-picked squadron, led by Wing-Commander Gibson (*Richard Todd*) is set up

Richard Todd in The Dam Busters *(1954)*

and achieves the impossible; but 56 of its men do not come back. Exciting, nearly outstanding war film; Redgrave superb. The popular 'Dam Busters' march was composed by Eric Coates.

RoC *Ursula Jeans, Derek Farr, Patrick Barr, John Fraser, George Baker, Brewster Mason, Anthony Doonan, Basil Sydney, Ernest Clark, Nigel Stock, Raymond Huntley, Bill Kerr, Robert Shaw, Harold Goodwin, Laurence Naismith, Frank Phillips, Stanley Van Beers, Colin Tapley, Brian Nissen, Peter Assinder, Richard Leech, Richard Thorp, David Morell, Ronald Wilson, Denys Graham, Basil Appleby, Tim Turner, Ewen Solon, Patrick McGoohan.*

DANCE HALL (1950)   [3]
Dir *Charles Crichton.* (Associate) Prod *E. V. H. Emmett.* Scr *Emmett, Diana Morgan, Alexander Mackendrick.* Ph *Douglas Slocombe.* PC *Ealing Studios.* Dis *General Film Distributors.* 80 mins. Cert *A*

Four factory girls (*Natasha Parry, Petula Clark, Diana Dors, Jane Hylton*) let their hair down on the floor of the local palais de danse on weekend evenings. Two find romance there, two enter a competition. Eve (*Parry*) is attracted by a smoothie (*Bonar Colleano*), with whom she enters the contest, but eventually goes back to Phil (*Donald Houston*) her old boyfriend. Efficiently made drama with insufficiently persuasive atmosphere.

RoC *Sydney Tafler, Douglas Barr, Gladys Henson, Fred Johnson, James Carney, Kay Kendall, Eunice Gayson, Hy Hazell, Dandy Nichols, Grace Arnold, Thomas Heathcote, Harold Goodwin, Christopher Kane, Tonie Macmillan, Alec Finter, Doris Hare, Michael Trubshawe, Geraldo and His Orchestra, Ted Heath and His Music, Wally Fryer and Margaret Barnes.*

DANCE LITTLE LADY (1954)   [3]
Dir *Val Guest.* Prod and PC *George Minter.* Scr *Guest, Doreen Montgomery.* Ph *Wilkie Cooper.* Dis *Renown.* Eastman Colour. 87 mins. Cert *A*

Furious that his ballerina wife (*Mai Zetterling*) has discovered his mistress, Mark (*Terence Morgan*) drives recklessly, crashing their car. His wife breaks her leg and, although her career is over, becomes a dancing teacher. Mark wants to make their daughter (*Mandy [Miller]*) a Hollywood child star and tries to trick his wife into it. But when the little girl is trapped in a fire, he gives his life to save her. Very highly coloured tear-jerker; climax is exciting.

RoC *Guy Rolfe, Eunice Gayson, Reginald Beckwith, Ina de la Haye, Harold Lang, Jane Aird, Richard O'Sullivan, William Kendall, Alexander Gauge, Lisa Gastoni, David Poole, Maryon Lane, Joan Hickson, Marianne Stone, Vera Day.*

DANGEROUS ASSIGNMENT (1950)   [2]
Dir and Ph *Ben R. Hart.* Prod *Miriam Crowdy.* Scr *Chick Messina.* PC *Target.* Dis *Apex.* 58 mins. Cert *A*

An American reporter, Joe (*Lionel Murton*) comes to Britain to find material for 'human crime stories'. He decides to investigate a racket in stolen cars and gets himself beaten up and mixed up in a couple of murders. With

the help of insurance investigator L. P. Cummings (*Pamela Deeming*), who proves to be a woman, Joe clears himself and gets his story. Rough and ready thick-ear, indifferently acted.
RoC *Ivan Craig, MacDonald Parke, Michael Hogarth, Bill Hodge, Edward Evans.*

DANGEROUS CARGO (1954) [3]
Dir *John Harlow*. Prod and Scr *Stanley Haynes*. Ph *Lionel Banes*. PC *ACT Films*. Dis *Monarch*. 61 mins. Cert U
Tim (*Jack Watling*), a London Airport security guard, is tricked by a wartime friend (*Terence Alexander*), now working for a big-time racketeer (*Karel Stepanek*), then blackmailed into revealing details of a gold shipment. Tim's resourceful wife Janie (*Susan Stephen*) resolves to save her husband, and has police waiting for the crooks when they try to steal the bullion. Bright performances lift ordinary melodrama.
RoC *Richard Pearson, John le Mesurier, Ballard Berkeley, John Longden, Genine Graham, Trevor Reid, Arthur Rigby, John H. Watson.*

DANGEROUS EXILE (1957) [2]
Dir *Brian Desmond Hurst*. Prod *George H. Brown*. Scr *Robin Estridge, from a novel by Vaughan Wilkins*. Ph *Geoffrey Unsworth*. PC and Dis *Rank*. Eastman Colour. VistaVision. 90 mins. Cert A
1795. The young Dauphin of France (*Richard O'Sullivan*) is smuggled by balloon from France to Wales by his uncle, de Beauvais (*Louis Jourdan*), who substitutes his own son in the Dauphin's prison cell. He is befriended in Wales by Virginia (*Belinda Lee*), whose maid (*Anne Heywood*) is in the pay of agents of the Republic. Finding his son killed, de Beauvais races back to Wales just in time to prevent the Dauphin's assassination by St Gerard (*Keith Michell*). Throwback to Gainsborough days is far-fetched, wanly-acted.
RoC *Terence Longdon, Martita Hunt, Finlay Currie, Jean Mercure, Jean Claudio, Frederick Leister, Laurence Payne, Austin Trevor, Jacques Brunius, Raymond Gerome, Brian Rawlinson, Derek Oldham, John Dearth, Lisa Lee, André Mikhelson, Sam Kydd, Richard Clarke.*

DANGEROUS VOYAGE (1954) [2]
(USA: *Terror Ship*)
Dir *Vernon Sewell*. Prod *W. H. Williams*. Scr *Julia Ward*. Ph *Jo(e) Ambor*. PC *Merton Park*. Dis *Anglo-Amalgamated*. 72 mins. Cert U
A mystery yacht is found drifting at sea. The three people who examine the boat, thinking it might have been used for smuggling, find burns accumulating on their arms. They discover the burns are caused by stolen uranium, hidden in the mast of the yacht. The thieves return for the uranium, and pursued by sea, set off an explosion which blows them out of the water. Same old British 'B' problem: good ideas, but mediocre execution. Laughs in the wrong places.
LP *William Lundigan, Naomi Chance, Vincent Ball, Jean Lodge, Kenneth Henry, Richard Stewart, John Warwick, Beresford Egan, Frank Littlewood, Armand Guinle, Peter Bathurst, Stanley Van Beers, Oliver Johnston, Hugh Morton, Michael Ingrams, Frank Henderson.*

DANGER WITHIN (1958) [4]
(USA: *Breakout*)
Dir *Don Chaffey*. Prod and PC *Colin Lesslie*. Scr *Bryan Forbes, Frank Harvey, from a novel by Michael Gilbert*. Ph *Arthur Grant*. Dis *British Lion*. 101 mins. Cert U
Attempted escapers at a North Italy prison camp in 1943 are dying, and it's clear that there is a traitor among Allied ranks. The Escape Committee, headed by Lt-Col Baird (*Richard Todd*) turns its attention to unmasking him, and do so during a mass escape bid. Although some way behind *Stalag 17*, film carries a good share of tension, excitement and humour.
RoC *Richard Attenborough, Michael Wilding, Bernard Lee, Dennis Price, Donald Houston, Peter Arne, William Franklyn, Vincent Ball, Ronnie Stevens, Peter Jones, Terence Alexander, Andrew Faulds, Steve Norbert, Cyril Shaps, Eric Lander, John Dearth, Robert Bruce, Harold Siddons, Ian Whittaker, David Williams, David Graham, Howard Williams, Dino Galvani, Michael Caine.*

THE DARK AVENGER (1955) [3]
(USA: *The Warriors*)
Dir *Henry Levin*. Prod *Vaughan N. Dean*. Scr *Daniel B. Ullman, (uncredited) Phil Park*. Ph *Guy Green*. PC *Monogram*. Dis *20th Century-Fox*. Eastman Colour. CinemaScope. 85 mins. Cert U
1350. To break a truce and get rid of the English during the Hundred Years' War, the French Count de Ville (*Peter Finch*) abducts English Lady Joan (*Joanne Dru*), hoping that Prince Edward (*Errol Flynn*) will launch a disastrous English attack. Edward, disguised, enlists in de Ville's army and eventually brings about the downfall and death of the French nobleman and the rescue of Lady Joan. Flynn again ripping regardless through the history books in strained historical romp.
RoC *Yvonne Furneaux, Patrick Holt, Michael Hordern, Moultrie Kelsall, Robert Urquhart, Vincent Winter, Noel Willman, Frances Rowe, Richard O'Sullivan, Alastair Hunter, Rupert Davies, Ewen Solon, Jack Lambert, John Welsh, Harold Kasket, Leslie Linder, Robert Brown, John Phillips, Sam Kydd.*

Peter Finch, Joanne Dru and Errol Flynn in The Dark Avenger *(1955)*

DARK INTERVAL (1950) [1]
Dir *Charles Saunders*. Prod *Arthur Reynolds*.

Scr *John Gilling*. Ph *E. Lloyd*. PC *Present Day*. Dis *Apex*. 60 mins. Cert A
Walter Jordan (*Andrew Osborn*), in whose family insanity runs, returns from his honeymoon and soon becomes unreasonably suspicious of his bride (*Zena Marshall*). He thinks that she and the family doctor are in love (true, on the doctor's part) and plotting to murder him. He tries to kill both his wife and the chauffeur. Cedric the butler (*John le Mesurier*), who has always protected Walter, shoots him, then poisons himself. Small cast struggles hard with another unintentionally comic British 'B'.
RoC *John Barry, Mona Washbourne, Wallas Eaton, Charmian Innes.*

THE DARK LIGHT (1951) [2]
Dir and Scr *Vernon Sewell*. Prod *Michael Carreras*. Ph *Walter Harvey*. PC *Hammer*. Dis *Exclusive*. 66 mins. Cert A
A lighthouse is found to be deserted, and a flashback reveals the answer. Bank robbers, two men and a girl, have landed there, the keeper agreeing to put them ashore. Three people meet sticky ends before the assistant keeper (*David Greene*) decides to surrender the girl (*Katherine Blake*) - and himself - to the authorities. Slow and grim.
RoC *Albert Lieven, Martin Benson, John Longden, Norman MacOwan, John Harvey, Jack Stewart, Joan Carol.*

THE DARK MAN (1950) [4]
Dir and Scr *Jeffrey Dell*. Prod *Julian Wintle*. Ph *Eric Cross*. PC *Independent Artists*. Dis *General Film Distributors*. 91 mins. Cert A
A thief (*Maxwell Reed*) kills a man while robbing a safe. Later he murders the cab-driver who takes him to the South Coast. He is seen by Molly (*Natasha Parry*), a girl cyclist, and sets out to add her to his victims, only narrowly failing twice before police corner and kill him on an artillery range. Good camerawork and direction of chase scenes paper over some of the weaknesses in script.
RoC *Edward Underdown, William Hartnell, Barbara Murray, Cyril Smith, Leonard White, John Singer, Geoffrey Sumner, Sam Kydd, Geoffrey Bond, Gerald Anderson, Betty Cooper, Robert Lang, Grace Denbigh Russell, Norman Claridge, John Hewer.*

DATE AT MIDNIGHT (1959) [2]
Dir *Godfrey Grayson*. Prod *Edward J. Danziger, Harry Lee Danziger*. Scr *Mark Grantham*. Ph *Jimmy Wilson*. PC *Danzigers*. Dis *Paramount*. 57 mins. Cert A
Ace New York reporter Bob Dillon (*Paul Carpenter*) comes to England to interview a famous criminal lawyer (*Ralph Michael*). But he finds himself involved in a murder mystery, eventually proving, with the help of a girl photographer (*Jean Aubrey*) that the lawyer's nephew didn't kill an ex-flame, but that the lawyer's possessive wife did. Standard crime drama.
RoC *Harriette Johns, John Charlesworth, Philip Ray, Robert Ayres, Howard Lang, Vernon Smythe, Carole Lorimer, Totti Truman Taylor, Janet Rowell, Paddy Webster.*

DATE WITH DISASTER (1957)   [2]

Dir *Charles Saunders*. Prod *Guido Coen*. Scr *Brock Williams*. Ph *Brendan Stafford*. PC *Fortress*. Dis *Eros*. 61 mins. Cert U

Two of the three partners in a garage business plan to relieve it of £20,000 with the help of a professional criminal (*William Hartnell*). The plan is carried out while senior partner Miles (*Tom Drake*) is away, but things go wrong for the crooks, one of them being killed and another captured. The third kidnaps Miles' girl (*Shirley Eaton*) but is traced and overpowered by Miles himself. Follows a well-worn second-feature path.

RoC *Maurice Kaufmann, Michael Golden, Richard Shaw*.

DAVY (1957)   [2]

Dir *Michael Relph*. Prod *Basil Dearden*. Scr *William Rose*. Ph *Douglas Slocombe*. PC *Ealing Films*. Dis *M-G-M*. Technicolor. Technirama. 85 mins. Cert U

Davy (*Harry Secombe*), a member of a successful knockabout comedy group called The Mad Morgans, finds that his powerful singing voice brings him to the attention of the Royal Opera House in London. His sister Gwen (*Susan Shaw*) is fearful that her husband George (*Ron Randell*) will leave her if the act breaks up. Sir Giles (*Alexander Knox*), an impresario, tries to persuade Davy to opt for a singing career, but he decides to return to The Mad Morgans. All pretty corny.

RoC *George Relph, Bill Owen, Adèle Leigh, Isabel Dean, Kenneth Connor, Peter Frampton, Gladys Henson, Joan Sims, George Moon, Clarkson Rose, Elizabeth (Liz) Fraser, Charles Lamb, Arnold Marle, Campbell Singer, Bernard Cribbins, Rachel Roberts*.

Bill Owen and Harry Secombe in Davy *(1957)*

THE DAY THEY ROBBED THE BANK OF ENGLAND (1959)   [5]

Dir *John Guillermin*. Prod *Jules Buck*. Scr *Howard Clewes, Richard Maibaum, from the novel by John Brophy*. Ph *Georges Périnal*. PC *Summit*. Dis *M-G-M*. 85 mins. Cert U

1901. Irish patriots fighting for home rule hire an American adventurer, Norgate (*Aldo Ray*), to help them rob the Bank of England. Burgling a museum to steal plans of the vaults, Norgate discovers a disused sewer running beneath the bank, and uses it to carry out the robbery – a million pounds in gold. Norgate is caught by Fitch (*Peter O'Toole*), officer of the guards at the bank, and the plan to get the gold away is abandoned when the chance of peaceful negotiations arises. Exciting adventure with its roots in fact.

RoC *Elizabeth Sellars, Kieron Moore, Hugh Griffith, Albert Sharpe, John le Mesurier, Joseph Tomelty, Wolf Frees, Miles Malleson, Colin Gordon, Michael Golden, Peter Myers, Arthur Lowe*.

A DAY TO REMEMBER (1953)   [3]

Dir *Ralph Thomas*. Prod and PC *Betty Box*. Scr *Robin Estridge, from a novel by Jerrard Tickell*. Ph *Ernest Steward*. Dis *General Film Distributors*. 92 mins. Cert U

The Hand and Flower darts team decides on Boulogne for its annual outing. A smuggling bid is foiled; an ex-soldier falls for a girl he knew in the war; a man super-conscious of his lack of height joins the Foreign Legion. The organizer (*James Hayter*) finally gives up track of his party and goes off jitterbugging. Working-class version of *Innocents in Paris* (qv). Cast works hard and with some success.

RoC *Donald Sinden, Stanley Holloway, Odile Versois, Joan Rice, Harry Fowler, Edward Chapman, Bill Owen, Peter Jones, Meredith Edwards, George Coulouris, Vernon Gray, Thora Hird, Theodore Bikel, Brenda de Banzie, Lilly Kann, Arthur Hill, Patricia Raine, Marianne Stone, Harold Lang, Germaine Delbat, Robert Le Beal, Georgette Anys, Marcel Poncin, Jacques Cey, Jacqueline Robert, Richard Molinas*.

DEADLY NIGHTSHADE (1952)   [3]

Dir *John Gilling*. Prod *Robert S. Baker, Monty Berman*. Scr *Laurence Huntington*. Ph *Berman*. PC *Kenilworth-Mid-Century*. Dis *General Film Distributors*. 61 mins. Cert U

Reading about Matthews, a man who was arrested in his place and proved to be his double, Barlow (*Emrys Jones*), a convict on the run, resolves to find Matthews and switch places. Matthews, who is accidentally killed in a struggle with Barlow, proves to have been a double-agent. By rounding up his confederates, Barlow escapes an extension of his sentence. Conventional 'B' feature with plenty of incident.

RoC *Zena Marshall, John Horsley, Joan Hickson, Hector Ross, Victor Platt, Roger Maxwell, Lesley Deane, Edward Evans, Alan Gordon, Ian Fleming, Martyn Wyldeck*.

DEADLY RECORD (1959)   [3]

Dir *Lawrence Huntington*. Prod *Vivian A. Cox*. Scr *Cox, Huntington*. Ph *Eric Cross*. PC *Independent Artists*. Dis *Anglo-Amalgamated*. 59 mins. Cert A

When his faithless wife is killed, pilot Trevor Hamilton (*Lee Patterson*) finds himself the chief suspect. In finding that a jealous airport receptionist (*Jane Hylton*) was the real killer, Trevor strikes up a friendship with Susan (*Barbara Shelley*), his wife's best friend, that promises well for the future. Very familiar plot at least moves with pace and confidence.

RoC *Peter Dyneley, Geoffrey Keen, John Paul, Everley Gregg, Edward Cast, George Pastell, Ferdy Mayne, April Olrich, Edward Cast, Percy Herbert, Geoffrey Tyrrell, Peter Dolphin, Doreen Dawne*.

DEATH GOES TO SCHOOL (1953)   [2]

Dir *Stephen Clarkson*. Prod *Victor Hanbury*. Scr *Clarkson, Maisie Sharman*. Ph *Eric Cross*. PC *Independent Artists*. Dis *Eros*. 65 mins. Cert U

A teacher is found murdered in the school grounds, and the suspects include colleagues who were jealous of her success, and the married man with whom she had been having an affair. Helped by one of the school mistresses (*Barbara Murray*), Inspector Campbell (*Gordon Jackson*) succeeds in sorting out the killer. Verbose, monotonous whodunnit.

RoC *Pamela Alan, Jane Aird, Beatrice Varley, Ann Butchart, Jenine Matto, Imogene Moynihan, Robert Long, Stanley Rose, Sam Kydd, Pauline Winter, Enid Stewart, Sandra Whipp, Nina Parry, Julie Stewart*.

DEATH IS A NUMBER (1951)   [2]

Dir and Prod *Robert Henryson*. Scr *Charles K. Shaw*. Ph *Phil Grindrod, Harry Long*. PC *Delman*. Dis *Adelphi*. 50 mins. Cert A

A 'numerologist' tries to prove that there is some evidence to support the validity of his 'science' by relating the tragic part played by the number nine in the family history of his friend, a racing-driver whose death in a crash fulfilled a 300-year-old curse. Silly 'B'-feature.

LP *Terence Alexander, Lesley Osmond, Denis Webb, Ingeborg Wells, Peter Gawthorne, Isabel George*.

DEATH OF AN ANGEL (1951)   [3]

Dir *Charles Saunders*. Prod *Anthony Hinds, Julian Lesser*. Scr *Reginald Long, from a play by Frank King*. Ph *Walter Harvey*. PC *Hammer/Lesser*. Dis *Exclusive*. 64 mins (later 59). Cert A

Young Dr Boswell (*Raymond Young*) becomes assistant to country doctor Welling (*Patrick Barr*) but, on the night Boswell goes to London to collect the rest of his things, Mrs Welling (*Jane Baxter*) is murdered. Suspected are Welling, Boswell, the surgery nurse (*Jean Lodge*), the Wellings' daughter (*Julie Somers*) and the bank manager (*Russell Waters*) who turns out to be the killer and falls to his death after a chase through a water mill. Some suspense; rather slow for a short film.

RoC *Russell Napier, James Mills, Frank Tickle, Katie Johnson, Robert Brown, John Kelly, Duggie Ascot, Hal Osmond, June Bardsley, David Stoll*.

THE DEATH OF MICHAEL TURBIN (1954)   [1]

Dir *Bernard Knowles*. Prod *Tom D. Connachie*. Scr *Guy Morgan; Paul Vincent Carroll and Larry Marcus*. Ph *Jimmy Wilson*. PC *Douglas Fairbanks Jr*. Dis *British Lion*. 52 mins. Cert U

Two stories. (1) A political prisoner is missed by a firing squad's bullets, and completes his remarkable escape from eastern Europe with the connivance of two frontier guards. (2) Spurned by his sweetheart, an Irishman goes to America and becomes a hated moneylender. Through the advice of a priest, he learns humility and is reunited with the original girl. Slow 'shorties' whose sentiment is hard to take.

LP *Christopher Rhodes, Elizabeth Wallace, Christopher Lee, Martin Benson; Tommy Duggan, June Thorburn, Barbara Mullen, Joseph Tomelty.*

DEATH OVER MY SHOULDER (1957) [2]

Dir *Arthur Crabtree.* Prod *Frank Bevis.* Scr *Norman Hudis.* Ph *Jimmy Harvey.* PC *Orb/Vicar.* Dis *Orb.* 89 mins. Cert A

Jack Regan (*Keefe Brasselle*), an American detective in London, tries to commit suicide when he learns his son has a rare disease, then sells his life to Longo (*Bonar Colleano*), a crook, to pay for treatment through life insurance. Longo hires deadly Evelyn Connors (*Jill Adams*), but Regan comes into a legacy and runs for his life. In a gun battle, Longo and Evelyn shoot each other. Tired and tedious; seems very long.

RoC *Arlene de Marco, Charles Farrell, Al Mulock, Sonia Dresdel, Peter Swanwick.*

DECAMERON NIGHTS (1952) [3]

Dir *Hugo Fregonese.* Prod *M.J. Frankovitch.* Scr *George Oppenheimer, from stories by Giovanni Boccaccio.* Ph *Guy Green.* PC *Film Locations.* Dis *Eros.* Technicolor. 93 mins. Cert A

A widow (*Joan Fontaine*), her lady friends, and Boccaccio (*Louis Jourdan*) flee from Florence in 1350 to escape the plague. In her country house, Boccaccio flirts with her and tells stories of sexual intrigue: a pretty wife gets herself kidnapped by a pirate and makes her husband cough up a ransom; a wife outwits her husband on a wager over her faithfulness; a young woman doctor 'given' a courtier husband as reward for saving a king's life proves her love for him. Well-set and photographed, otherwise mild doses of naughtiness.

RoC *Binnie Barnes, Joan Collins, Mara Lane, Melissa Stribling, Stella Riley; Godfrey Tearle, Eliot Makeham; Meinhart Maur, George and Bert Bernard, Van Boolen, Gordon Bell; Noel Purcell, Marjorie Rhodes, Hugh Morton.*

THE DEEP BLUE SEA (1955) [3]

Dir and Prod *Anatole Litvak.* Scr *Terence Rattigan, from his play.* Ph *Jack Hildyard.* PC *London Films.* Dis *20th Century-Fox.* Eastman Colour. CinemaScope. 99 mins. Cert A

Saving Hester (*Vivien Leigh*) from her second suicide attempt, Miller (*Eric Portman*) finds out that she has been enduring a fraught affair with Freddie (*Kenneth More*), a weak, feckless, likeable ex-RAF pilot with whom she is passionately in love, although he cannot respond on the same level. Miller tells her Freddie will always return and eventually destroy her; when he does so, having been offered a job in Canada, Hester manages to send him away for good. Disappointingly passionless adaptation of sombre hit play.

RoC *Emlyn Williams, Moira Lister, Arthur Hill, Jimmy Hanley, Miriam Karlin, Dandy Nichols, Heather Thatcher, Bill Shine, Alec McCowen, Sidney James, Gibb McLaughlin, Brian Oulton.*

THE DELAVINE AFFAIR (1954) [3]

Dir *Douglas Pierce.* Prod and PC *John Croydon, Henry Passmore.* Scr *George Fisher, from* a novel by Robert Chapman. Ph *Jonah Jones.* Dis *Monarch.* 64 mins. Cert U

The murder of a local character, Gospel Joe, leads reporter Rex Banner (*Peter Reynolds*) and his wife (*Honor Blackman*) on to the trail of jewel thieves. A femme fatale (*Valerie Vernon*) and a deserted farmhouse also figure in the plot before Rex corners the killer and, incidentally, clears his own name. Witty comedy-thriller with over-familiar plot but polished performances.

RoC *Gordon Jackson, Peter Neil, Michael Balfour, Laurie Main, Katie Johnson, Mark Daly, Anna Turner, Mai Bacon, Vernon Kelso, Christie Humphrey.*

DELAYED ACTION (1954) [1]

Dir *John Harlow.* Prod *Robert S. Baker, Monty Berman.* Scr *Geoffrey Orme.* Ph *Gerald Gibbs.* PC *Kenilworth-Mid-Century.* Dis *General Film Distributors.* 60 mins. Cert A

Failed novelist Ned Ellison (*Robert Ayres*) delays his suicide at the behest of a financier (*Alan Wheatley*), who wants to use the corpse for his own ends in his own time. Ellison is to be well paid, but the inevitable happens: he discovers a reason for living and wants out. Fortunately, police rescue him from his own folly. Very slow and ragged 'thriller' that well and truly lives up to its title.

RoC *June Thorburn, Bruce Seton, Michael Kelly, Michael Balfour, Ballard Berkeley, John Horsley, Dennis Chinnery, Ian Fleming, Olive Kirby, Charles Lamb, Ryck Rydon, Emrys Leyshon, Myrtle Reed, Derek Prentice, Trevor Reid, Myles Rudge, Donald Vowles, Arthur Hewlett.*

THE DEPRAVED (1957) [1]

Dir *Paul Dickson.* Prod *Edward J. Danziger, Harry Lee Danziger.* Scr *Brian Clemens, Edith Dell.* Ph *Jimmy Wilson.* PC *Danzigers.* Dis *United Artists.* 71 mins. Cert A

Dave (*Robert Arden*) an American Army officer, becomes involved with tempestuous Laura (*Anne Heywood*) and they murder her husband together, pushing him, in his car, into a river. Satisfied that Dave has done the job for her, Laura gives him to the police and prepares to make off with her lover, her chauffeur. But Dave escapes and shoots her dead. Very poor. Said one critic: 'The script does not call for good acting and it doesn't get it'.

RoC *Carroll Levis, Basil Dignam, Robert Ayres, Gary Thorne, Denis Shaw, Hal Osmond, Gilbert Winfield.*

DERBY DAY (1952) [3]

(USA: *Four Against Fate*)

Dir *Herbert Wilcox.* Prod *Wilcox, Maurice Cowan.* Scr *Monckton Hoffe, John Baines, Alan Melville.* Ph *Max Greene (Mutz Greenbaum).* PC *Wilcox-Neagle.* Dis *British Lion.* 85 mins. Cert U

Lady Helen (*Anna Neagle*) and David Scott (*Michael Wilding*) go to see the Derby to fulfil promises to their husband and fiancée, killed in the same air crash. Tommy (*John McCallum*) and Betty (*Googie Withers*) are there on the run, after he has killed her husband. Film star Gerald (*Peter Graves*) enjoys the day with a French girl (*Suzanne Cloutier*) whose employer 'won' him in a raffle. Taxi driver Joe (*Gordon*

Alfie Bass and John McCallum in Derby Day *(1952)*

Harker) drags along his grumbling wife (*Gladys Henson*). The day ends; Tommy is captured. Neagle-Wilding formula wearing thin.

RoC *Edwin Styles, Nigel Stock, Ralph Reader, Tom Walls Jr, Alfie Bass, Josephine Fitzgerald, Arthur Hambling, Myrette Morven, Richard Wattis, Ewan Roberts, Tonie Edgar Bruce, Leslie Weston, H. R. Hignett, Robert Brown, Gerald Anderson, Sam Kydd, Hugh Moxey, Derek Prentice, Michael Ripper, Philip Ray, Cyril Conway, Cicely Wolper, John Chandos, Jan Pilbeam, Mary Gillingham, Frank Webster, Raymond Glendenning, Bryan Johnston.*

DESERT MICE (1959) [3]

Dir *Michael Relph.* Prod *Relph, Basil Dearden.* Scr *David Climie.* Ph *Kenneth Hodges.* PC *Artna.* Dis *Rank.* 83 mins. Cert U

1941. A hastily assembled, woefully untalented group of entertainers is sent to the Middle East to give shows to far-flung bases. Its officers, Poskett (*Alfred Marks*) and Ribstone (*Kenneth Fortescue*) are asked to find a German commando group masquerading as British soldiers. They do so, and capture its leader (*Marius Goring*) by a conjuring trick. Good-hearted farce not too skilfully handled. Funny moments.

RoC *Patricia Bredin, Sidney James, Dick Bentley, Dora Bryan, Irene Handl, Reginald Beckwith, Joan Benham, Liz Fraser, Nigel Davenport.*

Dora Bryan (with spanner) and Irene Handl in Desert Mice *(1959)*

THE DESPERATE MAN (1959) [1]

Dir *Peter Maxwell.* Prod *Jack Greenwood.* Scr *James Eastwood, from a novel by Paul Somers.*

Ph *Gerald Moss*. PC *Merton Park*. Dis *Anglo-Amalgamated*. *58 mins. Cert U*

Curtis (*Conrad Phillips*) a reporter on holiday in Sussex, meets Carol (*Jill Ireland*), a local newsgirl, and they stumble across a murder. The killer, a jewel thief (*William Hartnell*) takes Carol hostage in a castle, but finally falls to his death from the battlements. Desperate is right.

RoC *Charles Gray, Peter Swanwick, Arthur Gomez, John Warwick, Patricia Burke, Ernest Butcher, Doris Yorke, Jean Aubrey, Brian Weske, Marian Collins.*

DESPERATE MOMENT (1953) [2]

Dir *Compton Bennett*. Prod *George H. Brown*. Scr *Brown, Patrick Kirwan, from the novel by Martha Albrand*. Ph *C. Pennington-Richards*. PC *Fanfare*. Dis *General Film Distributors*. *88 mins. Cert U*

Feeling he has nothing to live for when told his girlfriend Anna (*Mai Zetterling*) is dead, Simon (*Dirk Bogarde*) falsely confesses to murder and is sentenced to life. When Anna reappears, and he realizes the man who had told him she had died is the killer, Simon escapes, and, with Anna, tracks his quarry, now a Berlin racketeer, to earth. Takes some believing, doesn't it?

RoC *Albert Lieven, Philip Friend, Walter Rilla, Simone Silva, Frederick Wendhousen, Carl Jaffe, Gerard Heinz, André Mikhelson, Harold Ayer, Walter Gotell, Theodore Bikel, Friedrich Joloff, Ferdy Mayne, Antonio Gallardy, Paul Hardtmuth.*

DESTINATION MILAN (1954) [2]

Dir *Lawrence Huntington, Leslie Arliss, John Gilling*. Prod *Tom D. Connochie*. Scr *Lawrence Huntington and Robert Hall; Paul Vincent Carroll; Doreen Montgomery*. Ph *Jimmy Wilson, Ken Talbot, Brendan J. Stafford*. PC *Douglas Fairbanks Jr*. Dis *British Lion*. *78 mins. Cert U*

Three stories. (1) A rich American is saved by the guard on the Orient Express from a family of confidence tricksters. (2) Son and daughter of a miserly Scot and an Irish rogue respectively cannot get permission to marry until the skinflint is summoned for tax evasion and the Irishman rescues him. (3) A Norwegian artist murders his brother for money, but is trapped by his wife, who was his brother's mistress. TV-style stories lack character.

LP *Douglas Fairbanks Jr; Tommy Duggan, Lorraine Clewes, Christopher Lee, Paul Sheridan, Ann Stephens, Yusef Crandall; Cyril Cusack, John Laurie, Barbara Mullen; Greta Gynt, Peter Reynolds, John Horsley, Mary Merrall.*

DEVIL GIRL FROM MARS (1954) [3]

Dir *David Macdonald*. Prod *Edward J. Danziger, Harry Lee Danziger*. Scr *John C. Maher, James Eastwood, from their play*. Ph *Jack Cox*. PC *Danzigers*. Dis *British Lion*. *76 mins. Cert U*

Nyah (*Patricia Laffan*), a leader in the woman-dominated society of Mars, comes to Earth to take some men back to her planet. Landing (by error) in the Scottish Highlands, she enters a hotel and menaces the inhabitants,

who include an escaped convict (*Peter Reynolds*) being sheltered by the barmaid (*Adrienne Corri*). The convict goes with Nyah and a flash in the sky tells them he has blown up her spaceship. Talky science-fiction film runs like an early serial.

RoC *Hugh McDermott, Joseph Tomelty, Hazel Court, John Laurie, Sophie Stewart, Anthony Richmond, James Edmond, Stuart Hibberd* (voice).

DEVIL ON HORSEBACK (1954) [3]

Dir *Cyril Frankel*. Prod *John Grierson, Isobel Pargiter*. Scr *Neil Paterson, Montagu Slater, Geoffrey Orme*. Ph *Denny Densham*. PC *Group 3*. Dis *British Lion*. *89 mins. Cert U*

Miner's son Moppy Parfitt (*Jeremy Spenser*) proves a natural jockey, but develops a cruel and cynical streak and kills a failing horse by flogging it too hard; his subsequent suspension indirectly causes serious injury to fellow jockey Darky (*Sam Kydd*). A drunken ex-jockey, O'Hara (*Liam Redmond*) puts Moppy to rights, and he is actually sad when his skill sees him to victory against a recovered Darky on Moppy's old horse in a big race. Slow, atmospheric racing drama, well-acted; below-par racing sequences.

RoC *Googie Withers, John McCallum, Meredith Edwards, Vic Wise, George Rose, Malcolm Knight, Peter Lindsay, Eric Francis, Betty Hardy, Arthur Lovegrove, Harry Locke.*

DEVIL'S BAIT (1959) [4]

Dir *Peter Graham Scott*. Prod *Arthur Alcott*. Scr *Peter Johnston, Diana K. Watson*. Ph *Michael Reed*. PC *Independent Artists*. Dis *Rank*. *58 mins. Cert U*

A baker and his wife (*Geoffrey Keen, Jane Hylton*), not on the best of terms, hire an exterminator (*Dermot Kelly*) to rid their bakehouse of rats. Getting drunk after the job, he leaves cyanide dregs in the bottom of a tin which is later packed with dough. Picnickers buy the lethal loaf, and the hard but finally successful struggle to trace them in time draws the baker and his wife closer together. Distinctive, quite suspenseful little drama, with well-drawn characters.

RoC *Gordon Jackson, Eileen Moore, Shirley Lawrence, Molly Urquhart, Rupert Davies, Gillian Vaughan, Barbara Archer, Timothy Bateson, Noel Hood, Vivienne Bennett, Jack Stewart.*

THE DEVIL'S DISCIPLE (1959) [4]

Dir *Guy Hamilton*. Prod *Harold Hecht*. Scr *John Dighton, Roland Kibbee, from the play by George Bernard Shaw*. Ph *Jack Hildyard*. PC *Hecht-Hill-Lancaster/Brynaprod*. Dis *United Artists*. *83 mins. Cert U*

1777. Dick Dudgeon (*Kirk Douglas*), whose father was hanged by the British, is mistaken by them for the outspoken Parson Anderson (*Burt Lancaster*) and arrested. Meanwhile Anderson rides off to (successfully) help the American colonists fight a battle, before arriving at the gallows to save Dick from the hangman's rope. Unsuitably-cast slice of Shaw which mixes (good) action scenes uneasily with Shavian wit.

RoC *Janette Scott, Laurence Olivier, Eva Le*

Gallienne, Basil Sydney, Harry Andrews, George Rose, Neil McCallum, David Horne, Mervyn Johns, Erik Chitty, Jenny Jones.

THE DEVIL'S JEST (1954) [1]

Dir *Alfred Goulding*. Prod *Paul King*. Scr *Vance Uhden*. Ph *Hal Young*. PC *Terra Nova*. Dis *Equity British*. *61 mins. Cert A*

Scotland, in World War II. Following the deaths of two intelligence officers at a camp near a gloomy castle, MI5 investigates. Lady Enderby (*Mara [Russell-] Tavernan*) recognizes Major Seton (*Ivan Craig*) as her ex-lover, a German baron, and the father of her son. Trying to escape to a waiting U-boat, they are both shot. Remake of 1947's *Castle Sinister*, with the same star (but the emphasis in villainy shifted from Germany to Russia) and still as bad as ever.

RoC *Valentine Dyall, Derek Aylewood (Aylwood), Julian Sherrier, Lee Fox, Hamilton Keene.*

THE DEVIL'S PASS (1957) [2]

Dir, Scr and PC *Darcy Conyers*. Prod *David Henley*. Ph *S. D. Onions*. Dis *AB-Pathé*. *57 mins. Cert U*

Bill Buckle (*John Slater*), a handyman at an orphanage, dreams of regaining the fishing smack he was forced to sell. Learning that the present owners plan to scuttle the vessel for the insurance money, Bill gets aboard the abandoned boat and, with a boy stowaway (*Christopher Warbey*) steers her through rocks to safety, claiming salvage money and regaining the boat. Agreeable though most improbable. Shot at Brixham, Devon.

RoC *Joan Newell, Richard George, Archie Duncan, Charles Leno, Ewen Solon, Joy Rodgers.*

DEVIL'S POINT (1954) [2]
(USA: *Devil's Harbor*)

Dir *Montgomery Tully*. Prod, Scr and PC *Charles Deane*. Ph *Uncredited*. Dis *Monarch*. *65 mins. Cert U*

An American launch owner (*Richard Arlen*) accidentally comes into possession of some stolen cortisone, which the gang who stole it are desperate to recover. With the American's help, police trap the thieves' leader as Williams (*Vincent Ball*). The protagonists in the affair fight on top of an empty warehouse and Williams falls to his death. Very artificial thriller of little interest.

RoC *Greta Gynt, Donald Houston, Mary Germaine, Michael Balfour, Victor Baring, John Dunbar, John Lewis, Howard Lang, Anthony Viccars, Stella Andrews, Reginald Hearne, Doreen Halliday, Neil Gibson, Michael Mulcaster.*

DIAL 999 (1955) [4]
(USA: *The Way Out*)

Dir and Scr *Montgomery Tully, from the novel by Bruce Graeme*. Prod *Alec C. Snowden*. Ph *Philip Grindrod*. PC *Merton Park*. Dis *Anglo-Amalgamated*. *87 mins. Cert A*

Greg (*Gene Nelson*) tells his wife Terry (*Mona Freeman*) that he has accidentally killed a man in a fight. She and her brother (*Michael Goodliffe*) fight to get him out of the country by a criminals' escape route known as The Way

Gene Nelson and (background, in raincoat) John Bentley in Dial 999 *(1955)*

Out – even after she discovers that he really killed the man in cold blood. Freedom looks close until Greg panics; trapped by police, he runs in front of a bus. Seat-gripper thriller whose tension increases nicely.

RoC *John Bentley, Sydney Tafler, Charles Victor, Paula Byrne, Cyril Chamberlain, Arthur Lovegrove, Michael Golden, Tony Simpson, Jack MacNaughton, Charles Mortimer.*

THE DIAMOND (1954) [3]
(USA: *Diamond Wizard*)

Dir *Montgomery Tully.* Prod *Steven Pallos.* Scr *John C. Higgins, from a novel by Maurice Procter.* Ph *Arthur Grahame.* PC *Gibraltar.* Dis *United Artists.* 83 mins. Cert A

An American detective (*Dennis O'Keefe*), on the trail of bullion thieves, and a British police inspector (*Philip Friend*), hunting a vanished atom scientist, find their paths cross over a man making perfect synthetic diamonds. The crooks plan to buy them with their loot, and the process was invented by the scientist. The crooks are blown to pieces in their Kent castle HQ and the boffin rescued. Intricately developed thriller, though only the end is exciting. Originally made for 3D, but shown 'flat'.

RoC *Margaret Sheridan, Alan Wheatley, Ann Gudrun, Francis de Wolff, Eric Berry, Paul Hardtmuth, Colin Tapley, Donald Gray, Cyril Chamberlain, Hugh Morton, Gordon McLeod, Seymour Green, Paul Whitsun-Jones, Larry Burns, Michael Balfour, Don Cunningham, Victor Wood, Alastair Hunter.*

THE DIAMOND EXPERT (1955) [1]

Dir *David Macdonald.* Prod *Edward J. Danziger, Harry Lee Danziger.* Scr *Paul Tabori, Kate Barlay.* Ph *Jimmy Wilson.* PC *Danzigers.* Dis *United Artists.* 51 mins. Cert A

Two stories. (1) Phillips (*Paul Carpenter*), a wanted man, murders a diamond expert on board ship and assumes his identity. But it is the wrong identity – for he himself becomes the target for a killer. (2) A doctor (*Clifford Evans*) saves a man (*Lee Patterson*) from suicide, only to find the man trying to turn everyone against him – until the would-be suicide meets an accidental death. Very low-budget TV-originated stuff; not cinema material.

RoC *Ron Randell; Hugh Latimer, Leslie Linder; Mona Washbourne, Mary Parker.*

DICK BARTON AT BAY (1950) [2]

Dir *Godfrey Grayson.* Prod *Henry Halstead.* Scr *Ambrose Grayson, from a radio serial by Edward J. Mason.* Ph *Stanley Clinton.* PC *Marylebone/Hammer.* Dis *Exclusive.* 68 mins. Cert U

Police call in detective Dick Barton (*Don Stannard*) to look into the disappearance of a scientist and his daughter and the theft of a death ray, invented by the scientist. They have been kidnapped by Volkoff (*Meinhart Maur*), a sinister foreign agent, who imprisons them in a lighthouse at Beachy Head. Dick and the police trace and rescue them. The end of the line for Dick: strictly for younger schoolboys.

RoC *Tamara Desni, Percy Walsh, George Ford, Joyce Linden, Campbell Singer, John Arnatt, Richard George, Beatrice Kane, Patrick Macnee, George Crawford, Fred Owen, Paddy Ryan, Yoshihide Yanai, Ted Butterfield.*

THE DIPLOMATIC CORPSE (1958) [3]

Dir *Montgomery Tully.* Prod *Francis Searle.* Scr *Sidney Nelson, Maurice Harrison.* Ph *Phil Grindrod.* PC *ACT Films.* Dis *Rank.* 65 mins. Cert U

A foreign embassy in London is being used as the front for drug trafficking. Both reporters Billings (*Robin Bailey*) and Jenny (*Susan Shaw*) and Inspector Corcoran (*Liam Redmond*) come up against the problem of diplomatic immunity, but when Jenny proves too nosy and is kidnapped and held at the embassy, it gives the reporter and policeman the chance to use a ruse which both rescues Jenny and cracks the ring. Thriller with a sense of humour.

RoC *Harry Fowler, Maya Koumani, André Mikhelson, Bill Shine, Charles Farrell, Peter Bathurst, Johnny Briggs, Frank Hawkins, George Street, Nicholas Bruce.*

DIPLOMATIC PASSPORT (1954) [1]

Dir *Gene Martel.* Prod *Martel, Burt Balaban.* Scr *Paul Tabori.* Ph *James Wilson.* PC *Rich and Rich.* Dis *Eros.* 66 mins. Cert U

An American diplomat (*Paul Carpenter*) and his wife (*Marsha Hunt*) arrive in London and fall into the hands of international crooks, who use them as dupes in their smuggling activities. When they realize it, they are kidnapped, but the diplomat succeeds in escaping and alerting the police, who capture the gang. Visiting American Miss Hunt is more talented than most, but stands no chance against this plot, with its funny fight scenes and speeded-up chases.

RoC *Henry Oscar, Honor Blackman, Marne Maitland, John MacLaren, Henry Longhurst, John Welsh, David Conville.*

DISTANT TRUMPET (1952) [2]

Dir *Terence Fisher.* Prod *Derek Elphinstone, Harold Richmond.* Scr *Elphinstone.* Ph *Gordon Lang.* PC *Meridian.* Dis *Apex.* 63 mins. Cert U

In London to launch an appeal for his medical mission in Africa, Richard (*Derek Elphinstone*) is unfit to return, and takes over his doctor brother's (*Derek Bond*) rich practice, giving wealthy patients with imaginary illnesses short shrift. The young doctor has gone to Africa in Richard's place. When Richard is fit, he goes to Africa married to his brother's secretary (*Jean Patterson*) and they go into partnership. So poorly acted it loses one's interest.

RoC *Anne Brooke, Grace Gavin (Gaven), Keith Pyott, Jean Webster-Brough, Grace Denbigh-Russell, Constance Fraser, Alban Blakelock, John Howlett, Peter Fontaine, Gwynne Whitby, Anne Hunter.*

THE DIVIDED HEART (1954) [5]

Dir *Charles Crichton.* Prod *Michael Truman.* Scr *Jack Whittingham.* Ph *Otto Heller.* PC *Ealing Studios.* Dis *General Film Distributors.* 89 mins. Cert U

A 10-year-old war orphan (*Michel Ray*) becomes the centre of a court battle when his real mother (*Yvonne Mitchell*), having suffered terribly in the war, is found to be alive. His foster-parents (*Cornell Borchers, Armin Dahlen*) fight to keep him, and the boy wants to stay with them, but, after an emotive hearing, a majority decision hands him back to his real mother. Poignant drama was a great critical hit, less successful with the paying public.

RoC *Alexander Knox, Geoffrey Keen, Eddie Byrne, Liam Redmond, Theodore Bikel, Ferdy Mayne, André Mikhelson, Pamela Stirling, Martin Stephens, Martin Keller, Krystyna Rumistrzewicz, Mark Guebhard, Gilgi Hauser, Maria Leontovitsch, Marianne Walla, Dorit Welles, Hans Kuhn, Philo Hauser, Guy Stephen Deghy, Carl Duering, Dora Lavrencic, Richard Molinas, John Welsh, John Schlesinger, Nicholas Stuart, Hans Elwenspoek, Frederick Schrecker, Alec McCowen, Orest Orloff, Ilona Ference, Randal Kinkead, Arthur Cortez.*

DOCTOR AT LARGE (1957) [4]

Dir *Ralph Thomas.* Prod *Betty E. Box.* Scr *Nicholas Phipps, Richard Gordon, from Gordon's novel.* Ph *Ernest Steward.* PC and Dis *Rank.* Eastman Colour. VistaVision. 104 mins. Cert U

Third film in the 'doctor' series. Simon Sparrow (*Dirk Bogarde*) loses the post of house surgeon to a rival, takes a junior partnership in a country practice, but is forced to flee from his partner's amorous wife. In Harley Street, he deals with the rich, then goes on a Riviera spree with his colleague Benskin (*Donald Sinden*) who has come into money. Back at St Swithin's, where he started, he is offered a post as surgeon after all. Corny-copia of medical jokes raises quite a few laughs.

RoC *Muriel Pavlow, James Robertson Justice, Derek Farr, Michael Medwin, Shirley Eaton, Edward Chapman, George Coulouris, Gladys Henson, Anne Heywood, Lionel Jeffries, Mervyn Johns, Geoffrey Keen, Dilys Laye, A. E. Matthews, Guy Middleton, Barbara Murray, Nicholas Phipps, Frederick Piper, George Relph, Athene Seyler, Ernest Thesiger, Noel Purcell, Ernest Jay, Junia Crawford, Freda Bamford, Abe Barker, Martin Benson, Cyril Chamberlain, John Chandos, Peggyann Clifford, Campbell Cotts, Judith Furse, Harry Locke, Terence Longdon, Nicholas Phipps, Donald Pickering, Wensley Pithey, Maureen Pryor, Carol Richmond, Beth Rogan, Barbara Roscoe, Jean St Clair, Ronnie Stevens, Michael Trubshawe, Molly Urquhart.*

DOCTOR AT SEA (1955)   [4]

Dir *Ralph Thomas*. Prod *Betty Box*. Scr *Nicholas Phipps, Jack Davies, Richard Gordon, from Gordon's book*. Ph *Ernest Steward*. PC *Group/J. Arthur Rank*. Dis *Rank*. Technicolor. VistaVision. 93 mins. Cert U

Young doctor Simon Sparrow (*Dirk Bogarde*) signs as medical officer on a cargo steamer, falls foul of the captain (*James Robertson Justice*) and lands in jail after a drunken revel on arrival in South America. Two new passengers, Muriel (*Brenda de Banzie*), daughter of the shipping-line owner, and Hélène (*Brigitte Bardot*), a singer, pursue the captain and Simon amid further misadventures. Often amusing series of gags threaded together as a successor to *Doctor in the House*.

RoC *Maurice Denham, Michael Medwin, Hubert Gregg, Geoffrey Keen, James Kenney, Jill Adams, Raymond Huntley, Joan Sims, George Coulouris, Noel Purcell, Toke Townley, Cyril Chamberlain, Abe Barker, Thomas Heathcote, Frederick Piper, Michael Shepley, Felix Felton, Joan Hickson, Eugene Deckers, Mary Laura Wood, Ekali Solou, Martin Benson, Harold Kasket, Stuart Saunders, Paul Carpenter*.

Brigitte Bardot and Dirk Bogarde in Doctor at Sea *(1955)*

DOCTOR IN THE HOUSE (1954)   [4]

Dir *Ralph Thomas*. Prod *Betty Box*. Scr *Nicholas Phipps, Richard Gordon, from Gordon's novel*. Ph *Ernest Steward*. PC *Group*. Dis *General Film Distributors*. Technicolor. 91 mins. Cert U

Four medical students, Sparrow (*Dirk Bogarde*), Grimsdyke (*Kenneth More*), Benskin (*Donald Sinden*) and Taffy (*Donald Houston*) get into an incredible series of scrapes in their bids to become doctors. In the final exams, Sparrow and Taffy pass, while Benskin and Grimsdyke – not for the first time – fail. Catalogue of venerable medical jokes trotted out like new in this enormously successful comedy, the top British moneymaker of its year; several sequels followed.

RoC *Muriel Pavlow, James Robertson Justice, Kay Kendall, Suzanne Cloutier, Geoffrey Keen, George Coulouris, Jean Taylor-Smith, Harry Locke, Ann Gudrun, Joan Sims, Shirley Eaton, Nicholas Phipps, Amy Veness, Richard Wattis, Maureen Pryor, Geoffrey Sumner, Lisa Gastoni, Shirley Burniston, Joan Hickson, George Benson, Martin Boddey, Cyril Chamberlain, Ernest Clark, Mark Dignam, Eliot Makeham, Felix*

Felton, *Wyndham Goldie, Douglas Ives, Anthony Marlowe, Brian Oulton, Mona Washbourne*.

THE DOCTOR'S DILEMMA (1958)   [3]

Dir *Anthony Asquith*. Prod and Scr *Anatole de Grunwald, from the play by George Bernard Shaw*. Ph *Robert Krasker*. PC *Comet*. Dis *M-G-M*. 99 mins. Cert U

1900. Sir Colenso (*John Robinson*), inventor of a new treatment for TB, must decide whether to take on Dubedat (*Dirk Bogarde*), an artist of wayward genius, or Blenkinsop (*Michael Gwynn*), a dull doctor. He is struck by Dubedat's wife Jennifer (*Leslie Caron*), but discovers they are not married. After Dubedat steals a cigarette case at a party, Colenso refuses to treat him; he dies soon afterwards. Jennifer refuses Colenso's offer of marriage. Quiet drama, shorn of original satire, not really strong enough for full-length film.

RoC *Alastair Sim, Robert Morley, Felix Aylmer, Maureen Delany, Alec McCowen, Colin Gordon, Terence Alexander, Gwenda Ewen, Derek Prentice, Peter Sallis, Clifford Buckton*.

THE DOG AND THE DIAMONDS (1953)   [4]

Dir *Ralph Thomas*. Prod *Peter Rogers*. Scr *Patricia Latham*. Ph *Gordon Lang*. PC *London Independent/Children's Film Foundation*. Dis *Associated British*. 55 mins. Cert U

Forbidden to keep pets in their council flats, a gang of children haunts the local pet store run by Mrs Fossett (*Kathleen Harrison*). They turn the large garden of a deserted mansion into a menagerie, little realizing that the place houses a gang of jewel thieves, who are caught as a result of the children's activities. Good children's film, a prizewinner at the Venice festival.

RoC *George Coulouris, Geoffrey Sumner, Brian Oulton, Michael McGuire, Robert Sandford, Robert Scroggins, Barbara Brown, Molly Osborne, Hal Osmond, Arthur Lane, Dennis Wyndham*.

DON GIOVANNI (1955)   [3]

Dir and Prod *Paul Czinner, Alfred Travers*. Ph *S.D. Onions*. PC *Harmony*. Dis *Maxwell*. Eastman Colour. 170 mins. Cert U

A straightforward record of Mozart's opera, as performed at the 1954 Salzburg Festival, on a wide open-air stage. A valuable memento of the occasion, although not cinema, and such shortcomings as there are in the performance are highlighted by the approach.

LP *Cesare Siepi, Elizabeth Grümmer, Lisa della Casa, Anton Dermots, Otto Edelmann, Erna Berger, Walter Berry, Deszo Ernster*. Conductor: *Dr Wilhelm Furtwängler*.

DON'T BLAME THE STORK (1953)   [2]

Dir *Akos Rathony*. Prod *David Dent, Victor Katona*. Scr *Wolfgang Wilhelm, Talbot Rothwell, Katona*. PC *Advance/Objective*. Dis *Adelphi*. 80 mins. Cert A

When a Shakespearean actor (*Ian Hunter*) says he loves babies, he soon finds one on his doorstep. To be near him, Katie O'Connor (*Veronica Hurst*) says it's hers, which annoys the

actor's fiancée (*Patricia Laffan*). Though Katie's deception is rumbled, she gets her man in the end, and the baby goes back to its rightful mother. Capable players caught in very low farce.

RoC *Reginald Beckwith, Thora Hird, Howard Marion Crawford, Mark Daly, Avril Angers, Brenda de Banzie, Harry Fowler*.

DON'T PANIC CHAPS! (1959)   [2]

Dir *George Pollock*. Prod *Teddy Baird*. Scr *Jack Davies, from the radio play by Michael Corston, Ronald Holroyd*. Ph *Arthur Graham*. PC *ACT/Hammer*. Dis *Columbia*. 84 mins. Cert U

British and German army units, forgotten by their respective commands, sit out World War II on a small Adriatic island in a state of mutual armistice. Then a glamorous Italian castaway (*Nadja Regin*) is washed ashore and hostilities resume almost at once. British and German submarines eventually take off the now warring troops. Opportunities for satirical comedy are largely missed in this damp farce, originally called *Carry on Chaps!*, but changed for obvious reasons.

RoC *George Cole, Dennis Price, Thorley Walters, Harry Fowler, Nicholas Phipps, Percy Herbert, George Murcell, Gertan Klauber, Terence Alexander, Thomas Foulkes*.

DON'T SAY DIE (1950)   [2]

Dir *Vivian Milroy*. Prod *Milroy, Margot Lovell*. Scr *Dido and Vivian Milroy*. Ph *James Wilson*. PC *International/X Films*. Dis *Independent Film Distributors*. 61 mins. Cert U

Despite a blonde (*Sandra Dorne*) hiding in his trunk while her husband ransacks the flat, rakish Bertie (*Desmond Walter-Ellis*) is able to satisfy lawyers that he is a paragon of virtue, and thereby inherit the title Lord Blarney. Unfortunately this brings with it an Irish castle being used by smugglers. But Bertie drives them off and flees back to England with their spoils. Briefly released as *Never Say Die*, this Jeeves-type farce begins well, but tails off.

RoC *Charles Heslop, Tony Quinn, Constance Smith, Stanley Rose, Derek Tansley, Thomas Gallagher, Kenneth Connor, Raymond Rollett, Michael Raghan, Harry Lane, Denis McCarthy*.

DOUBLE CONFESSION (1950)   [2]

Dir *Ken Annakin*. Prod and PC *Harry Reynolds*. Scr *William Templeton, Ralph Keene, from a novel by John Garden*. Ph *Geoffrey Unsworth*. Dis *AB-Pathé*. 85 mins. Cert A

Jim (*Derek Farr*), a disillusioned war veteran, comes to the coast to see his estranged wife and finds her dead. Following a false confession of murder, he sets out to kill his wife's lover, or frame him for murder. He becomes involved with the real killers, who make attempts on his life. Inspector Tenby (*Naunton Wayne*) steps in and clears up the affair. Thriller seems to have bewildered most reviewers: one remarked that it told him more about Bexhill and Hastings than its own plot.

RoC *Peter Lorre, William Hartnell, Kathleen Harrison, Joan Hopkins, Ronald Howard, Leslie Dwyer, Henry Edwards, Vida Hope, George Woodbridge, Esma Cannon, Mona Washbourne,*

William Hartnell, Peter Lorre (dead) and Naunton Wayne in Double Confession (*1950*)

Jennifer Cross, Andrew Leigh, Fred Griffiths, Diana Connell, Jane Griffiths, Hal Osmond, Roy Plomley, Norman Astridge, Betty Nelson, Sidney Vivian.

DOUBLE CROSS (1956)   [2]
Dir *Anthony Squire.* Prod *Donald Taylor.* Scr *Squire, Kem Bennett, from a novel by Bennett.* Ph *Kenneth Talbot.* PC *Beaconsfield.* Dis *British Lion. 71 mins. Cert U*
Fisherman-cum-salmon poacher Albert Pascoe (*Donald Houston*) accepts a large sum of money to get three people across the English Channel. Warned by the female member (*Delphi Lawrence*) of the trio that they are enemy agents and his life is in danger, Albert strands the men in a cove. He returns with the girl to a hero's welcome – but narrowly escapes prosecution for poaching. Comedy-thriller delivers neither element.
RoC *Fay Compton, Anton Diffring, William Hartnell, Allan Cuthbertson, John Blythe, Frank Lawton, Ann Stephens, Harry Towb, Gene Anderson, Raymond Francis, Robert Shaw, Bruce Gordon, Helena Pickard, Toby Perkins.*

DOUBLE EXPOSURE (1954)   [2]
Dir and Scr *John Gilling.* Prod *Robert S. Baker, Monty Berman.* Ph *Berman.* PC *Kenilworth-Mid-Century.* Dis *General Film Distributors. 63 mins. Cert U*
Hired to find a missing girl, detective Pete Fleming (*John Bentley*) finds that his employer is only interested in finding the girl because she took some photographs of his house at the time of his wife's 'suicide'. It transpires she was pushed from a window by a man who now kills the husband and tries to shoot the girl photographer (*Rona Anderson*) before Fleming intervenes. Good premise, but thriller becomes less convincing as it progresses.
RoC *Garry Marsh, Alexander Gauge, Ingeborg Wells, Ryck Rydon, Frank Forsythe, John Horsley, Sally Newton, Alan Robinson.*

DOUBLE JEOPARDY (1955)   [1]
Dir *John Guillermin.* Prod *Michael Sadleir.* Scr *Ernest Borneman.* Ph *Geoffrey Faithfull.* PC *Mid-Ocean.* Dis *Eros. 56 mins. Cert A*
Two adventures of Mitch (*Lorne Greene*), skipper of the trading vessel *Shipwreck*, operating off North Africa. He helps a nationalist leader regain his rightful place, then sails to Tangiers, where he has to clear his engineer (*Michael Balfour*) of a murder charge. Innocuous TV adventures, hardly suitable for the larger screen.
RoC *Frederick Valk, Paul Carpenter, Michael Goodliffe, Alec Mango, Jacques Brunius, Sheila Burrell, Andrea Malandrinos.*

DOWN AMONG THE Z MEN (1952)   [3]
Dir *Maclean Rogers.* Prod and PC *E. J. Fancey.* Scr *Jimmy Grafton, Francis Charles.* Ph *Geoffrey Faithfull. New Realm. 71 mins. Cert U*
Harry Jones (*Harry Secombe*), grocer, 'Z' army reservist and amateur detective, trails mad Professor Pureheart (*Michael Bentine*), who has invented an atomic formula, to an army camp. Jones gets conscripted and in the way of a female MI5 agent (*Carole Carr*), as well as tangling with a gang of crooks, before preventing the formula from falling into enemy hands. Crazy comedy with musical interludes introduces 'Goons'; could have done with their radio scriptwriters.
RoC *Peter Sellers, Spike Milligan, Robert Cawdron, Graham Stark, Andrew Timothy, Elizabeth Kearns, Miriam Karlin, Eunice Gayson, Jane Morrison, The Television Toppers, Richard Turner, Judy Horton, Adrienne Scott.*

DRACULA (1958)   [4]
(USA: *Horror of Dracula*)
Dir *Terence Fisher.* Prod *Anthony Hinds.* Scr *Jimmy Sangster, from the novel by Bram Stoker.* Ph *Jack Asher.* PC *Hammer.* Dis *Rank/Universal-International. Eastman Colour. 81 mins. Cert X*
Transylvania in the 19th century. Working for Count Dracula (*Christopher Lee*) as librarian, Jonathan Harker (*John Van Eyssen*) is bitten by a vampire woman and finished off by Dracula himself. Harker's colleague, Dr Van Helsing (*Peter Cushing*) releases his soul, enraging Dracula, who vampirizes Harker's fiancée (*Carol Marsh*) and sister Mina (*Melissa Stribling*). Van Helsing saves Mina from complete destruction, then does battle with the Count, finally catching him in a shaft of sunlight which disintegrates him. Scary, plushly made new version of classic horror, oozing with atmosphere; brilliant special effects were much copied.
RoC *Michael Gough, Olga Dickie, Valerie*

Melissa Stribling and Christopher Lee in Dracula (*1958*)

Gaunt, Geoffrey Bayldon, Paul Cole, Miles Malleson, Charles Lloyd Pack, Janina Faye, George Woodbridge, Barbara Archer, George Benson, Guy Mills, George Merritt, William Sherwood, John Mossman, Stedwell Fletcher, Judith Nelmes, Humphrey Kent, Dick Morgan.

THE DRAGON OF PENDRAGON
CASTLE (1950)   [2]
Dir and Prod *John Baxter.* Scr *Mary Cathcart Borer.* Ph *Arthur Grant.* PC *Elstree Independent.* Dis *General Film Distributors. 52 mins. Cert U*
Peter, Judy and Bobby live in a castle. Their aristocratic but hard-up grandfather takes in paying guests. One day, while collecting wood on the beach, the children meet a young sea-dragon. They take him to the cold castle where, from his hideout in the dungeon, the dragon breathes out enough fire and smoke to heat the whole place. He also frightens some nasties, and uncovers buried treasure before returning to the sea. Rudimentary children's film, okay for tinies.
LP *Robin Netscher, Hilary Rennie, Jane Welsh, J. Hubert Moffatt, David Hannaford, Leslie Bradley, C. Denier Warren, Lily Lapidus, David Miller, Anne Blake, Suzanne Gibbs.*

DRY ROT (1956)   [2]
Dir *Maurice Elvey.* Prod *Jack Clayton.* Scr *John Chapman, from his play.* Ph *Arthur Grant.* PC *Romulus/Remus.* Dis *Independent Film Distributors/British Lion. 87 mins. Cert U*
To revive their flagging fortunes, three bookmakers, Alf (*Ronald Shiner*), Fred (*Brian Rix*) and Flash Harry (*Sidney James*) aim to fix a race, but the doped horse they want to substitute for the favourite is overdoped and Fred is forced to take the place of the favourite's jockey. It still wins, and the hapless trio exit left, pursued by the law. Amazingly bungled version of runaway stage farce; very slow.
RoC *Peggy Mount, Heather Sears, Lee Patterson, Joan Sims, Michael Shepley, Joan Haythorne, John Chapman, Joan Benham, Christian Duvaleix, Miles Malleson, Raymond Glendenning, Shirley Ann Field.*

DUBLIN NIGHTMARE (1958)   [3]
Dir *John Pomeroy.* Prod *Jon Penington, David Eady.* Scr *John Tully.* Ph *Eric Cross.* PC *Penington-Eady.* Dis *Rank. 64 mins. Cert U*
John (*William Sylvester*), a photographer, arrives in Dublin for a reunion with his wartime friend Steve (*Richard Leech*), to be told that Steve was killed in a car accident. Steve's girl Anna (*Marla Landi*), who thinks he was murdered, reveals that he was part of a terrorist group. Finally Steve proves to be alive, but is shot down by his own organisation as an embezzler and a traitor. Irish version of *The Third Man.* The two critics who wrote 'sluggish' and 'moves with swift sense of purpose' might have been reviewing two different films.
RoC *William Sherwood, Harry Hutchinson, Jack Cunningham, Pat O'Sullivan, Paddy Hayes, Helen Lindsay, Richard Curnoch, Anne Blake, Dermot Kelly, Peddy Joyce, Gerald C. Lawson.*

DUEL IN THE JUNGLE (1954) [3]

Dir *George Marshall*. Prod *Marcel Hellman*. Scr *Sam Marx, T. J. Morrison*. Ph *Erwin Hillier*. PC *Associated British*. Dis *AB-Pathé*. Technicolor. 102 mins. Cert U

Adventurer Perry Henderson (*David Farrar*) fakes his own suicide and disappears into the African jungle, planning to dive for diamonds in coastal waters on the proceeds of a fat insurance policy. His fiancée (*Jeanne Crain*) arrives, but the man (*Dana Andrews*) who travels with her is an insurance investigator and Henderson, unwittingly giving the game away, consequently tries to kill them both. He fails. Nothing if not lively, but light on credibility. Assistant director Tony Kelly was killed in the making of the film.

RoC *Patrick Barr, George Coulouris, Charles Goldner, Wilfrid Hyde White, Mary Merrall, Heather Thatcher, Michael Mataka, Paul Carpenter, Delphi Lawrence, Mary Mackenzie, Bea Duffell, Alec Finter, Patrick Parnell, John Salew, Walter Gotell, Charles Carson, Bill Fraser, Lionel Ngakane, Robert Sansom*.

THE DUKE WORE JEANS (1958) [4]

Dir *Gerald Thomas*. Prod *Peter Rogers*. Scr *Norman Hudis, from a story by Lionel Bart, Michael Pratt*. Ph *Otto Heller*. PC and Dis *Anglo-Amalgamated*. 90 mins. Cert U

Married without his parents' knowledge, the Hon. Tony Whitecliffe (*Tommy Steele*) is horrified when they ask him to woo a European princess (they're after her money). He sends his cockney double, Tommy (also *Steele*) in his place. The princess (*June Laverick*) takes an initially dim view of it all, but falls for Tommy, who wins over the court by proving he is a prince – his parents being a Pearly King and Queen. Steele sees silly but happy story through; good songs too.

RoC *Michael Medwin, Eric Pohlmann, Alan Wheatley, Mary Kerridge, Ambrosine Phillpotts, Clive Morton, Noel Hood, Arnold Daimond, Elwyn Brook-Jones, Philip Leaver, Susan Travers, Cyril Chamberlain*.

DUNKIRK (1958) [4]

Dir *Leslie Norman*. (Associate) Prod *Michael Forlong*. Scr *W. P. Lipscomb, David Divine, from books by Ewan Butler and Selby Bradford, and by Elleston Trevor*. Ph *Paul Beeson*. PC *Ealing Films*. Dis *M-G-M*. 134 mins. Cert U

Cut off from their unit in 1940 in the retreat to the French coast, a group of British soldiers led by Cpl Binns (*John Mills*) fights and dodges its way back to Dunkirk. Here they meet Holden (*Richard Attenborough*), a garageman, and Foreman (*Bernard Lee*), a reporter, who are among hundreds of small-boat owners evacuating British troops. Foreman is killed but, after a hair-raising breakdown at sea, Binns and Holden get away. Carefully made; exciting in a routine way; a bit disappointing.

RoC *Patricia Plunkett, Maxine Audley, Robert Urquhart, Ray Jackson, Ronald Hines, Sean Barrett, Roland Curran, Meredith Edwards, Eddie Byrne, Lionel Jeffries, Victor Maddern, Rodney Diak, Michael Shillo, Bud Flanagan, Chesney Allen, Michael Gwynn, Kenneth Cope, Joss Ambler, Frederick Piper, William Squire,*

Harry Landis, Anthony Nicholls, Denys Graham, Barry Foster, Nicholas Hannen, Michael Bates, Christopher Rhodes, John Horsley, Patrick Allen, Cyril Raymond, Warwick Ashton, Peter Halliday, Lloyd Lamble, Fred Griffiths, Dan Cressy, Bernard Cribbins.

DUST AND GOLD (1955) [2]

Dir *John Guillermin*. Prod *Michael Sadleir*. Scr *Lindsay Galloway, Knight Hassler*. Ph *Geoffrey Faithfull*. PC *Mid-Ocean*. Dis *Eros*. 64 mins. Cert U

Two adventures of Mitch (*Lorne Greene*), the itinerant skipper of a trading ship. In Italy, he has trouble with a lovely teenager (*Jackie Lane*), before getting her to the dustman she really loves. In Egypt, he clashes with an international thief, and restores a priceless artefact to a museum. TV episodes of *Sailor of Fortune* issued as a film. Not too bad but hardly cinema.

RoC *Paul Carpenter, Eric Pohlmann, Ferdy Mayne, Harold Kasket, Reginald Beckwith, Anna Valentina, Michael Balfour, Bruno Barnabe, Andrea Malandrinos, Michael Mellinger, Michael Macguire, Jack MacGowran, Lisa Gastoni, Marne Maitland, John Cazabon, John Salew, Jean Muir*.

E

EIGHT O'CLOCK WALK (1953) [3]

Dir *Lance Comfort*. Prod *George King*. Scr *Katherine Strueby, Guy Morgan*. Ph *Brendan Stafford*. PC *British Aviation/George King Productions*. Dis *British Lion*. 87 mins. Cert A

A taxi-driver (*Richard Attenborough*) is accused of murdering an eight-year-old girl. His wife (*Cathy O'Donnell*) firmly believes him innocent, but the evidence is damning and the case looks lost until counsel for the defence (*Derek Farr*) seizes on a sweet as the vital clue to unmask the real murderer. Promising suspense situation not credibly written, although sturdily acted.

RoC *Maurice Denham, Ian Hunter, Bruce Seton, Lilly Kann, Harry Welchman, Kynaston Reeves, Eithne Dunne, David Hannaford, Cheryl Molyneaux, Totti Truman Taylor, Robert Adair, Grace Arnold, Sally Stephens, Vernon Kelso, Robert Sydney, Max Brimmell, Humphrey Morton, Arthur Hewlett, Philip King, Jean St Clair, Enid Hewitt, Noel Dyson, Dorothy Darke, Bartlett Mullins, Sue Thackeray*.

THE ELUSIVE PIMPERNEL (1950) [2]
(USA: *The Fighting Pimpernel*)

Dir and Scr *Michael Powell, Emeric Pressburger, from a novel by Baroness Orczy*. Prod *Samuel Goldwyn, Alexander Korda*. Ph *Christopher Challis*. PC *London Films/The Archers*. Dis *British Lion*. Technicolor. 109 mins. Cert U

Jack Hawkins, Peter Copley and David Niven in The Elusive Pimpernel (*1950*)

The 1790s. Foppish Englishman Sir Percy Blakeney (*David Niven*) is the secret leader of a league planning to rescue French aristocrats from the guillotine. Chauvelin (*Cyril Cusack*) works on Percy's wife Marguerite's (*Margaret Leighton*) fears for her brother's safety and persuades her to help him trap the Pimpernel. Realizing it is Percy, she goes to France to warn him, but is captured by Chauvelin. Percy agrees to exchange his life for hers, but by a ruse they trick Chauvelin and escape to England. Perfect casting and credits somehow result in weak and bloodless film.

RoC *Jack Hawkins, Robert Coote, Edmond Audran, Danielle Godet, Arlette Marchal, Gérard Nery, Charles Victor, David Hutcheson, Eugene Deckers, John Longden, Arthur Wontner, David Oxley, Raymond Rollett, Philip Stainton, Robert Griffiths, George de Warfaz, Jane Gill-Davis, Richard George, Cherry Cottrell, John Fitzgerald, Patrick Macnee, Terence Alexander, Tommy Duggan, John Fitchen, John Hewitt, Hugh Kelly, Richmond Nairne, Sally Newland, Peter Copley*.

THE EMBEZZLER (1954) [3]

Dir and Scr *John Gilling*. Prod *Robert S. Baker, Monty Berman*. Ph *Jonah Jones*. PC *Kenilworth-Mid-Century*. Dis *General Film Distributors*. 61 mins. Cert A

Told he has only a short time to live, failed bank clerk Henry Paulson (*Charles Victor*) robs his own bank but is caught in the act. He flees to the coast, where he is befriended by the young bride (*Zena Marshall*) of a doctor, and saves her from the blackmailing attentions of a former lover, at the cost of his own life.

Zena Marshall and Charles Victor in The Embezzler (*1954*)

Victor's performance in Eliot Makeham/Edmund Gwenn style is redeeming feature of ingenuous drama.

RoC *Cyril Chamberlain, Leslie Weston, Avice Landone, Peggy Mount, Michael Gregson, Frank Forsyth, Patrick Jordan, Martin Wyldeck, Olive Kirby, Tony Lennon, Chris Bank, Lesley Carol (Carole Lesley), Phyllis Morris, Sam Kydd, Alastair Hunter, Dennis Chinnery, Ronnie Stevens, Ian Fleming, Michael Craig.*

EMERGENCY CALL (1952)   4
(USA: *Hundred Hour Hunt*)
Dir *Lewis Gilbert*. Prod *Ernest G. Roy*. Scr *Gilbert, Vernon Harris*. Ph *Wilkie Cooper, Dudley Lovell*. PC *Nettlefold*. Dis *Butchers*. 90 mins. Cert U

To find rare blood needed to save a little girl's life, the hospital authorities, aided by Scotland Yard, launch a nationwide hunt. A black stoker (*Earl Cameron*), a boxer (*Freddie Mills*) and a man on the run (*Sydney Tafler*) are found to be the only three with the child's rare blood group. All three have to be persuaded but, after the criminal is trapped, the last few pints of the precious liquid are secured. Economical thriller keeps going quite well.

RoC *Jack Warner, Anthony Steel, Joy Shelton, Sidney James, Eric Pohlmann, John Robinson, Henry Hewitt, Geoffrey Hibbert, Thora Hird, Avis Scott, Vida Hope, Peggy Bryan, Bruce Seton, Anna Turner, Fred Powell, Campbell Singer, Nigel Clarke, Michael Brennan, Anthony Oliver, Duncan Lamont, Arthur Lovegrove, Richard Gale, Dandy Nichols, Jennifer Tafler, Carman Manley, Michael Ward, Iris Vandeleur, Phil Ray, Peter Swanwick, Graham Stark, Freda Bamford, Hazel Sutton, Eric Davies, Ed Powell, Derek Prentice, Pat Hagate.*

ENCORE (1951)   4
Dir *Harold French, Pat Jackson, Anthony Pelissier*. Prod *Antony Darnborough*. Scr *T.E.B. Clarke, Arthur Macrae, Eric Ambler, from stories by W. Somerset Maugham*. Ph *Desmond Dickinson*. PC *Two Cities/Paramount British*. Dis *General Film Distributors*. 86 mins. Cert A

Three short stories. (1) Smooth con-man Tom (*Nigel Patrick*) triumphs over his hard-working brother (*Roland Culver*); (2) a garrulous spinster (*Kay Walsh*) bores the pants off everyone on a winter cruise, is almost outwitted by the captain's scheme, but still gets the last word; (3) a daredevil high-diver (*Glynis Johns*) who plunges nightly into a blazing tank loses then regains her nerve. Generally entertaining mixture.

RoC *Alison Leggatt, Charles Victor, Peter Graves, Margaret Vyner, Margaret Withers, Dorothy Bramhall, Patricia Raine, Campbell Cotts, Michael Trubshawe, Noel Purcell, Ronald Squire, John Laurie, Jacques François, John Horsley, Joan Harben, Brenda Hogan, Vincent Ball, Carol Wolveridge, John Warren, Terence Morgan, David Hutcheson, Charles Goldner, Mary Merrall, Heather Thatcher, Daphne Barker, Martin Miller, Guido Lorraine, Ferdy Mayne, Guy du Monceau, John Boxer.*

THE END OF THE AFFAIR (1954)   4
Dir *Edward Dmytryk*. Prod *David Lewis, David E. Rose*. Scr *Lenore Coffee, from the novel by Graham Greene*. Ph *Wilkie Cooper*. PC *Coronado*. Dis *Columbia*. 104 mins. Cert A

A passionate wartime affair develops between Bendrix (*Van Johnson*) and Sarah (*Deborah Kerr*), wife of a civil servant (*Peter Cushing*). In a bombing raid, Bendrix is seemingly killed, and only when Sarah vows in prayer (to a God in Whom she has never believed) that she will never see him again if he lives, does he miraculously recover. She keeps her vow until her death, a few months later, from pneumonia. Her last letter tells Bendrix all and gives him strength to face the future. Carefully made epic love-story - quite touching; but lacks the spark of passion.

RoC *John Mills, Stephen Murray, Nora Swinburne, Charles Goldner, Michael Goodliffe, Joyce Carey, Frederick Leister, Mary Williams, Elsie Wagstaff, Christopher Warbey, Nan Munro, Josephine Wilson, O'Donovan Shiell, Shela Ward, Stanley Rose, Robert Gregory.*

THE END OF THE LINE (1957)   2
Dir *Charles Saunders*. Prod *Guido Coen*. Scr *Paul Erickson*. Ph *Walter J. Harvey*. PC *Fortress*. Dis *Eros*. 66 mins. Cert A

With the help of an intricate alibi involving a fake phone call, cooked up by his mistress Liliane (*Barbara Shelley*), Mike (*Alan Baxter*) robs Crawford (*Arthur Gomez*), a 'fence', of a fortune in stolen jewels. Crawford is found dead, and Liliane and Mike are blackmailed. Mike decides to give himself up and thereby learns that *he* was the victim - of a plot between Liliane and Edwards (*Ferdy Mayne*), Crawford's associate, who are brought to book. Very far-fetched, stickily acted thriller.

RoC *Jennifer Jayne, Geoffrey Hibbert, Jack Melford, Marianne Brauns, Charles Clay, Harry Towb, Stella Bonheur, Colin Rix, Barbara Cochran.*

THE END OF THE ROAD (1954)   4
Dir *Wolf Rilla*. Prod *Alfred Shaughnessy*. Scr *James Forsyth, Geoffrey Orme, from a radio play by Forsyth*. Ph *Arthur Grant*. PC *Group 3*. Dis *British Lion*. 77 mins. Cert U

Mick-Mack (*Finlay Currie*) resents his enforced retirement and the strain it places on his relationship with his son Barney (*Duncan Lamont*) and daughter-in-law (*Naomi Chance*), with whom he lives. When Barney loses his job, Mick-Mack becomes nightwatchman at the factory that employed him as a plater. He is fired, but reinstated as a timekeeper after he finds the cause of plate contamination at the factory. Interesting study of the problems of old age.

RoC *Edward Chapman, David Hannaford, George Merritt, Gordon Whiting, Edie Martin, Herbert C. Walton, Claude Bonser, Eugene Leahy, Pauline Winter, Michael Bird, Tony Kilshawe, Hilda Fenemore, Kenneth Henry, Sam Kydd, Hugh Munro, Bert Sims, John Baker, Ewen Solon, Edward Malin.*

ESCAPADE (1955)   3
Dir *Philip Leacock*. Prod *Daniel M. Angel*,

Hannah Weinstein. Scr *Gilbert Holland, from the play by Roger Macdougall*. PC *Pinnacle*. Dis *Eros*. 88 mins. Cert U

John Hampden (*John Mills*), a fervent worker for world peace, has three boys at boarding school who have their own ways of helping him. The headmaster (*Alastair Sim*) arrives with the intention of expelling one boy for firing at a master with a blunderbuss; then comes news that the boys have run off and stolen a plane. It turns out that they are carrying a petition for peace, signed by boys all over the country, which is duly presented to the great powers meeting in Vienna. Rather unbelievable comedy with didactic undertones.

RoC *Yvonne Mitchell, Marie Lohr, Colin Gordon, Jeremy Spenser, Andrew Ray, Peter Asher, Nicky Edmett, Christopher Ridley, Sean Barrett, Sonia Williams, Mark Dignam, Kit Terrington, Colin Freear, Stephen Abbott, Anne Allan, John Rae.*

ESCAPE BY NIGHT (1953)   3
Dir and Scr *John Gilling*. Prod *Robert S. Baker, Monty Berman*. Ph *Berman*. PC *Tempean*. Dis *Eros*. 79 mins. Cert A

Tough, hard-drinking newsman Buchan (*Bonar Colleano*) aims to get an exclusive on vice king Rossini (*Sidney* - billed as 'Sydney' - *James*), with whom he plays a dangerous game of cat-and-mouse. Rossini captures Buchan, who escapes when the crook goes gunning for Rosetta (*Simone Silva*) whom he thinks has double-crossed him. Buchan saves Rosetta, the police shoot Rossini and the newsman gets his story. Speedy if not-too-credible thriller.

RoC *Andrew Ray, Ted Ray, Patrick Barr, Peter Sinclair, Avice Landone, Ronald Adam, Eric Berry, Martin Benson, Ronan O'Casey.*

ESCAPE IN THE SUN (1956)   4
Dir *George Breakston*. Prod *Breakston, John R. Carter*. Scr *Breakston*. Ph *Bernard Davies*. PC *Phoenix*. Dis *Paramount*. Eastman Colour. 86 mins. Cert A

Millionaire Michael O'Dell (*Martin Boddey*) takes his wife (*Vera Fusek*) when he goes with hunter Jim Harrison (*John Bentley*) on an elephant hunt. The reason: he knows his wife and Harrison are lovers and plans to make them his prey. He gives them a head start and, after many narrow escapes, the tables are turned and O'Dell dies. Melodramatic but very exciting jungle thriller.

RoC *Alan Tarlton, Frankie Vaughan (singing commentary).*

ESCAPEMENT (1957)   2
(USA: *Zex/The Electronic Monster*)
Dir *Montgomery Tully*. Prod *Alec C. Snowden*. Scr *Charles Eric Maine, J. McLaren Ross, from Maine's novel*. Ph *Bert Mason*. PC *Merton Park*. Dis *Anglo-Amalgamated*. 77 mins. Cert A

Dr Maxwell (*Meredith Edwards*) uses his expensive new electronic equipment to send neurosis sufferers into a coma, under which they can be subjected to soothing hallucinations. His backer Zakon (*Peter Illing*) plans to use the equipment to control key people all over

the world, but his plot is foiled by Keenan (*Rod Cameron*), an American insurance investigator. Main sufferers are the audience who have to sit through this unconvincing tosh.
RoC *Mary Murphy, Kay Callard, Carl Jaffe, Roberta Huby, Carl Duering, Larry Cross.*

ESCAPE ROUTE (1952) [2]
(USA: *I'll Get You*)
Dir *Seymour Friedman, Peter Graham Scott.* Prod *Ronald Kinnoch.* Scr *John V. Baines,* (uncredited) *Nicholas Phipps.* Ph *Eric Cross.* PC *Banner.* Dis *Eros. 79 mins. Cert U*
Steve Rossi (*George Raft*), undercover FBI agent, comes to England on the trail of Grand (*Clifford Evans*), a man believed to be behind world-wide kidnappings of scientists. He pretends he wants to work with Grand, discovers the 'escape route' by which he smuggles the boffins into eastern Europe and, with the help of a pretty MI5 secretary (*Sally Gray*), smashes the racket. Slow and hardly credible.
RoC *Reginald Tate, Patricia Laffan, Frederick Piper, John Warwick, Roddy Hughes, June Ashley.*

Sally Gray and George Raft in Escape Route *(1953)*

EXPRESSO BONGO (1959) [3]
Dir and Prod *Val Guest.* Scr *Wolf Mankowitz, from his play.* Ph *John Wilcox.* PC *Conquest.* Dis *British Lion/Britannia. DyaliScope. 111 mins. Cert A*
Johnny (*Laurence Harvey*), an aspiring agent, spots a teenage singer (*Cliff Richard*) in a coffee bar and, on 50 per cent of his earnings, steers him to the top. Dixie (*Yolande Donlan*), furious at his exploitation of the boy, exposes Johnny's contracts as illegal and takes his singer away from him. Johnny, wiser and unabashed, looks around for another golden goose. Rather dull film version of brilliantly satirical stage show; never quite makes up its mind where it's going.
RoC *Sylvia Syms, Meier Tzelniker, Ambrosine Phillpotts, Eric Pohlmann, Hermione Baddeley, Reginald Beckwith, Wilfrid Lawson, Martin Miller, Gilbert Harding, Avis Bunnage, Kenneth Griffith, Barry Lowe, Susan Hampshire, Susan Barnet, Peter Myers, Norma Parnell, Roy Everson, Patricia Lewis, Copeland Lawrence, Lisa Peake, Katherine Keeton, Christine Phillips, Sylvia Steele, Paula Barry, Rita Burke, Maureen O'Connor, Patty Dalton, Pamela Morris, Wolf Mankowitz, Esma Cannon.*

THE EXTRA DAY (1956) [4]
Dir, Scr and PC *William Fairchild.* Prod *E.M. Smedley Aston.* Ph *Arthur Grant.* Dis *British Lion. Eastman Colour. 83 mins. Cert U*
A film is finished. The director (*Laurence Naismith*) flies to America; the star (*Simone Simon*) jets off to Paris; an extra, Toni (*Josephine Griffin*) is getting married; another extra, Steve (*George Baker*) is off to a reunion. Then a can of film is lost. The assistant director (*Richard Basehart*) has the massive job of getting everyone back together again. He encounters various problems, falls for Toni and ruins her romance with a singer (*Denis Lotis*). Steve gets drunk and spends the night with the star! The film is finished again. Nice idea; entertaining though very fragmented.
RoC *Colin Gordon, Charles Victor, Joan Hickson, David Hannaford, Sidney James, Olga Lindo, Jill Bennett, Beryl Reid, Shani Wallis, Bryan Forbes, Eddie Byrne, Philip Ray, Meier Tzelniker, Doreen Dawne, John Humphrey, Peter Coke, Tommy Clegg, Hugh Dempster, Gerald Harper, Frank Williams, Elizabeth Wright, Jessie Evans.*

EYEWITNESS (1956) [2]
Dir *Muriel Box.* Prod *Sydney Box.* Scr *Janet Green.* Ph *Reginald Wyer.* PC and Dis *Rank. 82 mins. Cert A*
Wade (*Donald Sinden*) and Barney (*Nigel Stock*) rob a cinema. Wade kills the manager, but is seen by Lucy (*Muriel Pavlow*) who has just walked out on her husband (*Michael Craig*) after a tiff. Lucy flees from the killer, is knocked down by a bus and is taken to hospital, where Wade tries to finish her off. Thanks to Barney's conscience, he fails. Spotty thriller with miscast stars; Stock, though, is very good.
RoC *Belinda Lee, David Knight, Susan Beaumont, Ada Reeve, Avice Landone, Richard Wattis, George Woodbridge, Leslie Dwyer, Allan Cuthbertson, John Stuart, Nicholas Parsons, Charles Victor, Gillian Harrison, Anthony Oliver, Anna Turner, Harry Towb, Lionel Jeffries, Thomas Heathcote, Martin Boddey.*

Muriel Pavlow, Donald Sinden and Nigel Stock in Eyewitness *(1956)*

FABIAN OF THE YARD (1954) [3]
Dir *Edward Thompson, Anthony Beauchamp.* Prod and PC *Beauchamp.* Scr *Rex Rienits, John Davenport, from a book by Robert Fabian.* Ph *Hilton Craig.* Dis *Eros. 75 mins. Cert A*
Three stories from the casebook of Superintendent Fabian (*Bruce Seton*). (1) A lorry driver strangles a hitchhiker, but is traced by the law. (2) An actress is blackmailed by a threat of kidnapping her small son, but the crook is trapped collecting the 'ransom' money. (3) 1939. IRA men threatening to bomb Piccadilly are rounded up. Routine crime yarns with the emphasis on documentary detail.
RoC *Richard Pearson, Gwen Cherrill, Viola Lyel, Diana Beaumont, Howard Connell, Sarah Churchill, Victor Maddern, Margaret Boyd, Malcolm Kindell, Ann Hanslip, Jack Crowley, James Raglan*

FACE IN THE NIGHT (1956) [3]
(USA: *Menace in the Night*)
Dir *Lance Comfort.* Prod *Charles A. Leeds.* Scr *Norman Hudis, John Sherman, from a novel by Bruce Graeme.* Ph *Arthur Graham.* PC *Gibraltar.* Dis *Grand National. 75 mins. Cert A*
Jean (*Lisa Gastoni*) is the only witness to a mail-van robbery in a London side-street. She goes to the police. The gangleader, Rapson (*Griffith Jones*) threatens to kill Jean's young sister if she testifies. Jean acquiesces, but the mail-van driver dies, and a reporter (*Vincent Ball*) confronts her with his widow. Jean changes her mind again, and Rapson makes a run for it, plunging to his death off Tower Bridge. Fairish thriller with some good acting.
RoC *Eddie Byrne, Clifford Evans, Victor Maddern, Joan Miller, Leslie Dwyer, Leonard Sachs, Barbara Couper, Jenny Laird, Marie Burke, André Van Gyseghem, Angela White.*

FACE THE MUSIC (1954) [2]
(USA: *The Black Glove*)
Dir *Terence Fisher.* Prod *Michael Carreras.* Scr *Ernest Borneman, from his novel.* Ph *Jimmy Harvey.* PC *Hammer.* Dis *Exclusive. 84 mins. Cert A*
Suspected of murdering a singer, trumpeter James Bradley (*Alex Nicol*) sets out to clear his name. Finally he uses a tape-recorder and some snapshots to prove that recording studio manager Maurice Green (*Geoffrey Keen*) is a dangerous psychopath and the real killer. Slow-paced whodunnit with phoney showbiz atmosphere. Star seems ill-at-ease,
RoC *Eleanor Summerfield, John Salew, Paul Carpenter, Ann Hanslip, Fred Johnson, Martin Boddey, Arthur Lane, Gordon Crier, Paula Byrne, Leo Phillips, Fred Tripp, Ben Williams, Frank Birch, Jeremy Hawk, James Carney,*

Melvyn Hayes, Mark Singleton, Tony Hilton, Pat Jorden, Robert Sansom, Frank Pettitt, Kenny Baker's Dozen.

THE FAKE (1953)   [3]

Dir *Godfrey Grayson.* Prod *Steven Pallos.* Scr *Patrick Kirwan,* (uncredited) *Bridget Boland, from a story by James Daplyn.* Ph *Cedric Williams.* PC *Pax.* Dis *United Artists.* 81 mins. Cert U

Mitchell (*Dennis O'Keefe*), an American detective hired to guard a da Vinci painting on exhibition in London, is unable to prevent its theft. Suspicion falls on an embittered artist (*John Laurie*), skilled in copying. Mitchell falls for his daughter (*Coleen Gray*). Then the painter is found murdered and the thief proves to be a wealthy collector (*Hugh Williams*) who had tricked the painter into making a fake. Stolid crime drama.

RoC *Guy Middleton, Gerald Case, Eliot Makeham, Ellen Pollock, Dora Bryan, Billie Whitelaw, Seymour Green, Stanley van Beers, Morris Sweden, Arnold Bell, Philip Ray, Michael Ward, Clifford Buckton, Leslie Phillips, Marianne Noelle, John Wadham.*

FAKE'S PROGRESS (1950)   [2]

Dir *Ken Fairbairn.* Prod *Hilary Long.* Scr *Fairbairn, Long.* Ph *Alan Blowey.* PC *Falcon Films.* Dis *Arrow.* 52 mins. Cert U

A downtrodden clerk joins forces with a spiv-on-the-make and they try various schemes to get rich quick. Largely silent, this independent effort attempts to emulate early silent comedies without much success; the forerunner of such later comedies-without-words as *A Home of Your Own* and *The Plank.*

LP *Lou Cass, Harry Nova, Harry Secombe and Humphrey Lestocq* (commentators).

FAMILY DOCTOR (1958)   [2]
(USA: *RX Murder*)

Dir and Scr *Derek Twist, from a novel by Joan Fleming.* Prod *John Gossage.* Ph *Arthur Grant.* PC *Templar.* Dis *20th Century-Fox.* 85 mins. Cert A

Investigating the death of his divorced wife, American Jethro Jones (*Rick Jason*) finds that her husband Dr Dysert's (*Marius Goring*) three previous wives have also come to mysterious ends. Still a respected resident of an exclusive seaside resort, Dysert plans to marry Kitty (*Lisa Gastoni*). But when Jethro confronts him with gathered evidence, Dysert's effort to dispose of the American ends in his own death. Thriller might have gone places with a better script.

RoC *Sandu Scott, Mary Merrall, Vida Hope, Helen Shingler, Phyllis Neilson-Terry, Nicholas Hannen, Kynaston Reeves, Avice Landone, Frederick Leister, Patrick Waddington, Totti Truman Taylor, Noel Hood.*

FAST AND LOOSE (1954)   [2]

Dir *Gordon Parry.* Prod *Teddy Baird.* Scr *Ben Travers, A.R. Rawlinson, from a play by Travers.* Ph *Jack Asher.* PC *Group.* Dis *General Film Distributors.* 75 mins. Cert A

Peter (*Brian Reece*) misses the train his wife (*June Thorburn*) is on and finds himself stranded at a country inn with a glamorous ex-flame (*Kay Kendall*). Chaos ensues when their respective spouses arrive the following morning, but in the end Peter's marriage is saved. Supposed comedy is much inferior remake of *A Cuckoo in the Nest* (1934).

RoC *Stanley Holloway, Charles Victor, Vida Hope, Dora Bryan, Reginald Beckwith, Joan Young, Fabia Drake, Aubrey Mather, Toke Townley, Alexander Gauge, Eliot Makeham, John Warren.*

FATHER BROWN (1954)   [4]
(USA: *The Detective*)

Dir *Robert Hamer.* Prod *Vivian A. Cox.* Scr *Thelma Schnee, Hamer, from stories by G.K. Chesterton.* Ph *Harry Waxman.* PC *Facet.* Dis *Columbia.* 91 mins. Cert U

Priest-detective Father Brown (*Alec Guinness*) travels to Rome to protect a priceless cross, on its way to a Congress; but he is tricked by Flambeau (*Peter Finch*), a master of disguise, who steals the cross. Father Brown gets wealthy Lady Warren (*Joan Greenwood*) to put up a valuable chess set as bait for the crook, but Flambeau again gets away with it. The Father tracks Flambeau to a château in Burgundy and recovers the cross, and, more important, Flambeau's immortal soul. Engaging, stylish, gently humorous piece.

RoC *Cecil Parker, Bernard Lee, Sidney James, Gérard Oury, Ernest Thesiger, Ernest Clark, Everley Gregg, Austin Trevor, Marne Maitland, Eugene Deckers, Jim Gerald, Noel Howlett, John Salew, John Horsley, Launce Marschal, Daniel Clerice, Guido Lorraine, Sam Kydd, Hugh Dempster, Betty Baskcomb, Jack McNaughton, Diana von Prosody, Dino Galvani.*

FATHER'S DOING FINE (1952)   [4]

Dir *Henry Cass.* Prod *Victor Skutezky.* Scr *Anne Burnaby, from a play by Noel Langley.* Ph *Erwin Hillier.* PC *Associated British/Marble Arch.* Dis *AB-Pathé.* Technicolor. 83 mins. Cert U

Lady Buckering (*Heather Thatcher*) is a widow with four daughters, mostly as scatterbrained as herself, to say nothing of the fact that one of their husbands (*Richard Attenborough*) is a newly expectant father. There are love affairs, a share-buying disaster, unpaid rent and a crooked butler. When all is straightened out, and the twins are born, Lady B. settles for peace and quiet by marrying the family doctor (*George Thorpe*). Busy, boisterous comedy, chock-full of entrances and exits. Funny, too.

RoC *Diane Hart, Virginia McKenna, Susan Stephen, Mary Germaine, Noel Purcell, Jack Watling, Peter Hammond, Brian Worth, Sidney James, Ambrosine Phillpotts, Harry Locke, Jonathan Field, Wensley Pithey.*

THE FEMININE TOUCH (1956)   [3]
(USA: *The Gentle Touch*)

Dir *Pat Jackson.* (Associate) Prod *Jack Rix.* Scr (uncredited) *Ian McCormick, from a novel by Sheila Mackay Russell.* Ph *Paul Beeson.* PC *Ealing Studios.* Dis *Rank.* Technicolor. 91 mins. Cert U

Five girls (*Belinda Lee, Delphi Lawrence,*

George Baker and Belinda Lee in The Feminine Touch (*1956*)

Adrienne Corri, Henryetta Edwards, Barbara Archer) train to become nurses. Susan (*Lee*) falls in love with Jim (*George Baker*), a house doctor, and, after passing her final exams decides to share his intended life in the wilds of Canada. Episodic tribute to nursing profession has too much soft soap, not enough meat. Very good colour camerawork, though.

RoC *Diana Wynyard, Christopher Rhodes, Joan Haythorne, Beatrice Varley, Richard Leech, Dandy Nichols, Newton Blick, Mandy (Miller), Dorothy Alison, Joss Ambler, Constance Fraser, Joan Carol, Vivienne Drummond.*

FERRY TO HONG KONG (1959)   [2]

Dir *Lewis Gilbert.* Prod *George Maynard.* Scr *Vernon Harris, Gilbert, from a novel by Max Catto.* Ph *Otto Heller.* PC and Dis *Rank.* Eastman Colour. CinemaScope. 113 mins. Cert U

Mark (*Curt Jurgens*) is an Austrian adrift in the Far East; thrown out of Hong Kong and Macao, he finds himself a permanent passenger on a ferryboat skippered by pompous Hart (*Orson Welles*). A schoolmistress, Liz (*Sylvia Sims*) tries to befriend the grouchy Mark, who turns up trumps during a typhoon, keeping the ship afloat and helping to defend it against pirates. Hart and Liz, too, have learned something. Failed adventure story doesn't get interesting 'til too late.

RoC *Jeremy Spenser, Noel Purcell, Margaret Withers, John Wallace, Roy Chiao, Shelley Shen, Milton Reid, Louis Seto, Ronald Decent, Don Carlos, Nick Kendall, Kwan Shan Lam.*

FIEND WITHOUT A FACE (1958)   [3]

Dir *Arthur Crabtree.* Prod *John Croydon.* Scr *Herbert J. Leder, from a story by Amelia Reynolds Long.* Ph *Lionel Banes.* Sp eff *Ruppel and Nordhoff, Peter Neilson.* PC *Producers Associates.* Dis *Eros.* 74 mins. Cert X

Canada. It is discovered that corpses from which the brain and spinal cord have been removed are the victims of brain-like creatures which have resulted from a scientist's experiment in the field of materialized thought. Major Cummings (*Marshall Thompson*) of a nearby military radar station kills the creatures by switching off the station's atomic energy, which has been feeding them. Dreary horror film whose only (considerable) interest lies in the special effects, ahead of their time.

RoC *Kim Parker, Terence Kilburn, Kynaston*

Kim Parker in Fiend without a Face *(1958)*

Reeves, Stanley Maxted, James Dyrenforth, Peter Madden, Michael Balfour, Robert Mac-Kenzie, Gilbert Winfield, Launce Maraschal, R. Meadows White, Lala Lloyd, Tom Watson, Kerrigan Prescott, Alexander Archdale, Sheldon Allan, Shane Cordell, Sandra Glen.

FIGHTING MAD (1956) [1]

Dir *Denis Kavanagh.* Prod *Edwin J. Fancey.* Scr *Jennifer Wyatt.* Ph *Hal Morey.* PC *Border.* Dis *New Realm. 53 mins. Cert U*

Muscles Tanner (*Joe Robinson*), a boxer, who has accidentally killed two of his ring opponents, gives up boxing and emigrates to Canada - where he soon becomes embroiled with crooked lumbermen out to prevent his uncle from registering an oil claim. Their attempts to kill Muscles are unsuccessful and, with the help of the Mounties, he brings the timber terrors to justice. Very amateurish; with a hero called Muscles, its chances weren't high to begin with.

RoC *Adrienne Scott, Jack Taylor, Beckett Bould, Colin Cleminson.*

FILES FROM SCOTLAND YARD (1951) [2]

Dir *Anthony Squire.* Prod *Henry Hobhouse. No further credits issued.* PC *Parthian.* Dis *Independent Film Distributors. 58 mins. Cert U*

Three short stories based on real cases investigated by Scotland Yard. Episode titles: *The Lady's Companion, The Telephone* and *The Interrogation.* A forerunner of the long-running 'Scotland Yard' featurettes soon to come.

LP *Moira Lister, John Harvey, Dora Bryan, Reginald Purdell, Louise Hampton, Ben Williams.*

FINAL APPOINTMENT (1954) [2]

Dir *Terence Fisher.* Prod *Francis Searle.* Scr *Kenneth R. Hayles.* Ph *Jonah Jones.* PC *ACT Films.* Dis *Monarch. 69 mins. Cert U*

Alleged injustice in a wartime court-martial is the link between murders on successive July 10ths, discovered by reporter Mike Billings (*John Bentley*) whose assistant Jenny (*Eleanor Summerfield*) is always getting in his hair in her efforts to beat him to a scoop. Finally, she prevents another victim from being shot by the aggrieved villain (*Meredith Edwards*) who has pretended to be his own brother. Silly comedy-thriller; characters repeated in *Stolen Assignment* (1955).

RoC *Hubert Gregg, Liam Redmond, Jean Lodge,*

Sam Kydd, Charles Farrell, Peter Bathurst, Arthur Lowe.

THE FINAL COLUMN (1955) [1]

Dir *David Macdonald.* Prod *Edward J. Danziger, Harry Lee Danziger.* Scr *James Eastwood; Paul Tabori.* Ph *Jimmy Wilson.* PC *Danzigers.* Dis *Paramount. 51 mins. Cert A*

Two stories of deadly plans. (1) A newspaperman, framed and blackmailed over his mistress's death, plans to do away with himself and the blackmailer, with whom his daughter has fallen in love. But the police save him. (2) A doctor hypnotizes his wife's lover into breaking in to her room, and she shoots him. But, seeing what she has done, she turns the gun on the doctor. TV-slanted dramas, very weak. Said one critic: 'Meatless, the sandwich crumbles and is hard to swallow.'

LP *Ron Randell; John Longden, Jeannette Sterke, Christopher Lee, Kay Callard, Laurence Naismith, Sandra Dorne, Brian Worth, Robert Sansom.*

THE FINAL TEST (1953) [4]

Dir *Anthony Asquith.* Prod *R.J. Minney.* Scr *Terence Rattigan, from his TV play.* Ph *Bill McLeod.* PC *ACT Films.* Dis *General Film Distributors. 91 mins. Cert U*

Sam Palmer (*Jack Warner*), at odds with a son (*Ray Jackson*) who prefers poetry to cricket, is a veteran England batsman playing in his last test match. Instead of watching the game, his son goes to see Whitehead (*Robert Morley*), a fashionable playwright, who proves to be a cricket fanatic and insists on going to the test. Sam is out for a duck, but father and son are reconciled. Touching, amusing little story, not very deep, but with real cricketers thrown in for good measure.

RoC *Brenda Bruce, George Relph, Adrianne Allen, Stanley Maxted, Joan Swinstead, Richard Bebb, Valentine Dyall, Audrey White, Richard Wattis, Len Hutton, Denis Compton, Alec Bedser, Godfrey Evans, Jim Laker, Cyril Washbrook.*

FIND THE LADY (1956) [3]

Dir *Charles Saunders.* Prod *John Temple-Smith, Francis Edge.* Scr *Kenneth R. Hayles.* Ph *Brendan J. Stafford.* PC *Major.* Dis *Rank. 56 mins. Cert U*

June (*Beverley Brooks*), a model, visits her godmother in the country - to find that she has disappeared. She enlists the help of the local doctor (*Donald Houston*), but gets herself trapped by a gang of thieves who are using the house as both base and cover for their planned bank robbery. With the help of the doctor, June and her godmother are rescued by the police. Neatly plotted comedy-thriller rather short on genuine humour.

RoC *Mervyn Johns, Kay Callard, Maurice Kaufman(n), Edwin Richfield, Enid Lorimer, Ferdy Mayne, Moray Watson, Anne Heywood, John Drake, Edgar Driver, Nigel Green.*

FIRE DOWN BELOW (1957) [3]

Dir *Robert Parrish.* Prod *Irving Allen, Albert R. Broccoli, Ronald Kinnoch.* Scr *Irwin Shaw, from the novel by Max Catto.* Ph *Desmond*

Dickinson. PC *Warwick.* Dis *Columbia. Technicolor. CinemaScope. 115 mins. Cert A*

Trapped in a stricken freighter, refusing to have his leg amputated to save him, the truth about Tony's (*Jack Lemmon*) past is revealed. He and his partner Felix (*Robert Mitchum*) fell out over a woman (*Rita Hayworth*); they were hired to get her across frontiers and Felix gave their mutual smuggling game away to get rid of Tony, whom the girl had agreed to marry. Now Felix arrives in time to effect a reconciliation and haul Tony away from the freighter as it blows up. Rusty old script bogs down vivid adventure tale.

RoC *Herbert Lom, Bernard Lee, Bonar Colleano, Edric Connor, Anthony Newley, Peter Illing, Joan Miller, Eric Pohlmann, Lionel Murton, Maya Koumani, Murray Kash, Vivian Matalon, Gordon Tanner, Maurice Kaufmann, Philip Baird, Keith Banks.*

FIRE MAIDENS FROM OUTER SPACE (1956) [1]

Dir and Scr *Cy Roth.* Prod *George Fowler.* Ph *Ian Struthers.* PC *Criterion.* Dis *Eros. 80 mins. Cert U*

Five space scientists land on Jupiter's 13th moon to find it inhabited by girls in bikinis, an aged 'patriarch' and the Creature, who terrorizes the moon. Luther (*Anthony Dexter*) saves Hestia (*Susan Shaw*) from the Creature, and must marry her. But when the girls kill the Creature and put the patriarch to sleep, the scientists fly off, promising to return. Amazingly potty sci-fi romp, one of the cinema's great bad films.

RoC *Harry Fowler, Owen Berry, Paul Carpenter, Sydney Tafler, Rodney Diak, Jacqueline Curtiss.*

FIRST MAN INTO SPACE (1958) [3]

Dir *Robert Day.* Prod *John Croydon, Charles Vetter Jr.* Scr *John C. Cooper, Lance Z. Hargreaves.* Ph *Geoffrey Faithfull.* PC *Producers Associates.* Dis *M-G-M. 77 mins. Cert X*

Headstrong Dan Prescott (*Bill Edwards*), an American astronaut, repeatedly defies orders of his older brother Chuck (*Marshall Thompson*). On one occasion, he hits a cloud of meteor dust which, on his return to earth, turns him into a monster lusting for blood. Chuck gets Dan back to base, but the attempt to restore him kills him. Passable *Quatermass*-type adventure.

RoC *Marla Landi, Robert Ayres, Bill Nagy, Carl Jaffe, Roger Delgado, John McLaren, Helen Forrest, Spencer Teakle, Chuck Keyser, Jon Fabian, Richard Shaw, Bill Nick, Rowland Brand, Barry Shawzin, Mark Sheldon, Michael Bell, Sheree Winton, Franklyn Fox, Laurence Taylor.*

FIVE DAYS (1954) [3]
(USA: *Paid to Kill*)

Dir *Montgomery Tully.* Prod *Anthony Hinds.* Scr *Paul Tabori.* Ph *Jimmy Harvey.* PC *Hammer.* Dis *Executive. 72 mins. Cert A*

Nevill (*Dane Clark*), a financier faced with ruin, blackmails a friend, Paul (*Paul Carpenter*), into killing him within five days so that his wife (*Thea Gregory*) can collect the insurance. Within that time, things change, Nevill wants to live and frantically searches for Paul, narrowly escaping death several times. He finds his wife and his business partner (*Anthony Forwood*) out to kill him, having framed a kidnapped Paul. But the treacherous pair are both shot at the end. Good plot, assorted acting, poor script.

RoC *Cecile Chevreau, Howard Marion Crawford, Avis Scott, Peter Gawthorne, Leslie Wright, Hugo Schuster, Arthur Young, Martin Lawrence, Charles Hawtrey.*

THE FLANAGAN BOY (1953)   3
(USA: *Bad Blonde*)
Dir *Reginald LeBorg.* Prod *Anthony Hinds.* Scr *Richard Landau, Guy Elmes, from the novel by Max Catto.* Ph *Walter Harvey.* PC *Hammer.* Dis *Exclusive.* 81 mins. Cert A

Johnny Flanagan (*Tony Wright*), a hefty seaman, wins a fairground booth fight and is persuaded to turn professional by Charlie (*John Slater*), who introduces him to Vecchi (*Frederick Valk*), a promoter. Johnny's affair with Vecchi's blonde wife Lorna (*Barbara Peyton*) wrecks his career. After Lorna has persuaded him to kill Vecchi, he commits suicide. Retribution waits for Lorna too. Lurid stuff, quite strongly made.

RoC *Sidney James, Marie Burke, Selma Vaz Dias, George Woodbridge, Enzo Coticchia, Joe Quigley, Tom Clegg, Chris Adcock, Bob Simmonds, Ray Catthouse, Ralph Moss, Laurence Naismith, John Brooking, Bettina Dickson.*

FLANNELFOOT (1953)   2
Dir *Maclean Rogers.* Prod and PC *E.J. Fancey.* Scr *Carl Heck.* Ph *Geoffrey Faithfull.* Dis *New Realm.* 74 mins. Cert A

Crime reporter Mitchell (*Jack Watling*) is assigned to discover the identity of notorious jewel thief Flannelfoot and secure a scoop. His 'grass', Ginger (*Graham Stark*), is murdered and another killing is committed before Flannelfoot is unmasked at a house party. Only thing thriller does well is conceal its villain.

RoC *Ronald Howard, Mary Germaine, Gene Anderson, Ronald Adam, Adrienne Scott, Kim Peacock, Vanda Godsell, Edwin Richfield, Ronald Leigh-Hunt.*

THE FLAW (1955)   2
Dir *Terence Fisher.* Prod *Geoffrey Goodhart, Brandon Fleming.* Scr *Fleming.* Ph *Cedric Williams.* PC *Cybex.* Dis *Renown.* 61 mins. Cert A

A suave racing driver, Paul (*John Bentley*) marries an heiress (*Rona Anderson*) and plans to kill her on a climbing holiday. Her lawyer John (*Donald Houston*), who loves her, discovers the plot, but Paul slips him poison, then tells him of his 'double-murder alibi'. He takes John's body out to sea on his yacht, but the lawyer has been faking, there is a fight and Paul drowns. Apart from the odd directorial touch and the three stars, very amateurish.

RoC *Tonia Bern, Doris Yorke, J. Trevor Daivies, Cecilia Cavendish, Vera Mechechnie, Ann Sullivan, June Dawson, Langley Howard, Gerry Levy, Herbert St John, Christine Bocca, Derek Barnard, Andrew Leigh, Eric Aubrey.*

FLESH AND BLOOD (1951)   3
Dir *Anthony Kimmins.* Prod *Anatole de Grunwald.* Scr *de Grunwald, from a play by James Bridie.* Ph *Otto Heller.* PC *Harefield.* Dis *British Lion.* 102 mins. Cert A

The 1860s. Cameron (*Richard Todd*), a young Scots doctor, thought by his friend Dr Marshall (*André Morell*) to be a genius, dies from TB after making Marshall's daughter (*Ursula Howells*) pregnant. She too dies, and Marshall brings up the child (*Joan Greenwood*) who, grown, has an affair with a student whom she murders when he tries blackmail. Her son (*Todd*) has a stormy youth, but is a hero in World War I, and later develops a new serum to combat an epidemic. Marshall feels the genius is reborn. Complex, rambling saga.

RoC *Glynis Johns, Freda Jackson, James Hayter, George Cole, Ronald Howard, Walter Fitzgerald, Michael Hordern, Muriel Aked, Helen Christie, Lilly Kann, Patrick Macnee, Molly Weir, Hugh Dempster, Betty Paul, Alexander Gauge, Peter MacDonnell, Hector MacGregor, Archie Duncan, Anna Canitano, John Kelly, Joan Heal, Nina Parry, Billy Newsbury, Sally Owen, William Chappell, Jock McKay, Fred Johnson, John Vere.*

♦ THE FLESH AND THE FIENDS (1959)   3
(USA: *Mania*)
Dir *John Gilling.* Prod *Robert S. Baker, Monty Berman.* Scr *Gilling, Leon Griffiths.* Ph *Berman.* PC *Triad.* Dis *Regal. DyaliScope.* 97 mins. Cert X

1820. In Edinburgh, unscrupulous rogues Burke (*George Rose*) and Hare (*Donald Pleasence*) make a living out of robbing graves to keep the medical profession, especially Dr Knox (*Peter Cushing*), in dissecting material. Later, they decide to cash in on the law of supply and demand by murdering people unlikely to be missed. Eventually, they overstep the mark: Burke hangs; Hare is pursued by a mob and blinded. Busy, grisly shocker whose best asset is its period feel.

RoC *June Laverick, Dermot Walsh, Renee Houston, John Cairney, Billie Whitelaw, Melvyn Hayes, June Powell, Geoffrey Tyrrell, Beckett Bould.*

THE FLESH IS WEAK (1957)   2
Dir *Don Chaffey.* Prod and PC *Raymond Stross.* Scr *Leigh Vance.* Ph *Stephen Dade.* Dis *Eros.* 88 mins. Cert X

Marissa (*Milly Vitale*) is drawn into London's vice rackets through her friendship with Tony (*John Derek*), who forces her to become a prostitute, and has her framed and sent to prison when he thinks she might talk to a reporter (*William Franklyn*) whom Tony has beaten up. On her release, she tells the reporter she is ready to help him and the police make a case against Tony and his brother (*Martin Benson*), who control the vice ring. Lip-smacking exploitation, as dreary as it is sleazy.

RoC *Freda Jackson, Norman Wooland, Harold Lang, Patricia Jessel, Patricia Plunkett, Vera Day, Shirley Ann Field, John Paul, Denis Shaw, Joe Robinson, Roger Snowden, Charles Lloyd Pack.*

FLIGHT FROM VIENNA (1955)   3
Dir and Scr *Denis Kavanagh.* Prod and PC *E.J. Fancey.* Ph *Hal Morey.* Dis *New Realm.* 58 mins. Cert U

When Kosice (*Theodore Bikel*), a high-ranking Hungarian official, asks for asylum in the west, he finds himself forced to go back to Hungary to bring out a scientist to prove his sincerity. The hazardous mission is accomplished, and Kosice flown to London, where an attempt on his life is foiled. He is granted asylum. Reasonably convincing drama with good performance by Bikel.

RoC *John Bentley, Donald Gray, Adrienne Scott, Carina Helm.*

THE FLOATING DUTCHMAN (1953)   3
Dir and Scr *Vernon Sewell, from the novel by Nicolas Bentley.* Prod *W.H. Williams,* Ph *Joe Ambor.* PC *Merton Park.* Dis *Anglo-Amalgamated.* 76 mins. Cert A

Detective Alexander James (*Dermot Walsh*) works undercover to find the link between Otto (*Arnold Marlé*), a jeweller and fence, Skinner (*Sydney Tafler*), a jewel thief, and a Dutch jeweller whose body has been found in the Thames. On a jewel raid, police hold Skinner, but Snow White (*Guy Verney*), another gangster, gets away and tries to kill James, shooting Skinner instead. Otto reveals that both Snow White and Skinner were being blackmailed by the Dutchman. Formula thriller.

RoC *Mary Germaine, Hugh Morton, James Raglan, Nicolas Bentley, Derek Blomfield, Orest Olaff, Ian Wilson, Walter Horsbrugh, Frank Hawkins, Lindsay Hooper, Marjorie Gresley, Ken Midwood, Kathleen Page, Anna Turner, Howard Lang, John Cunningham, Jack Sands.*

FLOODS OF FEAR (1958)   4
Dir *Charles Crichton.* Prod *Sydney Box.* Scr *Crichton, Vivienne Knight, from the novel by John and Ward Hawkins.* Ph *Christopher Challis.* PC and Dis *Rank.* 84 mins. Cert A

America. During a disastrous flood, two men and a girl (*Anne Heywood*) are rescued by Donovan (*Howard Keel*) and find temporary safety on the second floor of her home. Donovan and Peebles (*Cyril Cusack*) are convicts, the other (*Harry H. Corbett*) their warder. Donovan rescues the girl when Peebles tries to rape her, and again when the house collapses under the floods. Serving time for a murder he

Howard Keel and Anne Heywood in Floods of Fear *(1958)*

didn't commit, Donovan is eaten up with revenge, but the girl finds proof of his innocence. Rugged, uncompromising thriller.

RoC *John Crawford, Eddie Byrne, John Phillips, James Dyrenforth, Peter Madden, Guy Kingsley Poynter, Jack Lester, Marie Devereux, Robert MacKenzie, Gordon Tanner, Vivian Matalon, Bill Edwards, Graydon Gould, Gordon Sterne, Kevin Scott.*

THE FLYING EYE (1955)   [4]

Dir *William Hammond*. Prod *William Weedon*. Scr *Hammond, Ken Hughes, Darrell Catling, from a novel by John Newton Chance*. Ph *Hone Glendinning*. PC *British Films/Children's Film Foundation*. Dis *British Lion*. 54 mins. Cert U
The efforts of foreign agents to steal the formula for a new, lightweight fuel are thwarted by the efforts of Colonel Audacious (*Geoffrey Sumner*) and his young assistant, Bunstuffer (*David Hannaford*) with the aid of a model aircraft which carries a tiny 'flying eye' TV inside it. With the help of the eye, the spies are traced and trapped. Enjoyable children's film with able performances and good special effects.

RoC *Julia Lockwood, Harcourt Williams, Ivan Craig.*

THE FLYING SCOT (1957)   [4]
(USA: *Mailbag Robbery*)

Dir and Prod *Compton Bennett*. Scr *Norman Hudis*. Ph *Insignia*. Dis *Anglo-Amalgamated*. 69 mins. Cert U
Ronnie (*Lee Patterson*), Jackie (*Kay Callard*) and Phil (*Alan Gifford*) launch an elaborate plan to rob the Flying Scot, an express train. Nothing goes right for them, but they surmount one unexpected obstacle after another, only to walk out into the arms of the law because of a neglected detail. Famous little second feature concentrates tightly on the matter in hand, builds suspense nicely.

RoC *Margaret Withers, Mark Baker, Jeremy Bodkin, Gerald Case, Kerry Jordan, John Dearth, Patsy Smart, John Lee*

Alan Gifford, Kay Callard and Lee Patterson in The Flying Scot *(1957)*

FOLLOW A STAR (1959)   [3]

Dir *Robert Asher*. Prod *Hugh Stewart*. Scr *Jack Davies, Henry Blyth, Norman Wisdom*. Ph *Jack Asher*. PC and Dis *Rank*. 103 mins. Cert U
Discovering that nervous but persistent would-be singer Norman Truscott (*Norman*

Wisdom) has a good voice, fading star Vernon Carew (*Jerry Desmonde*) has released Norman's recordings as his own. As Norman cannot sing without the company of his crippled girlfriend (*June Laverick*), his music teacher (*Hattie Jacques*) cannot prove the fraud. But Carew is finally unmasked on a stage where he is miming to Norman's recorded voice. Unhappy blend of comedy of embarrassment with mawkish sentiment.

RoC *Richard Wattis, Eddie Leslie, John le Mesurier, Sydney Tafler, Fenella Fielding, Ron Moody, Joe Melia, Charles Heslop, Charles Gray, Dick Emery, Michael Ward, Jess Conrad.*

FOLLOW THAT HORSE! (1959)   [3]

Dir *Alan Bromly*. Prod *Thomas Clyde*. Scr *Alfred Shaughnessy, William Douglas Hume, Howard Mason, from a novel by Mason*. Ph *Norman Warwick*. PC *Cavalcade/Associated British*. Dis *Warner-Pathé*. 80 mins. Cert U
Dick (*David Tomlinson*), an addle-brained Whitehall pen-pusher, is assigned to look after Spiegel (*Cyril Shaps*), a physicist, at a NATO conference, not realizing he is a spy. Spiegel steals a vital microfilm, but it is swallowed by a horse. The spies outbid Dick for the horse after it wins a selling race, but he and Susan (*Mary Peach*), the horse's ex-owner's daughter, outwit Spiegel and his contacts in the end. Vigorous playing by cast of scene-stealers just gets antiquated farce by.

RoC *Cecil Parker, Dora Bryan, Raymond Huntley, Richard Wattis, Sam Kydd, John Welsh, George Pravda, Peter Copley, Victor Brooks, Vic Wise, George A. Cooper, Tony Thawnton, Arthur Lowe.*

FOLLY TO BE WISE (1952)   [4]

Dir *Frank Launder*. Prod *Launder, Sidney Gilliat*. Scr *Launder, John Dighton, from a play by James Bridie*. Ph *Jack Hildyard*. PC *London Films*. Dis *British Lion*. 91 mins. Cert U
A brains trust for a service audience, chaired by chaplain Captain Paris (*Alastair Sim*), is thrown into confusion when a question about marriage reveals the illicit relationship between the wife (*Elizabeth Allan*) of another panellist (*Ronald Culver*) and a professor (*Colin Gordon*) also on the panel. Paris, Lady Dodds (*Martita Hunt*) and the questioner (*Janet Brown*) all pursue the husband, thinking he is going to kill himself, and all nearly go over a cliff. Funny-in-parts version of stage hit. Performances are amusing.

RoC *Miles Malleson, Edward Chapman, Peter Martyn, Robin Bailey, Clement McCallin, Michael Ripper, Leslie Watson, Michael Kelly, George Hurst, Cyril Chamberlain, Jo Powell, Catherine Finn, Enid McCall, Ann Varley, Myrette Morven, Harold Lang, George Cole (guest), Martin Boddey.*

FOOTSTEPS IN THE FOG (1955)   [3]

Dir *Arthur Lubin*. Prod *Maxwell Setton, M.J. Frankovitch*. Scr *Dorothy Reid, Lenore Coffee, Arthur Pierson, from a novel by W.W. Jacobs*. Ph *Christopher Challis*. PC *Film Locations*. Dis *Columbia*. Technicolor. 89 mins. Cert A
1905. London maid Lily (*Jean Simmons*) discovers that her employer, Lowry (*Stewart*

Granger), whom she loves, poisoned his wife, and blackmails her way to becoming housekeeper. Lowry tries to kill her, but in the fog gets the wrong girl, and finds himself on trial for the murder of someone he never knew. Acquitted, he gives himself small doses of poison, hoping that Lily, who wants to marry him, will be accused of attempted murder. But he dies, and Lily is indeed held – for a crime she did not commit. Well-acted but slow.

RoC *Bill Travers, Ronald Squire, Finlay Currie, Belinda Lee, Marjorie Rhodes, William Hartnell, Peter Bull, Barry Keegan, Sheila Manahan, Frederick Leister, Victor Maddern, Percy Marmont, Peter Williams.*

FOR BETTER, FOR WORSE (1954)   [4]
(USA: *Cocktails in the Kitchen*)

Dir *J. Lee Thompson*. Prod *Kenneth Harper*. Scr *Thompson, Peter Myers, Alec Grahame, from the play by Arthur Watkyn*. Ph *Guy Green*. PC *Kenwood*. Dis *AB-Pathé*. Eastman Colour. 84 mins. Cert U
Anne's (*Susan Stephen*) parents are full of foreboding when, at 19, she marries jobless university graduate Tony (*Dirk Bogarde*) and sets up in a small flat. The couple's trials and tribulations are numerous but they win through. Simple plotline packed full of amusing incident; in warm, human and charmingly funny domestic comedy.

RoC *Cecil Parker, Dennis Price, Eileen Herlie, Athene Seyler, Thora Hird, James Hayter, Charles Victor, Sidney James, Pia Terri, George Woodbridge, Robin Bailey, Peter Jones, Digby Wolfe, Jackie Lane, Edwin Styles, Mary Law, Leonard Sharp, Dennis Wyndham, Geoffrey Hibbert, Ronnie Stevens, Edmund Hockridge, Isobel George, Alma Cogan (voice).*

FORBIDDEN CARGO (1954)   [3]

Dir *Harold French*. Prod and Scr *Sydney Box*. Ph *C. Pennington-Richards*. PC *London Independent*. Dis *General Film Distributors*. 85 mins. Cert U
A birdwatcher (*Joyce Grenfell*) puts a customs investigator (*Nigel Patrick*) on the track of brother-and-sister smugglers (*Elizabeth Sellars, Terence Morgan*) and their gang. An attempt to dispatch the customs man by tampering with his diving equipment fails and when the girl realizes her brother in dealing not in currency but drugs, she gives him away, and he is killed after a car chase. Not-too-interesting story falls between documentary and thriller.

RoC *Greta Gynt, Jack Warner, Theodore Bikel, Eric Pohlmann, Michael Hordern, Martin Boddey, Jacques Brunius, James Gilbert, Hal Osmond.*

FORCES' SWEETHEART (1953)   [2]

Dir *Maclean Rogers*. Prod and PC *E.J. Fancey*. Scr *Rogers, Michael Bentine*. Ph *Geoffrey Faithfull*. Dis *New Realm*. 76 mins. Cert U
Judy James (*Hy Hazell*), a singer known as the 'forces' sweetheart', returns from a tour of Korea to be pursued by three suitors – all using the same name. Each ends up with one girl – though not all, of course, with Judy! Goon-style comedy struggles unsuccessfully to

overcome shoddy production standards; very awkward.

RoC *Harry Secombe, Michael Bentine, John Ainsworth, Molly Weir, Freddie Frinton, Graham Stark, Adrienne Scott, Kenneth Henry, John Fitzgerald, Michael McCarthy, Robert Moore, Russ Allen, The Leslie Roberts Television Girls.*

FOREVER MY HEART (1954) [1]

Dir *Leslie Arliss, Bernard Knowles.* Prod and PC *Douglas Fairbanks Jr.* Scr *Selwyn Jepson and Doreen Montgomery, Larry Marcus.* Ph *Ken Talbot, Eric Cross.* Dis *British Lion. 52 mins. Cert A*

Two stories. (1) A Cromwellian officer extracts information from a Royalist widow in adjoining cells at the Tower of London. He falls in love with her and gives his life to help her escape. (2) A prostitute believes that the ghost of her younger sister has come to kill her, but a psychiatrist is able to save her from suicide. Too talky; both stories cry out for more visual treatment.

LP *Douglas Fairbanks Jr, Muriel Pavlow, Stuart Lindsell, Anouk (Aimée), Dermot Palmer, Pierre Lefèvre.*

FORTUNE IS A WOMAN (1956) [4]
(USA: *She Played With Fire*)

Dir *Sidney Gilliat.* Prod *Frank Launder, Gilliat.* Scr *Launder, Gilliat, Val Valentine, from the novel by Winston Graham.* Ph *Gerald Gibbs.* PC *John Harvel/Launder-Gilliat.* Dis *Columbia. 94 mins. Cert A*

Branwell (*Jack Hawkins*), an insurance assessor, visits Lowis Manor, where Tracey and Sarah Moreton tell him a valuable painting has been destroyed by a fire; he later discovers the real painting has been sold and a fake burned. Returning, Branwell finds another fire – and the dead body of Tracey (*Dennis Price*). Sarah (*Arlene Dahl*) clears herself and marries Branwell, whom she knew before. In the ruins of the manor, the mystery is solved.... Thriller lacks a little drive, remains polished, satisfying.

RoC *Ian Hunter, Greta Gynt, Patrick Holt, Bernard Miles, Violet Farebrother, Michael Goodliffe, Christopher Lee, Malcolm Keen, John Robinson, Geoffrey Keen, Martin Lane, John Phillips, Patricia Marmont, George A. Cooper, Eileen Way, Edwina Carroll.*

FOUR DAYS (1951) [2]

Dir *John Guillermin.* Prod *Roger Proudlock.* Scr *Lindsay Galloway, J. McLaren Ross, from the play by Monckton Hoffe.* Ph *Ray Elton.* PC *Vandyke.* Dis *Grand National. 55 mins. Cert A*

Francis (*Hugh McDermott*), a businessman in trouble, flies to America for financial aid. His wife (*Kathleen Byron*) foolishly has an affair with a playboy, Johnny (*Peter Reynolds*), who has forged cheques on Francis' firm. Returning, Francis discovers the affair, throws himself off a cliff but survives. A repentant wife nurses him back to health and, when Johnny tries to blackmail her, Francis gives him a beating. Pretty silly, although mildly gripping in places.

RoC *Gordon McLeod, H.G. Stoker, John Harvey, Petra Davies, Francis Roberts.*

FOUR-SIDED TRIANGLE (1952) [2]

Dir *Terence Fisher.* Prod *Michael Carreras, Alexander Paal.* Scr *Paul Tabori, Fisher.* Ph *Reginald Wyer.* PC *Hammer.* Dis *Exclusive. 81 mins. Cert A*

Returning from America after 10 years, Lena (*Barbara Payton*) finds her friends Bill (*Stephen Murray*) and Robin (*John Van Eyssen*) creating a machine that will reproduce objects exactly. Robin and Lena fall in love, and Bill produces a replica of Lena from the machine, and calls her Helen. When Helen also falls for Robin, Bill and Lena try to destroy her memory, but Helen and Bill perish in a fire. Early Hammer excursion into horror field: laboratory scenes good, rest ludicrous.

RoC *James Hayter, Percy Marmont, Jennifer Dearman, Sean Barrett, Glyn Dearman, Kynaston Reeves, John Stuart, Edith Saville.*

THE FRANCHISE AFFAIR (1950) [3]

Dir *Lawrence Huntington.* Prod *Robert Hall.* Scr *Huntington, Hall, from the novel by Josephine Tey.* Ph *Günther Krampf.* PC *Associated British.* Dis *AB-Pathé. 88 mins. Cert A*

A mother and daughter living a reclusive life in their large house, The Franchise, are thrown into the public eye when Betty (*Ann Stephens*), a young girl, accuses them of kidnapping and beating her. Despite the efforts of their lawyer (*Michael Denison*), evidence builds against the women (*Marjorie Fielding, Dulcie Gray*) until they are brought to trial where, to their relief, Betty is proved a liar. Modest, rather interesting drama with occasional script highlights.

RoC *Anthony Nicholls, Athene Seyler, John Bailey, Hy Hazell, Kenneth More, Avice Landone, Maureen Glynne, Peter Jones, Moultrie Kelsall, John Warwick, Martin Boddey, Patrick Troughton, Hugh Moxey, Ernest Jay, Everley Gregg, Ambrosine Phillpotts, Jean Anderson, Harold Lang, John Forrest, Lawrence Ray, Olive Sloane, Victor Maddern, Doris Yorke, Will Ambro.*

FRIENDS AND NEIGHBOURS (1959) [3]

Dir *Gordon Parry.* Prod *Bertram Ostrer.* Scr *Val Valentine, Talbot Rothwell, from the play by Austin Steele.* Ph *Arthur Grant.* PC *Valiant.* Dis *British Lion. 79 mins. Cert U*

Albert (*Arthur Askey*), a bus conductor, and his family, by winning a draw, are able to play host to two visiting Russian social workers (*Peter Illing, Tilda Thamar*). It's a prize they soon find they would like to let slip through their fingers, even when the Russians sort out their daughter's love affair. Chaos soon reigns, and the Russians leave – only to return with a whole party to study this extraordinary British working-class family. Vigorous farce along old-fashioned lines.

RoC *Megs Jenkins, Reginald Beckwith, June Whitfield, Danny Ross, Catherine Feller, Jess Conrad, Linda Castle, George Wheeler, Max Robertson, Ken Parry, Steven Scott, Richard Walter, Donald Bisset, Anatole Smirnoff, Laurence Herder, Arthur Howard, Paul Bogdan, Alan Scott.*

THE FRIGHTENED MAN (1951) [3]

Dir and Scr *John Gilling.* Prod *Robert S. Baker, Monty Berman.* Ph *Berman.* PC *Tempean.* Dis *Eros. 69 mins. Cert A*

Julius (*Dermot Walsh*), ne'er-do-well son of junk dealer Rosselli (*Charles Victor*), is sent down from Oxford and joins a gang of jewel thieves. Rosselli, who is secretly the 'fence' for the gang, tries to stop his son from taking part in a foolhardy raid on a Hatton Garden jewel store, but Julius does so, falls from a roof and is killed. Adequate thriller of passing interest, quite well developed.

RoC *Barbara Murray, John Blythe, Michael Ward, Thord Hird, John Horsley, Annette Simmonds, Martin Benson.*

FRONT PAGE STORY (1953) [5]

Dir *Gordon Parry.* Prod and PC *Jay Lewis.* Scr *Lewis, Jack Howells, William Fairchild, Guy Morgan, from a novel by Robert Gaines.* Ph *Gilbert Taylor.* Dis *British Lion. 99 mins. Cert A*

A day in the life of the *Daily World*. An atomic scientist (*Martin Miller*), misguidedly passing on secrets in the cause of peace, is arrested in the paper's office. The editor, Grant (*Jack Hawkins*), has the task of telling five Cockney kids their mother has been killed. The World 'adopts' the children. A woman (*Eva Bartok*) cleared of euthanasia is hounded by reporters outside the court and run over by a bus. Grant's wife (*Elizabeth Allan*), who was leaving him, is listed missing on a crashed plane. It turns out she did not take the plane. Vivid newspaper drama pulls no punches on emotional and moral issues.

RoC *Derek Farr, Jenny Jones, Walter Fitzgerald, Patricia Marmont, Joseph Tomelty, Stephen Vercoe, Helen Haye, Michael Howard, Guy Middleton, Henry Mollison, Ronald Adam, Joan Stuart, Bruce Beeby, Gordon Bell, Tristram Rawson.*

FUN AT ST FANNY'S (1955) [1]

Dir *Maurice Elvey.* Prod *David Dent.* Scr *Anthony Verney, Fred Emney.* Ph *Eric Cross.* PC *Grand Alliance.* Dis *British Lion. CameraScope. 80 mins. Cert U*

Cardew the Cad (*Douglas 'Cardew' Robinson*), at 25 the oldest pupil at St Fanny's, will inherit a fortune unless he is expelled – in which case the money will pass to the school. Needless to say, the head, Dr Jankers (*Fred Emney*), plans to get Cardew expelled, by framing him for a theft with the help of some crooks; the sister (*Vera Day*) of one of them, in love with the Cad, foils the plan. Competent cast routed by what must be one of film history's worst comedy screenplays.

RoC *Claude Hulbert, Davy Kaye, Miriam Karlin, Freddie Mills, Johnny Brandon, Kynaston Reeves, Gerald Campion, Gabrielle Brune, Peter Butterworth, Dino Galvani, Stanley Unwin, Marianne Stone, Francis Langford's Singing Scholars.*

FURTHER UP THE CREEK (1958) [3]

Dir *Val Guest.* Prod *Henry Halsted.* Scr *Guest, John Warren, Len Heath.* Ph *Gerry Gibbs.* PC *Byron/Hammer.* Dis *Columbia. 91 mins. Cert U*

The rascally crew of the antiquated frigate *Aristotle* see their chance when it is sold to the president of Algerocco. Led by the Bosun (*Frankie Howerd*), they abandon their bookmaking business in favour of advertising a Mediterranean cruise. Only because their new commander, Lt Fairweather (*David Tomlinson*), foils a revolution in Algerocco, do the entire ship's roster evade court martial. Variation on previous comedy hit (*Up the Creek*; qv) works that much less well.

RoC *Shirley Eaton, Lionel Jeffries, Thora Hird, Lionel Murton, Sam Kydd, David Lodge, Eric Pohlmann, John Warren, Edwin Richfield, Stanley Unwin, Michael Goodliffe, Patrick Holt, Walter Hudd, Harry Landis, Ian Whittaker, Howard Williams, Peter Collingwood, Amy Dalby, Esma Cannon, Tom Gill, Jack Le White, Max Day, Mary Wilson, Katherine Byrne.*

G

THE GALLOPING MAJOR (1951)   4

Dir *Henry Cornelius.* Prod *Monja Danischewsky.* Scr *Danischewsky, Cornelius, Basil Radford.* Ph *Stanley Pavey.* PC *Sirius/Romulus.* Dis *Independent Film Distributors.* 82 mins. Cert U

Sporty Major Hill (*Basil Radford*) forms a syndicate of ordinary folk to buy a racehorse. He gets the wrong horse at an auction, but it proves a natural jumper, and the syndicate decides to enter it in the Grand National. The horse vanishes but is found again. At the last moment, Hill has to ride it himself. All the other horses fall and he wins. Mildly funny, warmly characterized romp.

RoC *Jimmy Hanley, Janette Scott, René Ray, A.E. Matthews, Joyce Grenfell, Hugh Griffith, Sydney Tafler, Charles Hawtrey, Sidney James, Charles Victor, Alfie Bass, Julien Mitchell, Charles Lamb, Gilbert Davis, Kenneth Evans, Tom Walls Jr, James Lomas, Ellen Pollock, Raymond Rollett, Arthur Denton, Sam Kydd, Michael Ward, Leslie Phillips, Clifford Cobbe, Dick Courtenay, Mary Matthews, Jacqueline Maude, Billy Russell, Duncan Lamont, Donovan Winter, Arthur Lovegrove, Derek Ensor, Roy Carr, Thora Hird, Ernie Metcalfe, Joe Day, Pat Ray, Joe Clarke, Dan Malvern, Ben Williams, Charlie Smirke, Raymond Glendenning, Bruce Belfrage, Marion Harris Jr, Mr Hawkins.*

THE GAMBLER AND THE LADY (1952)   2

Dir *Pat Jenkins,* (uncredited) *Sam Newfield.* Prod *Anthony Hinds.* Scr *Uncredited.* Ph *Walter Harvey.* PC *Hammer.* Dis *Exclusive.* 74 mins. Cert A

American gambler Jim Forster (*Dane Clark*), successful with a string of Mayfair casinos, throws over his dancer mistress Pat (*Kathleen Byron*) for a titled lady (*Naomi Chance*). While

his mind is on other things (like investing in a dud goldmine), Jim's 'joints' are wrecked, and his partner (*Meredith Edwards*) killed by the Colonna brothers, who want in. In a gun battle, Jim deals the Colonnas out; as he staggers away wounded, Pat runs him down in her car. Unconvincingly set drama, typical Dane Clark gloom.

RoC *Eric Pohlmann, Enzo Cottichia, Anthony Forwood, Jane Griffiths, Percy Marmont, Julian Somers, Anthony Ireland, Thomas Gallagher, Max Bacon, Eric Boon, Mona Washbourne, Richard Shaw, George Pastell, Martin Benson, Felix Osmond, Robert Adair, Mark Singleton, Peter Hutton, Andre Mikhelson, Paul Sheridan, Robert Brown, David Keir, Irissa Cooper, Laurie Taylor, The Valencia Trio.*

THE GAMMA PEOPLE (1955)   2

Dir *John Gilling.* Prod *John Gossage.* Scr *Gilling, Gossage.* Ph *Ted Moore.* PC *Warwick.* Dis *Columbia.* 78 mins. Cert A

A sinister scientist (*Walter Rilla*) in a small European state is using children for brain experiments, bombarding them with gamma rays that can make them geniuses or idiots. Two journalists (*Paul Douglas, Leslie Phillips*) who come there by chance, manage to put an end to the experiments after one of them persuades the villagers to storm the castle, which goes up in smoke. Ludicrous plot does raise some excitement.

RoC *Eva Bartok, Philip Leaver, Martin Miller, Michael Caridia, Pauline Drewett, Jackie Lane, Rosalie Crutchley, Olaf Pooley, Leonard Sachs, StJohn Stuart, Cyril Chamberlain, Paul Hardtmuth.*

THE GAY DOG (1954)   3

Dir *Maurice Elvey.* Prod *Ernest Gartside.* Scr *Peter Rogers, from a play by Joseph H. Colton.* Ph *James Wilson.* PC *Coronet.* Dis *Eros.* 87 mins. Cert U

Jim Gay (*Wilfred Pickles*) a north-country miner, loves his racing greyhound, Raving Beauty, more than his family. The dog is so successful that good odds are no longer available at local tracks. Jim takes the dog to an out-of-town track, discovers a high-class dog is in the same race, and backs it without telling his friends, who lose heavily on Raving Beauty, but force Jim to cough up their losses. Straightforward version of stage success lacks charm.

RoC *Petula Clark, Megs Jenkins, John Blythe, Margaret Barton, Russell Enoch (William Russell), Cyril Raymond, Harold Goodwin, Douglas Ives, Nuna Davey.*

THE GELIGNITE GANG (1956)   2
(USA: *The Dynamiters*)

Dir *Terence Fisher, Francis Searle.* Prod *Geoffrey Goodh(e)art, Brandon Fleming.* Scr *Fleming.* Ph *Cedric Williams.* PC *Cybex.* Dis *Renown.* 76 mins. Cert U

In spite of the disapproval of his senior partner, Rutherford (*Patrick Holt*), private eye Jimmy Baxter (*Wayne Morris*) accepts an assignment to find the Gelignite Gang, safe-cracking crooks. Sally (*Sandra Dorne*), Jim's sleuthing secretary, gets a clue which leads to the gang's HQ, but she is captured by its

leader - Rutherford. Jimmy and the police soon arrive, however, and clean up the criminal ring. Fast-moving crime drama is short on actual action, has unintentional laughs in shoals.

RoC *James Kenney, Simone Silva, Eric Pohlmann, Arthur Young, Lloyd Lamble, Hugh Miller, Ossie Waller, Bertha Russell, Leigh Crutchley, Bernadette Milnes, Mark Daly, Tony Doonan.*

GENEVIEVE (1953)   5

Dir and Prod *Henry Cornelius.* Scr *William Rose.* Ph *Christopher Challis.* PC *Sirius/Rank.* Dis *General Film Distributors.* Technicolor. 86 mins. Cert U

The annual 'old crocks' rally from London to Brighton sorely tries the patience of Wendy (*Dinah Sheridan*), wife of Alan (*John Gregson*), who is preparing Genevieve, his 1904 car, for the run. Rivalry between Alan and his friend Ambrose (*Kenneth More*) who brings his sophisticated girl Rosalind (*Kay Kendall*) culminates in a full-scale race on the return trip. Alan wins, and his relationship with Wendy resumes normality. Unusual comedy gem, well-written, enjoyable all the way through, with a hit harmonica theme, played by Larry Adler. British Oscar for best British film.

RoC *Geoffrey Keen, Harold Siddons, Joyce Grenfell, Arthur Wontner, Reginald Beckwith, Michael Medwin, Leslie Mitchell, Michael Balfour, Edie Martin.*

John Gregson and Dinah Sheridan in Genevieve *(1953)*

THE GENIE (1953)   3

Dir *Lance Comfort, Lawrence Huntington.* Prod and PC *Douglas Fairbanks Jr.* Scr *Noel Charles, Peter Gordon Scott, Doreen Montgomery,* Ph *Eric Cross, Brendan J. Stafford.* Dis *British Lion.* 75 mins. Cert A

Three stories about love. (1) Two prisoners-of-war fight over who shall go on an escape plane. Later one learns that the other, whom he has knocked out, has cheated anyway. (2) A widower's son will accept no-one in his beloved mother's place - until he learns she left them when he was a year old. (3) A genie assumes human form when he falls for a girl. But to save her grandfather from prison, he has to become a genie again. Last episode the best; others slow.

LP *Bill Travers, Scott McKay, Patricia Cutts, Tom Duggan, Sean Barrett, Bernadette O'Farrell, Douglas Fairbanks Jr, Yvonne Furneaux, Martin Miller.*

THE GENTLE GUNMAN (1952) [3]

Dir *Basil Dearden*. Prod *Michael Relph*. Scr *Roger Macdougall, from his play*. Ph *Gordon Dines*. PC *Ealing Studios*. Dis *General Film Distributors*. 86 mins. Cert A

1941. IRA men come to London to blow up underground stations. Terence (*John Mills*), appalled by the war damage, changes his mind. His brother Matt (*Dirk Bogarde*) takes his place, but his cohorts (*Liam Redmond, Jack MacGowran*) are captured. Terence carries out a daring rescue plan, but is only saved from execution by the IRA leader (*Robert Beatty*) when the rescued men turn up. Matt, too, decides to desert the cause of violence. Rambling dissertation with occasional thrills.

RoC *Elizabeth Sellars, James Kenney, Joseph Tomelty, Gilbert Harding, Barbara Mullen, Eddie Byrne, Michael Golden, Patric Doonan, John Orchard, Michael Dunne, Patricia Stewart, Tony Quinn, Edward Byrne, Seamus Kavanagh, Terence Alexander, Jean StClair, Doris Yorke, E.J. Kennedy, Harry Brogan.*

Dirk Bogarde in The Gentle Gunman *(1952)*

GEORDIE (1955)
(USA: *Wee Geordie*) [4]

Dir *Frank Launder*. Prod *Launder, Sidney Gilliat*. Scr *Gilliat, Launder, from the novel by David Walker*. Ph *Wilkie Cooper*. PC *Argonaut*. Dis *British Lion*. Technicolor. 99 mins (US:93). Cert U

After winning the hammer-throwing event at the Highland Games, Geordie (*Bill Travers*), a gamekeeper who has built up his physique with a physical culture course, is selected to throw the hammer for Britain in the Olympics in Australia. He is fancied there by the Danish lady shot-putter (*Doris Goddard*), wins the hammer and returns to his local girlfriend (*Norah Gorsen*). Charmingly fresh comedy.

RoC *Alastair Sim, Molly Urquhart, Jameson Clark, Francis de Wolff, Alex Mackenzie, Raymond Huntley, Brian Reece, Miles Malleson, Stanley Baxter, Jack Radcliffe, Duncan Macrae, Paul Young, Anna Ferguson, Margaret Boyd, Michael Ripper, Alex McCrindle, Eric Woodburn, Jack Short.*

GHOST SHIP (1952) [3]

Dir, Prod and Scr *Vernon Sewell*. Ph *Stanley Grant*. PC and Dis *Anglo-Amalgamated*. 74 mins. Cert A

Ex-naval-officer Guy (*Dermot Walsh*) and his wife Margaret (*Hazel Court*) buy a large motor yacht, *The Cyclops*, and prepare to live there. But crew members are hard to find and rumours soon abound that *The Cyclops* is haunted. Consulting a medium, Margaret finds that a previous owner has shot his wife and lover on board. The grim clue enables Guy to catch the 'ghost', who proves to be flesh and blood and with a special reason for getting rid of them. Eerie dose of maritime mystery.

RoC *Hugh Burden, John Robinson, Hugh Latimer, Patricia Owens, Melissa Stribling, Joan Carol, Mignon O'Doherty, Joss Ambler, Laidman Browne, Meadows White, Pat McGrath, Joss Ackland, John King-Kelly, Colin Douglas, Jack Stewart, Anthony Marlowe, Geoffrey Dunn, Ian Carmichael, Anthony Hayes, Barry Phelps, Robert Moore, Ewen Solon, Jock Finlay, Madoline Thomas, Graham Stuart, Gordon Bell.*

GIDEON'S DAY (1958)
(GB: *Gideon of Scotland Yard*) [4]

Dir *John Ford*. Prod *Michael Killanin*. Scr *T.E.B. Clarke, from the novel by J.J. Marric* (*John Creasey*). Ph *F.A. Young*. PC and Dis *Columbia British*. Technicolor. 91 mins. Cert A

Being booked for speeding by Simon, a zealous young policeman (*Andrew Ray*), Inspector Gideon's (*Jack Hawkins*) day gets off to a shaky start. It further includes a maniac killer (captured by Simon), a hit-and-run killing, bribery, robbery with violence and three murders. Home for the night, Gideon again crosses Simon (who is dating his daughter), but permits himself a smile when the youngster is booked for speeding. Quick-paced, likeable crime compendium in Ealing style with more than a tinge of humour.

RoC *Anna Lee, Anna Massey, Dianne Foster, Cyril Cusack, James Hayter, John Loder, Ronald Howard, Frank Lawton, Derek Bond, Howard Marion Crawford, Laurence Naismith, Grizelda Hervey, Doreen Madden, Miles Malleson, Marjorie Rhodes, Jack Watling, Michael Trubshawe, Michael Shepley, Barry Keegan, Hermione Bell, Donal Donnelly, Billie Whitelaw, Malcolm Ranson, Mavis Ranson, Francis Crowdy, David Aylmer, Brian Smith, Maureen Potter, John le Mesurier.*

Jack Hawkins and Dianne Foster in Gideon's Day *(1958)*

GIFT HORSE (1952)
(USA: *Glory at Sea*) [4]

Dir *Compton Bennett*. Prod *George Pitcher*. Scr *William Fairchild, Hugh Hastings, William*

Rose. Ph *Harry Waxman*. PC *Molton*. Dis *British Lion/Independent Film Distributors*. 100 mins. Cert U

1940. Fraser (*Trevor Howard*), unpopular captain of an aged destroyer, given to Britain by America, brings himself close to a (second) courtmartial, before an encounter with a U-boat, which he rams and sinks, brings him closer to his crew. Under heavy fire, the 'gift horse' leads the St-Nazaire raid and blows up the dock gates; its men are taken prisoner. Well-made war film with obvious strengths expertly exploited.

RoC *Richard Attenborough, Sonny Tufts, James Donald, Joan Rice, Bernard Lee, Dora Bryan, Hugh Williams, Robin Bailey, Meredith Edwards, John Forrest, Patric Doonan, Sidney James, James Kenney, James Carney, Russell Enoch* (*William Russell*), *Anthony Oliver, Harold Siddons, Harry Towb, George Street, Glyn Houston, John Gabriel, Michael Ashlin, Peter Hobbes, John Warren, Hugh Hastings, Tony Quinn, David Oake, Gwenda Wilson, Peter Bathurst, Lyn Evans, Robert Moore, John Wynn, Harold Ayer, Alan Rolfe, Michael Mulcaster, John Brooking, Tim Turner, Cyril Conway, Ann Wheatley, Charles Lloyd Pack, John Clevedon, Olaf Pooley.*

GILBERT HARDING SPEAKING OF MURDER (1953) [2]

Dir *Paul Dickson*. Prod *Edward J. and Harry Lee Danziger*. Scr *Paul Tabori, James Eastwood, Kate Barlay*. Ph *Jack Cox*. PC *Danzigers*. Dis *Paramount*. 76 mins. Cert A

Three short stories introduced by radio personality Gilbert Harding. (1) Two spinsters trap a former man-friend in an attic for 20 years as revenge for his having jilted them both. (2) An actor has the coat of his dreams made, only to find the design is the invention of thieves. (3) A writer exacts murderous retribution on a critic for condemning his play. Slow and portentous, possibly designed with TV in mind.

RoC *Kay Walsh, Betty Ann Davies, Patrick Barr, Frank Tilton, John Dunbar, Howard Marion Crawford, Wilfred Caithness, Andrea Malandrinos, Robert Raglan, Robert Adair, Harold Jamieson, Peter Bathurst, Hubert Gregg, Laurence Naismith, Jenny Laird, Philip Ray, Henry Longhurst, Alex McCrindle, Gabriel Toyne, Mark Singleton, Arthur Lowe.*

THE GILDED CAGE (1954) [3]

Dir *John Gilling*. Prod *Robert S. Baker, Monty Berman*. Scr *Brock Williams*. Ph *Berman*. PC *Tempean*. Dis *Eros*. 77 mins. Cert A

Steve (*Alex Nicol*), a US security officer, finds that his brother in London is involved in a plot to smuggle a priceless painting out of the country – a situation that leads to murder. Steve and his brother find themselves involved in some very rough stuff before they manage to expose the ruthless gang behind it. Standard thriller, vigorously played.

RoC *Veronica Hurst, Clifford Evans, Ursula Howells, Michael Alexander, Elwyn Brook-Jones, John Stuart, Ronan O'Casey, Trevor Reid, Patrick Jordan.*

GIRDLE OF GOLD (1952)   [2]

Dir *Montgomery Tully*. Prod *Darcy Conyers, Audrey Hirst*. Scr *Jack Dawe*. Ph *Jack Asher*. PC *Screenplays, London/Audrey Hirst*. Dis *Eros*. 62 mins. Cert U

A Welsh village. Griffiths, the undertaker (*Meredith Edwards*) hides his savings in his wife's corsets. But she (*Maudie Edwards*) is planning to run away with Evans the Milk (*Esmond Knight*). Getting herself a new corset, she gives the old one away, and Griffiths is soon engaged on a frantic chase which eventually ends with his recovery of both corset and wife. Good comedy idea ploddingly handled.
RoC *Petra Davies, Glyn Houston, Tonie MacMillan, Kenneth Evans*.

THE GIRL IN THE PICTURE (1956)   [3]

Dir *Don Chaffey*. Prod *Edward Lloyd*. Scr *Paul Rogers*. Ph *Ian Struthers*. PC *Cresswell*. Dis *Eros*. 61 mins. Cert U

John (*Donald Houston*), a crime reporter, fights to find a girl in a snapshot waving to a car known to contain a murderer. He finds her, falls for her, but she cannot help with identification. The killer doesn't know this and, in his attempt to dispose of her, meets his own death at the hands of the reporter. Straightforward, old-hat crime stuff, but brightly pushed along.
RoC *Junia Crawford, Patrick Holt, Maurice Kaufmann, Paddy Joyce, John Miller, Tom Chatto, Colin Cleminson, Lloyd Lamble*.

THE GIRL IS MINE (1950)   [2]

Dir and Scr *Marjorie Deans*. Prod *Freda Stock*. Ph *Ben Hart*. PC *Touchstone*. Dis *British Lion*. 51 mins. Cert U

An American, Jim (*Lionel Murton*) helps Hugh (*Patrick Macnee*) and Betty (*Pamela Deeming*) to hang on to their boat, the *Winkle*, in spite of the machinations of the crooked dock-owner (*Arthur Melton*) to whom they owe money. The villain removes their propeller, but they confound him by getting the money to pay their debt. Jim has fallen for Betty, but Hugh's anger is short-lived when he finds a dishy new girlfriend. Unambitious trifle, a rare example for the time of a film directed by a woman.
RoC *Richard Pearson, Ben Williams, Leonard Sharp, Elwyn Stock, Simon de Wardener, Patricia Dickson, Valerie Agnew*.

THE GIRL ON THE PIER (1953)   [2]

Dir *Lance Comfort*. Prod *John Temple-Smith*. Scr *Guy Morgan*. Ph *Bill McLeod*. PC *Major*. Dis *Apex*. 65 mins. Cert A

When ex-convict Nick Lane (*Ron Randell*) tracks down former associate Joe Hammond (*Campbell Singer*), now running a waxworks on Brighton pier, he soon seduces Joe's bored wife (*Veronica Hurst*). Hammond decides to kill him. A policeman's son on holiday reports suspicious circumstances but too late to prevent Lane's death. Chased by police, Hammond falls from the pier and drowns. Drama is mostly sombre, slow.
RoC *Charles Victor, Marjorie Rhodes, Brian Roper, Eileen Moore, Anthony Valentine, Steve Conway, Thorp Devereaux, Diana Wilding, Raymond James*.

GIRLS AT SEA (1958)   [2]

Dir *Gilbert Gunn*. Prod *Vaughan N. Dean, Gunn*. Scr *T.J. Morrison, Gunn, from a play by Stephen King-Hall and Ian Hay*. Ph *Erwin Hillier*. PC and Dis *Associated British*. Technicolor. 80 mins. Cert U

Three girls are stranded on board HMS *Scottia* after an engagement party there. The Admiral (*Michael Hordern*) pays an unexpected midnight visit, and the crew, led by the Captain (*Guy Rolfe*) and Marine Ogg (*Ronald Shiner*), try frantically to conceal the girls. They finally fail, but the arrival of the Admiral's jealous wife (*Fabia Drake*) saves their skins. Creaky old farce (*The Middle Watch*) hardly seaworthy even without the vigorous overplaying of most of cast.
RoC *Alan White, Anne Kimbell, Nadine Tallier, Mary Steele, Richard Coleman, Lionel Jeffries, Daniel Massey, David Lodge, Teddy Johnson, Warren Mitchell, Mercy Haystead, Michael Ripper, Marie Devereux, Brian Wilde, Harold Goodwin, David Aylmer, Richard Briers, Shane Cordell, Josephine Lisle*.

Anne Kimbell and Ronald Shiner in Girls at Sea *(1958)*

GLAD TIDINGS (1953)   [2]

Dir and Scr *Walter Rilla, from the play by R.F. Delderfield*. Prod *Victor Hanbury*. Ph *Eric Cross*. PC *Insignia*. Dis *Eros*. 68 mins. Cert U
Col. Tom Forester (*Raymond Huntley*) decides to retire from the Army, but his four children object to his marrying an attractive American widow (*Barbara Kelly*). She soon settles their hashes by finding husbands for two of the three girls and settling problems all round. When she storms off after a row, the offspring are soon begging her to come back. Not much fun in potted version of successful play.
RoC *Ronald Howard, Jean Lodge, Terence Alexander, Diana Calderwood, Laurence Payne, Arthur Howard, Brian Smith, Harry Green, Roger Maxwell, Yvette Wyatt, Doris Yorke*.

THE GLASS CAGE (1955)   [1]

Dir *Montgomery Tully*. Prod *Anthony Hinds*. Scr *Richard Landau, from a novel by A.E. Martin*. Ph *Walter Harvey*. PC *Hammer*. Dis *Exclusive*. 59 mins. Cert A
Murders at a fairground on a London bombsite centre around Sapolio (*Eric Pohlmann*), 'world champion starving man', whose next fast is to be staged there in a glass cage. The third victim is Sapolio himself and showman

Pel (*John Ireland*) suggests he be left 'asleep' in his cage to trap the murderer (*Geoffrey Keen*) - a scheme which comes off. Fragmented, unsatisfactory thriller bears signs of heavy cutting.
RoC *Honor Blackman, Sydney Tafler, Sidney James, Liam Redmond, Valerie Vernon, Arnold Marle, Stan Little, Tonia Bern, Anthony Richmond, Norah Gordon*.

THE GOLDEN DISC (1958)   [2]
(USA: *The Inbetween Age*)

Dir *Don Sharp*. Prod *W.G. Chalmers*. Scr *Sharp, Don Nicholl*. Ph *Geoffrey Faithfull*. PC and Dis *Butchers*. 78 mins. Cert U

Two young people (*Lee Patterson, Mary Steele*) turn a café into a coffee bar, and find a star on the doorstep in the form of their jack-of-all-trades (*Terry Dene*). His records and those of other bar artists start selling well, but the new 'firm' is threatened by the company that presses their discs, who want to take over their successful singers. A merger with an American company, however, solves the problem. Halting pop musical with a lot of inhibited acting.
RoC *Linda Gray, Ronald Adam, Peter Dyneley, David Jacobs, David Williams, Richard Turner, Marianne Stone, Olive Milbourne, Redmond Phillips, Raymond Hodge, Stanley Platts, Peter Godsell, Dennis Lotis, Nancy Whiskey, Sheila Buxton, Les Hobeaux, Murray Campbell, Phil Seamon Jazz Group, Sonny Stewart's Skiffle Kings, Teddy Kennedy Group, Don Rendell's Six*.

GOLDEN IVORY (1954)   [2]
(USA: *White Huntress*)

Dir *George Breakston*. Prod *John Croydon, Peter Crane, Breakston, Ray Stahl*. Scr *Dermot Quinn*. Ph *John Lawrence*. PC *Summit*. Dis *AB-Pathé*. Technicolor. 86 mins. Cert U

British East Africa, 1890. Two brother hunters (*John Bentley, Robert Urquhart*) escort a wagon-train of settlers through the jungle, and fall for the colonists' leader's daughter (*Susan Stephen*). Seth (*Alan Tarlton*) joins the convoy after killing two men in a quarrel over diamonds. Lured by gold, Paul (*Bentley*) diverts the convoy, but he and Seth fall victim to native warriors. Rough-edged action yarn with too much footage for its slim story.
RoC *Howarth Wood, Tom Lithgow, Morea Soutter, Maureen Connell, Reginald Smart, Kip Kamoi*.

THE GOLDEN LINK (1954)   [3]

Dir *Charles Saunders*. Prod *Guido Coen*. Scr *Allan Mackinnon*. Ph *Harry Waxman*. PC *Parkside*. Dis *Archway*. 83 mins. Cert A

A woman falls from the fourth floor, down the well of a block of flats. The three flats there are occupied by Supt Blake (*André Morell*), the woman's husband (*Patrick Holt*), with whom Blake's daughter (*Thea Gregory*) is in love, and Bill (*Jack Watling*), who assists in the investigation, but ultimately proves to be the killer. Thriller is a bit padded, but well worked out.
RoC *Arnold Bell, Olive Sloane, Bruce Beeby, Alexander Gauge, Ellen Pollock, Dorinda Stevens, Elsie Wagstaff, Edward Lexy, Marla Landi, Charlie Drake*.

THE GOLD EXPRESS (1955)   [1]

Dir *Guy Fergusson.* Prod *Frank Wells.* Scr *Jackson Budd.* Ph *Frank North.* PC *Gaumont-British.* Dis *Rank. 58 mins. Cert U*

Two newly-wed reporters, Bob and Mary (*Vernon Gray, Ann Walford*) are forced to forego their honeymoon and return to London on a train carrying a shipment of gold, which Rover (*Patrick Boxill*) plans to steal. With the help of two old ladies who write penny-dreadful crime novels, Bob foils Rover's plot - but Mary gets the story. Terrible crime story even the old ladies would be ashamed of.

RoC *May Hallatt, Ivy St Helier, Charles Rolfe, Delphi Lawrence, John Serret.*

GONE TO EARTH (1950)   [2]
(USA: *The Wild Heart*)

Dir and Scr *Michael Powell, Emeric Pressburger, from the novel by Mary Webb.* Prod *David O. Selznick.* Ph *Christopher Challis.* PC *London Films/Vanguard.* Dis *British Lion. Technicolor. 110 mins (US: 82). Cert A*

1897. Hazel Woodus (*Jennifer Jones*), a country innocent devoted to her pet fox, is pursued by the local squire (*David Farrar*), but marries a clergyman (*Cyril Cusack*) who makes no sexual demands on her. Seduced by the squire, she goes back to her husband because her lover ill-treats the fox. Trying to rescue the beast from a hunt led by the squire, she plunges to her death down a mineshaft. No chance; as one critic put it, 'the original novel was absurd enough'. The American version, with extra scenes directed by Rouben Mamoulian, is an almost entirely different film.

RoC *Sybil Thorndike, Edward Chapman, Esmond Knight, Hugh Griffith, George Cole, Beatrice Varley, Frances Clare, Raymond Rollett, Gerald C. Lawson, Valentine Dunn, Richmond Nairne, Owen Holder, Bartlett Mullins, Arthur Reynolds, Ann Tetheradge, Peter Dunlop, Louis Phillip, Joseph Cotten (narrator).*

Jennifer Jones in Gone to Earth *(1950)*

THE GOOD BEGINNING (1953)   [2]

Dir *Gilbert Gunn.* Prod *Robert Hall.* Scr *Gunn, Hall, Janet Green.* Ph *Lionel Banes.* PC *Associated British.* Dis *AB-Pathé. 65 mins. Cert U*

Johnny (*John Fraser*), a struggling clerk married to ambitious but careful Kit (*Eileen Moore*) is envious of the never-never lifestyle of their friends Brian (*Peter Reynolds*) and Evie (*Lana Morris*). When he gets a small bonus, he buys Kit a fur coat on hire purchase, soon falls behind with the payments and loses more money gambling. After borrowing money from his firm to settle his debts, Brian persuades him to sell the coat. Too modest to be either comedy or drama.

RoC *Humphrey Lestocq, Hugh Pryse, Peter Jones, Ann Stephens, Robert Raglan, David Kossoff, Victor Maddern, Roland Curram, Virginia Clay, Oliver Johnston, Lou Jacobi, Ronnie Harries, Barbara Cavan, Rosemary Whitfield, Eddie Vitch, Alma Cookson.*

THE GOOD COMPANIONS (1956)   [4]

Dir *J. Lee Thompson.* Prod *Lee Thompson, Hamilton G. Inglis.* Scr *T.J. Morrison, John Whiting, J.L. Hodson, from the novel by J.B. Priestley.* Ph *Gilbert Taylor.* PC *Associated British.* Dis *AB-Pathé. Technicolor. Cinema-Scope. 104 mins. Cert U*

Miss Trant (*Celia Johnson*), a spinster, Jess Oakroyd (*Eric Portman*), a dissatisfied Yorkshireman, and Inigo (*John Fraser*), a schoolteacher-composer, inject new money - and life - into a second-rate concert party called The Dinky Doos. The musical talents of Susie (*Janette Scott*) and Jerry (*Paddy Stone*) are brought to the fore and, when Inigo is offered a West End contract, he insists that his 'stars' must be seen by the impresario concerned. Despite sabotage attempts by hired thugs, Susie and Jerry win through to stardom, and Inigo gets Susie. Very decent remake of the Jessie Matthews classic, full of youthful zest.

RoC *Hugh Griffith, Bobby Howes, Joyce Grenfell, Rachel Roberts, Thora Hird, Mona Washbourne, Irving Davies, John Salew, Beatrice Varley, Alec McCowen, John le Mesurier, Fabia Drake, Anthony Newley, Shirley Ann Field, Margaret Simons, Kim Parker, Beryl Kaye, Jimmy Caroll, Jeremy Burnham, Anna Turner, Brian Oulton, Lloyd Pearson, Ralph Truman, Agnes Bernelle, Lloyd Lamble, Campbell Cotts, Leslie Carol (Carole Lesley), Larry Cross, Nicholas Bruce, Shane Cordell, Tom Gill, Marianne Stone, Max Butterfield, Marjorie Rhodes, Richard Leech, Barbara Archer, George Rose, Ian Wilson, Melvyn Hayes, Claude Bonser, Olwen Brookes, Richard Thorp, George Woodbridge.*

Janette Scott and Paddy Stone in The Good Companions *(1957)*

THE GOOD DIE YOUNG (1954)   [3]

Dir *Lewis Gilbert.* Prod *Jack Clayton.* Scr *Gilbert, Vernon Harris, from the novel by Richard Macauley.* Ph *Jack Asher.* PC *Remus.* Dis *Independent Film Distributors/British Lion. 98 mins. Cert A*

Three men down on their luck, Mike, a boxer (*Stanley Baker*), Joe, a broke ex-GI (*Richard Basehart*) and Eddie, an AWOL USAF sergeant (*John Ireland*) are persuaded by Rave (*Laurence Harvey*), a playboy whose wife refuses to pick up any more bills, to rob a mail-van. The robbery goes wrong, and the psychotic Rave murders Mike and Eddie. Joe escapes to the airport, but Rave follows and shoots him. Joe shoots Rave, who dies under a 'No Way Out' sign. Dark, gloomy thriller.

RoC *Joan Collins, Gloria Grahame, René Ray, Margaret Leighton, Robert Morley, Freda Jackson, Lee Patterson, Walter Hudd, Susan Shaw, Sandra Dorne, James Kenney, Leslie Dwyer, George Rose, Patricia Owens, Joan Heal, Thomas Gallagher, Patricia McCarron, Alf Hinds, MacDonald Parke, Marianne Stone, Alexander Davion, Patsy Hagate, Sheila McCormack, Zena Barry, Hugh Moxey, Harold Siddons, John McRae, Stella Hamilton, Philip Ray, Joe Bloom, Edward Judd.*

GRAND NATIONAL NIGHT (1953)   [3]
(USA: *Wicked Wife*)

Dir *Bob McNaught.* Prod *Phil C. Samuel.* Scr *McNaught, from the play by Dorothy and Campbell Christie.* Ph *Jack Asher.* PC *Talisman/George Minter.* Dis *Renown. 80 mins. Cert A*

Rejected by her lover, Babs Coates (*Moira Lister*) attacks her racehorse owner husband Gerald (*Nigel Patrick*) in a drunken rage, and is accidentally killed. Inspector Ayling (*Michael Hordern*) tries hard to bring Gerald, who has driven the body to Liverpool, to trial for murder - but fate and Gerald's friends decree otherwise. Middling but well-crafted thriller, from a highly successful play.

RoC *Beatrice Campbell, Betty Ann Davies, Noel Purcell, Colin Gordon, Gibb McLaughlin, Barry Mackay, Leslie Mitchell, Richard Grayden, May Hallatt, George Sequira, Ernest Jay, Russell Waters, George Rose, Harold Goodwin, Arthur Howard, Edward Evans, Maria Mercedes.*

THE GREAT GAME (1952)   [3]

Dir *Maurice Elvey.* Prod *David Dent.* Scr *Wolfgang Wilhelm, from a play by Basil Thomas.* Ph *Phil Grindrod.* PC *Advance.* Dis *Adelphi. 80 mins. Cert U*

Joe Lawson (*James Hayter*), grasping chairman of First Division football team Burnville United, cares little about the happiness and welfare of his players as long as relegation is avoided. His crooked deals to buy a new striker are found out, and he is forced to resign, returning to the printing business he has neglected, to find it has gone to the dogs. Good central performance in a film that never makes up its mind which targets to aim for.

RoC *Diana Dors, Thora Hird, Sheila Shand Gibbs, John Laurie, Glyn Houston, Geoffrey Toone, Jack Lambert, Meredith Edwards, Alexander Gauge, Frank Pettingell, Glenn Melvyn, Roddy Hughes, Sydney Vivian, Charles Leno, Tommy Lawton, Brentford Football Club.*

THE GREAT VAN ROBBERY (1958)   ☐ 3

Dir *Max Varnel.* Prod *Edward J. Danziger, Harry Lee Danziger.* Scr *Brian Clemens, Eldon Howard.* Ph *Nick Roeg.* PC *Danzigers.* Dis *United Artists. 71 mins. Cert U*

Interpol detective Caesar Smith (*Denis Shaw*), whose bulk conceals his prowess at judo, tracks robbers who have stolen £150,000 from London, through Rio de Janeiro, Rome and Paris back to London. He establishes the guilt of a coffee importer (*Tony Quinn*), who meets the sticky end that was intended for Smith. Routine crooks' tour with an unusual hero.

RoC *Kay Callard, Vera Fusek, Philip Saville, Carl Duering, Tony Doonan, Geoffrey Hibbert, Peter Elliott, Bob Simmons, Gordon Sterne, Guido Lorraine, Hal Osmond, June Rodney, Brian Weske, Carl Conway, Michael Bell, Jacques Cey, Julian Orchard, John Mackin, Robert Raglan, Paul Stassino, Peter Allenby.*

THE GREEN BUDDHA (1954)   ☐ 2

Dir *John Lemont.* Prod *William N. Boyle.* Scr *Paul Erickson.* Ph *Basil Emmott.* PC and Dis *Republic. 62 mins. Cert U*

An American charter pilot (*Wayne Morris*) falls victim to a gang of international thieves who have just stolen a jade Buddha from a London exhibition. The pilot pursues the trail of the thieves to Battersea Fun Fair, where they are both killed. What seems to be a quadruple cross is the only new element in this very familiar-looking material.

RoC *Mary Germaine, Walter Rilla, Mary Merrall, Lloyd Lamble, Kenneth Griffith, Arnold Marle, Leslie Linder, George Woodbridge, Percy Herbert, Marcia Ashton, Victor Platt, Wolf Frees, Frank Atkinson, Bartlett Mullins, Dan Lester.*

GREEN GROW THE RUSHES (1951)   ☐ 3

Dir *Derek Twist.* Prod *John Gossage.* Scr *Howard Clewes, Twist, from Clewes' novel.* Ph *Harry Waxman.* PC *ACT Films.* Dis *British Lion. 79 mins. Cert U*

Government inspectors discover that an entire Kent coast community (protected by an ancient charter) is smuggling brandy. The inspectors try to get solid evidence, but fail, until a cargo of brandy is washed over the sea wall into a field. When the locals drink every last drop, the Ministry men have to admit defeat. Much-troubled technicians' venture (refused a release for months) emerges as an atmospheric but otherwise pale copy of Ealing comedy.

LP *Roger Livesey, Honor Blackman, Richard Burton, Frederick Leister, John Salew, Colin Gordon, Geoffrey Keen, Eliot Makeham, Vida Hope, Cyril Smith, Russell Waters, Archie Duncan, Jack McNaughton, Bryan Forbes,*

Arnold Ridley, Gilbert Davis, Harcourt Williams, John Stamp, Harold Goodwin, Henrik Jacobsen, Betty Shale.

THE GREEN MAN (1956)   ☐ 4

Dir *Robert Day,* (uncredited) *Basil Dearden.* Prod *Frank Launder, Sidney Gilliat.* Scr *Launder, Gilliat, from their play* Meet a Body. Ph *Gerald Gibbs.* PC *Grenadier.* Dis *British Lion. 80 mins. Cert A*

For Hawkins (*Alastair Sim*), a professional assassin and master of disguise, life has been dull for ages until a commission comes along to dispose of Sir Gregory (*Raymond Huntley*), a pompous politician. Hawkins chooses The Green Man, a country inn where Sir Gregory is spending an illicit weekend with a girl (*Eileen Moore*). Thanks to the unwitting interference of a vacuum salesman (*George Cole*), Hawkins is foiled. Laughter builds up steadily; Sim irresistible.

RoC *Terry-Thomas, Avril Angers, Dora Bryan, John Chandos, Colin Gordon, Cyril Chamberlain, Doris Yorke, Vivienne Wood, Arthur Brough, Marie Burke, Peter Bull, Willoughby Goddard, Arthur Lowe, Michael Ripper, Leslie Weston, Terence Alexander, Lucy Griffiths.*

THE GREEN SCARF (1954)   ☐ 3

Dir *George More O'Ferrall.* Prod *Bertram Ostrer, Albert Fennell.* Scr *Gordon Wellesley, from a novel by Guy des Cars.* Ph *Jack Hildyard.* PC *B & A.* Dis *British Lion. 96 mins. Cert A*

An elderly French lawyer (*Michael Redgrave*) takes on the seemingly hopeless case of a murder on board ship, to which a deaf and blind mute (*Kieron Moore*) has already confessed. It transpires that he did so because he felt his wife (*Ann Todd*) had committed the crime, and that the real killer is a ship's steward. Competent-plus cast and interesting plot, although drama doesn't touch many emotional chords.

RoC *Leo Genn, Jane Griffiths, Michael Medwin, Anthony Nicholls, Phil Brown, George Merritt, Evelyn Roberts, Ella Milne, Jane Henderson, Richard O'Sullivan, Michael Golden, Tristan Rawson, Peter Burton, Walter Horsbrugh, Terence Alexander, Jane Lamb, Neil Wilson, Henry Caine, Launce Mareschal.*

GRIP OF THE STRANGLER (1958)   ☐ 3
(USA: *The Haunted Strangler*)

Dir *Robert Day.* Prod *John Croydon.* Scr *Jan Read, John C. Cooper.* Ph *Lionel Banes.* PC *Producers Associates.* Dis *Eros. 79 mins. Cert X* 1880. Novelist James Rankin (*Boris Karloff*) reopens the case of Styles, a man hanged 20 years before as the Haymarket Strangler. Rankin becomes convinced of the man's innocence, and of the guilt of a Dr Tennant, who disappeared. He discovers that *he* is Tennant; a knife he finds in Styles' coffin takes possession of him. He murders his wife and other women. Trapped, he dies clutching Styles' tombstone in one hand and the knife in the other. Gruesome horror film, quite scary.

RoC *Elizabeth Allan, Jean Kent, Vera Day, Anthony Dawson, Tim Turner, Diane Aubrey, Leslie Perrins, Dorothy Gordon.*

GUILT IS MY SHADOW (1950)   ☐ 3

Dir *Roy Kellino.* Prod *Ivan Foxwell.* Scr *Foxwell, Kellino, John Gilling, from a novel by Peter Curtis.* Ph *William McLeod.* PC *Associated British.* Dis *AB-Pathé. 86 mins. Cert A*

On the run after a bank robbery, Jamie (*Peter Reynolds*) makes for his Uncle Kit's farm in Devon, where he steals from Kit (*Patrick Holt*) and is joined by his wife Linda (*Elizabeth Sellars*). In a fight, Linda accidentally kills the worthless Jamie and she and Kit, by now in love, tip the body down a disused tin mine. Linda is plagued by guilt and nightmares and they confess to the 'crime'. Slow, pretty miserable drama has a certain glum fascination.

RoC *Lana Morris, Lawrence O'Madden, Avice Landone, Esma Cannon, Wensley Pithey, Aubrey Woods, Willoughby Gray.*

GUILTY? (1956)   ☐ 3

Dir *Edmond T. Greville.* Prod *Charles A. Leeds.* Scr *Maurice J. Wilson, Ernest Dudley, from a novel by Michael Gilbert.* Ph *Stan Pavey.* PC *Gibraltar.* Dis *Grand National. 93 mins. Cert A*

Convinced that a wartime resistance heroine is innocent of a murder charge, Nap Rumbold (*John Justin*), a solicitor-cum-detective, travels to France, where he not only unearths the evidence that will clear her, but, with the help of a glamorous police agent (*Barbara Laage*) exposes a counterfeiting ring. Plot's not too hot, but thriller is at least lively, well-acted.

RoC *Donald Wolfit, Norman Wooland, Stephen Murray, Betty Stockfeld, Sydney Tafler, Andrée Debar, Russell Napier, Frank Villard, Leslie Perrins, Kynaston Reeves, André Mikhelson, Margo Lion.*

THE GYPSY AND THE GENTLEMAN (1957)   ☐ 3

Dir *Joseph Losey.* Prod *Maurice Cowan.* Scr *Janet Green, from a novel by Nina Warner Hooke.* Ph *Jack Hildyard.* PC and Dis *Rank. Eastman Colour. 107 mins. Cert A*

Sir Paul (*Keith Michell*), a Regency rake, falls under the spell of wild gipsy Belle (*Melina Mercouri*), who marries him without realizing he is penniless, and that his sister Sarah (*June Laverick*) stands to inherit the family fortune. Belle and her lover Jess (*Patrick McGoohan*) send her to an asylum, Sir Paul signing committal papers while drunk. But Sarah is rescued by a suitor (*Lyndon Brook*) and Sir Paul, Belle and Jess all drown when their coach crashes into a river. Another echo of Gainsborough days; lurid melodrama.

RoC *Mervyn Johns, Clare Austin, Helen Haye, Newton Blick, John Salew, Gladys Boot, Edna Morris, Catherine Feller, Laurence Naismith, David Hart, Louis Aquilina, Nigel Green, Lawrence (Larry) Taylor.*

H

HAMMER THE TOFF (1952)   [3]

Dir *Maclean Rogers*. Prod *Ernest G. Roy*. Scr *Uncredited, from the novel by John Creasey*. Ph *Geoffrey Faithfull*. PC *Nettlefold*. Dis *Butchers*. 71 mins. Cert U

Society sleuth the Hon. Richard Rollison (*John Bentley*), known as The Toff, meets pretty Susan Lancaster (*Patricia Dainton*) on a train and helps her to prove that a 'Robin Hood' crook, who had been blamed for killing her uncle for a secret steel formula, did not commit the crime. Good source material, but just another thick-ear thriller results.

RoC *Valentine Dyall, John Robinson, Roddy Hughes, Katherine Blake, Wally Patch, Basil Dignam, Lockwood West, Charles Hawtrey, John Powe, Andrea Malandrinos, Ben Williams, Patricia Page, Monte di Lyle, John Mansi, Max Brent, Vivienne Burgess, Michael Mulcaster, Gordon Craig, Ian Fleming, Vi Stevens.*

HANDCUFFS, LONDON (1955)   [2]

Dir *Bernard Knowles*. Prod *John Larkin*. Scr *Brock Williams*. Ph *Brendan Stafford*. PC *Trinity*. Dis *Eros*. 76 mins. Cert U

After obtaining advice from an art expert, Bardwill (*Alexander Gauge*) about a rare stamp which turns out to be a fake, Superintendent Fabian (*Bruce Seton*) chases the art forger through three separate cases, only to find in the end that the culprit is Bardwill himself. Undistinguished thriller, originally intended as a three-parter for TV.

RoC *Robert Raglan, Noel Howlett, Ursula Howells, Kathleen Byron, Isabel Dean, Maurice Kaufman(n), Dorinda Stevens, C. Denier Warren, Michael Craig, Gladys Boot, Derek Aylward.*

HANDS OF DESTINY (1954)   [1]

Dir/Prod *Tony Young*. Scr/Dr *Josef Ranald*. Ph *Phil Grindrod*. PC *Grosvenor*. Dis *Adelphi*. 61 mins. Cert U

Tedious semi-documentary about the work of a cheiromancer. In one story, he has convinced a suicidal young woman that her hand foretold happiness. In a second instance, he helps reunite a mother with her long-lost son.

LP *Dr Josef Ranald, Hilda Fenemore, Terence Alexander, Benedicta Leigh, Asta Bredigand, Richard Burrell.*

HA' PENNY BREEZE (1950)   [4]

Dir *Frank Worth*. Prod *Darcy Conyers, Don Sharp*. Scr *Sharp, Worth*. Ph *George Stretton, Gordon Lang*. PC *Storytellers*. Dis *AB-Pathé*. 72 mins. Cert U

Returning to his near-derelict Suffolk village after the war, David (*Edwin Richfield*), with his Australian friend Johnny (*Don Sharp*), decides to revive the place by starting a yachting industry. He converts his own yacht into a flyer

and organizes a big race. When his sister (*Gwyneth Vaughan*), who's in love with Johnny, falls overboard, he loses – but the winner commissions him to build a new boat. Fresh, invigorating second-feature with nice characters.

RoC *Terry Everett, Eva Rowland, Roger Maxwell, John Powe, Natalie Raine, Frank Hawkins, Arthur Goullet, Bartlett Mullins, Owen Reynolds, Darcy Conyers, Chris Halward, Michael Gough.*

THE HAPPIEST DAYS OF YOUR LIFE (1950)   [5]

Dir *Frank Launder*. Prod *Launder, Sidney Gilliat*. Scr *Launder, John Dighton, from Dighton's play*. Ph *Stan Pavey*. PC *Individual*. Dis *British Lion*. 81 mins. Cert U

Nutbourne Boys' School suddenly discovers that, thanks to a ministerial error, it has to billet the girls of St Swithin's. The two heads (*Alastair Sim, Margaret Rutherford*) are soon at loggerheads – and in despair, particularly Pond, who spends his first night in a co-ed school sleeping in the bath. When girls' parents and Nutbourne governors pay visits, things go from bad to disastrous. Pond and Miss Whitchurch decide to start a school in Tanganyika. Lively, richly-characterized comedy is really very funny throughout.

RoC *Joyce Grenfell, Edward Rigby, Guy Middleton, John Bentley, Bernadette O'Farrell, Muriel Aked, John Turnbull, Richard Wattis, Arthur Howard, Millicent Wolf, Myrette Morven, Russell Waters, Patience Rentoul, John Boxer, Alan Broadhurst, Vivienne Wood, Kenneth Downey, Laurence Naismith, Stringer Davis, Stanley Lemin, Olwen Brookes, Nan Munro, Beryl Ede, Percy Walsh, Harold Goodwin, Gladys Henson, George Benson, Angela Glynne, Pat(ricia) Owens, Margaret Anderson, Betty Blackler, Fred Marshall, John Rhodes, Jim Davies, Keith Faulkner, William Symons, Lilian Stanley.*

Margaret Rutherford, Joyce Grenfell and Alastair Sim in The Happiest Days of Your Life *(1950)*

THE HAPPINESS OF THREE WOMEN (1954)   [3]

Dir *Maurice Elvey*. Prod *David Dent*. Scr *E. Eynon Evans, Maufy Davies, from a play by Evans*. Ph *Stan Pavey*. PC *Advance*. Dis *Adelphi*. 79 mins. Cert U

The postman-poet (*Eynon Evans*) of a Welsh

village is a patcher-up of broken romances. He helps a cripple who is to marry a local girl; a widow who lost her husband in the war; a young couple separated by his absence in Korea; and a wealthy woman who finds happiness in hard work at the inn. Rather overcrowded amalgam of sentiment and fun. The title's a misnomer – there are four women.

RoC *Brenda de Banzie, Petula Clark, Patricia Cutts, Patricia Burke, Donald Houston, Bill O'Connor, Gladys Hay, Glyn Houston, Emrys Leyshon, Hugh Pryse, Jessie Evans, John Lewis, Mary Jones, Julie Milton, Eira Griffiths, Ronnie Harris.*

HAPPY EVER AFTER (1954)   [5]
(USA: *O'Leary Night*/*Tonight's the Night*)

Dir/Prod *Mario Zampi*. Scr *Jack Davies, Michael Pertwee*. Ph *Stanley Pavey*. PC *Associated British*. Dis *AB-Pathé*. Technicolor. 86 mins. Cert U

In the Irish village of Rathbarney, the aged squire is killed while hunting. His successor (*David Niven*) proves to be a grasping nasty who collects debts, sacks old retainers, persecutes poachers, evicts tenants and refuses to buy rounds at the local! The villagers draw lots for murdering him, but in the midst of their disastrous attempts, the new squire is discovered trying to burn his manor down for the insurance. Achingly funny comedy, full of hilarious incident.

RoC *Yvonne de Carlo, Barry Fitzgerald, George Cole, A. E. Matthews, Robert Urquhart, Noelle Middleton, Michael Shepley, Joseph Tomelty, Eddie Byrne, James (Jimmy) Mageean, Liam Redmond, Patrick McAlinney, Anthony Nicholls, Brian O'Higgins, Patrick Westwood, Fred Johnson, Ronan O'Casey, Michael Martin-Harvey, Denis Martin, Bill Shine, Harry Hutchinson, Tommy Duggan.*

THE HAPPY FAMILY (1952)   [2]
(USA: *Mr Lord Says No*)

Dir *Muriel Box*. Prod *Sydney Box, William MacQuitty*. Scr *Muriel and Sydney Box, from the play by Michael Clayton Hutton*. Ph *Reginald H. Wyer*. PC *London Independent*. Dis *Apex*. 86 mins. Cert U

Thanks to an architect's mistake, the Lord family's grocery shop with flat above (known as the House of Lords) must be pulled down to make way for a road into the Festival of Britain site. The Lords (*Stanley Holloway, Kathleen Harrison*) resist by all means possible, ending by barricading themselves in. They are on the point of giving in when the Government does so, and builds the road round their home. Ealing-style comedy whose central situation wears thin rather quickly.

RoC *Naunton Wayne, George Cole, Eileen Moore, Dandy Nichols, John Stratton, Margaret Barton, Miles Malleson, Tom Gill, Geoffrey Sumner, Shirley Mitchell, Laurence Naismith, Edward Lexy, Cameron Hall, Hal Osmond, John Salew, Ernest Butcher, Lyn Evans, Michael Ward, Richard Wattis, David Keir, Anthony Oliver, Campbell Singer, Peter Martyn, Arthur Hambling, Eileen Way.*

HAPPY GO LOVELY (1950)   [4]

Dir *Bruce Humberstone*. Prod *Marcel Hellman*.

Vera-Ellen and David Niven in Happy Go
Lovely *(1950)*

Scr *Val Guest, Arthur Macrae.* Ph *Erwin Hillier.* PC *Excelsior.* Dis *AB-Pathé. Technicolor.
97 mins. Cert U*
Chorus girl Janet (*Vera-Ellen*) is wrongly
thought to be the girlfriend of eccentric Scots
millionaire B. G. Bruno (*David Niven*). The
producer of her show seizes on this, and pro-
motes her to stardom, hoping to influence his
creditors with Bruno's 'interest' in the show.
Bruno poses as a reporter to find out what's
going on, falls for Janet and ends up really
backing the show. A remake of 1937's *Paradise
for Two*, this pleasant musical doesn't really
compare with the Hollywood model, though
rapturously received by some critics.
RoC *Cesar Romero, Bobby Howes, Diane Hart,
Gordon Jackson, Sandra Dorne, Joyce Carey,
John Laurie, Barbara Couper, Henry Hewitt,
Gladys Henson, Hugh Dempster, Wylie Watson,
Joan Heal, Hector Ross, Ambrosine Phillpotts,
Molly Urquhart, David Lober, Jonathan Lucas,
Jack Billings, Rolf Alexander, Ian Stuart, Leon
Biedryski, Kay Kendall, Douglas Scott and His
Debonair Boys.*

HAPPY IS THE BRIDE (1957) [4]
Dir *Roy Boulting.* Prod *Paul Soskin.* Scr *Jeffrey Dell, Boulting, from a play by Esther
McCracken.* Ph *Ted Scaife.* PC *Panther Productions.* Dis *British Lion. 85 mins. Cert U*
It seems a romantic idyll when David (*Ian
Carmichael*) proposes to Janet (*Janette Scott*)
during a cricket match. But when the wedding
is announced, Janet's parents (*Cecil Parker,
Edith Sharpe*) take over. Aunt Florence (*Joyce
Grenfell*) forecasts disaster. Janet's sister (*Vir-
ginia Maskell*) arrives, claiming to have left her
husband. Janet and David try to escape, but
he is arrested for a driving offence, and a police
car takes them to their wedding. Hectic co-
medy with delightful cameos, a remake of
Quiet Wedding (1940).
RoC *Terry-Thomas, Eric Barker, Elvi Hale,
Miles Malleson, Athene Seyler, John le Mesur-
ier, Irene Handl, Thorley Walters, Nicholas
Parsons, Richard Bennett, Sarah Drury, Brian
Oulton, Rolf Lefebvre, Pauline Winters, Joan
Hickson, Ian Wilson, Douglas 'Cardew' Robin-
son, Victor Maddern, Sam Kydd, Peggyann
Clifford, Margaret Lacey, Enid Hewitt, Olive
Milbourne.*

THE HARASSED HERO (1954) [2]
Dir *Maurice Elvey.* Prod *Clive Nicholas.* Scr

Brock Williams. Ph *Hone Glendinning.* PC *Corsair.* Dis *AB-Pathé. 61 mins. Cert U*
Murray Selwyn (*Guy Middleton*), a wealthy
hypochondriac, accidentally gets mixed up in
a counterfeit racket on the eve of his departure
for a rest cure. The leader (*Elwyn Brook-Jones*)
of the gang makes frenzied attempts to recover
the printing plates Murray unwittingly has,
even kidnapping his nurse (*Joan Winmill*). But
she sets off signal flares from the gang's yacht
and brings about their capture. Likeable romp
could have been much funnier.
RoC *Mary Mackenzie, Harold Goodwin, Joss
Ambler, Clive Morton, Hugh Moxey, Gabrielle
Brune, Gaylord Cavallaro, Alfred Maron, Stafford Byrne, Simone Lovell, Harold Malin, Alan
Rolfe.*

HARRY BLACK (1958) [4]
(USA: *Harry Black and the Tiger*)
Dir *Hugo Fregonese.* Prod *John Brabourne.* Scr
*Sydney Boehm, from the novel by David
Walker.* Ph *John Wilcox.* PC *Mersham.* Dis
*20th Century-Fox. Technicolor. CinemaScope.
116 mins. Cert U*
India. Hunter Harry Black (*Stewart Granger*)
finds that his new neighbour is Tanner (*Anthony Steel*), the man whose panic was responsible for Harry losing a leg in the war. Tanner
begs to come along on a tiger hunt to prove
himself to his small son, but panics again, and
Harry is badly mauled. He is nursed back to
health by Tanner's wife (*Barbara Rush*), and,
with Tanner away, they fall in love; however,
they part on his return. Harry kills his tiger
and continues with his solitary life. Well-acted
jungle yarn with a cracking climax; a fillip for
three fading stars.
RoC *I. S. Johar, Martin Stephens, Frank Olegario, Kamala Devi, Gladys Boot, George Curzon, Archie Duncan, Harold Siddons, Allan
McClelland, Jan Conrad, André Maranne, John
Rae.*

THE HEADLESS GHOST (1959) [2]
Dir *Peter Graham Scott.* Prod *Jack Greenwood.*
Scr *Kenneth Langtry, Herman Cohen.* Ph *John
Wiles.* PC *Merton Park.* Dis *Anglo-Amalga-
mated. DyaliScope. 61 mins. Cert U*
Three American teenagers on holiday in Bri-
tain decide to stay the night in an old castle
when they hear it is haunted. One ghost asks
them to help another ghost find his head – and
this they do, in spite of the appearance of a
third ghost who keeps upsetting the applecart.
Bull-at-a-gate ghost comedy for younger au-
diences.
LP *Richard Lyon, Liliane Sottane, David Rose,
Clive Revill, Jack Allen, Alexander Archdale,
Carl Bernard.*

HEART OF A CHILD (1958) [3]
Dir *Clive Donner.* Prod *Alfred Shaughnessy.*
Scr *Leigh Vance, from the novel by Phyllis
Bottome.* Ph *Peter Hennessy.* PC *Beaconsfield.*
Dis *Rank. 76 mins. Cert U*
1918, the Austrian Tyrol. Ill-treated by his
father (*Donald Pleasence*), who threatens to sell
his St Bernard dog to a butcher, 11-year-old
Karl (*Richard Williams*) runs off to Innsbruck,
where a friendly vet buys the dog. On his re-

turn, his father beats him senseless. Karl later
gets the dog back, from the Red Cross, but is
trapped on a cliff in snow, and then rescued
by the dog and Maria (*Jean Anderson*), a spinster, who marries the vet. This time, Karl's
father allows him to keep his pet. Heavily
made tear-jerker doesn't touch the emotions.
RoC *John Glyn Jones, Maureen Pryor, Carla
Challoner, Andrew Keir, Norman MacOwan,
Willoughby Goddard, John Boxer.*

THE HEART OF A MAN (1959) [2]
Dir *Herbert Wilcox.* Prod *Anna Neagle.* Scr
Jack Trevor Story, Pamela Bower. Ph *Reginald
Wyer.* PC *Everest.* Dis *Rank. 92 mins. Cert U*
Frankie (*Frankie Vaughan*), an out-of-work
seaman, meets a tramp (*Peter Sinclair*) who
promises him £1,000 if he can earn £100 in a
month. The seaman tries his hand as a boun-
cer, boxer and commissionaire, but fails at
everything until finding success as a singer. He
finds the tramp in hospital, patently broke, and
gives him the £100, having also found a wife
(*Anne Heywood*) in the process. Dated vehicle
for Vaughan; the title song was a big hit.
RoC *Tony Britton, Anthony Newley, Michael
Medwin, George Rose, Harry Fowler, Leslie
Mitchell, Kent Walton, Hogan 'Kid' Bassey,
Harold Kasket, Vanda Hudson.*

THE HEART OF THE MATTER
(1953) [4]
Dir *George More O'Ferrall.* Prod *Ian Dalrymple.* Scr *Ian Dalrymple, Lesley Storm, from the
novel by Graham Greene.* Ph *Jack Hildyard.* PC
London Films. Dis *British Lion. 105 mins.
Cert A*
To pay for a holiday for the ailing wife (*Elizabeth Allan*) he no longer loves, Scobie (*Trevor Howard*), the disliked but fair deputy police commissioner in 1942 Sierra Leone, rashly
borrows money from a trader. The man blackmails Scobie over his relationship with an Austrian refugee (*Maria Schell*) and the policeman
is considering suicide when he is killed in a
street fracas. A bit unrelenting, but it does
capture the atmosphere and Howard is good.
RoC *Gerard Oury, Denholm Elliott, George
Coulouris, Peter Finch, Earl Cameron, Michael
Hordern, Cyril Raymond, Colin Gordon, Orlando Martins, Gillian Lind, Evelyn Roberts,
John Rae, Peter Burton, Eileen Thorndike, Anthony Snell, Jane Henderson, Stanley Lemin,
Eugene Leahy, Christopher Rhodes, Judith
Furse, Ewan Roberts, Jack Allen, John Akar,
John Glyn-Jones, Assany Kamara Wilson,
Saidu Fofana, Errol John.*

THE HEART WITHIN (1957) [3]
Dir *David Eady.* Prod *Jon Penington.* Scr *Geof-
frey Orme.* Ph *Ernest Palmer.* PC *Penington
Eady.* Dis *Rank. 61 mins. Cert U*
Danny (*David Hemmings*), 13-year-old son of
a dockside junk dealer (*James Hayter*), helps
Victor (*Earl Cameron*), a West Indian on the
run for a murder he didn't commit. By chance,
Danny learns that a narcotics king, Johnson
(*Clifford Evans*) is responsible, but is kid-
napped by the killer. When Victor storms to
the rescue, Johnson is killed and Victor

Clifford Evans and David Hemmings in The Heart Within *(1957)*

Alan Ladd and Jill Bennett in Hell Below Zero *(1953)*

cleared. Variably acted, quite pleasing racial-problem thriller.
RoC *Betty Cooper, Dan Jackson, Frank Sin-guineau, Gloria Simpson, Jack Stewart, Janice Hughes, Paula Henriques, Denton de Gray, Wally Thomas, Brian Tyler, Dawson France, Frank Pettit, Glynn Edwards, Ivor Salter.*

HEAVEN KNOWS, MR ALLISON
(1957)   [5]
Dir *John Huston.* Prod *Buddy Adler, Eugene Frenke.* Scr *John Lee Mahin, Huston, from the novel by Charles Shaw.* Ph *Oswald Morris.* PC/Dis *20th Century-Fox. 106 mins. Cert U*
An American marine, Allison (*Robert Mitchum*) is washed ashore on a Pacific island in World War II. The only other occupant is a nun, Sister Angela (*Deborah Kerr*). They co-exist quite happily until Allison celebrates the departure of a Japanese weather unit by getting drunk and assaulting the nun who flees into the jungle and catches fever. Remorseful, Allison nurses her, but then a major Jap force arrives, Allison kills an officer while stealing blankets, and, when US troops arrive, a full-scale battle ensues. Allison blows up Jap artillery, but is badly wounded. The unlikely duo is taken aboard a hospital ship, with Sister Angela praying by Allison's side. Exciting and tender in turn; unusual and entertaining.
No supporting cast.

HEIGHTS OF DANGER (1952)   [3]
Dir *Peter Bradford.* Prod *Howard Thomas.* Scr *Betty Davies.* Ph *Reg W. Cavender.* PC *Associated British/Pathé Documentary Unit/Children's Film Foundation.* Dis *AB-Pathé. 60 mins. Cert U*
Croudson (*Jack Melford*), a businessman, tries to buy the Burton family garage, knowing that its business will boom once a by-pass is built. In an effort to get the money to see them through, the Burtons compete in an Alpine car rally, and despite sabotage attempts by Croudson's hirelings, they win it. Mild children's entertainment.
RoC *Basil Appleby, Freda Bamford, Wilfred Downing, Annette Cabot, Christopher Cabot, Richard Goolden, Sebastian Cabot, Roger Snowden.*

HELL BELOW ZERO (1953)   [3]
Dir *Mark Robson, Anthony Bushell.* Prod *Irv-*ing *Allen, Albert R. Broccoli, (uncredited) George Willoughby.* Scr *Alec Coppel, Max Trell, Richard Maibaum, from a novel by Hammond Innes.* Ph *John Wilcox.* PC *Warwick.* Dis *Columbia. Technicolor. 90 mins. Cert U*
Attracted to Judie (*Joan Tetzel*), who is on her way to the Antarctic to investigate her father's death, adventurer Craig (*Alan Ladd*) signs on the icebreaker taking her there. He finds out that Erik (*Stanley Baker*) is the killer, but is transferred to a whaler skippered by a girl (*Jill Bennett*). Aboard the icebreaker, Erik rams the whaler and both vessels sink. Marooned on an icepack, Craig and Erik fight to the death with ice picks. Craig survives. Rugged thriller; locations lift it a little above the routine.
RoC *Basil Sydney, Joseph Tomelty, Niall MacGinnis, Peter Dyneley, Susan Rayne, Philo Hauser, John Witty, Genine Graham, Ivan Craig, Paddy Ryan, Cyril Chamberlain, Paul Homer, Edward Hardwicke, Brandon Toomey, Basil Cunard, Fred Griffiths, John Warren, Philip Ray, Paul Connell, Glyn Houston.*

HELL DRIVERS (1957)   [4]
Dir *Cy Endfield.* Prod *S. Benjamin Fisz.* Scr *John Kruse, C. Raker (Cy) Endfield.* Ph *Geoffrey Unsworth.* PC *Aqua.* Dis *Rank. VistaVision. 108 mins. Cert A*
Just out of prison, Tom Yately (*Stanley Baker*) gets a dangerous job driving rattletrap lorries along cliff roads, where a certain number of loads have to be carried each day, and the weak are soon weeded out. Red (*Patrick McGoohan*), the sadistic 'champion' driver,

Sean Connery, Sidney James, Stanley Baker (on floor) and Patrick McGoohan in Hell Drivers *(1957)*

soon has it in for Tom and, after a terrific fight between them, attempts to force Tom's lorry over the cliff. But it is Red who hurtles to his death. Rough, tough stuff; basically unconvincing perhaps, but still a good thriller.
RoC *Herbert Lom, Peggy Cummins, William Hartnell, Wilfrid Lawson, Sidney James, Jill Ireland, Gordon Jackson, Alfie Bass, David McCallum, Sean Connery, Vera Day, Marjorie Rhodes, Robin Bailey, Wensley Pithey, George Murcell, Beatrice Varley, Jean St Clair, Jerry Stovin, John Horsley, Marianne Stone, Ronald Clarke.*

HELL IS A CITY (1959)   [4]
Dir/Scr *Val Guest, from the novel by Maurice Proctor.* Prod *Michael Carreras.* Ph *Arthur Grant.* PC *Hammer.* Dis *Warner-Pathé. HammerScope. 98 mins. Cert A*
To the consternation of Inspector Martineau (*Stanley Baker*), Starling (*John Crawford*), a ruthless jewel thief, breaks jail and is soon involved in a raid in which a bookie's clerk is killed. Escaping from the bookie (*Donald Pleasence*) after forcing his wife (*Billie Whitelaw*), an old flame, to harbour him, Starling silences a mute girl witness (*Sarah Branch*), but is finally taken after a rooftop struggle with Martineau. With its tough approach and patchwork of small scenes, this exciting thriller was the forerunner of much British TV cops-and-robbers to follow. Manchester was reported to be not too pleased about the title.
RoC *Maxine Audley, Joseph Tomelty, George A. Cooper, Geoffrey Frederick, Vanda Godsell, Charles Houston, Russell Napier, Joby Blanshard, Charles Morgan, Peter Madden, Dickie Owen, Lois Daine, Warren Mitchell, Alister Williamson.*

HELL IS SOLD OUT (1951)   [3]
Dir *Michael Anderson.* Prod *Raymond Stross.* Scr *Guy Morgan, Moie Charles, from the novel by Maurice Dekobra.* Ph *Jack Asher.* PC *Zelstro.* Dis *Eros. 84 mins. Cert A*
Presumed dead in World War II, novelist Dominic Danges (*Herbert Lom*) returns from a prison camp to find that a new novel under his name is on the bookstalls and selling fast. He discovers the writer, Valerie (*Mai Zetterling*), but his publisher persuades him to continue the deception, and the two eventually marry. Curious title (actually that of the fictional novel) for a mixture of romance, drama and farce.
RoC *Richard Attenborough, Kathleen Byron, Hermione Baddeley, Zena Marshall, Nicholas Hannen, Joan Hickson, Eric Pohlmann, Laurence Naismith, Joan Young, Olaf Pooley, Hal Osmond, Aletha Orr, Virginia Bedard, George Margo, Ronald Adam, Joan Elan.*

HELLO LONDON (1958)   [1]
Dir *Sidney Smith.* Prod *George Fowler.* Scr *Fowler, Herb Sargent, Ken Englund, Guy Elmes.* Ph *Otto Heller.* PC *Kinran.* Dis *Regal. Eastman Colour. 78 mins. Cert U*
Hoping to persuade her to take part in a charity concert, *Michael Wilding* and *Eunice Gayson* take international ice skater *Sonja Henie* on a tour of London, finishing off the plot by caus-

ing her manager (*Ronnie Graham*) to miss his plane. Heavily dated patchwork musical.

RoC *Lisa Gastoni, Charles Heslop, Dora Bryan, Oliver Johnston, Trefor Jones, Stanley Holloway, Dennis Price, Robert Coote, Roy Castle, Joan Regan, Oliver Reed.*

HER FAVOURITE HUSBAND (1950) [2]
(USA: *The Taming of Dorothy*)

Dir *Mario Soldati*. Prod *John Sutro, Colin Lesslie*. Scr *Noel Langley, W. F. Templeton, from the play by Pepine de Felipe*. Ph *Mario Bava*. PC *Orlux*. Dis *Renown*. 79 mins. Cert A

Antonio (*Robert Beatty*), a timid Italian bank clerk beset by a dominant English wife (*Jean Kent*) and mother-in-law (*Margaret Rutherford*), is the double of lawless Leo (also *Beatty*), who robs his bank and frames him. While Antonio is in jail, Leo makes violent love to his wife, who likes it. Antonio is cleared but decides to model his life on Leo. In the end, his wife is not sure which of the two is her 'husband'. Film mistakes noise and muddle for comedy.

RoC *Gordon Harker, Rona Anderson, Walter Crisham, Max Adrian, Tamara Lees, Norman Shelley, Michael Balfour, Jack McNaughton, Danny Green, Joss Ambler, Mary Hinton, Peter Illing, Jimmy Vientola.*

Robert Beatty and Jean Kent in Her Favourite Husband *(1950)*

THE HIDE-OUT (1956) [2]

Dir *Peter Graham Scott*. Prod *John Temple-Smith, Francis Edge*. Scr *Kenneth R. Hayles*. Ph *Brendan J. Stafford*. PC *Major*. Dis *Rank*. 57 mins. Cert U

Investigating a case of banknotes that comes into his possession, Steve (*Dermot Walsh*) discovers that the money belongs to Robert Grant (*Ronald Howard*) who is buying diseased furs to save his bankrupt business. Robert is killed and the murderer – Tim (*Sam Kydd*), Steve's ex-convict friend – himself dies when the lorry in which he is making his escape with the furs crashes and is destroyed by fire. Adequate, rather muddled thriller.

RoC *Rona Anderson, Howard Lang, Edwin Richfield, Arnold Diamond, Trevor Reid, Frank Hawkins, Richard Shaw, Tommy Clegg, Jessica Cairns, Jack Taylor, Angela Krefeld.*

HIGH FLIGHT (1957) [3]

Dir *John Gilling*. Prod *Phil C. Samuel*. Scr *Joseph Landon, Kenneth Hughes, Gilling*. Ph

Ted Moore. PC *Warwick*. Dis *Columbia*. Technicolor. CinemaScope. 101 mins. Cert U

At an air cadet's training college, big-headed Tony Winchester (*Kenneth Haigh*) is soon at loggerheads with the CO, Rudge (*Ray Milland*), who was partly responsible for Winchester's father's death in World War II. After various scrapes – he is severely reprimanded by Rudge for one mid-air exploit – Winchester passes the course, and finds a new understanding with Rudge, when the older man 'nurses' him to safety after his engine fails. Superb flying scenes fail to compensate for ridiculous plot.

RoC *Helen Cherry, Anthony Newley, Leslie Phillips, Bernard Lee, Kenneth Fortescue, Sean Kelly, Duncan Lamont, Kynaston Reeves, John le Mesurier, Jan Brooks, Anne Aubrey, Jan Holden, Barry Foster, Glyn Houston.*

HIGH HELL (1958) [1]

Dir *Burt Balaban*. Prod *William N. Boyle, Arthur Mayer*. Scr *Irve Tunick, from the novel by Steve Frazee*. Ph *Jimmy Wilson*. PC *Rich & Rich*. Dis *Paramount*. 85 mins. Cert A

Trapped by a snowdrift high in the Canadian Rockies while visiting her estranged husband, one of a group of rugged gold miners, Lenore (*Elaine Stewart*) soon finds her presence sets the men on edge. The drunken Luke (*Patrick Allen*) tries to rape her, but she is saved by Craig (*John Derek*). Gold is struck; Luke and Lenore's husband (*Al Mullock*) attempt to dynamite the vein, but are killed after a battle with the rest of the miners. Foolishly plotted, gratingly acted; laughs are strictly unintentional.

RoC *Rodney Burke, Jerold Wells, Colin Croft, Nicholas Stuart.*

HIGH JUMP (1958) [2]

Dir *Godfrey Grayson*. Prod *Edward J. Danziger, Harry Lee Danziger*. Scr *Brian Clemens, Eldon Howard*. Ph *Jimmy Wilson*. PC *Danzigers*. Dis *United Artists*. 66 mins. Cert A

A trapeze artist who has lost his nerve (*Richard Wyler* – the former *Richard Stapley* in his first film under his new name) is seduced by a sultry widow (*Lisa Daniely*) into helping with a jewel robbery. When two men are killed, he sees the error of his ways and turns queen's evidence. Uninteresting thriller.

RoC *Leigh Madison, Michael Peake, Arnold Bell, Norah Gordon, Tony Doonan, Robert Raglan, Colin Tapley, Stuart Hillier.*

HIGHLY DANGEROUS (1950) [3]

Dir *Roy Baker*. Prod *Antony Darnborough*. Scr *Eric Ambler*. Ph *Reginald Wyer*. PC *Two Cities*. Dis *General Film Distributors*. 88 mins. Cert U

Frances (*Margaret Lockwood*), an entomologist, is sent to Eastern Europe to check rumours that insects are being bred for use in bacteriological warfare. Her contact is murdered and she is given a truth drug under which she sees herself as the death-defying heroine of a radio serial. She hatches a crazy plan which, with the help of an American reporter (*Dane Clark*), actually works: they destroy the lab., steal the insects and escape. The drug wears off and she wonders how she did

Dane Clark and Margaret Lockwood in Highly Dangerous *(1950)*

it. Some chuckles and thrills delivered by comprehensively silly story.

RoC *Marius Goring, Naunton Wayne, Wilfrid Hyde White, Eugene Deckers, Olaf Pooley, Gladys Henson, Paul Hardtmuth, Michael Hordern, George Benson, Eric Pohlmann, Joan Haythorne, Patric Doonan, Anthony Newley, Jill Balcon, Ernest Butcher, Lance Secretan, Toni Frost, Michael Ritterman, John Gabriel, John Horsley, Anton Diffring, Noel Johnson (voice).*

THE HIGH TERRACE (1956) [3]

Dir *Henry Cass*. Prod *Robert S. Baker*. Scr *Alfred Shaughnessy, Norman Hudis, Brock Williams*. Ph *Eric Cross*. PC *CIPA*. Dis *RKO Radio*. 82 mins. Cert A

Impresario Kellner (*Eric Pohlmann*) is found murdered by actress Stephanie (*Lois Maxwell*), whose ex-husband John (*Derek Bond*), a fellow-member of the company, helps her to establish an alibi. American Bill Lang (*Dale Robertson*) tries to sniff out the truth and, when John disappears, Stephanie realizes he has gone too far trying to shield her and that she must admit that she is the killer. Whodunnit is slow-moving, but keeps you guessing.

RoC *Mary Laura Wood, Lionel Jeffries, Jameson Clark, Carl Bernard, Garard Green, Olwen Brookes, Benita Lydal, Marianne Stone, Frederick Treves, Jonathan Field, Gretchen Franklin, Alan Robinson, Jack Cunningham, Arthur Lowe.*

HIGH TIDE AT NOON (1957) [3]

Dir *Philip Leacock*. Prod *Julian Wintle*. Scr *Neil Paterson, from the novel by Elizabeth Ogilvie*. Ph *Eric Cross*. PC/Dis *Rank*. 109 mins. Cert A

On a remote Nova Scotia island where the only trade is lobster fishing, Joanna (*Betta St John*) is wooed by Nils, a fisherman (*Michael Craig*), the brutish Simon (*Patrick McGoohan*) and a newcomer Alec (*William Sylvester*), whom she marries. Alec, however, becomes a gambler, deep in debt to Simon, and drowns in an accident. Simon tries to force himself on Joanna and Nils drives him from the island; but it is five years before Joanna realizes that it is Nils she now loves. At times pleasant, if rather distant and variably scripted romantic drama.

RoC *Flora Robson, Alexander Knox, Peter Arne, Patrick Allen, John Hayward, Jill Dixon, Susan Beaumont, Stella Bonheur, Stuart Nichol, George Murcell, Bernard Bresslaw,*

Errol MacKinnon, Anthony Bate, Victor Che-net, Franklin Fox, John Stevenson Lang, Gerald Lawson, Arthur Massey, Bill Nagy, Charles Richardson, Ewan Roberts, Ryck Rydon, Richard Shaw, Nicholas Stuart, Garry Thorne, Paul Massie.

HIGH TREASON (1951) [4]

Dir *Roy Boulting*. Prod *Paul Soskin*. Scr *Frank Harvey*, *Roy Boulting*. Ph *Gilbert Taylor*. PC *Conqueror*. Dis *General Film Distributors*. 93 mins. Cert U

Sabotage in the London docks. A foreman is, rightly, suspected by the police. He appeals to his secret confederates, who kill him off. The police track the saboteurs' headquarters to a London business college, and suspect an MP may be involved. They are, however, unaware of the saboteurs' plans to blow up the country's major power stations until one of their number, shocked by the docker's murder, squeals before being shot. A gun battle in Battersea Power Station results in the ring being wiped out. Unbelievable but tense and exciting thriller.

LP *Liam Redmond*, *André Morell*, *Mary Morris*, *Kenneth Griffith*, *Patric Doonan*, *Anthony Bushell*, *Joan Hickson*, *Anthony Nicholls*, *Geoffrey Keen*, *John Bailey*, *Dora Bryan*, *Charles Lloyd Pack*, *Laurence Naismith*, *Sam Kydd*, *Tony Quinn*, *Lockwood West*, *Bruce Seton*, *Stephen Jack*, *Helen Harvey*, *Frank Harvey*, *Robert Brennan*, *Harry Fowler*, *R. Stuart Lindsell*, *Alfie Bass*, *Cyril Conway*, *Mickey Wood*.

A HILL IN KOREA (1956) [4]
(USA: Hell in Korea)

Dir *Julian Amyes*. Prod *Anthony Squire*. Scr *Ian Dalrymple*, *Squire*, *Ronald Spencer*, *from the novel by Max Catto*. Ph *Freddie Francis*. PC *Wessex*. Dis *British Lion*. 81 mins. Cert A

The Korean War. After a foray into a village to see if it is occupied by the enemy, a small patrol of British soldiers is cut off by a Chinese advance. The soldiers are forced to take refuge in a hillside temple. The national service lieutenant (*George Baker*) worries that they are trapped and Wyatt (*Ronald Lewis*), a coward, tries to make a getaway. Their own aircraft bomb the temple but, under cover of the raid, they get away, although Wyatt panics and is killed. Goodish sweat-and-blood war film.

RoC *Harry Andrews*, *Stanley Baker*, *Michael Medwin*, *Stephen Boyd*, *Victor Maddern*, *Harry Landis*, *Robert Brown*, *Barry Lowe*, *Robert Shaw*, *Charles Laurence*, *Percy Herbert*, *Michael Caine*, *Eric Corrie*, *David Morrell*.

HINDLE WAKES (1952) [3]
(USA: Holiday Week)

Dir *Arthur Crabtree*. Prod *William J. Gell*, *Phil Brandon*. Scr *John Baines*, *from the play by Stanley Houghton*. Ph *Geoffrey Faithfull*. PC/Dis *Monarch*. 88 mins. Cert A

Mill girls Jenny (*Lisa Daniely*) and Mary (*Sandra Dorne*) take off for Blackpool from their home town of Hindle for the Wakes Week holiday. Jenny meets the mill-owner's son (*Brian Worth*) and they go off for a week together. Mary agrees to cover for Jenny, but is killed in an accident. Jenny's parents insist that she

marry the boy, but she refuses to do so. Strangely cast old chestnut has dated emotional appeal.

RoC *Leslie Dwyer*, *Joan Hickson*, *Michael Medwin*, *Ronald Adam*, *Mary Clare*, *Bill Travers*, *Lloyd Pearson*, *Tim Turner*, *Diana Hope*, *Beatrice Varley*, *Rita Webb*, *Ian Wilson*, *Cyril Smith*, *Alistair Hunter*, *Lionel Grose*.

HIS EXCELLENCY (1951) [2]

Dir *Robert Hamer*. Prod *Michael Truman*. Scr *Hamer*, *W. P. Lipscomb*, *from the play by Dorothy and Campbell Christie*. Ph *Douglas Slocombe*. PC *Ealing Studios*. Dis *General Film Distributors*. 83 mins. Cert U

George Harrison (*Eric Portman*), ex-leader of the dockers' union, is appointed governor of a British island colony. He faces much scepticism and prejudice, and upsets people with his blunt attitudes, but wins his spurs when his experience of dockyard politics enables him to nip an incipient riot in the bud. Disappointing, condescending comedy-drama, partly made on location in Sicily.

RoC *Cecil Parker*, *Helen Cherry*, *Susan Stephen*, *Edward Chapman*, *Clive Morton*, *Geoffrey Keen*, *Alec Mango*, *John Salew*, *Robin Bailey*, *Eric Pohlmann*, *Howard Marion Crawford*, *Paul Demel*, *Elspeth March*, *Henry Longhurst*, *Gerard Heinz*, *Barbara Leake*, *Barbara Cavan*, *Basil Dignam*, *Laurence Naismith*, *Victor Maddern*.

Clive Morton and Eric Portman in His Excellency (*1951*)

HIS MAJESTY O'KEEFE (1953) [2]

Dir *Byron Haskin*. Prod *Harold Hecht*. Scr *Borden Chase*, *James Hill*, *from a novel by Lawrence Kingman*, *Gerald Green*. Ph *Otto Heller*. PC/Dis *Warner Bros.* Technicolor. 90 mins. Cert U

Cast ashore by his mutinous crew, Captain O'Keefe (*Burt Lancaster*) finds himself on Yap, an island under German rule. He sees that a fortune could be made from Yap's copra, but the islanders will not work it, and the only thing they value is fei, a stone from a far-off island. To cut a long and tedious story short, O'Keefe gets the fei and then the copra, killing a pirate (*Charles Horvath*) who has enslaved Yap, and becoming king of the island.

RoC *Joan Rice*, *André Morell*, *Abraham Sofaer*, *Archie Savage*, *Benson Fong*, *Tessa Prendergast*, *Philip Ahn*, *Guy Doleman*, *Grant Taylor*, *Alexander Archdale*, *Lloyd Berrell*, *Harvey Adams*, *Warwick Ray*, *Paddy Mullely*, *Jim Crawford*.

HOBSON'S CHOICE (1953) [4]

Dir/Prod *David Lean*. Scr *Lean*, *Norman Spencer*, *Wynyarde Browne*, *from the play by Harold Brighouse*. Ph *Jack Hildyard*. PC *London Films*. Dis *British Lion*. 107 mins. Cert U

Prosperous Lancashire bootmaker Henry Hobson (*Charles Laughton*) refuses to give dowries for his three daughters, whereupon strongwilled Maggie (*Brenda de Banzie*), the oldest, marries Hobson's talented but downtrodden bootmaker, Willie (*John Mills*). She connives dowries for her two weaker sisters, then sets up with Willie in opposition to her father, making such a success of the business that the ailing Hobson is forced to take Willie on as a partner. Mostly delightful version of famous old story, with memorable moments.

RoC *Daphne Anderson*, *Prunella Scales*, *Richard Wattis*, *Derek Blomfield*, *Helen Haye*, *Joseph Tomelty*, *Jack Howarth*, *Julien Mitchell*, *Gibb McLaughlin*, *Philip Stainton*, *Dorothy Gordon*, *Madge Brindley*, *John Laurie*, *Raymond Huntley*, *Herbert C. Walton*.

Brenda de Banzie and John Mills in Hobson's Choice (*1954*)

THE HOLLY AND THE IVY (1952) [4]

Dir *George More O'Ferrall*. Prod/Scr *Anatole de Grunwald*, *from the play by Wynyard Browne*. Ph *Ted Scaife*. PC *London Films*. Dis *British Lion*. 83 mins. Cert U

Christmas Eve at the Vicarage. The elder daughter (*Celia Johnson*) fears that she must look after her father, the Vicar (*Ralph Richardson*) now that her mother has died, and not marry David (*John Gregson*). Son Mick (*Denholm Elliott*) returns from National Service, and younger daughter Margaret (*Margaret Leighton*) unexpectedly from London and her lonely flat. Home truths are told – mostly about Margaret's wartime affair and her son, recently dead. The Vicar proves surprisingly understanding: Margaret agrees to move there and her sister is free to marry. Pleasant, meaty drama, disliked by some for its theatricality.

RoC *Hugh Williams*, *William Hartnell*, *Robert Flemyng*, *Margaret Halstan*, *Maureen Delany*, *Roland Culver*, *John Barry*, *Dandy Nichols*.

HOME AND AWAY (1956) [3]

Dir *Vernon Sewell*. Prod *George Maynard*. Scr *Heather McIntyre*, *Sewell*, *R. F. Delderfield*, *from a play by McIntyre*. Ph *Basil Emmott*. PC *Guest-Conquest*. Dis *Eros*. 81 mins. Cert U

George and Elsie Knowles (*Jack Warner*,

Kathleen Harrison) think they have won the football pools, but the winning line belongs to their son and his friend. The friend's mother plans to deprive Master Knowles of his share, but the boys are minors, and cannot claim their jackpot. As a consolation, George helps to set the two teenagers up in a little business. The Huggetts live again in this comedy from the archives; some fun though.

RoC *Lana Morris, Charles Victor, Thora Hird, Leslie Henson, Harry Fowler, Valerie White, Merrie Carroll, Sam Kydd, Bernard Fox, Margaret St Barbe West, Ross Pendleton.*

HOME AT SEVEN (1952) [3]
(USA: *Murder on Monday*)

Dir *Ralph Richardson.* Prod *Maurice Cowan.* Scr *Anatole de Grunwald, from the play by R. C. Sherriff.* Ph *Jack Hildyard, Edward Scaife.* PC *London Films.* Dis *British Lion. 85 mins. Cert U*

David Preston (*Ralph Richardson*) fails to return 'home at seven' for the first time in many years. A bank clerk, he discovers that the safe of the local social club, with which he is involved, has been rifled and the caretaker murdered. And 24 hours are missing from his life. Feeling he may be guilty, he finally traces his movements in the lost hours, and establishes his innocence. Made for a pittance in 15 days, this fairly interesting drama was Richardson's only film as director.

RoC *Margaret Leighton, Jack Hawkins, Meriel Forbes, Campbell Singer, Frederick Piper, Diana Beaumont, Michael Shepley, Margaret Withers, Gerald Case.*

HOME TO DANGER (1951) [3]

Dir *Terence Fisher.* Prod *Lance Comfort.* Scr *John Temple-Smith, Francis Edge.* Ph *Reg Wyer.* PC *New World.* Dis *Eros. 66 mins. Cert A*

Barbara (*Rona Anderson*) returns from abroad on her father's suicide. A new will leaves her his estates, previously willed to his partner Wainwright (*Francis Lister*). Other beneficiaries are Robert (*Guy Rolfe*), a childhood friend, and an orphanage headed by the mysterious Hughes (*Alan Wheatley*). Events indicate Barbara is in danger, and a shooting party is arranged to have her killed. The assassin is found murdered in a marsh. A drugs-dealer involved is also killed. Later, Barbara is attacked by a man with a withered arm. Wain-

Rona Anderson and Alan Wheatley in Home to Danger (*1951*)

wright appears and tries to save her, but dies in the attempt. It is Willie (*Stanley Baker*), the family retainer, who kills the attacker (and her father's killer): it proves to be Hughes. Not too good, but lively.

RoC *Bruce Belfrage, Dennis Harkin, Peter Jones, Betty Henderson, Cyril Conway, Amy Dalby, Christopher Hodge, Joe Stern, Glyn Houston, Toni Frost, Frederick Buckland.*

HONEYMOON DEFERRED (1951) [3]

Dir *Mario Camerini.* Prod *John Sutro, Joseph Janni.* Scr *John Hunter, Franco Brusati, C. Denis Freeman.* Ph *Geoffrey Faithfull.* PC *Vic Films.* Dis *British Lion. 79 mins. Cert A*

A young English couple on honeymoon (*Griffith Jones, Sally Ann Howes*) find themselves in the same Italian village he had liberated 'single-handed' during the war. He is not, however, welcomed with exactly open arms, and not until he has cleared himself of all the charges levelled against him can the honeymoon proceed. English comedy situations pitchforked into a foreign setting; moves along all right, but just isn't funny.

RoC *Kieron Moore, Lea Padovani, Anna Dondini, David Keir, Moneta, Little Freddie Meloni, L. Rivanera, Helen Goss, W. E. Holloway.*

AN HONOURABLE MURDER (1959) [2]

Dir *Godfrey Grayson.* Prod *Edward J. Danziger, Harry Lee Danziger.* Scr *Brian Clemens, Eldon Howard, from a play by William Shakespeare.* Ph *Jimmy Wilson.* PC *Danzigers.* Dis *Warner-Pathé. 69 mins. Cert U*

Cassius (*Douglas Wilmer*) and other directors jealous of chairman Julian Caesar's (*John Longden*) success plan a coup. They enlist the reluctant help of a vital director, Brutus (*Norman Wooland*) and vote Caesar off the board. He dies from a heart attack. Later Caesar's friend Anthony (*Philip Saville*) becomes chairman and, in time, gets rid of all the old board. Brutus commits suicide. Wretched attempt to do *Julius Caesar* in a modern context, made on far too low a budget.

RoC *Margaretta Scott, Lisa Daniely, Marion Mathie, Colin Tapley, Kenneth Edwards, Arnold Bell, Stuart Saunders, Olive Kirby, Elizabeth Saunders, John Brooking, Shirley Cain, Sandra Yelland, Diana Chesney, Vernon Smythe.*

THE HORNET'S NEST (1955) [2]

Dir *Charles Saunders.* Prod *Guido Coen.* Scr *Allan Mackinnon.* Ph *Harry Waxman.* PC *Kenilworth.* Dis *Rank. 64 mins. Cert U*

A crook (*Charles Farrell*) hides the proceeds from a jewel robbery on a deserted barge, but is jailed for a week for assault. The barge is taken over by two model girls (*Marla Landi, June Thorburn*). After a fake message takes their male helper (*Paul Carpenter*) away, the girls almost sink the boat. The crook returns but fails to find the jewels, which have been 'lifted' by two old ladies (*Christine Silver, Nora Nicholson*) who help the models claim the reward money. Weak comedy-thriller on *Arsenic and Old Lace* lines.

RoC *Larry Burns, Alexander Gauge, Colin Douglas, Wilfred Fletcher, Gaylord Cavallaro,*

Jan Holden, Christopher Steele, Ronnie Stevens, Anita Sharp Bolster, Max Brimmell, Trevor Reid, Stuart Nichol.

HORRORS OF THE BLACK MUSEUM (1959) [2]

Dir *Arthur Crabtree.* Prod *Jack Greenwood.* Scr *Aben Kandel, Herman Cohen.* Ph *Desmond Dickinson.* PC *Herman Cohen.* Dis *Anglo-Amalgamated. Eastman Colour. CinemaScope. 80 mins. Cert X*

Bancroft (*Michael Gough*), a crippled journalist with a fascination for grisly murder (he has a 'black museum' in his home), manufactures a crime wave for himself to report by inducing his young assistant (under the influence of drugs) to kill people in horrifying ways. After Bancroft has despatched a blackmailing antiques dealer (*Beatrice Varley*) and a nosy doctor (*Gerald Anderson*), his assistant bungles his next killing and is trapped at a funfair, plunging from on high to bury his dagger in Bancroft's heart. Some critics attacked the censors for allowing this very nasty horror offering a certificate.

RoC *Geoffrey Keen, Graham Curnow, Shirley Ann Field, June Cunningham, John Warwick, Austin Trevor, Malou Pantera, Howard Greene, Dorinda Stevens, Stuart Saunders, Maya Koumani, Hilda Barry, Norah Gordon.*

THE HORSE'S MOUTH (1958) [4]

Dir *Ronald Neame.* Prod *John Bryan.* Scr *Alec Guinness, from the novel by Joyce Cary.* Ph *Arthur Ibbetson.* PC *Knightsbridge.* Dis *United Artists. Technicolor. 95 mins. Cert U*

Just out of jail, ragamuffin artist Gulley Jimson (*Alec Guinness*) harangues his wife (*Renée Houston*), who has been selling his early work, but is distracted by the opportunity to paint a mural in the flat of a wealthy collector who has gone away after expressing an interest in his work. With his disreputable friends, Gulley finds a giant blank wall and paints an even bigger mural, 'The Last Judgment'. Learning that the building has to be demolished, Gulley himself drives the bulldozer. Offbeat comedy, even blacker than *The Ladykillers*, was selected for the Royal Film Performance and, despite a mixed critical reception, did quite well. Paintings were by John Bratby.

RoC *Kay Walsh, Mike Morgan, Robert Coote, Arthur Macrae, Veronica Turleigh, Michael Gough, Reginald Beckwith, Ernest Thesiger, Gillian Vaughan, Richard Caldicot, Richard*

Alec Guinness in The Horse's Mouth (*1958*)

Leech, John Kidd, Elton Olivierre, May Hallatt, Rose Howlett, Jeremy Judge.

THE HOSTAGE (1956) 2

Dir *Harold Huth.* Prod *Thomas Clyde.* Scr *Alfred Shaughnessy.* Ph *Brendan Stafford.* PC *Douglas Fairbanks/Westridge.* Dis *Eros.* 80 mins. Cert *A*

Revolutionaries threatened with the hanging of their leader kidnap the President's daughter (*Mary Parker*) and an American pilot, Bill (*Ron Randell*) who gets in the way. The girl refuses to cooperate and the rebel leader dies. Before his followers can execute the girl, Bill, who has escaped, leads the police in to overcome them in a hand to hand battle. Laughably plotted thriller.

RoC *Carl Jaffe, Margaret Diamond, Cyril Luckham, Anne Blake, John Bailey, Victor Brooks.*

HOTEL SAHARA (1951) 4

Dir *Ken Annakin.* Prod *George H. Brown.* Scr *Brown, Patrick Kirwan.* Ph *Jack Hildyard.* PC *Tower.* Dis *General Film Distributors.* 96 mins. Cert *U*

1942. A wartime desert hotel finds itself in No Man's Land. Visited in turn by British, Italian, Free French and German forces, not to mention a few Arabs, it changes its appearance and attitudes for each new group, two of which inevitably collide. Just as the proprietor Emad (*Peter Ustinov*) and his beautiful and inventive mistress (*Yvonne de Carlo*) have got back to normal, the Americans arrive ... Artless, rollicking farce hardly pauses for breath. Pretty good fun.

RoC *David Tomlinson, Albert Lieven, Eugene Deckers, Roland Culver, Bill Owen, Sydney Tafler, Mireille Perrey, Ferdy Mayne, Tom Gill, Anton Diffring, Guido Lorraine, Rolf Richards, Henrik Jacobsen, Massimo Coen, Enzo Plazzotta, Bettina Hayes, John Salew, Harold Kasket, Olga Lowe, AC2 Lewis (goat).*

Yvonne de Carlo and Peter Ustinov in Hotel Sahara *(1951)*

HOT ICE (1952) 3

Dir/Scr *Kenneth Hume, from a play by Alan Melville.* Prod *Charles Reynolds.* Ph *Ted Lloyd.* PC *Present Day.* Dis *Apex.* 85 mins. Cert *A*

Invited for a weekend with Edwin Carson (*Ivor Barnard*), Jim Henderson (*John Justin*) finds that his fellow-guests are all owners of famous diamonds, due to be 'pressured' so that

Carson can add to his own collection. With the help of Carson's adopted daughter (*Barbara Murray*), Jim tries to outwit him, but Carson locks her in the jewel room and escapes with the diamonds. The butler (*Michael Balfour*), double-crossed by Carson, turns on the current surrounding the grounds, and Carson is electrocuted. Implausible comedy-thriller, neatly written and directed.

RoC *John Penrose, Gabrielle Brune, Anthony Pendrell, Bill Shine, Fred Gray, Dorothy Wheatley, Sam Kydd, Derek Sidney, Archie Duncan, Keith Grieve, Billy Howard, Ida Patlanski, Freddie Tripp, Kendal Chalmers.*

THE HOUND OF THE BASKERVILLES (1959) 2

Dir *Terence Fisher.* Prod *Anthony Hinds.* Scr *Peter Bryan, from the novel by Sir Arthur Conan Doyle.* Ph *Jack Asher.* PC *Hammer.* Dis *United Artists.* Technicolor. 86 mins. Cert *A*

1897. Detective Sherlock Holmes (*Peter Cushing*) sends his associate Dr Watson (*André Morell*) down to Baskerville Hall on the edge of Dartmoor to look after Sir Henry (*Christopher Lee*), in danger of becoming the latest Baskerville to be killed by a ghostly hound that lurks on the moors. Holmes, in various disguises, roots out the truth, and the perpetrator of the plot (*Marla Landi*) sinks to her death in Grimpen Mire. Unsuccessful, dully acted version of much-filmed chiller.

RoC *David Oxley, Miles Malleson, Francis de Wolff, Ewen Solon, John le Mesurier, Sam Kydd, Helen Goss, Judi Moyens, Michael Hawkins, Dave Birks, Ian Hewitson, Elizabeth Dott, Michael Mulcahy.*

HOUR OF DECISION (1957) 2

Dir *C. Pennington Richards.* Prod *Monty Berman.* Scr *Norman Hudis.* Ph *Stan Pavey.* PC *Tempean.* Dis *Eros.* 81 mins. Cert *A*

Investigating the death of a blackmailing columnist, reporter Joe Sanders (*Jeff Morrow*) finds that the mystery woman for whom the police are looking is his own wife Peggy (*Hazel Court*). In his efforts to clear Peggy from suspicion, Joe unmasks the real killer. Too-leisurely whodunnit at least hides its villian well.

RoC *Mary Laura Wood, Lionel Jeffries, Anthony Dawson, Carl Bernard, Vanda Godsell, Alan Gifford, Robert Sansom, Garrard Green, Margaret Allworthy, Richard Shaw, Marne Maitland, Anthony Snell, Michael Balfour.*

THE HOUR OF 13 (1952) 3

Dir *Harold French.* Prod *Hayes Goetz.* Scr *Leon Gordon, Howard Emmett Rogers, from a novel by Philip Macdonald.* Ph *Guy Green.* PC/Dis *MGM-British.* 78 mins. Cert *A*

The murder of ten policemen in identical circumstances has terrified Edwardian London. A pendant found near one body points to the killer being gentleman thief Nicholas Revel (*Peter Lawford*). Revel conducts his own investigation to clear himself, despatches the murderer in a savage struggle, and leaves stolen jewels by his body, clearing the way for him to marry his lady (*Dawn Addams*) and 'go straight'. Polished if hardly full-blooded period

thriller, a remake of the 1934 Hollywood film, *The Mystery of Mr X.*

RoC *Roland Culver, Derek Bond, Heather Thatcher, Leslie Dwyer, Colin Gordon, Fabia Drake, Michael Hordern, Jack McNaughton, Campbell Cotts, Michael Goodliffe, Moultrie Kelsall, Richard Shaw, Peter Copley, Sam Kydd.*

THE HOUSE ACROSS THE LAKE (1954) 4
(USA: *Heatwave*)

Dir/Scr *Ken Hughes, from his novel* High Wray. Prod *Anthony Hinds.* Ph *Jimmy Harvey.* PC *Hammer.* Dis *AB-Pathé.* 68 mins. Cert *A*

Pulp writer Kendrick (*Alex Nicol*) meets his rich neighbours across the lake and is soon seduced by Carol (*Hillary Brooke*), wife of Forrest (*Sidney James*), whom Kendrick likes, and just finishing with another lover, Vince (*Paul Carpenter*). Forrest is badly injured when his launch has an accident in fog, and Carol throws him overboard. When Kendrick finds she has gone back to Vince, he goes to the police. Smooth thriller, sharply characterized.

RoC *Susan Stephen, Cleo Rose, Peter Illing, Howard Lang, Gordon McLeod, Hugh Dempster, Joan Hickson, Harry Brunnings, John Sharpe, Peter Evans, Angela Glynne, Christine Adrian, Monti de Lyle.*

THE HOUSE IN THE SQUARE (1951) 3
(USA: *I'll Never Forget You*)

Dir *Roy Baker.* Prod *Sol C. Siegel.* Scr *Ranald MacDougall, from a play by John L. Balderston.* Ph *Georges Périnal.* PC/Dis *20th Century-Fox.* Technicolor. 91 mins. Cert *U*

Peter (*Tyrone Power*), an American atomic research chemist living in London, believes he is about to exchange places with an ancestor of the same name, and that the past, present and future exist on parallel planes. Transported back to 1784 on a bolt of lightning, he falls for his fiancée's sister Helen (*Ann Blyth*, who took over the role when Constance Smith fell ill with pneumonia) and tries to improve conditions in the era, but is thought mad. Returning in another flash of lightning, Peter meets his friend's sister, the image of Helen who, he learns, died soon after he 'left' the 18th century. Disappointing remake of *Berkeley Square* (1933), itself partly based on Henry James' *The Sense of the Past.* The whole thing vaguely reworked in 1978 as *Somewhere in Time.*

RoC *Michael Rennie, Dennis Price, Beatrice Campbell, Kathleen Byron, Raymond Huntley, Irene Browne, Robert Atkins, Felix Aylmer, Alex McCrindle, Gibb McLaughlin, Hamlyn Benson, Ronald Adam, Ronald Simpson, Diane Hart, Tom Gill, Jill Clifford, Victor Maddern, Peter Drury, Alec Finter, Anthony Pelly, Catherine Carlton (Boyle), Richard Carrickford, Rose Howlett, Arthur Denton.*

THE HOUSE IN THE WOODS (1957) 4

Dir/Scr *Maxwell Munden, from a short story by Walter C. Brown.* Prod *Geoffrey Goodhart.* Ph *Cedric Williams.* PC *Film Workshop.* Dis *Archway.* 60 mins. Cert *A*

Writer Geoffrey Carter (*Michael Gough*) and his wife Carol (*Patricia Roc*) rent a country cottage for Geoff's work, from a rather strange painter, Rowland (*Ronald Howard*). Geoff learns that Rowland is suspected of doing away with his wife, and is just in time to prevent Carol from meeting the same fate. Crisp, creepy thriller compels belief despite holes in the plot.

RoC *Bill Shine, Andrea Troubridge, Norah Hammond, Tony Doonan, Leigh Crutchley, Geoffrey Goodhart.*

HOUSE OF BLACKMAIL (1953)   2

Dir *Maurice Elvey*. Prod *Phil Brandon*. Scr *Allan Mackinnon*. Ph *Phil Grindrod*. PC *ACT Films*. Dis *Monarch*. 72 mins. Cert U
In a lonely mansion, army officer Jimmy (*William Sylvester*) and Carol (*Mary Germaine*), a spirited young woman, only escape a charge of murdering a blackmailer by sorting out the real killer from among a shoal of suspects. Very modest version of traditional thriller.

RoC *Alexander Gauge, John Arnatt, Denis Shaw, Ingeborg Wells, Patricia Owens, C. Denier Warren, Barry Wynne, Hugo Schuster.*

HOUSE OF SECRETS (1956)   3
(USA: *Triple Deception*)

Dir *Guy Green*. Prod *Julian Wintle, Vivian A. Cox*. Scr *Robert Buckner, Bryan Forbes, from the novel by Sterling Joel*. Ph *Harry Waxman*. PC/Dis *Rank*. Technicolor. 97 mins. Cert A
Larry Ellis (*Michael Craig*), a naval officer, is the double of a famous counterfeiter who, unknown to his criminal confederates, has just been killed in a car crash. Larry is sent in to infiltrate the counterfeit ring, but only just escapes death (by baling out) when the boss of the ring explodes a plane with all his colleagues on board. However, Larry brings him to justice. Thick-ear *Boys' Own*-style thriller with limited acting but good fight scenes and photography.

RoC *Brenda de Banzie, Julia Arnall, Barbara Bates, David Kossoff, Geoffrey Keen, Gerard Oury, Anton Diffring, Eric Pohlmann, Eugene Deckers, Jacques Brunius, Carl Jaffe, Balbina, Alan Tilvern, Gordon Tanner, David Lander, Violet Gould, John Serret, Jean Driant, Patrick Westwood, Yves Chanteau.*

THE HOUSE OF THE ARROW (1953)   4

Dir *Michael Anderson*. Prod *Vaughan M. Dean*. Scr *Edward Dryhurst, from the novel by A. E. W. Mason*. Ph *Erwin Hillier*. PC *Associated British*. Dis *AB-Pathé*. 73 mins. Cert A
Third screen version of the famous thriller in which the poisoning of a wealthy French widow provides a case for the inimitable Inspector Hanaud (*Oscar Homolka*). He discovers she was murdered by an arrow tipped with an untraceable African poison - and a whisper gives away the killer: her adopted niece, Betty (*Yvonne Furneaux*). Laughs and thrills skilfully handled: Homolka steals the show.

RoC *Josephine Griffin, Robert Urquhart, Harold Kasket, Pierre le Fèvre, Anthony Nicholls, Jacques Cey, Pierre Chaminade, Andrea Lea, Jeanne Pali, Ruth Lodge, Keith Pyott, René Leplat, Colette Wilde, René Poirier.*

THE HOUSE OF THE SEVEN HAWKS
(1959)   3

Dir *Richard Thorpe*. Prod/PC *David E. Rose*. Scr *Jo Eisinger, from a novel by Victor Canning*. Ph *Ted Scaife*. Dis *M-G-M*. 91 mins. Cert U
Nordley (*Robert Taylor*), a charter-boat skipper, agrees to a spot of smuggling between Britain and Holland. When his hush-hush cargo turns out to be a sack of money, a map and a corpse (of the charterer), he tangles with international crooks and Dutch police, all of whom are after a fortune in diamonds stolen by the Nazis. The resourceful Nordley comes out on top. Rapid-fire, complex thriller; only half as good as the book.

RoC *Nicole Maurey, Donald Wolfit, Linda Christian, David Kossoff, Gerard Heinz, Eric Pohlmann, Philo Hauser.*

HOW TO MURDER A RICH UNCLE
(1957)   4

Dir *Nigel Patrick*, (*uncredited*) *Max Varnel*. Prod *Ronald Kinnock*. Scr *John Paxton, from a play by Didier Vaix*. Ph *Ted Moore*. PC *Warwick*. Dis *Columbia*. CinemaScope. 79 mins. Cert U
This being a black comedy, it does, of course, deal with how *not* to murder a rich uncle. Crippled with debts and taxation, noble Sir Henry (*Nigel Patrick*) decides to polish off his rich American uncle George (*Charles Coburn*), disguising it as an accident. But, while uncle stays in good health, Sir Henry's aunt, son, mother and wife fall into the traps laid for him. Sir Henry is the last to go, whereupon Uncle George marries Aunt Alice (*Katie Johnson*), who is last seen putting something in his champagne ... Pleasant caper with some good chuckles.

RoC *Wendy Hiller, Anthony Newley, Athene Seyler, Noel Hood, Kenneth Fortescue, Michael Caine, Trevor Reid, Cyril Luckham, Patricia Webster, Johnson Bayly, Martin Boddey, Kevin Stoney, Anthony Shaw, Ian Wilson.*

HUNTED (1952)   4
(USA: *The Stranger in Between*)

Dir *Charles Crichton*. Prod *Julian Wintle*. Scr *Jack Whittingham*. Ph *Eric Cross*. PC *Independent Artists/British Film Makers*. Dis *General Film Distributors*. 84 mins. Cert A
Accidentally setting fire to his home, six-year-old Robbie (*Jon Whiteley*) runs away - into the arms of killer-on-the-run Chris (*Dirk Bogarde*) who, knowing the boy can identify him, takes him along, northwards, first to the Midlands, then to the Scottish border. Through their various scrapes, a bond of friendship grows between them. When Robbie falls seriously ill, Chris gives himself up to save him. Quite tense, quite touching; good location-shot chases.

RoC *Kay Walsh, Elizabeth Sellars, Frederick Piper, Julian Somers, Jane Aird, Jack Stewart, Geoffrey Keen, Joe Linnane, Leonard White, Gerald Anderson, Denis Webb, Gerald Case, Katherine Blake, Molly Urquhart, Grace Arnold, Alec Finter, Harry Quashie, Ian Hunter.*

THE HYPNOTIST (1957)   2
(USA: *Scotland Yard Dragnet*)

Dir/Scr *Montgomery Tully, from the play by*

Falkland L. Cary. Prod *Alec C. Snowden*. Ph *Philip Grindrod*. PC/Dis *Anglo-Amalgamated*. 89 mins. Cert A
Psychiatric hypnotist Francis Pelham (*Roland Culver*), receiving for treatment Val Neal (*Paul Carpenter*) a test pilot suffering from blackouts, uses the opportunity to rid himself of an unwanted wife. But Val will not obey Pelham's commands to murder, and the hypnotist is forced to do it himself, and frame Val. Val's fiancée Mary (*Patricia Roc*), whom Pelham fancies, turns the tables on the hypnotist. Unlikely tale does ramble on.

RoC *William Hartnell, Kay Callard, Ellen Pollock, Martin Wyldeck, Gordon Needham, Mary Jones, John Serret, Oliver Johnston, Edgar Driver, Robert Sansom, Douglas Hayes, Calvin Stewart, Gordon Harris, Jill Nicholls, Jessica Cairns, Hilda Barry, Tim Fitzgerald, Tom Tann, Dennis McCarthy.*

I

I ACCUSE! (1957)   3

Dir *José Ferrer*. Prod *Sam Zimbalist*. Scr *Gore Vidal, from the book by Nicholas Halasz*. Ph *F. A. Young*. PC/Dis *M-G-M British*. CinemaScope. 99 mins. Cert U
1894. On trumped-up evidence, Dreyfuss (*José Ferrer*), a French Army officer, is found guilty of treason and sentenced to life. His wife (*Viveca Lindfors*) and brother (*David Farrar*) discover proof of his innocence, but the war minister (*Donald Wolfit*) refuses to listen. The real culprit (*Anton Walbrook*) is court-martialled and acquitted, but when he sells his confession to an English paper, Dreyfuss is at last reinstated, having already received a condescending pardon. Passionless re-telling of famous true injustice.

RoC *Leo Genn, Emlyn Williams, Herbert Lom, Felix Aylmer, Harry Andrews, Peter Illing, George Coulouris, Ronald Howard, Eric Pohlmann, Carl Jaffe, John Chandos, Ernest Clark, Anthony Ireland, John Phillips, Laurence Naismith, Michael Hordern, Keith Pyott, Arthur Howard, Charles Gray, Michael Anthony, Michael Trubshawe, Malcolm Keen.*

I AM A CAMERA (1955)   3

Dir *Henry Cornelius*. (*Associate*) Prod *Jack Clayton*. Scr *John Collier, from the play by John Van Druten and stories by Christopher Isherwood*. Ph *Guy Green*. PC *Romulus/Remus*. Dis *Independent Film Distributors/British Lion*. 99 mins. Cert X
Berlin 1932. Tutor Christopher Isherwood (*Laurence Harvey*) shares his lodgings platonically with Sally (*Julie Harris*), a third-rate nightclub-singer. They foster an affair between two Jews (*Shelley Winters, Anton Diffring*), who flee the oncoming Nazis, and are themselves fostered by wealthy Clive (*Ron Randell*),

who becomes Sally's lover but eventually deserts them. Twenty years later, Chris and Sally meet again. She has written her memoirs ... Kaleidoscopic, atmospheric, but rather irritating nostalgia piece.

RoC *Lea Seidl, Jean Gargoet, Frederick Valk, Tutte Lemkow, Stanley Maxted, Patrick McGoohan, Zoë Newton, André Mikhelson, Richard Wattis, Julia Arnall, Peter Prowse, The Stan Bernard Trio, Harold Siddons, Frederick Valk.*

I BELIEVE IN YOU (1951) [4]

Dir *Basil Dearden.* Prod *Michael Relph.* Scr *Relph, Dearden, Jack Whittingham, Nicholas Phipps, from a book by Sewell Stokes.* Ph *Gordon Dines.* PC *Ealing Studios.* Dis *General Film Distributors.* 95 mins. Cert U

Phipps (*Cecil Parker*), a retired civil servant looking, at 55, for something to occupy his time, stumbles into the probation service. He and Matty (*Celia Johnson*), who helps him come to terms with the work, become involved with Norma (*Joan Collins*) and Hooker (*Harry Fowler*), in love and trying to go straight, and the unregenerate Jordie (*Laurence Harvey*). Events tempt Hooker to take part in a robbery. Phipps' headstrong action in preventing him results not in the sack he expects, but promotion. Rather cosy view of its subject, but interesting and entertaining.

RoC *Godfrey Tearle, George Relph, Ernest Jay, Ursula Howells, Sidney James, Katie Johnson, Ada Reeve, Brenda de Banzie, Alex McCrindle, Laurence Naismith, Gladys Henson, Stanley Escane, Cyril Waites, John Orchard, David Hannaford, Herbert C. Walton, Gwynne Whitby, Fred Griffiths, Richard Hart, Judith Furse.*

Cecil Parker and Laurence Harvey in I Believe in You *(1952)*

ICE COLD IN ALEX (1958) [4]
(USA: *Desert Attack*)

Dir *J. Lee Thompson.* Prod *W. A. Whittaker.* Scr *T. J. Morrison, Christopher Landon, Lee Thompson, from Landon's novel.* Ph *Gilbert Taylor.* PC *Associated British.* Dis *AB-Pathé.* 129 mins. Cert A

1942. As Tobruk collapses, Captain Anson (*John Mills*), who now leans more on the whisky bottle than on his sergeant (*Harry Andrews*) has to evacuate two nurses, Diana (*Sylvia Syms*) and Denise (*Diane Clare*) in a battered ambulance. They are joined by a South African (*Anthony Quayle*) whom they suspect

Harry Andrews, Anthony Quayle, Sylvia Syms and John Mills in Ice Cold in Alex *(1958)*

to be a German spy. But he helps them battle through minefields, German patrols and sandstorms. Denise is killed; Diana and Anson fall in love; the South African almost dies in a sand bog and is proved to be a German. Reaching Alexandria, they cannot bring themselves to hand him over, and drink ice-cold lager together before parting. Long but gripping war film, based on true events.

RoC *Richard Leech, Liam Redmond, Allan Cuthbertson, David Lodge, Michael Nightingale, Basil Hoskins, Walter Gotell, Frederick Jaeger, Richard Marner, Peter Arne, Paul Stassino, Vivian Pickles.*

IDLE ON PARADE (1959) [3]
(USA: *Idol on Parade*)

Dir *John Gilling.* Prod *Harold Huth.* Scr *John Antrobus, from the novel by William Camp.* Ph *Ted Moore.* PC *Warwick.* Dis *Columbia.* CinemaScope. 92 mins. Cert U

'Rock 'n' roll idol Jeep Jackson (*Anthony Newley*) is inducted into the Army, where he soon falls foul of the bellowing Sgt Lush (*William Bendix*). He romances the CO's daughter (*Anne Aubrey*) to the fury of her other suitor (*Lionel Jeffries*), and finally decides the army's okay – only to be re-posted to a weather station on the Outer Hebrides. Makeshift comedy has good pop songs (notably two by Gerry Laudan and Len Praverman) that helped make Newley a star.

RoC *David Lodge, Sidney James, Dilys Laye, Bernie Winters, William Kendall, Harry Fowler, Sean Kelly, Roderick Cook, Gordon Needham, Tom Bowman, Carl Conway, Michael Bell, Percy Herbert, Stanley Beard, Lester Nixon, Ian MacNaughtan, John Cowley, Eric Corrie, Norman Atkyns, Jane Navello, André Charisse, Rosamund Greenwood, Maureen Riscoe, Marigold Russell, Martin Boddey, Rupert Davies, Ian Wilson, John Wood, Rosemary Davis.*

I'LL GET YOU FOR THIS (1951) [4]
(USA: *Lucky Nick Cain*)

Dir *Joseph M. Newman.* Prod *Joseph Kaufman.* Scr *George Callahan, William Rose, from a novel by James Hadley Chase.* Ph *Otto Heller.* PC *Romulus/Kaydor.* 83 mins. Cert A

'Lucky' Nick Cain, a gambler (*George Raft*), visits San Paolo for a rest, but finds himself framed for the murder of a US Treasury

agent, thanks to Kay (*Coleen Gray*) who unwittingly leads him into a trap laid by a crooked casino manager (*Walter Rilla*). Nick escapes with the girl, and hides her in a ruined town while he clears his name, in the process exposing a ruthless counterfeiting gang. Fast-paced, thrill-crammed compendium of familiar situations.

RoC *Charles Goldner, Greta Gynt, Enzo Staiola, Hugh French, Elwyn Brook-Jones, Martin Benson, Peter Illing, Peter Bull, Constance Smith, Donald Stewart, Martin Miller, Prope Riello, Norman Shelley, Hannah Watt, Anthony Dawson, Valerie de Cadenet.*

ILL MET BY MOONLIGHT (1956) [4]
(USA: *Night Ambush*)

Dir/Prod/Scr *Michael Powell, Emeric Pressburger, from the book by W. Stanley Moss.* Ph *Christopher Challis.* PC *Vega.* Dis *Rank.* 104 mins. Cert U

1944. To encourage Cretan freedom fighters and demoralize the Germans, British agents working with partisans in Crete decide to kidnap a German general (*Marius Goring*). Led by 'Philidem' (*Dirk Bogarde*), they capture the general disguised as Nazi military policemen, and set off for a ship that will take him to Cairo. The general leaves a trail of buttons, medals, his hat and other things; these are all returned to him by Philidem when they reach the ship. Humorous, 'chummy' treatment of true-life exploit. Mikis Theodorakis' striking score was his first for an international film.

RoC *David Oxley, Cyril Cusack, Laurence Payne, Michael Gough, John Cairney, Brian Worth, Demitri Andreas, Adeeb Assaly, Wolfe Morris, Rowland Bartrop, Paul Stassino, George Egeniou, Theo Moreas, Andrea Malandrinos, Takis Frangofinos.*

I'M ALL RIGHT, JACK (1959) [4]

Dir *John Boulting.* Prod *Roy Boulting.* Scr *Frank Harvey, John Boulting, Alan Hackney, from a novel by Hackney.* Ph *Max Greene (Mutz Greenbaum).* PC *Charter.* Dis *British Lion.* 105 mins. Cert U

Stanley Windrush (*Ian Carmichael*), aspiring to a career in industry, is an amiable blunderer who soon finds himself caught between the devil of organized labour and the deep blue sea of organized big business. Pursued – on somewhat different levels – by shop steward Fred Kite (*Peter Sellers*) and his daughter Cynthia (*Liz Fraser*), Stanley, duped by his superiors and the scapegoat of a nation, finally seeks refuge in a nudist colony. Good performances and funny moments cloak the dislikeability of a film 'with something to offend everyone'. British Oscars for best British screenplay and best British actor (Sellers).

RoC *Terry-Thomas, Dennis Price, Richard Attenborough, Margaret Rutherford, Irene Handl, Miles Malleson, Victor Maddern, Marne Maitland, John le Mesurier, Raymond Huntley, Kenneth Griffith, Cardew Robinson, Terry Scott, Brian Oulton, Malcolm Muggeridge, Frank Phillips, Muriel Young, Fred Griffiths, Donal Donnelly, John Comer, Tony Comer, Bruce Wightman, Billy Rayment, Ronnie Stevens, John Glyn-Jones, Pauline Winter, Maurice Col-*

bourne, *Jeremy White, John Van Eyssen, Michael Bates, Robert Bruce, Robin Hay, Michael Ward, Sam Kydd, Stringer Davis, Tony Spear, Arthur Skinner, William Leacock, Eynon Evans, Esma Cannon, Robert Young, Roy Purcell, Marianne Stone, Edie Martin, Marion Shaw, Wally Patch, Alun Owen, Ian Wilson, Margaret Lacey, George Selway, Alan Wilson, David Lodge, Keith Smith, Kenneth J. Warren, Basil Dignam, Harry Locke, Martin Boddey, E.V.H. Emmett* (narrator).

I'M A STRANGER (1952)   [2]

Dir/Scr *Brock Williams*. Prod *Harold Richmond*. Ph *Gordon Lang*. PC *Corsair*. Dis *Apex*. 60 mins. Cert U

George (*Patric Doonan*) arrives in London from India to claim a sizeable inheritance only to discover that his grandfather's will is missing. A film star (*Greta Gynt*), a window cleaner (*James Hayter*) and a police inspector (*Hector Ross*) help him defeat a disinherited branch of the family and find the will. Very light comedy-drama; cast helps a little, not much.
RoC *Jean Cadell, Charles Lloyd Pack, Martina Mayne, Fulton Mackay, Raymond Young, John Kelly*.

THE IMPORTANCE OF BEING EARNEST (1952)   [5]

Dir *Anthony Asquith*. Prod *Teddy Baird*. Scr *Asquith, from the play by Oscar Wilde*. Ph *Desmond Dickinson*. PC *British Film Makers/Two Cities/Javelin/Asquith*. Dis *General Film Distributors*. Technicolor. 95 mins. Cert U

1895. Two men-about-town (*Michael Redgrave, Michael Denison*) both squire their ladies (*Joan Greenwood, Dorothy Tutin*) under the pseudonym of 'Ernest'. Eventually unmasked, the two smitten suitors are quite happy to be rechristened Ernest, but the intervention of the formidable Lady Bracknell (*Edith Evans*), mother of one of the girls, reveals that one of the men actually *is* the legendary Ernest. Sunny, stylish, witty comedy with some marvellous performances.
RoC *Margaret Rutherford, Miles Malleson, Richard Wattis, Aubrey Mather, Walter Hudd, Ivor Barnard*.

IMPULSE (1954)   [3]

Dir *Charles de la Tour* (uncredited), *Cy Endfield*. Prod *Robert S. Baker, Monty Berman*. Scr *Jonathan Roach (Endfield), Laurence Huntington*. Ph *Jonah Jones*. PC *Tempean*. Dis *Eros*. 80 mins. Cert A

While his wife (*Joy Shelton*) is away, Alan (*Arthur Kennedy*) has an affair with Lila (*Constance Smith*), a nightclub singer who claims to be trying to help her brother out of involvement with a diamond robbery, but later proves to be double-crossing everyone in a bid to get the diamonds herself. Alan, who had bought passage out of the country for them, decides to stay and face the music. Lila stays too – to clear him of complicity in a 'murder' that never was. Ordinary thriller at least keeps you guessing.
RoC *Jack Allen, James Carney, Cyril Chamberlain, Cameron Hall, Jean St Clair, Bruce Beeby*.

INDISCREET (1958)   [4]

Dir *Stanley Donen*. Prod *Donen, Cary Grant*. Scr *Norman Krasna, from his play* Kind Sir. Ph *Frederick A. Young*. PC *Grandon*. Dis *Warner Bros*. Technicolor. 99 mins. Cert A

American Philip Adams (*Cary Grant*), in London for a job with NATO, falls in love with his colleague's sister-in-law Anna (*Ingrid Bergman*), but uses his customary defence mechanism of saying that his wife will not give him a divorce. When Anna finds out he isn't married, she's furious, but he mars her plans to get even by telling her his wife has changed her mind. Glossy, entertaining comedy of manners, with stars expertly dispensing surface charm.
RoC *Cecil Parker, Phyllis Calvert, David Kossoff, Megs Jenkins, Oliver Johnston, Michael Anthony, Frank Hawkins, Richard Vernon, Eric Francis, Diane Clare*.

INN FOR TROUBLE (1959)   [2]

Dir *C. M. Pennington-Richards*. Prod *Ted Lloyd*. Scr *Fred Robinson, from his TV series* The Larkins. Ph *Eric Cross*. PC *Film Locations*. Dis *Eros*. 90 mins. Cert U

The Larkins (*Peggy Mount, David Kossoff*), a London family, inherit a village pub. It never seems to have any customers, and a big local brewery aims to keep it that way. But, with the aid of a specially potent beer, the Larkins family puts the place back on its feet, putting paid to the opposition's crooked schemes in the process. Home-made farce, broad in humour.
RoC *Leslie Phillips, Glyn Owen, Yvonne Monlaur, A. E. Matthews, Ronan O'Casey, Shaun O'Riordan, Gerald Campion, Alan Wheatley, Willoughby Goddard, Stanley Unwin, Charles Hawtrey, Graham Moffatt, Irene Handl, Fred Robinson, Graham Stark, Arthur Lawrence, Esma Cannon, Frank Williams, John Woodnutt, Edward Malin, Barbara Mitchell, Edwin Richfield, Alan Rolfe, Paddy Edwards, Edward Woodward*.

INNOCENT MEETING (1958)   [3]

Dir *Godfrey Grayson*. Prod *Edward J. Danziger, Harry Lee Danziger*. Scr *Brian Clemens, Eldon Howard*. Ph *Jimmy Wilson*. PC *Danzigers*. Dis *United Artists*. 62 mins. Cert A

On probation for robbery, Johnny (*Sean Lynch*) meets Connie (*Beth Rogan*), an upper-class girl who gets him a job in her father's textile firm. When Connie's father loses his wallet, Johnny is suspected, robs a shop and is cornered (with a gun) by police. The wallet is found, and Connie persuades Johnny to give himself up. Interesting film, well characterized; but its characters' actions lack credibility.
RoC *Raymond Huntley, Ian Fleming, Howard Lang, Arnold Bell, Denis Shaw, Tony Doonan, Gordon Needham, Colin Tapley, Robert Raglan, Robert Raikes, Robert Dorning, Brian Haines, Vernon Smythe, David Coote, Walter Horsbrugh, Hal Osmond, Frank Forsyth, Adrian Cairns, Edwin Richfield, Mark Singleton*.

INNOCENT SINNERS (1958)   [5]

Dir *Philip Leacock*. Prod *Hugh Stewart*. Scr *Neil Paterson, Rumer Godden, from a book by*

Godden. Ph *Harry Waxman*. PC/Dis *Rank*. 95 mins. Cert U

Hoydenish London teenager Lovejoy Mason (*June Brooks*), looked after by Mr and Mrs Vincent (*David Kossoff, Barbara Mullen*) while her mother is away (actually, gone for good), longs to own a garden and, with the help of Tip (*Christopher Hey*), a street-gang leader, creates one in the grounds of a bombed-out church. A lonely spinster (*Flora Robson*) befriends her, and proves Lovejoy's salvation when she is taken to court for stealing earth and flowers – providing a trust fund for the hard-up Vincents to adopt her. Charming, heart-warming drama, a real tear-jerker with natural child performers.
RoC *Brian Hammond, Catherine Lacey, Susan Beaumont, Edward Chapman, Lyndon Brook, Vanda Godsell, John Rae, Hilda Fenemore, Pauline Delany, Vanda Hudson, Andrew Cruickshank, Marianne Stone*.

INNOCENTS IN PARIS (1953)   [3]

Dir *Gordon Parry*. Prod/Scr *Anatole de Grunwald*. Ph *Gordon Lang*. PC *Romulus*. Dis *Independent Film Distributors/British Lion*. 102 mins. Cert A

Seven British tourists go to Paris. Most of them are out for a good time with the opposite sex. Sir Norman (*Alastair Sim*), a stuffy Treasury official, has an unexpected drunken night out with a Russian diplomat which brings to fruition a long-delayed economic conference. A typically British look at Paris, jumping, grasshopper-like, from story to story. Much at its best when being funny at the expense of the English.
RoC *Ronald Shiner, Margaret Rutherford, Claire Bloom, Claude Dauphin, Laurence Harvey, Jimmy Edwards, James Copeland, Mara Lane, Gaby Bruyère, Monique Gérard, Gregoire Aslan, Peter Illing, Colin Gordon, Kenneth Kove, Philip Stainton, Peter Jones, Richard Wattis, Reginald Beckwith, Alf Goddard, Frank Muir, Stringer Davis, Georgette Anys, Albert Dinan, Louise de Funès, Miles Joyce, Christopher Lee, Peter Randall, John Brooking, Joan Winmill, Kenneth Williams*.

THE INN OF THE SIXTH HAPPINESS (1958)   [4]

Dir *Mark Robson*. Prod *Robson, Buddy Adler*. Scr *Isobel Lennart, from a book by Alan Burgess*. Ph *F. A. Young*. PC/Dis *20th Century-*

Curt Jurgens, Robert Donat and Ingrid Bergman in The Inn of the Sixth Happiness *(1958)*

Fox. Eastman Colour. CinemaScope. 158 mins. Cert U

1930. Gladys Aylward (*Ingrid Bergman*), a serving-girl with a burning desire to become a missionary, journeys across Asia, enduring great hardship before reaching a north Chinese town, where she gradually earns the friendship of the aged missionary (*Athene Seyler*), the love of the people, the affection of a Eurasian officer in the Chinese army (*Curt Jurgens*) and the respect of the local Mandarin (*Robert Donat*) who, when the Japanese invade, tells her he has decided to become a Christian. As refugees pour through, Gladys leads a party of children on a hazardous journey over mountains to safety. True story, although somewhat romanticized; inspiring stuff.

RoC *Ronald Squire, Noel Hood, Richard Wattis, Joan Young, Moultrie Kelsall, Edith Sharpe, Peter Chong, Michael David, Burt Kwouk, Tsai Chin, Zed Zakari, Frank Blaine, Ronald Kyaing, Louise Lin, Michael Wee.*

AN INSPECTOR CALLS (1954) [4]

Dir *Guy Hamilton*. Prod *A. D. Peters*. Scr *Desmond Davis, from the play by J. B. Priestley*. Ph *Ted Scaife*. PC *Watergate*. Dis *British Lion*. 80 mins. Cert A

An inspector (*Alastair Sim*) calls on a wealthy provincial family in 1912, investigating the death of a girl who poisoned herself. Each member of the family is partly to blame. The father sacked her; the daughter had her dismissed from a store; the daughter's fiancé misused her as a mistress; the son got her pregnant; the mother refused her charity. The 'inspector' is proved to be bogus, maybe even an apparition. Then the police telephone ... Nicely-crafted drama always holds the interest.

RoC *Arthur Young, Olga Lindo, Eileen Moore, Bryan Forbes, Brian Worth, Jane Wenham, Pat Neal, Norman Bird, John Welsh, Barbara Everest, Jenny Jones, Amy Green, Catherine Willmer, Olwen Brookes, Bill Raymond, Walter Cross, George Hirste, Brenda Duncan, Helen Cleverley, Winnie Wiblin, Mabel Etherington, Charles Saynor, Vi Endean, George Woodbridge.*

INTENT TO KILL (1958) [4]

Dir *Jack Cardiff*. Prod *Adrian Worker*. Scr *Jimmy Sangster, from the novel by Michael Bryan*. Ph *Desmond Dickinson*. PC *Zonic*. Dis *20th Century-Fox*. CinemaScope. 89 mins. Cert A

The subject of a successful brain operation in Canada by Dr Bob McLaurin (*Richard Todd*), Juan Menda (*Herbert Lom*), a South American president, then suffers assassination attempts from a faction opposing his regime. The intention is to make it look as if he died from the operation. One person is killed, but the wrong one, and Menda recovers sufficiently to foil the final attempt himself. Fast-moving, tense thriller, with unexpected developments.

RoC *Betsy Drake, Warren Stevens, Carlo Justini, Paul Carpenter, Alexander Knox, Lisa Gastoni, Peter Arne, Kay Callard, John Crawford, Catherine Boyle, John McLaren, Jackie Collins, Maggie McGrath, John Carson, Stella Bonheur, Brenda Dunrich, Natalie Lynn, Kath-*

ryn *Sadler, Nancy Lewis, Ann Stephens, Hedger Wallace, Mark Baker, William Sherwood, Diana Hammond, Edouard Assaly, Michelle Aslanoff.*

INTERPOL (1957) [3]
(USA: *Pick-Up Alley*)

Dir *John Gilling, Max Varnel*. Prod *Irving Allen, Albert R. Broccoli*. Scr *John Paxton, from the novel by A. J. Forrest*. Ph *Ted Moore, Stan Pavey*. PC *Warwick*. Dis *Columbia*. 92 mins. Cert A

Obsessed with finding the man who killed his sister, Interpol agent Charles Sturgis (*Victor Mature*) gets his chance when he is sent to Europe to crack a dope ring headed by the very man, McNally (*Trevor Howard*), he's after. Captured and beaten, Sturgis is rescued by a fellow Interpol man, and pursues McNally to the docks, where he finally falls to his death from a crane. Howard dominates rather sloppy thriller.

RoC *Anita Ekberg, Bonar Colleano, Dorothy Alison, Sydney Tafler, André Morell, Martin Benson, Eric Pohlmann, Peter Illing, Lionel Murton, Danny Green, Sidney James, Yana, Marne Maitland, Harold Kasket, Van Boolen, Brian Nissen, Peter Elliott, Charles Lloyd Pack, Al Mullock, Alfred Burke, Maurice Browning, Cyril Shaps, Paul Stassino, Gaylord Cavallaro, Yvonne Romain.*

IN THE NICK (1959) [4]

Dir/Scr *Ken Hughes, from a story by Frank Norman*. Prod *Harold Huth*. Ph *Ted Moore*. PC *Warwick*. Dis *Columbia*. CinemaScope. 105 mins. Cert U

The Spider Kelly (*James Booth*) gang enters a prison without bars and immediately clashes with the rival Ted Ross (*Ian Hendry*) outfit. New psychiatrist Dr Newcombe (*Anthony Newley*) is handed the task of reforming Spider and his boys, and enlists the help of Spider's ex-girl Doll (*Anne Aubrey*). Things go well until Spider is suspected of stealing presents at a Christmas party. Newcombe proves Ross is guilty and Spider agrees to marry Doll. Comedy with music borrows characters from *Jazzboat* (qv), but benefits from warm and witty script.

RoC *Bernie Winters, Harry Andrews, Al Mullock, Derren Nesbitt, Niall MacGinnis, Victor Brooks, Kynaston Reeves, Barry Keegan.*

IN THE WAKE OF A STRANGER (1959) [1]

Dir *David Eady*. Prod *Jon Penington*. Scr *John Tully, from the novel by Ian Stuart Black*. Ph *Eric Cross*. PC *Crest*. Dis *Butchers*. 64 mins. Cert U

Suspected of killing a man while on a drunken shore leave, seaman Tom Cassidy (*Tony Wright*) has a tough time trying to prevent the real killers from convincing the police that he did it. But with the help of a schoolteacher (*Shirley Eaton*), with whom he falls in love, and the dead man's partner (*Willoughby Goddard*), Tom proves his innocence. Unpersuasive thriller.

RoC *Danny Green, Harry H. Corbett, Peter Sinclair, Tom Bowman, Alun Owen, David Hemmings.*

INTIMATE RELATIONS (1953) [3]

Dir/Scr *Charles Frank, from a play by Jean Cocteau*. Prod *David Dent*. Ph *Willie Cooper*. PC/Dis *Adelphi*. 86 mins. Cert X

Yvonne (*Marian Spencer*) is a possessive drab, jealous of her molly-coddled son's (*Russell Enoch – William Russell*) new girlfriend (*Elsy Albiin*), who turns out to be Yvonne's husband's (*Harold Warrender*) ex-mistress. Yvonne's suicide eventually clears the way for the lovers' future. Doomed attempt to make Cocteau's *Les parents terribles* (filmed by him in 1949) into an English movie makes a classic tragi-comedy seem merely foolish.

RoC *Ruth Dunning.*

THE INTIMATE STRANGER (1956) [4]
(USA: *Finger of Guilt*)

Dir *Joseph Walton* (*Losey*). Prod *Alec C. Snowdon*. Scr *Peter Howard, from his novel* Pay the Piper. Ph *Gerry Gibbs*. PC *Anglo-Guild*. Dis *Anglo-Amalgamated*. 95 mins. Cert A

Reggie (*Richard Basehart*), a young film producer married to the daughter (*Faith Brook*) of the head (*Roger Livesey*) of the studio, gets not only tantrums from his star (*Constance Cummings*), but letters from Evelyn (*Mary Murphy*), whom he insists he has never met, but whose story is so convincing that his wife leaves him. It turns out that Evelyn has been supplied with details of Reggie's life by Chapple (*Mervyn Johns*), Reggie's sacked predecessor, who hoped to discredit him. Reggie and his wife are reunited. Ingenious, if overlong, film conundrum.

RoC *Vernon Greeves, André Mikhelson, Basil Dignam, David Lodge, Jay Denyer, Katherine Page, Grace Denbigh-Russell, Frederick Steger, Wilfrid Downing, Edna Landor, Jack Stewart, Michael Ward.*

INTO THE BLUE (1950) [2]
(USA: *The Man in the Dinghy*)

Dir *Herbert Wilcox*. Prod *Wilcox, Michael Wilding*. Scr *Pamela Wilcox Bower, Donald Taylor, Nicholas Phipps*. Ph *Max Greene (Mutz Greenbaum)*. PC *Imperadio*. Dis *British Lion*. 83 mins. Cert U

Nicholas (*Michael Wilding*) has been duped into smuggling watches into England. He stows away with the Fergussons (*Jack Hulbert, Constance Cummings*) on their Norwegian cruise and persuades them to change course for Paris so that he can get his own back on the smugglers. He also falls in love with their adopted daughter (*Odile Versois*). Dreadful backdrops, soggy script; lots of talent thoroughly water-logged.

RoC *Edward Rigby.*

THE INTRUDER (1953) [5]

Dir *Guy Hamilton*. Prod/PC *Ivan Foxwell*. Scr *Robin Maugham, John Hunter, Anthony Squire, from a novel by Maugham*. Ph *Ted Scaife*. Dis *British Lion*. 84 mins. Cert U

Disturbing a burglar, Colonel Merton (*Jack Hawkins*) is appalled to see it is Ginger (*Michael Medwin*), one of his best troopers in the war. He traces the circumstances that led the man to take up a life of crime, in which, inevitably, a girl (*Susan Shaw*) was involved.

Jack Hawkins and Dennis Price in The Intruder *(1953)*

Tracking Ginger to a farm, Merton tries to persuade him to give himself up, which Ginger does only after Merton has offered to help him escape. Solid, thoughtful drama works well both in its war flashbacks and as social conscience thriller.

RoC *George Cole, Dennis Price, Hugh Williams, Duncan Lamont, Edward Chapman, Dora Bryan, Nicholas Phipps, Arthur Howard, Campbell Singer, Patrick Barr, Harold Lang, Richard Wattis, George Baker, Michael Ripper, Marc Sheldon, Charles Lamb, Peter Martyn, Robert Adair, Leonard Sharp, Elizabeth Digby-Smith, Rowena Gregory, Sydney Linton, Gene Anderson, David Horne, Norman Hargood, Michael McGuire, Graham Tunbridge, Richard Morris, Bette Vivian, Frances Gowans.*

INVITATION TO THE DANCE (1954) 3

Dir/Scr *Gene Kelly.* Prod *Arthur Freed.* Ph *Frederick A Young.* PC/Dis *MGM British. Technicolor. 62 mins. Cert U*
Two musical short stories, which in America were combined with a third – the cartoon/live action *The Magic Lamp* – to make one film. The first, *Ring Around the Rosy*, is a variation on *La Ronde*, centring on a jewelled bracelet that passes from hand to hand. The second, *Circus*, deals with the doomed love of a clown for the pretty equestrienne. *Gene Kelly* stars in both but undoubtedly, as an item, *The Magic Lamp* (made in America) was the more popular.

RoC *Igor Youskevitch, Claire Sombert, David Paltenghi, Daphne Dale, Claude Bessy, Tommy Rall, Belita, Irving Davies, Diana Adams, Tamara Toumanova.*

I ONLY ARSKED! (1958) 3

Dir *Montgomery Tully.* Prod *Anthony Hinds.* Scr *Sid Colin, Jack Davies, from Colin's TV series The Army Game.* Ph *Lionel Banes.* PC *Hammer/Granada.* Dis *Columbia. 82 mins. Cert U*
Horrified when they are posted to the British Middle-East protectorate of Darawa, the malingering occupants of 'Hut 29', Popeye (*Bernard Bresslaw*), Springer (*Michael Medwin*), Excused Boots (*Alfie Bass*), Professor (*Charles Hawtrey*) and Cupcake (*Norman Rossington*) cheer up no end when they discover a secret passage to the king's harem. With the help of the harem girls, they put down a revolution

and discover an oil well. Hit TV series goes east to mix satire with slapstick.
RoC *Geoffrey Sumner, David Lodge, Michael Bentine, Arthur Howard, Francis Matthews, Marie Devereux, Michael Ripper, Wolfe Morris, Ewen McDuff, Martin Boddey.*

THE IRON PETTICOAT (1956) 4

Dir *Ralph Thomas.* Prod *Betty Box, Harry Saltzman.* Scr *Ben Hecht.* Ph *Ernest Steward.* PC *Romulus/Remus.* Dis *Independent Film Distributors/British Lion. Technicolor. VistaVision. 90 mins. Cert A*
Russian pilot Vinka (*Katharine Hepburn*) flies across the Iron Curtain in a fit of pique, and is forced down in the American sector of Germany by American pilot Chuck (*Bob Hope*) who is given the job of converting her to western ideals; she tries to convert him to communism. Vinka is kidnapped by Russians and sentenced to death – then a change in policy finds her marrying Chuck as a symbol of peace between east and west. Sparkling *Ninotchka*-style joke.
RoC *James Robertson Justice, Noelle Middleton, Robert Helpmann, David Kossoff, Paul Carpenter, Sidney James, Alexander Gauge, Sandra Dorne, David Kossoff, Alan Gifford, Ritchard Wattis, Tutte Lemkow, Martin Boddey, Nicholas Phipps, Doris Goddard, Maria Antippas.*

ISLAND IN THE SUN (1957) 2

Dir *Robert Rossen.* Prod *Darryl F. Zanuck.* Scr *Alfred Hayes, from the novel by Alec Waugh.* Ph *F. A. Young.* PC/Dis *20th Century-Fox. Technicolor. CinemaScope. 119 mins. Cert A*
An election approaches on the Caribbean island of Santa Mara. Wealthy Maxwell Fleury (*James Mason*) stands against native leader David Boyeur (*Harry Belafonte*). Fleury turns the revelation of his coloured ancestry to his own advantage, but gets involved with a war hero (*Michael Rennie*) having an affair with his wife (*Patricia Owens*) and kills him. Boyeur rejects his white mistress (*Joan Fontaine*) as she will be a hindrance to his political career. A sort of Jamaican *Peyton Place*; hopelessly disjointed with far too many major characters.
RoC *Joan Collins, Dorothy Dandridge, John Justin, Diana Wynyard, Stephen Boyd, Basil Sydney, Hartley Power, John Williams, Ronald Squire.*

ISN'T LIFE WONDERFUL! (1952) 4

Dir *Harold French.* Prod *Warwick Ward.* Scr *Brock Williams from his novel* Uncle Willie and the Bicycle Shop. Ph *Erwin Hillier.* PC *Associated British.* Dis *AB-Pathé. Technicolor. 83 mins. Cert U*
1902. Before the rich American fiancée (*Dianne Foster*) of their son (*Robert Urquhart*) can arrive, a stuffy Victorian family decides that its black sheep, Uncle Willie (*Donald Wolfit*), must be whitewashed. So they set him up with a bicycle shop. Before long, the entire family, even Mother (*Eileen Herlie*) and Father (*Cecil Parker*), has caught the cycle craze. The lovers meet and fall out but, thanks to Willie, all ends well. Sunny, fun-filled comedy, a bit static.
RoC *Eleanor Summerfield, Peter Asher, Cecil Trouncer, Russell Waters, Edwin Styles, Fabia*

Drake, Arthur Young, Viola Lyel, Philip Stainton, George Woodbridge, Wensley Pithey, Alec Finter, Cecily Paget-Bowman, Basil Cunard, John Welsh, Margot Lister, Henry Hewitt.

IS YOUR HONEYMOON REALLY NECESSARY? (1953) 3

Dir *Maurice Elvey.* Prod *David Dent.* Scr *Talbot Rothwell, from the play by E. V. Tidmarsh.* Ph *Phil Grindrod.* PC *Advance.* Dis *Adelphi. 79 mins. Cert U*
An American airman (*Bonar Colleano*) comes to England with his bride (*Diana Decker*), to be met by his first wife (*Diana Dors*), not merely claiming alimony, but sowing seeds of doubt as to whether their divorce was valid. After numerous complications, the airman sorts it out, only to be confronted by a new candidate for his affections ... Routine farce.
RoC *David Tomlinson, Sidney James, MacDonald Parke, Audrey Freeman.*

IT'S A GRAND LIFE (1953) 2

Dir/Prod *John E. Blakeley.* Scr *H. F. Maltby, Frank Randle.* Ph *Ernest Palmer.* PC *Film Studios Manchester.* Dis *Mancunian. 102 mins. Cert U*
Accident-prone Private Randle can't even make a success of making the tea for his army unit – but he does succeed in saving a comely corporal from the lecherous clutches of his sergeant-major, and steers her into the arms of the private soldier who really loves her. Artless combination of comedy routines and musical interludes. Well-worn gags galore.
LP *Frank Randle, Diana Dors, Dan Young, Michael Brennan, Jennifer Jayne, John Blythe, Anthony Hulme, Charles Peters, Arthur White, Ian Fleming, Ruth Taylor, Winifred Atwell, Jack Pye.*

IT'S A GREAT DAY (1955) 2

Dir *John Warrington.* Prod *Victor Lyndon.* Scr *Roland and Michael Pertwee, from their TV series* The Groves. Ph *Cedric Williams.* PC *Grove.* Dis *Butchers. 71 mins. Cert U*
Racing to finish the flooring in a new housing estate before it is opened by a princess, builder Bob Grove (*Edward Evans*) accepts some tiles which prove to be stolen. Already selected to entertain the princess to tea, he now comes under suspicion of theft. But the thief's girl-friend (*Vera Day*) clears him, although chaos still reigns in his household when the princess make her appearance. Harmless comedy from a monumentally successful TV show; certainly there's a lot going on.
RoC *Ruth Dunning, Peter Bryant, Sheila Sweet, Nancy Roberts, Margaret Downs, Sidney James, Christopher Beeny, Victor Maddern, John Stuart, Henry Oscar, Marjorie Rhodes, Michael Balfour, Nan Braunton, Spencer Hale, Donald Finlay, Patrick Jordan, Ian Whittaker, Peggyann Clifford, Jack May, Stanley Rose, Vi Stevens.*

IT'S A WONDERFUL WORLD (1956) 4

Dir/Scr *Val Guest.* Prod/PC *George Minter.* Ph *Wilkie Cooper.* Dis *Renown. Technicolor. SpactaScope. 89 mins. Cert U*
Songwriters Ray (*Terence Morgan*) and Ken

(*George Cole*), languishing because their kind of music is out of style, hit the jackpot when Ken starts recording old music backwards as ultra-modern stuff, and Georgie, a young French singer, makes an enormous commercial success out of one of their other songs. Bright, noisy, inventive musical, sensibly not imitative of Hollywood.

RoC *Mylene Nicole* (*Demongeot*), *Kathleen Harrison, James Hayter, Harold Lang, Maurice Kaufmann, Richard Wattis, Reginald Beckwith, Derek Blomfield, Dennis Lotis, Maya Koumani, Walter Crisham, Charles Clay, Jock McKay, Hal Osmond, Sam Kydd, George Moon, Douglas Blackwell, Keith Sawbridge, Angela Braemar, Stan Thomason, Charles Brodie, Brian Sunners, Leslie Weston, Patricia Ryan, Avril Sadler, Jeanette Pearce, Howard Williams, Shirley Ann Field, Colin Croft, Roger Snowden, Douglas Bradley-Smith, Bernard Rebel, Francesco Russo, Lellah Sabarathy.*

IT'S GREAT TO BE YOUNG (1956) [5]
Dir *Cyril Frankel*. Prod *Viktor Skutezky*. Scr *Ted Willis*. Ph *Gilbert Taylor*. PC *Marble Arch*. Dis *AB-Pathé. Eastman Colour. 93 mins. Cert U*

At Angel Hill Grammar School, Mr Dingle (*John Mills*) is training the Upper Sixth for the National Festival of School Orchestras. An impromptu jazz session arouses the wrath of headmaster Frome (*Cecil Parker*) and starts a chain of events which ends in the resignation of Dingle and the siege of the Upper Sixth who barricade themselves in the gymnasium. Frome finally sees the value of compromise and he and Dingle are carried off on the shoulders of cheering children. Tremendous comedy-with-music that only lets its swinging pace drop for a touch of sappy teenage romance. Bubbling, joyous stuff.

RoC *Jeremy Spenser, Dorothy Bromily, Eleanor Summerfield, John Salew, Brian Smith, Dawson France, Wilfred Downing, Carole Shelley, Richard O'Sullivan, Robert Dickens, Elizabeth Kentish, Mona Washbourne, Mary Merrall, Derek Blomfield, Norman Pierce, Bryan Forbes, Marjorie Rhodes, Eddie Byrne, Russell Waters; Edna Savage, Ruby Murray, The Coronets* (*voices*).

John Mills and Jeremy Spenser (*background left*) *in* It's Great To Be Young! (*1956*)

IT'S NEVER TOO LATE (1956) [4]
Dir *Michael McCarthy*. Prod *George Pitcher*. Scr *Edward Dryhurst, from the play by Felicity*

Douglas. Ph *C. Pennington-Richards*. PC *Park Lane*. Dis *AB-Pathé. Eastman Colour. 95 mins. Cert U*

Housewife Laura (*Phyllis Calvert*) not only copes with a husband (*Patrick Barr*) who does nothing but read the paper, a grannie (*Jean Taylor-Smith*) who does nothing but grumble, a daughter (*Susan Stephen*) who endures hourly emotional crises, and a married daughter who spends her time throwing things at her husband, but also writes in her spare time. Summoned to Hollywood to work on a script, she soon returns to her family, realizing she can only work properly within its turmoil. Bright, frothy, if stagy comedy with many a chuckle.

RoC *Guy Rolfe, Sarah Lawson, Richard Leech, Peter Hammond, Delphi Lawrence, Robert Ayres, Barbara Cavan, Irene Handl, John Fernald, Peter Illing, Stanley Maxted, Shirley Ann Field.*

IT STARTED IN PARADISE (1952) [2]
Dir *Compton Bennett*. Prod *Sergei Nolbandov, Leslie Parkyn*. Scr *Marghanita Laski*. Ph *Jack Cardiff*. PC *British Film Makers*. Dis *General Film Distributors. Technicolor. 94 mins. Cert U*

In pre-war days, Martha (*Jane Hylton*), an ambitious fashion designer, elbows aside Madame Alice (*Martita Hunt*) and takes over their salon. During World War II, she loses her best designer Alison (*Muriel Pavlow*) and falls for a womanizing French count (*Terence Morgan*) and her standing in the trade slips. Realizing her mistakes by the early 1950s, Martha brings back Alison on her own terms, in a successful show financed by Turner (*Ian Hunter*), Martha's ex-lover. Uninteresting subject needed more depth and bite.

RoC *Kay Kendall, Brian Worth, Ronald Squire, Harold Lang, Lucienne Hill, Joyce Barbour, Diana Decker, Jack Allen, Mara Lane, Margaret Withers, Frank Tickle, Helen Forrest, Venora McIndoe, Diana Salisbury, Arthur Lane, Alan Gifford, Dorinda Stevens, Conrad Phillips, Bill Travers, Avis Scott, Douglas Muir, Basil Hoskins, June Brown, Teresa Dunnien, Naomi Chance.*

IVANHOE (1952) [4]
Dir *Richard Thorpe*. Prod *Pandro S. Berman*. Scr *Aeneas Mackenzie, Noel Langley, from the novel by Sir Walter Scott*. Ph *F. A. Young*. PC/Dis *MGM British. Technicolor. 107 mins. Cert U*

1190. In return for saving rich Jewish merchant Isaac from robbers, Saxon knight Wilfrid of Ivanhoe (*Robert Taylor*) is promised the rest of the money he needs for the ransom of Richard the Lionheart from the Austrians. Ivanhoe upholds Saxon honour against the Normans and Richard's treacherous brother John (*Guy Rolfe*), especially in tournaments; he and the merchant's daughter Rebecca (*Elizabeth Taylor*) are captured by Norman nobles, but rescued by Saxon friends. Villainous De Bois-Guilbert (*George Sanders*) and de Bracy (*Robert Douglas*) are killed, and Ivanhoe marries Rowena (*Joan Fontaine*), leaving Re-

Robert Taylor and Elizabeth Taylor in Ivanhoe (*1952*)

becca to return sadly to her people. Rousingly made, staidly acted.

RoC *Emlyn Williams, Finlay Currie, Felix Aylmer, Norman Wooland, Basil Sydney, Harold Warrender, Patrick Holt, Francis de Wolff, Roderick Lovell, John Ruddock, Michael Brennan, Megs Jenkins, Valentine Dyall, Lionel Harris, Sebastian Cabot, Carl Jaffe, John Richardson.*

I WAS MONTY'S DOUBLE (1958) [4]
(USA: *Monty's Double*)
Dir *John Guillermin*. Prod *Maxwell Setton*. Scr *Bryan Forbes, from the book by M. E. Clifton James*. Ph *Basil Emmott*. PC *FilmTraders/Maxwell Setton*. Dis *AB-Pathé. 100 mins. Cert U*

British officers Harvey (*John Mills*) and Logan (*Cecil Parker*) see the actor *Clifton James* (as himself), who bears a remarkable resemblance to General Montgomery, as an ideal opportunity, in 1944, to fool the Germans as to the location of the Allied invasion in Europe. The actor, although nervous, carries off the deception superbly, but is then kidnapped by Nazi commandos, Harvey having to launch a counter raid to get him back. Tense, amusing real-life story has plenty of excitement.

RoC *Marius Goring, Michael Hordern, Patrick Allen, Bryan Forbes, Leslie Phillips, James Hayter, Barbara Hicks, Sidney James, Vera Day, Victor Maddern, Marne Maitland, Alfie Bass, MacDonald Parke, Duncan Lamont, Patrick Holt, John le Mesurier, Anthony Sagar, John Gale, Kenneth J. Warren, Geoffrey Hibbert, Harry Fowler, Bill Nagy, Edward Judd, Victor Beaumont, Walter Gotell, David Lodge, Fred Nicholas, Maureen Connell, Sam Kydd, Allan Cuthbertson, Ronnie Stevens, Max Butterfield, Michael Oliver, Ian Whittaker, Alfred Maron, Patrick Connor, Michael Bird, Diana Beaumont, Brian Weske, Martin Shaban, Eric Francis, Derek Briggs, Desmond Roberts, Ronald Wilson, John G. Heller, Frederick Jaeger, David Davies.*

J

JACK THE RIPPER (1959) [3]

Dir *Robert S. Baker.* Prod *Baker, Monty Berman.* Scr *Jimmy Sangster.* Ph *Berman.* PC *Mid Century.* Dis *Regal. 85 mins. Cert X*

1888. American detective Sam Lowry (*Lee Patterson*) joins forces with Inspector O'Neill (*Eddie Byrne*) in investigating the murder of London prostitutes by Jack the Ripper. Lowry falls in love with Anne (*Betty McDowall*), niece of a surgeon (*John le Mesurier*), who proves to be the killer (in spite of a mob nearly lynching his mute assistant) and kills the girl he was after all the time before being crushed in a lift-shaft. Fair chiller; quite good atmosphere.

RoC *Ewen Solon, George Rose, Philip Leaver, Barbara Burke, Denis Shaw, Endre Muller, Anne Sharp, Esma Cannon, George Woodbridge, Bill Shine, Garard Green, Jack Allen, Jane Taylor, Dorinda Stevens, Marianne Stone, Hal Osmond, George Street, Olwen Brookes, Montparnasse Ballet.*

JACQUELINE (1956) [4]

Dir *Roy Baker.* Prod *George H. Brown.* Scr *Patrick Kirwan, Liam O'Flaherty, Patrick Campbell, Catherine Cookson.* Ph *Geoffrey Unsworth.* PC/Dis *Rank. 93 mins. Cert U*

Labourer Mike McNeil (*John Gregson*) would like to work on a farm, but is forced to work on the scaffolding in the Belfast shipyards, where his attacks of vertigo bring on crises and eventually get him fired. Always fond of a drop, he becomes a heavy drinker, but his young daughter Jacqueline (*Jacqueline Ryan*) still believes in him, marches up to hard-headed businessman Lord (*Liam Redmond*) and wrings a farm job out of him for her father. Likeable drama with atmospheric background detail.

RoC *Kathleen Ryan, Noel Purcell, Cyril Cusack, Richard O'Sullivan, Marie Kean, Maureen Delany, Tony Wright, Maureen Swanson, Sam Kydd, Agnes Brantford, Jack MacGowran, Barry Keegan, Rita Begley.*

JAZZBOAT (1959) [3]

Dir *Ken Hughes.* Prod *Harold Huth.* Scr *Hughes, John Antrobus.* Ph *Ted Moore, Nick Roeg.* PC *Warwick.* Dis *Columbia. CinemaScope. 96 mins. Cert A*

Bert (*Anthony Newley*) gets involved with a gang of crooks by posing as a cat burglar to meet their girl, The Doll (*Anne Aubrey*). He finds himself masterminding a big jewellery robbery. Getting away with the loot, he plans to return it, but the gang pursues him on a jazzboat trip to Margate with his girlfriend (*Joyce Blair*). Police arrest them after a hectic chase through a funfair. Sadistic streak mars this rough-edged comedy-musical with authentic south-east England backgrounds.

RoC *James Booth, Lionel Jeffries, David Lodge, Bernie Winters, Leo McKern, Al Mulock, Jean Philippe, Liam Gaffney, Henry Webb, Ted Heath and His Music*

JET STORM (1959) [3]

Dir *C. Raker (Cy) Endfield.* Prod *Steven Pallos.* Scr *Endfield, Sigmund Muller.* Ph *Jack Hildyard.* PC *Pendennis.* Dis *British Lion/Britannia. 99 mins. Cert A*

Bardow (*Stanley Baker*), captain of a jet flight from London to New York, discovers a bomb has been planted by Tilley (*Richard Attenborough*) to kill Brock (*George Rose*), the hit-and-run driver who killed his child. A group of passengers are prepared to kill Brock to appease Tilley but, after Brock dies accidentally, Tilley is still unmoved – until a small boy persuades him to defuse the bomb. Tilley kills himself. Familiar crisis-in-mid-air drama kept reasonably entertaining by all-star cast.

RoC *Hermione Baddeley, Bernard Braden, Diane Cilento, Barbara Kelly, David Kossoff, Virginia Maskell, Harry Secombe, Elizabeth Sellars, Sybil Thorndike, Marty Wilde, Mai Zetterling, Neil McCallum, Patrick Allen, Paul Carpenter, Megs Jenkins, Jackie Lane, Cec Linder, Lana Morris, Peter Bayliss, John Crewdson, Paul Eddington, Glyn Houston, Peter Illing, Jeremy Judge, George Murcell, Alun Owen, Irene Prador.*

JOE MACBETH (1955) [4]

Dir *Ken Hughes.* Prod *M. J. Frankovitch, George Maynard.* Scr *Philip Yordan.* Ph *Basil Emmott.* PC *Film Locations.* Dis *Columbia. 90 mins. Cert A*

Joe Macbeth (*Paul Douglas*) is happy being number two to an underworld kingpin (*Gregoire Aslan*). But his wife Lily (*Ruth Roman*) urges him to kill his boss and become number one. He knifes him while swimming, but his friend Banky's (*Sidney James*) son Lennie (*Bonar Colleano*) resents his assumption of leadership. Joe sends out hoodlums to get Lennie but they kill Banky by mistake. In another bungle, Lennie's wife and baby are killed when they should have been abducted. Joe accidentally kills Lily and is himself gunned down by Lennie. Blood-chilling gangster version of Shakespeare; but a bit arty at times.

RoC *Harry Green, Minerva Pious, Walter Crisham, Kay Callard, Robert Arden, George Margo, Nicholas Stuart, Beresford Egan, Victor*

Gregoire Aslan, Paul Douglas and Ruth Roman in Joe Macbeth (*1955*)

Baring, Bill Nagy, Kay Callard, Walter Crisham, Mark Baker, Alfred (Al) Mulock, Philip Vickers, Robert O'Neill, Johnny Ross, Launce Maraschal, Shirley Douglas, Louise Grant, Sheila Woods.

JOHN AND JULIE (1955) [4]

Dir and Scr *William Fairchild.* Prod *Herbert Mason.* Ph *Arthur Grant.* PC *Group 3.* Dis *British Lion. Eastman Colour. 82 mins. Cert U*

1953. Determined to see the coronation of Elizabeth II, John (*Colin Gibson*) aged 11, and Julie (*Lesley Dudley*) aged six, run away from their village and set out for London. Various people help them on their way and they find a further friend in London in the form of a kindly field-marshal (*Wilfred Hyde White*), who arranges for them to see the procession. But Julie falls asleep. Gentle comedy of considerable charm. Eddie Calvert's trumpet theme was a big hit.

RoC *Moira Lister, Noelle Middleton, Constance Cummings, Megs Jenkins, Sidney James, Peter Sellers, Joseph Tomelty, Patric Doonan, Andrew Cruickshank, Colin Gordon, Peter Jones, Mona Washbourne, Richard Dimbleby, Wynford Vaughan Thomas.*

JOHNNY ON THE RUN (1953) [4]

Dir and Prod *Lewis Gilbert.* Scr *Patricia Latham.* Ph *Gerald Gibbs.* PC *International Realist/Children's Film Foundation.* Dis *Associated British. 68 mins. Cert U*

Jan, a Polish orphan (*Eugeniusz Chylek*), runs away from his cruel foster-mother with some vague idea of getting to Poland. He unwittingly becomes the accomplice of thieves and seeks refuge in a Scottish village, where he is befriended by the children of an 'international village'. Both crooks and foster-mother track him down, but are trapped and outwitted respectively; Jan stays in the village. Exciting, intelligent children's film thunders along; one of the best CFF movies.

RoC *Sydney Tafler, Michael Balfour, Jean Anderson, Moultrie Kelsall, Mona Washbourne, Margaret McCourt, Edna Wynn, David Coote, Cleopatra Sylvestre, Louis Alexander, Elizabeth Saunders, Keith Faulkner, John Levitt.*

JOHNNY ON THE SPOT (1954) [2]

Dir *Maclean Rogers.* Prod and PC *E. J. Fancey.* Scr *Rogers, from a novel by Michael Cronin.* Ph *Geoffrey Faithfull.* Dis *New Realm. 72 mins. Cert U*

Johnny (*Hugh McDermott*) returns from a prison sentence in South America to get the man who framed him. When he reaches his house, the man and a girl are dead; a blind pianist is playing in the drawing-room. A man and a woman flee from the house. From this bizarre set of circumstances, Johnny rescues a kidnapped girl, cracks a criminal gang and clears his own name. Difficult to follow – or to care.

RoC *Elspet Gray, Paul Carpenter, Jean Lodge, Valentine Dyall, Ronald Adam, Adrienne Scott, Graham Stark, Pauline Olsen.*

JOHNNY, YOU'RE WANTED (1955) [3]

Dir *Vernon Sewell.* Prod *George Maynard.* Scr *Michael Leighton, Frank Driscoll, from the TV* serial by Maurice McLoughlin. Ph *Basil Emmott*. PC *Merton Park*. Dis *Anglo-Amalgamated. 71 mins. Cert A*

When a girl to whom he has given a lift is murdered, lorry-driver Johnny (*John Slater*) finds himself involved with a drug-smuggling gang who run their business under cover of a travelling fortune-telling show and a joke shop. Quite sprightly whodunnit rather obviously devised for Slater and *Alfred Marks* to shine. Exciting climax.

RoC *Garry Marsh, Chris Halward, Joan Rhodes, John Stuart, Thelma Ruby, Jack Stewart, John Helier, Joan Carol, Ann Lynn, Frank Thornton, Peter Burton, Eric Corrie, Jimmy Vyvyan, Thelma Ruby.*

JOSEPHINE AND MEN (1955) [2]

Dir *Roy Boulting*. Prod *John Boulting*. Scr *Nigel Balchin, Roy Boulting, Frank Harvey*. Ph *Gilbert Taylor*. PC *Charter*. Dis *British Lion. Eastman Colour. 98 mins. Cert U*

Josephine's (*Glynis Johns*) maternal instincts lead her to throw over businessman Alan (*Donald Sinden*) to marry struggling writer David (*Peter Finch*). When Alan gets into trouble following a massive swindle, she decides to flee with him. Then Alan is cleared – and Josephine returns to David. Comedy as limp (and slow) as it sounds. Good cast can't do much.

RoC *Jack Buchanan, William Hartnell, Heather Thatcher, Ronald Squire, Victor Maddern, Thorley Walters, Hugh Moxey, Laurence Naismith, John le Mesurier, Lisa Gastoni, Leo Ciceri, Pauline David, Sam Kydd.*

JUDGMENT DEFERRED (1951) [3]

Dir *John Baxter*. Prod *Baxter, John Grierson*. Scr *Geoffrey Orme, Barbara K. Emary, Walter Meade*, from a screenplay by *Herbert Ayres*. Ph *Arthur Grant*. PC *Group 3*. Dis *Associated British. 88 mins. Cert A*

The first Group 3 film is an expanded remake by Baxter of his own *Doss House* (1933): a reporter (*Hugh Sinclair*) investigating a drug ring comes across a strange group of derelicts operating from the crypt of a Dorset church. They are working to expose the leader of the drug racket, who has framed one of their number. With the reporter's help, they do so, and bring him to 'trial'. Bizarre story still runs very much like a 1930s movie.

RoC *Helen Shingler, Abraham Sofaer, Leslie Dwyer, Joan Collins, Harry Locke, Elwyn Brook-Jones, Martin Benson, Bransby Williams, Michael Martin-Harvey, Harry Welchman, Wilfrid Walter, Marcel Poncin, Maire O'Neill, Mary Merrall, Edgar Driver, Billy Russell, Bud Flanagan, June Elvin, Harold Goodwin, Fred Griffiths, Ann Lancaster, Cyril Smith, Freddie Watts, John Wynn, Herbert C. Walton, Michael Hogarth, Edmundo Ros and His Orchestra.*

JUMPING FOR JOY (1955) [2]

Dir *John Paddy Carstairs*. Prod *Raymond Stross*. Scr *Jack Davies, Henry E. Blyth*. Ph *Jack Cox*. PC/Dis *Rank. 88 mins. Cert U*

Willie (*Frankie Howerd*), oddjob boy at a greyhound track, gets fired over suspicion of involvement in a doping scandal. He buys a sick greyhound, nurses it back to health and, with

the assistance of 'Captain' Montague (*Stanley Holloway*), a confidence trickster, and the eccentric Lord and Lady Cranfield (*A.E. Matthews, Joan Hickson*), not only enters it for a big race that it wins, but proves his innocence as well. Comedy runs less well than dog, finishes lame.

RoC *Tony Wright, Alfie Bass, Lionel Jeffries, Susan Beaumont, Terence Longdon, Colin Gordon, Richard Wattis, Danny Green, Ewen Solon, A. J. 'Man Mountain' Dean, Jack Lambert, John Warren, Barbara Archer, William Kendall, Reginald Beckwith, Bill Fraser, Michael Ward, Beatrice Varley, Tom Gill, Charles Hawtrey, David Hannaford.*

JUST MY LUCK (1957) [4]

Dir *John Paddy Carstairs*. Prod *Hugh Stewart*. Scr *Alfred Shaughnessy, Peter Blackmore*. Ph *Jack Cox*. PC and Dis *Rank. 86 mins. Cert U*

To win enough money to propose to the girl (*Jill Dixon*) he loves, Norman (*Norman Wisdom*), a jeweller's oddjob boy, places £1 on a jockey to win all six of his races in one day. The odds are thousands to one. The jockey wins the first five races, but is on a no-hoper in the last. Norman tries to buy the horse but fails, and it comes in last before he realizes the jockey had switched mounts and has won. Pleasant Wisdom comedy, if hardly tailored to his talents.

RoC *Leslie Phillips, Margaret Rutherford, Delphi Lawrence, Edward Chapman, Joan Sims, Peter Copley, Michael Ward, Bill Fraser, Campbell Cotts, Robin Bailey, Sabrina, Marjorie Rhodes, Felix Felton, Sam Kydd, Frank Atkinson, James Bree, Lynne Cole, Joan Ingram, Beth Rogan, Marigold Russell, John Warwick, Leslie Davenport, Sylvia Childs, Eddie Dillon, Stringer Davis, Michael Brennan, Marianne Stone, Eddie Leslie, Ian Wilson, Ballard Berkeley, Jill Clifford, Vic Wise, Tom Naylor.*

K

KEEP IT CLEAN (1955) [2]

Dir *David Paltenghi*. Prod *Maxwell Setton, James R. Sloan*. Scr *Carl Nystrom, R. F. Delderfield*. PC *Marksman*. Dis *Eros. 75 mins. Cert U*

To market his brother-in-law's miracle cleaning invention, Bert (*Ronald Shiner*), an advertising agent, has to get financial support from clean-up-the-arts campaigner Pat Anstey (*Ursula Howells*). After becoming involved in a chaotic series of brawls and disasters, Bert achieves his aim. Shiner floundering outside auspices of big studios; time-honoured slapstick situations litter unfunny comedy.

RoC *James Hayter, Diane Hart, Jean Cadell, Tonia Bern, Colin Gordon, Benny Lee, Joan Sims, Gerald Campion, Albert Whelan, Denis Shaw, Mark Daly, Arthur Goullet, Norman*

Rossington, Violet Gould, Bert Brownbill, Tony Sympson, Pauline Winter, Lillemor Knudsen, Henry Longhurst, Roger Maxwell.

THE KEY (1958) [4]

Dir *Carol Reed*. Prod *Aubrey Baring*. Scr *Carl Foreman*, from a novel by *Jan de Hartog*. Ph *Oswald Morris*. PC *Open Road*. Dis *Columbia. CinemaScope. 127 mins. Cert A*

1941. Both Stella (*Sophia Loren*), a Swiss refugee, and her flat have been owned by a succession of tugboat skippers, each killed after a 'warning'. Chris's (*Trevor Howard*) warning is wine spilled on his chest; he hands Stella's key to David (*William Holden*). Chris is killed and Stella and David fall in love. When David's 'warning' comes, he hands the key to Kane (*Kieron Moore*) – but survives. Stella flees, with David swearing to follow; but Kane knows he cannot. Well-acted (especially by Howard, who won a British Oscar), but oh-so-gloomy.

RoC *Oscar Homolka, Bernard Lee, Beatrix Lehmann, Noel Purcell, Bryan Forbes, Russell Waters, James Heyter, Irene Handl, John Crawford, Rupert Davies, Sidney Vivian, Jameson Clark, Michael Caine, Carl Mohner.*
*Scenes deleted from final release print.

Sophia Loren and Trevor Howard in The Key *(1958)*

THE KEY MAN (1957) [2]

Dir *Montgomery Tully*. Prod *Alec C. Snowden*. Scr *J. McLaren Ross*, from his play. Ph *Philip Grindrod*. PC *Insignia*. Dis *Anglo-Amalgamated. 63 mins. Cert U*

Lionel Hulme (*Lee Patterson*) who runs a radio crime programme, buys himself a packet of trouble when he tries to reconstruct an old murder. It leads to an equally distant robbery from which the loot was never recovered. And the release of a long-term jailbird pitches Lionel into the middle of the hunt for a fortune in a safe-deposit box. But the criminal and his associates are rounded up after a car crash, before they can lay hands on the loot. Brisk but very ordinary thriller.

RoC *Hy Hazell, Colin Gordon, Philip Leaver, Henry Vidon, Paula Byrne, Harold Kasket, Maudie Edwards, George Margo, Ian Wilson, Billy Milton, Dennis Castle, Dave Rhodes, Rex Rashley, James McLoughlin.*

A KID FOR TWO FARTHINGS (1955) [4]

Dir and Prod *Carol Reed*. Scr *Wolf Mankowitz*, from his novel. Ph *Edward Scaife*. PC *Lon-*

don Films/Big Ben Films. Dis *Independent Film Distributors/British Lion. Eastman Colour. 96 mins. Cert U*
Most of the people in London's Petticoat Lane street market have problems – until little Joe (*Jonathan Ashmore*) buys a kid which, because of its one horn, he assumes to be the unicorn of the stories told to him by tailor Kandinsky (*David Kossoff*). Young wrestler Sam (*Joe Robinson*) wins a vital match and buys Sonia (*Diana Dors*) a ring, Kandinsky gets a new steam-press and other 'miracles' happen. The kid dies ... and the boy gets a new pet. Enjoyable fairy-tale; bustling life of the Lane is good, characters likeable.
RoC *Celia Johnson, Sidney James, Sydney Tafler, Brenda de Banzie, Primo Carnera, Vera Day, Lou Jacobi, Daphne Anderson, Harold Berens, Danny Green, Irene Handl, Rosalind Boxall, Eddie Byrne, Joseph Tomelty, Harry Purvis, Harry Baird, Lilly Kann, Arthur Lovegrove, Madge Brindley, Harold Goodwin, George Hirste, Eddie Malin, Derek Sydney, Sam Kydd, Peter Taylor, Marigold Russell, Max Denne, Norah Gordon, James Lomas, Charles Saynor, Mollie Palmer, Barbara Denney, Barbara Archer, Ann Chaplin, Anita Arley, Judith Nelmes, Arthur Skinner, Raymond Rollett, Bruce Beeby, Asher Day, Bart Allison, Norman Mitchell, Lew Mara, Frank Blake.*

THE KID FROM CANADA (1957) [4]
Dir *Kay Mander*. Prod *Ralph May*. Scr *John Eldridge*. Ph *Paddy Carey*. PC *Anvil/Children's Film Foundation*. Dis *British Lion. 57 mins. Cert U*
In Scotland on a visit to his cousins, 10-year-old Andy (*Christopher Braden*), a Canadian, soon falls out with them over alleged chicanery at a horse show. He proves his worth, though, when rescuing an injured shepherd on a mountainside, and the children become friends again. Well-made children's film; professionalism in all departments creates a convincing story.
RoC *Pamela Stirling, Bernard Braden, Bobby Stevenson, Elinor Laing, David Caldwell, Alex Mackenzie, Peter Macdonell, Katherine Page.*

KIDNAPPED (1959) [3]
Dir and Scr *Robert Stevenson, from the novel by Robert Louis Stevenson.* (Associate) Prod *Hugh Attwooll*. Ph *Paul Beeson*. PC and Dis *Walt Disney. Technicolor. 95 mins. Cert U*
Scotland 1750. Cheated out of his inheritance by his uncle (*John Laurie*), David Balfour (*James MacArthur*) is taken on a brig by Capt Hoseason (*Bernard Lee*) to be sold as a slave in America. Alan Breck Stewart (*Peter Finch*), a Jacobite fleeing the English, comes aboard, and helps David defeat Hoseason and his crew. After getting involved in a political murder case, they also put paid to David's uncle. Faithful to the book, but a little slow in the telling.
RoC *Niall MacGinnis, Finlay Currie, Peter O'Toole, Andrew Cruickshank, Duncan Macrae, Miles Malleson, Oliver Johnston, Alex Mackenzie, Norman MacOwan, Eileen Way, Jack Stewart, Edie Martin, Abe Barker, John Pike.*

THE KIDNAPPERS (1953) [5]
(USA: *The Little Kidnappers*)
Dir *Philip Leacock*. Prod *Sergei Nolbandov, Leslie Parkyn*. Scr *Neil Paterson*. Ph *Eric Cross*. PC *Group*. Dis *General Film Distributors. 93 mins. Cert U*
Nova Scotia. 1904. Mackenzie (*Duncan Macrae*), an elderly puritan, mistreats the orphan grandsons (*Jon Whiteley, Vincent Winter*) with whom he is saddled. They find a baby in the woods and feed it with goat's milk. A posse searching for the baby accidentally injures Mackenzie's eloping daughter Kirsty (*Adrienne Corri*). The older child is accused of kidnapping, but the baby's father defends him, and Mackenzie's heart softens. Comedy weepie of immense charm; the two boys both won special Academy Awards.
RoC *Jean Anderson, Theodore Bikel, Francis de Wolff, James Sutherland, John Rae, Jack Stewart, Jameson Clark, Eric Woodburn, Howard Connell, Christopher Beeny.*

KILLERS OF KILIMANJARO (1959) [2]
Dir *Richard Thorpe*. Prod *John R. Sloan*. Scr *John Gilling, with Richard Maibaum, Cyril Hume, Earl Fenton, from a book by John A. Hunter, Dan P. Mannkx*. Ph *Ted Moore*. *Technicolor. Cinemascope. 91 mins. Cert U*
East Africa 1900. Adamson, an engineer making a survey for the region's first railroad, has to take along Jane (*Anne Aubrey*), whose father and fiancé have disappeared in the interior, and Hooky (*Anthony Newley*), the rail company's chief clerk, as well as suffers attacks from slaver Ben Ahmed (*Gregoire Aslan*) who wants the rail monopoly. Adamson wins over a hostile tribe who help him defeat Ahmed and his men, but finds Jane's father dead and fiancé an embittered alcoholic. Hilarious *Boys Own* antics; abuzz with action if nothing else.
RoC *Allan Cuthbertson, Martin Benson, John Dimech, Orlando Martins, Martin Boddey, Earl Cameron, Harry Baird, Donald Pleasence, Anthony Jacobs, Joyce Blair, Barbara Joyce, Christine Pockett.*

A KILLER WALKS (1952) [1]
Dir, Prod and Scr *Ronald Drake, from a play by Gordon Glennon and a novel by Rayner Barton*. Ph *Jack Asher, Phil Grindrod*. PC *Leontine Entertainments*. Dis *Grand National. 57 mins. Cert A*
Slow-witted Frankie (*Trader Faulkner*) and his discontented brother Ned (*Laurence Harvey*) live with their grandmother on a farm. Desperate for money to keep his city girlfriend (*Susan Shaw*) in the style to which she's accustomed, Ned murders his grandmother and tries to pin it on Frankie. But he bungles the 'frame' and police take him away. Terrible, heavy rural tragedy reminiscent of a violent *East Lynne*.
RoC *Laurence Naismith, Sheila Shand Gibbs, Ethel Edwards.*

KILL HER GENTLY (1957) [2]
Dir *Charles Saunders*. Prod *Guido Coen*. Scr *Paul Erickson*. Ph *Walter J. Harvey*. PC *Fortress*. Dis *Columbia. 63 mins (originally 75). Cert A*
Jeff (*Griffith Jones*), an ex-mental patient in-

sanely jealous of his rich young wife Kay (*Maureen Connell*), picks up two escaped convicts and enlists them in a plan to murder her, promising them money and help to flee the country. When he has trouble raising the cash, things start to go wrong, and eventually he is the one who is caught by his own plot. Dreary thriller, severely cut before its release in 1960.
RoC *Marc Lawrence, George Mikell, Shay Gorman, Marianne Brauns, Frank Hawkins, Patrick O'Connell, David Lawton, John Gayford, Roger Avon.*

KILL ME TOMORROW (1957) [3]
Dir *Terence Fisher*. Prod *Francis Searle*. Scr *Robert Falconer, Manning O'Brine*. Ph *Geoffrey Faithfull*. PC *Delta*. Dis *Renown. 81 mins. Cert U*
Crosbie (*Pat O'Brien*), an alcoholic reporter, learning that his son needs an expensive operation, goes to ask for the job back that he has just lost, only to find his ex-editor murdered. He discovers the killer, but agrees to confess to the murder himself in return for the money to pay for his son's operation. When police refuse to believe him and release him, the real killer tries to kidnap his ailing son. Crosbie foils them at the cost of being shot in a gun battle. Sombre drama, adequately acted.
RoC *Lois Maxwell, George Coulouris, Wensley Pithey, Freddie Mills, Ronald Adam, Tommy Steele, April Olrich, Robert Brown, Richard Pasco, Peter Swanwick, George Eugeniou, Al Mulock, Stuart Nichol, Vic Wise, Claude Kingston.*

Pat O'Brien in Kill Me Tomorrow (*1957*)

THE KILTIES ARE COMING (1951) [2]
Dir, Prod and Deviser *Robert Jordan Hill*. Ph *Phil Grindrod*. PC *Advance*. Dis *Adelphi. 52 mins. Cert U*
A succession of variety acts featuring members of the Royal Kiltie Juniors, interspersed with interviews with the parents of the young Scottish entertainers. Acts are spirited, but presentation shows little skill.
LP *Peter Sinclair, MacDonald Hobley, Margaret Thomson, Molly Booth, Agnes Quinn, Ralph Bryson, Fran Lawrence, Molly Morrell, Kim Haughton and members of the Royal Kiltie Juniors.*

A KING IN NEW YORK (1957) [4]
Dir, Prod and Scr *Charles Chaplin*. Ph *Georges Périnal*. PC *Attica*. Dis *Archway. 109 mins. Cert U*

Dawn Addams and Charles Chaplin in A King in New York (*1957*)

An exiled European king (*Charles Chaplin*) flees to America where, shorn of the royal purse by his embezzling ex-premier, he is reduced to making television commercials. Called before the House Un-American Activities Committee, he accidentally soaks them with a fire-hose, but is cleared of Communist affiliations. A young boy (*Michael Chaplin*), whom he has befriended, is not so lucky in his encounters with the committee. The king, who is returning to Europe, consoles him that some day things will be all right. Satire is bitterly effective, though not too funny. Chaplin also wrote the music.
RoC *Dawn Addams, Maxine Audley, Jerry Desmonde, Oliver Johnston, Harry Green, Sidney James, Phil Brown, Shani Wallis, Joy Nichols, Robert Arden, John McLaren, Alan Gifford, Lauri Lupino Lane & George Truzzi, Joan Ingram, Nicholas Tanner, George Woodbridge, Macdonald Parke, Benice Swanson.*

KING OF THE UNDERWORLD (1952) [2]
Dir *Victor M. Gover*. Prod *Gilbert Church*. Scr *John Gilling*. Ph *S.D. Onions*. PC *Bushey*. Dis *Ambassador*. 82 mins. Cert A
Three adventures of genial but ruthless criminal kingpin Terence Riley (*Tod Slaughter*), as he steals jewels and a secret formula and becomes involved in a little blackmail. Morley of the Yard (*Patrick Barr*) is in hot pursuit, but Riley lives to fight another day. Slight change of pace for barnstorming star, but film not widely shown.
RoC *Tucker McGuire, Ingeborg Wells, Frank Hawkins, Len Sharp, Ann Valery, Larry Burns.*

KING'S RHAPSODY (1955) [3]
Dir and Prod *Herbert Wilcox*. Scr *Pamela Bower, Christopher Hassall, A.P. Herbert, from the musical play by Ivor Novello*. Ph *Max Greene (Mutz Greenbaum)*. PC *Everest*. Dis *British Lion. Eastman Colour. CinemaScope.* 92 mins. Cert U
After seven years' exile living with the woman (*Anna Neagle*) he loves, a European prince, Richard (*Errol Flynn*), succeeds to the throne and accepts a marriage to a foreign princess (*Patrice Wymore*). Popular feeling soon forces him to abdicate in favour of his young son, but years later the royal couple are reunited with the connivance of his ex-mistress. Rusty Rur-

itanian romance with music, apparently made on a fairly low budget.
RoC *Martita Hunt, Finlay Currie, Francis de Wolff, Joan Benham, Reginald Tate, Miles Malleson, Lionel Blair, Jon Gregory, Terence Theobald, Edmund Hockridge (voice).*

KNAVE OF HEARTS (1954) [4]
(USA: *Lovers, Happy Lovers*)
Dir *René Clément*. Prod *Paul Graetz*. Scr *Hugh Mills, Clement, Raymond Queneau, from a novel by Louis Hémon*. Ph *Oswald Morris*. PC *Transcontinental*. Dis *AB-Pathé*. 103 mins. Cert X
André (*Gérard Philipe*), a French clerk married to wealthy Catherine (*Valerie Hobson*) lays siege to her friend Pat (*Natasha Parry*), and tells her he lived with his boss (*Margaret Johnston*), fled from Norah (*Joan Greenwood*) when she suggested marriage, and was kept by a prostitute (*Germaine Montero*). Threatening to throw himself from a window if Pat doesn't give in, André slips, falls and is crippled, carrying on his philandering from a bathchair wheeled by Catherine and Pat. Witty, acerbic, incisive sex comedy with a Gallic touch.
RoC *Diana Decker, Percy Marmont, Eric Pohlmann, Bill Shine, Mai Bacon, Margot Field, Julie Anslow, Harry Towb, Gerald Campion, Martin Benson, Eileen Way, Arthur Howard, Beryl Cooke, Judith Nelmes, David Coote, Richard Hart.*

KNIGHTS OF THE ROUND TABLE (1953) [3]
Dir *Richard Thorpe*. Prod *Pandro S. Berman*. Scr *Talbot Jennings, Jan Lustig, Noel Langley, from Sir Thomas Malory's* Le Mort d'Arthur. Ph *F.A. Young*. PC and Dis *MGM British. Eastman Colour. CinemaScope.* 115 mins. Cert U
Arthur Pendragon (*Mel Ferrer*), King of England in the sixth century, befriends Lancelot (*Robert Taylor*) and forms the Knights of the Round Table at Camelot. When Lancelot is attracted to Queen Guinevere (*Ava Gardner*), the evil Modred (*Stanley Baker*) seeks to discredit him. Lancelot is exiled, but is eventually reconciled to a dying Arthur, and kills Modred in battle. Spectacular but rather heartless action film takes plenty of liberties with legend.
RoC *Anne Crawford, Felix Aylmer, Maureen Swanson, Gabriel Woolf, Anthony Forwood, Robert Urquhart, Niall MacGinnis, Ann Hanslip, Jill Clifford, Stephen Vercoe, Dagmar (Dana) Wynter, Patricia Owens, Doreen Dawne, Julia Arnall.*

L

THE LADY CRAVED EXCITEMENT (1950) [2]
Dir *Francis Searle*. Prod *Anthony Hinds*. Scr *Edward J. Jason, John Gilling, Searle, from a*

radio serial by Mason. Ph *Walter Harvey*. PC *Hammer*. Dis *Exclusive*. 69 mins. Cert U
Pat (*Hy Hazell*), a cabaret star, is constantly seeking more excitement in life. This leads her and her partner Johnny (*Michael Medwin*) into the thick of an unbalanced crook's plot to smuggle stolen works of art out of the country. They foil his plans. Light comedy-thriller has plenty of plot, but is a trifle dull considering the source is a radio serial.
RoC *Sidney James, John Longden, Andrew Keir, Danny Green, Thelma Grigg, Ian Wilson, Barbara Hamilton, Jasmine Dee, Gordon Mulholland.*

LADY GODIVA RIDES AGAIN (1951) [4]
Dir *Frank Launder*. Prod *Launder, Sidney Gilliat*. Scr *Launder, Val Valentine*. Ph *Wilkie Cooper*. PC *London Films*. Dis *British Lion*. 90 mins. Cert U
Marjorie (*Pauline Stroud*), a pretty waitress, enters a 'Lady Godiva' beauty contest and, much to her surprise, wins. She is persuaded to enter a big beauty contest, which is fixed in her favour. Marjorie now has dreams of becoming a film star, but her contract is scrapped after she is innocently involved in a minor scandal. She ends up as a nude in a vaudeville show, but is rescued by her family, and the Australian (*John McCallum*) who loves her. Broad comic satire, well constructed; darker possibilities of the plot are ignored.
RoC *Dennis Price, Stanley Holloway, Gladys Henson, George Cole, Diana Dors, Bernadette O'Farrell, Kay Kendall, Eddie Byrne, Renee Houston, Dora Bryan, Alastair Sim, Sidney James, Dagmar (Dana) Wynter, Tommy Duggan, Eddie Leslie, Walford Hyden, Lisa Lee, Lyn Evans, Edward Forsyth, Peter Martyn, Fred Berger, Henry Longhurst, Felix Felton, Arthur Brander, Sidney Vivian, Arthur Howard, Clive Baxter, Paul Connell, John Harvey, Tom Gill, Rowena Gregory, Michael Ripper, Charlotte Mitchell, Toke Townley, Patricia Goddard, Richard Wattis, Googie Withers, Trevor Howard, Myrette Morven, Leslie Mitchell, Russell Waters, Joan Collins, Violet Pretty (Anne Heywood), Jimmy Young, Greta Gray, Dorothy Hocking, Madeleine Mona, Dawn Chapple, Deirdre de Peyer, Rita Wheatley, June Charlier, Simone Silva, June Hart, Maureen O'Neill, Sylvia Wren, Kismet Shahani, Marlene Ann Dee, Suzanne Levesi, Ann Hanslip, Diana Russell, Gina Egan, Evelyn Buyers, Johnnie Johnston, Enid Smeedon, Phyllis Garnett, Noel Scott-Gorman, Peter O'Farrell, Cyril Chamberlain, Syd Dean and His Band.*

LADY IN THE FOG (1952) [3]
(USA: *Scotland Yard Inspector*)
Dir *Sam Newfield*. Prod *Anthony Hinds*. Scr *Orville Hampton, from the radio serial by Lester Powell*. Ph *Jimmy Harvey*. PC *Hammer/Lippert*. Dis *Exclusive*. 83 mins. Cert A
A man is run down by a car in a London fog. The victim's sister (*Bernadette O'Farrell*) believes it was murder, and gets an American reporter (*Cesar Romero*) to help her investigate. The trail leads through a dance hall and night-

club, to a shoot-out on a deserted film set, where the murderer is finally revealed. Fascinating radio serial turned into routine and hard-to-follow crime thriller.

RoC *Lois Maxwell, Geoffrey Keen, Campbell Singer, Lloyd Lamble, Mary Mackenzie, Alastair Hunter, Frank Birch, Lisa Lee, Wensley Pithey, Reed de Rouen, Bill Fraser, Peter Swanwick, Lionel Harris, Betty Cooper, Katie Johnson, Clare James, Stuart Sanders, Robert Moore, Jacques Cey, Jean Bayliss, Richard Johnson, Robert Dorning, Jack Howarth, Laurie Taylor, Stuart Nichol, Josephine Douglas, Marguerite Brennan, Terry Carney, Christina Forrest, Hazel Sutton, Dorinda Stevens, Robert Adair.*

THE LADY IS A SQUARE (1958) [3]
Dir/Prod *Herbert Wilcox.* Scr *Harold Purcell, Pamela Bower, Nicholas Phipps.* Ph *Gordon Dines.* PC *Associated British.* Dis *AB-Pathé.* 98 mins. Cert U

Unaware that her daughter's (*Janette Scott*) new boy-friend (*Frankie Vaughan*) is an aspiring pop singer, aristocratic Frances (*Anna Neagle*) mistakes him for the new butler when he comes to tune the piano. She realizes the truth when he has a hit record, and kicks him out not knowing he has given £3,000 in royalties to her orchestral charity. At a big National Youth Orchestra concert, pop and classical are reconciled. The Wilcoxes trying hard to be with-it. Just about bearable.

RoC *Anthony Newley, Wilfrid Hyde White, Ted Lune, Christopher Rhodes, Kenneth Cope, Josephine Fitzgerald, Mary Peach, Marguerite Brennan, Bruno Barnabe, Harold Kasket, John Carson, John le Mesurier, Walter Horsbrugh, Jeremy White, Robert Desmond, Gwynneth Tighe, Frederick Schiller, Derek Prentice, Myrette Morven, Gerald Case.*

THE LADYKILLERS (1955) [5]
Dir *Alexander Mackendrick.* (Associate) Prod *Seth Holt.* Scr *William Rose.* Ph *Otto Heller.* PC *Ealing Studios.* Dis *Rank.* Technicolor. 97 mins. Cert U

Old Mrs Wilberforce (*Katie Johnson*) gets a new tenant, 'The Professor' (*Alec Guinness*) the leader of a 'chamber ensemble' who are in fact robbers planning a big job. They bring it off, but the landlady discovers the loot. They plot to kill her, but cannot decide who shall do the deed and instead bump each other off one by one, The Professor being accidentally eliminated by a railway signal as he is disposing of the last body. Mrs Wilberforce is laughed at by the police, who are used to her fantasies, and is left wondering what to do with £60,000. Delightful black comedy with an atmosphere all its own. British Oscars: best actress, best screenplay.

RoC *Cecil Parker, Herbert Lom, Peter Sellers, Danny Green, Jack Warner, Frankie Howerd, Philip Stainton, Fred Griffiths, Kenneth Connor, Edie Martin, Jack Melford, Ewan Roberts, Harold Goodwin, Helen Burls, Evelyn Kerry, Pheobe Hodgson, Leonard Sharp, Stratford Johns, Sam Kydd, Neil Wilson, Michael Corcoran, Robert Moore, John Rudling, Madge*

Brindley, Lucy Griffiths, Peter Williams, George Roderick.

A LADY MISLAID (1958) [3]
Dir *David Macdonald.* Prod *Robert Hall.* Scr *Frederick Gotfurt, from the play by Kenneth Horne.* Ph *Norman Warwick.* PC *Welwyn.* Dis *AB-Pathé.* 60 mins. Cert U

Spinster sisters Esther (*Phyllis Calvert*) and Jennifer (*Gillian Owen*) are surprised when a policeman turns up at their country cottage searching for the body of the previous tenant's wife. A skeleton in the chicken-run turns out to be that of an ancient Briton and the 'killer' (*Thorley Walters*), although admitting to several wives, proves that this one is very much alive. Potted version of an old-fashioned black farce.

RoC *Alan White, Richard Leech, Constance Fraser, Sheila Shand Gibbs.*

LADY OF VENGEANCE (1957) [2]
Dir *Burt Balaban.* Prod *William N. Boyle, Balaban, Bernard Donnenfield.* Scr *Irve Tunick.* Ph *Ian Struthers.* PC *Princess.* Dis *United Artists.* 74 mins. Cert A

Marshall (*Dennis O'Keefe*), a wealthy publisher, seeks vengeance after the wishes of his ward, who committed suicide. He bribes a master crook (*Anton Diffring*) with one of the world's rarest stamps in order to kill the man responsible for the girl's death. He doesn't realize that the crook, Karnak, is the man he should be after. Marshall fails to go through with the plan, but Karnak dies accidentally because of it. Wretched, rambling thriller has only a plot twist to save it.

RoC *Ann Sears, Patrick Barr, Vernon Greeves, Eileen Elton, Frederick Schiller, G.H. Mulcaster, Jacqueline Curtiss, Gerald Case, Jack McNaughton, Colin Croft, Andy Ho, Humphrey Morton.*

THE LADY WITH A LAMP (1951) [4]
Dir/Prod *Herbert Wilcox.* Scr *Warren Chetham Strode, from the play by Reginald Berkeley.* Ph *Max Greene (Mutz Greenbaum).* PC *Imperadio.* Dis *British Lion.* 110 mins. Cert U

Episodes in the life of Florence Nightingale (*Anna Neagle*). Shocking her family by her resolve to be a nurse, she becomes superintendent at a hospital for gentlewomen. During the Crimean War of the 1850s, she and her nurses become angels of mercy to thousands of wounded. Herself ill, she returns, recovers and champions hospital reform. Usual careful, sedate Neagle/Wilcox biopic; sincere but lacking toughness.

RoC *Michael Wilding, Gladys Young, Felix Aylmer, Sybil Thorndike, Peter Graves, Julian d'Albie, Arthur Young, Edwin Styles, Barbara Couper, Helen Shingler, Helena Pickard, Rosalie Crutchley, Maureen Pryor, Henry Edwards, Andrew Osborn, Clement McCallin, Monckton Hoffe, Mary Mackenzie, Cecil Trouncer, Colin Gordon, Gordon Jackson, Charles Carson, Leslie Weston, Nigel Stock, Michael Brennan, Edie Martin, Peter Hobbes, Liam Gaffney, Ann Codrington, Betty Cooper, Edward Lexy, John Vere, Olive Bonham-Carter, Basil Dignam, Florence Nightingale Allebeury.*

THE LARGE ROPE (1953) [2]
Dir *Wolf Rilla.* Prod *Victor Hanbury.* Scr *Ted Willis.* Ph *Geoffrey Faithfull.* PC *Insignia.* Dis *United Artists.* 72 mins. Cert A

Tom Penney (*Donald Houston*) serves a long prison sentence for murder. On his release, he returns to his home village determined to clear himself - only to find himself suspected of another murder. Both old and new crimes are eventually solved - with Tom innocent on both counts. Leisurely, rather wearisome 'whodunnit'.

RoC *Susan Shaw, Robert Brown, Vanda Godsell, Leonard White, Margaret Anderson, Richard Warner, Peter Byrne, Barbara Cavan, Carl Bernard, Natalie Kent, Michael Mulcaster, Christine Finn, Thomas Heathcote, Douglas Herald, Edward Judd.*

THE LARK STILL SINGS (1954) [1]
Dir/Prod/Scr *Hugh Wedderburn.* Ph *Gordon Lang.* PC *Waverley.* Dis *Equity British.* 46 mins. Cert U

Michael (*Hugh Wedderburn*) returns, as a hotel waiter, to the seaside town he had known as a boy. He falls in love with Mollie (*Dorothy Dewhurst*), who works at the hotel, and she tells him about her farm in Ireland. They plan to live there together, but suddenly Mollie dies. Later, Michael finds the farm was a figment of her imagination. Amateurish, over-arty anecdote.

RoC *Roddy Hughes, Peggyann Clifford, Iris Vandeleur, Clement Hamelin.*

LAST HOLIDAY (1950) [4]
Dir *Henry Cass.* Prod *Stephen Mitchell, A.D. Peters, J.B. Priestley.* Scr *Priestley.* Ph *Ray Elton.* PC *Associated British/Watergate.* Dis *AB-Pathé.* 88 mins. Cert U

George Bird (*Alec Guinness*), a mild, hardworking northerner with few friends, is told he has a month to live. He spends his savings on a holiday at a fashionable seaside hotel. He finds relationships difficult at first, but spends his time helping people in trouble. He is offered attractive jobs and, when the hotel staff go on strike, leads the guests in do-it-yourselfing which brings everyone out of their shells. When the original diagnosis proves incorrect, George is overjoyed. Returning to the hotel, he swerves his car to avoid an accident and is

Alec Guinness and Helen Cherry in Last Holiday *(1950)*

killed. Sympathetically characterized, well-written film.

RoC *Beatrice Campbell, Kay Walsh, Bernard Lee, Wilfrid Hyde White, Muriel George, Helen Cherry, Jean Colin, Brian Worth, Sidney James, Coco (Gregoire) Aslan, Ernest Thesiger, Esma Cannon, Campbell Cotts, Moultrie Kelsall, David McCallum (Sr), Madame E. Kirkwood-Hackett, Eric Maturin, Harry Hutchinson, Hal Osmond, Norman Astridge, Brian Oulton, Heather Wilde, Ronald Simpson, Arthur Howard, Meier Tzelniker, Lockwood West, Leslie Weston.*

THE LAST MAN TO HANG? (1956) [2]

Dir *Terence Fisher.* Prod *John Gossage.* Scr *Ivor Montagu, Max Trell, Gerald Bullett, Maurice Elvey, from a novel by Bullett.* Ph *Desmond Dickinson.* PC *ACT Films.* Dis *Columbia. 75 mins. Cert A*

Framed by his housekeeper (*Freda Jackson*), who hated him, Sir Roderick Strood (*Tom Conway*) is charged with the murder of his neurotic wife (*Elizabeth Sellars*). Only one juryman believes in his innocence, but gradually convinces the others. A verdict of not guilty is returned and later it transpires that the housekeeper had seized the opportunity to identify a dead body as that of Lady Strood, who is still alive. Dullish, highly unlikely thriller.

RoC *Hugh Latimer, Raymond Huntley, Margaretta Scott, Eunice Gayson, David Horne, Victor Maddern, Anthony Newley, Walter Hudd, Anna Turner, Russell Napier, Olive Sloane, Tony Quinn, Hal Osmond, Bill Shine, Leslie Weston, Harold Goodwin, Jack Lambert, Michael McKeag, John Stuart, Joan Newall, Thomas Heathcote, Joan Hickson, Shelagh Fraser, Dan Cunningham, Charles Lloyd Pack, John Warren, Martin Boddey.*

Elizabeth Sellars and Tom Conway in The Last Man to Hang? *(1956)*

THE LAST MOMENT (1954) [1]

Dir *Lance Comfort.* Prod *Tom D. Connochie, Roy Goddard.* Scr *Selwyn Jepson, Paul Vincent Carroll.* Ph *Jimmy Wilson, Brendan J. Stafford.* PC *Douglas Fairbanks Jr.* Dis *British Lion. 51 mins. Cert A*

Two stories. (1) Inventing a new drug, George Griffin (*Douglas Fairbanks Jr*) is sickened by the grasping attitudes around him, and contemplates suicide – until his new drug is able to cure a severely crippled boy. (2) Gloom reigns in an Irish family after its head (*Cyril*

Cusack), under the influence of a Svengali-like campaigner, obliges his family to sign the pledge. Everyone is happy when he receives contrary advice from his local clergy. Slow and tedious.

RoC *Greta Gynt, Paul Carpenter, MacDonald Parke, Mary Merrall, Barbara Mullen, Fulton Mackay, Valerie Carton.*

THE LAST PAGE (1952) [3]
(USA: *Manbait*)

Dir *Terence Fisher.* Prod *Anthony Hinds.* Scr *Frederick Knott, from the play by James Hadley Chase.* Ph *Walter Harvey.* PC *Hammer/Lippert.* Dis *Exclusive. 84 mins. Cert A*

Shop assistant Ruby (*Diana Dors*) is convinced by her lover Jeff (*Peter Reynolds*) that a mild flirtation with her boss Harman (*George Brent*) presents a chance for blackmail. When Harman ignores the threat, Ruby's letter to his invalid wife (*Isabel Dean*) brings about her death. Harman pays up, Jeff accidentally kills Ruby for the money, and Harman is suspected, thanks to his jealous under-manager (*Raymond Huntley*). His assistant (*Marguerite Chapman*) tracks Jeff down, and police are just in time to prevent him strangling her. Efficient crime yarn could have been even better without fading Hollywood stars.

RoC *Eleanor Summerfield, Meredith Edwards, Harry Fowler, Conrad Phillips, Lawrence Ward, Nelly Arno, David Keir, Eleanor Brown, Jack Faint, John Mann, Harold Goodwin, Archie Duncan, Cyril Saxon, Leslie Weston, Lawrence O'Madden, Ian Wilson.*

THE LATE EDWINA BLACK (1951) [3]
(USA: *Obsessed*)

Dir *Maurice Elvey.* Prod *Ernest Gartside.* Scr *Charles Frank, David Evans, from the play by William Dinner, William Morum.* Ph *Stephen Dade.* PC *Elvey-Gartside.* Dis *Independent Film Distributors. 78 mins. Cert A*

Edwina Black's housekeeper (*Jean Cadell*) reports her mistress poisoned. Suspicion falls on the dead woman's husband (*David Farrar*) and companion (*Geraldine Fitzgerald*), but the inspector (*Roland Culver*) discovers the housekeeper administered the poison as her mistress wanted to commit suicide. Competent, rather muted version of stage success.

RoC *Mary Merrall, Harcourt Williams, Charles Heslop, Ronald Adam, Sydney Monckton, Irene Arnaud, Ernest Metcalfe.*

LAUGHING ANNE (1953) [3]

Dir/Prod *Herbert Wilcox.* Scr *Pamela Bower, from a novel by Joseph Conrad.* Ph *Max Greene (Mutz Greenbaum).* PC *Republic/Wilcox-Neagle.* Dis *Republic. Technicolor. 90 mins. Cert A*

Anne (*Margaret Lockwood*), a singer prone to laughing fits, and her lover Jem (*Forrest Tucker*), a boxer (once of Paris) who lost the use of his hands, now drift together through Javanese waterfront saloons of the 1890s. She falls in love with Captain Davidson (*Wendell Corey*), but returns to Jem. Years later, Davidson returns; Jem tries to steal his cargo and Anne, 'laughing' a warning, is killed by Jem, who is shot by Davidson. Turgid 'pop' version of a Joseph Conrad story (*Between the Tides*).

RoC *Ronald Shiner, Robert Harris, Jacques Brunius, Daphne Anderson, Helen Shingler, Danny Green, Harold Lang, Maurice Bush, Dave Crowley, Sean Lynch, Edgar Norfolk, Gerard Lohan, Andy Ho, Jack Cooper, Rudolph Offenbach.*

LAUGHTER IN PARADISE (1951) [4]

Dir/Prod *Mario Zampi.* Scr *Michael Pertwee, Jack Davies.* Ph *William McLeod.* PC *Transocean.* Dis *AB-Pathé. 93 mins. Cert U*

A practical joker leaves £50,000 each to four relatives, on condition that: his spinster sister (*Fay Compton*) earns her living for a month as a maid; a rakish cousin (*Guy Middleton*) marries the first girl he meets; a meek clerk (*George Cole*) pretends to hold up his bank; a retired army officer/novelist (*Alastair Sim*) commits a petty theft and spends a month in jail. They fulfil (or try to) the conditions, but find the money was a hoax. Surefire comedy idea; execution doesn't leave many dull moments.

RoC *Beatrice Campbell, Veronica Hurst, A.E. Matthews, Joyce Grenfell, Anthony Steel, John Laurie, Eleanor Summerfield, Ronald Adam, Leslie Dwyer, Ernest Thesiger, Hugh Griffith, Michael Pertwee, Mackenzie Ward, Audrey Hepburn, Charlotte Mitchell, Colin Gordon, Mary Germaine, Noel Howlett, Martin Boddey.*

LAUGHING IN THE SUNSHINE 1955 [3]

Dir *Dan Birt.* Prod *John Martin.* Scr *Tim Carew, from a play by Sven Cederstrand.* Ph *Sven Nykvist.* PC *Martin Films/Swint Film.* Dis *United Artists. Eastman Colour. 81 mins. Cert U*

A princess (*Jane Hylton*) takes a holiday in Sweden and falls in love with Gustav (*Bengt Logardt*) without realizing he is a prince. She is also incognito, and they reluctantly agree to part, meeting later at a gala royal ball, finding out the truth and falling in love all over again. Unabashed romance filmed in beautiful colour. An Anglo-Swedish co-production.

RoC *Peter Dyneley, Gene Anderson, Marjorie Fielding, Adolf Jahr, Stanley Maxted.*

THE LAVENDER HILL MOB (1951) [5]

Dir *Charles Crichton.* (Associate) Prod *Michael Truman.* Scr *T.E.B. Clarke.* Ph *Douglas Slocombe.* PC *Ealing Studios.* Dis *General Film Distributors. 78 mins. Cert U*

Holland (*Alec Guinness*), 20 years a mild bank clerk, plans the perfect robbery. He will steal a million pounds in gold bars, melt them down into gold statuettes of the Eiffel Tower and, with the help of associates, smuggle them out of the country. When six of the 'souvenirs' are bought by English schoolgirls in Paris, Holland's troubles escalate. Unlike his colleagues, he gets away to Brazil, but the law catches up with him. Delightful, inventive comedy rips riotously along. British Film Oscar as best film 1951. Academy Award for best screenplay.

RoC *Stanley Holloway, Sidney James, Alfie Bass, Marjorie Fielding, John Gregson, Clive Morton, Ronald Adam, Sydney Tafler, Edie Martin, Jacques Brunius, Meredith Edwards, Gibb McLaughlin, Patrick Barr, Marie Burke,*

Alfie Bass, Alec Guinness and Sidney James in The Lavender Hill Mob (*1951*)

John Salew, Ronald Adam, Audrey Hepburn, Arthur Hambling, William (James) Fox, Michael Trubshawe, Ann Hefferman, Eugene Deckers, Paul Demel, Andrea Malandrinos, Cyril Chamberlain, Tony Quinn, Moultrie Kelsall, Christopher Hewitt, David Davies, Frederick Piper, Peter Bull, Alanna Boyce, Joe Clarke, Charles Lamb, Archie Duncan, Fred Griffiths, Frank Forsyth, Arthur Mullard, Jacques Cey, Marie Ney, John Warwick, Robert Shaw.

LAW AND DISORDER (1958) [4]

Dir *Charles Crichton.* Prod *Paul Soskin, George Pitcher.* Scr *T.E.B. Clarke, Patrick Campbell, Vivienne Knight, from a novel by Denys Roberts.* Ph *Ted Scaife.* PC *Hotspur.* Dis *British Lion.* 76 mins. Cert U

Confidence trickster Percy (*Michael Redgrave*) decides to 'retire' when his son (*Jeremy Burnham*), who believes him to be a clergyman, becomes a judge's marshal. Unfortunately, at his retirement village on the coast, Percy becomes involved with smugglers. His ex-'colleagues' try but fail to prevent the case coming up when his son is in court, and it is only Percy's relationship with the judge (*Robert Morley*) that saves the day. An Ealing film in all but name, and not unworthy of the studio, if some way below their best.

RoC *Elizabeth Sellars, Ronald Squire, George Coulouris, Joan Hickson, Lionel Jeffries, Harold Goodwin, Meredith Edwards, Brenda Bruce, David Hutcheson, John le Mesurier, Michael Trubshawe, Reginald Beckwith, Moultrie Kelsall, Mary Kerridge, Irene Handl, Allan Cuthbertson, Sam Kydd, John Hewer, John Warwick, Nora Nicholson, Anthony Sagar, John Paul, Alfred Burke, Michael Brennan, Arthur Howard.*

LAXDALE HALL (1952) [3]
(USA: *Scotch on the Rocks*)

Dir *John Eldridge.* Prod *John Grierson, Alfred Shaughnessy, John Baxter.* Scr *Eldridge, Shaughnessy, from the novel by Eric Linklater.* Ph *Arthur Grant.* PC *Group 3.* Dis *Associated British.* 77 mins. Cert U

The five car owners of Laxdale, a Hebridean village, refuse to pay their road fund licences until a decent road has been constructed there. A parliamentary committee, led by Pettigrew (*Raymond Huntley*), a zealous MP, comes to investigate. The committee members are soon won over and when, through a complex series

of accidents, Pettigrew is arrested for poaching, he is blackmailed by one of his own colleagues into bringing the road to fruition. Charming, though not consistently funny addition to a then-familiar genre.

RoC *Kathleen Ryan, Ronald Squire, Sebastian Shaw, Fulton Mackay, Prunella Scales, Andrew Keir, Jameson Clark, Jean Colin, Kynaston Reeves, Keith Falkner, Grace Gavin (Gaven), Nell Ballantyne, Roddy Macmillan, Meg Buchanan, Ian MacNaughton, Tom Baird-Ferguson, Eric Woodburn, Rikki Fulton, James Gilbert, Howard Connell, James Copeland, Archie Duncan, Margaret Boyd, Norman MacOwan, James Anderson, Julian D'Albie, Walter Horsbrugh, Anthony Kilshawe, Lionel Harris, Keith Faulkner.*

Ronald Squire, Sebastian Shaw (rear) and Raymond Huntley in Laxdale Hall (*1953*)

LEASE OF LIFE (1954) [3]

Dir *Charles Frend.* Prod *Jack Rix.* Scr *Eric Ambler.* Ph *Douglas Slocombe.* PC *Ealing Studios.* Dis *General Film Distributors.* Eastman Colour. 94 mins. Cert U

Given a year to live, William Thorne (*Robert Donat*), a Yorkshire vicar, conceals it from his wife (*Kay Walsh*) and daughter (*Adrienne Corri*). He loses the chance of a well-paid chaplaincy by giving a 'controversial' address. His wife, desperate for money to enter her daughter for a music scholarship, appropriates £100 from a fund entrusted to Thorne, who replaces it by writing 'sermons' for a Sunday paper. Sincere, quiet, close-to-dull drama.

RoC *Denholm Elliott, Walter Fitzgerald, Vida Hope, Reginald Beckwith, Cyril Raymond, Jean Anderson, Mark Daly, Russell Waters, Richard Wattis, Beckett Bould, Frank Atkinson, Robert Sandford, Alan Webb, Frederick Piper, John Salew, Richard Leech, Edie Martin, Mark Dignam, Charles Saynor, Sheila Raynor.*

LEFT, RIGHT and CENTRE (1959) [4]

Dir *Sidney Gilliat.* Prod *Frank Launder, Gilliat.* Scr *Gilliat, Val Valentine.* Ph *Gerald Gibbs.* PC *Vale.* Dis *British Lion.* 95 mins. Cert U

TV personality Robert Wilcot (*Ian Carmichael*), for the Conservatives, opposes forthright Stella Stoker (*Patricia Bredin*) for Labour, at a by-election. After shouting each other down at public meetings, they fall in love, to the consternation of their agents, who arrange to get a couple of old flames on the

Ian Carmichael in Left, Right and Centre (*1959*)

scene. Robert wins after three recounts, but quickly ascends to the peerage, involving another by-election. He and Stella marry. Polished comedy with a few loud laughs.

RoC *Alastair Sim, Richard Wattis, Eric Barker, Moyra Fraser, Jack Hedley, Gordon Harker, William Kendall, Leslie Dwyer, George Benson, Frederick Leister, John Salew, Irene Handl, Jeremy Hawk, Eamonn Andrews, Gilbert Harding, Carole Carr, Josephine Douglas, Anthony Sharp, Moultrie Kelsall, Olwen Brookes, Peter Elliott, Philip Morant, Russell Waters, Fred Griffiths, Hattie Jacques, Bill Shine, Erik Chitty, Frank Atkinson, Redmond Phillips, John Sharp, Olaf Pooley, Douglas Ives, Sidney Gilliat.*

LET'S BE HAPPY (1957) [3]

Dir *Henry Levin.* Prod and PC *Marcel Hellman.* Scr *Diana Morgan, from a play by Aimee Stuart.* Ph *Erwin Hillier.* Dis *AB-Pathé.* Technicolor. CinemaScope. 106 mins. Cert U

A musical remake of *Jeannie* (1941), switching nationalities and locales. Jeannie (Vera-Ellen) is now an American who decides to spend a legacy on a visit to Scotland. She's helped by Stanley, a salesman (*Tony Martin*) and squired by a penniless Scottish lord (*Robert Flemyng*) who thinks she's made of money. Disillusioned, she returns to America – where Stanley is waiting for her. A couple of good songs, but nothing much about the film rings true.

RoC *Zena Marshall, Guy Middleton, Katharine Kath, Carl Duering, Helen Horton, Jean Cadell, Gordon Jackson, Molly Weir, Peter Sinclair, Beckett Bould, Alfred Burke, Vernon Greeves, Richard Molinas, Eugene Deckers, Russell Waters, Paul Young.*

LET'S HAVE A MURDER (1950) [2]

Dir and Prod *John E. Blakeley.* Scr *Anthony Toner.* Ph *Ernest Palmer.* PC *Film Studios Manchester.* Dis *Mancunian.* 95 mins. Cert U

Jimmy and Ben (*Jimmy Jewel, Ben Warriss*), two clumsy detectives investigating the murder of a singer, scare themselves more than the killer, whom they accidentally reveal to be a respectable psychiatrist, secretly a notorious jewel-thief. Second (and last) film venture by top radio comedy team again failed to crack the mainline film market.

RoC *Lesley Osmond, Kitty Blewett (Bluett), Claude Dampier, Stewart Rome, Anthony Pendrell, Eva Eacott.*

LIBEL (1959) [3]

Dir *Anthony Asquith*. Prod and PC *Anatole de Grunwald*. Scr *de Grunwald, Karl Tunberg, from the play by Edward Wooll*. Ph *Robert Krasker*. Dis *M-G-M*. 99 mins. Cert A

Sir Mark Loddon (*Dirk Bogarde*), living in gracious luxury, is accused by a former fellow-inmate (*Paul Massie*) in a wartime P-o-W camp of being an imposter. He sues for libel, but his case is hampered by his own intermittent loss of memory and soon seems to be going against him. His reaction to a surprise witness (the 'double', now a shambling wreck) causes his wife (*Olivia de Havilland*) to denounce him. The shock clears his memory, and he is able to prove that he is really Sir Mark. Uncomfortably improbable courtroom drama. RoC *Robert Morley, Wilfrid Hyde White, Anthony Dawson, Richard Wattis, Martin Miller, Millicent Martin, Toke Townley, Deering Wells, Bill Shine, Ivan Samson, Richard Dimbleby, Richard Pearson, Sam Kydd, Sebastian Saville, Robert Shaw, Geoffrey Bayldon, Gordon Sterne, Arthur Howard, Joyce Carey, Josephine Middleton, Kenneth Griffith, Barbara Archer, Anthony Doonan, Vanda Hudson.*

LIFE IN DANGER (1959) [3]

Dir *Terry Bishop*. Prod *Jack Parsons*. Scr *Malcolm Hulke, Eric Paice*. Ph *Peter Hennessy*. PC *Parroch*. Dis *Butchers*. 63 mins. Cert A

A child-murderer escapes from an asylum. A few miles away Hazel (*Julie Hopkins*), an emotionally unstable girl, takes up with a casual labourer (*Derren Nesbitt*). A group of locals, led by a major (*Howard Marion Crawford*) track them to a barn and become convinced the girl's life is in danger. Seeing the crowd, Hazel gets hysterical and the major fires his shotgun, wounding the man. News comes that the escaped killer has been captured miles away. Rather halting drama well performed by the two young leads. RoC *Victor Brooks, Jack Allen, Christopher Witty, Mary Manson, Bruce Seton, Carmel McSharry, Peter Swanwick, Bryan Coleman, Humphrey Lestocq, Richard Pearson, Celia Hewitt, Brian Rawlinson.*

LIFE IN EMERGENCY WARD 10 (1958) [3]

Dir *Robert Day*. Prod *Ted Lloyd*. Scr *Tessa Diamond, Hazel Adair, from their TV series*. Ph *Geoffrey Faithfull*. PC *Artistes' Alliance/Norman J. Hyams*. Dis *Eros*. 86 mins. Cert U

Familiar crises at a provincial hospital. A hole-in-the-heart boy is given new hope by a revolutionary heart-lung machine but, when it is used on an elderly Irishman, the patient dies. Meanwhile Dr Russell (*Michael Craig*) is fending off the attentions of his doctor landlord's wife (*Sheila Sweet*) and building a friendship with Sister Janet (*Dorothy Alison*). Quads are delivered the night the boy has his operation - it's a success. Soapy situations are expertly dispensed, but it's too unreal for tears to flow. RoC *Wilfrid Hyde White, Charles Tingwell, Frederick Bartman, Glyn Owen, Rosemary Miller, Rupert Davies, Joan Sims, David Lodge, Dorothy Gordon, Christopher Witty, Douglas Ives, Pauline Stroud, Tony Quinn, Jean Aubrey, Maurice Kaufmann, Christina Gregg, Geoffrey Adams, George Tovey, John Baker, Enid Lindsey, Peter Greenspan, Henry Momberg. Howard Knight, Mark Mylam.*

LIFE IN HER HANDS (1951) [3]

Dir *Philip Leacock*. Prod *Frederick Wilson*. Scr *Monica Dickens, Anthony Stevens*. Ph *Fred Gamage*. PC *Crown Film Unit*. Dis *United Artists*. 58 mins. Cert A

A young widow (*Kathleen Byron*), overcome with grief when her husband is killed, decides to become a nurse. She passes her training, but rebels against discipline in a fit of hysteria after the death of a patient. Her assistance in bringing new life into the world at a cesarian operation restores her faith in her choice of vocation. Sketchy semi-documentary, quite well acted. RoC *Bernadette O'Farrell, Jenny Laird, Jacqueline Charles, Robert Long, Grace Gaven, Jean Anderson, Joan Maude, Elwyn Brook-Jones, Grace Arnold, Audrey Teasdale.*

LIFE IS A CIRCUS (1958) [2]

Dir and Scr *Val Guest*. Prod *M. Smedley Aston*. Ph *Arthur Graham*. PC *Vale*. Dis *British Lion*. CinemaScope. 84 mins. Cert U

Joe Winter's Monster Circus has hit hard times. Its six sweeperuppers (*Bud Flanagan, Jimmy Nervo, Teddy Knox, Jimmy Gold, Charlie Naughton, 'Monsewer' Eddie Gray*) try to put on their own show but it is a shambles. Then Bud meets a rag-and-bone man (*Chesney Allen*) who sells him a lamp that produces a genie (*Lionel Jeffries*) when Bud rubs it. The genie gets things confused at first, but eventually proves the salvation of the circus. The Crazy Gang reworking an earlier hit, *Alf's Button Afloat* (qv). Bud and Ches reprise *Underneath the Arches*; otherwise a sad reminder of past farcical glories. RoC *Shirley Eaton, Michael Holliday, Joseph Tomelty, Eric Pohlmann, Fred Johnson, Harold Kasket, Maureen Moore, Edwin Richfield, Vava Peters, Ballard Berkeley, Geoffrey Denton, Peter Glaze, Danny Gray, Marion Collins, Howard Williams, Howard Greene, Marie Devereux, Sam Kydd, Ann Aylward, Jill Burrows, Andrea Loren.*

LIFE WITH THE LYONS (1953) [4]
(USA: *Family Affair*)

Dir *Val Guest*. Prod *Robert Dunbar*. Scr *Guest, Dunbar*. Ph *Walter Harvey*. PC *Hammer*. Dis *Exclusive*. 81 mins. Cert U

The Lyon family look forward to moving into their new home, but create such chaos that the landlord refuses to sign the lease. They try to persuade him, but disasters pile one on another: a broken chandelier, a flooded basement, jive parties, craters in the garden, explosions in the kitchen. But the landlord finally signs. Domestic pandemonium at the double, from the hit radio series; laughs all the way. LP *Ben Lyon, Bebe Daniels, Barbara Lyon, Richard Lyon, Hugh Morton, Horace Percival, Doris Rogers, Molly Weir, Gwen Lewis, Arthur Hill, Belinda Lee.*

LIGHT FINGERS (1957) [2]

Dir *Terry Bishop*. Prod *Roger Proudlock*. Scr *Alfred Shaughnessy*. Ph *Jimmy Harvey*. PC *Parkside*. Dis *Archway*. 86 mins. Cert U

Rose (*Eunice Gayson*) has a passion for auction sales, but her miserly husband Humphrey (*Roland Culver*) thinks she is a kleptomaniac. He engages a 'watchdog' (*Guy Rolfe*) to keep an eye on her, and sends her to a psychiatrist (*Ronald Howard*). When Rose exposes the watchdog as an opportunistic thief, Humphrey sees the truth and agrees to be less of a Scrooge in future. Very mild romantic comedy; seems endless. RoC *Hy Hazell, Avril Angers, Charles Lamb, Olga Dickie, Lonnie Donegan (who also composed the music).*

LILACS IN THE SPRING (1954) [3]
(USA: *Let's Make Up*)

Dir and Prod *Herbert Wilcox*. Scr *Miles Malleson (uncredited), from a play by Harold Purcell*. Ph *Max Greene (Mutz Greenbaum)*. PC *Everest/Wilcox-Neagle*. Dis *Republic*. Trucolor. 94 mins. Cert U

Injured in a bomb explosion in 1943, Carole (*Anna Neagle*) an entertainer, fantasizes herself as Queen Victoria and Nell Gwyn. Deciding between two suitors as she recovers, she remembers her mother, a stage and film star who married equally famous John Beaumont (*Errol Flynn*), split from him and was killed in an air crash on her way to a reconciliation. With Beaumont's help, Carole makes her decision. Stagy cavalcade of Neagliana with the star in four roles. Trucolor for once well used. RoC *David Farrar, Kathleen Harrison, Peter Graves, Helen Haye, Scott Sanders, Jennifer Mitchell, Alan Gifford, Gillian Harrison, George Margo, Alma Taylor, Hetty King, Sean Connery (extra).*

LILLI MARLENE (1950) [3]

Dir *Arthur Crabtree*. Prod *William Gell*. Scr *Leslie Wood*. Ph *Jack Asher*. PC and Dis *Monarch*. 85 mins. Cert U

Lilli (*Lisa Daniely*), the French girl whose song *Lilli Marlene* is loved by Germans and Allies alike, is kidnapped by the Nazis and made to broadcast for them in German. Rescued by British troops, she is later cleared of all suspicion of collaboration and reunited with the American reporter (*Hugh McDermott*) who had always had faith in her. Winds its way agreeably through a series of rather implausible situations. RoC *Richard Murdoch, Leslie Dwyer, John Blythe, Rufus Cruickshank, Michael Ward, Carl Jaffe, Irene Prador, Estelle Brody, Stanley Baker, Russell Hunter, Arthur Lawrence, Aud Johansen, Philo Hauser, Walter Gotell, Richard Marnery, Olaf Olsen, Judith Warden, Cecil Brock, Ben Williams, Marcel Poncin, Lawrence O'Madden, R. Stuart Lindsell, Barbara Cummings, Kenneth Cleveland, Conrad Phillips.*

THE LIMPING MAN (1953) [3]

Dir *Charles de Latour, (uncredited) Cy Endfield*. Prod *Donald Ginsberg*. Scr *Ian Stuart Black, Reginald Long*. Ph *Pat Kelly, Ron Robson*. PC *Banner*. Dis *Eros*. 74 mins. Cert U

Frank Prior (*Lloyd Bridges*), an American, returns to England to resume his wartime romance with Pauline (*Moira Lister*), an actress. As he leaves the plane, another passenger is shot by a limping man. The murdered man is identified as Brown (*Bruce Beeby*), who had been blackmailing Pauline, and later proves very much alive. Just as he is about to dispatch Frank, the latter wakes up. It was a dream ... Competent thriller spoiled by terrible ending.

RoC *Helene Cordet, Alan Wheatley, Leslie Phillips, André Van Gyseghem, Rachel Roberts, Irissa Cooper, Tom Gill, Robert Harben, Lionel Blair, Raymond Rollett, Marjorie Hume, Verne Morgan.*

LINKS OF JUSTICE (1958) [3]

Dir *Max Varnel.* Prod *Edward J. Danziger, Harry Lee Danziger.* Scr *Brian Clemens, Eldon Howard.* Ph *Jimmy Wilson.* PC *Danzigers.* Dis *Paramount.* 68 mins. Cert *U*

Clare (*Sarah Lawson*), a textile magnate, keeps her profligate husband Edgar (*Jack Watling*) short of money to a degree that drives him and his mistress Stella (*Kay Callard*) to hatch a murder plot. The plot is carried out, but it is Edgar who is found dead. Clare is arrested, but the evidence of a burglar proves she killed Edgar in self-defence. Thriller has some ingenuity; treatment is serviceable.

RoC *Denis Shaw, Robert Raikes, Geoffrey Hibbert, Michael Kelly, Jacques Cey, Jan Holden, Honor Shepherd, Hal Osmond, Totti Truman Taylor, Diana Chesney, Vernon Smythe, Andrea Malandrinos, Frank Henderson, Graydon Gould, John Drake, Peter Bathurst, Brian Weske, Adrian Cairns, Robert Dorning, Harold Lang.*

LITTLE BIG SHOT (1952) [2]

Dir *Jack Raymond.* Prod *Henry Halsted.* Scr *John Paddy Carstairs, from the play by Janet Allan.* Ph *James Wilson, Gerald Moss.* PC *Byron.* Dis *Associated British.* 90 mins. Cert *U*

Harry Hawkwood (*Ronald Shiner*) wants to follow in his father's fingerprints as a big-shot crook. But the gang only keeps the inept Harry on out of respect for his father. He is entrusted with casing a mansion as 'inside man' on a jewel raid. But he is soon suspected and all the gang except Harry caught with the assistance of the owner's troop of Girl Guides. Harry decides to go straight. Tiresome knockabout comedy.

RoC *Derek Farr, Marie Lohr, Manning Whiley, Danny Green, Yvette Wyatt, Digby Wolfe, Marjorie Stewart, Victor Baring, Cyril Conway, Gabrielle Daye, Daphne Barker, Lawrence Douglas, Steve Knight, Arthur Dibbs, Tony Bradley.*

LITTLE RED MONKEY (1954) [3]
(USA: *The Case of the Red Monkey*)

Dir *Ken Hughes.* Prod *Alec C. Snowden.* Scr *Hughes, James Eastwood, from a TV serial by Eric Maschwitz.* Ph *Josef Ambor.* PC *Merton Park.* Dis *Anglo-Amalgamated.* 73 mins. Cert *A*

Top British scientists are being killed and the only clue is a little red monkey seen at the scene of every crime. US State Department

agent Locklin (*Richard Conte*) and Harrington (*Russell Napier*) of the Special Branch track a missing scientist to the HQ of an 'international friendship club', where they engage and shoot the midget head of the gang – and owner of the monkey. Conte and the direction a cut above the rest in moderately exciting thriller.

RoC *Rona Anderson, Colin Gordon, Arnold Marle, Sylva Langova, Bernard Rebel, Donald Bisset, Noel Johnson, Colin Tapley, John Horsley, Geoffrey Denys, John King-Kelly, Leonard Frank, Peter Bathurst, Roland Brand, Jane Welch, Joan Plant, Weyman Mackay, Elizabeth Wallace, Richard Marner.*

LONDON ENTERTAINS (1951) [2]

Dir, Prod and PC *Edwin J. Fancey.* Scr *Jimmy Grafton.* Ph *Jeff Davis.* Dis *New Realm.* 49 mins. Cert *U*

Many of Britain's 'new' post-war radio favourites pop in and out of this undisciplined, madcap comedy-musical about two girls from a Swiss finishing school (*Christina Forrest, Pamela Bygrave*) who start an escort agency in London and, after going out with a number of unlikely clients, both find the 'right man'.

RoC *Vincent Ball, Eamonn Andrews, Peter Sellers, Harry Secombe, Spike Milligan, Tony Fayne, David Evans, Bobby Breen, Diana Coupland, Paul Adam, The Eastbourne Girls' Choir.*

THE LONG ARM (1956) [5]
(USA: *The Third Key*)

Dir *Charles Frend.* (Associate) Prod *Tom Morahan.* Scr *Janet Green, Robert Barr, Dorothy & Campbell Christie.* Ph *Gordon Dines.* PC *Ealing Studios.* Dis *Rank.* 96 mins. Cert *U*

Ingeniously foiling the police by pretending to be a nightwatchman at the scene of his own crime, a master safecracker (*Richard Leech*) slips up by killing a man on his next robbery, and finds weary but dogged Superintendent Halliday (*Jack Hawkins*) on his trail. Halliday discovers that the burgled safes were all of the same make, and that the thief is a former employee of the safe company, long thought dead. He traps him at the London Festival Hall. Solid, well-knit police thriller: *Dragnet* with British accents. The last Ealing film actually made at Ealing Studios.

Roc *John Stratton, Dorothy Alison, Geoffrey Keen, Ursula Howells, Sydney Tafler, Newton Blick, Meredith Edwards, Michael Brooke, Ralph Truman, George Rose, Maureen Delaney, Ian Bannen, Alec McCowen, Peter Burton, Sam Kydd, Glyn Houston, Joss Ambler, Maureen Davis, Nicholas Parsons, John Welsh, Gillian Webb, Harry Locke, William Mervyn, Harold Goodwin, Stratford Johns, John Warwick, Barry Keegan, Warwick Ashton, David Davies, Julie Milton, Jameson Clark.*

THE LONG DARK HALL (1951) [3]

Dir *Anthony Bushell, Reginald Beck.* Prod *Peter Cusick.* Scr *Nunnally Johnson, William Fairchild.* Ph *Wilkie Cooper.* PC *Five Oceans/Cusick International.* Dis *British Lion.* 86 mins. Cert *A*

Arthur Groome (*Rex Harrison*), a married man with two children, is arrested for the murder

of his mistress. He at first denies knowledge of her, hoping to spare his wife (*Lilli Palmer*), but is cornered, sent for trial, convicted on strong circumstantial evidence and sentenced to hang. The murderer confesses by letter – but, by a freak chance, Groome has not been hanged as arranged and police are now able to track the real killer (*Anthony Dawson*) down. Indifferent suspense drama.

RoC *Denis O'Dea, Raymond Huntley, Patricia Wayne (Cutts), Anthony Bushell, Meriel Forbes, Brenda de Banzie, William Squire, Michael Medwin, Colin Gordon, Eric Pohlmann, Tania Heald, Henrietta Barry, Dora Stevening, Ronald Simpson, Ballard Berkeley, Henry Longhurst, Douglas Jefferies, Fletcher Lightfoot, Anthony Shaw, Lily Molnar, Frank Tickle, Tom Macauley, Richard Littledale, Jenny Laird, Tony Quinn, Jill Bennett.*

THE LONG HAUL (1957) [3]

Dir and Scr *Ken Hughes, from the novel by Mervyn Mills.* Prod *Maxwell Setton.* Ph *Basil Emmott.* PC *Marksman.* Dis *Columbia.* 100 mins. Cert *A*

To please his wife (*Gene Anderson*) who doesn't want to go to America, ex-US army man Harry Miller (*Victor Mature*) becomes a truck driver. He comes up against Joe Easy (*Patrick Allen*), a haulage racketeer, after Joe's mistress (*Diana Dors*) has seduced him, and is forced to work for Joe after losing his own job. During a long haul with stolen furs, Joe is killed after a fight and Harry, shocked to find his small son is dangerously ill, gives himself up. Unsavoury thriller, well photographed.

RoC *Peter Reynolds, Liam Redmond, Meier Tzelniker, Michael Wade, Dervis Ward, Murray Kash, Jameson Clark, John Harvey, John Welsh, Roland Brand, Stanley Rose, Raymond Barry, Susan Campbell, Freddie Watts, Harcourt Curacao, Van Boolen, Norman Rossington, Martin Shaban, Madge Brindley.*

Patrick Allen and Victor Mature in The Long Haul *(1957)*

THE LONG KNIFE (1958) [3]

Dir *Montgomery Tully.* Prod *Jack Greenwood.* Scr *Ian Stuart Black, from a novel by Seldon Truss.* PC *Merton Park.* Dis *Anglo-Amalgamated.* 57 mins. Cert *U*

The operations of a gang of extortionists within a private clinic are discovered by Jill (*Joan Rice*), a nurse there. When wealthy Mrs

Cheam is found stabbed to death, Jill has trouble clearing herself of suspicion, but she is helped by the victim's lawyer (*Sheldon Lawrence*), who discovers that his client was killed by a woman (*Dorothy Brewster*) dressed as a man. Competent, lively thriller holds the interest, isn't too long.
RoC *Ellen Pollock, Victor Brooks, Arthur Gomez, Alan Keith.*

THE LONG MEMORY (1952) [3]
Dir *Robert Hamer.* Prod *Hugh Stewart.* Scr *Hamer, Frank Harvey, from the novel by Howard Clewes.* Ph *Harry Waxman.* PC *Europa.* Dis *General Film Distributors. 96 mins. Cert A*
Having done 12 years for a murder he didn't commit, Davidson (*John Mills*) is resolved to 'get' those who committed perjury to put him away, including his girl (*Elizabeth Sellars*), now married to the detective on the case (*John McCallum*). He rejects the friendship of a tramp (*Michael Martin-Harvey*) and a refugee girl (*Eva Bergh*) and finds the perjurers beneath his contempt. But his 'victim', Boyd (*John Chandos*), a crook, is alive and prospering; Boyd tries to shoot Davidson, but is killed by the tramp. Tough, but slow and disjointed.
RoC *Geoffrey Keen, John Slater, Thora Hird, Vida Hope, Harold Lang, Mary Mackenzie, Laurence Naismith, Peter Jones, Henry Edwards, John Glyn-Jones, John Horsley, Fred Johnson, Christopher Beeny, Julian Somers, Denis Shaw, Russell Waters.*

LOOK BACK IN ANGER (1959) [5]
Dir *Tony Richardson.* Prod *Gordon L.T. Scott.* Scr *Nigel Kneale, John Osborne, from Osborne's play.* Ph *Oswald Morris.* PC *Woodfall.* Dis *AB-Pathé. 100 mins. Cert X*
Jimmy Porter (*Richard Burton*) is a state-aided university graduate living with his wife Alison (*Mary Ure*) in squalor, and reviling society, the upper classes, the State, the Church and everything else that he sees as governed by hypocrisy. For a living, he runs a sweet stall. An actress, Helena (*Claire Bloom*), induces Alison to leave him. Later, Helena and Jimmy become lovers. Alison returns, having lost the baby she was expecting. Helena leaves. With *Room at the Top*, this tough-talking film lent impetus to a new wave of realist film-making in which honest dialogue won favour over action.
RoC *Edith Evans, Gary Raymond, Glen Byam-*

Mary Ure, Richard Burton and Claire Bloom in Look Back in Anger *(1959)*

Shaw, Phyllis Neilson-Terry, Donald Pleasence, Stanley Van Beers, Jordan Lawrence, John Dearth, Michael Balfour, George Devine, Anne Dickins, Nigel Davenport, Alfred Lynch, Toke Townley, Maureen Swanson, Jane Eccles, Shashi Kapoor, Walter Hudd, Chris Barber and His Jazz Band.

LOSER TAKES ALL (1956) [2]
Dir *Ken Annakin.* Prod and PC *John Stafford.* Scr *Graham Greene, from his novel.* Ph *Georges Périnal.* Dis *British Lion. Eastman Colour. Cinemascope. 88 mins. Cert A*
Bertrand (*Rossano Brazzi*), a mild accountant, so impresses his boss (*Robert Morley*) with his mathematical talent that he arranges for Bertrand and his fiancée Cary (*Glynis Johns*) to honeymoon on his Monte Carlo yacht. Once there, Bertrand evolves a system for winning at the casinos, and becomes estranged from Cary, who is squired by a fortune hunter (*Tony Britton*). The boss effects a reconciliation. Slack-paced comedy; the two leading male roles (*Brazzi, Britton*) would have been better cast the other way round.
RoC *Albert Lieven, Felix Aylmer, A.E. Matthews, Joyce Carey, Geoffrey Keen, Peter Illing, Walter Hudd, Charles Lloyd Pack, Guido Lorraine, Joan Benham, Carl Bernard, Shirley Ann Field.*

LOST (1955) [4]
(USA: *Tears for Simon*)
Dir *Guy Green.* Prod *Vivian A. Cox, (uncredited) Sydney Box.* Scr/*Janet Green.* Ph/*Harry Waxman.* PC and Dis *Rank. Eastman Colour. 89 mins. Cert A*
The baby son of a well-to-do American (*David Knight*) and his dress designer wife (*Julia Arnall*) is snatched from his pram, left momentarily unattended. Despite warnings from the police to leave well alone, the parents get involved with some dangerous red herrings, especially crooks who demand a ransom but haven't got the child – which is eventually traced to an unbalanced widow and recovered. Gripping weepie-thriller that never drags its feet.
RoC *David Farrar, Eleanor Summerfield, Anthony Oliver, Thora Hird, Anne Paige, Marjorie Rhodes, Anna Turner, Everley Gregg, Meredith Edwards, Irene Prador, Shirley Ann(e) Field, Eileen Peel, Barbara Shotter, Alma Taylor, Anita Sharp Bolster, Beverly Brooks, Robert Brown, Harry Brunning, Fanny Carby, Cyril Chamberlain, Peggyann Clifford, Glenda Davies, Guy Deghy, Michael Ward, Dorothy Gordon, Fred Griffiths, Joan Hickson, Brenda Hogan, Glyn Houston, Ray Jackson, Shirley Jenkins, Freda Bamford, Jack Lambert, Margot Lister, Arthur Lovegrove, William Lucas, Barry McCourmick, Jack McNaughton, Charlotte Mitchell, Hugh Morton, Dandy Nichols, Eileen Peel, Grace Denbigh Russell, Joan Sims, Ewen Solon, Marianne Stone, Mike Ward, Ronald Ward, Mona Washbourne, John Welsh, Leonard White, Barbara Windsor.*

THE LOST HOURS (1952) [2]
(USA: *The Big Frame*)
Dir *David Macdonald.* Prod *Robert S. Baker,*

Monty Berman. Scr *John Gilling.* Ph *Berman, Eric Bersche.* PC *Tempean.* Dis *Eros. 72 mins. Cert U*
Paul (*Mark Stevens*), an American pilot in England for an RAF reunion, is drugged and wakes to find himself a murder suspect. His investigations reveal a number of wartime pilots now involved in crime, and there are two more killings. The murderer is revealed to be Clark (*John Bentley*), Paul's rival for Louise (*Jean Kent*); he is caught by police after a chase. Quite fast-moving; script and acting undistinguished.
RoC *Dianne Foster, Garry Marsh, Jack Lambert, Leslie Perrins, Duncan Lamont, Thora Hird, Bryan Coleman, John Horsley, Cyril Smith, John Harvey, John Gabriel, Alastair Hunter, Sam Kydd.*

LOVE IN PAWN (1953) [2]
Dir *Charles Saunders.* Prod *Robert S. Baker, Monty Berman.* Scr *Guy Morgan, Frank Muir, Denis Norden.* Ph *Berman.* PC *Tempean.* Dis *Eros. 81 mins. Cert U*
Penniless artist Roger Fox (*Bernard Braden*) will be given £10,000 by an uncle if he can prove a profitable, sober existence. His wife Jean (*Barbara Kelly*) pawns him for £5 so she can entertain a solicitor handling uncle's affairs. The daughter (*Jean Carson*) of the pawnbroker (*Reg Dixon*) tries to seduce Roger; Jean loses the ticket, gets jealous and refuses to redeem him. All ends well, with the Foxes in the money. Popular radio husband-and-wife team in comedy that is just silly, not funny.
RoC *John Laurie, Walter Crisham, Avice Landone, Laurence Naismith, Tom Gill, Alan Robinson, Dorothy Gordon, Benita Lydell, Hal Osmond.*

THE LOVE LOTTERY (1953) [3]
Dir *Charles Crichton.* Prod *Monja Danischewsky.* Scr *Harry Kurnitz.* Ph *Douglas Slocombe.* PC *Ealing Studios.* Dis *General Film Distributors. Technicolor. 89 mins. Cert U*
Forever fleeing from female fans, film star Rex Allerton (*David Niven*) is persuaded to offer himself as first prize in a giant lottery, run by a gambling syndicate whose employee Jane (*Anne Vernon*) falls for Rex and buys up hundreds of tickets. In spite of her efforts, he is won by Sally (*Peggy Cummins*), a typist. Sally, however, finds that Rex doesn't match up to her dreams, and returns, to Jane's relief, to her boyfriend. Light, inconsequential comedy tends to muff its good ideas.
RoC *Herbert Lom, Gordon Jackson, Charles Victor, Hugh McDermott, June Clyde, Stanley Maxted, Felix Aylmer, John Chandos, Theodore Bikel, Sebastian Cabot, Eugene Deckers, Hattie Jacques, Andrea Malandrinos, Nicholas Stuart, Michael Ward, Helena Pickard, Marcel Poncin, Alexis Chesnakov, Nellie Arno, Gabrielle Blunt, Mark Baker, Boscoe Holder, Michael Craig, John Glyn-Jones, Humphrey Bogart (guest).*

THE LOVE MATCH (1954) [4]
Dir *David Paltenghi.* Prod *Maclean Rogers.* Scr *Geoffrey Orme, Glenn Melvyn, from Melvyn's play.* Ph *Arthur Grant.* PC *Group 3.* Dis *British Lion. 86 mins. Cert U*

Arrested for assaulting the referee at a soccer match, Bill (*Arthur Askey*) and Wally (*Glenn Melvyn*) find themselves in trouble after 'borrowing' the money from a railwaymen's holiday fund to pay the fine. They are robbed of £50, Bill's daughter (*Shirley Eaton*) twists her ankle just before entering a dance contest she might have won, and Bill's wife (*Thora Hird*) takes in the referee as a lodger! Bill and Wally recoup by betting on their local football team. Good, noisy north country comedy. Old jokes notch remarkably high scoring-rate.

RoC *James Kenney, Edward Chapman, Danny Ross, Robb Wilton, Maurice Kaufmann, Anthea Askey, William Franklyn, Patricia Hayes, Derek Kirby, Russell Waters, Peter Swanwick, Vi Stevens, Jill Adams, Dorothy Blythe, Ben Williams, Reginald Hearne, George Hirste, Iris Vandeleur, Sydney Bromley, June Martin, Bob Vossler, Leonard Williams, Richard Ford, Peter Godsell, Isabel George.*

LOVE'S A LUXURY (1952) [2]
(USA: *The Caretaker's Daughter*)
Dir *Francis Searle*. Prod *Thomas A. Blakeley*. Scr *Hugh Wakefield, Elwyn Ambrose, Guy Paxton, Edward V. Hole, from the play by Paxton and Hole*. Ph *Ernest Palmer*. PC *Mancunian*. Dis *Butchers*. 88 mins. Cert A

An impresario (*Hugh Wakefield*) heads for the country after a row with his prim wife (*Helen Shingler*). He is accompanied by an actor, Bobby (*Derek Bond*); when they arrive, they find the caretaker's pretty daughter (*Patricia Raine*) in charge. When the wife, with her son (*Michael Medwin*) and his girlfriend (*Zena Marshall*) turn up, the actor dresses up as the caretaker. A scoutmaster and his troop camped in the grounds get involved with bogus police officers. After frantic complications, peace reigns again in the country. Typically long and hoary Mancunian farce.

RoC *Bill Shine, Grace Arnold, David Hannaford, Peter Bathurst.*

LUCKY JIM (1957) [5]
Dir *John Boulting*. Prod *Roy Boulting*. Scr *Patrick Campbell, Jeffrey Dell, from the novel by Kingsley Amis*. Ph *Max Greene (Mutz Greenbaum)*. PC *Charter*. Dis *British Lion*. 95 mins. Cert U

Jim Dixon (*Ian Carmichael*), brash history lecturer of working-class origin at a provincial university, finds little problem in offending everyone there. He crosses a professor's (*Hugh*

Ian Carmichael in Lucky Jim *(1957)*

Griffith) pseudo-intellectual son (*Terry-Thomas*) and pinches his girlfriend (*Sharon Acker*), then embarks on a series of disasters, culminating in his 'Merrie England' lecture, which ends as a drunken harangue. Fired, Jim is rescued by his girlfriend's uncle, who offers him a good job. Wild, funny, nicely written farce (originally a social satire) hit the box-office jackpot.

RoC *Maureen Connell, Kenneth Griffith, Jean Anderson, Clive Morton, John Welsh, Reginald Beckwith, Jeremy Hawk, Harry Fowler, John Cairney, Charles Lamb, Jeremy Longhurst, Henry Longhurst, Ian Wilson, Ronald Cardew, Penny Morrell.*

THE LYONS IN PARIS (1954) [3]
Dir and Scr *Val Guest*. Prod *Robert Dunbar*. Ph *Jimmy Harvey*. PC *Hammer*. Dis *Exclusive*. 81 mins. Cert U

Ben Lyon's children *Barbara* and *Richard* suspect that their father is having an affair with Fifi le Fleur (*Martine Alexis*), but she has merely obtained the tickets for their holiday in Paris. Once there, however, both Ben and Richard become involved with her, and Ben finds himself fighting a duel, which fortunately ends with honour and flesh intact. Brisk, simple comedy frolic.

RoC *Bebe Daniels, Reginald Beckwith, Pierre Dudan, Dino Galvani, Horace Percival, Molly Weir, Doris Rogers, Gwen Lewis, Hugh Morton.*

M

MAD ABOUT MEN (1954) [4]
Dir *Ralph Thomas*. Prod *Betty Box*. Scr *Peter Blackmore*. Ph *Ernest Steward*. PC *Group*. Dis *General Film Distributors*. Technicolor. 90 mins. Cert U

A sequel to *Miranda* (1948). Caroline (*Glynis Johns*) is persuaded by Miranda (also Johns), a mermaid who resembles her facially, to go on a cycling trip so that Miranda can take her place for a while, with the aid of a wheelchair and an obliging nurse (*Margaret Rutherford*). Miranda is mad about men, and when the fiancée of one of them threatens her exposure, Caroline steps back into her own life to save the day. Amusing comedy, played with wit.

RoC *Donald Sinden, Anne Crawford, Dora Bryan, Nicholas Phipps, Peter Martyn, Noel Purcell, Irene Handl, Joan Hickson, Judith Furse, David Hurst, Martin Miller, Deryck Guyler, Anthony Oliver, Harry Welchman, Meredith Edwards, Marianne Stone, Douglas Ives, George Woodbridge, Lawrence Ward, Dandy Nichols, Martin Boddey, Ken Richmond, Stringer Davis, Henry Longhurst, John Horsley.*

MADAME LOUISE (1951) [2]
Dir *Maclean Rogers*. Prod *Ernest G. Roy*. Scr *Michael Pertwee, from the play by Vernon*

Sulvaine. Ph *Wilkie Cooper*. PC *Nettlefold*. Dis *Butchers*. 83 mins. Cert U

A bookmaker wins a fashionable Mayfair dress salon in a bet, and immediately sets about erasing its old-fashioned ways and bringing things bang up to date, especially its oldest inhabitant Mr Pastry (*Richard Hearne*). After sundry misadventures, the bookie admits defeat, and 'Madame Louise' goes back to its original owner. Sounds promising (and play was a hit), but fails dismally on screen.

RoC *Petula Clark, Garry Marsh, Hilda Bayley, Richard Gale, Doris Rogers, Harry Fowler, Charles Farrell, Vic Wise, John Powe, Robert Adair, Doorn van Steyn, Anita (Sharp) Bolster, Pauline Goodwin, Mavis Greenaway, Pat Raphael, Mackenzie Ward, Gerald Rex.*

Richard Hearne and Petula Clark in Madame Louise *(1951)*

MADE IN HEAVEN (1952) [3]
Dir *John Paddy Carstairs*. Prod *George H. Brown*. Scr *William Douglas Home, Brown*. Ph *Geoffrey Unsworth*. PC *Fanfare*. Dis *General Film Distributors*. Technicolor. 81 mins. Cert U

A young couple's (*David Tomlinson, Petula Clark*) efforts to win the famous Dunmow Flitch for a recently wed pair who haven't had a quarrel are put to a serious test with the arrival of a delectable Hungarian maid called Marta (*Sonja Ziemann*). A win will accelerate the building of their new house, and this is duly achieved, especially with the advent of Marta's Hungarian fiancé. Frothy romp strains for its laughs.

RoC *A.E. Matthews, Charles Victor, Sophie Stewart, Richard Wattis, Athene Seyler, Philip Stainton, Ferdy Mayne, Alfie Bass, Dora Bryan, Michael Brennan, Harold Kasket, George Bishop, Margot Lister, John Warren, Ronnie Stevens, Gilbert Davis, Stuart Latham.*

THE 'MAGGIE' (1953) [5]
(USA: *High and Dry*)
Dir *Alexander Mackendrick*. Prod *Michael Truman*. Scr *William Rose*. Ph *Gordon Dines*. PC *Ealing Studios*. Dis *General Film Distributors*. 92 mins. Cert U

The *Maggie*, a puffer boat plying the waters of the Western Scottish islands, is down on its luck when its wily captain, Mactaggart (*Alex Mackenzie*) cons the agent of an American businessman into entrusting him with a valuable cargo for a long trip. The American (*Paul Douglas*) is furious when he hears, finally

catching up with the puffer and trying to re-possess his cargo. But the crew continually outwit him and, falling under the *Maggie's* spell, he even agrees to jettison the cargo when the puffer runs on to some rocks. Warm, whimsical comedy, occasionally very funny.
RoC *James Copeland, Tommy Kearins, Abe Barker, Hubert Gregg, Geoffrey Keen, Dorothy Alison, Andrew Keir, Meg Buchanan, Fiona Glyne, Jameson Clark, Mark Dignam, Moultrie Kelsall, Sheila Shand Gibbs, Betty Henderson, Russell Waters, Duncan McIntyre, Roddy Mac-Millan, Jack Macguire, John Rae, Jack Ste-wart, Eric Woodburn, Douglas Robin, R.B. Wharrie, David Cameron, Catherine Fletcher, William Crichton, Andrew Downie, Herbert C. Cameron, Gilbert Stevenson.*

THE MAGIC BOX (1951)   [4]
Dir *John Boulting.* Prod *Ronald Neame.* Scr *Eric Ambler, from a book by Ray Allister.* Ph *Jack Cardiff.* PC *Festival.* Dis *British Lion.* Technicolor. 118 mins. Cert U
The 1870s. William Friese-Greene (*Robert Donat*) makes a name as a portrait photographer, but forsakes financial security to concentrate on inventing a motion picture camera. The ensuing financial hardships kill his wife (*Maria Schell*); finally successful, he gains little credit, his second wife (*Margaret Johnston*) leaving him in the face of bankruptcy. Speaking for film trade unity at a meeting in 1921, he collapses and dies, forgotten by all but a few. Character study has integrity, is well mounted and saved from the threat of tedium by a long list of guest stars. The industry's contribution to the Festival of Britain.
RoC (alphabetical order) *Renee Asherson, Richard Attenborough, Robert Beatty, Martin Boddey, Edward Chapman, John Charlesworth, Maurice Colbourne, Roland Culver, John Howard Davies, Michael Denison, Joan Dowling, Henry Edwards, Mary Ellis, Marjorie Fielding, Robert Flemyng, Leo Genn, Marius Goring, Everley Gregg, Joyce Grenfell, Robertson Hare, Kathleen Harrison, William Hartnell, Joan Hickson, Thora Hird, Stanley Holloway, Patrick Holt, Michael Hordern, Jack Hulbert, Sidney James, Glynis Johns, Mervyn Johns, Barry Jones, Peter Jones, James Kenney, Ann Lancaster, Herbert Lomas, John Longden, Bessie Love, Miles Malleson, Garry Marsh, Muir Matheson, A.E. Matthews, John McCallum, Bernard Miles, Richard Murdoch, David Oake, Laurence Olivier, Cecil Parker, Frank Pettingell, Norman Pierce, Eric Portman, Dennis Price, Michael Redgrave, Peter Reynolds, Margaret Rutherford, Janette Scott, Ronald Shiner, Sheila Sim, Madame Slobodskaya, Marianne Stone, John Stuart, Basil Sydney, Ernest Thesiger, Sybil Thorndike, David Tomlinson, Cecil Trouncer, Michael Trubshawe, Peter Ustinov, Frederick Valk, Amy Veness, Charles Victor, Kay Walsh, Norma Watson, Emlyn Williams, Harcourt Williams, Googie Withers, Joan Young.*

THE MAGIC GARDEN (1951)   [4]
Dir and Prod *Donald Swanson.* Scr *Ferdinand Webb, Swanson, Cyril Pennington-Richards.* Ph

Pennington-Richards. PC *Swan Films.* Dis *British Lion.* 63 mins. Cert U
A small South African town. A priest receives £40 from a parishioner, but a young thief steals it. Pursued, he hides the money in a garden, whence it falls into the hands of a poor family, who buy provisions and entrust the balance to the storekeeper. The thief retrieves it, only to have to hide it again; a young couple, finding the money, are able to get married. The thief keeps taking the ever-diminishing bankroll until it finally ends up back at the church. Low-budget feature has freshness and charm, highly original jazz score.
LP *Tommy Machaka, Harriet Qubeka, David Mnkwanazi, Dolly Rathebe, Victor Gwai, Grinsell Nogauza, Lucas Khosa, Linda Mⁿdikisa, Jonathan Mzamo.*

THE MAGNET (1950)   [3]
Dir *Charles Frend.* (Associate) Prod *Sidney Cole.* Scr *T.E.B. Clarke.* Ph *Lionel Banes.* PC *Ealing Studios.* Dis *General Film Distributors.* 79 mins. Cert A
Johnny (*William [James] Fox*) cheats a younger boy out of a super outsize magnet. His conscience troubling him, he gives it to a man collecting money for an iron lung. The man appeals to people to emulate the boy's generosity and the money is raised. A hunt for the boy is launched but, thinking the police are after him, he lies low. Finally, he is given a gold medal – which he allows himself to be done out of by his original victim. Slow picture has some charm, is finally too improbable.
RoC *Stephen Murray, Kay Walsh, Meredith Edwards, Gladys Henson, Wylie Watson, Thora Hird, Julien Mitchell, Michael Brooke Jr, Keith Robinson, Thomas Johnson, Bryan Michie, Anthony Oliver, Molly Hamley-Clifford, Harold Goodwin, Edward Davies, David Boyd, Geoffrey Yin, Joan Hickson, Grace Arnold, Jane Bough, Joss Ambler, Sam Kydd, Russell Waters, Thea Gregson (Gregory), Elsie Lowenthal, Seamus Mor Na Feasag (James Robertson Justice).*

MAKE ME AN OFFER (1954)   [3]
Dir *Cyril Frankel.* Prod *W.P. Lipscomb.* Scr *Lipscomb, Wolf Mankowitz, from Mankowitz's novel.* Ph *Denny Densham.* PC *Group 3.* Dis *British Lion.* Eastman Colour. 89 mins. Cert U
An impecunious antiques dealer (*Peter Finch*) has the chance of pulling off the coup of his life by buying a priceless Wedgwood vase for £100 from its eccentric young owner (*Adrienne Corri*). His problem is to raise even that much money. He does it by playing off dealers one against the other at an auction. Strenuous comedy has some ripe character cameos, but a slow pace.
RoC *Rosalie Crutchley, Finlay Currie, Ernest Thesiger, Wilfrid Lawson, Anthony Nicholls, Guy Middleton, Alfie Bass, Vic Wise, Meier Tzelniker, Richard O'Sullivan, Jane Wenham, Mark Baker.*

MAKE MINE A MILLION (1959)   [3]
Dir *Lance Comfort.* Prod *John Baxter.* Scr *Peter Blackmore, Talbot Rothwell, Arthur Askey.* Ph *Arthur Grant.* PC *Jack Hylton.* Dis *British Lion.* 82 mins. Cert U

Sid (*Sidney James*) intends to advertise his phenomenally unsuccessful detergent Bonko on National TV, which has no commercials. With the help of Arthur (*Arthur Askey*), a make-up man, he does just that, losing Arthur his job in the process. When thieves steal their 'pirate' broadcasting van, however, thinking it contains gold, Arthur is responsible for their capture and becomes a national hero, a situation Sid soon turns to his advantage. Enjoyable broad comedy, with good-natured performances.
RoC *Dermot Walsh, Sally Barnes, Clive Morton, Martin Benson, Kenneth Connor, Lionel Murton, Olga Lindo, Leigh Madison, Bruce Seton, George Margo, David Nettheim, Bernard Cribbins, Tom Gill, Richard Caldicot, Gillian Lynne, Anthea Askey, Tommy Trinder, Dickie Henderson, Evelyn Laye, Dennis Lotis, Raymond Glendenning, Patricia Bredin, Leonard Weir, Sabrina, Peter Noble, Sam Kydd, Bill Shine, Television Toppers, Penge Formation Dancers.*

MALAGA (1954)   [2]
(USA: *Fire Over Africa*)
Dir *Richard Sale.* Prod *Colin Lesslie, Montagu Marks (M.J. Frankovitch).* Scr *Robert Westerby.* Ph *Christopher Challis.* PC *Film Locations.* Dis *British Lion.* Technicolor. 84 mins. Cert U
A vast organization is smuggling contraband goods into Malaga. Agent Joanna Dane (*Maureen O'Hara*) comes to Tangier to try to discover the brains behind the ring. She gets a job in a gambling club, and suspects American Van Logan (*Macdonald Carey*), who turns out to be a fellow-agent. Suave hijacker Dupont (*Leonard Sachs*) finally gives her the information which enables her to round up the ring. Wildly improbable adventure, often unintentionally funny. Very good photography.
RoC *Guy Middleton, Binnie Barnes, James Lilburn, Harry Lane, Bruce Beeby, Meinhart Maur, Ferdy Mayne, Hugh McDermott, Gérard Tichy, Eric Corrie, Mike Brendall, Derek Sydney, Jacques Cey.*

MALTA STORY (1953)   [4]
Dir *Brian Desmond Hurst.* Prod *Peter de Sarigny.* Scr *William Fairchild, Nigel Balchin, de Sarigny, Thorold Dickinson.* Ph *Robert Krasker.* PC *British Film Makers.* Dis *General Film Distributors.* 103 mins. Cert U
World War II. Peter Ross (*Alec Guinness*), an archaeologist serving as a reconnaissance pilot, comes to Malta when it is hard pressed by German and Italian planes. Through disobeying an order on a flight, Ross puts his superiors on to a new Italian stratagem. He falls in love with Maria (*Muriel Pavlow*), but her brother proves to be secretly working for the Italians. Paving the way for the bombing of a German convoy, Ross is killed. Staunch war film doesn't create memorable characters, but has vivid action scenes.
RoC *Anthony Steel, Jack Hawkins, Flora Robson, Renee Asherson, Hugh Burden, Nigel Stock, Reginald Tate, Ralph Truman, Rosalie Crutchley, Michael Medwin, Ronald Adam, Stuart Burge, Jerry Desmonde, Ivor Barnard, Harold Siddons, Colin Loudan, Edward Chaffers, Noel*

Willman, Peter Bull, Richard Leven, Thomas Heathcote, Michael Craig, Lee Patterson, Maurice Denham (voice only).

MAN ACCUSED (1959)   [1]

Dir *Montgomery Tully.* Prod *Edward J. Danziger, Harry Lee Danziger.* Scr *Mark Grantham.* Ph *Jimmy Wilson.* PC *Danzigers.* Dis *United Artists. 58 mins. Cert U*

Just after he has become engaged to a baronet's daughter (*Carol Marsh*), Bob Jenson (*Ronald Howard*) is arrested for robbery and murder. He breaks jail, tracks down the real criminals and hands them over to the authorities. Careless presentation and a tired formula that's played out.

RoC *Ian Fleming, Catharina Ferraz, Colin Tapley, Howard Lang, Brian Nissen, Robert Dorning, Stuart Saunders, Gordon Needham, Graham Ashley, Diana Chesney, Kenneth Edwardes.*

THE MAN BETWEEN (1953)   [3]

Dir and Prod *Carol Reed.* Scr *Harry Kurnitz, Eric Linklater, from a novel by Walter Ebert.* Ph *Desmond Dickinson.* PC *London Films.* Dis *British Lion. 101 mins. Cert U*

Visiting her brother (*Geoffrey Toone*) and his wife (*Hildegarde Neff*) in West Berlin, Susanne (*Claire Bloom*) soon encounters Ivo Kern (*James Mason*), a shady 'go-between' who secures 'wanted' West Berliners for the east. Susanne and Ivo fall in love; when she is snatched by the east in mistake for her sister-in-law, Ivo helps her escape, but is killed in so doing. Atmospheric thriller lacks emotional appeal.

RoC *Aribert Waescher, Ernst Schroeder, Karl John, Hilde Sessak, Dieter Krause.*

MANDY (1952)   [4]
(USA: *Crash of Silence*)

Dir *Alexander Mackendrick.* Prod *Leslie Norman.* Scr *Jack Whittingham, Nigel Balchin, from a novel by Hilda Lewis.* Ph *Douglas Slocombe.* PC *Ealing Studios.* Dis *General Film Distributors. 93 mins. Cert A*

Christine (*Phyllis Calvert*) disagrees with her husband Harry (*Terence Morgan*) on keeping their deaf-and-dumb young daughter (*Mandy Miller*) at home. When Christine takes her north to a special school Harry leaves her, and sets a divorce detective on her trail when rumours reach him about Christine and Mandy's

Jack Hawkins, Phyllis Calvert and Mandy Miller in Mandy *(1952)*

teacher (*Jack Hawkins*). But when he sees for himself the child's progress, to speak a few words and play with others, he is reconciled both to the decision and to Christine. Beautiful central story in unconvincing marital drama framework.

RoC *Godfrey Tearle, Marjorie Fielding, Patricia Plunkett, Dorothy Alison, Nancy Price, Edward Chapman, Eleanor Summerfield, Colin Gordon, Julian Amyes, Gabrielle Brune, John Cazabon, Gwen Bacon, W.E. Holloway, Phyllis Morris, Gabrielle Blunt, Jean Shepheard, Jane Asher, Marlene Maddox.*

MAN FROM TANGIER (1957)   [2]
(USA: *Thunder Over Tangier*)

Dir *Lance Comfort.* Prod *W.G. Chalmers.* Scr *P. Manning O'Brine.* Ph *Geoffrey Faithfull.* PC and Dis *Butchers. 67 mins. Cert U*

Chuck Collins (*Robert Hutton*), a film stuntman, finds himself accidentally involved in passport and forgery rackets just through taking the wrong overcoat. Armstrong (*Emerton Court*), an international crook, steals a set of engraving plates, but is killed by the gang that made them – and Chuck finds himself under suspicion. With the help of a girl (*Lisa Gastoni*) who is being blackmailed by the gang, he clears himself. Lots of huff and puff bursts paper-thin plot.

RoC *Martin Benson, Derek Sydney, Jack Allen, Leonard Sachs, Robert Raglan, Harold Berens, Richard Shaw, Michael Balfour, Frank Forsyth, Reginald Hearne, Fred Lake, Marianne Stone, Adeeb Assaly, Alex Gallier, Frank Singuineau, James Lomas, Ronald Clark, Victor Beaumont.*

THE MAN INSIDE (1958)   [2]

Dir *John Gilling.* Prod *Harold Huth.* Scr *Gilling, David Shaw, Richard Maibaum, from the novel by M.E. Chaber.* Ph *Ted Moore, Cyril Knowles.* PC *Warwick,* Dis *Columbia.* CinemaScope. *96 mins. Cert A*

After 30 years with the same jewellery firm, Sam Carter (*Nigel Patrick*) takes his own pension -- the Tyrahna Blue diamond. A detective, March (*Jack Palance*) is soon on his trail across Europe, as is an adventuress, Trudie (*Anita Ekberg*) and criminals Lomer (*Bonar Colleano*) and Rizzio (*Sean Kelly*). Sam falls for Trudie, but realizes she is only after the diamond, and flees to London, where he, Lomer and Rizzio are all killed. Trudie gets the diamond – but decides to return it to its owners. Plenty going on in a thriller that only lacks a plot that makes sense.

RoC *Anthony Newley, Sidney James, Donald Pleasence, Eric Pohlmann, Josephine Brown, Gerard Heinz, Anne Aubrey, Naomi Chance, Alec Mango, Alfred Burke.*

THE MAN IN THE ROAD (1956)   [3]

Dir *Lance Comfort.* Prod *Charles A. Leeds.* Scr *Guy Morgan, from a novel by Anthony Armstrong.* Ph *Stan Pavey.* PC *Gibraltar.* Dis *Grand National. 84 mins. Cert U*

An injured man (*Derek Farr*), also suffering from amnesia, wakes up in a nursing home to be told he is an accountant who was about to leave for Russia. Suspicious, he eventually finds out that he is a scientist, whom enemy

agents are hoping to persuade peaceably to 'disappear' behind the Iron Curtain. With the help of an American girl (*Ella Raines*) he frees himself and police trap the ring of spies. Nothing new here, but well acted by solid cast.

RoC *Donald Wolfit, Lisa Daniely, Cyril Cusack, Karel Stepanek, Olive Sloane, Russell Napier, Frederick Piper, Bruce Beeby.*

MAN IN THE SHADOW (1957)   [2]

Dir *Montgomery Tully.* Prod *Alec C. Snowden.* Scr *Stratford Davis.* Ph *Philip Grindrod.* PC and Dis *Anglo-Amalgamated. 86 mins. Cert U*

When Alan Peters (*John Horsley*) is sentenced to death for a murder committed by Sullivan (*Zachary Scott*), his wife (*Faith Domergue*), an antique shop owner, sets out to prove his innocence, falling victim to a blackmailer and crossing wits with a number of shady characters before she finally succeeds, and Sullivan dies. Disappointing vehicle for visiting stars.

RoC *Gordon Jackson, Kay Callard, Peter Illing, Faith Brook, John Welsh, Fabia Drake, Julian Strange, Derek Sydney, Catharina Ferraz, Harold Siddons, Basil Dignam.*

THE MAN IN THE SKY (1956)   [4]

Dir *Charles Crichton.* (Associate) Prod *Seth Holt.* Scr *William Rose, John Eldridge.* Ph *Douglas Slocombe.* PC *Ealing Studios.* Dis *M-G-M. 87 mins. Cert U*

A hard-up test pilot (*Jack Hawkins*), whose livelihood depends on his struggling company's selling their new plane to an important buyer, is on a test flight when an engine catches fire. The crew and passengers bale out, but the pilot knows that if he does so hopes of a sale will be dashed. Against the odds, he lands the plane, although he is bitterly berated by his wife (*Elizabeth Sellars*). He insists that he was right to take the risk. Excellent at both ends, film is not quite so hot in the middle.

RoC *Walter Fitzgerald, Eddie Byrne, John Stratton, Victor Maddern, Lionel Jeffries, Donald Pleasence, Catherine Lacey, Megs Jenkins, Ernest Clark, Russell Waters, Howard Marion Crawford, Jeremy Bodkin, Gerard Lohan, Raymond Francis.*

THE MAN IN THE WHITE SUIT (1951)   [5]

Dir *Alexander Mackendrick.* (Associate) Prod *Sidney Cole.* Scr *Roger Macdougall, Alexander Mackendrick, John Dighton, from Macdougall's play.* Ph *Douglas Slocombe.* PC *Ealing Studios.* Dis *General Film Distributors. 85 mins. Cert U*

Sidney Stratton (*Alec Guinness*), a menial in textile research, is working on a new white fabric that will not get dirty or wear out. When he appears to have found it, after many hiccups, his employer (*Cecil Parker*) gives him funds to develop it. Industry is up in arms, thinking that the new cloth will create unemployment. Chased by everyone, Sidney finds his 'white suit' comes to pieces in their hands. He resolves to try again. Gloriously inventive social comedy.

RoC *Joan Greenwood, Michael Gough, Ernest Thesiger, Vida Hope, Howard Marion Crawford, John Rudling, Henry Mollison, Patric Doonan, Miles Malleson, Duncan Lamont, Har-*

old *Goodwin, Colin Gordon, Joan Harben, Mandy Miller, Brian Worth, Billy Russell, Arthur Howard, Roddy Hughes, Stuart Latham, Edie Martin, Charlotte Mitchell, Olaf Olsen, Desmond Roberts, Ewan Roberts, Charles Saynor, Russell Waters, George Benson, Frank Atkinson, Charles Cullum, F.B.J. Sharp, Scott Harold, Jack Howard, Jack McNaughton, Judith Furse.*

MAN OF THE MOMENT (1955) [4]

Dir *John Paddy Carstairs.* Prod *Hugh Stewart.* Scr *Carstairs, Vernon Sylvaine.* Ph *Jack Cox.* PC *Group.* Dis *Rank.* 95 mins (later 88). Cert *U*

Norman (*Norman Wisdom*), a junior filing clerk at the Foreign Office, makes up the numbers at a Geneva conference after dropping a washbasin on the head of one of the delegates. His unintentional deeds there cause the Tawaki Islanders to put their fate in his hands, and he becomes an international figure. Fêted with honours - and attempted assassinations - he must decide whether Tawaki shall become a strategic base, and whose. Now knighted, he journeys to Tawaki - but the island erupts and sinks into the sea. Very original comedy, probably Wisdom's funniest. Full of comic possibilities, at times uproarious.

RoC *Lana Morris, Belinda Lee, Jerry Desmonde, Karel Stepanek, Garry Marsh, Inia Te Wiata, Evelyn Roberts, Violet Farebrother, Martin Miller, Eugene Deckers, Hugh Morton, Lisa Gastoni, Charles Hawtrey, A.J. 'Man Mountain' Dean, Bruce Seton, Philip Gilbert, Julia Arnall, Doreen Dawne, Edward Evans, Ruth Dunning, Sheila Sweet, Peter Bryant, Margaret Downs, Macdonald Hobley, Philip Harben, Ronnie Waldman, The Beverley Sisters, Susan Beaumont, Harold Kasket, Beverly Brooks, Michael Ward, Derek Sydney, Peter Taylor, Peggyann Clifford, Ivan Craig, Joseph Behrman, Cyril Chamberlain.*

MANTRAP (1953) [2]

(USA: *Woman in Hiding*)

Dir *Terence Fisher.* Prod *Michael Carreras, Alexander Paal.* Scr *Fisher, Paul Tabori, from a novel by Elleston Trevor.* Ph *Reginald Wyer.* PC and Dis *Exclusive.* 79 mins. Cert *A*

Thelma (*Lois Maxwell*), wife of guilty-but-insane killer Speight (*Kieron Moore*), changes her identity - known only to her employer, Jerrard (*Hugh Sinclair*) - and marries Victor (*Bill Travers*). Speight escapes. Detective Hugo Bishop (*Paul Henreid*) and his secretary Vera (*Kay Kendall*) find him, discovering also that he is sane and seeking the real murderer who, in a showdown, turns out to be Jerrard, who is chased to his death. Good cast adrift in archly contrived thriller.

RoC *Lloyd Lamble, Anthony Forwood, Mary Laura Wood, John Penrose, Liam Gaffney, Conrad Phillips, John Stuart, Anna Turner, Christina Forrest, Arnold Diamond, Jane Welsh, Geoffrey Murphy, Terry Carney, Sally Newland, Barbara Kowin (Shelley).*

MANUELA (1957) [4]

(USA: *Stowaway Girl*)

Dir *Guy Hamilton.* Prod and PC *Ivan Foxwell.*

Scr *Hamilton, Foxwell, William Woods, from the novel by Woods.* Ph *Otto Heller.* Dis *British Lion.* 95 mins. Cert *A*

When his loutish first mate (*Pedro Armendariz*) brings aboard Manuela, a 17-year-old halfcaste girl (*Elsa Martinelli*), Prothero (*Trevor Howard*), the embittered skipper of their tramp-steamer plying the South American coasts, falls in love with her. His passion becomes so all-consuming that he fails to respond in time when fire breaks out; the ship goes down. Seeing no future for him with Manuela, Prothero returns to sea without her. Overall quite powerful romantic drama somewhat after Joseph Conrad in tone.

RoC *Donald Pleasence, Peter Illing, Leslie Weston, Jack MacGowran, Roger Delgado, Warren Mitchell, Harold Kasket, Barry Lowe, Max Butterfield, Harcourt Curacao, Juan Carolilla, John Rae, Andy Ho, Amando Guinle, Michael Peake.*

THE MAN UPSTAIRS (1958) [5]

Dir *Don Chaffey.* Prod *Robert Dunbar.* Scr *Alun Falconer, Dunbar, Chaffey.* Ph *Gerald Gibbs.* PC *ACT Films.* Dis *British Lion.* 84 mins. Cert *A*

There's trouble in a rooming house when the man upstairs (*Richard Attenborough*) seems to have a breakdown and goes berserk, throwing a policeman down the stairs. The police and welfare authorities are at odds on how to get the man, who seems to be on the brink of suicide, out; apparently, he blames himself for the death of a colleague at work. Finally a young housewife (*Dorothy Alison*) succeeds where others have failed, and brings him down. Nerve-racking suspense is sensibly kept tight.

RoC *Bernard Lee, Donald Houston, Virginia Maskell, Kenneth Griffith, Patricia Jessel, Maureen Connell, Charles Houston, Walter Hudd, Amy Dalby, Edward Judd, Patrick Jordan, Alfred Burke, David Griffith, Polly Clark, Graham Stewart, John Charlesworth, Raymond Ray, Arthur Gross, Dan Cressy, Victor Brooks.*

Richard Attenborough and Dorothy Alison in The Man Upstairs *(1958)*

THE MAN WHO COULD CHEAT DEATH (1959) [3]

Dir *Terence Fisher.* Prod *Michael Carreras.* Scr *Jimmy Sangster, from a play by Barre Lyndon.* Ph *Jack Asher.* PC *Hammer.* Dis *Paramount.* Technicolor. 83 mins. Cert *X*

1890. Paris doctor Georges Bonner (*Anton Diffring*) is 104, but looks 35, thanks to tenyearly gland operations performed by an aged colleague Ludwig (*Arnold Marle*). When Ludwig is killed in a falling-out, Bonner kidnaps Janine (*Hazel Court*) to force her surgeon lover (*Christopher Lee*) to do his upcoming operation. But Bonner dies, now looking his age, in a fire started by one of his disfigured victims. Lurid horror piece, confidently made but stolidly played.

RoC *Delphi Lawrence, Francis de Wolff, Gerda Larsen, Middleton Woods, Michael Ripper, Denis Shaw, Ian Hewitson, Frederick Rawlings, Marie Burke, Charles Lloyd-Pack, John Harrison, Lockwood West, Ronald Adam, Barry Shawzin.*

THE MAN WHO LIKED FUNERALS (1958) [2]

Dir *David Eady.* Prod *Jon Penington.* Scr *Margot Bennett.* Ph *Eric Cross.* PC *Penington-Eady.* Dis *Rank.* 64 mins. Cert *U*

Simon (*Leslie Phillips*), a wily printer, aims to save his favourite boys' club by attending funerals and blackmailing the bereaved over scandalous books he alleges he will keep secret concerning the departed. The scheme backfires when he crosses swords with a notorious gangster, and he has to get his employer to help him out of trouble. The 'victims' have pity on him, and the boys' club survives. Delightful idea given heavy-handed treatment.

RoC *Susan Beaumont, Bill Fraser, Jimmy Thompson, Mary Mackenzie, Anita SharpBolster, Lily Lapidus, Charles Clay, Alastair Hunter, Hester Paton-Brown, Thelma Ruby, Shaun O'Riordan, Paul Stassino, Etain O'Dell, James Ottaway, Arthur Mullard, Laurence Taylor, Paul Bogdan, Marianne Stone, Michael Bird, Anthony Green, Brian Tyler.*

THE MAN WHO LOVED REDHEADS (1954) [3]

Dir *Harold French.* Prod *Josef Somlo.* Scr *Terence Rattigan, from his play* Who is Sylvia? Ph *Georges Périnal.* PC *London Films.* Dis *British Lion.* Eastman Colour. 89 mins. Cert *A*

Despite being married to Caroline (*Gladys Cooper*), Mark (*John Justin*) has four great red-headed loves in his life - and they have all looked the same (*Moira Shearer*). When he, as an elderly man, is caught out in his involvement with the last of these, he finds out that Caroline has known all along. That night, he fails to recognize the aged first redhead among his guests. Gently witty romantic comedy rather lacking charm and personality.

RoC *Roland Culver, Denholm Elliott, Harry Andrews, Patricia Cutts, Moyra Fraser, John Hart, Joan Benham, Jeremy Spenser, Melvyn Hayes.*

THE MAN WHO NEVER WAS (1955) [4]

Dir *Ronald Neame.* Prod *André Hakim.* Scr *Nigel Balchin, from the book by Ewen Montagu.* Ph *Oswald Morris.* PC *Sumar.* Dis *20th Century-Fox.* Eastman Colour. CinemaScope. 103 mins. Cert *U*

1943. A body is washed ashore off the Spanish coast, its pockets bearing secret papers telling of an Allied invasion through Greece. The Germans send O'Reilly (*Stephen Boyd*) to check their authenticity. Through his visits to the parents of Commander Montagu (*Clifton Webb*) who thought up the scheme, and Lucy (*Gloria Grahame*), genuinely grieving over a dead fiancé that O'Reilly believes to be the drowned man, the Germans are fooled. True story, riveting all through. British Oscar for best screenplay.

RoC *Robert Flemyng, Josephine Griffin, Laurence Naismith, Geoffrey Keen, Moultrie Kelsall, Cyril Cusack, André Morell, Michael Hordern, Allan Cuthbertson, Joan Hickson, Terence Longdon, Gibb McLaughlin, Miles Malleson, William Russell, Richard Wattis, Wolf Frees, Brian Oulton, Ronald Adam, Peter Williams, D.A. Clarke-Smith, Ewen Montagu, Peter Sellers (voice), Michael Brill, John Welsh, Cecily Paget-Bowman, Robert Brown, Everley Gregg, Joan Hickson, Lloyd Lamble, Gordon Bell, Gerhard Puritz.*

Laurence Naismith, Clifton Webb and Robert Flemyng in The Man Who Never Was *(1955)*

THE MAN WHO WATCHED TRAINS GO BY (1952)   3
(USA: *Paris Express*)
Dir and Scr *Harold French, from the novel by George Simenon.* Prod and PC *Raymond Stross-Joseph Shaftel.* Ph *Otto Heller.* Dis *Eros.* Technicolor. 80 mins. Cert A

Kees (*Claude Rains*), head clerk of a highly respected Dutch firm, is shattered to discover that his boss (*Herbert Lom*) is spending the company's assets on a woman in Paris. They fight, and the boss accidentally drowns. Kees flees to Paris, and contacts the girl (*Marta Toren*), who betrays him to the police. He kills her with a breadknife. Kees tries to commit suicide, but the train he throws himself under switches to another track. His mind cracks up, and he is taken away by the authorities. Downbeat drama, oddly in colour.

RoC *Marius Goring, Anouk (Aimée), Lucie Mannheim, Felix Aylmer, Eric Pohlmann, Ferdy Mayne, Gibb McLaughlin, Joan St Clair, Mary Mackenzie, Robin Alalouf, Michael Alain, Jean Deveaux, Roy Purcell, MacDonald Parke, Michael Nightingale.*

THE MAN WHO WOULDN'T TALK (1957)   2
Dir and Prod *Herbert Wilcox.* Scr *Edgar Lustgarten, from a novel by Stanley Jackson.* Ph

Gordon Dines. PC *Everest.* Dis *British Lion.* 97 mins. Cert U

Following a visit to a Hungarian scientist who has sworn them to secrecy after telling them of germ warfare tests, Dr Smith (*Anthony Quayle*) and Eve (*Zsa Zsa Gabor*), a secret agent, surprise an intruder in their hotel. Smith's gun fires, Eve is killed and Smith, charged with her murder, refuses to talk because of his secrecy oath. Mary Randall (*Anna Neagle*), his QC, gets him off, in spite of his silence, with a brilliant defence. Dull, plodding drama.

RoC *Katherine Kath, Patrick Allen, Lloyd Lamble, Hugh McDermott, Dora Bryan, Leonard Sachs, John Welsh, John Paul, John le Mesurier, Edward Lexy, David Aylmer, Ballard Berkeley, Gordon Whiting, Anthony Sharp, Anthony Pendrell, Jan Conrad, Diana King, Jennifer Jayne, Graham Stewart, Anthony Woodruff, John Harvey, Cyril Chamberlain, Norman Mitchell, Alice Gachet, Neal Arden, Keith Banks, Lorraine Clewes, Jeff Shane, Middleton Woods.*

MAN WITH A GUN (1958)   3
Dir *Montgomery Tully.* Prod *Jack Greenwood.* Scr *Michael Winner.* Ph *John Wiles.* PC *Merton Park.* Dis *Anglo-Amalgamated.* 60 mins. Cert U

Investigating the burning-down of a nightclub, Mike (*Lee Patterson*), an insurance detective, at first suspects the owner (*John le Mesurier*) of arson. But, through the owner's niece (*Rona Anderson*), Mike comes to realize the fire is the work of a gang trying to start a London protection racket. With the help of the police, Mike destroys it. Embryo director's first script not a winner, but direction keeps brisk pace.

RoC *Warren Mitchell, Glen Mason, Harold Lang, Cyril Chamberlain, Carlo Borelli, Jack Taylor, Richard Shaw, Alec Finter, Joe Gibbons, Peter Thornton.*

THE MAN WITHOUT A BODY (1957)   1
Dir *W. Lee Wilder, Charles Saunders.* Prod *Wilder, Guido Coen.* Scr *William Grote.* Ph *Brendan Stafford.* PC *Filmplays,* Dis *Eros.* 78 mins. Cert X

Discovering that he has an inoperable brain tumour, and that a young surgeon has discovered a means of revitalizing dead tissue by brain manipulation, mad financier Karl Brussard (*George Coulouris*) steals the head of 16th-century astrologer Nostradamus. The 'head' leads him financially astray, however, and his wife (*Nadja Regin*) leaves him for the surgeon's assistant. Brussard kills her and maims her lover, whose head is severed by the surgeon in order to graft on the head of Nostradamus. The 'creature' then throws Brussard from the top of a bell-tower. Over-acted horror is even more absurd than synopsis sounds.

RoC *Julia Arnall, Robert Hutton, Sheldon Lawrence, Peter Copley, Michael Golden, Norman Shelley, Tony Quinn, Kim Parker.*

THE MARCH HARE (1956)   3
Dir *George More O'Ferrall.* Prod *Bertram Ostrer, Albert Fennell.* Scr *Gordon Wellesley, Allan Mackinnon, Paul Vincent Carroll, from*

a novel by *T.H. Bird.* Ph *Jack Hildyard.* PC *Achilles.* Dis *British Lion.* Eastman Colour. CinemaScope. 85 mins. Cert U

Impoverished Irish baronet Sir Charles Hare (*Terence Morgan*) has one racehorse left. Reared on eggs and cream, and trained by drunken Lazy Mangan (*Cyril Cusack*), who is allegedly in league with the 'Fairy Queen', the horse wins the Derby and Sir Charles the love of an American heiress. Curdled whimsy kept afloat by Cusack's sly playing. Philip Green's theme music was a big hit.

RoC *Peggy Cummins, Martita Hunt, Derrick de Marney, Wilfrid Hyde White, Charles Hawtrey, Maureen Delaney, Macdonald Parke, Ivan Samson, Reginald Beckwith, Stringer Davis, Clem Lister, Peter Swanwick, Charles Wade, John Gilbert, Fred Johnson, Bernard Rook.*

MARILYN (1953)
See Roadhouse Girl.

MARK OF THE PHOENIX (1957)   2
Dir *Maclean Rogers.* Prod *W.G. Chalmers.* Scr *Norman Hudis.* Ph *Geoffrey Faithfull.* PC and Dis *Butchers.* 64 mins. Cert U

A gang of international crooks kill a Belgian metallurgist, steal a sample of the radium-resistant alloy he's invented and force a jeweller to fashion a cigarette case from it. The case is planted on a jewel thief (*Sheldon Lawrence*), who will hopefully take it to East Germany. Instead, he tries to sell it to the leader of the gang – but survives to hand it over to the police. Feverishly complicated thriller, not too well acted.

RoC *Julia Arnall, Anton Diffring, Eric Pohlmann, George Margo, Martin Miller, Michael Peake, Roger Delgado, Bernard Rebel, Frederick Schrecker, Pierre Chaminade, Corinne Grey, Jennifer Jayne, Edouard Assaly, Victor Beaumont, Norma Parnell, Howard Green, Tom Clegg.*

MASK OF DUST (1954)   3
(USA: *Race for Life*)
Dir *Terence Fisher.* Prod *Mickey Delamar.* Scr *Paul Tabori, Richard Landau, from the novel by Jon Manchip White.* Ph *Jimmy Harvey.* PC *Hammer.* Dis *Exclusive.* 79 mins. Cert U

Bedevilled by injury and bad luck, Peter Wells (*Richard Conte*) continues his career as a racing driver in spite of the opposition of his wife Pat (*Mari Aldon*). After his best friend is killed, she leaves him; he is suspended for pulling out of the race to attend his dying friend, but is later reinstated and wins his next race heroically, despite being burned. He quits and Pat returns. Serviceable drama with well-integrated racing sequences.

RoC *George Coulouris, Peter Illing, Alec Mango, Meredith Edwards, James Copeland, Jeremy Hawk, Richard Marner, Edwin Richfield, Tim Turner, Stirling Moss, Reg Parnell, John Cooper, Alan Brown, Geoffrey Taylor.*

THE MASTER OF BALLANTRAE (1953)   4
Dir *William Keighley.* Prod *No credit.* Scr *Herb Meadow, Harold Medford, Robert Hall, T.J. Morrison, from the novel by Robert Louis Steven-*

Errol Flynn in The Master of Ballantrae *(1953)*

son. Ph *Jack Cardiff.* PC and Dis *Warner Bros. Technicolor. 88 mins. Cert U*
1745. Joining Bonnie Prince Charlie's rebellion on the toss of a coin with his brother Henry (*Anthony Steel*), Jamie Durisdeer (*Errol Flynn*) tastes defeat, escapes the English, sails off to pastures new, becomes a pirate captain, returns home to claim Alison (*Beatrice Campbell*) - now about to marry Henry, and is captured through the treachery of jealous Jessie (*Yvonne Furneaux*); later she dies to help him escape, and he and Alison ride away. Lively, beautifully photographed action yarn has very little to do with the book.
RoC *Roger Livesey, Mervyn Johns, Felix Aylmer, Jacques Berthier, Charles Goldner, Ralph Truman, Francis de Wolff, Moultrie Kelsall, Charles Carson, Jack Taylor, Stephen Vercoe.*

THE MASTER PLAN (1954)   3
Dir and Scr *Hugh Raker* (*Cy Endfield*), *from a TV play by Harold Bratt.* Prod *Charles A. Leeds, Steven Pallos.* Ph *Jonah Jones.* PC *Gibraltar.* Dis *Grand National. 78 mins. Cert U*
Baffled by security leaks, Col Cleaver (*Norman Wooland*) calls in American Major Brent (*Wayne Morris*), unaware that he suffers from blackouts which make him easy prey for enemy agents who make him their tool. Thanks to his secretary (*Mary Mackenzie*), Cleaver rumbles the game, revealing his own fiancée (*Tilda Thamar*) as the spies' leader. Quietly efficient, rather dialogue-heavy drama.
RoC *Arnold Bell, Marjorie Stewart, Laurie Main, Frederick Schrecker, Seymour Green, Lucienne Hill, Alan Tilvern, John Gabriel, Richard Marner.*

MEET ME TONIGHT (1952)   4
Dir *Anthony Pelissier.* Prod *Anthony Havelock-Allan.* Scr *Noël Coward, from his stage playlets.* Ph *Desmond Dickinson.* PC *British Film Makers.* Dis *General Film Distributors. Technicolor. 85 mins. Cert A*
Three 'playlets'. *Red Peppers*: backstage, music hall entertainers Lily (*Kay Walsh*) and George (*Ted Ray*) bicker continually, but present a united front against mutual enemies, causing a riot in the theatre. *Fumed Oak*: nagged by mother-in-law, wife and daughter, Henry (*Stanley Holloway*) eventually leaves and heads for the South Seas. *Ways and Means*: spongers Stella and Tony (*Valerie Hobson, Nigel Patrick*) scrounge, gamble and thieve on the Riviera.

Polished, amusing and talky: Coward also wrote the music.
RoC *Martita Hunt, Frank Pettingell, Bill Fraser, Toke Townley, Ian Wilson, Frank's Fox Terriers, Young China Troupe; Betty Ann Davies, Mary Merrall, Dorothy Gordon; Jack Warner, Jessie Royce Landis, Michael Trubshawe, Mary Jerrold, Yvonne Furneaux, Jacques Cey.*

MEET MR CALLAGHAN (1954)   3
Dir *Charles Saunders.* Prod *Guido Coen, Derrick de Marney.* Scr *Brock Williams, from the play by Gerald Verner and a novel by Peter Cheyney.* Ph *Harry Waxman.* PC *Pinnacle.* Dis *Eros. 89 mins. Cert A*
Cynthis (*Harriette Johns*) hires private eye Slim Callaghan (*Derrick de Marney*) when her uncle changes his will in her favour . . . she says. When Slim finds out uncle is already dead, he switches his suspicions from the three former beneficiaries to Cynthis herself - but finally tags Cynthis' fiancé (*Robert Adair*) as the killer. Sort of street-level *Thin Man* is effective thick ear, short on charm.
PoC *Peter Neil, Adrienne Corri, Delphi Lawrence, Belinda Lee, Larry Burns, John Longden, Trevor Reid, Roger Williams, Frank Henderson, Michael Balfour, Michael Partridge, Howard Douglas, Frank Sieman.*

MEET MR LUCIFER (1953)   3
Dir *Anthony Pelissier.* Prod *Monja Danischewsky.* Scr *Danischewsky, Peter Myers, Alec Graham, from a play by Arnold Ridley.* Ph *Desmond Dickinson.* PC *Ealing Studios.* Dis *General Film Distributors. 83 mins. Cert U*
Sam (*Stanley Holloway*), a pantomime demon king, is accidentally knocked out. He finds himself in Hell with Mr Lucifer (also Holloway). He tells Sam TV is making people too happy; he wants it to make them miserable. Sam sets to work with initial success, but the passing from hand to hand of a TV set only eventually leads to the reconciliation of a young couple. Sam finds himself back with Mr Lucifer . . . Satirical comedy has few teeth.
RoC *Peggy Cummins, Jack Watling, Joseph Tomelty, Barbara Murray, Humphrey Lestocq, Gordon Jackson, Jean Cadell, Kay Kendall, Charles Victor, Olive Sloane, Ernest Thesiger, Raymond Huntley, Frank Pettingell, Joan Sims, Ian Carmichael, Gilbert Harding, MacDonald Hobley, Philip Harben, Eddie Leslie, Gladys Henson, Edie Martin, Dandy Nichols, Roddy Hughes, Irene Handl, Eliot Makeham, Bill Fraser, Molly Hamley-Clifford, Toke Townley, Fred Griffiths, Herbert C. Walton, Diane Cilento.*

MEET MR MALCOLM (1953)   1
Dir *Daniel Birt.* Prod *Theo Lageard.* Scr *Brock Williams.* Ph *Hone Glendinning.* PC *Corsair.* Dis *AB-Pathé. 65 mins. Cert U*
The body of a successful business man is found at the foot of a cliff. The only clues are two cigarette-ends and an empty packet. A young detective-story writer (*Richard Gale*) helps the police on to the fact that the answer is involved with shady business deals and a stolen chemical formula. Dull, unimpressive thriller.
RoC *Sarah Lawson, Adrianne Allen, Duncan Lamont, Pamela Galloway, Meredith Edwards,*

John Horsley, John Blythe, Claude Dampier, Nigel Green, Simone Lovell, Jean St Clair, Derek Prentice.

MELBA (1953)   4
Dir *Lewis Milestone.* Prod *S.P. Eagle* (*Sam Spiegel*). Scr *Harry Kurnitz.* Ph *Ted Scaife, Arthur Ibbetson.* PC *Horizon.* Dis *United Artists. Technicolor. 120 mins. Cert U*
Nellie Mitchell (*Patrice Munsel*), an Australian farmer's daughter with a fine singing voice, trains in Paris in the early 1880s to become professional, eventually gaining a reputation as the finest soprano of her day. Her fiancé from Australia, Charles (*John McCallum*), arrives and marries her. But he cannot live with her fame, and they part. Rose-coloured view of singer's life; well-dressed, -directed and -sung.
RoC *Robert Morley, John Justin, Alec Clunes, Martita Hunt, Sybil Thorndike, Joseph Tomelty, Beatrice Varley, Cecile Chevreau, Violetta Elvin, Charles Craig.*

MEN AGAINST THE SUN (1953)   3
Dir and Ph *Brendan J. Stafford.* Prod and Scr *Alastair Scobie.* PC *Kenya Films.* Dis *Monarch. 65 mins. Cert U*
Hawker (*John Bentley*), a young engineer, undertakes to oversee the building of a railway from Mombasa to Uganda. His task is complicated by marauding lions and by a missionary doctor (*Zena Marshall*) who insists on coming along. He kills the lions, marries the doctor and sees the railway through. A Kenya-Britain co-production, the first. Drama is ordinary, but the settings make it worthwhile.
RoC *Alan Tarlton, Liam O'Laoghaire, Edward Johnson, Ambrose, Shanti Pandit, Flavia Andrade, K.A. Kolhatker.*

MEN OF SHERWOOD FOREST (1954)   4
Dir *Val Guest.* Prod *Michael Carreras.* Scr *Allan Mackinnon.* Ph *Jimmy Harvey.* PC *Hammer.* Dis *Exclusive. Eastman Colour. 77 mins. Cert U*
1150. Robin Hood (*Don Taylor*) is persuaded by two nobles whom he believes (falsely) to be loyal to the absent King Richard (*Patrick Holt*) to recover secret plans for the king's rescue from captivity in Germany. Though disguised as a troubadour, Robin is betrayed and captured. Lady Alys (*Eileen Moore*) and the merrie men help him escape in time to foil an intended ambush on the returning Richard. Good romp, in even lighter vein then usual.
RoC *Reginald Beckwith, David King-Wood, John Van Eyssen, Douglas Wilmer, Harold Lang, Leslie Linder, Vera Pearce, John Kerr (British), John Stuart, Raymond Rollett, Leonard Sachs, Toke Townley, Bernard Bresslaw, Jackie Lane.*

MIDNIGHT EPISODE (1950)   3
Dir *Gordon Parry.* Prod *Theo Lagard.* Scr *Rita Barisse, Reeve Taylor, Paul Vincent, from a novel by Georges Simenon.* Ph *Hone Glendinning.* PC *Triangle.* Dis *Columbia. 78 mins. Cert A*
A busker (*Stanley Holloway*) stumbles across a dead body and a lot of money in a wallet. He hands the money to police, but keeps the wallet, hoping to claim a reward. But the wallet contains an important clue to the identity of the

killer, who comes after the busker before police move in and rescue him. Remake of French film *Monsieur La Souris*: thriller content works better than the comedy.

RoC *Leslie Dwyer, Reginald Tate, Meredith Edwards, Wilfrid Hyde White, Joy Shelton, Natasha Parry, Leslie Perrins, Sebastian Cabot, Raymond Young, Campbell Copelin.*

THE MILLION POUND NOTE (1953) [4]
(USA: *Man with a Million*)
Dir *Ronald Neame.* Prod *John Bryan.* Scr *Jill Craigie, from the story by Mark Twain.* Ph *Geoffrey Unsworth.* PC *Group.* Dis *General Film Distributors.* Technicolor. 91 mins. Cert U

Two wealthy brothers (*Ronald Squire, Wilfrid Hyde White*) in England, 1900, make a bet over whether a man could live on a million pound note without actually spending any of it. They select a penniless American seaman (*Gregory Peck*) and at first the experiment is a wild success – until the note is stolen and the seaman finds himself beset by creditors. Later the note is returned and the seaman, having made money on the Stock Exchange, is able to settle down to a comfortable life. Zestful romp with mild satirical undertones; bland leading performances.
RoC *Jane Griffiths, A.E. Matthews, Joyce Grenfell, Maurice Denham, Reginald Beckwith, Brian Oulton, John Slater, Hartley Power, George Devine, Bryan Forbes, Ann Gudrun, Hugh Wakefield, Ernest Thesiger, Wilbur Evans, Ronald Adam, Joan Hickson, Eliot Makeham, Richard Caldicot, Hugh Latimer, Jack McNaughton, John Kelly, Harold Goodwin.*

THE MINIVER STORY (1950) [3]
Dir *H.C. Potter.* Prod *Sidney Franklin.* Scr *Ronald Millar, George Froeschel, from characters created by Jan Struther.* Ph *Joseph Ruttenberg.* PC and Dis *M-G-M British.* 104 mins. Cert U
A sequel to the Hollywood-made *Mrs Miniver*. It is 1945. Mrs M. (*Greer Garson*) welcomes her family back from the war, although knowing that she has only a year to live. She cures her daughter (*Cathy O'Donnell*) of an infatuation for a middle-aged man, and sees her married off to someone of her own age, before dying in the midst of her family. Sentiment piled on with a trowel.
RoC *Walter Pidgeon, John Hodiak, Leo Genn, Henry Wilcoxon, Reginald Owen, Anthony Bushell, Richard Gale, Peter Finch, William (James) Fox, Alison Leggatt, Cicely Paget-Bowman.*

MIRACLE IN SOHO (1957) [3]
Dir *Julian Amyes.* Prod and Scr *Emeric Pressburger.* Ph *Christopher Challis.* PC and Dis *Rank.* Eastman Colour. 98 mins. Cert U
Michael (*John Gregson*), the Casanova of his road gang, who loves the girls and leaves them when the roadmending job's done, moves into Soho, flirts with the local barmaid and captures the heart of Julia (*Belinda Lee*), the daughter of an Italian family about to emigrate to Canada. When his work is done, Julia prays for his return – and a water-main bursts, bringing Michael back. Sticky romantic comedy set in never-never Soho.
RoC *Cyril Cusack, Peter Illing, Rosalie Crutchley, Marie Burke, Ian Bannen, Brian Bedford,*

Barbara Archer, John Cairney, Billie Whitelaw, Lane Meddick, Julian Somers, Harry Brunning, Douglas Ives, George A. Cooper, Cyril Shaps, Richard Marner, Betty Shale, Junia Crawford, Michael Collins, Colin Douglas, George Eugeniou, Lucia Guillon, Gordon Humphris.

MISS ROBIN HOOD (1952) [2]
Dir *John Guillermin.* Prod *Donald Wilson.* Scr *Val Valentine, Patrick Campbell.* Ph *Arthur Grant.* PC *Group 3.* Dis *Associated British.* 78 mins. Cert U
Mild Henry Wrigley (*Richard Hearne*), who writes vivid adventure stories for girls, leads an orderly life until he encounters Miss Honey (*Margaret Rutherford*), an eccentric fan who involves him in a scheme to recover a secret whisky formula stolen from her forefathers. They succeed (and Wrigley quits his job), but ultimately return the formula in return for a distillery partnership. Miss Honey invades the publisher with scores of schoolgirls and Wrigley gets his job back. Would-be Ealing-style comedy is too silly for words.
RoC *Michael Medwin, Edward Lexy, Frances Rowe, Eunice Gayson, Sidney James, Peter Jones, James Robertson Justice, Dora Bryan, Eric Berry, Russell Waters, Reg Varney, Suzanne Gibbs, Francis de Wolff.*

MISS TULIP STAYS THE NIGHT
(1955) [1]
Dir *Leslie Arliss.* Prod *John O'Douglas.* Scr *Douglas, Bill Luckwell, Jack Hulbert.* Ph *Kent Talbot.* PC *Jaywell.* Dis *Adelphi.* 68 mins. Cert U
Andrew and Kate Dax (*Patrick Holt, Diana Dors*) are disturbed late at night by the eccentric Miss Tulip (*Cicely Courtneidge*) who demands a bed, and hands over a gun and some jewellery. In the morning, she is found dead. PC Feathers (*Jack Hulbert*) suspects Andrew, and is about to arrest him when Miss Tulip's twin sister Angela arrives. But Andrew deduces that the newcomer is Miss Tulip, who has murdered Angela for her money. Miss Tulip, now quite mad, is taken away. Hulbert and Courtneidge far from past glories in astoundingly cardboard comedy-thriller.
RoC *A.E. Matthews, Joss Ambler, Pat Terry-Thomas, George Roderick, Brian Oulton.*

MOBY DICK (1956) [4]
Dir *John Huston.* Prod *Huston, Vaughan N. Dean.* Scr *Huston, Ray Bradbury, from the book by Herman Melville.* Ph *Oswald Morris, Freddie Francis.* PC *Moulin.* Dis *Warner Bros.* Technicolor. 114 mins. Cert U
1840 in New Bedford. Ishmael (*Richard Basehart*), a young sailor, signs on with the whaling ship *Pequod*, whose captain, Ahab (*Gregory Peck*) is obsessed with killing a great white whale to which he has already lost a leg. The whale, Moby Dick, is tracked down but proves unkillable. Ahab is last sighted lashed to the whale's back still trying to kill it, while all his crew save Ishmael perish. Striking but slightly pretentious version of a famous yarn. Ending is very exciting if a long time coming.
RoC *Leo Genn, James Robertson Justice, Orson Welles, Harry Andrews, Bernard Miles, Noel*

Gregory Peck in Moby Dick *(1956)*

Purcell, Edric Connor, Mervyn Johns, Joseph Tomelty, Friedrich Ledebur, Philip Stainton, Royal Dano, Seamus Kelly, Tamba Alleney, Francis de Wolff, Ted Howard, Tom Clegg.

MODEL FOR MURDER (1959) [2]
Dir *Terry Bishop.* Prod *Robert Dunbar.* Scr *Bishop, Dunbar.* Ph *Petter Hennessy.* PC *Parroch.* Dis *British Lion.* 73 mins. Cert U
Searching for his late brother's girlfriend in London, David (*Keith Andes*), a US Navy officer, sees her murdered, is knocked out and wakes up to find himself framed for a jewellery theft and the girl's murder. With the help of the girl's friend (*Hazel Court*), David catches up with the real criminals at London Airport. Spirited cast can't do much with very routine thriller.
RoC *Michael Gough, Jean Aubrey, Peter Hammond, Patricia Jessel, Alfred Burke, Julia Arnall, Howard Marion Crawford, Edwin Richfield, Richard Pearson, George Benson, Neil Hallett, Diane Bester, Barbara Archer, Annabel Maule, Charles Lamb.*

MOMENT OF INDISCRETION (1958) [1]
Dir *Max Varnel.* Prod *Edward J. Danziger, Harry Lee Danziger.* Scr *Brian Clemens, Eldon Howard.* Ph *Jimmy Wilson.* PC *Danzigers.* Dis *United Artists.* 72 mins. Cert U
Going to say goodbye to an old flame before he leaves the country for good, Janet (*Lana Morris*) witnesses a murder. She drops her handkerchief by the body. Reluctant to tell her husband (*Ronald Howard*), she is compelled to when the handkerchief is traced and she is arrested for murder. Her husband gets cracking and helps trap the real killer. Inept thriller, passably acted but weakly written.
RoC *Denis Shaw, John Van Eyssen, John Witty, Ann Lynn, John Stone, Arnold Bell, Judy Bruce, Piers Keelan, Mark Singleton, Totti Truman Taylor, Walter Horsbrugh, Stuart Saunders, Robert Dorning, Brian Haines.*

THE MOONRAKER (1958) [4]
Dir *David Macdonald.* Prod *Hamilton G. Inglis.* Scr *Robert Hall, Wilfrid Eades, Alistair Bell, from the play by Arthur Watkyn.* Ph *Max Greene (Mutz Greenbaum).* PC *Associated British.* Dis *AB-Pathe.* Technicolor. 82 mins. Cert U
1651. As the mysterious Moonraker, the Earl of Dawlish (*George Baker*) helps fellow-Royalists escape the executioner's axe. Escorting Prince

Charles (*Gary Raymond*) en route to the Channel, he runs into a trap, but fights his way out. Danger looms again at a coastal inn, from Cromwellians Gregg (*Peter Arne*) and Beaumont (*Marius Goring*), whose fiancée (*Sylvia Syms*) falls for Dawlish. He allows himself to be taken so that the Prince may flee, then escapes and swims to a waiting ship. Enough action for a dozen swashbucklers; its director's best film for some years.

RoC *Richard Leech, Clive Morton, Paul Whitsun-Jones, Iris Russell, John le Mesurier, Patrick Troughton, Michael Anderson Jr, Patrick Waddington, Julian Somers, Sylvia Bidmead, Frances Rowe, Jennifer Browne, Richard Warner, George Woodbridge, Victor Brooks, Frank Hawkins, Keith Banks, Victor Platt, Gillian Vaughan, Edward Dentith, Leslie Linder, John Crocker.*

MORE DEADLY THAN THE MALE
(1958)   [1]
Dir, Prod, Scr and Ph *Robert Bucknell, from the novel by Paul Chevalier. PC UNA. Dis Cross-Channel. Eastman Colour. 60 mins. Cert X*
Saul (*Jeremy White*), an American on holiday in England, is seduced by Estelle (*Ann Davy*) and kills her husband. His fiancée arrives and is killed by Estelle. A vengeful Saul kills Estelle. He lines up all the bodies in a deserted blockhouse, in which he is irretrievably locked by the husband's mother. Saul shoots himself. Early sexploitationer, with a concentration on bodies, dead and alive.

RoC *Edna Doré, Lorraine Peters, John Mahoney.*

MORNING CALL (1957)   [1]
(USA: *The Strange Case of Dr Manning*)
Dir *Arthur Crabtree*. Prod *Derek Winn, Bill Luckwell*. Scr *Paul Tabori, Luckwell, Tom Waldron*. Ph *James Harvey*. PC *Winwell*. Dis *Astral. 75 mins. Cert A*
To the consternation of Annette Manning (*Greta Gynt*), whose husband has been kidnapped, the detective (*Ron Randell*) she hires calls in the police and, what with them and the Press, she finds it difficult to deliver the ransom without scaring the kidnapper away. She does so finally, but Dr Manning is then found dead, and the kidnapper falls to his death after a fight with the detective. Inept thriller, barely released.

RoC *Bruce Seton, Charles Farrell, Virginia Keiley, Garard Green, Wally Patch.*

MOTHER RILEY MEETS THE VAMPIRE (1952)   [2]
(USA: *Vampire Over London*)
Dir and Prod *John Gilling*. Scr *Val Valentine*. Ph *Stan Pavey, Dudley Lovell*. PC and Dis *Renown. 74 mins. Cert U*
Von Housen (*Bela Lugosi*), a sinister foreign scientist known as 'The Vampire', is wanted for questioning by Scotland Yard in connection with a number of mysterious disappearances. But the Yard cannot track him down and it is his housekeeper, Mrs Riley (*Arthur Lucan*) who brings both 'The Vampire' and his fiendish robot to destruction. Very poor script brought famous comedy series to a close.

RoC *Dora Bryan, Richard Wattis, Judith Furse,*

Philip Leaver, Maria Mercedes, Roderick Lovell, David Hurst, Hattie Jacques, Graham Moffatt, Dandy Nichols, Cyril Smith, Ian Wilson, Charles Lloyd-Pack, Arthur Brander, Peter Bathurst, George Benson, David Hannaford, Bill Shine, John le Mesurier.

MOULIN ROUGE (1952)   [4]
Dir *John Huston*. Prod *Huston, Jack Clayton*. Scr *Huston, Anthony Veiller, from the book by Pierre la Mure*. Ph *Oswald Morris*. PC *Romulus*. Dis *British Lion/Independent Film Distributors. Technicolor. 120 mins. Cert A*
1890. The dwarf painter Toulouse-Lautrec (*José Ferrer*) whose works depict the vivid nightlife of Paris's Montmartre, becomes infatuated with a prostitute (*Colette Marchand*), from whom he finally parts. He also becomes friends with an artist's model (*Suzanne Flon*) but, through his own self-doubt, loses the chance to marry her. Sinking ever deeper into alcohol, he is eventually taken home to his family château, to die at only 37. Brilliant recreation of the colourful scene painted by the artist, but the drama eventually becomes monotonous. Oscars for art direction and costume design; amazingly Oswald Morris failed to win for colour photography.

RoC *Zsa Zsa Gabor, Claude Nollier, Katherine Kath, Muriel Smith, Mary Clare, Walter Crisham, Harold Kasket, Jim Gerald, Georges Lannes, Lee Montague, Maureen Swanson, Tutte Lemkow, Jill Bennett, Theodore Bikel, Rupert John, Peter Cushing, Eric Pohlmann, Arissa Cooper, Charles Carson, Walter Cross, Francis de Wolff, Michael Balfour, Christopher Lee, Jean Landier, Robert Le Fort, René Poirier, Margaret Maxwell, Hilary Allen, Maria Samina, Sari Luzita, Sheila Nelson, Aleta Morrison, Hugh Dempster, Charles Perry, Tim Turner, Michael Seavers, Bernard Rebel, Christopher Rhodes, René Laplat, Maria Britneva, Charles Reynolds, Ina de la Haye, Richard Molinas, Isobel George, Donovan Winter, Madge Brindley, Peter Haddon, Everley Gregg, Raymond Rollett, David Garth, Anthony Gray, Terence O'Regan, Diane Cilento.*

José Ferrer in Moulin Rouge *(1953)*

THE MOUSE THAT ROARED (1959)   [4]
Dir *Jack Arnold*. Prod *Jon Penington*. Scr *Roger Macdougall, Stanley Mann, from the novel by Leonard Wibberley*. Ph *John Wilcox*. PC *Open Road*. Dis *Columbia. Technicolor. 90 mins. Cert U*
On the verge of bankruptcy because America

has successfully imitated its wine, the European duchy of Grand Fenwick declares war, expecting to be generously reimbursed in defeat. Tully Bascombe (*Peter Sellers*), who leads Fenwick's chainmailed invaders, is unaware he is supposed to lose and, capturing the Q-bomb, the world's deadliest weapon, brings America to its knees. He ousts Fenwick's scheming premier (also Sellers), negotiates a treaty between the USA and Queen Gloriana (also Sellers) and becomes a national hero – even though the Q-bomb proves to be a dud. Lots of funny moments in inventive satire.

RoC *Jean Seberg, William Hartnell, David Kossoff, Leo McKern, MacDonald Parke, Austin Willis, Timothy Bateson, Monty Landis, Colin Gordon, George Margo, Harold Krasker, Robin Gatehouse, Jacques Cey, Stuart Saunders, Ken Stanley, Bill Nagy, Mavis Villiers, Charles Clay, Harry de Bray, Bill Edwards.*

Peter Sellers in The Mouse That Roared *(1959)*

MR DENNING DRIVES NORTH
(1951)   [3]
Dir *Anthony Kimmins*. Prod *Kimmins, Stephen Mitchell*. Scr *Alec Coppel from his novel*. Ph *John Wilcox*. PC *London Films*. Dis *British Lion. 93 mins. Cert A*
Wealthy Tom Denning (*John Mills*), learning his daughter Liz (*Eileen Moore*) is having an affair with an international crook (*Herbert Lom*), goes to see the man to buy him off, but accidentally kills him. He dumps the body in a motorway ditch, but a gipsy finds it, steals a ring and is accused of murder. The daughter's lawyer fiancé (*Sam Wanamaker*) comes close to proving the truth, which is realized by Liz when she removes vital evidence which might have incriminated her father. Film walks tightrope between comedy and suspense with varying success.

RoC *Phyllis Calvert, Raymond Huntley, Bernard Lee, Wilfrid Hyde White, Freda Jackson, Sheila Shand Gibbs, Trader Faulkner, Russell Waters, John Stuart, Ronald Adam, Michael Shepley, Hugh Morton, David Davies, Ambrosine Phillpotts, Herbert C. Walton, John Stevens, Lyn Evans, John Warren, Raymond Francis, Edward Evans.*

MR DRAKE'S DUCK (1950)   [4]
Dir and Scr *Val Guest, from the radio play by Ian Messiter*. Prod *Daniel Angel, Douglas Fairbanks Jr*. Ph *Jack Cox*. PC *Angel Productions*. Dis *Eros. 85 mins. Cert U*

Newlywed city-dwellers Don and Penny Drake (*Douglas Fairbanks Jr, Yolande Donlan*) take on a Sussex farm and undergo a series of disasters in adapting to country life. At an auction, Penny unwittingly buys 60 ducks, one of which lays eggs with uranium content. The armed services move in while the authorities try to isolate the uranium duck. This has a devastating effect on the Drakes' farm – and even then the wrong duck is selected in the end. Popular, brightly-played farce.

RoC *A.E. Matthews, Jon Pertwee, Reginald Beckwith, Wilfrid Hyde White, Howard Marion Crawford, Peter Butterworth, Tom Gill, John Boxer.*

MR H.C. ANDERSEN (1950) [1]

Dir and Prod *Ronald Haines*. Cartoon dir *Leon Boje*. Scr *Ronald and Jean Haines*. Ph *W.R. Hutchinson*. PC and Dis *British Foundation*. 62 mins. Cert U

The life story of Danish author Hans Christian Anderson, with animated versions of his fairy stories and *Ali Baba and the 40 Thieves* thrown in for good measure. Poorly done mini-biopic runs like a fifth-form play.

LP *Ashley Glynne, Constance Lewis, Terence Noble, Stuart Sanders, June Elvin, Edward Sullivan, Victor Rietty, Kenyon Jervis, Eric Kemp, Dafydd Havard, Mercedes Desmore, Nan Kearns, Madam van Deerbeck, Barbara Madock, Doreen Hughes, Billy Stuart, Frank Crawshaw, Jennifer Dearman, Kitty Kenehan, Charles Cooper, Charles Reynolds, Denise Hurst, Catherina Ferray, Zoë Monteanu, Marcus Innesley, Helen Hill, Eileen Cleveland.*

THE MUDLARK (1950) [3]

Dir *Jean Negulesco*. Prod and Scr *Nunnally Johnson, from the novel by Theodore Bonnet*. Ph *Georges Périnal*. PC and Dis *20th Century-Fox*. 100 mins. Cert U

Finding a medallion bearing Queen Victoria's portrait on a dead sailor by the banks of the Thames, urchin Wheeler (*Andrew Ray*) determines to meet her. Discovered and arrested, Wheeler is sent to school, but runs away and gets into Windsor Castle. He sees the Queen (*Irene Dunne*), wins royal favour, and helps bring her out of her self-imposed retirement. A little solemn and dull, but a popular if not critical hit.

RoC *Alec Guinness, Beatrice Campbell, Anthony Steel, Finlay Currie, Raymond Lovell, Marjorie Fielding, Constance Smith, Ronan O'Casey, Edward Rigby, Kynaston Reeves, Wilfrid Hyde White, Robin Stevens, William Strange, Ernest Clark, Patricia Hitchcock, Eric Messiter, Pamela Arliss, Ian Selby, Maurice Warren, Michael Brooke, Jane Short, Howard Douglas, Richmond Nairne, George Dillon, Leonard Sharp, Vi Kaley, Freddie Watts, Y. Yanai, Paul Gerrard, Leonard Morris, Marjorie Gresley, Bob Head, Vi Stevens, Alan Gordon, Grace Denbigh-Russell.*

THE MUMMY (1959) [2]

Dir *Terence Fisher*. Prod *Michael Carreras*. Scr *Jimmy Sangster*. Ph *Jack Asher*. PC *Hammer*. Dis *Universal-International*. Technicolor. 88 mins. Cert X

1896. A team of British archaeologists break into the 4000-year-old tomb of Princess Anaka, and send the mummified body to the British Museum. But Kharis (*Christopher Lee*), a priest who was entombed with her after trying to restore her to life, now rises at the behest of Mehemet (*George Pastell*) who still worships ancient gods, and kills various expedition members before expiring in a swamp. This was never the strongest of horror legends, and even Hammer can't make it bite.

RoC *Peter Cushing, Yvonne Furneaux, Raymond Huntley, Felix Aylmer, Eddie Byrne, John Stuart, Harold Goodwin, Denis Shaw, Michael Ripper, Frederick Rawlings.*

MURDER AT SCOTLAND YARD (1952) [2]

Dir *Victor M. Gover*. Prod *Gilbert Church*. Scr *John Gilling*. Ph *Ted Lloyd*. PC *Bushey*. Dis *Ambassador*. 75 mins. Cert U

Three further adventures of crime king Terence Riley (*Tod Slaughter*): see also *King of the Underworld*. Possibly originally intended for television; did not gain wide release in cinemas.

RoC *Patrick Barr, Tucker McGuire, Dorothy Bramhall, Tom Macauley, Margaret Boyd, Larry Burns.*

MURDER AT SITE THREE (1958) [2]

Dir and PC *Francis Searle*. Prod *Charles A. Leeds*. Scr *Paddy Manning O'Brine, from a novel by W. Howard Baker*. Ph *Bert Mason*. Dis *Exclusive*. 68 mins. Cert U

Following the murder of an RAF security officer at an inter-continental ballistic missile site on England's east coast, detective Sexton Blake (*Geoffrey Toone*) and his assistant Tinker (*Richard Burrell*) use a truth drug to expose the site's security chief and one of his colleagues as spies. Characterization is good, but plot and treatment very uninteresting.

RoC *Barbara Shelley, John Warwick, Jill Melford, Reed de Rouen, Harry Towb, Theodore Wilhelm, Gordon Sterne.*

MURDER AT 3 A.M. (1953) [2]

Dir *Francis Searle*. Prod and Scr *John Ainsworth*. Ph *S.D. Onions*. PC *David Henley*. Dis *Renown*. 60 mins. Cert U

A series of assaults on wealthy women from night clubs culminates in a murder. Inspector Lawton (*Dennis Price*) suspects the killer may be his sister's (*Peggy Evans*) ex-commando boyfriend (*Philip Saville*). To his embarrassment, after he has used his sister to trap the man, it turns out the killer is the commando's half-brother. Shabby 'B' feature, tiresomely made.

RoC *Greta Mayaro, Rex Garner, Arnold Bell, Leonard Sharp, Norah Gordon, Renee Goddard, Arthur Lovegrove, Daphne Maddox, Robert Weedon, John Davis.*

MURDER BY PROXY (1955) [3]
(USA: *Blackout*)

Dir *Terence Fisher*. Prod *Michael Carreras*. Scr *Richard Landau, from the novel by Helen Neilson*. Ph *Jimmy Harvey*. PC *Hammer*. Dis *Exclusive*. 87 mins. Cert A

A deadbeat American drunk, Casey (*Dane Clark*), finds himself suspected of murder after accepting £500 to marry a strange girl (*Belinda Lee*), then blacking out. Her father has been killed; shortly afterwards, her fiancé (*Andrew Osborn*) joins him. Casey pulls himself together to discover that his 'bride's' mother (*Betty Ann Davies*) is the killer. Grim, slightly dull thriller with some witty lines along the way. Made in 1953.

RoC *Eleanor Summerfield, Harold Lang, Michael Golden, Jill Melford, Delphi Lawrence, Alfie Bass, Norah Gordon, Alvys Maben, Martin Lawrence, Cleo Laine, Arnold Diamond, Verne Morgan, Charles Stanley, Arthur Lovegrove, Mark Singleton, Stafford Byrne, Alfred March, Ann Gow, Kim Mills, Frank Singuineau, Harry Brunning.*

MURDER IN THE CATHEDRAL (1951) [3]

Dir, Prod and Scr *George Hoellering, from play by T.S. Eliot*. Ph *David Kosky*. PC and Dis *Film Traders*. 136 mins. Cert U

1147. Thomas a Becket (*Father John Groser*), Archbishop of Canterbury, tussles with his conscience (represented by four tempters) on the question of the State's influence on the Church. He emerges triumphant against temptation, but is murdered by four knightly assassins. Experimental film is overlong, only partially successful.

RoC *Alexander Gauge, Donald Bisset, Clement McCallin, Michael Groser, Mark Dignam, Michael Aldridge, Leo McKern, Paul Rogers, Niall MacGinnis, David Ward, George Woodbridge, Basil Burton, Alban Blakelock, T.S. Eliot (voice).*

MURDER REPORTED (1957) [2]

Dir *Charles Saunders*. Prod *Guido Coen*. Scr *Doreen Montgomery, from a novel by Robert Chapman*. Ph *Brendan Stafford*. PC *Fortress*. Dis *Columbia*. 58 mins. Cert A

When the body of a murdered woman is found in a trunk, reporters Jeff Holly (*Paul Carpenter*) and Amanda North (*Melissa Stribling*) discover that a switch of bodies – the woman had died of natural causes – involves a local man (*Peter Swanwick*) who had murdered a councillor, listed as a missing person. Breezily acted, but crime drama evokes more laughs than thrills.

RoC *Patrick Holt, John Laurie, Trevor Reid, Georgia Brown, Maurice Durant, Yvonne Warren (Romain), Gladys Boot, David Coote, Ewen Solon, Anne Blake, Hal Osmond, Reginald Hearne.*

MURDER WITHOUT CRIME (1950) [2]

Dir and Scr *J. Lee Thompson, from his play Double Error*. Prod *Victor Skutezky*. Ph *William McLeod*. PC *Associated British*. Dis *AB-Pathé*. 97 mins (later 76). Cert A

A young author (*Derek Farr*) quarrels with his wife (*Patricia Plunkett*) who leaves him. He meets a girl (*Joan Dowling*) at a nightclub. He has a fight with her and apparently kills her. His landlord (*Dennis Price*) taunts and blackmails him, knowing the girl is still alive. The writer goes to take poison, but the suspicious

landlord switches the glasses and poisons himself. Strains credulity and patience.
No supporting cast.

MY DAUGHTER JOY (1950) [2]
(USA: *Operation X*)

Dir and Prod *Gregory Ratoff*. Scr *Robert Thoeren, William Rose, from a novel by Irene Nemirowsky*. Ph *Georges Périnal*. PC *British Lion/London Films*. Dis *British Lion*. 81 mins. Cert A

Financier George Constantin (*Edward G. Robinson*) dotes on his spoiled daughter Joy (*Peggy Cummins*) and plans a marriage for her with an eastern potentate that will start a 'new dynasty'. Joy, however, is in love with a newspaperman and when, to preserve her happiness, her mother (*Nora Swinburne*) reveals she is not George's child, the knowledge sends him out of his mind. Only marginally less silly than it sounds; Robinson's performance helps a little.

RoC *Richard Greene, Walter Rilla, Finlay Currie, James Robertson Justice, Ronald Adam, David Hutcheson, Peter Illing, Ronald Ward, Roberto Villa, Don Nehan, Harry Lane, Gregory Ratoff.*

MY DEATH IS A MOCKERY (1952) [2]

Dir *Tony Young*. Prod *David Dent*. Scr *Douglas Baber, from his novel*. Ph *Phil Grindrod*. PC *Park Lane*. Dis *Adelphi*. 75 mins. Cert A

Failing to make a go of his trawling business, John (*Donald Houston*) is induced into smuggling by Hansen (*Bill Kerr*), a racketeer who desires John's wife (*Kathleen Byron*). Caught by French police, John knocks out their French accomplice (*Edward Leslie*), accidentally killing him. Hansen thinks it murder, but helps dispose of the body. He breaks down under interrogation. John is tried and hanged. Drama is resolutely dark and glum, minimally entertaining.
No supporting cast.

MYSTERY JUNCTION (1951) [2]

Dir and Scr *Michael McCarthy*. Prod *William H. Williams*. Ph *Bob Lapresle*. PC *Merton Park*. Dis *Anglo-Amalgamated*. 67 mins. Cert A

Larry (*Sydney Tafler*), a novelist, outlines the plot of a train thriller to a fellow-traveller. A man (*Martin Benson*) being escorted to his murder trial escapes at a snowbound stop and seizes a gun. He proves, however, not to be the one who kills two others during the night, though both he and the murderer die before the police arrive. 'Novel' thriller doesn't need credibility, but lacks pace too.

RoC *Barbara Murray, Pat(ricia) Owens, Christine Silver, Philip Dale, Pearl Cameron, John Salew, Denis Webb, David Davies, Charles Irwin, Ewen Solon, Cyril Smith, Sidney Monckton, Stanley Rose.*

MYSTERY ON BIRD ISLAND (1954) [3]

Dir and Scr *John Haggerty*. Prod *Anthony Gilkison*. Ph *William Pollard*. PC *Rayant/Children's Film Foundation*. Dis *British Lion*. 57 mins. Cert U

Two holidaying children in the Channel Islands make friends with two children from Alderney, and the quartet gets itself involved with a band of smugglers (and egg thieves),

using an island bird sanctuary as base for their operations. Despite the efforts of the landowner (*Alexander Gauge*) who controls the gang, the children contact Guernsey state authorities, and put an end to the villains' activities. Breezy children's adventure with nice backgrounds.

RoC *Mavis Sage, Vernon Morris, Nicky Edmett, Jennifer Beech, Roddy Hughes, John Drake, Howard Connell, Peter Arne, Alan Mackay.*

MY TEENAGE DAUGHTER (1956) [3]
(USA: *Teenage Bad Girl*)

Dir and Prod *Herbert Wilcox*. Scr *Felicity Douglas*. Ph *Max Greene (Mutz Greenbaum)*. PC *Everest*. Dis *British Lion*. 100 mins. Cert A

Widow Valerie Carr (*Anna Neagle*) has problems with her 17-year-old daugher Jan (*Sylvia Syms*). The girl's involved with upper class ne-er-do-well Tony (*Kenneth Haigh*) who, deep in debt, tries to squeeze money out of an elderly aunt, who inconsiderately dies from a heart attack, leaving Tony facing a manslaughter charge and Jan, after a short time in prison, contrite and running home to mother. Tearstained, very English variety of the 'Rebel' film.

RoC *Norman Wooland, Wilfrid Hyde White, Helen Haye, Julia Lockwood, Josephine Fitzgerald, Wanda Ventham, Murray Mayne, Michael Shepley, Avice Landone, Michael Meacham, Grizelda Hervey, Ballard Berkeley, Edie Martin, Myrette Morven, Betty Cooper, Lesley Osmond, Launce Maraschal, Diana King, Daphne Cave, Laidman Browne.*

Sylvia Syms, Anna Neagle and Julia Lockwood in My Teenage Daughter

MY WIFE'S FAMILY (1956) [2]

Dir *Gilbert Gunn*. Prod *Hamilton Inglis*. Scr *Talbot Rothwell, Gunn, from the play by Fred Duprez*. Ph *Gilbert Taylor*. PC *Forth Films*. Dis *AB-Pathé*. Eastman Colour. 76 mins. Cert U

Dreading the arrival of his mother-in-law, Jack Gay (*Ted Ray*) enlists the aid of his friend Doc Knott (*Ronald Shiner*). The arrival of Jack's old flame Gloria (*Greta Gynt*) makes matters worse, to say nothing of a 'baby grand' that gets mistaken in people's minds for a real baby. Never mind, mother-in-law in the end is humbled by her hitherto henpecked husband. Third screen version of hoary old farce is crashingly overplayed.

RoC *Diane Hart, Fabia Drake, Robertson Hare, Zena Marshall, Jessica Cairns, Benny Lee, James Mageean, Virginia Clay, Gilbert Harding, Martin Wyldeck, Patrick Westwood, Robert*

Dickens, Charles Wright, Peggyann Clifford, Laurie Main, Frank Hawkins, Ian Whittaker, Audrey Nicholson, Ian Wilson, Charles Doran, Frank Royde.

Ted Ray and Ronald Shiner in My Wife's Family *(1956)*

MY WIFE'S LODGER (1952) [2]

Dir *Maurice Elvey*. Prod *David Dent*. Scr *Dominic Roche, Stafford Dickens, from Roche's play*. Ph *Len Harris*. PC *Advance*. Dis *Adelphi*. 80 mins. Cert A

Willie (*Dominic Roche*) returns home after six years' overseas service in the army to find his house in an uproar and a lodger firmly installed. He goes out and gets drunk, but later learns from Tex, an American, that he has inherited a ranch in Texas. The lodger is revealed to be a crook and kicked out, and Willie is master in his own home. Vulgar northern farce with ancient jokes; enthusiastically played.

RoC *Diana Dors, Leslie Dwyer, Olive Sloane, Alan Sedgwick, Vincent Downing, Vi Kaley.*

N

NAKED EARTH (1957) [3]

Dir *Vincent Sherman*. Prod *Adrian Worker*. Scr *Milton Holmes*. Ph *Erwin Hillier*. PC *Foray Films*. Dis *20th Century-Fox*. CinemaScope. 96 mins. Cert A

1894. Danny (*Richard Todd*), an Irish farmer, comes to Africa to find that his intended partner has been eaten by crocodiles. Helped by David (*John Kitzmiller*), an African Christian, and Maria (*Juliette Gréco*), the dead partner's girl, Danny persuades the natives to help plant tobacco, but they refuse to harvest it and it dies. Danny marries Maria, becomes a crocodile-hunter, but has his skins stolen by traders. David saves the skins at the cost of his own life. Depressing jungle tale.

RoC *Finlay Currie, Laurence Naismith, Christopher Rhodes, Orlando Martins, Harold Kasket, Modesta, Blasio Kiyaga.*

NAKED FURY (1959) [3]

Dir *Charles Saunders*. Prod *Guido Coen*. Scr

Brock Williams. Ph *Geoffrey Faithfull.* PC *Coenda.* Dis *Butchers.* 60 mins. Cert A

After a successful bank raid in which they kill a nightwatchman, the four robbers take his daughter hostage and hold her in an old warehouse. One of them (*Kenneth Cope*) falls in love with the girl (*Leigh Madison*); then the squabbles and in-fighting begin . . . and all four robbers end up dead. Second-feature is better than it sounds, holds the attention.

RoC *Reed de Rouen, Arthur Lovegrove, Thomas (Tommy) Eytle, Alexander Field, Ann Lynn, Arthur Gross, Marianne Brauns, Redmond Phillips, Michael Collins, Eric Woodburn, Anne Sharp, Eric Corrie, Geoffrey Denton, Denis Shaw, Katy Cashfield, Vickie Gray, Julie Cavall, Mary Deighan, Sheree Winton, Eve Eden, Jill Burrows, Norma Parnell.*

THE NAKED HEART (1950)
(Canada: *Maria Chapdelaine*)
Dir *Marc Allégret.* Prod *Nelson Scott.* Scr *Allégret, Hugh Mills, Roger Vadim, J. McLaren-Ross, C.K. Jaeger, from a novel by Louis Hémon.* Ph *Armand Thirard.* PC *Everest.* Dis *British Lion.* 96 mins. Cert U

After five years in a convent, Maria (*Michèle Morgan*) returns to her native Canadian backwoods village. She attracts her childhood sweetheart, a carefree young trapper and a man on the run. One is frozen to death, another shot, and the third looks forward to, as one critic put it, 'a lifetime of boredom with Maria'. Badly acted and atrociously scripted, this was a turkey of truly remarkable proportions. Also known as *The Naked Earth.*

RoC *Kieron Moore, Françoise Rosay, Jack Watling, Philippe Lemaire, Brian Roper, Fred Johnson, Michael Mulcaster, Nancy Price, Francis de Wolff, George Woodbridge, Catherine Bradshaw, George (G.H.) Mulcaster, Rufus Cruickshank, Harry Locke, Ewen Solon, Richard George.*

THE NAKED TRUTH (1957)
(USA: *Your Past is Showing!*)
Dir/Prod *Mario Zampi.* Scr *Michael Pertwee.* Ph *Stanley Pavey.* PC *Anglofilm/Rank.* Dis *Rank.* 92 mins. Cert U

Threatened with the exposure of their private lives in a scandal magazine run by Michael Dennis (*Dennis Price*), a novelist (*Peggy Mount*), a peer (*Terry-Thomas*), an entertainer (*Peter Sellers*) and a model (*Shirley Eaton*)

Terry-Thomas and Dennis Price in The Naked Truth *(1957)*

separately decide to bump him off. When each attempt misfires, they band together and, after he has been arrested, spring him from jail and smuggle him across the Atlantic in an airship. But it crashes. Ealing-style black comedy, full of laughs.

RoC *Joan Sims, Georgina Cookson, Miles Malleson, Kenneth Griffith, Moultrie Kelsall, Wilfrid Lawson, Wally Patch, John Stuart, George Benson, Bill Edwards, Henry Hewitt, David Lodge, John Hurley, Marianne Stone, Peter Noble, Victor Rietti, Jerrold Wells.*

THE NARROWING CIRCLE (1955) [3]
Dir *Charles Saunders.* Prod *Frank Bevis.* Scr *Doreen Montgomery, from the novel by Julian Symons.* Ph *Jonah Jones.* PC *Fortress.* Dis *Eros.* 66 mins. Cert A

Rivals for an important post on a magazine are also after the same girl. When one is found dead in the other's flat, he cannot prove an alibi, and has to do some sleuthing on his own account. Each trail seems to lead to another murder, but in the end a simple clue reveals the real killer. Competently acted 'B' with a lot of plot for its running time.

LP *Paul Carpenter, Hazel Court, Russell Napier, Ferdy Mayne, Trevor Reid, Basil Dignam, June Ashley, Alan Robinson, Hugh Latimer, Paula Byrne, Ronald (Ronnie) Stevens, Mary Jones.*

THE NAVY LARK (1959) [2]
Dir *Gordon Parry.* Prod *Herbert Wilcox.* Scr *Sid Colin, Laurie Wyman, from Wyman's radio series.* Ph *Gordon Dines.* PC *Wilcox-Neagle.* Dis *20th Century-Fox.* CinemaScope. 82 mins. Cert U

Threatened by a naval busybody who wants their base declared redundant, the conniving commander (*Cecil Parker*) and crew of a minesweeper on a tiny Channel Island invent a yellow-fever outbreak and a phoney minesweeping exercise, topped off by a local uprising that develops into a real one. Much chastened, the busybody tears up his report. Clean but a bit clodhopping, comedy has much of its material literally transferred from radio.

RoC *Leslie Phillips, Ronald Shiner, Elvi Hale, Nicholas Phipps, Gordon Jackson, Cardew Robinson, Harold Kasket, Hattie Jacques, Reginald Beckwith, Kenneth J. Warren, Wanda Ventham, Richard Coleman, Llewellyn Rees, Clive Morton, Gordon Harris, Van Boolen, Gordon Whiting, Tom Gill, Walter Hudd.*

THE NET (1952) [3]
(USA: *Project M7*)
Dir *Anthony Asquith.* Prod *Antony Darnborough.* Scr *William Fairchild, from the novel by John Pudney.* Ph *Desmond Dickinson, Stanley Grant.* PC *Two Cities.* Dis *General Film Distributors.* 86 mins (*US:79*). Cert U

Aviation inventor Heathley (*James Donald*) is unaware that both his new jet plane and his marriage are in danger. His neglected wife (*Phyllis Calvert*) is wooed by a smooth colleague (*Herbert Lom*), while the plane is under threat from Dr Bord (*Noel Willman*), an enemy agent. After a near-fatal test, Heathley is taken off the project, and Bord is able to persuade

him to try another test with him. It succeeds, Bord pulls a gun and orders Heathley to fly east. They struggle and Bord dies. Heathley's wife, sick with worry, comes back to him. Thrills aloft, plot otherwise well grounded.

RoC *Robert Beatty, Muriel Pavlow, Patric Doonan, Walter Fitzgerald, Maurice Denham, Marjorie Fielding, Caven Watson, Herbert Lomas, Cyril Chamberlain, Tucker McGuire, Hartley Power, Hal Osmond, Geoffrey Denton, Marianne Stone, Johnnie Schofield, Patricia Glyn, John Warren, Philip Ray, Douglas Bradley-Smith, John Martin, John Lorrell.*

NEVER LET ME GO (1953) [3]
Dir *Delmer Daves.* Prod *Clarence Brown.* Scr *Ronald Millar, George Froeschel, from a novel by Roger Bax.* Ph *Robert Krasker.* PC and Dis *MGM-British.* 94 mins. Cert U

An American reporter (*Clark Gable*) meets and marries a Russian ballerina (*Gene Tierney*). Despite her exit permit, she is prevented from leaving the country. In England, he meets a man (*Richard Haydn*) in a similar fix, and they launch a daring, and somewhat harebrained scheme to get their wives back. With the help of a Cornish fisherman (*Bernard Miles*), they succeed. Far-fetched farrago with ageing stars.

RoC *Belita, Kenneth More, Frederick Valk, Anton Diffring, Karel Stepanek, Theodore Bikel, Anna Valentina, Peter Illing, Meinhart Maur, Robert Henderson, Stanley Maxted, Alexis Chesnakov, Anton Dolin, London Festival Ballet.*

NEVER LOOK BACK (1952) [3]
Dir *Francis Searle.* Prod *Michael Carreras, James Brennan.* Scr *John Hunter, Guy Morgan, Francis Searle.* Ph *Reginald Wyer.* PC *Hammer.* Dis *Exclusive.* 73 mins. Cert A

When old flame Guy (*Guy Middleton*) lies rather than say he spent the evening chatting to her, newly appointed King's Counsel Anne (*Rosamund John*) decides to defend him on a charge of killing his mistress that night. The prosecutor turns out to be Nigel (*Hugh Sinclair*), a KC she won't marry because of her career. Anne wins, but only at the expense of revealing the entire truth. Worse still, Guy does prove to be the killer. Her career in ruins, Anne is at least free to marry Nigel. Contrived thriller with a good climax; first half pretty slow.

RoC *Henry Edwards, Terence Longdon, John Warwick, Brenda de Banzie, Arthur Howard, Bruce Belfrage, Frances Rowe, H.S. Hills, Helene Burls, Bill Shine, June Mitchell, Barbara Shaw, David Scase, Norman Somers.*

NEVER SAY DIE (1950)
See Don't Say Die (1950)

NEVER TAKE NO FOR AN ANSWER (1951) [5]
Dir *Maurice Cloche, Ralph Smart.* Prod *Anthony Havelock-Allan.* Scr *Paul Gallico, Pauline Gallico, Cloche, Smart, from a novel by Paul Gallico.* Ph *Otto Heller.* PC *Constellation.* Dis *Independent Film Distributors.* 82 mins. Cert U. Bilingual versions

Assisi, Italy. Little Peppino's (*Vittorio Man-*

unta) best friend is his donkey Violetta. He begs the clergy for permission to take her to the crypt of St Francis, patron saint of animals, where he knows she will be cured. After countless refusals, Peppino goes to Rome, and gets a letter from the Pope. He leads Violetta into the crypt. Charming little film, a real heart-breaker.

RoC *Denis O'Dea, Frank Coulson, Guido Celano, Nerio Bernardi, Robert Adamina, John Murphy, Harry Weedon, Edward Hitchcock, Elisa della Vedova, Alessandro Tasca, Charles Borelli, Giorgio Riganti, Mino Billi, Gorella Gori, Clelia Matania, Ricardo Foti, John Myhers, Joop van Hulzen, John le Mesurier.*

NEXT TO NO TIME! (1958)   4

Dir and Scr *Henry Cornelius, from a novel by Paul Gallico.* Prod *Albert Fennell.* Ph *Freddie Francis.* PC *Montpelier.* Dis *British Lion.* Eastman Colour. 92 mins. Cert U

Needing finance for David Webb's (*Kenneth More*) scheme to convert to automation, his firm sends him on an Atlantic crossing to woo industrialist Sir Godfrey (*Roland Culver*). Nervous at first, David gains in confidence when an Irish barman tells him that anything can happen in the 'magic hour' lost every day on board. With the help of a friendly Hollywood star (*Betsy Drake*), he pulls off the deal. Pleasant, if uneasy mixture of genres. Smiles rather than guffaws.

RoC *Harry Green, Patrick Barr, Maureen Connell, Reginald Beckwith, Bessie Love, John Welsh, Howard Marion Crawford, Clive Morton, John Laurie, Irene Handl, Raymond Huntley, Ferdy Mayne, Sidney James, Shandra Walden, Barbara Cavan, Paul Whitsun-Jones, Fred Griffiths, Sally Travers, Eleanor Bryan, Arthur Lovegrove, Stanley Escane, Valerie Buckley, Paul Cole, Terry Burton, Fiona Chislett, Maurice Lane, Christopher Sandford, Russell Waters, Anthony Sagar, Kenneth Evans, Grace Chang, Anthony Chinn, Yvonne Buckingham.*

NIGHT AND THE CITY (1950)   3

Dir *Jules Dassin.* Prod *Samuel G. Engel.* Scr *Jo Eisinger, from the novel by Gerald Kersh.* Ph *Max Greene (Mutz Greenbaum).* PC and Dis 20th Century-Fox. 101 mins. Cert A

Harry (*Richard Widmark*), an American sharpster on the edge of London's underworld, dreams of controlling the city's 'wrestling racket'. He tries to promote bouts in opposition to Greek gangster Kristo (*Herbert Lom*) who bosses the capital's wrestling, by taking

Francis L. Sullivan and Richard Widmark in Night and the City (*1950*)

Kristo's father as partner. When the old man dies, Harry's life isn't worth a nickel; despite efforts by Mary (*Gene Tierney*) to save him, he is hunted down by Kristo's hit-man (*Mike Mazurki*), strangled and dumped in the Thames. Widmark's excellence and dry ice on Thameside can't lift routine thriller.

RoC *Googie Withers, Francis L. Sullivan, Hugh Marlowe, Stanley Zbyszko, Charles Farrell, Edward Chapman, James Hayter, Ken Richmond, Ada Reeve, Gibb McLaughlin, Aubrey Dexter, Russell Westwood, Maureen Delaney, Thomas Gallagher, Derek Blomfield, Kay Kendall.*

THE NIGHT MY NUMBER CAME UP (1955)   5

Dir *Leslie Norman.* (Associate) Prod *Tom Morahan.* Scr *R.C. Sherriff, based on the newspaper feature by Victor Goddard.* Ph *Lionel Banes.* PC Ealing Studios. Dis General Film Distributors. 94 mins. Cert U

A naval officer recounts a nightmare about an air marshal (*Michael Redgrave*) on a plane to Tokyo that crashes. When the air marshal boards a similar plane, details of the dream start to come unnervingly true. But disaster, as foreseen in the end of the dream, is averted by a forced landing and the passengers are rescued by a search party. Suspense drama holds the attention all the way.

RoC *Sheila Sim, Alexander Knox, Denholm Elliott, Ursula Jeans, Ralph Truman, Michael Hordern, Nigel Stock, Bill Kerr, Alfie Bass, George Rose, Victor Maddern, David Orr, David Yates, Doreen Aris, Richard Davies, Charles Perry, Geoffrey Tyrrell, Hugh Moxey, Nicholas Stuart, John Fabian, Percy Herbert, Robert Bruce, Philip Vickers, Stratford Johns.*

NIGHT OF THE DEMON (1957)   4
(USA: *Curse of the Demon*)

Dir *Jacques Tourneur.* Prod *Frank Bevis, Hal E. Chester.* Scr *Charles Bennett, Hal E. Chester, from a story by M.R. James.* Ph *Ted Scaife, S. D. Onions.* PC Sabre. Dis Columbia. 82 mins. Cert X

Professor Harrington (*Maurice Denham*) threatens to expose the occult activities of Dr Karswell (*Niall MacGinnis*). That night Karswell evokes a demon and, on the way home, Harrington dies. His niece (*Peggy Cummins*) calls in psychologist Dr Holden (*Dana Andrews*). Karswell gives Holden a parchment similar to that he gave Harrington and tells him he will die in four days. Holden manages to return the parchment to Karswell, who is devoured by the demon. Pretty scary thriller; a pity they had to show the demon.

RoC *Athene Seyler, Ewan Roberts, Liam Redmond, Peter Elliott, Reginald Beckwith, Richard Leech, Rosamund Greenwood, Lynn Tracy, Brian Wilde, Lloyd Lamble, Peter Hobbes, Charles Lloyd Pack, John Salew, Percy Herbert, Janet Barrow.*

THE NIGHT OF THE FULL MOON (1954)   1

Dir and Prod *Donald Taylor.* Scr *Taylor, Carl Koch.* Ph *Gerald Gibbs.* PC Hedgerley. Dis United Artists. 67 mins. Cert U

An American secret agent, Merritt (*Philip Saville*), crash-lands near an English farmhouse,

which is soon ringed by enemy spies out to regain the information Merritt has lifted from a foreign power. The locals agree to help but fail. Merritt is captured and only the unwitting intervention of the village bobby saves him. Pretty ridiculous; the cast deserves sympathy.

RoC *Kathleen Byron, Dermot Walsh, Anthony Ireland, Everley Gregg, Tim Turner, Elizabeth Wallace, George Merritt.*

A NIGHT TO REMEMBER (1958)   5

Dir *Roy Baker.* Prod *William MacQuitty.* Scr *Eric Ambler, from the book by Walter Lord.* Ph *Geoffrey Unsworth.* PC and Dis Rank. 122 mins. Cert U

1912. The giant liner *Titanic*, acclaimed as 'unsinkable', leaves England on her maiden voyage across the Atlantic. Carrying over 2000 passengers, the ship strikes an iceberg off Newfoundland, ripping a 300-foot-gash below sea level. Distress rockets are ignored by a ship ten miles away as fireworks. Less than three hours later, the ship is abandoned. Despite the efforts of Second Officer Lightoller (*Kenneth More*) in marshalling lifeboats, only 705 are saved. Enthralling, often impressive, sometimes moving reconstruction of true-life drama.

RoC *David McCallum, Michael Goodliffe, Ronald Allen, George Rose, Anthony Bushell, Ralph Michael, Robert Ayres, John Cairney, Honor Blackman, Jane Downs, Kenneth Griffith, Frank Lawton, Michael Bryant, Jill Dixon, Joseph Tomelty, Jack Watling, Alec McCowen, Richard Clarke, Ralph Michael, James Dyrenforth, Harriette Johns, Richard Leech, Tucker McGuire, John Merivale, Laurence Naismith, Russell Napier, Redmond Phillips, Patrick Waddington, Geoffrey Bayldon, Cyril Chamberlain, Bea Duffell, Harold Goldblatt, Gerald Harper, Richard Hayward, Thomas Heathcote, Danuta Karell, Andrew Keir, Christina Lubicz, Barry MacGregor, Eddie Malin, Patrick McAlinney, Helen Misener, Mary Monahan, Howard Pays, Philip Ray, Harold Siddons, Julian Somers, Tim Turner, Meier Tzelniker, Alan Frank, Tom Naylor, John Richardson, Sean Connery.*

NIGHT TRAIN FOR INVERNESS (1959)   2

Dir *Ernest Morris.* Prod *Edward J. Danziger, Harry Lee Danziger.* Scr *Mark Grantham.* Ph *Jimmy Wilson.* PC Danzigers. Dis Paramount. 69 mins. Cert U

The diabetic son (*Dennis Waterman*) of a released prisoner (*Norman Wooland*) is snatched by his father and taken on a train travelling to the north of Scotland. But the man does not realize the boy needs insulin injections every 12 hours, and the police launch a desperate hunt and pursuit before tragedy is averted.

RoC *Jane Hylton, Silvia Francis, Valentine Dyall, Howard Lang, Colin Tapley, Irene Arnold, Nancy Nevinson, Kaplan Kaye, Arnold Bell, Alastair Hunter, Rosamund Lesley, John Moulder-Brown, Josephine Stuart, Anton Rodgers, Larry Noble, Brian Nissen, Eric Dodson, Paddy Webster, Jack Melford, Adrian Blount.*

NIGHT WAS OUR FRIEND (1951)   2

Dir *Michael Anderson.* Prod *Gordon Parry.* Scr *Michael Pertwee, from his play.* Ph *Moray Grant.* PC ACT Films. Dis Monarch. 61 mins. Cert A

Missing for two years, Martin Raynor (*Michael Gough*) returns from the 'dead' (the Brazilian jungle) with his mind virtually unhinged. His wife (*Elizabeth Sellars*), although now in love with a doctor (*Ronald Howard*), looks after Martin, but, after he brutally attacks a man, realizes he belongs in a mental home. Martin commits suicide, and his wife is accused of murdering him, but cleared. Unrelentingly sombre melodrama, indifferently executed.

RoC *Marie Ney, Edward Lexy, Norah Gordon, John Salew, Cyril Smith, Cecil Bevan, Felix Felton, Linda Gray, Edie Martin, Roger Maxwell, Michael Pertwee.*

THE NIGHT WE DROPPED A CLANGER (1959)   [2]

Dir *Darcy Conyers*. Prod *David Henley*. Scr *John Chapman*. Ph *Ernest Steward*. PC *Four Star*. Dis *Rank*. 86 mins. Cert U

Wing Commander Blenkinsop (*Brian Rix*) is chosen to go on a secret mission to occupied France, while his double, Atwood, a latrine orderly, is sent to Africa as a decoy. By an error, their identities are switched, but Atwood becomes a hero (as Blenkinsop) when he captures a flying bomb. In post-war years, the two men meet and resume their real identities. Tired, broad and unpolished farce.

RoC *Cecil Parker, William Hartnell, Leslie Phillips, Leo Franklyn, Liz Fraser, Hattie Jacques, John Welsh, Sarah Branch, Toby Perkins, Vera Pearce, Charles Cameron, Oliver Johnston, Larry Noble, Julian D'Albie, Arthur Brough, Ray Cooney, John Langham, Rowland Bartrop, Julie Mendez, Harry Lane, Paul Bogdan, Victor Beaumont, John Chapman, Gilbert Harrison, Denis Shaw, Patrick Cargill, Stanley Coghan, Edward Ogden, Peter Burton, David Conville, Keith Banks, Arnold Bell, David Williams, Andrew Sachs, Robert Bruce, Geoffrey Denys.*

NIGHT WITHOUT STARS (1951)   [2]

Dir *Anthony Pelissier*. Prod *Hugh Stewart*. Scr *Winston Graham, from his novel*. Ph *Guy Green*. PC *Europa*. Dis *General Film Distributors*. 86 mins. Cert A

A near-blind lawyer (*David Farrar*) on holiday in Nice falls for a girl whose fiancé is killed in mysterious circumstances. Back in England, he recovers his sight, and returns, to discover that the dead man was head of a smuggling ring, and killed for wartime treachery. One of the gang (*Maurice Teynac*) wants to kill the lawyer despite his oath of silence, and the police have to step in. Humourless, rather incredible mystery-drama.

RoC *Nadia Gray, Gilles Quéant, Gérard Landry, June Clyde, Robert Ayres, Clive Morton, Eugene Deckers, Martin Benson, Ina de la Haye, Richard Molinas, Jehanne Pali, Marcel Poncin.*

THE NIGHT WON'T TALK (1952)   [3]

Dir *Daniel Birt*. Prod *Harold Richmond*. Scr *Brock Williams*. Ph *Brendan J. Stafford*. PC *Corsair*. Dis *AB-Pathé*. 61 mins. Cert U

The murder of an artist's model in London's Chelsea throws suspicion on Hawkes, her fiancé (*John Bailey*), and his new love Hazel (*Mary Germaine*), also a model. When Hazel almost becomes the killer's next victim, the police set

a trap, revealing the murderer to be Theo (*Hy Hazell*), a noted sculptress, herself in love with Hawkes. Although the ending is obvious, not bad for a British crime 'B' of the time.

RoC *Sarah Lawson, Elwyn Brook-Jones, Ballard Berkeley, Helene Burns, Leslie Weston, Grey Blake, Duncan Lamont, Raymond Young, Stuart Pearson.*

1984 (1955)   [3]

Dir *Michael Anderson*. Prod *N. Peter Rathvon*. Scr *William P. Templeton, Ralph Gilbert Bettinson, from the novel by George Orwell*. Ph *C. Pennington-Richards*. PC *Holiday*. Dis *AB-Pathé*. 90 mins. Cert X

1984. London, which is in Oceania, one of three world powers, is ruled by Big Brother, who sees all. Love is forbidden. Winston Smith (*Edmond O'Brien*), who works at the Ministry of Truth, falls in love with Julia (*Jan Sterling*) and they try to beat the system. But the junk-man who helps them set up a love nest is one of the Thought Police and O'Connor (*Michael Redgrave*), who gets them to join the anti-government underground, an Inner Party chief. Winston is shot after torture; so is Julia as she tries to reach him. Rather depressing, none-too-successful version of famous book.

RoC *David Kossoff, Mervyn Johns, Donald Pleasence, Carol Wolveridge, Ernest Clark, Ronan O'Casey, Kenneth Griffith, Michael Ripper, Ewen Solon.*

Edmond O'Brien and Michael Redgrave in 1984 *(1956)*

NODDY IN TOYLAND (1958)   [3]

Dir *Maclean Rogers*. Prod *Kay Luckwell*. Scr and PC *Bill & Michael Luckwell, from the book by Enid Blyton*. Dis *Luckwell*. Eastman Colour. 87 mins. Cert U

Live-action version of one of Enid Blyton's tales of little Noddy's adventures in Toyland. Here, Toyland is nearly wrecked by a series of acts of sabotage for which Noddy is arrested by PC Plod. But the crimes have been committed by the Red Goblins, who are finally shown to be the real culprits.

LP *Colin Spaull, Gloria Johnson, Peter Elliott, Leslie Sarony.*

NO HAUNT FOR A GENTLEMAN (1952)   [2]

Dir *Leonard Reeve*. Prod *Charles Reynolds*. Scr *Julian Caunter, Gerard Bryant, Reeve*. Ph *Ted Lloyd*. PC *Anglo-Scottish*. Dis *Apex*. 58 mins. Cert U

Newlyweds John and Miriam (*Anthony Pendrell, Sally Newton*) would be happy if it weren't for her mother (*Patience Rentoul*). Fortunately, on a Scottish honeymoon, they encounter FitzCholmondley (*Jack MacNaughton*), a restless ghost, who agrees to frighten mother-in-law away in return for eternal peace – which is what John and Miriam get as well. Tiresome comedy.

RoC *Dorothy Summers, Peter Swanwick, Rufus Cruickshank, Joan Hickson, Hattie Jacques, Joan Sterndale-Bennett, Barbara Shaw, David King-Wood.*

NO HIGHWAY (1951)   [4]
(USA: *No Highway in the Sky*)

Dir *Henry Koster*. Prod *Louis D. Lighton*. Scr *Oscar Milland, R.C. Sherriff, Alec Coppel, from the novel by Nevil Shute*. Ph *Georges Périnal*. PC and Dis *20th Century-Fox*. 99 mins. Cert U

Mr Honey (*James Stewart*), a research worker, is convinced that a metal used in the manufacture of aircraft is liable to crack up after a certain number of flying hours. When he finds himself travelling in a plane that will reach 'danger level' in flight, he insists on turning back and is eventually proved right. Slightly more than adequate transference of best-seller to screen; both a character study and a suspense thriller.

RoC *Marlene Dietrich, Glynis Johns, Jack Hawkins, Elizabeth Allan, Janette Scott, Ronald Squire, Niall MacGinnis, Kenneth More, Wilfrid Hyde White, Maurice Denham, David Hutcheson, Dora Bryan, Ben Williams, Hector MacGregor, Basil Appleby, Michael Kingsley, Peter Murray, Jill Clifford.*

James Stewart and Jack Hawkins in No Highway *(1951)*

NOOSE FOR A LADY (1953)   [3]

Dir *Wolf Rilla*. Prod *Victor Hanbury*. Scr *Rex Rienits, from a novel by Gerald Verner*. Ph *Jimmy Harvey*. PC *Insignia*. Dis *Anglo-Amalgamated*. 73 mins. Cert A

Margaret (*Pamela Alan*) has been convicted of murdering her husband, a man hated by all who knew him. Her cousin Simon (*Dennis Price*), on holiday from Uganda, enlists the aid of her stepdaughter Jill (*Rona Anderson*), who helps him discover the dead man was a blackmailer – but Simon also finds out Jill is the real killer. Competently acted and directed whodunnit weighed down by talk.

RoC *Ronald Howard, Melissa Stribling, Charles Lloyd Pack, Colin Tapley, Alison Leggatt, George Merritt, Robert Brown, Doris Yorke, Esma Cannon, Joe Linnane, Ian Wallace, Gabriel Blount, Marguerite Young, Millicent Wolf, Alexis Milne.*

NO RESTING PLACE (1951) [5]

Dir *Paul Rotha.* Prod and PC *Colin Lesslie.* Scr *Rotha, Lesslie, Michael Orrom, Gerard Healy, from the novel by Ian Niall.* Ph *Wolfgang Suschitzky.* Dis *Associated British.* 77 mins. Cert A

Alec Kyle (*Michael Gough*), an Irish tinker, kills a gamekeeper by accident, then assaults a policeman in a drunken brawl. This determines the officer to bring Kyle to the hangman for the death of the 'keeper. This he eventually does, although not before Kyle has enjoyed a brief countryside idyll with his wife and son. Critically acclaimed low-budget feature has sympathetic performances, vividly captures the outdoor life.

RoC *Eithne Dunne, Noel Purcell, Brian O'Higgins, Jack MacGowran, Christy Lawrence, Diana Campbell, Maureen O'Sullivan (not the Hollywood star), Esther O'Connor, Billy O'Gorman, Fred Johnson, Robert Hennessey, Austin Meldon.*

NO ROAD BACK (1956) [2]

Dir *Montgomery Tully.* Prod *Steven Pallos, Charles A. Leeds.* Scr *Leeds, Tully, from a play by Falkland L. Cary and Philip Weathers.* Ph *Lionel Banes.* PC *Gibraltar.* Dis *RKO Radio.* 83 mins. Cert A

Mrs Railton (*Margaret Rawlings*), though blind and deaf, runs a club and acts as fence for a gang of jewel thieves led by Clem (*Paul Carpenter*). Her son John (*Skip Homeier*) determines to break this up but only succeeds in being arrested in connection with the gang's latest raid. Clem kills a panicky associate (*Alfie Bass*), then Mrs Railton, after she has forced him to sign a confession, but is trapped by the police. Gloomy, dull drama, uneventful apart from a good safecracking sequence.

RoC *Patricia Dainton, Norman Wooland, Eleanor Summerfield, Sean Connery, Robert Bruce, Philip Ray, Thomas Gallagher.*

NOR THE MOON BY NIGHT (1958) [3]
(USA: *Elephant Gun*)

Dir *Ken Annakin.* Prod *John Stafford.* Scr *Guy Elmes, from the novel by Joy Packer.* Ph *Harry Waxman.* PC and Dis *Rank.* Eastman Colour. 92 mins. Cert U

Pen-friend for several years of African game warden Andrew Miller (*Patrick McGoohan*), Alice (*Belinda Lee*) is able to visit him at last when her sick mother dies. Andrew sends his brother (*Michael Craig*) to meet her, and they find themselves strongly attracted. Andrew, who is loved by Thea (*Anna Gaylor*) daughter of a poacher, is badly injured by lions. Alice finds herself torn by conflicting loyalties, slightly alleviated when she is cleared of suspicion of hastening her mother's death. But Andrew has decided it is Thea he loves. Rose-coloured romance, capably acted, fizzles out before fadeout.

RoC *Eric Pohlmann, Pamela Stirling, Lionel Ngakane, Joan Brickhill, Ben Heydenrych, Alfred Kumalo, Doreen Hlantie, John Willen, Ken Delofse, Gordon McPherson.*

NORTH WEST FRONTIER (1959) [5]
(USA: *Flame Over India*)

Dir *J. Lee Thompson.* Prod *Marcel Hellman.* Scr *Robin Estridge, Frank Nugent, Robert Westerby, from a novel by Patrick Ford.* Ph *Geoffrey Unsworth.* PC and Dis *Rank.* Eastman Colour. CinemaScope. 128 mins. Cert U

1905. British officer Scott (*Kenneth More*) rescues Prince Kishnan (*Govind Raja Ross*) and his governess Catherine (*Lauren Bacall*) from a rebellion of Moslem tribesmen. They clamber aboard an old locomotive, the Empress of India, and embark on a 300-mile journey to safety through rebel-held country. Numerous hazards are surmounted only for Van Leyden (*Herbert Lom*), a Moslem journalist, to seize a machine-gun. But Scott and Catherine see him off, and the Empress of India comes through. Hot, exciting, old-fashioned action film, More's last really big hit in the year he was voted most popular British star.

RoC *Wilfrid Hyde White, I.S. Johar, Ursula Jeans, Ian Hunter, Eugene Deckers, Jack Gwillim, Basil Hoskins, Moultrie Kelsall, Lionel Murton, S.M. Asgaralli, S.S. Chowdhary, Jaron Yalton, Homi Bode, Frank Olegario, Ronald Cardew.*

Laurel Bacall, Kenneth More and Ursula Jeans in North West Frontier (*1959*)

NO SAFETY AHEAD (1958) [1]

Dir *Max Varnel.* Prod *Edward J. Danziger, Harry Lee Danziger.* Scr *Robert Hirst.* Ph *Jimmy Wilson.* PC *Danzigers.* Dis *Paramount.* 68 mins. Cert U

Clem, a bank clerk (*James Kenney*), desperate for money to marry his girl (*Susan Beaumont*), falls in with his crooked brother and joins a gang that robs a bank. The raid ends in murder and Clem, on the run, decides to give himself up. The gang is brought to book after a running gun battle with police. Terrible; script is worst offender, with other departments almost equally guilty.

RoC *Denis Shaw, Tony Doonan, Gordon Needham, John Charlesworth, Brian Weske, Robert Raglan, Mark Singleton, William Hodge, Terence Cooper, Vanda Godsell, Robert Dorning, Ursula Camm, Walter Horsburgh, Hal Osmond, Neil Wilson, Garard Green, John Brooking,*

Frank Coda, Tom Naylor, Tony Harrison, Edward Judd, Walter Gotell.

NO SMOKING (1955) [2]

Dir *Henry Cass.* Prod *Robert S. Baker, Monty Berman.* Scr *Kenneth R. Hayles, from a TV play by Rex Rienits, George Moresby-White.* Ph *Berman.* PC *Tempean.* Dis *Eros.* 73 mins. Cert U

A village chemist (*Reg Dixon*) invents a pill that stops people smoking – and creates world-wide repercussions. The tobacco industry is up in arms. The Prime Minister intervenes. The chemist finally agrees to discontinue production of the pill; he starts work on a formula to make people give up drinking. Potty comedy doesn't catch fire.

RoC *Belinda Lee, Lionel Jeffries, Ruth Trouncer, Myrtle Rowe, Peter Martyn.*

NO TIME FOR TEARS (1957) [4]

Dir *Cyril Frankel.* Prod *W.A. Whittaker.* Scr *Anne Burnaby.* Ph *Gilbert Taylor.* PC and Dis *Associated British.* Eastman Colour. CinemaScope. 86 mins. Cert U

A children's hospital. Nurse Margaret (*Sylvia Syms*) falls for Dr Nigel (*George Baker*); his interest is passing and she finds consolation in her work. The Matron (*Anna Neagle*) cannot bring herself to return two children to their slum home, and adopts them. A little boy's sight hangs in the balance. A pair of twins – one with appendicitis – fool the doctors. Hospital soap opera largely steers clear of stickiness into warmth.

RoC *Anthony Quayle, Alan White, Daphne Anderson, Michael Hordern, Flora Robson, Joan Hickson, Patricia Marmont, Sophie Stewart, Rosalie Crutchley, Joan Sims, Angela Baddeley, Marjorie Rhodes, Christopher Witty, Lucille Mapp, Victor Brooks, Adrienne Poster, Jonathan Ley, Josephine Stuart, Mary Steele, Judith Stott, Viola Keats, Brian Smith, Richard O'Sullivan, Jessie Evans, Cyril Chamberlain, George Rose, Jessica Cairns, Gillian Owen, Loretta Parry, Christopher Frost, Carla Challenor.*

NO TIME TO DIE! (1958) [2]
(USA: *Tank Force*)

Dir *Terence Young.* Prod *Phil C. Samuel.* Scr *Richard Maibaum, Young.* Ph *Ted Moore.* PC *Warwick.* Dis *Columbia.* Technicolor. CinemaScope. 102 mins. Cert U

1942, the Libyan desert. Thatcher (*Victor Mature*), Kendall (*Leo Genn*), Noakes (*Anthony Newley*), Bartlett (*Sean Kelly*) and The Pole (*Bonar Colleano*) escape from an Italian P-o-W camp. They survive desert skirmishes with the enemy, only to be captured by a sheik in league with the Nazis. Bartlett dies, but Thatcher survives torture to escape with the rest. But, as freedom looms so does a German tank and Kendall and The Pole are killed before it is destroyed. Only Noakes and the injured Thatcher make it back. Laughable war film; script is dreadful.

RoC *Luciana Paluzzi, Kenneth Fortescue, Anne Aubrey, George Coulouris, Alfred Burke, David Lodge, Percy Herbert, Maxwell Shaw, Alan Tilvern, George Pravda.*

NO TRACE (1950) [3]

Dir and Scr *John Gilling*. Prod *Robert S. Baker, Monty Berman*. Ph *Berman*. PC *Tempean*. Dis *Eros*. 76 mins. Cert A

Southley (*Hugh Sinclair*), threatened by a blackmailer, disguises himself as a bewhiskered seaman, goes to the rogue's dreary dockside lodgings, and kills him. He has friends in the police, and is sure he has got away with it. But his secretary (*Dinah Sheridan*) discovers his guilt and is nearly throttled by him before police rescue her. Unlikely, but competently-done thriller.

RoC *John Laurie, Barry Morse, Dora Bryan, Michael Brennan, Michael Ward, Michael Evans, Madoline Thomas.*

NO TREES IN THE STREET (1958) [2]

Dir *J. Lee Thompson*. Prod *Frank Godwin*. Scr *Ted Willis, from his play*. Ph *Gilbert Taylor*. PC *Allegro*. Dis *AB-Pathé*. 96 mins. Cert X (later: A)

1938, a London slum. Jess (*Joan Miller*) encourages her son Tommy (*Melvyn Hayes*) into a life of crime with a crooked bookie (*Herbert Lom*) who fancies her daughter Hetty (*Sylvia Syms*); Jess gets the girl drunk so that he can seduce her. Later, the bookie humiliates her. Tommy moves from petty theft to murder. To save him from hanging, Hetty shoots him. Good play gone wrong on screen; direction and most of the performances take it right over the top.

RoC *Stanley Holloway, Ronald Howard, Liam Redmond, Carole Lesley, Lana Morris, Lilly Kann, Marianne Stone, Edwin Richfield, Campbell Singer, David Hemmings, Lloyd Lamble, Richard Shaw, Rita Webb, Fred Griffiths, Victor Brooks.*

NOT SO DUSTY (1956) [2]

Dir and Scr *Maclean Rogers, from a scenario by Kathleen Butler, H.F. Maltby*. Prod *Bill Luckwell, D.E.A. Winn*. Ph *Jimmy Wilson*. PC *Jaywell*. Dis *Eros*. 81 mins. Cert U

Two dustmen (*Bill Owen, Leslie Dwyer*) come into possession of a valuable book – thanks to a good deed. The donor's sneaky sister (*Ellen Pollock*) tries various tricks to get the book back, but the 'dusties' finally succeed in selling it to a wealthy man who will treasure it. Remake of 1936 film of same title, brought up to date in rather laboured fashion.

RoC *Joy Nichols, Dandy Nichols, Harold Berens, William Simons, Totti Truman Taylor, Tony Quinn, Roddy Hughes, Bill Shine, Wally Patch.*

NOT WANTED ON VOYAGE (1957) [2]

Dir *Maclean Rogers*. Prod *Henry Halsted, Jack Marks*. Scr *Michael Pertwee, Evadne Price, Roland Pertwee, Marks, from a play by Price and Ken Attiwill*. Ph *Arthur Grant*. PC *Byron/Ronald Shiner Productions*. Dis *Renown*. 82 mins. Cert U

Steward Higgins (*Ronald Shiner*), an expert on shady deals on his ocean liner, has his suspicions about who has taken a priceless diamond lost by a wealthy passenger. He and the gormless Steward Hollebone (*Brian Rix*) follow their noses through Tangier and, after sundry disasters, bring the thief to book. Broad remake of the 1933 comedy *Trouble* (qv), from which Price and Attiwill's play was adapted.

RoC *Griffith Jones, Catherine Boyle, Fabian Drake, Michael Brennan, Michael Shepley, Dorinda Stevens, Martin Boddey, Therese Burton, Janet Barrow, John Chapman, Michael Ripper, Hugh Moxey, Eric Pohlmann, Larry Noble, Peter Prowse.*

NOW AND FOREVER (1955) [3]

Dir and Prod *Mario Zampi*. Scr *R.F. Delderfield, Michael Pertwee, from a play by Delderfield*. Ph *Erwin Hillier*. PC *Associated British*. Dis *AB-Pathé*. Technicolor. 91 mins. Cert U

Teenagers Janette (*Janette Scott*) and Mike (*Vernon Gray*) fall in love but get a parental thumbs down to wedding plans. When Janette's attempt to fling herself from the school tower is foiled, they decide to elope. After many adventures, they are captured by police on the Scottish border; but their respective sets of parents now take a more sympathetic attitude. Wishy-washy romance full of stock characters gains some charm from Scott's fresh performance.

RoC *Kay Walsh, Jack Warner, Pamela Brown, David Kossoff, Wilfrid Lawson, Ronald Squire, Sonia Dresdel, Guy Middleton, Charles Victor, Marjorie Rhodes, Moultrie Kelsall, Bryan Forbes, Michael Pertwee, Jacqueline Curtiss, Jean Patterson, Henry Hewitt, Harold Goodwin.*

NOWHERE TO GO (1958) [4]

Dir *Seth Holt*. (Associate) Prod *Eric Williams*. Scr *Holt, Kenneth Tynan, from the novel by Donald MacKenzie*. Ph *Paul Beeson*. PC *Ealing Films*. Dis *M-G-M*. 87 mins. Cert U

Jailed for stealing a coin collection (the proceeds from which he has hidden away), Greg (*George Nader*) escapes with the help of an associate (*Bernard Lee*), whom he double-crosses and accidentally kills – thus outlawing him from the underworld, which refuses to help. Meeting Bridget (*Maggie Smith*), a socialite, Greg goes with her to her Welsh farm where, misunderstanding her words with detectives, he flees and is shot by a farmer. He steals a lorry but, weak from loss of blood, dies alone in a field. Thriller is bleak, but remains watchable.

RoC *Geoffrey Keen, Bessie Love, Andrée Melly, Howard Marion Crawford, Arthur Howard, John Welsh, Harry H. Corbett, Margaret McGrath, Harry Locke, Lionel Jeffries, Lilly Kann, John Turner, Lane Merrick, Charles Price.*

NUDIST PARADISE (1958) [1]

Dir *Charles Saunders*. Prod *Nat Miller, Geoffrey Bernerd*. Scr *Denise Kaye, Leslie Bell*. Ph *Henry Hall*. PC and Dis *Orb International*. Eastman Colour. NudiScope. 75 mins. Cert A

Joan (*Anita Love*), a secretary, converts her friend Pat (*Katy Cashfield*) to the wonders of nudist weekends. Here, Joan meets Mike (*Carl Conway*), an American art student. By the time they attend the first Naturist World Congress at Woburn Abbey, they are married and have a baby. First British nudist film in this wave sets depressing standards for the rest.

RoC *Dennis Carnell, Celia Hewitt, Emma Young, Walter Randall.*

THE NUDIST STORY (1959) [1]

Dir *Ramsey Herrington*. Prod *John P. Wyler*. Scr *Norman Armstrong*. Ph *Jimmy Wilson*. PC *Danzigers*. Dis *Eros*. Technicolor. 91 mins. Cert A

Jane (*Shelley Martin*) inherits a nudist camp which she at first regards as beneath her, but to which she is converted through an affair with the camp's director (*Brian Cobby*). The path of true love runs rough through the jealous efforts of his old flame (*Jacqueline D'Orsay*), but Jane's Aunt Meg steps in to reunite the bare lovers. Very long for this sort of thing. The photographer, at least, has worked on better films.

RoC *Anthony Oliver, Natalie Lynn, Joy Hinton, Paul Kendrick.*

OCTOBER MOTH (1959) [2]

Dir and Scr *John Kruse*. Prod *Julian Wintle, Leslie Parkyn*. Ph *Michael Reed*. PC *Independent Artists*. Dis *Rank*. 54 mins. Cert A

Finlay (*Lee Patterson*), a mentally retarded man living on a moorland farm with his sister Molly (*Lana Morris*), accidentally causes a woman motorist to crash and brings her home believing her to be his dead mother. Molly gets a telephone linesman, Tom (*Peter Dyneley*), to help. Finlay, believing him to be his sadistic father, tries to kill him, but is accidentally shot by Molly. Resolutely glum.

RoC *Sheila Raynor, Robert Cawdron.*

ODETTE (1950) [4]

Dir and Prod *Herbert Wilcox*. Scr *Warren Chetham Strode, from the book by Jerrard Tickle*. Ph *Max Greene (Mutz Greenbaum)*. PC *Imperadio*. Dis *British Lion*. 123 mins. Cert A

Trevor Howard and Anna Neagle in Odette *(1950)*

By chance (a wrongly addressed packet of holiday snaps), Marie-Céline (*Anna Neagle*), a Frenchwoman married to a Briton, comes into contact with the War Office in World War II, and accepts the hazardous job of a British agent in Nazi-occupied France, codenamed Odette. Captured and tortured, she refuses to talk, along with her commanding officer, Peter Churchill (*Trevor Howard*). The subsequent sentence of death is never carried out, and she is freed from a concentration camp by the arrival of the Americans. Later, she and Churchill marry. Stolid, sincere biography of wartime heroine.
RoC *Marius Goring, Peter Ustinov, Bernard Lee, Alfred Shieske, Gilles Quéant, Maurice Buckmaster, Marianne Waller, Frederick Wendhausen, Marie Burke, Guyri Wagner, Wolf Frees, Catherine Paul, John Hunter, Campbell Gray, Derrick Penley.*

OH, ROSALINDA!! (1955)   [2]
Dir, Prod and Scr *Michael Powell, Emeric Pressburger, from an opera by Johann Strauss.* Ph *Christopher Challis.* PC *Powell & Pressburger.* Dis *AB-Pathé.* Technicolor. CinemaScope. 101 mins. Cert U
Post-war Vienna. Dr Falke (*Anton Walbrook*), man-about-town known as 'The Bat', plans revenge on French colonel Eisenstein (*Michael Redgrave*) and his wife Rosalinda (*Ludmilla Tcherina*) for a fiendish practical joke. They go to a masked ball and flirt with each other, unaware of their identities. When Eisenstein later accuses Rosalinda of being fickle, she produces his watch to show that he was the one who was flirting with her. Very complicated romp, adapted from *Die Fledermaus.* Just doesn't work. Redgrave, Anthony Quayle and Anneliese Rothenberger sing their own roles.
RoC *Mel Ferrer, Dennis Price, Oska Sima, Richard Marner, Olga Lowe, Nicholas Bruce, Ray Buckingham, Jill Ireland.* Voices: *Sari Barabas, Alexander Young, Denis Dowling, Walter Berry.*

OLD MOTHER RILEY, HEADMISTRESS (1950)   [1]
Dir *John Harlow.* Prod and PC *Harry Reynolds.* Scr *Con West, Jack Marks.* Ph *Ken Talbot.* Dis *Renown.* 75 mins. Cert U
Mother Riley (*Arthur Lucan*), an Irish washerwoman, finds herself the owner of a laundry, which she barters for the school where her daughter Kitty instructs the choir. Mother Riley becomes headmistress, thwarting speculators who want to run a railway through the school grounds, and Kitty, who had been sacked, the music mistress. Mother Riley as a headmistress somewhat hard to take; one of the briefest and weakest of the series.
RoC *Kitty McShane, Enid Hewitt, Jenny Mathot, Ethel Royale, Harry Herbert, Cyril Smith, Paul Sheridan, Willer Neal, C. Denier Warren, Alfred Waller, Bill Stevens, Eve Dewhurst, Graham Tunbridge, Myrette Morven, Dorothy Darke, Beth Ross, Madge Brindley, Vi Kaley, Jacqueline Stanley, Catherine Carleton (Boyle), Patricia Owens, Luton Girls' Choir, George Melachrino and His Orchestra.*

OLD MOTHER RILEY'S JUNGLE TREASURE (1951)   [3]
Dir *Maclean Rogers.* Prod *George Minter.* Scr *Val Valentine.* Ph *James Wilson.* PC *Oakland Films.* Dis *Renown.* 75 mins. Cert U
Mother Riley (*Arthur Lucan*) and her daughter Kitty (*Kitty McShane*) work in an antique shop, where they find an ancient treasure map. Encountering all sorts of adventures in the jungle where the loot is supposedly located, they end up on a South Sea Island, loaded with hidden booty. Mother Riley is crowned queen by the local natives. Rumbustious nonsense just about passes muster.
RoC *Garry Marsh, Sebastian Cabot, Cyril Chamberlain, Anita d'Ray, Willer Neal, Roddy Hughes, Robert Adams, Peter Butterworth, Peter Swannwick, Harry Lane, Michael Ripper, Bill Shine, Maria Marcedes, Gerald Rex.*

ONCE A SINNER (1950)   [3]
Dir *Lewis Gilbert.* Prod and PC *John Argyle.* Scr *David Evans, from a novel by Ronald Marsh.* Ph *Frank North.* Dis *Butchers.* 80 mins. Cert A
John (*Jack Watling*), a bank clerk engaged to a nice girl (*Joy Shelton*), becomes enamoured of adventuress Irene (*Pat Kirkwood*), and marries her. She eventually deserts him for a former lover, but he follows her, and becomes tied up in a murder. To keep his name out of it, Irene commits suicide. Kirkwood surprisingly good in straight role, but film lacks basic credibility.
RoC *Sydney Tafler, Thora Hird, Humphrey Lestocq, Harry Fowler, Gordon McLeod, Edith Sharpe, Danny Green, R. Stuart Lindsell, Olive Sloane, George Street, Charles Paton, Stuart Latham, Rose Howlett.*

ONE GOOD TURN (1954)   [4]
Dir *John Paddy Carstairs.* Prod *Maurice Cowan.* Scr *Cowan, Carstairs, Ted Willis.* Ph *Jack Cox.* PC *Two Cities.* Dis *General Film Distributors.* 90 mins. Cert U
Norman (*Norman Wisdom*), an orphan who has stayed on at his collapsing orphanage as odd-job man, foolishly promises a boy a very expensive model car. In his efforts to raise the money, he wins the London to Brighton walk, conducts a symphony orchestra, almost wins a boxing contest and ends by not only getting the car, but saving the orphanage from the clutches of a greedy estate agent. Delightfully funny comedy with a gaggle of likeable characters.
RoC *Joan Rice, Shirley Abicair, Thora Hird, William Russell, Joan Ingram, Richard Caldicot, David Hurst, Harold Kasket, Keith Gilman, Marjorie Fender, Fred Kitchen Jr, Michael Balfour, Ricky McCullough, Harold Goodwin.*

ONE JUMP AHEAD (1955)   [3]
Dir *Charles Saunders.* Prod *Guido Coen.* Scr *Doreen Montgomery, from the novel by Robert Chapman.* Ph *Brendan J. Stafford.* PC *Kenilworth/Fortress.* Dis *General Film Distributors.* 66 mins. Cert A
Paul Carpenter and *Diane Hart* assume the roles previously played by Peter Reynolds and Honor Blackman in another adventure of reporter Banner, who is always one jump ahead of the police, this time in a case of the murder of an unidentified woman and a boy whom the killer thought

was a witness. An old flame (*Jill Adams*) of Banner's is revealed as the murderess. He leaves her a gun and one bullet . . . Dialogue occasionally crackles with humour; not bad of its type.
RoC *Freddie Mills, Peter Sinclair, Arnold Bell, Roddy Hughes, David Hannaford, Edward French, Jane Ashley, Rose Howlett, Freddie Watts, Mary Jones, Charles Lamb, Arthur Gross.*

ONE JUST MAN (1955)   [1]
Dir *David Macdonald.* Prod *Edward J. Danziger, Harry Lee Danziger.* Scr *James Eastwood, Kate Barley.* Ph *Jimmy Wilson.* PC *Danzigers.* Dis *AB-Pathé.* 55 mins. Cert A
Two stories. Judge Craig (*Alexander Knox*), the 'hanging' judge, decides to take the law into his own hands to right an injustice – with tragic results. An unscrupulous playboy (*Peter Reynolds*) undertakes an insurance fraud which ends in a double tragedy. Bigger tragedy is this badly scripted, TV-oriented film.
RoC *Ron Randell, Joan Haythorne, Maureen Swanson, Cyril Raymond, Eunice Gayson, John Warwick.*

THE ONE THAT GOT AWAY (1957)   [4]
Dir *Roy Baker.* Prod *Julian Wintle.* Scr *Howard Clewes, from the book by Kendal Burt and James Leasor.* Ph *Eric Cross.* PC and Dis *Rank.* 110 mins. Cert U
World War II. Captured in the Battle of Britain, pilot Franz von Werra is confident in his own ability to escape. Twice he nearly makes it, on one occasion getting into the cockpit of a plane before being stopped. Sent to Canada, he jumps from a train and flees across snow and ice to (then) neutral United States. A postscript states that he got back to Germany via Mexico, Peru and Spain, but was killed in action on the Russian front. Interesting war story with nail-biting climax.
RoC *Michael Goodliffe, Terence Alexander, Colin Gordon, Jack Gwillin, Andrew Faulds, Julian Somers, Alec McCowen, John Van Eyssen, Harry Lockart, Robert Crewdson, George Mikell, George Roubicek, Frederick Jaeger, Richard Marner, Paul Hansard, Stratford Johns, Glyn Houston.*

Hardy Kruger in The One That Got Away *(1957)*

ONE WAY OUT (1955)   [3]
Dir *Francis Searle.* Prod *John Temple-Smith, Francis Edge.* Scr *Jonathan Roche.* Ph *Walter Harvey.* PC *Major.* Dis *Rank.* 61 mins. Cert U
Superintendent Harcourt (*Eddie Byrne*) is de-

termined to nail racketeer Danvers (*John Chandos*), responsible for a girl's suicide. But Danvers' young partner Parrish (*Lyndon Brook*) involves Harcourt's daughter Shirley (*Jill Adams*) in a robbery, exposing the cop to blackmail. Shirley confesses, Harcourt leaves the force and, Parrish, having been trapped on a robbery, confronts Danvers, who guns Harcourt down, but fails to escape the following police. Good acting vitiated by implausible situations. RoC *Olive Milbourne, Arthur Howard, Arthur Lowe, Ryck Rydon, Anne Valery, Doris Gilmore, Nicholas Tanner.*

ONE WILD OAT (1951)   [3]

Dir *Charles Saunders*. Prod *John Croydon*. Scr *Vernon Sylvaine, Lawrence Huntington, from Sylvaine's play*. Ph *Robert Navarro*. PC *Coronet*. Dis *Eros*. 78 mins. Cert A

Proudfoot (*Robertson Hare*), a solicitor, investigates the past of his enemy Gilbey (*Stanley Holloway*), a greyhound owner, when his daughter decides to marry Gilbey's son. Gilbey retaliates by discovering a 'wild oat' from Proudfoot's own past, but the girl concerned proves to be an imposter playing her own game. Competently routine adaptation of hit stage farce; a little dated. RoC *June Sylvaine, Andrew Crawford, Sam Costa, Vera Pearce, Robert Moreton, Irene Handl, Constance Lorne, Ingeborg Wells, Charles Groves, Gwen Cherrill, Joan Rice, Audrey Hepburn, Fred Berger, William (James) Fox.*

Robertson Hare and Stanley Holloway in One Wild Oat *(1951)*

ONE WISH TOO MANY (1956)   [3]

Dir *John Durst*. Prod *Basil Wright*. Scr *John Eldridge*. Ph *Adrian Jeakins*. PC *Realist Film Unit/Children's Film Foundation*. Dis *British Lion*. 56 mins. Cert U

In the East End of London, young Peter (*Anthony Richmond*) discovers a marble which, like Aladdin's Lamp, makes his every wish come true. Peter has a high time until he wishes his toy steamroller were a real one. The steamroller thunders its way through the docks, doing untold damage, with Peter unable to stop it, until it finally crashes into the Thames. The marble has disappeared . . . Pleasant children's film with adequate trick effects. RoC *Arthur Howard, Gladys Young, Sam Costa, Rosalind Gourgey, John Pike, Terry Cooke, Bay White, Frank Hayden.*

ON THE RUN (1957)   [3]

Dir *Ernest Morris*. Prod *Edward J. Danziger, Harry Lee Danziger*. Scr *Brian Clemens, Eldon Howard*. Ph *Jimmy Wilson*. PC *Danzigers*. Dis *United Artists*. 70 mins. Cert A

Wesley (*Neil McCallum*) takes a job at a country garage, working for Tom (*William Hartnell*) and falling for his daughter Kitty (*Susan Beaumont*). Sensing he is running away from something, Kitty discovers that a gang is after Wesley, an ex-boxer, for refusing to throw a fight. She urges him to stand up to them and, when they arrive, he does so, beating them. Predictable thriller with better punch-ups than usual. RoC *Philip Saville, Gordon Tanner, Gilbert Winfield.*

OPERATION AMSTERDAM (1959)   [3]

Dir *Michael McCarthy*. Prod *Maurice Cowan*. Scr *McCarthy, John Eldridge, from a novel by David E. Walker*. Ph *Reginald Wyer*. PC and Dis *Rank*. 104 mins. Cert U

1940. As the Germans sweep through Holland, the British launch a mission to rescue a million pounds' worth of diamonds from a vault. As its members arrive, Amsterdam Harbour is already under heavy bombardment; it is also a bank holiday and the vaults, time-locked, have to be blown open. After a pitched battle with German forces, the British get away with the gems, but their Dutch contact (*Eva Bartok*) decides to stay to fight with the resistance. Slapdash and under-characterized, thriller does go at a tremendous pace for its length. RoC *Peter Finch, Tony Britton, Alexander Knox, Malcolm Keen, Christopher Rhodes, Tim Turner, John Horsley, Keith Pyott, Melvyn Hayes, Oscar Quitak, John Bailey, John Richardson.*

OPERATION BULLSHINE (1959)   [3]

Dir *Gilbert Gunn*. Prod *Frank Godwin*. Scr *Anne Burnaby, Rupert Lang, Gunn*. Ph *Gilbert Taylor*. PC *Associated British*. Dis *AB-Pathé. Technicolor*. 83 mins. Cert U

1942. On arrival at an anti-aircraft unit overpopulated with girls, Betty (*Barbara Murray*), an ATS girl, finds the competition is hottest for the charms of 'Killer' Brown (*Donald Sinden*) . . . her husband. Chaos ensues after 'Killer' is found (innocently) at a flat with his wife *and* another woman (*Carole Lesley*), but all ends well after the girls move into action to shoot down an enemy plane. Farce has its funny moments but did little to forward anyone's career, and possesses, as one critic put it, 'large numbers of underclad starlets'. RoC *Ronald Shiner, Naunton Wayne, Dora Bryan, John Cairney, Joan Rice, Daniel Massey, Fabia Drake, Peter Jones, John Welsh, Barbara Hicks, Cyril Chamberlain, Ambrosine Phillpotts, Naomi Chance, Judy Grinham, Marianne Stone, Harry Landis, Brian Weske, George Mikell.*

OPERATION CUPID (1959)   [2]

Dir *Charles Saunders*. Prod *Guido Coen*. Scr *Brock Williams*. Ph *Jimmy W. Harvey*. PC *Twickenham/Alliance*. Dis *Rank*. 65 mins. Cert U

Three shady characters, Charlie (*Charles Farrell*), Cecil (*Wallas Eaton*) and Mervyn (*Harold Goodwin*) find themselves the unwilling proprietors of a matrimonial agency. A millionairess (*Avice Landone*) looks fair game to Charlie, who marries her himself – then finds out she is as penniless as he. Never mind, they love each other. Weak comedy wastes good idea. RoC *Beth Rogan, Norma Parnell, Wally Patch, Pauline Shepherd, Bruce Seton, David Saire, Charles Clay, Martin Sterndale, Eddie Malin, Colin Rix, Neil Hallett, Audrey Nicholson, George Patterson, Roy Jefferies.*

OPERATION DIPLOMAT (1953)   [3]

Dir *John Guillermin*. Prod *Ernest G. Roy*. Scr *Guillermin, A.R. Rawlinson, from the TV serial by Francis Durbridge*. Ph *Gerald Gibbs*. PC *Nettlefold*. Dis *Butchers*. 70 mins. Cert U

Forced to operate on a mystery patient, surgeon Mark Fenton (*Guy Rolfe*) finds that the police do not believe his story. The nurse (*Lisa Daniely*) who assisted gives him the identity of his patient, but is murdered by a gang, who plan to smuggle the man, a diplomat, out of the country. Fenton and the now-compliant police reach the docks in time to prevent that happening. Unlikely, but vigorous thriller. RoC *Patricia Dainton, Sydney Tafler, Brian Worth, Anton Diffring, Ballard Berkeley, Edward Dain, James Raglan, Michael Golden, Avice Landone, Eric Berry, Ann Bennett, Jean Hardwicke, Alexis Chesnakov.*

OPERATION MURDER (1956)   [1]

Dir *Ernest Morris*. Prod *Harry Lee Danziger, Edward J. Danziger*. Scr *Brian Clemens*. Ph *Jimmy Wilson*. PC *Danzigers*. Dis *AB-Pathé*. 66 mins. Cert A

Doctors Wayne (*Tom Conway*) and Bowen (*Patrick Holt*) hatch a murderous plan to get their private hospital out of a financial hole. Wayne will murder his rich cousin (whose heir he is) while Bowen poses as him at an operation. The killing goes as planned – but Wayne's alibi is destroyed because of a name written on the dust of his car. Dull drama, described by one critic as 'clinical claptrap'. RoC *Sandra Dorne, Rosamund John, Robert Ayres, Virginia Keiley, John Stone, Alastair Hunter, Frank Hawkins, Gilbert Winfield, Timothy Fitzgerald, Tony Quinn.*

THE ORACLE (1952)   [3]
(USA: *The Horse's Mouth*)

Dir *(C.) Pennington Richards*. Prod *Colin Lesslie*. Scr *Patrick Campbell*. Ph *Wolfgang Suschitzky*. PC *Group 3*. Dis *General Film Distributors*. 84 mins. Cert U

A reporter (*Michael Medwin*) on holiday on an island off the Irish coast discovers an 'oracle' at the bottom of a well that can forecast anything. At first he is sacked for the story, but when the oracle starts forecasting racehorse winners, all racing in Britain is abandoned. The paper's readers want the oracle to tell them if there will be another war but the oracle, daunted, beats a retreat to the bottom of the sea. Apart from a few shafts at yellow journalism, comedy is resolutely whimsical. RoC *Robert Beatty, Mervyn Johns, Virginia McKenna, Joseph Tomelty, Gillian Lind, Ursula*

Michael Medwin, Joseph Tomelty and Virginia McKenna in The Oracle (1952)

Howells, Arthur Macrae, Louise Hampton, John Charlesworth, Maire O'Neill, Lockwood West, John McBride, Derek Tansley, Patrick McAlinney, Lionel Marson, Jean St Claire, Jack May, Gilbert Harding (voice).

ORDERS ARE ORDERS (1954)   [2]

Dir *David Paltenghi*. Prod *Donald Taylor*. Scr *Taylor, Geoffrey Orme, Eric Sykes, from the play by Ian Hay, Anthony Armstrong.* Ph *Arthur Grant.* PC *Group 3.* Dis *British Lion. 78 mins. Cert U*

An American film unit descends on a British army camp to make a science-fiction film, and the soldiers all chase the unit's girls – until a snap inspection by the divisional commander results in the expulsion of the Americans to a nearby haunted house to finish their film. Crude farce, a remake of 1933's *Orders is Orders,* interesting chiefly for the coincidental teaming of later-partners *Tony Hancock* and *Sidney James,* who give the two most amusing performances in the film.

RoC *Margot Grahame, Brian Reece, Raymond Huntley, Peter Sellers, Maureen Swanson, June Thorburn, Bill Fraser, Donald Pleasence, Peter Martyn, Edward Lexy, Eric Sykes, Barry Mackay, Clive Morton, Michael Trubshawe, Reggie (Reginald) Hearne, Barry Steele, Maureen Pryor, Mark Baker, Stephen Vercoe.*

ORDERS TO KILL (1958)   [5]

Dir *Anthony Asquith*. Prod *Asquith, Anthony Havelock-Allan*. Scr *Paul Dehn, George St George*. Ph *Desmond Dickinson*. PC *Lynx*. Dis *British Lion. 111 mins. Cert A*

Gene Summers (*Paul Massie*), an American flyer, is selected to go into France and assassinate a suspected traitor. Trained by MacMahon (*Eddie Albert*), who is worried about his lack of concern, Gene reaches Paris, and the target, Lafitte (*Leslie French*), a mild, kindly man with a family. The assassin begins to have doubts about the man's guilt, but accomplishes the killing, albeit messily. Two years later, having become an alcoholic, Summers learns Lafitte was innocent. He goes to his widow, gives her his two years' army back-pay and leaves, filled with remorse. Grim war film recovers well from leisurely start. British Academy Awards for best actress (*Irene Worth*) and best screenplay.

RoC *James Robertson Justice, Lillian Gish, John*

Crawford, Lionel Jeffries, Sandra Dorne, Jacques Brunius, Nicholas Phipps, Anne Blake, Lillie Bea Gifford, Sam Kydd, Miki Iveria, Henzie Raeburn, Robert Henderson, Andrea Malandrinos.

OUR GIRL FRIDAY (1953)   [2]
(USA: *The Adventures of Sadie*)

Dir and Scr *Noel Langley from a novel by Norman Lindsay*. Prod *George Minter*. Ph *Wilkie Cooper*. PC and Dis *Renown. Eastman Colour. 88 mins. Cert U*

Four shipwreck survivors find themselves on a desert island – millionaire's daughter Sadie (*Joan Collins*), cynical journalist Jimmy (*George Cole*), a lecturer (*Robertson Hare*) and the ship's stoker Pat (*Kenneth More*). The three men vow not to touch the girl, but Jimmy and the professor try it. When a ship rescues them, Sadie wants to marry Pat, who refuses. After another wreck, Pat and Sadie find themselves back on the island. Flimsy comedy just about gets by on the characters of the stars. First film in Eastman Colour.

RoC *Hermione Gingold, Walter Fitzgerald, Hattie Jacques, Felix Felton, Lionel Murton, Anthony Tancred, Michael Meacham.*

OUR MAN IN HAVANA (1959)   [4]

Dir and Prod *Carol Reed*. Scr *Graham Greene, from his novel*. Ph *Oswald Morris*. PC *Kinsmead*. Dis *Columbia. CinemaScope. 111 mins. Cert A*

Wormold (*Alec Guinness*), a vacuum-cleaner salesman in Cuba, with a daughter (*Jo Morrow*) to keep happy, allows himself to be recruited as a British secret agent. Stumped for genuine secrets to pass, but loath to say 'no' to the money involved, Wormold invents some, including a sinister weapon base in the mountains, based on vacuum-cleaner designs. When Wormold's best friend (*Burl Ives*) is murdered, and he himself narrowly escapes poisoning, he realizes he must call a halt to his new career. In London, he is awarded the OBE. Sardonic comedy-thriller with good cameo roles.

RoC *Maureen O'Hara, Ernie Kovacs, Ralph Richardson, Noël Coward, Paul Rogers, Gregoire Aslan, Duncan Macrae, Maurice Denham, Raymond Huntley, José Prieto, Timothy Bateson, Hugh Manning, Karel Stepanek, Ferdy Mayne, Maxine Audley, Rachel Roberts.*

Maureen O'Hara and Alec Guinness in Our Man in Havana ((*1959*)

OUTCAST OF THE ISLANDS (1951)   [5]

Dir and Prod *Carol Reed*. Scr *William Fairchild, from the novel by Joseph Conrad*. Ph *John Wilcox*. Ph *London Films*. Dis *British Lion. 102 mins. Cert A*

The Far East. Fired for embezzlement, Willems (*Trevor Howard*) is taken by Lingard (*Ralph Richardson*), who helped him as a youth when he ran away to sea, to a remote trading post he owns in the islands. A local politician uses Willems' passion for Aissa (*Kerima*) to get him to betray the secret channel to the post. Willems flees, and Lingard ultimately finds him living with Aissa, whom he no longer loves. She urges him to kill Lingard, to no avail, and Lingard leaves them there. Intelligent, atmospheric adaptation, the best Conrad available.

RoC *Robert Morley, Wendy Hiller, George Coulouris, Wilfrid Hyde White, Frederick Valk, Betty Ann Davies, Peter Illing, James Kenney, A.V. Bramble, Dharma Emmanuel, Annabel Morley, Marne Maitland.*

Robert Morley and Trevor Howard in Outcast of the Islands (*1951*)

OUT OF THE CLOUDS (1954)   [4]

Dir *Basil Dearden*. Prod *Michael Relph*. Scr *Relph, John Eldridge, Rex Rienits, from a novel by John Fores*. Ph *Paul Beeson*. PC *Ealing Studios*. Dis *General Film Distributors. Eastman Colour. 88 mins. Cert U*

Incidents at a fogbound airport. The duty officer (*Robert Beatty*) is convinced he has lost his girl, a stewardess (*Eunice Gayson*), to a pilot (*Anthony Steel*) involved in smuggling. But he is wrong. Bill (*David Knight*) meets Leah (*Margo Lorenz*), settling for security with a wealthy middle-aged American. When the fog lifts, Bill flies off, but changes his mind in Rome and returns – to find Leah waiting. Good entertainment if nothing special, with a not-too-distinguished cast giving of their best, and some ripe cameo roles.

RoC *James Robertson Justice, Marie Lohr, Gordon Harker, Isabel Dean, Abraham Sofaer, Bernard Lee, Megs Jenkins, Melissa Stribling, Michael Howard, Sidney James, Nicholas Phipps, Esma Cannon, Jill Melford, Arthur Howard, Cyril Luckham, Jack Lambert, Katie Johnson, William Franklyn.*

OVER THE GARDEN WALL (1950)   [1]

Dir and Prod *John E. Blakeley*. Scr *Anthony Toner*. Ph *Ernest Palmer*. PC *Film Studios*

Manchester. Dis Mancunian. 95 mins. Cert U
A working-class couple (*Jimmy James, Norman Evans*) are bent on giving their only daughter (*Sonya O'Shea*) and their ex-GI son-in-law (*John Wynn*) a right royal welcome. Trouble flares when father's boss's son (*Frederick Bradshaw*) arrives and flirts with the girl. The stars spend too much time off screen in this extension of Norman Evans's famous variety act. Interesting that when it was reissued ten years later, 40 minutes were taken out of it. Nobody complained.
RoC *Dan Young, Alec Pleon.*

P

PACIFIC DESTINY (1956) [4]
Dir *Wolf Rilla.* Prod and PC *James Lawrie.* Scr *Richard Mason, from a book by Sir Arthur Grimble.* Ph *Martin Curtis.* Dis *British Lion. Eastman Colour. CinemaScope. 97 mins. Cert U*
Arthur Grimble (*Denholm Elliott*), a young colonial officer, goes to serve in the South Seas in 1912 with his wife Olivia (*Susan Stephen*). The commissioner (*Michael Hordern*) gives him a baptism of fire by sending him off to look into land disputes. After he has his arms tattooed, helps to kill a shark, discredits the local witch doctor and starts, with Olivia, a baby clinic, the natives accept him. The commissioner finds the natives at peace and the Grimbles with a new baby. Pleasantly episodic true-life adventure from *A Pattern of Islands.*
RoC *Gordon Jackson, Inia Te Wiata, Moira Macdonald, Henrietta Godinet, Ollie Crichton, Hans Kruse, Felix Felton, Peter Bathurst, Clifford Buckton, Rosie Leavasa.*

PANDORA AND THE FLYING DUTCHMAN (1950) [3]
Dir, Prod and Scr *Albert Lewin.* Ph *Jack Cardiff.* PC *Romulus.* Dis *Independent Film Distributors. Technicolor. 122 mins. Cert A*
1930. On the coast of Spain, beautiful heartbreaker Pandora (*Ava Gardner*), toying with the affections of a racing-driver (*Nigel Patrick*)

James Mason and Mario Cabré in Pandora and the Flying Dutchman *(1951)*

and a bullfighter (*Mario Cabre*) encounters Hendrik (*James Mason*), the Flying Dutchman, doomed to roam the seas but granted six months ashore every seven years until the love of a girl willing to die for him ends his eternal suffering. He and Pandora are eventually united in a suicide pact. Long, ornate, dry, beautiful romantic fantasy split the critics.
RoC *Sheila Sim, Harold Warrender, Marius Goring, Pamela Kellino, John Laurie, Patricia Raine, Margarita d'Alvarez, Abraham Sofaer, Francisco Igual, Lila Moinar (Lily Molnar), Phoebe Hodgson, John Carew, Edward Leslie, Christina Forbes, Helen Cleveley, Gerald Welsh, Antonio Martin, La Pillina, Guillermi Beltran, Gabriel Carmona.*

PARK PLAZA 605 (1953) [2]
(USA: *Norman Conquest*)
Dir *Bernard Knowles.* Prod *Bertram Ostrer, Albert Fennell.* Scr *Knowles, Fennell, Ostrer, Clifford Witting, from a novel by Berkeley Gray.* Ph *Eric Cross.* PC *B & A.* Dis *Eros. 75 mins. Cert U*
Summoned to a hotel room, private-eye Norman Conquest (*Tom Conway*) is drugged and framed for murder by the mysterious Nadina (*Eva Bartok*), involved in diamond smuggling. Nadina is double-crossed by ex-Nazi von Henschel (*Robert Adair*), the real killer, and eventually gives her life helping Norman round up the smuggling ring. Indifferent thriller with tired performances.
RoC *Joy Shelton, Sidney James, Richard Wattis, Carl Jaffe, Frederick Schiller, Anton Diffring, Ian Fleming, Edwin Richfield, Michael Balfour, Martin Boddey, Terence Alexander, Victor Platt, Leon Davey, Richard Marner, Tony Hilton, Alan Rolfe, Derek Prentice, Frank Seiman, Brian Moorhead, Billie Hill, Anthony Woodruff.*

PASSAGE HOME (1955) [4]
Dir *Roy Baker.* Prod *Julian Wintle.* Scr *William Fairchild, from the novel by Richard Armstrong.* Ph *Geoffrey Unsworth.* PC *Group.* Dis *General Film Distributors. 102 mins. Cert A*
1931. A British merchant ship returning home from South America is forced to give passage to Ruth (*Diane Cilento*), an attractive governess. During the 30-day voyage, she is propositioned by the martinet skipper (*Peter Finch*), who takes to his cabin and the bottle after she is rescued by Vosper (*Anthony Steel*). The captain reasserts his authority in a storm, but Ruth has chosen Vosper. Lusty, gritty sea story, pushed along at a pace that disguises its creakiness.
RoC *Cyril Cusack, Geoffrey Keen, Hugh Griffith, Duncan Lamont, Bryan Forbes, Gordon Jackson, Michael Craig, Michael Bryant, Robert Brown, Martin Benson, Patrick McGoohan, Sam Kydd, Glyn Houston, Patrick Westwood, George Woodbridge, John Warren, Ian Whittaker, Scott Harold, Arthur Lovegrove, Leonard White, Peter Ventham, Gerald Andersen, Philip Ray.*

THE PASSING STRANGER (1954) [3]
Dir *John Arnold.* Prod *Anthony Simmons, Ian Gibson-Smith.* Scr *Arnold, Simmons.* Ph *Walter Lassally.* PC *Harlequin.* Dis *Independent Film Distributors/British Lion. 67 mins. Cert A*
Chick (*Lee Patterson*), a US Army deserter who has joined a gun-running gang, quits them after a killing and holes up in a roadside cafe run by two sisters, one of whom, Jill (*Diane Cilento*) falls for him. When they cannot afford to fly to America, Chick rejoins the gang and gets the robbery money despite a double-cross. Jill's ex-boyfriend (*Duncan Lamont*) sees to it that police catch Chick at the airport. Ambitious second-feature lacks basic material.
RoC *Olive Gregg, Liam Redmond, Harold Lang, Mark Dignam, Alfie Bass, Paul Whitsun-Jones, Cameron Hall, George Cooper, Lyndon Brook, Charles Leno, Leonard Williams, John Garside, Warren Mitchell, George Luscombe, Harry (H.) Corbett, Patrick Westwood, Russell Waters, Joe Sterne, John Pitt, John Fabian, Joby Blanshard.*

THE PASSIONATE STRANGER (1956) [3]
(USA: *A Novel Affair*)
Dir *Muriel Box.* Prod *Peter Rogers.* Scr *Muriel and Sydney Box.* Ph *Otto Heller.* PC *Beaconsfield.* Dis *British Lion. Partly Eastman Colour. 97 mins. Cert A*
When an easy-going Italian (*Carlo Justini*) arrives as chauffeur to a wheelchair-bound scientist (*Ralph Richardson*), the boffin's novelist wife (*Margaret Leighton*) writes the household characters into a lurid romantic novel. Reading it, the chauffeur imagines - to his cost - that it is a reflection of her true feelings. He is soon on his way, but a romance looms with the scientist's pretty maid (*Patricia Dainton*). Mildly funny comedy.
RoC *Marjorie Rhodes, Thorley Walters, Frederick Piper, Megs Jenkins, Alexander Gauge, John Arnatt, George Woodbridge, Allan Cuthbertson, Ada Reeve, Andrée Melly, Michael Shepley, Barbara Archer, Michael Trubshawe, Barbara Graley, Christopher Witty, Fred Tooze, Pat Ryan.*

PASSIONATE SUMMER (1958) [3]
Dir *Rudolph Cartier.* Prod *Kenneth Harper, George Willoughby.* Scr *Joan Henry, from a novel by Richard Mason.* Ph *Ernest Steward.* PC *Briar.* Dis *Rank. Eastman Colour. 104 mins. Cert A*
Jamaica. Douglas (*Bill Travers*), a teacher, loves Judy (*Virginia McKenna*), an air hostess still half in love with a married lothario (*Carl Mohner*). Silvia (*Ellen Barrie*), a precocious pupil, is infatuated with Douglas and, when she sees him seduced by Mrs Pawley (*Yvonne Mitchell*), his head's wife, she runs into a tropical storm and falls to her death in a quarry. At the inquest, Douglas is absolved from blame. Cardboard characters soon get soggy in overheated melodrama.
RoC *Alexander Knox, Guy Middleton, Bruce Pitt, Martin Stephens, Gordon Heath, Pearl Prescod, Harry Quashie, Roscoe Holder, Danny*

Daniels, Jan Holden, John Harrison, Waveney Lee.

PASSPORT TO SHAME (1958)   [2]
(USA: *Room 43*)
Dir *Alvin Rakoff.* Prod *John Clein.* Scr *Patrick Alexander.* Ph *Jack Asher.* PC *United Co-Productions.* Dis *British Lion.* 91 mins. Cert X

Tricked into coming to England from France by the 'madame' (*Brenda de Banzie*) of a brothel and her boss, Nick (*Herbert Lom*), Malou (*Odile Versois*) believes she is being employed as a companion. Cab-driver Johnny (*Eddie Constantine*), with whom she has had a one-day 'marriage' to get a passport, realizes she will be coerced into prostitution, and leads London's cabbies to her rescue. Nick falls to his death from a blazing building. As a thriller okay; as a social document exploitative and ridiculous.

RoC *Diana Dors, Robert Brown, Elwyn Brook-Jones, Cyril Shaps, Percy Cartwright, Denis Shaw, Joan Sims, James Ottaway, Lana Morris, Jackie Collins, Margaret Tyzack, Pat Pleasence, Steve Plytas, Charles Price, Robert Fabian, Michael Caine.*

PASSPORT TO TREASON (1956)   [3]
Dir *Robert S. Baker.* Prod *Baker, Monty Berman.* Scr *Kenneth R. Hayles, Norman Hudis, from the novel by Manning O'Brine.* Ph *Berman.* PC *Mid-Century.* Dis *Eros.* 80 mins. Cert U

After his colleague is murdered, private eye Mike O'Kelly (*Rod Cameron*) finds that an international peace league, headed by Syms (*Clifford Evans*) is the cloak for a neo-fascist ring. Diane (*Lois Maxwell*), a secretary in the league, and subsequently revealed as an MI5 agent, is kidnapped by Syms. Amid a nest of truth drugs, murder and double-dealing, O'Kelly finally rescues her and captures Syms. Resolute thriller reminiscent of the late 1930s.

RoC *John Colicos, Barbara Burke, Douglas Wilmer, Ballard Berkeley, Peter Illing, Marianne Stone, Andrew Faulds, Derek Sydney, Trevor Reid, Neil Wilson.*

PAUL TEMPLE RETURNS (1952)   [3]
Dir *Maclean Rogers.* Prod *Ernest G. Roy.* Scr *Francis Durbridge, from his radio serial* Paul Temple Intervenes. Ph *Geoffrey Faithfull.* PC *Nettlefold.* Dis *Butchers.* 71 mins. Cert U

Novelist and amateur sleuth Paul Temple (*John Bentley*) and his wife Steve (*Patricia Dainton*) investigate the Marquis murders. The trail leads from dockland to a bizarre mansion, full of eastern exotica – and snakes. By setting a trap, Temple catches the murderer. Good cast, but lack of professionalism in technical departments ensures mediocrity again; the film brought Temple series to a close.

RoC *Peter Gawthorne, Valentine Dyall, Christopher Lee, Arthur Hill, Ronald Leigh Hunt, Grey Blake, Robert Urquhart, Ben Williams, Dan Jackson, Andrea Malandrinos, George Patterson, Vi Kaley, Elizabeth Gilbert, Gerald Rex, Michael Mulcaster, Dennis Holmes, Sylvia Pugh.*

PAUL TEMPLE'S TRIUMPH (1950)   [2]
Dir *Maclean Rogers.* Prod *Ernest G. Roy.* Scr *A.R. Rawlinson, from a radio serial by Francis Durbridge.* Ph *Brendan J. Stafford.* PC *Nettlefold.* Dis *Butchers.* 80 mins. Cert U

Novelist Paul Temple (*John Bentley*) and his wife Steve (*Dinah Sheridan*) get involved with a secret atomic invention. When the professor with the formula is kidnapped, Temple sets out to find him. The trail leads through the New Forest to the leader of the mysterious 'Z' organization, whom Temple unmasks. Runs like a radio script on screen; no triumph for the famous sleuth this time.

RoC *Jack Livesey, Beatrice Varley, Barbara Couper, Jenny Mathot, Andrew Leigh, Hugh Dempster, Bruce Seton, Ivan Samson, Dino Galvani, Leo de Pokorny, Michael Brennan, Joseph O'Conor, Shaym Bahadur, Gerald Rex, Ben Williams, Anne Hayes, Peter Butterworth, Hamilton Keene, Jean Packer, Frederick Morant, Denys Val Norton, Michael Hogarth.*

PEEPING TOM (1959)   [4]
Dir, Prod and PC *Michael Powell.* Scr *Leo Marks.* Ph *Otto Heller.* Dis *Anglo-Amalgamated.* Eastman Colour. 108 mins. Cert X

Unhinged because his father had used him as a terrified guinea pig in a study of fear, Mark Lewis (*Carl Boehm*) takes pornographic pictures as a sideline to his work in a film studio, but consummates his relationships with women by stabbing them to death with the point of his tripod, filming their agony. Genuinely in love with Helen (*Anna Massey*), he is tormented by the desire to kill her when she discovers his secret. But the police arrive and Mark turns the tripod on himself, filming his own suicide. Splendid nightmare thriller much frowned upon in its day.

RoC *Moira Shearer, Maxine Audley, Brenda Bruce, Martin Miller, Esmond Knight, Bartlett Mullins, Michael Goodliffe, Jack Watson, Shirley Ann Field, Pamela Green, Nigel Davenport, Brian Wallace, Susan Travers, Maurice Durant, Brian Worth, Veronica Hurst, Miles Malleson, Alan Rolfe, Michael Powell.*

Carl Boehm in Peeping Tom *(1959)*

PENNY POINTS TO PARADISE (1951)   [2]
Dir *Tony Young.* Prod *Alan Cullimore.* Scr *John Ormonde.* PC *Advance/PYL Productions.* Dis *Adelphi.* 77 mins. Cert U

Harry Flakers (*Harry Secombe*) wins a fortune on a treble-chance football pool and is relieved of his winnings, temporarily, by a couple of slick seaside counterfeiters, who switch false banknotes for the real money. Early Goon-type effort is directionless, has just a few good chuckles.

RoC *Peter Sellers, Alfred Marks, Spike Milligan, Bill Kerr, Paddie O'Neil, Freddie Frinton, Vicki Page, Sam Kydd, Joe Linnane, Felix Mendelssohn and His Hawaiian Serenaders.*

PENNY PRINCESS (1952)   [3]
Dir, Prod and Scr *Val Guest.* Ph *Geoffrey Unsworth.* PC *Conquest.* Dis *General Film Distributors.* Technicolor. 93 mins. Cert U

Lindy (*Yolande Donlan*), an American shopgirl, inherits a tiny – and bankrupt – European republic. An English cheese salesman (*Dirk Bogarde*) helps her discover that the Lampidorrans manufacture an alcoholic cheese, which she turns into a best-selling export, restoring the economy. Neighbouring countries try a prohibitive import tax, but everything ends happily for Lampidorra and its 'penny princess'. Very slight comedy with music; enthusiastically played.

RoC *A.E. Matthews, Mary Clare, Edwin Styles, Reginald Beckwith, Kynaston Reeves, Peter Butterworth, Desmond Walter-Ellis, Laurence Naismith, Eric Pohlmann, Fletcher Lightfoot, Paul Sheridan, Robert Henderson, J. MacDonald Parke, Alexander Gauge, Anthony Oliver, Derek Prentice, Raf de la Torre, Richard Wattis.*

PERIL FOR THE GUY (1956)   [3]
Dir and Scr *James Hill, from the novel by John Kennett.* Prod *Hindle Edgar.* Ph *James Allen.* PC *World Wide/Children's Film Foundation.* Dis *British Lion.* 56 mins. Cert U

Four children and a scientist are kidnapped by crooks who want the scientist's oil detector invention. One of the children escapes and brings the police, the crooks eventually being routed by a combination of fireworks and fire hoses. Ritter (*Peter Copley*), the ringleader, falls from a helicopter into a lake and is captured. Predictable, lively frolics; parents might be disturbed at some of the things the kids get up to with fireworks!

RoC *Frazer Hines, Christopher Warbey, Amanda Coxall, Ali Alleney, Paul Daneman, Meredith Edwards, Kathrine Kath.*

PERSONAL AFFAIR (1953)   [3]
Dir *Anthony Pelissier.* Prod *Antony Darnborough.* Scr *Lesley Storm, from her play* A Day's Mischief. Ph *Reginald Wyer.* PC *Two Cities.* Dis *General Film Distributors.* 83 mins. Cert A

A 17-year-old schoolgirl (*Glynis Johns*) has a violent crush on her handsome teacher (*Leo Genn*). The interference of his wife (*Gene Tierney*) only makes things worse, the girl runs away and the teacher loses his job and is suspected of her murder. His wife is contemplating suicide when her husband prevents her, telling her the girl has returned. Rather hysterical and pretentious, though the plot is neatly developed.

RoC *Pamela Brown, Walter Fitzgerald, Megs Jenkins, Thora Hird, Michael Hordern, Martin*

Boddey, Norah Gaussen (Gorsen), Nanette Newman.

THE PICKWICK PAPERS (1952) [4]

Dir and Scr *Noel Langley, from the novel by Charles Dickens.* Prod *Langley, George Minter.* Ph *Wilkie Cooper.* PC and Dis *Renown.* 115 mins (later 109). Cert U

Mr Pickwick (*James Hayter*), plump, jovial chairman of the Pickwick club, sets out to tour England with fellow-members Tupman (*Alexander Gauge*), Winkle (*James Donald*) and Snodgrass (*Lionel Murton*). They meet the cavalier Jingle (*Nigel Patrick*), who gets them into all sorts of scrapes, put Pickwick into a debtors' prison, after a trumped-up breach-of-promise suit. But problems are solved, and Jingle gets enough money to start a new life. Jolly adaptation of Dickens classic; gets a bit too serious towards the end.

RoC *Kathleen Harrison, Joyce Grenfell, Hermione Gingold, Donald Wolfit, Hermione Baddeley, Harry Fowler, George Robey, William Hartnell, Joan Heal, Diane Hart, Sam Costa, Athene Seyler, D.A. Clarke-Smith, Alan Wheatley, June Thorburn, Gerald Campion, Mary Merrall, Raymond Lovell, Cecil Trouncer, Felix Felton, Max Adrian, Barry Mackay, Hattie Jacques, Noel Purcell, Gibb McLaughlin, Walter Fitzgerald, Helen Goss, Dandy Nichols, Jack McNaughton, Noel Willman, Helen Burls, May Hallatt, Raf de la Torre, David Hannaford, Jessie Evans, Linda Grey, Joan Benham, Marianne Stone, Pamela Deeming, John Vere, John Kelly, William Strange.*

Hermione Gingold and James Hayter in The Pickwick Papers *(1952)*

THE PLANTER'S WIFE (1952) [3]
(USA: *Outpost in Malaya*)

Dir *Ken Annakin.* Prod *John Stafford.* Scr *Peter Proud, Guy Elmes.* Ph *Geoffrey Unsworth.* PC *Pinnacle.* Dis *General Film Distributors.* 91 mins. Cert A

On his rubber plantation in Malaya, Jim Frazer (*Jack Hawkins*) makes continual plans for defence against a terrorist attack, ignoring his wife (*Claudette Colbert*) to the extent that she plans to take herself and their son (*Peter Asher*) back to England. The attack comes, however, before she can do so and, in the desperate but eventually successful fight to hold out, husband and wife are reunited. Domestic drama clouds important issues, making this average stuff.

RoC *Anthony Steel, Ram Gopal, Tom Macauley,*

Helen Goss, Jeremy Spenser, Sonya Hana, Andy Ho, Don Sharp, Bill Travers, Bryan Coleman, Alfie Bass, Shaym Bahadur, Maria Baillie, John Stamp, John Martin, Myrette Morven, Patrick Westwood, Ng Cheuk Kwong, Yah Ming, Victor Maddern.

PLEASE TURN OVER (1959) [3]

Dir *Gerald Thomas.* Prod *Peter Rogers.* Scr *Norman Hudis, from a play by Basil Thomas.* Ph *Ted Scaife.* PC and Dis *Anglo-Amalgamated.* 87 mins. Cert A

Bored teenager Jo (*Julia Lockwood*), irritated by the paragons of virtue around her, writes a lurid novel in which they all appear in thinly disguised form. Her father (*Ted Ray*) becomes an embezzling dipsomaniac, her mother (*Jean Kent*) an adultress, her staid aunt (*June Jago*) a frustrated, gin-soaked spinster, and so forth. When the book is published and becomes a best-seller, all hell is let loose. But things soon return to normal. Fair comedy; a few laughs.

RoC *Leslie Phillips, Joan Sims, Tim Seely, Charles Hawtrey, Dilys Laye, Lionel Jeffries, Colin Gordon, Joan Hickson, Victor Maddern, Ronald Adam, Cyril Chamberlain, George Street, Marianne Stone, Leigh Madison, Anthony Sagar, Celia Hewitt, Myrtle Reed, Lucy Griffiths, Ursula Hirst, Beryl Hardy, Noel Dyson, Patrick Durkin, Dominica More O'Ferrall, Paul Cole, George Howell.*

POLICE DOG (1955) [2]

Dir and Scr *Derek Twist.* Prod *Harold Huth.* Ph *Cedric Williams.* PC *Douglas Fairbanks Jr.* Dis *Eros.* 72 mins. Cert U

After his partner has been shot by a robber, PC Frank Mason (*Tim Turner*) is put in charge of Rex, a stray alsatian being trained for police duty. The killer has taken an everyday job, but the chance presence of two detectives panics him, and he decides to rob a safe and get away from the area. Mason and Rex are called in to the theft, and together track down their man.

RoC *Joan Rice, Charles Victor, Sandra Dorne, John le Mesurier, Cecil Brock, Nora(h) Gordon, Jimmy Gilbert, Ian Fleming, Norman Mitchell, Michael Scott.*

POOL OF LONDON (1950) [3]

Dir *Basil Dearden.* (Associate) Prod *Michael Relph.* Scr *Jack Whittingham, John Eldridge.* Ph *Gordon Dines.* PC *Ealing Studios.* Dis *General Film Distributors.* 85 mins. Cert U

A story of disillusion – for Johnny (*Earl Cameron*), a Jamaican seaman. His longtime friend Dan (*Bonar Colleano*) uses him to smuggle diamonds. A girl (*Susan Shaw*) befriends him, but only out of pity. Finally Dan, who has decided to give himself up as police and double-crossed associates chase him, has to insult Johnny badly to force him to yield the diamonds and save himself from involvement. Interesting thriller with dockside settings in the Ealing realism tradition.

RoC *Renee Asherson, Moira Lister, Max Adrian, Joan Dowling, James Robertson Justice, Michael Golden, John Longden, Alfie Bass, Leslie Phillips, George Benson, Christopher Hewitt, Beckett Bould, Laurence Naismith, Victor Maddern, Sam Kydd, Michael Ward, George Merritt.*

PORT AFRIQUE (1956) [2]

Dir *Rudolph Maté.* Prod *John R. Sloan, David E. Rose.* Scr *Frank Partos, John Cresswell, from the novel by Bernard Victor Dryer.* Ph *Wilkie Cooper.* PC *Coronado.* Dis *Columbia.* Technicolor. 91 mins. Cert A

Returning to Morocco and his estranged wife, after a period in the States, crippled flier Rip Reardon (*Phil Carey*) finds her dead. The local police call it suicide, but Rip is convinced she was killed. He investigates but wishes he hadn't bothered when he finds out she was murdered by a wife (*Rachel Gurney*) whose husband she was about to steal. Rip seeks to forget the past with singer Ynez (*Pier Angeli*). Plodding mystery with ill-at-ease stars.

RoC *Dennis Price, James Hayter, Eugene Deckers, Anthony Newley, Guido Lorraine, Christopher Lee, Denis Shaw, Guy de Monceau.*

PORT OF ESCAPE (1955) [3]

Dir *Tony Young.* Prod *Lance Comfort.* Scr *Barbara Harper, Young, Abby Mann, from a story by Harper.* Ph *Philip Grindrod.* PC *Wellington.* Dis *Renown.* 76 mins. Cert A

Two Australians, Mitch (*John McCallum*) and Dinty (*Bill Kerr*), the latter suffering from brainstorms, are wartime comrades bound for America. After Dinty nearly kills a man, they are thrown off their ship at London. Dinty again gets into a fight, and Mitch accidentally kills his adversary. They hide out on a boat owned by Anne (*Googie Withers*), a reporter, but Dinty's panic leads to his death when police chase him. Mitch gives himself up. Very modest farewell to British films for Withers and McCallum.

RoC *Alexander Gauge, Hugh Pryse, Joan Hickson, Wendy Danielli, Ingeborg Wells, Ewan Roberts, Simon Lack, Carl Jaffe, Gerald Andersen, Basil Dignam, Cameron Hall, Douglas Robinson, Jack Lester, George Rose, Robert Bruce, Norman Pierce, Len Llewellyn.*

PORTRAIT OF ALISON (1955) [3]
(USA: *Postmark for Danger*)

Dir *Guy Green.* Prod *Frank Godwin.* Scr *Green, Ken Hughes, from the TV serial by Francis Durbridge.* Ph *Wilkie Cooper.* PC *Insignia.* Dis *Anglo-Amalgamated.* 84 mins. Cert A

Commercial artist Tim Forrester (*Robert Beatty*) finds himself enmeshed in intrigue after his brother dies in a car crash (the police

Terry Moore and Allan Cuthbertson in Portrait of Alison *(1955)*

suspect murder) and Alison (*Terry Moore*), believed dead in the same smash, appears and asks him for help. A model (*Josephine Griffin*) is murdered in Tim's flat, the deaths being the work of an international smuggling ring, whose leader (*Allan Cuthbertson*) almost dispatches Alison before Tim rescues her. Smoothly-made jigsaw-type thriller.
RoC *William Sylvester, Geoffrey Keen, Henry Oscar, William Lucas, Terence Alexander, Stuart Saunders, Frank Thornton, Neil Wilson, Eric Corrie, Bruno Barnabe, Reginald Hearne, Patrick Dowling, Raymond Francis.*

PORTRAIT OF CLARE (1950) [3]
Dir *Lance Comfort.* Prod *Leslie Landau.* Scr *Landau, Adrian Arlington, from the novel by Francis Brett Young.* Ph *Günther Krampf.* PC *Associated British.* Dis *AB-Pathé. 98 mins. Cert A*
Clare (*Margaret Johnston*) tells her granddaughter the story of her love life to save the young girl making a big mistake. Clare's first husband (*Ronald Howard*) is drowned; the second (*Robin Bailey*) does not prove the kindly man he once seemed. Rid of him, she marries her barrister friend (*Richard Todd*) and finds true love again. Unoriginal romantic drama failed to establish Miss Johnston.
RoC *Mary Clare, Marjorie Fielding, Anthony Nicholls, Lloyd Pearson, Jeremy Spenser, Bruce Seton, Campbell Copelin, Molly Urquhart, Beckett Bould, S. Griffiths-Moss, Yvonne André, Hugh Morton, David Keir, Hugh Gort, Robert Adair, Grace Arnold, Ann Codrington, Andrew Leigh, Cameron Miller, Una Venning, Brian Peck, Charles Paton, Scott Harold, Amy Veness, Ann Gunning.*

PRELUDE TO FAME (1950) [3]
Dir *Fergus McDonell.* Prod *Donald B. Wilson.* Scr *Robert Westerby, from a novel by Aldous Huxley.* Ph *George Stretton.* PC *Two Cities.* Dis *General Film Distributors. 88 mins. Cert U*
A child music prodigy (*Jeremy Spenser*) is discovered in Italy, and an ambitious Englishwoman (*Kathleen Byron*) takes him away from his parents and makes him world-famous. The pressures of her ever-increasing demands almost drive the boy to suicide, but he is rescued and restored to his family by the man who originally discovered his talent. Some lovely music and the performance of the child star help partly to obscure the fact that this is a very slow film.
RoC *Guy Rolfe, Kathleen Ryan, James Robertson Justice, Henry Oscar, Rosalie Crutchley, John Slater, Ferdy Mayne, Robert Rietti, Robin Dowell, Hugo Schuster, Michael Balfour, David McCallum (Sr), Christopher Lee, Michael Crowdson, Dora Hyde, Don Liddel, Ben Williams, Alex Fields, Penny Dane, Leonard Trolley.*

THE PRICE OF SILENCE (1959) [1]
Dir *Montgomery Tully.* Prod and Scr *Maurice J. Wilson, from a novel by Laurence Maynell.* Ph *Geoffrey Faithfull.* PC and Dis *Grand National. 73 mins. Cert U*
Roger (*Gordon Jackson*) forges a new life for himself at an estate agency, following his re-

lease from prison. He fends off the attentions of his employer's wife (*Maya Koumani*) and falls instead for an artist (*June Thorburn*). But then he is blackmailed by his ex-cellmate Slug (*Sam Kydd*). When a murder is committed, Roger is suspected, but Slug is exposed as the killer, having strangled an old lady for her money. Quite unconvincing. Moral: don't let your producer write his own screenplay.
RoC *Terence Alexander, Mary Clare, Victor Brooks, Joan Heal, Olive Sloane, Llewellyn Rees, Annette Kerr, Norman Shelley, Norman Mitchell.*

THE PRINCE AND THE SHOWGIRL (1957) [4]
Dir *Laurence Olivier, Anthony Bushell.* Prod *Olivier.* Scr *Terence Rattigan, from his play The Sleeping Prince.* Ph *Jack Cardiff.* PC *Marilyn Monroe Productions.* Dis *Warner Bros. Technicolor. 116 mins. Cert A*
1911. The Regent of Carpathia (*Laurence Olivier*), in Britain for the coronation of George V, admires showgirl Elsie (*Marilyn Monroe*), who is invited to meet him. Rejecting his clumsy advances, she later wins his affection, is invited to the coronation, reconciles him with his son (*Jeremy Spenser*), the king, and returns to the stage. A few laughs and a tear or two, although the stars seem not quite at their ease.
RoC *Sybil Thorndike, Richard Wattis, Jean Kent, Esmond Knight, David Horne, Charles Victor, Daphne Anderson, Vera Day, Gillian Owen, Maxine Audley, Gladys Henson, Paul Hardwicke, Andrea Malandrinos, Margot Lister, Aubrey Dexter, Harold Goodwin, Rosamund Greenwood, Dennis Edwards.*

Sybil Thorndike and Marilyn Monroe in The Prince and the Showgirl *(1956)*

THE PRISONER (1955) [5]
Dir *Peter Glenville.* Prod *Vivian A. Cox, Sydney Box.* Scr *Bridget Boland, from her play.* Ph *Reg Wyer.* PC *London Independent/Facet.* Dis *Columbia. 94 mins. Cert A*
A nameless European state. A cardinal (*Alec Guinness*) who is required to confess to 'crimes' for political reasons, is handed over to his interrogator (*Jack Hawkins*), a psychologist. At first the men are evenly matched, but the state's man eventually detects a chink in the cardinal's armour when it emerges he did not love his mother. After confinement in the dark,

he admits he became a priest through pride. He signs the confession and, to avoid 'martyrdom', goes unpunished. The interrogator resigns. Moving, brilliantly acted dramatic duel only narrowly misses escaping its stage origins.
RoC *Raymond Huntley, Wilfrid Lawson, Jeannette Sterke, Ronald Lewis, Kenneth Griffith, Mark Dignam, Gerard Heinz, Richard Leech.*

PRIVATE INFORMATION (1952) [2]
Dir *Fergus McDonell.* Prod *Ronald Kinnoch.* Scr *Gordon Glennon, John Baines, Kinnoch, from a play by Glennon.* Ph *Eric Cross.* PC *ACT Films.* Dis *Monarch. 66 mins. Cert U*
Charlotte (*Jill Esmond*), tenant of a jerry-built council house, discovers a confidential report written by her son (*Jack Watling*), assistant to the borough surveyor. Suspecting bribery and corruption, she storms to the town hall, and accuses the mayor and the surveyor of taking bribes to pass defective drains. When a typhoid epidemic breaks out, she is proved right, though her daughter (*Carol Marsh*) nearly dies. Sincerity of intention not enough; film is badly acted and boring.
RoC *Gerard Heinz, Norman Shelley, Mercy Haystead, Lloyd Pearson, Henry Caine, Brenda de Banzie, Peter Swanwick.*

PRIVATE'S PROGRESS (1956) [3]
Dir *John Boulting.* Prod *Roy Boulting.* Scr *Frank Harvey, John Boulting, from the novel by Alan Hackney.* Ph *Eric Cross.* PC *Charter.* Dis *British Lion. 102 mins. Cert U*
Undergraduate Stanley Windrush (*Ian Carmichael*), an inept undergraduate called up for army service in World War II, is soon taught the secrets of work dodging by such ace scroungers as Cox (*Richard Attenborough*). An unscrupulous uncle involves Windrush in a scheme to steal art treasures from behind Nazi lines. Somehow, Windrush brings it off, but retribution catches up with both him and Cox. Very popular comedy has its moments, though none of them very original. Characters resolutely dislikeable.
RoC *Dennis Price, Terry-Thomas, William Hartnell, Jill Adams, Peter Jones, Thorley Walters, Ian Bannen, Victor Maddern, Kenneth Griffith, George Coulouris, Derrick de Marney, Miles Malleson, Michael Trubshawe, John le Mesurier, Brian Oulton, John Warren, Nicholas Bruce, David Lodge, David King-Wood, Frank Hawkins, Basil Dignam, Henry Longhurst, Henry Oscar, Theodore Zichy, Michael Ward, Robert Bruce, Ludwig Lawinski, Sally Miles, Irlyn Hall, Marianne Stone, Lockwood West, Jack McNaughton, Eynon Evans, Glyn Houston, Ronald Adam, Lloyd Lamble.*

A PRIZE OF GOLD (1954) [3]
Dir *Mark Robson.* Prod *Phil C. Samuel.* Scr *Robert Buckner, John Paxton, from the novel by Max Catto.* Ph *Ted Moore.* PC *Warwick.* Dis *Columbia. Technicolor. 99 mins. Cert A*
To help Maria (*Mai Zetterling*), a German girl he loves, take the orphan she has adopted to Brazil, USAF sergeant Joe Lawrence (*Richard Widmark*) plans to steal a consignment of gold being flown from Berlin to London. He hand-

picks his helpers, and brings off the job; but thieves fall out, then die one by one. The only consolation for Lawrence, who ultimately gives himself up, is that Maria gets to South America. Jaded action yarn shored up by good character cameos (*Nigel Patrick, George Cole, Donald Wolfit*).

RoC *Andrew Ray, Joseph Tomelty, Karel Stepanek, Eric Pohlmann, Robert Ayres, Olive Sloane, Ivan Craig, Alan Gifford, Leslie Linder, Harry Towb, Nelly Arno.*

PROFILE (1954) [2]

Dir *Francis Searle*. Prod *John Temple-Smith*. Scr *John Gilling*. Ph *Brendan Stafford*. PC *Major*. Dis *Monarch*. 66 mins. Cert A

Armstrong (*John Bentley*), new editor of the magazine *Profile*, is interested in the publisher's daughter (*Thea Gregory*), but the publisher's wife Margot (*Kathleen Byron*) is interested in *him*. The publisher dies from a heart attack; Armstrong is falsely accused of embezzlement, then suspected of murder when Margot is slain. The real killer is caught after a chase through the printing works. Tortuous thriller.

RoC *Stuart Lindsell, Garard Green, Ivan Craig, Lloyd Lamble, Arnold Bell, Frank Henderson, Bruce Beeby, John Parkes, June Charlier, Derek Prentice, Patrick Jordan, John Blake.*

THE PURPLE PLAIN (1954) [5]

Dir *Robert Parrish*. Prod *John Bryan*. Scr *Eric Ambler*, from the novel by *H.E. Bates*. Ph *Geoffrey Unsworth*. PC *Two Cities*. Dis *General Film Distributors*. Technicolor. 100 mins. Cert A

Forrester (*Gregory Peck*), a nerve-shot Canadian pilot in the Burma of 1945, is rehabilitated with the help of Anna (*Win Min Than*) and Miss McNab (*Brenda de Banzie*), a missionary. On a transport flight, his plane crashes and he and his passenger, Blore (*Maurice Denham*) have to trek through jungle with their injured navigator (*Lyndon Brook*). Blore, despairing, shoots himself, but Forrester, with the wounded man on his back, makes it. Gripping film, the dramatic sequences more effective than the romantic ones.

RoC *Bernard Lee, Anthony Bushell, Jack McNaughton, Josephine Griffin, Ram Gopal, Peter Arne, Dorothy Alison, Mya Mya Spencer, Harold Siddons, Lane Meddick, John Tinn, Soo Ah Song.*

Q

THE QUATERMASS EXPERIMENT (1955) [4]

(**USA**: *The Creeping Unknown*)

Dir *Val Guest*. Prod *Anthony Hinds*. Scr *Guest*,

Richard Landau, from the TV serial by *Nigel Kneale*. Ph *Jimmy Harvey*. Sp eff *Leslie Bowie*. PC *Hammer*. Dis *Exclusive*. 82 mins. Cert X

A space rocket crash lands back in Britain with two of its three-man crew gone and the third (*Richard Wordsworth*) in a state of shock. Professor Quatermass (*Brian Donlevy*) concludes that an alien force has taken possession of the astronaut's body, but the man's wife (*Margia Dean*) helps him 'escape'; already he is turning into a fungoid vegetable, killing numerous people before being trapped and destroyed in the rafters of Westminster Abbey. Hammer's greatest success to date, an effective version of TV shocker that gripped millions.

RoC *Jack Warner, David King-Wood, Gordon Jackson, Harold Lang, Thora Hird, Lionel Jeffries, Maurice Kaufmann, Frank Phillips, Gron Davies, Stanley Van Beers, Henry Longhurst, Michael Godfrey, Frank Phillips, Arthur Lovegrove, John Stirling, Eric Corrie, Margaret Anderson, Fred Johnson, George Roderick, Ernest Hare, John Kerr, John Wynn, Toke Townley, Bartlett Mullins, Molly Glessing, Mayne Lynton, Basil Dignam, Marianne Stone.*

QUATERMASS II (1957) [3]

(**USA**: *Enemy from Space*)

Dir *Val Guest*. Prod *Anthony Hinds*. Scr *Nigel Kneale, Guest*, from Kneale's TV serial. Ph *Gerald Gibbs*. PC *Hammer*. Dis *United Artists*. 85 mins. Cert X

Meteorites are releasing unknown forces which plant a fungus growth on the faces of humans, then take over their minds. Professor Quatermass (*Brian Donlevy*) discovers a research station in the middle of nowhere, manned with victims who have been taken over. He realizes it is an acclimatization centre for space aliens. With local townsfolk, he attacks the centre and, by increasing its oxygen supply, destroys the aliens. Not as good as the TV serial, but moves speedily and with purpose.

RoC *John Longden, Sidney James, Bryan Forbes, Vera Day, William Franklyn, Charles Lloyd Pack, Tom Chatto, John Van Eyssen, Percy Herbert, Michael Ripper, John Rae, Marianne Stone, Ronald Wilson, Jane Aird, Betty Impey, Lloyd Lamble, John Stuart, Gilbert Davies, Joyce Adams, Edwin Richfield, Howard Williams, Philip Baird, Robert Raikes, John Fabian, George Merritt, Arthur Blake, Michael Balfour, Jan Holden.*

A QUESTION OF ADULTERY (1958) [1]

Dir *Don Chaffey*. Prod *Raymond Stross*. Scr *Anne Edwards, Denis Freeman*. Ph *Stephen Dade*. PC *Connaught Place*. Dis *Eros*. 85 mins. Cert A

Discovering he is sterile after a car crash, Mark (*Anthony Steel*) suggests his wife Mary (*Julie London*) should have a child by artificial insemination. But after she becomes friendly with another man (*Anton Diffring*) at a Swiss clinic, he instigates divorce proceedings. He later regrets his action and, after the jury has failed to reach a verdict, drops the case and asks Mary's forgiveness. Sensationalistic treatment of sensitive theme. Feeble.

RoC *Basil Sydney, Donald Houston, Andrew*

Cruickshank, Frank Thring, Conrad Phillips, Kynaston Reeves, Mary Mackenzie, Georgina Cookson, Trader Faulkner, Vola Van Dere, Richard Caldicot, Arthur Gomez, Phillip Holles, John Rae, Trevor Reid, John Fabian, Rodney Burke, Michael Logan, John Charlesworth, Alan Welch, Michael Anthony, Max Brimmell, Van Boolen.

THE QUIET WOMAN (1950) [2]

Dir and Scr *John Gilling*. Prod *Robert S. Baker, Monty Berman*. Ph *Berman, E. Besche*. PC *Tempean*. Dis *Eros*. 71 mins. Cert U

Janie (*Jane Hylton*), a girl with a past, takes over a coastal inn called *The Quiet Woman*, and becomes attracted to a smuggler (*Derek Bond*). Her escaped-convict husband catches up with her, and insists she help him. The smuggler attempts to get him to France in his boat but they are thwarted by customs officers and the convict killed. Dullish drama; good photography its only plus-point.

RoC *Dora Bryan, Dianne Foster, Michael Balfour, John Horsley, Harry Towb, Campbell Singer.*

R

RADIO CAB MURDER (1954) [3]

Dir and Scr *Vernon Sewell*. Prod *George Maynard*. Ph *Geoffrey Faithfull*. PC *Insignia*. Dis *Eros*. 70 mins. Cert A

Ex-safecracker (convicted) Fred (*Jimmy Hanley*), working for a radio cab firm, seizes a chance to live down his past when asked to act as the police's 'inside man' in a robber gang who recruit ex-cons by getting them fired from their jobs. When the gang discover Fred's deception, they lock him in a deep-freeze. But his fellow cabbies come to the rescue and help round up the crooks. Stars and direction enliven cut-price, coincidence-stretching thriller.

RoC *Lana Morris, Sonia Holm, Jack Allen, Sam Kydd, Pat McGrath, Bruce Beeby, Elizabeth Seal, Rupert Evans, Michael Mellinger, Jack Stewart, Frank Thornton, Ian Wilson.*

THE RAINBOW JACKET (1954) [4]

Dir *Basil Dearden*. Prod *Michael Relph*. Scr *T.E.B. Clarke*. Ph *Otto Heller*. PC *Ealing Studios*. Dis *General Film Distributors*. Technicolor. 99 mins. Cert U

Trained by Sam (*Bill Owen*), an ex-jockey warned off the track for five years, young Georgie (*Fella Edmonds*) is taken on as an apprentice. But he is forced to throw a race to help Sam, who has fallen foul of a razor gang, and Sam's mother, who has lost her employer's money trying to help Sam. When Sam regains his licence, the gang menace him and Georgie again, but Sam forces Georgie to win a race he is meant to lose. Racecourse drama seems like

Fella Edmonds and Bill Owen in The Rainbow Jacket *(1954)*

a whiff of the real thing, apart from poor process work.

RoC *Kay Walsh, Edward Underdown, Robert Morley, Wilfrid Hyde White, Charles Victor, Ronald Ward, Howard Marion Crawford, Honor Blackman, Sidney James, Michael Trubshawe, Frederick Piper, Brian Roper, Eliot Makeham, George Thorpe, Herbert C. Walton, Michael Ripper, Colin Kemball, Sam Kydd, Katie Johnson, David Hemmings, Glyn Houston.*

RAISING A RIOT (1955)   [4]

Dir *Wendy Toye.* Prod *Ian Dalrymple, Hugh Perceval.* Scr *Dalrymple, Perceval, James Matthews, from the novel by Alfred Toombs.* Ph *Christopher Challis.* PC *London Films/Wessex.* Dis *British Lion.* Technicolor. 91 mins. Cert U

Tony (*Kenneth More*), a naval officer left in charge of his three children while his wife flies off to see her sick mother in Canada, takes them to his father's converted windmill in the country. Tony uses naval discipline to cope with his problems as head cook, bottle-washer, nurse, mother and teacher, and all goes well until a children's party, which ends with everyone throwing food at each other. His wife returns – but Tony finds he has been posted to Canada. Engaging, refreshing comedy, full of assorted comic incident.

RoC *Jan Miller, Shelagh Fraser, Mandy (Miller), Gary Billings, Fusty Bentine, Ronald Squire, Olga Lindo, Lionel Murton, Mary Laura Wood, Robin Brown, Nora Nicholson, Anita Sharp Bolster, Dorothy Dewhurst, Arthur Hill, Erik Chitty, Fred Griffiths, Sam Kydd, Bill Shine, Jessie Evans, Michael Bentine,*

Mandy (Miller), Kenneth More and Gary Billings in Raising a Riot *(1954)*

Charles Lamb, Cyril Chamberlain, Patricia Cree, Victor Maddern, Donald Pascoe.

RAMSBOTTOM RIDES AGAIN (1956) [3]

Dir and Prod *John Baxter.* Scr *Baxter, Basil Thomas, Geoffrey Orme, Arthur Askey, Glenn Melvyn, from the play by Harold G. Robert.* Ph *Arthur Grant.* PC *Jack Hylton Productions.* Dis *British Lion.* 93 mins. Cert U

Bill Ramsbottom (*Arthur Askey*) sells up his pub and takes his family off to Lonesome, in Canada, where he has inherited property from Wild Bill Ramsbottom, his grandpa. Once there, he soon tangles with Black Jake (*Sidney James*), a mean *hombre* the townsfolk all fear. More by luck than judgment, Bill cleans up the town. Broad English version of *Destry Rides Again*, on the juvenile side; *Jerry Desmonde* very funny as an Indian named Blue Eagle.

RoC *Glenn Melvyn, Betty Marsden, Shani Wallis, Frankie Vaughan, Danny Ross, Anthea Askey, June Grant, Sabrina, Donald Stewart, Billy Percy, Dennis Wyndham, Gary Wayne, Campbell Singer, Marne Maitland, Beckett Bould, Sam Kydd, Deryck Guyler, Edie Martin, Leonard Williams, John Carson.*

A RAY OF SUNSHINE (1950)   [2]

Dir *Horace Shepherd.* Prod *Phyllis Shepherd.* Scr *Uncredited.* PC *Delmar.* Dis *Adelphi.* 55 mins. Cert U

Variety show introduced by popular radio comedian *Ted Ray*, who, commented one critic, 'should have insisted on better material' for his film debut.

RoC *Lucille Gaye, Freddie Bamberger and Pam, Janet Brown, Wilson, Keppel and Betty, Morton Frazer's Harmonica Gang, Anita and Armand, Roberta, Ivy Benson and Her All-Girls Band.*

REACH FOR THE SKY (1956)   [5]

Dir *Lewis Gilbert.* Prod *Daniel M. Angel.* Scr *Gilbert, Vernon Harris, from the book by Paul Brickhill.* Ph *Jack Asher.* PC *Pinnacle.* Dis *Rank.* 135 mins. Cert U

A promising RAF flyer, Douglas Bader (*Kenneth More*) sustains injuries in an air crash in 1931 that mean the amputation of both legs. Against agonizing odds, he learns to walk with 'tin' legs and to fly again. With World War II, he finds himself needed again by the RAF and leads five Battle of Britain squadrons before being taken prisoner. His numerous attempts

Kenneth More and Dorothy Alison in Reach for the Sky *(1956)*

to escape are thwarted, but, in 1945, he leads the victory air parade over London in a Spitfire. Enthralling drama; war scenes familiar, but a very superior performance by the star. British Oscar as best British film.

RoC *Muriel Pavlow, Lyndon Brook, Lee Patterson, Alexander Knox, Dorothy Alison, Sydney Tafler, Howard Marion Crawford, Jack Watling, Michael Warre, Nigel Green, Anne Leon, Walter Hudd, Eddie Byrne, Charles Carson, Ronald Adam, Eric Pohlmann, Michael Gough, Basil Appleby, Philip Stainton, Beverly Brooks, Michael Ripper, Derek Blomfield, Avice Landone, Harry Locke, Sam Kydd, Anton Diffring, Michel Clément, Clive Revill, Michael Balfour.*

RECOIL (1953)   [3]

Dir and Scr *John Gilling.* Prod *Robert S. Baker, Monty Berman.* Ph *Berman.* PC *Tempean.* Dis *Eros.* 79 mins. Cert A

A jeweller's daughter, Jean (*Elizabeth Sellars*) tracks down the gang that robbed and beat her father. She gets in with the crooks, who fall out, split up and eventually shoot it out with each other, while police and one of the crooks' doctor brother (*Edward Underdown*) rescue Jean. Compact low-budget thriller.

RoC *Kieron Moore, John Horsley, Robert Raglan, Ethel O'Shea, Martin Benson, Michael Kelly, Iam Fleming, Bill Lowe, Tony Pelly, Derek Blomfield, Louise Grainger, Michael Balfour, Daphne Newton, Marguerite Brennan.*

THE RED BERET (1953)   [3]
(USA: *Paratrooper*)

Dir *Terence Young.* Prod *Irving Allen, Albert R. Broccoli, Anthony Bushell.* Scr *Richard Maibaum, Frank Nugent, from the book by Hilary St George Sanders.* Ph *John Wilcox.* PC *Warwick.* Dis *Columbia.* 88 mins. Cert U

McKendrick (*Alan Ladd*), an American on the run after causing the death of a friend in a flying accident, masquerades as a Canadian to join the British Parachute Regiment in World War II. He refuses to accept a commission until he has proved himself under fire in a desperate situation in North Africa in which he saves his patrol. One of the better Warwick productions, dramatically actionful, although with the usual deficiencies in script and character-drawing.

RoC *Susan Stephen, Leo Genn, Harry Andrews, Donald Houston, Anthony Bushell, Patric Doonan, Stanley Baker, Lana Morris, Tim Turner, Michael Kelly, Anton Diffring, Thomas Heathcote, Carl Duering, Walter Gotell, Yvonne Stein, Harry Locke, David Orr, John Boxer, Michael Balfour.*

THE RED DRESS (1954)   [3]

Dir *Lawrence Huntington, Charles Saunders.* Prod and PC *Douglas Fairbanks Jr.* Scr *Guy Morgan, Selwyn Jepson, Larry Marcus and Peter Quinn.* Ph *Ken Talbot, Brendan J. Stafford, Jimmy Wilson.* Dis *British Lion.* 76 mins. Cert A

Three stories. (1) A miner's wife (*Renee Asherson*) whose hated husband is missing in a pit disaster goes on a spending spree and meets another man. But her husband is still alive ... (2) A girl (*Joan Tetzel*) locks a man up to

prevent him marrying her sister. But she has the wrong man ... (3) A saboteur (*James Kenney*) plants a bomb and sweats over getting away from his factory before it goes off. He leaves with a co-worker, who produces the bomber's lunchbox with the bomb in it ... Very good last story lifts sandwich fare.
RoC *Clifford Evans, John Warwick, Meredith Edwards, Paul Carpenter, Deborah Turnbull, Warren Stanhope, John Salew, Peter Jones, Bartlett Mullins.*

THE RELUCTANT BRIDE (1955)   3
(USA: *Two Grooms for a Bride*)
Dir *Henry Cass.* Prod *Robert S. Baker, Monty Berman.* Scr *Frederick Stephani.* Ph *Berman.* PC *Tempean.* Dis *Eros.* 73 mins. Cert A.
When their parents disappear on a hunting expedition, the children try to get their father's brother (*John Carroll*) and wife's sister (*Virginia Bruce*) together, even though they are both engaged to other people. The children finally dispose of both unwanted fiancés and bring the couple together, just as it is announced that the missing parents have been found alive in the Congo. Two Hollywood stars polish up some familiar comedy material. Made in 1952; not released in Britain until 1955, in America until 1957.
RoC *Brian Oulton, Kay Callard, Michael Caridia, Barbara Brown, Kit Terrington, Alexander Gauge, Donald Stewart, Anita Sharp Bolster, Arthur Lowe, Tom Gill, Ann Doran, Tucker McGuire, Ernest Jay, Michael Balfour, Karen Greer.*

RELUCTANT HEROES (1951)   3
Dir *Jack Raymond.* Prod *Henry Halstead.* Scr *Colin Morris from his play.* Ph *James Wilson.* PC *Byron.* Dis *Associated British.* 80 mins. Cert U
Drill Sergeant Bell (*(Ronald Shiner*) finds himself with the awkward squad to end them all when the latest batch of National Service recruits arrives. They include gormless northerner Horace (*Brian Rix*) and playboy Michael (*Derek Far*) who eventually gets his ex-flame (*Christine Norden*) to say 'yes' to marriage during a headlong runaway tank ride. Rough-edged humour rattles along: hit the box-office bullseye.
RoC *Larry Noble, Betty Impey, Angela Wheatland, Anthony Baird, Colin Morris, Elspet Gray, Joan Henley, George Radford.*

THE RELUCTANT WIDOW (1950)   2
Dir *Bernard Knowles.* Prod *Gordon Wellesley.* Scr *Wellesley, J.B. Boothroyd, from the novel by Georgette Heyer.* Ph *Jack Hildyard.* PC *Two Cities.* Dis *General Film Distributors.* 91 mins. Cert A
The Napoleonic Wars. Elinor (*Jean Kent*), on her way to be a governess, gets in the wrong carriage, and falls under the influence of Lord Carlyon (*Guy Rolfe*) who marries her to a dying man for his own purposes, then instals her at the man's sinister country home, where her life is punctuated by the advent of spies, smugglers and suitors. She outwits Napoleon's agents for vital plans, and the story ends with a duel. Carlyon wins the duel – and Elinor.

Incident-filled tale hovers unhappily between comedy and adventure.
RoC *Paul Dupuis, Lana Morris, Kathleen Byron, Julian Dallas, Anthony Tancred, Peter Hammond, Jean Cadell, Andrew Cruickshank, George Thorpe, Ralph Truman, James Carney, Allan Jeayes, Hector MacGregor, Noel Howlett, Roddy Hughes, Cecil Bevan, Peter Bull, Johnnie Schofield, Ernest Jay, Maxwell Foster, John Warren, Jack Vyvyan, H.G. Stoker, Barry Denville, Janet Kaye, Peter Dunlop, John Bell.*

THE REVENGE OF FRANKENSTEIN
(1958)   2
Dir *Terence Fisher.* Prod *Anthony Hinds.* Scr *Jimmy Sangster, Hurford Janes, from characters created by Mary Shelley.* Ph *Jack Asher.* PC *Hammer.* Dis *Columbia. Technicolor.* 89 mins. Cert X
The 19th century. Escaping his persecutors, and still obsessed with creating a living being, Baron Frankenstein (*Peter Cushing*) uses his position at a charity clinic to obtain limbs, and gets a brain transplanted from the body of a dwarf. The resulting creature escapes before the brain has been 'programmed' and goes on a killing rampage. Learning what has happened, the patients at the clinic turn on Frankenstein and maul him. He survives – to pop up in London as Dr Frank of Harley Street. Often unintentionally funny, the weakest of the early Hammer horrors.
RoC *Eunice Gayson, Francis Matthews, Michael Gwynn, John Welsh, Lionel Jeffries, Oscar Quitak, Richard Wordsworth, Charles Lloyd Pack, John Stuart, Margery Gresley, Arnold Diamond, Avril Leslie, George Woodbridge, Anna Walmsley, Michael Ripper, Ian Whittaker.*

RICHARD III (1955)   6
Dir *Laurence Olivier, Anthony Bushell.* Prod *Olivier.* Text adviser *Alan Dent, from the play by William Shakespeare.* Ph *Otto Heller.* PC *London Films.* Dis *Independent Film Distributors/British Lion. Technicolor. VistaVision.* 161 mins. Cert U
Fifteenth-century England. Richard Crookback (*Laurence Olivier*) murders those who stand in his way to the throne, including the young princes in the Tower; and he marries Lady Anne (*Claire Bloom*), widow of Edward V. In 1485, he is killed at the Battle of Bosworth Field by the forces of Henry Tudor (*Stanley Baker*), who becomes king. Magnetic central performance by Olivier dominates what is probably the most commercial Shakespeare on record. British Oscars for best film and best actor (Olivier).
RoC *John Gielgud, Ralph Richardson, Alec Clunes, Cedric Hardwicke, Norman Wooland, Laurence Naismith, Pamela Brown, Mary Kerridge, Helen Haye, John Laurie, Esmond Knight, Michael Gough, Andrew Cruickshank, Clive Morton, Nicholas Hannen, Russell Thorndike, Paul Huson, Stewart Allen, Wally Bascoe, Norman Fisher, Terence Greenidge, Dan Cunningham, Douglas Wilmer, Michael Ripper, Andy Shine, Roy Russell, George Woodbridge, Peter Williams, Bill Shine, Ann Wilton, Timothy Bateson, Willoughby Gray, Derek Prentice,*

Deering Wells, Richard Bennett, Patrick Troughton, John Phillips, Brian Nissen, Alexander Davion, Lane Meddick, Robert Bishop.

THE RINGER (1952)   3
Dir *Guy Hamilton.* Prod *Hugh Perceval.* Scr *Val Valentine, Lesley Storm, from the play by Edgar Wallace.* Ph *Ted Scaife.* PC *London Films.* Dis *British Lion.* 78 mins. Cert U
The Ringer, a dangerous master of disguise, is after crooked lawyer Meister (*Herbert Lom*), who was responsible for the suicide of The Ringer's sister. The police close in, and Meister employs ex-convict Sam Hackitt (*William Hartnell*) as bodyguard. The police doctor (*Donald Wolfit*) proves to be The Ringer, and he kills Meister with the aid of a wire from the burglar alarm, then escapes. Good cast gets ancient thriller by.
RoC *Mai Zetterling, Greta Gynt, Norman Wooland, Denholm Elliott, Charles Victor, Dora Bryan, Walter Fitzgerald, John Stuart, John Slater, Campbell Singer.*

RIVER BEAT (1954)   4
Dir *Guy Green.* Prod *Victor Hanbury.* Scr *Rex Rienits.* Ph *Geoffrey Faithfull.* PC *Insignia.* Dis *Eros.* 70 mins. Cert U
Judy (*Phyllis Kirk*), radio operator aboard an American ship, is duped into smuggling diamonds into Britain in packets of cigarettes. Held by the customs, Judy's in trouble – especially when the body of the man who gave her the packages is fished out of the river. A police inspector (*John Bentley*) helps Judy trace the receiver of the gems – who kidnaps her before the law catches him after a river chase. Well-acted, well-paced, well-set thriller: well-above-average 'B'.
RoC *Robert Ayres, Ewan Roberts, Leonard White, Harold Ayer, Glyn Houston, Charles Lloyd Pack, David Hurst, Patrick Jordan, Margaret Anderson, Isabel George, Michael Balfour.*

Phyllis Kirk and John Bentley in River Beat *(1954)*

ROADHOUSE GIRL (1953)   2
Dir and Scr *Wolf Rilla, from a play by Peter Jones.* Prod *Ernest G. Roy.* Ph *Geoffrey Faithfull.* PC *Nettlefold.* Dis *Butchers.* 70 mins. Cert A
Tempted by Marilyn, the wife (*Sandra Dorne*) of a garage-owner (*Leslie Dwyer*), Tom (*Maxwell Reed*) kills him. The guilty couple cover

up the crime, and Marilyn starts a successful roadhouse adjoining the garage, helped by rich, smooth Nicky (*Ferdy Mayne*), who leaves her when he gets wind of what she has done. She reverts to Tom, but the police are on to them. Briefly released as *Marilyn*, this cutprice *The Postman Always Rings Twice* is not very good under either title.
RoC *Vida Hope, Hugh Pryse, Kenneth Connor, Ben Williams.*

ROBBERY UNDER ARMS (1957)   3

Dir *Jack Lee*. Prod *Joseph Janni*. Scr *Alexander Baron, W.P. Lipscomb, from the novel by Rolf Boldrewood*. Ph *Harry Waxman*. PC and Dis *Rank*. Eastman Colour. 99 mins. Cert A
1850, Australia. The adventurous Marston brothers, Dick (*Ronald Lewis*) and Jim (*David McCallum*), seeking to escape their dull lives, join wanted bushranger Captain Starlight (*Peter Finch*) in cattle-stealing, which leads to bank robbery and a price on their heads. Dick is betrayed by a woman and he and Starlight killed in the subsequent attempted rescue. Jim's wife Jean (*Jill Ireland*) talks him out of shooting it out with the law, and he gives himself up. Some of the acting is pretty bad in this 'Australian western', which made a better radio serial.
RoC *Maureen Swanson, Laurence Naismith, Vincent Ball, Jean Anderson, Johnny Cadell, Ursula Finlay, Larry Taylor, Russell Napier, Dudy Nimmo, Yvonne Buckingham, George Cormack, Doris Goddard.*

David McCallum and Peter Finch in Robbery Under Arms *(1957)*

ROBBERY WITH VIOLENCE (1958)   1

Dir, Prod and Ph *Ivan Barnett*. Scr *David Cumming*. PC *GIB Films*. Dis *Regal*. 67 mins. Cert A
Bank robber Peter Frayne (*Ivan Craig*) double-crosses his associates, scoots with the money and, hiding out as a hop-picker, resumes a love affair with an old flame (*Sally Day*), now the wife of a publican, whose body is soon found bundled up in a hopsack. Trapped by his associates in a fence's shop, Frayne's escape is cut off by the advent of the police, and he is shot dead by one of his 'partners'. Amateurish, very low-budget thriller provided a rare but unworthy star role for Ivan Craig.
RoC *Michael Golden, John Martin, John Trevor-Davis.*

ROB ROY, THE HIGHLAND ROGUE (1953)   4

Dir *Harold French*. Prod *Perce Pearce*. Scr *Lawrence E. Watkin*. Ph *Guy Green*. PC *Walt Disney*. Dis *RKO Radio*. Technicolor. 81 mins. Cert U
1715. Scottish rebel Rob Roy MacGregor (*Richard Todd*) escapes twice from his English captors, headed by the treacherous Duke of Montrose (*Michael Gough*). The Duke of Argyll (*James Robertson Justice*) tells King George I (*Eric Pohlmann*) that he will secure both Rob Roy and peace. But MacGregor has just captured an important stronghold, and it is on his own terms that he ultimately comes to London. Simple, lively, colourful Highland western; hasn't a lot to do with history.
RoC *Glynis Johns, Finlay Currie, Geoffrey Keen, Jean Taylor Smith, Archie Duncan, Michael Goodliffe, Marjorie Fielding, Russell Waters, Malcolm Keen, Ina de la Haye, Martin Boddey, Max Gardner, Ewen Solon, John McEvoy, Ian McNaughton, James Sutherland, Stevenson Lang, Charles Hubbard, Campbell Godley, Howard Douglas, Douglas Bradley-Smith, May Hallatt, Hamilton Keene, Henry Hewitt, David Keir, Hal Osmond, Middleton Woods, Andrew Laurence, Rupert Evans, Paddy Ryan, Kitty and Marietta MacLeod.*

ROCKETS GALORE (1958)   3
(USA: *Mad Little Island*)

Dir *Michael Relph*. Prod *Basil Dearden*. Scr *Monja Danischewsky, from the novel by Compton Mackenzie*. Ph *Reginald Wyer*. PC and Dis *Rank*. Eastman Colour. 94 mins. Cert U
The Hebridean islanders of Todday are determined to stop a rocket base being built there. Sabotage efforts are topped by the capture of a crashed guided missile, which government officials led by Hugh Mander (*Donald Sinden*) are unable to recover. The coup-de-grâce to Whitehall plans is delivered by schoolteacher Janet Macleod, who gets local seagulls painted pink and creates a rare bird. Sequel to the riotous *Whisky Galore!* (qv) is pleasant comedy, but the fun doesn't set the adrenalin flowing.
RoC *Roland Culver, Noel Purcell, Ian Hunter, Duncan Macrae, Jean Cadell, Gordon Jackson, Alex Mackenzie, James Copeland, Carl Jaffe, Nicholas Phipps, Catherine Lacey, John Laurie, Reginald Beckwith, Ronald (Ronnie) Corbett, Alex Mackenzie, Jameson Clark, John Stevenson Lang, Arthur Howard, Neil Ballantyne, Jack Short, Gabrielle Blunt.*

ROCK YOU SINNERS (1957)   1

Dir *Denis Kavanagh*. Prod *B.C. Fancey, Jeffrey Kruger*. Scr *Beatrice Scott*. Ph *Hal Morey*. PC and Dis *Small Films*. 59 mins. Cert U
A disc jockey (*Philip Gilbert*) gets his big break when he successfully arranges a television show about rock 'n' roll – but he nearly loses his girl-friend in his dedication to the job in hand. All ends well, however, when TV programme chiefs agree to turn the show into a series. Monumentally inept British rock 'n' roll offering. Said one critic: 'The acting is so wooden you could light a fire with it.'
RoC *Adrienne Scott, Colin Croft, Jackie Collins, Beckett Bould, Michael Duffield, Tony Hall, Diana Chesney, Martin Lyder, Red Montgomery, and Art Baxter 'n' His Rockin' Sinners, Tony Crombie and His Rockets, Rory Blackwell and the Blackjacks, Joan Small, Dickie Bennett, Curly Pat Barry, Tony Hall, Don Sollash and His Rockin' Horses, George (Calypso) Brown.*

ROGUE'S YARN (1956)   3

Dir *Vernon Sewell*. Prod *George Maynard*. Scr *Ernle Bradford, Sewell*. Ph *Hal Morey*. PC *Cresswell*. Dis *Eros*. 81 mins. Cert A
Urged on by his mistress (*Nicole Maurey*) to murder his invalid wife, John Marsden (*Derek Bond*) sets up a watertight alibi involving him crossing the Channel in his yacht. He kills his wife, but the nagging tenacity of a Scotland Yard inspector (*Elwyn Brook-Jones*) in picking up the finer details of the case finally nails both Marsden and his female accomplice. Intriguing will-they-get-him yarn with some offbeat characterization in supporting roles.
RoC *Hugh Latimer, John Serret, John Salew, Joan Carol, Nigel Fitzgerald, Madoline Thomas, Agatha Carroll, Barbara Christie, Hugh Morton, John Helier, Eric Corrie, Vernon Sewell.*

ROMEO AND JULIET (1954)   4

Dir and Scr *Renato Castellani, from the play by William Shakespeare*. Prod *Sandro Ghenzi, Joseph Janni*. Ph *Robert Krasker*. PC *Verona*. Dis *General Film Distributors*. Technicolor. 138 mins. Cert U
In 15th-century Verona, Juliet (*Susan Shentall*) and Romeo (*Laurence Harvey*), offspring of feuding families, fall in love. But their affair is doomed, and they end by committing suicide. Truly lovely to look at and quite liked by most critics. Frankly, though, it drags more than a bit, and the public were indifferent. The leading lady's only film role.
RoC *Flora Robson, Mervyn Johns, Bill Travers, Enzo Fiermonte, Aldo Zollo, Giovanni Rota, Sebastian Cabot, Lydia Sherwood, Norman Wooland, Guilio Garbinetti, Nietta Zocchi, Dagmar Josipovich, Luciano Bodi, Thomas Nicholls, John Gielgud (voice).*

ROOM AT THE TOP (1958)   6

Dir *Jack Clayton*. Prod *John and James Woolf*. Scr *Neil Paterson, from the novel by John Braine*. Ph *Freddie Francis*. PC *Remus*. Dis *Independent Film Distributors/British Lion*. 117 mins. Cert X
Joe Lampton (*Laurence Harvey*) a humble employee in a north-country town hall, is determined to get to the top. He fastens his attentions on Susan (*Heather Sears*), daughter of a rich businessman (*Donald Wolfit*), whose father sends her abroad. Joe has an affair with unhappily married Alice (*Simone Signoret*) but when Susan returns, he gets her pregnant, and her father has to agree to the marriage. Joe has to give up Alice, who drunkenly crashes her car and is killed. Biting exposé of bed and brass: British Oscar as best film, Academy Awards for writer Neil Paterson and actress Simone Signoret.
RoC *Donald Houston, Allan Cuthbertson, Hermione Baddeley, John Westbrook, Raymond*

Heather Sears and Laurence Harvey in Room at the Top *(1958)*

Huntley, Ambrosine Phillpotts, Richard Pasco, Beatrice Varley, Delena Kidd, Mary Peach, Miriam Karlin, Wilfrid Lawson, Ian Hendry, Prunella Scales, Katherine Page, Thelma Ruby, Anne Leon, Wendy Craig, Anthony Elgar, Kenneth Waller, Anthony Newlands, Andrew Irvine, Stephen Jack, April Olrich, John Welsh, Everley Gregg, Basil Dignam, Derry (Derren) Nesbitt, May Hallatt, Sheila Raynor, Gilda Emmanueli, Jane Eccles, Denis Linford, Edward Palmer, Michael Atkinson, Julian Somers, Richard Caldicot, Pat Lanski, Paul Whitsun-Jones, Yvonne Buckingham, Doreen Dawne, Harry Moore, Joan Leake, Honoria Burke, Allan Bracewell, Brian Worth, Ann Gunning, Linda Leon, Mandy Priestly, Bob Palmer, Bill Morgan, Eric Louro, Pamela Manson, Ruth Kettlewell, Derek Benfield, Isla Cameron, Sandra Thompson, Kendrick Owen, Bonita Bridgeman, Kathleen Fox, Angela Culbert.

ROOM IN THE HOUSE (1955)   [2]

Dir *Maurice Elvey*. Prod and Scr *Alfred Shaughnessy, from a play by E. Eynon Evans.* Ph *Gerald Gibbs*. PC *ACT Films*. Dis *Monarch*. *74 mins. Cert U*

Betsy (*Marjorie Rhodes*), a hard-working widow, goes to live with each of her sons in turn – and solves their family problems. Ending with the one she likes best, clergyman Hugh (*Hubert Gregg*), she is disappointed when he and his wife decide to emigrate to America - but finds her three sons have clubbed together to buy her old village cottage back for her. Rhodes is good, but makeshift comedy isn't much.

RoC *Patrick Barr, Rachel Gurney, Leslie Dwyer, Josephine Griffin, Helen Shingler, Margaret Anderson, Anthony Marlowe, Billie Whitelaw, Oliver Johnston, Julian d'Albie.*

ROONEY (1958)   [4]

Dir *George Pollock*. Prod *George H. Brown*. Scr *Patrick Kirwan, from the novel by Catherine Cookson.* Ph *Christopher Challis*. PC and Dis *Rank. 88 mins. Cert U*

Rooney (*John Gregson*), a carefree Irish dustman, flees from an amorous landlady into the stuffy O'Flynn house, where he takes a fancy to Maire (*Muriel Pavlow*), the family drudge. Grandfather (*Barry Fitzgerald*) leaves his money to her but, on the day of his funeral, she is accused of stealing a necklace. Rooney

tells police that he gave it to her and, on her release, proposes. Irish fable has realistic backgrounds, some charm.

RoC *Marie Kean, Noel Purcell, June Thorburn, Liam Redmond, Jack MacGowran, Eddie Byrne, Philip O'Flynn, Irene Browne, Harold Goldblatt, Pauline Delany, Godfrey Quigley, Joan Phillips, Maureen Toal.*

THE ROSSITER CASE (1950)   [2]

Dir *Francis Searle*. Prod *Anthony Hinds*. Scr *Kenneth Hyde, John Gilling, Searle, from a play by Hyde*. Ph *Jimmy Harvey*. PC *Hammer*. Dis *Exclusive. 75 mins. Cert A*

Peter Rossiter (*Clement McCallin*) is having an affair with his sister-in-law Honor (*Sheila Burrell*), which he is anxious to end. Unaware of this, his paralysed wife Liz (*Helen Shingler*) goes to confront Honor, who produces a gun. In the ensuing struggle, Honor is shot. Peter is suspected but Liz, who has been cured of her paralysis, decides to tell the truth. Talky drama rambles on.

RoC *Frederick Leister, Henry Edwards, Ann Codrington, Dorothy Batley, Gabrielle Blunt, Eleanore Bryan, Ewen Solon, Stanley Baker, Robert Percival, Dennis Castle, Frederic Steger, Anthony Allen.*

THE ROUGH AND THE SMOOTH (1959)   [2]

(USA: *Portrait of a Sinner*)

Dir *Robert Siodmak*. Prod and PC *George Minter*. Scr *Audrey Erskine-Lindop, Dudley Leslie, from the novel by Robin Maugham*. Ph *Otto Heller*. Dis *Renown. 99 mins (later 93). Cert X*

Although engaged to the niece of a press magnate, Mike (*Tony Britton*) becomes obsessed with Ila (*Nadja Tiller*), a mysterious nymphomaniac. He accepts various unlikely explanations of her behaviour, including her 'business relationship' with her boss Reg (*William Bendix*), until, through her efforts to get money for an ex-lover, he finds her in bed with Reg. She then leaves Reg, who shoots himself, but is in turn deserted by a disillusioned Mike. Risibly scripted sexual farrago, a setback for a good few careers.

RoC *Natasha Parry, Tony Wright, Donald Wolfit, Norman Wooland, Joyce Carey, Edward Chapman, Adrienne Corri, Beatrice Varley, Martin Miller, John Welsh, Michael Ward, Norman Pierce, Myles Eason, Cyril Smith, Geoffrey Bayldon.*

ROUGH SHOOT (1952)   [3]

(USA: *Shoot First*)

Dir *Robert Parrish*. Prod and PC *Raymond Stross*. Scr *Eric Ambler, from the novel by Geoffrey Household*. Ph *Stanley Pavey*. Dis *United Artists. 87 mins. Cert U*

Taine (*Joel McCrea*), an American colonel, rents a house in Dorset and some rough shooting. He fires a charge of buckshot and a poacher (in reality a spy) is killed. Taine finds himself enmeshed in a web of foreign agents who are finally rounded up in a battle at Madame Tussaud's waxworks museum. A few chuckles, some thrills, not much credibility. Confused plot needed a Hitchcock.

RoC *Herbert Lom, Evelyn Keyes, Marius Goring, Roland Culver, Karel Stepanek, Frank*

Lawton, Patricia Laffan, Megs Jenkins, David Hurst, Laurence Naismith, Cyril Raymond, Ellis Irving, Clement McCallin, Jack McNaughton, Arnold Bell, Joan Hickson, Powys Thomas, Robert Dickens, Denis Lehrer.

THE ROYAL BALLET (1959)   [3]

Dir and Prod *Paul Czinner*. Ph *S.D. Onions*. PC *Poetic Films*. Dis *Rank. Eastman Colour. 132 mins. Cert U*

Slightly disappointing record of the Royal Ballet's performances of *Swan Lake* (Act Two) and (shortened versions) *The Firebird* and *Ondine*. Lacks the passion of Czinner's previous record of *The Bolshoi Ballet* (qv); even so, for balletomanes, there are some fine moments.

LP *Margot Fonteyn, Michael Somes, Bryan Ashbridge, Rosemary Lindsay, Julia Farron, Franklin White, Alexander Grant, Covent Garden Orchestra.*

THE RUNAWAY BUS (1953)   [3]

Dir, Prod and Scr *Val Guest*. Ph *Stan Pavey*. PC *Conquest/Guest*. Dis *Eros. 78 mins. Cert U*

Relief bus 13, driven by hapless Percy Lamb (*Frankie Howerd*), tries to get passengers from fogbound London Airport to another aerodrome, thanks to the demands of trenchant Miss Beeston (*Margaret Rutherford*). Percy is horrified to find that the bus contains £200,000 in gold bars from an airport robbery. He misroutes into an army training ground with explosions all round. Police take a hand and the robber chief - Miss Beeston! Tepid star comedy with colourful supporting cast.

RoC *Belinda Lee, George Coulouris, Petula Clark, Toke Townley, Reginald Beckwith, Terence Alexander, Stringer Davis, Lisa Gastoni, John Horsley, Anthony Oliver, Frank Phillips, Sam Kydd, Michael Gwynne, Marianne Stone, Lionel Murton, Jimmy Young, Tedwell Chapman, Richard Beynon, Cyril Conway, Arthur Lovegrove, James Brown, Alistair Hunter.*

S

SAFARI (1956)   [3]

Dir *Terence Young*, Prod *Adrian D. Worker*. Scr *Anthony Veiller, from a novel by Robert Buckner*. Ph *John Wilcox, Ted Moore, Fred Ford*. PC *Warwick*. Dis *Columbia. Technicolor. CinemaScope. 91 mins. Cert A*

After the Mau Mau murder his wife and son, Kenya hunter Duffield (*Victor Mature*) agrees to lead a dangerous safari into guerilla territory for millionaire Sir Vincent (*Roland Culver*), who is determined to pot a legendary lion, and brings along his unloving mistress (*Janet Leigh*) who gets into all kinds of scrapes. Sir Vincent foolishly faces the lion alone and is mauled. The Mau Mau attack and Duffield

Janet Leigh and Victor Mature in Safari *(1956)*

kills their leader, but Sir Vincent dies. Almost a parody of such films, but lush and quite fun.
RoC *John Justin, Earl Cameron, Orlando Martins, Estelle Brody, Liam Redmond, Juma, Lionel Ngakane, Cy Grant, Brian May, John Cook, Bob Isaacs.*

THE SAFECRACKER (1957)   ☐4

Dir *Ray Milland.* Prod *John R. Sloan, David E. Rose.* Scr *Paul Monash, from the book by Lt-Col Rhys Davies and Bruce Thomas.* Ph *Gerald Gibbs.* PC *Coronado.* Dis *M-G-M.* 95 mins. Cert U
Colley Dawson (*Ray Milland*), a locksmith-turned-safecracker, jailed for ten years for his part in a string of antique thefts, is offered his freedom in 1940 in return for cracking a safe in Belgium containing a list of Nazi agents in London. After training as a commando, Colley, with his colleagues, carries out the raid successfully. In stopping to admire an antique, he is trapped and shot dead by German soldiers. Often tense drama, with an amusing account of Dawson's commando training. Based on fact.
RoC *Barry Jones, Jeannette Sterke, Victor Maddern, Ernest Clark, Cyril Raymond, Melissa Stribling, Percy Herbert, Barbara Everest, Anthony Nicholls, David Horne, Colin Gordon, Clive Morton, Colin Tapley, John Welsh, Pamela Stirling, Henry Vidon, Ian McNaughton, Bernard Fox, Charles Lloyd Pack, Barry Keegan, Sam Kydd.*

Ray Milland and Barry Jones in The Safecracker *(1957)*

SAIL INTO DANGER (1957)   ☐3

Dir and Scr *Kenneth Hume.* Prod *Steven Pal-*
los. Ph *Phil Grindrod.* PC *Patria.* Dis *Grand National.* 73 mins. Cert U
Blackmailed into sailing Lena (*Kathleen Ryan*), an ex-smuggling comrade, and her three Spanish 'associates' to Tangier, Steve (*Dennis O'Keefe*) pays for his past when the gang kills his boy, Angel (*John Bull*), in stealing a priceless madonna, and wounds his mate, Monty (*James Hayter*). Steve pursues and kills two of the gang, before the police capture Lena and the remaining robber. Interesting in plot but variable in performance.
RoC *Ana Luisa Peluffo, Pedro de Cordoba, Barta Barry, Felix de Pommes, Miguel Fleta.*

SAILOR BEWARE! (1956)   ☐3
(USA: *Panic in the Parlor*)

Dir *Gordon Parry.* Prod *Jack Clayton.* Scr *Philip King, Falkland L. Cary, from their play.* Ph *Douglas Slocombe.* PC *Romulus/Remus.* Dis *Independent Film Distributors/British Lion.* 80 mins. Cert U
The prospect of having fearsome Emma Hornett (*Peggy Mount*), his prospective mother-in-law, living only three doors away, is enough to make sailor Albert (*Ronald Lewis*) jilt her daughter Shirley (*Shirley Eaton*). Pa Hornett (*Cyril Smith*) seeks consolation in his ferrets. When Emma apologizes to everyone for her constant shouting and nagging, the wedding goes ahead. Broad farce from enormous stage hit, with rampaging central performance.
RoC *Esma Cannon, Gordon Jackson, Thora Hird, Geoffrey Keen, Jack MacGowran, Joy Webster, Peter Collingwood, Henry McGee, Eliot Makeham, Charles Houston, Anne Blake, Fred Griffiths, Douglas Blackwell, Edie Martin, Margaret Moore, Barbara Hicks.*

SAINT JOAN (1957)   ☐3

Dir and Prod *Otto Preminger.* Scr *Graham Greene from the play by George Bernard Shaw.* Ph *Georges Périnal.* PC *Preminger Productions/ Wheel Films.* Dis *United Artists.* 110 mins. Cert A
Joan (*Jean Seberg*), a French farm girl of 1429, who hears 'voices' and has inspiring qualities of leadership, is made a commander of the Dauphin's army against the English, wins a memorable battle at Orleans, but is captured by the Burgundians at Paris. After nine months of inquisition and imprisonment, she signs a confession of heresy – which she retracts when told she will still be sentenced to life. She is burnt to death at the stake. Colourless pageant has some good acting, but doesn't escape theatrical origins.
RoC *Richard Widmark, Richard Todd, Anton Walbrook, John Gielgud, Felix Aylmer, Harry Andrews, Barry Jones, Kenneth Haigh, Finlay Currie, Bernard Miles, Margot Grahame, Patrick Barr, Archie Duncan, Francis de Wolff, Victor Maddern, David Oxley, Sydney Bromley, David Langton, David Hemmings.*

THE SAINT'S RETURN (1953)   ☐3
(USA: *The Saint's Girl Friday*)

Dir *Seymour Friedman.* Prod *Anthony Hinds.* Scr *Allan Mackinnon.* Ph *Walter Harvey.* PC *Hammer.* Dis *Exclusive.* 73 mins. Cert U
American sleuth Simon Templar (*Louis Hay-*
ward), alias 'The Saint', comes to England after a telegram for help from an old friend. On arrival, he discovers she has been killed in an 'accident' and decides to investigate the shady waterfront gambling crowd with which she was mixed up. He succeeds in unmasking an evil blackmailer behind a gang of gambling racketeers. Little bite in disappointing tailpiece to 'Saint' films; just about average.
RoC *Naomi Chance, Sydney Tafler, Charles Victor, Harold Lang, Thomas Gallagher, Jane Carr, Fred Johnson, Russell Enoch (William Russell), Ian Fleming, John Wynn, Russell Napier, George Margo, Johnnie Schofield, Diana Dors.*

SALUTE THE TOFF (1951)   ☐3

Dir *Maclean Rogers.* Prod *Ernest G. Roy.* Scr *Uncredited, from the novel by John Creasey.* Ph *Geoffrey Faithfull.* PC *Nettlefold.* Dis *Butchers.* 75 mins. Cert A
Responding to an appeal from Fay (*Carol Marsh*) to find her missing boss Draycott (*Tony Britton*), society sleuth 'The Toff' (*John Bentley*) finds a dead body, is attacked in a hotel, and finally runs Draycott to earth, hiding from an insurance swindler who means to kill him. With the help of Inspector Grice (*Valentine Dyall*) and The Toff's butler (*Roddy Hughes*), the case is closed. Amiable thriller-comedy.
RoC *Shelagh Fraser, Wally Patch, June Elvin, Arthur Hill, Michael Golden, John Forbes-Robertson, Andrea Malandrinos, Jill Allen, Ian Fleming.*

THE SALVAGE GANG (1958)   ☐4

Dir and Scr *John Krish.* Prod *P. Hindle Edgar.* Ph *James Allen.* PC *World Wide/Children's Film Foundation.* Dis *British Lion.* 52 mins. Cert U
In their efforts to raise money to repair a broken saw, four children fail at painting, dog-washing and car-cleaning, and junk-dealing as well when it proves an iron bedstead they had sold was needed after all. They dash across London to get it back, and encounter sundry misadventures in getting it home. Inventive children's film with well-used backgrounds.
LP *Christopher Warbey, Ali Allen, Amanda Coxell, Frazer Hines, Richard Molinas.*

SAPPHIRE (1959)   ☐4

Dir *Basil Dearden.* Prod *Michael Relph.* Scr *Janet Green, Lukas Heller.* Ph *Harry Waxman.* PC *Artna.* Dis *Rank.* Eastman Colour. 92 mins. Cert A
A beautiful girl is found dead on Hampstead Heath. Through her vivid scarlet petticoat, the police team of Hazard (*Nigel Patrick*) and Learoyd (*Michael Craig*) identify her as Sapphire, a half-black girl passing for white. The white man (*Paul Massie*), whose child she was expecting, is one of the suspects who also include a couple of shady characters from the black underworld. Well-made manhunt drama gets a lift from its background; a surprise winner of the British Oscar for best British film, over *Tiger Bay* and other strong contenders.
RoC *Yvonne Mitchell, Bernard Miles, Earl Cameron, Olga Lindo, Gordon Heath, Jocelyn*

Britton, Orlando Martins, Rupert Davies, Robert Adams, Yvonne Buckingham, Freda Bamford, Harry Baird, Ronald Adam, Vanda Hudson, Peter Vaughan, Basil Dignam.

SATELLITE IN THE SKY (1956) [2]

Dir *Paul Dickson*. Prod *Edward J. Danziger, Harry Lee Danziger*. Scr *John C. Mather, J.T. McIntosh, Edith Dell*. Ph *Georges Périnal*. PC *Tridelta*. Dis *Warner Bros. Warnercolor. CinemaScope. 84 mins. Cert U*
An experimental rocketship takes off with a lady reporter (*Lois Maxwell*) as stowaway. The plan - to explode a new bomb outside the earth's atmosphere - goes wrong and the bomb attaches itself to the ship. The chief professor (*Donald Wolfit*) goes berserk, but two more of the scientists give their lives to save the rest. Laughable space-age heroics.
RoC *Lois Maxwell, Kieron Moore, Jimmy Hanley, Bryan Forbes, Thea Gregory, Barry Keegan, Walter Hudd, Donald Gray, Shirley Lawrence, Alan Gifford, Peter Neil, Carl Jaffe, Ryck Rydon, Ronan O'Casey, Robert O'Neil, Charles Richardson, Trevor Reid, Alastair Hunter, John Baker.*

SATURDAY ISLAND (1951) [3]
(USA: *Island of Desire*)

Dir *Stuart Heisler*. Prod *David E. Rose*. Scr *Stephanie Nordli, Heisler (uncredited)*. Ph *Oswald Morris, Arthur Ibbetson*. PC *Coronado*. Dis *RKO Radio. Technicolor. 102 mins. Cert A*
Shipwrecked in World War II when their supply ship is torpedoed, Chicken, a marine (*Tab Hunter*) and Elizabeth, a nurse (*Linda Darnell*) reach a desert island, where they eventually fall in love. The arrival of an RAF pilot (*Donald Gray*) whose arm Elizabeth has to amputate complicates things and, by the time help arrives, she has chosen the pilot. Darnell and camerawork only good things in flabby paradise romance.
RoC *John Laurie, Russell Waters, Sheila Chong, MacDonald Parke, Diana Decker, Peter Butterworth, Michael Newell, Lloyd Lamble, Harold Ayer, Hilda Fenemore, Joan Benham, Brenda Hogan, Katherine Blake.*

THE SAVAGE INNOCENTS (1959) [4]

Dir *Nicholas Ray, Baccio Bandini*. Prod *Joseph Janni, Maleno Malenotti*. Scr *Ray, Hans Ruesch, from a novel by F. Solinas*. Ph *Peter Hennessy, Aldo Tonti*. PC *Magic Film/Playart*. Dis *Rank. Technicolor. SuperTechnirama 70. 107 mins. Cert A*
Eskimos Inuk (*Anthony Quinn*) and Asiak (*Yoko Tani*), rejecting white man's civilization, build a traditional igloo, but Inuk is soon afterwards unwittingly responsible for the death of a missionary. Two troopers (*Peter O'Toole, Carlo Justini*) pursue the couple, who have by now had a baby. One freezes to death, the other comes to realize Inuk's innocence, but has to trick him into escaping to evade civilized 'justice', which he knows will convict him. Moving, if rather sanitized offbeat adventure.
RoC *Marie Yang, Andy Ho, Kaida Horiuchi, Yvonne Shima, Lee Montague, Francis de Wolff, Anthony Chinn, Anna May Wong (not the Hollywood star), Ed Devereaux, Marco Guglielmi, Michael Chow.*

THE SCAMP (1957) [4]

Dir and Scr *Wolf Rilla, from a play by Charlotte Hastings*. Prod *James Lawrie*. Ph *Freddie Francis*. PC *George Minter/Lawrie Productions*. Dis *Renown. 89 mins. Cert A*
Tod (*Colin Peterson*), a wild ten-year-old, is left with Stephen (*Richard Attenborough*), a teacher, and his wife, while his drunken father is abroad. Stephen shows Tod a better life, but he continues to run wild and Stephen feels compelled to give him a thrashing. Tod, now worse than ever, ends in juvenile court, and is restored to his returning father (*Terence Morgan*). But, after he thinks he has killed his father when the latter attacks him in an alcoholic rage, Tod is returned to Stephen's care, this time happily. Generally entertaining tear-jerker.
RoC *Dorothy Alison, Jill Adams, Geoffrey Keen, Margaretta Scott, Maureen Delany, Charles Lloyd Pack, Victor Brooks, June Cunningham, David Franks, Sam Kydd, Cyril Wheeler, Kenneth Edwards, David Evans, Marc Sheldon, Sidney Vivian, Hugh Russell, Peter Soule, Kenneth Collins, Garry Leeman, Oliver MacGreevy, Roger Avon.*

THE SCAPEGOAT (1958) [3]

Dir *Robert Hamer*. Prod *Michael Balcon*. Scr *Hamer, Gore Vidal, from the novel by Daphne du Maurier*. Ph *Paul Beeson*. PC *Guinness-du Maurier*. Dis *M-G-M. 92 mins. Cert A*
John Barratt (*Alec Guinness*), a quiet Englishman on holiday in France, is tricked by his double, an aristocrat, into assuming his identity. He inherits a chateau, a crazy mother (*Bette Davis*), an unhappy wife Françoise (*Irene Worth*) and a teenage daughter. Barratt is getting to grips with it all when the Frenchman returns, murders Françoise for her money and tells Barratt to go. There is a duel which Barratt wins. Then he does go - with the Frenchman's mistress (*Nicole Maurey*) in tow. Stylish, rather over-elaborate drama.
RoC *Pamela Brown, Geoffrey Keen, Annabel Bartlett, Leslie French, Noel Howlett, Peter Bull, Alan Webb, Maria Britneva, Eddie Byrne, Alexander Archdale, Peter Sallis.*

Alec Guinness and Bette Davis in The Scapegoat *(1958)*

THE SCARLET SPEAR (1953) [3]

Dir and Scr *George Breakston, Ray Stahl*. Prod *Charles Reynolds*. Ph *Bernard Davies*. PC *Present Day*. Dis *United Artists. Technicolor. 78 mins. Cert U*

Tribal Africa. District officer Jim Barnenson (*John Bentley*) fights to prevent a young chief (*Morasi*) from committing a ritual murder (to prove his worthiness) which would start a tribal war. A girl reporter (*Martha Hyer*) is caught up in the chase, which ends when the chief saves Jim's life at the cost of his own. Dying, he snaps his spear to break the primitive tradition. Serviceable jungle thrills.
Native supporting cast.

SCARLET THREAD (1951) [3]

Dir *Lewis Gilbert*. Prod *Ernest G. Roy*. Scr *A.R. Rawlinson, Moie Charles, from their play*. Ph *Geoffrey Faithfull*. PC *Nettlefold/International Realist*. Dis *Butchers. 85 mins. Cert A*
Cambridge. A shabby petty thief (*Laurence Harvey*) links up with a deformed but suave gangster (*Sydney Tafler*), and kills a passer-by during a jewellery raid. The thief falls for a university professor's daughter (*Kathleen Byron*) before realizing it was her father he shot. He and his boss are shot dead after being pursued by police. Unpleasant characters effectively drawn; above average for British co-feature.
RoC *Eliot Makeham, Arthur Hill, Dora Bryan, Harry Fowler, Cyril Chamberlain, Renee Kelly, Bill Shine, Hylton Allen, Vi Kaley, Ben Williams, Joyce Boorman, Gerald Rex, John Powe, Sheila Aza.*

THE SCARLET WEB (1954) [3]

Dir *Charles Saunders*. Prod *Frank Bevis*. Scr *Doreen Montgomery*. Ph *Hone Glendining*. PC *Fortress*. Dis *Eros. 64 mins. Cert A*
An insurance investigator (*Griffith Jones*) finds himself framed for murder after seductive Laura Vane (*Zena Marshall*) pays him to recover a letter from a blackmailer. His boss, Susan (*Hazel Court*) connects Laura with the dead girl's husband, but nearly loses her own life before the police arrive to collar the killers. Very familiar story but more professionally put together than most of its kind.
RoC *Robert Perceval, Molly Raynor, Ronald (Ronnie) Stevens, Stuart Douglass, Johnnie Schofield, Michael Balfour, John Fitzgerald.*

SCROOGE (1951) [4]
(USA: *A Christmas Carol*)

Dir *Brian Desmond Hurst*. Prod *George Minter*. Scr *Noel Langley, from a novel by Charles Dickens*. Ph *C. Pennington-Richards*. PC and Dis *Renown. 86 mins. Cert U*
Miserly old Victorian Ebenezer Scrooge (*Alastair Sim*), who keeps his clerk Bob Cratchit (*Mervyn Johns*) in penury, is visited first by the ghost of his partner, Jacob Marley (*Michael Hordern*), now doomed to wander in agony, and then by the spirits of Christmas past, Christmas present and Christmas yet-to-come. Scrooge emerges from the nightmare a new man, and helps save Cratchit's crippled son Tiny Tim. Now regarded as the classic version of the story, but not unanimously praised in its day.
RoC *Kathleen Harrison, Hermione Baddeley, George Cole, Jack Warner, Rona Anderson, Clifford Mollison, Carol Marsh, Brian Worth, John Charlesworth, Glyn Dearman, Francis de*

Mervyn Johns and Alastair Sim in Scrooge *(1951)*

Wolff, Michael Dolan, Miles Malleson, Ernest Thesiger, Olga Edwardes, Hattie Jacques, Roddy Hughes, Eliot Makeham, Louise Hampton, Noel Howlett, Fred Johnson, Peter Bull, Douglas Muir, Henry Hewitt, Hugh Dempster, Patrick Macnee.

SEA DEVILS (1952)   3

Dir *Raoul Walsh*. Prod *David E. Rose, (uncredited) John R. Sloan*. Scr *Borden Chase, from a novel by Victor Hugo*. Ph *Wilkie Cooper*. PC *Coronado*. Dis *RKO-Radio*. Technicolor. 90 mins. Cert U

1805. England sends a woman spy, Drouette (*Yvonne De Carlo*) to learn of Napoleon's invasion plans. Gilliatt (*Rock Hudson*), smuggler and skipper of the boat that takes her to France, mistakes her for a French spy, but she completes her mission, only to be captured by the French authorities. Gilliatt, now aware of her identity, rescues her. Fast-moving, slackly scripted, highly coloured adventure yarn.

RoC *Maxwell Reed, Denis O'Dea, Bryan Forbes, Michael Goodliffe, Jacques Brunius, Ivor Barnard, Arthur Wontner, Gerard Oury, Keith Pyott, René Poirier, Laurie Taylor, Reed de Rouen, Michael Mulcaster.*

SEA FURY (1958)   2

Dir *C. Raker Endfield*. Prod *S. Benjamin Fisz*. Scr *Endfield, John Kruse*. Ph *Reginald Wyer*. PC and Dis *Rank*. 98 mins. Cert A

Stranded in Spain, Abel Hewson (*Stanley Baker*) gets a job on a salvage tug, but soon becomes the rival of the ageing skipper, Bellew (*Victor McLaglen*) for a fiery Spanish girl (*Luciana Paluzzi*). Bellew, seeing that he is too old to compete, gets drunk, and Hewson has to take the tug out in a fierce gale to rescue a ship. His heroic success brings about a reconciliation with Bellew. Brilliant sea scenes, but foolish plot.

RoC *Gregoire Aslan, David Oxley, Rupert Davies, Robert Shaw, Joe Robinson, Dermot Walsh, Francis de Wolff, George Murcell, Percy Herbert, Roger Delgado, Barry Foster, Richard Pearson, Fred Johnson, Jack Taylor.*

SEAGULLS OVER SORRENTO (1954)   4
(USA: *Crest of the Wave*)

Dir and Prod *John and Roy Boulting*. Scr *Frank Harvey, Roy Boulting, from the play by*

Hugh Hastings. Ph *Gilbert Taylor*. PC and Dis *MGM British*. 92 mins. Cert U

Tensions, both comic and dramatic, rise between British and American naval scientists working on experimental torpedoes at a remote research station off the Scottish coast. Tests result in the deaths of three British personnel, but Lt Wharton (*John Justin*) discovers the cause just as the government cancels the project. A final test by Bradville (*Gene Kelly*) and Turner (*Bernard Lee*) is successful. Well-mixed blend of laughter and thrills.

RoC *Sidney James, Jeff Richards, Patric Doonan, Ray Jackson, Fredd Wayne, Patrick Barr, David Orr.*

SEA OF SAND (1958)   5

Dir *Guy Green*. Prod *Robert S. Baker, Monty Berman*. Scr *Robert Westerby*. Ph *Wilkie Cooper*. PC *Tempean*. Dis *Rank*. 97 mins. Cert U

Williams (*John Gregson*) and Cotton (*Michael Craig*), contrasting officers who cannot get on, lead a North African expedition in 1943 to destroy a huge fuel dump. They achieve their aim, only to find the dump conceals an army of new tanks, which will now pursue them. Struggling back through minefields, sandstorms and many other hazards, Cotton and Williams are eventually both killed, although their men get back. Excellent war film full of incident; familiar types come sweatingly to life.

RoC *Richard Attenborough, Dermot Walsh, Vincent Ball, Percy Herbert, Barry Foster, Andrew Faulds, George Murcell, Ray McAnally, Harold Goodwin, Tony Thawnton, Wolf Frees, George Mikell.*

THE SEA SHALL NOT HAVE THEM (1954)   3

Dir *Lewis Gilbert*. Prod and PC *Daniel M. Angel*. Scr *Gilbert, Vernon Harris*. Ph *Stephen Dade*. Dis *Eros*. 91 mins. Cert U

1944. Four survivors from a downed plane (*Michael Redgrave, Dirk Bogarde, Bonar Colleano, Jack Watling*) drift in the North Sea in a dinghy. One of them possesses vital information about new German missiles. Rescue attempts fail frustratingly and the men weaken. But finally they are picked up in the middle of a minefield near the coast, in the face of heavy shelling from Nazi shore batteries. Repetitive war film with the actors getting few chances.

RoC *Anthony Steel, Nigel Patrick, James Kenney, Sydney Tafler, Griffith Jones, Guy Middleton, Paul Carpenter, Anton Diffring, Rachel Kempson, Ian Whittaker, George Rose, Joan Sims, Victor Maddern, Michael Ripper, Glyn Houston, Jack Taylor, Michael Balfour, Eddie Byrne, Jack Lambert, Moultrie Kelsall, Nigel Green, Ann Gudrun.*

SEA WIFE (1957)   3

Dir *Bob McNaught*. Prod *André Hakim*. Scr *George K. Burke, from a novel by J.M. Scott*. Ph *Ted Scaife*. PC *Sumar*. Dis *20th Century-Fox*. Technicolor. CinemaScope. 81 mins. Cert A

1942. A passenger ship loaded with refugees from war-torn Singapore is torpedoed. On one life-raft, the four survivors are Biscuit (*Richard*

Richard Burton and Joan Collins in Sea Wife *(1957)*

Burton), a flyer, Sea Wife (*Joan Collins*), a nun, Bulldog (*Basil Sydney*), a businessman, and Number Four (*Cy Grant*), the black purser. Biscuit falls in love with Sea Wife and cannot understand why she will not respond. Bulldog tricks them into leaving Number Four on an island; he is eaten by sharks. They drift on for days, being picked up on the point of death. Later Biscuit searches for Sea Wife, but passes her by on the street. Incongruously cast melodrama doesn't touch the emotions.

RoC *Ronald Squire, Harold Goodwin, Gibb McLaughlin, Roddy Hughes, Lloyd Lamble, Ronald Adam, Nicholas Hannen, Beatrice Varley, Otokichi Ikeda, Tenji Takagi.*

SECOND FIDDLE (1957)   3

Dir *Maurice Elvey*. Prod *Robert Dunbar*. Scr *Allan Mackinnon, Dunbar*. Ph *Arthur Graham*. PC *ACT Films*. Dis *British Lion*. 73 mins. Cert U

Deborah (*Adrienne Corri*) and Charles (*Thorley Walters*) are so popular at their advertising agency that the staff successfully petition for the revoking of a company rule about the employment of married women, when they decide to wed. Deborah's career moves faster than her new husband's, and when she goes to America, he falls into an affair with a slinky secretary (*Lisa Gastoni*). He realizes her worthlessness just in time to welcome Deborah home. Minor but quite bright comedy frolic.

RoC *Richard Wattis, Bill Fraser, Aud Johansen, Madoline Thomas, Brian Nissen, Ryck Rydon, Jill Melford, Jay (Joy) Webster, Dino Galvani, Johnny Briggs, Launce Maraschal, Frederick Piper, Beckett Bould, Frederick Victor, Christina Lubics (Lubitz), Yah Ming, Ian Whittaker, Doreen Dawne, Cyril Renison.*

THE SECOND MATE (1950)   2

Dir and Prod *John Baxter*. Scr *Barbara K. Emary, Jack Francis*. Ph *Arthur Grant*. PC *Elstree Independent*. Dis *Associated British*. 76 mins. Cert U

Determined to avenge the death of a friend killed by a smuggling gang, bargee Bill Tomkins (*Gordon Harker*) joins them. Rumbling his game, the gang kidnaps his adopted son and second mate, Bobby (*David Hannaford*) and Bill takes the bait. Bobby escapes, saves Bill from a delayed action bomb, and the gang is brought to book. Slow, rather crudely made comedy-thriller that even Harker's experience can't save.

RoC *Graham Moffatt, Byrl Walkley, Charles Sewell, Anne Blake, Charles Heslop, Jane Welsh, Howard Douglas, Hamilton Keene, Sam Kydd, Johnnie Schofield, Pat Keogh, Pauline Drewett, Tom Fallon.*

THE SECOND MRS TANQUERAY (1952) [2]

Dir *Dallas Bower.* Prod *Roger Proudlock.* Scr *Uncredited, from the play by Arthur Wing Pinero.* Ph *Gerald Gibbs.* PC *Vandyke.* Dis *Associated British. 76 mins. Cert A*

Despite warnings from his friends, Aubrey Tanqueray (*Hugh Sinclair*) marries Paula (*Pamela Brown*), a woman with a scarlet past. Paula's own reputation causes Aubrey's friends to ostracize her and she fights continually with his daughter Ellean (*Virginia McKenna*), whose fiancé proves to be one of Paula's many lovers. Seeing that she has no future, Paula commits suicide. Well-written but now completely outdated piece.

RoC *Ronald Ward, Andrew Osborn, Mary Hinton, Peter Haddon, Peter Bull, Bruce Seton, Shelagh Frazer, Charles Perry.*

THE SECRET (1955) [3]

Dir and Scr *C Raker (Cy) Endfield, from the play by Robert Brenon.* Prod *S. Benjamin Fisz.* Ph *Jack Asher.* PC *Golden Era.* Dis *Eros. Eastman Colour. 80 mins. Cert A*

Nick (*Sam Wanamaker*), a shiftless American hoping to get back to New York, plays up to a widow who has smuggled diamonds to England in a teddy bear, but when she accidently falls over a cliff, he is suspected of murder. Finding the diamonds, he tries to sell them but is beaten up and loses the stones. Katie (*Mandy Miller*) tells the police on the case that her bear has been switched, and, when Nick chases her in a fairground, is knocked down by a dodgem. But she forgives him, he admits his part in the affair and the law catches up with the crooks. Slow thriller with one or two striking performances.

RoC *André Morell, Jan Miller, Richard O'Sullivan, Marian Spencer, Wyndham Goldie, Henry Caine, Harold Berens, Aimee Delamain, John Miller.*

THE SECRET CAVE (1953) [1]

Dir *John Durst.* Prod *Frank A. Hoare.* Scr *Joe Mendoza, from a novel by Thomas Hardy.* Ph *Martin Curtis.* PC *Merton Park/Children's Film Foundation.* Dis *Associated British. 62 mins. Cert U*

Discovering the source of their village stream, two boys try to divert it when their mother is threatened with eviction from her farm, so that the value of her land will go up. But they are trapped by rising water and, to prevent further escapades, dynamite the entrance to the cave where they found the source. Limply directed children's adventure with musical sequences thrown in. A fair disaster.

LP *Nicholas Edmett, David Coote, Susan Ford, Lewis Gedge, Trevor Hill, Johnny Morris.*

THE SECRET MAN (1958) [3]

Dir and Prod *Ronald Kinnoch.* Scr *Tony O'Grady.* Ph *Geoffrey Faithfull.* PC *Amalgamated.* Dis *Butchers. 68 mins. Cert U*

A physicist (*Marshall Thompson*) and his assistant – and fiancée (*Anne Aubrey*) – find themselves drawn into a Special Branch investigation to track down a spy at their research station. By posing as a security risk himself, the physicist is able to help Major Anderson (*John Loder*) and his men draw the culprit out into the open. Old-fashioned espionage drama, tiredly written but well performed; good surprise ending.

RoC *John Stuart, Henry Oscar, Magda Miller, Murray Kash, Michael Mellinger, Robert MacKenzie, Bernard Archard, Tom Bowman, Peter Elliott, Stan Simmons, Shirley Thieman, Robert Dorning, Harcourt Curacao.*

THE SECRET OF THE FOREST (1955) [3]

Dir *Darcy Conyers.* Prod *Anthony Gilkison.* Scr *Conyers, Gerry (Gerard) Bryant.* Ph *Sydney Samuelson.* PC *Rayant/Children's Film Foundation.* Dis *British Lion. 61 mins. Cert U*

Two spoilt children, Henry (*Kit Terrington*) and Caroline (*Jacqueline Cox*) take a holiday with an uncle in Suffolk and are befriended by two foresters' children (*Barry Knight, Diana Day*) who soon knock stuffy ideas out of them. The children become involved with crooks who have stolen a valuable gold cup. Henry and Caroline are captured by them, but their friends are watching from a forest 'firetower' and send for help, bringing the crooks to book. Enid Blyton-style children's yarn.

RoC *Michael Balfour, Vincent Ball, Arthur Lovegrove.*

SECRET PEOPLE (1951) [3]

Dir *Thorold Dickinson.* Prod *Sidney Cole.* Scr *Dickinson, Wolfgang Wilhelm, Christianna Brand.* Ph *Gordon Dines.* PC *Ealing Studios.* Dis *General Film Distributors. 96 mins. Cert A*

London, 1937. Two sisters (*Valentina Cortesa, Audrey Hepburn*) become involved in a bomb plot by fellow-exiles against the tyrants who have taken over their country. The elder sister realizes that she is being used, and gives her life to save her sister from the same fate. Drama is slackly constructed but interesting; alas, pleased few members of the critics or public.

RoC *Serge Reggiani, Charles Goldner, Megs Jenkins, Irene Worth, Reginald Tate, Michael Shepley, Athene Seyler, Geoffrey Hibbert, Sydney Tafler, John Ruddock, Michael Allan, Norman Williams, John Field, Angela Fouldes, Charlie Cairoli and Paul, Hugo Schuster, Lionel Harris, Rollo Gamble, John Penrose, John Chandos, Michael Ripper, Yvonne Coulette, John Mansi, John Gabriel, Olga Landiak, Frederick Schiller, Phaedros Antonio, Gaston Richer, Derek Elphinstone, Edward Evans, Ingeborg Wells, Bob Monkhouse, Helen Ford, Ann Lancaster, Grace Draper, Bertram Shuttleworth, Pamela Harrington, John Allen, Joe Linnane, Bay White, Sam Kydd, Simone Silva.*

THE SECRET PLACE (1956) [5]

Dir *Clive Donner.* Prod *John Bryan, Anthony Perry.* Scr *Linette Perry.* Ph *Ernest Steward.* PC and Dis *Rank. 98 mins. Cert A*

Idolized by policeman's son Freddie (*Michael Brooke*), East Ender Molly (*Belinda Lee*) is involved with crooks Gerry (*Ronald Lewis*) and Steve (*Michael Gwynn*) and, through Freddie, gets them a PC's uniform they need to carry out a daring jewel raid. A fence refuses to take uncut diamonds, which are hidden by Mike, Molly's brother (*David McCallum*) in an old gramophone which, unknowingly, Molly gives to Freddie. Realizing he has been used, a devastated Freddie hides the diamonds, but is chased by Gerry. Faced with a choice, Molly sides with Freddie and watches Gerry taken away by the police. Convincingly set drama with tingling climax.

RoC *Geoffrey Keen, Maureen Pryor, George Selway, George A. Cooper, John Welsh, Hugh Manning, Anne Blake, Brendon Hanley, Philip Ray, Wendy Craig.*

SECRET TENT (1956) [2]

Dir *Don Chaffey.* Prod *Nat Miller, Frank Bevis.* Scr *Jan Read, from the play by Elizabeth Addeyman.* Ph *Harry Waxman.* PC *Forward Films.* Dis *British Lion. 69 mins. Cert A*

Ruth (*Andrée Melly*), a reformed 'bad girl' now happily married, disappears at the same time as a burglary in the vicinity. Her husband (*Donald Gray*) turns against her – and later incorrectly identifies the body of a murdered girl as hers – although it turns out that she had been forced to help her brother, a petty thief, escape after the robbery. The killer is apprehended and husband and wife reconciled. Popular TV favourites star, but melodrama is just another 'B'.

RoC *Jean Anderson, Sonia Dresdel, Peter Hammond, Andrew Cruickshank, Dinah Ann Rogers, Conrad Phillips, Shirley Jacobs.*

SECRET VENTURE (1954) [2]

Dir *R.G. Springsteen.* Prod *William N. Boyle.* Scr *Paul Erickson, Kenneth R. Hayles.* Ph *Basil Emmott.* PC and Dis *Republic. 69 mins. Cert U*

A famous scientist is kidnapped, but his vital briefcase, containing a secret formula for a new jet fuel, falls into the hands of American Ted O'Hara (*Kent Taylor*). Subsequently, O'Hara is offered a large sum of money for the case and determines to sort things out for himself, to the consternation of Scotland Yard, to whom he proves a thorn in the side before they close the case and arrest the kidnappers. US star and director, but result is just like any other minor hunt-the-scientist thriller.

RoC *Jane Hylton, Kathleen Byron, Karel Stepanek, Martin Boddey, John Boxer, Frederick Valk, Maurice Kaufmann, Arthur Lane, Michael Balfour, Hugo Schuster, John Warren, Fred Griffiths, Terence Brook, Patrick Dowling, Arthur Bentley, Michael Ripper, Vivienne Martin, Alexander Field.*

SEE HOW THEY RUN (1955) [3]

Dir *Leslie Arliss.* Prod *Bill Luckwell, D.E.A. Winn.* Scr *Arliss, Val Valentine, Roy Miller, from the play by Philip King.* PC *Winwell.* Dis *British Lion.* 84 *mins. Cert U*

To spend a night 'off limits' with an old flame (*Greta Gynt*) from the acting profession, Corporal Wally Winton (*Ronald Shiner*) dresses in her husband's (vicar's) clothes. A complicated evening ensues, after Basher (*Charles Farrell*), an escaped convict, robs a bishop of *his* clothes, ending with five clerics, real and fake, on the loose while the authorities try to sort them out. Wally's efforts get him promoted to sergeant, by which he inherits a legacy. Crazy but obvious comedy; a good cast has to work hard to force the laughs.

RoC *James Hayter, Wilfrid Hyde White, Dora Bryan, Richard Wattis, Ian Wilson, Roddy Hughes, Ballard Berkeley, Michael Brennan, Viola Lyel, Gloria Haig, Stuart Latham, Hamilton Keene, Fred Griffiths, Will Cruft, Tony Quinn, George Roderick, Ken Buckle, Johnnie Schofield, Arthur Cortez.*

THE SEEKERS (1954) [2]
(USA: *Land of Fury*)

Dir *Ken Annakin.* Prod *George H. Brown.* Scr *William Fairchild, from a novel by John Guthrie.* Ph *Geoffrey Unsworth.* PC *Group/Fanfare.* Dis *General Film Distributors. Eastman Colour.* 90 *mins.* (*US:75*) *Cert A*

New Zealand, 1820. Philip Wayne (*Jack Hawkins*), a British sailor, determines to make a new life for himself and his bride (*Glynis Johns*), with the help of his friend, an enlightened chieftain (*Inia Te Wiata*), who even forgives Philip an indiscretion with his sultry wife (*Laya Raki*). But a medicine man incites a tribe to attack the British settlers, who are massacred. Only the Waynes' baby survives. Rather embarrassing British attempt at an Antipodean western.

RoC *Noel Purcell, Kenneth Williams, Patrick Warbrick, Thomas Heathcote, Tony Erstich, Francis de Wolff, Edward Baker, James Copeland, Norman Mitchell, Ian Fleming, Maharaia Winiata, Henry Gilbert, Patrick Rawiri, Mac Hata, J. Ward Holmes, Fred Johnson, F.B.J. Sharp, Kim Parker.*

SENTENCED FOR LIFE (1959) [2]

Dir *Max Varnel.* Prod *Edward J. Danziger, Harry Lee Danziger.* Scr *Eldon Howard, Mark Grantham.* Ph *S.D. Onions.* PC *Danzigers.* Dis *United Artists.* 64 *mins. Cert U*

The man who is sentenced to life is engineer John Richards (*Jack Gwillim*), alleged to have sold secrets to enemy agents. He believes he was framed by his ex-partner (*Basil Dignam*), but when his law student son Jim (*Francis Matthews*) investigates he reveals treachery from an unexpected source. Very modest drama.

RoC *Jill Williams, Lorraine Clewes, Mark Singleton, Nyree Dawn Porter, Arnold Bell, John M. Moore, Garard Green, Norah Gordon, Jack Taylor, Eric Dodson, Vernon Smythe, Reginald Hearne, Jack Melford, Charles Maunsell.*

SERIOUS CHARGE (1959) [4]
(USA: *A Touch of Hell*)

Dir *Terence Young.* Prod *Mickey Delamar.* Scr *Delamar, Guy Elmes, from the play by Philip*

King. Ph *Georges Périnal.* PC *Alva.* Dis *Eros.* 99 *mins. Cert X*

A new vicar's (*Anthony Quayle*) skill at football and open-mindedness go a long way towards making inroads into Bellington's juvenile delinquency problem. But he rebuffs the advances of frustrated Hester (*Sarah Churchill*) and this costs him dear when she maliciously confirms the charge (untrue) by Larry (*Andrew Ray*) - accused by the vicar of causing a girl's death - that the priest has assaulted him. At length, Larry is proved a liar and the vicar, on the brink of resigning, is cleared. Good drama with (less successful) serious undertones. Also Cliff Richard's debut: he sings *Livin' Doll* and *No Turning Back.*

RoC *Liliane Brousse, Irene Browne, Percy Herbert, Noel Howlett, Wensley Pithey, Leigh Madison, Judith Furse, Jean Cadell, Wilfred Pickles, Olive Sloane, Wilfrid Brambell, George Roderick, Jess Conrad.*

SEVEN DAYS TO NOON (1950) [5]

Dir *John Boulting.* Prod *Roy Boulting.* Scr *Roy Boulting, Frank Harvey.* Ph *Gilbert Taylor.* PC *Boulting Brothers/London Films.* Dis *British Lion.* 94 *mins. Cert A*

A professor (*Barry Jones*) working on the atomic bomb cracks under the strain of knowing the use to which it will be put. He steals a bomb and threatens to blow up London within a week if all atomic work is not stopped. The authorities evacuate the city while police hunt for the professor. He is found just in time, and the bomb rendered harmless. Suspenseful thriller with a sense of urgency in every foot. Academy Award for best original story - by Paul Dehn and James Bernard.

RoC *Olive Sloane, André Morell, Sheila Manahan, Hugh Cross, Joan Hickson, Ronald Adam, Marie Ney, Geoffrey Keen, Merrill Mueller, Russell Waters, Wyndham Goldie, Martin Boddey, Frederick Allen, Victor Maddern, Ian Wilson.*

Barry Jones and Olive Sloane in Seven Days to Noon (*1950*)

SEVEN THUNDERS (1957) [3]
(USA: *The Beasts of Marseilles*)

Dir *Hugo Fregonese.* Prod *Daniel M. Angel.* Scr *John Baines, from the novel by Rupert Croft-Cooke.* Ph *Wilkie Cooper.* PC *Dial.* Dis *Rank.* 100 *mins. Cert A*

Dave (*Stephen Boyd*) and Jim (*Tony Wright*), two escaped English prisoners-of-war, hide out in Marseilles in 1943, until the chance comes

to escape to England. Dave falls in love with Lise (*Anna Gaylor*), an enterprising orphan, but both men nearly fall foul of Martout (*James Robertson Justice*), ostensibly a smuggler of men, but in reality a dealer in double-cross who poisons fugitives for their money. In the German destruction of the city, Martout is killed and Dave, Jim and Lise board a boat bound for Spain. Improbable but vigorous escape yarn.

RoC *Kathleen Harrison, Eugene Deckers, Rosalie Crutchley, Katherine Kath, James Kenney, Anton Diffring, Martin Miller, George Coulouris, Carl Duering, Edric Connor, Marcel Pagliero, Leonard Sachs, Gaylord Cavallaro, Denis Shaw, Gerard Heinz, Jacques Cey, Vanda Hudson, Yvonne Warren (Romain), Christina Lubitz, Shirley Ann Field, June Ramsay, Andrea Malandrinos, Conchita Macauley, Marne Maitland, June Cowell, Françoise Martinelli, Peter Augustine, Michel Clément.*

SEVEN WAVES AWAY (1956) [3]
(USA: *Abandon Ship!*)

Dir and Scr *Richard Sale.* Prod *John R. Sloan, Ted Richmond.* Ph *Wilkie Cooper.* PC *Copa.* Dis *Columbia.* 95 *mins. Cert A*

A luxury liner sinks after striking a World War II mine, leaving 27 passengers and crew on a lifeboat in mid Atlantic. Holmes (*Tyrone Power*), an officer, orders the weak and wounded to be thrown overboard, coming to be regarded as a saviour by the rest - until they are rescued by a ship that has already picked up most of those Holmes forced off the lifeboat. He is left to live with his actions. Stark drama has brilliant idea, but is not too well written or acted.

RoC *Mai Zetterling, Lloyd Nolan, Stephen Boyd, Moira Lister, James Hayter, Marie Löhr, Moultrie Kelsall, Noel Willman, Gordon Jackson, Clive Morton, Laurence Naismith, John Stratton, Eddie Byrne, Clare Austin, Orlando Martins, Finlay Currie, Victor Maddern, Ralph Michael.*

SHADOW OF A MAN (1954) [3]

Dir *Michael McCarthy.* Prod and PC *E.J. Fancey.* Scr *Paul Erickson, McCarthy.* Ph *Geoffrey Faithfull.* Dis *New Realm.* 69 *mins. Cert A*

When a drunk-about-town has a fight with a nightclub manager and is found dead next morning, the verdict is heart failure. The police, though, suspect murder, and the killer, a diabetic given away by a hypodermic syringe, is eventually cornered and caught on a seaside pier. Average low-key drama with stronger-than-usual love interest.

LP *Paul Carpenter, Rona Anderson, Jane Griffiths, Ronald Leigh Hunt, Tony Quinn, Jack Taylor, Robert O'Neill, Rose Alba.*

SHADOW OF THE EAGLE (1950) [3]

Dir *Sidney Salkow.* Prod *Anthony Havelock-Allan.* Scr *Doreen Montgomery, Hagar Wilde.* Ph *Erwin Hillier.* PC *Valiant-Tuscania.* Dis *Independent Film Distributors.* 92 *mins. Cert U*

1770. One of the favoured officers of Catherine the Great (*Binnie Barnes*), Count Orloff (*Richard Greene*), goes to Venice to capture a princess (*Valentina Cortesa*) who claims to be heir to the Russian throne. He falls in love with her, but his plan to get her to waive her claims and go to Paris with him is thwarted by his rival, Gen Korsakov (*Charles Goldner*), who gets them both back to Russia and a condemned cell. But against overwhelming odds, Orloff and the princess escape to freedom. Potentially 'big' British film is little more than Greene schoolboy adventure.

RoC *Greta Gynt, Walter Rilla, Hugh French, Dennis Vance.*

SHADOW OF THE PAST (1950)   [3]

Dir *Mario Zampi.* Prod *Zampi, Mae Murray.* Scr *Aldo di Benedetti, Ian Stuart Black.* Ph *Hone Glendinning.* PC *Anglofilm.* Dis *Columbia. 83 mins. Cert A*

While staying with friends, a young man sees a mysterious woman in black in a house locked up for two years. Finding the owner of the house, he discovers the woman is the image of the owner's wife, who was killed in a car crash. The woman in black is in fact the twin of the dead woman, who was murdered by her husband. The young man helps her get her revenge. Modest but quite tense; twists in the plot are well concealed.

LP *Terence Morgan, Joyce Howard, Michael Medwin, Andrew Osborn, Wylie Watson, Marie Ney, Ella Retford, Ronald Adam, Louise Gainsborough, Ian Fleming, W.E. Holloway, Eve Ashley, Meadows White, Willoughby Gray, Francis Roberts, John Warren, Richard Neller, Anthony Pendrell, Dervis Ward.*

THE SHAKEDOWN (1959)   [2]

Dir *John Lemont.* Prod *Norman Williams.* Scr *Leigh Vance, Lemont.* Ph *Brendan Stafford.* PC *Ethiro/Alliance.* Dis *Rank. 92 mins. Cert X*

Just out of jail, rakish but ruthless crook Augie (*Terence Morgan*) finds a new racket: a portrait studio that is the front for a peep show in which nudes are photographed by amateur cameramen, a stituation which leads to blackmail. Mildred (*Hazel Court*), a policewoman, goes undercover to bust the racket, but nearly loses her life before the police move in. Augie is shot dead by one of his victims. Exploitative tough thriller.

RoC *Donald Pleasence, Robert Beatty, Bill Owen, Harry H. Corbett, Gene Anderson, Eddie Byrne, John Salew, Georgina Cookson, Jack Lambert, Dorinda Stevens, Linda Castle, Joan*

Hazel Court and Terence Morgan in The Shakedown (*1959*)

Haythorne, Sheila Buxton, Larry Burns, Laurence Taylor, Edward Judd, Charles Lamb, Jack Taylor, Douglas Bradley-Smith, Patty Dalton, Lynn Curtis, Leila Williams, Pauline Dukes, Angela Douglas, Julia Rogers, Arthur Lovegrove, Paul Whitsun-Jones, Diana Chesney, Timothy Bateson, Frank Hawkins, Robert Sansom, Neal Arden, Candy Scott, Wendy Peters.

SHAKE HANDS WITH THE DEVIL
(1959)   [4]

Dir and Prod *Michael Anderson.* Scr *Ivan Goff, Ben Roberts, Marion Thompson, from the novel by Reardon Conner.* Ph *Erwin Hillier.* PC *Troy Films.* Dis *United Artists, 111 mins. Cert A*

Dublin, 1921. Kerry (*Don Murray*), a medical student, finds, after he has been beaten up by British 'black-and-tans', that his superior, Professor Lenihan (*James Cagney*), is an IRA leader. In retaliation for Lady FitzHugh's (*Sybil Thorndike*) starving herself in prison, Leniham kidnaps Jennifer (*Dana Wynter*), daughter of a top British official, but Kerry eventually sees that Lenihan's devotion to violence has gone beyond idealism; he is forced to kill him before he can shoot Jennifer and jeopardize a peace treaty. Strong thriller liked by most critics; a few complained that it cheapened and caricatured the conflict.

RoC *Michael Redgrave, Glynis Johns, Cyril Cussack, Marianne Benet, Peter Reynolds, Harry Brogan, Allan Cuthbertson, John Cairney, Lewis Casson, Christopher Rhodes, John Breslin, Harry H. Corbett, Richard Harris, William Hartnell, Niall MacGinnis, Ray McAnally, Noel Purcell, Alan White, Robert Brown, Eithne Dunne, Eileen Crowe, John le Mesurier, Patrick McAlinney, Clive Morton, Christopher Casson, Donal Donnelly, Wilfrid Downing, Paul Farrell, Ronald Walsh.*

James Cagney in Shake Hands with the Devil (*1958*)

SHE DIDN'T SAY NO! (1958)   [3]

Dir *Cyril Frankel.* Prod *Sergei Nolbandov.* Scr *T.J. Morrison, Una Troy, from a novel by Troy.* Ph *Gilbert Taylor.* PC *GW Films.* Dis *AB-Pathé. Technicolor. 97 mins. Cert A*

Bridget (*Eileen Herlie*), an Irish widow, has six children by five different fathers. A court case brought by local do-gooders only proves that Bridget is a fit mother, so the fathers get together to buy her a farm a good way away. Jamesey (*Niall MacGinnis*) is appointed to the actual purchase, which he makes - then marries Bridget. Comedy of embarrassment has some charm, is occasionally touching.

RoC *Ray McAnally, Perlita Neilson, Liam Redmond, Betty McDowell, Ian Bannen, Jack MacGowran, Wilfred Downing, Ann Dickens, Teresa Scoble, Lesley Scoble, Raymond Manthorpe, Patrick McAlinney, Joan O'Hara, Eithne Dunne, Hilton Edwards, Maureen Halligan, Harry Hutchinson, Paul Farrell, Shirley Joy, Viola Keats, Anna Manahan, Michael O'Brien, Joan Welsh.*

THE SHERIFF OF FRACTURED JAW
(1958)   [4]

Dir *Raoul Walsh.* Prod and PC *Daniel M. Angel.* Scr *Arthur Dales, from the story by Jacob Hay.* Ph *Otto Heller.* Dis *20th Century-Fox. Eastman Colour. CinemaScope. 110 mins. Cert U*

Travelling by stagecoach to the far west town of Fractured Jaw in the 1850s, English gunsmith Jonathan Tibbs (*Kenneth More*) unwittingly routs an Indian raid and befriends the local chief. When he finds himself elected sheriff, saloon gal Kate (*Jayne Mansfield*) teaches him how to handle a gun and they fall in love. After Tibbs sells the Indians guns for furs, the local ranchers revolt, but Tibbs is saved by the Indians, whom he makes his deputies. Sunny, fun-filled comedy; More at his most popular.

RoC *Henry Hull, William Campbell, Bruce Cabot, Reed de Rouen, Ronald Squire, Charles Irwin, Robert Morley, Donald Stewart, David Horne, Sheldon Lawrence, Gordon Tanner, Sidney James, Eynon Evans, Clancy Cooper, Tucker McGuire, Nick Brady, Larry Taylor, Jack Lester, Nicholas Stuart, Susan Denny, Charles Farrell, Chief Jonas Applegarth, Deputy Chief Joe Buffalo, Connie Francis (voice).*

Kenneth More and Jayne Mansfield in The Sheriff of Fractured Jaw (*1958*)

SHE SHALL HAVE MURDER (1950)   [2]

Dir *Daniel Birt.* Prod *Derrick de Marney, Guido Coen.* Scr *Allan Mackinnon, from the novel by Delano Ames.* Ph *Robert Navarro.* PC *Concanen.* Dis *Independent Film Distributors. 90 mins. Cert U*

Jane (*Rosamund John*), a law clerk with ambitions to be a thriller writer, looks into the murder of one of her firm's clients, an eccentric old lady. After discovering that everyone in her office has a motive, she breaks a vital alibi by finding out that the firm's senior partner (*Felix Aylmer*) was in the office at midnight, and unmasks the killer. Slow, unconvincingly acted film has most of the faults typical of second-rate British thrillers of the time.

RoC *Derrick de Marney, Mary Jerrold, Joyce Heron, Jack Allen, Harry Fowler, John Bentley, Beatrice Varley, Henryetta Edwards, Duncan Lamont, June Elvin, Jack McNaughton, Olaf Pooley, Leon Davey, Denys Val Norton, Francis de Wolff, Jonathan Field, Jimmy Rhodes, Anthony Hilton, Frances Leak, Wanda Rands.*

THE SHIP THAT DIED OF SHAME (1955)   3
(USA: *PT Raiders*)

Dir *Basil Dearden.* Prod *Michael Relph.* Scr *Relph, Dearden, John Whiting, from the novel by Nicholas Monsarrat.* Ph *Gordon Dines.* PC *Ealing Studios.* Dis *General Film Distributors. 91 mins. Cert A*

After the war, the crew of Motor Gun Boat 1087, Bill (*George Baker*), Hoskins (*Richard Attenborough*) and Birdie (*Bill Owen*) take to smuggling spirits, nylons and other black market items across the Channel – very profitably. But when Hoskins involves them in arms and counterfeit currency, 1087 becomes more difficult to handle. Their boss (*Roland Culver*) is killed, and Hoskins falls overboard in a fight with Bill, shortly before 1087 dashes itself against the rocks. Fable is well-set but hard to swallow.

RoC *Virginia McKenna, Bernard Lee, Ralph Truman, John Chandos, John Longden, Harold Goodwin, David Langton, Stratford Johns.*

THE SHIRALEE (1957)   4

Dir *Leslie Norman.* (Associate) Prod *Jack Rix.* Scr *Norman, Neil Paterson, from the novel by D'Arcy Niland.* Ph *Paul Beeson.* PC *Ealing Films.* Dis *M-G-M. 99 mins. Cert A*

Macauley (*Peter Finch*), an itinerant Australian swagman, returning from his travels to find his wife (*Elizabeth Sellars*) with her lover, seizes his small daughter Buster (*Dana Wilson*) and takes to the road. They move from friend to friend, until Macauley is forced to return to town after Buster has been hurt in an accident. He is beaten up by hoodlums hired by his wife's lover. But, as Buster recovers, there is hope for the future in Macauley's renewed relationship with Lily (*Rosemary Harris*), mother of his other child. Unevenly acted, but touching, sympathetically handled drama.

RoC *George Rose, Tessie O'Shea, Sidney James, Russell Napier, Niall MacGinnis, Reg Lye, Barbara Archer, Charles Tingwell, John Phillips, Alec Mango.*

THE SIEGE OF PINCHGUT (1959)   4

Dir *Harry Watt.* (Associate) Prod *Eric Williams.* Scr *Watt, Jon Cleary, Alexander Baron.* Ph *Gordon Dines.* PC *Ealing Films.* Dis *AB-Pathé. 104 mins. Cert U*

Australia. Four convicts escape and are forced to hole up on the tiny island of Pinchgut in Sydney Harbour, where they take hostage the keeper and his family (*Gerry Duggan, Barbara Mullen, Heather Sears*) and the leader (*Aldo Ray*) trains a naval gun on an ammunition ship in the port. But, after sharpshooters pick off two of his fellows, he is cornered on a tower and shot down, still protesting his innocence.

Tremendously exciting action scenes make up for lack of definition elsewhere. The last Ealing film.

RoC *Neil McCallum, Victor Maddern, Carlo Justini, Alan Tilvern, Kenneth J. Warren, Grant Taylor, Derek Barnes, Richard Vernon, Martin Boddey, Ewan Macduff, Max Robertson, John Pusey, Fred Abbot.*

THE SILENT ENEMY (1958)   4

Dir and Scr *William Fairchild, from a book by Marshall Pugh.* Prod *Bertram Ostrer.* Ph *Otto Heller,* (underwater) *Egil Nystrom.* PC *Romulus.* Dis *Independent Film Distributors/British Lion. 112 mins. Cert A*

1941. British ships in Gibraltar are being blown up by limpet mines. The unorthodox Lt 'Buster' Crabb (*Laurence Harvey*) talks his way into the leadership of the British diving team, and finds that the Italian saboteurs are based at a nearby neutral Spanish port. Crabb and Knowles (*Michael Craig*) get a midget submarine, stack it with explosives and guide it into the Italians' base, blowing it up. Undemanding war film with excitement and a vein of humour.

RoC *Dawn Addams, John Clements, Gianna Maria Canale, Arnoldo Foa, Massimo Serato, Sidney James, Alec McCowen, Howard Marion Crawford, Ewen Solon, Nigel Stock, Brian Oulton, Carlo Justini, Giacomo Rossi-Stuart, Ian Whittaker, Raymond Young, David Lodge, Cyril Shaps, Ian McNaughton, Lee Montague, John Lee, John Longden, Alan Webb, John Moffatt, Harold Siddons, Michael Brill, Sydney King, Hugh Moxey, Jerome Willis, Desmond Jordan, Tom Watson, Jack May, Derren Nesbitt, Laurence Brooks, Peter Welsh, Yvonne Romain.*

THE SILKEN AFFAIR (1956)   3

Dir *Roy Kellino.* Prod *Fred Feldkamp.* Scr *Robert Lewis Taylor.* Ph *Gilbert Taylor.* PC *Dragon.* Dis *RKO Radio. 96 mins. Cert U*

Married for 18 dull years to a dull wife (*Dorothy Alison*), dull accountant Roger Tweakham (*David Niven*) undergoes a complete change of outlook after meeting a carefree French girl (*Geneviève Page*). He doctors the accounts of a bankrupt firm to give it an air of prosperity and fixes the books of a firm he hates to set it on the slide. He is sent to prison but, on his release, finds that, thanks to wheeler-dealing by his fellow conspirator (*Wilfrid Hyde White*), he now has a controlling interest in both companies. Would-be frolic never gets off the ground.

RoC *Ronald Squire, Beatrice Straight, Howard Marion Crawford, Richard Wattis, Miles Malleson, Joan Sims, Irene Handl, Charles Carson, Harry Locke, Martin Boddey, Colin Morris, Leonard Sharp, John Carroll, Shirley Ann Field.*

SIMBA (1955)   4

Dir *Brian Desmond Hurst.* Prod *Peter de Sarigny.* Scr *John Baines, Robin Estridge.* Ph *Geoffrey Unsworth.* PC *Group.* Dis *General Film Distributors. Eastman Colour. 99 mins. Cert A*

Howard (*Dirk Bogarde*) arrives in East Africa with Mary (*Virginia McKenna*), an English

friend, to discover that his brother has been killed by Mau Mau terrorists. He suspects the local doctor, Karanja (*Earl Cameron*) to be the leader of the Mau Mau group, but it is in fact Karanja's father (*Orlando Martins*), a tribal chief. In a final siege of Howard's farm, both blacks die. Strong, meaty drama, if faintly unreal.

RoC *Donald Sinden, Basil Sydney, Marie Ney, Joseph Tomelty, Frank Singuineau, Ben Johnson (not US actor), Huntley Campbell, Slim Harris, Glyn Lawson, Harry Quash, John Chandos, Desmond Roberts, Errol John, Willy Sholanke.*

SIMON AND LAURA (1955)   4

Dir *Muriel Box.* Prod *Teddy Baird.* Scr *Peter Blackmore, from the play by Alan Melville.* Ph *Ernest Steward.* PC *Group.* Dis *Rank. Technicolor. VistaVision. 91 mins. Cert U*

A warring stage couple, Simon (*Peter Finch*) and Laura (*Kay Kendall*), who are on the edge of bankruptcy as well as divorce, stay together for the sake of what proves to be a successful television series. Just as the programme's fortunes are flagging, the couple's private lives erupt in front of the cameras. The production team gets involved in the 'live' free-for-all and audience reaction ensures the future of the series. Familiar plotline rejigged to provide some witty jibes at TV.

RoC *Muriel Pavlow, Ian Carmichael, Hubert Dregg, Maurice Denham, Thora Hird, Clive Parritt, Alan Wheatley, Richard Wattis, Terence Longdon, Joan Hickson, Cyril Chamberlain, Marianne Stone, Muriel George, Charles Hawtrey, Susan Beaumont, Philip Gilbert, Gilbert Harding, John Ellison, Isobel Barnett, George Cansdale, Peter Haigh, Shirley Ann Field, Julia Arnall, Hal Osmond, Jill Ireland.*

SING ALONG WITH ME (1952)   2

Dir *Peter Graham Scott.* Prod *John Croydon.* Scr *Scott, Dennis Vance.* Ph *Gerald Gibbs.* PC *HH Films.* Dis *British Lion. 78 mins. Cert U*

Welsh grocer David Parry's (*Donald Peers*) success in a songwriting contest brings him a contract with a music publisher. Lonely in London, he cannot write new material, but gets by on the strength of songs he has already written. He prevents a crooked music publisher from stealing his first new song, and is reconciled with the young widow (*Dodo Watts*) back home who had previously refused to marry him. Modest musical with curiously dislikeable characters.

RoC *Dennis Vance, Jill Clifford, Mercy Haystead, Cyril Chamberlain, Humphrey Morton, George Curzon, Leonard Morris, Michael Bilton, Ben Williams, Bryan Royceston, Norah Gordon, Leonard Sharp, Sam Kydd, Elsie Monks, Helen Forrest, Dorothy King, Marian Edwards-Greene, Maureen Allen, Dennis Castle, Dennis Brian.*

SINGLE-HANDED (1953)   4
(USA: *Sailor of the King*)

Dir *Roy Boulting.* Prod *Frank McCarthy.* Scr *Valentine Davies, from a novel by C.S. Forester.* Ph *Gilbert Taylor.* PC and Dis *20th Century-Fox. 84 mins. Cert U*

Brown (*Jeffrey Hunter*), offspring of a World

War I romance between a naval officer (*Michael Rennie*) and a prim girl (*Wendy Hiller*), plays a lone hand in a delaying action in World War II. As a seaman, he escapes his German captors and holes up on a rocky island, pinning the German ship in harbour. He is eventually killed, but a British ship has arrived (captained by Brown's father, who does not know him) and sinks the German vessel as it tries to put to sea. Sturdy, low-key remake of 1935's *Brown On Resolution/For Ever England*.

RoC *Bernard Lee, Peter Van Eyck, Patrick Barr, Victor Maddern, Robin Bailey, John Horsley, James Copeland, Sam Kydd, Nicholas Bruce, Martin Boddey, Guido Lorraine, Lockwood West, James Drake, Robert Dean, John Schlesinger, Derek Prentice.*

6-5 SPECIAL (1958) [3]

Dir *Alfred Shaughnessy*. Prod *Herbert Smith*. Scr *Norman Hudis*. Ph *Leo Rogers*. PC and Dis *Anglo-Amalgamated*. 85 mins. Cert U

Ann (*Diane Todd*) and Judy (*Avril Leslie*) take the 6-5 special train to London, where they hope to break into show business. They find it crammed with entertainers, plus two show business scouts (*Josephine Douglas, Pete Murray*) on a nationwide talent-spotting tour. Ann does an audition in the dining car and her lovely singing voice persuades the scouts to give her a permanent spot in their TV pop series. Performers are enthusiastic, but it's not enough for the uninitiated.

RoC *Finlay Currie, Freddie Mills, Lonnie Donegan, Jim Dale, Petula Clark, Dickie Valentine, Joan Regan, Russ Hamilton, The King Brothers, Don Lang and His Frantic 5, Johnny Dankworth and His Orchestra, Cleo Laine, Mike and Bernie Winters, Jackie Dennis, Victor Soverall, The Kentones, Desmond Lane, The John Barry Seven, Jimmy Lloyd.*

THE SIX MEN (1951) [2]

Dir *Michael Law*. Prod *Roger Proudlock*. Scr *Reed de Rouen, Law, Richard Eastham, from a story by E. and M.A. Radford*. Ph *S.D. Onions*. PC *Planet*. Dis *Eros*. 65 mins. Cert A

A series of major crimes, perpetrated by a gang known as The Six Men, is baffling Scotland Yard. A blind man called The Mole (*Louis Weichart*) leads detectives Holroyd (*Harold Warrender*) and Hunter (*Michael Evans*) to a club where Christina (*Olga Edwardes*), an actress, proves to be a link with the gang. Holroyd adopts offbeat methods which lead to the crooks' killing each other one by one, until the last is captured. Some excitement; actors stoically suffer poor dialogue.

RoC *Peter Bull, Avril Angers, Desmond Jeans, Ivan Craig, Reed de Rouen, Christopher Page, Edward Malin.*

SKID KIDS (1952) [3]

Dir *Don Chaffey*. Prod *Gilbert Church*. Scr *Jack Howells*. Ph *S.D. Onions*. PC *Bushey/Children's Film Foundation*. Dis *Associated British*. 65 mins. Cert U

Incensed when they are evicted from their cycle track because of thefts (of which they are innocent) at the cycle factory nearby, the Burton Road Bullets, training for the final of an East End of London junior track competition, determine to track down those responsible. After a car chase, two 'spivs', Spike and Sam, are held, and their garage-owner boss also caught. The Bullets are promised a new and better track. Lively junior stuff but with rather stiff children.

LP *Barry McGregor, Anthony Lang, Peter Neal, Tom Walls (Jr), Angela Monk, Frank Hawkins, Tom Macauley, A.E. Matthews.*

THE SLEEPING TIGER (1954) [3]

Dir *Victor Hanbury* (*Joseph Losey*). Prod *Hanbury*. Scr *Derek Frye* (*Carl Foreman*). Ph *Harry Waxman*. PC *Insignia*. Dis *Anglo-Amalgamated*. 89 mins. Cert A.

When petty crook Frank Clements (*Dirk Bogarde*) tries to hold up Dr Esmond (*Alexander Knox*), a psychiatrist, Esmond takes him into his home to find out what makes a criminal tick. Frank seduces Esmond's all-too-willing wife Glenda (*Alexis Smith*), but has a change of heart when Esmond provides him with an alibi for another robbery. She pretends Frank has attacked her; Esmond pretends to shoot him. Frank flees, but Glenda picks him up in her car and crashes it over a cliff. Foolish but full-blooded stuff in the old Warner style.

RoC *Hugh Griffith, Patricia McCarron, Maxine Audley, Glyn Houston, Harry Towb, Russell Waters, Billie Whitelaw, Fred Griffiths, Esma Cannon.*

Alexis Smith and Dirk Bogarde in The Sleeping Tiger *(1954)*

THE SMALLEST SHOW ON EARTH (1957) [4]

Dir *Basil Dearden*. Prod *Michael Relph*. Scr *William Rose, John Eldridge*. Ph *Douglas Slocombe*. PC *Hallmark/Launder-Gilliat*. Dis *British Lion*. 80 mins. Cert U

Matt and Jean Spenser (*Bill Travers, Virginia McKenna*) inherit a fleapit cinema, the Bijou, whose screen shakes each time a train goes past and whose staff consists of a drunken projectionist (*Peter Sellers*), an Edwardian cashier (*Margaret Rutherford*) and a doddery doorman (*Bernard Miles*). The Grand offers to buy them out for £500, which would barely pay off their debts – so they reopen the Bijou. Sabotage (slipping scotch into the projectionist) is afoot, but when the doorman burns down the Grand, its owners are forced to increase their offer 20-fold. Too-short comedy gets lots of laughs from its character stars.

RoC *Leslie Phillips, Francis de Wolff, Sidney James, June Cunningham, George Cross, Stringer Davis, George Cormack, Sam Kydd, Michael Corcoran.*

SMALL HOTEL (1957) [3]

Dir *David Macdonald*. Prod *Robert Hall*. Scr *Wilfred Eades, from the play by Rex Frost*. Ph *Norman Warwick*. PC *Welwyn*. Dis *AB-Pathé*. 59 mins. Cert U

Life in a hotel for genteel guests. When Albert (*Gordon Harker*), the old head waiter, the world's greatest expert on tipping and fiddling, learns he is to be replaced by a young, efficient woman, he moves into action. He uses blackmail and other chicanery to settle the hash of a nosey inspector and maintain his position. Successful play telescoped into typical Harker vehicle of 20 years earlier. Inoffensive comedy.

RoC *Janet Munro, John Loder, Marie Lohr, Billie Whitelaw, Francis Matthews, Irene Handl, Dora Bryan, Frederick Schiller, Dorothy Bromily, Derek Blomfield, Ruth Trouncer.*

SMALL TOWN STORY (1953) [2]

Dir *Montgomery Tully*. Prod *Otto Kreisler*. Scr *George Fisher, Franz Marischka, Maurice Weissberger*. Ph *Jo Jago, Peter Hamilton*. PC *Almanack*. Dis *General Film Distributors*. 69 mins. Cert U

Bob Regan (*Kent Walton*), Canadian ex-Serviceman and footballer, joins a struggling soccer team which stands to come into a large sum of money if it wins promotion to a higher division. His ex-girlfriend (*Susan Shaw*), paid by other interests, tries to lure him away to a bigger club, but is unsuccessful. Woeful drama boosted by good soccer scenes.

RoC *Donald Houston, Alan Wheatley, George Merritt, Margaret Harrison, Norman Williams, Arthur Rigby, Raymond Glendenning, Billy Milne, Richard Wattis, Michael Balfour, Johnnie Schofield, Denis Compton; members of Arsenal, Millwall and Hayes Football Clubs, and Middlesex Cricket Club.*

SMART ALEC (1951) [2]

Dir *John Guillermin*. Prod *Roger Proudlock*. Scr *Alec Coppel*. Ph *Ray Elton*. PC *Vandyke*. Dis *Grand National*. 58 mins. Cert A

Alec (*Peter Reynolds*) sets himself up in a flat over that of his rich uncle, invites the police commissioner, and tells him of his premonition that his uncle will be killed. Alec then murders his uncle using a boreless gun and an ice bullet, but a twist of fate sees him brought to justice even after he has been tried and acquitted. Fair thriller takes itself too lightly.

RoC *Mercy Haystead, Leslie Dwyer, Edward Lexy, Kynaston Reeves, Charles Hawtrey, John Harvey.*

SMILEY (1956) [5]

Dir and Prod *Anthony Kimmins*. Scr *Kimmins, Moore Raymond*. Ph *Ted Scaife, Ross Wood*. PC *London Films*. Dis *20th Century-Fox*. Colour by De Luxe. CinemaScope. 105 mins. Cert U

Smiley (*Colin Petersen*), a lovable scamp from

a small Australian bush town, has ambitions to own a bicycle. He can expect nothing from his drunken father or overworked mother, so the vicar (*Ralph Richardson*) gives him a Sunday job ringing church bells, the police sergeant (*Chips Rafferty*) finds him some sheep-shearing and the publican (*John McCallum*) gives him some packages (dope) for local aborigines. Although Smiley's father steals his savings, all ends well; he gets the bike. Sunny, charming family adventure story.

RoC *Jocelyn Hernfield, Bruce Archer, Margaret Christensen, Reg Lye, Charles Tingwell, Marion Johns, William Rees, Guy Doleman, Gavin Davies, Bob Sunin, Chow Sing, Reggie Weigand.*

SMILEY GETS A GUN (1958)   3

Dir and Prod *Anthony Kimmins.* Scr *Kimmins, Rex Rienits, from a novel by Moore Raymond.* Ph *Ted Scaife.* PC *Canberra.* Dis *20th Century-Fox. Technicolor. CinemaScope. 90 mins. Cert U*

Tearaway Smiley Greevins (*Keith Calvert*), who lives in a small Australian town, is promised a gun by the local policeman (*Chips Rafferty*) if he earns it. He befriends fearsome old Granny McKinley (*Sybil Thorndike*), but when her hoard of gold is stolen, Smiley is suspected. Smiley helps to find the real culprit – a city reporter – and gets his gun. Friendly, unpolished children's romp.

RoC *Bruce Archer, Margaret Christensen, Reg Lye, Grant Taylor, Verena Kimmins, Guy Doleman, Leonard Teale, Jannine Dinnen, Brian Farley, Richard Pusey, Barbara Eather, Ruth Cracknell, Bruce Beeby, Charles Tasman, Frank Ransom, John Fegan, John Tate, Val Cooney, William Rees, Gordon Chater.*

THE SNORKEL (1958)   3

Dir *Guy Green.* Prod *Michael Carreras.* Scr *Peter Myers, Jimmy Sangster, from the novel by Anthony Dawson.* Ph *Jack Asher.* PC *Hammer.* Dis *Columbia. 90 mins. Cert A*

Having drowned his wife's first husband, Jacques (*Peter Van Eyck*) now plans to get rid of her for her money. He gasses her, making sure she cannot escape by staying with her and wearing a snorkel. His resourceful stepdaughter Candy (*Mandy Miller*) proves to disbelieving police how the murder could have been committed, then brings about the death of Jacques, caught in one of his own traps. Intriguing but slow-moving suspense drama.

Peter Van Eyck and Mandy Miller in The Snorkel *(1958)*

RoC *Betta St John, Gregoire Aslan, William Franklyn, Marie Burke, Irene Prador, Henry Vidon, Robert Rietty, Armando Guinle, David Ritch.*

SOAP-BOX DERBY (1957)   4

Dir and Scr *Darcy Conyers.* Prod *Anthony Gilkison.* Ph *Douglas Ransom.* PC *Rayant/Children's Film Foundation.* Dis *CFF. 64 mins. Cert U*

Great rivalry exists between the Battersea Bats and the Victoria Victors, two sets of London boys who build cars for the forthcoming Soapbox Derby. The Victors resort to chicanery to steal the Bats' revolutionary new design, and blame the designer (*Roy Townshend*), who is thrown out by the Bats. At the last moment the car is retrieved from where the Victors had hidden it, and wins for the Bats. Vigorous melodrama, enthusiastically played by the kids.

RoC *Michael Crawford, Keith Davis, Alan Coleshill, Carla Challenor, Denis Shaw, Harry Fowler, Mark Daly, Malcolm Kirby, Raymond Dudley, Jean Ireland, David Williams.*

SOHO CONSPIRACY (1950)   2

Dir *Cecil H. Williamson.* Prod *Edwin J. Fancey.* Scr *Williamson, Ralph Dawson.* Ph *Jeff Davis, R. Densham.* PC and Dis *DUK Films. 85 mins. Cert U*

A press agent and a Soho restaurateur's daughter plan to put on a charity concert in aid of the restoration of a bombed church. When a lawyer who wants to gain control of the restaurant for nefarious ends steps in to thwart their plans, the inhabitants of Soho take a hand, and see that the show goes on. Cut-price film 'borrows' wholesale from earlier movies for its distinguished 'guest stars'.

LP *Jacques Labreque, Zena Marshall, John Witty, Peter Gawthorne, Syd and Max Harrison and (from other films) Tito Gobbi, Tito Schipa, Beniamino Gigli, Gino Becchi.*

SOHO INCIDENT (1956)   3
(USA: *Spin a Dark Web*)

Dir *Vernon Sewell.* Prod *George Maynard,* (*uncredited*) *M.J. Frankovitch.* Scr *Ian Stuart Black, from a novel by Robert Westerby.* Ph *Basil Emmott.* PC *Film Locations.* Dis *Columbia. 77 mins. Cert A*

Jim (*Lee Patterson*), a beefy Canadian out to make an easy living, joins a crooked Soho betting gang headed by Rico (*Martin Benson*) and his sister Bella (*Faith Domergue*). When the gang murders a boxer who refused to throw a fight, Jim wants out, but he is forced to stay when the gang threatens the life of the boxer's sister (*Rona Anderson*), of whom he is fond. Police close in on the gang, who shoot it out: Rico is killed and the others captured. But the law deals leniently with Jim. Standard thriller of fair pace and good backgrounds.

RoC *Robert Arden, Peter Hammond, Joss Ambler, Peter Burton, Sam Kydd, Bernard Fox, Peter Benson.*

SO LITTLE TIME (1952)   3

Dir *Compton Bennett.* Prod *Maxwell Setton, Aubrey Baring.* Scr *John Cresswell, from a novel by Noelle Henry.* Ph *Oswald Morris.* PC *May-*

flower. Dis *Associated British-Pathé. 88 mins. Cert U*

World War II. Through a mutual love of music, Nicole (*Maria Schell*), daughter of an aristocratic Belgian family whose sons and father have been killed by the Nazis, falls in love with the German military governor (*Marius Goring*). A cousin in the resistance forces her to betray him. Nicole is killed, and the governor commits suicide. Slow, well-acted, rather touching, unusual love story just misses being a good film.

RoC *Gabrielle Dorziat, Barbara Mullen, John Bailey, Lucie Mannheim, Harold Lang, David Hurst, Andrée Melly, Oscar Quitak, Stanley van Beers, Olga Lowe, Wolf Frees, Alison Peline, Jeremy Geidt.*

SO LONG AT THE FAIR (1950)   4

Dir *Antony Darnborough, Terence Fisher.* Prod *Betty Box.* Scr *Hugh Mills, Anthony Thorne, from Thorne's novel.* Ph *Reginald Wyer.* PC *Gainsborough.* Dis *General Film Distributors. 86 mins. Cert U*

Vicky (*Jean Simmons*) and her brother Johnny (*David Tomlinson*) come to Paris for the Great Exhibition of 1889. After a night out, Vicky wakes up in their hotel next morning to find that Johnny has disappeared. His bedroom is now a bathroom. The staff deny all knowledge of him. Failing to get help from the police or British consul, Vicky is in a state of panic but an English artist (*Dirk Bogarde*) helps her. Together, they discover the truth: Johnny was taken ill that night with plague; if the news had got out, the whole Exhibition would have been endangered. Quite suspenseful: certainly a mystery with a difference.

RoC *Honor Blackman, Cathleen Nesbitt, Felix Aylmer, Betty Warren, Marcel Poncin, Austin Trevor, André Morell, Zena Marshall, Eugene Deckers, Natasha Sokolova, Nelly Arno.*

SOLUTION BY PHONE (1953)   2

Dir *Alfred Travers.* Prod *Brandon Fleming, Geoffrey Goodhart.* Scr *Fleming.* Ph *Hilton Craig.* PC *Pan.* Dis *AB-Pathé. 59 mins. Cert A*

A successful crime novelist (*Clifford Evans*) is tricked by the murderer (*John Witty*) of the author's faithless wife (*Georgina Cookson*) into giving advice on the disposal of a body – with the result that he finds himself suspected of murder, especially in view of his own affair with his secretary (*Thea Gregory*). It's the detective work of the secretary which leads police to pinpoint the right man. Ingenious plot, but poorly done.

RoC *Enid Hewitt, Geoffrey Goodhart, Max Brimmell, Charles Lamb, Jessica Cairns, Diana Payan, Johnnie Schofield.*

SOMEONE AT THE DOOR (1950)   3

Dir *Francis Searle.* Prod *Anthony Hinds.* Scr *A.R. Rawlinson, from the play by Dorothy and Campbell Christie.* Ph *Walter Harvey.* PC *Hammer.* Dis *Exclusive. 66 mins. Cert U*

Reporter Ronnie (*Michael Medwin*) and his sister Sally (*Yvonne Owen*) live in a reputedly haunted house she has inherited. Ronnie plans to make a name for himself by 'murdering' his sister (who will go into hiding), standing trial and then producing the 'corpse'. Her fiancé, a medical student, provides a body, but things go awry and Ronnie finds himself in danger of being hanged. Close remake of 1936 version. RoC *Garry Marsh, Hugh Latimer, Danny Green, Campbell Singer, John Kelly.*

SOMETHING IN THE CITY (1950)   ③

Dir *Maclean Rogers.* Prod *Ernest G. Roy.* Scr *H.F. Maltby.* Ph *Brendan J. Stafford.* PC *Nettlefold.* Dis *Butchers.* 76 mins. Cert U

Ningle (*Richard Hearne*) leads his wife and grown-up daughter to think that he is a city businessman, and keeps up the deception by leaving at the same time each morning, and taking up his real occupation – pavement artist. Eventually, he is accused of murdering his other 'self' and has a tough time clearing things up. Harmless comedy, a remake of the same writer and director's 1937 film, *The Strange Adventures of Mr Smith.*

RoC *Ellen Pollock, Garry Marsh, Betty Sinclair, Tom Gill, Diana Calderwood, Bill Shine, Dora Bryan, George Merritt, Horace Kenney, Molly Weir, Stanley Vilven, Gerald Rex, Vi Kaley, Ben Williams, Esmé Beringer, Kenneth Henry, Mackenzie Ward.*

Richard Hearne and Horace Kenney in Something in the City (*1950*)

SOMETHING MONEY CAN'T BUY (1952)   ②

Dir *Pat Jackson.* Prod *Joseph Janni.* Scr *Jackson, James Lansdale Hodson.* Ph *C. Pennington-Richards.* PC *Vic/Rank/British Film Makers.* Dis *General Film Distributors.* 83 mins. Cert U

Harry Wilding (*Anthony Steel*) finds it hard to settle down to a 'Civvy Street' career after army life. His wife Anne (*Patricia Roc*) launches a successful secretarial agency, and Harry fumes as a housewife until, with two brother officers-in-trouble and an impoverished lord (*A.E. Matthews*), he starts a mobile catering business which, after initial disasters, gets off the ground. With some reluctance, Anne quits her agency, and reverts to being a wife at home. Occasionally funny comedy hasn't sufficient comic situations or invention in script.

RoC *Moira Lister, David Hutcheson, Michael Trubshawe, Diane Hart, Charles Victor, Henry Edwards, Mary Hinton, D.A. Clarke-Smith, Mara Lane, John Barry, Dennis Arundell, Joss Ambler, Michael Brennan, Helen Goss, Joe Lin-*

nane, *Oscar Quitak, Irene Prador, Johnnie Schofield, Olwen Brookes, Margaret Vyner.*

SONG OF PARIS (1952)   ④
(USA: *Bachelor in Paris*)

Dir *John Guillermin.* Prod *Roger Proudlock.* Scr *Allan Mackinnon, Frank Muir, Denis Norden.* Ph *Ray Elton, Len Harris.* PC *Vandyke.* Dis *Adelphi.* 80 mins. Cert A

Englishman Matthew (*Dennis Price*), a mother-dominated stomach-pill salesman, meets Clementine (*Anne Vernon*), a Parisian cabaret star, when his taxi door rips off her skirt. In love, they go to England, where Matthew tells his mother that Clementine is an aristocrat, and is challenged to a duel by her pursuing fiancé (*Mischa Auer*). Fortunately for Matthew, police intervene, and the Frenchman settles for Matthew's mother. Champagne comedy fizzes most of the way.

RoC *Hermione Baddeley, Joan Kenny, Brian Worth, Duncan Lamont, Tessa Prendergast, Anton Diffring.*

SON OF A STRANGER (1957)   ②

Dir *Ernest Morris.* Prod *Edward J. Danziger, Harry Lee Danziger.* Scr *Stanley Miller.* Ph *Jimmy Wilson.* PC *Danzigers.* Dis *United Artists.* 68 mins. Cert A.

Tom (*James Kenney*), who beats up old women for his living, hates his dying mother but dreams his unknown father is well-to-do. An anonymous letter sets him off on a search for his father, which leads to Cornwall, where he murders an old woman before finding out his father is the local doctor. Having learned about Tom, the man grabs a rifle and is accidentally shot. Tom is found guilty and hangs. Squalid, very low-budget morality play is ludicrously unconvincing. Kenney still playing cosh boys (but well).

RoC *Ann Stephens, Victor Maddern, Basil Dignam, Catherine Finn, Diana Chesney, Mona Washbourne.*

SON OF ROBIN HOOD (1958)   ③

Dir *George Sherman.* Prod *Sherman, Jack Lamont.* Scr *George W. George, George Slavin.* Ph *Arthur Grant.* PC *Argo.* Dis *20th Century-Fox.* Eastman Colour. CinemaScope. 77 mins. Cert U

When the Black Duke (*David Farrar*), planning to seize the English throne in 1200, imprisons the Regent (*Marius Goring*), the ageing outlaws of Sherwood Forest call on the offspring of Robin Hood, who turns out to be a girl (*June Laverick*) and the Regent's younger brother Jamie (*Al Hedison*) to lead them. The Duke's castle is stormed and Jamie kills him in a duel. Juvenile frolic with lively action.

RoC *Philip Friend, Delphi Lawrence, George Coulouris, George Woodbridge, Jack Lambert, Humphrey Lestocq, Noel Hood, Shelagh Fraser, Maya Koumani, Oliver Johnston, Russell Napier, Alastair Hunter, Robert Bruce, Jack Taylor, Christine Halward, Richard Walters, Doreen Dawne.*

S.O.S. PACIFIC (1959)   ③

Dir *Guy Green.* Prod *John Nasht, Patrick Filmer-Sankey.* Scr *Robert Westerby.* Ph *Wilkie*

Cooper. PC *Sydney Box Associates.* Dis *Rank.* 91 mins. Cert A

The Pacific. Mark (*Eddie Constantine*), a smuggler, is turned in by stoolpigeon Whitey (*Richard Attenborough*). Both are passengers on a plane piloted by drunken Bennett (*John Gregson*), which catches fire and crashes in the sea. The adjoining island is the site of an H-bomb test due in a few hours; Bennett gives his life to help Mark swim to it and stop the mechanism. Whitey is also killed. Pretty ludicrous drama at least keeps busy, is well acted.

RoC *Pier Angeli, Eva Bartok, Clifford Evans, Jean Anderson, Cec Linder, Gunnar Moller, Harold Kasket.*

SOULS IN CONFLICT (1954)   ②

Dir and Scr *Leonard Reeve, Dick Ross.* Prod *Ross.* Ph *Guy Green.* PC *Anglo-Scottish.* Dis *Billy Graham Evangelistic Films.* Eastman Colour. 75 mins. Cert U

Three people, a country vicar's daughter who has become an actress, a test pilot and a factory worker who has failed to win the pools because a friend failed to post his coupon, all find new faith and hope when the Billy Graham religious crusade visits London. Very syrupy forced-dose of religion, with only *Billy Graham* himself registering with conviction.

RoC *Joan Winmill, Eric Micklewood, Charles Leno, Hilda Fenemore, Frederick Leister, Daphne Abbott, Neal Arden, Colleen Townsend Evans, Don Moomaw.*

THE SOUND BARRIER (1952)   ④
(USA: *Breaking the Sound Barrier*)

Dir and Prod *David Lean.* Scr *Terence Rattigan.* Ph *Jack Hildyard.* PC *London Films.* Dis *British Lion.* 118 mins. Cert A

Susan Ridgefield (*Ann Todd*), daughter of a ruthless, ambitious aircraft-factory owner (*Ralph Richardson*), watches first her brother (*Denholm Elliott*), then her husband (*Nigel Patrick*) killed, one trying to please his father in a solo flight, the other trying to break the sound barrier. A third pilot (*John Justin*) succeeds in breaking the barrier and Susan, seeing human chinks in her father's armour, returns to him with her baby. Good flying film touches the emotions more in the air than on the ground. British Oscar as best film of 1952.

RoC *Dinah Sheridan, Joseph Tomelty, Jack Allen, Ralph Michael, Donald Harron, Vincent Holman, Douglas Muir, Leslie Phillips, Robert*

Ann Todd and Nigel Patrick in The Sound Barrier (*1952*)

Brooks Turner, Anthony Snell, Jolyon Jackley (baby).

SOUTH OF ALGIERS (1952) 3
(USA: *The Golden Mask*)
Dir *Jack Lee*. Prod *Maxwell Setton, Aubrey Baring*. Scr *Robert Westerby*. Ph *Oswald Morris*. PC *Mayflower*. Dis *AB-Pathé*. Technicolor. *95 mins. Cert U*

Rival parties cross the Sahara desert to find a fabled golden mask, to be found with other art treasures in a tomb. One is interested for archaeological reasons, the other for monetary gain. There are deadly Arab bandits and sandstorms to face, and the money-grabbing party is wiped out, the last member in the very act of clutching the prize he sought. Colourful adventure with rambling, *Schoolboys' Own* plot.
LP *Eric Portman, Van Heflin, Wanda Hendrix, Charles Goldner, Jacques François, Jacques Brunius, Alec Mango, Marne Maitland, George Pastell, Marie France, Aubrey Mather, Noelle Middleton, Simone Silva, Alec Finter, René Leplat, Pierre Chaminade, Arnold Diamond, Messaoud, Michael Mellinger, Maxwell Setton, Aubrey Baring*.

SPACEWAYS (1953) 2
Dir *Terence Fisher*. Prod *Michael Carreras*. Scr *Paul Tabori, Richard Landau, from a radio play by Charles Eric Maine*. Ph *Reginald Wyer*. PC *Hammer*. Dis *Exclusive. 76 mins. Cert U*

An American scientist (*Howard Duff*) working on a three-stage space rocket, is suspected of having murdered his wife and her lover – they have in fact run away together – and shot their bodies into space. The American goes up into space to prove everyone wrong and, on his return, finds he is free to marry the mathematician (*Eva Bartok*) who stowed away with him – his wife has been shot by her lover. Pretty lame British entry into science-fiction.
RoC *Andrew Osborn, Cecile Chevreau, Michael Medwin, Alan Wheatley, Philip Leaver, Anthony Ireland, Hugh Moxey, David Horne, Jean Webster-Brough, Leo Philips, Marianne Stone*.

THE SPANIARD'S CURSE (1958) 3
Dir *Ralph Kemplen*. Prod *Roger Proudlock*. Scr *Kenneth Hyde, from a novel by Edith Pargiter*. Ph *Arthur Grant*. PC *Wentworth*. Dis *Independent Film Distributors/British Lion. 79 mins. Cert U*

Unjustly condemned to death for murder, Stevenson (*Basil Dignam*) invokes an old Spanish curse on those responsible – and two deaths follow almost at once. When Stevenson himself dies, the judge (*Michael Hordern*) and his daughter (*Susan Beaumont*) realize they must settle the matter – and the real killer is found after a meeting of interested parties in a deserted churchyard. Interesting yarn lacks fullblooded treatment.
RoC *Tony Wright, Lee Patterson, Henry Oscar, Ralph Truman, Brian Oulton, Roddy Hughes, Olga Dickie*.

THE SPANISH GARDENER (1956) 4
Dir *Philip Leacock*. Prod *John Bryan*. Scr *Les-*

ley Storm, Bryan, from the novel by A.J. Cronin*. Ph *Chris(topher) Challis*. PC and Dis *Rank. Technicolor. 97 mins. Cert U*

Smothered by his diplomat father (*Michael Hordern*), whose wife has left him, Nicholas (*Jon Whiteley*) becomes friends with a gardener, José (*Dirk Bogarde*) at a consulate in a small Spanish port. Nicholas' father resents the friendship and is quick to have José arrested when the sneaky chauffeur (*Cyril Cusack*) frames him for theft. José escapes and, wounded, is eventually found by Nicholas, whose father sees the error of his ways and clears matters up. Fresh, entertaining drama.
RoC *Maureen Swanson, Lyndon Brook, Josephine Griffin, Bernard Lee, Rosalie Crutchley, Ina de la Haye, Geoffrey Keen, Harold Scott, Jack Stewart, Richard Molinas, Susan Lyall Grant, John Adderley, David Lander*.

THE SQUARE PEG (1958) 3
Dir *John Paddy Carstairs*. Prod *Hugh Stewart*. Scr *Jack Davies, Henry Blyth, Norman Wisdom, Eddie Leslie*. Ph *Jack Cox*. PC and Dis *Rank. 89 mins. Cert U*

1943. Norman (*Norman Wisdom*), a roadmender, and borough-engineer Grimsdyke (*Edward Chapman*) are drafted into the Army as a result of Norman's mistakenly digging a huge hole outside the barracks. In error, they are transferred to the paratroops and dropped behind enemy lines, where Norman capitalizes on his likeness to a German general by impersonating him. They finally escape a firing squad by falling into a hole Norman has dug. Back home Norman is made mayor. Slapdash comedy; Wisdom hams strenuously to paper over the cracks.
RoC *Honor Blackman, Campbell Singer, Hattie Jacques, Brian Worth, Terence Alexander, John Warwick, Arnold Bell, Eddie Leslie, André Maranne, Frank Williams, Oliver Reed, Victor Beaumont, Martin Boddey, Harold Goodwin*.

THE SQUARE RING (1953) 4
Dir *Basil Dearden*. Prod *Michael Relph*. Scr *Robert Westerby, Peter Myers, Alec Grahame, from the play by Ralph W. Peterson*. Ph *Gordon Dines*. PC *Ealing Studios*. Dis *General Film Distributors. 83 mins. Cert A*

Various stories are played out concerning the contestants at a boxing hall – principally that of 'Kid' Curtis (*Robert Beatty*), a former champion trying for a comeback that has estranged him from his wife (*Bernadette O'Farrell*). In a savage

Kay Kendall and Robert Beatty in The Square Ring (*1953*)

battle, he wins – but dies from the pounding he has taken. Tremendous cast largely wasted on every boxing cliché in the book. Good ringside atmosphere and performances.
RoC *Jack Warner, Bill Owen, Maxwell Reed, Joan Collins, Kay Kendall, Eddie Byrne, Bill Travers, Sidney James, Alfie Bass, Sydney Tafler, Ronald Lewis, Joan Sims, George Rose, Alexander Gauge, Vic Wise, Michael Golden, Vernon Kelso, Michael Ingrams, Ivan Staff, Madoline Thomas, Ben Williams, Alf Hines, Harry Herbert, Joe Evans, Kid Berg, Joe Bloom, C.H. Nichols*.

STAGE FRIGHT (1950) 3
Dir and Prod *Alfred Hitchcock*. Scr *Whitfield Cook, Alma Reville, James Bridie, from a novel by Selwyn Jepson*. Ph *Wilkie Cooper*. PC and Dis *Warner Bros. 111 mins. Cert A*

Jonathan (*Richard Todd*), distraught, tells his friend Eve (*Jane Wyman*) that Charlotte (*Marlene Dietrich*), an actress with whom he is besotted, has killed her husband and asked him to destroy a bloodstained dress. Now the police suspect him. Eve poses as Charlotte's maid to try to get incriminating evidence against her, but a persistent police detective (*Michael Wilding*) proves that Jonathan was the killer. Muffled Hitchcock; actors seem unduly restrained.
RoC *Alastair Sim, Sybil Thorndike, Kay Walsh, Miles Malleson, Joyce Grenfell, Hector MacGregor, André Morell, Patrick Hitchcock, Cyril Chamberlain, Helen Goss, Everley Gregg, Irene Handl, Arthur Howard, Lionel Jeffries, Alfred Hitchcock*.

Richard Todd and Marlene Dietrich in Stage Fright (*1950*)

STAR OF INDIA (1953) 3
Dir *Arthur Lubin*. Prod and PC *Raymond Stross*. Scr *Herbert Dalmas, C. Denis Freeman, (uncredited) Seton I. Miller*. Ph C *Pennington-Richards*. Dis *Eros. Technicolor. 97 mins. Cert U*

1690. Returning to France after five years of fighting in India, Pierre St Laurent (*Cornel Wilde*) finds his lands have been confiscated by the evil Narbonne (*Herbert Lom*), who has also stolen the Star of India, a priceless emerald, from a Dutch collection in India. Recovering it from the hilt of Narbonne's sword for Dutch girl Katrina (*Jean Wallace*), Pierre flees. Narbonne catches up with him at the harbour, but Pierre kills him. Well-knit if sketchily acted swashbuckler.

RoC *Yvonne Sanson, Basil Sydney, Walter Rilla, John Slater, Leslie Linder, Arnold Bell.*

STAR OF MY NIGHT (1953)   2

Dir *Paul Dickson.* Prod *Edward J. Danziger, Harry Lee Danziger.* Scr *Paul Tabori.* Ph *Jack Cox.* PC *Kenilworth.* Dis *General Film Distributors. 71 mins. Cert U*

Michael (*Griffith Jones*), a cynical sculptor, falls for a ballerina (*Pauline Olsen*) and starts on a lifesize statue of her. Knocked out by her jealous boyfriend, Michael finds he is going blind. He throws away a chance of saving his sight to finish the statue, then tries to make Iris believe he doesn't love her. But she finds out the truth, and returns to devote her life to him. Gloomy, artily written drama.

RoC *Kathleen Byron, Hugh Williams, Harold Lang, Andre Mikhelson, Ilona Ference, Kenneth Edwards, Mona Washbourne, The Malcolm Mitchell Trio.*

STARS IN YOUR EYES (1956)   2

Dir *Maurice Elvey.* Prod *David Dent.* Scr *Talbot Rothwell, Hubert Gregg.* Ph *S.D. Onions.* PC *Grand Alliance.* Dis *British Lion. Eastman Colour. CameraScope. 96 mins. Cert U*

Four music-hall friends, all down on their luck, decide to put on a show at the derelict theatre one of them has inherited. Their first show is almost ruined by two sabotage-bent agents, but the second goes on TV live when a producer is faced with a sudden cancellation. It brings them a successful run, and estranged husband-and-wife David (*Bonar Colleano*) and Ann (*Dorothy Squires*) come together again. Poor material defeats energetic cast.

RoC *Pat Kirkwood, Nat Jackley, Jack Jackson, Vera Day, Joan Sims, Hubert Gregg, Meier Tzelniker, Jimmy Clitheroe, Freddie Frinton, Reginald Forsythe, Ronnie Clark, Gerald Harper, Gabrielle Brune.*

STATE SECRET (1950)   5
(USA: *The Great Manhunt*)

Dir and Scr *Sidney Gilliat*, from a novel by *Roy Huggins.* Prod *Frank Launder, Gilliat.* Ph *Robert Krasker.* PC *London Films.* Dis *British Lion. 104 mins (US: 97). Cert U*

Marlowe (*Douglas Fairbanks Jr*), a surgeon invited to Vosnia, finds that his patient is the head of state, who must be kept alive for the elections. When the man dies, Marlowe knows he must flee. Evading state police, he teams up with a cabaret artist (*Glynis Johns*) and a racketeer (*Herbert Lom*) is 'persuaded' to help them but, after narrow escapes, they are caught on the border. Ready for execution, Marlowe is saved by a political 'change' ... Thrilling, sharply scripted, atmospheric chase drama. Vosnian language created by Georgina Shield.

RoC *Jack Hawkins, Walter Rilla, Karel Stepanek, Carl Jaffe, Gerard Heinz, Hans Moser, Gerik Schjelderup, Guido Lorraine, Peter Illing, Olga Lowe, Therese van Kye, Robert Ayres, Howard Douglas, Martin Boddey, Russell Waters, Leonard Sachs, Arthur Howard, Anton Diffring, Leslie Linder, Leo Beiber, Nelly Arno, Paul Demel, Danny Green, Arthur Reynolds, Richard Molinas, Eric Pohlmann, Louis Wiech-*

ert, Henrik Jacobsen, Pat Rafael, Walter Magee, Anton Diffring.

THE STEEL BAYONET (1957)   2

Dir and Prod *Michael Carreras.* Scr *Howard Clewes.* Ph *Jack Asher.* PC *Hammer.* Dis *United Artists. HammerScope. 85 mins. Cert A*

Tunis, 1943. Battle-weary Company C, under Major Gerrard (*Leo Genn*) must try to hold a derelict farmhouse against enemy attack. They are joined by five raw recruits, headed by the arrogant Lt Vernon (*Michael Medwin*). At first they hold out against German infantry, but when the enemy bring in tanks, the farm is overrun. Lt Vernon escapes, and a dying Gerrard manages to radio artillery support to bomb the farm. Stereotyped war film.

RoC *Kieron Moore, Robert Brown, Michael Ripper, John Paul, Shay Gorman, Tom Bowman, Bernard Horsfall, John Watson, Arthur Lovegrove, Percy Herbert, Paddy Joyce, Jack Stewart, David Crowley, Barry Lowe, Michael Dear, Ian Whittaker, Michael Balfour, Raymond Francis, Anthony Warren, Rolf Carston, Garard Green, Wolf Frees, Jeremy Longhurst, David Ritch, Abdul Noor, Victor Platt.*

THE STEEL KEY (1953)   3

Dir *Robert S. Baker.* Prod *Baker, Monty Berman.* Scr *John Gilling, Roy Chanslor.* Ph *Gerald Gibbs.* PC *Tempean.* Dis *Eros. 70 mins. Cert A*

Professors Muller and Newman are working on a formula for hardening steel when Muller is murdered. Adventurer Johnny O'Flynne (*Terence Morgan*) arrives on the case in time for Newman's funeral. Johnny and Doreen (*Joan Rice*), a nurse, discover that Newman is alive and being held by a Dr Crabtree (*Colin Tapley*). Newman's wife (*Dianne Foster*) is killed and Johnny suspected. Police trail Crabtree, who is shot by Newman (*Esmond Knight*), unmasked as the king villain who killed everyone. Light thriller is quite unconvincing, but so hectic it almost gets away with it.

RoC *Raymond Lovell, Hector Ross, Arthur Lovegrove, Mark Baker, Mary Jones, Roger Maxwell, Sam Kydd, Esma Cannon.*

STOCK CAR (1955)   3

Dir *Wolf Rilla.* Prod *A.R. Rawlinson.* Scr *Rawlinson, Victor Lyndon.* Ph *Geoffrey Faithfull.* PC *Balblair.* Dis *Butchers. 68 mins. Cert A*

The daughter (*Rona Anderson*) of a stock-car owner killed while racing is dissuaded from selling his garage by fellow-racer Larry (*Paul Carpenter*) who helps her run it, and pay off her father's debts to the oily Turk (*Paul Whitsun-Jones*). Turk's mistress (*Susan Shaw*) takes a fancy to Larry, who is beaten up and nearly killed in a fixed race, before he wins the big one - and the heroine. Souped-up cars steal honours from stock plot.

RoC *Harry Fowler, Robert Rietty, Alma Taylor, Patrick Jordan, Sabrina, Lorrae Desmond, Eve Raymond, Frank Thornton, Doreen Locke, Kim Parker, Fraser Hines, Reginald Barrett, Ann Croft.*

THE STOLEN AIRLINER (1955)   3

Dir and Scr *Don Sharp*, from a novel by *John*

Pudney. Prod *Howard Thomas.* Ph *Jo Jago.* PC *AB-Pathé/Children's Film Foundation.* Dis *British Lion. 59 mins. Cert U*

Foreign delegates in Britain to place an order for a new airliner, are kidnapped and impersonated by criminals. Three children are hijacked with the plane, but two of them manage to bale out and warn the authorities. An air chase, during which the remaining boy and his uncle, a hostage on board, battle and overpower the enemy agents, ends the affair. Brisk children's film spoiled by too-comic villains.

LP *Fella Edmunds, Diana Day, Michael Macguire, Peter Dyneley, Ballard Berkeley, Nicola Braithwaite, Iris Russell, David King-Wood.*

STOLEN ASSIGNMENT (1955)   1

Dir *Terence Fisher.* Prod *Francis Searle.* Scr *Kenneth R. Hayles.* Ph *James Harvey.* PC *ACT Films.* Dis *British Lion. 62 mins. Cert U*

A woman is reported missing and rival journalists Mike (*John Bentley*) and Jenny (*Hy Hazell*) fight to be the first to unravel the mystery, both getting in the hair of the police led by Inspector Corcoran (*Eddie Byrne*). It's Jenny who finally picks up the vital clue that the woman's artist husband (*Patrick Holt*) is the killer. Comedy-thriller would have done well to stick to the thrills; pretty bad.

RoC *Joyce Carey, Kay Callard, Charles Farrell, Jessica Cairns, Violet Gould, Michael Ellison, Desmond Rayner, Graham Stuart, Frank Forsyth, Raymond Rollett.*

STOLEN FACE (1952)   2

Dir *Terence Fisher.* Prod *Anthony Hinds.* Scr *Martin Berkeley, Richard Landau.* Ph *Walter Harvey.* PC *Hammer/Lippert.* Dis *Exclusive. 72 mins. Cert A*

Plastic surgeon Philip Ritter (*Paul Henreid*) falls for pianist Alice Brent (*Lizabeth Scott*), but she is engaged to someone else. After a successful tour she returns to him, freed from her ex-fiancé, only to find that Philip has remodelled the face of a girl crook to look like hers and married her. It takes the death of his wife in an accidental fall from a train to bring the lovers back together. Grim.

RoC *André Morell, Susan Stephen, Mary Mackenzie, John Wood, Arnold Ridley, Everley Gregg, Cyril Smith, Diana Beaumont, Janet Burnell, Grace Gaven, Terence O'Regan, Alexis France, John Bull, Dorothy Bramhall, Ambrosine Phillpotts, Russell Napier, Hal Osmond, William Murray, Howard Douglas, Brookes Turner, Bartlett Mullins, Philip Viccars, James Valentine, John Warren, Frank Hawkins, Richard Wattis, Ben Williams.*

THE STOLEN PLANS (1952)   4

Dir and Scr *James Hill.* Prod *Frank Wells.* Ph *Frank North.* PC *Gaumont-British/Children's Film Foundation.* Dis *Associated British. 58 mins. Cert U*

A London boy (*Lance Secretan*) and his French pen-friend (*Mavis Sage*) become friendly with an aircraft-designer. But an invitation to visit him involves them with a gang of international spies who are after some secret aeroplane blueprints. The children resourcefully foil the spies, who are ultimately trapped by police. Exciting children's yarn; the first CFF film.

RoC *Peter Neil, Pamela Edmunds, Peter Burton, Patrick Boxill, Len Sharp, Geoffrey Goodheart, Ludmila Tchakalova, Larry Burns.*

STOLEN TIME (1955)   2
(USA: *Blonde Blackmailer*)

Dir, Prod, Scr and PC *Charles Deane.* Ph *Geoffrey Faithfull.* Dis *British Lion. 59 mins. Cert A*

Out of jail after seven years for a murder he didn't commit, Tony (*Richard Arlen*)) encounters a blonde blackmailer (*Susan Shaw*), a blind pickpocket and a gang of thugs in his efforts to find the killer and clear his name. He eventually corners the murderer, whose confession the police, tracking Tony, are on hand to hear. Draggy drama, performed without enthusiasm.

RoC *Vincent Ball, Constance Leigh, Andrea Malandrinos, Alathea Siddons, Clive St George, Reginald Hearne, Howard Lang, John Dunbar, Sydney Bromley, Claudia Carr, Dafydd Havard, Patricia Salonika, Arnold Adrian.*

STORM OVER THE NILE (1955)   4

Dir *Terence Young, Zoltan Korda.* Prod *Korda.* Scr *R.C. Sherriff, Lajos Biro, Arthur Wimperis, from a novel by A.E.W. Mason.* PC *London Films.* Dis *Independent Film Distributors/ British Lion. Technicolor. CinemaScope. 107 mins. Cert U*

Another remake of *The Four Feathers.* In 1895 Harry Faversham (*Anthony Steel*) resigns his commission rather than go to the Sudan, and is branded a coward by his fellow-officers (*Laurence Harvey, Ronald Lewis, Ian Carmichael*) and his fiancée (*Mary Ure*). Seeing his act in its true light, Faversham goes to the Sudan to redeem himself, and saves the life of all three of his comrades. Still a good yarn, but performances a little less effective than in the classic 1939 version.

RoC *James Robertson Justice, Geoffrey Keen, Jack Lambert, Ferdy Mayne, Michael Hordern, Christopher Lee, Sam Kydd, John Wynne, Avis Scott, Raymond Francis.*

Ronald Lewis, Christopher Lee, Ian Carmichael and Anthony Steel in Storm Over the Nile *(1955)*

STORMY CROSSING (1958)   2
(USA: *Black Tide*)

Dir *C. Pennington-Richards.* Prod *Monty Ber-*

man. Scr *Brock Williams, from a story by Sid Harris, Lou Dyer.* Ph *Berman.* PC *Tempean.* Dis *Eros. 69 mins. Cert U*

Kitty (*Joy Webster*), model and swimmer, is put in for a cross-channel race by her lover, Paul (*Derek Bond*). Danny (*Sheldon Lawrence*), another swimmer, falls in love with her during training, but Paul murders her during the swim so that his wife will not find out about their affair. Danny cannot convince his trainer, Griff (*John Ireland*), that it's murder, nor the police, but Griff acts when Danny, too, is nearly killed, and Paul is arrested. Unsubtle treatment sinks thriller.

RoC *Maureen Connell, Leslie Dwyer, Sam Rockett, Jack Taylor, Cameron Hall, Arthur Lowe.*

THE STORY OF ESTHER
COSTELLO (1957)   3
(USA: *Golden Virgin*)

Dir *David Miller.* Prod *Miller, Jack Clayton.* Scr *Charles Kaufman, Lesley Storm, from the novel by Nicholas Monsarrat.* Ph *Robert Krasker.* PC *Romulus.* Dis *Columbia. 104 mins. Cert A*

Socialite Margaret Landi (*Joan Crawford*) devotes her life to helping a deaf, dumb and blind girl, Esther Costello (*Heather Sears*), whom she finds living in abject squalor. Margaret's estranged husband Carlo (*Rossano Brazzi*) returns to turn Margaret's charity campaign into an exploitation carnival. When he tries to rape Esther, Margaret shoots first him and then herself. Pretty nasty emotional drama, always looking for sordid angles.

RoC *Lee Patterson, Ron Randell, Fay Compton, John Loder, Sidney James, Denis O'Dea, Bessie Love, Robert Ayres, Maureen Delaney, Estelle Brody, June Clyde, Megs Jenkins, Andrew Cruickshank, Sally Smith, Diana Day, Victor Rietti, Sheila Manahan, Tony Quinn.*

Joan Crawford, Heather Sears and Lee Patterson in The Story of Esther Costello (*1957*)

THE STORY OF GILBERT
AND SULLIVAN (1953)   4
(USA: *The Great Gilbert and Sullivan*)

Dir *Sidney Gilliat.* Prod *Frank Launder, Gilliat.* Scr *Gilliat, Leslie Baily, from a book by Baily.* Ph *Christopher Challis, Edward Scaife.* PC *London Films.* Dis *British Lion. Technicolor. 109 mins. Cert U*

1875. Composer Arthur Sullivan (*Maurice Evans*) and librettist W.S. Gilbert (*Robert*

Morley) join forces to write a series of enormously popular operattas. Their temperaments always clash, and when theatrical manager D'Oyly Carte (*Peter Finch*) builds a theatre to accommodate Sullivan's more serious ambitions, they quarrel and part. Only when Sullivan becomes seriously ill is there a reconciliation. Grand, lavish musical biopic. Enjoyable, but lacks highspots.

RoC *Eileen Herlie, Martyn Green, Dinah Sheridan, Isabel Dean, Wilfrid Hyde White, Muriel Aked, Michael Ripper, Bernadette O'Farrell, Ann Hanslip, Eric Berry, Yvonne Marsh, Lloyd Lamble, Ian Wallace, Anthony Snell, Richard Warner, Perlita Neilson, Leonard Sachs, Muriel Brunskill, Owen Brannigan, Harold Williams, Yvonne Marsh, Charlotte Mitchell, Stella Riley, Philip Ray, John Rae, George Cross, George Woodbridge, Robert Brooks Turner, Anthony Green, Tom Round, Gron Davies, John Banks, John Hughes.* Voices: *Webster Booth, Elsie Morison, Marjorie Thomas, John Cameron, Gordon Clinton, Jennifer Vyvyan, Joan Gillingham, Kenneth Downey.*

THE STORY OF ROBIN HOOD
AND HIS MERRIE MEN (1952)   4

Dir *Ken Annakin, Alex Bryce.* Prod *Perce Pearce.* Scr *Lawrence E. Watkin.* Ph *Guy Green.* PC *Walt Disney/RKO Radio.* Dis *RKO Radio. Technicolor. 84 mins. Cert U*

The 1190s. With King Richard away on the Crusades, his brother Prince John (*Hubert Gregg*) bleeds the country white with taxes. Robin Hood (*Richard Todd*), an outlawed earl, forms a band of men loyal to Richard, takes to Sherwood Forest and robs the rich to give to the poor. He is aided by Maid Marian (*Joan Rice*), who is imprisoned by John and the Sheriff of Nottingham (*Peter Finch*), but rescued by Robin. The king returns and John is exiled. Hearty, no-frills romp with some personable 'merrie men'.

RoC *James Hayter, James Robertson Justice, Martita Hunt, Elton Hayes, Bill Owen, Patrick Barr, Michael Hordern, Reginald Tate, Hal Osmond, Anthony Forwood, Anthony Eustrel, Clement McCallin, Louise Hampton.*

THE STRANGE AWAKENING (1958)   4
(USA: *Female Fiends*)

Dir *Montgomery Tully.* Prod *Alec C. Snowden.* Scr *J. McLaren Ross, from a novel by Patrick Quentin.* Ph *Philip Grindrod.* PC *Merton Park.* Dis *Anglo-Amalgamated. 68 mins. Cert U*

After giving a lift to Louis (*Richard Molinas*) in France, tourist Peter Chance (*Lex Barker*) finds himself in a villa, unable to recall what has happened. It seems he lives there and is married to Selena (*Carole Mathews*); he is also heir to a fortune. In a bid to escape, he finds the body of her real husband, and realizes he is a cog in a plot by Selena, her sister (*Lisa Gastoni*) and mother (*Nora Swinburne*) to get the money; Louis was a paid accomplice. The sister dies in a fire and Chance traps Louis. Genuinely atmospheric suspense film.

RoC *Peter Dyneley, Joe Robinson, Malou Pantera, John Serret, Stanley Maxted, Monica Grey, Yvonne André, Raf de la Torre.*

STRANGER AT MY DOOR (1950) [3]

Dir *Brendan J. Stafford, Desmond Leslie*. Prod *Paul King*. Scr *Leslie*. Ph *Stafford*. PC *Leinster Films*. Dis *Monarch*. 80 mins. Cert A
In Dublin, a young ex-commando takes unwillingly to burglary to provide his girl with luxuries (he thinks), but in effect to enable her to pay off a blackmailer. He emerges from the affair wiser but very much sadder. Thriller is complicated and rather jerky but quite persuasive.
LP *Michael Moore, Valentine Dyall, Joseph O'Conor, Maire O'Neill, Jill Raymond, Agnes Bernelle, Liam O'Leary, Harry Hutchinson, W.E. Holloway, Michael Seavers, Alan Gore-Lewis, Charles Mansell, Dorothy Dewhurst, Madalene Burgess, Bea Duffell, Jimmy Page, Charles Vance, Malachy Keegan, Katherine Mora, Nigel Neilson.*

THE STRANGER CAME HOME (1954) [3]
(USA: *The Unholy Four*)

Dir *Terence Fisher*. Prod/Scr *Michael Carreras, from a novel by George Sanders*. Ph *Jim Harvey*. PC *Hammer*. Dis *Exclusive*. 80 mins. Cert A
Shanghaied in Portugal, Philip (*William Sylvester*) returns after three years' loss of memory to find his three former business associates all courting his (presumed) widow (*Paulette Goddard*). Two murders are committed, for which suspicion falls on Philip and his wife; but he clears their names and finds the killer. Strength of character sees well-worn, fairly suspenseful thriller through.
RoC *Patrick Holt, Paul Carpenter, Alvys Maben, Russell Napier, David King-Wood, Pat(ricia) Owens, Kay Callard, Jeremy Hawk, Jack Taylor, Kim Mills, Owen Evans, Philip Lennard.*

STRANGER FROM VENUS (1954) [1]
(USA: *Immediate Decision*)

Dir *Burt Balaban*. Prod *Balaban, Gene Martel*. Scr *Hans Jacoby*. Ph *Kenneth Talbot*. PC *Princess/Rich and Rich*. Dis *Eros*. 75 mins. Cert U
A Venusian (*Helmut Dantine*) comes to earth to talk about galactic peace, concerned about the earth people's handling of atomic power. The earthmen plot to gain Venus's scientific secrets for their own ends, and only the alien's giving of his own life to prevent his comrades from being ambushed stops an inter-planetary disaster. Far-fetched and stilted.
RoC *Patricia Neal, Derek Bond, Cyril Luckham, Willoughby Gray, Marigold Russell, Arthur Young, Kenneth Edwards, David Garth, Stanley Van Beers, Nigel Green, Graham Stuart.*

STRANGER IN TOWN (1957) [3]

Dir *George Pollock*. Prod *Sidney Roberts, Robert S. Baker, Monty Berman*. Scr *Norman Hudis, Edward Dryhurst, from a novel by Frank Chittenden*. Ph *Geoffrey Faithfull*. PC *Tempean*. Dis *Eros*. 74 mins. Cert U
An American composer living in a sleepy English village is shot dead. A journalist (*Alex Nicol*) probes the death, the trail running to the local gossip (*Mona Washbourne*) who is found gassed. The composer turns out to have

been a blackmailer, philanderer and thief, one of his blackmail victims being Captain Nash (*Charles Lloyd Pack*), who killed him and the gossip, and is about to kill again when overpowered by the journalist. 'Clumsy and incoherent' or 'sharp and sound', according to which magazine you chose – this split the critics.
RoC *Anne Paige, Mary Laura Wood, Bruce Beeby, John Horsley, Colin Tapley, Betty Impey, Arthur Lowe.*

THE STRANGER'S HAND (1953) [4]

Dir *Mario Soldati*. Prod *John Stafford, Peter Moore, Graham Greene*. Scr *Guy Elmes, Giorgio Bassani, from the story by Greene*. Ph *Enzo Serafin*. PC *Independent Film Producers*. Dis *British Lion*. 86 mins. Cert U. Bilingual versions
Schoolboy Roger (*Richard O'Sullivan*) flies to Venice to join his British security-officer father (*Trevor Howard*), only to find that he has been kidnapped by Vivaldi (*Eduardo Ciannelli*), a foreign activist. Roger makes friends who try to help him, but fails to recognize his father at first is one of Vivaldi's 'typhoid patients'. Police are finally able to storm the ship on which the man is held after Roger's friend Joe (*Richard Basehart*) gives them an excuse to do so by setting fire to it. Vivaldi is killed. Not completely successful, but strongly atmospheric drama.
RoC *Alida Valli, Stephen Murray, Giorgio Constantini.*

STRANGERS' MEETING (1957) [1]

Dir *Robert Day*. Prod *E. Smedley Aston, Jack Parsons*. Scr *David Gordon*. Ph *Arthur Grant*. PC *Parroch Films*. Dis *Rank*. 64 mins. Cert A
Belair (*Peter Arne*), an acrobat wrongly convicted of manslaughter, escapes bent on clearing his name. Injured, he makes for an inn, where he meets a former colleague, who puts him on to the real killer – Rosie (*Barbara Archer*), ex-member of Belair's circus team. In a struggle, Rosie falls to her death down a flight of stairs, but Belair already has her confession on record. Totally unconvincing; quite a hiccup in the careers of all concerned.
RoC *Delphi Lawrence, Conrad Phillips, David Ritch, David Lodge, Selma Vaz Dias, Victor Maddern, John Kelly, Doris Hare, Kathleen Williams, Lesley Nunnerley, Reginald Hearne, George Tovey, Ernest Brightmore, Norman Rossington, Arthur Gomez, Arthur Sullivan, Dorita Curtis-Hayward.*

THE STRANGE WORLD OF PLANET X (1958) [2]
(USA: *Cosmic Monsters*)

Dir *Gilbert Gunn*. Prod and PC *George Maynard*. Scr *Paul Ryder, Jo Ambor, from the novel by René Ray*. Ph *Ambor*. Dis *Eros*. 74 mins. Cert X
When Dr Laird (*Alec Mango*) starts messing about with magnetic fields at his isolated forest laboratory, he not only causes insects around to grow to gigantic size, but attracts the attention of Smith (*Martin Benson*), a visitor from outer space. The military destroys the insects, and Smith blasts Laird and his laboratory into oblivion. Dully acted shocker with laughable process work.

RoC *Forrest Tucker, Gaby André, Hugh Latimer, Patricia Sinclair, Wyndham Goldie, Richard Warner, Geoffrey Chater, Catherine Lancaster, Hilda Fenemore, Susan Redway, Neil Wilson.*

THE STRANGLERS OF BOMBAY (1959) [3]

Dir *Terence Fisher*. Prod *Anthony Hinds*. Scr *David Zelag Goodman*. Ph *Arthur Grant*. PC *Hammer*. Dis *Columbia*. MegaScope. 80 mins. Cert A
India 1826. The British East India company resolves to act on the hundreds of passengers who are disappearing on its routes. Captain Lewis (*Guy Rolfe*) finds that responsibility lies with the T'hugs, a fanatical cult of stranglers. The arrogant officer (*Allan Cuthbertson*) assigned to investigate brings about his own death, and it is left to Lewis, after a narrow squeak, to clear up the murderous cult. Grisly thriller.
RoC *Andrew Cruickshank, George Pastell, Marne Maitland, Jan Holden, Paul Stassino, David Spenser, Tutte Lemkow, Marie Devereux, Roger Delgado, John Harvey, Michael Nightingale, Margaret Gordon, Steven Scott, Jack McNaughton, Ewen Solon.*

THE STRAW MAN (1953) [2]

Dir, Prod and Scr *Donald Taylor, from a novel by Doris Miles Disney*. Ph *Gerald Gibbs*. PC *Hedgerley*. Dis *United Artists*. 74 mins. Cert A
When a man with a big life policy is convicted of the murder of an old flame, the insurance company assigns Howard (*Clifford Evans*) to the case. The man's bride Ruth (*Lana Morris*) hires private eye Ferris (*Dermot Walsh*), but Howard soon suspects the two are connected. Trapped, Ferris threatens him. Ruth shoots Ferris, hoping to cover herself but, sure of his case, Howard hands her to the police. Thriller loses one's interest after tense beginning.
RoC *Amy Dalby, Ronald Ward, Josephine Stuart, Peter Williams, Philip Saville.*

STREET CORNER (1953) [3]
(USA: *Both Sides of the Law*)

Dir *Muriel Box*. Prod *William MacQuitty*. Scr *Muriel and Sydney Box*. Ph *Reginald H. Wyer*. PC *London Independent/Sydney Box*. Dis *General Film Distributors*. 94 mins. Cert U
Cases in the lives of policewomen in Chelsea, London. A WRAC deserter (*Eleanor Summerfield*) rescues a child from drowning and is let off lightly. A girl shoplifter (*Peggy Cummins*) leaves her husband and child for a flashy crook (*Terence Morgan*), who coshes a jeweller, and is hunted down. Documentary-style thriller with upper-class lady coppers. Good final chase, otherwise unreal.
RoC *Anne Crawford, Rosamund John, Barbara Murray, Ronald Howard, Sarah Lawson, Yvonne Marsh, Michael Medwin, Charles Victor, Dora Bryan, Eunice Gayson, Michael Hordern, Lloyd Lamble, John Warwick, Joyce Carey, Maurice Denham, Thora Hird, Marjorie Rhodes, Anthony Oliver, David Horne, John Stuart, Campbell Singer, Isabel George, Harold Lang, Archie Duncan, Russell Waters, Martin Wyldeck, James Gilbert, Jean Anderson, Nelly*

Arno, Lilly Kann, Myrtle Reed, Leo Bieber, Brian Kent, Basil Lord, Kathleen Michael, Charlotte Mitchell, Dandy Nichols, Peter Swanwick, Michael Ward, Brian Wilde, Francis Rowe, Pat Nye.

STREET OF SHADOWS (1953) [3]
(USA: *Shadow Man*)

Dir and Scr *Richard Vernon, from a novel by Gerald Verner.* Prod *W.H. Williams.* Ph *Phil Grindrod.* PC *Merton Park.* Dis *Anglo-Amalgamated.* 83 mins Cert A

After his sultry ex-mistress Angèle (*Simone Silva*) is murdered by his club-footed assistant (*Victor Maddern*), whom she has led on, nightclub owner Luigi (*Cesar Romero*) is in trouble. But when society girl Barbara (*Kay Kendall*), who has left her husband for him, dresses in Angèle's clothes, Limpy breaks down and confesses. Nice harmonica theme and Maddern's performance enliven routine thriller.

RoC *Edward Underdown, John Penrose, Molly Hamley-Clifford, Annaconda, Bill Travers, Eileen Way, Liam Gaffney, Robert Cawdron, Rose McLaren, Michael Kelly, Paul Hardtmuth.*

STRICTLY CONFIDENTIAL (1959) [2]

Dir *Charles Saunders.* Prod *Guido Coen.* Scr *Brock Williams.* Ph *Jimmy W. Harvey.* PC *Alliance/Twickenham.* Dis *Rank.* 62 mins. Cert U

Two old-school-tie con-artists (*Richard Murdoch, William Kendall*) are fooled by a shadier pair out to gain control of a thriving business concern. But the police, who have been keeping a check on the situation, move in and arrest the criminals, advising the two gentlemen con-men to disappear. Stars are moderate but deserve a little better than this unfunny comedy.

RoC *William Hartnell, Maya Koumani, Bruce Seton, Neil Hallett, Ellis Irving, Colin Rix, Beresford Egan, Llewellyn Rees, Larry Burns, Harry Ross, Paul Bogdan, Norman Pitt, Jean Trend, Denis Wood.*

STRYKER OF THE YARD (1953) [2]

Dir *Arthur Crabtree.* (Associate) Prod *William N. Boyle.* Scr *Guy Morgan, Lester Powell.* Ph *Basil Emmott.* PC/Dis *Republic.* 67 mins. Cert U

Two stories from the casebook of Inspector Stryker (*Clifford Evans*), made with half an eye to TV. A bank clerk (*Jack Watling*) pockets money in a raid, hoping to throw the blame on the thieves, who kidnap him before he turns the tables. A forger (*Eliot Makeham*) distributes fake fivers to those most in need; the law deals with him leniently. Lighthearted, light-weight sleuthing; only Makeham brings it to life.

RoC *George Woodbridge; Susan Stephen, Hugh Latimer, Ronald Adam, Irene Handl, Glyn Houston, Walter Gotell, Peter Swanwick, Ivan Craig, Sidney Vivian, Ben Williams, Frank Atkinson; John Salew, Brenda Hogan, Basil Appleby, Edwin Richfield, Dorothy Bramhall, Christina Forrest, Jack Stewart, Desmond Llewellyn, John Warren, Michael McKeag, Colin Campbell, Ian Fleming, Alfred Maron, Patrick Jordan, Gaylord Cavallaro.*

SUBWAY IN THE SKY (1958) [3]

Dir *Muriel Box.* Prod *John Temple-Smith, Patrick Filmer-Sankey, Sydney Box.* Scr *Jack Andrews, from the play by Ian Main.* Ph *Wilkie Cooper.* PC *Orbit.* Dis *British Lion/Britannia.* 87 mins. Cert A

Hiding from the authorities who want him for drug trafficking, Major Grant (*Van Johnson*) is helped by Lilli (*Hildegarde Neff*), a cabaret singer in whose apartment he has hidden, to prove his innocence. Grant's stepson (*Vivian Matalon*) proves to be the guilty party – he commits one murder and is about to kill Lilli when Grant and the authorities step in. Successful play makes mild, stagey movie.

RoC *Albert Lieven, Cec Linder, Katherine Kath, Edward Judd, Chuck Keyser, Carl Jaffe, Gaylord Cavallaro, Brian Wilde, Michael Bell, Bill Edwards, Kerrigan Prescott, James Maxwell, Gerda Larsen, Tom Watson.*

SUDDENLY, LAST SUMMER (1959) [4]

Dir *Joseph L. Mankiewicz.* Prod *Sam Spiegel.* Scr *Gore Vidal, Tennessee Williams, from Williams' play.* Ph *Jack Hildyard.* PC *Horizon.* Dis *Columbia.* 114 mins. Cert X

Summoned to perform a lobotomy on mad Catherine Holly (*Elizabeth Taylor*) by her cousin's mother Violet (*Katherine Hepburn*), Dr Cukrowicz (*Montgomery Clift*) finds the girl is insane only on the subject of her cousin Sebastian's death. With a truth drug, he discovers Sebastian was a homosexual, for whom Catherine unknowingly replaced an ageing Violet as 'bait' for boys. He had been torn apart and eaten by starving beggar boys on holiday in Spain. Catherine is cured and Violet retreats into fantasy. Gripping psychological drama, somewhat altered from the play.

RoC *Mercedes McCambridge, Gary Raymond, Mavis Villiers, Patricia Marmont, Joan Young, David Cameron, Maria Britneva, Sheila Robbins, Roberta Woolley.*

SUMMER MADNESS (1955) [5]
(USA: *Summertime*)

Dir *David Lean.* Prod *Ilya Lopert.* Scr *Lean, H.E. Bates, from a play by Arthur Laurents.* Ph *Jack Hildyard.* PC *London Films/Lopert Films.* Dis *British Lion/United Artists.* Eastman Colour. 100 mins. Cert A

Spinster secretary Jane Hudson (*Katharine Hepburn*) spends her first European holiday in Venice, where she is befriended by a persistent

Katharine Hepburn and Gaetano Autiero in Summer Madness *(1955)*

waif (*Gaetano Autiero*), falls into the canal and has an affair with a married antiques dealer (*Rossano Brazzi*). Realizing that there is no future in the relationship, Jane leaves Venice with her memories intact. Touching, charming romance, with the city wonderfully captured by director and cameraman.

RoC *Isa Miranda, Darren McGavin, Mari Aldon, Jane Rose, Jeremy Spenser, MacDonald Parke, Virginia Simeon, André Morell.*

SUPERSONIC SAUCER (1956) [3]

Dir *S.G. Ferguson.* Prod *Frank Wells.* Scr *Dallas Bower.* Ph *Frank North.* PC *Gaumont-British/Children's Film Foundation.* Dis *British Lion.* 50 mins. Cert U

Unable to go home for the holiday, Greta (*Gillian Harrison*) and Sumac (*Marcia Monolescu*), overseas pupils at an English boarding school, run into a baby flying saucer from Venus, which tries to help them get their fares home by stealing £1,000,000 from a bank. The saucer is captured by crooks intent on stealing the school trophies, but the girls foil them and are able to go home on the reward money, while the saucer returns to Venus. Engaging fantasy with tolerable trick work.

RoC *Fella Edmonds, Donald Gray, Tony Lyons, Raymond Rollett, Hilda Fenemore, Andrew Motte-Harrison.*

THE SURGEON'S KNIFE (1957) [2]

Dir *Gordon Parry.* Prod *Charles A. Leeds.* Scr *Robert Westerby, from a novel by Anne Hocking.* Ph *Lionel Banes.* PC *Gibraltar.* Dis *Grand National.* 84 mins. Cert A

Alex Waring (*Donald Houston*), a working-class man of ruthless ambition, has moved into a high society bracket as a successful surgeon. When he blunders during an operation, he soon disposes of both the important witnesses, a disapproving matron and a blackmailing anaesthetist. He plans to mete out the same treatment to his wife later, but fate hands him a lethal dose of his own medicine ... Turgid drama.

RoC *Adrienne Corri, Lyndon Brook, Sydney Tafler, Mervyn Johns, Jean Cadell, Marie Ney, Beatrice Varley, John Welsh, Ronald Adam, Noel Hood, André Van Gyseghem, Frank Forsyth, Tom Bowman, Susan Westerby, Betty Shale.*

SUSPENDED ALIBI (1956) [3]

Dir *Alfred Shaughnessy.* Prod *Robert Dunbar.* Scr *Kenneth R. Hayles.* Ph *Peter Hennessey.* PC *ACT Films.* Dis *Rank.* 65 mins. Cert U

Journalist Paul's (*Patrick Holt*) affair with Diana (*Naomi Chance*) leads to him being arrested for murder when the friend, with whom he had established an alibi before going to break it off with Diana, is stabbed. Paul's wife (*Honor Blackman*) stands by him when he is sentenced to hang, but it's his paper's crime reporter (*Andrew Keir*) who roots out a tiny piece of evidence which reveals the killer and saves Paul's life. Far-fetched, but efficiently made of its minor type.

RoC *Valentine Dyall, Lloyd Lamble, Viola Lyel, Frederick Piper, Bryan Coleman, Wally Patch, Jeanette Hutchinson, Tony Winterbot-*

tom, Madoline Thomas, Edgar Wreford, John Baker, Ian Whittaker, Brown Derby, Vincent Lawson, Walter Horsbrugh, Richard McNeff.

SVENGALI (1954)   3

Dir and Scr *Noel Langley, from the novel by George du Maurier*. Prod *George Minter*. Ph *Wilkie Cooper*. PC *Alderdale*. Dis *Renown*. Eastman Colour. 82 mins. Cert A

Paris 1890. Trilby (*Hildegarde Neff*), an artist's model, is friendly with three students, with one of whom, Billy (*Terence Morgan*) she falls in love. Under the hypnotic influence of Svengali (*Donald Wolfit*), whom Billy has been injured (by bolting horses) fighting, Trilby becomes a great singer, but Svengali dies at her opening concert and Trilby goes into a coma, woken only by the pleas of Billy. Wolfit's chew-the-scenery style suited to this role, but film is otherwise unsuccessful.

RoC *Derek Bond, Paul Rogers, Harry Secombe, David Kossoff, Hubert Gregg, Alfie Bass, Noel Purcell, Peter Illing, Hugh Cross, Michael Craig, Elizabeth Schwartzkopf, Toots Pound, Joan Haythorne, David Oxley, Richard Pearson, Rica Fox, Neville Philips, Arnold Bell, Joan Heal, Martin Boddey, Cyril Smith, Marne Maitland.*

Hildegarde Neff and Donald Wolfit in Svengali *(1954)*

SWEET BEAT (1959)   1

Dir *Ronnie Albert*. Prod *Jeffrey S. Kruger*. Scr *Ron Ahran*. Ph *S.D. Onions*. PC *Flamingo*. Dis *Archway*. 56 mins. Cert U

Bonnie (*Julie Amber*) wins a beauty contest, but comes to London to achieve her real ambition - to be a singer. Tricked into going to New York, Bonnie nearly ends up as a stripper, but is saved by her boyfriend Bill (*Sheldon Lawrence*). Bottom-budget pop musical/moral warning has that home-made look.

RoC *Irv Bauer, Leonie Page, David Browning.*

THE SWORD AND THE ROSE (1953)   3

Dir *Ken Annakin*. Prod *Perce Pearce*. Scr *Lawrence Edward Watkin, from a novel by Charles Major*. Ph *Geoffrey Unsworth*. PC *Walt Disney*. Dis *RKO-Radio*. Technicolor. 91 mins. Cert U

1514. Spirited Mary Tudor (*Glynis Johns*) is in love with an adventurous commoner, Charles (*Richard Todd*) and refusing to marry the aged Louis XII of France, elopes with Charles dressed as a pageboy. The king, Henry

VIII (*James Robertson Justice*) brings them back; to save Charles' life, Mary marries Louis, who soon dies. Charles sees off the rivalry of Buckingham (*Michael Gough*) for Mary's hand. Disney version of history; lively enough for those unconcerned with facts.

RoC *Jean Mercure, Jane Barrett, Peter Copley, Rosalie Crutchley, D.A. Clarke-Smith, Ernest Jay, Gérard Oury, John Vere, Philip Lennard, Bryan Coleman, Fernand Fabré, Thomas Heathcote, Russell Waters, John Serret, Bob Simmons, Philip Glasier, Robert Le Beal, Gaston Richer, Helen Goss, Patrick Cargill, Anthony Sharpe, Caven Watson, Hal Osmond, Richard Molinas, Norman Pierce, Douglas Bradley-Smith, Ewen Solon, Rupert Evans, Paddy Ryan, Arthur Brander.*

TAKE A POWDER (1953)   1

Dir *R.L. 'Tommy' Tomlinson, Julian Vedey*. Prod *Derrick Wynne*. Scr *Rex Diamond, Vedey*. Ph *Ernest Palmer*. PC *RLT*. Dis *Apex*. 58 mins. Cert U

Maxie (*Max Bacon*), a quack-medicine man selling 'Cure-All Atomic Powder', is mistaken for a kidnapped atomic scientist and placed in charge of a hospital. The scientist's daughter (*Isabel George*) helps to rescue her father and end Maxie's discomfort. Artless comedy lurches slowly along in vain search for laughs or thrills.

RoC *Maudie Edwards, Julian Vedey, Neville Gates, Fred Kitchen Jr, Alexis Chesnakov, Larry Taylor, Bobby Beaumont, Joe Cunningham, Mark Singleton, Gordon Craig, Muriel White, Diana Wynne.*

TAKE ME TO PARIS (1950)   2

Dir *Jack Raymond*. Prod *Henry Halstead*. Scr *Max Catto*. Ph *James Wilson*. PC *Byron*. Dis *AB-Pathé*. 72 mins. Cert U

Crooked French and British stable-lads make a deal to smuggle counterfeit money across the channel in a horse blanket. The horse concerned goes lame, and the 'no-hoper' of the stable, Dunderhead, is the last-minute substitute, together with his jockey Albert (*Albert Modley*). Dunderhead manages to win his race, and Albert foils the crooks' plans. Silly comedy has just the occasional nice moment.

RoC *Roberta Huby, Bruce Seton, Richard Molinas, George Bishop, Leonard Sharp, Jim Gerald, Claire Guilbert, Argus, Lottie Beck, Marc Valbel, Gerald Rex, Paul Bonifas.*

A TALE OF FIVE CITIES (1951)   2
(USA: *A Tale of Five Women*)

Dir *Montgomery Tully and* (uncredited) *R. Marcellini, Emil E. Reinert, Gyon Cziffra, M. Stuadte*. Prod *Alexander Paul, Boris Morros*. Scr *Patrick Kirwan, Maurice J. Wilson*. Ph

Gordon Lang. PC and Dis *Grand National*. 99 mins. Cert A

An airman (*Bonar Colleano*) suffering from amnesia in post-war Berlin has five banknotes of varying currency on him, each bearing the signature of a girl. He tries to trace his past life through them, backed by the editor (*Barbara Kelly*) of a New York magazine, who senses a good story. The last girl (*Lana Morris*) turns out to be a London trapeze artist who is his sister and partner. He is free to marry the editor, and resume his career. Some authentic atmosphere, otherwise a misfire.

RoC *Anne Vernon, Eva Bartok, Gina Lollobrigida, Karin Himbold, Geoffrey Sumner, Lily Kahn (Lilly Kann), Danny Green, Carl Jaffe, Philip Leaver, Annette Poivre, Charles Irwin, MacDonald Parke, Arthur Gomez, Aletha Orr, Andrew Irvine, Terence Alexander.*

A TALE OF THREE WOMEN (1954)   2

Dir *Paul Dickson, Thelma Connell*. Prod *Edward J. Danziger, Harry Lee Danziger*. Scr *Paul Tabori, James Eastwood, George Mikes*. Ph *Jack Cox, James Wilson*. PC *Danzigers*. Dis *Paramount*. 85 mins. Cert A

Three short stories. (1) A con-man (*Derek Bond*) gets his lady accomplice (*Hazel Court*) to marry a diamond merchant (*David Horne*), then murders him. But the girl develops a conscience ... (2) A kleptomaniac (*Jack Watling*), turned out by his rich father, turns to burglary, but is saved from prison by his fiancée (*Gene Anderson*). (3) A jeweller (*Karel Stepanek*) murders his book-keeper, but when his wife (*Catherine Finn*) finds he is having an affair, she gives him away. Heavily overplayed, TV-orientated collection.

RoC *Gilbert Harding (narrator), Oliver Johnston, Peter Gawthorne, Hélène Cordet, Michael Ripper, Philip Leaver, Patricia Owens, Gordon McLeod, Robert Perceval, Digby Wolfe.*

A TALE OF TWO CITIES (1958)   4

Dir *Ralph Thomas*. Prod *Betty Box*. Scr *T.E.B. Clarke, from the novel by Charles Dickens*. Ph *Ernest Steward*. PC and Dis *Rank*. 117 mins. Cert A

1795. Sydney Carton (*Dirk Bogarde*), a young lawyer usually the worse for drink, gives evidence at a trial which saves French aristocrat Darnay (*Paul Guers*) from a charge of treason. Married to Lucie (*Dorothy Tutin*), who is also adored by Carton, Darnay returns to France,

Stephen Murray, Dorothy Tutin, Dirk Bogarde and Athene Seyler in A Tale of Two Cities *(1958)*

is captured and sentenced to the guillotine. For love of Lucie, Carton takes his place in prison, and goes to his death. Steady version of Dickens' classic, told in simple, straightforward (slightly uninspired) way.

RoC *Cecil Parker, Stephen Murray, Athene Seyler, Ian Bannen, Alfie Bass, Ernest Clark, Rosalie Crutchley, Christopher Lee, Freda Jackson, Marie Versini, Duncan Lamont, Leo McKern, Donald Pleasence, Dominique Boschero, Eric Pohlmann.*

THE TALES OF HOFFMAN (1951) [3]

Dir, Prod and Scr *Michael Powell, Emeric Pressburger (libretto: Dennis Arundell) from the opera by Jacques Offenbach.* Ph *Christopher Challis.* PC *The Archers/London Films.* Dis *British Lion. Technicolor. 127 mins. Cert U*
In love with ballerina Stella (*Moira Shearer*), the poet Hoffman (*Robert Rounseville*) recalls three loves: a lifesize doll (*Shearer*) he believed to be real; a courtesan (*Ludmilla Tcherina*) who, with the aid of a magician, stole his soul (he regains it by breaking her magic mirror); and a girl (*Ann Ayars*) forbidden to sing, who dies when she does so. Realizing the fruitlessness of his pursuit of the eternal female, Hoffman cedes Stella to a rival. Vivid experiment in opera/ballet. Eyecatching if not very entertaining.

RoC *Robert Helpmann, Pamela Brown, Leonide Massine, Frederick Ashton, Meinhart Maur, Edmond Audran, John Ford, Richard Golding, Philip Leaver, Sir Thomas Beecham, Lionel Harris, Mogens Wreth. Singers and voices: Monica Sinclair, René Soames, Owen Brannigan, Fisher-Morgan, Dorothy Boyd, Grahame Clifford, Bruce Dargavel, Margherita Grandi, Murray Dickie, Joan Alexander.*

TALK OF A MILLION (1951) [3]
(USA: *You Can't Beat the Irish*)

Dir *John Paddy Carstairs.* Prod *Alex Boyd.* Scr *Frederic Gotfurt, from a play by Louis d'Alton.* Ph *Jack Hildyard.* PC *Associated British.* Dis *AB-Pathé. 78 mins. Cert U*
Lazy Irishman Murnahan (*Jack Warner*) finds a new way to make easy money when an American lawyer comes to his village looking for the heir to a fortune. Giving the impression that he's the heir, Murnahan runs up huge credit, buys a good portion of the village, and is able to retire a rich man before the truth comes out. Pleasant Irish whimsy: nothing special.
RoC *Barbara Mullen, Noel Purcell, Ronan O'Casey, Niall MacGinnis, Michael Dolan, Sidney James, Alfie Bass, Elizabeth Erskine, Joan Kenney, Vincent Ball, Milo O'Shea, Anita (Sharp) Bolster, Tony Quinn, Paul Connell, John McDarby, Fred Johnson, E.J. Kennedy, John Kelley, Joe Linnane, Gordon Tanner, Bill Shine, Christie Humphrey.*

TALL HEADLINES (1952) [2]

Dir *Terence Young.* Prod and PC *Raymond Stross.* Scr *Audrey Erskine Lindop, Dudley Leslie, from Erskine Lindop's novel.* Ph *C. Pennington-Richards.* Dis *Grand National. 100 mins. Cert A*
A family whose son was hanged for murder move to another district and change their

names. Their other son (*Michael Denison*) falls in love with a cashier (*Mai Zetterling*) and marries her, but is haunted by his brother and a fear that he may murder his wife. When he tells her she runs away and is killed in an accident. A 'picture of misery', not helped by the assortment of accents within its 'suburban' family.

RoC *Flora Robson, André Morell, Dennis Price, Jane Hylton, Naunton Wayne, Mervyn Johns, Celia Lipton, Olive Stone, Barbara Blair, Hugh Dempster, Michael Ward, Peter Burton, Don Philips, Joan Hickson, Sidney James.*

TANGIER ASSIGNMENT (1954) [1]

Dir and Scr *Ted Leversuch.* Prod *Cyril Parker.* Ph *Stanley Lipinski.* PC *Rock.* Dis *New Realm. 65 mins. Cert U*
A special agent tracks down a gun-running ring in Tangier, with the help of a pretty cabaret singer. They trail one member of the gang to the coastal caves that are their headquarters. The gang attack and overpower them, but the girl escapes and brings the police in the nick of time. Very minor and amateurish adventure, with speeded up action and a Spanish supporting cast.
LP *Robert Simmons, June Powell, Fernando Rey.*

TARZAN AND THE LOST SAFARI (1956) [3]

Dir *Bruce Humberstone.* Prod *John Croydon, Sy Weintraub.* Scr *Montgomery Pittman, Lillie Hayward, from characters by Edgar Rice Burroughs.* Ph *C.M. Pennington-Richards.* PC *Solar.* Dis *M-G-M. Technicolor. CinemaScope. 81 mins. Cert U*
A charter plane crash-lands in the African jungle. Diana (*Betta St John*) is kidnapped by the hostile Oparian tribe, but rescued by the hunter Tusker (*Robert Beatty*) who is in fact in league with the Oparians and has his eye on a hoard of priceless ivory tusks. Tarzan (*Gordon Scott*) joins the survivors and saves them when Tusker tries to lead them into an Oparian trap. Tusker gets a spear in the back, and Tarzan gets the rest – who have also solved some personal problems on the trek – to safety. Rather stagey jungle jinks.
RoC *Yolande Donlan, Wilfrid Hyde White, George Coulouris, Peter Arne, Orlando Martins.*

TARZAN'S GREATEST ADVENTURE (1959) [4]

Dir *John Guillermin.* Prod *Sy Weintraub.* Scr *Berne Giler, Guillermin, from characters by Edgar Rice Burroughs.* Ph *Skeets Kelly.* PC *Solar.* Dis *Paramount. Technicolor. 84 mins. Cert U*
Bad guys are after a diamond mine, and only Tarzan (*Gordon Scott*), aided by a girl (*Sara Shane*) whose plane has crashed in the jungle, can stop them. Eliminating his adversaries one by one, Tarzan defeats their leader (who plunges to his death) after a massive high-altitude struggle. Thrills galore in vivid adventure with superior cast.
RoC *Anthony Quayle, Sean Connery, Scilla Gabel, Niall MacGinnis, Al Mulock.*

THE TECKMAN MYSTERY (1954) [4]

Dir *Wendy Toye.* Prod *Josef Somlo.* Scr *Francis Durbridge, James Matthews, from Durbridge's TV serial.* Ph *Jack Hildyard.* PC *Corona/London Films.* Dis *British Lion. 89 mins. Cert U*
Commissioned to write a book on Teckman, who disappeared testing a new plane, Chance (*John Justin*) has his flat ransacked, is knocked out and is offered a lot of money to leave the country. The man who made the offer is murdered – then Teckman (*Michael Medwin*) reappears, having changed his mind about giving air secrets to a foreign power. He is shot by them, but survives to make a rendezvous with his sister (*Margaret Leighton*). Chance, realizing she is the head agent, follows them to the top of a building; slipping, she falls to her death. Typical Durbridge mystery with fine profusion of 'cliffhanger' endings.

RoC *Roland Culver, George Coulouris, Duncan Lamont, Raymond Huntley, Jane Wenham, Meier Tzelniker, Harry Locke, Barbara Murray, Frances Rowe, Warwick Ashton, Irene Lister, Andrea Malandrinos, Gwen Nelson, Mary Grant, Ben Williams, Peter Taylor, Dan Cressey, Peter Augustine, Maurice Lane, Mollie Palmer, Bruce Beeby, Gordon Morrison.*

TEN SECONDS TO HELL (1958) [3]

Dir *Robert Aldrich.* Prod *Michael Carreras.* Scr *Aldrich, Teddi Sherman, from a novel by Lawrence P. Bachmann.* Ph *Ernest Laszlo.* PC *Hammer/Seven Arts.* Dis *United Artists. 94 mins. Cert A*
Post-war Berlin. Six German soldiers form a bomb disposal squad with each to put half his earnings into a common pool, the last survivor to collect the money. Four are killed, leaving Körtner (*Jack Palance*) and Wirtz (*Jeff Chandler*) who are both in love with Margot (*Martine Carol*), a war widow. When they are asked to defuse a thousand-pound bomb, Wirtz tries to rig it to cause Körtner's death but is blown to pieces himself. Unusual theme in Anglo-American film falls victim to old-hat plot devices.
RoC *Robert Cornthwaite, Dave Willock, Wes Addy, Jimmy Goodwin, Virginia Baker, Richard Wattis, Nancy Lee.*

THAT LADY (1955) [2]

Dir *Terence Young.* Prod *Sy Bartlett.* Scr *Bartlett, Anthony Veiller, from the novel by Kate O'Brien.* Ph *Robert Krasker.* PC *Atlanta.* Dis *20th Century-Fox. Eastman Colour. CinemaScope. 100 mins. Cert A*
Spain, 1590. Ana, Princess of Eboli (*Olivia de Havilland*), who was once loved by King Philip (*Paul Scofield*) and fought a duel over him in which she lost an eye, has, years later, just lost her husband when she falls in love with the king's first minister Perez (*Gilbert Roland*). Philip has them thrown in separate prisons. Ana dies but Perez gets her young son to safety. Unrelieved gloom and doom; even the love affair doesn't catch fire.
RoC *Françoise Rosay, Dennis Price, Anthony Dawson, Robert Harris, Peter Illing, José Nieto, Christopher Lee, Andy Shine.*

THAT WOMAN OPPOSITE (1957)   [3]
(USA: *City After Midnight*)

Dir and Scr *Compton Bennett, from a novel by John Dickson Carr*. Prod *William Gell*. Ph *Lionel Banes*. PC *Monarch*. Dis *Monarch/British Lion*. Cert *A*. 83 mins. Cert *A*

In a French town, the murder of a gendarme is followed by that of Sir Maurice Lawes (*Wilfrid Hyde White*), an Englishman who may have witnessed it. Ned (*William Franklyn*), a jewel thief, his ex-wife Eve (*Phyllis Kirk*), now engaged to Sir Maurice's son Toby (*Jack Watling*), a two-timing Romeo, and Toby himself all come under suspicion. Private-eye Dermot Kinross (*Dan O'Herlihy*) not only solves the case but wins Eve. Dispassionate thriller; difficult, though, to guess the killer.

RoC *Petula Clark, Margaret Withers, Guido Lorraine, Jacques Cey, André Charisse, Robert Raikes, Tita Dane, Balbina, Irene Moore, Concepta Fennell, Campbell Gray, John Serret*.

THEM NICE AMERICANS (1958)   [3]

Dir *Anthony (Tony) Young*. Prod *Young, Richard Lawrence Griffith*. Scr *Gilbert Winfield*. Ph *Ernie Palmer*. PC *Chelsea Films*. Dis *Butchers*. 62 mins. Cert *U*

American-hating Inspector Adams (*Basil Dignam*) is incensed when his daughter Ann (*Vera Day*) falls for a GI, Johnny (*Sheldon Lawrence*). Johnny's well-meaning friend Joe (*Bonar Colleano*) tries to patch things up, with consequences increasingly disastrous. But when Johnny rescues Ann's young brother, trapped in a minefield, Adams changes his mind. Attractive little film, if very minor.

RoC *Renee Houston, Patti Morgan, Michael Wade, Ryck Rydon, Gilbert Winfield, Ron Gilliland, Ronald Brand, Bill Edwards, Robert Edwards, Chuck Keyser, John Evans, John Stacy, Jan Kent, Marian Collins, Anthony Wilson, Denis Gilmore*.

THERE IS ANOTHER SUN (1950)   [2]
(USA: *Wall of Death*)

Dir *Lewis Gilbert*. Prod *Ernest G. Roy*. Scr *Guy Morgan*. Ph *Wilkie Cooper*. PC *Nettlefold*. Dis *Butchers*. 95 mins. Cert *A*

Maguire (*Laurence Harvey*), the star of a fairground boxing booth, falls under the (bad) influence of Racer (*Maxwell Reed*), the ace wall-of-death rider, who involves him in a robbery and other crimes. Racer enters for a speedway trial to get back to the big time from

Laurence Harvey and Maxwell Reed in There is Another Sun (*1951*)

which he was kicked out, but is killed. Maguire's girl (*Susan Shaw*) can be sure that it is now her influence that will prevail. Gloomy, depressing number; long too.

RoC *Hermione Baddeley, Leslie Dwyer, Meredith Edwards, Robert Adair, Earl Cameron, Charles Farrell, Eric Pohlmann, Harry Fowler, Leslie Bradley, Laurence Naismith, Hal Osmond, Jennifer Jayne, Dennis Vance, Vic Wise, Peter Scott, Dennis Bowen, John Westbrook, Fred Powell, Stanley Rose, John Powe, J.H. Messham, Tom Messham, Jim Kynaston*.

THERE'S ALWAYS A THURSDAY (1957)   [4]

Dir *Charles Saunders*. Prod *Guido Coen*. Scr *Brandon Fleming*. Ph *Brendan Stafford*. PC *Associated Sound Film Industries*. Dis *Rank*. 62 mins. Cert *A*

Henpecked Potter (*Charles Victor*), glad to be rid of his awful family, takes £20 blackmail money for his employer (*Patrick Holt*) to Vera (*Frances Day*). His loud-mouth brother-in-law (*Bruce Seton*) gives Potter a philanderer's reputation and through it, he is offered a directorship on a prosperous form selling naughty lingerie. Vera, who is rather fond of Potter, demands an extra £20 - every Thursday. Bitter-sweet comedy nicely performed by Victor; rather above the average.

RoC *Marjorie Rhodes, Jill Ireland, Glen Alyn, Ewen Solon, Lloyd Lamble, Alex McIntosh, Deirdre Mayne, Lance George, Richard Thorp, Howard Green, Peter Fontain, Geoffrey Goodhart, Reginald Hearne, Martin Boddey, Alexander Field, Robert Raglan, Yvonne Savage, Margaret Rowe, Yvette Davis, Andrea Malandrinos*.

THERE WAS A YOUNG LADY (1952)   [3]

Dir and Scr *Lawrence Huntington, from a radio serial by Vernon Harris, John Jowett*. Prod *A.R. Rawlinson*. Ph *Gerald Gibbs*. PC *Nettlefold/Ernest G. Roy*. Dis *Butchers*. 84 mins. Cert *U*

Elizabeth (*Dulcie Gray*) is a super-efficient secretary at a diamond merchant's - too efficient for new owner David (*Michael Denison*), who knows nothing about diamonds, but fires her out of pique. Kidnapped by a gang of crooks, she gets a message to David who tracks her down and dispatches the crooks one by one, although she already has them under her thumb. Brightish comedy with Miss Gray at her most piquant.

RoC *Bill Owen, Sydney Tafler, Geraldine McEwan, Charles Farrell, Robert Adair, Bill Shine, Kenneth Connor, Tommy Duggan, Marcel Poncin, Basil Dignam, Ben Williams, Janet Butler, Gerald Rex*.

THESE DANGEROUS YEARS (1957)   [3]
(USA: *Dangerous Youth*)

Dir *Herbert Wilcox*. Prod *Anna Neagle*. Scr *Jack Trevor Story*. Ph *Gordon Dines*. PC *Everest/Anna Neagle Productions*. Dis *AB-Pathé*. 108 mins. Cert *A*

Dave (*Frankie Vaughan*), a Liverpool gangleader, is called up for Army service. He soon falls foul of Simpson (*Kenneth Cope*), the camp bully, who is indirectly responsible for the

Carole Lesley, George Baker and Frankie Vaughan in These Dangerous Years (*1957*)

death of Dave's friend Smiley (*Ray Jackson*). Dave severely wounds Simpson, and deserts. But an understanding padre (*George Baker*) persuades Dave to return and, at an enquiry, he is cleared. Amalgam of familiar elements for a new star tugs away at every discernible emotional string.

RoC *Carole Lesley, Jackie Lane, Eddie Byrne, Thora Hird, Katherine Kath, Robert Desmond, David Lodge, John le Mesurier, Reginald Beckwith, Richard Leech, Ralph Reader, Eric Morley, Marjorie Rhodes, Ray Jackson, Lloyd Lamble, Michael Ripper, Martin Boddey, John Breslin, Victor Brooks, David Gregory*.

THEY CAN'T HANG ME (1955)   [3]

Dir *Val Guest*. Prod *Roger Proudlock*. Scr *Guest, Val Valentine, from a novel by Leonard Mosley*. Ph *Michael Brandt*. PC *Vandyke*. Dis *Independent Film Distributors/British Lion*. 75 mins. Cert *A*

Convicted murderer Pitt (*André Morell*) bargains with the law: his life in exchange for top-secret information about atomic spies. But the police, led by Brown (*Terence Morgan*) track down the top enemy agent, then trick a traitor scientist into giving himself away. Brown feels it only fair to make one last visit to Pitt, who must now die after all. Familiar espionage elements slickly re-juggled.

RoC *Yolande Donlan, Anthony Oliver, Ursula Howells, Reginald Beckwith, Guido Lorraine, Basil Dignam, Raymond Rollett, Fred Johnson, Arnold Marle, John Maxwell, Nigel Sharpe, Barry Lowe, Diana Lambert, Cyril Renison, Petra Davies, Arthur Lovegrove, Michael Godfrey, Guy Mills*.

THEY NEVER LEARN (1956)   [1]

Dir *Denis Kavanagh*. Prod and PC *Edwin J. Fancey*. Scr *Kavanagh, Fancey*. Ph *Hal Morey*. Dis *New Realm*. 48 mins. Cert *U*

A policewoman (*Adrienne Scott*) goes undercover as a jailbird to win the confidence of a forger (*Jackie Collins*). On their release, the policewoman is able to lead her colleagues to the forger's associates (*John Blythe, Graham Stark*), one of whom is captured. The other jumps to his death from the tower of a cathedral. Rudimentary quota quickie, a throwback to the 1930s.

No further cast issued!

THEY WERE NOT DIVIDED (1950) [4]
Dir and Scr *Terence Young*. Prod *Herbert Smith*. Ph *Harry Waxman*. PC *Two Cities*. Dis *General Film Distributors. 102 mins. Cert A*
An Englishman (*Edward Underdown*), an American (*Ralph Clanton*) and an Irishman (*Michael Brennan*) all join the Welsh Guards in World War II; they become firm friends. The American falls for an English girl (*Stella Andrews*) and marries her on 48 hours' leave. The Englishman and the American both become officers but, on a reconnaissance, the American is hit by a shell. The Englishman refuses to leave his friend and they die together. Later they are buried side by side. Rambling but popular film with good battle scenes and a sense of comradeship.
RoC *Helen Cherry, Michael Trubshawe, John Wynn, Desmond Llewellyn, Rufus Cruickshank, Estelle Brody, Christopher Lee, R.S.M. Brittain, Anthony Dawson, Ian Murray, Rupert Gerard, Robert Ayres.*

THEY WHO DARE (1953) [4]
Dir *Lewis Milestone*. Prod *Aubrey Baring, Maxwell Setton*. Scr *Robert Westerby*. Ph *Wilkie Cooper*. PC *Mayflower*. Dis *British Lion. Technicolor. 106 mins. Cert U*
Lt Graham (*Dirk Bogarde*) of the Special Boat Service is to carry out a daring raid on the Greek island of Rhodes, to blow up two enemy air-fields. After a hazardous overland trek on which water is hard to find, he and his company succeed in their mission, but Graham makes a mistake which means the capture of some of his men. Back on the coast, Graham and Sgt Corcoran (*Denholm Elliott*), the last survivors, find their dinghies gone, but manage to swim to a waiting submarine. Tense if rather superficial wartime adventure.
RoC *Akim Tamiroff, Gérard Oury, Eric Pohlmann, Alec Mango, Kay Callard, Russell Enoch (William Russell), David Peel, Sam Kydd, Lisa Gastoni, Peter Burton, Michael Mellinger, Anthea Leigh, Eileen Way.*

THIRD MAN ON THE MOUNTAIN (1959) [3]
Dir *Ken Annakin*. Prod *William H. Anderson*. Scr *Eleanor Griffin, from a novel by James Ramsay Ullman*. Ph *Harry Waxman*. PC and Dis *Walt Disney. Technicolor. 103 mins. Cert U*
1865. Young Rudi (*James MacArthur*) dreams of climbing The Citadel, the mountain that killed his father. Getting a chance, he bungles it, but his girlfriend (*Janet Munro*) and an ex-guide (*Laurence Naismith*) help him train for another go. He follows rival-climbers Winter (*Michael Rennie*) and Saxo (*Herbert Lom*) and, when the latter falls, saves his life, leaving Winter to become the first man to climb The Citadel. Badly acted adventure with some exciting climbing tension towards the end.
RoC *James Donald, Lee Patterson, Walter Fitzgerald, Nora Swinburne, Ferdy Mayne, Helen Hayes.*

THIRD PARTY RISK (1955) [3]
(USA: *The Deadly Game*)
Dir and Scr *Daniel Birt, from the novel by Nicolas Bentley*. Prod *Robert Dunbar*. Ph

Jimmy Harvey. PC *Hammer*. Dis *Exclusive. 70 mins. Cert U*
Lured on by his interest in a girl (*Maureen Swanson*) involved, American songwriter Philip (*Lloyd Bridges*) delivers a package for a friend. But the friend is murdered, and the package contained microfilm of a formula in whose theft Philip is now involved. In Spain, he enlists the help of the local police to trap the killer, a financier (*Finlay Currie*), who is caught at a fiesta. Unimaginative thriller lifted by a number of capable performances.
RoC *Simone Silva, Ferdy Mayne, Peter Dyneley, Roger Delgado, George Woodbridge, Russell Waters, Mary Parker, Seymour Green, Toots Pound.*

THE THIRD VISITOR (1951) [2]
Dir *Maurice Elvey*. Prod *Ernest Gartside*. Scr *Gerald Anstruther, David Evans, from Anstruther's play*. Ph *Stephen Dade*. PC *Elvey-Gartside*. Dis *Eros. 85 mins. Cert A*
A number of people are suspected when crime king Carling (*Karel Stepanek*) is murdered. It seems as though Steffy (*Sonia Dresdel*) may be the killer, but then Inspector Mallory (*Guy Middleton*) discovers Carling is still alive and had killed the man whose body was identified as his. Before the police can step in, Carling is shot dead by another of his many enemies. Actors try hard with unconvincing material.
RoC *Hubert Gregg, Colin Gordon, Eleanor Summerfield, John Slater, Cyril Smith, Michael Martin-Harvey.*

13 EAST STREET (1952) [3]
Dir *Robert S. Baker*. Prod *Baker, Monty Berman*. Scr *John Gilling*. Ph *Berman*. PC *Tempean*. Dis *Eros. 71 mins. Cert A*
Detective Gerald Blake (*Patrick Holt*) goes undercover, joining a gang of thieves to get the evidence to smash it. The gang spot Blake with his contact man, whom they kill, planning to dispatch Blake after their next big haul. But the body is found and police arrive in time to save Blake and grab the gang. Conventional crime 'B' with good chase climax.
RoC *Sandra Dorne, Robert Ayres, Sonia Holm, Dora Bryan, Michael Balfour, Michael Brennan, Hector MacGregor, Alan Judd, Michael Ward, Alan Gordon. Harry Fowler.*

• **THE 39 STEPS** (1959) [3]
Dir *Ralph Thomas*. Prod *Betty E. Box*. Scr *Frank Harvey, from a scenario by Charles Bennett, Ian Hay, Alma Reville, and the novel by John Buchan*. Ph *Ernest Steward*. PC and Dis *Rank. Eastman Colour. 93 mins. Cert U*
The murder of a nanny (*Faith Brook*) in his London flat plunges Richard Hannay (*Kenneth More*) into a world of intrigue and espionage, with himself as the quarry, hunted to Scotland and back again. Dodging death at such contrasting locations as the Forth Bridge and a girls' school, he finds the answer to the mystery – a spy ring called The 39 Steps – at a London music-hall, where the ring's chief (*Barry Jones*) is killed. Serviceable thriller can't compare with Hitchcock original.
RoC *Taina Elg, Brenda de Banzie, James Hayter, Duncan Lamont, Michael Goodliffe, Regin-*

Taina Elg and Kenneth More in The 39 Steps (1959)

ald Beckwith, Sidney James, Jameson Clark, Andrew Cruickshank, Leslie Dwyer, Betty Henderson, Joan Hickson, Brian Oulton, John Richardson, Sam Kydd, Michael Brennan.

36 HOURS (1954) [2]
(USA: *Terror Street*)
Dir *Montgomery Tully*. Prod *Anthony Hinds*. Scr *Steve Fisher*. Ph *Jimmy Harvey*. PC *Hammer*. Dis *Exclusive. 80 mins. Cert A*
When his wife's letters stop, USAF pilot Bill (*Dan Duryea*) flies back to England – to find her (*Elsy Albiin*) installed in a sumptuous flat. He is knocked out and she is shot dead. He finds himself forced to find the murderer to establish his own innocence and, in so doing, discovers that his wife was mixed in diamond smuggling with the man (*John Chandos*) who killed her. Suspense moderate. Good acting (just) pulls it through.
RoC *Ann Gudrun, Eric Pohlmann, Kenneth Griffith, Jane Carr, Harold Lang, Michael Golden, Marianne Stone, John Wynn, Russell Napier, Lee Patterson, Jacqueline Mackenzie, John Warren, Stephen Vercoe, Robert Henderson, Gabrielle Blunt, Sheila Berry, Cleo Rose, Christine Adrian, Robert O'Neal. Angela Glynne, Richard Ford, Kenneth Brown.*

THIS OTHER EDEN (1959) [3]
Dir *Muriel Box*. Prod *Alec C. Snowden*. Scr *Patrick Kirwan, Blanaid Irvine, from the play by Louis d'Alton*. Ph *Gerald Gibbs*. PC *Emmet Dalton*. Dis *Regal. 81 mins. Cert U*
1945. Irish townsfolk decide to erect a statue to a rebel leader killed by the black-and-tans in the 1920s. Crispin (*Leslie Phillips*), one of two new arrivals, and son of the English colonel who shot the rebel, thinks it in bad taste. Conor (*Norman Rodway*), the other, finding he is the rebel's natural son, destroys the statue. Crispin gets the blame and is nearly lynched before Conor confesses. Irish whimsy too weak to hit its satirical targets.
RoC *Audrey Dalton, Niall MacGinnis, Milo O'Shea, Geoffrey Golden, Harry Brogan, Paul Farrell, Hilton Edwards, Philip O'Flynn, Gerald Sullivan, Ria Mooney, Eddie Golden, Isobel Couser.*

THOSE PEOPLE NEXT DOOR (1952) [1]
Dir *John Harlow*. Prod *Tom Blakeley*. Scr *Uncredited, from a play by Zelda Davees*. Ph *Roy*

Fogwell. PC *Film Studios Manchester.* Dis *Eros.* 77 mins. Cert U

1941. Sam Twigg (*Jack Warner*) is not only bothered by the Germans but by the escapades of two troublesome daughters and a son. His older daughter (*Patricia Cutts*) falls for the RAF officer son (*Peter Forbes-Robertson*) of titled parents, who come to sort the Twiggs out just as the flier is reported shot down. When he turns up with just a broken leg, the families are soon united. The Huggett comedy vein mined out; poor and stagey, with dislikeable characters.

RoC *Marjorie Rhodes, Charles Victor, Garry Marsh, Anthony Newley, Norah Gaussen (Gorsen), Gladys Henson, Jimmy James, Grace Arnold, Geoffrey Sumner.*

THOUGHT TO KILL (1953)   2

Dir *Leslie Arliss, Lawrence Huntington, Bernard Knowles.* Prod and PC *Douglas Fairbanks Jr.* Scr *Selwyn Jepson, Roland Pertwee, Larry Marcus & Robert Westerby.* Ph *Eric Cross, Ken Talbot.* Dis *British Lion.* 77 mins. Cert A

Three short stories. (1) A clerk thinks about killing an invalid with a hoard of cash under his bed. He decides against it. The man dies and leaves him his money. (2) A henpecked grocer finds a new wife and a better job. (3) A £5 note passes through the hands of a deadbeat, a cosh-boy, a woman alcoholic and a would-be suicide. An epilogue reveals it to have been counterfeit. Uninventive trilogy.

LP *Ernest Thesiger, James Thompson, Eileen Moore, Brian Worth, John Veer, Henry Longhurst, Dorothy Gordon; Bill Owen, Avice Landone, Lana Morris, Ronald Adam, John Warwick, Wally Patch, Douglas Fairbanks Jr, Percy Marmont, James Kenney, Doris Hare, Melissa Stribling, David Horne, Geoffrey Hibbert, Roderick Lovell, John Mann, Peter Elliott.*

THREE CASES OF MURDER (1954)   2

Dir *Wendy Toye, David Eady, George More O'Ferrall.* Prod *Ian Dalrymple, Hugh Perceval.* Scr *Ian Dalrymple, Sidney Carroll, Donald Wilson, from stories by Roderick Wilkinson, Brett Halliday and W. Somerset Maugham.* Ph *Georges Périnal.* PC and Wessex *London Films.* Dis *British Lion.* 99 mins. Cert A

(1) A museum guide (*Hugh Pryse*), fascinated by a picture of a house, finds himself inside it – permanently, thanks to the artist (*Alan Badel*) who painted it. (2) A romantic triangle seems to have been resolved when the girl (*Elizabeth Sellars*) is killed, and one suitor (*John Gregson*) 'kills himself'. But a barman (*Badel*) reveals the murderer. (3) Two MPs (*Orson Welles, Badel*) conduct a 'duel of dreams'. In the end, both die. First story the best; others disappointing.

RoC *Leueen McGrath, Eddie Byrne, John Salew, Ann Hanslip, Harry Welchman; Emrys Jones, Jack Lambert, Philip Dale, Colette Wilde, Christina Forrest, Maurice Kaufmann, Diana Morrison, Beau Edmonds, Ray Edmonds; Helen Cherry, Arthur Wontner, André Morell, Zena Marshall, Patrick Macnee, Peter Burton, John Humphrey, David Horne, Evelyn Hall, Mark Sheldon, Wilfrid Walter, Ronald Cardew,*

Henry Oscar, John Boxer, Vera Pearce, Judith Whittaker.

THREE CORNERED FATE (1954)   2

Dir *David Macdonald.* Prod *Edward J Danziger, Harry Lee Danziger.* Scr *Paul Tabori (1 and 2), James Eastwood and Kate Barlay.* Ph *Jack Cox.* PC *Danzigers.* Dis *Paramount.* 75 mins. Cert A

Three stories involving the threat of death. (1) A man and his son are poisoned by Malayan rebels and the wife has only enough antidote for one . . . (2) A refugee dancer comes between a producer and his fiancée. The fiancée tries to kill the ballerina, but the producer dies instead. (3) A schoolgirl in love with her music teacher hides in a chest to be near him and is almost asphyxiated. The teacher looks like taking the blame, until her diary is found. All heavy going.

LP *Ron Randell, Joyce Heron, Mark Dignam, Ian Whittaker, Maureen Swanson, Derek Bond, Joan Schofield, Jean Aubrey, Anthony Snell, Josephine Douglas, Helen Goss.*

THREE CROOKED MEN (1958)   3

Dir *Ernest Morris.* Prod *Edward J. Danziger, Harry Lee Danziger.* Scr *Brian Clemens, Eldon Howard,* Ph *Jimmy Wilson.* PC *Danzigers.* Dis *Paramount.* 71 mins. Cert U

Three crooks plan to rob a bank through the wall of the store next door. But the owner (*Gordon Jackson*) comes back unexpectedly and they are forced to capture him; they also bag a passer-by (*Warren Mitchell*) who responds to the owner's cries for help. The two victims are briefly suspected of the crime themselves, but eventually help police to bring the criminals to justice. Mixture of suspense drama and character studies; not too bad.

RoC *Eric Pohlmann, Philip Saville, Michael Mellinger, Kenneth Edwards, Frank Sieman, Noel Dyson, Arnold Bell, Alex Gallier, Michael Allinson, Peter Bathurst, Len Sharp.*

THREE MEN IN A BOAT (1956)   2

Dir *Ken Annakin.* Prod *Jack Clayton.* Scr *Hubert Gregg, Vernon Harris, from the book by Jerome K. Jerome.* Ph *Eric Cross.* PC *Romulus/Remus.* Dis *Independent Film Distributors/British Lion. Eastman Colour. CinemaScope.* 94 mins. Cert U

Three friends, George (*Laurence Harvey*), Harris (*Jimmy Edwards*) and J. (*David Tomlinson*) take a boating holiday on the Thames. They meet three pretty girls (*Shirley Eaton, Jill Ireland, Lisa Gastoni*), but apart from that pretty well everything goes wrong, including falling in the river and getting hopelessly lost in the Hampton Court maze. Colourful comedy lacks Jerome's original humour – just isn't funny.

RoC *Martita Hunt, Adrienne Corri, Noelle Middleton, Robertson Hare, Campbell Cotts, A.E. Matthews, Miles Malleson, Ernest Thesiger, Joan Haythorne, Charles Lloyd Pack, Stuart Saunders, Shane Cordell, Norman Rossington, Margot Lister, George Woodbridge, Esma Cannon, Toke Townley, Barbara Archer, Harold Goodwin, Sheila Raynor, Miranda Connell, Hal Osmond, Fred Griffiths, Neta (dog).*

THREE'S COMPANY (1953)   2

Dir *Terence Fisher (1 and 2), Charles Saunders.* Prod and PC *Douglas Fairbanks Jr.* Scr *Richard Alan Simmons, Larry Marcus, John Cresswell.* Ph *Jimmy Wilson, Brendan Stafford.* Dis *British Lion.* 78 mins. Cert A

Three suspense stories. A surgeon (*Basil Sydney*) has to operate on the lover his estranged daughter (*Elizabeth Sellars*) has nearly killed; a clerk (*George Benson*) becomes involved in a murder-by-phone after dialling a wrong number; a man and his faithless wife (*Fairbanks, Constance Cummings*) buy a haunted house that knows murder will be committed there. Slight fare, made for British cinemas, American TV.

No supporting cast.

THREE STEPS IN THE DARK (1953)   2

Dir *Daniel Birt.* Prod *Harold Richmond.* Scr *Brock Williams.* Ph *Hone Glendinning.* PC *Corsair.* Dis *AB-Pathé.* 60 mins. Cert A

When a wealthy and much-hated eccentric (*Nicholas Hannen*) announces that he has altered his will, you can bet he's not long for this world. It takes his detective story-writing niece Sophy (*Greta Gynt*) to sort out the killer from a clutch of greedy relations. Boring, very low-budget 'thriller'.

RoC *Hugh Sinclair, Sarah Lawson, Hélène Cordet, Elwyn Brook-Jones, John Van Eyssen, Alastair Hunter, Katie Johnson, Alan Robinson, Neil Hallett, Raymond Young.*

THREE STEPS TO THE GALLOWS (1953)   3
(USA: *White Fire*)

Dir and Scr *John Gilling.* Prod *Robert S. Baker, Monty Berman.* Ph *Berman.* PC *Tempean,* Dis *Eros.* 81 mins. Cert A

Stevens (*Scott Brady*) an American cargo-ship officer, docks in London to find his brother due to be executed for murder – the frame-up victim of a diamond-smuggling ring. They try to frame Stevens in much the same way, but he is too clever and tough for them, and brings them to justice. Very formula thriller, given a little gloss by its two Hollywood stars. Not released until 1955.

RoC *Mary Castle, Ferdy Mayne, Colin Tapley, John Blythe, Gabrielle Brune, Lloyd Lamble, Ballard Berkeley, Paul Erickson, Bill Lowe, Hal Osmond, Dennis Chinnery, Ronald Leigh-Hunt, Arthur Lovegrove, Harcourt Nicholls, Russell Westwood, Laurie Taylor, Alastair Hunter, Michael Balfour, Julian Somers, Ronan O'Casey, Johnnie Schofield.*

THREE SUNDAYS TO LIVE (1957)   1

Dir *Ernest Morris.* Prod *Edward J. Danziger, Harry Lee Danziger.* Scr *Brian Clemens.* Ph *Jimmy Wilson.* PC *Danzigers.* Dis *United Artists.* 71 mins. Cert U

Frank (*Kieron Moore*), a dance-band leader, is framed for murder and sentenced to death, the only witness, Ruth Chapman (*Sandra Dorne*), being reported killed in America. But she is still alive (though not for long), as Frank finds out with the help of his girlfriend (*Jane Griffiths*) when he escapes. The killer thinks he has disposed of the wrong girl, and is trapped when he makes a second attempt. 'Thriller', both dreary and ridiculous.

RoC *Basil Dignam, Hal Ayer, John Longden, John Stone, Mona Washbourne, Norman Mitchell, Ferdy Mayne.*

THE THREE WORLDS OF GULLIVER (1959) 3

Dir *Jack Sher.* Prod *Charles H. Schneer.* Scr *Sher, Arthur Ross, from a book by Jonathan Swift.* Ph *Wilkie Cooper.* Sp eff *Ray Harryhausen.* PC *Morningside.* Dis *Columbia.* Technicolor. SuperDynamation. *97 mins. Cert U*

In the 18th century, ship's surgeon Lemuel Gulliver (*Kerwin Mathews*) is washed overboard and encounters adventures in lands where he is, first, a giant (Lilliput) and next a pigmy surrounded by giants (Brobdignag). Eventually he and his fiancée Elizabeth (*June Thorburn*), who has been stranded in Brobdignag, float back to England in a giant basket. Harryhausen's effects hadn't yet hit their stride in this adventure. There is no sign of the 'third world' of Gulliver.

RoC *Jo Morrow, Lee Patterson, Gergoire Aslan, Basil Sydney, Sherri Alberoni, Charles Lloyd-Pack, Martin Benson, Mary Ellis, Peter Bull, Marian Spencer, Alec Mango.*

TIGER BAY (1959) 5

Dir *J. Lee Thompson.* Prod *John Hawkesworth, Julian Wintle, Leslie Parkyn.* Scr *Hawkesworth, Shelley Smith, from a novel by Noel Calef.* Ph *Eric Cross.* PC *Independent Artists.* Dis *Rank. 105 mins. Cert A*

In the Tiger Bay docks of South Wales, Korchinsky (*Horst Buchholz*) kills the girl (*Yvonne Mitchell*) who has been unfaithful to him. He is witnessed by 12-year-old tomboy Gillie (*Hayley Mills*) who is chiefly interested in stealing the gun. Later Korchinsky kidnaps her, and a strong friendship springs up between them. Spt Graham (*John Mills*) traps her into giving him away but, on his skip, she refuses to identify him. When she falls overboard, Korchinsky betrays himself by saving her. Thriller has movingly human performances, generates great tension.

RoC *Megs Jenkins, Anthony Dawson, George Selway, George Pastell, Meredith Edwards, Paul Stassino, Shari, Marne Maitland, Christopher Rhodes, Marianne Stone, Rachel Thomas, Brian Hammond, Kenneth Griffith, Eynon Evans, Edward Cast, David Davies.*

John Mills and Hayley Mills in Tiger Bay *(1959)*

TIGER BY THE TAIL (1955) 3 (USA: *Crossup*)

Dir *John Gilling.* Prod *Robert S. Baker, Monty Berman.* Scr *Gilling, Willis Goldbeck.* Ph *Eric Cross.* PC *Tempean.* Dis *Eros. 83 mins. Cert A*

Through a friendship with a nightclub girl (*Lisa Daniely*), a reporter, Desmond (*Larry Parks*) becomes the prey of those running a counterfeit currency racket. With his secretary Jane (*Constance Smith*), he is kidnapped by a gang, but he manages to free Jane, who escapes and fetches the police. Standard British thriller with familiar situations leaves its competent cast little chance to shine.

RoC *Cyril Chamberlain, Ronan O'Casey, Donald Stewart, Marie Bryant, Alexander Gauge, Russell Westwood, Daphne Newton, Thora Hird, Joan Heal, Ronald Leigh-Hunt, Doris Hare, Frank Forsyth, Robert Moore, John Easton.*

TIGER IN THE SMOKE (1956) 4

Dir *Roy Baker.* Prod *Leslie Parkyn.* Scr *Anthony Pelissier, from the novel by Margery Allingham.* Ph *Geoffrey Unsworth.* PC and Dis *Rank. 94 mins. Cert A*

In the fog of a London winter, a group of itinerant musicians wanders, ex-servicemen all, dedicated to finding Havoc (*Tony Wright*), the ex-sergeant who stole their loot from a wartime commando raid. Havoc is now in jail, but escapes bent on looking for the treasure himself. Meg (*Muriel Pavlow*), widow of the man who led the raid, escapes Havoc's murder attempt and, with her fiancé Geoffrey (*Donald Sinden*), uncovers the loot. Havoc intervenes but, after a fight with Geoffrey, police take him into custody. Thriller loses its grip after brilliant first hour.

RoC *Bernard Miles, Alec Clunes, Laurence Naismith, Christopher Rhodes, Charles Victor, Sam Kydd, Kenneth Griffith, Gerald Harper, Wensley Pithey, Thomas Heathcote, Beatrice Varley, Stanley Rose, Stratford Johns, Brian Wilde, Hilda Barry.*

TIM DRISCOLL'S DONKEY (1954) 1

Dir *Terry Bishop.* Prod *Gilbert Church.* Scr *Bishop, Patricia Latham.* Ph *S.D. Onions.* PC *Bushey/Children's Film Foundation.* Dis *British Lion. 59 mins. Cert U*

Orphan Tim (*David Coote*) lives with his grandfather in Ireland, rearing donkeys. His own donkey, Patchy, is sold by accident, and Tim follows him to England, where he rides him to victory in a donkey race, being rewarded by getting Patchy back for good. Pretty scrappy, lacklustre affair, a rare disappointment from the CFF. This donkey is a turkey.

RoC *John Kelly, Peggy Marshall, Carole Lorimer, Anthony Green, Shay Gordon, Hugh Latimer.*

TIME BOMB (1952) 3 (USA: *Terror on a Train*)

Dir *Ted Tetzlaff.* Prod *Richard Goldstone.* Scr *Kem Bennett, from his novel* Death at Attention. Ph *F.A. Young.* PC and Dis *MGM-British. 72 mins. Cert U*

A bomb is placed in a trainload of naval mines en route to Portsmouth. Lyncort, a Canadian engineer (*Glenn Ford*), hunts, finds and defuses the mine, despite the worry that his wife (*Anne*

Glenn Ford in Time Bomb *(1953)*

Vernon) may leave him. The saboteur (*Victor Maddern*) is caught by police in Portsmouth. It is learned that he has placed a second bomb. Rather drab thriller with some built-in excitements.

RoC *Maurice Denham, Harcourt Williams, Harold Warrender, John Horsley, Campbell Singer, Bill Fraser, Herbert C. Walton, Frank Atkinson, Ernest Butcher, Ada Reeve, Martin Wyldeck, Harry Locke, Sam Kydd.*

—

TIME GENTLEMEN PLEASE! (1952) 4

Dir *Lewis Gilbert.* Prod *Herbert Mason.* Scr *Peter Blackmore, from a novel by R.J. Minney.* Ph *Wilkie Cooper.* PC Group 3. Dis *Associated British. 83 mins. Cert U*

The Prime Minister is about to visit Britain's perfect village, Little Hayhoe, which decides to throw the village tramp, Dan Dance (*Eddie Byrne*) into an almshouse. The new vicar discovers that, as the only inhabitant of the almshouse, Dan is entitled to £6,000 from village funds. The council tries to oust Dan but, at the next elections, a new council is elected, with Dan as chairman. He decides to turn the almshouse into a day nursery, while the council finds him a job - as a mattress tester. Brisk, amusing comedy curio.

RoC *Jane Barrett, Raymond Lovell, Hermione Baddeley, Marjorie Rhodes, Sidney James, Sydney Tafler, Dora Bryan, Robert Brown, Thora Hird, Ivor Barnard, Patrick McAlinney, Edie Martin, Joan Young, Peter Jones, Marianne Stone, Julian d'Albie, Nigel Clarke, Henry Longhurst, Peter Swanwick, Thomas Gallagher, Freda Bamford, Ian Carmichael, Brian Roper, Harry Herbert, Jack May, Toke Townley, Tristram Rawson, Donovan Winter, Sheila Aza, Julie Millan, Michael Edmunds, Cora Bennett, Audrey Noble, Virginia Winter, Neil Gemmell, Helen Boursnell.*

TIME IS MY ENEMY (1954) 3

Dir *Don Chaffey.* Prod *Roger Proudlock.* Scr *Allan Mackinnon, from a play by Ella Adkins.* Ph *Geoffrey Faithfull.* PC *Vandyke.* Dis *Independent Film Distributors/British Lion. 64 mins. Cert A*

Suave Martin Radley (*Dennis Price*) goads his ex-wife Barbara (*Renee Asherson*) into shooting him (with blanks), so that she will confess to the murder of the man she thinks he is - but who, in reality, has been killed by Radley. An astute inspector (*Duncan Lamont*) guesses Radley's game, and arrests him as he tries to flee the country. Good cast well in character, but dialogue and situations make it routine.

RoC *Susan Shaw, Patrick Barr, William Franklyn, Brenda Hogan, Bonar Colleano, Alfie Bass, Agnes Laughlan, Bruce Beeby, Mavis Villiers, Barbara Grayley, Dandy Nichols, Nigel Neilson, Neil Wilson, Alastair Hunter, Erik Chitty, Audrey Hessey, Ian Wilson.*

TIME LOCK (1957)   [4]

Dir *Gerald Thomas.* Prod and Scr *Peter Rogers, from the TV play by Arthur Hailey.* Ph *Peter Hennessy.* PC *Romulus/Beaconsfield.* Dis *Independent Film Distributors/British Lion.* 73 mins. Cert A

Toronto, Canada. A small boy (*Vincent Winter*) is accidentally locked in a bank vault that cannot be opened for nearly three days. Doctors calculate he cannot survive longer than 12 hours. The boy's frantic parents (*Lee Patterson, Betty McDowall*) watch in anguish as police, labourers and welders all fail, but finally a vault expert (*Robert Beatty*) does the trick, and the boy is brought out unconscious but alive. Taut, economical thriller.

RoC *Robert Ayres, Alan Gifford, Larry Cross, Sandra Francis, Gordon Tanner, Victor Wood, Jack Cunningham, Sean Connery, Murray Kash, John Paul, Don Ewer.*

THE TIME OF HIS LIFE (1955)   [3]

Dir *Leslie Hiscott.* Prod *Elizabeth Hiscott, W.A. Smith.* Scr *Leslie Hiscott, Richard Hearne.* Ph *Kenneth Talbot.* PC *Shaftesbury.* Dis *Renown.* 74 mins. Cert U

Unhappy to be released from Wandsmoor Prison, where he had been happy, Charles Pastry (*Richard Hearne*) is locked away by his social-climbing daughter (*Ellen Pollock*) until she can ship him off to Australia to avoid a scandal. After several forays from his attic prison, causing chaos and embarrassment to the household, he returns to Wandsmoor - as handyman to the governor. Unusual comedy with touches of pathos; quite acceptable.

RoC *Robert Moreton, Richard Wattis, John Downing, Frederick Leister, Anne Smith, Darcy Conyers, Arthur Hewlett, Andrea Troubridge, Peter Sinclair, Yvonne Hearne, Neil Wilson, Alan Whittaker, Edgar Driver, Jessica Cairns, Peggyann Clifford.*

TIMESLIP (1955)   [4]

Dir *Ken Hughes.* Prod *Alec C. Snowden.* Scr *Hughes, Charles Eric Maine, from Maine's TV play.* PC *Anglo-Guild.* Dis *Anglo-Amalgamated.* 93 mins. Cert A

An almost-dead man fished out of the Thames is the double of a top scientist (*Peter Arne*). But reporter Mike Delaney (*Gene Nelson*) is convinced the wounded man is the scientist and the man at the research institute a fake. Clinically dead for a short while, the injured man's brain, working several seconds ahead of 'real' time, enables Delaney to save the institute from being blown up. For unlikely plot to succeed, film has to be fast and exciting: it is.

RoC *Faith Domergue, Joseph Tomelty, Donald Gray, Vic Perry, Launce Maraschal, Roland Brand, Charles Hawtrey, Susan Chester, Muriel Young, Martin Wyldeck, Carl Jaffe, Barry Mackay.*

A TIME TO KILL (1955)   [3]

Dir *Charles Saunders.* Prod *Clive Nicholas, Fred Swann.* Scr *Doreen Montgomery.* Ph *James Wilson.* PC *Fortress.* Dis *AB-Pathé.* 64 mins. Cert A

Peter (*John Horsley*), chemist and philanderer, realizes that the drinks of himself and his mistress Madeline (*June Ashley*) have been poisoned. He phones Dr Cole (*Keneth Kent*), but Madeline dies. The doctor's wife (*Mary Jones*) tells Peter's reporter friend Denis (*Jack Watling*) that Madeline and a mystery man were blackmailers. Peter's fiancée (*Rona Anderson*) takes up the case, and, despite the murder of Mrs Cole, proves that the mystery man - and killer - is Denis. Complex thriller is very average, but does muster a few moments of tension.

RoC *Russell Napier, Alastair Hunter, Joan Hickson, John le Mesurier, Edward Frency, Arthur Gross.*

TIME WITHOUT PITY (1957)   [3]

Dir *Joseph Losey.* Prod *John Arnold, Anthony Simmons, Leon Clore.* Scr *Ben Barzman, from a play by Emlyn Williams.* Ph *Freddie Francis.* PC *Harlequin.* Dis *Eros.* 88 mins. Cert A

Graham (*Michael Redgrave*), an alcoholic half-way through 'drying out', has 24 hours to help his son (*Alec McCowen*), condemned for a murder he didn't commit. He becomes involved with a neurotic family, finding that the wife (*Ann Todd*) loved his son, and that the father (*Leo McKern*) is the real killer. Graham forces the man to shoot him, knowing it will save his son. Stylishly acted, but over-directed drama. Very sombre.

RoC *Peter Cushing, Lois Maxwell, Paul Daneman, Richard Wordsworth, Renee Houston, George Devine, Joan Plowright, Ernest Clark, Dickie Henderson, Peter Copley, Hugh Moxey, Julian Somers, John Chandos.*

Ann Todd and Michael Redgrave in Time Without Pity *(1957)*

THE TITFIELD THUNDERBOLT (1952)   [4]

Dir *Charles Crichton.* Prod *Michael Truman.* Scr *T.E.B. Clarke.* Ph *Douglas Slocombe.* PC *Ealing Studios.* Dis *General Film Distributors.* Technicolor. 84 mins (*US:82*). Cert U

British Railways decides to close down the single-line railway which connects the village of Titfield to its nearest town and run a bus service instead. The villagers take over the rail-

Hugh Griffith (rear), John Gregson, Naunton Wayne (rear), George Relph and Stanley Holloway in The Titfield Thunderbolt *(1953)*

way themselves, and run it despite the skulduggery of the bus company, which is finally driven to wreck the train at night. The villagers, however, bring out an old engine, The Thunderbolt, from their museum, and make a triumphant run, gaining BR sanction for the line's continuance. Pleasing, rib-tickling comedy, if not the riot it might have been.

LP *Stanley Holloway, George Relph, John Gregson, Naunton Wayne, Godfrey Tearle, Gabrielle Brune, Hugh Griffith, Sidney James, Reginald Beckwith, Edie Martin, Michael Trubshawe, Nancy O'Neil, Jack MacGowran, Ewan Roberts, Campbell Singer, Wensley Pithey, Harold Alford, Herbert C. Walton, John Rudling, Ted Burbidge, Frank Green.*

TO DOROTHY, A SON (1954)   [4]
(USA: *Cash on Delivery*)

Dir *Muriel Box.* Prod *Sydney Box, Peter Rogers, Ben Schrift.* Scr *Rogers, from the play by Roger Macdougall.* Ph *Ernest Steward.* PC *Welbeck.* Dis *Independent Film Distributors/British Lion.* 84 mins. Cert U

Showgirl Myrtle La Mar (*Shelley Winters*) heads from America to Britain and her ex-husband (*John Gregson*) when she hears he has inherited £2,000,000, which will go to her if he has no son by a certain deadline. Horror of horrors, he is remarried to Dorothy (*Peggy Cummins*), who is on the verge of giving birth. Who gets the money? There's a twist in the tail of this fairly funny romp, as Myrtle and her 'ex' get to share the millions.

RoC *Wilfrid Hyde White, Mona Washbourne, Hartley Power, Martin Miller, Hal Osmond, Anthony Oliver, Joan Sims, Aubrey Mather, Ronald Adam, Charles Hawtrey, Alfie Bass, Meredith Edwards, Marjorie Rhodes, Maurice Kaufman(n), John Warren, Dorothy Bramhall, Grace Denbigh Russell, Bartlett Mullins, Joan Newall, Campbell Singer, Joan Hickson, Fred Berger, Nicholas Parsons, Ann Gudrun.*

TO HAVE AND TO HOLD (1950)   [3]

Dir *Godfrey Grayson.* Prod *Anthony Hinds.* Scr *Reginald Long, from the play by Lionel Brown.* Ph *James Harvey.* PC *Hammer.* Dis *Exclusive.* 63 mins. Cert A

Learning that he has only a brief time to live, Brian Harding (*Patrick Barr*), crippled by a fall from a horse, devotes his remaining days to securing the future happiness of his wife and daughter, to the exclusion of his own and to the extent of encouraging his wife's relationship with another man of whom she is fond. Odd, strained little drama, almost redeemed by the acting.

RoC *Avis Scott, Eunice Gayson, Robert Ayres, Ellen Pollock, Richard Warner, Harry Fine, Peter Neil.*

TOM BROWN'S SCHOOLDAYS
(1951) 3

Dir *Gordon Parry.* Prod *Brian Desmond Hurst.* Scr *Noel Langley, from the novel by Thomas Hughes.* Ph *C. Pennington-Richards.* PC *Talisman.* Dis *Renown.* 96 mins. Cert U

The 1830s. At 11, Tom Brown (*John Howard Davies*) goes to Rugby, a public school. He makes friends with East (*John Charlesworth*), but soon falls foul of Flashman (*John Forrest*), the school bully. Despite various tortures by older boys, Tom survives; he and East have a fight with Flashman, who is thrashed. As a result of a further incident in which the weakling Arthur (*Glyn Dearman*) nearly dies, Flashman is expelled. The Head (*Robert Newton*) continues his programme of reform; Tom scores a try in the house rugby contest. Faithful but uninspired version of classic story: a popular success however.

RoC *Diana Wynyard, James Hayter, Hermione Baddeley, Kathleen Byron, Michael Hordern, Francis de Wolff, Max Bygraves, Amy Veness, Brian Worth, Rachel Gurney, Geoffrey Goodheart, Michael Ward, Michael Brennan, Peter Madden, Anthony Doonan, Neil North, Ben Aris, Peter Scott, Robin Dowell, John Campbell, Gabriel Woolf, Roland Dallas, David Jenks, Derek Stephens.*

THE TOMMY STEELE STORY (1957) 4
(USA: *Rock Around the World*)

Dir *Gerard Bryant.* Prod *Herbert Smith.* Scr *Norman Hudis.* Ph *Peter Hennessy.* PC/Dis *Anglo-Amalgamated.* 82 mins. Cert U

South London youth Tommy Steele (*himself*) buys a guitar from a junk dealer (*Mark Daly*) and learns to play it during a spell in hospital. Later, as a ship's steward, he entertains the passengers and, on returning to London, gets a job as a singer in a coffee bar frequented by show business scouts. He is 'discovered' and his records quickly take the charts by storm. Interesting account of the entertainer's early years, dominated by his own engaging personality. Hit songs include *Butterfingers* and *Freight Train.*

RoC *Lisa Daniely, Patrick Westwood, Hilda Fenemore, Charles Lamb, Peter Lewison, John Boxer, Cyril Chamberlain, Humphrey Lyttelton and His Band, Chas McDevitt Skiffle Group with Nancy Whiskey, Tommy Eytle Calypso Band, Chris O'Brien's Caribbeans, The Steelmen, Dennis Price, Tom Littlewood.*

TOMMY THE TOREADOR (1959) 4

Dir *John Paddy Carstairs.* Prod *George H. Brown.* Scr *Nicholas Phipps, Sid Colin, Talbot Rothwell, Patrick Kirwan, Brown.* Ph *Gilbert Taylor.* PC *Fanfare.* Dis *Warner-Pathé.* Technicolor. 87 mins. Cert U

On shore leave in Spain, Tommy (*Tommy Steele*), a seaman, fortuitously saves the life of a famous bullfighter (*Virgilio Texera*), who in turn helps Tommy out of a trumped-up smuggling charge by starting a fight. Impresario Cadena (*Sidney James*) persuades Tommy to take the jailed toreador's place in the bullring, but gives him a ferocious bull instead of the tame animal he had promised. Tommy is again rescued by his friend the toreador. Bright, unpolished fiesta with a good variety of songs.

RoC *Janet Munro, Bernard Cribbins, Noel Purcell, Pepé Nieto, Ferdy Mayne, Kenneth Williams, Eric Sykes, Harold Kasket, Manolo Blazquez, Warren Mitchell, Charles Grey, Andrea Malandrinos, José Valero, Francis de Wolff, Tutte Lemkow, Edwin Richfield, Pilarin San Clemente, Michel Andel Rodriguez.*

tom thumb (1958) 4

Dir and Prod *George Pal.* Scr *Ladislas Fodor, from a story by the Brothers Grimm.* Ph *Georges Périnal.* Sp eff *Tom Howard.* PC *Galaxy.* Dis *M-G-M.* Eastman Colour. 92 mins. Cert U

The Forest Queen (*June Thorburn*) takes childless Anna (*Jessie Matthews*) at her wish, and gives her and Jonathan the woodsman (*Bernard Miles*), a son (*Russ Tamblyn*) two inches tall. He makes friends with the village piper (*Alan Young*), but is conned by two wicked villains (*Peter Sellers, Terry-Thomas*) into helping them rob the treasury vault. His parents are arrested, but Tom and the piper bring the culprits to book. Delightful fairy story with some good songs and trick effects; occasionally very funny too. Won Academy Award for its special effects.

RoC *Ian Wallace, Barbara Ferris, Stan Freberg (voices), The Puppetoons.*

TONS OF TROUBLE (1956) 3

Dir *Leslie Hiscott.* Prod *Elizabeth Hiscott, Richard Hearne.* Scr *Leslie Hiscott, Hearne.* Ph *Norman Warwick.* PC *Shaftesbury.* Dis *Renown.* 77 mins. Cert U

Pastry (*Richard Hearne*), eccentric oddjob man at a London block of flats, is devoted to his two giant boilers, Mavis and Ethel, both of them over 40 years old. For the love of Mavis and Ethel, he gets mixed up in a big business deal, and with the police. Sacked by the horrid Miss Shaw (*Joan Marion*), he is reinstated – and rewarded – just in time to stop Mavis blowing her top. Farce, pathos and story blended tolerably well.

RoC *William Hartnell, Robert Moreton, Austin Trevor, Ralph Truman, Ronald Adam, Junia Crawford, Tony Quinn, John Stuart, Yvonne Hearne.*

TONY DRAWS A HORSE (1950) 3

Dir *John Paddy Carstairs.* Prod *Brock Williams, Harold Richmond.* Scr *Williams, from the play by Lesley Storm.* Ph *Jack Hildyard.* PC *Pinnacle.* Dis *General Film Distributors.* 91 mins. Cert A

Tony (*Anthony Lang*), son of a Harley Street surgeon (*Cecil Parker*), is allowed by his mother (*Anne Crawford*) to behave as he likes. When he draws 'rude' pictures on his father's consulting room door, the parents have a fight, and she storms off to her mother's. Here she creates havoc on the eve of her sister's wedding, before being reconciled with her husband. In the end, Tony gets a good whacking. Sometimes amusing, rather talkative comedy.

RoC *Mervyn Johns, Derek Bond, Barbara Murray, Edward Rigby, Barbara Everest, Dandy Nichols, Kynaston Reeves, David Hurst, Ann Smith, Susan Dudley, Marjorie Gresley, Gabrielle Blunt, Harold Richmond, Michael Ward.*

TOO MANY CROOKS (1958) 3

Dir and Prod *Mario Zampi.* Scr *Michael Pertwee.* Ph *Stanley Pavey.* PC and Dis *Rank.* 87 mins. Cert U

The latest project of a bungling bunch of crooks, Fingers (*George Cole*), Snowdrop (*Bernard Bresslaw*), Sid (*Sidney James*) and Whisper (*Joe Melia*), is to kidnap a millionaire's daughter. But they get his wife (*Brenda de Banzie*); her husband (*Terry-Thomas*) doesn't want her back. Miffed, she helps them lay hands on his hidden fortune. But they lose it again in the end. Crazy comedy not always paced as well as riotous car chase at the end.

RoC *Vera Day, Delphi Lawrence, John le Mesurier, Sydney Tafler, Rosalie Ashley, Nicholas Parsons, Terry Scott, John Stuart, Vilma Ann Leslie, Edie Martin, Tutte Lemkow.*

TOO YOUNG TO LOVE (1959) 2

Dir *Muriel Box.* Prod *Herbert Smith.* Scr *Sydney and Muriel Box, from a play by Elsa Shelley.* Ph *Gerald Gibbs.* PC *Beaconsfield/Welbeck.* Dis *Rank.* 88 mins. Cert X

Brooklyn. Elizabeth (*Pauline Hahn*), a 15-year-old, is brought to juvenile court, which hears of her procurement by a pimp following wild parties, her abortion, her often absent parents and her final contraction of syphilis. The judge (*Thomas Mitchell*) persuades a chastened Elizabeth that she should go to hospital and approved school. Modern-day morality play, heavy going.

RoC *Joan Miller, Austin Willis, Jess Conrad, Cec Linder, Bessie Love, Alan Gifford, Vivian Matalon, Sheila Gallagher, Cal McCord, Miki Iveria, Robert Henderson, Charles Farrell, Ilona Ference, Roma Miller, Bill O'Connor, Ian Hughes, Bee Duffell, Margaret Griffin, Robert Desmond, Tom Gerrard, Michael Bell, Eric Hewitson, Larry Martyn, Nicholas Evans, Malcolm Knight.*

TO PARIS WITH LOVE (1954) 4

Dir *Robert Hamer.* Prod *Anthony Darnborough.* Scr *Robert Buckner.* Ph *Reginald Wyer.* PC *Two Cities.* Dis *General Film Distributors.* Technicolor. 78 mins. Cert A

A father and son (*Alec Guinness, Vernon Gray*) go to Paris for a holiday, each planning an amorous adventure for the other. The 'pairings' get switched, then back again. But not quite, as the son falls for a girl of his own age, while his original choice (*Odile Versois*) goes back to her childhood sweetheart. Complicated comedy of some charm, most noticeably in Guinness's performance.

RoC *Elina Labourdette, Claude Romain, Maureen Davis, Austin Trevor, Jacques François, Jacques Brunius, Pamela Stirling, Michael Anthony, Mollie Hartley Milburn, Claude Nollier,*

Jacques Cey, André Mikhelson, Nicholas Bruce, Toni Frost, Georges Lafaye Company.

TOP FLOOR GIRL (1959) [2]

Dir *Max Varnel.* Prod *Edward J. Danziger, Harry Lee Danziger.* Scr *Brian Clemens, Eldon Howard.* Ph *Jimmy Wilson.* PC *Danzigers.* Dis *Paramount. 71 mins. Cert U*

Connie (*Kay Callard*) joins an advertising agency and, to further her executive ambitions, makes use of the men she meets. Soon, she has become engaged to the son of the agency's wealthiest client. Shortly before the wedding, however, she throws him over for a young executive with his own agency. The old, old story – on a budget.

RoC *Neil Hallett, Maurice Kaufmann, Robert Raikes, Brian Nissen, Diana Chesney, Elizabeth (Liz) Fraser, Arnold Bell, Robert Dorning, William Hodge, Mark Singleton, Terence Cooper, Vilma Ann Leslie, Ian Wilson, Norah Gordon, Totti Truman Taylor, Olive Kirby, Jan Holden, Hal Osmond, Pauline Arden, Hilary Tindall, Derek Prentice.*

TOP OF THE FORM (1952) [2]

Dir *John Paddy Carstairs.* Prod *Paul Soskin.* Scr *Carstairs, Patrick Kirwan, Ted Willis, from an original screenplay by Anthony Kimmins, Leslie Arliss, Val Guest, and Marriott Edgar.* Ph *Ernest Steward.* PC *British Film Makers.* Dis *General Film Distributors. 75 mins. Cert U*

'Professor' Fortescue (*Ronald Shiner*), a racing tipster, accidentally becomes head of a boys' school. The boys prove adept students of betting, cheating and gambling, but, when he takes them on an 'educational' trip to Paris, they help the 'Professor' save the Mona Lisa from a gang of thieves. Broad, galumphing comedy remake of *Good Morning, Boys* (1937).

RoC *Harry Fowler, Alfie Bass, Anthony Newley, Jacqueline Pierreux, Mary Jerrold, Richard Wattis, Howard Marion Crawford, Roland Curram, Terence Mitchell, Gerald Campion, Oscar Quitak, Kynaston Reeves, Martin Benson, Eddie Sutch, Ronald (Ronnie) Corbett, Marcel Poncin, Ina de la Haye.*

Ronald Shiner, Ronnie Corbett and Alfie Bass in Top of the Form *(1953)*

TOP SECRET (1952) [4]
(USA: *Mr Potts Goes to Moscow*)

Dir and Prod *Mario Zampi.* Scr *Jack Davies, Michael Pertwee.* Ph *Stanley Pavey.* PC *Transocean.* Dis *AB-Pathé. 93 mins. Cert U*

A bumbling sanitary engineer (*George Cole*) picks up the wrong briefcase and finds himself whisked off to Moscow. The case he contains atomic secrets, although at first he thinks the Russians are fascinated by his design for a new toilet. When he finds out, he has a tough time getting out, but does so, helped by the Russian interpreter (*Nadia Gray*) who loves him. Broad satire with some outstandingly funny moments.

RoC *Oscar Homolka, Wilfrid Hyde White, Charles Goldner, Irene Handl, Gerard Heinz, Frederick Leister, Michael Medwin, Olaf Pooley, Edwin Styles, Geoffrey Sumner, Frederick Valk, Eleanor Summerfield, Kynaston Reeves, Richard Wattis, Ronald Adam, Ernest Jay, Henry Hewitt, Walter Horsbrugh, Anthony Shaw, Tim Turner, Gibb McLaughlin, Michael Balfour, Hal Osmond, Ronnie Stevens, Phyllis Morris, Myrtle Reed, Ina de la Haye, David Hurst, Bernard Rebel, Guido Lorraine, Terence Alexander, Richard Marner, Martin Boddey, Fred Berger, Victor Maddern, Reed de Rouen, Johnny Catcher, Willoughby Gray, Stanislaus Zienciakiewicz, Christopher Lee.*

TOTO AND THE POACHERS (1957) [3]

Dir *Brian Salt.* Prod *Henry Geddes.* Scr *Salt, John Coquillon, Michael Johns.* Ph *Coquillon.* PC *World Safari/Children's Film Foundation.* Dis *British Lion. Eastman Colour. 50 mins. Cert U*

An African version of the boy-who-cried-wolf theme. No-one believes little Toto's (*John Aloisi*) tall stories any more, so when he sees three strangers behaving suspiciously, it takes a dead elephant to convince his game scout uncle that ivory poachers are on the loose. After a hectic chase, the villains are caught and taken away. Rather amateurishly made adventure, but enjoyable for junior schoolchildren.

RoC *David Betts, Mpigano, Shabani Hamisi, Obago, Ansi Shaibu, Kiplagat.*

TOUCH AND GO (1955) [3]
(USA: *The Light Touch*)

Dir *Michael Truman.* (Associate) Prod *Seth Holt.* Scr *William Rose.* Ph *Douglas Slocombe.* PC *Ealing Studios.* Dis *Rank. Technicolor. 84 mins. Cert U*

Fletcher (*Jack Hawkins*), a furniture designer, decides to emigrate to Australia with his wife Helen (*Margaret Johnston*) and daughter Peggy (*June Thorburn*). There's the problem of finding a home for the family's huge black cat, Heathcliff, and the bigger problem of Peggy's new boyfriend (*John Fraser*). Other obstacles pile up. Fletcher is offered a new position with his old firm. Heathcliff disappears. The Fletchers decide to remain. Heathcliff watches from their roof. Wafer-thin comedy with the wrong players.

RoC *Roland Culver, James Hayter, Alison Leggatt, Margaret Halstan, Henry Longhurst, Basil Dignam, Bessie Love, Gabrielle Brune, Heather Sears, Arthur Howard, Peter Hunt, Jill Dixon, Margaret Courtenay, Alfred Burke, Elizabeth Winch (Liz Fraser), Heathcliff (cat).*

A TOUCH OF LARCENY (1959) [4]

Dir *Guy Hamilton.* Prod and PC *Ivan Foxwell.*

Scr *Roger Macdougall, Foxwell, Hamilton, Paul Winterton, from a novel by Andrew Garve.* Dis *Paramount. 91 mins. Cert U*

Max (*James Mason*), an ex-submarine officer now bored at the Admiralty, hits on a plan to whisk the money-minded fiancée (*Vera Miles*) of a diplomat (*George Sanders*) from under his rival's nose. He will fool the Press into believing he is a traitor about to flee to Russia with secrets, then hide on a remote island, emerge and sue for libel. Although the plan goes wrong (he is really marooned), he gets the girl in the end. Smooth, witty, lightly handled comedy.

RoC *William Kendall, Harry Andrews, Duncan Lamont, Barbara Hicks, Peter Barkworth, Robert Flemyng, Ernest Clark, Percy Herbert, John le Mesurier, Jimmy Lloyd, Mavis Villiers, MacDonald Parke, Stanley Zevic, André Mikhelson, Frederick Piper, Dickie Owen, William Mervyn, Gordon Harris, Charles Carson, Basil Dignam, Rosemary Dorken, Rachel Gurney, Waveney Lee, Martin Stephens, Alexander Archdale, Richard Marner, John Horsley, Ronald Leigh-Hunt.*

A TOUCH OF THE SUN (1956) [2]

Dir *Gordon Parry.* Prod and PC *Raymond Stross.* Scr *Alfred Shaughnessy.* Ph *Arthur Grant.* Dis *Eros. 81 mins. Cert U*

A hotel porter (*Frankie Howerd*) wanting the sack so that he can spend a £10,000 legacy on the Riviera causes chaos at his hotel for fun and is promptly fired. Soon back disillusioned with a life of leisure, he buys the hotel, disguises the staff as guests to impress potential backers, and makes a roaring success of his new venture. Corny comedy does disservice to its talented cast.

RoC *Dorothy Bromily, Dennis Price, Ruby Murray, Gordon Harker, Reginald Beckwith, Richard Wattis, Alfie Bass, Willoughby Goddard, Katherine Kath, Colin Gordon, Naomi Chance, Pierre Dudan, Miriam Karlin, Esma Cannon, Edna Morris, Ian Whittaker, Brian Summers, Lee Young, George Margo, Ann George, Jed Brown, Lucy Griffiths, Evelyn Roberts, John Vere.*

A TOWN LIKE ALICE (1956) [4]

Dir *Jack Lee.* Prod *Joseph Janni.* Scr *W.P. Lipscomb, Richard Mason, from the novel by Nevil Shute.* Ph *Geoffrey Unsworth.* PC *Vic/Rank.* Dis *Rank. 117 mins. Cert A*

Virginia McKenna and Takagi in A Town Like Alice *(1956)*

World War II. When their men are taken prisoner, women and children of British civilians in Malaya are forced to set off on a long trek. No Japanese officer will take responsibility for them, and many die from starvation and disease. Their leader, Jean (*Virginia McKenna*) becomes involved with an Australian (*Peter Finch*) who steals food for them but is tortured for his pains. After the war, Jean learns that he survived, and they are reunited at his home town, Alice Springs. Grim, moving saga of survival. British Oscars: best actor, best actress.
RoC *Takagi, Tran Van Khe, Jean Anderson, Marie Lohr, Maureen Swanson, Renee Houston, Nora Nicholson, Eileen Moore, John Fabian, Tim Turner, Vi Ngoc Tuan, Geoffrey Keen, Vincent Ball, June Shaw, Armine Sandford, Mary Allen, Virginia Clay, Bay White, Philippa Morgan, Dorothy Moss, Gwenda Ewen, Josephine Miller, Edwina Carroll, Sanny Bin Hussein, Yamada, Nakamishi, Ikada, Charles Marshall, Cameron Moore, Jane White, Margaret Eaden, Meg Buckingham, Domenic Lieven, Peter John, Geoffrey Hawkins.*

TOWN ON TRIAL! (1956)   ☐4
Dir *John Guillermin*. Prod *Maxwell Setton*. Scr *Robert Westerby, Ken Hughes*. Ph *Basil Emmott*. PC *Marksman*. Dis *Columbia. 96 mins. Cert A*

When the local good-time girl of a country village is found strangled, Scotland Yard's Halloran (*John Mills*) is called in and, his brusque manner soon alienating the locals, suspects the mayor, Dixon (*Geoffrey Keen*) and his daughter (*Elizabeth Seal*) – who is the next victim – as well as Dr Fenner (*Charles Coburn*), blackmailer Roper (*Derek Farr*) whose baby the first victim was expecting and Crowley (*Alec McCowen*), a sensitive young man who proves to be a dangerous schizoid and the real killer. Halloran arrests him after a chase up the local steeple. Well-made mystery with frightening murders and a tense climax.
RoC *Barbara Bates, Fay Compton, Margaretta Scott, Meredith Edwards, Magda Miller, Maureen Connell, Harry Locke, David Quitak, Dandy Nichols, Raymond Huntley.*

TRACK THE MAN DOWN (1954)   ☐1
Dir *R.G. Springsteen*. Prod *William N. Boyle*. Scr *Paul Erickson, Kenneth R. Hayles*. Ph *Basil*

Emmott. PC and Dis *Republic 75 mins. Cert A*
Rick (*George Rose*) double-crosses his accomplices after a racetrack robbery. The case with the money is passed from Rick's girl Mary (*Ursula Howells*) to her sister (*Petula Clark*) who takes it to the coast to the suspicion of reporter Don Ford (*Kent Taylor*) who shares the same coach. Rick captures the coach, but his associate – whom he shoots – and the police arrive in time for a showdown. Fragmented, silly thriller; a few unintentional laughs. Virtually the end of Petula Clark's British screen career.
RoC *Renee Houston, Charles Lloyd Pack, Arthur Lane, Mary Mackenzie, Walter Rilla, Kenneth Griffith, John Pike, Lloyd Lamble, Michael Balfour, Grahame Ashley, Michael Golden, John Singer, Bartlett Mullins, Frank Atkinson, John Welsh, Iris Vandeleur, Mona Lilian, Jack Lambert, Richard Molinas, Noel Hood, Brian Franklin, Eric Lander, Hugh Cameron, Ted Palmer.*

THE TRAITOR (1957)   ☐2
(USA: *The Accused*)
Dir and Scr *Michael McCarthy*. Prod *E.J. Fancey*. Ph *Bert Mason*. PC *Fantur Films*. Dis *New Realm. 88 mins. Cert A*
Colonel Price (*Donald Wolfit*), a wartime resistance leader, invites wartime colleagues to a reunion to find out which one of them betrayed the unit to the Gestapo. An agent who knows the identity of the traitor is murdered before he can talk. And Price has to face responsibility for a second killing that night before the betrayer is unmasked. Talky enough for a radio script, this drama drags on screen.
RoC *Jane Griffiths, Robert Bray, Anton Diffring, Carl Jaffe, Oscar Quitak, Rupert Davies, John Van Eyssen, Karel Stepanek, Christopher Lee.*

TREAD SOFTLY (1952)   ☐2
Dir *David Macdonald*. Prod *Donald Ginsberg, Vivian Cox*. Scr *Gerald Verner, from his radio serial* The Show Must Go On. Ph *Reginald Wyer*. PC *Albany*. Dis *Apex. 71 mins. Cert A*
Madeleine (*Frances Day*), star of an upcoming London musical, walks out on the orders of her impresario friend (*Olaf Olsen*), who hopes to buy up the show. But the producer (*John Bentley*) rents a 'haunted' theatre – on the owner's condition that the dressing-room of her husband, murdered there, remains locked. The owner's son is killed on stage, and the locked room opened: inside is the body of Madeleine. Police trap the killer on opening night. Lifeless musical thriller.
RoC *Patricia Dainton, John Laurie, Nora Nicholson, Harry Locke, Betty Baskcomb, Robert Urquhart, Michael Ward, Betty Hare, Ronald Leigh-Hunt, Hamilton Keene, Anthony Verner, Colin Croft, Nelly Arno.*

TREAD SOFTLY STRANGER (1958)   ☐2
Dir *Gordon Parry*. Prod and Scr *George Minter, Denis O'Dell, from the play by Jack Popplewell*. Ph *Douglas Slocombe*. PC *Alderdale*. Dis *Renown. 91 mins. Cert A*
A Yorkshire town. Dave (*Terence Morgan*), who has embezzled £300 to keep his flighty

girlfriend Calico (*Diana Dors*) in goodies, is joined by his brother Johnny (*George Baker*), on the run from racetrack creditors. Dave decides to solve their problems in a robbery, but he panics and kills a nightwatchman, whose son traces a missing witness, bringing a confession from Dave, who is unaware the man is blind. Thriller has silly dialogue, fails to make use of its Rotherham backgrounds. Theme song sung by Jim Dale.
RoC *Patrick Allen, Jane Griffiths, Maureen Delany, Betty Warren, Thomas Heathcote, Russell Napier, Wilfrid Lawson, Norman MacOwan, Joseph Tomelty, Chris Fay, Terry Baker, Timothy Bateson, John Salew, Michael Golden, George Merritt, Jack McNaughton, Andrew Keir, Hal Osmond, Norman Pierce, Patrick Crean, Sandra Francis.*

TREASURE AT THE MILL (1957)   ☐4
Dir *Max Anderson*. Prod *A.V. Curtice*. Scr *Mary Cathcart Borer, from a story by Malcolm Saville*. Ph *Jimmy Ewins*. PC *Wallace/Children's Film Foundation*. Dis *British Lion. 61 mins. Cert U*
Adams (*Richard Palmer*) and Wilson (*John Ruddock*) both hunt for treasure one of Adams' ancestors is supposed to have hidden in a mill. Adams befriends the Pettits, the new owners of the mill, who help him discover the treasure and outwit Wilson, who employs Adams' mother, for whom Adams will now be able to buy a cottage. Refreshingly shot against natural backgrounds (mainly Dedham in Essex) and crisply acted; a good children's film.
RoC *Merrilyn Pettit, Hilary Pettit, Harry Pettit Jr, Mr and Mrs Harry Pettit Sr.*

TREASURE HUNT (1952)   ☐3
Dir *John Paddy Carstairs*. Prod and Scr *Anatole de Grunwald, from the play by M.J. Farrell and John Perry*. Ph *C. Pennington-Richards*. PC *Romulus*. Dis *British Lion/Independent Film Distributors. 79 mins. Cert U*
In an Irish mansion whose owner has proved to be penniless, paying guests are invited to restore the family fortunes, to the discomfort of the largely potty older members of the family, who lay various traps to get rid of the Americans who descend on them. When Anna Rose (*Martita Hunt*) discovers a nest of valuable rubies in her gigantic hat, the need for visitors is over. Cast play with spirit but on several different levels: farce varies between flat and fizzy.
RoC *Jimmy Edwards, Naunton Wayne, Athene Seyler, June Clyde, Miles Malleson, Susan Stephen, Brian Worth, Mara Lane, Maire O'Neill, Toke Townley, Bee Duffell, Joseph Tomelty, John McDarby, Tony Quinn, Wilfred Caithness, Hamlyn Benson, Irene Handl, Sheila Carty, Kendrick Owen, Marguerite Brennan, Diana Campbell, John Kelly, Kenneth Kove, Patrick O'Connor, James Page, Roger Maxwell, Nella Occleppo, Michael Ripper, Fred Johnson, Alfie Bass.*

TREASURE ISLAND (1950)   ☐4
Dir *Byron Haskin*. Prod *Perce Pearce*. Scr *Lawrence E. Watkin, from the novel by Robert*

Louis Stevenson. Ph *F.A. Young*. PC *Walt Disney-RKO British*. Dis *RKO Radio*. Technicolor. 96 mins. Cert U

1750s. An old sea captain, Billy Bones (*Finlay Currie*), receives two pirate visitors at his inn, Black Dog (*Francis de Wolff*), and Blind Pew (*John Laurie*), who gives him the Black Spot, frightening him to death. Bones' map of Captain Flint's treasure falls into the hands of innkeeper's son Jim Hawkins (*Bobby Driscoll*) who takes part in an expedition to the island where it is buried. A rascally sea cook, Long John Silver (*Robert Newton*) leads a mutiny, but later switches sides and escapes to the high seas with a bag of gold. Full-blooded version of the famous yarn with an unforgettable central performance.

RoC *Basil Sydney, Walter Fitzgerald, Denis O'Dea, Ralph Truman, Geoffrey Keen, Geoffrey Wilkinson, John Gregson, William Devlin, Harry Locke, Jim O'Brady, Stephen Jack, Reginald Drummond, David Davies, Andrew Blackett, Eddie Moran, Howard Douglas, Sam Kydd, Harold Jamieson, Bob Head, Ken Buckle, Paddy Brannigan, Jack Arrow, Freddie Clark*.

Robert Newton and Bobby Driscoll in Treasure Island (*1950*)

THE TREASURE OF SAN TERESA

(1959) [2]

Dir *Alvin Rakoff*. Prod *John Nasht, Patrick Filmer-Sankey*. Scr *Jack Andrews, Jeffrey Dell*. Ph *Wilkie Cooper*. PC *Orbit*. Dis *British Lion/Britannia*. 81 mins. Cert A

Larry (*Eddie Constantine*), an American ex-secret serviceman, returns to Europe to retrieve jewels he had hidden for a dying Nazi general in 1944. He is helped by the general's daughter (*Dawn Addams*), now a prostitute, but double-crossed by a lawyer (*Marius Goring*) also in on the secret. Getting away with the gems, Larry is held by 'policemen' who prove to be fakes, finds the lawyer shot and finally sees the jewels sink to the bottom of a river. Confused, over-complicated thriller.

RoC *Nadine Tallier, Christopher Lee, Walter Gotell, Gaylord Cavallaro, Georgina Cookson, Willy Witte, Clive Dunn, Sheldon Lawrence, Penelope Horner, Derek Sydney, Hubert Mittendorf, Anna Turner, Leslie 'Hutch' Hutchinson, Marie Devereux, Thomas Gallagher, Susan Travers, Stella Bonheur, Tsai Chin, Diana Potter, Tom Bowman, Steve Plytas, Margaret Boyd, Egon Mohr, Walter Buhler*.

TRENT'S LAST CASE (1952) [2]

Dir and Prod *Herbert Wilcox*. Scr *Pamela Wilcox Bower*, from the novel by *E.C. Bentley*. Ph *Max Greene (Mutz Greenbaum)*. PC *Wilcox-Neagle*. Dis *British Lion*. 90 mins. Cert U

Philip Trent (*Michael Wilding*), reporter-turned-detective, sets out to prove that the death of wealthy financier Manderson (*Orson Welles*) was not suicide, but murder by his wife (*Margaret Lockwood*) and secretary (*John McCallum*) who were in love. But he is wrong: Manderson did kill himself, his attempt to frame Marlowe being foiled by his wife. Unwise, talky remake of story first filmed in 1920.

RoC *Miles Malleson, Hugh McDermott, Jack McNaughton, Sam Kydd, Eileen Joyce, Kenneth Williams*.

TRIO (1950) [4]

Dir *Ken Annakin, Harold French*. Prod *Antony Darnborough*. Scr *R.C. Sherriff, Noel Langley*, from stories by *W. Somerset Maugham*. Ph *Reginald Wyer, Geoffrey Unsworth*. PC *Gainsborough*. Dis *General Film Distributors*. 91 mins. Cert A

(1) A verger (*James Hayter*) is discharged when his vicar (*Michael Hordern*) finds out he is illiterate. The verger buys a small shop and in a few years is running a chain of stores. He turns the tables on the vicar. (2) A ship's bore, Mr Knowall (*Nigel Patrick*), a jeweller, saves a lady's blushes by saying that her real pearls are fake. (3) In a TB sanatorium, a girl and a retired army officer marry, knowing that one or both may die, and one of two quarrelling old men does die, leaving the other without purpose in life. Fairly good entertainment, doesn't quite make the most of source material. First two stories directed by Annakin, final segment by French.

RoC *Kathleen Harrison, Felix Aylmer, Lana Morris, Henry Edwards, Glyn Houston, Eliot Makeham, Harry Fowler, Anne Crawford, Naunton Wayne, Wilfrid Hyde White, Michael Medwin, Clive Morton, Bill Linden-Travers, Dennis Harkin, Jean Simmons, Michael Rennie, John Laurie, Finlay Currie, Roland Culver, Raymond Huntley, Betty Ann Davies, André Morell, Mary Merrall, Marjorie Fielding, Joan Schofield, Michael Ward*.

TRIPLE BLACKMAIL (1955) [1]

Dir *Paul Gerrard, David Macdonald*. Prod *Edward J. Danziger, Harry Lee Danziger*. Scr *Paul Tabori, Kate Barlay, James Eastwood, Elizabeth Berridge, Reginald Moore*. Ph *Jimmy Wilson*. PC *Danzigers*. Dis *Paramount*. 76 mins. Cert A

Three tales of blackmail. (1) A financier (*Philip Friend*) thinks his lovely young bride is being blackmailed, but she and her lover are plotting to kill him, which they do. (2) Depressed because her younger sisters are getting married, Gwen (*Marjorie Stewart*) sends herself flowers and love letters – which leads to a narrow escape from a blackmailer. (3) A bigamist (*Robert Ayres*) is suspected of killing a blackmailing detective hired by his first wife (*Adrienne Corri*) who is herself the killer. More poor TV drama piped into cinemas.

RoC *Betta St John, Philip Friend, Nicholas*

Hill, Mona Washbourne, Peter Neil, Ann Stephens, Mary Parker, George Howe, Ronan O'Casey, Robert O'Neil, Nanette Newman, Conrad Phillips, Ron Randell.*

THE TROLLENBERG TERROR

(1958) (USA: *The Crawling Eye*) [3]

Dir *Quintin Lawrence*. Prod *Robert S. Baker, Monty Berman*. Scr *Jimmy Sangster*, from a TV serial by *Peter Key*. Ph *Bergman*, Sp eff *Les Bowie*. PC *Tempean*. Dis *Eros*. 83 mins. Cert X

Something from outer space is lurking in a radioactive cloud at the top of a Swiss mountain. Victims' heads are wrenched from their bodies. With the help of two telepathic sisters (*Jennifer Jayne, Janet Munro*), UNO scientific investigator Alan Brooks (*Forrest Tucker*) prevents the aliens from spreading their influence. They are destroyed in a bombing raid. Fast rip-off of TV success.

RoC *Laurence Payne, Warren Mitchell, Andrew Faulds, Stuart Saunders, Frederick Schiller, Colin Douglas, Derek Sydney, Richard Golding, George Herbert, Anne Sharp, Caroline Glazier, Garard Green, Jeremy Longhurst, Anthony Parker, Leslie Heritage, Theodor Wilhelm*.

TROUBLE IN STORE (1953) [4]

Dir *John Paddy Carstairs*. Prod *Maurice Cowan*. Scr *Carstairs, Cowans, Ted Willis*. Ph *Ernest Steward*. PC *Two Cities/J. Arthur Rank*. Dis *General Film Distributors*. 85 mins. Cert U

A minion in a big London store, Norman's (*Norman Wisdom*) attempts to become a window dresser all end in chaos. At the staff social, he sets himself alight and ruins his boss's (*Jerry Desmonde*) speech. Trying to help a dreadnought shoplifter (*Margaret Rutherford*) with her ill-gotten gains doesn't help. But finally he thwarts a plot to rob the store and wins promotion and his shopgirl friend (*Lana Morris*). Cautiously received slapstick comedy produced nationwide queues.

RoC *Derek Bond, Moira Lister, Megs Jenkins, Joan Sims, Michael Brennan, Michael Ward, John Warwick, Perlita Nielson, Eddie Leslie, Cyril Chamberlain, Ronan O'Casey, John Warren, Ian Wilson, Esma Cannon*.

TROUBLE IN THE GLEN (1954) [2]

Dir and Prod *Herbert Wilcox*. Scr *Frank S. Nugent*. Ph *Max Greene (Mutz Greenbaum)*. PC *Republic/Wilcox-Neagle*. Dis *Republic*. Trucolor. 91 mins. Cert U

A South American tycoon (*Orson Welles*) takes up residence as a Highland laird in Scotland. He soons upsets locals, especially a little girl (*Margaret McCourt*) who asks a visiting American (*Forrest Tucker*) who is, unknowing, her father, to champion her cause. He falls in love with the laird's daughter (*Margaret Lockwood*) and prevents a possible battle between evicted tinkers and imported Glasgow thugs. Peace is restored to the glen. Curdled whimsy with Lockwood far from *Owd Bob*; Trucolor adds to the air of unreality.

RoC *John McCallum, Victor McLaglen, Eddie Byrne, Archie Duncan, Ann Gudrun, Moultrie Kelsall, Alex McCrindle, Mary Mackenzie, Jack Watling, Peter Sinclair, Janet Barrow,*

Albert Chevalier, George Cormack, Dorothea Dell, Grizelda Hervey, Alastair Hunter, William Kelly, Stevenson Lang, Robin Lloyd, Duncan McIntyre, Jock McKay, Michael Shepley, Jack Stewart, F.A. Vinyals.

TROUBLE WITH EVE (1959)   [1]

Dir *Francis Searle*. Prod *Tom Blakeley*. Scr *Brock Williams, from a play by June Garland.* Ph *James Harvey*. PC *Blakeley's*. Dis *Butchers*. 65 mins. Cert A

Blonde widow Louise (*Hy Hazell*) causes ripples in Warlock village with her plans to turn her cottage into a tearoom. Things seem to be settling back to normal when the chairman (*Robert Urquhart*) of the council falls for her, but the arrival of Louise's daughter Eve (*Sally Smith*) with her 'beatnik' friends from Paris ends in a riot, with Louise winning through in the end. Slapstick farce devoid of inspiration.

RoC *Garry Marsh, Vera Day, Tony Quinn, Brenda Hogan, Denis Shaw, Bill Shine, Bruce Seton, Iris Vandeleur, Kim Shelley, Grace D. Russell, Frank Atkinson, David Grahame.*

TRUE AS A TURTLE (1956)   [3]

Dir *Wendy Toye*. Prod *Peter de Sarigny*. Scr *Jack Davies, John Coates, Nicholas Phipps, from Coates' novel.* Ph *Reginald Wyer*. PC and Dis *Rank*. Eastman Colour. 96 mins. Cert U

A channel voyage on the yacht *Turtle* includes the owners (*Cecil Parker, Avice Landone*), a honeymooning couple (*John Gregson, June Thorburn*), the owners' cousin (*Elvi Hale*) and a friend of the family (*Keith Michell*), who is suspected of being a crook, but turns out to be a casino security officer out to get the owner's wife for using fake counters. She proves to be innocent, and all concerned are rescued in the end from a *Turtle* broken down in thick fog. Happy-go lucky, if slackly paced comedy.

RoC *Betty Stockfeld, Jacques Brunius, Charles Clay, Gabrielle Brune, Michael Bryant, Pauline Drewett, John Harvey, Beth Rogan.*

THE TRUTH ABOUT WOMEN (1957)   [4]

Dir *Muriel Box*. Prod *Sydney Box*. Scr *Muriel and Sydney Box*. Ph *Otto Heller*. PC *Beaconsfield*. Dis *British Lion*. Eastman Colour. 107 mins. Cert A

To guide his son-in-law through a problem with his daughter, diplomat Humphrey (*Laurence Harvey*) recounts his own amorous adventures. He is bewildered by suffragette

Eva Gabor and Laurence Harvey in The Truth About Women (*1957*)

Ambrosine (*Diane Cilento*); banished from Yekrut for trying to smuggle out a slave girl (*Jackie Lane*); bamboozled by Parisienne Louise (*Eva Gabor*) whose husband challenges him to a duel; jilted by an American heiress (*Lisa Gastoni*); married by a painter (*Julie Harris*), who dies in childbirth; nursed through war wounds by Julie (*Mai Zetterling*) whom he loves but loses. Humphrey's life comes full circle when he re-encounters Ambrosine and marries her. In-and-out, but warmly elegant, richly coloured charade.

RoC *Michael Denison, Derek Farr, Roland Culver, Elina Labourdette, Wilfrid Hyde White, Marius Goring, Christopher Lee, Griffith Jones, Catherine Boyle, Thorley Walters, Ernest Thesiger, Ambrosine Phillpotts, Robert Rietty, Balbina, Aletha Orr, Hal Osmond, John Glyn-Jones.*

TURN THE KEY SOFTLY (1953)   [3]

Dir *Jack Lee*. Prod *Maurice Cowan*. Scr *Lee, Cowan, John Brophy, from Brophy's novel.* Ph *Geoffrey Unsworth*. PC *Chiltern*. Dis *General Film Distributors*. 81 mins. Cert A

Three women are released from Holloway Prison: Monica (*Yvonne Mitchell*), a burglar's mistress; Mrs Quilliam (*Kathleen Harrison*), an elderly dog-loving kleptomaniac; and Stella (*Joan Collins*), a high-class prostitute. Both Stella and Monica are almost sucked back into crime but escape. Mrs Quilliam, after a shoplifting spree, loses her dog and is run over looking for it. It is cared for by Monica. Melodrama given its head; realism scarcely gets a look in.

RoC *Terence Morgan, Dorothy Alison, Thora Hird, Glyn Houston, Geoffrey Keen, Russell Waters, Clive Morton, Richard Massingham.*

24 HOURS OF A WOMAN'S LIFE (1952)   [2]

Dir *Victor Saville*. Prod *Ivan Foxwell*. Scr *Warren Chetham Strode, from the novel by Stefan Zweig*. Ph *Christopher Challis*. PC *Associated British*. Dis *AB-Pathé*. Technicolor. 89 mins. Cert A

The Riviera. Seeing a café-owner's daughter elope with a stranger, novelist Robert Stirling (*Leo Genn*) tells a story of the past, in which a young widow (*Merle Oberon*) was befriended by a young gambler (*Richard Todd*) on the verge of ruin. They fell in love, but she was unable to save him from his addiction, or suicide. Stirling's wife walks in: it is the ex-widow. Very slow tear-jerker with lush settings.

RoC *Stephen Murray, Peter Reynolds, Joan Dowling, June Clyde, Isabel Dean, Robert Ayres, Mara Lane, Peter Illing, Jacques Brunius, Peter Jones, Yvonne Furneaux, Madame d'Alvarez, Jeanne Pili, Peter Hobbes, Trader Faulkner, Pierre Le Fèvre, Moultrie Kelsall, Jacques Cey, Jill Clifford.*

TWICE UPON A TIME (1953)   [2]

Dir, Prod and Scr *Emeric Pressburger, from a novel by Erich Kastner.* Ph *Christopher Challis*. PC *London Films*. Dis *British Lion*. 76 mins. Cert U

Twins (*Yolande and Charmian Larthe*), long-parted from each other by divorced parents, meet at a Tyrolean holiday camp, find out who they are, switch places, and contrive to bring their parents back together again. A remake of the 1951 German film *Das doppelte Löttchen*, and remade by Disney in Hollywood in 1961 as *The Parent Trap*. This version is sticky and not well acted.

RoC *Jack Hawkins, Elizabeth Allan, Hugh Williams, Violetta Elvin, Isabel Dean, Michael Gough, Walter Fitzgerald, Eileen Elton, Kenneth Melville, Norah Gordon, Isabel George, Cecily Wager, Molly Terraine, Martin Miller, Lilly Kann, Jean Stuart, Margaret Boyd, Myrette Morven, Elizabeth Arnold, Jack Lambert, Archie Duncan, Colin Wilcox, Monica Thomson, Pat Baker, Margaret McCourt, Alanna Boyce, Isla Richardson.*

THE TWO-HEADED SPY (1958)   [2]

Dir *André De Toth*. Prod *Hal E. Chester, Bill Kirby*. Scr *James O'Donnell*. Ph *Ted Scaife*. PC *Sabre*. Dis *Columbia*. 93 mins. Cert U

Schottland (*Jack Hawkins*), a 'plant' in the German officer corps for many years, is an Englishman working for the Allies, steering clear of romantic involvements, and sharing a passion for clocks with his contact, Cornaz (*Felix Aylmer*), who is eventually discovered by the Gestapo and murdered. His new contact is Lili (*Gia Scala*) and, despite danger from a young Nazi officer (*Erik Schumann*) attracted to her, Schottland remains undiscovered until the times comes in 1945 to make his escape. Fascinating true story, but rather badly made.

RoC *Alexander Knox, Laurence Naismith, Edward Underdown, Donald Pleasence, Martin Benson, Kenneth Griffith, Walter Hudd, Harriette Johns, Geoffrey Bayldon, Richard Grey, Michael Caine, Victor Woolf, Ronald Hines, Martin Boddey, Desmond Roberts, Victor Fairley, Thorp Devereaux, Peter Swanwick, Deering Wells, John McClaren, Peter Welch, John Dunmar, Martin Sterndale.*

TWO ON THE TILES (1951)   [3]

Dir *John Guillermin*. Prod *Roger Proudlock*. Scr *Alec Coppel*. Ph *Ray Elton*. PC *Vandyke*. Dis *Grand National*. 72 mins. Cert A

A young wife (*Brenda Bruce*) is forced to spend a night on a ship when she fails to leave a party there on time. Her husband (*Hugh McDermott*), who is in Paris, is given the same room as an attractive young woman, with whose problems he becomes involved. Later, both are blackmailed by their butler (*Herbert Lom*), until they unite against him, and reveal the woman in Paris to have been his wife. Comedy has slim material, but is well performed.

RoC *Ingeborg Wells, Humphrey Lestocq, G.A. Guinle, Les Compagnons de la Chanson.*

U

THE UGLY DUCKLING (1959) [3]

Dir *Lance Comfort*. Prod *Michael Carreras, Tommy Lyndon-Haynes*. Scr *Sid Colin, Jack Davies, from characters by Robert Louis Stevenson*. Ph *Michael Reed*. PC *Hammer*. Dis *Columbia*. 84 mins. Cert U

Henry (*Bernard Bresslaw*), gormless descendant of the infamous Jekyll family, accidentally triggers an explosion which reveals his great grandfather's famous formula for personality change. In no time, Henry is transforming himself into suave, fearless criminal Teddy Hyde. Reverting to Jekyll, he finds the proceeds of a jewel robbery in his pockets, and proceeds to round up the gang. Comedy fails to build on its original good idea.

RoC *Jean Muir, Jon Pertwee, Reginald Beckwith, Maudie Edwards, Richard Wattis, Elwyn Brook-Jones, Michael Ripper, David Lodge, Harold Goodwin, Norma Marla, Keith Smith, Michael Ward, John Harvey, Jess Conrad, Mary Wilson, Geremy Philips, Vicky Marshall, Jill Carson, Cyril Chamberlain, Alan Coleshill, Jean Driant, Nicholas Tanner, Shelagh Dey, Ian Wilson, Verne Morgan, Sheila Hammond, Ian Ainsley, Reginald Marsh, Roger Avon, Richard Statman, Robert Desmond, Alexander Doré*.

Jean Muir and Bernard Bresslaw in The Ugly Duckling *(1959)*

UNDERCOVER GIRL (1957) [1]

Dir *Francis Searle*. Prod *Kay Luckwell, D.E.A. Winn*. Scr *Bernard Lewis, Bill Luckwell*. Ph *Jimmy Harvey*. PC *Bill & Michael Luckwell*. Dis *Butchers*. 68 mins. Cert A

A reporter on the verge of exposing a drugpeddling ring is killed before he can write his story. His brother (*Paul Carpenter*) is helped in his efforts to avenge his death by a girl (*Kay Callard*) who works undercover at the nightclub whose owner proves to be not only a blackmailer but the brains behind the narcotics ring. Capable cast swamped by truly dreadful treatment of story, including a fight where the 'punches' miss by miles. Deplorable.

RoC *Bruce Seton, Monica Grey, Tony Quinn, Jackie Collins, Kim Parker, Maya Koumani, John Boxer, Alexander Field, Paddy Ryan, Milton Reid, Eleanor Leigh, Robert Raglan, George Roderick, Michael Moore, Totti Truman Taylor, Mark Hashfield, Gerry Collins*.

UP FOR THE CUP (1950) [4]

Dir *Jack Raymond*. Prod *Henry Halstead*. Scr *Con West, Jack Marks*. Ph *Henry Harris*. PC *Citadel/Byron*. Dis *Associated British*. 76 mins. Cert U

Yorkshire mill-worker Albert Entwhistle (*Albert Modley*) takes his wife to London to see the shops (and the Cup Final). He loses first her, then his wallet with his ticket for the match. But everything comes right in the end. Wild comedy never lets up throughout, is one of the best of the 'regional' farces.

RoC *Mai Bacon, Harold Berens, Wallas Eaton, Charmian Innes, Helen Christie, Jack Melford, Fred Groves, John Warren, Arthur Gomez, Lilli Molnar*.

UP IN THE WORLD (1956) [4]

Dir *John Paddy Carstairs*. Prod *Hugh Stewart*. Scr *Jack Davies, Henry E. Blyth, Peter Blackmore*. Ph *Jack Cox*. PC and Dis *Rank* 91 mins. Cert U

There are lots of windows for Norman (*Norman Wisdom*) to clean at Banderville Manor, and plenty of time for him to become the butt of young Sir Reggie (*Michael Caridia*), who forces Norman to take him to a nightclub. At the club, Norman foils an attempt to kidnap the little bart, who is knocked out and loses his memory – as a result of which Norman is convicted of kidnapping and gets 25 years. He escapes and Sir Reggie gets another bump on the head which restores his memory. Comedy is uninventive, but Wisdom makes it funny in parts.

RoC *Maureen Swanson, Jerry Desmonde, Ambrosine Phillpotts, Michael Ward, Jill Dixon, Edwin Styles, William Lucas, Lionel Jeffries, Cyril Chamberlain, Eddie Leslie, Bernard Bresslaw, Ian Wilson*.

Maureen Swanson, Norman Wisdom and Colin Gordon in Up in the World *(1956)*

UPSTAIRS AND DOWNSTAIRS (1959) [2]

Dir *Ralph Thomas*. Prod *Betty E. Box*. Scr *Frank Harvey, from the novel by Ronald Scott*

Thorne. Ph *Ernest Steward*. PC and Dis *Rank*. Eastman Colour. 101 mins. Cert A

When he marries the boss's daughter (*Anne Heywood*), Richard (*Michael Craig*) finds he has to take over the entertaining of important clients. Unfortunately, he and his wife seem to get through more maids than dinners. There's an Italian nymphomaniac, an alcoholic, a disaster-prone Welsh girl, a bank robber and a Swede (*Mylene Demongeot*) who wreaks havoc with the clients. Finally, they find the perfect servant – an ex-policeman! Fairly dire comedy almost saved by Demongeot's sparkle in the last half-hour.

RoC *James Robertson Justice, Daniel Massey, Claudia Cardinale, Sidney James, Joan Hickson, Joan Sims, Joseph Tomelty, Nora Nicholson, Reginald Beckwith, Irene Handl, Austin Willis, Margalo Gillmore, Cyril Chamberlain, Dilys Laye, William Mervyn, Eric Pohlmann, Jean Cadell, Barbara Everest, Barbara Steele, Stephen Gregson, Nicholas Phipps, Jeremy Burnham, Nicholas Parsons, Hal Osmond, Madge Ryan, Betty Henderson, Gaylord Cavallaro, Bill Edwards, David Cargill, Shirley Lawrence, Shirley Ann Field, Susan Hampshire*.

UP THE CREEK (1958) [4]

Dir *Val Guest*. Prod *Henry Halstead*. Scr (*all uncredited*) *Guest, John Warren, Len Heath*. Ph *Arthur Grant*. PC *Byron*. Dis *Warner Bros*. HammerScope. 83 mins. Cert U

Rocket-mad Lt Fairweather (*David Tomlinson*), having conducted disastrous experiments at naval stations all over the country, is finally assigned to a mothballed cruiser at the end of a creek, where he finds the crew, led by the wily bo'sun (*Peter Sellers*), have established a thriving black-market for ship's stores with nearby villagers. They are all saved from court martial when a visiting admiral (*Wilfrid Hyde White*) fires off Fairweather's home-made rocket and sinks the ship. Broad but funny traditional farce; could have done with lighter handling.

RoC *Liliane Sottane, Lionel Jeffries, Lionel Murton, Vera Day, Reginald Beckwith, Sam Kydd, John Warren, David Lodge, Michael Goodliffe, Frank Pettingell, Tom Gill, Howard Williams, Peter Collingwood, Barry Lowe, Edwin Richfield, Max Butterfield, Malcolm Ransom, Donald Bisset, Leonard Fenton, Basil Dignam, Peter Coke, Jack McNaughton, Larry Noble, Patrick Cargill, Michael Ripper*.

UP TO HIS NECK (1954) [3]

Dir *John Paddy Carstairs*. Prod *Hugh Stewart*. Scr *Patrick Kirwan, Carstairs, Ted Willis* (*uncredited*), *Maurice Cowan*. Ph *Ernest Steward*. PC *Group*. Dis *General Film Distributors*. 91 mins. Cert U

Seaman Carter (*Ronald Shiner*), left in charge of naval stores on a South Sea island, has been forgotten for 10 years. The islanders have made him king. Then a naval landing party 'rescues' him and details him to train jungle commandos out to recapture a submarine from bandits. Tagged as a deserter, Carter panics and is taken by the bandits; but his Polynesian cutie (*Laya Raki*) helps him turn the tables and become a hero. Laboured remake of *Jack Ahoy!* (1934).

RoC *Harry Fowler, Brian Rix, Bryan Forbes, Anthony Newley, Colin Gordon, Michael Brennan, Gerald Campion, John Warwick, Martin Boddy, Alec Mango, Hattie Jacques, Roland Curram, Jan Miller, Norman Mitchell, Kim Parker, Shirley Burniston, Ruth Sheal, Eileen Sands, Harold Kasket.*

V

VALLEY OF EAGLES (1951) [2]

Dir and Scr *Terence Young*. Prod *Nat A. Bronsten, George Willoughby*. Ph *Harry Waxman*. PC *Independent Sovereign*. Dis *General Film Distributors*. 86 mins. Cert U

The wife (*Mary Laura Wood*) and assistant (*Anthony Dawson*) of Swedish scientist Nils (*John McCallum*) run off together, taking part of his machinery for extracting power from sound waves. With a police inspector (*Jack Warner*), Nils pursues them to Lapland, where, joined by a girl school-inspector (*Nadia Gray*) and two children, they are besieged by wolves until rescued by a Lapp tribe who hunt with eagles trained like falcons. The fugitives are killed by an avalanche. Flatly written thriller wastes locations and action scenes.

RoC *Norman MacOwan, Martin Boddey, Christopher Lee, Ewen Solon, Alfred Maurstad, Niama Wiwstrand, George Willoughby, Peter Blitz, Sarah Crawford, Molly Warner, Triliot Billqvist, Gosta Cederlund, Sten Lindgren, Kurt Sundström, Holger Kax.*

VALLEY OF SONG (1952) [4]
(USA: *Men Are Children Twice*)

Dir *Gilbert Gunn*. Prod *Vaughan N. Dean*. Scr *Phil Park, Cliff Gordon, from a play by Gordon*. Ph *Lionel Banes*. PC *Associated British*. Dis *AB-Pathé*. 74 mins. Cert U

A small Welsh village is dominated by the Davies and Lloyd families. A feud arises between them after the choice of a Mrs Davies to sing contralto in Handel's *Messiah*, which a Mrs Lloyd has sung for 15 years. Young lovers Cliff Lloyd (*John Fraser*) and Olwen Davies (*Maureen Swanson*), failing to elope, help to bring about a reconciliation between the families. The choirmaster (*Clifford Evans*) decides the ladies shall share the part. Extremely pleasant comedy, affectionately done.

RoC *Mervyn Johns, Rachel Thomas, Betty Cooper, Rachel Roberts, Hugh Pryse, Edward Evans, Kenneth Evans, Kenneth Williams, Howell Davis, Emrys Leyshon, Prysor Williams, Desmond Llewellyn, Ronnie Harries, John Wynn, Dudley Jones, John Glyn Jones, Madoline Thomas, Olwen Brookes, Ben Williams, Ann Elsden, Sarah Davies, Valentine Dunn, Eric Francis, Alun Owen, Denys Graham, Lane Meddick.*

VALUE FOR MONEY (1955) [3]

Dir *Ken Annakin*. Prod *Sergei Nolbandov*. Scr *R.F. Delderfield, William Fairchild, from the novel by Derrick Boothroyd*. Ph *Geoffrey Unsworth*. PC *Group*. Dis *Rank*. Technicolor. VistaVision. 93 mins. Cert U

After a spat with his girl Ethel (*Susan Stephen*), North Country rag millionaire Chayley (*John Gregson*) takes himself off to London, becoming involved with showgirl Ruthine (*Diana Dors*), who believes him to be poor and refuses his proposal. Discovering the truth, Ruthine rushes to accept. Chayley gets cold feet when she goes on a spending spree and, although Ethel gets him back, Ruthine does get another rich Yorkshireman. Quite lively comedy along traditional British lines.

RoC *Derek Farr, Frank Pettingell, Jill Adams, Charles Victor, Donald Pleasence, Joan Hickson, Hal Osmond, Ernest Thesiger, James Gregson, Sheila Raynor, Ronald Chesney, Leslie Phillips, Paddy Stone, Irving Davies, Sheila O'Neil, Ruth Shiel, Carol Day, Eleanor Fazan, Jane Doré, Oliver Reed, Mavis Greenaway, Julia Arnall.*

VENETIAN BIRD (1952) [3]
(USA: *The Assassin*)

Dir *Ralph Thomas*. Prod *Betty Box*. Scr *Victor Canning, from his novel*. Ph *Ernest Steward*. PC *British Film Makers*. Dis *General Film Distributors*. 95 mins. Cert A

Edward Mercer (*Richard Todd*) is hired by an American to trace a patriot who helped him in the war. In Venice, Mercer finds himself wandering in a maze of political intrigue, and eventually discovers the man he is looking for is now a hired assassin (*John Gregson*). He imprisons Mercer and frames him for murder. The detective escapes and the assassin is hunted to his death. Grade C relative of *The Third Man*, talkative but briskly directed.

RoC *Eva Bartok, George Coulouris, Margot Grahame, Walter Rilla, John Bailey, Sidney James, Martin Boddey, Michael Balfour, Sydney Tafler, Miles Malleson, Eric Pohlmann, David Hurst, Raymond Young, Ferdy Mayne, Jill Clifford, Eileen Way, Toni Lucarda, Janice Kane, Meier Tzelniker.*

THE VICIOUS CIRCLE (1957) [4]
(USA: *The Circle*)

Dir *Gerald Thomas*. Prod *Peter Rogers*. Scr *Francis Durbridge, from his TV serial* The Brass Candlestick. Ph *Otto Heller*. PC *Romulus/Beaconsfield*. Dis *Independent Film Distributors/British Lion*. 84 mins. Cert U

Dr Latimer (*John Mills*), acting for a film producer friend, meets Frieda (*Lisa Daniely*), a film star, at the airport, where he is helped by Windsor (*Lionel Jeffries*), an odd reporter, who drives her off to Claridges, while Latimer meets Laura (*Noelle Middleton*), his fiancée, and Ken Palmer (*Derek Farr*), his friend. He is rung by Dr Kimber (*Mervyn Johns*) for advice on a patient, Mrs Ambler (*René Ray*), who tells him she's seen a body with a candlestick nearby. Frieda is found dead in Latimer's flat (with half a candlestick nearby), but Mrs Ambler who is later also murdered, says Latimer's story is all lies and she doesn't know Kimber.

John Mills and Roland Culver in The Vicious Circle (*1957*)

Further, the producer never called him, Windsor doesn't exist, Frieda never went to Claridges and half a candlestick is found in Latimer's car. He suspects Laura, and the mysterious Brady (*Wilfrid Hyde White*), who turns out to be a special agent using Latimer as bait to catch an international crook – Ken, who tries to gas Latimer (who is saved by Laura) before police trap him. Fast-paced, fiendishly complicated whodunnit.

RoC *Roland Culver, Diana Lambert, David Williams, John Gordon.*

THE VILLAGE (1953) [3]

Dir *Leopold Lindtberg*. Prod *Lazar Wechsler, Kenneth Maidment*. Scr *David Weschler, Elizabeth Montagu, Lindtberg*. Ph *Emil Berna*. PC *Rosslyn*. Dis *AB-Pathé*. 83 mins. Cert U

Alan (*John Justin*) and Wanda (*Eva Dahlbeck*), teachers at the Pestalozzi Children's Village for war orphans, fall in love. Two of the children, Anja and Andrzej (*Krystina Bragiel, Voytek Dolinsky*) become great friends and are desolate at the thought of being parted. They run away together, but Andrzej falls from a ledge of the castle in which they are hiding, and is killed. Sincere story of real-life village fails to stir the emotions.

RoC *Trevor Hill, Mary Hinton, Guido Lorraine, W. Woytecki, Sigfrit Steiner.*

VIOLENT MOMENT (1958) [2]

Dir *Sidney Hayers*. Prod *Bernard Coote*. Scr *Peter Barnes*. Ph *Phil Grindrod*. PC *Independent Artists*. Dis *Anglo-Amalgamated*. 61 mins. Cert A

Deserting the army in war, Baines (*Lyndon Brook*) strangles his mistress (*Jane Hylton*) on discovering she has sold their son for adoption. He takes the child's tumbler doll; years later, when he is a successful businessman engaged to his secretary (*Jill Browne*), the doll, following a burglary at her flat, is his final undoing. Contrived, shabbily acted (apart from Brook) drama.

RoC *John Paul, Rupert Davies, Moira Redmond, Bruce Seton, Martin Miller, Frederick Piper, Martin Boddey, Gerald Anderson, Leonard White.*

VIOLENT PLAYGROUND (1957) [3]

Dir *Basil Dearden*. Prod *Michael Relph*. Scr *James Kennaway from his novel*. Ph *Reginald Wyer*. PC and Dis *Rank*. 108 mins. Cert U

Moved into the juvenile crime department, Liverpool detective Truman (*Stanley Baker*) suspects that Johnny (*David McCallum*), the older brother of the two tearaways he's keeping an eye on, is responsible for the cases of arson on which he was working before his transfer. Killing a van-driver in attempting a getaway, Johnny takes the two children hostage, but is persuaded to give himself up by his older sister (*Anne Heywood*) with whom Truman is in love. Social conscience thriller doesn't bite deep enough.
RoC *Peter Cushing, John Slater, Clifford Evans, Moultrie Kelsall, George A. Cooper, Brona Boland, Fergal Boland, Michael Chow, Tsai Chin, Gerrard Gibson, Benice Swanson, Sean Lynch, Fred Fowell, Sheila Raynor, Christopher Cooke, Irene Arnold, Oonagh Quinn.*

VIRGIN ISLAND (1958)   4
(USA: *Our Virgin Island*)
Dir *Pat Jackson*. Prod *Leon Clore, Grahame Tharp*. Scr *Philip Rush, Jackson, from a book by Robb White*. Ph *Freddie Francis*. PC *Countryman*. Dis *British Lion*. Eastman Colour. *94 mins. Cert U*
Falling in love at first sight with American archaeologist Evan (*John Cassavetes*) in the Virgin Islands, Briton Tina Lomax (*Virginia Maskell*) marries and joins him on a tiny off-shore island he has bought for a song. A brass bedstead is their only furniture, and a fisherman (*Sidney Poitier*) their only neighbour. After an idyllic six months of sun, sea, triumphs and disasters, they have a baby and decide to spend half their time on the mainland, half on their island. Warm, happy film that occasionally gets a bit preachy.
RoC *Isabel Dean, Colin Gordon, Howard Marion Crawford, Edric Connor, Ruby Dee, Gladys Boot, Julian Mayfield, Reginald Hearne, Arnold Bell, Alonzo Bozan.*

THE VOICE OF MERRILL (1952)   3
(USA: *Murder Will Out*)
Dir and Scr *John Gilling*. Prod *Robert S. Baker, Monty Berman*. Ph *Berman*. PC *Tempean*. Dis *Eros. 84 mins. Cert U*
A blackmailer is murdered. Suspected are Jonathan (*James Robertson Justice*), an author with only months to live, and his wife Alycia (*Valerie Hobson*), who doesn't know he is dying,

Edward Underdown, Valerie Hobson and James Robertson Justice in The Voice of Merrill *(1952)*

but loves Hugh (*Edward Underdown*), a struggling writer who wins radio fame reading some of Jonathan's early work Alycia has submitted under her maiden name. Jonathan, the killer, plans to frame Hugh for the murder; Alycia fails to poison him but he dies anyway, Hugh intends to confess. Alycia, running to stop him, is killed by a lorry. Hugh is cleared. Long, complex thriller.
RoC *Henry Kendall, Garry Marsh, Daniel Wherry, Sam Kydd, Daphne Newton, Ian Fleming, Johnnie Schofield.*

THE WALLET (1952)   2
Dir and Prod *Morton M. Lewis*. Scr *Ted Willis*. Ph *Brendan J. Stafford*. PC *Sunset*. Dis *Archway. 64 mins. Cert A*
A fight between police and foreign agents: a wallet containing £120 and priceless microfilm is thrown from a window. Its trail is followed by a stranger (*John Longden*). It passes through the hands of a dance hostess longing to escape her life, a cashier with a demanding mistress and a clerk who blackmails the cashier for the sake of his crooked child. The stranger gets the wallet and the microfilm - but is arrested: he is the leader of the enemy agents. Idea is good, execution very moderate.
RoC *Chili Bouchier, Roberta Huby, Alfred Farrell, Hilda Fenemore, Diana Calderwood, John Gatrell, Leslie French, Peter Prowse, Shawn O'Riordan, Robert Moore, Leslie Parker, Geoffrey Denys, Bernard Davies, Hilary Dean, Wanda Rands, Jimmy Brown.*

WATERFRONT (1950)   3
(USA: *Waterfront Women*)
Dir *Michael Anderson*. Prod *Paul Soskin*. Scr *John Brophy, Soskin, from Brophy's novel*. Ph *Harry Waxman*. PC *Conqueror*. Dis *General Film Distributors. 80 mins. Cert A*
McCabe (*Robert Newton*), a ship's fireman whose main pleasure is drink, deserts his wife and two (soon to be three) children for a life at sea. Years later, he returns to Liverpool, in trouble and with a grudge against the ship's engineer, whom he kills in an alcoholic fury. His wife (*Kathleen Harrison*) visits him in prison with the son he has never seen. Dark drama free from sideline issues; rare straight role for Miss Harrison.
RoC *Susan Shaw, Richard Burton, Avis Scott, Kenneth Griffith, Robin Netscher, Olive Sloane, Charles Victor, James Hayter, Michael Brennan, Allan Jeayes, Hattie Jacques, Duncan Lamont, Anthony Oliver.*

THE WEAK AND THE WICKED
(1953)   3
Dir *J. Lee Thompson*. Prod *Victor Skutezky*. Scr *Lee Thompson, Anne Burnaby, Joan Henry, from Henry's book* Who Lie in Gaol. Ph *Gilbert*

Taylor. PC *Associated British/Marble Arch*. Dis *AB-Pathé. 88 mins. Cert A*
Her huge gambling debts land Jean (*Glynis Johns*) in jail for 12 months. She meets Betty (*Diana Dors*), a good-time girl 'taking the rap' for a boyfriend, Babs (*Jane Hylton*) whose heedlessness had caused her child's death, Nellie (*Oliver Sloane*), a shoplifter, and later Millie (*Athene Seyler*), a genteel old lady doing time on a trumped-up blackmail charge. On an evening out before transfer to another prison, Jean thinks Betty has absconded - but she returns, like the man (*John Gregson*) Jean thought she had lost. Familiar types in rose-coloured view of prison life.
RoC *Sidney James, Sybil Thorndike, A.E. Matthews, Anthony Nicholls, Barbara Couper, Joyce Heron, Ursula Howells, Mary Merrall, Rachel Roberts, Marjorie Rhodes, Simone Silva, Josephine Griffin, Josephine Stuart, Bessie Love, Sandra Dorne, Edwin Styles, Cecil Trouncer, Paul Carpenter, Eliot Makeham, Joan Haythorne, Jean Taylor-Smith, Thea Gregory, Tom Gill, Irene Handl, Marjorie Stewart, Hannah Watt, Kathleen Michael, Maureen Pryor, Ruth Denning, Margaret Diamond.*

THE WEAPON (1956)   4
Dir *Val Guest*. Prod *Hal E. Chester, Frank Bevis*. Scr *Fred Freiburger*. Ph *Reg Wyer*. PC *Periclean*. Dis *Eros. SuperScope 235. 81 mins. Cert A*.
A boy, Erik (*Jon Whiteley*) finds a gun on a bomb site and accidentally wounds his friend with it. He flees, hiding the gun again. His mother (*Lizabeth Scott*) is distraught and the police are annoyed - they believe the gun was one used in an unsolved murder. The murderer (*George Cole*) forces Erik to reveal the new hiding place, but is pursued by police and falls to his death from the top of a gutted building. Workmanlike thriller.
RoC *Steve Cochran, Herbert Marshall, Nicole Maurey, Laurence Naismith, John Horsley, Denis Shaw, Stanley Maxted, Basil Dignam, Fred Johnson, Richard Goolden, Arthur Lovegrove, Felix Felton, Joan Schofield, Myrtle Reed, Roland Brand, Ryck Rydon, Vivian Matalon, Peter Augustine, George Bradford, Peter Godsell, Fraser Hines.*

WEB OF SUSPICION (1959)   2
Dir *Max Varnel*. Prod *Edward J. Danziger, Harry Lee Danziger*. Scr *Brian Clemens, Eldon Howard*. Ph *Jimmy Wilson*. PC *Danzigers*. Dis *Paramount. 70 mins. Cert A*
PT instructor Bradley (*Philip Friend*) is forced to flee from a lynch mob after being suspected of a schoolgirl's murder. Assisted by his girlfriend (*Susan Beaumont*), the art mistress, he discovers the real killer is the secretly psychotic music master (*John Martin*) whom he bests in a hand-to-hand struggle, proving his own innocence in the process. Killer is obvious but script has enough unintentional humour to stifle yawns.
RoC *Peter Sinclair, Robert Raglan, Ian Fleming, Peter Elliott, Rolf Harris, Hal Osmond, John Brooking, Diana Chesney, Jack Melford, Vivienne Lacey, Ann Taylor, Carol White, girls of the Corona Stage School.*

THE WEDDING OF LILLI MARLENE (1953) [1]

Dir *Arthur Crabtree*. Prod *William Gell*. Scr *John Baines*. Ph *Arthur Grant*. PC and Dis *Monarch*. 89 mins. Cert U

Lilli Marlene (*Lisa Daniely*) of wartime fame is determined to make a success in show business before she will marry the broadcaster (*Hugh McDermott*) she loves. She gets a job in the chorus and bags the star role when Maggie (*Gabrielle Brune*) leaves to get married. Maggie is soon back and causes Lilli to break down on opening night. The Eighth Army boys in the gallery come to her rescue and she scores a triumph. Long, stiff and tedious.

RoC *Jack Billings, Joan Heal, Robert Ayres, Sidney James, Wally Patch, Irene Handl, John Blythe, Mairhi Russell, Tom Gill, Ernst Ulman, Ben Williams, Dandy Nichols, Ann Bennett, Jacques Cey, Patricia Somerset, Jacqueline Mackenzie, Ann Duran, Lou Matto, Charmian Buchel.*

WEST OF SUEZ (1956) [3]
(USA: *Fighting Wildcats*)

Dir *Arthur Crabtree*. Prod *Kay Luckwell, D.E.A. Winn*. Scr *Norman Hudis*. Ph *Jimmy Harvey*. PC *Winwell*. Dis *Astral*. 85 mins. Cert A

Brett (*Keefe Brasselle*), a mercenary American explosives expert, is hired to blow up a visiting Arab ruler in a London street – for a sky high price. He and his employer Langford (*Karel Stepanek*) escape after a gunfight with MI5 men, but Brett's girlfriend Pat (*Kay Callard*) saves the Arab target at the expense of her own life. Demented with grief, Brett guns for Langford, and they kill each other. Interesting suspense drama slowed down by love interest.

RoC *Ursula Howells, Bruce Seton, Maya Koumani, Harry Fowler, Sheldon Lawrence, Richard Shaw, Alex Gallier.*

WEST OF ZANZIBAR (1954) [3]

Dir *Harry Watt*. Prod *Leslie Norman*. Scr *Jack Whittingham, Max Catto*. Ph *Paul Beeson*. PC *Ealing Studios*. Dis *General Film Distributors*. Technicolor. 94 mins. Cert U

The young men of an African tribe seeking new land succumb to the lure of the money involved in ivory-poaching. Gamewarden Bob Payton (*Anthony Steel*) is determined to put a stop to this and tracks down the white smugglers involved, whose leader (*Martin Benson*) is brought to justice when the tribe turns against him. Slow-moving, beautifully shot sequel to *Where No Vultures Fly*; the heroine (*Sheila Sim*) has an amazing wardrobe for the African bush.

RoC *Edric Connor, Orlando Martins, William Simons, Peter Illing, Juma, Howard Marion Crawford, R. Stuart Lindsell, David Osieli, Bethlehem Sketch, Edward Johnson, Joanna Kitau, Roy Cable, Sheikh Abdullah, Fatuma.*

WHAT EVERY WOMAN WANTS (1954) [3]

Dir *Maurice Elvey*. Prod *David Dent*. Scr *Talbot Rothwell, from a play by Edwin Lewis*. Ph *Wilkie Cooper*. PC *Advance*. Dis *Adelphi*. 88 mins. Cert A

Tired of living with relatives, and of her pol-itically orientated husband (*Patric Doonan*), Midlands girl Jane (*Elsy Albiin*) flirts with the idea of an affair with her Korean War-wounded cousin (*William Sylvester*). She splits from her husband, but her grandfather brings the young couple together again, and they promise to look for a home of their own. Broad down-to-earth drama.

RoC *Brenda de Banzie, Dominic Roche, Joan Hickson, Brian Rix, Beckett Bould, Edwin Richfield, Douglas Ives, Joan Sims, Prunella Scales.*

WHAT THE BUTLER SAW (1950) [3]

Dir *Godfrey Grayson*. Prod *Anthony Hinds*. Scr *A.R. Rawlinson, Edward J. Mason, from the story by Roger and Donald Good*. Ph *Walter Harvey*. PC *Hammer*. Dis *Exclusive*. 63 mins. Cert U

The Earl (*Edward Rigby*), retiring as the governor of a group of British-owned tropical islands, returns to England to discover that the native princess (*Mercy Haystead*) in love with his butler (*Henry Mollison*) has stowed away in a trunk. The Earl's family try to get her out of the country, but only a series of comic disasters ensues. Rigby's valiant efforts keep farce going.

RoC *Michael Ward, Eleanor Hallam, Peter Burton, Ann Valery, Tonie MacMillan, Mollie Palmer, Howard Charlton, Alfred Harris, George Bishop, Norman Pitt.*

WHEEL OF FATE (1953) [1]

Dir and Prod *Francis Searle*. Scr *Guy Elmes, from the play by Alex Atkinson*. Ph *Reg(inald) Wyer*. PC *Kenilworth*. Dis *General Film Distributors*. 70 mins. Cert A

Johnny (*Patric Doonan*) and his half-brother Ted (*Bryan Forbes*) run a garage. Ted's tastes run to dog-racing and a dance-hall singer Lucky (*Sandra Dorne*), who falls for Johnny. To get her back, Ted decides to let his miserly, bedridden father die by withdrawing his medicine, and steal his money. Trapped by police, Ted tries to jump under a train, but it stops in time and he has to face the music. A low-point even of British 'B's of the 1950s – alternately ludicrous and depressing.

RoC *John Horsley, Martin Benson, Johnnie Schofield, Cyril Smith.*

WHERE NO VULTURES FLY (1951) [3]
(USA: *Ivory Hunter*)

Dir *Harry Watt*. (Associate) Prod *Leslie Nor-

Anthony Steel, Dinah Sheridan and William Simons in Where No Vultures Fly *(1951)*

man*. Scr *Ralph Smart, W.P. Lipscomb, Norman*. Ph *Geoffrey Unsworth, Paul Beeson*. PC *Ealing Studios*. Dis *General Film Distributors*. Technicolor. 107 mins. Cert U

Game warden Bob Payton (*Anthony Steel*), sickened by the slaughter of wildlife in East Africa, starts a drive for a national safari park. He and his wife (*Dinah Sheridan*) have to tangle with ivory poachers, whose leader (*Harold Warrender*) is eventually killed fleeing from the law, before his dream of a land 'where no vultures fly' comes true. Royal Performance film received thumbs-down from critics, thumbs up from public: it proved the top British moneymaker of 1952.

RoC *Meredith Edwards, Orlando Martins, William Simons, Philip Birkinshaw, Jack Arundell Mallett, Kenneth Augustus Jeremy, Wallace Needham-Clark, Andrew Cruickshank.*

WHERE'S CHARLEY? (1952) [4]

Dir *David Butler*. Prod *Ernest Martin, Cy Feuer*. Scr *John Monks Jr, from Frank Loesser and George Abbott's stage musical from a play by Brandon Thomas*. Ph *Erwin Hillier*. Dance dir *Michael Kidd*. PC and Dis *Warner Bros.* Technicolor. 97 mins. Cert U

1890. Oxford undergraduate Charley Wykeham (*Ray Bolger*) is forced to impersonate his own aunt from Brazil as chaperone to himself and his friend Jack (*Robert Shackleton*) while they court Amy (*Allyn McLerie*) and Kitty (*Mary Germaine*). One of the girls' fathers falls in love with 'auntie' and matters rapidly come to a frantic head when the real aunt (*Margaretta Scott*) turns up. Sunny, funny musical with at least one memorable tune; Bolger is brilliant.

RoC *Horace Cooper, Howard Marion Crawford, Henry Hewitt, H.G. Stoker, Martin Miller, Arthur Mason.*

Ray Bolger in Where's Charley? *(1952)*

WHERE THERE'S A WILL (1955) [3]

Dir *Vernon Sewell*. Prod *George Maynard*. Scr *R.F. Delderfield, from his play*. Ph *Basil Emmott*. PC *Film Locations*. Dis *Eros*. 78 mins. Cert U

A cockney family inherits a run-down Devon farm. Alfie (*Leslie Dwyer*) wants to make a go of it. His sisters (*Thelma Ruby, Dandy Nichols*) and workshy brother-in-law (*George Cole*) aren't so keen. But, with the help of the farm's housekeeper (*Kathleen Harrison*) and a missing will, Alfie keeps his country life. The corn is as high as the weeds on the farm, but lively playing keeps the laughs coming. Not for high-brows.

RoC *Michael Shepley, Hugh Morton, Edward Lexy, Norman MacOwan, Edward Woodward, Sam Kydd, Philip Ray, Bill Shine.*

WHIRLPOOL (1959) [1]

Dir *Lewis Allen.* Prod *George Pitcher.* Scr *Lawrence P. Bachmann,* from his novel The Lorelei. Ph *Geoffrey Unsworth.* PC and Dis *Rank. Eastman Colour. 95 mins. Cert A*

On the run with her murderer love (*William Sylvester*), Lora (*Juliette Greco*) falls in love with the captain (*O.W. Fischer*) of the tanker she has taken down the Rhine and with river life itself. Her lover also boards the vessel but, in a struggle with the skipper, falls overboard, Lora is arrested but vows to return to the Rhine. Slow, miserable drama; one of the Rank Organization's more comprehensive disasters.

RoC *Muriel Pavlow, Marius Goring, Lilly Kann, Peter Illing, Richard Palmer, Geoffrey Bayldon, Victor Brooks, Arthur Howell, Harold Kasket.*

WHISPERING SMITH HITS LONDON (1951) [3]
(USA: *Whispering Smith Versus Scotland Yard*)

Dir *Francis Searle.* Prod *Anthony Hinds, Julian Lesser.* Scr *John Gilling.* Ph *Walter Harvey.* PC *Hammer/Lesser.* Dis *Exclusive. 82 mins. Cert A*

'Whispering' Smith (*Richard Carlson*), an American detective on holiday in London, is hired by Anne (*Rona Anderson*) to look into her boss's daughter's suspect suicide. Smith at first encounters a wall of silence, but later uncovers a conspiracy involving blackmail, and including Louise (*Greta Gynt*) who proves to be the 'dead' daughter. She fires at Smith but only kills her accomplice Roger (*Herbert Lom*). Exciting enough crime drama for those who can keep track of the plot.

RoC *Alan Wheatley, Dora Bryan, Reginald Beckwith, Danny Green, Daniel Wherry, James Raglan, Michael Ward, Stuart Nichol, Laurence Naismith, Christine Silver, Vic Wise, Middleton Woods, Ben Williams, Sidney Vivian, Tony Frost, June Bardsley, Michael Hogarth, John Wynn, Anthony Warner, Ian Wilson, Stanley Baker, Lionel Grose, John Singer, John Kyle.*

WHITE CORRIDORS (1951) [5]

Dir *Pat Jackson.* Prod *Joseph Janni, John Croyden.* Scr *Jackson, Jan Read from a novel by Helen Ashton.* Ph *C. Pennington-Richards.* PC *Vic Films.* Dis *General Film Distributors. 102 mins (US: 85). Cert A*

At a Midlands hospital, a young boy is brought in with blood poisoning. The serum on which Dr Marriner (*James Donald*) is working cannot be perfected in time to save the boy and Marriner accidentally infects himself as well. Acting against instructions, Dr Dean (*Googie Withers*), who loves him, injects Marriner with the serum. As the boy dies, Marriner begins to recover. Intelligently handled, episodic medical drama always carries urgency at its core.

RoC *Geoffrey Tearle, Petula Clark, Moira Lis-*

ter, *Jack Watling, Barry Jones, Basil Radford, Megs Jenkins, Henry Edwards, Brand Inglis, Dagmar (Dana) Wynter, Gerard Heinz, Avice Landone, Jean Anderson, Fabia Drake, H.F. Hills, Bruce Seton, Johnnie Schofield, Grace Gaven, Helen Harvey, Lyn Evans, Jean Lodge, Timothy Bateson, Patrick Troughton, Dandy Nichols, Deirdre Doyle, Mignon O'Doherty, Mary Minton, Philip Stainton, Joan Winmill, Humphrey Howorth.*

THE WHITE TRAP (1959) [3]

Dir *Sidney Hayers.* Prod *Julian Wintle, Leslie Parkyn.* Scr *Peter Barnes.* Ph *Eric Cross.* PC *Independent Artists.* Dis *Anglo-Amalgamated. 58 mins. Cert U*

Paul Langley (*Lee Patterson*), a war hero now in jail, breaks out to be with his fragile wife Joan (*Felicity Young*), expecting their first baby. With the help of a wartime friend, Paul evades both police and press cordons thrown around the hospital and reaches his wife's ward – just as she dies giving birth to a son. After a bitter exchange with the authorities, Paul gives himself up. Some tension in later stages.

RoC *Michael Goodliffe, Conrad Phillips, Jack Allen, Yvette Wyatt, Gillian Vaughan, Trevor Maskell, Harold Siddons, Charles Leno, Ian Colin, Helen Towers.*

WHO DONE IT? (1955) [4]

Dir *Basil Dearden.* Prod *Michael Relph.* Scr *T.E.B. Clarke.* Ph *Otto Heller.* PC *Ealing Studios.* Dis *Rank. 85 mins. Cert U*

When he wins £100 and a bloodhound in a competition, ice-rink sweeper Hugo Dill (*Benny Hill*) sets up his own detective agency. He soon becomes involved with Iron Curtain spies plotting to blow up British scientists, and only the help of variety strong-girl Frankie (*Belinda Lee*) helps prevent both the assassinations and the transmission of a microfilm containing the scientists' invention to enemy agents. Believable characters help in wildly comic story. Unpolished, but very funny.

RoC *David Kossoff, Garry Marsh, George Margo, Ernest Thesiger, Denis Shaw, Frederick Schiller, Thorley Walters, Nicholas Phipps, Gibb McLaughlin, Irene Handl, Charles Hawtrey, Jeremy Hawk, Philip Stainton, Warwick Ashton, Stratford Johns, Ernest Jay, Harold Scott, Arthur Lowe, Robert McDermott, Norah Blaney, Fabian (dog), Dagenham Girl Pipers.*

Benny Hill and Belinda Lee in Who Done It? *(1956)*

WHO GOES THERE! (1952) [4]
(USA: *The Passionate Sentry*)

Dir and Prod *Anthony Kimmins.* Scr *John Dighton,* from his play. Ph *John Wilcox, Ted Scaife.* PC *London Films.* Dis *British Lion. 85 mins. Cert U*

Christina Deed (*Peggy Cummins*) comes to England to see her fiancé, Arthur (*George Cole*), a Guardsman who seems to be on almost permanent sentry duty outside royal residences. This gives philandering Miles (*Nigel Patrick*), a chance to try to seduce Christina in his Grace-and-Favour house by St James's Palace, which complicates his sister's (*Valerie Hobson*) romance with another guardsman (*Anthony Bushell*). The right couples get together in the end. Well-oiled class-distinctions farce; a popular success.

RoC *A.E. Matthews, Joss Ambler.*

THE WHOLE TRUTH (1958) [4]

Dir *John Guillermin.* Prod *Jack Clayton.* Scr *Jonathan Latimer,* from the TV play by Philip Mackie. Ph *Wilkie Cooper.* PC *Romulus Valiant.* Dis *Columbia. 84 mins. Cert A*

Film producer Max (*Stewart Granger*) is told that his mistress (*Gianna Maria Canale*) has been murdered. Going to her chalet, he is amazed to find her alive. The 'detective' (*George Sanders*) who told him proves to be her husband, Carliss. Then the girl really is murdered – and Max arrested. But his wife (*Donna Reed*) proves Carliss to be the killer; fleeing, his car crashes and he is killed. Competent thriller, suitably mystifying if occasionally unconvincing.

RoC *Michael Shillo, Peter Dyneley, Richard Molinas, Jimmy Thompson, John Van Eyssen, Philip Vickers, Carlo Justini, Hy Hazell.*

Herbert Marshall and Arlene Dahl in Wicked As They Come *(1956)*

WICKED AS THEY COME (1956) [2]

Dir *Ken Hughes.* Prod *Maxwell Setton,* (uncredited) *M.J. Frankovitch.* Scr *Hughes, Robert Westerby, Sigmund Miller,* from a novel by Bill S. Ballinger. Ph *Basil Emmott.* PC *Film Locations.* Dis *Columbia. 94 mins. Cert A*

Born in a New York slum, Kathy Allen's (*Arlene Dahl*) aims are to make a success of life and suckers of men. Two of them fix a beauty contest for her, then she milks another of his money. After an affair with her employer, Kathy marries the boss of her corporation. She accidentally kills him and is charged with murder. But after the truth comes out, Kathy is free to look for more rich pickings. Thirties-sytle story (cf *Baby Face*) looks thin; not played with much flair.

RoC *Phil Carey, Herbert Marshall, Michael Goodliffe, David Kossoff, Ralph Truman, Sidney James, Faith Brook, Marvin Kane, Patrick Allen, Jacques Brunius, Gilbert Winfield, Alastair Hunter, Larry Cross.*

WIDE BOY (1952)   2

Dir *Ken Hughes.* Prod *W.H. Williams.* Scr *Rex Rienits.* Ph *Jo Ambor.* PC *Merton Park.* Dis *Anglo-Amalgamated. 67 mins. Cert A*

Benny (*Sydney Tafler*), a small-time racketeer, has a girlfriend, Molly (*Susan Shaw*), whose expensive tastes lead him into bigger crime. The theft of a wallet proves an entrée to blackmail – but also to murder when the victim rebels. But Molly's retention of the handbag that held the wallet is their undoing, and Benny the 'wide boy' is hounded to his death by police. Story stretches the arm of coincidence to inordinate lengths.

RoC *Ronald Howard, Melissa Stribling, Colin Tapley, Laidman Browne, Helen Christie, Glyn Houston.*

WILL ANY GENTLEMAN...? (1953)   4

Dir *Michael Anderson.* Prod *Hamilton G. Inglis.* Scr *Vernon Sylvaine, from his play.* Ph *Erwin Hillier.* PC *Associated British.* Dis *AB-Pathé. Technicolor. 84 mins. Cert U*

Henry (*George Cole*), a meek bank clerk, is unwillingly pushed up on stage, and hypnotized by the Great Mendoza (*Alan Badel*). Failing to emerge from the trance after the show, Henry becomes a devil-may-care philanderer, shocking his wife (*Veronica Hurst*), making advances to the maid (*Joan Sims*) and 'borrowing' the bank's money for riotous living. It takes the return of Mendoza to bring things back to normal. Bright, funny, well-produced comedy.

RoC *Jon Pertwee, James Hayter, Heather Thatcher, William Hartnell, Diana Decker, Sidney James, Brian Oulton, Alexander Gauge, Peter Butterworth, Wally Patch, Lionel Jeffries, Josephine Douglas, Wilfred Boyle, Jill Melford, Diana Hope, Martyn Wyldeck, Richard Massingham, Frank Birch, Arthur Howard, Brian Wilde, Nan Braunton, Lucy Griffiths, Harry Herbert, Russ Allen, Sylvia Russell, Jackie Joyner, Joan Sims, Eleanor Fazan, Lillemor Knudsen.*

THE WIND CANNOT READ (1958)   4

Dir *Ralph Thomas.* Prod *Betty E. Box.* Scr *Richard Mason, from his novel.* Ph *Ernest Steward.* PC and Dis *Rank. Eastman Colour. 114 mins. Cert U*

1943. Posted to India on a Japanese language course, flier Michael Quinn (*Dirk Bogarde*) falls deeply in love with Sabby (*Yoko Tani*), an instructor. They marry in secret, but Michael has to leave and is captured in Burma. When word comes that Sabby is ill with a brain disease, Michael makes a desperate escape from his prison camp and gets back to India. A few days later, Sabby has a sudden

Yoko Tani and Dirk Bogarde in The Wind Cannot Read *(1958)*

relapse and dies. Sensitively-played, warmly human weepie.

RoC *John Fraser, Ronald Lewis, Anthony Bushell, Henry Okawa, Marne Maitland, Michael Medwin, Richard Leech, Anthony Wager, Tadeshi Ikeda, Donald Pleasence, Yoichi Matsue, Joy Michael, Avice Landone.*

WINDFALL (1955)   3

Dir *Henry Cass.* Prod *Robert S. Baker, Monty Berman.* Scr *John Gilling.* Ph *Berman.* PC *Mid-Century.* Dis *Eros. 64 mins. Cert U*

Arthur, an elderly shop assistant (*Lionel Jeffries* at 29!) finds a case containing £2000 and hangs on to it for a possible reward. He lends his own savings to his son (*Jack Watling*) who is conned out of them. His daughter's flashy new boyfriend steals the £2000, but it proves to be counterfeit and he is arrested, while Arthur joins his son in a suddenly prospering business. Pleasant unpretentious parable.

RoC *Gordon Jackson, Avice Landone, Patricia Owens, Cyril Chamberlain, Brian Worth, Arthur Lowe, Erik Chitty, Alastair Hunter, Peter Swanwick.*

WINDOM'S WAY (1957)   4

Dir *Ronald Neame.* Prod *John Bryan.* Scr *Jill Craigie, from the novel by James Ramsey Ullman.* Ph *Christopher Challis.* PC and Dis *Rank. Eastman Colour. 108 mins. Cert U*

Dr Windom (*Peter Finch*), idealistic head of a small Malay hospital, is reconciled with his wife (*Mary Ure*) after a trial separation, but becomes involved in the local strife involving workers, the police and the military. Time and again he attempts to act as mediator and to steer people in the way of peace, but is consistently let down by the underhand tactics of the authorities. He escapes from a rebel army that has captured him, and bitterly prepares to leave. But his wife persuades him to stay and fight on. Courageous, unflinching film whose heart rules its head; thus not always as effective as it might be.

RoC *Natasha Parry, Robert Flemyng, Michael Hordern, John Cairney, Gregoire Aslan, Marne Maitland, George Margo, Kurt Siegenberg, Martin Benson, Sanny Bin Hussan, Olaf Pooley.*

WINGS OF DANGER (1952)   3
(USA: *Dead on Course*)

Dir *Terence Fisher.* Prod *Anthony Hinds.* Scr

John Gilling, from a novel by Elleston Trevor. Ph *Walter Harvey.* PC *Hammer/Lippert.* Dis *Exclusive. 73 mins. Cert U*

Counterfeit dollar smuggling runs between London and the Channel Islands, on an airline owned by Boyd Spencer (*Arthur Lane*). Pilot Van (*Zachary Scott*) is in love with the sister (*Naomi Chance*) of a pilot (*Robert Beatty*) involved in the racket. The latter fakes a crash and is presumed dead. Van gets in touch with a detective and between them they close the racket, Spencer himself proving to be the counterfeiter in chief. Lacklustre thriller.

RoC *Kay Kendall, Diane Cilento, Colin Tapley, Harold Lang, Jack Allen, Sheila Raynor, Courtney Hope, June Ashley, Natasha Sokolova, June Mitchell, James Steel, Russ Allen, Darcy Conyers.*

THE WITNESS (1959)   2

Dir *Geoffrey Muller.* Prod *Jack Greenwood.* Scr *Julian Bond.* Ph *John Wiles.* PC *Merton Park.* Dis *Anglo-Amalgamated. 58 mins. Cert U*

Tormented by other children because his father (*Dermot Walsh*) has been in prison, ten-year-old Peter (*Martin Stephens*) witnesses a crime (of which his father is suspected) and is used by the police to trap the real criminals, who try to silence him but fail. He is returned to his father, now cleared of implication in the crime. Weak story with appealing child performance.

RoC *Greta Gynt, Russell Napier, John Chandos, Derek Sydney, Hedger Wallace, Tom Bowman, Geoffrey Denton, Ronald Wood, Rupert Osborne, Stewart Guidotti, Malcolm Knight.*

WITNESS IN THE DARK (1959)   2

Dir *Wolf Rilla.* Prod *Norman Williams.* Scr *Leigh Vance, John Lemont.* Ph *Brendan Stafford.* PC *Ethiro/Alliance.* Dis *Rank. 62 mins. Cert U*

Jane (*Patricia Dainton*), a blind switchboard operator, inherits a valuable old brooch from a murdered neighbour. But the killer, who had brushed against her on the stairs, fears her sense of touch and resolves to 'get' her and the trinket. But Jane is working with the police, and when the murderer returns to the scene of his crime, he is caught. Nice performance by Dainton, but thriller is pretty ropy overall.

RoC *Conrad Phillips, Madge Ryan, Nigel Green, Enid Lorimer, Richard O'Sullivan, Stuart Saunders, Ian Colin, Noel Trevarthen, Maureen O'Reilly, Larry Burns, Ann Wrigg, Frazer Hines.*

WOMANEATER (1957)   1
(USA: *The Woman Eater*)

Dir *Charles Saunders.* Prod *Guido Coen.* Scr *Brandon Fleming.* Ph *Ernest Palmer.* PC *Fortress.* Dis *Eros. 71 mins. Cert X*

A mad scientist (*George Coulouris*) returns from the Amazon with a man-eating tree, or, as one critic put it, 'a tree peckish only for young girls whose statistics are ever so vital'. Fed by nubile beauties, the tree gives out a liquid which the scientist believes will restore the dead. It does – but they are out of their minds. The scientist and his tree are eventually destroyed by fire. Daft without being horrific; the tree is a better actor than some of the cast.

RoC *Vera Day, Peter Wayn, Joyce Gregg, Joy Webster, Sara Leighton, June Ashley, Rachel Lofting, Maxwell Foster, Jimmy Vaughan, Edward Higgins.*

THE WOMAN FOR JOE (1955)   3

Dir *George More O'Ferrall.* Prod *Leslie Parkyn.* Scr *Neil Paterson, from his story And Delilah.* Ph *Georges Périnal.* PC *Group.* Dis *Rank.* Technicolor. VistaVision 91 mins. Cert U

George (*Jimmy Karoubi*), a midget, boosts the fortunes of a fair run by Joe (*George Baker*) with his cunning and insight, but the two fall out over a singer, Mary (*Diane Cilento*), with whom they both fall in love. Mary, who has joined the fair singing to lions in their cage, imports the same female midget for George that Joe has unsuccessfully tried; but when George is fatally injured in a trapeze fall, he lies to save Mary's feelings. Difficult subject, not too cleverly handled; fairground atmosphere is good.

RoC *David Kossoff, Violet Farebrother, Earl Cameron, Sydney Tafler, Man Mountain Dean, Patrick Westwood, Derek Sydney, Verna Gilmore, Martin Miller, Meier Tzelniker, Miriam Karlin, Frank Paulo, Amy Veness, Terence Longdon, Jill Ireland, Arthur Lowe.*

WOMAN IN A DRESSING GOWN (1957)   5

Dir *J. Lee Thompson.* Prod *Thompson, Frank Godwin.* Scr *Ted Willis, from his TV play.* Ph *Gilbert Taylor.* PC *Godwin-Willis.* Dis *AB Pathé.* 93 mins. Cert A

Slatternly Amy Preston (*Yvonne Mitchell*) is losing her husband Jim (*Anthony Quayle*) to another woman (*Sylvia Syms*). Stunned when Jim asks for a divorce, she tries to set up a confrontation with him and the girl, but gets drunk and can only make a bitter, screeching attack on the girl before packing Jim's bags and sending him away. Appalled at the anguish he has caused, Jim returns home. Superior kitchen sink soaper whose power overcomes even the casting of upper-class stars in working-class roles.

RoC *Andrew Ray, Carole Lesley, Olga Lindo, Harry Locke, Marianne Stone, Michael Ripper, Norah Gordon, Max Butterfield, Roberta Woolley.*

Sylvia Syms, Yvonne Mitchell and Anthony Quayle in Woman in a Dressing Gown *(1957)*

THE WOMAN IN QUESTION (1950)   3
(USA: *Five Angles on Murder*)

Dir *Anthony Asquith.* Prod *Teddy Baird.* Scr *John Cresswell.* Ph *Desmond Dickinson.* PC *Javelin.* Dis *General Film Distributors.* 88 mins. Cert A

Astra (*Jean Kent*), a fairground fortune-teller of easy virtue, is found strangled. In police interviews, suspects see her in different lights. To the shopkeeper (*Charles Victor*) who wanted to marry her, she's an innocent; to her char (*Hermione Baddeley*) the perfect lady; to her sister (*Susan Shaw*) a schemer; to the sister's fiancé (*Dirk Bogarde*), having dallied with her, a brazen hussy. A sailor (*John McCallum*) doesn't understand her complex character. Superintendent Lodge (*Duncan Macrae*) sorts out the killer. Interesting thriller; doesn't quite work.

RoC *Lana Morris, Joe Linnane, Vida Hope, Duncan Lamont, Anthony Dawson, Albert Chevalier, John Boxer, Julian d'Albie, Bobbie Scroggins, Richard Pearson, Richard Dunn, John Martin, Ian Fleming, Josephine Middleton, Everley Gregg, Helen Goss, Norah Gordon, Merle Tottenham, Tom Macauley.*

A WOMAN OF MYSTERY (1957)   2

Dir *Ernest Morris.* Prod *Edward J. Danziger, Harry Lee Danziger.* Scr *Brian Clemens, Eldon Howard.* Ph *Jimmy Wilson.* PC *Danzigers.* Dis *United Artists.* 71 mins. Cert U

Reporter Ray Savage (*Dermot Walsh*) has no appetite for the facts behind a young girl's suicide – until he discovers it was murder. He not only finds the killer, but uncovers a counterfeit ring into the bargain. Flat presentation nullifies a crisp, well-constructed screenplay.

RoC *Hazel Court, Jennifer Jayne, Ferdy Mayne, Ernest Clark, Diana Chesney, Paul Dickson, David Lander, Gordon Tanner, Robert Hunter.*

A WOMAN POSSESSED (1958)   3

Dir *Max Varnel.* Prod *Edward J. Danziger, Harry Lee Danziger.* Scr *Brian Clemens, Eldon Howard.* Ph *Jimmy Wilson.* PC *Danzigers.* Dis *United Artists.* 68 mins. Cert U

When Dr John Winthrop (*Francis Matthews*) returns from America with his new fiancée Ann (*Kay Callard*), his domineering mother (*Margaretta Scott*) soon makes it clear that she opposes the match. She demands that John and Ann live with her, as Ann has a weak heart, then gives Ann the wrong pills when she has an attack. John saves Ann's life and turns on his mother, only to find that the housekeeper (*Alison Leggatt*) switched the pills. All three resolve to work towards a better relationship. Well-acted, but not-too-interesting drama.

RoC *Ian Fleming, Jan Holden, Denis Shaw, Totti Truman Taylor, Tony Thawnton, Edith Saville.*

THE WOMAN'S ANGLE (1952)   2

Dir *Leslie Arliss.* Prod *Walter C. Mycroft.* Scr *Arliss, Mabbie Poole, from a novel by Ruth Feiner.* Ph *Erwin Hillier.* PC *Bow Bells.* Dis *AB-Pathé.* 86 mins. Cert A

Head and manager of a family of musicians, Robert (*Edward Underdown*) has a complex love life which includes a failed marriage to his brother's nurse (*Lois Maxwell*), a torrid affair with a ballerina (*Claude Farell*) and a cerebral relationship with a young music critic (*Cathy O'Donnell*) who settles him down. Arliss still making films to a Gainsborough formula that no longer works; novelettish stuff.

RoC *Peter Reynolds, Isabel Dean, John Bentley, Marjorie Fielding, Anthony Nicholls, Olaf Pooley, Joan Collins, Ernest Thesiger, Eric Pohlmann, Dagmar (Dana) Wynter, Geoffrey Toone, Anton Diffring, Miles Malleson, Malcolm Knight, Frederick Berger, Leslie Weston, Lea Seidl, Thelma d'Aguilar, Peter Illing, Sylva Langova, Bill Shine, Norah Gordon, Wensley Pithey, Rufus Cruickshank, Fred Griffiths.*

A WOMAN'S TEMPTATION (1959)   3

Dir *Godfrey Grayson.* Prod *Edward J. Danziger, Harry Lee Danziger.* Scr *Brian Clemens, Eldon Howard.* Ph *Jimmy Wilson.* PC *Danzigers.* Dis *British Lion.* 60 mins. Cert U

Betty (*Patricia Driscoll*), a struggling young widow, finds a wad of notes and has visions of giving her young son the expensive education of which she has always dreamed. Before she can use the money, the crooks who stole the money trace her, but her friend Mike is nearby and beats them up. Betty hands the money to the police. 'Drab and dispirited' or 'exciting fare', according to what you read. Certainly offbeat, though, and Driscoll is sympathetic.

RoC *John Longden, Neil Hallett, John Pike, Robert Raglan, Gordon Needham, Frazer Hines, Kenneth J. Warren, Ross Yeo, Michael Saunders, Malcolm Ranson, Howard Lang, Ian Wilson, Joey White, Christopher Cooke, Claude Kingston, Carl Conway, Raymond Hodge.*

THE WOMAN WITH NO NAME (1950)   2
(USA: *Her Panelled Door*)

Dir *Ladislas Vajda, George More O'Ferrall.* Prod *John Stafford.* Scr *Vajda, Guy Morgan, from a novel by Theresa Charles.* Ph *Otto Heller.* PC *Independent Film Producers.* Dis *AB-Pathé.* 83 mins. Cert A

1940. Yvonne (*Phyllis Calvert*) loses her memory in the Blitz. Marrying a Norwegian RAF officer (*Richard Burton*) who is shot down, she discovers she has an (estranged) husband (*Edward Underdown*) and half-sister (*Helen Cherry*) in the country. They refuse to believe in her amnesia, but, after she finds that her half-sister had jealously caused the rift between herself and her crippled husband, everything ends happily. Calvert's return to British films not a a happy one. American title change takes some believing.

RoC *Anthony Nicholls, James Hayter, Betty Ann Davies, Amy Veness, Andrew Osborn, Olive Milbourne, June Bardsley, Patrick Troughton, Will Ambro, Harold Scott, Willoughby Gray, Vi Stevens, David Keir, Kathleen Boutall, Irlin Hall, Leslie Phillips, Terence Alexander, Bill Shine, Richard Pearson, Jean Shepheard.*

WOMEN OF TWILIGHT (1952)   5
(USA: *Twilight Women*)

Dir *Gordon Parry.* Prod. *Daniel M. Angel.* Scr *Anatole de Grunwald, from the play by Sylvia Rayman.* Ph *Jack Asher.* PC *Romulus/Daniel*

M. Angel. Dis British Lion. 89 mins. Cert X
A blackmailer and baby-farmer, Helen Allistair (*Freda Jackson*) is a landlady who specializes in taking in unmarried mothers-to-be. Her latest victim, Vivianne (*Reńe Ray*), mistress of a condemned killer (*Laurence Harvey*), is befriended by another boarder Christine (*Lois Maxwell*), whose own baby dies when Helen refuses to call a doctor. Vivianne confronts Helen, who pushes her downstairs and leaves her to die. Helen's fellow-worker Jess (*Vida Hope*) turns on her and helps her bring her to justice. Grim, sordid, unrelenting drama, Britain's first 'X'.
RoC *Joan Dowling, Dora Bryan, Mary Germaine, Ingeborg Wells, Dorothy Gordon, Clare James, Cyril Smith, Betty Henderson, Ben Williams, Bruce Beeby, Marguerite Brennan, Katherine Page, Edna Morris, Dandy Nichols, Michael Corkran, Arnold Bell, Gordon Craig, Cyril Conway, Geoffrey Goodheart, Harry Brunning, Robin Dowell, Liam Gaffney, Roy Russell.*

WOMEN WITHOUT MEN (1956)   ③
(USA: *Blonde Bait*)
Dir *Elmo Williams.* Prod *Anthony Hinds.* Scr *Val Guest, Richard Landau.* Ph *Walter Harvey.* PC *Hammer.* Dis *Exclusive. 73 mins. Cert A*
Jailed for injuring a man in self-defence, Angie (*Beverly Michaels*) makes a break during a Christmas concert to keep a tryst with her boy-friend (*Paul Carpenter*), who discharges himself from hospital to keep the date himself. Angie also helps fellow-escapee Marguerite (*April Olrich*) prevent her baby being sent to an orphanage, before giving herself up. Women's prison drama with welcome vein of humour; silly plot, lively performances.
RoC *Joan Rice, Thora Hird, Avril Angers, Hermione Baddeley, Gordon Jackson, Ralph Michael, Sheila Burrell, Valerie White, Maurice Kaufmann, David Lodge, John Welsh, Olwen Brookes, Betty Cooper, Doris Gilmore, Fanny Carby, Yvonne Manners, Peter Welsh, Oscar Nation, Katherine Feliaz, Michael Golden, Anthony Miles, Bill Shine, Muriel Young, Mark Kingston, Verne Morgan, Charles Saynor.*

WONDERFUL THINGS! (1958)   ③
Dir *Herbert Wilcox.* Prod *Anna Neagle.* Scr *Jack Trevor Story.* Ph *Gordon Dines.* PC *Everest.* Dis *AB-Pathé. 85 mins. Cert U*
Carmello (*Frankie Vaughan*) and Mario (*Jer-*

Frankie Vaughan and Jackie Lane in Wonderful Things! *(1958)*

emy Spenser), Catalan fishermen working off the coast of Gibraltar, are not making a go of their trade. Carmello goes to London, promising to send for his girl Pepita (*Jackie Lane*) later. He meets a socialite (*Jean Dawnay*) who falls in love with him and, after Mario secretly sells his boat to send Pepita to London, she realizes that it is Mario she loves. Simple, ingenuous romance, a little amateurish in parts. A popular success.
RoC *Wilfrid Hyde White, Eddie Byrne, Harold Kasket, Christopher Rhodes, Cyril Chamberlain, Nancy Nevinson, Barbara Goalen, Elizabeth (Liz) Fraser, Ronnie Barker.*

THE WONDER KID (1951)   ②
Dir and Prod *Karl Hartl.* Scr *Gene Markey.* Ph *Robert Krasker, Günther Anders.* PC *London Films.* Dis *British Lion. 85 mins. Cert U*
Child-pianist Sebastian (*Bobby Henrey*) is exploited by his manager Gorik (*Elwyn Brook-Jones*), who plans to adopt him. His governess enlists help to get him away, but unwittingly picks a gang of crooks who kidnap the boy and hold him to ransom. With them, however, Sebastian learns to stand on his own feet and when he is eventually restored to his friends, compels Gorik to sign a reasonable contract. Comedy-drama in bilingual versions hasn't the charm to spring to life.
RoC *Robert Shackleton, Christa Winter, Muriel Aked, Paul Hardtmuth, Oskar Werner, Sebastian Cabot, June Elvin, Klaus Birsch, Lowe (dog).*

THE WOODEN HORSE (1950)   ⑤
Dir *Jack Lee.* Prod *Ian Dalrymple.* Scr *Eric Williams, from his book.* Ph *C. M. Pennington-Richards.* PC *Wessex.* Dis *British Lion. 101 mins. Cert U*
The Allied prisoners of Stalag Luft III, a World War II German P-o-W camp, devise a novel method of escape. They dig their tunnel beneath a large vaulting horse, which is placed in full view of the enemy, and vigorously used much of the day. Peter (*Leo Genn*) and John (*Anthony Steel*) are assisted by the French resistance to get to Denmark, and then to Sweden, where they meet up again with the third escapee. Exciting, ingenious true-life story set the pattern for several such films to come.
RoC *David Tomlinson, David Greene, Peter Burton, Patrick Waddington, Michael Goodliffe, Anthony Dawson, Bryan Forbes, Franz Schaftheitlin, Hans Meyer, Jacques Brunius, Dan Cunningham, Philip Dale, Russell Waters, Ralph Ward, Johannes Johanson, Herbert Kilitz, Helga Erickssen, Lis Lowert, Peter Finch, Meinhart Maur, Walter Gotell, Walter Hertner, Bill Travers.*

WORM'S EYE VIEW (1951)   ③
Dir *Jack Raymond.* Prod *Henry Halstead.* Scr *R. F. Delderfield, Jack Marks, from Delderfield's play.* Ph *James Wilson.* PC *Byron.* Dis *Associated British. 77 mins. Cert U*
Events in the lives of five RAF men billeted in a suburban household during World War II. Led by Porter (*Ronald Shiner*), a malingering 'spiv' always on the make, the quintet

John Blythe, Diana Dors and Ronald Shiner in Worm's Eye View *(1950)*

plagues the life out of the vinegary landlady (*Everley Gregg*), her henpecked husband, objectionable stepson and pretty daughter, to say nothing of the saucy maid (*Diana Dors*). Limited fun from salty conversational exchanges; a big box-office winner, it made Shiner a star.
RoC *Garry Marsh, John Blythe, Bruce Seton, Digby Wolfe, Eric Davies, Christina Forrest, William Percy, Jonathan Field.*

WRONG NUMBER (1959)   ②
Dir *Vernon Sewell.* Prod *Jack Greenwood.* Scr *James Eastwood, from the play by Norman Edwards.* Ph *Josef Ambor.* PC *Merlin.* Dis *Anglo-Amalgamated. 60 mins. Cert U*
A man is killed in a mail-van robbery, and the killer (*Peter Reynolds*) seems to have got away with it, until an old dear's (*Olive Sloane*) remembrance of a snatch of conversation from dialling a wrong number puts the police on the trail of him and the gang for whom he works. Most unconvincing minor thriller; Olive Sloane's ripe performance at least punctuates the groans.
RoC *Lisa Gastoni, Peter Elliott, Paul Whitsun-Jones, Barry Keegan, John Horsley, Harold Goodwin, Arthur Lovegrove, Catherina Ferraz, Christopher Trace.*

X THE UNKNOWN (1956)   ③
Dir *Leslie Norman.* Prod *Anthony Hinds.* Scr *Jimmy Sangster.* Ph *Gerald Gibbs.* PC *Hammer.* Dis *Exclusive. 78 mins. Cert X*
After a mysterious explosion on the Scottish moors, a number of soldiers training there are found to be suffering from radiation. A bubbly horror lies in the chasm resulting from the blast, from whence it periodically sucks the life out of soldiers guarding it. Scientists conclude that it feeds on radiation and set a baited trap which results in it being exterminated in a belt of atomic flame. Well-photographed and well-

acted horror which just isn't very entertaining. LP *Dean Jagger, Edward Chapman, Leo McKern, William Lucas, John Harvey, Peter Hammond, Michael Ripper, Anthony Newley, Ian McNaughton, Kenneth Cope, Edwin Richfield, Jameson Clark, Michael Brooke, Marianne Brauns, Fraser Hines, Jane Aird, Neil Hallett, Norman MacOwan, Edward Judd.*

Y

YANGTSE INCIDENT (1957)
(USA: *Battle Hell*)

Dir *Michael Anderson*. Prod *Herbert Wilcox*. Scr *Eric Ambler, from a book by Laurence Earl*. Ph *Gordon Dines*. PC *Everest/Wilcox-Neagle*. Dis *British Lion. 112 mins. Cert U*
1949. Civil war rages in China and, crippled by heavy shellfire, HMS *Amethyst* is trapped on the Yangtse river. The captain is killed. Endless negotiations with the Chinese eventually lead the new captain, Kerans (*Richard Todd*), into making a break for freedom. Despite heavy harassment and constant shellfire, he guides the ship 140 miles down river to the open sea. Long and passionless film only rarely catches the inspiration of actual events; sturdily acted.
RoC *William Hartnell, Akim Tamiroff, Donald Houston, Keye Luke, Sophie Stewart, Robert Urquhart, James Kenney, Richard Leech, Michael Brill, Barry Foster, Thomas Heathcote, Sam Kydd, Ewen Solon, Ian Bannen, Gene Anderson, Ray Jackson, Bernard Cribbins, Brian Smith, John Charlesworth, Kenneth Cope, Alfred Burke, John A Tinn, Karl Rawlings, Andy Ho, Cesar Da' Rocha, Dennis Clinton, Anthony Chinn, Richard Coleman, Murray Kash, Yah Ming, A Chong Choy, Gordon Whiting, Donald Bradley, Garcia Tay, John Paul, Basil Dignam, Peter Hutton, Edward Dentith, Ralph Truman, N. C. Doo, Tom Tann, John Horsley, Tom Bowman, David Aylmer, Jeremy Burnham, Cyril Luckham, Allan Cuthbertson.*

A YANK IN ERMINE (1955)

Dir *Gordon Parry*. Prod *William Gell*. Scr *John Paddy Carstairs, from his novel* Solid, Said the Earl. Ph *Arthur Grant*. PC and Dis *Monarch. Eastman Colour. 85 mins. Cert U*
Hearing he is now the Earl of Beverlow, American flier Joe (*Peter Thompson*) comes to Britain with friends to look over his new estate. He falls in love with an English girl (*Noelle Middleton*) and, although an old flame (*Diana Decker*) threatens to upset the applecart, she falls for an impeccable Englishman (*Guy Middleton*) and there is a double wedding. Very broad comedy, missing few chances for obvious fun.
RoC *Harold Lloyd Jr, Jon Pertwee, Edward Chapman, Richard Wattis, Reginald Beckwith,*

Jennifer Jayne, Sidney James, Harry Locke, George Woodbridge, John MacLaren.

THE YELLOW BALLOON (1952)

Dir *J. Lee Thompson*. Prod *Victor Skutezky*. Scr *Anne Burnaby, Lee Thompson*. Ph *Gilbert Taylor*. PC *Marble Arch/Associated British*. Dis *AB-Pathé. 80 mins. Cert X*
A schoolboy struggle over a balloon ends in one falling to his death. Len (*William Sylvester*), a crook, tells Frankie (*Andrew Ray*), the survivor, that he saw him push his friend to his death. Having forced Frankie to help in a robbery, Len then tries to dispatch him, but after chilling chases in a lift shaft and a disused tube station, plunges to his doom. Edge-of-seat thriller, Britain's second 'X'.
RoC *Kathleen Ryan, Kenneth More, Bernard Lee, Hy Hazell, Veronica Hurst, Sandra Dorne, Campbell Singer, Sidney James, Marjorie Rhodes, Eliot Makeham, Stephen Fenemore, Peter Jones, Laurie Main.*

THE YELLOW ROBE (1954)

Dir *David Macdonald*. Prod *Edward J. Danziger, Harry Lee Danziger*. Scr *George St George, James Eastwood*. Ph *Jimmy Wilson*. PC *Danzigers*. Dis *AB-Pathé. 51 mins. Cert U*
Two stories of murder. (1) Penniless Frank (*Tony Penderell*) is suspected of the murder of a man with evidence to prove he is *not* inheriting a fortune. But the police prove a solicitor had a stronger motive … (2) A young widow (*Honor Blackman*) traps the two men who murdered her husband because he threatened their financial future. First story poor; second played with drive and conviction.
RoC *Ron Randell; Robert Raglan, Iris Russell, Peter Neil, Mona Washbourne, Nicholas Hill; Clifford Evans, Martin Boddey, Bill Nagy.*

YESTERDAY'S ENEMY (1959)

Dir *Val Guest*. Prod *Michael Carreras*. Scr *Peter Newman, from his TV play*. Ph *Arthur Grant*. PC *Hammer*. Dis *Columbia. MegaScope. 95 mins. Cert A*
Burma 1942. Puzzled by the presence of a Japanese colonel and a mysterious map among enemy dead in a village, ruthless British officer Langford (*Stanley Baker*) shoots two civilians to expose a spy. The padre (*Guy Rolfe*) and war correspondent (*Leo McKern*) in his party see this as a war crime. Later, the situation is reversed, and Langford and his men die to protect the information they have learned. Grim, grisly war film.
RoC *Gordon Jackson, David Oxley, Richard Pasco, Bryan Forbes, Philip Ahn, Percy Herbert, Edwina Carroll, Russell Waters, Wolf(e) Morris, David Lodge, Barry Lowe, Alan Keith, Howard Williams, Timothy Bateson, Arthur Lovegrove, Donald Churchill, Nicholas Brady, Barry Steele.*

YIELD TO THE NIGHT (1956)
(USA: *Blonde Sinner*)

Dir *J. Lee Thompson*. Prod *Kenneth Harper*. Scr *John Cresswell, Joan Henry, from Henry's novel*. Ph *Gilbert Taylor*. PC *Associated British*. Dis *AB-Pathé. 100 mins. Cert X*
Awaiting hanging for murder, Mary (*Diana*

Yvonne Mitchell and Diana Dors in Yield to the Night *(1956)*

Dors) reflects on her past. She recalls falling in love with Jim (*Michael Craig*), a nightclub pianist for whom she leaves her husband. He in turn falls for another woman and, when she rejects him, commits suicide. Filled with desire for revenge, Mary kills her rival. In the condemned cell, she hears that there is to be no reprieve. Convincing, if unrelievedly grim drama that proved its glamorous leading lady could really act.
RoC *Yvonne Mitchell, Geoffrey Keen, Olga Lindo, Mary Mackenzie, Joan Miller, Marie Ney, Liam Redmond, Marjorie Rhodes, Athene Seyler, Molly Urquhart, Hary Locke, Michael Ripper, Joyce Blair, Charles Clay, Peggy Livesey, Mona Washbourne, Alec Finter, Marianne Stone, Mercia Shaw, Charles Lloyd Pack, Dandy Nichols, John Charlesworth, Frank Hawkins, Shirley Ann Field.*

YOU CAN'T ESCAPE (1955)

Dir *Wilfred Eades*. Prod *Robert Hall*. Scr *Hall, Doreen Montgomery, from a novel by Alan Kennington*. Ph *Norman Warwick*. PC *Forth Films*. Dis *AB-Pathé. 77 mins. Cert A*
Darwin (*Robert Urquhart*), a novelist, kills an ex-mistress and persuades his fiancée (*Noelle Middleton*) to help bury the body. He also murders a blackmailer (*Peter Reynolds*), tries to incriminate his friend David (*Guy Rolfe*) and plans to murder his fiancée when she threatens to save David by coming clean. She is rescued by police in the nick of time. Very lacklustre thriller.
RoC *Martin Boddey, Elizabeth Kentish, Barbara Cavan, Thorley Walters, Jacqueline Mackenzie, Llewellyn Rees, Paddy Brannigan, Hal Osmond, Sam Kydd, Barbara Leake, Oliver Johnston, Wensley Pithey, Edward Forsyth, Alec Finter, Walter Horsbrugh, Gerald Andersen.*

YOU KNOW WHAT SAILORS ARE
(1953)

Dir *Ken Annakin*. Prod *Peter Rogers, Julian Wintle*. Scr *Rogers, from a novel by Edward Hyams*. Ph *Reginald Wyer*. PC *Group*. Dis *General Film Distributors. Technicolor. 89 mins. Cert U*
Naval lieutenant Sylvester Green (*Donald Sinden*) crowns a drunken spree by making a contraption from a pawnbroker's sign and a pram and welding it to the deck of a foreign destroyer. Panicked by the furore it causes, he

identifies it as '998', a radar detector. The top scientist of nearby Agraria prevents his country from being invaded by his pretended knowledge of the 'deadly' weapon. Beautiful girls abound in a comedy that sounds ridiculous but is actually quite good fun.

RoC *Sarah Lawson, Akim Tamiroff, Naunton Wayne, Bill Kerr, Dora Bryan, Martin Miller, Michael Shepley, Ferdy Mayne, Michael Hordern, Peter Arne, Bryan Coleman, Peter Martyn, Shirley Lorrimer, Cyril Chamberlain, Hal Osmond, Eileen Sands, Janet Richards, Marianne Stone, Peter Dyneley, Shirley Eaton, Lisa Gastoni, Jan Miller.*

YOU LUCKY PEOPLE (1955)   [3]

Dir *Maurice Elvey.* Prod *David Dent.* Scr *Anthony Verney, with Tommy Trinder.* Ph *Gordon Dines.* PC *Advance.* Dis *Adelphi.* CameraScope. 79 mins. Cert U

Arriving for his two weeks' reserve training, Tommy Smart (*Tommy Trinder*), an ex-serviceman who has got on through selling army surplus goods, soon meets an old enemy in Sgt-Major Thickpenny (*Rufus Cruickshank*). In the midst of such escapades as blundering into the WRACs' barracks, Smart sorts out a love triangle and proves his cunning matches his name by outwitting Thickpenny. Ancient army farce, but Trinder squeezes some laughs out of the time-honoured material.

RoC *Mary Parker, Dora Bryan, RSM Brittain, James Copeland, Derek Prentice, Harold Goodwin, Michael Kelly, Michael Trubshawe, Mark Singleton, Charles Rolfe, Mignon O'Doherty, Rolf Harris.*

THE YOUNG AND THE GUILTY (1958)   [3]

Dir *Peter Cotes.* Prod *Warwick Ward.* Scr *Ted Willis, from his TV play.* Ph *Norman Warwick.* PC *Welwyn.* Dis *AB-Pathé.* 67 mins. Cert A

Two 'A' level students (*Andrew Ray, Janet Munro*) conceive an innocent crush on each other. One of their 'love letters' is intercepted by misunderstanding parents, and the teenagers are forbidden to see each other. They are caught in the middle of an illicit tryst in the girl's bedroom at night, but this leads, after a talk with both sets of parents, to a situation where they can meet openly again. Rather strained for effect but is occasionally touching in a naive way.

RoC *Phyllis Calvert, Edward Chapman, Campbell Singer, Hilda Fenemore, Jean StClair, Sonia Rees*

THE YOUNG LOVERS (1954)   [5]
(USA: *Chance Meeting*)

Dir *Anthony Asquith.* Prod *Anthony Havelock-Allan.* Scr *Robin Estridge, George Tabori.* Ph *Jack Asher.* PC *Group.* Dis *General Film Distributors.* 96 mins. Cert A

After a chance encounter at a ballet, Ted (*David Knight*), a US intelligence officer in London, falls in love with Anna (*Odile Versois*), daughter of an Eastern European minister. Both are accused of treachery, mental and actual; they are hounded and their phones tapped. Anna gets pregnant and fixes a final meeting with Ted before she is sent home; through it, Ted is arrested. He escapes, con-

Odile Versois and David Knight in The Young Lovers *(1954)*

tacts Anna and they flee, stealing a boat and heading out to sea. Wreckage is washed up and a poignant note from Anna found. But the boat has survived the storm ... Movingly acted, grippingly told; the best film of Asquith's later years. Some critics disliked the happy ending. British Oscar for best screenplay.

RoC *David Kossoff, Joseph Tomelty, Paul Carpenter, Theodore Bikel, Jill Adams, John McClaren, Betty Marsden, Peter Illing, Peter Dyneley, Bernard Rebel.*

YOUNG WIVES' TALE (1951)   [4]

Dir *Henry Cass.* Prod *Victor Skutezky.* Scr *Anne Burnaby, from the play by Ronald Jeans.* Ph *Erwin Hillier.* PC *Associated British.* Dis *AB-Pathé.* 79 mins. Cert A

Sabina (*Joan Greenwood*) is a temperamental dilly who lives with her author husband (*Nigel Patrick*) in the same house as Mary (*Helen Cherry*) and her husband Bruce (*Derek Farr*). Then there's a lodger (*Audrey Hepburn*). And nannies, who keep resigning. Some households seem built for disaster. In this one, kettles whistle vainly, milk boils over, and the dog steals the dinner. Bits of comic business follow fast one upon another in this successful - almost slapstick - comedy.

RoC *Guy Middleton, Athene Seyler, Fabia Drake, Irene Handl, Anthony Deamer, Carol James, Joan Sanderson, Selma vaz Dias, Jack McNaughton, Brian Oulton.*

YOU PAY YOUR MONEY (1956)   [2]

Dir and Scr *Maclean Rogers, from a novel by Michael Cronin.* Prod *W. G. Chalmers.* Ph *Jimmy Harvey.* PC and Dis *Butchers.* 68 mins. Cert U

A financier who smuggles valuable books gets more trouble than he needs when a couple of the books prove to be wanted by a fanatical Arab league. His assistant Bob (*Hugh McDermott*) finds his wife (*Honor Blackman*) kidnapped by the league. But, with the help of an Arab diplomat, and a Soho gangster who 'owes him', Bob manages to turn the tables, rescue his wife and keep the books. Thriller is vigorous, but you never quite forget how silly the plot is.

RoC *Jane Hylton, Ivan Samson, Ferdy Mayne, Hugh Moxey, Shirley Deane, Gerard Heinz, Basil Dignam, Peter Swanwick, Fred Griffiths, Ben Williams, Elsie Wagstaff, Vincent Holman, Mark Daly.*

YOU'RE ONLY YOUNG TWICE! (1952)   [2]

Dir *Terry Bishop.* Prod *John Grierson, John Baxter, Barbara K. Emary.* Scr *Bishop, Lindsay Galloway, Reginald Beckwith, from a play by James Bridie.* Ph *Jo Jago.* PC *Group 3.* Dis *Associated British.* 81 mins. Cert U

Pretty Ada (*Diane Hart*) comes to a Scottish university looking for her uncle, is mistaken for someone else and becomes secretary to the Principal (*Patrick Barr*), with whom she falls in love. Uncle, a famous rebel Irish poet, turns out to be masquerading as the university gatekeeper and running a nightclub and bookmaking businesses on the side. Their chief opponent, a professor (*Duncan Macrae*) is brought low when his son (*Charles Hawtrey*) gets drunk at the club. Uncle is offered the 'Chair' in Celtic poetry. Too foolish for words, this comedy fell between all sorts of stools.

RoC *Joseph Tomelty, Robert Urquhart, Edward Lexy, Jacqueline Mackenzie, Eric Woodburn, Molly Urquhart, Reginald Beckwith, Moultrie Kelsall, Roddy MacMillan, Wendy Noel, Archie Duncan, Alistair Hunter, Andrew Downie, Russell Waters.*

YOUR MONEY OR YOUR WIFE (1959)   [1]

Dir *Anthony Simmons.* Prod *Norman Williams.* Scr *Ronald Jeans.* Ph *Brendan Stafford.* PC *Ethiro/Alliance.* Dis *Rank.* 91 mins. Cert A

When their inheritance of money through a will proves troublesome, Gay (*Peggy Cummins*) and Pel (*Donald Sinden*) Butterworth take in some (rather extraordinary) paying guests. When this fails, they discover that, by divorcing, they can get their hands on half the money from the will. Thanks to a technicality, the divorce becomes a reality, but Gay keeps her husband - as a paying guest. Very heavy farce; the performances smack of desperation.

RoC *Richard Wattis, Peter Reynolds, Georgina Cookson, Barbara Steele, Gladys Boot, Betty Baskcomb, Olive Sloane, Ian Fleming, Candy Scott, Noel Trevarthen.*

YOUR WITNESS (1950)   [3]
(USA: *Eye Witness*)

Dir *Robert Montgomery.* Prod *David E. Rose, Joan Harrison.* Scr *Hugo Butler, Ian Hunter, William Douglas Home.* Ph *Gerald Gibbs.* PC *Coronado.* Dis *Warner Bros.* 100 mins. Cert A

A New York lawyer (*Robert Montgomery*) flies to England to help the wartime friend (*Michael Ripper*) who saved his life, but now stands accused of taking someone else's. His plea of self-defence hinges on a girl who was in the murdered man's house at the time. The lawyer narrows this down to three; finally a book of poems enables him to pinpoint the right one. Sometimes suspenseful and well directed, but long and rather slow thriller.

RoC *Leslie Banks, Felix Aylmer, Andrew Cruickshank, Patricia Wayne (Cutts), Harcourt Williams, Jenny Laird, Ann Stephens, Wylie Watson, Noel Howlett, James Hayter, Shelagh Fraser. Philip Dale, Hal Osmond, Lyonel Watts, Derrick Penley, Erik Chitty, Ruth Lee, Stanley Baker, Richard Wattis, John Sharp.*

Z

ZARAK (1956)   2

Dir *Terence Young*. Prod *Phil C. Samuel*. Scr *Richard Maibaum*. Ph *John Wilcox, Ted Moore, Cyril Knowles*. PC *Warwick*. Dis *Columbia*. *Technicolor. CinemaScope. 95 mins. Cert A*

Zarak Khan (*Victor Mature*) and his band of outlaws roaming India's northwest frontier are captured by Major Ingram (*Michael Wilding*) and his men. Zarak escapes and, with the vicious Ahmad Khan (*Peter Illing*) besieges the British garrison. After Ingram is tortured by Ahmad, Zarak saves him at the cost of his own

Anita Ekberg and Victor Mature in Zarak *(1956)*

life. Ridiculous eastern dust-rouser – from the team that was later to make James Bond!
RoC *Anita Ekberg, Bonar Colleano, Finlay Currie, Eunice Gayson, Eddie Byrne, Frederick Valk, Eric Pohlmann, André Morell, Bernard Miles, Yana, Patrick McGoohan, Harold Goodwin, Geoffrey Keen, Alec Mango, Oscar Quitak, George Margo, Arnold Marle.*

ZOO BABY (1957)   2

Dir *David Eady*. Prod *Jon Penington*. Scr *Jan Read*. Ph *Ernest Palmer*. PC *Penington Eady*. Dis *Rank. 59 mins. Cert U*

Young Pip (*Gerald Lohan*), son of a big game hunter, loves all animals, but longs to own a coatimundi, with its long ringed tail. When a 'coati' disappears from Chessington Zoo, a newsreel cameraman is suspected, but Pip is the culprit. Not released until 1960, but it has a certain unpretentious charm.
RoC *Angela Baddeley, Maurice Kaufmann, Dorothy Bromily, Bruce Seton, Ronald Leigh-Hunt, Peter Sinclair, Doreen Keogh, Erik Chitty, Peter Allenby, June Clarke, Alan Penn, Garard Green, Robert Raglan, Michael Peake.*

SHORTS

Entertainment feature films of the 1950s between 20 minutes' and 44 minutes' duration

1950
The Clown (34)
An International Affair (27)
Irish Melody (37)
Mr Pastry Does the Laundry (29)
The Mystery of the Snakeskin Belt (serial. Eight episodes, 16 mins each)
Return Fare to Laughter (38)
Round Rainbow Corner (32)
*The Starfish (38. Co-director: John Schlesinger)

1951
*The Case of the Missing Scene (41)
Change of Heart (21)
Cookery Nook (28) with Terry-Thomas
David (38)
Let's Go Crazy (33) with Peter Sellers
Looking for Trouble (44)
The Man with the Twisted Lip (35)
Mirth and Melody (36)
One Good Turn (28)
*Out of True (40)
The Queen Steps Out (20) with Terry-Thomas
Return to Glannascaul (23) with Orson Welles
Trek to Mashomba (44)

1951
At Home with the Hardwickes (series of six. 17–20 mins)
A Ghost for Sale (31)
Giselle (31)
Highlights of Radio (20)
Made for Laughs (34)
Murder at the Grange (31)
Potter of the Yard (30)

Say Abracadabra (28)
To the Rescue (21)
What a Husband! (20)

1953
All Hallowe'en (34)
Betty Slow Drag (26)
*The Blakes Slept Here (38) Technicolor
The Bo'sun's Mate (30)
Bunty Wins a Pup (26)
The Candlelight Murder (32. Director: Ken Hughes)
The Case of Canary Jones (34)
The Case of Express Delivery (35)
The Case of Gracie Budd (34)
The Case of Soho Red (33)
The Case of the Black Falcon (36)
The Case of the Last Dance (35)
The Case of the Marriage Bureau (34)
The Drayton Case (26. Director: Ken Hughes)
The Mask (28) Cert X
Master of Laughter (33)
The Missing Man (30)
Mr Beamish Goes South (33)
Out of the Bandbox (30)
A Prince for Cynthia (28)
*The Stranger Left No Card (23)
Strange Stories (44)
The Super Secret Service (25) with Peter Sellers
*The Tell Tale Heart (20) with Stanley Baker. Cert X
Too Many Detectives (33)

1954
The Blazing Caravan (32. Director: Ken Hughes)
Calling All Cars (44)
The Case of Diamond Annie (35)
The Case of Uncle Henry (35)

The Case of the Bogus Count (34)
The Case of the Pearl Payroll (34)
*The Case of the Second Shot (36)
*The Dark Stairway (32. Director: Ken Hughes)
*Fatal Journey (30)
Five O'Clock Finish (20)
Harmony Lane (25) in 3-D
Late Night Final (29)
The Missing Princess (31)
Mystery at Monstein (28)
Night Plane to Amsterdam (31. Director: Ken Hughes)
Passenger to Tokyo (32. Director: Ken Hughes)
The Silent Witness (32)
The Strange Case of Blondie (32. Director: Ken Hughes)
Variety Half Hour (30)

1955
All Living Things (30)
*The Bespoke Overcoat (35. Director: Jack Clayton)
The Case of the Mukkinese Battlehorn (30)
Cyril Stapleton and the Show Band (28) In colour
Dead on Time (27)
Dollars for Sale (36)
Eric Winstone Band Show (28) In colour
Just for You (31) Eastman Colour. CinemaScope
The Man on the Cliff (23)
Murder Anonymous (31. Director: Ken Hughes)
The Mysterious Bullet (31)
No Love for Judy (31)
*On Such a Night (37) Eastman Colour. Director: Anthony Asquith

The Right Person (30) Eastman Colour. CinemaScope
Song of Norway (32)
The Stateless Man (29)

1956
Bullet from the Past (33)
The Case of the River Morgue (34)
Destination Death (31)
Dick Turpin - Highwayman (25) with Philip Friend. Eastman Colour. CinemaScope
*The Door in the Wall (29) Technicolor. Dynamic Frame
Eric Winstone's Stagecoach (30) Eastman Colour. CinemaScope
Faithful to the Rescue (25)
Five Guineas a Week (33) Eastman Colour. CinemaScope
The Gentle Corsican (25) Trucolor
Invitation to Magic (20)
The Lonely House (33)
A Man on the Beach (30) Eastman Colour. CinemaScope
The Message (31)
On the Twelfth Day (23) Eastman Colour
Parade of the Bands (28) Eastman Colour. CinemaScope

Person Unknown (32)
Raiders of the River (serial. Eight episodes, 16–20 mins each)

1957
All Square Aft (29) Eastman Colour
The Awakening Hour (21)
The Case of the Smiling Widow (31)
Danger List (22) with Philip Friend, Honor Blackman, Mervyn Johns
Day of Grace (26) Eastman Colour. CinemaScope
Dearth of a Salesman (29) with Peter Sellers
Edmundo Ros Half Hour (28) Eastman Colour
Five Clues to Fortune (serial. Eight episodes, 15–18 mins each)
Five on a Treasure Island (serial. Eight episodes, 14–18 mins each)
Inside Information (32)
*Insomnia is Good for You (26) with Peter Sellers
Jack Trent Investigates (28)
The Mail Van Murder (29)
Night Crossing (32)
The Tyburn Case (32)
The White Cliffs Mystery (32)

1958
A Clean Sweep (27)
Crime of Honour (27)
The Crossroad Gallows (29)
Death Was a Passenger (20)
Mingaloo (21)
Portrait of a Matador (22)
Print of Death (26)

1959
The Adventures of Rex (series. Five episodes, 12–15 mins each)
The Dawn Killer (serial. Eight episodes, 10–16 mins each)
The Ghost Train Murder (32)
The Great Expedition (29)
Men of Tomorrow (40)
Mystery in the Mine (serial. Eight episodes, 14–18 mins each)
Stars of a Summer Night (24) Eastman Colour
The Unseeing Eye (28)
The Young Jacobites (serial. Eight episodes, 15–20 mins each)
The Visit (39)

*indicates a film of above average merit
Minutes in brackets

Bibliography

For reference and research, I am indebted to many magazines and newspapers from the period 1928–59, but especially *Picturegoer, Picture Show, Kinematograph Weekly* and the *Monthly Film Bulletin*. The following books have also proved valuable in building up a portrait of the British cinema during these years.

ARMES, Roy. *A Critical History of British Cinema*. Secker and Warburg, 1978.

BALCON, Michael, LINDGREN, Ernest, HARDY, Forsyth and MANVELL, Roger. *Twenty Years of British Films*. Falcon, 1947.

BALCON, Michael. *Michael Balcon Presents . . . A Lifetime of Films*. Hutchinson, 1969.

BARKER, Felix. *The House That Stoll Built*. Frederick Muller, 1957.

BARR, Charles. *Ealing Studios*. David and Charles, 1977.

BOX, Muriel. *Odd Woman Out*. Leslie Frewin, 1974.

BROWN, Geoff. *Launder and Gilliat*. British Film Institute, 1977.

BROWN, Geoff. *Walter Forde*. British Film Institute, 1977.

CLARKE, T.E.B. *This is Where I Came In*. Michael Joseph, 1974.

CLERKE and COCKERAN (Publishers). *The Elstree Story: 21 Years of Film Making* (various contributors).

COTTRELL, John. *Laurence Olivier*. Weidenfeld and Nicolson, 1975.

CURRAN, James, and PORTER, Vincent, eds. *British Cinema History*. Weidenfeld and Nicolson, 1983.

DANISCHEWSKY, Monja. *White Russian, Red Face*. Victor Gollancz, 1966.

FIELDS, Gracie. *Sing As We Go*. Frederick Muller, 1960.

GIFFORD, Denis. *British Cinema*. Zwemmer, 1968.

GIFFORD, Denis. *Catalogue of British Films, 1895–1970*. David and Charles, 1973.

GIFFORD, Denis. *The Illustrated Who's Who in British Films*. B.T. Batsford, 1978.

HALLIWELL, Leslie. *Halliwell's Film Guide*. Granada Publishing, 1977, 1980, 1983.

HINXMAN, Margaret, and D'ARCY, Susan. *The Films of Dirk Bogarde*. LSP, 1974.

HUNTLEY, John. *British Technicolor Films*. Skelton Robinson, 1948.

HULBERT, Jack. *The Little Woman's Always Right*. W.H. Allen, 1975.

KATZ, Ephraim. *The International Film Encyclopedia*. Macmillan, 1980.

KULIK, Karol. *Alexander Korda – the Man Who Could Work Miracles*. W.H. Allen, 1975.

LOW, Rachael. *Films of Comment and Persuasion in the 1930s*. George Allen and Unwin, 1979.

LOW, Rachael. *The History of the British Film 1918–1929*. George Allen and Unwin, 1971.

MARSHALL, Michael. *Top Hat and Tails*. Elm Tree, 1978.

MINNEY, R. J. *Puffin Asquith*. Leslie Frewin, 1973.

NOBLE, Peter, ed. *International Film and TV Year Book*. 1946 through 1960. British and American Film Press/Holdings Ltd. Dates as given.

PALMER, Scott. *A Who's Who of British Film Actors*. The Scarecrow Press, 1981.

PERRY, George. *Forever Ealing*. Pavilion/Michael Joseph, 1981.

PERRY, George. *The Great British Picture Show*. Hart-Davis, MacGibbon, 1974.

PERRY, George. *Hitchcock*. Macmillan, 1975.

PERRY, George. *Movies from the Mansion*. Elm Tree Books/Hamish Hamilton, 1976.

POWELL, Dilys. *Films Since 1939*. The British Council, 1947.

PRATLEY, Gerald. *The Cinema of David Lean*. Tantivy, 1974.

QUINLAN, David. *The Illustrated Directory of Film Stars*. B.T. Batsford, 1981.

QUINLAN, David. *The Illustrated Guide to Film Directors*. B.T. Batsford, 1983.

RHODE, Eric. *A History of the Cinema*. Penguin, 1976.

ROUD, Richard, ed. *Cinema: a Critical Dictionary*. Two volumes. Secker and Warburg, 1980.

SPEED, F. Maurice. *Film Review*. 1944 though 1960–61. Macdonald, dates as given.

THOMSON, David. *A Biographical Dictionary of the Cinema*. Secker and Warburg, 1975.

THORNTON, Michael. *Jessie Matthews*. Hart-Davis, MacGibbon, 1974.

VERMILYE, Jerry. *The Great British Films*. Citadel, 1978.

WALKER, Alexander. *Hollywood, England*. Michael Joseph, 1974.

WARREN, Patricia. *Elstree, the British Hollywood*. Elm Tree/Hamish Hamilton, 1983.

WILCOX, Herbert. *25,000 Sunsets*. The Bodley Head, 1967.

WOOD, Alan. *Mr Rank*. Hodder and Stoughton, 1952.

WRIGHT, Basil. *The Long View*. Secker and Warburg, 1974.